How to Use the Maps in *Western Civilization: A Brief History, Fourth Edition*

Here are some basic map concepts that will help you to get the most out of the maps in this textbook.

- Always look at the scale, which allows you to determine the distance in miles or kilometers between locations on the map.

- Examine the legend carefully. It explains the colors and symbols used on the map.

- Note the locations of mountains, rivers, oceans, and other geographic features, and consider how these would affect such human activities as agriculture, commerce, travel, and warfare.

- Read the map caption thoroughly. It provides important information, sometimes not covered in the text itself, and poses a thought question to encourage you to think beyond the mere appearance of the map and make connections across chapters, regions, and concepts.

- Several "spot maps" appear in each chapter, to allow you to view in detail smaller areas that may not be apparent in larger maps. For example, a spot map in Chapter 1 lets you zoom in on Hammurabi's Empire.

- Many of the text's maps also carry a globe icon alongside the title, which indicates that the map appears in interactive form on the text's website:

http://www.thomsonedu.com/history/spielvogel

Western Civilization:
A Brief History

COMPREHENSIVE VOLUME
FOURTH EDITION

Western Civilization: A Brief History

JACKSON J. SPIELVOGEL

The Pennsylvania State University

THOMSON

WADSWORTH

Australia • Brazil • Canada • Mexico • Singapore • Spain
United Kingdom • United States

THOMSON
WADSWORTH

Publisher *Clark Baxter*
Senior Acquisitions Editor *Ashley Dodge*
Development Editor *Margaret McAndrew Beasley*
Assistant Editor *Kristen Tatroe*
Editorial Assistant *Ashley Spicer*
Associate Development Project Manager *Lee McCracken*
Senior Marketing Manager *Janise Fry*
Marketing Assistant *Teresa Jessen*
Senior Marketing Communications Manager *Tami Strang*
Content Project Managers *Katy German, Karol Jurado*
Creative Director *Rob Hugel*
Executive Art Director *Maria Epes*

Senior Print Buyer *Karen Hunt*
Production Service *Jonathan Peck, Dovetail Publishing Services*
Text Designer *Kathleen Cunningham*
Photo Researcher *Abigail Baxter*
Copy Editor *Bruce Emmer*
Permissions Editor *Sarah D'Stair*
Cover Designer *Kathleen Cunningham*
Cover Image *A detail from* Master of the Half Figures *(15th century),*
Hermitage, St. Petersburg, Russia, Scala/Art Resource, NY
Cover Printer *Courier Corporation/Kendallville*
Compositor *International Typesetting and Composition*
Printer *Courier Corporation/Kendallville*

Thomson Higher Education
10 Davis Drive
Belmont, CA 94002-3098
USA

Library of Congress Control Number: 2006939302

Student Edition:
ISBN-13: 978-0-495-09973-4
ISBN-10: 0-495-09973-2

ABOUT THE AUTHOR

*J*ACKSON J. SPIELVOGEL is associate professor emeritus of history at The Pennsylvania State University. He received his Ph.D. from The Ohio State University, where he specialized in Reformation history under Harold J. Grimm. His articles and reviews have appeared in such journals as *Moreana, Journal of General Education, Catholic Historical Review, Archiv für Reformationsgeschichte,* and *American Historical Review.* He has also contributed chapters or articles to *The Social History of the Reformation, The Holy Roman Empire: A Dictionary Handbook,* the *Simon Wiesenthal Center Annual of Holocaust Studies,* and *Utopian Studies.* His work has been supported by fellowships from the Fulbright Foundation and the Foundation for Reformation Research. At Penn State, he helped inaugurate the Western civilization courses as well as a popular course on Nazi Germany. His book *Hitler and Nazi Germany* was published in 1987 (fifth edition, 2005). He is the author of *Western Civilization,* first published in 1991 (sixth edition, 2006) and the coauthor (with William Duiker) of *World History,* first published in 1994 (fifth edition, 2007). Professor Spielvogel has won five major universitywide teaching awards. During the year 1988–1989, he held the Penn State Teaching Fellowship, the university's most prestigious teaching award. In 1996, he won the Dean Arthur Ray Warnock Award for Outstanding Faculty Member, and in 2000, he received the Schreyer Honors College Excellence in Teaching Award.

*T*o Diane,
whose love and support made it all possible
J.J.S.

BRIEF CONTENTS

DETAILED CONTENTS

29 THE CONTEMPORARY WESTERN WORLD SINCE 1973 560

MAPS

CHRONOLOGIES

DOCUMENTS

These pages constitute an extension of the copyright page. We have made every effort to trace the ownership of all copyrighted material and to secure permission from copyright holders. In the event of any question arising as to the use of any material, we will be pleased to make the necessary corrections in future printings. Thanks are due to the following authors, publishers, and agents for permission to use the material indicated.

Continues on page 603

PREFACE

We are often reminded how important it is to understand today's world if we are to deal with our growing number of challenges. And yet that understanding will be incomplete if we in the Western world do not comprehend the meaning of Western civilization and the role it has played in the world. Despite modern progress, we still greatly reflect our religious traditions, our political systems and theories, our economic and social structures, and our cultural heritage. I have written this brief history of Western civilization to assist a new generation of students in learning more about the past that has shaped them and the world in which they live.

For the fourth edition, as in the third, I have added considerable new material on world history to show the impact other parts of the world have had on the West. Certainly, the terrorist attacks on the World Trade Center towers in New York and the Pentagon outside Washington, D.C., on September 11, 2001, have dramatized the intricate relationship between the West and the rest of the world. In this edition, I have attempted to show not only how Western civilization has affected the rest of the world but also how it has been influenced since its beginnings by contact with other peoples around the world.

Another of my goals was to write a well-balanced work in which the political, economic, social, religious, intellectual, cultural, and military aspects of Western civilization would be integrated into a chronologically ordered synthesis. Moreover, I wanted to avoid the approach that is quite common in other brief histories of Western civilization—an approach that makes them collections of facts with little continuity from section to section. Instead, I sought to keep the story in history. Narrative history effectively transmits the knowledge of the past and is the form that best enables students to remember and understand the past. At the same time, I have not overlooked the need for the kind of historical analysis that makes students aware that historians often disagree in their interpretations of the past.

Features of the Text

To enliven the past and let readers see for themselves the materials that historians use to create their pictures of the past, I have included in each chapter **primary sources** (boxed documents) that are keyed to the discussion in the text. The documents include examples of the religious, artistic, intellectual, social, economic, and political aspects of Western life. Such varied sources as a description of the life of an upper-class Roman, advice from a Carolingian

mother to her son, marriage negotiations in Renaissance Italy, a debate in the Reformation era, and the diary of a German soldier at Stalingrad all reveal in vivid fashion what Western civilization meant to the individual men and women who shaped it by their activities.

Each chapter has a **lengthy introduction and conclusion** to help maintain the continuity of the narrative and to provide a synthesis of important themes. Anecdotes in the chapter introductions convey more dramatically the major theme or themes of each chapter. **Detailed chronologies** reinforce the events discussed in the text, and **illustrated timelines** at the end of each chapter enable students to see at a glance the major developments of an era. Many of the timelines have been revised to show parallel developments in different cultures or nations. An **annotated bibliography** at the end of each chapter reviews the most recent literature on each period and also points readers to some of the older "classic" works in each field.

Updated maps and illustrations serve to deepen readers' understanding of the text. **Detailed map captions** are designed to enrich students' awareness of the importance of geography to history, and numerous spot maps enable students to see at a glance the region or subject being discussed in the text. To facilitate understanding of cultural movements, illustrations of artistic works discussed in the text are placed near the discussions. **Chapter outlines and focus questions, including critical thinking questions,** at the beginning of each chapter give students a useful overview and guide them to the main subjects of each chapter. A **glossary of important terms** (now boldfaced within the text) and a **pronunciation guide** are included to maximize reader comprehension and aid in review.

New to This Edition

As preparation for the revision of *Western Civilization: A Brief History,* I reexamined the entire book and analyzed the comments and reviews of colleagues who have found the book to be a useful instrument for introducing their students to the history of Western civilization. In making revisions for the fourth edition, I sought to build on the strengths of the first three editions and above all to maintain the balance, synthesis, and narrative qualities that characterized those editions. To keep up with the ever-growing body of historical scholarship, new or revised material has been added throughout the book on many topics, including Paleolithic painting; Hammurabi; the Hittites; the Hanging Gardens of Babylon; Athenian democracy; the decline of the Greek city-states; Greek interaction with India; Hellenistic monarchies; the Celts and their threat to the Hellenistic kingdoms; Hannibal;. Greek influence on the Romans; Cicero; crises in the third century; late antiquity; Germans during the Late Roman Empire; the end of the Roman Empire; the cultural shift brought by the conversion of Europe to Christianity; Augustine and Boethius; Islam; Alcuin and the Carolingian Renaissance; Muslim libraries and intellectual life; revival of Roman law; cross-cultural contacts between Western and Eastern translators and scholars; aristocratic women; the reconquest of Spain; the Hundred Years' War; the Great Schism; the Serb-Ottoman conflict in the fourteenth century; expansion of the Ottoman Empire and the fall of Constantinople; Michelangelo; Wyclif; Luther; Zwingli; the theology of the Anabaptists; the Council of Trent; the revived papacy in the Catholic Reformation; Jesuit missionaries to Asia; the slave trade; decline of the Ming in China; European ideas of cultural superiority; chemistry in the Scientific Revolution; Tahiti and Diderot; deism; Baron d'Holbach's atheism; the role of social divisions in the American Revolution; revolt in Saint-Domingue; the military conquests of Napoleon; Germaine de Staël; industrialization on the European continent; Chartism; Napoleon III's imperialistic adventure in Mexico; Florence Nightingale and nursing in the Crimean War; the spread of industrialization to Japan; the political history of Britain, Italy, Austria-Hungary, Russia, and France in the nineteenth century; causal factors in the rise of imperialism; Africa and Asia before imperialism; the response to imperialism by indigenous peoples; World War I as a global conflict; the Stalinist era; the Japanese home front in World War II; decolonization; the Cold War; women in the Soviet Union and Eastern Europe; politics since 1989; the reunification of Germany; the disintegration of Yugoslavia; and art, varieties of religious life, and science and popular culture since the 1970s. Throughout the revising process, I rewrote some sections and added many new subheadings to facilitate comprehension of the content of the chapters.

Chapters 6 and 7 were reorganized; Chapter 6 now focuses on the Roman Empire to 284, and Chapter 7 is a mostly new chapter on late antiquity and the emergence of the medieval world. The post–World War II material in Chapters 28 and 29 was reorganized to make the chapters chronologically consistent. Chapter 29 was also expanded and updated. New sections were added to a number of chapters: "Transformation of the Roman World: Crises in the Third Century" in Chapter 6; "The Spread of Industrialization to Japan" in Chapter 23; "The Casualties of War" in Chapter 25; "European States and the World: The Colonial Empires" in Chapter 26; "The Path to War in Asia" and "The New Order in Asia" in Chapter 27; "Europe and the World: Decolonization" in Chapter 28; and "The Unification of Europe" and "Postmodern Thought" in Chapter 29. The Suggestions for Further Reading at the end of each chapter were updated, and new illustrations were added throughout the book.

The enthusiastic response to the primary sources (boxed documents) led me to evaluate the content of each document carefully and add new documents throughout the text, including "An Italian Banker Discusses Trading Between Europe and China"; "The Childhood of Catherine the Great"; and "Soldier and Peasant Voices in the Russian Revolution." I also added questions to help guide students in analyzing the documents.

Because courses in Western civilization at American and Canadian colleges and universities follow different chronological divisions, a one-volume edition and a two-volume edition of this text are available to fit the needs of instructors. Teaching and learning ancillaries include the following:

For the Instructor

Instructor's Resource CD-ROM with ExamView® Includes the Instructor's Manual, Test Bank, Resource Integration Grid, ExamView® testing, and PowerPoint® slides with lecture outlines and images that can be used as offered, or customized by importing personal lecture slides or other material. ExamView allows instructors to create, deliver, and customize tests and study guides (both print and online) in minutes with this easy-to-use assessment and tutorial system. Instructors can build tests with as many as 250 questions using up to 12 question types. Using ExamView's complete word-processing capabilities, they can enter an unlimited number of new questions or edit existing ones.

ThomsonNOW This powerful and interactive web-based resource allows instructors to manage large classes with ease—student results flow directly to an instructor's gradebook—and it allows students to gauge their own unique study needs through pre-tests, personalized study plans, and more. Visit www.thomsonedu.com/thomsonnow

Full-Color Map Acetate Package Includes all maps from the text and other sources. More than 100 images. Map commentary is provided by James Harrison, Siena College.

History Video Library A completely new selection of videos for this edition, from *Films from the Humanities & Sciences* and other sources. Over fifty titles to choose from, with coverage spanning from "Egypt: A Gift to Civilization" to "Children of the Holocaust." Available to qualified adoptions.

Music of Western Civilization Available free to adopters, and for a small fee to students, this CD contains many of the musical selections highlighted in the text and provides a broad sampling of the important musical pieces of Western civilization.

JoinIn™ on TurningPoint® Combined with a choice of keypad systems, *JoinIn* turns PowerPoint® applications into audience response software. With a click on a handheld device, students can respond to multiple choice questions, short polls, interactive exercises, and peer review questions. Instructors can take attendance, check student comprehension of concepts, collect student demographics to better assess student needs, and even administer quizzes. This tool is available to qualified adopters.

For the Student

Map Exercise Workbook Prepared by Cynthia Kosso, Northern Arizona University. Thoroughly revised and upgraded. Over twenty maps and exercises ask students to identify important cities and countries. Available in two volumes.

MapTutor CD-ROM This interactive map tutorial helps students learn geography by having them locate geographical features, regions, cities, and sociopolitical movements. Each map exercise is accompanied by questions that test their knowledge and promote critical thinking. Animations vividly show movement such as the conquests of the Romans, the spread of Christianity, invasions, medieval trade routes, and the spread of the Black Death.

Document Exercise Workbook Prepared by Donna Van Raaphorst, Cuyahoga Community College. A collection of exercises based around primary sources. Available in two volumes.

Magellan Atlas of Western Civilization Available to bundle with any Western civilization text; contains forty-four full-color historical maps, including "The Conflict in Afghanistan, 2001" and "States of the World, 2001."

Gregory, Documents of Western Civilization This reader can accompany any Western civilization text. Contains a broad selection of carefully chosen documents.

InfoTrac® College Edition A Wadsworth exclusive. Students receive four months of real-time access to InfoTrac College Editions' online database of continuously updated, full-length articles from more than 900 journals and periodicals. By doing a simply keyword search, users can quickly generate a powerful list of related articles from thousands of possibilities, then select relevant articles to explore or print out for reference or further study. For professors, InfoTrac articles offer opportunities to ignite discussions or augment their lectures with the latest developments in the discipline. For students, InfoTrac's virtual library allows Internet access to sources that extend their learning far beyond the pages of a text.

Wadsworth History Resource Center

http://history.wadsworth.com

Both instructors and students will enjoy the Wadsworth History Resource Center, with access to the chapter-by-chapter resources for Spielvogel's Western civilization texts. Text-specific content for students includes interactive maps, interactive timelines, simulations, "At the Movies" film activities, tutorial quizzes, glossary, hyperlinks, InfoTrac exercises, and Internet activities. Instructors also have access to the Instructor's Manual, lesson plans, and PowerPoint slides (access code required). From the History home page, instructors and students can access many selections, such as an Internet Guide for History, a career center, lessons on surfing the Web, the World History image bank, and links to great history-related Web sites.

ACKNOWLEDGMENTS

I would like to thank the many teachers and students who have used the first three editions of *Western Civilization: A Brief History*. I am gratified by their enthusiastic response to a textbook that was intended to put the story back in history and capture the imagination of the reader. I especially thank the many teachers and students who made the effort to contact me personally to share their enthusiasm. I am deeply grateful to John Soares for his assistance in preparing the map captions and to Charmarie Blaisdell of Northeastern University for her detailed suggestions on women's history. Daniel Haxall and Kathryn Spielvogel of The Pennsylvania State University provided valuable assistance with materials on postwar art, popular culture, and Postmodern art and thought. Thanks to Wadsworth's comprehensive review process, many historians were asked to evaluate my manuscript and review each edition. I am grateful to the following for the innumerable suggestions for previous editions, which have greatly improved my work:

Paul Allen
University of Utah

Gerald Anderson
North Dakota State University

Susan L. H. Anderson
Campbell University

Letizia Argenteri
University of San Diego

Roy A. Austensen
Illinois State University

James A. Baer
Northern Virginia Community College–Alexandria

James T. Baker
Western Kentucky University

Patrick Bass
Morningside College

John F. Battick
University of Maine

Frederic J. Baumgartner
Virginia Polytechnic Institute

Phillip N. Bebb
Ohio University

Anthony Bedford
Modesto Junior College

F. E. Beemon
Middle Tennessee State University

Joel Benson
Northwest Missouri State University

Leonard R. Berlanstein
University of Virginia

Douglas T. Bisson
Belmont University

Charmarie Blaisdell
Northeastern University

Stephen H. Blumm
Montgomery County Community College

Hugh S. Bonar
California State University

Werner Braatz
University of Wisconsin–Oshkosh

Alfred S. Bradford
University of Missouri

Maryann E. Brink
College of William & Mary

Blaine T. Browne
Broward Community College

J. Holden Camp, Jr.
Hillyer College, University of Hartford

Jack Cargill
Rutgers University

Martha Carlin
University of Wisconsin–Milwaukee

Elizabeth Carney
Clemson University

Kevin K. Carroll
Arizona State University

Yuan-Ling Chao
Middle Tennessee State University

Eric H. Cline
Xavier University

Robert Cole
Utah State University

William J. Connell
Rutgers University

Nancy Conradt
College of DuPage

Marc Cooper
Southwest Missouri State

Richard A. Cosgrove
University of Arizona

David A. Crain
South Dakota State University

Michael A. Crane Jr. (student)
Everett Community College

Steve Culbertson
Owens Community College

Luanne Dagley
Pellissippi State Technical Community College

Michael F. Doyle
Ocean County College

Michael Duckett
Dawson College

Roxanne Easley
Central Washington University

James W. Ermatinger
University of Nebraska–Kearney

Charles T. Evans
Northern Virginia Community College

Porter Ewing
Los Angeles City College

Carla Falkner
Northeast Mississippi Community College

Steven Fanning
University of Illinois–Chicago

Ellsworth Faris
California State University–Chico

Gary B. Ferngren
Oregon State University

Mary Helen Finnerty
Westchester Community College

A. Z. Freeman
Robinson College

Marsha Frey
Kansas State University

Frank J. Frost
University of California–Santa Barbara

Frank Garosi
California State University–Sacramento

Lorettann Gascard
Franklin Pierce College

Richard M. Golden
University of North Texas

Manuel G. Gonzales
Diablo Valley College

Amy G. Gordon
Denison University

Richard J. Grace
Providence College

Hanns Gross
Loyola University

John F. Guilmartin
Ohio State University

Jeffrey S. Hamilton
Gustavus Adolphus College

J. Drew Harrington
Western Kentucky University

James Harrison
Siena College

A. J. Heisserer
University of Oklahoma

Rowena Hernández-Múzquiz
Old Dominion University

Betsey Hertzler
Mesa Community College

Robert Herzstein
University of South Carolina

Shirley Hickson
North Greenville College

Martha L. Hildreth
University of Nevada

Boyd H. Hill, Jr.
University of Colorado–Boulder

Michael Hofstetter
Bethany College

Donald C. Holsinger
Seattle Pacific University

Frank L. Holt
University of Houston

W. Robert Houston
University of South Alabama

Paul Hughes
Sussex County Community College

Richard A. Jackson
University of Houston

Fred Jewell
Harding University

Jenny M. Jochens
Towson State University

William M. Johnston
University of Massachusetts

Allen E. Jones
Troy State University

Jeffrey A. Kaufmann
Muscatine Community College

David O. Kieft
University of Minnesota

Patricia Killen
Pacific Lutheran University

William E. Kinsella Jr.
Northern Virginia Community College–Annandale

James M. Kittelson
Ohio State University

Doug Klepper
Santa Fe Community College

Cynthia Kosso
Northern Arizona University

Clayton Miles Lehmann
University of South Dakota

Diana Chen Lin
Indiana University, Northwest

Ursula W. MacAffer
Hudson Valley Community College

Harold Marcuse
University of California–Santa Barbara

Mavis Mate
University of Oregon

T. Ronald Melton
Brewton Parker College

Jack Allen Meyer
University of South Carolina

Eugene W. Miller Jr.
The Pennsylvania State University–Hazleton

David Mock
Tallahassee Community College

John Patrick Montano
University of Delaware

Rex Morrow
Trident Technical College

Thomas M. Mulhern
University of North Dakota

Pierce Mullen
Montana State University

Frederick I. Murphy
Western Kentucky University

William M. Murray
University of South Florida

Otto M. Nelson
Texas Tech University

Sam Nelson
Willmar Community College

John A. Nichols
Slippery Rock University

Lisa Nofzinger
Albuquerque Technical Vocational Institute

Chris Oldstone-Moore
Augustana College

Donald Ostrowski
Harvard University

James O. Overfield
University of Vermont

Matthew L. Panczyk
Bergen Community College

Kathleen Parrow
Black Hills State University

Carla Rahn Phillips
University of Minnesota

Keith Pickus
Wichita State University

Linda J. Piper
University of Georgia

Janet Polasky
University of New Hampshire

Thomas W. Porter
Randolph-Macon College

Charles A. Povlovich
California State University–Fullerton

Nancy Rachels
Hillsborough CommunityCollege

Charles Rearick
University of Massachusetts–Amherst

Jerome V. Reel Jr.
Clemson University

Paul Reuter
Jefferson State Community College

Joseph Robertson
Gadsden State Community College

Jonathan Roth
San Jose State University

Constance M. Rousseau
Providence College

Julius R. Ruff
Marquette University

Richard Saller
University of Chicago

Magdalena Sanchez
Texas Christian University

Jack Schanfield
Suffolk County Community College

Roger Schlesinger
Washington State University

Joanne Schneider
Rhode Island College

Thomas C. Schunk
University of Wisconsin–Oshkosh

Denise Scifres
Hinds Community College

Kyle C. Sessions
Illinois State University

Linda Simmons
Northern Virginia Community College–Manassas

Donald V. Sippel
Rhode Island College

Glen Spann
Asbury College

John W. Steinberg
Georgia Southern University

Paul W. Strait
Florida State University

James E. Straukamp
California State University–Sacramento

Brian E. Strayer
Andrews University

Fred Suppe
Ball State University

Roger Tate
Somerset Community College

Tom Taylor
Seattle University

Jack W. Thacker
Western Kentucky University

David S. Trask
Guilford Technical Community College

Thomas Turley
Santa Clara University

John G. Tuthill
University of Guam

Maarten Ultee
University of Alabama

Donna L. Van Raaphorst
Cuyahoga Community College

Allen M. Ward
University of Connecticut

Richard D. Weigel
Western Kentucky University

Michael Weiss
Linn-Benton Community College

Richard S. Williams
Washington State University

Arthur H. Williamson
California State University–Sacramento

Katherine Workman
Wright State University

Judith T. Wozniak
Cleveland State University

Walter J. Wussow
University of Wisconsin–Eau Claire

Edwin M. Yamauchi
Miami University

The following individuals contributed suggestions for the fourth edition:

Robert L. Bergman
Glendale Community College

Michael Clinton
Gwynedd Mercy College

Caitlin Corning
George Fox University

Marion F. Deshmukh
George Mason University

Laura Dull
Delta College

Eve Fisher
South Dakota State University

Lucien Frary
Rider University

Derek Hastings
Oakland University

David R. C. Hudson
Texas A&M University

George Kaloudis
Rivier College

Mark Klobas
Scottsdale Community College

Anthony Makowski
Delaware County Community College

Tom Maulucci
State University of New York–Fredonia

David Mock
Tallahassee Community College

Heather O'Grady-Evans
Elmira College

Jonathan Perry
University of Central Florida

Bonnie F. Saunders
Glendale Community College

Richard Schellhammer
University of West Alabama

Colleen M. Shaughnessy Zeena
Endicott College

Douglas R. Skopp
State University of New York–Plattsburgh

Ruth Suyama
Los Angeles Mission College

Janet A. Thompson
Tallahassee Community College

Thomas Turley
Santa Clara University

Nancy G. Vavra
University of Colorado–Boulder

The editors at Thomson Wadsworth have been both helpful and congenial at all times. I especially wish to thank Clark Baxter, whose clever wit, wisdom, gentle prodding, and good friendship have added much depth to our working relationship. Margaret Beasley thoughtfully, wisely, efficiently, and pleasantly guided the overall development of the fourth edition. I also want to express my gratitude to Jon Peck, of Dovetail Publishing Services, whose good humor, well-advised suggestions, and generous verbal support made the production process such a delight. Bruce Emmer, an outstanding copyeditor, taught me much about the fine points of the English language. Abbie Baxter provided valuable assistance in obtaining permissions for the illustrations and also made superb suggestions for new illustrations.

Above all, I thank my family for their support. The gifts of love, laughter, and patience from my daughters, Jennifer and Kathryn; my sons, Eric and Christian; my daughters-in-law, Liz and Laurie; and my son-in-law, Daniel, were enormously appreciated. My wife and best friend, Diane, contributed editorial assistance, wise counsel, good humor, and the loving support that made it possible for me to accomplish a project of this magnitude. I could not have written the book without her.

INTRODUCTION TO
STUDENTS OF WESTERN CIVILIZATION

*C*ivilization, as historians define it, first emerged between five and six thousand years ago when people in different parts of the world began to live in organized communities with distinct political, military, economic, and social structures. Religious, intellectual, and artistic activities assumed important roles in these early societies. The focus of this book is on Western civilization, a civilization that many people identify with the continent of Europe.

Defining Western Civilization

Western civilization itself has evolved considerably over the centuries. Most historians trace the origins of Western civilization to the classical world of Rome and Greece and even farther back to the Mediterranean basin, including lands in North Africa and the Middle East. Nevertheless, people in these civilizations viewed themselves as subjects of states or empires, not as members of Western civilization. Later, with the rise of Christianity, peoples in Europe began to identify themselves as part of a civilization different from others, such as that of Islam, leading to a concept of a Western civilization different from other civilizations. In the fifteenth century, Renaissance intellectuals began to identify this civilization not only with Christianity but also with the intellectual and political achievements of the ancient Greeks and Romans.

Important to the development of the idea of a distinct Western civilization were encounters with other peoples. Between 700 and 1500, encounters with the world of Islam helped define the West. But after 1500, as European ships began to move into other parts of the world, encounters with peoples in Asia, Africa, and the Americas not only had an impact on the civilizations found there but also affected how people in the West defined themselves. At the same time, as they set up colonies, Europeans began to transplant a sense of Western identity to other areas of the world, especially North America and parts of Latin America, that have come to be considered part of Western civilization.

As the concept of Western civilization has evolved over the centuries, so have the values and unique features associated with that civilization. Science played a crucial role in the development of modern Western civilization. The societies of the Greeks, the Romans, and the medieval Europeans were based largely on a belief in the existence of a spiritual order; a dramatic departure to a natural or material view of the universe occurred in the seventeenth-century Scientific Revolution. Science and technology have been important in the growth of today's modern and largely secular Western civilization, although antecedents to scientific development also existed in Greek and medieval thought and practice, and spirituality remains a component of the Western world today.

Many historians have viewed the concept of political liberty, belief in the fundamental value of every individual, and a rational outlook based on a system of logical, analytical thought as unique aspects of Western civilization. Of course, the West has also witnessed horrendous negations of liberty, individualism, and reason. Racism, slavery, violence, world wars, totalitarian regimes—these, too, form part of the complex story of what constitutes Western civilization.

The Dating of Time

In our examination of Western civilization, we need also to be aware of the dating of time. In recording the past, historians try to determine the exact time when events occurred. World War II in Europe, for example, began on September 1, 1939, when Hitler sent German troops into Poland, and ended on May 7, 1945, when Germany surrendered. By using dates, historians can place events in order and try to determine the development of patterns over periods of time.

If someone asked you when you were born, you would reply with a number, such as 1987. In the United States, we would all accept that number without question because it is part of the dating system followed in the Western world (Europe and the Western Hemisphere). In this system, events are dated by counting backward or forward from the birth of Jesus Christ (assumed to be the year 1). An event that took place four hundred years before the birth of Jesus would be dated 400 B.C. (before Christ). Dates after the birth of Jesus are labeled A.D. These letters stand for the Latin words *anno Domini,* which mean "in the year of the Lord." Thus an event that took place two hundred years after the birth of Jesus is written A.D. 200, or "in the year of the Lord 200." It can also be written as 200, just as you would not give your birth year as A.D. 1987 but simply as 1987. Historians also make use of other terms to refer to time. A decade is ten years, a century is one hundred years, and a millennium is one thousand years. Thus "the fourth century B.C." refers to the fourth period of one hundred years counting backward from 1, the assumed date of the birth of Jesus. Since the first century B.C. would be the years 100 B.C. to 1 B.C., the fourth century B.C. would be the years 400 B.C. to 301 B.C. We could say, then, that an event in 350 B.C. took place in the fourth century B.C.

"The fourth century A.D." refers to the fourth period of one hundred years after the birth of Jesus. Since the first period of one hundred years would be the years 1 to 100, the fourth period or fourth century would be the years 301 to 400. We could say, then, that an event in 350 took place in the fourth century. Likewise, the first millennium B.C. refers to the years 1000 B.C. to 1 B.C.; the second millennium A.D. refers to the years 1001 to 2000. Some historians now prefer to use the abbreviations B.C.E. ("before the Common Era") and C.E. ("Common Era") instead of B.C. and A.D. This is especially true of world historians, who prefer to use symbols that are not so Western- or Christian-oriented. The dates, of course, remain the same. Thus 1950 B.C.E. and 1950 B.C. would be the same year. In keeping with current usage by many historians of Western civilization, this book uses the notations B.C. and A.D.

The dating of events can also vary from people to people. Most people in the Western world use the Western calendar, also known as the Gregorian calendar after Pope Gregory XIII, who refined it in 1582. The Hebrew calendar uses a different system in which the year 1 is the equivalent of the Western year 3760 B.C., considered to be the date of the creation of the world according to the Bible. Thus the Western year 2006 is the year 5766 on the Hebrew calendar. The Islamic calendar begins year 1 on the day Muhammad fled Mecca, which is the year 622 on the Western calendar.

THE ANCIENT NEAR EAST: THE FIRST CIVILIZATIONS

Ruins of the ancient Sumerian city of Uruk

© Nik Wheeler / CORBIS

$\mathcal{I}$N 1849, A DARING YOUNG Englishman made a hazardous journey into the deserts and swamps of southern Iraq. Moving south down the banks of the Euphrates River while braving high winds and temperatures that reached 120 degrees Fahrenheit, William Loftus led a small expedition in search of the roots of civilization. As he said, "From our childhood we have been led to regard this place as the cradle of the human race."

Guided by native Arabs into the southernmost reaches of Iraq, Loftus and his small group of explorers were soon overwhelmed by what they saw. He wrote, "I know of nothing more exciting or impressive than the first sight of one of these great piles, looming in solitary grandeur from the surrounding plains and marshes." One of these piles, known to the natives as the mound of Warka, contained the ruins of Uruk, one of the first cities in the world and part of the world's first civilization.

Southern Iraq, known to ancient peoples as Mesopotamia, was one area in the world where civilization began. Western civilization can be traced back to the ancient Near East, where people in Mesopotamia and Egypt developed organized societies and created the ideas and institutions that we associate with civilization. The later Greeks and

Romans, who played such a crucial role in the development of Western civilization, were themselves nourished and influenced by these older societies in the Near East. It is appropriate, therefore, to begin our story of Western civilization in the ancient Near East with the early civilizations of Mesopotamia and Egypt. Before considering them, however, we must briefly examine prehistory and observe how human beings made the shift from hunting and gathering to agricultural communities and ultimately to cities and civilization.◆

The First Humans

Historians rely primarily on documents to create their pictures of the past, but no written records exist for the prehistory of humankind. In their absence, the story of early humanity depends on archaeological and, more recently, biological information, which anthropologists and archaeologists use to formulate theories about our early past.

The earliest humanlike creatures—known as hominids—existed in Africa as long as three to four million years ago. Known as Australopithecines, they flourished in East and South Africa and were the first hominids to make simple stone tools.

A second stage in early human development occurred around 1.5 million years ago when HOMO ERECTUS ("upright human being") emerged. *Homo erectus* made use of larger and more varied tools and was the first hominid to leave Africa and to move into both Europe and Asia.

Around 250,000 years ago, a third and crucial stage in human development began with the emergence of *Homo sapiens* ("wise human being"). By 100,000 B.C., two groups of *Homo sapiens* had developed. One type was the Neanderthal, whose remains were first found in the Neander valley in Germany. Neanderthal remains have since been found in both Europe and the Middle East and have been dated to between 100,000 and 30,000 B.C. Neanderthals relied on a variety of stone tools and were the first early people to bury their dead.

The first analtomically modern humans, known as *Homo sapiens sapiens* ("wise, wise human being"), appeared in Africa between 200,000 and 150,000 years ago. Recent evidence indicates that they began to spread outside Africa around 70,000 years ago. Map 1.1 shows probable dates for different movements, although many of these are still controversial. By 30,000 B.C., *Homo sapiens sapiens* had replaced the Neanderthals, who had largely become extinct, and by 10,000 B.C., members of the *Homo sapiens sapiens* species could be found throughout the world. By that time, it was the only human species left. All humans today, be they Europeans, Australian aborigines, or Africans, belong to the same subspecies.

The Hunter-Gatherers of the Old Stone Age

One of the basic distinguishing features of the human species is the ability to make tools. The earliest tools were made of stone, and the term **Paleolithic** (Greek for "old stone") **Age** is used to designate this early period of human history (c. 2,500,000–10,000 B.C.).

For hundreds of thousands of years, humans relied on hunting and gathering for their daily food. Paleolithic peoples had a close relationship with the world around them, and over a period of time, they came to know which animals to hunt and which plants to eat. They did not know how to grow crops or raise animals, however. They gathered wild nuts, berries, fruits, and a variety of wild grains and green plants. Around the world, they hunted and consumed different animals, including buffalo, horses, bison, wild goats, and reindeer. In coastal areas, fish were a rich source of nourishment.

The hunting of animals and the gathering of wild plants no doubt led to certain patterns of living. Archaeologists and anthropologists have speculated that Paleolithic people lived in small bands of twenty to thirty. They were nomadic, moving from place to place to follow animal migrations and vegetation cycles. Hunting depended on careful observation of animal behavior patterns and required a group effort for success. Over the years, tools became more refined and more useful. The invention of the spear, and later the bow and arrow, made hunting considerably easier. Harpoons and fishhooks made of bone increased the catch of fish.

Both men and women were responsible for finding food—the chief work of Paleolithic people. Since women bore and raised the children, they generally stayed close to the camps, but they played an important role in acquiring food by gathering berries, nuts, and grains. Men hunted wild animals, an activity that took them far from camp. Because both men and women played important roles in providing for the band's survival, scientists believe that a rough equality existed between men and women. Indeed, some speculate that both men and women made the decisions that affected the activities of the Paleolithic band.

Some groups of Paleolithic peoples, especially those who lived in cold climates, found shelter in caves. Over time, they created new types of shelter as well. Perhaps the most common was a simple structure of wood poles or sticks covered with animal hides. The systematic use of fire, which archaeologists believe began around 500,000 years ago, made it possible for the caves and human-made structures to have a source of light and

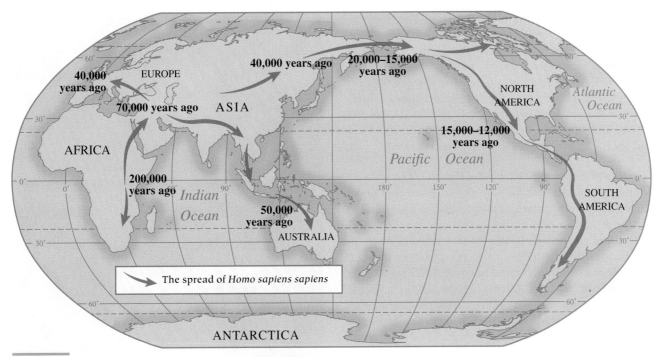

MAP 1.1 **The Spread of *Homo sapiens sapiens*.** *Homo sapiens sapiens* spread from Africa beginning about 70,000 years ago. Living and traveling in small groups, these anatomically modern humans were hunter-gatherers. Although groups of people advanced beyond their old hunting grounds at a rate of only 2 or 3 miles per generation, this was enough to populate the world in tens of thousands of years. **?** Given that some diffusion of humans occurred during ice ages, how would such climate change affect humans and their movements, especially from Asia to Australia and Asia to North America? View an animated version of this map or related maps at http://thomsonedu.com/history/spielvogel

heat. Fire also enabled early humans to cook their food, making it taste better, last longer, and in the case of some plants, such as wild grain, easier to chew and digest.

The making of tools and the use of fire—two important technological innovations of Paleolithic peoples—remind us how crucial the ability to adapt was to human survival. But Paleolithic peoples did more than just survive. The cave paintings of large animals found in southwestern France and northern Spain bear witness to the cultural activity of Paleolithic peoples. A cave discovered in southern France in 1994 (known as the Chauvet Cave, after the leader of the expedition that found it) contains more than three hundred paintings of lions, oxen, owls, panthers, and other animals. Most of these are animals that Paleolithic people did not hunt, which suggests to some scholars that the paintings were made for religious or even decorative purposes. The discoverers were overwhelmed by what they saw: "There was a moment of ecstasy. . . . They overflowed with joy and emotion. . . . These were moments of indescribable madness."[1]

The Neolithic Revolution (c. 10,000–4000 B.C.)

The end of the last ice age around 10,000 B.C. was followed by what is called the **Neolithic Revolution**, a significant change in living patterns that occurred in the New Stone Age (*Neolithic* is Greek for "new stone"). The name New Stone Age is misleading, however. Although Neolithic peoples made a new type of polished stone ax, this was not the major change that occurred after 10,000 B.C.

An Agricultural Revolution The biggest change was the shift from hunting animals and gathering plants for sustenance to producing food by systematic agriculture. The planting of grains and vegetables provided a regular supply of food, while the taming of animals, such as sheep, goats, cattle, and pigs, added a steady source of meat, milk, and fibers such as wool for clothing. Larger animals could also be used as beasts of burden. The growing of crops and the taming of food-producing animals created a new relationship between humans and nature. Historians speak of this as an agricultural revolution. Revolutionary change is dramatic and requires great effort, but the ability to acquire food on a regular basis gave humans greater control over their environment. It also allowed them to give up their nomadic ways of life and begin to live in settled communities.

Systematic agriculture probably developed independently between 8000 and 7000 B.C. in various parts of the world. Different plants were cultivated in each: wheat, barley, and lentils in the Near East; rice and millet in southern Asia; millet and yams in western Africa; and beans, potatoes, and corn in the Americas. The Neolithic agricultural revolution needed a favorable environment. In the Near East, the upland areas above the Fertile Crescent (present-day northern Iraq and southern Turkey) were more conducive to systematic farming than the river valleys. This region received the necessary rainfall and was the home of two wild plant species (barley and wheat) and four wild animal species (pigs, cows, goats, and sheep) that humans eventually domesticated.

Consequences of the Neolithic Revolution The growing of crops on a regular basis gave rise to more permanent settlements, which historians refer to as Neolithic farming villages or towns. One of the oldest and most extensive agricultural villages was Çatal Hüyük, located in modern-day Turkey. Its walls enclosed 32 acres, and its population probably reached six thousand inhabitants during its high point from 6700 to 5700 B.C. People lived in simple mudbrick houses that were built so close to one another that there were few streets. To get to their homes, people had to walk along the rooftops and then enter the house through a hole in the roof.

Archaeologists have discovered twelve cultivated products in Çatal Hüyük, including fruits, nuts, and three kinds of wheat. Artisans made weapons and jewelry that were traded with neighboring people. Religious shrines housing figures of gods and goddesses have been found at Çatal Hüyük, as have a number of female statuettes. Molded with noticeably large breasts and buttocks, these "earth mothers" perhaps symbolically represented the fertility of both "mother earth" and human mothers. The shrines and the statues point to the role of religion in the lives of these Neolithic peoples.

The Neolithic Revolution had far-reaching consequences. Once people settled in villages or towns, they built permanent houses for protection and other structures for the storage of goods. As organized communities stockpiled food and accumulated material goods, they began to engage in trade. People also began to specialize in certain crafts, and a division of labor developed. Pottery was made from clay and baked in a fire to make it hard. The pots were used for cooking and to store grains. Woven baskets were also used for storage. Stone tools became refined as flint blades were employed to make sickles and hoes for use in the fields. In the course of the Neolithic Age, many of the food plants still in use today began to be cultivated. Moreover, fibers from plants such as flax were used to make thread that was woven into cloth.

The change to systematic agriculture in the Neolithic Age also had consequences for the relationship between men and women. Men assumed the primary responsibility for working in the fields and herding animals, jobs that kept them away from the home. Although women also worked in the fields, many remained behind to care for the children, weave clothes, and perform other tasks that required labor close to home. In time, as work outside the home was increasingly perceived as more

Statue from Ain Ghazal. This life-size statue made of plaster, sand, and crushed chalk dating from 6500 B.C. was discovered in 1984 in Ain Ghazal, an archaeological site near Amman, Jordan. It is among the oldest known statues of the human figure. Although it appears lifelike, its features are considered generic rather than a portrait of an individual face. The purpose and meaning of this sculpture may never be known.

important than work done at home, men came to play the more dominant role in society, a basic pattern that would persist until our own times.

Other patterns set in the Neolithic Age also proved to be enduring elements of human history. Fixed dwellings, domesticated animals, regular farming, a division of labor, men holding power—all of these are part of the human story. For all of our modern scientific and technological progress, human survival still depends on the growing and storing of food, an accomplishment of people in the Neolithic Age. The Neolithic Revolution was truly a turning point in human history.

New Developments Between 4000 and 3000 B.C., significant technical developments began to transform the Neolithic towns. The invention of writing enabled records to be kept, and the use of metals marked a new level of human control over the environment and its resources. Already before 4000 B.C., craftspeople had discovered that certain rocks could be heated to liquefy metals embedded in them. The metals could then be cast in molds to produce tools and weapons that were more refined than stone instruments. Although copper was the first metal to be made into tools, after 4000 B.C., craftspeople in western Asia discovered that combining copper and tin created bronze, a much harder and more durable metal than copper. Its widespread use has led historians to call the period from around 3000 to 1200 B.C. the **Bronze Age**; thereafter, bronze was increasingly replaced by iron.

At first, Neolithic settlements were mere villages. But as their inhabitants mastered the art of farming, more complex human societies began to emerge. As wealth increased, these societies began to develop armies and to build walled towns and cities. By the beginning of the Bronze Age, the concentration of larger numbers of people in the river valleys of Mesopotamia and Egypt was leading to a whole new pattern for human life.

The Emergence of Civilization

As we have seen, early human beings formed small groups that developed a simple culture that enabled them to survive. As human societies grew and developed greater complexity, a new form of human existence—called *civilization*—came into being. A **civilization** is a complex culture in which large numbers of human beings share a number of common elements. Historians have identified a number of basic characteristics of civilization. These include (1) an urban focus: cities became the centers of political, economic, social, cultural, and religious development; (2) a distinct religious structure: the gods were deemed crucial to the community's success, and professional priestly classes regulated relations with the gods; (3) new political and military structures: an organized government bureaucracy arose to meet the administrative demands of the growing population, and armies were organized to gain land and power; (4) a new social structure based on economic power: while kings and an upper class of priests, political leaders, and warriors dominated, there also existed a large group of free men (farmers, artisans, craftspeople) and at the very bottom, socially, a class of slaves; (5) the development of writing: kings, priests, merchants, and artisans used writing to keep records; and (6) new forms of significant artistic and intellectual activity: for example, monumental architectural structures, usually religious, occupied a prominent place in urban environments.

The civilizations that developed in Mesopotamia and Egypt, the forerunners of Western civilization, will be examined in detail in this chapter. But civilization also developed independently in other parts of the world. Between 3000 and 1500 B.C., the valleys of the Indus River in India supported a flourishing civilization that extended hundreds of miles from the Himalayas to the coast of the Arabian Sea. Two major cities, Harappa and Mohenjo-Daro, were at the heart of this South Asian civilization. Many written records of the Indus valley civilization exist, but their language has not yet been deciphered. This Indus valley civilization carried on extensive trade with cities in Mesopotamia.

Harappa and Mohenjo-Daro

Another river valley civilization emerged along the Yellow River in northern China about 4,000 years ago. Under the Shang dynasty of kings, which ruled from 1750 to 1122 B.C., this civilization contained impressive cities with huge city walls, royal palaces, and large royal tombs. A system of irrigation enabled this early Chinese civilization to maintain a prosperous farming society ruled by an aristocratic class whose major concern was war.

The Yellow River, China

Scholars have believed for a long time that civilization emerged only in four areas, in the fertile river valleys of the Tigris and Euphrates, the Nile, the Indus, and the Yellow River—that is, in Mesopotamia, Egypt, India, and China. Recently, however, archaeologists have discovered two other early civilizations. One of these flourished in Central Asia (in what are now the republics of Turkmenistan and Uzbekistan)

Central Asian Civilization

around 4,000 years ago. People in this civilization built mudbrick buildings, raised sheep and goats, had bronze tools, used a system of irrigation to grow wheat and barley, and had a writing system.

Another early civilization was discovered in the Supe River valley of Peru. At the center of this civilization was

Caral, Peru

the city of Caral, which flourished around 2600 B.C. It contained buildings for officials, apartment buildings, and grand residences, all built of stone. The inhabitants of Caral also developed a system of irrigation by diverting a river more than a mile upstream into their fields.

Why early civilizations developed remains difficult to explain. One theory maintains that challenges forced human beings to make efforts that resulted in the rise of civilization. Some scholars have argued that material forces, such as the growth of food surpluses, made possible the specialization of labor and development of large communities with bureaucratic organization. But the area of the Fertile Crescent (see Map 1.2), in which Mesopotamian civilization emerged, was not naturally conducive to agriculture. Abundant food could be produced only with a massive human effort to manage the water, an undertaking that required organization and led to civilized societies. Other historians have argued that nonmaterial forces, primarily religious, provided the sense of unity and purpose that made such organized living possible. And some scholars doubt that we will ever discover the actual causes of early civilization.

Civilization in Mesopotamia

The Greeks spoke of the valley between the Tigris and Euphrates rivers as Mesopotamia, the "land between the rivers." The region receives little rain, but the soil of the plain of southern Mesopotamia was enlarged and enriched over the years by layers of silt deposited by the rivers. In late spring, the Tigris and Euphrates overflow their banks and deposit their fertile silt, but since this flooding depends on the melting of snows in the upland mountains where the rivers begin, it is irregular and sometimes catastrophic. In such circumstances, farming could be accomplished only with human intervention in the form of irrigation and drainage ditches. A complex system was required to control the flow of the rivers and produce the crops. Large-scale irrigation made possible the expansion of agriculture in this region, and the abundant food provided the material base for the emergence of civilization in Mesopotamia.

The City-States of Ancient Mesopotamia

The creators of Mesopotamian civilization were the Sumerians, a people whose origins remain unclear. By 3000

B.C., they had established a number of independent cities in southern Mesopotamia, including Eridu, Ur, Uruk, Umma, and Lagash. As cities expanded in size, they came to exercise political and economic control over the surrounding countryside, forming city-states. These city-states were the basic units of Sumerian civilization.

Sumerian Cities Sumerian cities were surrounded by walls. Uruk, for example, occupied an area of approximately 1,000 acres encircled by a wall 6 miles long with defense towers located every 30 to 35 feet along the wall. City dwellings, built of sun-dried bricks, included both the small flats of peasants and the larger dwellings of the civic and priestly officials. Although Mesopotamia had little stone or wood for building purposes, it did have plenty of mud. Mudbricks, easily shaped by hand, were left to bake in the hot sun until they were hard enough to use for building. People in Mesopotamia were remarkably inventive with mudbricks, constructing some of the largest brick buildings in the world.

The most prominent building in a Sumerian city was the temple, which was dedicated to the chief god or goddess of the city and often built atop a massive stepped tower called a **ziggurat**. The Sumerians believed that gods and goddesses owned the cities, and much wealth was used to build temples as well as elaborate houses for the priests and priestesses who served the gods. Priests and priestesses, who supervised the temples and their property, had great power. The temples owned much of the city land and livestock and served not only as the physical center of the city but also its economic and political center. In fact, historians believe that in the early stages of the city-states, priests and priestesses played an important role in ruling. The Sumerians believed that the gods ruled the cities, making the state a theocracy (government by a divine authority). Eventually, however, ruling power was shared with worldly figures known as kings.

Kingship Sumerians viewed kingship as divine in origin; they believed kings derived their power from the gods and were the agents of the gods. As one person said in a petition to his king: "You in your judgment, you are the son of Anu [god of the sky]; your commands, like the word of a god, cannot be reversed; your words, like rain pouring down from heaven, are without number."[2] Regardless of their origins, kings had power—they led armies, initiated legislation, supervised the building of public works, provided courts, and organized workers for the irrigation projects on which Mesopotamian agriculture depended. The army, the government bureaucracy, and the priests and priestesses all aided the kings in their rule.

Economy and Society The economy of the Sumerian city-states was primarily agricultural, but commerce and industry became important as well. The people of

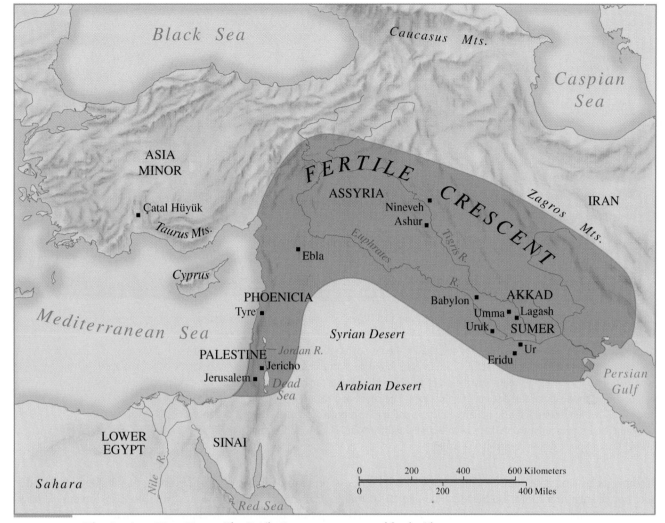

MAP 1.2 **The Ancient Near East.** The Fertile Crescent encompassed land with access to water. Employing flood management and irrigation systems, the peoples of the region established civilizations based on agriculture. These civilizations developed writing, law codes, and economic specialization. ❓ What geographical aspects of the Mesopotamian city-states made conflict between them likely? 🌎 **View an animated version of this map or related maps at** http://thomsonedu.com/history/spielvogel

Mesopotamia produced woolen textiles, pottery, and metalwork. Foreign trade, which was primarily a royal monopoly, could be extensive. Royal officials imported luxury items, such as copper and tin, aromatic woods, and fruit trees, in exchange for dried fish, wool, barley, wheat, and goods produced by Mesopotamian metalworkers. Traders traveled by land to the Mediterranean in the west and by sea to India in the east. The invention of the wheel around 3000 B.C. led to carts with wheels that made the transport of goods easier.

Sumerian city-states contained three major social groups: nobles, commoners, and slaves. Nobles included royal and priestly officials and their families. Commoners included the nobles' clients who worked for the palace and temple estates and other free citizens who worked as farmers, merchants, fishers, scribes, and craftspeople. At least 90 percent of the population were farmers. They

could exchange their crops for the goods of the artisans in town markets. Slaves belonged to palace officials, who used them mostly in building projects; temple officials, who used mostly female slaves to weave cloth and grind grain; and rich landowners, who used them for farming and domestic work.

Empires in Ancient Mesopotamia

As the number of Sumerian city-states grew and the states expanded, conflicts arose as city-state fought city-state for control of land and water. The fortunes of various city-states rose and fell over the centuries. The constant wars, with their burning and sacking of cities, left many Sumerians in deep despair, as is evident in the words of this Sumerian poem from the city of Ur: "Ur is destroyed,

The "Royal Standard" of Ur. This detail is from the "Royal Standard" of Ur, a box dating from around 2700 B.C. that was discovered in a stone tomb from the royal cemetery of the Sumerian city-state of Ur. The scenes on one side of the box depict the activities of the king and his military forces. Shown in the bottom panel are four Sumerian battle chariots. Each chariot held two men, one who held the reins and the other armed with a spear for combat. A special compartment in the chariot held a number of spears. The charging chariots are seen defeating the enemy. In the middle band, the Sumerian soldiers round up the captured enemies. In the top band, the captives are presented to the king, who has alighted from his chariot and is shown standing above all the others in the center of the panel.

bitter is its lament. The country's blood now fills its holes like hot bronze in a mold. Bodies dissolve like fat in the sun. Our temple is destroyed; the gods have abandoned us, like migrating birds. Smoke lies on our city like a shroud."

Located on the flat land of Mesopotamia, the Sumerian city-states were also open to invasion. To the north of the Sumerian city-states lived the Akkadians. We call them a Semitic people because of the type of language they spoke (see Table 1.1). Around 2340 B.C., Sargon, leader of the Akkadians, overran the Sumerian city-states and established an empire that included most of Mesopotamia as well as lands westward to the Mediterranean. But the Akkadian empire eventually disintegrated, and its end by 2100 B.C. brought a return to the system of warring city-states until Ur-Nammu of Ur succeeded in reunifying most of Mesopotamia. But this final flowering of Sumerian

culture collapsed with the coming of the Amorites. Under Hammurabi, the Amorites, or Old Babylonians, a large group of Semitic-speaking seminomads, created a new empire.

Hammurabi (1792–1750 B.C.) employed a well-disciplined army of foot soldiers who carried axes, spears, and copper or bronze daggers. He learned to divide his opponents and subdue them one by one. Using such methods, he gained control of Sumer and Akkad and reunified Mesopotamia almost to the old borders created by Sargon of Akkad. After his conquests, he called himself "the sun of Babylon, the king who has made the four quarters of the world subservient," and established a new capital at Babylon, north of Akkad. He also built temples, defensive walls, and irrigation canals; encouraged trade; and brought about an economic revival. Indeed, Hammurabi saw himself as a shepherd to his people: "I am indeed the shepherd who brings

Hammurabi's Empire

TABLE 1.1	**Some Semitic Languages**
Akkadian	Canaanitic
Arabic	Hebrew
Aramaic	Phoenician
Assyrian	Syriac
Babylonian	

NOTE: Languages in italic type are no longer spoken.

THE CODE OF HAMMURABI

*ammurabi's is the most complete Mesopotamian law code, although not the earliest. It was inscribed on a stone stele topped by a bas-relief picturing Hammurabi receiving the inspiration for the law code from the sun god Shamash, who was also the god of justice. The law code emphasizes the principle of an eye for an eye and punishments that vary according to social status. Punishments could be severe. The following examples illustrate these concerns.

The Code of Hammurabi

25. If fire broke out in a free man's house and a free man, who went to extinguish it, cast his eye on the goods of the owner of the house and has appropriated the goods of the owner of the house, that free man shall be thrown into that fire.

129. If the wife of a free man has been caught while lying with another man, they shall bind them and throw them into the water. If the husband of the woman wishes to spare his wife, then the king in turn may spare his subject.

131. If a free man's wife was accused by her husband, but she was not caught while lying with another man, she shall make affirmation by god and return to her house.

196. If a free man has destroyed the eye of a member of the aristocracy, they shall destroy his eye.

198. If he has destroyed the eye of a commoner or broken the bone of a commoner, he shall pay one mina of silver.

199. If he has destroyed the eye of a free man's slave or broken the bone of a free man's slave, he shall pay one-half his value.

209. If a free man struck another free man's daughter and has caused her to have a miscarriage, he shall pay ten shekels of silver for her fetus.

210. If that woman has died, they shall put his daughter to death.

211. If by a blow he has caused a commoner's daughter to have a miscarriage, he shall pay five shekels of silver.

212. If that woman has died, he shall pay one-half mina of silver.

213. If he struck a free man's female slave and has caused her to have a miscarriage, he shall pay two shekels of silver.

214. If that female slave has died, he shall pay one-third mina of silver.

What do these points of law from the Code of Hammurabi reveal to you about Mesopotamian society?

peace, whose scepter is just. My benevolent shade was spread over my city. I held the people of the lands of Sumer and Akkad safely on my lap."[3] Hammurabi left his dynasty strong enough that it survived until the 1550s B.C. when the Kassites from the northeast took over.

The Code of Hammurabi Hammurabi is best remembered for his law code, a collection of 282 laws. For centuries, laws had regulated people's relationships with one another in the lands of Mesopotamia, but only fragments of these earlier codes survive. Although many scholars today view Hammurabi's collection less as a code of laws and more as the attempt of Hammurabi to portray himself as the source of justice to the people, the code still gives us a glimpse of the Babylonian society of his time (see the box above).

The Code of Hammurabi reveals a society with a system of strict justice. Penalties for criminal offenses were severe and varied according to the social class of the victim. A crime against a member of the upper class (a noble) was punished more severely than the same offense against a member of the lower class. Moreover, the principle of "an eye for an eye, a tooth for a tooth" was fundamental to this system of justice. This meant that punishments should fit the crime: "If a freeman has destroyed the eye of a member of the aristocracy, they shall destroy his eye." Hammurabi's code also had an

impact on legal ideas in southwestern Asia for hundreds of years, as the following verse from the Hebrew Bible demonstrates: "If anyone injures his neighbor, whatever he has done must be done to him: fracture for fracture, eye for eye, tooth for tooth. As he has injured the other, so he is to be injured" (Leviticus 24:19–20).

Hammurabi's code took the responsibilities of public officials very seriously. The governor of an area and city officials were expected to catch burglars. If they failed to do so, the officials in the district where the crime was committed had to replace the lost property. If murderers were not found, the officials had to pay a fine to the relatives of the murdered person.

The law code also furthered the proper performance of work with what amounted to consumer protection laws. Builders were held responsible for the buildings they constructed. If a house collapsed and caused the death of the owner, the builder was put to death. If the collapse caused the death of the son of the owner, the son of the builder was put to death. If goods were destroyed by the collapse, they had to be replaced and the house itself reconstructed at the builder's expense.

The largest number of laws in the Code of Hammurabi focused on marriage and the family. Parents arranged marriages for their children. After marriage, the parties involved signed a marriage contract; without it, no one was considered legally married. The husband provided a bridal payment, and the woman's parents were responsible for a dowry to the new husband.

As in many patriarchal societies, women had far fewer privileges and rights in marriage than men. A woman's place was in the home, and failure to fulfill her expected duties was grounds for divorce. If she was not able to bear children, her husband could divorce her, but he did have to return the dowry to her family. If his wife tried to leave home to engage in business, thus neglecting her house, her husband could divorce her and did not have to repay the dowry. Furthermore, a wife who was a "gadabout, . . . neglecting her house [and] humiliating her husband," could be drowned. We do know that in practice not all women remained at home. Some worked in the fields and others in business, where they were especially prominent in the running of taverns.

Women were guaranteed some rights, however. If a woman was divorced without good reason, she received the dowry back. A woman could seek divorce and get her dowry back if her husband was unable to show that she had done anything wrong. In theory, a wife was guaranteed use of her husband's property in the event of his death. The mother could also decide which of her sons would receive an inheritance.

Sexual relations were strictly regulated as well. Husbands, but not wives, were permitted sexual activity outside marriage. A wife and her lover caught committing adultery were pitched into the river, although if the husband pardoned his wife, the king could pardon the guilty man. Incest was strictly forbidden. If a father had incestuous relations with his daughter, he would be banished. Incest between a son and mother resulted in both being burned.

Fathers ruled their children as well as their wives. Obedience was duly expected: "If a son has struck his father, they shall cut off his hand." If a son committed a serious enough offense, his father could disinherit him, although fathers were not permitted to disinherit their sons arbitrarily.

The Culture of Mesopotamia

A spiritual worldview was of fundamental importance to Mesopotamian culture. To the peoples of Mesopotamia, the gods were living realities who affected all aspects of life. It was crucial, therefore, that the correct hierarchies be observed. Leaders could prepare armies for war, but success depended on a favorable relationship with the gods. This helps explain the importance of the priestly class and is the reason why even the kings took great care to dedicate offerings and monuments to the gods.

The Importance of Religion The Mesopotamians viewed their city-states as earthly copies of a divine model and order. Each city-state was sacred because it was linked to a god or goddess. Hence Nippur, the earliest center of Sumerian religion, was dedicated to Enlil, the

god of wind. Moreover, located at the heart of each city-state was a temple complex. Occupying several acres, this sacred area consisted of a ziggurat with a temple at the top dedicated to the god or goddess who owned the city. The temple complex was the true center of the community. The main god or goddess dwelt there symbolically in the form of a statue, and the ceremony of dedication included a ritual that linked the statue to the god or goddess and thus supposedly harnessed the power of the deity for the city's benefit. Considerable wealth was poured into the construction of temples and other buildings used for the residences of priests and priestesses who helped the gods. Although the gods literally owned the city, the temple complex used only part of the land and rented out the remainder. The temples dominated individual and commercial life, an indication of the close relationship between Mesopotamian religion and culture.

The physical environment had an obvious impact on the Mesopotamian view of the universe. Ferocious floods, heavy downpours, scorching winds, and oppressive humidity were all part of the local climate. These conditions and the resulting famines easily convinced Mesopotamians that this world was controlled by supernatural forces and that the days of human beings "are numbered; whatever he may do, he is but wind," as *The Epic of Gilgamesh* laments. In the presence of nature, Mesopotamians could easily feel helpless, as this poem relates:

> The rampant flood which no man can oppose,
> Which shakes the heavens and causes earth to tremble,
> In an appalling blanket folds mother and child,
> Beats down the canebrake's full luxuriant greenery,
> And drowns the harvest in its time of ripeness.[4]

The Mesopotamians discerned cosmic rhythms in the universe and accepted its order but perceived that it was not completely safe because of the presence of willful, powerful cosmic powers that they identified with gods and goddesses.

With its numerous gods and goddesses animating all aspects of the universe, Mesopotamian religion was **polytheistic**. The four most important deities were An, Enlil, Enki, and Ninhursaga. An was the god of the sky and hence the most important force in the universe. Since his basic essence was authority, he was also viewed as the source or active principle of all authority, including the earthly power of rulers and fathers alike. Enlil, god of wind, was considered the second greatest power of the visible universe. In charge of the wind and thus an expression of the legitimate use of force, Enlil became the symbol of the proper use of force on earth as well. Enki was god of the earth. Since the earth was the source of life-giving waters, Enki was also god of rivers, wells, and canals. More generally, he represented the waters of creativity and was responsible for inventions and crafts. Ninhursaga began as a goddess associated with soil, mountains, and vegetation. Eventually, however, she was worshiped as a mother goddess, a "mother of all children," who manifested her power by giving birth to kings and conferring the royal insignia on them.

Human beings' relationship with their gods was based on subservience since, according to Sumerian myth, human beings were created to do the manual labor the gods were unwilling to do for themselves. Moreover, humans were insecure because they could never be sure what the gods would do. But humans did make attempts to circumvent or relieve their anxiety by discovering the intentions of the gods; these efforts gave rise to the development of the arts of **divination**.

Divination took a variety of forms. A common form, at least for kings and priests who could afford it, in-volved killing animals, such as sheep or goats, and examining their livers or other organs. Supposedly, features seen in the organs of the sacrificed animals foretold events to come. One handbook predicted that if the animal organ had shape *x*, the outcome of the military campaign would be *y*. Private individuals relied on cheaper divinatory techniques. These included interpreting patterns of smoke from burning incense or the pattern formed when oil was poured into water. The Mesopotamian arts of divination arose out of the desire to discover the purposes of the gods: if people could decipher the signs that foretold events, the events would be predictable, and humans could act wisely.

The Cultivation of New Arts and Sciences The realization of writing's great potential was another aspect of Mesopotamian culture. The oldest Mesopotamian texts date to around 3000 B.C. and were written by the Sumerians, who used a **cuneiform** ("wedge-shaped") system of writing. Using a reed stylus, they made wedge-shaped impressions on clay tablets, which were then baked or dried in the sun. Once dried, these tablets were virtually indestructible, and the several hundred thousand that have been discovered have served as a valuable source of information for modern scholars. Sumerian writing evolved from pictures of physical objects to simplified and stylized signs, leading eventually to a phonetic system that made possible the written expression of abstract ideas.

Mesopotamian peoples used writing primarily for record keeping. They also produced monumental texts, documents that were intended to last forever, such as

Hervé Lewandowski/Réunion des Musées Nationaux/Art Resource, NY

The Development of Cuneiform Writing. Pictured here is the cone of Uruinimgina, an example of cuneiform writing from an early Sumerian dynasty. The inscription announces reductions in taxes. The table shows the development of writing from pictographic signs to cuneiform characters.

Courtesy Andromeda Oxford Limited, Oxford, England (Louvre, Paris)

Pictographic sign, c. 3100 B.C.									
Interpretation	star	?sun over horizon	?stream	ear of barley	bull's head	bowl	head + bowl	lower leg	?shrouded body
Cuneiform sign, c. 2400 B.C.									
Cuneiform sign c. 700 B.C. (turned through 90°)									
Phonetic value*	dingir, an	u_4, ud	a	še	gu_4	nig_2, ninda	ku_2	du, gin, gub	lu_2
Meaning	god, sky	day, sun	water, seed, son	barley	ox	food, bread	to eat	to walk, to stand	man

*Some signs have more than one phonetic value and some sounds are represented by more than one sign; for example, u_4 means the fourth sign with the value u.

THE GREAT FLOOD

The great poem of Mesopotamian literature, *The Epic of Gilgamesh,* includes an account by Utnapishtim (a Mesopotamian forerunner of the biblical Noah), who had built a ship and survived the flood unleashed by the gods to destroy humankind. This selection recounts how the god Ea advised Utnapishtim to build a boat and how he came to land his boat at the end of the flood. In this section, Utnapishtim is telling his story to Gilgamesh.

The Epic of Gilgamesh

"In those days the world teemed, the people multiplied, the world bellowed like a wild bull, and the great god was aroused by the clamor. Enlil heard the clamor and he said to the gods in council, 'The uproar of mankind is intolerable and sleep is no longer possible by reason of the babel.' So the gods agreed to exterminate mankind. Enlil did this, but Ea [Sumerian Enki, god of the waters] because of his oath warned me in a dream . . . , 'Tear down your house and build a boat, abandon possessions and look for life, despise worldly goods and save your soul alive. Tear down your house, I say, and build a boat. . . . Then take up into the boat the seed of all living creatures. . . .' [Utnapishtim did as he was told, and then the destruction came.]

"For six days and six nights the winds blew, torrent and tempest and flood overwhelmed the world, tempest and flood raged together like warring hosts. When the seventh day dawned the storm from the south subsided, the sea grew calm, the flood was stifled; I looked at the face of the world and there was silence, all mankind was turned to clay. The surface of the sea stretched as flat as a rooftop; I opened a hatch and the light fell on my face. Then I bowed low, I sat down and I wept, the tears streamed down my face, for on every side was the waste of water. I looked for land in vain, but fourteen leagues distant there appeared a mountain, and there the boat grounded; on the mountain of Nisir the boat held fast, she held fast and did not budge. . . . When the seventh day dawned I loosed a dove and let her go. She flew away, but finding no resting-place she returned. Then I loosed a swallow, and she flew away but finding no resting-place she returned. I loosed a raven, she saw that the waters had retreated, she ate, she flew around, she cawed, and she did not come back. Then I threw everything open to the four winds, I made a sacrifice and poured out a libation on the mountain top."

What does this selection from The Epic of Gilgamesh *tell you about the relationship between the Mesopotamians and their gods? How might you explain the difference between this account and the biblical flood story in Genesis?*

---

inscriptions etched in stone on statues and royal buildings. Numerous texts were prepared for teaching purposes. Schools for scribes were in operation by 2500 B.C. They were necessary because much time was needed to master the cuneiform system of writing. The primary goal of scribal education was to produce professionally trained scribes for careers in the temples and palaces, the military, and government. Pupils were male and primarily from wealthy families.

Writing was important because it enabled a society to keep records and maintain knowledge of previous practices and events. Writing also made it possible for people to communicate ideas in new ways, which is especially evident in Mesopotamian literary works. The most famous piece of Mesopotamian literature was *The Epic of Gilgamesh,* an elaborate poem that records the exploits of a legendary king of Uruk. Gilgamesh—wise, strong, and perfect in body, part man, part god—befriends a hairy beast named Enkidu. Together they set off in pursuit of heroic deeds. When Enkidu dies, Gilgamesh experiences the pain of mortality and embarks on a search for the secret of immortality. But his efforts fail (see the box above), and Gilgamesh remains mortal. The desire for immortality, one of humankind's great searches, ends in complete frustration. Everlasting life, this Mesopotamian epic makes clear, is only for the gods.

Mesopotamians also made outstanding achievements in mathematics and astronomy. In math, the Sumerians devised a number system based on 60, using combinations of 6 and 10 for practical solutions. Geometry was used to measure fields and erect buildings. In astronomy, the Sumerians made use of units of 60 and charted the heavenly constellations. Their calendar was based on twelve lunar months and was brought into harmony with the solar year by adding an extra month from time to time.

Egyptian Civilization: "The Gift of the Nile"

Although contemporaneous with Mesopotamia, civilization in Egypt evolved along somewhat different lines. Of central importance to the development of Egyptian civilization was the Nile River. That the Egyptian people recognized its significance is apparent in this Hymn to the Nile (also see the box on p. 13): "The bringer of food, rich in provisions, creator of all good, lord of majesty, sweet of fragrance. . . . He who . . . fills the magazines, makes the granaries wide, and gives things to the poor. He who makes every beloved tree to grow. . . ."[5] Egypt, like Mesopotamia, was a river valley civilization.

SIGNIFICANCE OF THE NILE RIVER AND THE PHARAOH

*T*wo of the most important sources of life for the ancient Egyptians were the Nile River and the pharaoh. Egyptians perceived that the Nile River made possible the abundant food that was a major source of their well-being. This *Hymn to the Nile*, probably from the nineteenth and twentieth dynasties in the New Kingdom, expresses the gratitude Egyptians felt for the Nile.

Hymn to the Nile

Hail to you, O Nile, that issues from the earth and comes to keep Egypt alive! . . .

He that waters the meadows which Re created, in order to keep every kid alive.

He that makes to drink the desert and the place distant from water: that is his dew coming down from heaven. . . .

The lord of fishes, he who makes the marsh-birds to go upstream. . . .

He who makes barley and brings emmer [wheat] into being, that he may make the temples festive.

If he is sluggish, then nostrils are stopped up, and everybody is poor. . . .

When he rises, then the land is in jubilation, then every belly is in joy, every backbone takes on laughter, and every tooth is exposed.

The bringer of good, rich in provisions, creator of all good, lord of majesty, sweet of fragrance. . . .

He who makes every beloved tree to grow, without lack of them.

The Egyptian king, or pharaoh, was viewed as a god and the absolute ruler of Egypt. His significance and the gratitude of the Egyptian people for his existence are evident in this hymn from the reign of Sesotris III (c. 1880–1840 B.C.).

Hymn to the Pharaoh

He has come unto us that he may carry away Upper Egypt; the double diadem [crown of Upper and Lower Egypt] has rested on his head.

He has come unto us and has united the Two Lands; he has mingled the reed with the bee [symbols of Lower and Upper Egypt].

He has come unto us and has brought the Black Land under his sway; he has apportioned to himself the Red Land.

He has come unto us and has taken the Two Lands under his protection; he has given peace to the Two Riverbanks.

He has come unto us and has made Egypt to live; he has banished its suffering.

He has come unto us and has made the people to live; he has caused the throat of the subjects to breathe. . . .

He has come unto us and has done battle for his boundaries; he has delivered them that were robbed.

How do these hymns underscore the importance to Egyptian civilization of the Nile River and the institution of the pharaoh?

The Impact of Geography

The Nile is a unique river, beginning in the heart of Africa and coursing northward for thousands of miles. It is the longest river in the world. Thanks to the Nile, an area several miles wide on both banks of the river was capable of producing abundant harvests. The "miracle" of the Nile was its annual flooding. The river rose in the summer from rains in Central Africa, crested in Egypt in September and October, and left a deposit of silt that enriched the soil. The Egyptians called this fertile land the "Black Land" because it was dark from the silt and the lush crops that grew on it. Beyond these narrow strips of fertile fields lay the deserts (the "Red Land").

Unlike the floods of Mesopotamia's rivers, the flooding of the Nile was gradual and usually predictable, and the river itself was seen as life-enhancing, not life-threatening. Although a system of organized irrigation was still necessary, the small villages along the Nile could make the effort without the massive state intervention that was required in Mesopotamia. Egyptian civilization consequently tended to remain more rural, with many small population centers congregated along a narrow band on both sides of the Nile. About 100 miles before it empties into the Mediterranean, the river splits into two major branches, forming the delta, a triangular-shaped territory called Lower Egypt to distinguish it from Upper Egypt, the land upstream to the south (see Map 1.3). Egypt's important cities developed at the tip of the delta. Even today, most of Egypt's people are crowded along the banks of the Nile River.

The surpluses of food that Egyptian farmers grew in the fertile Nile valley made Egypt prosperous. But the Nile also served a unifying factor in Egyptian history. In

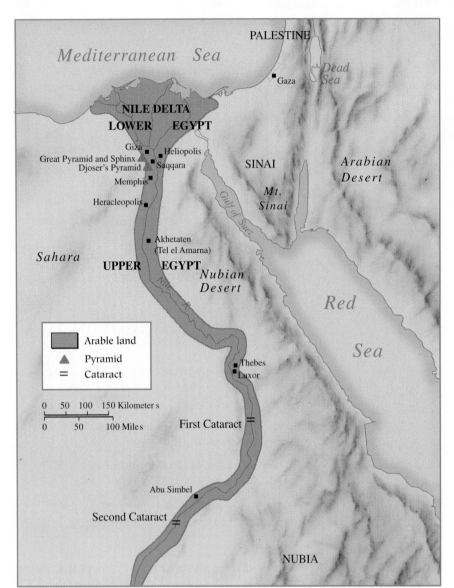

MAP 1.3 **Ancient Egypt.**
Egyptian civilization centered on the life-giving water and flood silts of the Nile River, with most of the population living in Lower Egypt, where the river splits to form the Nile delta. Most of the pyramids, built during the Old Kingdom, are clustered at the entrance to the delta.
? How did the lands to the east and west of the river make invasions of Egypt difficult? View an animated version of this map or related maps at http:// thomsonedu.com/history/spielvogel

ancient times, the Nile was the fastest way to travel through the land, making both transportation and communication easier. Winds from the north pushed sailboats south, and the current of the Nile carried them north. Often when they headed downstream (north), people used long poles or paddles to propel their boats forward.

Unlike Mesopotamia, which was subject to constant invasion, Egypt was blessed by natural barriers that fostered isolation, protected it from invasion, and gave it a sense of security. These barriers included the deserts to the west and east; the cataracts (rapids) on the southern part of the Nile, which made defense relatively easy; and the Mediterranean Sea to the north. These barriers, however, did not prevent the development of trade.

In essence, Egyptian geography and topography played important roles in the early history of the country. The regularity of the Nile floods and the relative isolation of the Egyptians created a sense of security that was accompanied by a feeling of changelessness. Egyptian civilization was characterized by a remarkable degree of continuity over thousands of years. It was no accident that Egyptians believed in cyclical rather than linear progress. Just as the sun passed through its daily cycle and the Nile its annual overflow, Egyptian kings reaffirmed the basic, unchanging principles of justice at the beginning of each new cycle of rule.

The Old and Middle Kingdoms

The basic framework for the study of Egyptian history was provided by Manetho, an Egyptian priest and historian who lived in the early third century B.C. He divided Egyptian history into thirty-one dynasties of kings. Using Manetho's and other lists of kings, modern historians have divided Egyptian history into three major periods known as the Old Kingdom, the Middle Kingdom, and the New Kingdom. These were periods of long-term stability characterized by strong monarchical authority, competent bureaucracy, freedom from invasion, the construction of temples and pyramids, and

Early Dynastic Period (dynasties 1–2)	c. 3100–2686 B.C.
Old Kingdom (dynasties 3–6)	c. 2686–2125 B.C.
First Intermediate Period (dynasties 7–10)	c. 2125–2055 B.C.
Middle Kingdom (dynasties 11–12)	c. 2055–1650 B.C.
Second Intermediate Period (dynasties 13–17)	c. 1650–1550 B.C.
New Kingdom (dynasties 18–20)	c. 1550–1070 B.C.
Postempire Egypt (dynasties 21–31)	1070–30 B.C.

considerable intellectual and cultural activity. But between the periods of stability were times of political chaos known as the Intermediate Periods, characterized by weak political structures and rivalry for leadership, invasions, a decline in building activity, and a restructuring of society.

According to the Egyptians' own tradition, their land consisted initially of numerous populated areas ruled by tribal chieftains. Around 3100 B.C., the first Egyptian royal dynasty, under a king called Menes, united Upper and Lower Egypt into a single kingdom. Henceforth the king would be called "King of Upper and Lower Egypt," and the royal crown would be a double diadem, signifying the unification of all Egypt. Just as the Nile served to unite Upper and Lower Egypt physically, kingship served to unite the two areas politically.

The Old Kingdom The Old Kingdom encompassed the third through sixth dynasties of Egyptian kings, lasting from around 2686 to 2125 B.C. It was an age of prosperity and splendor, made visible in the construction of the greatest and largest pyramids in Egypt's history. The capital of the Old Kingdom was located at Memphis, south of the delta.

Kingship was a divine institution in ancient Egypt and formed part of a universal cosmic scheme (see the box on p. 13): "What is the king of Upper and Lower Egypt? He is a god by whose dealings one lives, the father and mother of all men, alone by himself, without an equal."[6] In obeying their king, subjects helped maintain the cosmic order. A breakdown in royal power could only mean that citizens were offending divinity and weakening the universal structure. Among the various titles of Egyptian kings, pharaoh (originally meaning "great house" or "palace") eventually came to be the most common.

Although they possessed absolute power, Egyptian kings were supposed to rule not arbitrarily but according to set principles. The chief principle was called *Ma'at,* a spiritual precept that conveyed the idea of truth and justice, especially right order and harmony. To ancient Egyptians, this fundamental order and harmony had existed throughout the universe since the beginning of time. Pharaohs were the divine instruments who maintained it and were themselves subject to it.

Although theoretically absolute in their power, in practice Egyptian kings did not rule alone. Initially, members of the king's family performed administrative tasks, but by the fourth dynasty, a bureaucracy with regular procedures had developed. Especially important was the office of vizier, "steward of the whole land." Directly responsible to the king, the vizier was in charge of the bureaucracy, with its numerous departments, including police, justice, river transport, and public works. Agriculture and the treasury were the most important departments. Agriculture was, of course, the backbone of Egyptian prosperity, and the treasury collected taxes, which were paid in kind. A careful assessment of land and tenants was undertaken to provide the tax base.

For administrative purposes, Egypt was divided into provinces or nomes, as they were later called by the Greeks—twenty-two in Upper and twenty in Lower Egypt. A governor, called by the Greeks a nomarch, was head of each nome and was responsible to the king and vizier. Nomarchs, however, tended to build up large holdings of land and power within their nomes, creating a potential rivalry with the pharaohs.

The Middle Kingdom Despite the theory of divine order, the Old Kingdom eventually collapsed, ushering in a period of chaos. Eventually, a new royal dynasty managed to pacify all Egypt and inaugurated the Middle Kingdom, a new period of stability lasting from around 2055 to 1650 B.C. Several factors contributed to its vitality. The nome structure was reorganized. The boundaries of each nome were now settled precisely, and the obligations of the nomes to the state were clearly delineated. Nomarchs were confirmed as hereditary officeholders but with the understanding that their duties must be performed faithfully. These included the collection of taxes for the state and the recruitment of labor forces for royal projects, such as stone quarrying.

The Middle Kingdom was characterized by a new concern on the part of the pharaohs for the people. In the Old Kingdom, the pharaoh had been viewed as an inaccessible god-king. Now he was portrayed as the shepherd of his people with the responsibility to build public works and provide for the public welfare. As one pharaoh expressed it, "He [a particular god] created me as one who should do that which he had done, and to carry out that which he commanded should be done. He appointed me herdsman of this land, for he knew who would keep it in order for him."[7]

Society and Economy in Ancient Egypt

Egyptian society had a simple structure in the Old and Middle Kingdoms; basically, it was organized along hierarchical lines with the god-king at the top. The king was surrounded by an upper class of nobles and priests who participated in the elaborate rituals of life that surrounded the pharaoh. This ruling class ran the government and managed its own landed estates, which provided much of its wealth.

Below the upper classes were merchants and artisans. Merchants engaged in active trade up and down the Nile as well as in town and village markets. Some merchants also engaged in international trade; they were sent by the king to Crete and Syria, where they obtained wood and other products. Expeditions traveled into Nubia for ivory and down the Red Sea to Punt for incense and spices. Egyptian artisans displayed unusually high standards of craftsmanship and beauty and produced an incredible variety of goods: stone dishes; beautifully painted boxes made of clay; wooden furniture; gold, silver, and copper tools and containers; paper and rope made of papyrus; and linen clothing.

The largest number of people in Egypt simply worked the land. In theory, the king owned all the land but granted portions of it to his subjects. Large sections were in the possession of nobles and the temple complexes. Most of the lower classes were serfs or common people who were bound to the land and cultivated the estates. They paid taxes in the form of crops to the king, nobles, and priests, lived in small villages or towns, and provided military service and forced labor for building projects.

The Culture of Egypt

Egypt produced a culture that dazzled and awed its later conquerors. The Egyptians' technical achievements alone, especially visible in the construction of the pyramids, demonstrated a measure of skill unique in the world at that time. To the Egyptians, all of these achievements were part of a cosmic order suffused with the presence of the divine.

Spiritual Life in Egyptian Society   The Egyptians had no word for religion because it was an inseparable element of existence in the world in which they lived. The Egyptians had a remarkable number of gods associated with heavenly bodies and natural forces. Two groups, sun gods and land gods, came to have special prominence, hardly unusual in view of the importance to Egypt's well-being of the sun, the river, and the fertile land along its banks. The sun was the source of life and hence worthy of worship. A sun cult developed, and the sun god took on different forms and names, depending on his specific function. He was worshiped as Atum in human form and as Re, who had a human body but the head of a falcon. The pharaoh took the title "Son of Re" because he was regarded as the earthly embodiment of Re.

River and land deities included Osiris and Isis with their child Horus, who was related to the Nile and to the sun as well. Osiris became especially important as a symbol of resurrection. A famous Egyptian myth told of the struggle between Osiris, who brought civilization to Egypt, and his evil brother Seth, who killed him, cut his body into fourteen parts, and tossed them into the Nile. Osiris's faithful wife, Isis, found the pieces and, with help from other gods, restored Osiris to life. As a symbol of resurrection and as judge of the dead, Osiris took on an important role for the Egyptians. By identifying with Osiris, one could hope to gain new life, just as Osiris had done. The dead, embalmed and mummified, were placed in tombs (in the case of kings, in pyramidal tombs), given the name of Osiris, and by a process of magical identification became Osiris. Like Osiris, they would then be reborn. The flood of the Nile and the new life it brought to Egypt were symbolized by Isis gathering all of Osiris' parts together and were celebrated each spring in the festival of the new land.

Later Egyptian spiritual practice began to emphasize morality by stressing Osiris' role as judge of the dead. The dead were asked to give an account of their earthly deeds to show whether they deserved a reward. Other means were also employed to gain immortality. Magical incantations, preserved in the *Book of the Dead*, were used to ensure a favorable journey to a happy afterlife. Specific instructions explained what to do when confronted by the judge of the dead. These instructions had two aspects. The negative confession gave a detailed list of what one had not done:

> *I have not committed evil against men.*
> *I have not mistreated cattle.*
> *I have not blasphemed a god. . . .*
> *I have not done violence to a poor man. . . .*
> *I have not made anyone sick. . . .*
> *I have not killed. . . .*
> *I have not caused anyone suffering. . . .*
> *I have not had sexual relations with a boy.*
> *I have not defiled myself.*[8]

Later the supplicant made a speech listing his good actions: "I have done that which men said and that with which gods are content. . . . I have given bread to the hungry, water to the thirsty, clothing to the naked, and a ferry-boat to him who was marooned. I have provided divine offerings for the gods and mortuary offerings for the dead."[9]

The Pyramids   One of the great achievements of Egyptian civilization, the building of pyramids, occurred in the time of the Old Kingdom. Pyramids were not built in isolation but as part of a larger complex dedicated to the dead—in effect, a city of the dead. The area included a large pyramid for the king's burial, smaller pyramids for his family, and mastabas, rectangular structures with flat roofs, as tombs for the pharaoh's noble officials. The tombs were well prepared for their residents. The rooms were furnished and stocked with numerous supplies, including chairs, boats, chests, weapons, games, dishes, and a variety of foods. The Egyptians believed that human beings had two bodies, a physical one and a

Osiris as Judge of the Dead. According to the *Book of the Dead*, after making a denial of offenses (the "negative confession"), the deceased experienced the "weighing of the heart." Shown here is a judgment scene from the *Book of the Dead* of Hunefer, a royal scribe who died around 1285 B.C. Hunefer's heart is placed on one side of a balance scale; on the other side is the feather of Ma'at, the goddess of truth. For Hunefer, heart and feather are of equal weight, so the god Anubis ushers him into the presence of Osiris, seated on his throne at the right. A "swallowing monster," a hybrid creature of crocodile, lion, and hippopotamus, stood ready at the scale to devour the deceased if he failed the test.

spiritual one, which they called the *ka*. If the physical body was properly preserved (that is, mummified) and the tomb furnished with all the various objects of regular life, the *ka* could return and continue its life despite the death of the physical body.

To preserve the physical body after death, the Egyptians practiced mummification, a process of slowly drying a dead body to prevent it from rotting. Special workshops, run by priests, performed this procedure, primarily for the wealthy families who could afford it. According to Herodotus, an ancient Greek historian (see Chapter 3) who visited Egypt around 450 B.C., "The most refined method is as follows: first of all they draw out the brain through the nostrils with an iron hook. . . . Then they make an incision in the flank with a sharp Ethiopian stone through which they extract all the internal organs."[10] The liver, lungs, stomach, and intestines were placed in four special jars that were put in the tomb with the mummy. The priests then covered the corpse with a natural salt that absorbed the body's water. Later, they filled the body with spices and wrapped it with layers of linen soaked in resin. At the end of the process, which took about seventy days, a lifelike mask was placed over the head and shoulders of the mummy, which was then sealed in a case and placed in its tomb in a pyramid.

The largest and most magnificent of all the pyramids was built under King Khufu. Constructed at Giza around 2540 B.C., this famous Great Pyramid covers 13 acres, measures 756 feet at each side of its base, and stands 481 feet high. Its four sides are almost precisely oriented to the four points of the compass. The interior included a grand gallery to the burial chamber, which was built of granite with a lidless sarcophagus for the pharaoh's body. The Great Pyramid still stands as a visible symbol of the power of Egyptian kings and the spiritual conviction that underlay Egyptian society. No later pyramid ever matched its size or splendor. But an Egyptian pyramid was not just the king's tomb; it was also an important symbol of royal power. It could be seen for miles as a visible reminder of the glory and might of the ruler, who was a living god on earth.

Art and Writing Commissioned by kings or nobles for use in temples and tombs, Egyptian art was largely functional. Wall paintings and statues of gods and kings in temples served a strictly spiritual purpose. They were an integral part of the performance of ritual, which was thought necessary to preserve the cosmic order and hence the well-being of Egypt. Likewise, the mural scenes and sculptured figures found in the tombs had a specific

The Pyramids at Giza. The three pyramids at Giza, across the Nile River from Cairo, are the most famous in Egypt. At the rear is the largest of the three pyramids—the Great Pyramid of Khufu. Next to it is the pyramid of Khafre. In the foreground is the smaller pyramid of Menkaure standing behind the even smaller pyramids for the pharaohs' wives. Covering almost 13 acres, the Great Pyramid of Khufu is immense. It is estimated that the Great Pyramid contains 2.3 million stone blocks, each weighing about 2.5 tons.

function. They were supposed to aid the journey of the deceased into the afterworld.

Egyptian art was also formulaic. Artists and sculptors were expected to observe a strict canon of proportions that determined both form and presentation. This canon gave Egyptian art a distinctive appearance for thousands of years. Especially characteristic was the convention of combining the profile, semiprofile, and frontal views of the human body in relief work and painting in order to represent each part of the body accurately. The result was an art that was highly stylized yet still allowed distinctive features to be displayed.

Writing in Egypt emerged during the first two dynasties. The Greeks later labeled Egyptian writing **hieroglyphics**, meaning "priest carvings" or "sacred writings." Hieroglyphs were symbols that depicted objects and had a sacred value at the same time. Although hieroglyphs were later simplified into two scripts for writing purposes, they never developed into an alphabet. Egyptian hieroglyphs were initially carved in stone, but later the two simplified scripts were written on papyrus, a paper made from the papyrus reed that grew along the Nile. Most of the ancient Egyptian literature that has come down to us was written on papyrus rolls and wooden tablets.

Chaos and a New Order: The New Kingdom

The Middle Kingdom was brought to an end by a new period of instability. An incursion into the delta region by a people known as the Hyksos initiated this second age of chaos. The Hyksos, a Semitic-speaking people, infiltrated Egypt in the seventeenth century B.C. and came to dominate much of Egypt. However, the presence of the Hyksos was not entirely negative for Egypt. They taught the Egyptians to make bronze for use in new agricultural tools and weapons. The Hyksos also brought new aspects of warfare to Egypt, including the horse-drawn war chariot, a heavier sword, and the compound bow. Eventually, a new line of pharaohs—the eighteenth dynasty—made use of the new weapons to throw off Hyksos domination, reunite Egypt, establish the New Kingdom (c. 1550–1070 B.C.), and launch the Egyptians along a new militaristic and imperialistic path. During the period of the New Kingdom, Egypt became the most powerful state in the Middle East. The Egyptians occupied Palestine and Syria but permitted local princes to rule under Egyptian control. Egyptian armies also moved westward into Libya and expanded Egypt's border to the south by conquering the African kingdom of Nubia.

The eighteenth dynasty was not without its own troubles, however. Amenhotep IV (c. 1364–1347 B.C.) introduced the worship of Aten, god of the sun disk, as the chief god and pursued his worship with great enthusiasm. Changing his own name to Akhenaten ("it is well with Aten"), the pharaoh closed the temples of other gods and especially endeavored to lessen the power of Amon-Re and his priesthood at Thebes. Akhenaten strove to reduce the priests' influence by replacing Thebes as the capital of Egypt with Akhetaten ("dedicated to Aten"), a new city located near modern Tel el Amarna, 200 miles north of Thebes.

Akhenaten's attempt at religious change failed. It was too much to ask Egyptians to ignore their traditional ways and beliefs, especially since they saw the destruction of the old gods as subversive of the very cosmic order on which Egypt's survival and continuing prosperity depended. Moreover, the priests at Thebes were unalterably opposed to the changes, which diminished their influence and power. At the same time, Akhenaten's preoccupation with religion caused him to ignore foreign affairs and led to the loss of both Syria and Palestine. Akhenaten's changes were soon undone after his death by those who influenced his successor, the boy-pharaoh Tutankhamen (1347–1338 B.C.). Tutankhamen returned the government to Thebes and restored the old gods. The Aten experiment had failed to take hold, and the eighteenth dynasty itself came to an end in 1333 B.C.

The nineteenth dynasty managed to restore Egyptian power one more time. Under Rameses II (c. 1279–1213 B.C.), the Egyptians regained control of Palestine but were unable to reestablish the borders of their earlier empire. New invasions in the thirteenth century by the "Sea Peoples," as the Egyptians called them, destroyed Egyptian power in Palestine and drove the Egyptians back within their old frontiers. The days of Egyptian empire were ended, and the New Kingdom itself expired with the end of the twentieth dynasty in 1070 B.C. For the next thousand years, despite periodical revivals of strength, Egypt was dominated by Libyans, Nubians, Persians, and finally Macedonians after the conquest of Alexander the Great (see Chapter 4). In the first century B.C., Egypt became a province in Rome's mighty empire.

Daily Life in Ancient Egypt: Family and Marriage

Ancient Egyptians had a very positive attitude toward daily life on earth and followed the advice of the wisdom literature, which suggested that people marry young and establish a home and family. Monogamy was the general rule, although a husband was allowed to keep additional wives if his first wife was childless. Pharaohs were entitled to harems; the queen, however, was acknowledged as the Great Wife, with a status higher than that of the other wives. The husband was master in the house, but wives were very much respected and in charge of the household and education of the children. From a book of wise sayings came this advice:

> If you are a man of standing, you should found your household and love your wife at home as is fitting. Fill her belly; clothe her back. Ointment is the prescription for her body. Make her heart glad as long as you live. She is a profitable field for her lord. You should not contend with her at law, and keep her far from gaining control. . . . Let her heart be soothed through what may accrue to you; it means keeping her long in your house.[11]

Women's property and inheritance remained in their hands, even in marriage. Although most careers and public offices were closed to women, some did operate businesses. Peasant women worked long hours in the

The Egyptian Diet. The diet of the upper and lower classes in ancient Egypt varied considerably. Meat and fowl, including beef, goat, pork, goose, and pigeons, were on the tables of the rich. Although done for sport as well as food, hunting waterfowl in the stands of papyrus reeds that grew along the river's banks was a favourite pastime of the Egyptian upper classes. Shown on the left is a hunting scene from the eighteenth-dynasty tomb of Nebamun in Thebes. Nebamun, a nobleman, is seen standing in his boat using his throwstick to hunt birds. He holds three birds in his right hand while a cat retrieves two in its claws and holds the wings of another in its teeth. The basic diet of the poor consisted chiefly of bread, and the baking of bread was an important task in all households. The tomb painting on the right from the eighteenth-century dynasty tomb of Mennah shows two men carrying grain while slave girls fight over leftovers in the background.

A FATHER'S ADVICE

*U*pper-class Egyptians enjoyed compiling collections of wise sayings to provide guidance for leading an upright and successful life. This excerpt is taken from *The Instruction of the Vizier Ptah-hotep* and dates from around 2450 B.C. The vizier was the pharaoh's chief official. In this selection, Ptah-hotep advises his son on how to be a successful official.

The Instruction of the Vizier Ptah-hotep

Then he said to his son:

Let not your heart be puffed-up because of your knowledge; be not confident because you are a wise man. Take counsel with the ignorant as well as the wise. The full limits of skill cannot be attained, and there is no skilled man equipped to his full advantage. Good speech is more hidden than the emerald, but it may be found with maidservants at the grindstones. . . .

If you are a leader commanding the affairs of the multitude, seek out for yourself every beneficial deed, until it may be that your own affairs are without wrong. Justice is great, and its appropriateness is lasting; it has been disturbed since the time of him who made it, whereas there is punishment for him who passes over its laws. It is the right path before him who knows nothing. Wrongdoing has never brought its undertaking into port. It may be that it is fraud that gains riches, but the strength of justice is that it lasts. . . .

If you are a man of intimacy, whom one great man sends to another, be thoroughly reliable when he sends you. Carry out the errand for him as he has spoken. Do not be reserved about what is said to you, and beware of any act of forgetfulness. Grasp hold of truth, and do not exceed it. Mere gratification is by no means to be repeated. Struggle against making words worse, thus making one great man hostile to another through vulgar speech. . . .

If you are a man of standing and found a household and produce a son who is pleasing to god, if he is correct and inclines toward your ways and listens to your instruction, while his manners in your house are fitting, and if he takes care of your property as it should be, seek out for him every useful action. He is your son, . . . you should not cut your heart off from him.

But a man's seed often creates enmity. If he goes astray and transgresses your plans and does not carry out your instruction, so that his manners in your household are wretched, and he rebels against all that you say, while his mouth runs on in the most wretched talk, quite apart from his experience, while he possesses nothing, you should cast him off: he is not your son at all. He was not really born to you. Thus you enslave him entirely according to his own speech. He is one whom god has condemned in the very womb. . . .

What does this passage reveal about Egyptian bureaucrats?

---

fields and at numerous domestic tasks, especially weaving cloth. Upper-class women could function as priestesses, and a few queens even became pharaohs in their own right. Most famous was Hatshepsut in the New Kingdom. She served as regent for her stepson Thutmosis III but assumed the throne for herself and remained in power until her death.

Hatshepsut's reign was a prosperous one, as is especially evident in her building activity. She is most famous for the temple dedicated to herself at Deir el Bahri on the west bank of the Nile at Thebes. As pharaoh, Hatshepsut sent out military expeditions, encouraged mining, fostered agriculture, and sent a trading expedition to lower Africa. Because pharaohs were almost always male, Hatshepsut's official statues show her clothed and bearded like a king. She was referred to as "His Majesty." That Hatshepsut was aware of her unusual position is evident from an inscription she had placed on one of her temples. It read, "Now my heart turns to and fro, in thinking what will the people say, they who shall see my monument in after years, and shall speak of what I have done."

Marriages were arranged by parents. The primary concerns were family and property, and clearly the chief purpose of marriage was to produce children, especially sons (see the box above). From the New Kingdom came this piece of wisdom: "Take to yourself a wife while you are a youth, that she may produce a son for you."[12] Only sons could carry on the family name. Daughters were not slighted, however. Numerous tomb paintings show the close and affectionate relationship parents had with both sons and daughters. Although marriages were arranged, some of the surviving love poems from ancient Egypt indicate an element of romance in some marriages. Marriages could and did end in divorce, which was allowed, apparently with compensation for the wife. Adultery, however, was strictly prohibited, and punishments were severe, especially for women, who could have their noses cut off or be burned at the stake.

CONCLUSION

Although early civilizations emerged in different parts of the world, the foundations of Western civilization were laid by the Mesopotamians and Egyptians. They developed cities and struggled with the problems of organized states. They developed writing to keep records and created literature. They constructed monumental architecture to please their gods, symbolize their power, and preserve their culture for all time. They developed new political, military, social, and religious structures to deal with the basic problems of human existence and organization. These first literate civilizations left detailed records that allow us to view how they grappled with three of the fundamental problems that humans have pondered: the nature of human relationships, the nature of the universe, and the role of divine forces in the cosmos. Although later peoples in Western civilization would provide different answers from those of the Mesopotamians and Egyptians, it was they who first posed the questions, gave answers, and wrote them down. Human memory begins with these two civilizations.

By the middle of the second millennium B.C., the creative impulse of the Mesopotamian and Egyptian civilizations was beginning to wane. The invasion of the Sea Peoples around 1200 B.C. ushered in a whole new pattern of petty states and new kingdoms that would lead to the largest empires the ancient Near East had seen.

TIMELINE

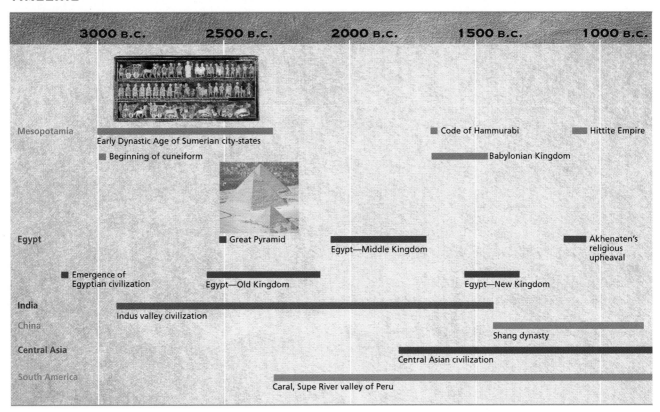

	3000 B.C.	2500 B.C.	2000 B.C.	1500 B.C.	1000 B.C.

Mesopotamia

Early Dynastic Age of Sumerian city-states
Beginning of cuneiform
Code of Hammurabi
Babylonian Kingdom
Hittite Empire

Egypt

Emergence of Egyptian civilization
Great Pyramid
Egypt—Old Kingdom
Egypt—Middle Kingdom
Egypt—New Kingdom
Akhenaten's religious upheaval

India

Indus valley civilization

China

Shang dynasty

Central Asia

Central Asian civilization

South America

Caral, Supe River valley of Peru

NOTES

1. J.-M. Chauvet et al., *Dawn of Art: The Chauvet Cave* (New York, 1996), pp. 49–50.
2. Quoted in A. Kuhrt, *The Ancient Near East, c. 3000–330 B.C.* (London, 1995), vol. 1, p. 68.
3. Quoted in M. van de Mieroop, *A History of the Ancient Near East, ca. 3000–323 B.C.* (Oxford, 2004), p. 106.
4. T. Jacobsen, "Mesopotamia," in H. Frankfort et al., *Before Philosophy* (Baltimore, 1949), p. 139.
5. J. B. Pritchard, *Ancient Near Eastern Texts*, 3d ed. (Princeton, N.J., 1969), p. 372.
6. Quoted in M. Covensky, *The Ancient Near Eastern Tradition* (New York, 1966), p. 51.
7. Quoted in B. G. Trigger, B. J. Kemp, D. O'Connor, and A. B. Lloyd, *Ancient Egypt: A Social History* (Cambridge, 1983), p. 74.
8. Pritchard, *Ancient Near Eastern Texts*, p. 34.
9. Ibid., p. 36.
10. Quoted in R.-M. Hagen and R. Hagen, *Egypt: People, Gods, Pharaohs* (Cologne, 2002), p. 148.
11. Pritchard, *Ancient Near Eastern Texts*, p. 413.
12. Ibid., p. 420.

SUGGESTIONS FOR FURTHER READING

For a beautifully illustrated introduction to the ancient world, see *Past Worlds: The Times Atlas of Archaeology* (Maplewood, N.J., 1988), written by an international group of scholars. A detailed history of the ancient world with chapters written by different specialists is available in the twelve volumes of *The Cambridge Ancient History*, now in its third edition. A less detailed but sound survey can be found in

L. De Blois and R. J. van der Spek, *An Introduction to the Ancient World,* trans. S. Mellor (London, 1997). The following works are of considerable value in examining the prehistory of humankind: **R. Leakey,** *The Making of Mankind* (London, 1981); **R. J. Wenke,** *Patterns in Prehistory: Humankind's First Three Million Years,* 4th ed. (New York, 1999); **P. Mellars and C. Stringer,** *The Human Revolution* (Edinburgh, 1989); and **D. O. Henry,** *From Foraging to Agriculture* (Philadelphia, 1989). For a study of the role of women in early human society, see **E. Barber,** *Women's Work: The First 20,000 Years* (New York, 1994).

Excellent reference tools on the ancient Near East can be found in **P. Bienkowski** and **A. Milward, eds.,** *Dictionary of the Ancient Near East* (Philadelphia, 2000), and **G. Leick,** *Who's Who in the Ancient Near East* (London, 1999). General surveys of Mesopotamia and Egypt include **A. B. Knapp,** *The History and Culture of Ancient Western Asia and Egypt* (Chicago, 1987), and **W. von Soden,** *The Ancient Orient: An Introduction to the Study of the Ancient Near East* (Grand Rapids, Mich., 1994). For a detailed survey, see **A. Kuhrt,** *The Ancient Near East, c. 3000–330 B.C.,* 2 vols. (London, 1995). A brief recent survey can be found in **M. van de Mieroop,** *A History of the Ancient Near East, ca. 3000–323 B.C.* (Oxford, 2004). **H.W.F. Saggs,** *Babylonians* (Norman, Okla., 1995), and **G. Leick,** *The Babylonians* (London, 2003), provide an overview of the peoples of ancient Mesopotamia. On the economic and social history of the ancient Near East, see **D. C. Snell,** *Life in the Ancient Near East* (New Haven, Conn., 1997).

General works on ancient Mesopotamia include **J. N. Postgate,** *Early Mesopotamia: Society and Economy at the Dawn of History* (London, 1992), and **A. L. Oppenheim,** *Ancient Mesopotamia,* 2d ed. (Chicago, 1977). A beautifully illustrated survey can be found in **M. Roaf,** *Cultural Atlas of Mesopotamia and the Ancient Near East* (New York, 1996). The world of the Sumerians has been well described in **S. N. Kramer,** *The Sumerians* (Chicago, 1963) and *History Begins at Sumer* (New York, 1959). See also the summary of the historical and archaeological evidence by **H. Crawford,** *Sumer and the Sumerians* (Cambridge, 1991). The fundamental work on the spiritual perspective of ancient Mesopotamia is **T. Jacobsen,** *The Treasures of Darkness: A History of Mesopotamian Religion* (New Haven, Conn., 1976). On daily life, see **S. Bertman,** *Handbook to Life in Ancient Mesopotamia* (New York, 2003).

For a good introduction to ancient Egypt, see the beautifully illustrated works by **M. Hayes,** *The Egyptians* (New York, 1997), and **D. P. Silverman,** ed., *Ancient Egypt* (New York, 1997). Other general surveys include **I. Shaw,** ed., *The Oxford History of Ancient Egypt* (New York, 2000); **N. Grant,** *The Egyptians* (New York, 1996); and **N. Grimal,** *A History of Ancient Egypt,* trans. I. Shaw (Oxford, 1992). On Akhenaten and his religious changes, see **D. Redford,** *Akhenaten: The Heretic King* (Princeton, N.J., 1984). Egyptian religion is covered in **S. Quirke,** *Ancient Egyptian Religion* (London, 1992). On Egyptian culture in general, see **J. A. Wilson,** *The Culture of Ancient Egypt* (Chicago, 1956). An important study on women is **G. Robins,** *Women in Ancient Egypt* (Cambridge, Mass., 1993). Daily life can be examined in **E. Strouhal,** *Life of the Ancient Egyptians* (Norman, Okla., 1992).

Thomson NOW! Enter *ThomsonNOW* using the access card that is available for *Western Civilization: A Brief History.* *ThomsonNOW* will help you understand this chapter with lesson plans generated for your needs. In addition, you can read the following documents, and many more, online:

Enuma Elish
Herodotus, *History,* **Book 2, Chapters 124–127**

WESTERN CIVILIZATION RESOURCES

Visit the Web site for *Western Civilization: A Brief History* for resources specific to this book:

http://www.thomsonedu.com/history/spielvogel

For a variety of tools to help you succeed in this course, visit the Western Civilization Resource Center at

http://history.wadsworth.com/spielvogel

Included are quizzes, images, documents, interactive simulations, maps and timelines, movie explorations, and a wealth of other sources.

THE ANCIENT NEAR EAST: PEOPLES AND EMPIRES

A medieval Italian manuscript version of the judgment of Solomon

Alinari/Regione Umbria/Art Resource, NY (Archivio di Stato, Gubbio, Italy)

ROUND 970 B.C., Solomon came to the throne of Israel, a small state in western Asia. He was lacking in military prowess but excelled in many other ways. Through trade and a series of foreign alliances, he created a strong, flourishing state. But he was especially famed for his skill as a judge. When two women came before him, each claiming that the same infant was her natural child, Solomon ordered his servant to cut the child in half and give half to each woman. The first woman objected: "Please, my lord, give her the living baby! Don't kill him!" The second woman replied, "Neither I nor you shall have him. Cut him in two!" Then Solomon rendered his judgment: "Give the living baby to the first woman. Do not kill him; she is his mother." According to the biblical account, "When all Israel heard the verdict the king had given, they held the king in awe, because they saw that he had wisdom from God to administer justice." After Solomon's death, Israel's power began to crumble. But how had such a small nation been able to survive as long as it did in a Near East dominated by mighty empires?

The weakening of Egypt around 1200 B.C. left no dominant powers in the Near East, allowing a patchwork of petty kingdoms and city-states to emerge, especially in Syria and

Palestine. One of these small states, the Hebrew nation known as Israel, has played a role in Western civilization completely disproportionate to its size. The Hebrews played a minor part in the politics of the ancient Near East, but their spiritual heritage, in the form of Judeo-Christian values, is one of the basic pillars of Western civilization.

The small states did not last. Ever since the first city-states had arisen in the Near East around 3000 B.C., there had been an ongoing movement toward the creation of larger territorial states with more sophisticated systems of control. This process reached a high point in the first millennium B.C. with the appearance of vast empires. Between 1000 and 500 B.C., the Assyrians, the Chaldeans, and the Persians all forged empires that encompassed large areas of the ancient Near East. Each had impressive and grandiose capital cities that emphasized the power and wealth of its rulers. Each brought peace and order for a time by employing new administrative techniques. Each eventually fell to other conquerors. In the long run, these large empires had less impact on Western civilization than the Hebrew people. In human history, the power of ideas is often more significant than the power of empires.

On the Fringes of Civilization

Our story of the beginnings of Western civilization has been dominated so far by Mesopotamia and Egypt. But significant developments were also taking place on the fringes of these civilizations. Farming had spread into the Balkan peninsula of Europe by 6500 B.C., and by 4000 B.C. it was well established in southern France, central Europe, and the coastal regions of the Mediterranean. Although migrating farmers from the Near East may have brought some farming techniques into Europe, historians now believe that the Neolithic peoples of Europe domesticated animals and began to farm largely on their own.

One outstanding feature of late Neolithic Europe was the building of megalithic structures. *Megalith* is Greek for "large stone." Radiocarbon dating, a technique that allows scientists to determine the age of objects, shows that the first megalithic structures were built around 4000 B.C., more than a thousand years before the great pyramids were built in Egypt. Between 3200 and 1500 B.C., standing stones that were placed in circles or lined up in rows were erected throughout the British Isles and northwestern France. Other megalithic constructions have been found as far north as Scandinavia and as far south as the islands of Corsica, Sardinia, and Malta. Some archaeologists have demonstrated that the stone circles were used as observatories to detect not only such simple astronomical phenomena as the midwinter and midsummer sunrises but also such sophisticated observations as the major and minor standstills of the moon.

By far the most famous of these megalithic constructions is Stonehenge in England. Stonehenge consists

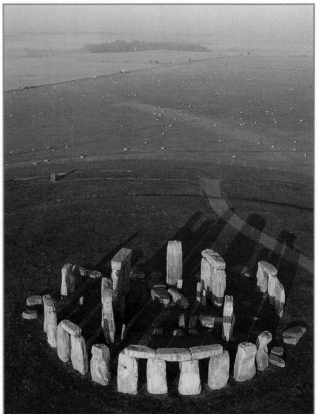

© Adam Woolfitt / CORBIS

Stonehenge. The Bronze Age in northwestern Europe is known for its megaliths, or large standing stones. Between 3200 and 1500 B.C., standing stones arranged in circles or lined up in rows were erected throughout the British Isles and northwestern France. The most famous of these megalithic constructions is Stonehenge in England.

of a series of concentric rings of standing stones. Its construction sometime between 2100 and 1900 B.C. was no small accomplishment. The eighty bluestones used at Stonehenge, for example, weigh 4 tons each and were transported to the site from their original source 135 miles away. Like other megalithic structures, Stonehenge indicates a remarkable awareness of astronomy on the part of its builders, as well as an impressive coordination of workers.

The Impact of the Indo-Europeans

For many historians, both the details of construction and the purpose of the megalithic structures of Europe remain a mystery. Also puzzling is the role of Indo-European people. The name *Indo-European* refers to people who used a language derived from a single parent tongue. Indo-European languages include Greek, Latin, Persian, Sanskrit, and the Germanic languages (see Table 2.1). It has been suggested that the original Indo-European-speaking peoples were based somewhere in the steppe region north of the Black Sea or in southwestern Asia, in modern Iran or Afghanistan. Although there had

TABLE 2.1	Some Indo-European Languages
SUBFAMILY	**LANGUAGES**
Indo-Iranian	*Sanskrit,* Persian
Balto-Slavic	Russian, Serbo-Croatian, Czech, Polish, Lithuanian
Hellenic	Greek
Italic	*Latin,* Romance languages (French, Italian, Spanish, Portuguese, Romanian)
Celtic	Irish, Gaelic
Germanic	Swedish, Danish, Norwegian, German, Dutch, English

NOTE: Languages in italic type are no longer spoken.

been earlier migrations, around 2000 B.C. these people began major nomadic movements into Europe (including present-day Italy and Greece), India, and western Asia. One group of Indo-Europeans who moved into Asia Minor and Anatolia (modern Turkey) around 1750 B.C. coalesced with the native peoples to form the Hittite kingdom with its capital at Hattusha (Bogazköy in modern Turkey).

Starting around 1600 B.C., the Hittites assembled their own empire in western Asia and even threatened the power of the Egyptians. The Hittites were the first of the Indo-European peoples to make use of iron, enabling them to construct weapons that were stronger and cheaper to make because of the widespread availability of iron ore. Hittite power faltered around 1200 B.C., in part due to internal problems but also as a result of attacks from the west by the Sea Peoples, groups of unknown origin who moved across the Mediterranean in the late thirteenth and early twelfth centuries B.C., and also by an aggressive tribe known as the Gasga, who raided Hittite cities. By 1190 B.C., Hittite power was at an end.

During its heyday, however, the Hittite Empire was one of the great powers in western Asia. The Hittite ruler, known as the Great King, controlled the core areas of the kingdom but in western and southern Anatolia and Syria allowed local rulers to swear allegiance to him as vassals. Constant squabbling over succession to the throne, however, tended to weaken royal authority at times.

During its height, the Hittite Empire also demonstrated an interesting ability to assimilate other cultures into its own. In languages, literature, art, law, and religion, the Hittites borrowed much from Mesopotamia as well as the native peoples that they had subdued. Recent scholarship has stressed the important role of the Hittites in transmitting Mesopotamian culture, as they transformed it, to later Western civilization in the Mediterranean area, especially to the Mycenaean Greeks (See Chapter 3).

The crumbling of the Hittite kingdom and the weakening of Egypt after 1200 B.C. left a power vacuum in western Asia, allowing a patchwork of petty kingdoms and city-states to emerge, especially in the area at the eastern end of the Mediterranean Sea. The Hebrews were one of these peoples.

The Hebrews: "The Children of Israel"

The Hebrews were a Semitic-speaking people who had a tradition concerning their origins and history that was eventually written down as part of the Hebrew Bible, known to Christians as the Old Testament. Describing themselves originally as nomads organized in clans, the Hebrews' tradition states that they were descendants of the patriarch Abraham, who had migrated from Mesopotamia to Palestine, where they became identified as the "Children of Israel." Again according to tradition, a drought in Palestine caused many Hebrews to migrate to Egypt, where they lived peacefully until they were enslaved by pharaohs who used them as laborers on building projects. These Hebrews remained in bondage until Moses led them eastward out of Egypt in the Exodus, which some historians have argued would have occurred in the first half of the thirteenth century B.C. According to the biblical account, the Hebrews then wandered for many years in the desert until they entered Palestine. Organized into twelve tribes, they became embroiled in conflict with the Philistines, a people who had settled in the coastal area of Palestine but were beginning to move into the inland areas.

Many scholars today doubt that the early books of the Hebrew Bible reflect the true history of the early Israelites. They argue that the early books of the Bible, written centuries after the events described, preserve only what the Israelites came to believe about themselves and that recent archaeological evidence often contradicts the details of the biblical account. Some of these scholars have even argued that the Israelites were not nomadic invaders but indigenous peoples in the Palestinian hill country. What is generally agreed, however, is that between 1200 and 1000 B.C., the Israelites emerged as a distinct group of people, possibly organized in tribes or a league of tribes, who established a united kingdom known as Israel.

The United Kingdom

The first king of the Israelites was Saul (c. 1020–1000 B.C.), who initially achieved some success in the ongoing struggle with the Philistines. But after his death in a disastrous battle with this enemy, a brief period of anarchy ensued until one of Saul's lieutenants, David (c. 1000–970 B.C.), reunited the Israelites, defeated the Philistines, and established control over all of Palestine (see Map 2.1). According to the biblical account, some of his conquests led to harsh treatment for the conquered people: "David also defeated the Moabites. He made them lie down on the ground and measured them off with a length of cord. Every two lengths of them were put to death, and the third length was allowed to live. So the Moabites became subject to David and brought tribute."[1] Among David's conquests was the city of

MAP 2.1   **Palestine in the First Millennium** B.C.   United under Saul, David, and Solomon, greater Israel split into two states—Israel and Judah—after the death of Solomon. With power divided, the Israelites could not resist invasions that dispersed many Jews from Palestine. Some, such as the "ten lost tribes," never returned. Others were sent to Babylon but were later allowed to return under the rule of the Persians. **?** Why was Israel more vulnerable to the Assyrian Empire than Judah was?

🔍 **View an animated version of this map or related maps at**
http://thomsonedu.com/history/spielvogel

Jerusalem, which he made into the capital of a united kingdom. David centralized Israel's political organization and accelerated the integration of the Israelites into a settled community based on farming and urban life.

David's son Solomon (c. 970–930 B.C.) did even more to strengthen royal power. He expanded the political and military establishments and was especially active in extending the trading activities of the Israelites. Solomon is best known for his building projects, of which the most famous was the Temple in Jerusalem. The Israelites viewed the Temple as the symbolic center of their religion and hence of the kingdom of Israel itself. The Temple now housed the Ark of the Covenant, a holy chest containing the sacred relics of the Hebrew religion and, symbolically, the throne of the invisible God of Israel. Under Solomon, ancient Israel was at the height

Exiles from Judah.   The Assyrians overran the kingdom of Israel in 722 or 721 B.C., destroyed the capital city of Samaria, and then began an assault on the kingdom of Judah. In this eighth-century relief from the palace of Sennacherib at Nineveh, captives with animals and baggage are shown on their way into exile after the Assyrian conquest of the fortified town of Lachish in Judah in 701 B.C. A woman and child have been allowed to travel on the cart. The Assyrians failed, however, to take Jerusalem, and Judah remained independent, although it was forced to pay tribute to the Assyrians.

of its power, but his efforts to extend royal power throughout his kingdom led to dissatisfaction among some of his subjects.

The Divided Kingdom

After Solomon's death, tensions in Israel between the northern and southern tribes led to the establishment of two separate kingdoms—the kingdom of Israel, composed of the ten northern tribes, with its capital eventually at Samaria, and the southern kingdom of Judah, consisting of two tribes, with its capital at Jerusalem. In 722 or 721 B.C., the Assyrians destroyed Samaria, overran the kingdom of Israel, and deported many Israelites to other parts of the Assyrian Empire. These dispersed Israelites (the "ten lost tribes") merged with neighboring peoples and gradually lost their identity.

The southern kingdom of Judah was also forced to pay tribute to Assyria but managed to retain its independence as Assyrian power declined. A new enemy, however, appeared on the horizon. The Chaldeans brought the final destruction of Assyria, conquered the kingdom of Judah, and completely destroyed Jerusalem in 586 B.C. Many people from Judah were deported to Babylonia; the memory of their exile is still evoked in the stirring words of Psalm 137:

> *By the rivers of Babylon, we sat and wept when we remembered Zion....*

Saul—first king	c. 1020–1000 B.C.
King David	c. 1000–970 B.C.
King Solomon	c. 970–930 B.C.
Northern kingdom of Israel destroyed by Assyria	722 or 721 B.C.
Southern kingdom of Judah falls to Chaldeans; destruction of Jerusalem	586 B.C.
Return of exiles to Jerusalem	538 B.C.

How can we sing the songs of the Lord while in a
foreign land?
If I forget you, O Jerusalem, may my right hand forget
its skill.
May my tongue cling to the roof of my mouth if I do
not remember you, if I do not consider Jerusalem
my highest joy.[2]

But the Babylonian captivity of the people of Judah did not last. A new set of conquerors, the Persians, destroyed the Chaldean kingdom but allowed the people of Judah to return to Jerusalem and rebuild their city and temple. The revived kingdom of Judah remained under Persian control until the conquests of Alexander the Great in the fourth century B.C. The people of Judah survived, eventually becoming known as the Jews and giving their name to Judaism, the religion of Yahweh, the Jewish God.

The Spiritual Dimensions of Israel

The spiritual perspective of the Israelites evolved over time. Early Israelites probably worshiped many gods, including nature spirits dwelling in trees and rocks. For some Israelites, Yahweh was the chief god of Israel, but many, including kings of Israel and Judah, worshiped other gods as well. It was among the Babylonian exiles that Yahweh, the God of Israel, came to be regarded as the only God. After the return of these exiles to Judah, their point of view eventually became dominant, and pure **monotheism**, or the belief that there is only one God for all peoples, came to be the major tenet of Judaism.

"I Am the Lord Your God": Ruler of the World According to the Jewish conception, there is but one God, whom the Jews called Yahweh. God is the creator of the world and everything in it. Indeed, Yahweh means "he causes to be." To the Jews, the gods of all other peoples were idols. The Jewish God ruled the world; he was subject to nothing. All peoples were his servants, whether they knew it or not. This God was also transcendent. He had created nature but was not in nature. The stars, moon, rivers, wind, and other natural phenomena were not divinities or suffused with divinity, as other peoples of the ancient Near East believed, but they were God's handiwork. All of God's creations could be admired for their awesome beauty but not worshiped as gods.

This omnipotent creator of the universe was not removed from the life he had created, however, but was a just and good God who expected goodness from his people. If they did not obey his will, they would be punished. But he was also a God of mercy and love: "The Lord is gracious and compassionate, slow to anger and rich in love. The Lord is good to all; he has compassion on all he has made."[3] Despite the powerful dimensions of God as creator and sustainer of the universe, the Jewish message also emphasized that each person could have a personal relationship with this powerful being. As the psalmist sang, "My help comes from the Lord, the Maker of heaven and earth. He will not let your foot slip—he who watches over you will not slumber."[4]

"You Only Have I Chosen": Covenant and Law Three aspects of the Hebrew religious tradition had special significance: the covenant, law, and the prophets. The Israelites believed that during the Exodus from Egypt, when Moses supposedly led his people out of bondage into the "promised land," a special event occurred that determined the Jewish experience for all time. According to tradition, God entered into a covenant or contract with the tribes of Israel who believed that Yahweh had spoken to them through Moses (see the box on p. 28). The Israelites promised to obey Yahweh and follow his law. In return, Yahweh promised to take special care of his chosen people, "a peculiar treasure unto me above all people."

This covenant between Yahweh and his chosen people could be fulfilled, however, only by obedience to the law of God. Law became a crucial element of the Jewish world and had a number of different dimensions. In some instances, it set forth specific requirements, such as payments for offenses. Most important, since the major characteristic of God was his goodness, ethical concerns stood at the center of the law. Sometimes these took the form of specific standards of moral behavior: "You shall not murder. You shall not commit adultery. You shall not steal."[5] But these concerns were also expressed in decrees that regulated the economic, social, and political life of the community since God's laws of morality applied to all areas of life. These laws made no class distinctions and emphasized the protection of the poor, widows, orphans, and slaves.

The Prophets The Israelites believed that certain religious leaders or "holy men," called prophets, were sent by God to serve as his voice to his people. The golden age of the prophets began in the mid-eighth century B.C. and continued during the time when the people of Israel and Judah were threatened by Assyrian and Chaldean conquerors. These "men of God" went through the land warning the Israelites that they had failed to keep God's commandments and would be punished for breaking the

THE COVENANT AND THE LAW: THE BOOK OF EXODUS

uring the Exodus from Egypt, the Hebrews are said to have made a covenant with Yahweh. They agreed to obey their God and follow his law. In return, Yahweh promised to take special care of his chosen people. This selection from the biblical book of Exodus describes the making of the covenant and God's commandments to the Hebrews.

Exodus 19:1–8

In the third month after the Israelites left Egypt—on the very day—they came to the Desert of Sinai. After they set out from Rephidim, they entered the desert of Sinai, and Israel camped there in the desert in front of the mountain. Then Moses went up to God, and the Lord, called to him from the mountain, and said, "This is what you are to say to the house of Jacob and what you are to tell the people of Israel: 'You yourselves have seen what I did to Egypt, and how I carried you on eagles's wings and brought you to myself. Now if you obey me fully and keep my covenant, then out of all nations you will be my treasured possession. Although the whole earth is mine, you will be for me a kingdom of priests and a holy nation.' These are the words you are to speak to the Israelites." So Moses went back and summoned the elders of the people and set before them all the words the Lord had commanded him to speak. The people all responded together, "We will do everything the Lord has said." So Moses brought their answer back to the Lord.

Exodus 20:1–17

And God spoke all these words, "I am the Lord your God, who brought you out of Egypt, out of the land of slavery. You shall have no other gods before me. You shall not make for yourself an idol in the form of anything in heaven above or on the earth beneath or in the waters below. You shall not bow down to them or worship them; for I, the Lord your God, am a jealous God, punishing the children for the sin of the fathers to the third and fourth generation of those who hate, but showing love to a thousand generations of those who love me and keep my commandments. You shall not misuse the name of the Lord your God, for the Lord will not hold anyone guiltless who misuse his name. Remember the Sabbath day by keeping it holy. Six days you shall labor and do all your work, but the seventh day is a Sabbath to the Lord your God. On it you shall not do any work, neither you, nor your son or daughter, nor your manservant or maidservant, nor your animals, nor the alien within your gates. For in six days the Lord made the heavens and the earth, the sea, and all that is in them, but he rested on the seventh day. Therefore the Lord blessed the Sabbath day and made it holy. Honor your father and your mother, so that you may live long in the land the Lord your God is giving you. You shall not murder. You shall not commit adultery. You shall not steal. You shall not give false testimony against your neighbor. You shall not covet your neighbor's house. You shall not covet your neighbor's wife, or his manservant or maidservant, his ox or donkey, or anything that belongs to your neighbor.

What was the nature of the covenant between Yahweh and the Hebrews? What was its moral significance for the Hebrew people? How might you explain its differences from Hammurabi's Code?

---

covenant: "I will punish you for all your iniquities." Amos prophesied the fall of the northern kingdom of Israel to Assyria; twenty years later, Isaiah said the kingdom of Judah too would fall (see the box on p. 29).

Out of the words of the prophets came new concepts that enriched the Jewish tradition and ultimately Western civilization, including a notion of universalism and a yearning for social justice. Although the Jews' religious practices gave them a sense of separateness from other peoples, the prophets transcended this by embracing a concern for all humanity. All nations would someday come to the God of Israel: "All the earth shall worship you." A universal community of all people under God would someday be established by Israel's effort. This vision encompassed the elimination of war and the establishment of peace for all the nations of the world. In the words of the prophet Isaiah: "He will judge between the nations and will settle disputes for many people. They will beat their swords into plowshares and their spears into pruning hooks. Nation will not take up sword against nation, nor will they train for war anymore."[6]

The prophets also cried out against social injustice. They condemned the rich for causing the poor to suffer, denounced luxuries as worthless, and warned of dire punishments for these sins. God's command was to live justly, share with one's neighbors, care for the poor and the unfortunate, and act with compassion. When God's command was not followed, the social fabric of the community was threatened. These proclamations by Israel's prophets became a source for Western ideals of social justice, even if they have never been perfectly realized.

Although the prophets eventually developed a sense of universalism, the demands of the Jewish religion—the obligation to obey their God—encouraged a separation between the Jews and their non-Jewish neighbors. Unlike most other peoples of the Near East, Jews could not simply be amalgamated into a community by accepting the gods of their conquerors and their neighbors. To remain faithful to the demands of their God, they might even have to refuse loyalty to political leaders.

THE HEBREW PROPHETS: MICAH, ISAIAH, AND AMOS

*T*he Hebrew prophets warned the Israelites that they must obey God's commandments or face being punished for breaking their covenant with God. These selections from the biblical prophets Micah, Isaiah, and Amos make clear that God's punishment would fall on the Israelites for their sins. Even the Assyrians, as Isaiah indicated, would be used as God's instrument to punish them.

Micah 6:9–16

Listen! The Lord is calling to the city—and to fear your name is wisdom—"Heed the rod and the One who appointed it. Am I still to forget, O wicked house, your ill-gotten treasures . . . ? Shall I acquit a man with dishonest scales, with a bag of false weights? Her rich men are violent; her people are liars and their tongues speak deceitfully. Therefore, I have begun to destroy you, to ruin you because of your sins. You will eat but not be satisfied; your stomach will still be empty. You will store up but save nothing, because what you save I will give to the sword. You will plant but not harvest; you will press olives but not use the oil on yourselves, you will crush grapes but not drink the wine. . . . Therefore I will give you over to ruin and your people to derision; you will bear the scorn of the nations."

Isaiah 10:1–6

Woe to those who make unjust laws, to those who issue oppressive decrees, to deprive the poor of their rights and withhold justice from the oppressed of my people, making their prey and robbing the fatherless. What will you do on the day of reckoning, when disaster comes from afar? To whom will you run for help? Where will you leave your riches? Nothing will remain but to cringe among the captives or fall among the slain. Yet for all this, his anger is not turned away, his hand is still upraised. "Woe to the Assyrian, the rod of my anger, in whose hand is the club of my wrath! I send him against a godless nation, I dispatch him against a people who anger me, to seize loot and snatch plunder, and to trample them down like mud in the streets."

Amos 3:1–2

Hear this word the Lord has spoken against you, O people of Israel—against the whole family I brought up out of Egypt: "You only have I chosen of all the families of the earth; therefore, I will punish you for all your sins."

What did the Hebrew prophets focus on as the transgressions of the Hebrew people? What do these selections tell you about the nature of the Hebrews as a "chosen" people?

The Neighbors of the Israelites

The Israelites were not the only people living in Palestine. The Philistines, who invaded from the sea, established five towns on the coastal plain of the region. They settled down as farmers and eventually entered into conflict with the Israelites. Although the Philistines were newcomers to the area, the Phoenicians had resided there for some time but now found themselves with a new independence. A Semitic-speaking people, the Phoenicians resided along the Mediterranean coast on a narrow band of land 120 miles long. They had rebuilt their major cities after destruction by the Sea Peoples. Their newfound political independence helped the Phoenicians expand the trade that was already the foundation of their prosperity. In fact, the Phoenician city of Byblos had been the principal distribution center for Egyptian papyrus outside Egypt (the Greek word for book, *biblos*, is derived from the name Byblos).

Hebrew Law. Because of the supposed covenant between Yahweh and the Israelites, law became an important part of Jewish life. Seen here is a twelfth-century manuscript page of the *Mishneh Torah*, a fourteen-volume study of all of Jewish law by Moses Maimonides, the foremost Jewish philosopher of the Middle Ages.

Phoenician Colonies and Trade Routes, c. 800 B.C.

The chief cities of Phoenicia—Byblos, Tyre, and Sidon—were ports on the eastern Mediterranean, but they also served as distribution centers for the lands to the east in Mesopotamia. The Phoenicians themselves produced a number of goods for foreign markets, including purple dye, glass, wine, and lumber from the famous cedars of Lebanon. In addition, the Phoenicians improved their ships and became great international sea traders. They charted new routes, not only in the Mediterranean but also in the Atlantic Ocean, where they sailed south along the west coast of Africa. The Phoenicians established a number of colonies in the western Mediterranean, including settlements in southern Spain, Sicily, and Sardinia. Carthage, the Phoenicians' most famous colony, was located on the North African coast.

Culturally, the Phoenicians are best known as transmitters. Instead of using pictographs or signs to represent whole words and syllables as the Mesopotamians and Egyptians did, the Phoenicians simplified their writing by using twenty-two different signs to represent the sounds of their speech. These twenty-two characters or letters could be used to spell out all the words in the Phoenician language. Although the Phoenicians were not the only people to invent an alphabet, theirs would have special significance because it was eventually passed on to the Greeks. The Phoenicians achieved much while independent, but they ultimately fell subject to the Assyrians, Chaldeans, and Persians.

The Assyrian Empire

The existence of independent states in Palestine was possible only because of the power vacuum existing in the ancient Near East after the demise of the Hittite kingdom and the weakening of Egypt. But this condition did not last; new empires soon came to dominate vast stretches of the ancient Near East. The first of these empires emerged in Assyria, an area whose location on the upper Tigris River brought it into both cultural and political contact with southern Mesopotamia.

Although part of Mesopotamia, Assyria, with its hills and adequate, if not ample, rainfall, had a different terrain and climate. The Assyrians were a Semitic-speaking people who exploited the use of iron weapons to establish an empire by 700 B.C. that included Mesopotamia, parts of the Iranian plateau, sections of Asia Minor, Syria, Palestine, and Egypt down to Thebes (see Map 2.2). Ashurbanipal (669–626 B.C.) was one of the strongest Assyrian rulers, but it was already becoming apparent during his reign that the Assyrian Empire was greatly overextended. Internal strife intensified as powerful Assyrian nobles gained control of vast territories and waged their own private military campaigns. Moreover, subject peoples, such as the Babylonians, greatly resented Assyrian rule and rebelled against it. Soon after Ashurbanipal's reign, the Assyrian Empire began to disintegrate rapidly. The capital city of Nineveh fell to a coalition of Chaldeans and Medes in 612 B.C., and in 605 B.C. the rest of the empire was finally divided between the coalition powers.

Organization of the Empire

At its height, the Assyrian Empire was ruled by kings whose power was considered absolute. Under their leadership, the empire became well organized. By eliminating governorships held by nobles on a hereditary basis and instituting a new hierarchy of local officials directly responsible to the king, the Assyrian kings gained greater control over the resources of the empire. The Assyrians also developed an efficient system of communication to administer their empire more effectively. A network of posting stages was established throughout the empire that used relays of horses (mules or donkeys in mountainous terrain) to carry messages. The system was so effective that a provincial governor anywhere in the empire (except Egypt) could send a query and receive an answer from the king within a week.

The Assyrian Military Machine

The ability of the Assyrians to conquer and maintain an empire was due to a combination of factors. Over many years of practice, the Assyrians developed effective military leaders and fighters. They were able to enlist and deploy troops numbering in the hundreds of thousands, although most campaigns were not conducted on such a large scale. In 845 B.C., an Assyrian army of 120,000 men crossed the Euphrates on a campaign. Size alone was not decisive, however. The Assyrian army was extremely well organized and disciplined. It included a standing army of infantrymen as its core, accompanied by cavalrymen and horse-drawn war chariots that were used as mobile platforms for shooting arrows. Moreover, the Assyrians had the advantage of having the first large armies equipped with iron weapons. The Hittites had been the first to develop iron metallurgy, but iron came to be used extensively only after new methods for hardening it became common after 1000 B.C.

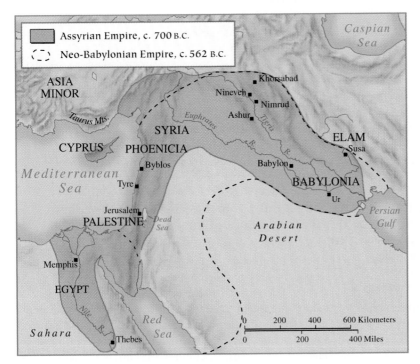

MAP 2.2 **The Assyrian and Neo-Babylonian Empires.** The Assyrian Empire expanded in large part due to its brutal military methods. It maintained its rule through use of a common language and religion, along with extremely violent suppression of internal revolts. It was overthrown by Chaldeans in Babylonia, leading to the Neo-Babylonian Empire epitomized by Nebuchadnezzar. [?] Why was control of Babylonia crucial to both empires? [View icon] **View an animated version of this map or related maps at** http://thomsonedu.com/history/spielvogel

Another factor in the army's success was its ability to use various military tactics (see the box on p. 32). The Assyrians were skilled at waging guerrilla war in the mountains and set battles on open ground and were especially renowned for siege warfare. They would hammer a city's walls with heavy, wheeled siege towers and armored battering rams while sappers dug tunnels to undermine the walls' foundations and cause them to collapse. The besieging Assyrian armies learned to cut off supplies so effectively that if a city did not fall to them, the inhabitants could be starved into submission.

A final factor in the effectiveness of the Assyrian military machine was its ability to create a climate of terror as an instrument of war. The Assyrians became famous for their terror tactics, although some historians believe that their policies were no worse than those of other conquerors. As a matter of regular policy, the Assyrians laid waste the land in which they were fighting, smashing dams, looting and destroying towns, setting crops on fire, and cutting down trees, particularly fruit trees. The Assyrians were especially known for committing atrocities on their captives. King Ashurnasirpal recorded this account of his treatment of prisoners:

> 3000 of their combat troops I felled with weapons. . . . Many of the captives taken from them I burned in a fire. Many I took alive; from some of these I cut off their hands to the wrist, from others I cut off their noses, ears and fingers; I put out the eyes of many of the soldiers. . . . I burned their young men and women to death.[7]

After conquering another city, the same king wrote: "I fixed up a pile of corpses in front of the city's gate. I flayed the nobles, as many as had rebelled, and spread their skins out on the piles. . . . I flayed many within my land and spread their skins out on the walls."[8] (Obviously not a king

to play games with!) Note that this policy of extreme cruelty to prisoners was not used against all enemies but was reserved primarily for those who were already part of the empire and then rebelled against Assyrian rule.

Assyrian Society and Culture

Unlike the Hebrews, the Assyrians were not fearful of mixing with other peoples. In fact, the Assyrian policy of deporting many prisoners of newly conquered territories to Assyria created a polyglot society in which ethnic differences were not very important. It has been estimated that over a period of three centuries, between four and five million people were deported to Assyria, resulting in a population that was very racially and linguistically mixed. What gave identity to the Assyrians themselves was their language, although even that was akin to that of their southern neighbors in Babylonia, who also spoke a Semitic tongue. Religion was also a cohesive force. Assyria was literally "the land of Ashur," a reference to its chief god. The king, as the human representative of the god Ashur, provided a unifying focus.

Agriculture formed the principal basis of Assyrian life. Assyria was a land of farming villages with relatively few significant cities, especially in comparison to southern Mesopotamia. Unlike the river valleys, where farming required the minute organization of large numbers of people to control irrigation, Assyrian farms received sufficient moisture from regular rainfall.

Trade was second to agriculture in economic importance. For internal trade, metals, such as gold, silver, copper, and bronze, were used as a medium of exchange. Various agricultural products also served as a form of payment or exchange. Because of their geographical

THE ASSYRIAN MILITARY MACHINE

The Assyrians won a reputation for having a mighty military machine. They were able to use a variety of military tactics and were successful whether they were employing guerrilla warfare, fighting set battles, or laying siege to cities. In these three selections, Assyrian kings describe their military conquests.

King Sennacherib (704–681 B.C.) Describes a Battle with the Elamites in 691

At the command of the god Ashur, the great Lord, I rushed upon the enemy like the approach of a hurricane. . . . I put them to rout and turned them back. I transfixed the troops of the enemy with javelins and arrows. . . . I cut their throats like sheep. . . . My prancing steeds, trained to harness, plunged into their welling blood as into a river; the wheels of my battle chariot were bespattered with blood and filth. I filled the plain with the corpses of their warriors like herbage. . . . As to the sheikhs of the Chaldeans, panic from my onslaught overwhelmed them like a demon. They abandoned their tents and fled for their lives, crushing the corpses of their troop as they went. . . . In their terror they passed scalding urine and voided their excrement into their chariots.

King Sennacherib Describes His Siege of Jerusalem (701 B.C.)

As to Hezekiah, the Jew, he did not submit to my yoke, I laid siege to forty-six of his strong cities, walled forts and to the countless small villages in their vicinity, and conquered them by means of well-stamped earth-ramps, and battering-rams brought thus near to the walls combined with the attack by foot soldiers, using mines, breeches as well as sapper work. I drove out of them 200,150 people, young and old, male and female, horses, mules, donkeys, camels, big and small cattle beyond counting, and considered them booty. Himself I made a prisoner in Jerusalem, his royal residence, like a bird in a cage. I surrounded him with earthwork in order to molest those who were leaving his city's gate.

King Ashurbanipal (669–626 B.C.) Describes His Treatment of Conquered Babylon

I tore out the tongues of those whose slanderous mouths had uttered blasphemies against my god Ashur and had plotted against me, his god-fearing prince; I defeated them completely. The others, I smashed alive with the very same statues of protective deities with which they had smashed my own grandfather Sennacherib—now finally as a belated burial sacrifice for his soul. I fed their corpses, cut into small pieces, to dogs, pigs, . . . vultures, the birds of the sky and also the fish of the ocean. After I had performed this and thus made quiet again the hearts of the great gods, my lords, I removed the corpses of those whom the pestilence had felled, whose leftovers after the dogs and pigs had fed on them were obstructing the streets, filling the places of Babylon, and of those who had lost their lives through the terrible famine.

As seen in their own descriptions, what did Assyrian kings believe was important for military success? Do you think their accounts may be exaggerated? Why?

location, the Assyrians served as middlemen and participated in an international trade in which they imported timber, wine, and precious metals and stones while exporting textiles produced in palaces, temples, and private villas.

Assyrian culture was a hybrid. The Assyrians assimilated much of Mesopotamian civilization and saw themselves as guardians of Sumerian and Babylonian culture. Ashurbanipal, for example, established a large library at Nineveh that included the available works of Mesopotamian history. Assyrian religion reflected this assimilation of other cultures as well. Although the Assyrians' national god Ashur was their chief deity, virtually all the other gods and goddesses were Mesopotamian.

Among the best-known objects of Assyrian art are the relief sculptures found in the royal palaces in three of the Assyrian capital cities, Nimrud, Nineveh, and Khorsabad. These reliefs, which were begun in the ninth century B.C. and reached their high point in the reign of Ashurbanipal in the seventh, depicted two different kinds of subject matter: ritual or ceremonial scenes, revolving around the person of the king, and scenes of hunting and war. The latter show realistic action scenes of the king and his warriors engaged in battle or hunting animals, especially lions. These pictures depict a strongly masculine world where discipline, brute force, and toughness are the enduring values, indeed, the very values of the Assyrian military monarchy.

The Persian Empire

The Chaldeans, a Semitic-speaking people, had gained ascendancy in Babylonia by the seventh century and came to form the chief resistance to Assyrian control of Mesopotamia. After the collapse of the Assyrian Empire, the Chaldeans, under their king Nebuchadnezzar II (605–562 B.C.), regained for Babylonia a position as the leading power in the ancient Near East.

Nebuchadnezzar rebuilt Babylon as the center of his empire, giving it a reputation as one of the great cities of the ancient world. Babylon was surrounded by great walls, 8 miles in length, encircled by a moat filled by the Euphrates River. The city was adorned with temples and

King Ashurbanipal's Lion Hunt. This relief, sculptured on alabaster as a decoration for the northern palace in Nineveh, depicts King Ashurbanipal engaged in a lion hunt. Lion hunts were not conducted in the wild but under controlled circumstances. The king and his retainers faced lions released from cages in an arena. The purpose was to glorify the king as a conqueror of the king of beasts. Relief sculpture, one of the best-known forms of Assyrian art, reached its high point under Ashurbanipal at about the time that the Assyrian Empire began to disintegrate.

palaces; most famous of all were the Hanging Gardens, known as one of the Seven Wonders of the ancient world. These were supposedly built to satisfy Nebuchadnezzar's wife, a princess from the land of Media, who missed the mountains of her homeland. A series of terraces led to a plateau, an artificial mountain, at the top of which grew the lush gardens irrigated by water piped to the top. According to the account of a first-century A.D. author, the impression of the gardens from a distance was quite remarkable:

> On the top of the citadel are the hanging gardens, a wonder celebrated in the tales of the Greeks. . . . Columns of stone were set up to sustain the whole work, and on these was laid a floor of squared blocks, strong enough to hold the earth which is thrown upon it to a great depth, as well as the water with which they irrigate the soil; and the structure supports trees of such great size that the thickness of their trunks equals a measure of eight cubits [about 12 feet]. They tower to a height of fifty feet, and they yield as much fruit as if they were growing in their native soil. . . . To those who look upon the trees from a distance, real woods seem to be overhanging their native mountains.[9]

But the splendor of the Neo-Babylonian Empire proved to be short-lived when Babylon fell to the Persians in 539 B.C.

The Persians were an Indo-European–speaking people who lived in southwestern Iran. Primarily nomadic, the Persians were organized in tribes or clans led by petty kings assisted by a group of warriors who formed a class of nobles. At the beginning of the seventh century B.C., the Persians became unified under the Achaemenid dynasty, based in Persis in southern Iran. One of the dynasty's members, Cyrus (559–530 B.C.), created a powerful Persian state that rearranged the political map of the ancient Near East.

Cyrus the Great

In 550 B.C., Cyrus established Persian control over Media, making it the first Persian **satrapy** or province. Three years later, Cyrus defeated the prosperous Lydian kingdom in western Asia Minor, and Lydia became another Persian satrapy. Cyrus' forces then went on to conquer the Greek city-states that had been established on the Ionian coast. Cyrus then turned eastward, subduing the eastern part of the Iranian plateau, Sogdiana, and even western India. His eastern frontiers secured, Cyrus entered Mesopotamia in 539 and captured Babylon. His treatment of Babylonia showed remarkable restraint and wisdom. Babylonia was made into a Persian province under a Persian satrap, but many government officials were kept in their positions. Cyrus took the title "King of All, Great King, Mighty King, King of Babylon, King of the Land of Sumer and Akkad, King of the Four Rims [of the earth], the Son of Cambyses the Great King, King of Anshan"[10] and insisted that he stood in the ancient, unbroken line of Babylonian kings. By appealing to the vanity of the Babylonians, he won their loyalty. Cyrus also issued an edict permitting the Jews, who had been brought to Babylon in the sixth century B.C., to return to Jerusalem with their sacred temple objects and to rebuild their temple as well.

To his contemporaries, Cyrus the Great was deserving of his epithet. The Greek historian Herodotus recounted that the Persians viewed him as a "father," a ruler who was "gentle, and procured them all manner of goods."[11] Certainly, Cyrus must have been an unusual ruler for his time, a man who demonstrated considerable wisdom and compassion in the conquest and organization of his empire. Cyrus gained the favor of the priesthoods in his conquered lands by restoring temples

MAP 2.3 **The Persian Empire at the Time of Darius.** Cyrus the Great united the Persians and led them in successful conquest of much of the Near East. By the time of Darius, the Persian Empire was the largest the world had yet seen. The Persians allowed religious tolerance and gave some government positions to natives of conquered territories. **?** How did Persian policies attempt to overcome the difficulties of governing far-flung provinces? **View an animated version of this map or related maps at** http://thomsonedu.com/history/spielvogel

and permitting religious toleration. He won approval by using not only Persians but also native peoples as government officials in their own states. Unlike the Assyrian rulers of an earlier empire, he had a reputation for mercy. Medes, Babylonians, and Hebrews all accepted him as their legitimate ruler. Indeed, the Hebrews regarded him as the anointed one of God:

> I am the Lord who says of Cyrus, "He is my shepherd and will accomplish all that I please"; he will say of Jerusalem, "Let it be rebuilt"; and of the temple, "Let its foundations be laid." This is what the Lord says to his anointed, to Cyrus, whose right hand I take hold of to subdue nations before him.[12]

Cyrus had a genuine respect for ancient civilizations—in building his palaces, he made use of Assyrian, Babylonian, Egyptian, and Lydian practices.

Expanding the Empire

Cyrus' successors extended the territory of the Persian Empire. His son Cambyses (530–522 B.C.) undertook a successful invasion of Egypt and made it into a satrapy with Memphis as its capital. Darius (521–486 B.C.) added

a new Persian province in western India that extended to the Indus River and moved into Europe proper, conquering Thrace and making the Macedonian king a vassal (see Map 2.3). A revolt of the Ionian Greek cities in 499 B.C. resulted in temporary freedom for these communities in western Asia Minor. Aid from the Greek mainland, most notably from Athens, encouraged the Ionians to invade Lydia and burn Sardis, center of the Lydian satrapy. This event led to Darius' involvement with the mainland Greeks. After reestablishing control of the Ionian Greek cities, Darius undertook an invasion of the Greek mainland, which culminated in the famous Athenian victory in the Battle of Marathon in 490 B.C. (see Chapter 3).

Governing the Empire

By the reign of Darius, the Persians had created the largest empire the world had yet seen. It not only included all the old centers of power in the Near East, Egypt, Mesopotamia, and Assyria but also extended into Thrace and Asia Minor in the west and into India in the east. For administrative purposes, the empire had been divided into around twenty satrapies. Each of these

CHRONOLOGY The Ancient Empires

The Assyrians	
Height of power	700 B.C.
Ashurbanipal	669–626 B.C.
Capture of Nineveh	612 B.C.
Destruction of the Assyrian Empire	605 B.C.
The Chaldeans	
Ascendancy in Babylonia	600s B.C.
Height of Neo-Babylonian Empire under King Nebuchadnezzar II	605–562 B.C.
Fall of Babylon	539 B.C.
The Persians	
Unification under Achaemenid dynasty	600s B.C.
Persian control over Medes	550 B.C.
Conquests of Cyrus the Great	559–530 B.C.
Cambyses and conquest of Egypt	530–522 B.C.
Reign of Darius	521–486 B.C.

Darius, the Great King. Darius ruled the Persian Empire from 521 to 486 B.C. He is shown here on his throne in Persepolis, a new capital city that he built. In his right hand, Darius holds the royal staff, in his left, a lotus blossom with two buds, a symbol of royalty.

provinces was ruled by a governor or satrap, literally a "protector of the kingdom." Although Darius had not introduced the system of satrapies, he organized it more rationally. He created a sensible system for calculating the tribute that each satrapy owed to the central government and gave satraps specific civil and military duties. They collected tributes, were responsible for justice and security, raised military levies for the royal army, and normally commanded the military forces within their satrapies. In terms of real power, the satraps were miniature kings with courts imitative of the Great King's.

From the time of Darius on, satraps were men of Persian descent. The major satrapies were given to princes of the royal family, and their position became essentially hereditary. The minor satrapies were placed in the hands of Persian nobles. Their offices, too, tended to pass from father to son. The hereditary nature of the governors' offices made it necessary to provide some checks on their power. Consequently, royal officials at the satrapal courts acted as spies for the Great King.

An efficient system of communication was crucial to sustaining the Persian Empire. Well-maintained roads facilitated the rapid transit of military and government personnel. One in particular, the so-called Royal Road, stretched from Sardis, the center of Lydia in Asia Minor, to Susa, the chief capital of the Persian Empire. Like the Assyrians, the Persians established staging posts equipped with fresh horses for the king's messengers.

The Great King Darius

In this vast administrative system, the Persian king occupied an exalted position. All subjects were the king's servants, and he was the source of all justice, possessing the power of life and death over everyone. Persian kings were largely secluded and not easily accessible. They resided in a series of splendid palaces. Darius in particular was a palace builder on a grand scale. His description of the construction of a palace in the chief Persian capital of Susa demonstrated what a truly international empire Persia was:

This is the . . . palace which at Susa I built. From afar its ornamentation was brought. . . . The cedar timber was brought from a mountain named Lebanon; the Assyrians brought it to Babylon, and from Babylon the Carians and Ionians brought it to Susa. Teakwood was brought from Gandara and from Carmania. The gold which was used here was brought from Sardis and from Bactria. The stone—lapis lazuli and carnelian—was brought from Sogdiana. . . . The silver and copper were brought from Egypt. The ornamentation with which the wall was

A Dinner with the Persian King

The Persian kings lived in luxury as a result of their conquests and ability to levy taxes from their conquered subjects. In this selection, we read a description of how a Persian king dined with his numerous guests.

Athenaeus, The Deipnosophists

Heracleides of Cumae, author of the *Persian History*, writes in the second book of the work entitled *Equipment*: "All who attend upon the Persian kings when they dine first bathe themselves and then serve in white clothes, and spend nearly half the day on preparations for the dinner. Of those who are invited to eat with the king, some dine outdoors, in full sight of anyone who wishes to look on; others dine indoors in the king's company. Yet even these do not eat in his presence, for there are two rooms opposite each other, in one of which the king has his meal, in the other the invited guests. The king can see them through the curtain at the door, but they cannot see him. Sometimes, however, on the occasion of a public holiday, all dine in a single room with the king, in the great hall. And whenever the king commands a symposium [drinking-bout following the dinner], which he does often, he has about a dozen companions at the drinking. When they have finished dinner, that is the king by himself, the guests in the other room, these fellow-drinkers are summoned by one of the eunuchs; and entering they drink with him, though even they do not have the same wine; moreover, they sit on the floor, while he reclines on a couch supported by feet of gold, and they depart after having drunk to excess. In most cases the king breakfasts and dines alone, but sometimes his wife and some of his sons dine with him. And throughout the dinner his concubines sing and play the lyre; one of them is the soloist, the others sing in chorus. And so ... the 'king's dinner,' as it is called, will appear prodigal to one who merely hears about it, but when one examines it carefully it will be found to have been got up with economy and even with parsimony; and the same is true of the dinners among other Persians of high station. For one thousand animals are slaughtered daily for the king; these comprise horses, camels, oxen, asses, deer, and most of the small animals; many birds are also consumed, including Arabian ostriches—and the creature is large—geese, and cocks. And of all these only moderate portions are served to each of the king's guests, and each of them may carry home whatever he leaves untouched at the meal. But the greater part of these meats and other foods are taken into the courtyard for the bodyguard and light-armed troopers maintained by the king; there they divide all the half-eaten remnants of meat and bread and share them in equal portions. . . ."

What does this description of a royal dinner tell you about the nature of Persian kingship?

---

adorned was brought from Ionia. The ivory was brought from Ethiopia, from India, and from Arachosia. The stone pillars were brought from ... Elam. The artisans who dressed the stone were Ionians and Sardians. The goldsmiths who wrought the gold were Medes and Egyptians. ... Those who worked the baked brick [with figures] were Babylonians. The men who adorned the wall were Medes and Egyptians. At Susa here a splendid work was ordered; very splendid did it turn out.[13]

But Darius was unhappy with Susa. He did not really consider it his homeland, and it was oppressively hot in the summer months. He built another residence at Persepolis, a new capital located to the southeast of the old one at a higher elevation.

The policies of Darius also tended to widen the gap between the king and his subjects. As the Great King himself said of all his subjects, "What was said to them by me, night and day it was done."[14] Over a period of time, the Great Kings in their greed came to hoard immense quantities of gold and silver in the various treasuries located in the capital cities. Both their hoarding of wealth and their later overtaxation of their subjects are seen as crucial factors in the ultimate weakening of the Persian Empire (see the box above).

In its heyday, however, the empire stood supreme, and much of its power depended on the military. By the time of Darius, the Persian monarchs had created a standing army of professional soldiers. This army was truly international, composed of contingents from the various peoples who made up the empire. At its core was a cavalry force of ten thousand and an elite infantry force of ten thousand Medes and Persians known as the Immortals because they were never allowed to fall below ten thousand in number. When one was killed, he was immediately replaced. The Persians made effective use of their cavalry, especially for operating behind enemy lines and breaking up lines of communication.

Persian Religion

Of all the Persians' cultural contributions, the most original was their religion, **Zoroastrianism**. According to Persian tradition, its founder, Zoroaster, was born in 660 B.C. After a period of wandering and solitude, he experienced revelations that caused him to be revered as a prophet of the "true religion." His teachings were eventually written down in the third century A.D. in the *Zend Avesta*.

Like the Hebrews', Zoroaster's spiritual message was monotheistic. To Zoroaster, Ahuramazda was the only god, and the religion he preached was the only perfect

Archers of the Persian Guard. One of the main pillars supporting the Persian Empire was the military. This frieze, composed of enameled brick, depicts members of the famous infantry force known as the Immortals, so called because their number was never allowed to drop below ten thousand. Anyone killed would be replaced immediately. The men in the frieze carry the standard lance and bow and arrow of the infantry.

one. Ahuramazda (the "Wise Lord") was the supreme deity who brought all things into being:

> *This I ask of You, O Ahuramazda; answer me well:*
> *Who at the Creation was the first father of Justice?—*
> *Who assigned their path to the sun and the stars?—*
> *Who decreed the waxing and waning of the moon, if*
> *   it was not You?—...*
> *Who has fixed the earth below, and the heaven above*
> *   with its clouds that it might not be moved?—*
> *Who has appointed the waters and the green things*
> *   upon the earth?—*
> *Who has harnessed to the wind and the clouds their*
> *   steeds?—...*
> *Thus do I strive to recognize in You, O Wise One,*
> *Together with the Holy Spirit, the Creator of all*
> *   things.*[15]

According to Zoroaster, Ahuramazda also possessed abstract qualities or states that all humans should aspire to, such as good thought, right, and piety. Although Ahuramazda was supreme, he was not unopposed. At the beginning of the world, the good spirit of Ahuramazda was opposed by the evil spirit, known as Ahriman.

Humans also played a role in this cosmic struggle between good and evil. Ahuramazda, the creator, gave all humans free will and the power to choose between right and wrong. The good person chooses the right way of Ahuramazda. Zoroaster taught that there would be an end to the struggle between good and evil. Ahuramazda would eventually triumph, and at the last judgment at the end of the world, the final separation of good and evil would occur. Individuals, too, would be judged. Each soul faced a final evaluation of its actions. If a person had performed good deeds, he or she would achieve paradise; if evil deeds, the soul would be thrown into an abyss of torment.

CONCLUSION

Around 1200 B.C., the decline of the Hittites and the Egyptians had created a void that allowed a number of small states to emerge and flourish temporarily. All of them were eventually overshadowed by the rise of the great empires of the Assyrians, Chaldeans, and Persians. The Assyrian Empire was the first to unite almost all of the ancient Near East. Even larger, however, was the empire of the Great Kings of Persia. Although it owed much to the administrative organization created by the Assyrians, the Persian Empire had its own peculiar strengths. Persian rule was tolerant as well as efficient. Conquered peoples were allowed to keep their own religions, customs, and methods of doing business. The many years of peace that the Persian Empire brought to the Near East facilitated trade and the general well-being of its peoples. It is no wonder that many peoples expressed their gratitude for being subjects of the Great Kings of Persia.

The Hebrews were one of these peoples. They created no empire and were dominated by the Assyrians, Chaldeans, and Persians. Nevertheless, they left a spiritual legacy that influenced much of the later development of Western civilization. The evolution of Hebrew monotheism helped Judaism become one of the world's great religions; it influenced the development of both Christianity and Islam. When we speak of the Judeo-Christian heritage of Western civilization, we refer not only to the concept of monotheism but also to ideas of law, morality, and social justice that have become important parts of Western culture.

On the western fringes of the Persian Empire, another relatively small group of people, the Greeks, were evolving cultural and political ideals that would also have an important impact on Western civilization. It is to the Greeks that we now turn.

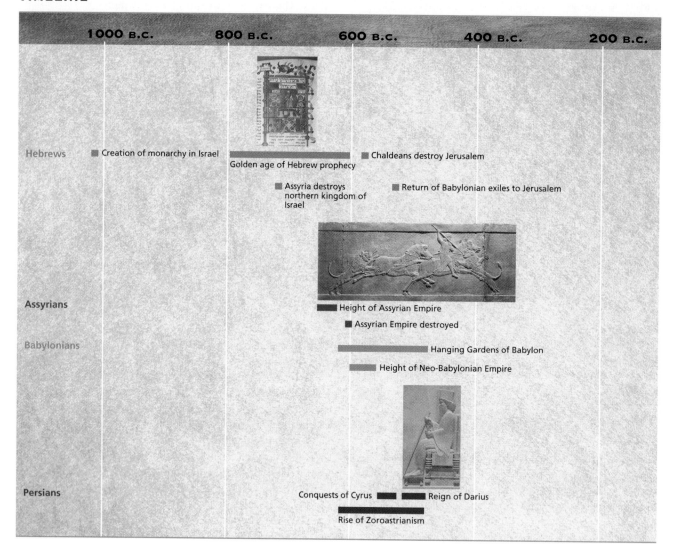

	1000 B.C.	800 B.C.	600 B.C.	400 B.C.	200 B.C.

Hebrews — Creation of monarchy in Israel

Golden age of Hebrew prophecy

— Chaldeans destroy Jerusalem

— Assyria destroys northern kingdom of Israel

— Return of Babylonian exiles to Jerusalem

Assyrians

Height of Assyrian Empire

Assyrian Empire destroyed

Babylonians

Hanging Gardens of Babylon

Height of Neo-Babylonian Empire

Persians

Conquests of Cyrus — Reign of Darius

Rise of Zoroastrianism

NOTES

1. 2 Samuel 8:2.
2. Psalms 137:1, 4–6.
3. Psalms 145:8–9.
4. Psalms 121:2–3.
5. Exodus 20:13–15.
6. Isaiah 2:4.
7. Quoted in H.W.F. Saggs, *The Might That Was Assyria* (London, 1984), p. 261.
8. Ibid., p. 262.
9. J. C. Rolfe, trans., *Quintus Curtius I* (Cambridge, Mass., 1971), pp. 337–339.
10. Quoted in J. M. Cook, *The Persian Empire* (New York, 1983), p. 32.
11. Herodotus, *The Persian Wars*, trans. G. Rawlinson (New York, 1942), p. 257.
12. Isaiah 44:28, 45:1.
13. Quoted in A. T. Olmstead, *History of the Persian Empire* (Chicago, 1948), p. 168.
14. Quoted in Cook, *The Persian Empire*, p. 76.

15. Yasna 44:3–4, 7, as quoted in A. C. Bouquet, *Sacred Books of the World* (Harmondsworth, England, 1954), pp. 111–112.

SUGGESTIONS FOR FURTHER READING

On the Sea Peoples, see the standard work by **N. Sandars**, *The Sea Peoples: Warriors of the Ancient Mediterranean* (London, 1978). Surveys on the Hittites can be found in **O. R. Gurney**, *The Hittites*, rev. ed. (Harmondsworth, England, 1990), and **T. Bryce**, *The Kingdom of the Hittites* (Oxford, 1998). See also **T. Bryce**, *Life and Society in the Hittite World* (Oxford, 2002). For an excellent general survey of the material covered in this chapter, see **A. Kuhrt**, *The Ancient Near East, c. 3000–330 B.C.*, vol. 2 (London, 1995), and **M. van de Mieroop**, *A History of the Ancient Near East, ca. 3000–323 B.C.* (Oxford, 2004).

There is an enormous literature on ancient Israel. Two good studies on the archaeological aspects are **A. Mazar**, *Archaeology of the Land of the Bible* (New York, 1992), and **A. Ben-Tor**, ed., *The Archaeology of Ancient Israel* (New Haven, Conn., 1992). For historical narratives, see especially **J. Bright**, *A History of Israel*, 3d ed. (Philadelphia, 1981), a fundamental study; **J. M. Miller and J. H. Hayes**, *A History of Ancient Israel and Judah* (Philadelphia, 1986); **M. Grant**, *The History of Ancient Israel* (New York, 1984); and **H. Shanks**, *Ancient Israel: A Short History from Abraham to the Roman Destruction of the Temple* (Englewood Cliffs, N.J., 1988). For a new perspective, see **N. P. Lemche**, *Ancient Israel: A New History of Israelite Society* (Sheffield, England, 1988). On the origins of the Israelites, see **W. G. Dever**, *Who Were the Early Israelites and Where Did They Come From?* (Grand Rapids, Mich., 2003).

For general studies on the religion of the Hebrews, see **R. Albertz**, *A History of Israelite Religion in the Old Testament Period* (Louisville, Ky., 1994), and **W. J. Doorly**, *The Religion of Israel* (New York, 1997). The role of the prophets is given a new interpretation in **N. Podhoretz**, *The Prophets* (New York, 2002).

For a good account of Phoenician domestic and overseas expansion, see **D. Harden**, *The Phoenicians*, rev. ed. (Harmondsworth, England, 1980). See also **M. E. Aubet**, *The Phoenicians and the West: Politics, Colonies and Trade* (Cambridge, 1993), and **G. Markoe**, *Phoenicians* (London, 2000), on Phoenician society.

A detailed account of Assyrian history is **H.W.F. Saggs**, *The Might That Was Assyria* (London, 1984). **A. T. Olmstead**, *History of Assyria* (Chicago, 1975), is a basic survey of the Assyrian Empire. The Neo-Babylonian Empire can be examined in **H. W. F. Saggs**, *Babylonians* (Norman, Okla., 1995).

The classic work on the Persian Empire is **A. T. Olmstead**, *History of the Persian Empire* (Chicago, 1948), but **J. M. Cook**, *The Persian Empire* (New York, 1983), provides new material and fresh interpretations. Also of value is **J. Curtis**, *Ancient Persia* (Cambridge, Mass., 1990). On the history of Zoroastrianism, see **S. A. Nigosian**, *The Zoroastrian Faith: Tradition and Modern Research* (New York, 1993).

Thomson NOW! Enter *ThomsonNOW* using the access card that is available for *Western Civilization: A Brief History*. *ThomsonNOW* will help you understand this chapter with lesson plans generated for your needs. In addition, you can read the following documents, and many more, online:

Book of Ezra
(Old Testament), Baal Myth of Ugarit

WESTERN CIVILIZATION RESOURCES

Visit the Web site for *Western Civilization: A Brief History* for resources specific to this book:
http://www.thomsonedu.com/history/spielvogel

For a variety of tools to help you succeed in this course, visit the Western Civilization Resource Center at
http://history.wadsworth.com/spielvogel

Included are quizzes, images, documents, interactive simulations, maps and timelines, movie explorations, and a wealth of other sources.

THE CIVILIZATION OF THE GREEKS

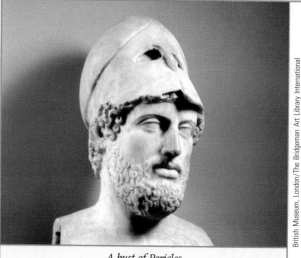

A bust of Pericles

British Museum, London/The Bridgeman Art Library International

*I*N 431 B.C., **WAR ERUPTED** as two very different Greek city-states—Athens and Sparta—fought for domination of the Greek world. The people of Athens felt secure behind their walls and in the first winter of the war held a public funeral to honor those who had died in battle. On the day of the ceremony, the citizens of Athens joined in a procession, with the relatives of the dead wailing for their loved ones. As was the custom in Athens, one leading citizen was asked to address the crowd, and on this day it was Pericles who spoke to the people. He talked about the greatness of Athens and reminded the Athenians of the strength of their political system: "Our constitution," he said, "is called a democracy because power is in the hands not of a minority but of the whole people. When it is a question of settling private disputes, everyone is equal before the law. Just as our political life is free and open, so is our day-to-day life in our relations with each other. . . . Here each individual is interested not only in his own affairs but in the affairs of the state as well."

In this famous Funeral Oration, Pericles gave voice to the ideal of democracy and the importance of the individual. It was the Greeks who constructed the intellectual foundations of our Western heritage. They asked some basic questions about human life that still dominate our own intellectual pursuits: What is the nature of the universe? What is the purpose of human existence? What is our relationship to divine forces? What constitutes a community? What constitutes a state? What is true education? What are the true sources of law? What is truth itself, and how do we realize it? Not only did the Greeks provide answers to these questions, but they created a system of logical, analytical thought to examine them. This rational outlook has remained an important feature of Western civilization.

The remarkable story of ancient Greek civilization begins with the arrival of the first Greeks around 1900 B.C. By the eighth century B.C., the characteristic institution of ancient Greek life, the polis or city-state, had emerged. Greek civilization flourished and reached its height in the Classical era of the fifth century B.C., which has come to be closely identified with the achievements of Athenian democracy.◆

Early Greece

Geography played an important role in Greek history. Compared to the landmasses of Mesopotamia and Egypt, Greece covered a small area. Its mountainous peninsula encompassed only 45,000 square miles of territory, about the same as the state of Louisiana. The mountains and the sea were especially significant. Much of Greece consists of small plains and river valleys surrounded by mountain ranges 8,000 to 10,000 feet high. The mountainous terrain had the effect of isolating Greeks from one another. Consequently, Greek communities tended to follow their own separate paths and develop their own way of life. As time went on, these communities became attached to their independence and were only too willing to fight one another to gain advantage. No doubt the small size of these independent Greek communities fostered participation in political affairs and unique cultural expressions, but the rivalry among these communities also led to the bitter warfare that ultimately devastated Greek society.

The sea also influenced the evolution of Greek society. Greece had a long seacoast, dotted by bays and inlets that provided numerous harbors. The Greeks also inhabited a number of islands to the west, south, and particularly the east of the Greek mainland. It is no accident that the Greeks became seafarers who sailed out into the Aegean and the Mediterranean first to make contact with the outside world and later to establish colonies that would spread Greek civilization throughout the Mediterranean region.

Topography helped determine the major territories into which Greece was ultimately divided. South of the Gulf of Corinth was the Peloponnesus, virtually an island (see Map 3.1). Consisting mostly of hills, mountains, and small valleys, the Peloponnesus was the location of Sparta, as well as the site of Olympia, where famous athletic games were held. Northeast of the Peloponnesus was the Attic peninsula (or Attica), the home of Athens,

hemmed in by mountains to the north and west and surrounded by the sea to the south and east. Northwest of Attica was Boeotia in central Greece with its chief city of Thebes. To the north of Boeotia was Thessaly, which contained the largest plains and became a great producer of grain and horses. To the north of Thessaly lay Macedonia, which was not of much importance in Greek history until 338 B.C., when a Macedonian king, Philip II, conquered the Greeks.

Minoan Crete

The earliest civilization in the Aegean region emerged on the large island of Crete, southeast of the Greek mainland. A Bronze Age civilization that used metals, especially bronze, in making weapons had been established there by 2800 B.C. This forgotten civilization was rediscovered at the turn of the twentieth century by the English archaeologist Arthur Evans, who named it "Minoan" after Minos, a legendary king of Crete. In language and religion, the Minoans were not Greek, although they did have some influence on the peoples of the Greek mainland.

Evans's excavations on Crete at the beginning of the twentieth century led to the discovery of an enormous palace complex at Knossus, near modern Heracleion, that was most likely the center of a far-ranging "sea empire," probably largely commercial. We know from archaeological remains that the people of Minoan Crete were accustomed to sea travel and had made contact with the more advanced civilization of Egypt.

The Minoan civilization reached its height between 2000 and 1450 B.C. The palace at Knossus, the royal seat of the kings, demonstrates the prosperity and power of this civilization. It was an elaborate structure built around a central courtyard and included numerous private living rooms for the royal family and workshops for making decorated vases, small sculptures, and jewelry. Even bathrooms, with elaborate drains, were part of the complex. The rooms were decorated with frescoes in bright colors showing sporting events and naturalistic scenes that have led some observers to conclude that the Cretans had a great love of nature.

The centers of Minoan civilization on Crete suffered a sudden and catastrophic collapse around 1450 B.C. The cause of this destruction has been vigorously debated. Some historians believe that a tsunami triggered by a powerful volcanic eruption on the island of Thera was responsible for the devastation. Most historians, however, maintain that the destruction was the result of invasion and pillage by mainland Greeks known as the Mycenaeans.

The First Greek State: Mycenae

The term *Mycenaean* is derived from Mycenae, a remarkable fortified site first excavated by the amateur German archaeologist Heinrich Schliemann. Mycenae

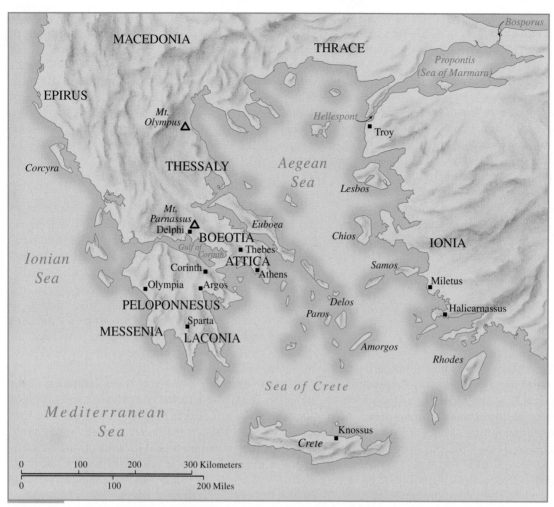

MAP 3.1 **Ancient Greece (c. 750–338 B.C.).** Between 750 and 500 B.C., the city-state emerged as the central institution in Greek life and the Greeks' colonization of the Mediterranean and Black Seas. Classical Greece lasted from about 500 to 338 B.C. and marked the high point of Greek civilization in the arts, science, philosophy, and politics but also the period of the Persian Wars and the Peloponnesian War. **?** How does the geography of Greece help explain the rise and development of the Greek city-state? **View an animated version of this map or related maps at** http://thomsonedu.com/history/spielvogel

was one center in a Greek civilization that flourished between 1600 and 1100 B.C. The Mycenaean Greeks were part of the Indo-European family of peoples (see Chapter 2) who spread from their original location into southern and western Europe, India, and Iran. One group entered the territory of Greece from the north around 1900 B.C. and managed to gain control of the Greek mainland and develop a civilization.

Mycenaean civilization, which reached its high point between 1400 and 1200 B.C., consisted of a number of powerful monarchies based in fortified palace complexes. Like Mycenae itself, the palaces were built on hills and surrounded by gigantic stone walls. These various centers of power probably formed a loose confederacy of independent states, with Mycenae being the strongest. Next in importance to the kings in these states were the army commanders, priests, and the bureaucrats who kept careful records. The free citizenry included peasants, soldiers,

and artisans, and the lowest rung of the social ladder consisted of serfs and slaves.

The Mycenaeans were, above all, a warrior people who prided themselves on their heroic deeds in battle. Some scholars believe that the Mycenaeans, led by Mycenae itself, spread outward militarily, conquering Crete and making it part of the Mycenaean world. The most famous of all their supposed military adventures has come down to us in the epic poetry of Homer (discussed in the next few pages). Did the Mycenaean Greeks, led by Agamemnon, king of Mycenae, indeed sack the city of Troy on the northwestern coast of Asia Minor around 1250 B.C.,

Minoan Crete and Mycenaean Greece

as Homer described? Since the excavations of Heinrich Schliemann, begun in 1870, scholars have debated this question. Many believe that Homer's account does have a basis in fact.

By the late thirteenth century B.C., Mycenaean Greece was showing signs of serious trouble. Mycenae itself was torched around 1190 B.C., and other Mycenaean centers show similar patterns of destruction as new waves of Greek-speaking invaders moved in from the north. By 1100 B.C., the Mycenaean culture was coming to an end, and the Greek world was entering a new period of considerable insecurity.

The Greeks in a Dark Age (c. 1100–c. 750 B.C.)

After the collapse of Mycenaean civilization, Greece entered a difficult period in which the population declined and food production dropped. Because of the dire conditions and our meager knowledge about the period, historians call it the Dark Age. Not until 850 B.C. did farming revive. At the same time, some new developments were forming the basis for a revived Greece.

During the Dark Age, large numbers of Greeks left the mainland and migrated across the Aegean Sea to various islands and especially to the western shores of Asia Minor, a strip of territory that came to be called Ionia. The Greeks who resided there were called Ionians. Two other major groups of Greeks settled in established parts of Greece. The Aeolian Greeks, located in northern and central Greece, colonized the large island of Lesbos and the adjacent territory of the mainland. The Dorians established themselves in southwestern Greece, especially in the Peloponnesus, as well as on some of the islands in the south Aegean Sea, including Crete.

Other important activities occurred in the Dark Age as well. Greece saw a revival of some trade and some economic activity besides agriculture. Iron came into use for the construction of weapons. And at some point in the eighth century B.C., the Greeks adopted the Phoenician alphabet to give themselves a new system of writing. Near the very end of this Dark Age appeared the work of Homer, who has come to be viewed as one of the greatest poets of all time.

Homer and Homeric Greece

The *Iliad* and the *Odyssey*, the great epic poems of early Greece, were based on stories that had been passed on from generation to generation. It is generally assumed that early in the eighth century B.C., Homer made use of these oral traditions to compose the *Iliad*, his epic of the Trojan War. The war was precipitated by Paris, a prince of Troy, whose kidnapping of Helen, wife of the king of the Greek state of Sparta, outraged all the Greeks. Under the leadership of the Spartan king's brother, Agamemnon

The Slaying of Hector. This scene from a Corinthian Greek vase painting depicts the final battle between Achilles and the Trojan hero Hector, a scene taken from Homer's *Iliad*. The *Iliad* is Homer's masterpiece and was important to later Greeks as a means of teaching the aristocratic values of courage and honor.

of Mycenae, the Greeks attacked Troy. Ten years later, the Greeks finally won and sacked the city.

But the *Iliad* is not so much the story of the war itself as it is the tale of the Greek hero Achilles and how the "wrath of Achilles" led to disaster. As is true of all great literature, the *Iliad* abounds in universal lessons. Underlying them all is the clear message, as one commentator has observed, that "men will still come and go like the generations of leaves in the forest; that [man] will still be weak, and the gods strong and incalculable; that the quality of a man matters more than his achievement; that violence and recklessness will still lead to disaster, and that this will fall on the innocent as well as on the guilty."[1]

The *Odyssey*, Homer's other masterpiece, is an epic romance that recounts the journeys of a Greek hero named Odysseus after the fall of Troy and his ultimate return to his wife. But there is a larger vision here as well: the testing of the heroic stature of Odysseus until, by both cunning and patience, he prevails. In the course of this testing, the underlying moral message is "that virtue is a better policy than vice."[2]

Although the *Iliad* and the *Odyssey* supposedly deal with the heroes of the Mycenaean age of the thirteenth century B.C., many scholars believe that they really describe the social conditions of the Dark Age. According to the Homeric view, Greece was a society based on agriculture in which a landed warrior-aristocracy controlled much wealth and exercised considerable power. Homer's world reflects the values of aristocratic heroes.

Homer's Enduring Importance

This explains the importance of Homer to later generations of Greeks. Homer did not so much record history as make it. The Greeks regarded the *Iliad* and the *Odyssey* as authentic history recorded by one poet, Homer. These masterpieces gave the Greeks an idealized past with a cast of heroes and came to be used as standard texts for the education of generations of Greek males. As one Athenian stated, "My father was anxious to see me develop into a good man . . . and as a means to this end he compelled me to memorize all of Homer."[3] The values Homer taught were essentially the aristocratic values of courage and honor (see the box on p. 45). A hero strives for excellence, which the Greeks called *arete*. In the warrior-aristocratic world of Homer, *arete* is won in struggle or contest. Through his willingness to fight, the hero protects his family and friends, preserves his own honor and that of his family, and earns his reputation.

In the Homeric world, aristocratic women, too, were expected to pursue excellence. Penelope, for example, the wife of Odysseus, the hero of the *Odyssey*, remains faithful to her husband and displays great courage and intelligence in preserving their household during her husband's long absence. Upon his return, Odysseus praises her for her excellence: "Madame, there is not a man in the wide world who could find fault with you. For your fame has reached heaven itself, like that of some perfect king, ruling a populous and mighty state with the fear of god in his heart, and upholding the right."[4] Homer gave the Greeks a model of heroism, honor, and nobility. But in time, as a new world of city-states emerged in Greece, new values of cooperation and community also transformed what the Greeks learned from Homer.

The World of the Greek City-States (c. 750–c. 500 B.C.)

In the eighth century B.C., Greek civilization burst forth with new energies. Two major developments stand out in this era: the evolution of the *polis* as the central institution in Greek life and the Greeks' colonization of the Mediterranean and Black Seas.

The *Polis*

The Greek **polis** (plural, *poleis*) developed slowly during the Dark Age and by the eighth century B.C. had emerged as a truly unique and fundamental institution in Greek society. In a physical sense, the *polis* encompassed a town or city or even a village and its surrounding countryside. But the town or city or village served as the focus or central point where the citizens of the *polis* could assemble for political, social, and religious activities. In some *poleis*, this central meeting point was a hill, which could serve as a place of refuge during an attack and later in some sites came to be the religious center on which temples and public monuments were erected. Below this *acropolis* would be an *agora*, an open place that served both as a place where citizens could assemble and as a market.

Poleis varied greatly in size, from a few square miles to a few hundred square miles. The larger ones were the product of consolidation. The territory of Attica, for example, had once had twelve *poleis* but eventually became a single *polis* (Athens) through a process of amalgamation. The population of Athens grew to about 250,000 by the fifth century B.C. Most *poleis* were much smaller, consisting of only a few hundred to several thousand people.

Although our word *politics* is derived from the Greek term *polis*, the *polis* itself was much more than just a political institution. It was, above all, a community of citizens in which all political, economic, social, cultural, and religious activities were focused. As a community, the *polis* consisted of citizens with political rights (adult males), citizens with no political rights (women and children), and noncitizens (slaves and resident aliens). All citizens of a *polis* possessed basic rights, but these were coupled with responsibilities. The Greek philosopher Aristotle argued that the citizen did not just belong to himself; "we must rather regard every citizen as belonging to the state." The unity of citizens was important and often meant that states would take an active role in directing the patterns of life. However, the loyalty that citizens had to their *poleis* also had a negative side. *Poleis* distrusted one another, and the division of Greece into fiercely patriotic sovereign units helped bring about its ruin. Greece was not a united country but a geographical expression. The cultural unity of the Greeks did not mean much politically.

A New Military System: The Hoplites

As the *polis* developed, so did a new military system. In earlier times, wars in Greece had been fought by aristocratic cavalry soldiers—nobles on horseback. These aristocrats, who were large landowners, also dominated the political life of their *poleis*. But by the end of the eighth century and beginning of the seventh, a new military order came into being that was based on **hoplites**, heavily armed infantrymen who wore bronze or leather helmets, breastplates, and greaves (shin guards). Each carried a round shield, a short sword, and a thrusting spear about 9 feet long. Hoplites advanced into battle as a unit, forming a phalanx (a rectangular formation) in tight order, usually eight ranks deep. As long as the hoplites kept their order, were not outflanked, and did not break, they either secured victory or, at the very least, suffered no harm. The phalanx was easily routed, however, if it broke its order. The safety of the phalanx depended on the solidarity and discipline of its members. As one seventh-century B.C. poet noted, a good hoplite was "a short man firmly placed upon his legs, with a courageous heart, not to be uprooted from the spot where he plants his legs."[5]

The hoplite force had political as well as military repercussions. The aristocratic cavalry was now outdated. Since each hoplite provided his own armor, men of

HOMER'S IDEAL OF EXCELLENCE

The *Iliad* and the *Odyssey* were used as basic texts for the education of Greeks for hundreds of years in antiquity. This passage from the *Iliad*, describing a conversation between Hector, prince of Troy, and his wife, Andromache, illustrates the Greek ideal of gaining honor through combat. At the end of the passage, Homer also reveals what became the Greek attitude toward women: women are supposed to spin and weave and take care of their households and their children.

Homer, *Iliad*

Hector looked at his son and smiled, but said nothing. Andromache, bursting into tears, went up to him and put her hand in his. "Hector," she said, "you are possessed. This bravery of yours will be your end. You do not think of your little boy or your unhappy wife, whom you will make a widow soon. Some day the Achaeans [Greeks] are bound to kill you in a massed attack. And when I lose you I might as well be dead. . . . I have no father, no mother, now. . . . I had seven brothers too at home. In one day all of them went down to Hades' House. The great Achilles of the swift feet killed them all. . . ."

"So you, Hector, are father and mother and brother to me, as well as my beloved husband. Have pity on me now; stay here on the tower; and do not make your boy an orphan and your wife a widow. . . ."

"All that, my dear," said the great Hector of the glittering helmet, "is surely my concern. But if I hid myself like a coward and refused to fight, I could never face the Trojans and the Trojan ladies in their trailing gowns. Besides, it would go against the grain, for I have trained myself always, like a good soldier, to take my place in the front line and win glory for my father and myself. . . ."

As he finished, glorious Hector held out his arms to take his boy. But the child shrank back with a cry to the bosom of his girdled nurse, alarmed by his father's appearance. He was frightened by the bronze of the helmet and the horsehair plume that he saw nodding grimly down at him. His father and his lady mother had to laugh. But noble Hector quickly took his helmet off and put the dazzling thing on the ground. Then he kissed his son, dandled him in his arms, and prayed to Zeus and the other gods: "Zeus; and you other gods, grant that this boy of mine may be, like me, preeminent in Troy; as strong and brave as I; a mighty king of Ilium. May people say, when he comes back from battle, 'Here is a better man than his father.' Let him bring home the bloodstained armor of the enemy he has killed, and make his mother happy."

Hector handed the boy to his wife, who took him to her fragrant breast. She was smiling through her tears, and when her husband saw this he was moved. He stroked her with his hand and said: "My dear, I beg you not to be too much distressed. No one is going to send me down to Hades before my proper time. But Fate is a thing that no man born of woman, coward or hero, can escape. Go home now, and attend to your own work, the loom and the spindle, and see that the maidservants get on with theirs. War is men's business; and this war is the business of every man in Ilium, myself above all."

What important ideals for Greek men and women are revealed in this passage from the Iliad?

---

property, both aristocrats and small farmers, made up the new phalanx. Those who could become hoplites and fight for the state could also challenge aristocratic control.

Colonization and the Growth of Trade

Between 750 and 550 B.C., large numbers of Greeks left to settle in distant lands. Poverty and land hunger created by the growing gulf between rich and poor, overpopulation, and the development of trade were all factors that led to the establishment of colonies. Some Greek colonies were simply trading posts or centers for the transshipment of goods to Greece. Most were larger settlements that included good agricultural land taken from the native populations in those areas. Each colony was founded as a *polis* and was usually independent of the *metropolis* ("mother *polis*") that had established it.

In the western Mediterranean, new Greek settlements were established along the coastline of southern Italy, southern France, eastern Spain, and northern Africa west of Egypt. To the north, the Greeks set up colonies in Thrace, where they sought good farmland to grow grains. Greeks also settled along the shores of the Black Sea and secured the approaches to it with cities on the Hellespont and Bosporus, most noticeably Byzantium, site of the later Constantinople (Istanbul). By establishing these settlements, the Greeks spread their culture throughout the Mediterranean basin. Colonization also led to increased trade and industry. The Greeks on the mainland sent their pottery, wine, and olive oil to these areas; in return, they received grains and metals from the west and fish, timber, wheat, metals, and slaves from the Black Sea region. In many *poleis*, the expansion of trade and industry created a new group of rich men who desired political privileges commensurate with their wealth but found them impossible to gain because of the power of the ruling aristocrats.

Tyranny in the Greek Polis

The desires of these new groups opened the door to the rise of **tyrants** in the seventh and sixth centuries B.C. They

The Hoplite Forces. The Greek hoplites were infantrymen equipped with large round shields and long thrusting spears. In battle, they advanced in tight phalanx formation and were dangerous opponents as long as this formation remained unbroken. This vase painting of the seventh century B.C. shows two groups of hoplite warriors engaged in battle. The piper on the left is leading another line of soldiers preparing to enter the fray.

were not necessarily oppressive or wicked, as our word *tyrant* connotes. Greek tyrants were rulers who seized power by force and who were not subject to the law. Support for the tyrants came from the new rich, who made their money in trade and industry, as well as from poor peasants, who were in debt to landholding aristocrats. Both groups were opposed to the domination of political power by aristocratic **oligarchies**.

Tyrants usually achieved power by a local coup d'état and maintained it by using mercenary soldiers. Once in power, they built marketplaces, temples, and walls that created jobs, glorified the city, and enhanced their own popularity. Tyrants also favored the interests of merchants and traders. Despite these achievements, however, tyranny fell out of favor by the end of the sixth century B.C. Its very nature as a system outside the law seemed contradictory to the ideal of law in a Greek community. Although tyranny did not last, it played a significant role in the course of Greek history by ending the rule of narrow aristocratic oligarchies. The end of tyranny opened the door to greater numbers of people in government. Although this trend culminated in the development of democracy in some communities, in other states expanded

oligarchies of one kind or another managed to remain in power. Greek states exhibited considerable variety in their governmental structures; this can perhaps best be seen by examining the two most famous and most powerful Greek city-states, Sparta and Athens.

Sparta

The Spartans originally occupied four small villages in the southwestern Peloponnesus, in an area known as Laconia, that eventually became unified into a single *polis.* This unification made Sparta a strong community in Laconia and enabled the Spartans to conquer the neighboring Laconians. Many Laconians became *periokoi,* free inhabitants but not citizens who were required to pay taxes and perform military service for Sparta. Other Laconians became **helots** (the name is derived from a Greek word for "capture"). They were bound to the land and forced to work on farms and as household servants for the Spartans.

When the land in Laconia proved unable to maintain the growing number of Spartan citizens, the Spartans looked for land nearby and, beginning around 730 B.C., undertook the conquest of neighboring Messenia despite its larger size and population. Messenia possessed a large, fertile plain ideal for growing grain. After its conquest, which was not completed until the seventh century B.C., the Messenians were made helots and forced to work for the Spartans.

The New Sparta To ensure control over their conquered Laconian and Messenian helots, the Spartans decided to create a military state. By the early sixth century B.C., they had transformed Sparta into a military camp (see the box on p. 48). The lives of all Spartans were now rigidly organized. At birth, each child was examined by state officials who decided whether it was fit to live. Infants judged unfit were left to die. Boys were taken from their mothers at the age of seven and put under control of the state. They lived in military-style barracks, where they were subjected to harsh discipline to make them tough and given an education that stressed military training and obedience to authority. At twenty, Spartan males were enrolled in the army for regular military service. Although allowed to marry, they continued to live in the barracks and ate all their meals in public dining halls with their fellow soldiers. Meals were simple; the famous Spartan black broth consisted of a piece of pork boiled in blood, salt, and vinegar, causing a visitor who ate in a public mess to remark that he now understood why Spartans were not afraid to die. At thirty, Spartan males were allowed to vote in the assembly and live at home, but they stayed in the army until the age of sixty.

While their husbands remained in military barracks until age thirty, Spartan women lived at home. Because of this separation, Spartan women had greater freedom of movement and greater power in the household than was common for women elsewhere in Greece. They were encouraged to exercise and remain fit to bear and raise healthy children. Like the men, Spartan women engaged in athletic exercises in the nude. Many Spartan women upheld the strict Spartan values, expecting their husbands and sons to be brave in war. The story is told that as a Spartan mother was burying her son, an old woman came up to her and said, "You poor woman, what a misfortune." "No," replied the other, "because I bore him so that he might die for Sparta and that is what has happened, as I wished."[6] Another Spartan woman, as she was handing her son his shield, told him to come back carrying his shield or being carried on it.

The Spartan State The Spartan government was headed by two kings, who led the Spartan army on its campaigns. A group of five men, known as the ephors, were elected each year and were responsible for the education of youth and the conduct of all citizens. A council of elders, composed of the two kings and twenty-eight citizens over the age of sixty, decided on the issues that would be presented to an assembly. This assembly of all male citizens did not debate but only voted on the issues put before it by the council of elders.

To make their new military state secure, the Spartans deliberately turned their backs on the outside world. Foreigners, who might bring in new ideas, were discouraged from visiting Sparta. Nor were Spartans, except for military reasons, encouraged to travel abroad where they might pick up new ideas that might prove dangerous to the stability of the state. Likewise, Spartan citizens were discouraged from studying philosophy, literature, or the arts—subjects that might encourage new thoughts. The art of war and of ruling was the Spartan ideal; all other arts were frowned on.

In the sixth century, Sparta used its military might and the fear it inspired to gain greater control of the Peloponnesus by organizing an alliance of almost all the Peloponnesian states. Sparta's strength enabled it to dominate this Peloponnesian League and determine its policies. By 500 B.C., the Spartans had organized a powerful military state that maintained order and stability in the Peloponnesus. Raised from early childhood to believe that total loyalty to the Spartan state was the basic reason for existence, the Spartans viewed their strength as justification for their militaristic ideals and regimented society.

Athens

By 700 B.C., Athens had established a unified *polis* on the peninsula of Attica. Although early Athens had been ruled by a monarchy, by the seventh century it had fallen under the control of its aristocrats. They possessed the best land and controlled political and religious life by means of a council of nobles, assisted by a board of nine archons. Although an assembly of full citizens did exist, it possessed few powers.

Near the end of the seventh century B.C., Athens faced political turmoil because of serious economic problems. Many Athenian farmers found themselves sold into slavery when they were unable to repay the loans they had borrowed from their aristocratic neighbors, pledging themselves as collateral. Over and over, cries arose to cancel the debts and give land to the poor. Athens seemed on the verge of civil war.

The Reforms of Solon The ruling Athenian aristocrats responded to this crisis by choosing Solon, a reform-minded aristocrat, as sole archon in 594 B.C. and giving him full power to make changes. Solon canceled all current land debts, outlawed new loans based on humans as collateral, and freed people who had fallen into slavery for debts. He refused, however, to carry out the redistribution of the land and hence failed to deal with the basic cause of the economic crisis.

Like his economic reforms, Solon's political measures were also a compromise. Though by no means eliminating the power of the aristocracy, they opened the door to the participation of new people, especially the nonaristocratic wealthy, in the government. But Solon's reforms, though popular, did not solve Athens' problems.

THE LYCURGAN REFORMS

To maintain control over the conquered Messenians, the Spartans instituted the reforms that created their military state. These reforms are associated with the name of the lawgiver Lycurgus, although historians are not sure of his historicity. In this account of Lycurgus, the ancient Greek historian Plutarch discusses the effect of these reforms on the treatment and education of boys.

Plutarch, *Lycurgus*

Lycurgus was of another mind; he would not have masters bought out of the market for his young Spartans, . . . nor was it lawful, indeed, for the father himself to breed up the children after his own fancy; but as soon as they were seven years old they were to be enrolled in certain companies and classes, where they all lived under the same order and discipline, doing their exercises and taking their play together. Of these, he who showed the most conduct and courage was made captain; they had their eyes always upon him, obeyed his orders, and underwent patiently whatsoever punishment he inflicted; so that the whole course of their education was one continued exercise of a ready and perfect obedience. The old men, too, were spectators of their performances, and often raised quarrels and disputes among them, to have a good opportunity of finding out their different characters, and of seeing which would be valiant, which a coward, when they should come to more dangerous encounters. Reading and writing they gave them just enough to serve their turn; their chief care was to make them good subjects, and to teach them to endure pain and conquer in battle. To this end, as they grew in years, their discipline was proportionately increased; their heads were close-clipped, they were accustomed to go barefoot, and for the most part to play naked.

After they were twelve years old, they were no longer allowed to wear any undergarments, they had one coat to serve them a year; their bodies were hard and dry, with but little acquaintance of baths and unguents; these human indulgences they were allowed only on some few particular days in the year. They lodged together in little bands upon beds made of the rushes which grew by the banks of the river Eurotas, which they were to break off with their hands with a knife; if it were winter, they mingled some thistledown with their rushes, which it was thought had the property of giving warmth. By the time they were come to this age there was not any of the more hopeful boys who had not a lover to bear him company. The old men, too, had an eye upon them, coming often to the grounds to hear and see them contend either in wit or strength with one another, and this as seriously . . . as if they were their fathers, their tutors, or their magistrates; so that there scarcely was any time or place without someone present to put them in mind of their duty, and punish them if they had neglected it.

[Spartan boys were also encouraged to steal their food.] They stole, too, all other meat they could lay their hands on, looking out and watching all opportunities, when people were asleep or more careless than usual. If they were caught, they were not only punished with whipping, but hunger, too, being reduced to their ordinary allowance, which was but very slender, and so contrived on purpose, that they might set about to help themselves, and be forced to exercise their energy and address. This was the principal design of their hard fare.

What does this passage from Plutarch's account of Lycurgus reveal about the nature of the Spartan state? Why would this whole program have been distasteful to the Athenians?

Aristocratic factions continued to vie for power, and the poorer peasants resented Solon's failure to institute land redistribution. Internal strife finally led to the very institution Solon had hoped to avoid—tyranny. Pisistratus, an aristocrat, seized power in 560 B.C. Pursuing a foreign policy that aided Athenian trade, Pisistratus remained popular with the merchants. But the Athenians rebelled against his son and ended the tyranny in 510 B.C. Although the aristocrats attempted to reestablish an oligarchy, Cleisthenes, another aristocratic reformer, opposed this plan and, with the backing of the Athenian people, gained the upper hand in 508 B.C. The reforms of Cleisthenes now established the basis for Athenian democracy.

The Reforms of Cleisthenes A major aim of Cleisthenes' reforms was to weaken the power of traditional localities and regions, which had provided the foundation for aristocratic strength. He made the *demes*, the villages and townships of Attica, the basic units of political life. Cleisthenes enrolled all the citizens of the demes in ten new tribes, each of which contained inhabitants located in the country districts of Attica, the coastal areas, and Athens. The ten tribes thus contained a cross section of the population and reflected all of Attica, a move that gave local areas a basic role in the political structure. Each of the ten tribes chose fifty members by lot each year for a new Council of Five Hundred, which was responsible for the administration of both foreign and financial affairs and prepared the business that would be handled by the assembly. This assembly of all male citizens had final authority in the passing of laws after free and open debate; thus Cleisthenes' reforms strengthened the central role of the assembly of citizens in the Athenian political system.

The reforms of Cleisthenes created the foundations for Athenian democracy. More changes would come in the fifth century when the Athenians themselves would

Sparta	
Conquest of Messenia	c. 730–710 B.C.
Beginning of Peloponnesian League	c. 560–550 B.C.
Athens	
Solon's reforms	594–593 B.C.
Tyranny of Pisistratus	c. 560–556 and 546–527 B.C.
Deposition of Hippias—end of tyranny	510 B.C.
Cleisthenes' reforms	c. 508–501 B.C.

begin to use the word *democracy* to describe their system (from the Greek words *demos,* "people," and *kratia,* "power," thus "power to the people"). By 500 B.C., Athens was more united than it had ever been and was about to assume a more important role in Greek affairs.

The High Point of Greek Civilization: Classical Greece

Classical Greece is the name given to the period from around 500 B.C. to the conquest of Greece by the Macedonian king Philip II in 338 B.C. It was a time of brilliant achievement, much of it associated with the flowering of democracy in Athens under the leadership of Pericles. Many of the lasting contributions of the Greeks occurred during this period. The age began with a mighty confrontation between the Greek states and the mammoth Persian Empire.

The Challenge of Persia

As Greek civilization expanded throughout the Mediterranean, it was inevitable that it would come into contact with the Persian Empire to the east. The Ionian Greek cities in western Asia Minor had already fallen subject to the Persian Empire by the mid-sixth century B.C. An unsuccessful revolt by the Ionian cities in 499, assisted by the Athenian navy, led the Persian ruler Darius to seek revenge by attacking the mainland Greeks in 490. The Persians landed an army on the plain of Marathon, only 26 miles from Athens. There a mostly Athenian army, though clearly outnumbered, went on the attack and defeated the Persians decisively.

Xerxes, the new Persian monarch after the death of Darius in 486 B.C., vowed revenge and renewed the invasion of Greece. In preparation for the attack, some of the Greek states formed a defensive league under Spartan leadership, while the Athenians pursued a new military policy by developing a navy. By the time of the Persian invasion in 480 B.C., the Athenians had produced a fleet of about two hundred vessels.

Xerxes led a massive invasion force into Greece: close to 150,000 troops, almost seven hundred naval ships, and hundreds of supply ships to keep their large army fed. The Greeks hoped to stop the Persians at the pass of Thermopylae along the main road into central Greece. A Greek force numbering close to nine thousand, under the leadership of the Spartan king Leonidas and his contingent of three hundred Spartans, held off the Persian army for several days. The Spartan troops were especially brave. When told that Persian arrows would darken the sky in battle, one Spartan warrior supposedly responded, "That is good news. We will fight in the shade!" Unfortunately for the Greeks, a traitor told the Persians how to use a mountain path to outflank the Greek force. King Leonidas and the three hundred Spartans fought to the last man.

The Athenians, now threatened by the onslaught of the Persian forces, abandoned their city. While the Persians sacked and burned Athens, the Greek fleet remained offshore near the island of Salamis and challenged the Persian navy to fight. Although the Greeks were outnumbered, they managed to outmaneuver the Persian fleet and utterly defeated it. A few months later, early in 479 B.C., the Greeks formed the largest Greek army seen up to that time and decisively defeated the Persian army at Plataea, northwest of Attica. The Greeks had won the war and were now free to pursue their own destiny.

The Growth of an Athenian Empire in the Age of Pericles

After the defeat of the Persians, Athens stepped in to provide new leadership against the Persians by forming a confederation called the Delian League. Organized in the winter of 478–477 B.C., the Delian League was dominated by the Athenians from the beginning. Its main headquarters was the island of Delos, but its chief officials, including the treasurers and commanders of the fleet, were Athenian. Under the leadership of the Athenians, the Delian League pursued the attack against the Persian Empire. Virtually all of the Greek states in the Aegean were liberated from Persian control. Arguing that the Persian threat was now over, some members of the Delian League wished to withdraw. But the Athenians forced them to remain in the league and to pay tribute. "No secession" became Athenian policy. The Delian League was rapidly becoming the nucleus of an Athenian empire.

At home, Athenians favored the new imperial policy, especially in the 450s B.C., when an aristocrat named Pericles began to play an important political role. Under Pericles, Athens embarked on a policy of expanding democracy at home while severing its ties with Sparta and expanding its new empire abroad. This period of Athenian and Greek history, which historians have subsequently labeled the Age of Pericles, witnessed the height of Athenian power and the culmination of its brilliance as a civilization.

In the Age of Pericles, the Athenians became deeply attached to their democratic system. The sovereignty of the people was embodied in the assembly, which consisted of all male citizens over eighteen years of age. In the 440s, that was probably a group of about 43,000. Not all attended, however, and the number present at the meetings, which were held every ten days on a hillside east of the Acropolis, seldom reached 6,000. The assembly passed all laws and made final decisions on war and foreign policy.

Routine administration of public affairs was handled by a large body of city magistrates, usually chosen by lot without regard to class and usually serving one-year terms. This meant that many male citizens held public office at some time in their lives. A board of ten officials known as generals (*strategoi*) were elected by public vote to guide affairs of state, although their power depended on the respect they had attained. Generals were usually wealthy aristocrats, even though the people were free to select others. The generals could be reelected, enabling individual leaders to play an important political role. Pericles' reelection fifteen times as a general made him one of the leading politicians between 461 and 429 B.C.

All public officials were subject to scrutiny and could be deposed from office if they lost the people's confidence. After 488 B.C., the Athenians occasionally made use of a tactic called ostracism. Members of the assembly could write on a broken pottery fragment (*ostrakon*) the name of the person they most disliked or considered most harmful to the *polis*. A person who received a majority (if at least six thousand votes were cast) was exiled for ten years.

Pericles expanded the Athenians' involvement in democracy, which was what Athenians had come to call their form of government (see the box on p. 51). Power was in the hands of the people: male citizens voted in the assemblies and served as jurors in the courts. Lower-class citizens were now eligible for public offices formerly closed to them. Pericles also introduced state pay for officeholders, including the widely held jury duty. This meant that even poor citizens could hold public office and afford to participate in public affairs. Nevertheless, although the Athenians developed a system of government that was unique in its time in which citizens had equal rights and the people were the government, aristocrats continued to hold the most important offices, and many people, including women, slaves, and foreigners residing in Athens, were not given the same political rights.

The Athenian pursuit of democracy at home was coupled with increasing imperialism abroad. Citing the threat of the Persian fleet in the Aegean, the Athenians moved the Delian League treasury from the island of Delos to Athens itself in 454 B.C. Members were charged a fee (tribute) for the Athenian claim of protection. Pericles also used the money in the league treasury, without the approval of its members, to build new temples in Athens, an arrogant reminder that the Delian League had become the Athenian Empire. But Athenian imperialism alarmed the other Greek states, and soon all Greece was confronted with a new war.

The Great Peloponnesian War

During the forty years after the defeat of the Persians, the Greek world divided into two major camps: Sparta and its supporters and the Athenian Empire. In his classic *History of the Peloponnesian War,* the great Greek historian Thucydides pointed out that the basic long-range cause of the Peloponnesian War was the fear that Sparta and its allies had of the growing Athenian Empire. Then, too, Athens and Sparta had built two very different kinds of societies, and neither state was able to tolerate the other's system. A series of disputes finally led to the outbreak of war in 431 B.C.

At the beginning of the war, both sides believed they had winning strategies. The Athenians planned to remain behind the protective walls of Athens while the overseas empire and the navy kept them supplied. Pericles knew perfectly well that the Spartans and their allies could beat the Athenians in pitched battles, which was the chief aim of the Spartan strategy. The Spartans and their allies attacked Athens, hoping that the Athenians would send out their army to fight beyond the walls. But Pericles was convinced that Athens was secure behind its walls and retaliated by sending out naval excursions to ravage the seacoast of the Peloponnesus.

In the second year of the war, however, plague devastated the crowded city of Athens and wiped out possibly one-third of the population. Pericles himself died the following year (429 B.C.), a severe loss to Athens. Despite the ravages of the plague, the Athenians fought on in a struggle that dragged on for another twenty-seven years. A crushing blow came in 405 B.C. when the Athenian fleet was destroyed at Aegospotami on the Hellespont. Athens was besieged and surrendered in 404. Its walls were torn down, the navy was disbanded, and the Athenian Empire was destroyed. The great war was finally over.

The Decline of the Greek States (404–338 B.C.)

The Great Peloponnesian War weakened the major Greek states and led to new alliances among the *poleis*. After the defeat of Athens in 404 B.C., the Spartans established control over Greece. Oligarchies of local leaders in cooperation with Spartan garrisons were imposed on states "liberated" from Athenian imperialism. But the harsh policies of the oligarchs soon led to a reaction. In Athens, rebellion enabled the Athenians to reestablish their democracy in 403 B.C. and even to rebuild their navy and again become an important force in the Greek world.

To maintain its newly organized leadership in Greek affairs, Sparta encouraged a Greek crusade against the

ATHENIAN DEMOCRACY: THE FUNERAL ORATION OF PERICLES

In his History of the Peloponnesian War, the Greek historian Thucydides presented his reconstruction of the eulogy given by Pericles in the winter of 431–430 B.C. to honor the Athenians killed in the first campaigns of the Great Peloponnesian War. It is a magnificent, idealized description of the Athenian democracy at its height.

Thucydides, *History of the Peloponnesian War*

Our constitution is called a democracy because power is in the hands not of a minority but of the whole people. When it is a question of settling private disputes, everyone is equal before the law; when it is a question of putting one person before another in positions of public responsibility, what counts is not membership of a particular class, but the actual ability which the man possesses. No one, so long as he has it in him to be of service to the state, is kept in political obscurity because of poverty. And, just as our political life is free and open, so is our day-to-day life in our relations with each other. We do not get into a state with our next-door neighbor if he enjoys himself in his own way, nor do we give him the kind of black looks which, though they do no real harm, still do hurt people's feeling. We are free and tolerant in our private lives; but in public affairs we keep to the law. This is because it commands our deep respect.

We give our obedience to those whom we put in positions of authority, and we obey the laws themselves, especially those which are for the protection of the oppressed, and those unwritten laws which it is an acknowledged shame to break. . . . Here each individual is interested not only in his own affairs but in the affairs of the state as well: even those who are mostly occupied with their own business are extremely well-informed on general politics—this is a peculiarity of ours: we do not say that a man who takes no interest in politics is a man who minds his own business; we say that he has no business here at all. We Athenians, in our own persons, take our decisions on policy or submit them to proper discussions: for we do not think that there is an incompatibility between words and deeds; the worst thing is to rush into action before the consequences have been properly debated. . . . Taking everything together then, I declare that our city is an education to Greece, and I declare that in my opinion each single one of our citizens, in all the manifold aspects of life, is able to show himself the rightful lord and owner of his own person and do this, moreover, with exceptional grace and exceptional versatility. And to show that this is no empty boasting for the present occasion, but real tangible fact, you have only to consider the power which our city possesses and which has been won by those very qualities which I have mentioned.

In the eyes of Pericles, what are the ideals of Athenian democracy? In what ways does Pericles exaggerate his claims? Why would the Athenian passion for debate described by Pericles have been distasteful to the Spartans?

Persians as a common enemy. But the Persians had learned the lessons of Greek politics and offered financial support to Athens and other Greek states to oppose Spartan power within Greece itself, thus beginning a new war that finally ended in 386 B.C.

The city-state of Thebes, in Boeotia, north of Athens, now began to exert its influence. Under the leader Epaminondas, the Thebans dramatically defeated the Spartan army at the Battle of Leuctra in 371 B.C. Spartan power declined, but Theban ascendancy was short-lived. After the death of Epaminondas in the Battle of Mantinea in 362 B.C., the Thebans could no longer dominate Greek politics. Yet the Greek states continued their petty wars, seemingly oblivious to the growing danger to the north, where King Philip II of Macedonia was developing a unified state that would finally end the destructive fratricide of the Greek states by imposing Macedonian authority.

The Culture and Society of Classical Greece

Classical Greece was a time of remarkable intellectual and cultural growth throughout the Greek world, and Peri-clean Athens was the most important center of classical Greek culture.

The Writing of History

History as we know it, the systematic analysis of past events, was a Greek creation. Herodotus (c. 484–c. 425 B.C.) was the author of *The Persian Wars,* a work commonly regarded as the first real history in Western civilization. The Greek word *historia* (from which we derive our word *history*) means "research" or "investigation," and it is in the opening line of Herodotus' *History* that we find the first recorded use of the word:

These are the researches [*historia*] of Herodotus of Halicarnassus, which he publishes, in the hope of thereby preserving from decay the remembrance of what men have done, and of preventing the great and wonderful actions of the Greeks and the Barbarians from losing their due meed [reward] of glory; and withal to put on record what were their grounds of feud.[7]

The central theme of Herodotus' work is the conflict between the Greeks and the Persians, which he viewed as a struggle between freedom and despotism. Herodotus traveled extensively and questioned many people to obtain his information. Although he was a master storyteller and sometimes included considerable fanciful material, Herodotus was also capable of exhibiting a critical attitude toward the materials he used.

Thucydides (c. 460–c. 400 B.C.) was a far better historian, indeed, the greatest of the ancient world. Thucydides was an Athenian and a participant in the Peloponnesian War. He had been elected a general, but a defeat in battle led the Athenian assembly to send him into exile, which gave him the opportunity to concentrate on writing his *History of the Peloponnesian War.*

Unlike Herodotus, Thucydides was not concerned with divine forces or gods as causal factors in history. He saw war and politics in purely rational terms, as the activities of human beings. He examined the causes of the Peloponnesian War in a clear and objective fashion, placing much emphasis on the accuracy of his facts. As he stated:

> And with regard to my factual reporting of the events of the war I have made it a principle not to write down the first story that came my way, and not even to be guided by my own general impressions; either I was present myself at the events which I have described or else I heard of them from eyewitnesses whose reports I have checked with as much thoroughness as possible.[8]

Thucydides also provided remarkable insight into the human condition. He believed that political situations recur in similar fashion and that the study of history is therefore of great value in understanding the present.

Greek Drama

Drama, as we know it, was created by the Greeks and was clearly intended to do more than entertain. It was used to educate citizens and was supported by the state for that reason. Plays were presented in outdoor theaters as part of a religious festival. The form of Greek plays remained rather stable. Three male actors who wore masks acted all the parts. A chorus, also male, played the role of groups of people or served as narrators. Action was very limited because the emphasis was on the story and its meaning.

The first Greek dramas were tragedies, plays based on the suffering of a hero and usually ending in disaster. Aeschylus (525–456 B.C.) is the first tragedian whose plays are known to us. Although he wrote ninety tragedies, only seven have survived. As was customary in Greek tragedy, his plots were simple. The entire drama focused on a single tragic event and its meaning. Greek tragedies were sometimes presented in a trilogy (a set of three plays) built around a common theme. The only complete trilogy we possess, called the *Oresteia,* was written by Aeschylus. The theme of this trilogy is derived from Homer. Agamemnon, the king of Mycenae, returns a hero from the defeat of Troy. His wife, Clytemnestra, avenges the sacrificial death of her daughter Iphigenia by

murdering Agamemnon, who had been responsible for Iphigenia's death. In the second play of the trilogy, Agamemnon's son Orestes avenges his father by killing his mother. Orestes is now pursued by the Furies, who torment him for killing his mother. Evil acts breed evil acts and suffering is one's lot, suggests Aeschylus. But Orestes is put on trial and acquitted by Athena, the patron goddess of Athens. Personal vendetta has been eliminated, and law has prevailed.

Another great Athenian playwright was Sophocles (c. 496–406 B.C.), whose most famous play was *Oedipus the King.* The oracle of Apollo foretells how a man (Oedipus) will kill his own father and marry his mother. Despite all attempts at prevention, the tragic events occur. Although it appears that Oedipus suffered the fate determined by the gods, Oedipus also accepts that he himself as a free man must bear responsibility for his actions: "It was Apollo, friends, Apollo, that brought this bitter bitterness, my sorrows to completion. But the hand that struck me was none but my own."[9]

The third outstanding Athenian tragedian, Euripides (c. 485–406 B.C.), tried to create more realistic characters. His plots also became more complex and reflected a greater interest in real-life situations. Perhaps the greatest of all his plays was *The Bacchae,* which dealt with the introduction of the hysterical rites associated with Dionysus, god of wine. Euripides is often seen as a skeptic who questioned traditional moral and religious values. Euripides was also critical of the traditional view that war was glorious. He portrayed war as brutal and barbaric.

Greek tragedies dealt with universal themes still relevant in our day. They probed such problems as the nature of good and evil, the conflict between spiritual values and the demands of the state or family, the rights of the individual, the nature of divine forces, and human nature. Over and over, the tragic lesson was repeated: humans were free and yet could operate only within limitations imposed by the gods. The real task was to cultivate the balance and moderation that led to awareness of one's true position. But the pride in human accomplishment and independence is real. As the chorus chants in Sophocles' *Antigone,* "Is there anything more wonderful on earth, our marvelous planet, than the miracle of man?"[10]

Greek comedy developed later than tragedy. The plays of Aristophanes (c. 450–c. 385 B.C.), who used both grotesque masks and obscene jokes to entertain the Athenian audience, are examples of Old Comedy, which was used to attack or savagely satirize both politicians and intellectuals. In *The Clouds,* for example, Aristophanes characterized the philosopher Socrates as the operator of a thought factory where people could learn deceitful ways to handle other people. Of special importance to Aristophanes was his opposition to the Peloponnesian War. *Lysistrata,* performed in 411 B.C., at a time when Athens was in serious danger of losing the war, conveyed a comic but effective message against the war.

The Arts: The Classical Ideal

The arts of the Western world have been largely dominated by the artistic standards established by the Greeks of the Classical period. Classical Greek art did not aim at experimentation for experiment's sake but was concerned with expressing eternally true ideals. The subject matter was the human being, presented as an object of great beauty. The Classical style, based on the ideals of reason, moderation, balance, and harmony in all things, was meant to civilize the emotions.

In architecture, the most important structure was the temple dedicated to a god or goddess. Because Greek religious ceremonies were held at altars in the open air, temples were not used to enclose the faithful, as modern churches are. At the center of Greek temples were walled rooms that housed the statues of deities and treasuries in which gifts to the gods and goddesses were safeguarded. These central rooms were surrounded by a screen of columns that give Greek temples their open structure. The columns were originally made of wood but were changed to limestone in the seventh century and to marble in the fifth century B.C.

Some of the finest examples of Greek Classical architecture were built in fifth-century Athens. The most famous building, regarded as the greatest example of the Classical Greek temple, is the Parthenon, built between 447 and 432 B.C. The master builders Ictinus and Callicrates directed the construction of this temple consecrated to Athena, the patron goddess of Athens. The Parthenon typifies the principles of Classical architecture: the search for calm, clarity, and freedom from superfluous detail. The individual parts of the temple were constructed in accordance with certain mathematical ratios also found in natural phenomena. The architects' concern with these laws of proportion is paralleled by the attempt of Greek philosophers to understand the general laws underlying nature.

Greek sculpture also developed a Classical style that differed significantly from the artificial stiffness of earlier periods. Statues of the male nude, the favorite subject of Greek sculptors, now exhibited more relaxed attitudes; their faces were self-assured; their bodies were flexible and smooth-muscled. Although the figures possessed natural features that made them lifelike, Greek sculptors sought to achieve not realism but a standard of ideal beauty. Polyclitus, a fifth-century sculptor, wrote a treatise (now lost) on a canon of proportions that he illustrated in a work known as the *Doryphoros*. His theory maintained that the use of ideal proportions, based on mathematical ratios found in nature, could produce an ideal human form, beautiful in its perfected and refined features. This search for ideal beauty was the dominant aspect of Classical sculpture.

The Greek Love of Wisdom

Philosophy is a Greek word that literally means "love of wisdom." Early Greek philosophers were concerned with the development of critical or rational thought about the nature of the universe and the place of divine forces in it. The **Sophists,** however, were a group of philosophical teachers in fifth-century Athens who rejected such speculation as foolish; they argued that understanding the universe was beyond the reach of the human mind. It was more important for individuals to improve themselves, so the only worthwhile object of study was human behavior. The Sophists were wandering scholars who sold their services as professional teachers to the young men of Greece, especially those of Athens. The Sophists stressed the importance of **rhetoric** (the art of persuasive speaking) in winning debates and swaying an audience, a skill that was especially valuable in democratic Athens. To the Sophists, there was no absolute right or wrong—what was right for one individual might be wrong for another. True wisdom consisted of being able to perceive and pursue one's own good. Because of these ideas, many people viewed the Sophists as harmful to society and especially dangerous to the values of young people.

One of the critics of the Sophists was Socrates (469–399 B.C.). Because he left no writing of his own, we know about him only from his pupils, especially his most

Doric   **Ionic**   **Corinthian**

Doric, Ionic, and Corinthian Orders. The size and shape of a column constituted one of the most important aspects of Greek temple architecture. The Doric order, with plain capitals and no base, developed first in the Dorian Peloponnesus and was rather simple in comparison to the slender Ionic column, which had an elaborate base and spiral-shaped capitals, and the Corinthian column, which featured leaf-shaped capitals.

© Photodisc Green/Getty Images

The Parthenon. The arts in Classical Greece were designed to express the eternal ideals of reason, moderation, symmetry, balance, and harmony. In architecture, the most important form was the temple, and the classic example of this kind of architecture is the Parthenon, built between 447 and 432 B.C. Located on the Acropolis in Athens, the Parthenon was dedicated to Athena, the patron goddess of the city, but it also served as a shining example of the power and wealth of the Athenian Empire.

famous one, Plato. By occupation, Socrates was a stonemason, but his true love was philosophy. He taught a number of pupils, but not for pay, because he believed that the goal of education was only to improve the individual. He made use of a teaching method that is still known by his name. The **Socratic method** employs a question-and-answer technique to lead pupils to see things for themselves using their own reason. Socrates believed that all real knowledge is within each person; only critical examination was needed to call it forth. This was the real task of philosophy, since "the unexamined life is not worth living."

Socrates' questioning of authority led him into trouble. Athens had had a tradition of free thought and inquiry, but defeat in the Peloponnesian War had created an environment much less tolerant of open debate and soul-searching. Socrates was accused and convicted of corrupting the youth of Athens by his teaching. An Athenian jury sentenced him to death.

One of Socrates' disciples was Plato (c. 429–347 B.C.), considered by many the greatest philosopher of Western civilization. Unlike his master Socrates, who wrote nothing, Plato wrote a great deal. He was fascinated with

Doryphoros. This statue, known as the *Doryphoros,* or spear carrier, is a Roman copy of the original work by the fifth-century B.C. sculptor Polyclitus, who believed it illustrated the ideal proportions of the human figure. Classical Greek sculpture moved away from the stiffness of earlier figures but retained the young male nude as the favorite subject matter. The statues became more lifelike, with relaxed poses and flexible, smooth-muscled bodies. The aim of sculpture, however, was not simply realism but rather the expression of ideal beauty.

Scala/Art Resource, NY (Museo Archeologico Nazionale, Naples)

the question of reality: How do we know what is real? According to Plato, a higher world of eternal, unchanging Ideas or Forms has always existed. To know these Forms is to know truth. These ideal Forms constitute reality and can only be apprehended by a trained mind, which, of course, is the goal of philosophy. The objects that we perceive with our senses are simply reflections of the ideal Forms. Hence they are shadows, while reality is found in the Forms themselves.

Plato's ideas of government were set out in a dialogue he titled *The Republic.* Based on his experience in Athens, Plato had come to distrust the workings of democracy. It was obvious to him that individuals could not attain an ethical life unless they lived in a just and rational state. Plato's search for the just state led him to construct an ideal state in which the population was divided into three basic groups. At the top was an upper class, a ruling elite, the philosopher-kings: "Unless either philosophers become kings in their countries or those who are now called kings and rulers come to be sufficiently inspired with a genuine desire for wisdom; unless, that is to say, political power and philosophy meet together . . . there can be no rest from troubles . . . for states, nor yet, as I believe, for all mankind."[11] The second group consisted of citizens who showed courage, the warriors who protected the society. All the rest made up the masses, essentially people driven not by wisdom or courage but by desire. They would be the producers of society—the artisans, tradesmen, and farmers.

In Plato's ideal state, each group fulfilled its assigned role, creating a society that functioned harmoniously. The needs of the community, rather than the happiness of the individual, were Plato's concern, and he focused on the need for the guardians or rulers, above all, to be removed from any concerns for wealth or prestige so that they could strive for what was best for the community. To rid the guardians of these desires, Plato urged that they live together, forgoing both private property and family life. Plato believed that women, too, could be rulers; in this he departed radically from the actual practices of the Greek states.

Plato established a school at Athens known as the Academy. One of his pupils, who studied there for twenty years, was Aristotle (384–322 B.C.), who later became a tutor to Alexander the Great. Aristotle did not accept Plato's theory of ideal Forms. Instead he believed that by examining individual objects, we can perceive their form and arrive at universal principles; however, these principles do not exist as a separate higher world of reality beyond material things but are a part of things themselves. Aristotle's interests, then, lay in analyzing and classifying things based on thorough research and investigation. His interests were wide-ranging, and he wrote treatises on an enormous number of subjects: ethics, logic, politics, poetry, astronomy, geology, biology, and physics.

Like Plato, Aristotle wished for an effective form of government that would rationally direct human affairs. Unlike Plato, he did not seek an ideal state based on the

embodiment of an ideal Form of justice; he tried to find the best form of government through a rational examination of existing governments. For his *Politics,* Aristotle examined the constitutions of 158 states and arrived at general categories for organizing governments. He identified three good forms of government: monarchy, aristocracy, and constitutional government. But based on his examination, he warned that monarchy can easily turn into tyranny, aristocracy into oligarchy, and constitutional government into radical democracy or anarchy. He favored constitutional government as the best form for most people.

Aristotle's philosophical and political ideas played an enormous role in the development of Western thought during the Middle Ages (see Chapter 9). So did his ideas on women. Aristotle believed that marriage was meant to provide mutual comfort between man and woman and contributed to the overall happiness of a community: "The community needs both male and female excellences or it can only be half-blessed."[12] Nevertheless, Aristotle maintained that women were biologically inferior to men: "A woman is, as it were, an infertile male. She is female in fact on account of a kind of inadequacy." Therefore, according to Aristotle, women must be subordinated to men, not only in the community but also in marriage: "The association between husband and wife is clearly an aristocracy. The man rules by virtue of merit, and in the sphere that is his by right; but he hands over to this wife such matters as are suitable for her."[13]

Greek Religion

Greek religion was intricately connected to every aspect of daily life; it was both social and practical. Public festivals, which originated in religious practices, served specific functions: boys were prepared to be warriors, girls to be mothers. Since religion was related to every aspect of life, citizens had to have a proper attitude toward the gods. Religion was a civic cult necessary for the well-being of the state. Temples dedicated to a god or goddess were the major buildings in Greek society.

Homer gave an account of the gods that provided Greek religion with a definite structure. Over a period of time, most Greeks came to accept a common religion based on twelve chief gods and goddesses who were thought to live on Mount Olympus, the highest mountain in Greece. Among the twelve were Zeus, the chief deity and father of the gods; Athena, goddess of wisdom and crafts; Apollo, god of the sun and poetry; Aphrodite, goddess of love; and Poseidon, brother of Zeus and god of the seas and earthquakes.

The twelve Olympian gods were common to all Greeks, who thus shared a basic polytheistic religion. Each *polis* usually singled out one of the twelve Olympians as a guardian deity of its community. Athena was the patron goddess of Athens, for example. Because it was desirable to have the gods look favorably on one's activities, ritual assumed enormous proportions in Greek religion. Prayers were often combined with gifts to the gods based on the principle "I give to you, the gods, so that you will give in return." Ritual also meant sacrifices of animals or food. Animals were burned on an altar in front of a temple or a small altar in front of a home.

Festivals also developed as a way to honor the gods and goddesses. Some of these (the Panhellenic celebrations) were important to all Greeks and were held at special locations, such as those dedicated to the worship of Zeus at Olympia or to Apollo at Delphi. Numerous events were held in honor of the gods at the great festivals, including athletic competitions to which all Greeks were invited. The first such games were held at the Olympic festival in 776 B.C. and then held every four years thereafter to honor Zeus. Initially, the Olympic contests consisted of foot races and wrestling, but later, boxing, javelin throwing, and various other contests were added.

The Greeks also had a great desire to know the will of the gods. To do so, they made use of the oracle, a sacred shrine dedicated to a god or goddess who revealed the future. The most famous was the oracle of Apollo at Delphi, located on the side of Mount Parnassus, overlooking the Gulf of Corinth. At Delphi, a priestess listened to questions while in a state of ecstasy that was believed to be induced by Apollo. Her responses were interpreted by the priests and given in verse form to the person asking questions. Representatives of states and individuals traveled to Delphi to consult the oracle of Apollo. States might inquire whether they should undertake a military expedition; individuals might raise such questions as "Heracleidas asks whether he will have offspring from the wife he has now." Responses were often enigmatic and at times even politically motivated. Croesus, the king of Lydia in Asia Minor, who was known for his vast wealth, sent messengers to the oracle at Delphi, asking whether he should go to war with the Persians. The oracle replied that if Croesus attacked the Persians, a mighty empire would be destroyed. Overjoyed to hear these words, Croesus made war on the Persians but was crushed by the enemy forces. A mighty empire was indeed destroyed—his own.

Daily Life in Classical Athens

The Greek city-state was, above all, a male community: only adult male citizens took part in public life. In Athens, this meant the exclusion of women, slaves, and foreign residents, or roughly 85 percent of the population in Attica. Of the 150,000 citizens in Athens, about 43,000 were adult males who exercised political power. Resident foreigners, who numbered about 35,000, received the protection of the laws but were also subject to some of the responsibilities of citizens, namely, military service and the funding of festivals. The remaining social group, the slaves, numbered around 100,000. Most slaves in Athens worked in the home as cooks and maids or toiled in the fields. Some were owned by the state and worked on public construction projects.

Economy and Lifestyle The Athenian economy was largely agricultural but highly diversified. Athenian farmers grew grains, vegetables, and fruit for local consumption; cultivated vines and olive trees for wine and olive oil, which were exportable products; and grazed sheep and goats for wool and milk products. Given the size of its population and the lack of abundant fertile land, Athens had to import between 50 and 80 percent of its grain, a staple in the Athenian diet. Trade was thus highly important to the Athenian economy. The building of the port at Piraeus and the Long Walls (a series of defensive walls nearly 5 miles long connecting Athens and Piraeus) created the physical conditions that made Athens the leading trade center in the fifth-century Greek world.

Artisans were more important to the Athenian economy than their relatively small numbers might suggest. Athens was the chief producer of high-quality painted pottery in the fifth century. Other crafts had moved beyond the small workshop into the factory through the use of slave labor. The shield factory of Lysias, for example, employed 120 slaves. Public works projects also provided jobs for Athenians. The building program of Pericles, financed from the Delian League treasury, made possible the hiring of both skilled and unskilled labor.

The Athenian lifestyle was simple. Houses were furnished with necessities bought from artisans, such as beds, couches, tables, chests, pottery, stools, baskets, and cooking utensils. Wives and slaves made clothes and blankets at home. The Athenian diet was rather plain and relied on such basic foods as barley, wheat, millet, lentils, grapes, figs, olives, almonds, bread made at home, vegetables, eggs, fish, cheese, and chicken. Olive oil was widely used, not only for eating but also for lighting lamps and rubbing on the body after washing and exercise. Although country houses kept animals, they were used for reasons other than their flesh: oxen for plowing, sheep for wool, goats for milk and cheese.

Family and Relationships The family was an important institution in ancient Athens. It was composed of husband, wife, and children (a nuclear family), although other dependent relatives and slaves were also part of the family economic unit. The family's primary social function was to produce new citizens. Strict laws of the fifth century had stipulated that a citizen must be the offspring of a legally acknowledged marriage between two Athenian citizens whose parents were also citizens.

Women were citizens who could participate in most religious cults and festivals but were otherwise excluded from public life. They could not own property beyond personal items and always had a male guardian. The function of the Athenian woman as wife was very clear. Her foremost obligation was to bear children, especially male children who would preserve the family line. The marriage formula that Athenians used put it succinctly: "I give this woman for the procreation of legitimate children." A wife was also expected to take care of her family and her house, either doing the household work herself

8. Thucydides, *History of the Pelop...*
   Warner (Harmondsworth, Eng...

9. Sophocles, *Oedipus the King*, tr...
   1959), pp. 68–69.

10. Sophocles, *Antigone*, trans. D. ...
    p. 146.

11. Plato, *The Republic*, trans. F. M...
    1945), pp. 178–179.

12. Aristotle, quoted in S. Blunde...
    (Cambridge, Mass., 1995), p. ...

13. Ibid., p. 186.

SUGGESTIONS FOR FUR

A standard one-volume reference wor...
and R. Meiggs, *A History of Greece t*
Great, 4th ed. (New York, 1975). For ...
introduction, see **F. Durando, *Ancien***
Western World (New York, 1997). For ...
see **J. Camp and E. Fisher, *The World***
2002). Other good general introducti...
T. R. Martin, *Ancient Greece* (New Ha...
The Cambridge Illustrated History o
1998); and **W. Donlan et al., *Ancient***
Cultural History (New York, 1998).

Early Greek history is examined ...
ed. (Cambridge, Mass., 1993); **M. I. F***
and Archaic Ages, 2d ed. (New York, ...
Discovery of the Greek Bronze Age (...
and his world, see the modern classic ...
Odysseus, 2d ed. (New York, 1979).

General works on Archaic Greec...
Archaic Greece (London, 1980), and **...**
(London, 1987). Economic and social ...
in **C. Starr, *The Economic and Socia***
500 B.C. (Oxford, 1977). On coloniza...
Greeks Overseas, rev. ed. (Baltimore, ...
McGlew, *Tyranny and Political Cult*
N.Y., 1993). On the culture of Archai...
Orientalizing Revolution: Near Easte
in the Early Archaic Age (Cambridge...
P. A. Cartledge, *Spartan Reflections*
Spartans (New York, 2003). On early ...
A. Jones, *Athenian Democracy* (Lon...
Demos (New York, 1985). The Persian ...
The Greco-Persian Wars (Berkeley, ...

A general history of Classical G...
Davies, *Democracy and Classical Gr*
1993).Valuable works on Athens incl...
and the Birth of Democracy (New Yo...
of Democratic Thinking: The Invent
Athens (Cambridge, 1988); **C. W. Fo***
Athens from Cleisthenes to Pericles

HOUSEHOLD MANAGEMENT AND THE ROLE OF THE ATHENIAN WIFE

*I*n fifth-century Athens, a woman's place was in the home. She had two major responsibilities: the bearing and raising children and the management of the household. In his dialogue on estate management, Xenophon relates the instructions of an Attican gentleman to his new wife.

Xenophon, *Oeconomicus*

[Ischomachus addresses his new wife:] For it seems to me, dear, that the gods with great discernment have coupled together male and female, as they are called, chiefly in order that they may form a perfect partnership in mutual service. For, in the first place that the various species of living creatures may not fail, they are joined in wedlock for the production of children. Secondly, offspring to support them in old age is provided by this union, to human beings, at any rate. Thirdly, human beings live not in the open air, like beasts, but obviously need shelter. Nevertheless, those who mean to win stores to fill the covered place, have need of someone to work at the open-air occupations; since plowing, sowing, planting and grazing are all such open-air employments; and these supply the needful food. . . . For he made

the man's body and mind more capable of enduring cold and heat, and journeys and campaigns; and therefore imposed on him the outdoor tasks. To the woman, since he had made her body less capable of such endurance, I take it that God has assigned the indoor tasks. And knowing that he had created in the woman and had imposed on her the nourishment of the infants, he meted out to her a larger portion of affection for newborn babes than to the man. . . .

Your duty will be to remain indoors and send out those servants whose work is outside, and superintend those who are to work indoors, and to receive the incomings, and distribute so much of them as must be spent, and watch over so much as is to be kept in store, and take care that the sum laid by for a year be not spent in a month. And when wool is brought to you, you must see that cloaks are made for those that want them. You must see too that the dry corn is in good condition for making food. One of the duties that fall to you, however, will perhaps seem rather thankless: you will have to see that any servant who is ill is cared for.

What does the selection from Xenophon tell you about the role of women in the Athenian household?

or supervising the slaves who did the actual work (see the box above).

Women were kept under strict control. Since they were married at fourteen or fifteen, they were taught about their responsibilities at an early age. Although many managed to learn to read and play musical instruments, they were often cut off from any formal education. And women were supposed to remain at home, out of sight, except when attending funerals or festivals. If they left the house, they were to be accompanied.

Male homosexuality was also a prominent feature of Athenian life. The Greek homosexual ideal was a rela-

tionship between a mature man and a young male. It is most likely that this was an aristocratic ideal and not one practiced by the common people. Although the relationship was frequently physical, the Greeks also viewed it as educational. The older male (the "lover") won the love of his "beloved" by his value as a teacher and by the devotion he demonstrated in training his charge. In a sense, this love relationship was seen as a way of initiating young men into the male world of political and military dominance. The Greeks did not feel that the coexistence of homosexual and heterosexual predilections created any special problems for individuals or their society.

Erich Lessing/Art Resource, NY (Louvre, Paris)

Women in the Loom Room. In Athens, women were considered citizens and could participate in religious cults and festivals, but they were barred from any political activity. Women were thought to belong in the house, caring for the children and the needs of the household. A principal activity of Greek women was the making of clothes. This scene from the side of a fifth-century B.C. Greek vessel shows one woman spinning and another holding a small hand loom.

CONCLUSION

The civilization of the anci
head of Western culture. So
established the foundations
rodotus and Thucydides cr
Our literary forms are large
and drama. Greek notions
beauty have remained the
Western art. A rational met
modern science, was conce
political terms are of Greek
of the rights and duties of
were conceived in Athens,
Athens gave the idea of de

NOTES

1. H. D. F. Kitto, *The Greeks*
   1951), p. 64.
2. Homer, *Odyssey*, trans. E.
   England, 1946), p. 337.
3. Xenophon, *Symposium*, tr
   Mass., 1968), III, 5.

CHAPTER 4

THE HELLENISTIC WORLD

CHAPTER OUTLINE AND FOCUS QUESTIONS

Macedonia and the Conquests of Alexander

☐ How was Alexander able to amass his empire, and what might his rule have been like if he had lived longer?

The World of the Hellenistic Kingdoms

☐ What were the main features of the political and military organization of the Hellenistic kingdoms, and how did the new political systems differ from those of the Greek city-states? What were the main social developments in the Hellenistic world?

Culture in the Hellenistic World

☐ What achievements in literature, art, science, and philosophy occurred during the Hellenistic period?

Religion in the Hellenistic World

☐ Which religions were prominent during the Hellenistic period, and what does their popularity suggest about Hellenistic society?

CRITICAL THINKING

☐ How was the Hellenistic period different from the Greek Classical Age?

Detail of Alexander from the Battle of Issus mosaic in Pompeii

Erich Lessing/Art Resource, NY (Museo Archeologico Nazionale, Naples)

IN 334 B.C., **ALEXANDER THE GREAT** led an army of Greeks and Macedonians into western Asia to launch his attack on the Persian Empire. Years of campaigning resulted in the complete defeat of the Persians, and in 327, Alexander and his troops pushed east into India. But two more years of fighting in an exotic and difficult terrain exhausted his troops, who rebelled and refused to go on. Reluctantly, Alexander turned back, leading his men across the arid lands of southern Persia. Conditions in the desert were appalling; the blazing sun and lack of water led to thousands of deaths. At one point, when a group of his soldiers found a little water, they scooped it up in a helmet and gave it to Alexander. Then, according to Arrian, an ancient Greek historian, Alexander, "with a word of thanks for the gift, took the helmet and, in full view of his troops, poured the water on the ground. So extraordinary was the effect of this action that the water wasted by Alexander was as good as a drink for every man in the army." Ever the great military leader, Alexander had found yet another way to inspire his troops.

Alexander the Great was the son of King Philip II of Macedonia, who in 338 B.C. had defeated the Greeks and established his control over the Greek peninsula. When Alexander became king after Philip's death, he led the

HOUSEHOLD MANAGEMENT AND THE ROLE OF THE ATHENIAN WIFE

*I*n fifth-century Athens, a woman's place was in the home. She had two major responsibilities: the bearing and raising children and the management of the household. In his dialogue on estate management, Xenophon relates the instructions of an Attican gentleman to his new wife.

Xenophon, *Oeconomicus*

[Ischomachus addresses his new wife:] For it seems to me, dear, that the gods with great discernment have coupled together male and female, as they are called, chiefly in order that they may form a perfect partnership in mutual service. For, in the first place that the various species of living creatures may not fail, they are joined in wedlock for the production of children. Secondly, offspring to support them in old age is provided by this union, to human beings, at any rate. Thirdly, human beings live not in the open air, like beasts, but obviously need shelter. Nevertheless, those who mean to win stores to fill the covered place, have need of someone to work at the open-air occupations; since plowing, sowing, planting and grazing are all such open-air employments; and these supply the needful food. . . . For he made

the man's body and mind more capable of enduring cold and heat, and journeys and campaigns; and therefore imposed on him the outdoor tasks. To the woman, since he had made her body less capable of such endurance, I take it that God has assigned the indoor tasks. And knowing that he had created in the woman and had imposed on her the nourishment of the infants, he meted out to her a larger portion of affection for newborn babes than to the man. . . .

Your duty will be to remain indoors and send out those servants whose work is outside, and superintend those who are to work indoors, and to receive the incomings, and distribute so much of them as must be spent, and watch over so much as is to be kept in store, and take care that the sum laid by for a year be not spent in a month. And when wool is brought to you, you must see that cloaks are made for those that want them. You must see too that the dry corn is in good condition for making food. One of the duties that fall to you, however, will perhaps seem rather thankless: you will have to see that any servant who is ill is cared for.

What does the selection from Xenophon tell you about the role of women in the Athenian household?

or supervising the slaves who did the actual work (see the box above).

Women were kept under strict control. Since they were married at fourteen or fifteen, they were taught about their responsibilities at an early age. Although many managed to learn to read and play musical instruments, they were often cut off from any formal education. And women were supposed to remain at home, out of sight, except when attending funerals or festivals. If they left the house, they were to be accompanied.

Male homosexuality was also a prominent feature of Athenian life. The Greek homosexual ideal was a rela-

tionship between a mature man and a young male. It is most likely that this was an aristocratic ideal and not one practiced by the common people. Although the relationship was frequently physical, the Greeks also viewed it as educational. The older male (the "lover") won the love of his "beloved" by his value as a teacher and by the devotion he demonstrated in training his charge. In a sense, this love relationship was seen as a way of initiating young men into the male world of political and military dominance. The Greeks did not feel that the coexistence of homosexual and heterosexual predilections created any special problems for individuals or their society.

Erich Lessing/Art Resource, NY (Louvre, Paris)

Women in the Loom Room. In Athens, women were considered citizens and could participate in religious cults and festivals, but they were barred from any political activity. Women were thought to belong in the house, caring for the children and the needs of the household. A principal activity of Greek women was the making of clothes. This scene from the side of a fifth-century B.C. Greek vessel shows one woman spinning and another holding a small hand loom.

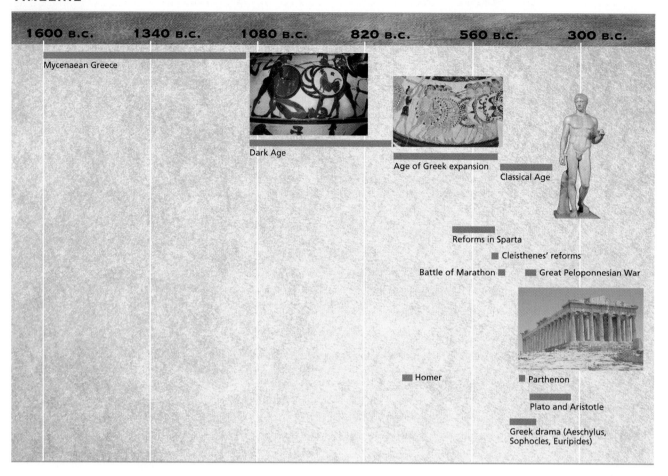

| 1600 B.C. | 1340 B.C. | 1080 B.C. | 820 B.C. | 560 B.C. | 300 B.C. |

Mycenaean Greece

Dark Age

Age of Greek expansion

Classical Age

Reforms in Sparta

Cleisthenes' reforms

Battle of Marathon

Great Peloponnesian War

Homer

Parthenon

Plato and Aristotle

Greek drama (Aeschylus, Sophocles, Euripides)

CONCLUSION

The civilization of the ancient Greeks was the fountainhead of Western culture. Socrates, Plato, and Aristotle established the foundations of Western philosophy. Herodotus and Thucydides created the discipline of history. Our literary forms are largely derived from Greek poetry and drama. Greek notions of harmony, proportion, and beauty have remained the touchstones for all subsequent Western art. A rational method of inquiry, so important to modern science, was conceived in ancient Greece. Many political terms are of Greek origin, and so are our concepts of the rights and duties of citizenship, especially as they were conceived in Athens, the first great democracy. Athens gave the idea of democracy to the Western world.

Especially during their Classical period, the Greeks raised and debated the fundamental questions about the purpose of human existence, the structure of human society, and the nature of the universe that have concerned Western thinkers ever since.

All of these achievements came from a group of small city-states in ancient Greece. And yet Greek civilization also contains an element of tragedy. For all of their brilliant accomplishments, the Greeks were unable to rise above the divisions and rivalries that caused them to fight each other and undermine their own civilization. Of course, their contributions to Western civilization have outlived their political struggles.

NOTES

1. H. D. F. Kitto, *The Greeks* (Harmondsworth, England, 1951), p. 64.
2. Homer, *Odyssey*, trans. E.V. Rieu (Harmondsworth, England, 1946), p. 337.
3. Xenophon, *Symposium*, trans. O. J. Todd (Cambridge, Mass., 1968), III, 5.
4. Homer, *Odyssey*, pp. 290–291.
5. Quoted in T. R. Martin, *Ancient Greece* (New Haven, Conn., 1996), p. 62.
6. Plutarch, quoted in E. Fantham, H. P. Foley, N. B. Kampen, S. B. Pomeroy, and H. A. Shapiro, *Women in the Classical World* (New York, 1994), p. 64.
7. Herodotus, *The Persian Wars*, trans. G. Rawlinson (New York, 1942), p. 3.

8. Thucydides, *History of the Peloponnesian War*, trans. R. Warner (Harmondsworth, England, 1954), p. 24.

9. Sophocles, *Oedipus the King*, trans. D. Grene (Chicago, 1959), pp. 68–69.

10. Sophocles, *Antigone*, trans. D. Taylor (London, 1986), p. 146.

11. Plato, *The Republic*, trans. F. M. Cornford (New York, 1945), pp. 178–179.

12. Aristotle, quoted in S. Blundell, *Women in Ancient Greece* (Cambridge, Mass., 1995), p. 106.

13. Ibid., p. 186.

SUGGESTIONS FOR FURTHER READING

A standard one-volume reference work for Greek history is **J. B. Bury and R. Meiggs**, ***A History of Greece to the Death of Alexander the Great***, 4th ed. (New York, 1975). For a beautifully illustrated introduction, see **F. Durando**, ***Ancient Greece: The Dawn of the Western World*** (New York, 1997). For a brief illustrated introduction, see **J. Camp and E. Fisher**, ***The World of the Ancient Greeks*** (London, 2002). Other good general introductions to Greek history include **T. R. Martin**, ***Ancient Greece*** (New Haven, Conn., 1996); **P. Cartledge**, ***The Cambridge Illustrated History of Ancient Greece*** (Cambridge, 1998); and **W. Donlan et al.**, ***Ancient Greece: A Political, Social, and Cultural History*** (New York, 1998).

Early Greek history is examined in **O. Murray**, ***Early Greece***, 2d ed. (Cambridge, Mass., 1993); **M. I. Finley**, ***Early Greece: The Bronze and Archaic Ages***, 2d ed. (New York, 1982); and **J. L. Fitton**, ***The Discovery of the Greek Bronze Age*** (Cambridge, 1995). On Homer and his world, see the modern classic by **M. I. Finley**, ***The World of Odysseus***, 2d ed. (New York, 1979).

General works on Archaic Greece include **A. M. Snodgrass**, ***Archaic Greece*** (London, 1980), and **M. Grant**, ***The Rise of the Greeks*** (London, 1987). Economic and social history of the period is covered in **C. Starr**, ***The Economic and Social Growth of Early Greece, 800–500 B.C.*** (Oxford, 1977). On colonization, see **J. Boardman**, ***The Greeks Overseas***, rev. ed. (Baltimore, 1980). On tyranny, see **J. F. McGlew**, ***Tyranny and Political Culture in Ancient Greece*** (Ithaca, N.Y., 1993). On the culture of Archaic Greece, see **W. Burkert**, ***The Orientalizing Revolution: Near Eastern Influence on Greek Culture in the Early Archaic Age*** (Cambridge, Mass., 1992). On Sparta, see **P. A. Cartledge**, ***Spartan Reflections*** (Berkeley, Calif., 2001) and ***The Spartans*** (New York, 2003). On early Athens, see the still valuable **A. Jones**, ***Athenian Democracy*** (London, 1957), and **R. Osborne**, ***Demos*** (New York, 1985). The Persian Wars are examined in **P. Green**, ***The Greco-Persian Wars*** (Berkeley, Calif., 1996).

A general history of Classical Greece can be found in **J. K. Davies**, ***Democracy and Classical Greece***, 2d ed. (Cambridge, Mass., 1993). Valuable works on Athens include **D. Kagan**, ***Pericles of Athens and the Birth of Democracy*** (New York, 1991); **C. Farrar**, ***The Origins of Democratic Thinking: The Invention of Politics in Classical Athens*** (Cambridge, 1988); **C. W. Fornara** and **L. J. Samons II**, ***Athens from Cleisthenes to Pericles*** (Berkeley, Calif., 1991); and

D. Stockton, ***The Classical Athenian Democracy*** (Oxford, 1990). An interesting work on the intellectual and political history of Athens in the late fifth century B.C. is **M. Munn**, ***The School of History: Athens in the Age of Socrates*** (Berkeley, Calif., 2000). On the development of the Athenian Empire, see **M. F. McGregor**, ***The Athenians and Their Empire*** (Vancouver, 1987). The best way to examine the Great Peloponnesian War is to read the work of **Thucydides**, ***History of the Peloponnesian War***, trans. **R. Warner** (Harmondsworth, England, 1954). An excellent recent history is **D. Kagan**, ***The Peloponnesian War*** (New York, 2003). On fourth-century Athens, see **M. H. Hansen**, ***The Athenian Democracy in the Age of Demosthenes*** (Oxford, 1991).

For a comprehensive history of Greek art, see **M. Robertson**, ***A History of Greek Art***, 2 vols. (Cambridge, 1975). On sculpture, see **A. Stewart**, ***Greek Sculpture: An Exploration*** (New Haven, Conn., 1990). A basic survey of architecture is **H. W. Lawrence**, ***Greek Architecture***, rev. ed. (Harmondsworth, England, 1983). On Greek drama, see the general work by **J. De Romilly**, ***A Short History of Greek Literature*** (Chicago, 1985). On Greek philosophy, a detailed study is available in **W. K. C. Guthrie**, ***A History of Greek Philosophy***, 6 vols. (Cambridge, 1962–1981).

On Greek religion, see **J. N. Bremmer**, ***Greek Religion*** (Oxford, 1994), and **R. Garland**, ***Religion and the Greeks*** (New York, 1994). On athletic competitions, see **S. G. Miller**, ***Ancient Greek Athletics*** (New Haven, Conn., 2004).

On the family and women, see **C. B. Patterson**, ***The Family in Greek History*** (New York, 1998); **E. Fantham et al.**, ***Women in the Classical World*** (New York, 1994); and **S. Blundell**, ***Women in Ancient Greece*** (London, 1995). On slavery, see **N.R.E. Fisher**, ***Slavery in Classical Greece*** (New York, 1995). On homosexuality, see **K. J. Dover**, ***Greek Homosexuality*** (London, 1978), and **E. Cantarella**, ***Bisexuality in the Ancient World*** (New Haven, Conn., 1992).

Thomson NOW! Enter *ThomsonNOW* using the access card that is available for *Western Civilization: A Brief History.* *ThomsonNOW* will help you understand this chapter with lesson plans generated for your needs. In addition, you can read the following documents, and many more, online:

Tyrtaeus, A War Song
Aeschylus, selection from the end of *Agamemnon*
Sophocles, excerpts from *Oedipus the King*
Euripides, excerpt from *Medea*
Plato, excerpts from *Apology* and *Republic*

WESTERN CIVILIZATION RESOURCES

Visit the Web site for *Western Civilization: A Brief History* for resources specific to this book:

http://www.thomsonedu.com/history/spielvogel

For a variety of tools to help you succeed in this course, visit the Western Civilization Resource Center at

http://history.wadsworth.com/spielvogel

Included are quizzes, images, documents, interactive simulations, maps and timelines, movie explorations, and a wealth of other sources.

4

THE HELLENISTIC WORLD

CHAPTER OUTLINE
AND FOCUS QUESTIONS

Macedonia and the Conquests of Alexander

▢ How was Alexander able to amass his empire, and what might his rule have been like if he had lived longer?

The World of the Hellenistic Kingdoms

▢ What were the main features of the political and military organization of the Hellenistic kingdoms, and how did the new political systems differ from those of the Greek city-states? What were the main social developments in the Hellenistic world?

Culture in the Hellenistic World

▢ What achievements in literature, art, science, and philosophy occurred during the Hellenistic period?

Religion in the Hellenistic World

▢ Which religions were prominent during the Hellenistic period, and what does their popularity suggest about Hellenistic society?

CRITICAL THINKING

▢ How was the Hellenistic period different from the Greek Classical Age?

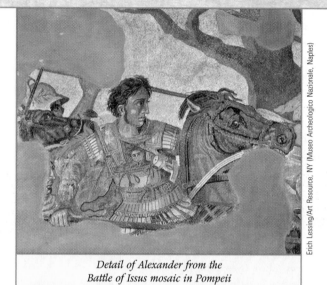

Detail of Alexander from the Battle of Issus mosaic in Pompeii

Erich Lessing/Art Resource, NY (Museo Archeologico Nazionale, Naples)

𝓘N 334 B.C., **ALEXANDER THE GREAT** led an army of Greeks and Macedonians into western Asia to launch his attack on the Persian Empire. Years of campaigning resulted in the complete defeat of the Persians, and in 327, Alexander and his troops pushed east into India. But two more years of fighting in an exotic and difficult terrain exhausted his troops, who rebelled and refused to go on. Reluctantly, Alexander turned back, leading his men across the arid lands of southern Persia. Conditions in the desert were appalling; the blazing sun and lack of water led to thousands of deaths. At one point, when a group of his soldiers found a little water, they scooped it up in a helmet and gave it to Alexander. Then, according to Arrian, an ancient Greek historian, Alexander, "with a word of thanks for the gift, took the helmet and, in full view of his troops, poured the water on the ground. So extraordinary was the effect of this action that the water wasted by Alexander was as good as a drink for every man in the army." Ever the great military leader, Alexander had found yet another way to inspire his troops.

Alexander the Great was the son of King Philip II of Macedonia, who in 338 B.C. had defeated the Greeks and established his control over the Greek peninsula. When Alexander became king after Philip's death, he led the

Macedonians and Greeks on a spectacular conquest of the Persian Empire, opening the door to the spread of Greek culture throughout the ancient Near East. Greek settlers poured into the lands of the ancient Near East as bureaucrats, traders, soldiers, and scholars. Alexander's triumph gave rise to a new series of kingdoms that blended the achievements of the eastern world with the cultural outlook and attitudes of the Greeks. We use the term **Hellenistic** to designate this new order. The Hellenistic world was the world of Greeks and non-Greek easterners, and it resulted, in its own way, in a remarkable series of accomplishments that are sometimes underestimated. They form the story of this chapter.◆

Macedonia and the Conquests of Alexander

While the Greek city-states were busy fighting each other, to their north a new and ultimately powerful kingdom was emerging. Its people, the Macedonians, were viewed as barbarians by their Greek neighbors to the south. The Macedonians were mostly rural folk and were organized in tribes, not city-states. Not until the end of the fifth century B.C. did Macedonia become an important kingdom. But when Philip II (359–336 B.C.) took control, he turned Macedonia into the chief power of the Greek world.

Philip and the Conquest of Greece

The Greeks had mixed reactions to Philip's growing strength. Some viewed Philip as a savior who would rescue the Greeks from themselves by uniting them. Many Athenians, however, especially the orator Demosthenes, portrayed Philip as ruthless, deceitful, treacherous, and barbaric and called on the Athenians to undertake a struggle against him. In a speech to the Athenian assembly, Demosthenes exclaimed: "[Philip] is not only no Greek, nor related to the Greeks, but not even a barbarian from any place that can be named with honor, but a pestilent knave from Macedonia, from where it was never yet possible to buy a decent slave."

Demosthenes' repeated calls for action, combined with Philip's rapid expansion, finally spurred Athens into action. Allied with a number of other Greek states, Athens fought the Macedonians at the Battle of Chaeronea, near Thebes, in 338 B.C. The Macedonian army crushed the Greeks, and Philip was now free to consolidate his control over the Greek peninsula. The independent Greek *polis*, long the basic political unit of the Greek world, came to an end as Philip formed an alliance of the Greek states that we call the Corinthian League because they met at Corinth. All members took an oath of loyalty: "I swear by Zeus, Earth, Sun, Poseidon, Athena, Ares, and all the gods and goddesses, I will abide by the peace, and I will not break the agreements with

Philip the Macedonian, nor will I take up arms with hostile intent against any one of those who abide by the oaths either by land or by sea."[1]

Although Philip allowed the Greek city-states autonomy in domestic affairs, he retained the general direction of their foreign affairs. Philip insisted that the Greek states end their bitter rivalries and cooperate with him in a war against Persia. Before Philip could undertake his invasion of Asia, however, he was assassinated, leaving the task to his son Alexander.

Alexander the Great

Alexander was only twenty when he became king of Macedonia. The illustrious conqueror was in many ways prepared for kingship by his father, who had taken Alexander along on military campaigns and had given him control of the cavalry at the important Battle of

Alexander the Great. This marble head of Alexander the Great was made in the second or first century B.C. The long hair and tilt of his head reflect the description of Alexander in the literary sources of the time. This portrait shows a youthful and even godlike appearance. Alexander claimed to be descended from Heracles, a Greek hero worshiped as a god, and as pharaoh of Egypt, he gained recognition as a living deity. It is reported that at the base of one of his statues, now lost, in which Alexander was shown gazing at Zeus, were the words "I place the earth under my sway; you, O Zeus, keep Olympus."

Chaeronea. After his father's assassination, Alexander moved quickly to assert his authority, securing the Macedonian frontiers and smothering a rebellion in Greece. He then turned to his father's dream, the invasion of the Persian Empire.

The Conquests of Alexander   There is no doubt that Alexander was taking a chance in attacking the Persian Empire. Although weakened in some respects, it was still a strong state. Alexander's fleet was inferior to the Persian navy, and his finances were shaky at best. In the spring of 334 B.C., Alexander entered Asia Minor with an army of some 37,000 men. About half were Macedonians, the rest Greeks and other allies. The cavalry, which would play an important role as a striking force, numbered about 5,000.

His first confrontation with the Persians, in a battle at the Granicus River in 334 B.C. (see Map 4.1), nearly cost him his life but resulted in a major victory. By spring 333, the entire western half of Asia Minor was in Alexander's hands, and the Ionian Greek cities of western Asia Minor had been "liberated" from the Persian oppressor. Meanwhile, the Persian king, Darius III, mobilized his forces to stop Alexander's army. Although the Persian troops outnumbered Alexander's, the Battle of Issus was fought on a narrow field that canceled the advantage of superior numbers and resulted in another Macedonian success. The Persian cause was certainly not helped when Darius made a spectacular exit from the battlefield before it was even clear who would win. After his victory at Issus in 333 B.C., Alexander turned south, and by the winter of 332, Syria, Palestine, and Egypt were under his domination. He took the traditional title of pharaoh of Egypt and founded the first of a series of cities named after him (Alexandria) as the Greek administrative capital of Egypt. It became (and remains today) one of Egypt's and the Mediterranean world's most important cities.

The next year, Alexander renewed his offensive, moving into the territory of the ancient Mesopotamian kingdoms and fighting a decisive battle with the Persians not far from Babylon. At Gaugamela, Alexander's men were clearly outnumbered by the Persian forces, which had established the battle site on a broad, open plain where their war chariots could maneuver to best advantage. Alexander was able to break through the center of the Persian line with his heavy cavalry, followed by the infantry.

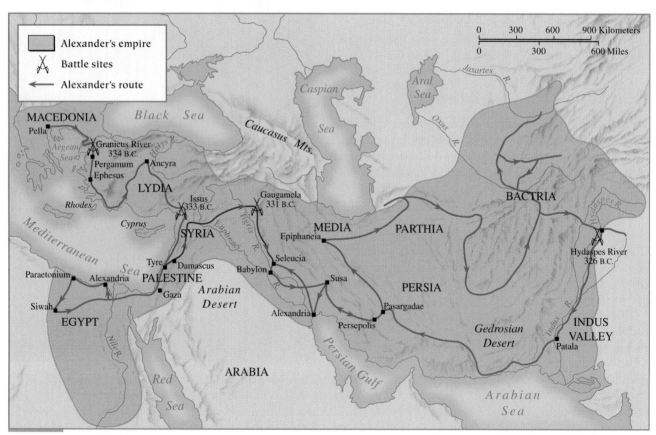

MAP 4.1   **The Conquests of Alexander the Great.**   In just twelve years, Alexander the Great conquered vast territories. Dominating lands from west of the Nile to east of the Indus, he brought the Persian Empire, Egypt, and much of the Middle East under his control and laid the foundations for the Hellenistic world. **?** Approximately how far did he and his troops travel during those twelve years? 🔊 **View an animated version of this map or related map at**
http://thomsonedu.com/history/spielvogel

The battle turned into a rout, although Darius managed to escape. After his victory, Alexander entered Babylon and then proceeded to the Persian capitals at Susa and Persepolis, where he acquired the Persian treasuries and took possession of vast quantities of gold and silver.

By 330, Alexander was again on the march. After Darius was killed by one of his own men, Alexander took the title and office of the Great King of the Persians. But he was not content to rest with the spoils of the Persian Empire. During the next three years, he moved east and northeast, as far as modern Pakistan. By summer 327 B.C., he had entered India, which at that time was divided into a number of warring states. In 326 B.C., Alexander and his armies arrived in the plains of north-western India. At the Battle of the Hydaspes River, Alexander won a brutally fought battle (see the box on p. 64). When Alexander made clear his determination to march east to conquer more of India, his soldiers, weary of campaigning year after year, mutinied and re-fused to go further. Alexander acceded to their demands and agreed to return, leading his troops through southern Persia across the Gedrosian Desert, where they suffered heavy losses from appalling desert conditions. Alexander and the remnant of his army went to Susa and then Babylon, where he planned still more campaigns. But in June 323 B.C., weakened from wounds, fever, and prob-ably excessive alcohol, he died at the age of thirty-two.

The Legacy of Alexander   Alexander is one of the most puzzling great figures in history. Historians relying on the

same sources give vastly different pictures of him. Some portray him as an idealistic visionary and others as a ruthless Machiavellian. No doubt he was a great military leader—a master of strategy and tactics, fighting in every kind of terrain and facing every kind of opponent. Alexander was a brave and even reckless fighter who was quite willing to lead his men into battle and risk his own life. His example inspired his troops to follow him into unknown lands and difficult situations. We know that he sought to imitate Achilles, the warrior-hero of Homer's *Iliad*, an important ideal in Greek culture. Alexander kept a copy of the *Iliad*—and a dagger—under his pillow. He also

Alexander and Darius at the Battle of Issus.   This late-second- or early-first-century B.C. mosaic from the floor of a Roman villa at Pompeii is thought to be a copy of a panel painting by Philoxenos of Eretria about 310 B.C. The mosaic depicts the battle between Alexander and Darius III, king of Persia, at Issus in 333 B.C. Alexander is seen at left on horseback, recklessly leading his troops into battle. Darius is shown in his chariot, already turning around to flee from the enemy.

Erich Lessing/Art Resource, NY (Museo Archeologico Nazionale, Naples)

ALEXANDER MEETS AN INDIAN KING

*I*n his campaigns in India, Alexander fought a number of difficult battles. At the Battle of the Hydaspes River, he faced a strong opponent in the Indian king Porus. After defeating Porus, Alexander treated him with respect, according to Arrian, Alexander's ancient biographer.

Arrian, *The Campaigns of Alexander*

Throughout the action Porus had proved himself a man indeed, not only as a commander but as a soldier of the truest courage. When he saw his cavalry cut to pieces, most of his infantry dead, and his elephants killed or roaming riderless and bewildered about the field, his behavior was very different from that of the Persian King Darius: unlike Darius, he did not lead the scramble to save his own skin, but so long as a single unit of his men held together, he fought bravely on. It was only when he was himself wounded that he turned the elephant on which he rode and began to withdraw. . . . Alexander, anxious to save the life of this great and gallant soldier, sent . . . [to him] an Indian named Meroes, a man he had been told had long been Porus' friend. Porus listened to Meroes' message, stopped his elephant, and dismounted; he was much distressed by thirst, so when he had revived himself by drinking, he told Meroes to conduct him with all speed to Alexander.

Alexander, informed of his approach, rode out to meet him. . . . When they met, he reined in his horse and looked at his adversary with admiration: he was a magnificent figure of a man, over seven feet high and of great personal beauty; his bearing had lost none of its pride; his air was of one brave man meeting another, of a king in the presence of a king, with whom he had fought honorably for his kingdom.

Alexander was the first to speak. "What," he said, "do you wish that I should do with you?" "Treat me as a king ought," Porus is said to have replied. "For my part," said Alexander, pleased by his answer, "your request shall be granted. But is there not something you would wish for yourself? Ask it." "Everything," said Porus, "is contained in this one request."

The dignity of these words gave Alexander even more pleasure, and he restored to Porus his sovereignty over his subjects, adding to his realm other territory of even greater extent. Thus he did indeed use a brave man as a king ought, and from that time forward found him in every way a loyal friend.

———————————

What do we learn from Arrian's account about Alexander's military skills and Indian methods of fighting?

---

claimed to be descended from Heracles, the Greek hero who came to be worshiped as a god. Alexander also aspired to divine honors; as pharaoh of Egypt, he became a living god according to Egyptian tradition and at one point even sent instructions to the Greek cities to "vote him a god."

Regardless of his ideals, motives, or views about himself, one fact stands out: Alexander created a new age, the Hellenistic era. The word *Hellenistic* is derived from a Greek word meaning "to imitate Greeks." It is an appropriate way, then, to describe an age that saw the extension of the Greek language and ideas to the non-Greek world of the Near East. Alexander's destruction of the Persian monarchy had extended Greco-Macedonian rule over an enormous area. It created opportunities for Greek engineers, intellectuals, merchants, soldiers, and administrators. While the Greeks on the mainland might remain committed to the ideals of their city-states, those who followed Alexander and his successors participated in a new political unity based on the principle of monarchy. Alexander had transformed his army from a Macedonian force into an international one, owing loyalty only to himself. His successors used force to establish military monarchies that dominated the Hellenistic world after his death. Autocratic power, based on military strength and pretensions of divine rule, became a regular feature of those Hellenistic monarchies and was part of Alexander's political legacy to the Hellenistic world. His vision of empire no doubt inspired the Romans, who were the ultimate heirs of Alexander's legacy.

But Alexander also left a cultural legacy. As a result of his conquests, Greek language, art, architecture, and literature spread throughout the Near East. The urban centers of the Hellenistic Age, many founded by Alexander and his successors, became springboards for the diffusion of Greek culture. Alexander had established a number of cities and military colonies named Alexandria to guard strategic points and supervise wide areas. Most of the settlers were Greek mercenaries. It has been estimated that in the course of his campaigns, Alexander summoned 60,000 to 65,000 additional mercenaries from Greece, at least 36,000 of whom took up residence in the garrisons and new cities. While the Greeks spread their culture in the East, they were also inevitably influenced by Eastern ways. Thus Alexander's legacy became one of the hallmarks of the Hellenistic world: the clash and fusion of different cultures.

The World of the Hellenistic Kingdoms

The united empire that Alexander created by his conquests disintegrated after his death. All too soon, Macedonian military leaders were engaged in a struggle for power. By 300 B.C., any hope of unity was dead.

MAP 4.2 The Hellenistic Kingdoms. Alexander died unexpectedly at the age of thirty-two and did not designate a successor. Upon his death, his generals struggled for power, eventually establishing four monarchies that spread Hellenistic culture and fostered trade and economic development. ❓ Which kingdom encompassed most of the old Persian Empire? 🌐 **View an animated version of this map or related maps at** http://thomsonedu.com/history/spielvogel

Hellenistic Monarchies

Eventually, four Hellenistic kingdoms emerged as the successors to Alexander (see Map 4.2). In Macedonia, the struggles for power led to the extermination of Alexander's dynasty. Not until 276 B.C. did Antigonus Gonatus, the grandson of one of Alexander's generals, succeed in establishing the Antigonid dynasty as rulers of Macedonia. The Antigonids viewed control of Greece as essential to their power but did not see outright conquest as necessary.

Another Hellenistic monarchy was founded by the general Seleucus, who established the Seleucid dynasty of Syria. This was the largest of the Hellenistic kingdoms and controlled much of the old Persian Empire from Turkey in the west to India in the east, although the Seleucids found it increasingly difficult to maintain control of the eastern territories. In fact, an Indian ruler named Chandragupta Maurya (324–301 B.C.) established a new Indian state, the Mauryan Empire, and drove out the Seleucid forces. However, the Seleucid rulers maintained relations with the Mauryan Empire. Trade was fostered, especially in such luxuries as spices and jewels.

A third Hellenistic kingdom came into being by freeing itself from the Seleucids. This was the kingdom of Pergamum in western Asia Minor under the Attalid dynasty. In 133 B.C., the last member of the Attalid dynasty bequeathed his kingdom to Rome in his will.

The fourth Hellenistic monarchy was Egypt, which had come under the control of Ptolemy, another Macedonian general. Named governor of Egypt after Alexander's death, Ptolemy had established himself as king by 305 B.C., founding the Ptolemaic dynasty of pharaohs. Hellenistic Egypt lasted longer than all the other Hellenistic monarchies; it was not until the reign of Cleopatra VII, who allied herself with the wrong side in the Roman civil wars (see Chapter 5), that Egypt fell to the Romans in 30 B.C.

The Threat from the Celts

The Celts, also known as the Gauls, were a people who had occupied large areas of Europe north of the Alps during the early Iron Age (c. 800–500 B.C.), especially the region to the south and west of the Rhine River, west of the Alps, and north of the Pyrenees (a region known as Gaul).

At the end of the fifth century B.C., possibly as the result of overpopulation, Celtic peoples began to migrate south and east. One group sacked the city of Rome in 390 B.C. (see Chapter 5). After the death of Alexander the Great, other groups of Celts began to threaten the Hellenistic world. Celts attacked Macedonia early in the third century B.C., as one ancient writer reported: "When the defeated Macedonians had fixed themselves within the walls of their cities, the victorious Brennus ravaged the fields of the whole of Macedonia with no one to oppose him."[2] Brennus also led a group of 30,000 Celts into Greece itself and caused considerable damage until being defeated in 278 B.C.

Other groups of Celts later attacked Asia Minor, where Attalus I defeated them in 230 B.C. After his victory, Attalus gained control of much of Asia Minor and declared himself king of Pergamum. Their attacks led the Celts to be feared everywhere in the Hellenistic world.

© Araldo de Luca/CORBIS|Museo Nazionale Romano (Palazzo Altemps), Rome)

A Celt and His Wife: Better a Martyr than a Slave. This statue of a Celtic chieftain and his wife is a Roman copy of a bronze original that was part of a larger monument erected in the 220s B.C. to commemorate the victory of Attalus I of Pergamum over the Celts, a victory that gave Pergamum control over much of Asia Minor. In this scene, the defeated Celtic leader plunges a sword into his chest just after he has killed his wife to prevent her from being sold into slavery.

Political Institutions

The Hellenistic monarchies provided a sort of stability for several centuries, even though Hellenistic kings refused to accept the new status quo and periodically engaged in wars to alter it. At the same time, an underlying strain always existed between the new Greco-Macedonian ruling class and the native populations. Together these factors generated a certain degree of tension that was never truly ended until the vibrant Roman state to the west stepped in and imposed a new order.

The Hellenistic kingdoms shared a common political system that represented a break with their Greek past. To the Greeks, monarchy was an institution for barbarians, associated in their minds with people like the Persians. Although they retained democratic forms of government in their cities, the Greeks of the Hellenistic world were forced to accept monarchy as a new fact of political life.

Although Alexander the Great had apparently hoped to fuse Greeks and easterners—he used Persians as administrators and encouraged his soldiers to marry easterners, as he himself did—Hellenistic monarchs relied primarily on Greeks and Macedonians to form the new ruling class. It has been estimated that in the Seleucid kingdom, for example, only 2.5 percent of the people in authority were non-Greek, and most of them were commanders of local military units. Those who did advance to important administrative posts had learned Greek (all government business was transacted in Greek) and had become Hellenized in a cultural sense. The policy of excluding non-Greeks from leadership positions, it should be added, was not due to the incompetence of the natives but to the determination of the Greek ruling class to maintain its privileged position. It was the Greco-Macedonian ruling class that provided the only unity in the Hellenistic world.

Hellenistic Cities

Cities played an especially important role in the Hellenistic kingdoms. Throughout his conquests, Alexander had founded a series of new cities and military settlements, and Hellenistic kings did likewise. The new population centers varied considerably in size and importance. Military settlements were meant to maintain order and might consist of only a few hundred men who were strongly dependent on the king. But there were also new independent cities with thousands of inhabitants. Alexandria in Egypt was the largest city in the Mediterranean region by the first century B.C.

Hellenistic rulers encouraged this massive spread of Greek colonists to the Near East because of their intrinsic value to the new monarchies. Greeks (and Macedonians) provided not only a recruiting ground for the army but also a pool of civilian administrators and workers who would contribute to economic development. Even architects, engineers, dramatists, and áctors were in demand in the new Greek cities. Many Greeks and Macedonians were quick to see the advantages of moving to the new urban centers and gladly sought their fortunes in the Near East. Greeks of all backgrounds joined the exodus, at least until around 250 B.C., when the outpouring began to slow.

In the Hellenistic cities, the culture was primarily Greek. The political institutions of the cities were modeled after those of the Greek *polis*. Greeks of the Classical period would easily have recognized the councils, assemblies, and codes of law. The physical layout of the new cities was also modeled after those of the Greek homeland. Using the traditional rectilinear grid, cities were laid out with temples, altars, and stone theaters.

Many of the new urban centers were completely dominated by Greeks while the native populations remained cut off from all civic institutions. The Greeks commissioned purely Greek sculpture, read literature of the Classical period, and had separate law courts for themselves. Complaints from resentful natives have been recorded. An Egyptian camel driver, for example, complained bitterly that he was not paid regularly because he did "not know how to behave like a Greek." Not only was it difficult for easterners to enter the ranks of the ruling class, but those who did so had to become thoroughly Hellenized. This often required alienation from one's own culture.

The Greeks' belief in their own cultural superiority provided an easy rationalization for their political dominance of the eastern cities. But Greek control of the new cities of the Near East was also necessary because the kings frequently used the cities as instruments of government, enabling them to rule considerable territory without an extensive bureaucracy. At the same time, for security reasons, the Greeks needed the support of the kings. After all, the Hellenistic cities were islands of Greek culture in a sea of non-Greeks. The relationship between rulers and cities, therefore, was a symbiotic one that bore serious consequences for the cities.

In the political system, religious practices, and architecture of their new cities, the Greeks tried to re-create the *poleis* of their homeland. But it was no longer possible to do so. The new cities were not autonomous entities and soon found themselves dependent on the power of the Hellenistic monarchies. Although the kings did not rule the cities directly, they restricted freedom in other ways. Cities knew they could not conduct an independent foreign policy and did not try to do so. The kings also demanded tribute, which could be a heavy burden.

The Greek cities of the Hellenistic era were the chief agents for the spread of Greek culture in the Near East, as far, in fact, as modern Afghanistan and India. These cities were also remarkably vibrant despite their subordination to the Hellenistic monarchies and persisted in being a focal point for the loyalty of their citizens.

Economic Trends in the Hellenistic World

Agriculture was still of primary importance to both the native populations and the new Greek cities of the Hellenistic world. The Greek cities continued their old agrarian patterns. A well-defined citizen body owned land and worked it with the assistance of slaves. But these farms were isolated units in a vast area of land ultimately owned by the king or assigned to large estate owners and worked by native peasants dwelling in villages. Overall, then, neither agricultural patterns nor methods of production underwent significant changes.

Few new products or manufacturing methods were introduced during the Hellenistic era, but the centers of manufacturing shifted significantly. Industry spread from Greece to the east—especially to Asia Minor, Rhodes, and Egypt. New textile centers were set up at Pergamum, while glass and silver crafts were developed in Syria. And busiest of all the cities in manufacturing was Alexandria in Egypt, center of the production of parchment, textiles, linens, oil, metalwork, and glass.

Commerce expanded considerably in the Hellenistic era. Indeed, trading contacts linked much of the Hellenistic world. The decline in the number of political barriers encouraged more commercial traffic. Although Hellenistic monarchs still fought wars, the conquests of Alexander and the policies of his successors made possible greater trade between east and west. Two major trade routes connected the east with the Mediterranean. The central route was the major one and led by sea from India to the Persian Gulf, up the Tigris River to Seleucia, which replaced Babylon as the center for waterborne traffic from the Persian Gulf and overland caravan routes as well. Overland routes from Seleucia then led to Antioch and Ephesus. A southern route wound its way from India by sea but went around Arabia and up the Red Sea to Petra or later Berenice. Caravan routes then led overland to Coptos on the Nile and from there to Alexandria and the Mediterranean.

An incredible variety of products was traded: gold and silver from Spain; iron from northern Armenia; salt from Asia Minor; timber from Macedonia; purple dye from Tyre; ebony, gems, ivory, and spices from India; frankincense (used on altars) from Arabia; slaves from Thrace, Syria, and Asia Minor; fine wines from Syria and western Asia Minor; olive oil from Athens; and numerous exquisite foodstuffs, such as the famous prunes of Damascus. The greatest trade, however, was in the basic staple of life—grain. The great exporting areas were Egypt, Sicily, and the Black Sea region.

New Opportunities For Women

One of the significant features of social life in the Hellenistic world was the emergence of new opportunities for women—at least, for upper-class women—especially in the economic area. Documents show increasing numbers of women involved in managing slaves, selling property, and making loans. Even then, legal contracts in which women were involved had to include their official male guardians, although in numerous instances these men no longer played an important function but were listed only to satisfy legal requirements. In Sparta, women

A NEW AUTONOMY FOR WOMEN

𝒰 pper-class women made noticeable gains in Hellenistic society. But even in the lives of ordinary women, a new assertiveness came to the fore despite the continuing domination of society by men. The first selection is taken from the letter of a wife to her husband, complaining about his failure to return home. In the second selection, a father complains that his daughter has abandoned him, contrary to Egyptian law providing that children who have been properly raised should support their parents.

Letter from Isias to Hephaistion, 168 B.C.

If you are well and other things are going right, it would accord with the prayer that I make continually to the gods. I myself and the child and all the household are in good health and think of you always. When I received your letter from Horos, in which you announce that you are in detention in the Serapeum at Memphis, for the news that you are well I straightway thanked the gods, but about your not coming home, when all the others who had been secluded there have come, I am ill-pleased, because after having piloted myself and your child through such bad times and been driven to every extremity owing to the price of wheat, I thought that now at least, with you at home, I should enjoy some respite, whereas you have not even thought of coming home nor given any regard to our circumstances, remembering how I was in want of everything while you were still here, not to mention this long lapse of time and these critical days, during which you have sent us nothing. As, moreover, Horos who delivered the letter has brought news of your having been released from detention, I am thoroughly ill-pleased. Notwithstanding, as your mother also is annoyed, for her sake as well as for mine please return to the city, if nothing more pressing holds you back. You will do me a favor by taking care of your bodily health. Farewell.

Letter from Ktesikles to King Ptolemy, 220 B.C.

I am wronged by Dionysios and by Nike my daughter. For though I raised her, my own daughter, and educated her and brought her to maturity, when I was stricken with bodily ill-health and was losing my eyesight, she was not minded to furnish me with any of the necessities of life. When I sought to obtain justice from her in Alexandria, she begged my pardon, and in the eighteenth year she swore me a written royal oath to give me each month twenty drachmas, which she was to earn by her own bodily labor. . . . But now corrupted by Dionysios, who is a comic actor, she does not do for me anything of what was in the written oath, despising my weakness and ill-health. I beg you, therefore, O King, not to allow me to be wronged by my daughter and by Dionysios the actor who corrupted her, but to order Diophanes the strategus [a provincial administrator] to summon them and hear us out; and if I am speaking the truth, let Diophanes deal with her corrupter as seems good to him and compel my daughter Nike to do justice to me. If this is done I shall no longer be wronged but by fleeing to you, O King, I shall obtain justice.

What specific complaints are contained in each letter? What do these complaints reveal about some women in the Hellenistic world?

---

were allowed to own land and manage their own economic affairs. Because many of their husbands were absent or had died in war, many Spartan women became wealthy; females owned 40 percent of the land in Sparta.

Spartan women, however, were an exception, especially on the Greek mainland. Women in Athens, for example, still remained highly restricted and supervised. Although a few philosophers welcomed female participation in men's affairs, many philosophers rejected equality between men and women and asserted that the traditional roles of wives and mothers were most satisfying for women. In her treatise "On Chastity," Phintys wrote that "serving as generals, public officials, and statesmen is appropriate for men," but "keeping house, remaining within, and taking care of husbands belongs to women."[3]

But the opinions of philosophers did not prevent upper-class women from making gains in areas other than the economic sphere (see the box above). New possibilities for females arose when women in some areas of the Hellenistic world were allowed to pursue education in the traditional fields of literature, music, and even athletics. Education, then, provided new opportunities for women: female poets appeared again in the third century B.C., and there are instances of women involved in both scholarly and artistic activities.

The creation of the Hellenistic monarchies, which represented a considerable departure from the world of the *polis*, also gave new scope to the role played by the monarchs' wives, the Hellenistic queens. In Macedonia, a pattern of alliances between mothers and sons provided openings for women to take an active role in politics, especially in political intrigue. In Egypt, opportunities for royal women were even greater because the Ptolemaic rulers reverted to an Egyptian custom of kings marrying their own sisters. Of the first eight Ptolemaic rulers, four wed their sisters. Ptolemy II and his sister-wife Arsinoë II were both worshiped as gods in their lifetimes. Arsinoë played an energetic role in government and was involved in the expansion of the Egyptian navy. She was also the first Egyptian queen whose portrait appeared on coins with her husband. Hellenistic queens also showed an intense interest in culture. They wrote poems, collected art, and corresponded with intellectuals.

Culture in the Hellenistic World

Although the Hellenistic kingdoms encompassed vast areas and many diverse peoples, the Greeks provided a sense of unity as a result of the diffusion of Greek culture throughout the region. The Hellenistic era was a period of considerable cultural accomplishment in many areas—literature, art, science, and philosophy. Although these achievements occurred everywhere in the Hellenistic world, certain centers, especially the great cities of Alexandria and Pergamum, stood out. In both cities, cultural developments were encouraged by the rulers themselves. Rich Hellenistic kings had considerable resources with which to patronize culture.

The Ptolemies in Egypt made Alexandria an especially important cultural center. The library became the largest in ancient times, housing more than half a million scrolls. The museum (literally, "temple of the Muses") created a favorable environment for scholarly research. Alexandria became home to poets, writers, philosophers, and scientists—scholars of all kinds.

New Directions in Literature

The Hellenistic Age produced an enormous quantity of literature, most of which has not survived. Hellenistic monarchs, who held literary talent in high esteem, subsidized writers on a grand scale. The Ptolemaic rulers of Egypt were particularly lavish. The combination of their largess and the famous library drew a host of scholars and authors to Alexandria, including a circle of poets. Theocritus (c. 315–250 B.C.), originally a native of the island of Sicily, wrote "little poems" or idylls dealing with erotic subjects, lovers' complaints, and pastoral themes expressing his love of nature and its beauty.

In the Hellenistic era, Athens remained the theatrical center of the Greek world. As tragedy withered, writers invented New Comedy, which rejected political themes and sought only to entertain and amuse. The Athenian playwright Menander (c. 342–291 B.C.) was perhaps the best representative of New Comedy. Plots were simple: typically, a hero falls in love with a not-really-so-bad prostitute who turns out eventually to be the long-lost daughter of a rich neighbor. The hero marries her, and they live happily ever after.

The Hellenistic period saw a great outpouring of historical and biographical literature. The chief historian of the Hellenistic Age was Polybius (c. 203–c. 120 B.C.), a Greek who lived for some years in Rome. He is regarded as second only to Thucydides among Greek historians. His major work consisted of forty books narrating the history of the "inhabited Mediterranean world" from 221 to 146 B.C. Only the first five books are extant, although long extracts from the other books survive. His history

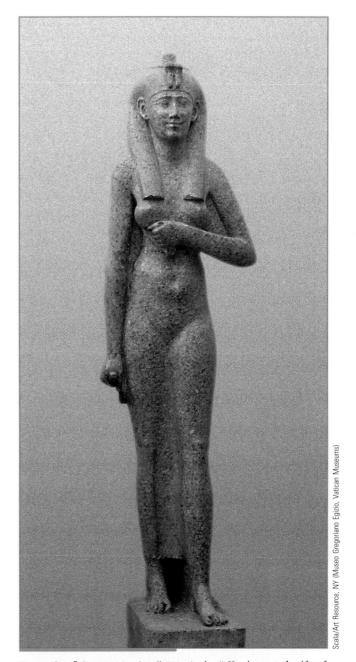

Portrait of Queen Arsinoë II. Arsinoë II, sister and wife of King Ptolemy II, played an active role in Egyptian political affairs. This statue from the Ptolemaic period depicts the queen in the traditional garb of a pharaoh's wife.

focuses on the growth of Rome from a city-state to a vast empire. It is apparent that Polybius understood the significance of the Romans' achievement. He followed Thucydides in seeking rational motives for historical events. He also approached his sources critically and used firsthand accounts.

Hellenistic Art

In addition to being patrons of literary talent, the Hellenistic monarchs were eager to spend their money to beautify and adorn the cities in their states. The founding of new cities and the rebuilding of old ones provided numerous opportunities for Greek architects and sculptors. The structures of the Greek homeland—gymnasia, baths, theaters, and, of course, temples—lined the streets of these cities. Most noticeable in the temples was the use of the more ornate Corinthian order, which became especially popular during the Hellenistic Age (see the illustration in Chapter 3 on p. 53).

Sculptors were commissioned by Hellenistic kings and rich citizens. Thousands of statues, many paid for by the people honored, were erected in towns and cities all over the Hellenistic world. While maintaining the technical skill of the classical period, Hellenistic sculptors moved away from the idealism of fifth-century classicism to a more emotional and realistic art, seen in numerous statues of old women, drunks, and little children at play.

Alexander the Great's incursion into the western part of India resulted in some Greek cultural influences there, especially during the Hellenistic era. In the first century B.C., Indian sculptors began to create statues of the Buddha. The impact of Greek sculpture was especially evident in the Buddhist statues made in Gandhara, which is today part of Pakistan.

A Golden Age of Science

The Hellenistic era witnessed a more conscious separation of science from philosophy. In Classical Greece, what we would call the physical and life sciences had been divisions of philosophical inquiry. Nevertheless, the Greeks, by the time of Aristotle, had already established an important principle of scientific investigation, empirical research, or systematic observation as the basis for generalization. In the Hellenistic Age, the sciences tended to be studied in their own right.

One of the traditional areas of Greek science was astronomy, and two Alexandrian scholars continued this exploration. Aristarchus of Samos (c. 310–230 B.C.) developed a heliocentric view of the universe, contending that the sun and the fixed stars remained stationary while the earth rotated around the sun in a circular orbit. This view was not widely accepted, and most scholars clung to the earlier geocentric view of the Greeks, which held that the earth was at the center of the universe. Another astronomer, Eratosthenes (c. 275–194 B.C.), determined that the earth was round and calculated the earth's circumference at 24,675 miles, within 200 miles of the actual figure.

A third Alexandrian scholar was Euclid, who lived around 300 B.C. He established a school in Alexandria but is primarily known for his *Elements*. This was a systematic organization of the fundamental elements of geometry as they had already been worked out; it became the standard textbook of plane geometry and was used up to modern times.

The most famous of the scientists of the Hellenistic period, Archimedes (287–212 B.C.), came from the western Mediterranean region. Archimedes was especially

© Araldo de Luca/CORBIS

Drunken Old Woman. Hellenistic sculptors no longer tried to capture ideal beauty in their sculpture, a quest that characterized Greek classicism, but moved toward a more emotional and realistic art. This statue of a drunken old woman is typical of this new trend in art. Old and haggard, mired in poverty, she struggles to just go on living.

important for his work on the geometry of spheres and cylinders, for establishing the value of the mathematical constant pi, and for creating the science of hydrostatics. Archimedes was also a practical inventor. He may have devised the so-called Archimedean screw, used to pump water out of mines and to lift irrigation water, as well as a compound pulley for transporting heavy weights. During the Roman siege of his native city of Syracuse, he constructed a number of devices to thwart the attackers. According to Plutarch's account, the Romans became so frightened "that if they did but see a little rope or a piece of wood from the wall, instantly crying out, that there it was again, Archimedes was about to let fly some device at them, they turned their backs and fled."[4] Archimedes' accomplishments inspired a wealth of semilegendary stories. Supposedly, he discovered specific gravity by observing the water he displaced in his bath and became so excited by his realization that he jumped out of the water and ran home naked, shouting "Eureka!" ("I have found it!"). He is said to have emphasized the importance of levers by proclaiming to the king of Syracuse, "Give me a

Hellenistic Sculpture and a Greek-Style Buddha.   Greek architects and sculptors were highly valued throughout the Hellenistic world. Shown on the left is a terra-cotta statuette of a draped young woman, made as a tomb offering near Thebes, probably around 300 B.C. The incursion of Alexander into the western part of India resulted in some Greek cultural influences there. During the first century B.C., Indian sculptors in Gandhara began to make statues of the Buddha in a style that combined Indian and Hellenistic artistic traditions, evident in the stone sculpture of Buddha on the right. Note the wavy hair topped by a bun tied with a ribbon, also a feature of earlier statues of Greek deities. This Buddha is also seen wearing a Greek-style toga.

lever and a place to stand on, and I will move the earth." The king was so impressed that he encouraged Archimedes to lower his sights and build defensive weapons instead.

Philosophy: New Schools of Thought

While Alexandria and Pergamum became the renowned cultural centers of the Hellenistic world, Athens remained the prime center for philosophy and continued to attract the most illustrious philosophers, who chose to establish their schools there. Two entirely new schools of philosophical thought reinforced Athens' reputation as a philosophical center.

Epicureanism   Epicurus (341–270 B.C.), the founder of **Epicureanism**, established a school in Athens before 300 B.C.

Epicurus' famous belief in a doctrine of pleasure began with his view of the world. Though he did not deny the existence of the gods, he did not believe they played any active role in the world. The universe ran on its own. This left human beings free to follow self-interest as a basic motivating force. Happiness was the goal of life, and the means to achieving it was the pursuit of pleasure, the only true good. But the pursuit of pleasure was not meant in a physical, hedonistic sense:

> When, therefore, we maintain that pleasure is the end, we do not mean the pleasures of profligates and those that consist in sensuality, as is supposed by some who are either ignorant or disagree with us or do not understand, but freedom from pain in the body and from trouble in the mind. For it is not continuous drinkings and revellings, nor the satisfaction of lusts, nor the enjoyment of fish and other luxuries of the

THE STOIC IDEAL OF HARMONY WITH GOD

The Stoic Cleanthes (331–232 B.C.) succeeded Zeno as head of this school of philosophy. One historian of Hellenistic civilization has called this work by Cleanthes the greatest religious hymn in Greek literature. Certainly, it demonstrates that Stoicism, unlike Epicureanism, did have an underlying spiritual foundation. This poem has been compared to the great psalms of the Hebrews.

Cleanthes, *Hymn to Zeus*

Nothing occurs on the earth apart from you, O God,

nor in the heavenly regions nor on the sea,

except what bad men do in their folly;

but you know to make the odd even,

and to harmonize what is dissonant; to you the alien is akin.

And so you have wrought together into one all things that are good and bad,

So that there arises one eternal logos [rationale] of all things,

Which all bad mortals shun and ignore,

Unhappy wretches, ever seeking the possession of good things

They neither see nor hear the universal law of God,

By obeying which they might enjoy a happy life.

Based on Cleanthes' poem, what are some of the beliefs of the Stoics. How do they differ from the beliefs of the Epicureans?

---

wealthy table, which produce a pleasant life, but sober reasoning, searching out the motives for all choice and avoidance, and banishing mere opinions, to which are due the greatest disturbance of the spirit.[5]

Pleasure was not satisfying one's desire in an active, gluttonous fashion but rather freedom from emotional turmoil, freedom from worry, the freedom that came from a mind at rest. To achieve this passive pleasure, one had to free oneself from public activity: "We must release ourselves from the prison of affairs and politics." They were too strenuous to give peace of mind. But this was not a renunciation of all social life, for to Epicurus, a life could be complete only when it was centered on the basic ideal of friendship: "Of all the things which wisdom acquires to produce the blessedness of the complete life, far the greatest is the possession of friendship."[6] Epicurus' own life in Athens was an embodiment of his teachings. He and his friends created their own private community where they could pursue their ideal of true happiness.

Stoicism   Epicureanism was eventually overshadowed by another school of thought known as **Stoicism**, which became the most popular philosophy of the Hellenistic world and later flourished in the Roman Empire as well. It was the product of a teacher named Zeno (335–263 B.C.), who came to Athens and began to teach in a public colonnade known as the Painted Portico (the *Stoa Poikile*—hence *Stoicism*). Like Epicureanism, Stoicism was concerned with how individuals find happiness. But Stoics took a radically different approach to the problem. To them, happiness, the supreme good, could be found only in virtue, which meant essentially living in harmony with the divine will. One achieved happiness by choosing to follow the divine will through the free exercise of one's

own will. To the Stoics, the divine will was the same thing as the will of nature because nature was simply a manifestation or expression of the gods. "Living according to nature," therefore, meant following the divine will or the natural laws that the gods established to run the universe.

Virtuous living, then, was living in accordance with the laws of nature or submitting to the divine will (see the box above). This led to the acceptance of whatever one received in life since the divine will for us was by its very nature good. By accepting divine law, people mastered themselves and gained inner peace. Life's problems could not disturb such individuals, and they could bear whatever life offered (hence our word *stoic*).

Unlike Epicureans, Stoics did not believe in the need to separate oneself from the world and politics. Public service was regarded as noble. The real Stoic was a good citizen and could even be a good government official. Because Stoics believed that a divine principle was present throughout the universe, each human being also contained a divine spark. This led to a belief in the oneness of humanity. The world constituted a single society of equal human beings. Although they were not equal in the outer world, because each contained the divine spark, all were free to follow the divine will (what was best for each individual). All persons then, even slaves, though unfree in body, were equal at the level of the soul.

Epicureanism and especially Stoicism appealed to large numbers of people in the Hellenistic world. Both of these philosophies focused primarily on the problem of human happiness. Their popularity would suggest a fundamental change in the character of the Greek lifestyle. In the Classical Greek world, the happiness of individuals and the meaning of life were closely associated with the life of the *polis*. One found fulfillment within the community. In the Hellenistic kingdoms, although the *polis* continued to exist, the sense that one could find satisfaction and fulfillment through life in the *polis* had weakened. Not only did individuals seek new philosophies that offered personal happiness, but in the cosmopolitan world of the Hellenistic states, with their mixtures of peoples, a new openness to thoughts of universality could also emerge. For some people, Stoicism embodied this larger sense of community. The appeal of new philosophies in the Hellenistic era can also be explained by the apparent decline in certain aspects of traditional religion.

Religion in the Hellenistic World

When the Greeks spread throughout the Hellenistic kingdoms, they took their gods with them. Although the construction of temples may have been less important than in classical times, there were still many demonstrations of a lively religious faith. But over a period of time, there was a noticeable decline in the vitality of the traditional Greek Olympian religion. The civic cults based on the traditional gods no longer seemed sufficient to satisfy people's emotional needs.

This left Greeks receptive to the numerous religious cults of the eastern world. The Greeks were always tolerant of other existing religious institutions. Hence in the Hellenistic cities of the Near East, the traditional civic cults of their own gods and foreign cults existed side by side. Alexandria had cults of the traditional Greek gods, Egyptian deities such as Isis and Horus, the Babylonian Astarte, and the Syrian Atargatis.

But for many people, the search for personal meaning remained unfulfilled. Among educated Greeks, the philosophies of Epicureanism and especially Stoicism offered help. Another source of solace came in the form of **mystery religions**.

Mystery Religions

Mystery cults, with their secret initiations and promises of individual salvation, were not new to the Greek world. But the Greeks of the Hellenistic era were strongly influenced by eastern mystery cults, such as those of Egypt, which offered a distinct advantage over the Greek mystery religions. The latter had usually been connected to specific locations (such as Eleusis), which meant that a would-be initiate had to undertake a pilgrimage in order to participate in the rites. In contrast, the eastern mystery religions were readily available since temples to their gods and goddesses were located throughout the Greek cities of the east.

All of the mystery religions were based on the same fundamental premises. Individuals could pursue a path to salvation and achieve eternal life by being initiated into a union with a savior god or goddess who had died and risen again. The ritual of initiation, by which the seeker identified with the god or goddess, was, no doubt, a highly emotional experience.

The Egyptian cult of Isis was one of the most popular of the mystery religions. The cult of Isis was very ancient but became truly universal in Hellenistic times. Isis was the goddess of women, marriage, and children, as one of her hymns states: "I am she whom women call goddess. I ordained that women should be loved by men: I brought wife and husband together, and invented the marriage contract. I ordained that women should bear children."[7] Isis was also portrayed as the giver of civilization who had brought laws and letters to all humankind. The cult of Isis offered a precious commodity to its initiates— the promise of eternal life. In many ways, the mystery religions of the Hellenistic era helped pave the way for Christianity.

The Jews In The Hellenistic World

In observing the similarities among their gods and goddesses, Greeks and easterners tended to assume they were the same beings with different names, giving rise to a process of **syncretism**. But a special position was occupied in the Hellenistic world by the Jews, whose monotheistic religion was exclusive and did not accommodate this kind of fusion of spiritual beings.

The Jewish province of Judaea (which embraced the lands of the old Hebrew Kingdom of Judah) was ruled by the Ptolemies until it fell under the control of the Seleucids by 200 B.C. In the reign of the Seleucid king Antiochus IV (175–163 B.C.), conflict erupted in Judaea. Hellenistic monarchs were generally tolerant of all religions, but problems with Rome prompted Antiochus to try to impose more cultural and religious unity throughout his kingdom. When he sent troops to Jerusalem and seized the Temple, he sparked a Jewish uprising led by Judas Maccabaeus (164 B.C.). The rebels succeeded in recapturing the Temple, a joyous event that has been celebrated every year since in the Jewish holiday of Hanukkah (Hebrew for "rededication"). Although the conflict in Judaea continued, the Seleucids ultimately made concessions and allowed the Jews considerable freedom.

But large numbers of Jews no longer lived in Judaea. There was a large Jewish population in Egypt, particularly in Alexandria, as well as Jewish settlements throughout the cities of Asia Minor and Syria. In each city, Jews generally set up a synagogue and formed a private association for worship as other foreigners did. But some city authorities also allowed the Jews to form a political corporation that gave them greater rights than other resident aliens. Most important, they gained the privilege to live by their own laws and their own judicial system. The Jews were not really interested in citizenship in the cities in which they resided because full citizenship required worship of the city's gods, anathema to Jews, who believed only in Yahweh.

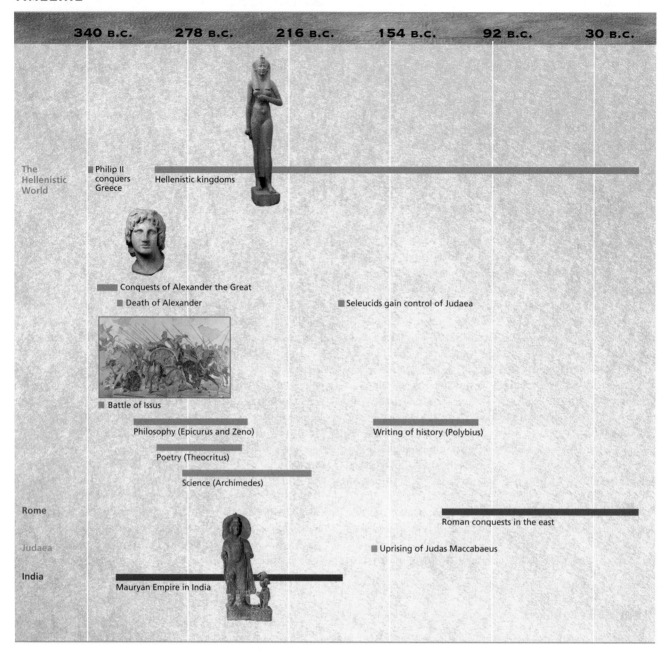

	340 B.C.	278 B.C.	216 B.C.	154 B.C.	92 B.C.	30 B.C.

The Hellenistic World

■ Philip II conquers Greece

Hellenistic kingdoms

Conquests of Alexander the Great

■ Death of Alexander

■ Seleucids gain control of Judaea

■ Battle of Issus

Philosophy (Epicurus and Zeno)

Writing of history (Polybius)

Poetry (Theocritus)

Science (Archimedes)

Rome

Roman conquests in the east

Judaea

■ Uprising of Judas Maccabaeus

India

Mauryan Empire in India

CONCLUSION

Although historians once viewed the Hellenistic era as a period of stagnation after the brilliant Greek civilization of the fifth century B.C., our survey of the Hellenistic world has shown the inaccuracy of that position. The Hellenistic period was vibrant in its own way. New cities arose and flourished. New philosophical ideas captured the minds of many. Significant achievements occurred in art, literature, and science. Greek culture spread throughout the Near East and made an impact wherever it was carried. In some areas of the Hellenistic world, queens played an active role in political life, and many upper-class women found new avenues for expressing themselves.

But serious problems remained. Hellenistic kings continued to engage in inconclusive wars. Much of the formal culture was the special preserve of the Greek conquerors, whose attitude of superiority kept them largely separated from the native masses of the Hellenistic kingdoms. Although the Hellenistic world achieved a degree of political stability, by the late third century B.C. signs of decline were beginning to multiply. Some of the more farsighted perhaps realized the danger presented to the Hellenistic world by the growing power of Rome. The Romans would ultimately inherit Alexander's empire, and we must now turn to them and try to understand what made them such successful conquerors.

NOTES

1. Quoted in S. B. Pomeroy, S. M. Burstein, W. Donlan, and J. T. Roberts, *Ancient Greece: A Political, Social, and Cultural History* (Oxford, 1999), p. 390.
2. Quoted in G. Shipley, *The Greek World After Alexander, 323–30 B.C.* (London, 2000), p. 53.
3. Quoted in M. B. Fant and M. R. Lefkowitz, *Women's Life in Greece and Rome: A Source Book in Translation* (Baltimore, 1992), no. 208.
4. Plutarch, *Life of Marcellus*, trans. J. Dryden (New York, n.d.), p. 378.
5. *Epicurus: The Extant Remains*, trans. C. Bailey (Oxford, 1926), pp. 89–90.
6. Ibid., pp. 115, 101.
7. Quoted in W. W. Tarn, *Hellenistic Civilization* (London, 1930), p. 324.

SUGGESTIONS FOR FURTHER READING

For a general introduction to the Hellenistic era, see **F. W. Walbank**, *The Hellenistic World* (Cambridge, Mass., 1993), and **G. Shipley**, *The Greek World After Alexander, 323–30 B.C.* (New York, 2000). Other studies include **W. W. Tarn** and **G. T. Griffith**, *Hellenistic Civilization*, 3d ed. (London, 1952); **M. Grant**, *From Alexander to Cleopatra: The Hellenistic World* (London, 1982); and **P. Green**, *Alexander to Actium: The Historic Evolution of the Hellenistic Age* (Berkeley, Calif., 1990).

For a good introduction to the early history of Macedonia, see **E. N. Borza**, *In the Shadow of Olympus: The Emergence of Macedon* (Princeton, N.J., 1990), and **R. M. Errington**, *A History of Macedonia* (Berkeley, Calif., 1990). There are considerable differences of opinion on Alexander the Great. Good biographies include **R. L. Fox**, *Alexander the Great* (London, 1973); **P. Cartledge**, *Alexander the Great* (New York, 2004); **N.G.L. Hammond**, *The Genius of Alexander the Great* (Chapel Hill, N.C., 1997); **P. Green**, *Alexander of Macedon* (Berkeley, Calif., 1991); and **G. M. Rogers**, *Alexander: The Ambiguity of Greatness* (New York, 2004).

Studies on the various Hellenistic monarchies include **N.G.L. Hammond** and **F. W. Walbank**, *A History of Macedonia, vol. 3, 336–167 B.C.* (Oxford, 1988); **S. Sherwin-White** and **A. Kuhrt**, *From Samarkand to Sardis: A New Approach to the Seleucid Empire* (Berkeley, Calif., 1993); **N. Lewis**, *Greeks in Ptolemaic Egypt* (Oxford, 1986); and **R. E. Allen**, *The Attalid Kingdom* (Oxford, 1983).

On the Celts, see **B. Cunliffe**, *The Ancient Celts* (London, 1997), and the beautifully illustrated brief study by **J. Davies**, *The Celts* (London, 2000).

A good survey of Hellenistic cities can be found in **A.H.M. Jones**, *The Greek City from Alexander to Justinian* (Oxford, 1940). On economic and social trends, see **M. I. Finley**, *The Ancient Economy*, 2d ed. (London, 1985), and the classic and still indispensable **M. I. Rostovtzeff**, *Social and Economic History of the Hellenistic World*, 3 vols., 2d ed. (Oxford, 1953). Hellenistic women are examined in **S. B. Pomeroy**, *Women in Hellenistic Egypt* (New York, 1984).

For a general introduction to Hellenistic culture, see **J. Onians**, *Art and Thought in the Hellenistic Age* (London, 1979). On art, see **J. J. Pollitt**, *Art in the Hellenistic Age* (New York, 1986). The best general survey of Hellenistic philosophy is **A. A. Long**, *Hellenistic Philosophy: Stoics, Epicureans, Skeptics*, 2d ed. (London, 1986). A superb work on Hellenistic science is **G.E.R. Lloyd**, *Greek Science After Aristotle* (London, 1973).

On various face of Hellenistic religion, see **L. Martin**, *Hellenistic Religions: An Introduction* (New York, 1987), and **R. E. Witt**, *Isis in the Graeco-Roman World* (London, 1971).

On the entry of Rome into the Hellenistic world, see the basic work by **E. S. Gruen**, *The Hellenistic World and the Coming of Rome*, 2 vols. (Berkeley, Calif., 1984).

Thomson NOW! Enter *ThomsonNOW* using the access card that is available for *Western Civilization: A Brief History*. *ThomsonNOW* will help you understand this chapter with lesson plans generated for your needs. In addition, you can read the following documents, and many more, online:

Plutarch, Life of Alexander
Aristotle, excerpt from *Nicomachean Ethics*
Aristotle, *Metaphysics*, Chapter 12

WESTERN CIVILIZATION RESOURCES

Visit the Web site for *Western Civilization: A Brief History* for resources specific to this book:

http://www.thomsonedu.com/history/spielvogel

For a variety of tools to help you succeed in this course, visit the Western Civilization Resource Center at

http://history.wadsworth.com/spielvogel

Included are quizzes, images, documents, interactive simulations, maps and timelines, movie explorations, and a wealth of other sources.

CHAPTER

5

THE ROMAN REPUBLIC

CHAPTER OUTLINE
AND FOCUS QUESTIONS

The Emergence of Rome

☐ What influence did the Etruscans and Greeks have on early Roman history?

The Roman Republic (c. 509–264 B.C.)

☐ What policies and institutions help explain the Romans' success in conquering Italy?

The Roman Conquest of the Mediterranean (264–133 B.C.)

☐ How did Rome achieve its empire from 264 to 133 B.C., and what is meant by the phrase "Roman imperialism"?

Society and Culture in the Roman World

☐ How did the acquisition of an empire affect Roman social and economic institutions, values and attitudes, and art and literature?

The Decline and Fall of the Roman Republic (133–31 B.C.)

☐ What were the main problems Rome faced during the last century of the Republic, and how were they ultimately resolved?

CRITICAL THINKING

☐ What did the Roman poet Horace mean when he wrote, "Captive Greece took captive her rude conqueror"?

Horatius defending the bridge as envisioned by Charles Le Brun, a seventeenth-century French painter

© Dulwich Picture Gallery, London/Bridgeman Art Library

*E*ARLY ROMAN HISTORY is filled with legendary tales of the heroes who made Rome great. One of the best known is the story of Horatius at the bridge. Threatened by attack from the neighboring Etruscans, Roman farmers abandoned their fields and moved into the city, where they would be protected by the walls. One weak point in the Roman defenses, however, was a wooden bridge over the Tiber River. Horatius was on guard at the bridge when a sudden assault by the Etruscans caused many Roman troops to throw down their weapons and flee. Horatius urged them to make a stand at the bridge to protect Rome; when they hesitated, as a last resort he told them to destroy the bridge behind him while he held the Etruscans back. Astonished at the sight of a single defender, the confused Etruscans threw their spears at Horatius, who caught them on his shield and barred the way. By the time the Etruscans had regrouped and were about to overwhelm the lone defender, the Roman soldiers brought down the bridge. When Horatius heard the bridge crash into the river behind him, he dived fully armed into the water and swam safely to the other side through a hail of arrows. Rome had been saved by the courageous act of a Roman who knew his duty and was determined to carry it out. Courage, duty, determination—these qualities would also serve the many

Romans who believed that it was their mission to rule nations and peoples.

In the first millennium B.C., a group of Latin-speaking people established a small community on the plain of Latium on the Italian peninsula. This community, called Rome, was one of the numerous communities founded by Latin-speaking peoples throughout Latium and the rest of Italy. Roman history is basically the story of the Romans' conquest of the plain of Latium, then Italy, and finally the entire Mediterranean region. How were the Romans able to do this? The Romans made the right decisions at the right time; in other words, they had political wisdom.

They were also practical. Unlike the Greeks, who reserved their citizenship for small, select groups, the Romans often offered citizenship to the peoples they conquered, thus laying the groundwork for a strong, integrated empire. The Romans also did not hesitate to borrow ideas and culture from the Greeks. Roman strength lay in government, law, and engineering. The Romans knew how to govern people, establish legal structures, and construct the roads that took them to the ends of the known world. Throughout their empire, they carried their law, their political institutions, their engineering skills, and their Latin language. And even after the Romans were gone, those same gifts continued to play an important role in the civilizations that came after them.◆

The Emergence of Rome

Italy is a peninsula extending about 750 miles from north to south (see Map 5.1). It is not very wide, however, averaging about 120 miles across. The Apennine Mountains traverse the peninsula from north to south, forming a ridge down the middle that divides west from east. Nevertheless, Italy has some fairly large fertile plains ideal for farming. Most important were the Po River valley in the north, probably the most fertile agricultural area; the plain of Latium, on which Rome was located; and Campania to the south of Latium. To the east of the Italian peninsula is the Adriatic Sea, and to the west, the Tyrrhenian Sea with the nearby large islands of Corsica and Sardinia. Sicily lies just west of the toe of the boot-shaped Italian peninsula.

Geography had an impact on Roman history. Although the Apennines bisect Italy, they are less rugged than the mountain ranges of Greece and so did not divide the peninsula into many small isolated communities. Italy also possessed considerably more productive farmland than Greece, enabling it to support a large population. Rome's location was favorable from a geographical point of view. Located 18 miles inland on the Tiber River, Rome had access to the sea and yet was far enough inland to be safe from pirates. Built on seven hills, it was easily defended. Situated where the Tiber could be readily forded, Rome became a natural crossing point for north-south traffic in western Italy. All in all, Rome had a good central location in Italy from which to expand.

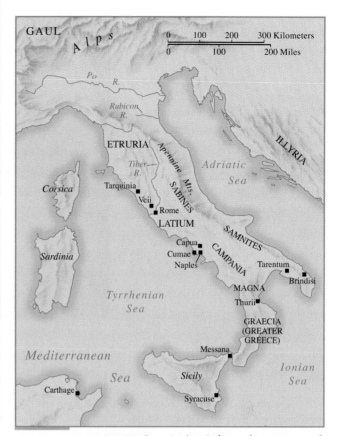

MAP 5.1 **Ancient Italy.** Ancient Italy was home to several groups. Both the Etruscans in the north and the Greeks in the south had a major influence on the development of Rome. ❓ Once Rome conquered the Etruscans, Sabines, Samnites, and other local groups, what aspects of the Italian peninsula helped make it defensible against outside enemies? ◉ **View an animated version of this map or related maps at** http://thomsonedu.com/history/spielvogel

Moreover, the Italian peninsula juts into the Mediterranean, making it an important crossroads between the western and eastern parts of that sea. Once Rome had unified Italy, involvement in affairs throughout the region was natural. And after the Romans had conquered their Mediterranean empire, Italy's central location made their task of governing that empire considerably easier.

The Greeks in Italy

We know little about the Indo-European peoples who moved into Italy during the second half of the second millennium B.C. By the first millennium B.C., other peoples had also settled in Italy, the two most notable being the Greeks and the Etruscans. The Greeks arrived on the Italian peninsula in large numbers during the age of Greek colonization (750–550 B.C.; see Chapter 3). Initially, the Greeks settled in southern Italy and gradually migrated around the coast and up the peninsula as far as Brindisi. They also occupied the eastern two-thirds of Sicily. Ultimately, the Greeks had considerable influence on Rome. They cultivated olives and grapes, passed on

Etruscan Tomb Mural. Like the Egyptians, the Etruscans filled their tombs with furniture, bowls, and other objects of daily life, as well as murals showing diversions experienced in life and awaiting the dead in the afterlife. Shown in this mural found in an Etruscan tomb at Tarquinia are servants and musicians at a banquet. This mural was painted in the first half of the fifth century B.C.

their alphabetic system of writing, and provided artistic and cultural models through their sculpture, architecture, and literature. Indeed, many historians view Roman culture as a continuation of Greek culture. Whereas Greek influence had initially touched Rome indirectly through the Etruscans, the Roman conquest of southern Italy and Sicily brought the Romans into direct contact with Greeks.

The Etruscans

The initial development of Rome was influenced most by the Etruscans, who had settled north of Rome in Etruria. The origins of the Etruscans are not clear, but after 650 B.C., they expanded in Italy and became the dominant cultural and economic force in a number of areas. To the north, they moved into north-central Italy, including the Po valley. To the south, according to Roman tradition and archaeological evidence, they controlled Rome and possibly all of Latium. From Latium they moved south and came into direct conflict with Greek colonists in southern Italy. In the sixth century B.C., the Etruscans were at the height of their power. But by 480 B.C., their power had begun to decline, and by 400 B.C., they were confined to Etruria itself. Later they were invaded by Celts from Gaul and then conquered by the Romans. But by then the Etruscans had made an impact. By transforming villages into towns and cities, they brought urbanization to northern and central Italy (as the Greeks had done in southern Italy). Rome was the Etruscans' most enduring product.

Early Rome

According to Roman legend, Rome was founded by twin brothers, Romulus and Remus, in 753 B.C., and archaeologists have found that around that time, there was a settlement consisting of huts on the tops of several of Rome's hills. The early Romans, basically a pastoral people, spoke Latin, which, like Greek, belongs to the Indo-European family of languages (see Table 2.1 in Chapter 2). The Roman historical tradition also maintained that early Rome (753–509 B.C.) had been under the control of seven kings and that two of the last three had been Etruscans. Some historians believe that the king list may have some historical accuracy. What is certain is that Rome did fall under the influence of the Etruscans for about one hundred years during the period of the kings.

By the beginning of the sixth century, under Etruscan influence, Rome began to change from a pastoral community to an actual city. The Etruscans were responsible for an outstanding building program. They constructed the first roadbed of the chief street through Rome—the Sacred Way—before 575 B.C. and oversaw the development of temples, markets, shops, streets, and houses. By 509 B.C., the date when the monarchy was supposedly overthrown and a republican form of government was established, a new Rome had emerged, essentially as a result of the fusion of Etruscan and native Roman elements. After Rome had expanded over its seven hills and the valleys in between, the Servian Wall was built to surround the city in the fourth century B.C.

The City of Rome

The Roman Republic (c. 509–264 B.C.)

The transition from a monarchy to a republican government was not easy. Rome felt threatened by enemies from every direction and, in the process of meeting these threats, embarked on a course of military expansion that led to the conquest of the entire Italian peninsula. During this period of expansion in Italy, the Roman Republic developed political institutions that were in many ways determined by the social divisions that existed within the community.

The Roman State

In politics and law, as in conquest, the Romans took a practical approach and fashioned political institutions in response to problems as they arose. Hence it is important to remember that the political institutions we will discuss evolved over a period of centuries.

Political Institutions   The chief executive officers of the Roman Republic were the **consuls** and **praetors**. Two consuls, chosen annually, administered the government and led the Roman army into battle. They possessed *imperium,* or "the right to command." In 366 B.C., a new office, that of the praetor, was created. The praetor also possessed *imperium* and could govern Rome when the consuls were away from the city and could also lead armies. The praetor's primary function, however, was the execution of justice. He was in charge of the civil law as it applied to Roman citizens. In 242 B.C., reflecting Rome's growth, another praetor was added to judge cases in which one or both people were noncitizens.

As Rome expanded into the Mediterranean, additional praetors were established to govern the newly conquered provinces (two in 227, two more in 197). But as the number of provinces continued to grow, the Romans devised a new system in which ex-consuls and ex-praetors who had served their one-year terms were given the title of proconsul and propraetor and sent out as provincial governors. This demonstrates once again the Romans' practical solution to an immediate problem. It was reasonable to assume that officials with governmental experience would make good provincial administrators, although this was not always true in practice due to the opportunities for financial corruption in the provinces.

The Roman state also had administrative officials with specialized duties. **Quaestors** were assigned to assist consuls and praetors in the administration of financial affairs. **Aediles** supervised the public games and watched over the grain supply of the city, a major problem for a rapidly growing urban community that relied on imported grain to feed its population.

The Roman **senate** held an especially important position in the Roman Republic. The senate or council of elders was a select group of about three hundred men who served for life. The senate was not a legislative body and could only advise the magistrates. This advice of the senate was not taken lightly, however, and by the third century B.C. it had virtually the force of law. No doubt the prestige of the senate's members furthered this development. But it also helped that the senate met continuously, while the chief magistrates changed annually and the popular assemblies operated slowly and met only periodically.

The Roman Republic possessed a number of popular assemblies. The most important was the **centuriate assembly,** essentially the Roman army functioning in its political role. Organized by classes based on wealth, it was structured in such a way that the wealthiest citizens always had a majority. The centuriate assembly elected the chief magistrates and passed laws. Another assembly, the council of the plebs, came into being in 471 B.C. as a result of the struggle of the orders (see next section).

The government of the Roman Republic, then, consisted of three major elements. Two consuls and later other elected officials served as magistrates and ran the state. An assembly of adult males (the centuriate assembly), controlled by the wealthiest citizens, elected these officials, while the senate, a small group of large landowners, advised them. The Roman state, then, was an aristocratic republic controlled by a relatively small group of privileged people.

The Struggle of the Orders: Social Divisions in the Roman Republic   The most noticeable element in the social organization of early Rome was the division between two groups—the **patricians** and the **plebeians**. The patrician class in Rome consisted of families who were descended from the original senators appointed during the period of the kings. Their initial prominence was probably due to their wealth as great landowners. Thus patricians constituted an aristocratic governing class. Only they could be consuls, other magistrates, and senators. Through their patronage of large numbers of dependent clients, they could control the centuriate assembly and many other facets of Roman life.

The plebeians constituted the considerably larger group of "independent, unprivileged, poorer, and vulnerable men" as well as large nonpatrician landowners, less wealthy landholders, craftspeople, merchants, and small farmers. Although they were citizens, they did not possess the same rights as the patricians. Both patricians and plebeians could vote, but only the patricians could be elected to governmental offices. Both had the right to make legal contracts and marriages, but intermarriage between patricians and plebeians was forbidden. At the beginning of the fifth century B.C., the plebeians began a struggle to seek both political and social equality with the patricians.

The first success of the plebeians came in 494 B.C., when they withdrew physically from the state. The patricians, realizing that they could not defend Rome by themselves, were forced to compromise. Two new officials known as **tribunes of the plebs** were instituted (later raised to five and then ten in number). These tribunes were given the power to protect plebeians against arrest by patrician

CINCINNATUS SAVES ROME: A ROMAN MORALITY TALE

here is perhaps no better account of how the virtues of duty and simplicity enabled good Roman citizens to prevail during the travails of the fifth century B.C. than Livy's account of Cincinnatus. He was chosen dictator, supposedly in 457 B.C., to defend Rome against the attacks of the Aequi. The position of dictator was a temporary expedient used only in emergencies; the consuls would resign, and a leader with unlimited power would be appointed for a fixed period (usually six months). In this account, Cincinnatus did his duty, defeated the Aequi, and returned to his simple farm in just fifteen days.

Livy, *The Early History of Rome*

The city was thrown into a state of turmoil, and the general alarm was as great as if Rome herself were surrounded. Nautius was sent for, but it was quickly decided that he was not the man to inspire full confidence; the situation evidently called for a dictator, and, with no dissenting voice, Lucius Quinctius Cincinnatus was named for the post.

Now I would solicit the particular attention of those numerous people who imagine that money is everything in this world, and that rank and ability are inseparable from wealth: let them observe that Cincinnatus, the one man in whom Rome reposed all her hope of survival, was at that moment working a little three-acre farm . . . west of the Tiber, just opposite the spot where the shipyards are today. A mission from the city found him at work on his land—digging a ditch, maybe, or plowing. Greetings were exchanged, and he was asked—with a prayer for divine blessing on himself

and his country—to put on his toga and hear the Senate's instructions. This naturally surprised him, and, asking if all were well, he told his wife Racilia to run to their cottage and fetch his toga. The toga was brought, and wiping the grimy sweat from his hands and face he put it on; at once the envoys from the city saluted him, with congratulations, as Dictator, invited him to enter Rome, and informed him of the terrible danger of Municius' army. A state vessel was waiting for him on the river, and on the city bank he was welcomed by his three sons who had come to meet him, then by other kinsmen and friends, and finally by nearly the whole body of senators. Closely attended by all these people and preceded by his lictors he was then escorted to his residence through streets lined with great crowds of common folk who, be it said, were by no means so pleased to see the new Dictator, as they thought his power excessive and dreaded the way in which he was likely to use it.

[Cincinnatus proceeds to raise an army, march out, and defeat the Aequi.]

In Rome the Senate was convened by Quintus Fabius the City Prefect, and a decree was passed inviting Cincinnatus to enter in triumph with his troops. The chariot he rode in was preceded by the enemy commanders and the military standards, and followed by his army loaded with its spoils. . . . Cincinnatus finally resigned after holding office for fifteen days, having originally accepted it for a period of six months.

What values did Livy emphasize in his account of Cincinnatus? How important were those values to Rome's success? Why did Livy say he wrote his history?

---

magistrates. Moreover, after a new popular assembly for plebeians only, called the **council of the plebs**, was created in 471 B.C., the tribunes became responsible for convoking it and placing proposals before it. If adopted, these measures became **plebiscita** ("it is the opinion of the plebs"), but they were binding only on the plebeians, not the patricians. Nevertheless, the council of the plebs gave the plebeians considerable political leverage. After 445 B.C., when a law allowed patricians and plebeians to intermarry, the division between the two groups became less important. In the fourth century B.C., the consulship was opened to the plebeians. The climax of the struggle between the orders came in 287 B.C. with passage of a law that stipulated that all *plebiscita* passed by the council of the plebs had the force of law and were binding on the entire community, including patricians.

The struggle between the orders, then, had a significant impact on the development of the Roman constitution. Plebeians could hold the highest offices of state, they could intermarry with the patricians, and they could pass laws binding on the entire Roman community. Although the struggle had been long, the Romans had handled it by

compromise, not violent revolution. Theoretically, by 287 B.C., all Roman citizens were equal under the law, and all could strive for political office. But in reality, as a result of the right of intermarriage, a select number of patrician and plebeian families formed a new senatorial aristocracy that came to dominate the political offices. The Roman Republic had not become a democracy.

The Roman Conquest of Italy

At the beginning of the Republic, Rome was surrounded by enemies, including the Etruscans to the north and the Sabines, Volscians, and Aequi to the east and south. The Latin communities on the plain of Latium posed an even more immediate threat. If we are to believe Livy, one of the chief ancient sources for the history of the early Roman Republic, Rome was engaged in almost continuous warfare with its neighbors for the next hundred years.

In his account of these years, Livy provided a detailed narrative of Roman efforts. Many of Livy's stories were legendary in character and indeed were modeled on events in Greek history. But Livy, writing in the first

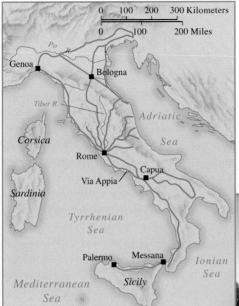

Roman Roads in Italy. The Romans built a remarkable system of roads. After laying a foundation with gravel, which allowed for drainage, the Roman builders placed flagstones, closely fitted together. Unlike other peoples who built similar kinds of roads, the Romans did not follow the contours of the land but made their roads as straight as possible to facilitate communications and transportation, especially for military purposes. Seen here is a view of the Via Appia (Appian Way), built in 312 B.C. under the leadership of the censor and consul Appius Claudius (Roman roads were often named after the great Roman families who encouraged their construction). The Via Appia (shown on the map) was meant to make it easy for Roman armies to march from Rome to the newly conquered city of Capua, a distance of 152 miles.

century B.C., used such stories to teach Romans the moral values and virtues that had made Rome great. These included tenacity, duty, courage, and especially discipline (see the box on p. 80). Indeed, Livy recounted stories of military leaders who executed their own sons for leaving their place in battle, a serious offense, since the success of the hoplite infantry depended on maintaining a precise order. These stories had little basis in fact, but like the story of George Washington and the cherry tree in American history, they provided mythic images to reinforce Roman patriotism.

By 340 B.C., Rome had crushed the Latin states in Latium. During the next fifty years, the Romans waged a fierce struggle with the Samnites, a hill people from the central Apennines, some of whom had settled in Campania, south of Rome. Rome was again victorious. The conquest of the Samnites gave Rome considerable control over a large part of Italy and also brought it into direct contact with the Greek communities of southern Italy. Soon after their conquest of the Samnites, the Romans were involved in hostilities with some of these Greek cities and by 267 B.C. had completed their conquest of southern Italy. After overrunning the remaining Etruscan states to the north in 264 B.C., Rome had conquered all of modern Italy except the extreme north.

To rule Italy, the Romans devised the Roman Confederation. Under this system, Rome allowed some peoples—especially the Latins—to have full Roman citizenship. Most of the remaining communities were made allies. They remained free to run their own local affairs but were required to provide soldiers for Rome. Moreover, the Romans made it clear that loyal allies could improve their status and even aspire to becoming Roman

citizens. Thus the Romans had found a way to give conquered peoples a stake in Rome's success.

The Romans' conquest of Italy can hardly be said to be the result of a direct policy of expansion. Much of it was opportunistic. The Romans did not hesitate to act when they felt that their security was threatened. And surrounded by potential enemies, Rome in a sense never felt secure. Yet once embarked on a course of expansion, the Romans pursued consistent policies that help explain their success. The Romans excelled at making wise diplomatic decisions. Though firm and even cruel when necessary—rebellions were put down without mercy—they were also shrewd in extending their citizenship and allowing autonomy in domestic affairs. In addition, the Romans were not only good soldiers but persistent ones as well. The loss of an army or a fleet did not cause them to quit but instead spurred them on to build new armies and new fleets. Finally, the Romans had a practical sense of strategy. As they conquered, they settled Romans and Latins in new communities outside Latium. By 264 B.C., the Romans had established fortified towns at all strategic locations. By building roads to these settlements and connecting them, the Romans assured themselves of an impressive military and communications network that enabled them to rule effectively and efficiently. By insisting on military service from the allies in the Roman

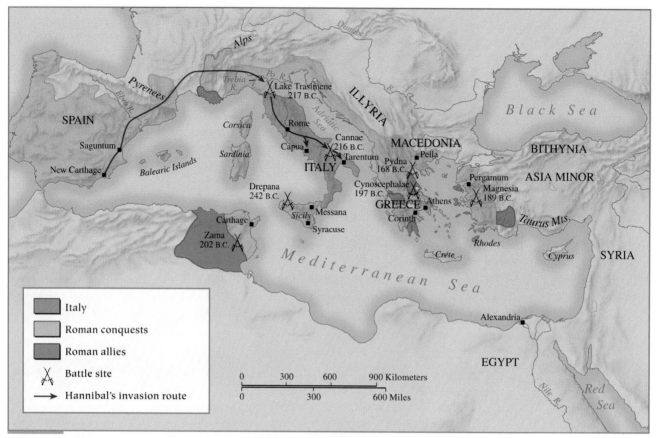

MAP 5.2 Roman Conquests in the Mediterranean, 264–133 B.C. Beginning with the Punic Wars, Rome expanded its holdings, first in the western Mediterranean at the expense of Carthage and later in Greece and western Asia Minor. ❓ What aspects of Mediterranean geography, combined with the territorial holdings and aspirations of Rome and the Carthaginians, made the Punic Wars more likely? 🌐 **View an animated version of this map or related maps at** http://thomsonedu.com/history/spielvogel

Confederation, Rome essentially mobilized the entire military manpower of all Italy for its wars.

The Roman Conquest of the Mediterranean (264–133 B.C.)

After their conquest of the Italian peninsula, the Romans found themselves face to face with a formidable Mediterranean power—Carthage. Founded around 800 B.C. by Phoenicians from Tyre, Carthage in North Africa was located in a favorable position for commanding Mediterranean trade routes and had become an important commercial center (see Map 5.2). It had become politically and militarily strong as well. By the third century B.C., the Carthaginian empire included the coast of northern Africa, southern Spain, Sardinia, Corsica, and western Sicily. With its monopoly of western Mediterranean trade, Carthage was the largest and richest state in the area. The presence of Carthaginians in Sicily made the Romans apprehensive about Carthaginian encroachment on the Italian coast. In 264 B.C., mutual suspicions drove the two powers into a lengthy struggle for control of the western Mediterranean.

The Struggle with Carthage

The First Punic War (264–241 B.C.) (the Latin word for Phoenician was *Punicus*) began when the Romans decided to intervene in a struggle between two Sicilian cities by sending an army to Sicily. The Carthaginians, who considered Sicily within their own sphere of influence, deemed this just cause for war. In going to war, both sides determined on the conquest of Sicily. The Romans realized that the war would be long and drawn out if they could not supplement land operations with a navy and promptly developed a substantial naval fleet. The Carthaginians, for their part, had difficulty finding enough mercenaries to continue the fight. After a long struggle in which both sides lost battles in northern Africa and Sicily, a Roman fleet defeated the Carthaginian navy off Sicily, and the war quickly came to an end. In 241 B.C., Carthage gave up all rights to Sicily and had to pay an indemnity.

Hannibal and the Second Punic War After the war, Carthage made an unexpected recovery and extended its domains in Spain to compensate for the territory lost to Rome. The Carthaginians proceeded to organize a formidable land army in the event of a second war with Rome, because they realized that defeating Rome on land was essential to victory. When the Romans encouraged one of Carthage's Spanish allies to revolt against Carthage, Hannibal, the greatest of the Carthaginian generals, struck back, beginning the Second Punic War (218–201 B.C.).

This time the Carthaginians decided to bring the war home to the Romans by fighting them in their own backyard. Hannibal went into Spain, moved east, and crossed the Alps with an army of thirty to forty thousand men and six thousand horses and elephants. The Alps took a toll on the Carthaginian army; most of the elephants did not survive the trip. The remaining army, however, posed a real threat. At Cannae in 216 B.C., the Romans lost an army of almost forty thousand men. Rome seemed on the brink of disaster but refused to give up, raised yet another army, and gradually recovered. Although Hannibal remained free to roam in Italy, he had neither the men nor the equipment to lay siege to the major cities, including Rome itself. The Romans began to reconquer some of the Italian cities that had rebelled against Roman rule after Hannibal's successes. More important, the Romans pursued a strategy that aimed at undermining the Carthaginian empire in Spain. By 206 B.C., the Romans had pushed the Carthaginians out of Spain.

The Romans then took the war directly to Carthage. Late in 204 B.C., a Roman army under Publius Cornelius Scipio, later known as Scipio Africanus, moved from Sicily into northern Africa and forced the Carthaginians to recall Hannibal from Italy. At the Battle of Zama in 202 B.C., the Romans decisively defeated Hannibal's forces, and the war was over. Eventually, Hannibal left Carthage and went to help Antiochus, the ruler of the Seleucid kingdom, in his struggle with Rome. After Antiochus made peace with the Romans, Hannibal fled to Bithynia, near the Black Sea. Pursued by the Romans, Hannibal killed himself after saying, "Let us free Rome of her dread of one old man."

By the peace treaty signed in 201 B.C. by the Carthaginians and Romans, Carthage lost Spain, agreed to pay an indemnity, and promised not to go to war without Rome's permission. Spain, like Sicily, Corsica, and Sardinia earlier, was made into a Roman province. Rome had become the dominant power in the western Mediterranean.

The Destruction of Carthage But some Romans wanted even more. A number of prominent Romans, especially the conservative politician Cato, advocated the complete destruction of Carthage. Cato ended every speech he made to the senate with the words, "And I think Carthage must be destroyed." When the Carthaginians technically broke their peace treaty with Rome by going to war against one of Rome's North African allies who had been encroaching on Carthage's home territory, the Romans declared war. Roman forces undertook their third and last war with Carthage (149–146 B.C.). This time Carthage was no match for the Romans, who in 146 B.C. seized this opportunity to carry out the final destruction of Carthage. The territory was made a Roman province called Africa.

The Eastern Mediterranean

During the Punic Wars, Rome had become acutely aware of the Hellenistic states of the eastern Mediterranean when the king of Macedonia made an alliance with Hannibal after the Roman defeat at Cannae. But Rome was preoccupied with the Carthaginians, and it was not until after the defeat of Carthage that Rome became involved in the world of Hellenistic politics as an advocate of the freedom of the Greek states. This support of the Greeks brought the Romans into conflict with both Macedonia and the kingdom of the Seleucids. Roman military victories and diplomatic negotiations rearranged the territorial boundaries of the Hellenistic kingdoms and brought the Greek states their freedom in 196 B.C. For fifty years, the Romans tried to be a power broker in the affairs of the Greeks without direct control of their lands. When the effort failed, the Romans changed their policy.

Macedonia was made a Roman province in 148 B.C., and when some of the Greek states rose in revolt against Rome's restrictive policies, Rome acted decisively. The city of Corinth, leader of the revolt, was destroyed in 146 B.C. to teach the Greeks a lesson, and Greece was placed under the control of the Roman governor of Macedonia. Thirteen years later, in 133 B.C., the king of Pergamum deeded his kingdom to Rome, giving Rome its first province in Asia. Rome was now master of the Mediterranean Sea.

The Nature of Roman Imperialism

Rome's empire was built in three stages: the conquest of Italy, the conflict with Carthage and expansion into the western Mediterranean, and the involvement with and domination of the Hellenistic kingdoms in the eastern Mediterranean. The Romans did not have a master plan for the creation of an empire; as it had been in Italy, much of their continued expansion was opportunistic, in response to perceived threats to their security. The more they expanded, the more threats to their security appeared on the horizon, involving them in yet more conflicts. Indeed, the Romans liked to portray themselves as declaring war only for defensive reasons or to protect allies. That is only part of the story, however. It is likely, as some historians have suggested, that at some point a group of Roman aristocratic leaders emerged who favored expansion both for the glory it offered and for the economic benefits it provided. Certainly, by the second century B.C., aristocratic senators perceived new opportunities for lucrative foreign commands, enormous spoils of war, and an abundant supply of slave labor for their growing landed estates. By that same time, the destruction

Alinari/Art Resource, NY (Mostra Augustea, Rome)

A Roman Legionary. The Roman legionaries, famed for their courage and tenacity, made possible Roman domination of the Mediterranean Sea. At the time of the Punic Wars, the Roman legionaries wore chain-mail armor and helmets with plumes and carried oval shields. Roman soldiers used heavy javelins and swords were their major weapons. This equipment, which is evident in this reconstruction of a Roman legionary from a museum in Rome, remained standard until the time of Julius Caesar.

of Corinth and Carthage indicated that Roman imperialism had become more arrogant and brutal as well. Rome's foreign success also had enormous repercussions for the internal development of the Roman Republic.

The Roman Conquest of Italy and the Mediterranean

Defeat of the Latin states	340–338 B.C.
Samnite Wars	343–290 B.C.
Defeat of Greek states in southern Italy	281–267 B.C.
First Punic War	264–241 B.C.
Second Punic War	218–201 B.C.
Battle of Cannae	216 B.C.
Completion of Roman seizure of Spain	206 B.C.
Battle of Zama	202 B.C.
Third Punic War	149–146 B.C.
Incorporation of Macedonia as a Roman province	148 B.C.
Destruction of Carthage	146 B.C.
Roman acquisition of Pergamum	133 B.C.

Society and Culture in the Roman World

One of the most noticeable aspects of Roman culture and society is the impact of the Greeks. The Romans had experienced Greek influence early on through the Greek cities in southern Italy. By the end of the third century B.C., however, Greek civilization was playing an ever-increasing role in Roman culture. Greek ambassadors, merchants, and artists traveled to Rome and spread Greek thought and practices. After their conquest of the Hellenistic kingdoms, Roman military commanders shipped Greek manuscripts and artworks back to Rome. Multitudes of educated Greek slaves were used in Roman households. Virtually every area of Roman life, from literature and philosophy to religion and education, was affected by Greek models. Rich Romans hired Greek tutors and sent their sons to Athens to study. As the Roman poet Horace said, "Captive Greece took captive her rude conqueror." Greek thought captivated the less sophisticated Roman mind, and the Romans became willing transmitters of Greek culture—not, however, without some resistance from Romans who had nothing but contempt for Greek politics and who feared the end of old Roman values. Even those who favored Greek culture blamed the Greeks for Rome's new vices, including a taste for luxury and homosexual practices.

Roman Religion

Every aspect of Roman society was permeated with religion. The official state religion focused on the worship of a pantheon of gods and goddesses, including Jupiter, Juno, Minerva, and Mars. As Rome developed and came into contact with other peoples and gods, the community simply adopted new deities. Hence the Greek Hermes became the Roman Mercury. Eventually, a complete amalgamation of Greek and Roman religion occurred, giving the Romans and the Greeks essentially a single "Greco-Roman" religion.

Roman religion focused on the worship of the gods for a very practical reason—human beings were thought to be totally dependent on them. The exact performance of ritual was crucial to establishing a right relationship with the gods. What was true for individuals was also valid for the state: it also had to observe correct ritual to receive its reward. Accurate performance of ritual was performed by a college of priests or pontiffs, who thus bore responsibility for maintaining the right relationship between the state and the gods. If the rituals were performed correctly, the Romans would obtain the "peace of the gods." No doubt the Roman success in creating an empire was a visible confirmation of divine favor. As Cicero, the first-century B.C. politician and writer, claimed, "We have overcome all the nations of the world, because we have realized that the world is directed and governed by the gods."[1]

Temple of Portunus. The Romans considered the proper worship of the gods an important key to success. Typical of Roman religious architecture was the small urban temple located in the midst of a crowded commercial center. Pictured here is a rectangular temple built in Rome in the late second or early first century B.C. and dedicated to Portunus, the god of harbors. The temple was located in the cattle market close to the Tiber River.

Just as the state had an official cult, so did families. Because the family was regarded as a small state within the state, it had its own household cults, which included Janus, the spirit of the doorway, and Vesta, goddess of the hearth. Here, too, proper ritual was important, and it was the responsibility of the **paterfamilias** as head of the family to ensure that religious obligations were properly fulfilled.

Religious festivals were an important part of Roman religious practice. There were two kinds: public festivals ordained and paid for by the state and private festivals celebrated by individuals and families. By the mid-second century B.C., six public festivals were celebrated annually, each lasting several days. The practice of holding games also grew out of religious festivals. The games were inaugurated in honor of Jupiter Optimus Maximus ("best and greatest"), the patron deity of Rome, but had become annual events by 366 B.C. In the late Republic, both the number of games and the number of days they lasted were increased. Originally, the games consisted of chariot racing in the Circus Maximus; later, animal hunts and theatrical performances were added. In the empire, gladiatorial contests would become the primary focus (see Chapter 6).

The Growth of Slavery

Slavery was a common institution throughout the ancient world, but no people possessed more slaves or relied so much on slave labor as the Romans eventually did. Before the third century B.C., a small Roman farmer might possess one or two slaves who would help farm his few acres and perform domestic chores. These slaves would most likely be from Italy and be regarded as part of the family household. Only the very rich would have large numbers of slaves.

The Roman conquest of the Mediterranean brought a drastic change in the use of slaves. Large numbers of foreign slaves were brought back to Italy. During the Republic, then, the chief source of slaves was from capture in war, followed by piracy. Of course, the children of slaves also became slaves. While some Roman generals brought back slaves to be sold to benefit the public treasury, ambitious generals of the first century B.C., such as Pompey and Caesar, made personal fortunes by treating slaves captured by their armies as private property.

Slaves were used in many ways in Roman society. The rich, of course, owned the most and the best. In the late Republic, it became a badge of prestige to be attended by many slaves. Greeks were in much demand as tutors, musicians, doctors, and artists. Roman businessmen would employ them as shop assistants or artisans. Slaves were also used as farm laborers; in fact, huge gangs of slaves living in pitiful conditions worked the large landed estates known as **latifundia**. Cato the Elder argued that it was cheaper to work slaves to death and then replace them than to treat them well. Many slaves of all nationalities were used as menial household workers, such

Household Slaves. It became a sign of status for upper-class Romans to have numerous specialist slaves at work in a household. This wall painting from central Italy depicts an elaborate dressing room where a female slave is arranging a girl's hair while the girl's mother and sister look on.

as cooks, valets, waiters, cleaners, and gardeners. Roads, aqueducts, and other public facilities were constructed by contractors using slave labor. The total number of slaves is difficult to judge—estimates vary from 20 to 30 percent of the population.

It is also difficult to generalize about the treatment of Roman slaves. There are numerous instances of humane treatment by masters and situations where slaves even protected their owners from danger out of gratitude and esteem. But slaves were also subject to severe punishments, torture, abuse, and hard labor that drove some to run away or even revolt against their owners. The Republic had stringent laws against aiding a runaway slave. The murder of a master by a slave might mean the execution of all the other household slaves. Near the end of the second century B.C., large-scale slave revolts occurred in Sicily, where enormous gangs of slaves were subjected to horrible working conditions on large landed estates. Slaves were branded, beaten, inadequately fed, worked in chains, and housed at night in underground prisons. It took three years (135–132 B.C.) to crush a revolt of seventy thousand slaves, and the great revolt on Sicily (104–101 B.C.) involved most of the island and took a Roman army of seventeen thousand men to suppress. The most famous revolt on the Italian peninsula occurred in 73 B.C. Led by Spartacus, a slave who had been a Thracian gladiator, the revolt broke out in southern Italy and involved seventy thousand slaves. Spartacus managed to defeat several Roman armies before he was finally trapped and killed in southern Italy in 71 B.C. Six thousand of his followers were crucified, the traditional form of execution for slaves.

The Roman Family

At the heart of the Roman social structure stood the family, headed by the *paterfamilias*—the dominant male. The household also included the wife, sons with their wives and children, unmarried daughters, and slaves. A family was virtually a small state within the state, and the power of the *paterfamilias* was parallel to that of the state magistrates over the citizens. Like the Greeks, Roman males believed that the weakness of the female sex necessitated male guardians (see the box on p. 87). The *paterfamilias* exercised that authority; on his death, sons or nearest male relatives assumed the role of guardians. By the late Republic, however, although the rights of male guardians remained legally in effect, upper-class women found numerous ways to circumvent the power of their guardians.

Fathers arranged the marriages of daughters, although there are instances of mothers and daughters having influence on the choice. In the Republic, women married *cum manu*, "with legal control" passing from father to husband. By the mid-first century B.C., the dominant practice had changed to *sine manu*, "without legal control," which meant that married daughters officially remained within the father's legal power. Since the fathers of most married women were dead, not being in the "legal control" of a husband made possible independent property rights that forceful women could translate into considerable power within the household and outside it. Traditionally, Roman marriages were intended to be for life, but divorce was introduced in the third century B.C. and became relatively easy to obtain since either party could initiate it and no one needed to prove the breakdown of the marriage. Divorce became especially prevalent in the first century B.C.—a period of political turmoil—when marriages were used to cement political alliances.

Some parents in upper-class families provided education for their daughters. Some girls had private tutors, and others may have gone to primary schools. But at the age when boys were entering secondary schools, girls were pushed into marriage. The legal minimum age was twelve, although fourteen was a more common age in practice. Although some Roman doctors warned that early pregnancies could be dangerous for young girls, early marriages persisted due to the desire to benefit from dowries as soon as possible and the reality of early mortality. A good example is Tullia, Cicero's beloved daughter. She was married at sixteen, widowed at twenty-two, remarried one year later, divorced at twenty-eight, remarried at twenty-nine, and divorced at thirty-three. She died at thirty-four, not unusual for females in Roman society.

The Evolution of Roman Law

One of Rome's chief gifts to the Mediterranean world of its day and to succeeding generations was its development of law. The Twelve Tables of 450 B.C. were the first codification of Roman law (see the box on p. 88), and although inappropriate for later times, they were never officially

CATO THE ELDER ON WOMEN

During the Second Punic War, the Romans enacted the Oppian Law, which limited the amount of gold women could possess and restricted their dress and use of carriages. In 195 B.C., an attempt was made to repeal the law, and women demonstrated in the streets on behalf of the effort. According to the Roman historian Livy, the conservative Roman official Cato the Elder spoke against repeal and against the women favoring it. Although the words are probably not Cato's own, they do reflect a traditional male Roman attitude toward women.

Livy, *The History of Rome*

"If each of us, citizens, had determined to assert his rights and dignity as a husband with respect to his own spouse, we should have less trouble with the sex as a whole; as it is, our liberty, destroyed at home by female violence, even here in the Forum is crushed and trodden underfoot, and because we have not kept them individually under control, we dread them collectively. . . . But from no class is there not the greatest danger if you permit them meetings and gatherings and secret consultations. . . .

"Our ancestors permitted no woman to conduct even personal business without a guardian to intervene in her behalf; they wished them to be under the control of fathers, brothers, husbands; we (Heaven help us!) allow them now even to interfere in public affairs, yes, and to visit the Forum and our informal and formal sessions. What else are they doing now on the streets and at the corners except urging the bill of the tribunes and voting for the repeal of the law?

Give loose rein to their uncontrollable nature and to this untamed creature and expect that they will themselves set bounds to their license; unless you act, this is the least of the things enjoined upon women by custom or law and to which they submit with a feeling of injustice. It is complete liberty or rather, if we wish to speak the truth, complete license that they desire.

"If they win in this, what will they not attempt? Review all the laws with which your forefathers restrained their license and made them subject to their husbands; even with all these bonds you can scarcely control them. What of this? If you suffer them to seize these bonds one by one and wrench themselves free and finally to be placed on a parity with their husbands, do you think you will be able to endure them? The moment they begin to be your equals, they will be your superiors. . . .

"Now they publicly address other women's husbands, and, what is more serious, they beg for law and votes, and from various men they get what they ask. In matters affecting yourself, your property, your children, you, Sir, can be importuned; once the law has ceased to set a limit to your wife's expenditures you will never set it yourself. Do not think, citizens, that the situation which existed before the law was passed will ever return. . . ."

What particular actions on the part of the women protesting this law have angered Cato? What more general concerns does he have about Roman women? What does he believe is women's ultimate goal in regard to men?

---

abrogated and were still memorized by schoolboys in the first century B.C. Civil law derived from the Twelve Tables proved inadequate for later Roman needs, however, and gave way to corrections and additions by the praetors. On taking office, a praetor issued an edict listing his guidelines for dealing with different kinds of legal cases. The praetors were knowledgeable in law, but they also relied on Roman jurists—amateur law experts—for advice in preparing their edicts. The interpretations of the jurists, often embodied in the edicts of the praetors, created a body of legal principles.

In 242 B.C., the Romans appointed a second praetor who was responsible for examining suits between a Roman and a non-Roman as well as between two non-Romans. The Romans found that although some of their rules of law could be used in these cases, special rules were often needed. These rules gave rise to a body of law known as the law of nations, defined by the Romans as "that part of the law which we apply both to ourselves and to foreigners." But the influence of Greek philosophy, primarily Stoicism, led Romans in the late Republic to develop the idea of the law of nature—or universal divine law derived from right reason. The Romans came to view their law of nations as

derived from or identical to this law of nature, thus giving Roman jurists a philosophical justification for systematizing Roman law according to basic principles.

The Development of Literature

The Romans produced little literature before the third century B.C., and the Latin literature that emerged in that century was strongly influenced by Greek models. The demand for plays at public festivals eventually led to a growing number of native playwrights. One of the best known was Plautus (c. 254–184 B.C.), who used plots from Greek New Comedy (see Chapter 4) for his own plays. The actors wore Greek costumes and Greek masks and portrayed the same basic stock characters: lecherous old men, skillful slaves, prostitutes, young men in love. Plautus wrote for the masses and became a very popular playwright in Rome.

In the last century of the Republic, the Romans began to produce a new poetry, less dependent on epic themes and more inclined to personal expression. Latin poets were now able to use various Greek forms to express their own feelings about people, social and political life, and love. The finest example of this can be seen in

THE TWELVE TABLES

In 451 B.C., plebeian pressure led to the creation of a special commission of ten men who were responsible for codifying Rome's laws and making them public. In so doing, the plebeians hoped that they could restrict the arbitrary power of the patrician magistrates, who alone had access to the laws. The Twelve Tables represent the first formal codification of Roman laws and customs. The laws dealt with litigation procedures, debt, family relations, property, and other matters of public and sacred law. The code was inscribed on bronze plaques, which were eventually destroyed. These selections are taken from reconstructions of the code preserved in later writings.

Selections from the Twelve Tables

Table III: Execution; Law of Debt

When a debt has been acknowledged, or judgment about the matter has been pronounced in court, thirty days must be the legitimate time of grace. After that, the debtor may be arrested by laying on of hands. Bring him into court. If he does not satisfy the judgment, or no one in court offers himself as surety in his behalf, the creditor may take the defaulter with him. He may bind him either in stocks or in fetters. . . .

Unless they make a settlement, debtors shall be held in bond for sixty days. During that time they shall be brought before the praetor's court in the meeting place on three successive market days, and the amount for which they are judged liable shall be announced; on the third market day they shall suffer capital punishment or be delivered up for sale abroad, across the Tiber.

Table IV: Rights of Head of Family

Quickly kill . . . a dreadfully deformed child.

If a father three times surrenders a son for sale, the son shall be free from the father.

A child born ten months after the father's death will not be admitted into legal inheritance.

Table V: Guardianship; Succession

Females shall remain in guardianship even when they have attained their majority.

A spendthrift is forbidden to exercise administration over his own goods. . . . A person who, being insane or a spendthrift, is prohibited from administering his own goods shall be under trusteeship of agnates [nearest male relatives].

Table VII: Rights Concerning Land

Branches of a tree may be lopped off all round to a height of more than 15 feet. . . . Should a tree on a neighbor's farm be bent crooked by a wind and lean over your farm, action may be taken for removal of that tree.

It is permitted to gather up fruit falling down on another man's farm.

Table VIII: Torts or Delicts

If any person has sung or composed against another person a song such as was causing slander or insult to another, he shall be clubbed to death.

If a person has maimed another's limb, let there be retaliation in kind unless he makes agreement for settlement with him.

Any person who destroys by burning any building or heap of corn deposited alongside a house shall be bound, scourged, and put to death by burning at the stake, provided that he has committed the said misdeed with malice aforethought, but if he shall have committed it by accident, that is, by negligence, it is ordained that he repair the damage.

Table IX: Public Law

The penalty shall be capital punishment for a judge or arbiter legally appointed who has been found guilty of receiving a bribe for giving a decision.

Table XI: Supplementary Laws

Intermarriage shall not take place between plebeians and patricians.

What do the selections from the Twelve Points reveal about Roman society? In what ways do these points of law differ from those found in the Code of Hammurabi? In what ways are they similar?

---

the work of Catullus (c. 87–54 B.C.), Rome's "best lyric poet" and one of the greatest in world literature.

Catullus became a master at adapting and refining Greek forms of poetry to express his emotions. He wrote a variety of poems on, among other things, political figures, social customs, the use of language, the death of his brother, and the travails of love. Catullus became infatuated with Clodia, the promiscuous sister of a tribune and wife of a provincial governor, and addressed a number of poems to her (he called her Lesbia), describing his passionate love and hatred for her (Clodia had many other lovers besides Catullus):

> *You used to say that you wished to know only Catullus,*
> *Lesbia, and wouldn't take even Jove before me!*
> *I didn't regard you just as my mistress then:*
> *I cherished you as a father does his sons or his*
> *daughters' husbands.*
> *Now that I know you, I burn for you even more fiercely,*
> *though I regard you as almost utterly worthless.*

How can that be, you ask? It's because such cruelty forces lust to assume the shrunken place of affection.²

The ability of Catullus to express in simple fashion his intense feelings and curiosity about himself and his world had a noticeable impact on later Latin poets.

The development of Roman prose was greatly aided by the practice of oratory. Romans had great respect for oratory since the ability to persuade people in public debate meant success in politics. Oratory was brought to perfection in a literary fashion by Cicero (106–43 B.C.), the best exemplar of the literary and intellectual interests of the senatorial elite of the late Republic and, indeed, the greatest prose writer of that period. For Cicero, oratory was not simply skillful speaking. An orator was a statesman, a man who achieved his highest goal by pursuing an active life in public affairs.

Later, when the turmoil of the late Republic forced him into semiretirement politically, Cicero became more interested in the writing of philosophical treatises. He served a most valuable purpose for Roman society by popularizing and making understandable the works of Greek philosophers. In his philosophical works, Cicero, more than anyone else, transmitted the classical intellectual heritage to the Western world. Cicero's original contributions came in the field of politics. His works *On the Laws* and *On the Republic* provided fresh insights into political thought, including the need for a mixed constitution: "a moderate and well-balanced form of government which is a combination of the three simple good forms (monarchy, aristocracy, and democracy) is preferable even to monarchy."³ His emphasis on the need to pursue an active life to benefit and improve humankind would greatly influence the later Italian Renaissance.

Roman Art

The Romans were also dependent on the Greeks for artistic inspiration. During the third and second centuries B.C., they adopted many features of the Hellenistic style of art. The Romans developed a taste for Greek statues, which they placed not only in public buildings but also in their homes. Once demand outstripped the supply of original works, reproductions of Greek statues became fashionable. The Romans' own portrait sculpture was characterized by an intense realism that included even unpleasant physical details. Wall paintings and frescoes in the houses of the rich realistically depicted landscapes, portraits, and scenes from mythological stories.

The Romans excelled in architecture, a highly practical art. Although they continued to employ Greek styles and made use of colonnades, rectangular structures, and post-and-lintel construction, the Romans were also innovative. They made considerable use of curvilinear forms: the arch, vault, and dome. The Romans were also the first people in antiquity to use concrete on an enormous scale. By combining concrete and curvilinear forms, they were able to construct massive buildings—public baths and amphitheaters, the most famous of which was the Coliseum in Rome, capable of seating fifty thousand spectators. These large buildings were made possible by Roman engineering skills. These same skills were put to use in constructing roads (the Romans built a network of 50,000 miles of roads throughout their empire), aqueducts (in Rome, almost a dozen aqueducts kept a population of one million supplied with water), and bridges.

Values and Attitudes

The Romans were by nature a conservative people. They were very concerned about maintaining the *mos maiorum*, the customs or traditions of their ancestors. They emphasized parental authority and, above all, their obligations to the state. The highest virtue was *pietas*—the dutiful execution of one's obligations to one's fellow citizens, to the gods, and to the state.

By the second century B.C., however, the assembling of an empire had begun to weaken the old values. The Romans began to focus more on affluence, status, and material possessions. Emphasis shifted toward individualism and away from collective well-being, the old public spirit that had served Rome so well. Observers worried about the decline of the old values blamed it on different causes. Some felt that after the destruction of Carthage, the Romans no longer had any strong enemies to challenge them. Others believed that the Romans had simply been overwhelmed by the affluence afforded by the new empire. And some blamed everything on the Greeks for importing ideas and practices baneful to the Romans. Of course, there were also many Romans who, though desirous of maintaining traditional values, were also well aware that the acquisition of an empire had created a new world with new demands and values.

The Decline and Fall of the Roman Republic (133–31 B.C.)

By the mid-second century B.C., Roman domination of the Mediterranean Sea was well established. Yet the process of building an empire had weakened and threatened the internal stability of Rome. This internal instability characterizes the period of Roman history from 133 until 31 B.C., when the armies of Octavian defeated Mark Antony and stood supreme over the Roman world. By that time, the constitution of the Roman Republic was in shambles.

Social, Economic, and Political Problems

By the second century B.C., the senate had become the effective governing body of the Roman state. It consisted of three hundred men, drawn primarily from the landed aristocracy; they remained senators for life and held the chief magistracies of the Republic. During the wars of the third and second centuries, the senate came to exercise enormous power. It directed the wars and took control of both foreign and domestic policy, including financial affairs.

Moreover, the magistracies and senate were increasingly controlled by a relatively select circle of wealthy and powerful families, both patrician and plebeian, called the **nobiles** ("nobles"). In the hundred years from 233 to 133 B.C., 80 percent of the consuls came from twenty-six families; moreover, 50 percent came from only ten families. Hence the *nobiles* constituted a governing oligarchy that managed, through its landed wealth, system of patronage, and intimidation, to maintain its hold over the magistracies and senate and thus guide the destiny of Rome while running the state in its own interests.

By the end of the second century B.C., two types of aristocratic leaders, called the **optimates** ("the best men") and the **populares** ("favoring the people"), became prominent. *Optimates* and *populares* were terms of political rhetoric that were used by individuals within the aristocracy against fellow aristocratic rivals to distinguish one set of tactics from another. The *optimates* controlled the senate and wished to maintain their oligarchical privileges, while the *populares* were usually other ambitious aristocrats who used the people's assemblies as instruments to break the domination of the *optimates*. The conflicts between these two types of aristocratic leaders and their supporters engulfed the first century B.C. in political turmoil.

Of course, the aristocrats formed only a tiny minority of the Roman people. The backbone of the Roman state and army had traditionally been the small farmers. But economic changes that began in the period of the Punic Wars increasingly undermined the position of that group. Their lands had been severely damaged during the Second Punic War when Hannibal invaded Italy. Moreover, in order to win the wars, Rome had to increase the term of military service from two to six years. When they returned home, many farmers found their farms so deteriorated that they chose to sell out instead of remaining on the land. By this time, capitalistic agriculture was also increasing rapidly. Landed aristocrats had been able to develop large estates (the *latifundia*) by taking over state-owned land and by buying out small peasant owners. These large estates relied on slave and tenant labor and frequently concentrated on cash crops, such as grapes for wine, olives, and sheep for wool, which small farmers could not afford to do. Thus the rise of the *latifundia* contributed to the decline in the number of small citizen farmers. Because the latter group traditionally provided the foundation of the Roman army, the number of men available for military service declined. Moreover, many of these small farmers drifted to the cities, especially Rome, forming a large class of day laborers who possessed no property. This new urban proletariat was a highly unstable mass with the potential for much trouble in depressed times.

The Reforms of the Gracchi

In 133 B.C., Tiberius Gracchus, himself a member of the aristocracy and a new tribune, came to believe that the underlying cause of Rome's problems was the decline of the small farmer. Consequently, Tiberius bypassed the senate, where he knew his rivals would oppose his proposal, and had the council of the plebs pass a land reform bill that authorized the government to reclaim public land held by large landowners and to distribute it to landless Romans. Many senators, themselves large landowners whose estates included large tracts of public land, were furious, and a group of them took the law into their own hands and assassinated Tiberius.

The efforts of Tiberius Gracchus were continued by his brother Gaius, elected tribune for both 123 and 122 B.C. Gaius, too, pushed for the distribution of land to displaced farmers. But he broadened his reform program with measures that would benefit the **equestrian order,** a rising group of wealthy people who wanted a share in the political power held by the ruling aristocracy. Many senators, hostile to Gaius' reforms and fearful of his growing popularity, instigated mob action that resulted in the death of the reformer and many of his friends in 121 B.C. The attempts of the Gracchus brothers to bring reforms had opened the door to more instability and further violence.

A New Role for the Roman Army: Marius and Sulla

In the closing years of the second century B.C., a series of military disasters gave rise to a fresh outburst of popular anger against the old leaders of the senate. Military defeats in northern Africa under a senate-appointed general encouraged Marius—a "new man" from the equestrian order—to run for the consulship on a "win the war" campaign slogan. Marius won and became a consul for 107 B.C. Marius took command of the army in Africa and brought the war to a successful conclusion. He was then called on to defeat the Celts, who threatened an invasion of Italy. Marius was made consul for five years, from 104 to 100 B.C., raised a new army, and decisively defeated the Celts, leaving him in a position of personal ascendancy in Rome.

In raising a new army, Marius initiated military reforms that proved to have drastic consequences. The Roman army had traditionally been a conscript army of small landholders. Marius recruited volunteers from both the urban and rural proletariat who possessed no property. These volunteers swore an oath of loyalty to the general, not the senate, and thus inaugurated a professional-type army that might no longer be subject to the state. Moreover, to recruit these men, a general would promise them land, so the generals had to play politics to get legislation passed that would provide the land for their veterans. Marius left a powerful legacy. He had created a new system of military recruitment that placed much power in the hands of the individual generals.

Lucius Cornelius Sulla was the next general to take advantage of the new military system. The senate had placed him in charge of a war in Asia Minor, but when the council of the plebs tried to transfer command of this war to Marius, a civil war ensued. Sulla won and seized Rome itself in 82 B.C. He forced the senate to grant him the title of dictator to "reconstitute the Republic." After conducting a reign of terror to wipe out all opposition, Sulla revised the constitution to restore power to the senate and eliminated most of the powers of the popular assemblies and the tribunes of the plebs. In 79 B.C., believing that he had created a firm foundation for the traditional Republic governed by a powerful senate, he retired. But his real legacy was quite different from what he had intended. His example of using an army to seize power would prove most attractive to ambitious men.

The Collapse of the Republic

For the next fifty years, Roman history would be characterized by two important features: the jostling for power by a number of strong individuals and the civil wars generated by their conflicts. Three men came to hold enormous military and political power—Crassus, Pompey, and Julius Caesar. Crassus, who was known as the richest man in Rome, had successfully put down the major slave rebellion led by Spartacus. Pompey had returned from a successful military command in Spain in 71 B.C. and had been hailed as a military hero. Julius Caesar had been a spokesman for the *populares* from the beginning of his political career and had a military command in Spain. In 60 B.C., Caesar joined with Crassus and Pompey to form a coalition that historians call the First Triumvirate.

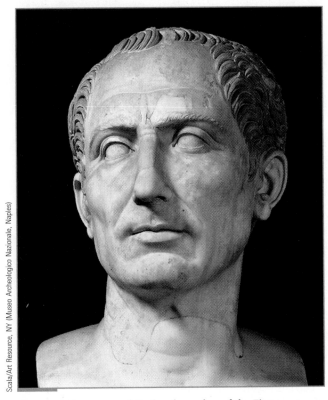

Scala/Art Resource, NY (Museo Archeologico Nazionale, Naples)

Caesar. Conqueror of Gaul and member of the First Triumvirate, Julius Caesar is perhaps the best-known figure of the late Republic. Caesar became dictator of Rome in 47 B.C. and after his victories in the civil war was made dictator for life. Some members of the senate who resented his power assassinated him in 44 B.C. Pictured is a marble copy of a bust of Caesar.

Though others had made political deals before, the combined wealth and power of these three men was enormous, enabling them to dominate the political scene and achieve their basic aims: Pompey received lands for his veterans and a command in Spain, Crassus was given a command in Syria, and Caesar was granted a special military command in Gaul (modern France). When Crassus was killed in battle in 53 B.C., his death left two powerful men with armies in direct competition. Caesar had used his time in Gaul wisely. He had conquered all of Gaul and gained fame, wealth, and military experience as well as an army of seasoned veterans who were loyal to him. When leading senators fastened on Pompey as the less harmful to their cause and voted for Caesar to lay down his command and return as a private citizen to Rome, Caesar refused. He chose to keep his army and moved into Italy by illegally crossing the Rubicon, the river that formed the southern boundary of his province. ("Crossing the Rubicon" is a phrase used to this day to mean taking a decisive action and being unable to turn back.) Caesar marched on Rome, starting a civil war between his forces and those of Pompey and his allies. The defeat of Pompey's forces left Caesar in complete control of the Roman government.

Caesar had officially been made dictator in 47 B.C., and three years later, he was made dictator for life. He continued to hold elections for offices but saw to it that his supporters chose the people he recommended. Upon becoming Rome's ruler, he quickly instituted a number of ambitious reforms. He increased the senate to nine hundred members by filling it with many of his supporters and granted citizenship to a number of people in the provinces who had helped him. By establishing colonies of Roman citizens in North Africa, Gaul, and Spain, he initiated a process of Romanization in those areas. He also reorganized the administrative structures of cities in Italy in an attempt to create a sense of order in their government. Caesar was a generous victor and pardoned

THE ASSASSINATION OF JULIUS CAESAR

When it became apparent that Julius Caesar had no intention of restoring the Republic as they conceived it, about sixty senators, many of them his friends or pardoned enemies, formed a conspiracy to assassinate the dictator. It was led by Gaius Cassius and Marcus Brutus, who naively imagined that this act would restore the traditional Republic. The conspirators set the Ides of March (March 15), 44 B.C., as the date for the assassination. Although warned about a plot against his life, Caesar chose to disregard it. This account of his death is taken from his biography by the Greek writer Plutarch.

Plutarch, *Life of Caesar*

Fate, however, is to all appearance more unavoidable than unexpected. For many strange prodigies and apparitions are said to have been observed shortly before this event. . . . One finds it also related by many that a soothsayer bade him [Caesar] prepare for some great danger on the Ides of March. When this day was come, Caesar, as he went to the senate, met this soothsayer, and said to him mockingly, "The Ides of March are come," who answered him calmly, "Yes, they are come, but they are not past. . . ."

All these things might happen by chance. But the place which was destined for the scene of this murder, in which the senate met that day, was the same in which Pompey's statue stood, and was one of the edifices which Pompey had raised and dedicated with his theater to the use of the public, plainly showing that there was something of a supernatural influence which guided the action and ordered it to that particular place. Cassius, just before the act, is said to have looked toward Pompey's statue, and silently implored his assistance. . . . When Caesar entered, the senate stood up to show their respect to him, and of Brutus' confederates, some came about his chair and stood behind it, others met him, pretending to add their petitions to those of Tillius Cimber, in behalf of his brother, who was in exile; and they followed him with their joint applications till he came to his seat. When he sat down, he refused to comply with their requests, and upon their urging him further began to reproach them severely for their demand, when Tillius, laying hold of his robe with both his hands, pulled it down from his neck, which was the signal for the assault. Casca gave him the first cut in the neck, which was not mortal nor dangerous, as coming from one who at the beginning of such a bold action was probably very much disturbed; Caesar immediately turned about, and laid his hand upon the dagger and kept hold of it. And both of them at the same time cried out, he that received the blow, in Latin, "Vile Casca, what does this mean?" and he that gave it, in Greek to his brother, "Brother, help!" Upon this first onset, those who were not privy to the design were astonished, and their horror and amazement at what they saw were so great that they dared not fly nor assist Caesar, nor so much as speak a word. But those who came prepared for the business enclosed him on every side, with their naked daggers in their hands. Which way soever he turned he met with blows, and saw their swords leveled at his face and eyes, and was encompassed like a wild beast in the toils on every side. For it had been agreed they should each of them make a thrust at him, and flesh themselves with his blood; for which reason Brutus also gave him one stab in the groin. Some say that he fought and resisted all the rest, shifting his body to avoid the blows, and calling out for help, but that when he saw Brutus' sword drawn, he covered his face with his robe and submitted, letting himself fall, whether it were by chance or that he was pushed in that direction by his murderers, at the foot of the pedestal on which Pompey's statue stood, and which was thus wetted with his blood. So that Pompey himself seemed to have presided, as it were, over the revenge done upon his adversary, who lay here at his feet, and breathed out his soul through his multitude of wounds, for they say he received three-and-twenty. And the conspirators themselves were many of them wounded by each other while they all leveled their blows at the same person.

What does the account of Caesar's assassination tell you about the character of Julius Caesar?

---

many of the republican leaders who had opposed him, allowing them to return to Rome. He also reformed the calendar by introducing the Egyptian solar year of 365 days (with changes implemented in 1582, it became the basis of our current calendar). He planned much more in the way of building projects and military adventures in the east, but in 44 B.C., a group of leading senators who resented his domination assassinated him in the belief that they had struck a blow for republican liberty (see the box above). In truth, they had set the stage for another civil war that delivered the death blow to the Republic.

Within a few years after Caesar's death, two men had divided the Roman world between them—Octavian, Caesar's heir and grandnephew, taking the west, and Antony, Caesar's ally and assistant, the east. But the empire of the Romans, large as it was, was still too small for two masters, and Octavian and Antony eventually came into conflict. Antony allied himself with the Egyptian queen Cleopatra VII, with whom, like Caesar before him, he fell in love. Octavian began a propaganda campaign, accusing Antony of catering to Cleopatra and giving away Roman territory to this "whore of the east." Finally, at the Battle of Actium in Greece in 31 B.C., Octavian's forces smashed the army and navy of Antony and Cleopatra. Both fled to Egypt, where, according to the account of the Roman historian Florus, they committed suicide a year later:

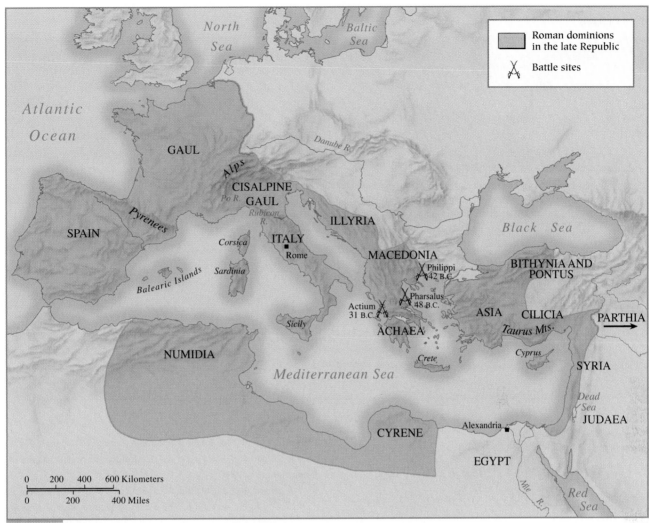

MAP 5.3 **Roman Dominions in the Late Republic, 31 B.C.** Rome expanded its empire not only in response to military threats on its borders but also for increased access to economic resources and markets, in addition to the vanity of conquest itself. ❓ For comparison, look back at Map 5.2. In what areas did the Romans gain the greatest amount of territory, and how? 🌐 **View an animated version of this map or related maps at** http://thomsonedu.com/history/spielvogel

Antony was the first to commit suicide, by the sword. Cleopatra threw herself at Octavian's feet, and tried her best to attract his gaze: in vain, for his self-control was impervious to her beauty. It was not her life she was after, for that had already been granted, but a portion of her kingdom. When she realized this was hopeless and that she had been earmarked to feature in Octavian's triumph in Rome, she took advantage of her guard's carelessness to get herself into the mausoleum, as the royal tomb is called.

Once there, she put on the royal robes which she was accustomed to wear, and lay down in a richly perfumed coffin beside her Antony. Then she applied poisonous snakes to her veins and slipped into death as though into a sleep.[4]

Octavian, at the age of thirty-two, stood supreme over the Roman world (see Map 5.3). The civil wars had ended. And so had the Republic.

CONCLUSION

In the eighth and seventh centuries B.C., the pastoral community of Rome emerged as a city. Between 509 and 264 B.C., the expansion of this city led to the union of almost all of Italy under Rome's control. Even more dramatically, between 264 and 133 B.C., Rome expanded to the west and east and became master of the Mediterranean Sea.

After 133 B.C., however, Rome's republican institutions proved inadequate for the task of ruling an empire. In the breakdown that ensued, ambitious individuals saw op-

portunities for power unparalleled in Roman history and succumbed to the temptations. After a series of bloody civil wars, peace was finally achieved when Octavian defeated Antony and Cleopatra. Octavian's real task was at hand: to create a new system of government that seemed to preserve the Republic while establishing the basis for a new order that would rule the empire in an orderly fashion. Octavian proved equal to the task of establishing a Roman imperial state.

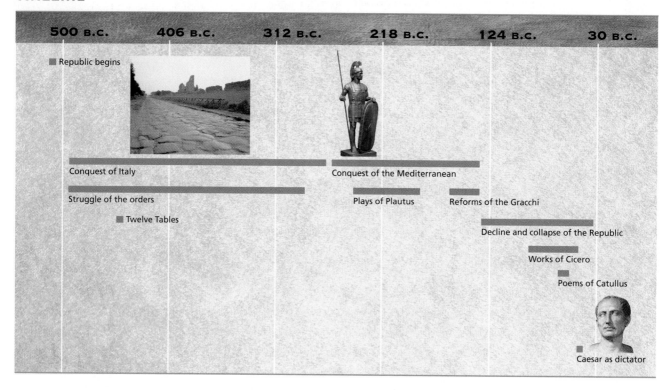

500 B.C.   406 B.C.   312 B.C.   218 B.C.   124 B.C.   30 B.C.

■ Republic begins

Conquest of Italy

Conquest of the Mediterranean

Struggle of the orders

Plays of Plautus

Reforms of the Gracchi

■ Twelve Tables

Decline and collapse of the Republic

Works of Cicero

Poems of Catullus

■ Caesar as dictator

NOTES

1. Quoted in C. Starr, *Past and Future in Ancient History* (Lanham, Md., 1987), pp. 38–39.
2. *The Poems of Catullus,* trans. C. Martin (Baltimore, 1990), p. 109.
3. Quoted in A. Everitt, *Cicero* (New York, 2001), p. 181.
4. Florus, *Epitome of Roman History,* trans. E. S. Forster (Cambridge, Mass., 1961), IV, ii, 149–151

SUGGESTIONS FOR FURTHER READING

For a general account of the Roman Republic, see **J. Boardman, J. Griffin, and O. Murray, *eds., The Oxford History of the Roman World*** (Oxford, 1991). Good surveys of Roman history include **M. H. Crawford, *The Roman Republic,*** 2d ed. (Cambridge, Mass., 1993); **H. H. Scullard, *History of the Roman World, 753–146 B.C.,*** 4th ed. (London, 1978) and ***From the Gracchi to Nero,*** 5th ed. (London, 1982); **M. Le Glay, J.-L. Voisin, and Y. Le Bohec, *A History of Rome,*** trans. **A. Nevill,** 2d ed. (Oxford, 2000); **M. T. Boatwright, D. J. Gargola, and R. J. A. Talbert, *The Romans: From Village to Empire*** (New York, 2004); and **A. Kamm, *The Romans*** (London, 1995). For beautifully illustrated surveys, see **J. F. Drinkwater and A. Drummond, *The World of the Romans*** (New York, 1993), and **G. Woolf,** ed., ***Cambridge Illustrated History of the Roman World*** (Cambridge, 2003). The history of early Rome is well covered in **T. J. Cornell, *The Beginnings of Rome: Italy and Rome from the Bronze Age to the Punic Wars (c. 1000–264 B.C.)*** (London, 1995).

Aspects of the Roman political structure can be studied in **R. E. Mitchell, *Patricians and Plebeians: The Origin of the Roman State*** (Ithaca, N.Y., 1990). Changes in Rome's economic life can be examined in **A. H. M. Jones, *The Roman Economy*** (Oxford, 1974). On the Roman social structure, see **G. Alföldy, *The Social History of Rome*** (London, 1985).

A general account of Rome's expansion in the Mediterranean is provided by **R. M. Errington, *The Dawn of Empire: Rome's Rise to World Power*** (Ithaca, N.Y., 1971). On the conquest of Italy, see **J.-M. David, *The Roman Conquest of Italy,*** trans. **A. Nevill** (Oxford, 1996). On Rome's struggle with Carthage, see **N. Bagnall, *The Punic Wars*** (Oxford, 2002), and **A. Goldsworthy, *The Punic Wars*** (New York, 2001). On Roman expansion in the eastern Mediterranean, see **A. N. Sherwin-White, *Roman Foreign Policy in the Greek East*** (London, 1984). On Roman military forces, see **A. Goldsworthy, *The Complete Roman Army*** (London, 2003).

Roman religion can be examined in **J. Liebeschuetz, *Continuity and Change in Roman Religion*** (Oxford, 1979), and **H. H. Scullard, *Festivals and Ceremonies of the Roman Republic*** (Ithaca, N.Y., 1981). A general study of daily life in Rome is available in **F. Dupont, *Daily Life in Ancient Rome*** (Oxford, 1994). On the Roman family, see **S. Dixon, *The Roman Family*** (Baltimore, 1992). Roman women are examined in **R. Baumann, *Women and Politics in Ancient Rome*** (New York, 1995), and **S. Dixon, *The Roman Mother*** (Norman, Okla., 1988). On slavery and its consequences, see **K. R. Bradley, *Slavery and Rebellion in the Roman World, 140–70 B.C.*** (Bloomington, Ind., 1989). For a brief and readable survey of Latin literature, see **R. M. Ogilvie, *Roman Literature and Society*** (Harmondsworth, England, 1980). On Roman art and architecture, see **R. Ling, *Roman Painting*** (New York, 1991); **D. E. Kleiner, *Roman Sculpture*** (New Haven, Conn., 1992); and **M. Wheeler, *Roman Art and Architecture*** (London, 1964).

An excellent account of basic problems in the history of the late Republic can be found in **M. Beard and M. H. Crawford, *Rome in the***

Late Republic (London, 1985). Also valuable are **D. Shotter,** *The Fall of the Roman Republic* (London, 1994), and **E. Hildinger,** *Swords Against the Senate: The Rise of the Roman Army and the Fall of the Republic* (Cambridge, Mass., 2002). Numerous biographies provide many details on the politics of the period. Especially worthwhile are **A. H. Bernstein,** *Tiberius Sempronius Gracchus: Tradition and Apostasy* (Ithaca, N.Y., 1978); **D. Stockton,** *The Gracchi* (Oxford, 1979); **C. Meier,** *Caesar* (London, 1995); **R. Seager,** *Pompey: A Political Biography* (Berkeley, Calif., 1980); and **A. Everitt,** *Cicero* (New York, 2001).

Thomson **Enter** *ThomsonNOW* using the access card that is **NOW!** available for *Western Civilization: A Brief History.* *ThomsonNOW* will help you understand this chapter with lesson plans generated for your needs. In addition, you can read the following documents, and many more, online:

Terence, *Phormio*
Plutarch, Life of Caesar
Cicero, Oration in Defense of Aulus Licinius Archias
Cicero, Tusculan Disputations

WESTERN CIVILIZATION RESOURCES

Visit the Web site for *Western Civilization: A Brief History* for resources specific to this book:

http://www.thomsonedu.com/history/spielvogel

For a variety of tools to help you succeed in this course, visit the Western Civilization Resource Center at

http://history.wadsworth.com/spielvogel

Included are quizzes, images, documents, interactive simulations, maps and timelines, movie explorations, and a wealth of other sources.

THE ROMAN EMPIRE

Hadrian (with outstretched arms) entering Rome

Nimatallah/Art Resource, NY (Palazzo dei Conservatori, Rome)

𝒲ITH THE VICTORIES OF OCTAVIAN, peace finally settled on the Roman world. Although civil conflict still erupted occasionally, the new imperial state constructed by Octavian experienced a period of remarkable stability for the next two hundred years. To the Romans, their divine mission was clearly to rule nations and peoples. Hadrian, an emperor during the second century A.D., was one of many Roman leaders who believed in Rome's mission. He was a strong and intelligent ruler who took his responsibilities seriously. Between 121 and 132, he visited all of the provinces in the empire. According to his Roman biographer, Aelius Spartianus, "Hardly any emperor ever traveled with such speed over so much territory." When he arrived in a province, Hadrian dealt firsthand with any problems and bestowed many favors on the local population. He also worked to establish the boundaries of the provinces and provide for their defense. New fortifications, such as the 80-mile-long Hadrian's Wall across northern Britain, were built to defend the borders. Hadrian insisted on rigid discipline for frontier armies and demanded that the soldiers be kept in training, "just as if war were imminent." He also tried to lead by personal example; according to his biographer, he spent time with the troops and "cheerfully ate out of doors such camp food as bacon, cheese, and vinegar." Moreover, he "would walk as much as twenty miles fully armed."

The Romans imposed their peace on the largest empire established in antiquity. Indeed, Rome's writers proclaimed that "by heaven's will my Rome shall be capital of the world."[1] Rome's writers were not quite accurate, but few Romans were aware of the Han Chinese Empire, which flourished at the same time (202 B.C.–A.D. 221) and extended from Central Asia to the Pacific. Although there was little contact between them, the Han and Roman Empires had remarkable similarities: they lasted for centuries; they had remarkable success in establishing centralized control; and they maintained their law and political institutions, their technical skills, and their languages throughout the empire.

By the third century A.D., however, Rome's ability to rule nations and people began to weaken as the empire began to experience renewed civil war, economic chaos, and invasions. At the same time, Christianity emerged in one of the most remarkable success stories of Western civilization.◆

The Age of Augustus (31 B.C.– A.D. 14)

In 27 B.C., Octavian proclaimed the "restoration of the Republic." He understood that only traditional republican forms would satisfy the senatorial aristocracy. At the same time, Octavian was aware that the Republic could not be fully restored and managed to arrive at a compromise that worked at least during his lifetime. In 27 B.C., the senate awarded him the title of Augustus, "revered one." He preferred the title *princeps*, meaning "chief citizen" or "first among equals." The system of rule that Augustus established is sometimes called the **principate**, conveying the idea of a constitutional monarch as coruler with the senate. But while Augustus worked to maintain this appearance, in reality power was heavily weighted in favor of the *princeps*.

The New Order

In the new constitutional order that Augustus created, the basic governmental structure consisted of the *princeps* (Augustus) and an aristocratic senate. Augustus retained the senate as the chief deliberative body of the Roman state. Its decrees, screened in advance by the *princeps*, now had the effect of law. The title of *princeps* carried no power in itself, but Augustus held the office of consul each year until 23 B.C., when he assumed the power of a tribune, which enabled him to propose laws and veto any item of public business. By observing proper legal forms for his power, Augustus proved highly popular. As the Roman historian Tacitus commented, "Indeed, he attracted everybody's goodwill by the enjoyable gift of peace.... Opposition did not exist."[2] No doubt the ending of the

Augustus. Octavian, Caesar's adopted son, emerged victorious from the civil conflict that rocked the Republic after Caesar's assassination. The senate awarded him the title Augustus. This marble statue from Prima Porta, an idealized portrait, is based on Greek rather than Roman models. The statue was meant to be a propaganda piece, depicting a youthful general addressing his troops. At the bottom stands Cupid, the son of Venus, goddess of love, meant to be a reminder that the Julians, Caesar's family, claimed descent from Venus, thus emphasizing the ruler's divine background.

civil wars had greatly bolstered Augustus' popularity (see the box on p. 98). At the same time, his continuing control of the army, while making possible the Roman peace, was a crucial source of his power.

The Military Augustus was especially eager to stabilize the military and administrative structures of the Roman Empire. The peace of the empire depended on the army, and so did the security of the *princeps*. While primarily responsible for guarding the frontiers of the empire, the

THE ACHIEVEMENTS OF AUGUSTUS

This excerpt is taken from a text written by Augustus and inscribed on a bronze tablet at Rome. Copies of the text were displayed in stone in many provincial capitals. Called "the most famous ancient inscription," the *Res Gestae* of Augustus summarizes his accomplishments in three major areas: his offices, his private expenditures on behalf of the state, and his exploits in war and peace. Though factual in approach, it is a highly subjective account.

Augustus, *Res Gestae*

Below is a copy of the accomplishments of the deified Augustus by which he brought the whole world under the empire of the Roman people, and of the moneys expended by him on the state and the Roman people, as inscribed on two bronze pillars set up in Rome.

1. At the age of nineteen, on my own initiative and at my own expense, I raised an army by means of which I liberated the Republic, which was oppressed by the tyranny of a faction [Mark Antony and his supporters]....

2. Those who assassinated my father [Julius Caesar, his adoptive father] I drove into exile, avenging their crime by due process of law; and afterwards when they waged war against the state, I conquered them twice on the battlefield.

3. I waged many wars throughout the whole world by land and by sea, both civil and foreign, and when victorious I spared all citizens who sought pardon....

5. The dictatorship offered to me ... by the people and the senate, both in my absence and in my presence, I refused to accept....

17. Four times I came to the assistance of the treasury with my own money, transferring to those in charge of the treasury 150,000,000 sesterces. And in the consulship of Marcus Lepidus and Lucius Arruntius I transferred out of my own patrimony 170,000,000 sesterces to the soldiers' bonus fund, which was established on my advice for the purpose of providing bonuses for soldiers who had completed twenty or more years of service....

22. I gave a gladiatorial show three times in my own name, and five times in the names of my sons or grandsons; at these shows about 10,000 fought....

25. I brought peace to the sea by suppressing the pirates. In that war I turned over to their masters for punishment nearly 30,000 slaves who had run away from their owners and taken up arms against the state....

26. I extended the frontiers of all the provinces of the Roman people on whose boundaries were peoples not subject to our empire....

27. I added Egypt to the empire of the Roman people....

28. I established colonies of soldiers in Africa, Sicily, Macedonia, in both Spanish provinces, in Achaea, Asia, Syria, Narbonese Gaul, and Pisidia. Italy, moreover, has twenty-eight colonies established by me, which in my lifetime have grown to be famous and populous....

35. When I held my thirteenth consulship, the senate, the equestrian order, and the entire Roman people gave me the title of "father of the country."...At the time I wrote this document I was in my seventy-sixth year.

What were the achievements of Augustus? To what extent did these accomplishments create the "job" of being emperor? In what sense could this document be called a piece of propaganda?

army was also used to maintain domestic order within the provinces. Augustus maintained a standing army of twenty-eight legions, or about 150,000 men. Roman legionaries were recruited only from the citizenry and, under Augustus, largely from Italy. Augustus also maintained a large contingent of auxiliary forces—around 130,000—enlisted from the subject peoples. Augustus was also responsible for establishing the **praetorian guard**. Although nominally a military reserve, these "nine cohorts of elite troops," roughly nine thousand men, had the important task of guarding the person of the *princeps*. Eventually the praetorian guard would play a weighty role in making and deposing emperors.

The role of the *princeps* as military commander gave rise to a title by which this ruler eventually came to be known. When victorious, a military commander was acclaimed by his troops as *imperator*. Augustus was so acclaimed on a number of occasions. *Imperator* is our word *emperor*. Although this title was applied to Augustus and his successors, Augustus himself preferred to use the title of *princeps*.

Roman Provinces and Frontiers Augustus inaugurated a new system for governing the provinces. Under the Republic, the senate had appointed the provincial governors. Now certain provinces were allotted to the *princeps*, who assigned deputies known as legates to govern them. These legates were from the senatorial class and held office as long as the emperor chose. The senate continued to designate the governors of the remaining provinces, but the authority of Augustus enabled him to overrule the senatorial governors and establish a uniform imperial policy.

Augustus also stabilized the frontiers of the Roman Empire. He conquered the central and maritime Alps and then expanded Roman control of the Balkan peninsula up to the Danube River. His attempt to conquer Germany failed when three Roman legions under Varus were massacred in A.D. 9 in the Teutoburg Forest by a coalition of German tribes. The defeat severely dampened Augustus' enthusiasm for continued expansion in central Europe. Thereafter, the Romans were content to use the Rhine as the frontier between the Roman province of

Gaul and the German tribes to the east. In fact, Augustus' difficulties had convinced him that "the empire should not be extended beyond its present frontiers."[3] His defeats in Germany taught Augustus that Rome's power was not unlimited. They also left him devastated; for months he beat his head against a door, shouting "Varus, give me back my legions."

Augustan Society

Society in the Early Roman Empire was characterized by a system of social stratification, inherited from the Republic, in which Roman citizens were divided into three basic classes: the senatorial, equestrian, and lower classes. Augustus had accepted the senatorial order as a ruling class for the empire. Senators filled the chief magistracies of the Roman government, held the most important military posts, and governed the provinces. One needed to possess property worth 1 million sesterces (an unskilled laborer in Rome received 3 sesterces a day; a Roman legionary, 900 sesterces a year in pay) to belong to the senatorial order. The equestrian order was open to all Roman citizens of good standing who possessed property valued at 400,000 sesterces. They, too, could now hold military and governmental offices, but the positions open to them were less important than those of the senators.

Citizens not of the senatorial or equestrian order belonged to the lower classes, who made up the overwhelming majority of the free citizens. The diminution of the power of the Roman assemblies ended whatever political power they may have possessed earlier in the Republic. Many of these people were provided with free grain and public spectacles to keep them from creating disturbances. Nevertheless, by gaining wealth and serving as lower officers in the Roman legions, it was sometimes possible for them to advance to the equestrian order.

Augustus' belief that Roman morals had been corrupted during the late Republic led him to initiate social legislation to arrest the decline. He thought that increased luxury had undermined traditional Roman frugality and simplicity and caused a decline in morals, evidenced by easy divorce, a falling birthrate among the upper classes, and lax behavior manifested in hedonistic parties and the love affairs of prominent Romans with fashionable women and elegant boys.

Through his new social legislation, Augustus hoped to restore respectability to the upper classes and reverse the declining birthrate as well. Expenditures for feasts were limited, and other laws made adultery a criminal offense. In fact, Augustus' own daughter Julia was exiled for adultery. Augustus also revised the tax laws to penalize bachelors, widowers, and married persons who had fewer than three children.

The Augustan Age

The Augustan Age was a lengthy one. Augustus died in A.D. 14 after dominating the Roman world for forty-five years. He had created a new order while placating the old by restoring and maintaining traditional values, a fitting combination for a leader whose favorite maxim was "make haste slowly." By the time of his death, his new order was so well established that few agitated for an alternative. Indeed, as the Roman historian Tacitus pointed out, "Actium had been won before the younger men were born. Even most of the older generation had come into a world of civil wars. Practically no one had ever seen truly Republican government. . . . Political equality was a thing of the past; all eyes watched for imperial commands."[4] The Republic was now only a memory and, given its last century of warfare, an unpleasant one at that. The new order was here to stay.

The Early Empire (14–180)

There was no serious opposition to Augustus' choice of his stepson Tiberius as his successor. By designating a family member as *princeps,* Augustus established the Julio-Claudian dynasty; the next four successors of Augustus were related either to his own family or to that of his wife, Livia.

The Julio-Claudians

Several major tendencies emerged during the reigns of the Julio-Claudians (14–68). In general, more and more of the responsibilities that Augustus had given to the senate tended to be taken over by the emperors, who also instituted an imperial bureaucracy, staffed by talented freedmen, to run the government on a daily basis. As the Julio-Claudian successors of Augustus acted more openly as real rulers rather than "first citizens of the state," the opportunity for arbitrary and corrupt acts also increased. Nero (54–68) freely eliminated people he wanted out of the way, including his own mother, whose murder he arranged. Without troops, the senators proved unable to oppose these excesses. However, Nero's extravagances did provoke a revolt of the Roman legions. Abandoned by the guards, Nero chose to commit suicide by stabbing himself in the throat after uttering his final words, "What an artist the world is losing in me." A new civil war erupted in 69, known as the year of the four emperors. The significance of the year 69 was summed up precisely by Tacitus when he stated that "a well-hidden secret of the principate had been revealed: it was possible, it seemed, for an emperor to be chosen outside Rome."[5]

The Five "Good Emperors" (96–180)

At the beginning of the second century, however, a series of five so-called **good emperors** created a period of peace and prosperity that lasted for almost a hundred years. These men treated the ruling classes with respect, cooperated with the senate, ended arbitrary executions, maintained peace throughout the empire, and supported domestic policies generally beneficial to the empire. Though absolute monarchs, they were known for their tolerance and diplomacy. By adopting capable men as their successors, the first four good emperors reduced the chances of succession problems.

Under the five good emperors, the powers of the emperor continued to be extended at the expense of the senate. Increasingly, imperial officials appointed and directed by the emperor took over the running of the government. The good emperors also extended the scope of imperial administration to areas previously untouched by the imperial government. Trajan (98–117) established a program that provided state funds to assist poor parents in raising and educating their children.

The good emperors were widely praised by their subjects for their extensive building programs. Trajan and Hadrian (117–138) were especially active in constructing public works—aqueducts, bridges, roads, and harbor facilities—throughout the provinces and in Rome. Trajan built a new forum in Rome to provide a setting for his celebrated victory column. Hadrian's Pantheon, a temple of "all the gods," is one of the grandest ancient buildings surviving in Rome.

The Roman Empire at Its Height: Frontiers and Provinces

Although Trajan broke with Augustus' policy of defensive imperialism by extending Roman rule into Dacia (modern Romania), Mesopotamia, and the Sinai peninsula, his conquests represent the high-water mark of Roman expansion (see Map 6.1). His successors recognized that the empire was overextended and pursued a policy of retrenchment. Hadrian withdrew Roman forces from much of Mesopotamia. Although he retained Dacia and Arabia, he went on the defensive in his frontier policy by reinforcing the fortifications along a line connecting the Rhine and Danube Rivers and by building a defensive wall 80 miles long to keep the Scots out of Roman Britain.

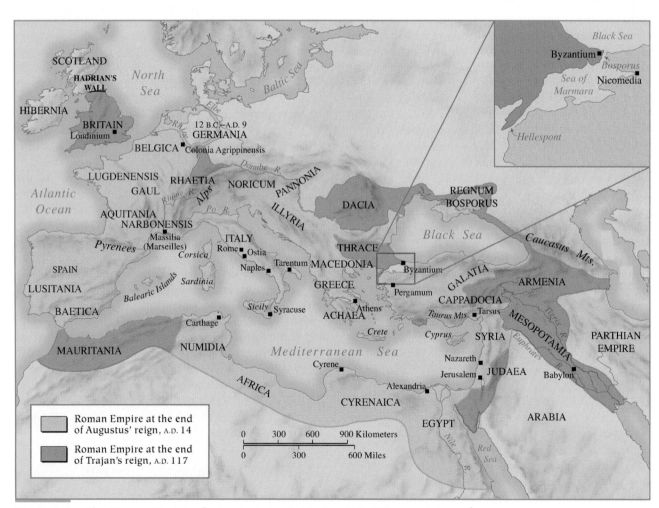

MAP 6.1   The Roman Empire from Augustus to Trajan (14–117). Augustus and later emperors continued the expansion of the Roman Empire, adding more resources but also increasing the tasks of administration and keeping the peace. Compare this map with Map 5.3 ❓ Which territories were conquered by Augustus, and which were added by the end of Trajan's reign? 🖱 **View an animated version of this map or related maps at** http://thomsonedu.com/history/ spielvogel

By the end of the second century, the vulnerability of the empire had become apparent. Frontiers were stabilized, and the Roman forces were established in permanent bases behind the frontiers. But when one frontier was attacked, troops had to be drawn from other frontiers, leaving them vulnerable to attack. The empire lacked a real strategic reserve, and in the next century its weakness would be ever more apparent.

At its height in the second century, the Roman Empire was one of the greatest states the world had seen. It covered about 3.5 million square miles and had a population, like that of Han China, estimated at more than 50 million. While the emperors and the imperial administration provided a degree of unity, considerable leeway was given to local customs, and the privileges of Roman citizenship were extended to many people throughout the empire. In 212, the emperor Caracalla completed the process by giving Roman citizenship to every free inhabitant of the empire. Latin was the language of the western part of the empire, while Greek was used in the east. Although Roman culture spread to all parts of the empire, there were limits to Romanization because local languages persisted and many of the empire's residents spoke neither Latin nor Greek.

The Importance of Cities   The administration and cultural life of the Roman Empire depended greatly on cities and towns. A provincial governor's staff was not large, so local city officials were expected to act as Roman agents in carrying out many government functions, especially those related to taxes. Most towns and cities were not large by modern standards. The biggest was Rome, but there were also some large cities in the east: Alexandria in Egypt numbered over 300,000 inhabitants, Ephesus in Asia Minor had 200,000, Antioch in Syria around 150,000. In the west, cities were usually small, with only a few thousand inhabitants. Cities were important in the spread of Roman culture, law, and the Latin language. They were also uniform in physical appearance with similar temples, markets, amphitheaters, and other public buildings.

Magistrates and town councillors chosen from the ranks of the wealthy upper classes directed municipal administration. These municipal offices were unsalaried but were nevertheless desired by wealthy citizens because they received prestige and power at the local level as well as Roman citizenship. Roman municipal policy effectively tied the upper classes to Roman rule and ensured that these classes would retain control over the rest of the population.

The process of Romanization in the provinces was reflected in significant changes in the governing classes of the empire. In the course of the first century, there was a noticeable decline in the number of senators from Italian families. Increasingly, the Roman senate was being recruited from wealthy provincial equestrian families. The provinces also provided many of the legionaries for the Roman army and, beginning with Trajan, supplied many of the emperors.

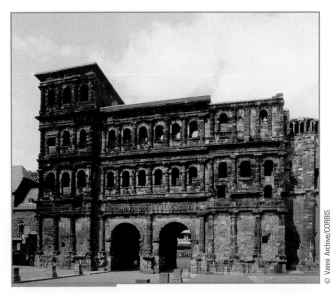

Rome in Germany.   The Roman army helped bring Roman culture and institutions to the provinces. Local production and trade grew up around the military camps to meet the soldiers' needs, and cities often developed from the bases themselves or from colonies located nearby. Pictured are the remains of the Porta Nigra, the gateway to the Roman city of Augusta Treverorum (modern Trier). In the Early Empire, Trier became the headquarters of the imperial procurator of Belgica and the two Germanies. Its close location to Roman military camps along the Rhine enabled it to flourish as one of the major cities in the western Roman Empire.

Prosperity in the Early Empire

The Early Empire was a period of considerable prosperity. Internal peace resulted in unprecedented levels of trade (see Map 6.2). Merchants from all over the empire came to the chief Italian ports of Puteoli on the Bay of Naples and Ostia at the mouth of the Tiber. Trade extended beyond the Roman boundaries and included even silk goods from China. The importation of large quantities of grain to feed the people of Rome and an incredible quantity of luxury items for the wealthy upper classes in the west led to a steady drain of gold and silver coins from Italy and the west to the eastern part of the empire.

Increased trade helped stimulate manufacturing. The cities of the east still produced the items made in Hellenistic times. The first two centuries of the empire also witnessed the high point of industrial development in Italy. Some industries became concentrated in certain areas, such as bronze work in Capua and pottery in Arretium in Etruria. Other industries, such as brickmaking, were pursued in rural areas on large landed estates. Much production remained small-scale and was done by individual craftsmen, usually freedmen or slaves. In the course of the first century, Italian centers of industry began to experience increasing competition from the provinces.

Despite the extensive trade and commerce, agriculture remained the chief occupation of most people and the underlying basis of Roman prosperity. While the large

MAP 6.2 Trade Routes and Products in the Roman Empire, c. 200. Although still primarily an agrarian economy, the Roman Empire provided the single currency and stable conditions necessary for an expansion of trade in various commodities and products. [?] An extensive system of roads and shipping routes also facilitated trade. What truth is there to the statement "All roads lead to Rome"? [icon] **View an animated version of this map or related maps at** http://thomsonedu.com/history/spielvogel

landed estates called *latifundia* still dominated agriculture, especially in southern and central Italy, small peasant farms persisted, particularly in Etruria and the Po valley. Although large estates concentrating on sheep and cattle raising used slaves, the lands of some *latifundia* were worked by free tenant farmers who paid rent in labor, produce, or sometimes cash.

In considering the prosperity of the Roman world, it is important to remember the enormous gulf between rich and poor (see the box on p. 103.). The development

Roman Trade. Trade was an important ingredient in the prosperity of the Early Empire. This third-century A.D. Roman mosaic from Sousse, Tunisia, shows workers unloading a cargo of iron ore from a ship.

THE DAILY LIFE OF AN UPPER-CLASS ROMAN

There was an enormous gulf between rich and poor in Roman society. The upper classes lived lives of great leisure and luxury in their villas and on their vast estates. Pliny the Younger (c. 62–c. 113) was an upper-class Roman who rose to the position of governor of Bithynia in Asia Minor. In this excerpt from one of his letters, Pliny describes a typical day vacationing at one of his Italian villas. Although Pliny owned four villas in Italy, he did not belong to the ranks of the really rich in Roman society.

Pliny, Letter to Fuscus Salinator

You want to know how I plan the summer days I spend in Tuscany. I wake when I like, usually about sunrise, often earlier but rarely later. My shutters stay closed, for in the stillness and darkness I feel myself surprisingly detached from any distractions and left to myself in freedom. . . . If I have anything on hand I work it out in my head, choosing and correcting the wording, and the amount I achieve depends on the ease or difficulty with which my thoughts can be marshaled and kept in my head. Then I call my secretary, the shutters are opened, and I dictate what I have put into shape; he goes out, is recalled, and again dismissed. Three or four hours after I first wake (but I don't keep to fixed times) I betake myself according to the weather either to the terrace or the covered arcade, work out the rest of my subject, and dictate it. I go for a drive, and spend the time in the same way as when walking or lying down; my powers of concentration do not flag and are in fact refreshed by the change. After a short sleep and another walk I read a Greek or Latin speech aloud and with emphasis, not so much for the sake of my voice as my digestion, though of course both are strengthened by this. Then I have another walk, am oiled, take exercise, and have a bath. If I am dining alone with my wife or with a few friends, a book is read aloud during the meal and afterward we listen to a comedy or some music; then I walk again with the members of my household, some of whom are educated. Thus the evening is prolonged with varied conversations, and even when the days are at their longest, comes to a satisfying end.

Sometimes I vary this routine, for, if I have spent a long time on my couch or taking a walk, after my siesta and reading I go out on horseback instead of a carriage so as to be quicker and take less time. Part of the day is given up to friends who visit me from neighboring towns and sometimes come to my aid with a welcome interruption when I am tired. Occasionally I go hunting, but not without my notebooks so that I shall have something to bring home even if I catch nothing. I also give some time to my tenants (they think it should be more) and the boorishness of their complaints gives fresh zest to our literary interests and the more civilized pursuits of town.

What does Pliny's letter tell you about the lifestyle of upper-class Romans? Could this lifestyle be related to the decline of the Roman Empire?

---

of towns and cities, so important to the creation of any civilization, is based in large degree on the agricultural surpluses of the countryside. In ancient times, the margin of surplus produced by each farmer was relatively small. Therefore, the upper classes and urban populations had to be supported by the labor of a large number of farmers who never found it easy to produce much more than for themselves. In lean years, when there were no surpluses, the townspeople often took what they wanted, leaving little for the peasants.

Roman Culture and Society in the Early Empire

The high point of Latin literature was reached in the time of Augustus. The literary accomplishments of the Augustan Age were such that the period has been called the golden age of Latin literature.

The Golden Age of Latin Literature

The most distinguished poet of the Augustan Age was Virgil (70–19 B.C.). The son of a small landholder in northern Italy, he welcomed the rule of Augustus and wrote his greatest work in the emperor's honor. Virgil's masterpiece was the *Aeneid*, an epic poem clearly meant to rival the work of Homer. The connection between Troy and Rome is made explicitly. Aeneas, the son of Anchises of Troy, survives the destruction of Troy and eventually settles in Latium; hence Roman civilization is linked to Greek history. The character of Aeneas is portrayed as the ideal Roman—his virtues are duty, piety, and faithfulness. Virgil's overall purpose was to show that Aeneas had fulfilled his mission to establish the Romans in Italy and thereby start Rome on its divine mission to rule the world.

> Let others fashion from bronze more lifelike, breathing images—
> For so they shall—and evoke living faces from marble;
> Others excel as orators, others track with their instruments
> The planets circling in heaven and predict when stars will appear.
> But, Romans, never forget that government is your medium!
> Be this your art:—to practise men in the habit of peace,
> Generosity to the conquered, and firmness against aggressors[6]

OVID AND THE ART OF LOVE

*O*vid has been called the last great poet of the Augustan golden age of literature. One of his most famous works was *The Art of Love,* a guidebook for the seduction of women. Unfortunately for Ovid, the work appeared at a time when Augustus was anxious to improve the morals of the Roman upper class. Augustus considered the work offensive, and Ovid soon found himself in exile.

Ovid, *The Art of Love*

Now I'll teach you how to captivate and hold the woman of your choice. This is the most important part of all my lessons. Lovers of every land, lend an attentive ear to my discourse; let goodwill warm your hearts, for I am going to fulfill the promises I made you.

First of all, be quite sure that there isn't a woman who cannot be won, and make up your mind that you will win her. Only you must prepare the ground. Sooner would the birds cease their song in the springtime, or the grasshopper be silent in the summer,...than a woman resist the tender wooing of a youthful lover....

Now the first thing you have to do is to get on good terms with the fair one's maid. She can make things easy for you. Find out whether she is fully in her mistress's confidence, and if she knows all about her secret dissipations. Leave no stone unturned to win her over. Once you have her on your side, the rest is easy....

In the first place, it's best to send her a letter, just to pave the way. In it you should tell her how you dote on her; pay her beauty compliments and say all the nice things lovers always say....Even the gods are moved by the voice of entreaty. And promise, promise, promise. Promises will cost you nothing. Everyone's a millionaire where promises are concerned....

If she refuses your letter and sends it back unread, don't give up; hope for the best and try again....

Don't let your hair stick up in tufts on your head; see that your hair and your beard are decently trimmed. See also that your nails are clean and nicely filed; don't have any hair growing out of your nostrils; take care that your breath is sweet, and don't go about reeking like a billy-goat. All other toilet refinements leave to the women or to perverts....

When you find yourself at a feast where the wine is flowing freely, and where a woman shares the same couch with you, pray to that god whose mysteries are celebrated during the night, that the wine may not overcloud your brain. 'Tis then you may easily hold converse with your mistress in hidden words whereof she will easily divine the meaning....

By subtle flatteries you may be able to steal into her heart, even as the river insensibly overflows the banks which fringe it. Never cease to sing the praises of her face, her hair, her taper fingers and her dainty foot....

Tears, too, are a mighty useful resource in the matter of love. They would melt a diamond. Make a point, therefore, of letting your mistress see your face all wet with tears.

Howbeit, if you can't manage to squeeze out any tears—and they won't always flow just when you want them to—put your finger in your eyes.

What were Ovid's principles of love? Why do you think Augustus found The Art of Love *so offensive?*

As Virgil expressed it, ruling was Rome's gift.

Another prominent Augustan poet was Horace (65–8 B.C.), a friend of Virgil's. Horace was a sophisticated writer whose overriding concern was to point out to his contemporaries the "follies and vices of his age." In the *Satires,* a medley of poems on a variety of subjects, Horace is revealed as a detached observer of human weaknesses. He directed his attacks against movements, not living people, and took on such subjects as sexual immorality, greed, and job dissatisfaction ("How does it happen, Maecenas, that no man alone is content with his lot?"). Horace mostly laughs at the weaknesses of humankind and calls for forbearance: "Supposing my friend has got liquored and wetted my couch,...is he for such a lapse to be deemed less dear as a friend, or because when hungry he snatched up before me a chicken from my side of the dish?"[7]

Ovid (43 B.C.–A.D. 18) was the last of the great poets of the golden age. He belonged to a youthful, privileged social group in Rome that liked to ridicule old Roman values. In keeping with the spirit of this group, Ovid wrote a frivolous series of love poems known as the *Amores.* Intended to entertain and shock, they achieved their goal.

Another of Ovid's works was *The Art of Love.* This was essentially a takeoff on didactic poems. Whereas authors of earlier didactic poems had written guides to farming, hunting, or some such subject, Ovid's work was a handbook on the seduction of women (see the box above).

The most famous Latin prose work of the golden age was written by the historian Livy (59 B.C.–A.D. 17). Livy's masterpiece was his *History of Rome* from the foundation of the city to 9 B.C. Only 35 of the original 142 books have survived, although we do possess brief summaries of the whole work from other authors. Livy perceived history in terms of moral lessons. He stated in the preface that

> the study of history is the best medicine for a sick mind; for in history you have a record of the infinite variety of human experience plainly set out for all to see; and in that record you can find for yourself and your country both examples and warnings: fine things to take as models, base things, rotten through and through, to avoid.[8]

For Livy, human character was the determining factor in history.

Livy's history celebrated Rome's greatness. He built scene upon scene that not only revealed the character of the chief figures but also demonstrated the virtues that had made Rome great. Of course, he had serious weaknesses as a historian. He was not always concerned about the factual accuracy of his stories. But he was an excellent storyteller, and his work remained the standard history of Rome for centuries.

The Silver Age of Latin Literature

In the history of Latin literature, the century and a half after Augustus is often labeled the "silver age" to indicate that the literary efforts of the period, though good, were not equal to the high standards of the Augustan golden age. The popularity of rhetorical training encouraged the use of clever literary expressions at the expense of original content. A good example of this trend can be found in the works of Seneca.

Educated in Rome, Seneca (c. 4 B.C.–A.D. 65) became strongly attached to the philosophy of Stoicism. In letters written to a young friend, he expressed the basic tenets of Stoicism: living according to nature, accepting events dispassionately as part of the divine plan, and universal love for all humanity. Thus "the first thing philosophy promises us is the feeling of fellowship, of belonging to mankind and being members of a community. . . . Philosophy calls for simple living, not for doing penance, and the simple way of life need not be a crude one."[9] Viewed in retrospect, Seneca displays some glaring inconsistencies. While preaching the virtues of simplicity, he amassed a fortune and was ruthless at times in protecting it. His letters show humanity, benevolence, and fortitude, but his sentiments are often undermined by an attempt to be clever with words.

The greatest historian of the silver age was Tacitus (c. 56–120). His main works included the *Annals* and *Histories,* which presented a narrative account of Roman history from the reign of Tiberius through the assassination of Domitian (14–96). Tacitus believed that history had a moral purpose: "It seems to me a historian's foremost duty to ensure that merit is recorded, and to confront evil deeds and words with the fear of posterity's denunciations."[10] As a member of the senatorial class, Tacitus was disgusted with the abuses of power perpetrated by the emperors and was determined that the "evil deeds" of wicked men would not be forgotten. Many historians believe he went too far in projecting the evils of his own day into his account of the past. His work *Germania* is especially important as a source of information about the early Germans. But it too is colored by Tacitus' attempt to show the Germans as noble savages in comparison with the decadent Romans.

Roman Law

The Early Empire experienced great progress in the study and codification of the law. The second and early third centuries A.D. witnessed the "classical age of Roman law," a period in which a number of great jurists classified and compiled basic legal principles that have proved extremely valuable to the Western world. Most jurists emphasized the emperor as the source of law: "What has pleased the emperor has the force of law."

In the "classical age of Roman law," the identification of the law of nations with natural law led to a concept of natural rights. According to the jurist Ulpian (d. 228), natural rights implied that all men are born equal and should therefore be equal before the law. In practice, however, that principle was not applied. The Romans did, however, establish standards of justice applicable to all people, many of which we would immediately recognize. A person was regarded as innocent until proved otherwise. People accused of wrongdoing were allowed to defend themselves before a judge. A judge was expected to weigh evidence carefully before arriving at a decision. These principles lived on in Western civilization long after the fall of the Roman Empire.

The Upper-Class Roman Family

By the second century A.D., significant changes were occurring in the Roman family. The foundations of the authority of the *paterfamilias* over his family, which had already begun to weaken in the late Republic, were further undermined. The *paterfamilias* no longer had absolute authority over his children; he could no longer sell his children into slavery or have them put to death. Moreover, the husband's absolute authority over his wife also disappeared, a process that had begun in the late Republic. In the Early Empire, the idea of male guardianship continued to weaken significantly, and by the late second century had become a formality.

Upper-class Roman women in the Early Empire had considerable freedom and independence. They had acquired the right to own, inherit, and dispose of property. Upper-class women could attend races, the theater, and events in the amphitheater, although in the latter two places they were forced to sit in sections apart from the men. Moreover, ladies of rank were still accompanied by maids and companions when they went out. Some women operated businesses, such as shipping firms. Women could still not participate in politics, but the Early Empire saw a number of important women who influenced politics through their husbands, including Livia, the wife of Augustus; Agrippina, the mother of Nero; and Plotina, the wife of Trajan.

Imperial Rome

At the center of the colossal Roman Empire was the ancient city of Rome (see Map 6.3). Truly a capital city, Rome had the largest population of any city in the empire. It is estimated that its population was close to one million by the time of Augustus. For anyone with ambitions, Rome was the place to be. A magnet to many people, Rome was extremely cosmopolitan. Nationalities from all over the

MAP 6.3 **Imperial Rome.** A large, overcrowded, and dirty city, Rome was the political, economic, social, and cultural hub of the Roman Empire. Squalid and desperate living conditions for the poor contrasted dramatically with the city's magnificent architectural works. ❓ How did roads from outside enter Rome, and what might explain this? 🔵 **View an animated version of this map or related maps at** http://thomsonedu.com/history/ spielvogel

empire resided there, with entire neighborhoods inhabited by specific groups, such as Greeks and Syrians.

Rome was an overcrowded and noisy city. Because of the congestion, cart and wagon traffic was banned from the streets during the day. The noise from the resulting vehicular movement at night often made sleep difficult. Evening pedestrian travel was dangerous. Although Augustus had organized a police force, lone travelers could be assaulted, robbed, or soaked by filth thrown out of the upper-story windows of Rome's massive apartment buildings.

An enormous gulf existed between rich and poor in the city of Rome. While the rich had comfortable villas, the poor lived in apartment blocks called *insulae,* which might be six stories high. Constructed of concrete, they were often poorly built and prone to collapse. The use of wooden beams in the floors and movable stoves, torches, candles, and lamps within the rooms for heat and light made the danger of fire constant. Once started, fires were extremely difficult to put out. The famous conflagration of 64, which Nero was unjustly accused of starting, devastated a good part of the city. Besides the hazards of collapse and fire, living conditions were also poor. High rents forced entire families into one room. The absence of plumbing and central heating made life so uncomfortable that poorer Romans spent most of their time outdoors in the streets.

Fortunately for these people, Rome boasted public buildings unequaled anywhere in the empire. Its temples, forums, markets, baths, theaters, triumphal arches, governmental buildings, and amphitheaters gave parts of the city an appearance of grandeur and magnificence.

Though the center of a great empire, Rome was also a great parasite. Beginning with Augustus, the emperors accepted responsibility for providing food for the urban populace, with about 200,000 people receiving free grain.

Even with the free grain, conditions were grim for the poor. Early in the second century, a Roman doctor noted that rickets was common among children in the city.

In addition to food, entertainment was provided on a grand scale for the inhabitants of Rome. The poet Juvenal said of the Roman masses, "But nowadays, with no vote to sell, their motto is 'Couldn't care less.' Time was when their plebiscite elected generals, heads of state, commanders of legions: but now they've pulled in their horns, there's only two things that concern them: Bread and Circuses."[11] Public spectacles were provided by the emperor and other state officials as part of the great festivals—most of them religious in origin—celebrated by the state. More than one hundred days a year were given over to these public holidays. The festivals included three major types of entertainment. At the Circus Maximus, horse and chariot races attracted hundreds of thousands of spectators, while dramatic and other performances were held in theaters. But the most famous of all the public spectacles were the gladiatorial shows.

The Gladiatorial Shows

The gladiatorial shows were an integral part of Roman society. They took place in amphitheaters, the first permanent one of which had been constructed at Rome in 29 B.C. Perhaps the most famous was the Flavian amphitheater, called the Colosseum, which could seat fifty thousand spectators. Similar amphitheaters were built throughout the empire, with capacities ranging from a few thousand to tens of thousands. In most cities and towns, the amphitheaters were the biggest buildings, rivaled only by the circuses for races and the public baths. Where a society invests its money gives an idea of its

The Gladiatorial Games. Although some gladiators were free men enticed by the possibility of rewards, most were condemned criminals, slaves, or prisoners of war who were trained in special schools. A great gladiator could win his freedom through the games. This mosaic from the fourth century A.D. depicts different aspects of gladiatorial fighting and clearly shows the bloody nature of the games.

priorities. Since the amphitheater was the primary location for the gladiatorial games, it is fair to say that public slaughter was an important part of Roman culture.

Gladiatorial games were held from dawn to dusk. Contests to the death between trained fighters formed the central focus of these games. Most gladiators were slaves or condemned criminals and were trained for combat in special gladiatorial schools.

Gladiatorial games included other forms of entertainment as well. Criminals of all ages and both sexes were sent into the arena without weapons to face certain death from wild animals who would tear them to pieces. Numerous kinds of animal contests were also staged: wild beasts against each other, such as bears against buffaloes; staged hunts with men shooting safely from behind iron bars; and gladiators in the arena with bulls, tigers, and lions. Reportedly, five thousand beasts were killed in one day of games when the emperor Titus inaugurated the Colosseum in A.D. 80. Enormous resources were invested in the capture and shipment of wild animals for slaughter, and whole species were hunted to extinction in parts of the empire.

These bloodthirsty spectacles were wildly popular with the Roman people. The Roman historian Tacitus said, "Few indeed are to be found who talk of any other subjects in their homes, and whenever we enter a classroom, what else is the conversation of the youths."[12] But the gladiatorial games served a purpose beyond mere entertainment. Like the other forms of public entertainment, they fulfilled both a political and a social need by diverting thoughts of the idle masses from political unrest. It was said of the emperor Trajan that he understood that although the distribution of grain and money satisfied the individual, spectacles were necessary for the "contentment of the masses."

Transformation of the Roman World: Crises in the Third Century

At the end of the second century, a number of natural catastrophes struck Rome. Floods of the Tiber, famine, and plague brought back from the east by the army led to considerable loss of population and a shortage of military manpower. To many Romans, these natural disasters seemed to portend an ominous future for Rome, and indeed, in the course of the third century, the Roman Empire came near to collapse.

Political and Military Woes

After a series of civil wars, Septimius Severus (193–211), who was born in North Africa and spoke Latin with an accent, used his legions to seize power. On his deathbed, Septimius Severus advised his sons, "Live in harmony, make the soldiers rich, and don't give a damn for anything else." His advice set the tone for the new dynasty he established. The Severan rulers (193–235) began to create a military monarchy. The army was expanded, soldiers' pay was increased, and military officers were appointed to important government positions. A new stability seemed at hand, but the increased power of the military led new military leaders to aspire to become emperor, and the military monarchy of the Severan rulers degenerated into military anarchy.

For the next fifty years (235–284), the empire was mired in the chaos of continual civil war. Contenders for the imperial throne found that bribing soldiers was an effective way to become emperor. In these five decades, there were twenty-two emperors, only two of whom did

Septimius Severus and His Family. This portrait painted on wood about A.D. 200, found in Egypt, is the only existing painted likeness of a Roman emperor. The emperor is portrayed with gray hair and beard in memory of Marcus Aurelius. To legitimize his authority, Septimius Severus had himself adopted into the Antonine dynasty, calling himself the son of Marcus Aurelius. The emperor stands next to his wife with their two sons in front of them. The face of his son Geta has been blotted out, no doubt by order of the other son standing next to him, Caracalla, who had his brother killed when he succeeded to the throne.

not meet a violent end. At the same time, the empire was beset by a series of invasions, no doubt encouraged by the internal turmoil. In the east, the Sassanid Persians made inroads into Roman territory. A fitting symbol of Rome's crisis was the capture of the Roman emperor, Valerian (253–260), by the Persians and his death in captivity, an event unprecedented in Roman history. Valerian's body was displayed in the chief towns of Persia. Germanic tribes also poured into the empire. The Goths overran the Balkans and moved into Greece and Asia Minor. The Franks advanced into Gaul and Spain. Not until the reign of Aurelian (270–275) were most of the boundaries restored. Although he abandoned the Danubian province of Dacia, Aurelian reconquered Gaul and reestablished order in the east and along the Danube. Grateful citizens hailed him as "restorer of the world."

As civil wars and invasion wore down the central government, provinces began to break away from the empire. A military commander named Postumus seized control of Gaul and then gained the support of Britain and Spain. He defended his "Gallic empire" until he was killed by his own soldiers in 269. In the east, Zenobia, the wife of the ruler of Syria, seized power after his death and then in 270 extended her control over Egypt and much of Asia Minor. In 272, Emperor Aurelian ended this threat to imperial power by defeating Zenobia and her forces in Syria.

Economic and Social Crises

Invasions, civil wars, and plague came close to causing an economic collapse of the Roman Empire in the third century. The population declined drastically, possibly by as much as one-third. There was a noticeable decline in trade and small industry. The labor shortage created by plague affected both military recruiting and the economy. Farm production deteriorated significantly. Fields were ravaged by Germanic tribes and even more often by the defending Roman armies. Many farmers complained that Roman commanders and their soldiers were confiscating produce and livestock. Provincial governors seemed powerless to stop these depredations, and some even joined in the extortion. The monetary system began to show signs of collapse as a result of debased coinage and the beginnings of serious inflation.

Armies were needed more than ever, but financial strains made it difficult to enlist and pay the necessary soldiers. Short of cash, the imperial government paid its soldiers with produce, causing bitter resentment. Whereas in the second century the Roman army had been recruited among the inhabitants of frontier provinces, by the mid-third century the state had to rely on hiring barbarians to fight under Roman commanders. These soldiers had no understanding of Roman traditions and no real attachment to either the empire or the emperors. By the end of the third century, a new political structure would emerge (see Chapter 7).

Transformation of the Roman World: The Rise of Christianity

The advent of Christianity marks a fundamental break with the dominant values of the Greco-Roman world. Christian views of God, human beings, and the world were quite different from those of the Greeks and Romans. Nevertheless, to understand the rise of Christianity, we must first examine both the religious environment of the Roman world and the Jewish background from which Christianity emerged.

The Religious World of the Roman Empire

Augustus had taken a number of steps to revive the Roman state religion, which had declined during the turmoil of the late Republic. The official state religion focused on the worship of a pantheon of gods and goddesses. Observance of proper ritual by state priests theoretically established the proper relationship between Romans and the gods and guaranteed security, peace, and prosperity. The polytheistic Romans were extremely tolerant of other religions. The Romans allowed the worship of native gods and goddesses throughout their provinces and even adopted some of the local gods. In addition, the imperial cult of Rome and Augustus was developed to bolster support for the emperors. After Augustus, deceased emperors deified by the Roman senate were included in the official imperial cult.

The desire for a more emotional spiritual experience led many people to the mystery religions of the Hellenistic east, which flooded into the western Roman world during the Early Empire. The mystery religions offered secret teachings that promised their followers advantages unavailable through Roman religion: an entry into a higher world of reality and the promise of a future life superior to the present one. They also featured elaborate rituals with deep emotional appeal. By participating in their ceremonies and performing their rites, an adherent could achieve communion with spiritual beings and undergo purification that opened the door to life after death.

Although many mystery cults competed for the attention of the Roman world, perhaps the most important was Mithraism. Mithras was the chief agent of Ahuramazda, the supreme god of light in Persian Zoroastrianism (see Chapter 2). In the Roman world, Mithras came to be identified with the sun god and was known by his Roman title, the Unconquered Sun. Mithraism had spread rapidly in Rome and the western provinces by the second century A.D. and was especially favored by soldiers, who viewed Mithras as their patron deity. Mithraists paid homage to the sun on the first day of the week (Sunday), commemorated the sun's birthday around December 25, and celebrated ceremonial meals. All of these practices had parallels in Christianity.

The Jewish Background

In Hellenistic times, the Jewish people had been granted considerable independence by their Seleucid rulers (see Chapter 4). Roman involvement with the Jews began in 63 B.C., and by A.D. 6, Judaea had been made a province and placed under the direction of a Roman procurator. But unrest continued, augmented by divisions among the Jews themselves. The Sadducees favored a rigid adherence to Hebrew law, rejected the possibility of personal immortality, and favored cooperation with the Romans. The Pharisees followed a strict adherence to Jewish ritual, and although they wanted Judaea to be free from Roman control, they did not advocate violent means to achieve this goal. The Essenes were a Jewish sect that lived in a religious community near the Dead Sea. As revealed in the Dead Sea Scrolls, a collection of documents first discovered in 1947, the Essenes, like many other Jews, awaited a Messiah who would save Israel from oppression, usher in the kingdom of God, and establish a true paradise on earth. A fourth group, the Zealots, were militant extremists who advocated the violent overthrow of Roman rule. A Jewish revolt in A.D. 66 was crushed by the Romans four years later. The Jewish Temple in Jerusalem was destroyed, and Roman power once more stood supreme in Judaea.

The Origins of Christianity

In the midst of the confusion and conflict in Judaea, Jesus of Nazareth (c. 6 B.C.–A.D. 30) began his public preaching. Jesus grew up in Galilee, an important center of the militant Zealots. Jesus' message was straightforward. He reassured his fellow Jews that he did not plan to undermine their traditional religion: "Do not think that I have come to abolish the Law or the Prophets; I have not come to abolish them but to fulfill them."[13] According to Jesus, what was important was not strict adherence to the letter of the law and attention to rules and prohibitions but the transformation of the inner person: "So in everything, do to others what you would have them do to you, for this sums up the Law and the Prophets."[14] God's command was simple—to love God and one another: "Love the Lord your God with all your heart and with all your soul and with all your mind and with all your strength. The second is this: Love your neighbor as yourself."[15] In the Sermon on the Mount (see the box on p. 110), Jesus presented the ethical concepts—humility, charity, and brotherly love—that would form the basis for the value system of medieval Western civilization. As we have seen, these were not the values of classical Greco-Roman civilization.

Although some Jews welcomed Jesus as the Messiah who would save Israel from oppression and establish God's kingdom on earth, Jesus spoke of a heavenly kingdom, not an earthly one: "My kingdom is not of this world."[16] In this he disappointed the radicals. At the same time, conservative religious leaders believed that Jesus was another false Messiah who was undermining respect for traditional Jewish religion. To the Roman authorities of Palestine and their local allies, the Nazarene was a potential revolutionary who might transform Jewish expectations of a messianic kingdom into a revolt against Rome. Jesus thus found himself denounced on many sides and was given over to the Roman authorities. The procurator Pontius Pilate ordered his crucifixion. But

CHRISTIAN IDEALS: THE SERMON ON THE MOUNT

*C*hristianity was one of many religions competing for attention in the Roman Empire during the first and second centuries. The rise of Christianity marked a fundamental break with the value system of the upper-class elites who dominated the world of classical antiquity. As these excerpts from the Sermon on the Mount in the Gospel of Matthew illustrate, Christians emphasized humility, charity, brotherly love, and a belief in the inner being and a spiritual kingdom superior to this material world. These values and principles were not those of classical Greco-Roman civilization as exemplified in the words and deeds of its leaders.

The Gospel According to Matthew

Now when he saw the crowds, he went up on a mountainside and sat down. His disciples came to him, and he began to teach them saying:

> *Blessed are the poor in spirit: for theirs is the kingdom of heaven.*
>
> *Blessed are those who mourn: for they will be comforted.*
>
> *Blessed are the meek: for they will inherit the earth.*
>
> *Blessed are those who hunger and thirst for righteousness: for they will be filled.*
>
> *Blessed are the merciful: for they will be shown mercy.*
>
> *Blessed are the pure in heart: for they will see God.*
>
> *Blessed are the peacemakers: for they will be called sons of God.*
>
> *Blessed are those who are persecuted because of righteousness for theirs is the kingdom of heaven....*

You have heard that it was said, "Eye for eye, and tooth for tooth." But I tell you, Do not resist an evil person. If someone strikes you on the right cheek, turn to him the other also....

You have heard that it was said, "Love your neighbor, and hate your enemy." But I tell you, Love your enemies and pray for those who persecute you....

Do not store up for yourselves treasures on earth, where moth and rust destroy, and where thieves break in and steal. But store up for yourselves treasures in heaven, where moth and rust do not destroy, and where thieves do not break in and steal. For where your treasure is, there your heart will be also....

No one can serve two masters. Either he will hate the one and love the other, or he will be devoted to the one and despise the other. You cannot serve both God and Money.

Therefore I tell you, do not worry about your life, what you will eat or drink; or about your body, what you will wear. Is not life more important than food, and the body more important than clothes? Look at the birds of the air; they do not sow or reap to store away in barns, and yet your heavenly Father feeds them. Are you not much more valuable than they?...So do not worry, saying, What shall we eat? or What shall we drink? or What shall we wear? For the pagans run after all these things, and your heavenly Father knows that you need them. But seek first his kingdom and his righteousness, and all these things will be given to you as well.

What were the ideals of early Christianity? How do they differ from the values and principles of classical Greco-Roman civilization?

---

that did not solve the problem. A few loyal disciples spread the story that Jesus had overcome death, had been resurrected, and had then ascended into heaven. The belief in Jesus' resurrection became an important tenet of Christian doctrine. Jesus was now hailed by his followers as the "anointed one" (*Christos* in Greek), the Messiah who would return and usher in the kingdom of God on earth.

The Importance of Paul   Christianity began, then, as a religious movement within Judaism and was viewed that way by Roman authorities for many decades. Although tradition holds that one of Jesus' disciples, Peter, founded the Christian church at Rome, the most important figure in early Christianity after Jesus was Paul of Tarsus (c. 5–c. 67). Paul reached out to non-Jews and transformed Christianity from a Jewish sect into a broader religious movement.

Called the "second founder of Christianity," Paul was a Jewish Roman citizen who had been strongly influenced by Hellenistic Greek culture. He believed that the message of Jesus should be preached not only to Jews but to Gentiles (non-Jews) as well. Paul was responsible for founding Christian communities throughout Asia Minor and along the shores of the Aegean.

It was Paul who provided a universal foundation for the spread of Jesus' ideas. He taught that Jesus was, in effect, a savior-God, the son of God, who had come to earth to save all humans who were basically sinners as a result of Adam's original sin of disobedience against God. By his death, Jesus had atoned for the sins of all humans and made it possible for all men and women to experience a new beginning with the potential for individual salvation. By accepting Jesus Christ as their Savior, they too could be saved.

The Spread of Christianity   At first, Christianity spread slowly. Although the teachings of early Christianity were mostly disseminated by the preaching of convinced Christians, written materials also appeared. Paul had written a series of letters, or epistles, outlining Christian

Jesus and His Apostles. Pictured is a fourth-century fresco from a Roman catacomb depicting Jesus and his apostles. Catacombs were underground cemeteries where early Christians buried their dead. Christian tradition holds that in times of imperial repression, Christians withdrew to the catacombs to pray and even hide.

beliefs for different Christian communities. Some of Jesus' disciples may also have preserved some of the sayings of the master in writing and would have passed on personal memories that became the basis of the written gospels—the "good news" concerning Jesus—which attempted to provide a record of Jesus' life and teachings and formed the core of the New Testament, the Christian Bible. Although Jerusalem was the first center of Christianity, its destruction by the Romans in A.D. 70 left individual Christian churches with considerable independence. By 100, Christian churches had been established in most of the major cities of the east and in some places in the western part of the empire. Many early Christians came from the ranks of Hellenized Jews and the Greek-speaking populations of the east. But in the second and third centuries, an increasing number of followers came from Latin-speaking people. A Latin translation of the Greek New Testament that appeared soon after 200 aided this process.

Although some of the fundamental values of Christianity differed markedly from those of the Greco-Roman world, the Romans initially did not pay much attention to the Christians, whom they regarded at first as simply another sect of Judaism. The structure of the Roman Empire itself aided the growth of Christianity. Christian missionaries, including some of Jesus' original twelve disciples, or apostles, used Roman roads to travel throughout the empire spreading their "good news."

As the popular appeal of Christianity grew, the Roman attitude toward it began to change. The Romans were tolerant of other religions except when they threatened public order or public morals. Many Romans came to view Christians as harmful to the order of the Roman state. Because Christians held their meetings in secret and seemed to be connected to Christian groups in distant areas, the government could view them as potentially dangerous to the state.

Some Romans felt that Christians were overly exclusive and hence harmful to the community and public order. The Christians did not recognize other gods and therefore abstained from public festivals honoring these divinities. Finally, Christians refused to participate in the worship of the state gods and the imperial cult. Since the Romans regarded these as important to the state, the Christians' refusal undermined the security of the state and hence constituted an act of treason, punishable by death. But to the Christians, who believed there was only one real God, the worship of state gods and the emperors was idolatry and would endanger their own salvation.

Roman persecution of Christians in the first and second centuries was never systematic but sporadic and local. Persecution began during the reign of Nero. After the fire that destroyed much of Rome, the emperor used the Christians as scapegoats, accusing them of arson and hatred of the human race and subjecting them to cruel deaths in Rome. In the second century, Christians were largely ignored as harmless. By the end of the reigns of the five good emperors, Christians still represented a small minority, but one of considerable strength.

The Growth of Christianity

The sporadic persecution of Christians by the Romans in the first and second centuries had done nothing to stop the growth of Christianity. It had, in fact, served to strengthen Christianity as an institution in the second and third centuries by causing it to shed the loose structure of the first century and move toward a more centralized organization of its various church communities. Crucial to this change was the emerging role of the bishops, who began to assume more control over church communities. The Christian church was creating a well-defined hierarchical structure in which the bishops and clergy were salaried officers separate from the laity or regular church members.

Christianity grew slowly in the first century, took root in the second, and had spread widely by the third. Why was Christianity able to attract so many followers? First of all, the Christian message had much to offer the Roman world. The promise of salvation, made possible by Jesus' death and resurrection, had immense appeal in a world full of suffering and injustice. Christianity seemed to imbue life with a meaning and purpose beyond the simple material things of everyday reality. Second, Christianity was not entirely unfamiliar. It could be viewed as simply another eastern mystery religion, offering immortality as the result of the sacrificial death of a savior-God. At the same time, it offered advantages that the other mystery religions lacked. Jesus had been a human figure, not a mythological one, such as Mithras. Moreover, Christianity had universal appeal. Unlike Mithraism, it was not restricted to men. Furthermore, it did not require a painful or expensive initiation rite as other mystery religions did. Initiation was accomplished simply by baptism—a purification by water—by which one entered into direct communion with Jesus. In addition, Christianity gave new meaning to life and offered what the Roman state religions could not—a personal relationship with God and a link to higher worlds.

Finally, Christianity fulfilled the human need to belong. Christians formed communities bound to one another in which people could express their love by helping each other and offering assistance to the poor, the sick, widows, and orphans. Christianity satisfied the need to belong in a way that the huge, impersonal, and remote Roman Empire could never do.

Christianity proved attractive to all classes. The promise of eternal life was for all—rich, poor, aristocrats, slaves, men, and women. As Paul stated in his Epistle to the Colossians: "And [you] have put on the new self, which is being renewed in knowledge in the image of its Creator. Here there is no Greek nor Jew, circumcised or uncircumcised, barbarian, Scythian, slave or free, but Christ is all, and is in all."[17] Although it did not call for revolution or social upheaval, Christianity emphasized a sense of spiritual equality for all people.

Many women, in fact, found that Christianity offered them new roles and new forms of companionship with other women. Christian women fostered the new religion in their own homes and preached their convictions to other people in their towns and villages. Many also died for their faith. Perpetua was an aristocratic woman who converted to Christianity. Her pagan family begged her to renounce her new faith, but she refused. Arrested by the Roman authorities, she chose instead to die for her faith and was one of a group of Christians who were slaughtered by wild beasts in the arena at Carthage on March 7, 203.

As the Christian church became more organized, some emperors in the third century responded with more systematic persecutions, but their schemes failed to work. The last great persecution was by Diocletian at the beginning of the fourth century. But even he had to admit what had become apparent in the course of the third century—Christianity had become too strong to be eradicated by force.

TIMELINE

CONCLUSION

The Roman Republic had created one of the largest empires in antiquity, but its republican institutions had proved inadequate for the task of ruling an empire. After a series of bloody civil wars, Augustus created a new order that began the Roman Empire, which experienced a lengthy period of peace and prosperity between 14 and 180. During this **Pax Romana**, trade flourished and the provinces were governed efficiently. In addition, within their empire, the Romans developed a remarkable series of achievements that were bequeathed to the future.

These achievements were fundamental to the development of Western civilization. The Romance languages of today (French, Italian, Spanish, Portuguese, and Romanian) are based on Latin. Western practices of impartial justice

and trial by jury owe much to Roman law. As great builders, the Romans left monuments to their skills throughout Europe, some of which, including aqueducts and roads, are still in use today. Other monuments provided models for public buildings in the West for hundreds of years. Aspects of Roman administrative practices survived in the Western world for centuries. The Romans also preserved the intellectual heritage of the Greco-Roman world of antiquity.

By the third century A.D., the Roman world was being buffeted by civil wars, invasions, and economic problems. At the same time, a new religion–Christianity–was spreading throughout the empire. As we shall see in the next chapter, the response to these developments slowly transformed the Roman Empire.

NOTES

1. Livy, *The Early History of Rome*, trans. A. de Sélincourt (Harmondsworth, England, 1960), p. 35.
2. Tacitus, *The Annals of Imperial Rome*, trans. M. Grant (Harmondsworth, England, 1956), p. 30.
3. Ibid., p. 37.
4. Ibid., p. 31.
5. Tacitus, *The Histories, trans.* K. Wellesley (Harmondsworth, England, 1964), p. 23.
6. Virgil, *The Aeneid*, trans. C. Day Lewis (Garden City, N.Y., 1952), p. 154.
7. Horace, *Satires,* in *The Complete Works of Horace*, trans. Lord Dunsany and M. Oakley (London, 1961), 1.1, p. 139; 1.3, p. 151.
8. Livy, *Early History of Rome*, p. 18.
9. Seneca, *Letters from a Stoic*, trans. R. Campbell (Harmondsworth, England, 1969), let. 5.
10. Tacitus, *Annals of Imperial Rome*, p. 147.
11. Juvenal, *The Sixteen Satires*, trans. P. Green (Harmondsworth, England, 1967), sat. 10, p. 207.
12. Tacitus, *A Dialogue on Oratory*, in *The Complete Works of Tacitus*, trans. A. Church and W. Brodribb (New York, 1942), 29, p. 758.
13. Matthew 5:17.
14. Matthew 7:12.
15. Mark 12:30–31.
16. John 18:36.
17. Colossians 3:10–11.

SUGGESTIONS FOR FURTHER READING

For a general account of the Roman Empire, see **J. Boardman, J. Griffin, and O. Murray, eds.,** *The Oxford History of the Roman World* (Oxford, 1991), and **G. Wolf, ed.,** *Cambridge Illustrated History of the Roman World* (Cambridge, 2003). Good surveys of the Early Empire include **P. Garnsey and R. P. Saller,** *The Roman Empire: Economy, Society and Culture* (London, 1987); **C. Wells,** *The Roman Empire*, 2d ed. (London, 1992); **M. Goodman,** *The Roman World,* *44 B.C.–A.D 180* (London, 1997); **J. Wacher,** *The Roman Empire* (London, 1987); and **F. Millar,** *The Roman Empire and Its Neighbours*, 2d ed. (London, 1981).

Studies of Roman emperors of the first and second centuries include **W. Eck,** *The Age of Augustus*, trans. **D. L. Schneider** (Oxford, 2003); **R. Seager,** *Tiberius* (London, 1972); **E. Champlin,** *Nero* (Cambridge, Mass., 2003); **E. Speller,** *Following Hadrian* (Oxford, 2003); and **M. Hammond,** *The Antonine Monarchy* (Rome, 1959). For brief biographies of all the Roman emperors, see **M. Grant,** *The Roman Emperors* (New York, 1985). On the wife of Augustus, see **A. A. Barrett,** *Livia: First Lady of Imperial Rome* (New Haven, Conn., 2002).

The Roman army is examined in **J. B. Campbell,** *The Emperor and the Roman Army* (Oxford, 1984). On the provinces and Roman foreign policy, see **E. N. Luttwak,** *The Grand Strategy of the Roman Empire from the First Century A.D. to the Third* (Baltimore, 1976); **B. Isaac,** *The Limits of Empire: The Roman Empire in the East* (Oxford, 1990); and **S. L. Dyson,** *The Creation of the Roman Frontier* (Princeton, N.J., 1985). On the battle in the Teutoburg Forest, see **P. S. Wells,** *The Battle That Stopped Rome: Emperor Augustus, Arminius, and the Slaughter of the Legions in the Teutoburg Forest* (New York, 2003).

A good survey of Roman literature can be found in **R. M. Ogilvie,** *Roman Literature and Society* (Harmondsworth, England, 1980). More specialized studies include **R. O. Lyne,** *The Latin Love Poets from Catullus to Horace* (Oxford, 1980), and **K. Galinsky,** *Augustan Culture* (Princeton, N.J., 1996).

Various aspects of Roman society are covered in **L. Adkins and R. A. Adkins,** *Handbook to Life in Ancient Rome* (New York, 1994). Also useful on urban life is **J. E. Stambaugh,** *The Ancient Roman City* (Baltimore, 1988). On public festivals, see **P. Veyne,** *Bread and Circuses* (London, 1992). On the gladiators, see **T. Wiedemann,** *Emperors and Gladiators* (New York, 1992). Studies on Roman women include **J.P.V.D. Balsdon,** *Roman Women: Their History and Habits* (London, 1969), and **S. B. Pomeroy,** *Goddesses, Whores, Wives, and Slaves: Women in Classical Antiquity* (New York, 1975), pp. 149–226. On slavery, see **K. Bradley,** *Slavery and Society at Rome* (New York, 1994).

For a general introduction to early Christianity, see **J. Court and K. Court**, *The New Testament World* (Cambridge, 1990). Useful works on early Christianity include **W. A. Meeks**, *The First Urban Christians* (New Haven, Conn., 1983); **W.H.C. Frend**, *The Rise of Christianity* (Philadelphia, 1984); and **R. MacMullen**, *Christianizing the Roman Empire* (New Haven, Conn., 1984). For a detailed analysis of Christianity in the 30s and 40s of the first century A.D., see **J. D. Crossan**, *The Birth of Christianity* (New York, 1998). On Christian women, see **D. M. Scholer, ed.,** *Women in Early Christianity* (New York, 1993), and **R. Kraemer**, *Her Share of the Blessings: Women's Religion Among the Pagans, Jews and Christians in the Graeco-Roman World* (Oxford, 1995).

Thomson NOW! Enter *ThomsonNOW* using the access card that is available for *Western Civilization: A Brief History*. *ThomsonNOW* will help you understand this chapter with lesson plans generated for your needs. In addition, you can read the following documents, and many more, online:

Virgil, Book 1 of *The Aeneid*
Horace, Satire 1 of Book 1
The Gospel of Mark (New Testament)
Ignatius, "Letter to the Ephesians"

WESTERN CIVILIZATION RESOURCES

Visit the Web site for *Western Civilization: A Brief History* for resources specific to this book:

http://www.thomsonedu.com/history/spielvogel

For a variety of tools to help you succeed in this course, visit the Western Civilization Resource Center at

http://history.wadsworth.com/spielvogel

Included are quizzes, images, documents, interactive simulations, maps and timelines, movie explorations, and a wealth of other sources.

LATE ANTIQUITY AND THE EMERGENCE OF THE MEDIEVAL WORLD

CHAPTER OUTLINE AND FOCUS QUESTIONS

The Late Roman Empire

▣ What reforms did Diocletian and Constantine institute, and to what extent were the reforms successful?

The Germanic Kingdoms

▣ What changes did the Germanic peoples make to the political, economic, and social conditions of the western Roman Empire?

Development of the Christian Church

▣ What were the chief characteristics of Benedictine monasticism, and what role did monks play in both the conversion of Europe to Christianity and the intellectual life of the Germanic kingdoms?

The Byzantine Empire

▣ How did the Byzantine Empire that had emerged by the eighth century differ from the empire of Justinian and from the Germanic kingdoms in the west?

The Rise of Islam

▣ What was the basic message of Islam, and why was it able to expand so successfully?

CRITICAL THINKING

▣ In what ways were the Byzantine and Islamic civilizations different from the civilization developing in western Europe? In what ways were they similar?

A fourteenth-century French manuscript illustration of the baptism of Clovis

Giraudon/The Bridgeman Art Library International (Bibliotheque Municipale, Castres, France)

𝓑Y THE THIRD CENTURY, the third century, the Roman Empire was experiencing a number of problems as well as witnessing the growth of a new religion–Christianity. To restore the empire, the emperors Diocletian and Constantine initiated a number of reforms, and Constantine converted to Christianity, starting a process that gave the Late Empire a new state religion.

After Constantine, the empire continued to survive, but it had to deal repeatedly with incursions of Germanic tribes in the west. By the second half of the fifth century, new political arrangements were undermining the old imperial structure in the west, leading to the emergence of a series of German kingdoms that would form the basis of a new civilization. The Christian church also played a role as it converted these Germanic tribes to its faith.

The conversion to Christianity of the pagan leaders of German tribes was sometimes dramatic, at least as reported by the sixth-century historian Gregory of Tours. Clovis, leader of the Franks, married Clotilde, daughter of the king of the Burgundians. She was a Christian, but Clovis refused her pleas to become a Christian, telling her, "Your god can do nothing." But during a battle with the Alemanni, when

Clovis' army was close to utter destruction, "He saw the danger; his heart was stirred; and he raised his eyes to heaven, saying, 'Jesus Christ, I beseech the glory of your aid. If you shall grant me victory over these enemies, I will believe in you and be baptized in your name.'" When he had uttered these words, the Alemanni began to flee. Clovis soon became a Christian.

While the Germanic kingdoms were establishing roots in the west, the eastern part of the old Roman Empire, increasingly Greek in culture, continued as the Byzantine Empire. Serving as a buffer between Europe and the peoples to the east, the Byzantine or Eastern Roman Empire also preserved the intellectual and legal accomplishments of Greek and Roman antiquity. At the same time, a new culture centered on Islam emerged in the east; it spread through large parts of the old Roman Empire, preserved much of Greek culture, and created its own flourishing civilization. This chapter concerns the dramatic transformations occurring in the Roman world in late antiquity, the heirs of the Roman Empire, and the medieval world they began to create.◆

The Late Roman Empire

At the end of the third and beginning of the fourth centuries, the Roman Empire gained a new lease on life through the efforts of two strong emperors, Diocletian and Constantine, who restored order and stability. The Roman Empire was virtually transformed into a new state: the Late Roman Empire, which included a new governmental structure, a rigid economic and social system, and a new state religion—Christianity.

The Reforms of Diocletian and Constantine

Diocletian had risen through the ranks to become a prominent military leader. After the murder of the emperor Numerian by his praetorian prefect, Diocletian executed the prefect and was then hailed as emperor by his soldiers. Diocletian's own rise to power led him to see the need for a new system for ruling the Roman Empire.

Political Reforms   Believing that the empire had grown too large for a single ruler, Diocletian (284–305) divided it into four administrative units (see Map 7.1), each with its own prefect. Despite the appearance of four-man rule, however, Diocletian's military seniority enabled him to claim a higher status and hold the ultimate authority. Constantine (306–337) continued and even expanded the autocratic policies of Diocletian. Both rulers greatly strengthened and enlarged the administrative bureaucracies of the Roman Empire. Henceforth, civil and military bureaucracies were sharply separated. Each contained a hierarchy of officials who exercised control at the various levels. The emperor presided over both hierarchies of officials and served as the only link between them. New titles of nobility—such as *illustres* ("illustrious ones") and

illustrissimi ("most illustrious ones")—were instituted to dignify the holders of positions in the civil and military bureaucracies.

Military Reforms   Additional military reforms were also instituted. The army was enlarged to almost 400,000 men, including units filled with Germans. By the end of Constantine's reign, a new organization of the army had also been put in place. Military forces were of two kinds: garrison troops, which were located on the frontiers and intended as a first line of defense against invaders, and mobile units, which were located behind the frontier but could be quickly moved to support frontier troops when the borders were threatened. This gave the empire greater flexibility in responding to invasion.

Economic and Social Trends   The political and military reforms of Diocletian and Constantine greatly enlarged two institutions—the army and the civil service—that drained most of the public funds. Though more revenues were needed to pay for the army and bureaucracy, the population was not growing, so the tax base could not be expanded. Diocletian and Constantine devised new economic and social policies to deal with these financial burdens, but like their political policies, they were all based on coercion and loss of individual freedom. To fight **inflation**, Diocletian resorted to issuing a price edict in 301 that established maximum wages and prices for the entire empire, but despite severe penalties, it was unenforceable and failed to work.

Coercion also came to form the underlying basis for numerous occupations in the Late Roman Empire. To ensure the tax base and keep the empire going despite the shortage of labor, the emperors issued edicts that forced people to remain in their designated vocations. Basic jobs, such as bakers and shippers, became hereditary. Free tenant farmers continued to decline and soon found themselves bound to the land by large landowners who took advantage of depressed agricultural conditions to enlarge their landed estates.

In general, the economic and social policies of Diocletian and Constantine were based on an unprecedented degree of control and coercion. Though temporarily successful, such authoritarian policies in the long run stifled the very vitality the Late Empire needed to revive its sagging fortunes.

Constantine's Building Program   Constantine was especially interested in building programs despite the strain they placed on the budget. Between 324 and 330, he engaged in his biggest project, the construction of a new capital city in the east, on the site of the Greek city of Byzantium, on the shores of the Bosporus. Named the "city of Constantine," or Constantinople (modern Istanbul), it was developed for defensive reasons; it had an excellent strategic location. Calling it his "New Rome," Constantine endowed the city with a forum, large palaces, and a vast amphitheater. It was officially dedicated on May 11,

MAP 7.1 **Divisions of the Late Roman Empire, c. 300.** Diocletian imposed order and a new economic and administrative structure on the Late Empire. He divided the Roman Empire into four regions, each ruled by either an "Augustus" or a "Caesar," although Diocletian retained supreme power. [?] Compare this map with Map 6.1. How much territory was lost by the time of Diocletian? View an animated version of this map or related maps at http://thomsonedu.com/history/spielvogel

330, "by the commandment of God," and in the following years, many Christian churches were built there.

The Empire's New Religion

Christianity flourished after Constantine became the first Christian emperor. According to the traditional story, before a crucial battle, he saw a vision of a Christian cross with the writing, "In this sign you will conquer." Having won the battle, the story goes, Constantine was convinced of the power of the Christian God. Although he was not baptized until the end of his life, in 313 he issued the famous Edict of Milan, officially tolerating the existence of Christianity. Under Theodosius "the Great" (378–395), it was made the official religion of the Roman Empire. Christianity had triumphed.

Organization and Religious Disputes By the fourth century, the Christian church had developed a system of government. The Christian community in each city was headed by a bishop, whose area of jurisdiction was known as a bishopric or diocese. The bishoprics of each Roman province were clustered together under the direction of an archbishop. The bishops of four great cities, Rome, Jerusalem, Alexandria, and Antioch, held positions of special power in church affairs because the churches in these cities all asserted that they had been founded by the original apostles sent out by Jesus.

One reason the church needed a more formal organization was the problem of **heresy**. As Christianity developed and spread, contradictory interpretations of important doctrines emerged. Heresy came to be viewed as a teaching different from the official catholic or universal beliefs of the

The Emperor Constantine. Constantine played an important role in restoring order and stability to the Roman Empire at the beginning of the fourth century. This marble head of Constantine, which is 8 feet 6 inches high, was part of an enormous 30-foot-tall seated statue of the emperor in the New Basilica in Rome. Constantine used these awe-inspiring statues throughout the empire to build support for imperial policies by reminding his subjects of his position as an absolute ruler with immense power. With his eyes turned toward heaven Constantine's special relationship with God is made clear.

church. In a world where people were concerned about salvation, the question of whether Jesus' nature was divine or human took on great significance. These doctrinal differences also became political issues, creating political factions that actually warred with one another. It is unlikely that ordinary people understood what these debates meant.

One of the major heresies of the fourth century was **Arianism**, which was a product of the followers of Arius, a priest from Alexandria in Egypt. Arius believed that Jesus Christ had been human and thus not truly God. Arius was opposed by Athanasius, a bishop of Alexandria, who argued that Jesus was human but also truly God. Emperor Constantine, disturbed by the controversy, called the first ecumenical council of the church, a meeting composed of representatives from the entire Christian community. The Council of Nicaea, held in 325, condemned Arianism and stated that Jesus was of "the same substance" as God:

> We believe in one God the Father All-sovereign, maker of all things visible and invisible; And in one Lord Jesus Christ, the Son of God, begotten of the Father, only-begotten, that is, of the substance of the Father, God of God, Light of Light, true God of true God, begotten not made, of one substance with the Father.[1]

The Council of Nicaea did not end the controversy, however; not only did Arianism persist in some parts of the Roman Empire for many years, but many of the Germanic Goths who established states in the west converted to Arian Christianity (see "The Germanic Kingdoms" later in this chapter). As a result of these fourth-century theological controversies, the Roman emperor came to play an increasingly important role in church affairs.

The End of the Western Empire

Constantine had reunited the Roman Empire and restored a semblance of order. After his death, however, the empire continued to divide into western and eastern parts, and by 395, they had become virtually two independent states. In the fifth century, the empire in the east remained intact under the Roman emperor in Constantinople (see "The Byzantine Empire" later in this chapter), but the administrative structure of the empire in the west collapsed and was replaced by a series of Germanic kingdoms.

During the first and second centuries A.D., the Romans had established the Rhine and Danube Rivers as the empire's northern boundary. The Romans called all the peoples to the north of the rivers "Germans" and regarded them as uncivilized barbarians. In fact, the Germans consisted of different groups with their own customs and identities, but these constantly changed as tribes broke up and came together in new configurations. At times, they formed larger confederations under strong warrior leaders. The Germans lived by herding and farming and also traded with people living along the northern frontiers of the Roman Empire.

Although the Romans had established political frontiers along the Rhine and Danube Rivers, Romans and Germans often came into contact across these boundaries. For some time, the Romans had hired Germanic tribes to fight other Germanic tribes that threatened Rome or enlisted groups of Germans to fight for Rome. In any case, until the fourth century, the empire had proved capable of absorbing these people without harm to its political structure. In the second half of the fourth century, however, the situation began to change.

In the late fourth century, the Germanic tribes came under new pressures when the Huns, a fierce tribe of nomads from Asia, moved into the Black Sea region and forced Germanic groups westward. One of the largest groups, which came to be known as the Visigoths, crossed the Danube into German territory and settled down as Roman allies. Ill-treated by Roman officials, the Visigoths soon revolted, and the attempt to stop them at Adrianople in 378 led to a crushing defeat for the Romans. Soon the Visigoths were again on the move. Under their king Alaric, they moved into Italy and sacked Rome in 410. Then, at the urging of the emperor, they moved into Spain and southern Gaul as Roman allies.

The Roman experience with the Visigoths established a precedent. The emperors in the first half of the fifth century made alliances with whole groups of Germanic

Diocletian	284–305
Constantine	306–337
Edict of Milan	313
Construction of Constantinople	324–330
Battle of Adrianople	378
Theodosius the Great	378–395
Division of the empire	395
Alaric and Visigoths sack Rome	410
Roman legions abandon Britain	410
Vandals sack Rome	455
Odoacer deposes Romulus Augustulus	476

peoples, who settled peacefully in the western part of the empire. The Burgundians settled themselves in much of eastern Gaul, just south of another German tribe called the Alemanni. Only the Vandals consistently remained hostile to the Romans. They sacked parts of Gaul and crossed the Pyrenees into Spain. Defeated by incoming Visigoths, the Vandals crossed the Strait of Gibraltar and conquered the province of Africa. In 455, the Vandals even attacked Rome, sacking it more ferociously than the Visigoths had in 410.

Increasingly, German military leaders dominated the imperial courts of the western empire, treating the Roman emperors as puppet rulers under their control. One such German leader finally ended the charade of Roman imperial rule. Odoacer deposed the Roman emperor, Romulus Augustulus, in 476 and began to rule on his own. Meanwhile, the Ostrogoths, another branch of the Goths, under their king Theodoric (493–526), marched into Italy, killed Odoacer, and established control of Italy in 493.

By the end of the fifth century, Roman imperial authority in the west had ceased. Nevertheless, the intellectual, governmental, and cultural traditions of the Late Roman Empire continued to live in the new Germanic kingdoms.

The Germanic Kingdoms

By 500, the western Roman Empire was being replaced politically by a series of kingdoms ruled by German monarchs (see Map 7.2). The pattern of settlement and the fusion of the Romans and Germans took different forms in the various kingdoms.

The Ostrogothic Kingdom of Italy

More than any other Germanic state, the Ostrogothic kingdom of Italy managed to maintain the Roman tradition of government. The Ostrogothic king, Theodoric, had received a Roman education while a hostage in Constantinople. After taking control of Italy, he was eager to create a synthesis of Ostrogothic and Roman practices.

In addition to maintaining the entire structure of imperial Roman government, he established separate systems of rule for the Ostrogoths and the Romans. The Italian population lived under Roman law administered by Roman officials. The Ostrogoths were governed by their own customs and their own officials.

After Theodoric's death in 526, it quickly became apparent that much of his success had been due to the force of his personality. His successors soon found themselves facing opposition from the imperial forces of the Byzantine or eastern Roman Empire. Under Emperor Justinian (527–565) (see "The Byzantine Empire" later in this chapter), Byzantine armies reconquered Italy between 535 and 554, devastating much of the peninsula and in the process destroying Rome as one of the great urban centers of the Mediterranean world. The Byzantine reconquest proved ephemeral, however. Another German tribe, the Lombards, invaded in 568 and conquered much of northern and central Italy. Unlike the Ostrogoths, the Lombards were harsh rulers who cared little for Roman structures and traditions.

The Visigothic Kingdom of Spain

The Visigothic kingdom in Spain demonstrated a number of parallels to the Ostrogothic kingdom of Italy. Both favored coexistence between the Roman and German populations, both featured a warrior caste dominating a larger native population, and both continued to maintain much of the Roman structure of government while largely excluding Romans from power. There were also noticeable differences, however. Laws preventing intermarriage were dropped, and the Visigothic and Hispano-Roman peoples began to blend. A new body of law common to both peoples also developed.

The Visigothic kingdom possessed one fatal weakness. With no established procedure for choosing new rulers, powerful Visigoths fought constantly to lay claim to the kingship. Church officials tried to help develop a sense of order, as this decree illustrates: "No one of us shall dare to seize the kingdom; no one shall arouse sedition among the citizenry; no one shall think of killing the king...." Church edicts failed to stop the feuds, however, and assassinations remained a way of life in Visigothic Spain. In 711, Muslim invaders destroyed the Visigothic kingdom itself (see "The Rise of Islam" later in this chapter).

The Frankish Kingdom

Only one of the German states on the European continent proved long-lasting—the kingdom of the Franks. The establishment of a Frankish kingdom was the work of Clovis (c. 482–511), a member of the Merovingian dynasty who became a Catholic Christian around 500. He was not the first German king to convert to Christianity, but the others had joined the Arian sect of

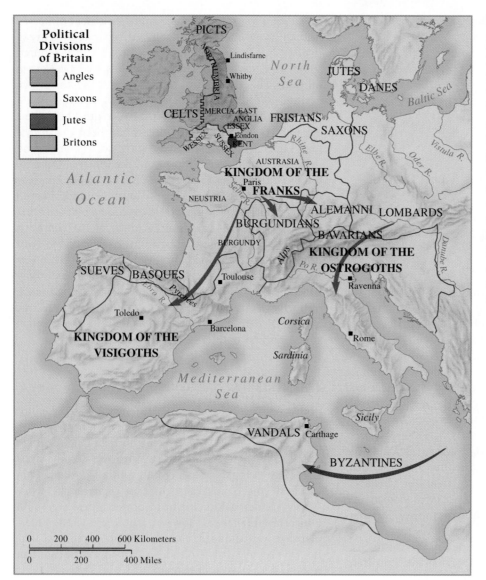

MAP 7.2 **The Germanic Kingdoms of the Old Western Empire.** The Germanic tribes filled the power vacuum caused by the demise of the Roman Empire, building states that blended elements of Germanic customs and laws with those of Roman culture, including large-scale conversions to Christianity. The Franks established the most durable of these Germanic states. **?** How did the movements of Franks during this period correspond to the borders of present-day France? 🐎 View an animated version of this map or related maps at http://thomsonedu.com/history/spielvogel

Christianity. The Christian church in Rome, which had become known as the Roman Catholic church, regarded the Arians as heretics, who believed in teachings different from the official church doctrine. Clovis' conversion to Catholic Christianity gained him the support of the Roman Catholic church, which was eager to obtain the friendship of a major Germanic ruler who was a Catholic Christian.

By 510, Clovis had established a powerful new Frankish kingdom stretching from the Pyrenees in the west to German lands in the east (modern-day France and western Germany). After the death of Clovis, however, his sons divided the newly created kingdom, as was the Frankish custom. During the sixth and seventh centuries, the once-united Frankish kingdom came to be partitioned into three major areas: Neustria in northern Gaul; Austrasia, consisting of the ancient Frankish lands on both sides of the Rhine; and the former kingdom of Burgundy.

During this time, the Frankish kingdom witnessed a process of fusion between Gallo-Roman and Frankish cultures and peoples, a process accompanied by a significant decline in Roman standards of civilization and commercial activity. The Franks were warriors and did little to encourage either urban life or trade. By 750, Frankish Gaul was basically an agricultural society in which the old Roman estates of the Late Empire had continued unimpeded. Institutionally, however, Germanic concepts of kingship and customary law replaced the Roman governmental structure.

Anglo-Saxon England

The barbarian pressures on the western Roman Empire had forced the emperors to withdraw the Roman armies and abandon Britain by the beginning of the fifth century. This opened the door to the Angles and Saxons, Germanic tribes from Denmark and northern Germany. Although these same peoples had made plundering raids for the past century, the withdrawal of the Roman armies

Baptism of Clovis. The conversion of Clovis to Roman Catholicism around 500 was an important factor in gaining papal support for his Frankish kingdom. In this illustration from a thirteenth-century Italian manuscript, Clovis is being baptized by Saint Remigius, the bishop of Rheims. Saint Remigius was known as a devout missionary; it was said, "by his signs and miracles, he brought low the heathen altars everywhere."

CHRONOLOGY The Germanic Kingdoms

Theodoric establishes Ostrogothic kingdom in Italy	493
Frankish king Clovis converts to Christianity	c. 500
Reconquest of Italy by Byzantines	535–552
Lombards begin conquest of Italy	568
Muslims shatter Visigoths in Spain	711

enabled them to make settlements instead. They met with resistance from the Celtic Britons, however, who still controlled the western regions of Cornwall, Wales, and Cumberland at the beginning of the seventh century. The German invaders eventually succeeded in carving out small kingdoms throughout the island, Kent in southeast England being one of them.

The Society of the Germanic Kingdoms

As Germans and Romans intermarried and began to create a new society, some of the social customs of the Germanic people began to play an important role. The crucial social bond among the Germanic peoples was the family, especially the extended or patriarchal family of husbands, wives, children, brothers, sisters, cousins, and grandparents. In addition to working the land together and passing it down to succeeding generations, the extended family provided protection, which was sorely needed in the violent atmosphere of Merovingian times.

The German conception of family affected the way Germanic law treated crime and punishment. In the Roman system, as in our own, a crime such as murder was considered an offense against society or the state and was handled by a court that heard evidence and arrived at a decision. Germanic law tended to be personal. An injury by one person against another could mean a blood feud in which the family of the injured party took revenge on the kin of the wrongdoer. Feuds could lead to savage acts of revenge, such as hacking off hands or feet, gouging

out eyes, or slicing off ears and noses. Because this system could easily get out of control, an alternative system arose that made use of a fine called **wergeld**, which was paid by a wrongdoer to the family of the person he had injured or killed. *Wergeld,* which means "man money," was the value of a person in monetary terms. That value varied considerably according to social status. An offense against a nobleman, for example, cost considerably more than one against a freeman or a slave.

Under German customary law, compurgation and the ordeal were the two most commonly used procedures for determining whether an accused person was guilty and should have to pay wergeld. Compurgation was the swearing of an oath by the accused person, backed up by a group of "oath helpers," numbering twelve or twenty-five, who would also swear that the accused person should be believed. The ordeal functioned in a variety of ways, all of which were based on the principle of divine intervention; divine forces (whether pagan or Christian) would not allow an innocent person to be harmed (see the box on p. 122).

The Frankish Family and Marriage For the Franks, like other Germanic peoples, the extended family was at the center of social organization. The Frankish family structure was simple. Males were dominant and made all the important decisions. A woman obeyed her father until she married and then fell under the legal domination of her husband. A widow, however, could hold property without a male guardian. In Frankish law, the wergeld of a wife of childbearing age—of value because she could bring forth children—was considerably higher than that of a man. The law stated, "If any one killed a free woman after she had begun bearing children, he shall be sentenced to 24,000 denars . . . After she can have no more children, he who kills her shall be sentenced to 8,000 denars."[2]

Because marriage affected the extended family group, fathers or uncles could arrange marriages for the good of the family without considering their children's wishes. Most important was the engagement ceremony in which a prospective son-in-law made a payment symbolizing the purchase of paternal authority over the bride. The essential feature of the marriage itself involved placing the married couple in bed to achieve their physical union. In first marriages, it was considered important that the wife be a virgin, which ensured that any children would

GERMANIC CUSTOMARY LAW: THE ORDEAL

In Germanic customary law, the ordeal came to be a means by which accused persons might clear themselves. Although the ordeal took different forms, all involved a physical trial of some sort, such as holding a red-hot iron. It was believed that God would protect the innocent and allow them to come through the ordeal unharmed. This sixth-century account by Gregory of Tours describes an ordeal by hot water.

Gregory of Tours, "An Ordeal of Hot Water" (c. 580)

An Arian presbyter disputing with a deacon of our religion made venomous assertions against the Son of God and the Holy Ghost, as is the habit of that sect [the Arians]. But when the deacon had discoursed a long time concerning the reasonableness of our faith and the heretic, blinded by the fog of unbelief, continued to reject the truth, . . . the former said: "Why weary ourselves with long discussions? Let acts approve the truth; let a kettle be heated over the fire and someone's ring be thrown into the boiling water. Let him who shall take it from the heated liquid be approved as a follower of the truth, and afterward let the other party be converted to the knowledge of the truth. And do you also understand, O heretic, that this our party will fulfill the conditions with the aid of the Holy Ghost; you shall confess that there is no discordance, no dissimilarity in the Holy Trinity." The heretic consented to the proposition and they separated after appointing the next morning for the trial. But the fervor of faith in which the deacon had first made this suggestion began to cool through the instigation of the enemy. Rising with the dawn he bathed his arm in oil and smeared it with ointment. But nevertheless he made the round of the sacred places and called in prayer on the

Lord. . . . About the third hour they met in the market place. The people came together to see the show. A fire was lighted, the kettle was placed upon it, and when it grew very hot the ring was thrown into the boiling water. The deacon invited the heretic to take it out of the water first. But he promptly refused, saying, "You who did propose this trial are the one to take it out." The deacon all of a tremble bared his arm. And when the heretic presbyter saw it besmeared with ointment he cried out: "With magic arts you have thought to protect yourself, that you have made use of these salves, but what you have done will not avail." While they were thus quarreling there came up a deacon from Ravenna named Iacinthus and inquired what the trouble was about. When he learned the truth he drew his arm out from under his robe at once and plunged his right hand into the kettle. Now the ring that had been thrown in was a little thing and very light so that it was thrown about by the water as chaff would be blown about by the wind; and searching for it a long time he found it after about an hour. Meanwhile the flame beneath the kettle blazed up mightily so that the greater heat might make it difficult for the ring to be followed by the hand; but the deacon extracted it at length and suffered no harm, protesting rather that at the bottom the kettle was cold while at the top it was just pleasantly warm. When the heretic beheld this he was greatly confused and audaciously thrust his hand into the kettle saying, "My faith will aid me." As soon as his hand had been thrust in all the flesh was boiled off the bones clear up to the elbow. And so the dispute ended.

What was the purpose of the ordeal of hot water? What does it reveal about the nature of the society that used it?

be the husband's. A virgin symbolized the ability of the bloodline to continue. Accordingly, adultery was viewed as pollution of the woman and her offspring, hence poisoning the future. Adulterous wives were severely punished (an adulterous woman could be strangled or even burned alive); adulterous husbands were not. Divorce was relatively simple and was initiated primarily by the husband. Divorced wives simply returned to their families.

For most women in the new Germanic kingdoms, their legal status reflected the material conditions of their lives. Archaeological evidence suggests that most women had life expectancies of only thirty to forty years, and 10 to 15 percent of women died in their childbearing years, no doubt due to complications associated with childbirth. For most women, life consisted of domestic labor: providing food and clothing for the household, caring for the children, and assisting with numerous farming chores. Of all women's labors, the most important was childbearing, because it was indispensable to perpetuating the family and its possessions.

Development of the Christian Church

By the end of the fourth century, Christianity had become the predominant religion of the Roman Empire. As the official Roman state disintegrated, the Christian church played an increasingly important role in the emergence and growth of the new European civilization.

The Power of the Pope

One of the far-reaching developments in the history of the Christian church was the emergence of one bishop— that of Rome—as the recognized leader of the western Christian church. According to church tradition, Jesus had given the keys to the kingdom of heaven to Peter, who was considered the chief apostle and the first bishop of Rome. Subsequent bishops of Rome were considered Peter's successors and came to be known as popes (from

THE LIFE OF SAINT ANTHONY

*I*n the third and early fourth centuries, the lives of martyrs had provided important models for early Christianity. But in the course of the fourth century, monks or desert fathers, who attempted to achieve spiritual perfection through asceticism, the denial of earthly life, and the struggle with demons became the new spiritual ideal for Christians. Consequently, spiritual biographies of early monks became a significant new form of Christian literature. Especially noteworthy was *The Life of Saint Anthony* by Saint Athanasius, the defender of Catholic orthodoxy against the Arians. His work had been translated into Latin before 386. This excerpt describes how Anthony fought off the temptations of Satan.

Athanasius, *The Life of Saint Anthony*

Now when the Enemy [Satan] saw that his craftiness in this matter was without profit, and that the more he brought temptation into Saint Anthony, the more strenuous the saint was in protecting himself against him with the armor of righteousness, he attacked him by means of the vigor of early manhood which is bound up in the nature of our humanity. With the goadings of passion he sued to trouble him by night, and in the daytime also he would vex him and pain him with the same to such an extent that even those who saw him knew from his appearance that he was waging war against the Adversary. But the more the Evil One brought unto him filthy and maddening thoughts, the more Saint Anthony took refuge in prayer and in abundant supplication,

and amid them all he remained wholly chaste. And the Evil One was working upon him every shameful deed according to his wont, and at length he even appeared unto Saint Anthony in the form of a woman; and other things which resembled this he performed with ease, for such things are a subject for boasting to him.

But the blessed Anthony knelt down upon his knees on the ground, and prayed before Him who said, "Before you criest unto Me, I will answer you," and said, "O my Lord, this I entreat you. Let not Your love be blotted out from my mind, and behold, I am, by Your grace, innocent before You." And again the Enemy multiplied in him the thoughts of lust, until Saint Anthony became as one who was being burned up, not through the Evil One, but through his own lusts; but he girded himself about with the threat of the thought of the Judgment, and of the torture of Gehenna, and of the worm which does not die. And while meditating on the thoughts which could be directed against the Evil One, he prayed for thoughts which would be hostile to him. Thus, to the reproach and shame of the Enemy, these things could not be performed; for he who imagined that he could be God was made a mock of by a young man, and he who boasted over flesh and blood was vanquished by a man who was clothed with flesh.

Based on the account by Athanasius, how would you characterize the ascetic ideals of early Christian monks? How important were those ideals to the growth of early Christianity?

---

the Latin word *papa*, meaning "father") of the Catholic church.

Although western Christians came to accept the bishop of Rome as head of the church in the fourth and fifth centuries, there was no unanimity on the extent of the powers the pope possessed as a result of this position. Nevertheless, the emergence in the sixth century of a strong pope, Gregory I, known as Gregory the Great, set the papacy and the Roman Catholic church on an energetic path that enabled the church in the seventh and eighth centuries to play an increasingly prominent role in civilizing the Germans and aiding the emergence of a distinctly new European civilization.

As pope, Gregory I (590–604) took charge of Rome and its surrounding area and made it into an administrative unit that eventually came to be known as the Papal States. Gregory also pursued a policy of extending papal authority over the Christian church in the west. He intervened in ecclesiastical conflicts throughout Italy and corresponded with the Frankish rulers, urging them to reform the church in Gaul. He successfully initiated the efforts of missionaries to convert England to Christianity and was especially active in converting the pagan peoples of Germanic Europe. His primary instrument was the monastic movement.

The Monks and Their Missions

A **monk** (Latin *monachus*, meaning "one who lives alone") was a person who sought to live a life divorced from the world, cut off from ordinary human society, in order to pursue an ideal of godliness or total dedication to the will of God. Christian **monasticism** was initially based on the model of the solitary hermit who forsakes all civilized society to pursue spirituality. Saint Anthony (c. 250–350) was a prosperous peasant in Egypt who decided to follow Jesus' injunction in the Gospel of Saint Mark: "Go your way, sell whatsoever you have, and give to the poor, and you shall have treasure in heaven: and come, take up the cross, and follow me." Anthony gave away his 300 acres of land to the poor and went into the desert to pursue his ideal of holiness (see the box above). Others did likewise, often to extremes. Saint Simeon the Stylite lived for three decades in a basket atop a pillar over 60 feet high. These spiritual gymnastics established a new ideal for Christianity. Whereas the early Christian model had been the martyr who died for the faith and achieved eternal life in the process, the new ideal was the monk who died to the world and achieved spiritual life through denial, asceticism, and mystical experience of God.

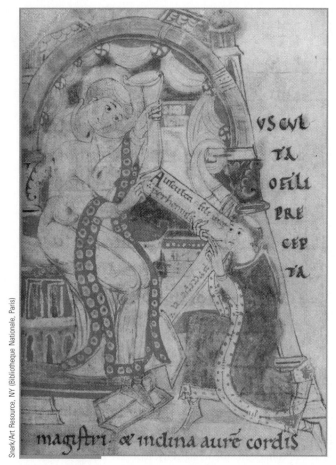

Snark/Art Resource, NY (Bibliotheque Nationale, Paris)

Saint Benedict. Benedict was the author of a set of rules that was instrumental in the development of monastic groups in the Catholic church. Shown in this medieval Latin manuscript is Benedict handing the rules of the Benedictine order to a monk.

These early monks, however, soon found themselves unable to live in solitude. Their feats of holiness attracted followers on a wide scale, and as the monastic ideal spread throughout the east, a new form of monasticism based on the practice of communal life soon became the dominant form. Monastic communities came to be seen as the ideal Christian society that could provide a moral example to the wider society around them.

Benedictine Monasticism Saint Benedict of Nursia (c. 480–c. 543), who founded a monastic house for which he wrote a set of rules sometime between 520 and 530, established the fundamental form of monastic life in the western Christian church. The Benedictine rule came to be used by other monastic groups and was crucial to the growth of monasticism in the western Christian world.

Benedict's rule favored an ideal of moderation. In chapter 40 of the rule, on the amount a monk should drink, this sense of moderation becomes apparent:

> "Every man has his proper gift from God, one after this manner, another after that." And therefore it is with some misgiving that we determine the amount of food for someone

else. Still, having regard for the weakness of some brothers, we believe that a hemina of wine [a quarter liter] per day will suffice for all. Let those, however, to whom God gives the gift of abstinence, know that they shall have their proper reward. But if either the circumstances of the place, the work, or the heat of summer necessitates more, let it lie in the discretion of the abbot to grant it. But let him take care in all things lest satiety or drunkenness supervene.[3]

At the same time, moderation did not preclude a disciplined existence based on the ideals of poverty, chastity, and obedience.

Benedict's rule divided each day into a series of activities, with primary emphasis on prayer and manual labor. Physical work of some kind was required of all monks for several hours a day because idleness was "the enemy of the soul." At the very heart of community practice was prayer, the proper "work of God." While this included private meditation and reading, all monks gathered together seven times during the day for common prayer and chanting of psalms. A Benedictine life was a communal one; monks ate, worked, slept, and worshiped together.

Each Benedictine monastery was strictly ruled by an **abbot**, or "father" of the monastery, who held complete authority over them; unquestioning obedience to the will of the abbot was expected of each monk. Each Benedictine monastery owned lands that enabled it to be a self-sustaining community, isolated from and independent of the world surrounding it. Within the monastery, however, monks were to fulfill their vow of poverty: "Let all things be common to all, as it is written, lest anyone should say that anything is his own or arrogate it to himself."[4] By the eighth century, Benedictine monasticism had spread throughout the west.

Although the original monks were men, women soon followed suit in withdrawing from the world to dedicate themselves to God. The first monastic rule for western women was produced by Caesarius of Arles for his sister in the fifth century. It strongly emphasized a rigid cloistering of these **nuns** to preserve them from dangers.

Monasticism played an indispensable role in early medieval civilization. Monks became the new heroes of Christian civilization. Their dedication to God became the highest ideal of Christian life. Monks copied Latin works and passed on the legacy of the ancient world to Western civilization in its European stage. Moreover, the monks played an increasingly significant role in spreading Christianity to the entire European world.

Monks as Missionaries The British Isles, in particular, became an important center of Christian culture and missionary fervor. After their conversion, the Celts of Ireland and Anglo-Saxons of England created new centers of Christian learning and in turn themselves became enthusiastic missionaries.

By the sixth century, Irish monasticism was a flourishing institution with its own unique characteristics. Unlike Benedictine monasticism, it was strongly ascetic. Monks performed strenuous fasts, prayed and meditated

IRISH MONASTICISM AND THE PENITENTIAL

Irish monasticism became well known for its ascetic practices. Much emphasis was placed on careful examination of conscience to determine if one had committed a sin against God. To facilitate this examination, penitentials were developed that listed possible sins with appropriate penances. Penance usually meant fasting a number of days each week on bread and water. Although these penitentials were eventually used throughout Christendom, they were especially important in Irish Christianity. This excerpt from the Penitential of Cummean, an Irish abbot, was written about 650 and demonstrates a distinctive feature of the penitentials, an acute preoccupation with sexual sins.

The Penitential of Cummean

A bishop who commits fornication shall be degraded and shall do penance for twelve years.

A presbyter or a deacon who commits natural fornication, having previously taken the vow of a monk, shall do penance for seven years. He shall ask pardon every hour; he shall perform a special fast during every week except in the days between Easter and Pentecost.

He who defiles his mother shall do penance for three years, with perpetual pilgrimage.

So shall those who commit sodomy do penance every seven years.

He who merely desires in his mind to commit fornication, but is not able, shall do penance for one year, especially in the three forty-day periods.

He who is willingly polluted during sleep shall arise and sing nine psalms in order, kneeling. On the following day, he shall live on bread and water.

A cleric who commits fornication once shall do penance for one year on bread and water; if he begets a son he shall do penance for seven years as an exile; so also a virgin.

He who loves any woman, but is unaware of any evil beyond a few conversations, shall do penance for forty days.

He who is in a state of matrimony ought to be continent during the three forty-day periods and on Saturday and on Sunday, night and day, and in the two appointed week days [Wednesday and Friday], and after conception, and during the entire menstrual period.

After a birth he shall abstain, if it is a son, for thirty-three [days]; if a daughter, for sixty-six [days].

Boys talking alone and transgressing the regulations of the elders [in the monastery], shall be corrected by three special fasts.

Children who imitate acts of fornication, twenty days; if frequently, forty.

But boys of twenty years who practice masturbation together and confess [shall do penance] twenty or forty days before they take communion.

What does the Penitential of Cummean reveal about the nature of Irish monasticism? What do you think was the theory of human sexuality held by early Irish Christianity?

frequently under extreme privations, and confessed their sins on a regular basis to their superiors. In fact, Irish monasticism gave rise to the use of penitentials or manuals that provided a guide for examining one's life to see what sins, or offenses against the will of God, one had committed (see the box above). A great love of learning also characterized Irish monasticism. The Irish eagerly absorbed both Latin and Greek culture and fostered education as a major part of their monastic life.

Their emphasis on asceticism led many Irish monks to go into voluntary exile. This "exile for the love of God" was not into isolation, however, but into missionary activity. Irish monks became fervid missionaries. Saint Columba (521–597) left Ireland in 565 as a "pilgrim for Christ" and founded an influential monastic community off the coast of Scotland on the island of Iona. From there Irish missionaries went to northern England to begin the process of converting the Angles and Saxons. Other Irish monks traveled to the European continent. New monasteries founded by the Irish became centers of learning wherever they were located.

At the same time the Irish monks were busy bringing their version of Christianity to the Anglo-Saxons of Britain, Pope Gregory the Great had set into motion an effort to convert England to Roman Christianity. His most important agent was Augustine, a monk from Rome, who arrived in England in 597. England at that time had a number of Germanic kingdoms. Augustine went first to Kent, where he converted King Ethelbert; most of the king's subjects then followed suit. Pope Gregory's conversion techniques emphasized persuasion rather than force, and as seen in this excerpt from one of his letters, he was willing to assimilate old pagan practices in order to coax the pagans into the new faith:

> We wish you [Abbot Mellitus] to inform him [Augustine] that we have been giving careful thought to the affairs of the English, and have come to the conclusion that the temples of the idols among that people should on no account be destroyed. The idols are to be destroyed, but the temples themselves are to be aspersed with holy water, altars set up in them, and relics deposited there. For if these temples are well-built, they must be purified from the worship of demons and dedicated to the service of the true God.[5]

Freed of their pagan past, temples had become churches, as one Christian commentator noted with joy: "The dwelling place of demons has become a house of God. The saving light has come to shine, where shadows covered all. Where sacrifices once took place and idols

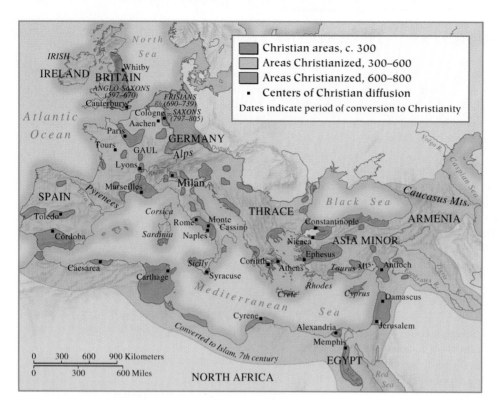

stood, angelic choirs now dance. Where God was angered once, now God is made content."[6] Likewise, old pagan feasts were given new names and incorporated into the Christian calendar. The Christian feast of Christmas, for example, was held on December 25, the day of the pagan celebration of the winter solstice.

As Roman Christianity spread northward in Britain, it encountered Irish Christianity moving southward. Roman Christianity prevailed, although the English church, despite its newfound unity and loyalty to Rome, retained some Irish features. Most important was the concentration on monastic culture with special emphasis on learning and missionary work. By 700, the English church had become the best trained and most learned in western Europe.

Following the Irish example, English monks spread to the European continent to carry on the work of conversion (see Map 7.3). Most important was Boniface (c. 680–755), who undertook the conversion of pagan Germans in Frisia, Bavaria, and Saxony. By 740, Saint Boniface, the "Apostle of the Germans," had become the most famous churchman in Europe. Fourteen years later, he was killed while trying to convert the pagan Frisians. Boniface was a brilliant example of the numerous Irish and English monks whose tireless efforts made Europe the bastion of the Roman Catholic faith.

Women and Monasticism Women played an important role in the monastic missionary movement and the conversion of the Germanic kingdoms. Double monasteries, where both monks and nuns lived in separate houses but attended church services together, were found in both the English and Frankish kingdoms. The monks and nuns followed a common rule under a common head. Frequently, this leader was an **abbess** rather than an abbot. Many of these abbesses belonged to royal houses, especially in Anglo-Saxon England. In the kingdom of Northumbria, for example, Saint Hilda founded the monastery of Whitby in 657. As abbess, she was responsible for giving learning an important role in the life of the monastery; five future bishops were educated under her tutelage. For female intellectuals, monasteries offered opportunities for learning not found elsewhere in the society of their day.

Nuns of the seventh and eighth centuries also played an important role in the spread of Christianity. The great English missionary Boniface relied on nuns in England for books and money. He also asked the abbess of Wimborne to send groups of nuns to establish convents in newly converted German lands. A nun named Leoba established the first convent in Germany at Bischofsheim.

The Path of Celibacy The monastic movement enabled some women to pursue a new path to holiness, Cloisters for both men and women offered the ideal place to practice the new Christian ideal of celibacy. This newfound emphasis on abstaining from sexual relations, especially evident in the emphasis on virginity, created a new image of the human body in late antiquity. To many Greeks and Roman, the human body had been a source of beauty, joy, and pleasure, noticeable in numerous works of art. To many Christians, the body was seen as a hindrance to a spiritual connection with God. The refusal to have sex was a victory over the desires of the flesh and thus an avenue to holiness.

In the fourth and fifth centuries, a cult of virginity also moved beyond the walls of monasteries and convents.

Throughout the Mediterranean world, groups of women got together to study the importance and benefits of celibacy. In Rome, a woman named Marcella supported a group of aristocratic women in their studies of celibacy.

Christianity and Intellectual Life

Many early Christians expressed considerable hostility toward the pagan culture of the classical world. Tertullian (c. 160–c. 225), a Christian writer from Carthage, had proclaimed: "What has Jerusalem to do with Athens, the Church with the Academy, the Christian with the heretic? . . . After Jesus Christ we have no need of speculation, after the Gospel no need of research."[7] To many early Christians, the Bible (see Chapter 6) contained all the knowledge anyone needed. Others, however, thought it was not possible to separate Christian thought from classical traditions and education and encouraged Christianity to absorb the classical heritage. As it spread in the eastern Roman world, Christianity adopted Greek as its language; the New Testament was written in Greek. Christians also turned to Greek thought for help in expressing complicated theological concepts. In many ways, then, Christianity served to preserve Greco-Roman culture.

The work of Augustine (354–430) provides one of the best examples of how Christianity used pagan culture in the service of Christianity. Augustine came to be seen as one of the Latin fathers of the Catholic church, intellectuals who wrote in Latin and profoundly influenced the development of Christian thought in the west.

Born in North Africa, Augustine was reared by his mother, an ardent Christian. He eventually became a professor of rhetoric at Milan in 384. After experiencing a profound and moving religious experience, he gave up his teaching position and went back to North Africa, where he became bishop of Hippo from 396 until his death in 430.

Augustine's most famous work, *The City of God,* was a profound expression of a Christian philosophy of government and history. In it, he theorized on the ideal relations between two kinds of societies existing throughout time—the City of God and the City of the World. Those who loved God would be loyal to the City of God, whose ultimate location was the kingdom of heaven. Earthly society would always be uncertain because of human beings' inclination to sin. And yet the City of the World was still necessary, for it was the duty of rulers to curb the depraved instincts of sinful humans and maintain the peace necessary for Christians to live in the world. Hence Augustine posited that secular government and authority were necessary for the pursuit of the true Christian life on earth; in doing so, he provided a justification for secular political authority that would play an important role in medieval thought.

Another important intellectual of the early church was Jerome (345–420), who pursued literary studies in Rome and became a master of Latin prose. Jerome had mixed feelings about his love for classical studies, however, and like Augustine, he experienced a spiritual conversion after which he tried to dedicate himself more fully to Jesus. Ultimately, Jerome found a compromise by purifying the literature of the pagan world and then using it to further the Christian faith. Jerome was a great scholar, and his extensive knowledge of both Hebrew and Greek enabled him to translate the Old and New Testaments into Latin. In the process, he created the so-called Latin Vulgate, or common text, of the Scriptures that became the standard edition for the Catholic church in the Middle Ages.

Although the Christian church came to accept classical culture, it was not easy to do so in the world of the new German kingdoms. Nevertheless, some Christian scholars managed to keep learning alive. Boethius and Cassiodorus, two important Christian intellectuals, both served as officials of the Ostrogothic king Theodoric. Boethius (c. 480–524) received the traditional education typical of the Roman aristocracy. His most famous work was written in prison, where he was kept for a year by Theodoric on a charge of treason before being executed. This work, *On the Consolation of Philosophy,* is a dialogue between Boethius and philosophy personified as a woman. Philosophy leads Boethius to a clear understanding of true happiness and the highest good, which she equates with God. These are not achieved by outward conditions, since the person who lives virtuously finds happiness within.

Cassiodorus (c. 490–c. 585) also came from an aristocratic Roman family and served as an official of the Ostrogothic king Theodoric. The conflicts that erupted after the death of Theodoric led Cassiodorus to withdraw from public life and retire to his landed estates in southern Italy, where he wrote his final work, *Divine and Human Readings.* This was a compendium of the literature of both Christian and pagan antiquity. Cassiodorus accepted the advice of earlier Christian intellectuals to make use of classical works while treasuring the Scriptures above all else.

Cassiodorus continued the tradition of late antiquity of classifying knowledge according to certain subjects. In assembling his compendium of authors, he followed the works of late ancient authors in placing all secular knowledge into the categories of the seven **liberal arts**, which were divided into two major groups: the *trivium,* consisting of grammar, rhetoric, and dialectic or logic, and the *quadrivium,* consisting of the mathematical subjects of arithmetic, geometry, astronomy, and music. The seven liberal arts would become the cornerstone of education until the seventeenth century.

The Byzantine Empire

As noted earlier, in the fourth century, the western and eastern parts of the Roman Empire began to go their separate ways. As the Germans moved into the western part

Justinian and His Court. Ravenna remained the center of the Byzantine presence in Italy for two hundred years. The Church of San Vitale at Ravenna contains some of the finest examples of sixth-century Byzantine mosaics (artworks created by cementing small colored pieces of glass or rock to a wall or floor). This mosaic depicts the Byzantine emperor Justinian and his court dressed in their elaborate robes. Justinian is seen with soldiers, his staff, and members of the clergy.

of the empire and established various kingdoms over the course of the next hundred years, the Roman Empire in the east, centered on Constantinople, solidified and prospered.

The Reign of Justinian (527–565)

When he became emperor of the eastern Roman Empire, Justinian was determined to reestablish the Roman Empire in the entire Mediterranean world. His army, commanded by Belisarius, probably the best general of the late Roman world, sailed to North Africa and quickly destroyed the Vandals in two major battles. From North Africa, Belisarius led his forces onto the Italian peninsula and defeated the Ostrogoths. By 552, Justinian appeared to have achieved his goal. His reconstituted empire included Italy, part of Spain, North Africa, Asia Minor, Palestine, and Syria (see Map 7.4). But his success proved fleeting. Only three years after Justinian's death, the Lombards conquered much of Italy. Although the eastern empire maintained the fiction of Italy as a province, its forces were limited to southern and central Italy, Sicily, and some coastal areas.

Justinian's most important contribution was his codification of Roman law. The eastern empire had inherited a vast quantity of legal materials connected to the development of Roman law, which Justinian wished to simplify. The result was the *Corpus Iuris Civilis* (Body of Civil Law), a codification of Roman law that remained in force in the eastern Roman Empire until its end in 1453. And because it was written in Latin (it was in fact the last product of eastern Roman culture to be written in Latin, which was soon replaced by Greek), it was also eventually used in the west and ultimately became the basis of the legal system of all of continental Europe.

Life in Constantinople: The Emperor's Building Program   After riots destroyed much of Constantinople in 532, Emperor Justinian rebuilt the city and gave it the

appearance it would keep for almost a thousand years. With a population estimated in the hundreds of thousands, Constantinople was the largest city in Europe during the Middle Ages. It viewed itself as the center of an empire and a special Christian city.

Until the twelfth century, Constantinople was Europe's greatest commercial center, the chief marketplace where western and eastern products were exchanged. Highly desired in Europe were the products of the East: silk from China, spices from Southeast Asia and India, jewelry and ivory from India (the latter used by artisans for church items), wheat and furs from southern Russia, and flax and honey from the Balkans. Many of these eastern goods were then shipped to the Mediterranean area and northern Europe. Moreover, imported raw materials were used in Constantinople for local industries. During Justinian's reign, two Christian monks smuggled silkworms from China to begin a Byzantine silk industry. The state controlled the production of silk cloth, and the workshops themselves were housed in Constantinople's royal palace complex. European demand for silk cloth made it the city's most lucrative product.

Much of Constantinople's appearance in the Middle Ages was due to Justinian's program of rebuilding in the sixth century. The city was dominated by an immense palace complex, hundreds of churches, and a huge arena known as the Hippodrome. No residential district was particularly fashionable; palaces, tenements, and slums ranged alongside one another. Justinian added many new buildings. His public works projects included roads, bridges, walls, public baths, law courts, and colossal underground reservoirs to hold the city's water supply. He also built hospitals, schools, monasteries, and churches. Churches were his special passion, and in Constantinople alone he built or rebuilt thirty-four of them. His greatest achievement was the famous Hagia Sophia, the Church of the Holy Wisdom, completed in 537. The center of Hagia Sophia consisted of four large piers crowned by

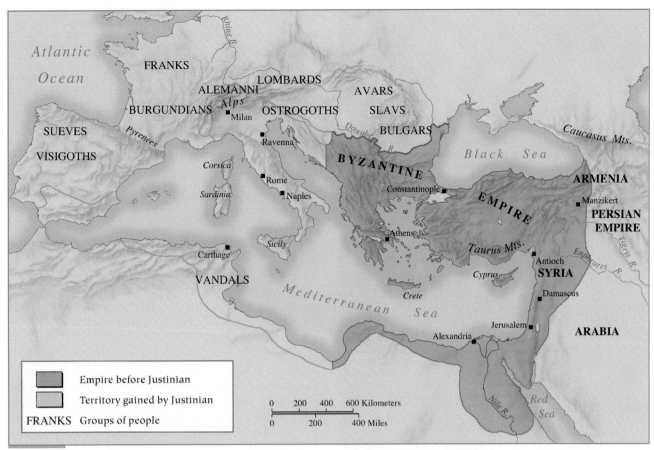

MAP 7.4 **The Byzantine Empire in the Time of Justinian.** The Byzantine emperor Justinian briefly restored much of the Mediterranean portion of the old Roman Empire. His general Belisarius quickly conquered the Vandals in North Africa but wrested Italy from the Ostrogoths only after a long and devastating struggle. ? Examine Map 6.1. What former Roman territories lay outside Justinian's control? View an animated version of this map or related maps at http://thomsonedu.com/history/spielvogel

an enormous dome, which seemed to be floating in space. In part this impression was created by ringing the base of the dome with forty-two windows, which allowed an incredible play of light within the cathedral. Light served to remind the worshipers of God. As invisible light illuminates darkness, so too was it believed that invisible spirit illuminates the world.

The Hippodrome was a huge amphitheater, constructed of brick covered by marble, holding between forty and sixty thousand spectators. Although gladiator fights were held there, the main events were the chariot races; twenty-four would usually be presented in one day. The citizens of Constantinople were passionate fans of chariot racing. Successful charioteers were acclaimed as heroes and honored with public statues.

From Eastern Roman to Byzantine Empire

Justinian's accomplishments had been spectacular, but when he died, he left the eastern Roman Empire with serious problems: too much territory to protect far from Constantinople, an empty treasury, a decline in population

after a plague, and renewed threats to its frontiers. In the first half of the seventh century, the empire faced attacks from the Persians to the east and the Slavs to the north.

The most serious challenge to the eastern Roman Empire came from the rise of Islam, which unified the Arab tribes and created a powerful new force that swept through the east (see the next section, "The Rise of Islam"). The defeat of an eastern Roman army at Yarmuk in 636 meant the loss of the provinces of Syria and Palestine. The Arabs also moved into the old Persian Empire and conquered it. Arabs and eastern Roman forces now faced each other along a frontier in southern Asia Minor.

Problems arose along the northern frontier as well, especially in the Balkans, where an Asiatic people known as the Bulgars had arrived earlier in the sixth century. In 679, the Bulgars defeated the eastern Roman forces and took possession of the lower Danube valley, establishing a strong Bulgarian kingdom.

By the beginning of the eighth century, the eastern Roman Empire was greatly diminished in size. Consisting only of the eastern Balkans and Asia Minor, it was no longer a major eastern Mediterranean state. The external

Interior of Hagia Sophia. This view of the interior of the Church of the Holy Wisdom, constructed under Justinian by Anthemius of Tralles and Isidore of Milan, gives an idea of how the windows around the base of the dome produced a special play of light within the cathedral. The pulpits and plaques bearing inscriptions from the Qur'an were introduced when the Turks converted this church to a mosque in the fifteenth century.

challenges had important internal repercussions as well. By the eighth century, the eastern Roman Empire had been transformed into what historians call the Byzantine Empire, a civilization with its own unique character that would last until 1453 (Constantinople was built on the site of an older city named Byzantium—hence the term *Byzantine*).

The Byzantine Empire, c. 750

© Digital Vision/Getty Images

CHRONOLOGY The Byzantine Empire	
Reign of Justinian	527–565
Justinian codifies Roman law	529–533
Reconquest of Italy by the Byzantines	535–552
Completion of Hagia Sophia	537
Arab defeat of Byzantines at Yarmuk	636
Defeat by the Bulgars; losses in the Balkans	679

The Byzantine Empire was both a Greek and a Christian state. Increasingly, Latin fell into disuse as Greek became both the common and the official language of the empire. The Byzantine Empire was also built on a faith in Jesus that was shared by almost all of its citizens. An enormous amount of artistic talent was poured into the construction of churches, church ceremonies, and church decoration. Spiritual principles deeply permeated Byzantine art.

The emperor occupied a crucial position in the Byzantine state. Portrayed as chosen by God, the emperor was crowned in sacred ceremonies, and his subjects were expected to prostrate themselves in his presence. His power was considered absolute and was limited in practice only by deposition or assassination. Because the emperor appointed the head of the church (known as the patriarch), he also exercised control over both church and state. The Byzantines believed that God had commanded their state to preserve the true Christian faith. Emperor, clergy, and state officials were all bound together in service to this ideal. It can be said that spiritual values truly held the Byzantine state together.

By 750, it was apparent that two of Rome's heirs, the Germanic kingdoms and the Byzantine Empire, were moving in different directions. Nevertheless, Byzantine influence on the Western world was significant. The images of a Roman imperial state that continued to haunt the west lived on in Byzantium. The legal system of the west owed much to Justinian's codification of Roman law. In addition, the Byzantine Empire served as a buffer state, protecting the west for a long time from incursions from the east. Although the Byzantine Empire would continue to influence the west until its demise in 1453, it went its own way. One of its bitterest enemies was the new power of Islam.

The Rise of Islam

Like the Hebrews and the Assyrians, the Arabs were a Semitic-speaking people of the Near East with a long history. In Roman times, the Arabian peninsula was dominated by Bedouin nomads who moved constantly to find water and food for themselves and their animals. Although some Arabs prospered from trading activities, especially in the north, most Arabs were poor Bedouins, whose tribes were known for their independence, their warlike qualities, and their dislike of urban-dwelling Arabs.

Although these early Arabs were polytheistic, there was a supreme God named Allah (Arabic for "God") who ruled over the other gods. Allah was symbolized by a sacred stone, and each tribe had its own stone. All tribes, however, worshiped a massive black meteorite, the Black Stone, which had been placed in a central shrine called the *Ka'ba* in the city of Mecca.

In the fifth and sixth centuries A.D., the Arabian peninsula took on new importance. As a result of political disorder in Mesopotamia and Egypt, the usual trade routes in the region began to change. A new trade route—from the Mediterranean through Mecca to Yemen and then by ship across the Arabian Sea and the Indian Ocean—became more popular, and communities in that part of the Arabian peninsula, including Mecca, began to prosper from this caravan trade. As a result, tensions arose between the Bedouins in the desert and the increasingly wealthy merchant classes in the towns. Into this intense world came Muhammad.

Muhammad

Born in Mecca to a merchant family, Muhammad (c. 570–632) was orphaned at the age of five. He grew up to become a caravan manager and eventually married a rich widow who was also his employer. In his middle years, he began to experience visions that he believed were inspired by Allah. Muhammad believed that although Allah had already revealed himself in part through Moses and Jesus—and thus through the Hebrew and Christian traditions—the final revelations were now being given to him. Out of these revelations, which were eventually written down, came the Qur'an (or Koran), which contained the guidelines by which followers of Allah were to live. Muhammad's teachings formed the basis for the religion known as Islam, which means "submission to the will of Allah." Allah was the all-powerful being who had created the universe and everything in it. Humans must subject themselves to Allah if they wished to achieve everlasting life. Those who became his followers were called Muslims, meaning "practitioners of Islam."

After receiving the revelations, Muhammad set out to convince the people of Mecca of the truth of his revelations. At first, many thought he was insane, and others feared that his attacks on the corrupt society around him would upset the established social and political order. Discouraged by the failure of the Meccans to accept his message, in 622 Muhammad and some of his closest supporters left the city and moved north to the rival city of Yathrib, later renamed Medina ("city of the Prophet"). The year of the journey to Medina, known in history as the *Hegira* ("departure"), became year 1 in the official calendar of Islam.

Muhammad, who had been invited to the town by a number of prominent residents, soon began to win support from people in Medina as well as from members of Bedouin tribes in the surrounding countryside. From these groups, he formed the first Muslim community (the **umma**). Muslims saw no separation between political and religious authority; submission to the will of Allah meant submission to his Prophet, Muhammad. Muhammad soon became both a religious and political leader. His political and military skills enabled him to put together a reliable military force, with which he returned to Mecca in 630, conquering the city and converting the

Muslims Celebrating the End of Ramadan. Ramadan is the holy month of Islam during which all Muslims must fast from dawn to sunset. Observance of Ramadan is one of the Five Pillars of Islam. Muhammad instituted the fast during his stay at Medina. It was designed to replace the single Jewish Day of Atonement. This Persian miniature depicts Muslims on horseback celebrating the end of Ramadan.

THE QUR'AN: THE PILGRIMAGE

*T*he Qur'an is the sacred book of the Muslims, comparable to the Bible in Christianity. This selection from Sura 22, titled "Pilgrimage," discusses the importance of making a pilgrimage to Mecca, one of the Five Pillars of Islam. The pilgrim's final destination was the *Ka'ba* at Mecca, containing the Black Stone.

Qur'an, Sura 22: "Pilgrimage"

Exhort all men to make the pilgrimage. They will come to you on foot and on the backs of swift camels from every distant quarter; they will come to avail themselves of many a benefit, and to pronounce on the appointed days the name of God over the cattle which He has given them for food. Eat of their flesh, and feed the poor and the unfortunate.

Then let the pilgrims tidy themselves, make their vows, and circle the Ancient House. Such is God's commandment. He that reveres the sacred rites of God shall fare better in the sight of his Lord.

The flesh of cattle is lawful for you, except for that which has been specified before. Guard yourselves against the filth of idols; and avoid the utterance of falsehoods.

Dedicate yourselves to God, and serve none besides Him. The man who serves other deities besides God is like him who falls from heaven and is snatched by the birds or carried away by the wind to some far-off region. Even such is he.

He that reveres the offerings made to God shows the piety of his heart. Your cattle are useful to you in many ways until the time of their slaughter. Then they are offered for sacrifice at the Ancient House.

For every community We have ordained a ritual, that they may pronounce the name of God over the cattle which He has given them for food. Your God is one God; to Him surrender yourselves. Give good news to the humble, whose hearts are filled with awe at the mention of God; who endure adversity with fortitude, attend to their prayers, and give in alms from what We gave them.

We have made the camels a part of God's rites. They are of much use to you. Pronounce over them the name of God as you draw them up in line and slaughter them; and when they have fallen to the ground eat of their flesh and feed the uncomplaining beggar and the demanding supplicant. Thus have We subjected them to your service, so that you may give thanks.

Their flesh and blood does not reach God; it is your piety that reaches Him. Thus has He subjected them to your service, so that you may give glory to God for guiding you.

Give good news to the righteous. God will ward off evil from true believers. God does not love the treacherous and the thankless.

What is the key purpose of undertaking a pilgrimage to Mecca? What is the historical importance of the sacred stone?

---

townspeople to the new faith. From Mecca, Muhammad's ideas spread quickly across the Arabian peninsula and within a relatively short time had resulted in both the religious and political unification of Arab society.

The Teachings of Islam

At the heart of Islam was the Qur'an, with the basic message that there is no God but Allah and Muhammad is his Prophet. Essentially, the Qur'an contains Muhammad's revelations of a heavenly book written down by secretaries. Consisting of 114 *suras* (chapters), the Qur'an is the sacred book of Islam, which recorded the beliefs of the Muslims and served as their code of ethics and law.

Islam was a direct and simple faith, emphasizing the need to obey the will of Allah. This meant following a basic ethical code consisting of the **Five Pillars of Islam:** belief in Allah and Muhammad as his Prophet; standard prayer five times a day and public prayer on Friday at midday to worship Allah; observance of the holy month of **Ramadan** (the ninth month on the Muslim calendar) with fasting from dawn to sunset; making a pilgrimage (known as the *hajj*), if possible, to Mecca at least once in one's lifetime (see the box above); and giving alms to the poor and unfortunate. The faithful who observed the law were guaranteed a place in an eternal paradise.

Islam was not just a set of religious beliefs but a way of life as well. After the death of Muhammad, Muslim scholars drew up a law code, called the *Shari'a,* to provide believers with a set of prescriptions to regulate their daily lives. Much of the *Shari'a* was drawn from existing legal regulations or from the *Hadith,* a collection of the sayings of Muhammad that was used to supplement the revelations contained in the Qur'an. Believers were subject to strict guidelines for their behavior. In addition to the Five Pillars, Muslims were forbidden to gamble, to eat pork, to drink alcoholic beverages, and to engage in dishonest behavior. Sexual practices were also strictly regulated. Marriages were to be arranged by parents, and contact between unmarried men and women was discouraged. In accordance with Bedouin custom, males were permitted to have more than one wife, but Muhammad attempted to limit the practice by restricting the number of wives to four.

The Spread of Islam

The death of Muhammad in 632 presented his followers with a dilemma. Muhammad had never named a successor, and although he had several daughters, he left no sons. In a male-oriented society, who would lead the community of the faithful? Shortly after Muhammad's death, some of his closest followers selected Abu Bakr, a wealthy merchant

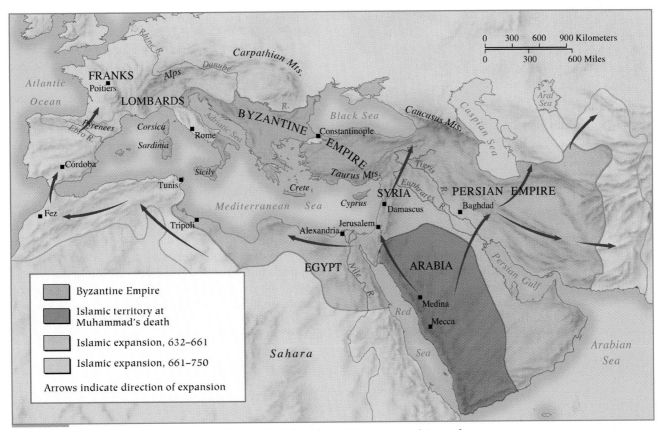

MAP 7.5 **The Spread of Islam.** Muhammad, the prophet of Islam, engaged in warfare against neighboring tribes. Militaristic expansion continued with great zeal under the Prophet's successors. Islamic rule spread rapidly in the decades after Muhammad's death, stopped finally by the Byzantine Empire and the Franks. ❓ Why was the continuance of the Byzantine Empire a key factor in stopping the spread of Islam into Europe? 🔍 **View an animated version of this map or related maps at** http://thomsonedu.com/history/spielvogel

who was Muhammad's father-in-law, as **caliph**, or temporal leader, of the Islamic community.

Muhammad and the early caliphs who succeeded him took up the Arabic tribal custom of the *razzia* or raid in the struggle against their enemies. Some people refer to this activity as *jihad*, which they misleadingly interpret as "holy war." *Jihad* actually means "striving in the way of the Lord" to achieve personal betterment, which can include a fair, defensive fight to preserve one's life and one's faith. Arab conquests were not carried out to convert others, since conversion to Islam was purely voluntary. Conquered people who did not convert were required only to submit to Muslim rule and pay taxes.

The Byzantines and the Persians were the first to feel the strength of the newly united Arabs. At Yarmuk in 636, the Muslims defeated the Byzantine army, and by 640 they had taken possession of the province of Syria (see Map 7.5). To the east, the Arabs went on to conquer the Persian Empire by 650. In the meantime, by 642, Egypt and other areas of northern Africa had been added to the new Muslim empire. Led by a series of brilliant generals, the Arabs had put together a large and highly motivated army whose valor was enhanced by the belief that Muslim warriors were guaranteed a place in paradise if they died in battle.

Early caliphs, ruling from Medina, organized their newly conquered territories into taxpaying provinces. By the mid-seventh century, problems arose again over the succession to the Prophet until Ali, Muhammad's son-in-law, was assassinated and the general Muawiya, the governor of Syria and one of Ali's chief rivals, became caliph in 661. He was known for one outstanding virtue: he used force only when necessary. As he said, "I never use my sword when my whip will do, nor my whip when my tongue will do."[8] Muawiya moved quickly to make the caliphate hereditary in his own family, thus establishing the Umayyad dynasty. As one of its first actions, the Umayyad dynasty moved the capital of the Muslim empire from Medina to Damascus in Syria. This internal dissension over the caliphate created a split in Islam between the Shi'ites, or those who accepted only the descendants of Ali, Muhammad's son-in-law, as the true rulers, and the Sunnites, who claimed that the descendants of the Umayyads were the true caliphs. This seventh-century split in Islam has lasted to the present day.

Birth of Muhammad	c. 570
Muhammad's flight from Mecca (*Hegira*)	622
Death of Muhammad	632
Defeat of Byzantines at Yarmuk	636
Seizure of Byzantine provinces of Syria and Egypt	640–642
Defeat of Persians	650
Invasion of Spain	c. 710

Internal dissension, however, did not stop the expansion of Islam. After sweeping across North Africa, the Muslims crossed the Strait of Gibraltar and moved into Spain around 710. The Visigothic kingdom collapsed, and by 725, most of Spain had become a Muslim state with its center at Córdoba. In 732, a Muslim army, making a foray into southern France, was defeated at the Battle of Tours near Poitiers. Muslim expansion in Europe came to a halt.

Meanwhile, in 717, another Muslim force had launched a naval attack on Constantinople with the hope of destroying the Byzantine Empire. In the spring of 718, the Byzantines destroyed the Muslim fleet and saved the Byzantine Empire and indirectly Christian Europe, because the fall of Constantinople would no doubt have opened the door to Muslim invasion of eastern Europe. The Byzantine Empire and Islam now established an uneasy frontier in southern Asia Minor.

The Arab advance had finally come to an end, but not before the southern and eastern Mediterranean parts of the old Roman Empire had been conquered. Islam had become heir to much of the old Roman Empire. The Umayyad dynasty at Damascus now ruled an enormous empire. While expansion had conveyed untold wealth and new ethnic groups into the fold of Islam, it also brought contact with Byzantine and Persian civilization. As a result, the new Arab empire would be influenced by Greek culture as well as the older civilizations of the ancient Near East.

TIMELINE

	250	350	450	550	650	750
Roman Empire	Diocletian and Constantine	■ Division of the empire	■ Odoacer deposes Romulus Augustulus			
Europe			Germanic kingdoms	■ Benedictine order established		
				■ Lombards begin conquest of Italy		
Byzantine Empire				Reign of Justinian / ■ Completion of Hagia Sophia	■ Arab defeat of Byzantines at Yarmuk / ■ Byzantine losses in the Balkans	
Arab Empire				Life of Muhammad / ■ Muhammad's flight to Medina	■ Muslim entry into Spain / Defeat of Muslims near Poitiers	

CONCLUSION

The period from the mid-third century to the mid-eighth century was both chaotic and creative. During late antiquity, the Roman world of the Mediterranean was gradually transformed. Three new entities fell heir to Roman civilization: the Germanic kingdoms of western Europe, the Byzantine Empire, and Islam. In the west, Roman elements combined with German and Celtic influences; in the east, Greek and eastern elements of late antiquity were of more consequence. Although the Germanic kingdoms of the west and the Byzantine civilization of the east came to share a common bond in Christianity, the faith proved incapable of keeping them in harmony politically, and the two civilizations continued to move apart. But Christianity remained a dominant influence in both civilizations and in the west was especially important as a civilizing agent that brought pagan peoples into the new European civilization that was slowly being born. The rise of Islam, Rome's third heir, resulted in the loss of the southern and eastern Mediterranean portions of the old Roman Empire to a religious power that was neither Roman nor Christian. The new Islamic empire forced Europe back on itself, and slowly there emerged a new culture that became the heart of what we know as Western civilization.

NOTES

1. "The Creed of Nicaea," in H. Bettenson, ed., *Documents of the Christian Church* (London, 1963), p. 35.
2. E. F. Henderson, *Select Historical Documents of the Middle Ages* (London, 1892), p. 181.
3. N. F. Cantor, ed., *The Medieval World, 300–1300* (New York, 1963), p. 104.
4. Ibid. p. 103.
5. Bede, *A History of the English Church and People*, trans. L. Sherley-Price (Harmondsworth, England, 1968), pp. 86–87.
6. Quoted in P. Brown, *The Rise of Western Christendom: Triumph and Adversity, A.D. 200–1000* (Oxford, 1997), p. 98.
7. Tertullian, "The Prescriptions Against the Heretics," in *The Library of Christian Classics*, vol. 5, *Early Latin Theology*, ed. and trans. S. L. Greenslade (Philadelphia, 1956), p. 36.
8. Quoted in A. Goldschmidt Jr., *A Concise History of the Middle East*, 4th ed. (Boulder, Colo., 1991), p. 56.

SUGGESTIONS FOR FURTHER READING

For good introductions to late antiquity, see **P. Brown, *The World of Late Antiquity, A.D. 150–750*** (New York, 1989); **J. Moorhead, *The Roman Empire Divided, 400–700*** (London, 2001); **A. Cameron, *The Mediterranean World in Late Antiquity, A.D. 395–600*** (London, 1993); and **R. Collins, *Early Medieval Europe, 300–1000*** (New York, 1991). There is an excellent collection of essays and encyclopedic entries in **G. W. Bowersock, P. Brown,** and **O. Grabar, *Late Antiquity: A Guide to the Postclassical World*** (Cambridge, Mass., 1999).

On the Late Roman Empire, see **A. Cameron, *The Later Roman Empire*** (Cambridge, Mass., 1993). On the fourth century, see **M. Grant, *Constantine the Great: The Man and His Times*** (New York, 1993), and **T. D. Barnes, *The New Empire of Diocletian and Constantine*** (Cambridge, Mass., 1982). Studies analyzing the aristocratic circles, the barbarian invasions, and the military problem include **E. A. Thompson, *Romans and Barbarians*** (Madison, Wis., 1982); **A. Ferrill, *The Fall of the Roman Empire: The Military Explanation*** (London, 1986); and **P. Heather, *The Fall of the Roman Empire: A New History of Rome and the Barbarians*** (New York, 2006).

For surveys of the German tribes and their migrations, see **T. S. Burns, *A History of the Ostrogoths*** (Bloomington, Ind., 1984); **P. Heather, *Goths and Romans*** (Oxford, 1991); **E. James, *The Franks*** (Oxford, 1988); and **I. N. Wood, *Merovingian Kingdoms*** (London, 1994). On the relationship between the Romans and the Germans, see **T. S. Burns, *Rome and the Barbarians, 100 B.C.–A.D 400*** (Baltimore, 2003).

For a superb introduction to early Christianity, see **P. Brown, *The Rise of Western Christendom: Triumph and Adversity, A.D. 200–1000,*** 2d ed. (Oxford, 2002). On Saints Augustine and Jerome, see **H. Chadwick, *Augustine*** (Oxford, 1986), and **J.N.D. Kelly, *Saint Jerome*** (London, 1975). For a good account of early monasticism, see **C. H. Lawrence, *Medieval Monasticism*,** 2d ed. (London, 1989). For women in monastic life, see **S. F. Wemple, *Women in Frankish Society: Marriage and the Cloister, 500–900*** (Philadelphia, 1981). On women in general, see **G. Clark, *Women in Late Antiquity: Pagan and Christian Life-Styles*** (Oxford, 1993).

A brief survey of the development of the papacy can be found in **G. Barraclough, *The Medieval Papacy*** (New York, 1968). **J. Richards, *The Popes and the Papacy in the Early Middle Ages, 476–752*** (Boston, 1979), is a more detailed study of the early papacy. On Pope Gregory the Great, see **C. Straw, *Gregory the Great: Perfection in Imperfection*** (Berkeley, Calif., 1988). On Irish monasticism, see **L. M. Bitel, *Isle of the Saints: Monastic Settlement and Christian Community in Early Ireland*** (Ithaca, N.Y., 1990).

Brief but good introductions to Byzantine history can be found in **J. Haldon, *Byzantium: A History*** (Charleston, S.C., 2000), and **W. Treadgold, *A Concise History of Byzantium*** (London, 2001). For a comprehensive survey of the Byzantine Empire, see **W. Treadgold, *A History of the Byzantine State and Society*** (Stanford, Calif., 1997). See also **C. Mango, ed., *The Oxford History of Byzantium*** (Oxford, 2002). On Justinian, see **J. Moorhead, *Justinian*** (London, 1995), and **J.A.S. Evans, *The Age of Justinian*** (New York, 1996). The role of the Christian church is discussed in **J. Hussey, *The Orthodox Church in the Byzantine Empire*** (Oxford, 1986).

Good brief surveys of the Islamic Middle East include **A. Goldschmidt Jr., *A Concise History of the Middle East*,** 7th ed. (Boulder, Colo., 2001), and **S. N. Fisher** and **W. Ochsenwald, *The Middle East: A History*** (New York, 2003). On the rise of Islam, see **F. E. Peters, *Muhammad and the Origins of Islam*** (Albany, N.Y., 1994); **M. Lings, *Muhammad: His Life Based on the Earliest Sources***

(New York, 1983); and **F. Donner**, *The Early Islamic Conquests* (Princeton, N.J., 1980).

Thomson **NOW!** Enter *ThomsonNOW* using the access card that is available for *Western Civilization: A Brief History.* *ThomsonNOW* will help you understand this chapter with lesson plans generated for your needs. In addition, you can read the following documents, and many more, online:

Saint Paul's First Epistle to the Corinthians
Pliny the Younger, Letter 97
Plotinus, excerpts from the first book of the Six Enneads

EUROPEAN CIVILIZATION IN THE EARLY MIDDLE AGES, 750–1000

CHAPTER OUTLINE AND FOCUS QUESTIONS

The World of the Carolingians

▢ How did the political, intellectual, and daily life in the Carolingian Empire represent a fusion of Gallo-Roman, Germanic, and Christian practices?

Disintegration of the Carolingian Empire

▢ What impact did the Vikings have on the history and culture of medieval Europe?

The Emerging World of Lords and Vassals

▢ What was fief-holding, and how was it related to manorialism?

The Zenith of Byzantine Civilization

▢ What were the chief developments in the Byzantine Empire between 750 and 1000?

The Slavic Peoples of Central and Eastern Europe

▢ What patterns of development occurred in central and eastern Europe as a result of the Slavic peoples?

The World of Islam

▢ What were the chief developments in the Islamic world between 750 and 1000?

CRITICAL THINKING

▢ In what ways can it be said the Islamic civilization was superior to the civilization of western Europe in the ninth and tenth centuries?

A medieval French manuscript illustration of the coronation of Charlemagne by Pope Leo III

N 800, CHARLEMAGNE, the king of the Franks, journeyed to Rome to help Pope Leo III, who was barely clinging to power in the face of rebellious Romans. On Christmas Day, Charlemagne and his family, attended by Romans, Franks, and even visitors from the Byzantine Empire, crowded into Saint Peter's Basilica to hear Mass. Quite unexpectedly, at least according to a Frankish writer, "as the king rose from praying before the tomb of the blessed apostle Peter, Pope Leo placed a golden crown on his head." In keeping with ancient tradition, the people in the church shouted, "Long life and victory to Charles Augustus, crowned by God the great and pacific Emperor of the Romans." Seemingly, the Roman Empire in the West had been reborn, and Charles had become the first western emperor since 476. But this "Roman emperor" was actually a German king, and he had been crowned by the head of the western Christian church. In truth, the coronation of Charlemagne was a sign not of the rebirth of the Roman Empire but of the emergence of a new European civilization.

By the year of Charlemagne's coronation, the contours of this new European civilization were beginning to emerge in western Europe. Increasingly, Europe would become the focus and center of Western civilization. Building on a fusion of Germanic, Greco-Roman, and Christian elements, the medieval European world first became visible in the Carolingian Empire of Charlemagne. The agrarian foundations of the eighth and ninth centuries proved inadequate to maintain a large monarchical system, however, and a new political and military order based on the decentralization of political power subsequently evolved to become an integral part of the political world of the Middle Ages.

European civilization began on a shaky and uncertain foundation, however. In the ninth century, Vikings, Magyars, and Muslims posed threats that could easily have stifled the new society. But European civilization absorbed the challenges. The Vikings and Magyars were assimilated, and recovery slowly began. By 1000, European civilization was ready to embark on a period of dazzling vitality and expansion.♦

The World of the Carolingians

By the eighth century, the Merovingian dynasty was losing its control of the Frankish lands. Charles Martel, the Carolingian mayor of the palace of Austrasia, became the virtual ruler of these territories. When Charles died in 741, Pepin, his son, deposed the Merovingians and assumed the kingship of the Frankish state, an action approved by the pope. In imitation of an Old Testament practice, Pepin (751–768) was crowned and formally anointed with holy oil by a representative of the pope. The anointing not only symbolized that the king had been entrusted with a sacred office but also provided yet another example of the fusion between Germanic institutions and Christian practices in the Early Middle Ages.

Charlemagne and the Carolingian Empire (768–814)

Pepin was succeeded on the throne of the Frankish kingdom by his son, a dynamic and powerful ruler known to history as Charles the Great, or Charlemagne (*Carolus magnus* in Latin—hence our word *Carolingian*). Charlemagne was a determined and decisive man, intelligent and inquisitive. A fierce warrior, he was also a wise patron of learning and a resolute statesman (see the box on p. 139). He greatly expanded the territory of the Carolingian Empire during his lengthy rule (see Map 8.1).

Expansion of the Carolingian Empire   In the tradition of the Germanic kings, Charlemagne was a determined warrior who undertook fifty-four military campaigns. Even though the Frankish army was relatively small—only eight thousand men gathered each spring for campaigning—supplying it and transporting it to distant areas could still present serious problems. The Frankish army consisted mostly of infantry, with some cavalry armed with swords and spears.

Charlemagne's campaigns took him to many parts of Europe. In 773, Charlemagne led his army into Italy, crushed the Lombards, and took control of the Lombard state. Although his son was crowned king of Italy, Charlemagne was its real ruler. Four years after his invasion of Italy, Charlemagne moved his forces into northern Spain. This campaign proved disappointing: not only did the Basques harass his army as it crossed the Pyrenees on the way home, but they also ambushed and annihilated his rear guard.

Charlemagne was considerably more successful with his eastern campaigns into Germany, especially against the Saxons living between the Elbe River and the North Sea. As Einhard, Charlemagne's biographer, recounted it:

> No war ever undertaken by the Frank nation was carried on with such persistence and bitterness, or cost so much labor, because the Saxons, like almost all the tribes of Germany, were a fierce people, given to the worship of devils, and hostile to our religion, and did not consider it dishonorable to transgress and violate all law, human and divine.[1]

Charlemagne's insistence that the Saxons convert to Christianity simply fueled their resistance. Not until 804, after eighteen campaigns, was Saxony finally pacified and added to the Carolingian domain.

In southeastern Germany, Charlemagne invaded the land of the Bavarians in 787 and brought them into his empire by the following year, an expansion that then brought him into contact with the southern Slavs and the Avars. The latter disappeared from history after their utter devastation at the hands of Charlemagne's army. Now at its height, Charlemagne's empire covered much of western and central Europe; not until the time of Napoleon in the nineteenth century would an empire of this size be seen again in Europe.

Governing the Empire   Charlemagne continued the efforts of his father in organizing the Carolingian kingdom. Because there was no system of public taxation, Charlemagne was dependent on the royal estates for the resources he needed to govern his empire. Food and goods derived from these lands provided support for the king, his household staff, and officials. To keep the nobles in his service, Charlemagne granted part of the royal lands as lifetime holdings to nobles who assisted him.

Besides the household staff, the administration of the empire was accomplished by counts, who were the king's chief representatives in local areas. Counts were members of the nobility who had already existed under the Merovingians. They had come to control public services in their own lands and thus acted as judges, military leaders, and agents of the king. Gradually, as the rule of the Merovingian kings weakened, many counts had simply attached the royal lands and services performed on behalf of the king to their own family possessions.

In an effort to gain greater control over his kingdom, Charlemagne attempted to limit the power of the counts. They were required to serve outside their own family

THE ACHIEVEMENTS OF CHARLEMAGNE

*E*inhard, the biographer of Charlemagne, was born in the valley of the Main River in Germany about 775. Raised and educated in the monastery of Fulda, an important center of learning, he arrived at the court of Charlemagne in 791 or 792. Although he did not achieve high office under Charlemagne, he served as private secretary to Louis the Pious, Charlemagne's son and successor. Einhard's *Life of Charlemagne* was modeled on Suetonius's *Lives of the Caesars*, especially his biography of Augustus. Einhard's work, written between 817 and 830, was the "first medieval biography of a lay figure." In this selection, he discusses some of Charlemagne's accomplishments.

Einhard, *Life of Charlemagne*

Such are the wars, most skillfully planned and successfully fought, which this most powerful king waged during the forty-seven years of his reign. He so largely increased the Frank kingdom, which was already great and strong when he received it at his father's hands, that more than double its former territory was added to it.... He subdued all the wild and barbarous tribes dwelling in Germany between the Rhine and the Vistula, the Ocean and the Danube, all of which speak very much the same language, but differ widely from one another in customs and dress....

He added to the glory of his reign by gaining the good will of several kings and nations.... The Emperors of Constantinople [the Byzantine emperors] sought friendship and alliance with Charles by several embassies; and even when the Greeks [the Byzantines] suspected him of designing to take the empire from them, because of his assumption of the title Emperor, they made a close alliance with him, that he might have no cause of offense. In fact, the power of the Franks was always viewed with a jealous eye, whence the Greek proverb, "Have the Frank for your friend, but not for your neighbor."

This King, who showed himself so great in extending his empire and subduing foreign nations, and was constantly occupied with plans to that end, undertook also very many works calculated to adorn and benefit his kingdom, and brought several of them to completion. Among these, the most deserving of mention are the basilica of the Holy Mother of God at Aix-la-Chapelle, built in the most admirable manner, and a bridge over the Rhine River at Mainz, half a mile long, the breadth of the river at this point.... Above all, sacred buildings were the object of his care throughout his whole kingdom; and whenever he found them falling to ruin from age, he commanded the priests and fathers who had charge of them to repair them, and made sure by commissioners that his instructions were obeyed.... Thus did Charles defend and increase as well as beautify his kingdom....

He cherished with the greatest fervor and devotion the principles of the Christian religion, which had been instilled into him from infancy. Hence it was that he built the beautiful church at Aix-la-Chapelle, which he adorned with gold and silver and lamps, and with rails and doors of solid brass. He had the columns and marbles for this structure brought from Rome and Ravenna, for he could not find such as were suitable elsewhere. He was a constant worshiper at this church as long as his health permitted, going morning and evening, even after nightfall, besides attending mass....

He was very forward in caring for the poor, so much so that he not only made a point of giving in his own country and his own kingdom, but when he discovered that there were Christians living in poverty in Syria, Egypt, and Africa, at Jerusalem, Alexandria, and Carthage, he had compassion on their wants, and used to send money over the seas to them.... He sent great and countless gifts to the popes, and throughout his whole reign the wish that he had nearest at heart was to reestablish the ancient authority of the city of Rome under his care and by his influence, and to defend and protect the Church of St. Peter, and to beautify and enrich it out of his own store above all other churches.

How long did Einhard know Charlemagne? Does this excerpt reflect close, personal knowledge of the man, his court, and his works or hearsay and legend?

---

lands and were moved about periodically rather than being permitted to remain in a county for life. By making the offices appointive, Charlemagne tried to prevent the counts' children from automatically inheriting their offices. Moreover, as another check on the counts, Charlemagne instituted the *missi dominici* ("messengers of the lord king"), a lay lord and a church official who were sent out to local districts to ensure that the counts were executing the king's wishes.

The Carolingian system was glaringly inefficient. Great distances had to be covered on horseback, making it impossible for Charlemagne and his household staff to exercise much supervision over local affairs. What held the system together was personal loyalty to the king—who was strong enough to ensure loyalty by force when necessary.

Charlemagne also realized that the Catholic church could provide valuable assistance in governing his kingdom. By the end of the seventh century, the system of ecclesiastical government within the Christian church that had been created in the Late Roman Empire had largely disintegrated. Many church offices were not filled or were held by grossly unqualified relatives of the royal family. Both Pepin and his son Charlemagne took up the cause of church reform by creating new bishoprics and archbishoprics, restoring old ones, and seeing to it that the clergy accepted the orders of their superiors and executed their duties.

Charlemagne as Emperor As Charlemagne's power grew, so did his prestige as the most powerful Christian ruler; one monk even wrote of his empire as the "kingdom of Europe."

MAP 8.1 **The Carolingian Empire.** Charlemagne inherited the Carolingian Empire from his father, Pepin. He expanded his territories in several directions, creating an empire that would not be rivaled in size until the conquests of Napoleon in the early nineteenth century. ❓ How might Charlemagne's holdings in northern Italy have influenced his relationship with the pope? 🌐 **View an animated version of this map or related maps at** http://thomsonedu.com/history/spielvogel

In 800, Charlemagne acquired a new title—emperor of the Romans—largely as a result of the ever-closer relationship between the papacy and the Frankish monarchs.

Already during the reign of Pepin, an alliance emerged between the kingdom of the Franks and the papacy. The popes welcomed this support, and in the course of the second half of the eighth century, they increasingly severed their ties with the Byzantine Empire and drew closer to the Frankish kingdom. Charlemagne encouraged this development. In 799, after a rebellion against his authority, Pope Leo III (795–816) managed to escape from Rome and flee to safety at Charlemagne's court. Charlemagne offered assistance, and when he went to Rome in November 800 to settle affairs, he was received by the pope like an emperor. On Christmas Day in 800, Pope Leo placed a crown on Charlemagne's head and declared him emperor of the Romans.

The significance of this imperial coronation has been much debated. Charlemagne's biographer Einhard claimed that Charlemagne "at first had such an aversion that he declared that he would not have set foot in the Church the day that it was conferred, although it was a great feast-day, if he could have foreseen the design of the Pope."[2] But Charlemagne also perceived the usefulness of the imperial title; after all, he was now on a level of equality with the Byzantine emperor. Moreover, the papacy now had a defender of great stature, although later popes in the Middle Ages would become involved in fierce struggles with emperors over who possessed the higher power.

In any case, Charlemagne's coronation as Roman emperor demonstrated the strength, even after three hundred years, of the concept of an enduring Roman Empire. More important, it symbolized the fusion of the Roman, Christian, and Germanic elements that constituted the foundation of European civilization. A Germanic king had been crowned emperor of the Romans by the spiritual leader of western Christendom. A new civilization had emerged.

The Carolingian Intellectual Renewal

Charlemagne had a strong desire to revive learning in his kingdom, an attitude that stemmed from his own intellectual curiosity as well as the need to provide educated clergy for the church and literate officials for the government. His efforts led to a revival of learning and culture that some historians have labeled the Carolingian Renaissance, or "rebirth" of learning.

For the most part, the revival of classical studies and the efforts to preserve Latin culture took place in the monasteries, many of which had been established by the Irish and English missionaries of the seventh and eighth centuries. By the ninth century, the work required of Benedictine monks was the copying of manuscripts. Monasteries established **scriptoria**, or writing rooms, where monks copied not only the works of early Christianity, such as the Bible, but also the works of Latin classical authors. The production of manuscripts in Carolingian monastic *scriptoria* was a crucial factor in the preservation of the ancient legacy. About eight thousand manuscripts survive from Carolingian times. Virtually 90 percent of the ancient Roman works that we have today exist because they were copied by Carolingian monks.

Charlemagne personally promoted learning by establishing a palace school and encouraging scholars from all over Europe to come to the Carolingian court. The best known of these scholars was Alcuin from the famous school at York, founded as part of a great revival of learning in the Anglo-Saxon kingdom of Northumbria. From 782 to 796, while serving at Charlemagne's court as an adviser on ecclesiastical affairs, Alcuin also provided

The Coronation of Charlemagne. After a rebellion in 799 forced Pope Leo III to seek refuge at Charlemagne's court, Charlemagne went to Rome to settle the affair. There, on Christmas Day 800, he was crowned emperor of the Romans by the pope. This manuscript illustration shows Leo III placing a crown on Charlemagne's head.

the leadership for the palace school. He concentrated on teaching classical Latin and adopted Cassiodorus' sevenfold division of knowledge known as the liberal arts (see Chapter 7), which became the basis for all later medieval education. All in all, the Carolingian Renaissance played a crucial role in keeping the classical heritage alive as well as maintaining the intellectual life of the Catholic church.

Life in the Carolingian World

In daily life as well as intellectual life, the newly emerging Europe of the Carolingian era witnessed an amalgamation of Roman, Germanic, and Christian practices. These last in particular seem to have exercised an ever-increasing influence.

Family and Marriage By Carolingian times, the Catholic church had begun to influence Frankish family life and marital and sexual attitudes. Marriages in Frankish society were arranged by fathers or uncles to meet the needs of the extended family. Although wives were expected to be faithful to their husbands, Frankish aristocrats often kept concubines, either slave girls or free women from their estates. Even the "most Christian king" Charlemagne kept a number of concubines.

To limit such sexual license, the church increasingly emphasized its role in marriage and attempted to Christianize it. Although marriage was a civil arrangement, priests tried to add their blessings and strengthen the concept of a special marriage ceremony. To stabilize marriages, the church also began to emphasize **monogamy** and permanence. A Frankish church council in 789 stipulated that marriage was "indissoluble" and condemned the practice of concubinage and easy divorce, and during the reign of Emperor Louis the Pious (814–840), the church formally prohibited divorce. Now a man who married was expected to remain with his wife "even though she were sterile, deformed, old, dirty, drunken, a frequenter of bad company, lascivious, vain, greedy, unfaithful, quarrelsome, abusive . . . , for when that man was free, he freely engaged himself."[3]

The acceptance and spread of the Catholic church's views on the indissolubility of marriage encouraged the development of the **nuclear family** at the expense of the extended family. Although the kin was still an influential social and political force, the conjugal unit came to be seen as the basic unit of society. The new practice of young couples establishing their own households brought a dynamic element to European society. It also had a significant impact on women (see the box on p. 142). In the extended family, the eldest woman controlled all the other female members; in the nuclear family, the wife was still dominated by her husband, but at least she now had control of her own household and children.

Christianity and Sexuality The early church fathers had stressed that celibacy and complete abstinence from sexual activity constituted an ideal state superior to marriage. Subsequently, the early church gradually developed a case for clerical celibacy, although it proved impossible to enforce in the Early Middle Ages. The early fathers had also emphasized, however, that not all people had the self-discipline to remain celibate. It was thus permissible to marry, as Paul had indicated in his first epistle to the Corinthians:

> It is good for a man not to touch a woman. Nevertheless, to avoid fornication, let every man have his own wife, and let every woman have her own husband. . . . I say therefore to the unmarried and widows, it is good for them if they abide even as I. But if they cannot contain, let them marry: for it is better to marry than to burn.[4]

The church thus viewed marriage as the lesser of two evils; it was a concession to human weakness and fulfilled

ADVICE FROM A CAROLINGIAN MOTHER

The wife of a Carolingian aristocrat bore numerous responsibilities. She was entrusted with the management of the household and even the administration of extensive landed estates while her husband was absent in the royal service or on a military campaign. A wife was also expected to bear larger numbers of children and to supervise their upbringing. This selection by Dhouda, wife of Bernard, marquis of Septimania (in southern France), is taken from a manual she wrote to instruct her son on his duties to his new lord, King Charles the Bald (840–877).

Dhouda of Septimania, *Handbook for William*

Direction on your comportment toward your lord.

You have Charles as your lord; you have him as lord because, as I believe, God and your father, Bernard, have chosen him for you to serve at the beginning of your career, in the flower of your youth. Remember that he comes from a great and noble lineage on both sides of his family. Serve him not only so that you please him in obvious ways, but also as one clearheaded in matters of both body and soul. Be steadfastly and completely loyal to him in all things....

This is why, my son, I urge you to keep this loyalty as long as you live, in your body and in your mind. For the advancement that it brings you will be of great value both to you and to those who in turn serve you. May the madness of treachery never, not once, make you offer an angry insult. May it never give rise in your heart to the idea of being disloyal to your lord. There is harsh and shameful talk about men who act in this fashion. I do not think that such will befall you or those who fight alongside you because such an attitude has never shown itself among your ancestors. It has not been seen among them, it is not seen now, and it will not be seen in the future.

Be truthful to your lord, my son William, child of their lineage. Be vigilant, energetic, and offer him ready assistance as I have said here. In every matter of importance to royal power take care to show yourself a man of good judgment—in your own thoughts and in public—to the extent that God gives you strength. Read the sayings and the lives of the holy Fathers who have gone before us. You will there discover how you may serve your lord and be faithful to him in all things. When you understand this, devote yourself to the faithful execution of your lord's commands. Look around as well and observe those who fight for him loyally and constantly. Learn from them how you may serve him. Then, informed by their example, with the help and support of God, you will easily reach the celestial goal I have mentioned above. And may your heavenly Lord God be generous and benevolent toward you. May he keep you safe, be your kind leader and your protector. May he deign to assist you in all your actions and be your constant defender.

What advice does Dhouda give her son? What does this selection tell us about aristocratic women in the Early Middle Ages and their relationship with power?

---

the need for companionship, sex, and children. In the church of the Early Middle Ages, it was generally agreed that marriage gave the right to indulge in sexual intercourse. Sex, then, was permissible within marriage, but only so long as it was used for the sole purpose of procreation, not for pleasure. The church condemned all forms of contraception and also strongly condemned abortion, although its prohibition failed to stop either practice. Various herbal potions were available to prohibit conception or cause abortion. The Catholic church accepted only one way to limit children: periodic or total abstinence from intercourse.

The Catholic church's condemnation of sexual activity outside marriage also included homosexuality. Neither Roman religion nor Roman law had recognized any real difference between homosexual and heterosexual eroticism, and the Roman Empire had taken no legal measures against homosexual relations between adults. Later, in the Byzantine Empire, the emperor Justinian in 538 condemned homosexuality, emphasizing that such practices brought down the wrath of God ("we have provoked Him to anger") and endangered the welfare of the state. Justinian recommended that the guilty parties be punished by castration. Although the church in the Early Middle Ages similarly condemned homosexuality, it also pursued a flexible policy in its treatment of homosexuals. In the Early Middle Ages, homosexuals were treated less harshly than married couples who practiced contraception.

Diet For both rich and poor, the fundamental staple of the Carolingian diet was bread. The aristocratic classes, as well as the monks, consumed it in large quantities. Ovens at the monastery of Saint Gall were able to bake a thousand loaves of bread. Sometimes a gruel made of barley and oats was substituted for bread in the peasant diet.

The upper classes in Carolingian society enjoyed a much more varied diet than the peasants. Pork was the primary meat. Domestic pigs, allowed to run wild in the forests to find their own food, were collected and slaughtered in the fall, then smoked and salted to be eaten during the winter months. Because Carolingian aristocrats were especially fond of roasted meat, hunting wild game became one of their favorite activities. They ate little beef and mutton, however, because cattle were kept as dairy cows and oxen to draw plows, and sheep were raised for wool.

Dairy products became prevalent in the Carolingian diet. Milk, which spoiled rapidly, was made into cheese and butter. Chickens were raised for their eggs. Vegetables also formed a crucial part of the diet of both the rich and the poor. These included legumes, such as beans, peas, and lentils, and roots, such as garlic, onions, and carrots.

Both gluttony and drunkenness were vices shared by many people in Carolingian society. Monastic rations were greatly enlarged in the eighth century to include a daily allotment of 3.7 pounds of bread (nuns were permitted only 3 pounds), 1.5 quarts of wine or ale, 2 to 3 ounces of cheese, and 8 ounces of vegetables (4 for nuns). These rations totaled 6,000 calories a day, and since only heavy and fatty foods—bread, milk, and cheese—were considered nourishing, we begin to understand why some Carolingians were known for their potbellies.

Everyone in Carolingian society, including abbots and monks, drank heavily and often to excess. Taverns became a regular feature of life and were found everywhere: in marketplaces, in pilgrimage centers, and on royal, episcopal, and monastic estates. Drinking contests were not unusual; one penitential stated, "Does drunken bravado encourage you to attempt to outdrink your friends? If so, thirty days's fast."

The aristocrats and monks favored wine above all other beverages, and much care was lavished on its production, especially by monasteries. Ale was especially popular in the northern and eastern parts of the

Carolingian world. Water was also drunk as a beverage, but much care had to be taken to obtain pure sources from wells or clear streams.

Health Medical practice in Carolingian times stressed the use of medicinal herbs and bleeding. Although the latter was practiced regularly, moderation was frequently recommended. Some advised carefulness as well: "Who dares to undertake a bleeding should see to it that his hand does not tremble." Physicians were also available when people faced serious illnesses. Many were clerics, and monasteries trained their own. Monasteries kept medical manuscripts copied from ancient works and grew herbs to provide stocks of medicinal plants. Carolingian medical manuscripts contained descriptions of illnesses, recipes for medical potions, and even gynecological advice, although monks in particular expended little effort on female medical needs.

Physicians of the Early Middle Ages supplemented their medicines and natural practices with appeals for otherworldly help. Magical rites and influences were carried over from pagan times; Germanic tribes had used magical medicine for centuries. But as pagans were converted to Christianity, miraculous healing through the intervention of God, Jesus, or the saints soon replaced pagan practices. Medieval chronicles abound with accounts of people healed by touching a saint's body.

Disintegration of the Carolingian Empire

The Carolingian Empire began to disintegrate soon after Charlemagne's death. Charlemagne was succeeded by his son Louis the Pious (814–840), who was unable to control either the Frankish aristocracy or his own four sons, who fought continually. In 843, after their father's death, the three surviving brothers signed the Treaty of Verdun. This agreement divided the Carolingian Empire among them into three major sections: Charles the Bald (843–877) obtained the west Frankish lands, which formed the core of the eventual kingdom of France; Louis the German (843–876) took the eastern lands, which became Germany; and Lothair (840–855) received the title of emperor and a "Middle Kingdom" extending from the North Sea to Italy, including the Netherlands, the Rhineland, and northern Italy. The territories of the Middle Kingdom became a source of incessant struggle between the other two Frankish rulers and their heirs. Indeed, France

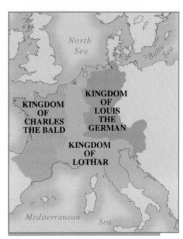

Division of the Carolingian Empire by the Treaty of Verdun, 843

Travelers at an Inn. Inns provided refuge for the many pilgrims, merchants, and others who traveled Europe's dangerous roads in the Middle Ages. In this illustration, two merchants are shown playing backgammon to while away the time.

and Germany would fight over the territories of the Middle Kingdom for centuries.

Although this division of the Carolingian Empire was made for political reasons (dividing landholdings among the male heirs was a traditional Frankish custom), two different cultures began to emerge. By the ninth century, inhabitants of the west Frankish area were speaking a Romance language derived from Latin that became French. Eastern Franks spoke a Germanic dialect. The later kingdoms of France and Germany did not yet exist, however. In the ninth century, the frequent struggles among the numerous heirs of the sons of Louis the Pious led to further disintegration of the Carolingian Empire. In the meantime, while powerful aristocrats acquired even more power in their own local territories at the expense of the squabbling Carolingian rulers, the process of disintegration was abetted by external attacks on various parts of the old Carolingian world.

Invasions of the Ninth and Tenth Centuries

In the ninth and tenth centuries, western Europe was beset by a wave of invasions of several non-Christian peoples—one old enemy, the Muslims, and two new ones, the Magyars and Vikings (see Map 8.2). The Muslims began a new series of attacks in the Mediterranean in the ninth century. They raided the southern coasts of Europe, especially Italy; occupied Sicily; destroyed the Carolingian defenses in northern Spain; and conducted forays into southern France. The Magyars were a people from western

MAP 8.2 Invasions of the Ninth and Tenth Centuries. Attacks by invading Vikings, Magyars, and Muslims terrorized much of Europe in the ninth and tenth centuries, disrupting the economy and spurring the development of fief-holding. The Vikings were the biggest problem, but they eventually formed settlements, converted to Christianity, and were assimilated. ❓ Why was it important for the marauding Vikings to build sound boats and develop good seafaring skills? 🔹 View an animated version of this map or related maps at http://thomsonedu.com/history/spielvogel

Asia who moved into eastern and central Europe at the end of the ninth century. They established themselves on the plains of Hungary and from there made raids into western Europe. The Magyars were finally crushed at the Battle of Lechfeld in Germany in 955. At the end of the tenth century, they were converted to Christianity and settled down to establish the kingdom of Hungary.

The Vikings By far the most devastating and far-reaching attacks of the time came from the Northmen or Norsemen of Scandinavia, also known as the Vikings. The Vikings were a Germanic people who had settled in Scandinavia. Why they invaded other areas of Europe is uncertain. Perhaps overpopulation and the emergence of more effective monarchs in Denmark, Norway, and Sweden caused some of the freedom-loving Scandinavians to seek escape from the growing order. The Vikings' great love of adventure and their search for booty and new avenues of trade may also have been important factors.

Two features of Viking society help explain what the Vikings accomplished. First, they were warriors. And second, they were superb shipbuilders and sailors. Their ships were the best of the period. Long and narrow with beautifully carved arched prows, the Viking "dragon ships" carried about fifty men. Their shallow draft enabled them to sail up European rivers and attack places at some distance inland. Vikings sacked villages and towns, destroyed churches, and easily defeated small local armies. Viking attacks frightened people and led many a clergyman to plead with them to change their behavior and appease God's anger, as is revealed in this sermon in 1014 by an English archbishop:

> Things have not gone well now for a long time at home or abroad, but there has been devastation and persecution in every district again and again, and the English have been for a long time now completely defeated and too greatly disheartened through God's anger; and the pirates [Vikings] so strong with God's consent that often in battle one puts to flight ten, and sometimes less, sometimes more, all because of our sins.... We pay them continually and they humiliate us daily; they ravage and they burn, plunder, and rob and carry on board; and lo, what else is there in all these events except God's anger clear and visible over this people?[5]

Because there were different groups of Scandinavians, Viking expansion varied a great deal. Norwegian Vikings moved into Ireland and western England, while the Danes attacked eastern England, Frisia, and the Rhineland and navigated rivers to enter western Frankish lands. Swedish Vikings dominated the Baltic Sea and progressed into the Slavic areas to the east. Moving into northwestern Russia, they went down the rivers to Novgorod and Kiev and established fortified ports throughout these territories.

Early Viking raids had been carried out largely in the summer; by the mid-ninth century, however, the Northmen had begun to establish winter settlements in Europe from which they could make expeditions to conquer and settle new lands. By 850, groups of Norsemen had settled in Ireland, and the Danes occupied an area known as the

Vikings Attacking England. This illustration from an eleventh-century English manuscript depicts a group of armed Vikings invading England. Two ships have already reached the shore, and a few Vikings are shown walking down a long gangplank onto English soil.

Danelaw in northeast England by 878. Beginning in 911, the ruler of the western Frankish lands gave one band of Vikings land at the mouth of the Seine River, forming a section of France that ultimately became known as Normandy. This policy of settling the Vikings and converting them to Christianity was a deliberate one, since the new inhabitants served as protectors against additional Norseman attacks.

The Vikings were also daring explorers. After 860, they sailed westward in their long ships across the north Atlantic, reaching Iceland in 874. Erik the Red, a Viking exiled from Iceland, traveled even farther west and discovered Greenland in 985. A Viking site in North America was founded in Newfoundland.

By the tenth century, Viking expansion was drawing to a close, but not before Viking settlements had been made in many parts of Europe. Like the Magyars, the Vikings were assimilated into European civilization. Once again, Christianity proved a decisive civilizing force. Europe and Christianity were becoming virtually synonymous.

The Viking raids and settlements also had important political repercussions. The inability of royal authorities to protect their peoples against these incursions caused local populations to turn instead to the local aristocrats who provided security for them. In the process, the landed aristocrats not only increased their strength and prestige but also assumed even more of the functions of local governments that had previously belonged to kings; over time these developments led to a new political and military order.

The Emerging World of Lords and Vassals

The renewed invasions and the disintegration of the Carolingian Empire led to the emergence of a new type of relationship between free individuals. When governments ceased to be able to defend their subjects, it became important to find some powerful lord who could offer protection in exchange for service. The contract sworn between a lord and his subordinate (known as a vassal) is the basis of a form of social organization that later generations of historians called feudalism. But feudalism was never a system, and many historians today prefer to avoid using the term.

Vassalage

The practice of **vassalage** was derived from Germanic society, in which warriors swore an oath of loyalty to their leader. They fought for their chief, and he in turn took care of their needs. By the eighth century, an individual who served a lord in a military capacity was known as a vassal.

With the breakdown of governments, powerful nobles took control of large areas of land. They needed men to fight for them, so the practice arose of giving grants of land to vassals who in return would fight for their lord. The Frankish army had originally consisted of foot soldiers, dressed in coats of mail and armed with swords. But in the eighth century, when larger horses and the stirrup were introduced, a military change began to occur. Earlier, horsemen had been throwers of spears. Now they wore armored coats of mail (the larger horse could carry the weight) and wielded long lances that enabled them to act as battering rams (the stirrups kept them on their horses). For almost five hundred years, warfare in Europe was

dominated by heavily armored cavalry, or knights, as they came to be called. The knights came to have the greatest social prestige and formed the backbone of the European aristocracy.

Of course, a horse, armor, and weapons were expensive to purchase and maintain, and learning to wield these instruments skillfully on horseback took much time and practice. Consequently, lords who wanted men to fight for them had to grant each vassal a piece of land that provided for the support of the vassal and his family. In return, the vassal provided fighting skills. In the Early Middle Ages, when trade was minimal and wealth was

A Medieval Knight. In return for his fighting skills, a knight received a piece of land from his lord that provided for his economic support. Pictured here is a bronze statue of a knight with his equipment. The introduction of the high saddle, stirrup, and larger horses allowed horsemen to wear heavier armor and to wield long lances, vastly improving the fighting ability of the cavalry.

based primarily on land holdings, land became the most important gift a lord could give to a vassal in return for military service.

The relationship between lord and vassal was made official by a public ceremony. To become a vassal, a man performed an act of homage to his lord, as described in this passage from a medieval digest of law:

> The man should put his hands together as a sign of humility, and place them between the two hands of his lord as a token that he vows everything to him and promises faith to him; and the lord should receive him and promise to keep faith with him. Then the man should say: "Sir, I enter your homage and faith and become your man by mouth and hands [that is, by taking the oath and placing his hands between those of the lord], and I swear and promise to keep faith and loyalty to you against all others, and to guard your rights with all my strength."[6]

As in the earlier Germanic band, loyalty to one's lord was the chief virtue.

Fief-Holding

The land granted to a vassal in return for military service came to be known as a **fief**. In time, many vassals who held such grants of land came to exercise rights of jurisdiction or political and legal authority within their fiefs. As the Carolingian world disintegrated politically under the impact of internal dissension and invasions, an increasing number of powerful lords arose. Instead of a single government, many people were now responsible for keeping order.

Fief-holding also became increasingly complicated with the development of **subinfeudation**. The vassals of a king, who were themselves great lords, might also have vassals who would owe them military service in return for a grant of land from their estates. Those vassals, in turn, might likewise have vassals, who at this low level would be simple knights with barely enough land to provide their equipment. The lord-vassal relationship, then, bound together both greater and lesser landowners. At all levels, the lord-vassal

relationship was always an honorable relationship between free men and did not imply any sense of servitude. Since kings could no longer provide security in the midst of the breakdown created by the invasions of the ninth century, the practice of subinfeudation became ever more widespread. With their rights of jurisdiction, fiefs gave lords virtual possession of the rights of government.

The new practice of lordship was basically a product of the Carolingian world, but it also spread to England, Germany, central Europe, and in some form to Italy. Fief-holding came to be characterized by a set of practices that determined the relationship between a lord and his vassal. The major obligation of a vassal to his lord was to perform military service, usually about forty days a year. A vassal was also required to appear at his lord's court when summoned to give advice to the lord. He might also be asked to sit in judgment in a legal case because the important vassals of a lord were peers and only they could judge each other. Finally, vassals were also responsible for aids, or financial payments to the lord on a number of occasions, including the knighting of the lord's eldest son, the marriage of his eldest daughter, and the ransom of the lord's person in the event he was captured.

In turn, a lord had responsibilities toward his vassals. His major obligation was to protect his vassal, either by defending him militarily or by taking his side in a court of law if necessary. The lord was also responsible for the maintenance of the vassal, usually by granting him a fief.

The Manorial System

The landholding class of nobles and knights comprised a military elite whose ability to function as warriors depended on having the leisure time to pursue the arts of war. Landed estates, worked by a dependent peasant class, provided the economic sustenance that made this way of life possible. A **manor** (see Map 8.3) was simply an agricultural estate operated by a lord and worked by peasants.

MAP 8.3 A Typical Manor. The manorial system created small, tightly knit communities in which peasants were economically and physically bound to their lord. Crops were rotated, with roughly one-third of the fields lying fallow at any one time, which helped replenish soil nutrients (see Chapter 9). **?** How does the area of the lord's manor, other buildings, garden, and orchard compare to that of the peasant holdings in the village? **View an animated version of this map or related maps at** http://thomsonedu.com/history/spielvogel

Manorialism grew out of the unsettled circumstances of the Early Middle Ages, when small farmers often needed protection or food in a time of bad harvests. Free peasants gave up their freedom to the lords of large landed estates in return for protection and use of the lord's land. Although a large class of free peasants continued to exist, increasing numbers of free peasants became serfs—peasants bound to the land and required to provide labor services, pay rents, and be subject to the lord's jurisdiction. By the ninth century, probably 60 percent of the population of western Europe had become serfs.

Labor services consisted of working the lord's **demesne**, the land retained by the lord, which might consist of one-third to one-half of the cultivated lands scattered throughout the manor. The rest would be used by the peasants for themselves. Building barns and digging ditches were also part of the labor services. Serfs usually worked about three days a week for their lord.

The serfs paid rents by giving the lord a share of every product they raised. Moreover, serfs paid the lord for the use of the manor's common pasturelands, streams, ponds, and surrounding woodlands. For example, if a serf fished in the pond or stream on a manor, he turned over part of the catch to his lord. Peasants were also obliged to pay a tithe (a tenth of their produce) to their local village church.

Lords possessed a variety of legal rights over their serfs as a result of their unfree status. Serfs were legally bound to the lord's lands and could not leave without his permission. Although free to marry, serfs could not marry anyone outside their manor without the lord's approval. Moreover, lords sometimes exercised public rights or political authority on their lands, which gave them the right to try peasants in their own court. In fact, the lord's manorial court provided the only law that most peasants knew. Peasants also had to pay the lord for certain services; for example, they might be required to bring their grain to the lord's mill and pay a fee to have it ground into flour. Thus the rights a lord possessed on his manor gave him virtual control over both the lives and the property of his serfs.

In the Early Middle Ages, whether free or unfree, a vast majority of men and women, possibly 90 percent, worked the land. Although trade declined precipitously in this period, it never entirely disappeared. Overall, however, compared to the Byzantine Empire or Muslim caliphates, western Europe in the Early Middle Ages was an underdeveloped, predominantly agricultural society.

The Zenith of Byzantine Civilization

In the seventh and eighth centuries, the Byzantine Empire had lost much of its territory to Slavs, Bulgars, and Muslims. By 750, the empire consisted only of Asia Minor, some lands in the Balkans, and the southern coast of Italy. Although Byzantium was beset with internal dissension and invasions in the ninth century, it was able to deal with them and not only endured but even expanded, reaching its high point in the tenth century, which some historians have called the "golden age of Byzantine civilization."

During the reign of Michael III (842–867), the Byzantine Empire continued to be plagued by problems. The Bulgars mounted new attacks, and the Arabs continued to harass the empire. Moreover, a new church problem with political repercussions erupted over differences between the pope as leader of the western Christian church and the patriarch of Constantinople as leader of the eastern (or Orthodox) Christian church. Patriarch Photius condemned the pope as a heretic for accepting a revised form of the Nicene Creed stating that the Holy Spirit proceeded from the Father and the Son instead of "The Holy Spirit, who proceeds from the Father." A council of eastern bishops followed Photius's wishes and excommunicated the pope, creating the so-called Photian schism. Although the differences were later

Peasants in the Manorial System. In the manorial system, peasants were required to provide labor services for their lord. This thirteenth-century illustration shows a group of English peasants harvesting grain. Overseeing them is a bailiff, or manager, who supervised the work of the peasants.

A WESTERN VIEW OF THE BYZANTINE EMPIRE

ishop Liudprand of Cremona undertook diplomatic missions to Constantinople on behalf of two western kings, Berengar of Italy and Otto I of Germany. This selection is taken from his description of his mission to the Byzantine emperor Constantine VII in 949 as an envoy for Berengar, king of Italy from 950 until his overthrow by Otto I of Germany in 964. Liudprand had mixed feelings about Byzantium: admiration, yet also envy and hostility because of its superior wealth.

Liudprand of Cremona, *Antapodosis*

Next to the imperial residence at Constantinople there is a palace of remarkable size and beauty which the Greeks called Magnavra...the name being equivalent to "fresh breeze." In order to receive some Spanish envoys, who had recently arrived, as well as myself..., Constantine gave orders that his palace should be got ready....

Before the emperor's seat stood a tree, made of bronze gilded over, whose branches were filled with birds, also made of gilded bronze, which uttered different cries, each according to its varying species. The throne itself was so marvelously fashioned that at one moment it seemed a low structure, and at another it rose high into the air. It was of immense size and was guarded by lions, made either of bronze or of wood covered over with gold, who beat the ground with their tails and gave a dreadful roar with open mouth and quivering tongue. Leaning upon the shoulders of two eunuchs I was brought into the emperor's presence. At my approach the lions began to roar and the birds to cry out, each according to its kind; but I was neither terrified nor surprised, for I had previously made enquiry about all these things from people who were well acquainted with them. So after I had three times made obeisance to the emperor with my face upon the ground, I lifted my head, and behold! The man whom just before I had seen sitting on a moderately elevated seat had now changed his raiment and was sitting on the level of the ceiling. How it was done I could not imagine, unless perhaps he was lifted up by some such sort of device as we use for raising the timbers of a wine press. On that occasion he did not address me personally...but by the intermediary of a secretary he enquired about Berengar's doings and asked after his health. I made a fitting reply and then, at a nod from the interpreter, left his presence and retired to my lodging.

It would give me some pleasure also to record here what I did then for Berengar....The Spanish envoys...had brought handsome gifts from their masters to the emperor Constantine. I for my part had brought nothing from Berengar except a letter and that was full of lies. I was very greatly disturbed and shamed at this and I began to consider anxiously what I had better do. In my doubt and perplexity it finally occurred to me that I might offer the gifts, which on my account I had brought for the emperor, as coming from Berengar, and trick out my humble present with fine words. I therefore presented him with nine excellent curaisses, seven excellent shields with gilded bosses, two silver gift cauldrons, some swords, spears and spits, and what was more precious to the emperor than anything, four carzimasia; that being the Greek name for young eunuchs who have had both their testicles and their penis removed. This operation is performed by traders at Verdun, who take the boys into Spain and make a huge profit.

What impressions of the Byzantine court do you receive from Liudprand of Cremona's account? What is the modern meaning of the word Byzantine? How does this account help explain the modern meaning of the word?

---

papered over, this controversy served to further the division between the eastern and western Christian churches.

The Macedonian Dynasty

The problems that arose during Michael's reign were effectively dealt with by the efforts of a new dynasty of Byzantine emperors, known as the Macedonians (867–1081). This dynastic line managed to repel the external enemies, go over to the offensive, and reestablish domestic order. Supported by the church, the emperors continued to think of the Byzantine Empire as a continuation of the Christian Roman Empire of late antiquity. Although for diplomatic reasons they occasionally recognized the imperial title of western emperors, such as Charlemagne, they still regarded them as little more than barbarian parvenus.

The Macedonian emperors could boast of a remarkable number of achievements in the late ninth and tenth centuries. They worked to strengthen the position of free farmers, who felt threatened by the attempts of landed aristocrats to expand their estates at the expense of the farmers. The emperors were well aware that the free farmers made up the rank and file of the Byzantine cavalry and provided the military strength of the empire. The Macedonian emperors also fostered a burst of economic prosperity by expanding trade relations with western Europe, especially by selling silks and metalworks. Thanks to this prosperity, the city of Constantinople flourished. Foreign visitors continued to be astounded by its size, wealth, and physical surroundings. To western Europeans, it was the stuff of legends and fables (see the box above).

In the midst of this prosperity, Byzantine cultural influence expanded due to the active missionary efforts of eastern Byzantine Christians. Eastern Orthodox Christianity was spread to eastern European peoples, including the Bulgars and the Serbs. Perhaps the greatest missionary success occurred when the prince of Kiev in Russia converted to Christianity in 987.

Under the Macedonian rulers, Byzantium enjoyed a strong civil service, talented emperors, and military advances. In the tenth century, these competent emperors combined with a number of talented generals to mobilize the empire's military resources and take the offensive. The Bulgars were defeated, and both the eastern and western parts of Bulgaria were annexed to the empire. The Byzantines went on to add the islands of Crete and Cyprus to the empire and defeat the Muslim forces in Syria, expanding the empire to the upper Euphrates. By the end of the reign of Basil II (976–1025), the Byzantine Empire was the largest it had been since the beginning of the seventh century.

The Byzantine Empire in 1025

The Slavic Peoples of Central and Eastern Europe

North of Byzantium and east of the Carolingian Empire lay a spacious plain through which a number of Asiatic nomads, including the Huns, Bulgars, Avars, and Magyars, had pushed their way westward, terrorizing and plundering the settled peasant communities. Eastern Europe was ravaged by these successive waves of invaders,

who found it relatively easy to create large empires that were in turn overthrown by the next invaders.Over a period of time, the invaders themselves were largely assimilated with the native Slavic peoples of the area.

The Slavs were originally a single people in central Europe who, through mass migrations and nomadic invasions, gradually divided into three major groups: the western, southern, and eastern Slavs (see Map 8.4).

Western Slavs

In the region east of the eastern Frankish or Germanic kingdom emerged the Polish and Bohemian kingdoms of the western Slavs. The Germans assumed responsibility for the conversion of these Slavic peoples since some German emperors considered it their duty to spread Christianity to the barbarians. Of course, it also gave them the opportunity to extend their political authority. German missionaries had converted the Czechs in Bohemia by the end of the ninth century, and a bishopric eventually occupied by a Czech bishop was established at Prague in the tenth. The Slavs in Poland were not converted until the reign of Prince Mieszko (c. 960–992). In 1000, an independent Polish archbishopric was set up at

MAP 8.4 The Migrations of the Slavs. Originally from east-central Europe, the Slavic people broke into three groups. The western Slavs converted to Catholic Christianity, while the eastern Slavs and southern Slavs, under the influence of the Byzantine Empire, embraced the Eastern Orthodox faith. **?** What connections do these Slavic migrations have with what we today characterize as eastern Europe? **View an animated version of this map or related maps at** http://thomsonedu.com/history/spielvogel

Gniezno by the pope. The non-Slavic kingdom of Hungary, which emerged after the Magyars settled down after their defeat at Lechfeld in 955, was also converted to Christianity by German missionaries. Saint Stephen, king of Hungary from 997 to 1038, facilitated the acceptance of Christianity by his people. The Poles, Czechs, and Hungarians all accepted Catholic or western Christianity and became closely tied to the Roman Catholic church and its Latin culture.

Southern Slavs

The southern and eastern Slavic populations largely took a different path because of their proximity to the Byzantine Empire. The Slavic peoples of Moravia were converted to the Eastern Orthodox Christianity of the Byzantine Empire by two Byzantine missionary brothers, Cyril and Methodius, who began their activities in 863. They created a Slavonic (Cyrillic) alphabet, translated the Bible into Slavonic, and created Slavonic church services. While the southern Slavic peoples accepted Christianity, a split eventually developed between the Croats, who accepted the Roman church, and the Serbs, who remained loyal to eastern Christianity.

Although the Bulgars were originally an Asiatic people who conquered much of the Balkan peninsula, they were eventually absorbed by the larger native south Slavic population. Together, by the ninth century, they formed a largely Slavic Bulgarian kingdom. Although the conversion to Christianity of this state was complicated by the rivalry between the Roman Catholic and Eastern Orthodox churches, the Bulgarians eventually accepted the latter. By the end of the ninth century, they embraced the Slavonic church services earlier developed by Cyril and Methodius. The acceptance of Eastern Orthodoxy by the southern Slavic peoples, the Serbs and Bulgarians, meant that their cultural life was also linked to the Byzantine state.

Eastern Slavs

The eastern Slavic peoples, from whom the modern Russians, White Russians (Belarusians), and Ukrainians are descended, had settled in the territory of present-day Ukraine and European Russia. There, beginning in the late eighth century, they began to contend with Viking invaders. Swedish Vikings, known to the eastern Slavs as Varangians, moved down the extensive network of rivers into the lands of the eastern Slavs in search of booty and new trade routes. After establishing trading links with the Byzantine state, the Varangians built trading settlements, became involved in the civil wars among the Slavic peoples, and eventually came to dominate the native peoples, just as their fellow Vikings were doing in parts of western Europe. According to the traditional version of the story, the semilegendary Rurik secured his ruling dynasty in the Slavic settlement of Novgorod in 862. Rurik and his fellow Vikings were called the Rus, from which Russia, the name eventually attached to the state they founded is derived (see the box on p. 152). Although much about Rurik is unclear, it is certain that his follower Oleg (c. 873–913) took up residence in Kiev and established the Rus state, a union of east Slavic territories known as the principality of Kiev. Oleg's successors extended their control over the eastern Slavs and expanded the territory of Kiev until it encompassed the lands between the Baltic and Black Seas and the Danube and Volga Rivers. By marrying Slavic wives, the Viking ruling class was gradually assimilated into the Slavic population, a process confirmed by their assumption of Slavic names.

The growth of the principality of Kiev attracted religious missionaries, especially from the Byzantine Empire. One Rus ruler, Vladimir (c. 980–1015), married the Byzantine emperor's sister and officially accepted Christianity for himself and his people in 987. His primary motive was probably not a spiritual one. By all accounts, Vladimir was a cruel and vicious man who believed an established church would be helpful in the development of an organized state. From the end of the tenth century on, Byzantine Christianity became the model for Russian religious life, just as Byzantine imperial ideals came to influence the outward forms of Russian political life.

The World of Islam

The Umayyad dynasty of caliphs had established Damascus as the center of an Islamic empire created by Arab expansion in the seventh and eighth centuries. But Umayyad rule created resentment, and the Umayyads also helped bring about their own end by their corrupt behavior. One caliph, for example, supposedly swam in a pool of wine and drank enough of it to lower the wine level considerably. Finally, in 750, Abu al-Abbas, a descendant of the uncle of Muhammad, brought an end to the Umayyad dynasty and established the Abbasid dynasty, which lasted until 1258.

The Abbasid rulers brought much change to the world of Islam. They tried to break down the distinctions between Arab and non-Arab Muslims. All Muslims, regardless of ethnic background, could now hold both civil and military offices. This helped open Islamic life to the influences of the civilizations they had conquered. Many Arabs now began to intermarry with the peoples they had conquered.

In 762, the Abbasids built a new capital city, Baghdad, on the Tigris River far to the east of Damascus. The new capital was well placed. It took advantage of river traffic to the Persian Gulf and was located on the caravan route from the Mediterranean to Central Asia. The move eastward allowed Persian influence to come to the fore, encouraging a new cultural orientation. Under the Abbasids, judges, merchants, and government officials, rather than warriors, were regarded as the ideal citizens.

The new Abbasid dynasty experienced a period of splendid rule well into the ninth century. Best known of

A MUSLIM'S DESCRIPTION OF THE RUS

*D*espite the difficulties that travel presented, some contact among the various cultures did occur through trade, diplomacy, and the conquest and migration of peoples. This document is a description of the Swedish Rus who eventually merged with the native Slavic peoples to form the principality of Kiev, commonly regarded as the first Russian state. This account was written by Ibn Fadlan, a Muslim diplomat sent from Baghdad in 921 to a settlement on the Volga River. His comments on the filthiness of the Rus reflect the Muslim preoccupation with cleanliness.

Ibn Fadlan, *Description of the Rus*

I saw the Rus folk when they arrived on their trading-mission and settled at the river Atul (Volga). Never had I seen people of more perfect physique. They are tall as date-palms, and reddish in color. They wear neither coat nor kaftan, but each man carried a cape which covers one half of his body, leaving one hand free. No one is ever parted from his axe, sword, and knife. Their swords are Frankish in design, broad, flat, and fluted. Each man has a number of trees, figures, and the like from the fingernails to the neck. Each woman carried on her bosom a container made of iron, silver, copper or gold—its size and substance depending on her man's wealth....

They [the Rus] are the filthiest of God's creatures. They do not wash after discharging their natural functions, neither do they wash their hands after meals. They are as lousy as donkeys. They arrive from their distant river, and there they build big houses on its shores. Ten or twenty of them may live together in one house, and each of them has a couch of his own where he sits and diverts himself with the pretty slave girls whom he had brought along for sale. He will make love with one of them while a comrade looks on; sometimes they indulge in a communal orgy, and, if a customer should turn up to buy a girl, the Rus man will not let her go till he has finished with her.

They wash their hands and faces every day in incredibly filthy water. Every morning the girl brings her master a large bowl of water in which he washes his hands and face and hair, then blows his nose into it and spits into it. When he has finished the girl takes the bowl to his neighbor—who repeats the performance. Thus the bowl goes the rounds of the entire household....

If one of the Rus folk falls sick they put him in a tent by himself and leave bread and water for him. They do not visit him, however, or speak to him, especially if he is a serf. Should he recover he rejoins the others; if he dies they burn him. But if he happens to be a serf they leave him for the dogs and vultures to devour. If they catch a robber they hang him to a tree until he is torn to threads by wind and weather....

What was Ibn Fadlan's impression of the Rus? Why do you think he was so critical of their behavior?

---

the caliphs of the time was Harun al-Rashid (786–809), whose reign is often described as the golden age of the Abbasid caliphate. His son al-Ma'mun (813–833) was a great patron of learning. He founded an astronomical observatory and created a foundation for translating classical Greek works. This was also a period of growing economic prosperity. The Arabs had conquered many of the richest provinces of the old Roman Empire, and they now controlled the trade routes to the east. Baghdad became the center of an enormous trade empire that extended into Europe, Asia, and Africa, greatly adding to the wealth of the Islamic world.

Despite the prosperity, all was not quite well in the empire of the Abbasids. There was much fighting over the succession to the caliphate. When Harun al-Rashid died, his two sons fought to succeed him in a struggle that almost destroyed the city of Baghdad. As the tenth-century Muslim historian al-Mas'udi wrote, "Mansions were destroyed,

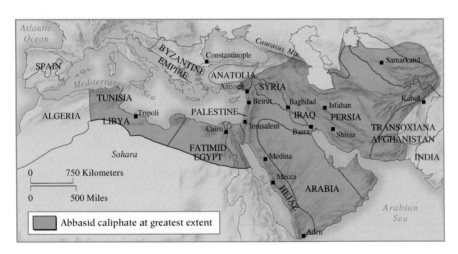

The Abbasid Caliphate at the Height of Its Power

most remarkable monuments obliterated; prices soared.... Brother turned his sword against brother, son against father, as some fought for Amin, others for Ma'mun. Houses and palaces fuelled the flames; property was put to the sack."[7]

Vast wealth also gave rise to financial corruption. By awarding important positions to court favorites, the Abbasid caliphs began to undermine the foundations of their own power and become figureheads. Rulers of the provinces of the empire broke away from the control of the caliphs and established their own independent dynasties. In the eighth century, Spain had already established its own caliphate when Abd al-Rahman of the Umayyad dynasty had fled there. In 756, he seized control of southern Spain and then expanded his power into the center of the peninsula. He took the title of emir, or commander, and set up the emirate of al-Andalus (the Arabic name for Spain), with its center at Córdoba. Under Abd-al-Rahman's successors, a unique society developed in which all religions were tolerated. The court also supported writers and artists, creating a brilliant and flourishing culture.

The fragmentation of the Islamic empire accelerated in the tenth century. A caliphate of the Fatimid family was established in Egypt in 973, and an independent dynasty also operated in North Africa. Despite the political disunity of the Islamic world, however, the underlying Islamic civilization was unified by two common bonds: the Qur'an and the Arabic language.

Islamic Civilization

From the beginning of their empire, Muslim Arabs had demonstrated a willingness to absorb the culture of their conquered territories. The Arabs were truly heirs to the remaining Greco-Roman culture of the Roman Empire. Just as readily, they assimilated Byzantine and Persian culture. In the eighth and ninth centuries, numerous Greek, Syrian, and Persian scientific and philosophical works were translated into Arabic. As the chief language in the southern Mediterranean and the Near East and the required language of Muslims, Arabic became a truly international tongue.

The Muslims created a brilliant urban culture at a time when western Europe was predominantly a rural world of petty villages. This can be seen in such new cities as Baghdad and Cairo, but also in Córdoba, the capital of the Umayyad caliphate in Spain. With a population of possibly 100,000, Córdoba was Europe's largest city after Constantinople. It had seventy public libraries, and the number of manuscripts in the caliph's private library reached 400,000. One caliph collected books from different parts of the world and then had them translated into Arabic and Latin. These included works on geography that later proved valuable to Western sailors and merchants. Schools were also established, and the Great Mosque of Córdoba became a center for scholars from all over the Islamic world. Large numbers of women served as teachers and librarians in Córdoba.

CHRONOLOGY	Byzantium, the Slavs, and the Islamic World
The Byzantine Empire	
Michael III	842–867
Macedonian dynasty	867–1081
Basil II	976–1025
The Slavs	
Establishment of Novgorod	c. 862
Conversion of Moravian Slavs by Cyril and Methodius	863
Founding of principality of Kiev	c. 873–913
Reign of Prince Mieszko; conversion of Slavs in Poland to Christianity	c. 960–992
Vladimir's conversion to Christianity	987
Saint Stephen, king of Hungary	997–1038
Islam	
Overthrow of Umayyad dynasty by Abbasids	750
Creation of emirate of al-Andalus	756
Harun al-Rashid	786–809
Establishment of Fatimid caliphate in Egypt	973

During the first few centuries of the Arab empire, it was the Islamic world that saved and spread the scientific and philosophical works of ancient civilizations. At a time when the ancient Greek philosophers were largely unknown in Europe, key works by Plato and Aristotle were translated into Arabic. They were put in a library called the House of Wisdom in Baghdad, where they were read and studied by Muslim scholars. Texts on mathematics were brought from India. This process was aided by the use of paper. The making of paper was introduced from China in the eighth century, and by the end of the century, paper factories had been established in Baghdad. Booksellers and libraries soon followed. European universities later benefited from this scholarship when these works were translated from Arabic into Latin.

Although Islamic scholars are rightly praised for preserving much of classical knowledge for the West, they also made considerable advances of their own. Nowhere is this more evident than in their contributions to mathematics and the natural sciences. The list of achievements in mathematics and astronomy alone is impressive. The Muslims adopted and passed on the numerical system of India, including the use of the zero. In Europe, it became known as the Arabic system. Al-Khwarizmi, a ninth-century Iranian mathematician, developed the mathematical discipline of algebra. In astronomy, the Muslims were aware that the earth was round, and they set up an observatory at Baghdad to study the stars, many of which they named. They also perfected the astrolabe, an instrument used by sailors to determine their location by observing the positions of heavenly bodies. It was the astrolabe that made it possible for Europeans to sail to the Americas.

Mosque at Córdoba. The first Great Mosque of Córdoba was built by Abd-al-Rahman, founder of the Umayyad dynasty of Spain, in the eighth century. The mosque was later enlarged in the tenth century. Shown here is the interior of the sanctuary, with its two levels of arches. Although the Umayyad caliphs of Damascus were overthrown and replaced by the Abbasid dynasty in the eighth century, the independent Umayyad dynasty in Spain lasted until the eleventh century.

Muslim scholars also made discoveries in chemistry and developed medicine as a field of scientific study. Especially renowned was Ibn Sina (980–1037), known as Avicenna in the West, who wrote a medical encyclopedia that, among other things, stressed the contagious nature of certain diseases and showed how they could be spread by contaminated water supplies. After its translation into Latin, Avicenna's work became a basic medical textbook for medieval European university students. Avicenna was but one of many Arabic scholars whose work was translated into Latin and helped the development of intellectual life in Europe in the twelfth and thirteenth centuries.

TIMELINE

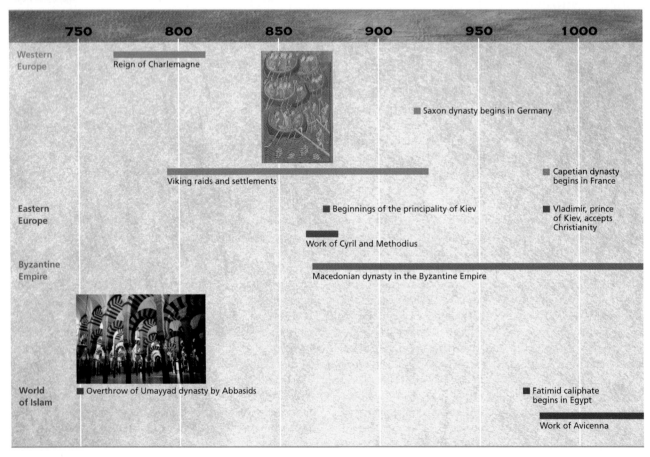

	750	800	850	900	950	1000
Western Europe		Reign of Charlemagne		■ Saxon dynasty begins in Germany		■ Capetian dynasty begins in France
		Viking raids and settlements				
Eastern Europe			■ Beginnings of the principality of Kiev		■ Vladimír, prince of Kiev, accepts Christianity	
			Work of Cyril and Methodius			
Byzantine Empire				Macedonian dynasty in the Byzantine Empire		
World of Islam		■ Overthrow of Umayyad dynasty by Abbasids			■ Fatimid caliphate begins in Egypt	
						Work of Avicenna

CONCLUSION

After the turmoil of the disintegration of the Roman Empire and the establishment of the Germanic states, a new European civilization began to emerge in the Early Middle Ages. The coronation of Charlemagne, descendant of a Germanic tribe converted to Christianity, as Roman emperor in 800 symbolized the fusion of the three chief components of the new European civilization: the German tribes, the classical tradition, and Christianity. In the long run, the creation of a western empire fostered the idea of a distinct European identity and marked the shift of power from the south to the north. Italy and the Mediterranean had been the center of the Roman Empire. The lands north of the Alps now became the political center of Europe.

With the disintegration of the Carolingian Empire, new political institutions began to develop in Europe, characterized by a decentralization of political control in which lords exercised legal, administrative, and military power. The practice of fief-holding transferred public authority into private hands and provided the security sorely lacking in a time of weak central government and repeated invasions by Muslims, Magyars, and Vikings. While Europe struggled, the Byzantine and Islamic worlds continued to prosper and flourish, the brilliance of their urban cultures standing in marked contrast to the under-developed rural world of Europe. By 1000, however, rural Europe had not only recovered but was beginning to expand in ways undreamed of by previous generations. Europe stood poised for a giant leap.

NOTES

1. Einhard, *The Life of Charlemagne,* trans. S. Turner (Ann Arbor, Mich., 1960), p. 30.
2. Ibid., p. 57
3. Quoted in P. Riché, *Daily Life in the World of Charlemagne,* trans. J. A. McNamara (Philadelphia, 1978), p. 56.
4. 1 Corinthians 7:1–2, 8–9.
5. Quoted in S. Keynes, "The Vikings in England, c. 790–1016," in P. Sawyer, ed., *The Oxford Illustrated History of the Vikings* (Oxford, 1997), p. 81.
6. Quoted in O. Thatcher and E. McNeal, eds., *A Source Book for Medieval History* (New York, 1905), p. 363.
7. al-Mas'sudi, *The Meadows of Gold: The Abbasids,* ed. P. Lunde and C. Stone (London, 1989), p. 151.

SUGGESTIONS FOR FURTHER READING

Good general histories of the entire medieval period can be found in **S. Painter and B. Tierney, *Western Europe in the Middle Ages, 300–1475*** (New York, 1983); **E. Peters, *Europe and the Middle Ages,*** 2d ed. (Englewood Cliffs, N.J., 1989); **D. Nicholas, *The Evolution of the Medieval World: Society, Government, and Thought in Europe, 312–1500*** (London, 1993); and **G. Holmes, ed., *The Oxford Illustrated History of Medieval Europe*** (Oxford, 1988). For a good general survey of the social history of the Middle Ages, see **C. B. Bouchard, *Life and Society in the West: Antiquity and the Middle Ages*** (San Diego, Calif., 1988). For a brief history of the period covered in this chapter, see **R. Collins, *Early Medieval Europe, 300–1000*** (New York, 1991). See also the brief work by **B. Rosenwein, *A Short History of the Middle Ages*** (Orchard Park, N.Y., 2002). For a good collection of essays, see **R. McKitterick, ed., *Early Middle Ages: Europe, 400–1000*** (Oxford, 2001).

Carolingian Europe is examined in **P. Riché, *The Carolingians: A Family Who Forged Europe*** (Philadelphia, 1993). On Charlemagne, see **A. Barbero, *Charlemagne: Father of a Continent,*** trans. A

Cameron (Berkeley, Calif., 2004). On Carolingian culture, see *Carolingian Culture: Emulation and Innovation* (New York, 1994) and the collection of essays titled *The Frankish Kings and Culture in the Early Middle Ages* (Brookfield, Vt., 1995) by **R. McKitterick.**

Various aspects of social life in the Carolingian world are examined in **P. Riché, *Daily Life in the World of Charlemagne,*** trans. **J. A. McNamara** (Philadelphia, 1978); **C. B. Bouchard, *Life and Society in the West: Antiquity and the Middle Ages*** (San Diego, Calif., 1988), ch. 5; and **S. F. Wemple, *Women in Frankish Society: Marriage and the Cloister*** (Philadelphia, 1981). On attitudes toward sexuality in the early Christian church, see the important works by **P. Brown, *The Body and Society*** (New York, 1988), and **E. Pagels, *Adam, Eve, and the Serpent*** (New York, 1988).

The Vikings are examined in **F. D. Logan, *The Vikings in History,*** 2d ed. (London, 1991); **G. Jones, *A History of the Vikings,*** rev. ed. (Oxford, 2001); and **P. Sawyer, ed., *The Oxford Illustrated History of the Vikings*** (New York, 1997).

Two introductory works on fief-holding are **J. R. Strayer, *Feudalism*** (Princeton, N.J., 1985), and the classic work by **M. Bloch, *Feudal Society,*** trans. **L. A. Manyon** (London, 1961). For an important revisionist view, see **S. Reynolds, *Fiefs and Vassals*** (Oxford, 1994).

Byzantine civilization in this period is examined in **R. Jenkins, *Byzantium: The Imperial Centuries, 610–1071*** (New York, 1969), and **W. Treadgold, *The Byzantine Revival, 780–842*** (Stanford, Calif., 1988). On the Slavic peoples of central and eastern Europe, see **F. Dvornik, *The Slavs in European History and Civilization*** (New Brunswick, N.J., 1962); **Z. Vana, *The World of the Ancient Slavs*** (London, 1983); and **S. Franklin** and **J. Shepard, *The Emergence of Rus, 750–1200*** (New York, 1996). The world of Islam in this period is discussed in **H. Kennedy, *The Prophet and the Age of the Caliphates: The Islamic Near East from the Sixth to the Eleventh Century*** (London, 1986), and **J. Lassner, *The Shaping of Abbasid Rule*** (Princeton, N.J., 1980). For a broad view on the relations between Islam and the West, see **B. Lewis, *Islam and the West*** (Oxford, 1994).

Enter *ThomsonNOW* using the access card that is available for *Western Civilization: A Brief History.* *ThomsonNOW* will help you understand this chapter with lesson plans generated for your needs. In addition, you can read the following documents, and many more, online:

Saint Benedict, Rule

Saint Finnian of Clonard, Penitential

Einhard, *Life of Charlemagne*

THE RECOVERY AND GROWTH OF EUROPEAN SOCIETY IN THE HIGH MIDDLE AGES

Street scene in a thirteenth-century English town

© Mary Evans Picture Library/The Image Works

𝒯HE NEW EUROPEAN CIVILIZATION that had emerged in the ninth and tenth centuries began to come into its own in the eleventh and twelfth centuries as Europeans established new patterns that reached their zenith in the thirteenth century. The High Middle Ages (1000–1300) was a period of recovery and growth for Western civilization, characterized by a greater sense of security and a burst of energy and enthusiasm. New agricultural practices that increased the food supply helped spur a commercial and urban revival that, accompanied by a rising population, gave a new dynamism to a formerly static society.

Townspeople themselves were often great enthusiasts for their new way of life. In the twelfth century, William Fitz-Stephen spoke of London as one of the noble cities of the world: "It is happy in the healthiness of its air, in the Christian religion, in the strength of its defences, the nature of its site, the honor of its citizens, the modesty of its women; pleasant in sports; fruitful of noble men." To Fitz-Stephen, London offered myriad opportunities and pleasures. Fairs and markets were held regularly, and "practically anything that man may need is brought daily not only into special places but even into the open squares." Any man, according to Fitz-Stephen, "if he is healthy and not a good-for-nothing, may earn his living expenses and esteem according to his station." Then, too, there are the happy inhabitants of the city: Where else has one "ever met such a wonderful show of people this side or the other side of the sea"? Sporting events and leisure activities are available in every season of the year: "In Easter holidays they fight battles on water." In summer, "the youths are exercised in leaping, dancing, shooting, wrestling, casting the stone; the maidens dance as long as they can well see." In winter, "when the great fen, or moor, which waters the walls of the city on the north side, is frozen, many young men play upon the ice; some, striding as wide as they may, do slide swiftly."[1] To Fitz-Stephen, "every convenience for human pleasure is known to be at hand" in London. One would hardly know from his cheerful description that medieval cities faced overcrowded conditions, terrible smells from rotting garbage and raw sewage, and the constant challenge of epidemics and fires.

By the twelfth and thirteenth centuries, both the urban centers and the urban population of Europe were experiencing a dramatic expansion. New forms of cultural and intellectual expression also arose in this new urban world. Although European society in the High Middle Ages remained overwhelmingly agricultural, the growth of trade and cities along with the development of a money economy and new commercial practices and institutions constituted a veritable commercial revolution that affected most of Europe.◆

Land and People in the High Middle Ages

In the Early Middle Ages, Europe was a sparsely populated expanse dotted with villages of farmers and warriors and covered with forests, which provided building and heating materials and food in the form of game. The climate had begun to improve around 700 after centuries of wetter and colder conditions, but natural disasters remained a threat. Drought or too much rain could mean bad harvests, famine, and dietary deficiencies that made people susceptible to a wide range of diseases. Life expectancy remained low.

The High Middle Ages, from 1000 to 1300, witnessed continued improvement in climate as a small rise in temperature made for longer and better growing seasons. At the same time, Europe experienced a dramatic increase in population, from 38.5 to 73.5 million people (see Table 9.1). This was physically evident in the growth of agricultural villages, towns, and cities and the increase in land under cultivation.

What accounted for this dramatic rise in population? For one thing, conditions in Europe were more settled and peaceful after the invasions of the Early Middle Ages had stopped. Agricultural production also rose dramatically after 1000. Were it not for this increase in food supplies, the greater population could never have been sustained.

TABLE 9.1   Population Estimates (in millions), 1000 and 1340

AREA	1000	1340
Mediterranean		
Greece and Balkans	5	6
Italy	5	10
Iberia	7	9
Total	17	25
Western and Central Europe		
France and Low Countries	6	19
British Isles	2	5
Germany and Scandinavia	4	11.5
Total	12	35.5
Eastern Europe		
Russia	6	8
Poland	2	3
Hungary	1.5	2
Total	9.5	13
Total	*38.5*	*73.5*

Source: J. C. Russell, *The Control of Late Ancient and Medieval Population* (Philadelphia: American Philosophical Society, 1985) p. 36. These are estimates; some figures, especially those for eastern Europe, could be radically revised by new research.

The New Agriculture

During the High Middle Ages, significant changes occurred in the way Europeans farmed. In addition to the improved growing conditions, another factor in increasing the output of food was the increase in arable land, achieved chiefly by clearing forested areas for cultivation (see the box on p. 159). Land-hungry peasants cut down trees and drained swamps. By the thirteenth century, the total acreage used for farming in Europe was greater than at any time before or since.

Technological Changes   Technological changes also furthered the development of agriculture. Many of these depended on the use of iron, which was mined in various areas of Europe. Iron was in demand to make swords and armor as well as scythes, axheads, and hoes for use on farms and saws, hammers, and nails for building purposes. Iron was crucial in making the **carruca,** a heavy, wheeled plow strong enough to turn over the dense clay soil north of the Alps and allow for drainage.

Because of the *carruca*'s weight, six or eight oxen were needed to pull it, but oxen were slow. Two new inventions for the horse made it possible to plow faster. A new horse collar, which appeared in the tenth century, distributed the weight around the shoulders and chest, rather than along the throat, and could be used to hitch up a series of horses, enabling them to pull the heavy new plow faster and cultivate more land. And horseshoes, iron pads nailed to the horses' hooves, gave them better traction in the rocky, clayey soil.

THE ELIMINATION OF MEDIEVAL FORESTS

*O*ne of the interesting environmental changes of the Middle Ages was the elimination of millions of acres of forest to create new areas of arable land and to meet the demand for timber. Timber was used as fuel and to build houses, mills of all kinds, bridges, fortresses, and ships. Incredible quantities of wood were burned to make charcoal for the iron forges. The clearing of the forests caused the price of wood to skyrocket by the thirteenth century. This document from 1140 illustrates the process. Suger, the abbot of Saint-Denis, needed 35-foot beams for the construction of a new church. His master carpenters told him that there were no longer any trees big enough in the area around Paris and that he would have to go far afield to find such tall trees. This selection recounts his efforts.

Suger's Search for Wooden Beams

On a certain night, when I had returned from celebrating Matins [a prayer service], I began to think in bed that I myself should go through all the forests of these parts.... Quickly disposing of all duties and hurrying up in the early morning, we hastened with our carpenters, and with the measurements of the beams, to the forest called Iveline. When we traversed our possession in the Valley of Chevreuse we summoned...the keepers of our own forests as well as men who know about the other woods, and questioned them under oath whether we would find there, no matter with how much trouble, any timbers of that measure. At this they smiled, or rather would have laughed at us if they had dared; they wondered whether we were quite ignorant of the fact that nothing of the kind could be found in the entire region, especially since Milon, the Castellan of Chevreuse,...had left nothing unimpaired or untouched that could be used for palisades and bulwarks while he was long subjected to wars both by our Lord the King and Amaury de Montfort. We however—scorning whatever they might say—began, with the courage of our faith as it were, to search through the woods; and toward the first hour we found one timber adequate to the measure. Why say more? By the ninth hour or sooner, we had, through the thickets, the depths of the forest and the dense, thorny tangles, marked down twelve timbers (for so many were necessary) to the astonishment of all.

What does Suger's search for wooden beams reveal about the environmental problems of the Middle Ages?

The use of the heavy, wheeled plow also led to cooperative agricultural villages. Because iron was expensive, the plow had to be purchased by the entire community. Similarly, an individual family could not afford a team of animals, so villagers shared their beasts. Moreover, the plow's size and weight made it hard to maneuver, so land was cultivated in long strips to minimize the amount of turning that would have to be done.

People in the High Middle Ages learned to harness the power of water and wind to do jobs formerly done by human or animal muscle. Mills, located along streams and powered by the rushing water, were used to grind grains and produce flour. Dams were built to increase the force of the water. Europeans also developed windmills to capture the power of the wind. These two types of mills were the most important inventions for the harnessing of power until the steam engine in the eighteenth century, and their spread had revolutionary consequences for producing more food.

The Three-Field System The shift from a two-field to a **three-field system** also contributed to the increase in agricultural production. In the Early Middle Ages, it was common to plant one field while allowing another of equal size to lie fallow to regain its fertility. Now estates were divided into three parts. One field was planted in the fall with winter grains, such as rye and wheat, while spring grains, such as oats and barley, and vegetables, such as peas, beans, or lentils, were planted in the second field. The third was allowed to lie fallow. By rotating the fields, only one-third, rather than one-half, of the land lay fallow at any time. The rotation of crops also prevented the soil from being exhausted so quickly, and more crops could now be grown.

By the thirteenth century, increasing demand for agricultural produce in the towns and cities led to higher food prices. This encouraged lords to try to grow more food for profit. One way to do this was to lease their demesne land to their serfs. Labor services were then transformed into money payments or fixed rents, thereby converting many unfree serfs into free peasants. Although many peasants still remained economically dependent on their lords, they were no longer legally tied to the land. Lords, in turn, became collectors of rents rather than operators of manors with both political and legal privileges. The political and legal powers once exercised by lords were increasingly reclaimed by the monarchical states.

Life of the Peasantry

Peasant activities were largely determined by the seasons of the year. Each season brought a new round of tasks appropriate for the time, although some periods were considerably more hectic than others, especially harvest time in August and September. A new cycle began in October, when the peasants prepared the ground for planting winter crops. In February and March, the land was plowed for spring crops—oats, barley, peas, beans, and lentils. Early summer was a comparatively relaxed time, although there was still weeding and sheepshearing

Peasant Activities. The kind of work that European peasants did was dictated by the month and the season. This French calendar of 1460 shows a number of medieval farming activities, including sowing seeds, harvesting crops, pruning plants, shearing sheep, threshing, pressing grapes, and taking care of animals.

to be done. In every season, serfs worked not only their own land but also the lord's demesne. They also tended the small gardens attached to their dwellings where they grew the vegetables that made up much of their diet.

Religious feast days, Sunday Mass, baptisms, marriages, and funerals all brought peasants into contact with the village church, a crucial part of manorial life. In the village church, the peasant was baptized as an infant, confirmed in his or her faith, sometimes married, and given the sacrament of Holy Communion as well as the last rites of the church before death. The village priest taught the peasants the basic elements of Christianity so that they would gain the Christian's ultimate goal, salvation.

The lifestyle of the peasants was very simple. Their cottages consisted of wood frames with walls made of laths or sticks; the spaces between the laths were stuffed with straw and rubble and then plastered over with clay. Roofs were thatched. The houses of poorer peasants consisted of a single room, but others had at least two rooms—a main room for cooking, eating, and other activities and another room for sleeping. There was little privacy in a medieval peasant household.

Peasant women occupied both an important and a difficult position in manorial society. They were expected to carry and bear their children and at the same time fulfill their obligation to labor in the fields. Their ability to manage the household might determine whether a peasant family would starve or survive in difficult times.

Though simple, a peasant's daily diet was nutritious when food was available. The basic staple of the peasant diet, and the medieval diet in general, was bread. After

the women made dough for the bread, the loaves were baked in community ovens, which were owned by the lord of the manor. Peasant bread generally contained not only wheat and rye but also barley, millet, and oats, giving it a dark appearance and a heavy, hard texture. Bread was supplemented by vegetables from the household gardens, cheese from cow's or goat's milk, nuts and berries from woodlands, and fruits such as apples, pears, and cherries. Chickens provided eggs and sometimes meat.

Grains were important not only for bread but also for making ale. In northern Europe, ale was the most common drink of the poor. If records are accurate, enormous quantities of it were consumed. A monastery in the twelfth century records a daily allotment to the monks of three gallons a day, far above the weekend consumption of many present-day college students. Peasants in the field undoubtedly consumed even more. This high consumption of alcohol might explain the large number of accidental deaths recorded in medieval court records.

The Aristocracy of the High Middle Ages

In the High Middle Ages, European society was dominated by a group of men whose chief preoccupation was warfare—the lords and vassals of medieval society. The lords were the kings, dukes, counts, barons, and viscounts (and even bishops and archbishops) who held extensive lands and considerable political power. They formed an **aristocracy** or nobility that held real political, economic, and social power. Nobles relied for military help on knights, mounted warriors who fought for them in return for

Art Resource, NY (Musée Condé, Chantilly, France)

Castle and Aristocrats. This illustration is from the *Très Riches Heures* (Very Sumptuous Hours) of Jean, duke of Berry. The three Limbourg brothers created this "book of hours," which was a book containing prayers to be recited at different times each day. This scene depicts the château at Dourdan, France, and its surrounding lands. In the foreground, elaborately dressed aristocratic men and women are seen amusing themselves.

kitchens, stables, and storerooms; a great hall for visitors, dining, and administrative business; and numerous rooms for sleeping and living. The growing wealth of the High Middle Ages made it possible for the European nobility to build more complex castles with thicker walls and more elaborately decorated interiors. As castles became more sturdily built, they proved to be more easily defended and harder to seize by force.

The Way of the Warrior At the age of seven or eight, the sons of the nobility were sent either to a clerical school to pursue a religious career or to another nobleman's castle, where they prepared for the life of a noble. Their chief lessons were military; they learned how to joust, hunt, ride, and handle weapons properly. After his apprenticeship in knighthood, at about the age of twenty-one, a young man formally entered the adult world in a ceremony of "knighting." A sponsor girded a sword on the young candidate and struck him on the cheek or neck with an open hand (or later touched him three times on the shoulder with the blade of a sword), possibly signifying the passing of the sponsor's military valor to the new knight.

In the eleventh and twelfth centuries, under the influence of the church, an ideal of civilized behavior called **chivalry** gradually evolved among the nobility. Chivalry represented a code of ethics that knights were supposed to uphold. In addition to defending the church and the defenseless, knights were expected to treat captives as honored guests instead of putting them in dungeons. Chivalry also implied that knights should fight only for glory, but this account of a group of English knights by a medieval writer reveals another motive for battle: "The whole city was plundered to the last farthing, and then they proceeded to rob all the churches throughout the city, . . . and seizing gold and silver, cloth of all colors, gold rings, goblets, and precious stones . . . they all returned to their own lords rich men."[2] Apparently, not all chivalric ideals were taken seriously.

After his formal initiation into the world of warriors, a young man returned home to find himself once again subject to his parents' authority. Young men were discouraged from marrying until their fathers died, at which time they could marry and become lords of the castle. Trained to be warriors but with no adult responsibilities, young knights had little to do but fight. As the church stepped up efforts to curb socially destructive fighting in the twelfth century, tournaments began to be organized. Initially, tournaments consisted of the melee, in which warriors on horseback fought with blunted weapons in free-for-all combat. By late in the century, the melee was preceded by the joust, or individual combat between two knights. Gradually, the joust became the main part of the tournament. Knights saw tournaments as an excellent way to train for war. As one knight explained, "A knight cannot distinguish himself in [war] if he has not trained for it in tourneys. He must have seen his blood flow, heard his teeth crack under fist blows, felt his opponent's weight bear down upon him as he lay on the ground and,

weapons and daily sustenance. As warriors united by the institution of knighthood, lords and knights came to form a common group, albeit a group with social divisions based on extremes of wealth and landholdings.

Medieval theory maintained that the warlike qualities of the nobility were justified by their role as defenders of society, and the growth of the European nobility in the High Middle Ages was made visible by an increasing number of castles scattered across the landscape. Although castle architecture varied considerably, castles did possess two common features: they were permanent residences for the noble family, its retainers, and servants, and they were defensible fortifications. For defensive purposes, castles were surrounded by open areas and large stone walls. At the heart of the castle was the keep, a large, multistoried building that housed

WOMEN IN MEDIEVAL THOUGHT

*W*hether a nun or the wife of an aristocrat, towns-man, or peasant, a woman in the Middle Ages was considered inferior to a man and by nature subject to a man's authority. Although there are a number of examples of strong women who ignored such attitudes, church teachings reinforced these notions. The first selection from Gratian, the twelfth-century jurist who wrote the first sys-tematic work on canon law, supports this view. The second selection was written by a wealthy fifty-year-old merchant in Paris who wanted to instruct his fifteen-year-old bride on how to be a good wife.

Gratian, *Decretum*

Women should be subject to their men. The natural order for mankind is that women should serve men and children their parents, for it is just that the lesser serve the greater.

The image of God is in man and it is one. Women were drawn from man, who has God's jurisdiction as if he were God's vicar, because he has the image of one God. Therefore woman is not made in God's image.

Woman's authority is nil; let her in all things be subject to the rule of man.... And neither can she teach, nor be a witness, nor give a guarantee, nor sit in judgment.

Adam was beguiled by Eve, not she by him. It is right that he whom woman led into wrongdoing should have her under his direction, so that he may not fail a second time through female-levity.

A Merchant of Paris on Marriage

I entreat you to keep his linen clean, for this is up to you. Because the care of outside affairs is men's work, a husband must look after these things, and go and come, run here and there in rain, wind, snow, and hail—sometimes wet, some-times dry, sometimes sweating, other times shivering, badly fed, badly housed, badly shod, badly bedded—and nothing harms him because he is cheered by the anticipation of the care his wife will take of him on his return—of the pleasures, joys, and comforts she will provide, or have provided for him in her presence: to have his shoes off before a good fire, to have his feet washed, to have clean shoes and hose, to be well fed, provided with good drink, well served, well honored, well bedded in white sheets and white nightcaps, well covered with good furs, and comforted with other joys and amusements, intimacies, affections, and secrets about which I am silent. And on the next day fresh linen and garments....

Also keep peace with him. Remember the country proverb that says there are three things that drive a good man from his home: a house with a bad roof, a smoking chimney, and a quarrelsome woman. I beg you, in order to preserve your husband's love and good will, be loving, amiable, and sweet with him.... Thus protect and shield your husband from all troubles, give him all the comfort you can think of, wait on him, and have him waited on in your home.... If you do what is said here, he will always have his affection and his heart turned toward you and your service, and he will forsake all other homes, all other women, all other help, and all other households.

What do these two documents reveal about male attitudes toward women in the Middle Ages? How were these atti-tudes justified?

---

after being twenty times unhorsed, have risen twenty times to fight."[3]

Aristocratic Women   Although women could legally hold property, most women remained under the control of men—their fathers until they married (usually at the age of fifteen or sixteen) and their husbands after they married. Nevertheless, aristocratic women had numerous opportunities for playing important roles. Because the lord was often away at war, on a Crusade (see Chapter 10), or at court, the lady of the castle had to manage the estate, a considerable responsibility in view of the fact that households, even of lesser aristocrats, could include large numbers of officials and servants. The lady of the castle was also responsible on a regular basis for overseeing the food supply and maintaining all other supplies for the smooth operation of the household.

Although women were expected to be subservient to their husbands (see the box above), there were many strong women who advised and sometimes even dominated their husbands. Perhaps the most famous was Eleanor of Aquitaine (c. 1122–1204), heiress to the duchy of Aquitaine in southwestern France. Married to King Louis VII of France (1137–1180), Eleanor accompanied her husband on a Crusade, but her alleged affair with her uncle during the Crusade led Louis to have their marriage annulled. Eleanor then married Henry, duke of Normandy and count of Anjou, who became King Henry II of England (1154–1189). She took an active role in politics, even assisting her sons in rebelling against Henry in 1173 and 1174.

Blanche of Castile (1188–1252) was another powerful medieval queen. She became regent while her son Louis IX was a boy and ruled France with a powerful hand during much of the 1220s and 1230s. She repelled the attempt of some rebellious French nobles to seize her son, the young king, and defeated Henry III of England when he tried to incite an uprising in France in an attempt to reconquer Normandy. Blanche's political sense was so astute that even when Louis IX came of age, he continued to rely on her as his chief adviser. One medieval chronicler gave her the highest compliment he could think of: "She ruled as a man."

The New World of Trade and Cities

Medieval Europe was an overwhelmingly agrarian society, with most people living in small villages. In the eleventh and twelfth centuries, however, new elements were introduced that began to transform the economic foundation of Western civilization: a revival of trade, considerable expansion in the circulation of money, a restoration of specialized craftspeople and artisans, and the growth and development of towns. These changes were made possible by the new agricultural practices and subsequent increase in food production, which freed some European families from the need to produce their own food. Merchants and artisans could now buy their necessities.

The Revival of Trade

The revival of commercial activity was a gradual process. During the chaotic conditions of the Early Middle Ages, large-scale trade had declined in western Europe except for Byzantine contacts with Italy and the Jewish traders who moved back and forth between the Muslim and Christian worlds. By the end of the tenth century, however, people with both the skills and the products for commercial activity were emerging in Europe.

Cities in Italy assumed a leading role in the revival of trade (see Map 9.1). By the end of the eighth century, Venice, on the northeastern coast, had emerged as a town with close trading ties to the Byzantine Empire. It developed a mercantile fleet and by the end of the tenth century had become the chief western trading center for

MAP 9.1   Medieval Trade Routes. Italian cities and Flanders were the centers of gradually expanding trade in Europe. They fostered the exchange of goods from the Byzantine Empire and the Far East with those of various regions of Europe. The diminishing threats of violence over time greatly helped trade. ❓ Look at Map 6.2. In what areas had trade expanded, and how can you account for this? ◈ **View an animated version of this map or related maps at** http://thomsonedu.com/history/spielvogel

AN ITALIAN BANKER DISCUSSES TRADING BETWEEN EUROPE AND CHINA

*W*orking on behalf of a banking guild in Florence, Francesco Balducci Pegolotti journeyed to England and Cyprus. As a result of his contacts with many Italian merchants, he acquired considerable information about long-distance trade between Europe and China. In this account, written in 1340, he provides advice for Italian merchants.

Francesco Balducci Pegolotti, *An Account of Traders Between Europe and China*

In the first place, you must let your beard grow long and not shave. And at Tana [modern Rostov] you should furnish yourself with a guide. And you must not try to save money in the matter of guides by taking a bad one instead of a good one. For the additional wages of the good one will not cost you so much as you will save by having him. And besides the guide it will be well to take at least two good menservants who are acquainted with the Turkish tongue....

The road you travel from Tana to China is perfectly safe, whether by day or night, according to what the merchants say who have used it. Only if the merchant, in going or coming, should die upon the road, everything belonging to him will become the possession of the lord in the country in which he dies.... And in like manner if he dies in China.... China is a province which contains a multitude of cities and towns. Among others there is one in particular, that is to say the capital city, to which many merchants are attracted, and in which there is a vast amount of trade; this city is called Khanbaliq [modern Beijing]. And the said city has a circuit of one hundred miles, and is all full of people and houses and of dwellers in the said city....

Whatever silver the merchants may carry with them as far as China, the emperor of China will take from them and put into his treasury. And to merchants who thus bring silver they give that paper money of theirs in exchange...and with this money you can readily buy silk and all other merchandise that you have a desire to buy. And all the people of the country are bound to receive it. And yet you shall not pay a higher price for your goods because your money is of paper.

What were Francesco Pegolotti's impressions of China? Were they positive or negative? Explain your answer.

Byzantine and Islamic commerce. Other coastal communities in western Italy, such as Genoa and Pisa, also opened new trade routes.

In the High Middle Ages, Italian merchants became even more daring in their trade activities. They established trading posts in Cairo, Damascus, and a number of Black Sea ports, where they acquired goods brought by Muslim merchants from India, China, and Southeast Asia. A few Italian merchants even journeyed to India and China in search of trade (see the box above).

While the northern Italian cities were busy trading in the Mediterranean, the towns of Flanders were doing likewise in northern Europe. Flanders, the area along the coast of present-day Belgium and northern France, was known for the production of a much desired, high-quality woolen cloth. The location of Flanders made it a logical entrepôt for the traders of northern Europe. Merchants from England, Scandinavia, France, and Germany converged there to trade their wares for woolen cloth. Flanders prospered in the eleventh and twelfth centuries, and such Flemish towns as Bruges and Ghent became centers for the trade and manufacture of woolen cloth.

By the twelfth century, it was almost inevitable that a regular exchange of goods would develop between Flanders and Italy. To encourage this trade, the counts of Champagne in northern France devised a series of six fairs held annually in the chief towns of their territory. Northern merchants brought the furs, woolen cloth, tin, hemp, and honey of northern Europe to the fairs of Champagne and exchanged them for the cloth and swords of northern Italy and the silks, sugar, and spices of the East.

As trade increased, both gold and silver came to be in demand at fairs and trading markets of all kinds. Slowly, a money economy began to emerge. New trading companies as well as banking firms were set up to manage the exchange and sale of goods. All of these new practices were part of the rise of **commercial capitalism,** an economic system in which people invested in trade and goods in order to make profits.

The Growth of Cities

The revival of trade led to a revival of cities. Merchants needed places where they could live and build warehouses to store their goods. Towns had greatly declined in the Early Middle Ages, especially in Europe north of the Alps. Old Roman cities continued to exist but had dwindled in size and population. With the revival of trade, merchants began to settle in these old cities, followed by craft workers or artisans, people who had developed skills on manors

Flanders as a Trade Center

or elsewhere and now perceived the opportunity to ply their trade producing objects that could be sold by the merchants. In the course of the eleventh and twelfth centuries, the old Roman cities came alive with new residents.

Founding of New Cities and Towns   Beginning in the late tenth century, many new cities and towns were founded, particularly in northern Europe. Usually, a group of merchants established a settlement near some fortified stronghold, such as a castle or monastery. The original meaning of the English *borough* or *burgh* and the German *Burg* as a fortress or walled enclosure is still evident in the names of many cities, such as Edinburgh and Hamburg. Castles were particularly favored because they were usually located along major routes of transportation or at the intersection of two important trade routes; the lords of the castle also offered protection. As the settlement prospered and expanded outward, new walls were built to protect it.

Most towns were closely tied to their surrounding territories because they were dependent on the countryside for their food supplies. In addition, they were often part of the territory belonging to a lord and were subject to his jurisdiction. Although lords wanted to treat towns and townspeople as they would their vassals and serfs, cities had totally different needs and a different perspective. Townspeople needed mobility to trade. Consequently, the merchants and artisans of these boroughs and burghs, who came to be called burghers or **bourgeois,** constituted a revolutionary group who needed their own unique laws to meet their requirements. Since the townspeople were profiting from the growth of trade and sale of their products, they were willing to pay for the right to make their own laws and govern themselves. In many instances, lords and kings saw the potential for vast new sources of revenues and were willing to grant (or sell) to the townspeople the liberties they were beginning to demand.

By 1100, burghers were obtaining charters of liberties from their territorial lords that granted them the privileges they wanted, including the right to bequeath goods and sell property, freedom from any military obligation to the lord, written urban law that guaranteed them their freedom, and the right to become a free person after residing a year and a day in the town. The last provision made it possible for a runaway serf who could avoid capture to become a free person in a city. Almost all new urban communities gained these elementary liberties, but only some towns obtained the right to govern themselves by choosing their own officials and administering their own courts of law.

City Governments   Over time, medieval cities developed their own governments for running the affairs of the community. Citizens (males who had been born in the city or who had lived there for some time) elected members of a city council that ran the affairs of the city and also served as judges and magistrates. The electoral process was carefully engineered to ensure that only members of the wealthiest and most powerful families, who came to be called the patricians, were elected.

City governments kept close watch over the activities of their community. To care for the welfare of the community, a government might regulate air and water pollution; provide water barrels and delegate responsibility to people in every section of the town to fight fires, which were an ever-present danger; construct warehouses to stockpile grain in the event of food emergencies; and set the standards of weights and measures used in the various local industries. Urban crime was not a major problem in the towns of the High Middle Ages because the relatively small size of communities made it difficult for criminals to operate openly. Nevertheless, medieval urban governments did organize town guards to patrol the streets by night and the city walls by day. People caught committing criminal acts were quickly tried for their offenses. Serious offenses, such as murder, were punished by execution, usually by hanging. Lesser crimes were punished by fines, flogging, or branding.

Medieval cities remained relatively small in comparison to either ancient or modern cities. A large trading city would number about 5,000 inhabitants. By 1300, London was the largest city in England, with almost 40,000 people. On the Continent north of the Alps, only a few great urban centers of commerce, such as Bruges and Ghent, had a population close to that. Italian cities tended to be larger, with Venice, Florence, Genoa, Milan, and Naples numbering almost 100,000 inhabitants each. Even the largest European city, however, seemed insignificant alongside the Byzantine capital of Constantinople or the Arab cities of Damascus, Baghdad, and Cairo. For a long time to come, Europe remained predominantly rural, but in the long run, the rise of towns and the growth of trade laid the foundations for the eventual transformation of Europe from a rural agricultural society to an urban industrial one.

Life in the Medieval City

Medieval towns were surrounded by stone walls that were expensive to build, so the space within was precious and tightly filled. This gave medieval cities their characteristic appearance of narrow, winding streets with houses crowded against each other and the second and third stories of the dwellings built out over the streets. Because dwellings were constructed mostly of wood before the fourteenth century and candles and wood fires were used for light and heat, the danger of fire was great. Medieval cities burned rapidly once a fire started.

Most of the people who lived in cities were merchants involved in trade and artisans engaged in manufacturing of some kind. Generally, merchants and artisans had their own sections within a city. The merchant area included warehouses, inns, and taverns. Artisan sections were usually divided along craft lines; each craft had its own street where its activity was pursued.

(Snark/Art Resource, NY (Bibliotheque de l'Arsenal, Paris, France))

Shops in a Medieval Town. Most urban residents were merchants involved in trade and artisans who manufactured a wide variety of products. Master craftsmen had their workshops in the ground-level rooms of their houses. In this illustration, two well-dressed burghers are touring the shopping districts of a French town. Tailors, furriers, a barber, and a grocer (from left to right) are visible at work in their shops.

The physical environment of many medieval cities was not pleasant. They were often dirty and rife with smells from animal and human waste deposited in backyard privies or on the streets. Air pollution was also a fact of life, not only from the ubiquitous wood fires but also from the use of a cheaper fuel, coal, employed industrially by lime burners, brewers, and dyers, as well as by poor people who could not afford to purchase wood. Cities were also unable to stop water pollution, especially from the tanning and animal-slaughtering industries. Butchers dumped blood and waste products from their butchered animals into the river, while tanners threw in tannic acids, dried blood, fat, hair, and wastes.

Because of the pollution, cities were not inclined to use the rivers for drinking water but relied instead on wells. Some communities repaired the system of aqueducts left over from Roman times, and some even constructed new ones. Private and public baths also existed in medieval towns. Paris, for example, had thirty-two public baths for men and women. City laws did not allow lepers and people with "bad reputations" to use them, but such measures did not prevent the public baths from being known for permissiveness. One contemporary commented on what occurred in public bathhouses: "Shameful things. Men make a point of staying all night in the public baths and women at the break of day come in and through 'ignorance' find themselves in the men's rooms."[4] Authorities came under increasing pressure to close the baths

down, and the great plague of the fourteenth century sealed their fate.

There were considerably more men than women in medieval cities. Women, in addition to supervising the household, purchasing food and preparing meals, raising the children, and managing the family finances, were also often expected to help their husbands in their trades. Some women also developed their own trades, such as brewing ale or making glass, to earn extra money. Sometimes when master craftsmen died, their widows carried on their trades. Some women in medieval towns were thus able to lead lives of considerable independence.

Industry in Medieval Cities

The revival of trade enabled cities and towns to become important centers for manufacturing a wide range of products, such as cloth, metalwork, shoes, and leather goods. A host of crafts were carried on in houses along the narrow streets of the medieval cities. From the twelfth century on, artisans began to organize themselves into **guilds,** which came to play a leading role in the economic life of the cities.

By the thirteenth century, virtually every group of craft workers, including tanners, carpenters, and bakers, had its own guild, and specialized groups of merchants, such as dealers in silk, spices, wool, or banking, had guilds as well. Craft guilds directed almost every aspect of the production process. They set standards for the articles produced, specified the methods of production to be used, and fixed the price at which the finished goods could be sold. Guilds also determined the number of men who could enter a specific trade and the procedure they must follow to do so.

A person who wanted to learn a trade first became an apprentice to a master craftsman, usually at around the age of ten. After five to seven years of service, in which they learned their craft, apprentices became journeymen (or journeywomen, although most were male), who then worked for wages for other masters. Journeymen aspired to become masters as well. To do so, they were expected to produce a "masterpiece," a finished piece in their craft that allowed the master craftsmen of the guild to judge whether the journeymen were qualified to become masters and join the guild.

The Intellectual and Artistic World of the High Middle Ages

The High Middle Ages was a time of tremendous intellectual and artistic vitality. The period witnessed the growth of educational institutions, a rebirth of interest in ancient culture, a quickening of theological thought, the development of a vernacular literature, and a burst of activity in architecture. While monks continued to play an important role in intellectual activity, the secular clergy, cities, and courts, whether of kings, princes, or high church officials, began to exert a newfound influence. Especially significant were the new cultural expressions that emerged in towns and cities.

The Rise of Universities

The university as we know it—with faculty, students, and degrees—was a product of the High Middle Ages. The word *university* is derived from the Latin word *universitas*, meaning a corporation or guild, and referred to either a guild of teachers or a guild of students. Medieval universities were educational guilds or corporations that produced educated and trained individuals.

The Origins of Universities The first European university was founded in Bologna, Italy, and coincided with the revival of interest in Roman law, especially the rediscovery of Justinian's *Body of Civil Law*. In the twelfth century, Irnerius (1088–1125), a great teacher of Roman law in Bologna, attracted students from all over Europe. Most of them were laymen, usually older individuals who served as administrators to kings and princes and were eager to learn more about law so they could apply it in their jobs. To protect themselves, students at Bologna formed a guild or *universitas*, which was recognized by Emperor Frederick Barbarossa and given a charter in 1158. Although the faculty also organized itself as a group, the *universitas* of students at Bologna was far more influential. It obtained a promise of freedom for students from

local authorities, regulated the price of books and lodging, and determined the curriculum, fees, and standards for their masters. Teachers were fined if they missed a class or began their lectures late.

In northern Europe, the University of Paris became the first recognized university. A number of teachers or masters who had received licenses to teach from the cathedral school of Notre-Dame in Paris began to take on extra students for a fee. By the end of the twelfth century, these masters teaching at Paris had formed a *universitas* or guild of masters. By 1200, the king of France, Philip Augustus, officially acknowledged the existence of the University of Paris. The University of Oxford in England, organized on the Paris model, appeared in 1208. A migration of scholars from Oxford led to the establishment of Cambridge University the following year. In the Late Middle Ages, kings, popes, and princes vied to found new universities. By the end of the Middle Ages, there were eighty universities in Europe, most of them located in England, France, Italy, and Germany (see Map 9.2).

Teachers and Students in the Medieval University A student's initial studies at a medieval university centered around the traditional liberal arts curriculum, which consisted of grammar, rhetoric, logic, arithmetic, geometry, astronomy, and music. All classes were conducted in Latin, which provided a common means of communication for students, regardless of their country of origin. Basically, medieval university instruction was done by a

MAP 9.2 **Main Intellectual Centers of Medieval Europe.** Education in the Early Middle Ages rested primarily with the clergy, especially the monks. Although monastic schools were the centers of learning from the ninth century to the early eleventh, they were surpassed in the course of the eleventh century by the cathedral schools organized by the secular (nonmonastic) clergy. In the twelfth and thirteenth centuries, the universities surpassed both monastic and cathedral schools as intellectual centers. ❓ In what ways did France qualify as the intellectual capital of Europe? 🖱 **View an animated version of this map or related maps at** http://thomsonedu.com/history/spielvogel

lecture method. The word *lecture* is derived from the Latin verb meaning "to read." Before the development of the printing press in the fifteenth century, books were expensive, and few students could afford them, so masters read from a text (such as a collection of laws if the subject were law) and then added their commentaries. No exams were given after a series of lectures, but when a student applied for a degree, he (women did not attend universities in the Middle Ages) was given a comprehensive oral examination by a committee of teachers. These exams were taken after a four- or six-year period of study. The first degree a student could earn was the *artium baccalaureus*, or bachelor of arts; later he might receive an *artium magister*, or master of arts. All degrees were technically licenses to teach, although most students receiving them did not become teachers.

After completing the liberal arts curriculum, a student could go on to study law, medicine, or theology, which was the most highly regarded subject of the medieval curriculum. The study of law, medicine, or theology could take a decade or more. A student who passed his final oral examinations was granted a doctoral degree, which officially allowed him to teach his subject. Students who received degrees from medieval universities could pursue other careers besides teaching that proved to be much more lucrative. A law degree was deemed essential for those who wished to serve as advisers to kings and princes. The growing administrative bureaucracies of popes and kings also demanded a supply of clerks with a university education who could keep records and draw up official documents. Medieval universities provided the teachers, administrators, lawyers, and doctors for medieval society.

Medieval universities shared in the violent atmosphere of the age. Records from courts of law reveal numerous instances of disturbances in European universities. One German professor was finally dismissed for stabbing one too many of his colleagues in faculty meetings. A student in Bologna was attacked in the classroom by another student armed with a sword. Oxford regulations attempted to dampen the violence by forbidding students to bring weapons to class. Not uncommonly, town and gown struggles ("gown" refers to the academic robe worn by teachers and students) escalated into bloody riots between townspeople and students (see the box on p. 169).

A Revival of Classical Antiquity

Another aspect of the intellectual revival of the High Middle Ages was a resurgence of interest in the works of classical antiquity—the works of the Greeks and Romans. In the twelfth century, western Europe was introduced to a large number of Greek scientific and philosophical works, including those of Galen and Hippocrates on medicine, Ptolemy on astronomy, and Euclid on mathematics. Above all, the West now had available the complete works of Aristotle. During the second half of the twelfth century, all of Aristotle's scientific works were translated into Latin. This great influx of Aristotle's works had an overwhelming impact on the West. He came to be viewed as the "master of those who know," the man who seemed to have understood every field of knowledge.

The recovery of Greek scientific and philosophical works was not a simple process, however. Little knowledge of Greek had survived in Europe. It was through the Muslim world, especially in Spain, that the West recovered the works of Aristotle and other Greeks. The translation of Greek works into Arabic was one aspect of the brilliant Muslim civilization; in the twelfth century, these writings were translated from Arabic into Latin, making them available to the West.

University Classroom. This illustration shows a university classroom in fourteenth-century Germany. As was customary in medieval classrooms, the master is reading from a text. The students vary considerably in age and in the amount of attention they are willing to give the lecturer.

University Students and Violence at Oxford

Medieval universities shared in the violent atmosphere of their age. Town-and-gown quarrels often resulted in bloody conflicts, especially during the universities' formative period. This selection is taken from an anonymous description of a student riot at Oxford at the end of the thirteenth century.

A Student Riot at Oxford

[The townsmen] seized and imprisoned all scholars on whom they could lay hands, invaded their inns [halls of residence], made havoc of their goods and trampled their books under foot. In the face of such provocation the Proctors [university officials] sent their assistants about the town, forbidding the students to leave their inns. But all commands and exhortations were in vain. By nine o'clock next morning, bands of scholars were parading the streets in martial array. If the Proctors failed to restrain them, the mayor was equally powerless to restrain his townsmen. The great bell of St. Martin's rang out an alarm; oxhorns were sounded in the streets; messengers were sent into the country to collect rustic allies. The clerks [students and teachers], who numbered three thousand in all, began their attack simultaneously in various quarters. They broke open warehouses in the Spicery, the Cutlery and elsewhere. Armed with bow and arrows, swords and bucklers, slings and stones, they fell upon their opponents. Three they slew, and wounded fifty or more. One band … took up a position in High Street between the Churches of St. Mary and All Saints', and attacked the house of a certain Edward Hales. This Hales was a long-standing enemy of the clerks. There were no half measures with him. He seized his crossbow, and from an upper chamber sent an unerring shaft into the eye of the pugnacious rector. The death of their valiant leader caused the clerks to lose heart. They fled, closely pursued by the townsmen and country-folk. Some were struck down in the streets, and others who had taken refuge in the churches were dragged out and driven mercilessly to prison, lashed with thongs and goaded with iron spikes.

Complaints of murder, violence and robbery were lodged straightway with the King by both parties. The townsmen claimed three thousand pounds' damage. The commissioners, however, appointed to decide the matter, condemned them to pay two hundred marks, removed the bailiffs, and banished twelve of the most turbulent citizens from Oxford.

Who do you think was responsible for this conflict between town and gown? Why? Why do you think the king supported the university?

The Islamic world had more to contribute intellectually to the West than translations, however. Scientific work in the ninth and tenth centuries had enabled it to forge far ahead of the Western world, and in the twelfth and thirteenth centuries, Arabic works on physics, mathematics, medicine, and optics became available to the West in Latin translations. Adelard of Bath (1090–1150) was one source of these works. Having traveled throughout the Mediterranean world, he later translated an Arabic version of Euclid's *Elements* (see Chapter 4) into Latin, as well as the mathematical works of al-Khwarizmi (see Chapter 8). Adelard also introduced to Europeans the astrolabe, an Arabic astronomical instrument of great value to sailors.

When Aristotle's works were brought into the West in the second half of the twelfth century, they were accompanied by commentaries written by outstanding Arabic and Jewish philosophers. One example was Ibn-Rushd, also known as Averroës (1126–1198), who lived in Córdoba and composed a systematic commentary on virtually all of Aristotle's surviving works.

The Revival of Roman Law

Another aspect of the revival of classical antiquity was the rediscovery of the great work of Justinian, the *Body of Civil Law*, known to the medieval West before 1100 only at second hand. Initially, teachers of law, such as Irnerius of Bologna, were content merely to explain the meaning of Roman legal terms to their students. Gradually, they became more sophisticated so that by the mid-twelfth century, "doctors of law" had developed commentaries and systematic treatises on the legal texts. Italian cities, above all Pavia and Bologna, became prominent centers for the study of Roman law. By the thirteenth century, Italian jurists were systematizing the various professional commentaries on Roman law into a single commentary known as the ordinary gloss. Study of Roman law at the universities came to consist of learning the text of the law along with this gloss.

The training of students in Roman law at medieval universities led to further application of its principles as these students became judges, lawyers, scribes, and councillors for the towns and monarchies of western Europe. By the beginning of the thirteenth century, the old system of the ordeal was being replaced by a rational decision-making process based on the systematic collection and analysis of evidence, a clear indication of the impact of Roman law on the European legal system.

The Development of Scholasticism

The importance of Christianity in medieval society probably made it certain that theology would play a central role in the European intellectual world. Theology, the formal study of religion, was "queen of the sciences" in the new universities. Beginning in the eleventh century, the effort to apply reason or logical analysis to the church's basic doctrines had a significant impact on the study of theology. The word **scholasticism** is used to refer to the philosophical and theological system of the medieval schools. A primary preoccupation of scholasticism was the attempt to reconcile faith and reason—to demonstrate that what was accepted on faith was in harmony with what could be learned by reason.

Scholasticism had its beginnings in the theological world of the eleventh and twelfth centuries but reached its high point in the thirteenth. The overriding task of scholasticism in the thirteenth century was to harmonize Christian revelation with the work of Aristotle. The great influx of Aristotle's works into the West in the High Middle Ages threw many theologians into consternation. Aristotle was so highly regarded that he was called simply "the Philosopher," yet he had arrived at his conclusions by rational thought—not revelation—and some of his doctrines, such as the mortality of the individual soul, contradicted the teachings of the church. The most famous attempt to reconcile Aristotle and the doctrines of Christianity was that of Saint Thomas Aquinas.

Thomas Aquinas (1225–1274) studied theology at Cologne and Paris and taught at both Naples and Paris, and it was at the latter that he finished his famous *Summa Theologica* (*Summa of Theology*—a summa was a compendium that attempted to bring together all existing knowledge on a given subject). Aquinas' masterpiece was organized according to the dialectical method of the scholastics. Aquinas first posed a question, cited sources that offered opposing opinions on the question, and then resolved them by arriving at his own conclusions. In this fashion, Aquinas raised and discussed some six hundred articles or issues.

Aquinas' reputation derives from his masterful attempt to reconcile faith and reason. He took it for granted that there were truths derived by reason and truths derived by faith. He was certain, however, that the two truths could not be in conflict:

> The light of faith that is freely infused into us does not destroy the light of natural knowledge [reason] implanted in us naturally. For although the natural light of the human mind is insufficient to show us these things made manifest by faith, it is nevertheless impossible that these things which the divine principle gives us by faith are contrary to these implanted in us by nature [reason]. Indeed, were that the case, one or the other would have to be false, and, since both are given to us by God, God would have to be the author of untruth, which is impossible.... It is impossible that those things which are of philosophy can be contrary to those things which are of faith.[5]

The natural mind, unaided by faith, could arrive at truths concerning the physical universe. Without the help of God's grace, however, reason alone could not grasp spiritual truths, such as the Trinity (the belief that God, Jesus, and the Holy Spirit are three manifestations of the same unique deity) or the Incarnation (the belief that Jesus in his lifetime was God in human form).

Literature in the High Middle Ages

Latin was the universal language of medieval European civilization. Used in the church and schools, it enabled learned people to communicate anywhere on the Continent. But in the twelfth century, much new literature was being written in the vernacular (the local language, such as Spanish, French, English, or German). A new market for vernacular literature appeared in the twelfth century when educated laypeople at court and in the new urban society sought fresh avenues of entertainment.

Perhaps the most popular vernacular literature of the twelfth century was troubadour poetry, which was chiefly the product of nobles and knights. This poetry focused on the love of a knight for a lady, generally a married noble lady, who inspires him to become a braver knight and a better poet. A good example is found in the laments of the crusading noble Jaufré Rudel, who cherished a dream lady from afar whom he said he would always love but feared he would never meet:

> Most sad, most joyous shall I go away,
> Let me have seen her for a single day,
>   My love afar,
> I shall not see her, for her land and mine
> Are sundered, and the ways are hard to find,
> So many ways, and I shall lose my way,
>   So wills it God.[6]

First appearing in southern France, troubadour poetry soon spread to northern France, Italy, and Germany.

Another type of vernacular literature was the **chanson de geste,** or heroic epic. The earliest and finest example is *The Song of Roland*, which appeared around 1100 and was written in a dialect of French, a language derived from Latin. The *chansons de geste* were written for a male-dominated society. The chief events described in these poems are battles and political contests. Their world is one of combat in which knights fight courageously for their kings and lords. Women play little or no role in this literary genre.

Romanesque Architecture: "A White Mantle of Churches"

The eleventh and twelfth centuries witnessed an explosion of building, both private and public. The construction of castles and churches absorbed most of the surplus resources of medieval society and at the same time reflected its basic preoccupations, God and warfare. The churches were by far the most conspicuous of the public buildings. A chronicler of the eleventh century commented:

> [After the] year of the millennium, which is now about three years past, people all over the world, but especially in Italy and France, began to rebuild their churches. Although most of them were well built and in little need of alterations, Christian nations were rivalling each other to have the most beautiful edifices. One might say the world was shaking herself, throwing off her old garments, and robing herself with a white mantle of

churches. Then nearly all the cathedrals, the monasteries dedicated to different saints, and even the small village chapels were reconstructed more beautifully by the faithful.[7]

Hundreds of new cathedrals, abbeys, and pilgrimage churches, as well as thousands of parish churches in rural villages, were built in the eleventh and twelfth centuries. This building spree reflected a revived religious culture and the increased wealth of the period produced by agriculture, trade, and the growth of cities.

The cathedrals of the eleventh and twelfth centuries were built in the **Romanesque** style, a truly international style. The construction of churches required the services of a cadre of professional master builders whose employment throughout Europe guaranteed international unity in basic features.

Romanesque churches were normally built in the basilica shape used in the construction of churches in the Late Roman Empire. Basilicas were simply rectangular buildings with flat wooden roofs. Elaborating on this basic plan, Romanesque builders made a significant innovation by replacing the flat wooden roof with a long, round stone vault called a barrel vault or a cross vault where two barrel vaults intersected (a vault is simply a curved roof made of masonry). The barrel vault was used when a transept was added to create a church plan in the shape of a cross. Although barrel and cross vaults were technically difficult to construct, they were considered aesthetically pleasing and technically proficient. They also had fine acoustics.

Because stone roofs were extremely heavy, Romanesque churches required massive pillars and walls to hold them up. This left little space for windows, making Romanesque churches quite dark inside. The massive walls and pillars gave Romanesque churches a sense of solidity and a look reminiscent of a fortress.

Barrel Vaulting. The eleventh and twelfth centuries witnessed an explosion of church construction. Using the basilica shape, master builders replaced flat wooden roofs with long, round stone vaults known as barrel vaults. As this illustration of a Romanesque church in Vienne, France, indicates, the barrel vault limited the size of the church and left little room for windows.

The Gothic Cathedral

Begun in the twelfth century and brought to perfection in the thirteenth, the **Gothic** cathedral remains one of the great artistic triumphs of the High Middle Ages. Soaring skyward, as if to reach heaven, it was a fitting symbol for medieval people's preoccupation with God.

Two fundamental innovations of the twelfth century made Gothic cathedrals possible. The combination of ribbed vaults and pointed arches replaced the barrel vault of Romanesque churches and enabled builders to make Gothic churches higher than their Romanesque counterparts. The use of pointed arches and ribbed vaults created an impression of upward movement, a sense of weightless upward thrust that implied the energy of God. Another technical innovation, the flying buttress, basically a heavy arched pier of stone built onto the outside of the walls, made it possible to distribute the weight of the church's vaulted ceilings outward and downward and thus reduce the thickness of the heavy walls used in Romanesque churches to hold the weight of the massive barrel vaults. The thinner walls of Gothic cathedrals could conse-

quently be filled with magnificent stained-glass windows, which created a play of light inside that varied with the sun at different times of the day. The preoccupation with colored light in Gothic cathedrals was inspired by the belief that natural light was a symbol of the divine light of God.

The first fully Gothic church was the abbey church of Saint-Denis near Paris, inspired by its famous Abbot Suger and built between 1140 and 1150. A product of northern France, the Gothic style had spread by the mid-thirteenth century to England, Spain, Germany, and virtually all the rest of Europe. The most brilliant Gothic cathedrals were still to be found in France—in Paris (Notre-Dame), Reims, Amiens, and Chartres.

A Gothic cathedral was the work of an entire community. All classes of society contributed to its construction. Money was raised from wealthy townspeople, who had profited from the new trade and industries, as well as from kings and nobles. Master masons, who were both architects and engineers, designed the cathedrals.

The Gothic Cathedral. The Gothic cathedral was one of the greatest artistic triumphs of the High Middle Ages. Shown here is the cathedral of Notre-Dame in Paris. Begun in 1163, it was not completed until the beginning of the fourteenth century.

Interior of a Gothic Cathedral. The use of ribbed vaults and pointed arches gave the Gothic cathedral a feeling of upward movement. Moreover, due to the flying buttress, the cathedral could have thin walls with stained-glass windows that filled the interior with light. The flying buttress was a heavy pier of stone built onto the outside of the walls to bear the brunt of the weight of the church's vaulted ceiling.

They drew up the plans and supervised the work of construction. Stonemasons and other craftspeople were paid a daily wage and provided the skilled labor to build the cathedrals. A Gothic cathedral symbolized the chief preoccupation of a medieval Christian community, its dedication to a spiritual ideal. As we have observed before, the largest buildings of an era reflect the values of its society. The Gothic cathedral, with its towers soaring toward heaven, gave witness to an age when a spiritual impulse still underlay most of existence.

CONCLUSION

The new European civilization that had emerged in the Early Middle Ages began to flourish in the High Middle Ages. Better growing conditions, an expansion of cultivated land, and technological and agricultural changes combined to enable Europe's food supply to increase significantly after 1000. This increase helped sustain a dramatic rise in population that was apparent in the expansion of towns and cities.

The High Middle Ages witnessed economic and social changes that some historians believe set European civilization on a path that lasted until the Industrial Revolution of the late eighteenth century created a new pattern. The revival of trade, the expansion of towns and cities, and the development of a money economy did not mean the end of a predominantly rural European society, but they did open the door to new ways to make a living and new opportunities for people to expand and enrich their lives. Eventually, they laid the foundations for the development of a mostly urban industrial society.

The High Middle Ages also gave birth to a cultural revival that led to a rediscovery of important aspects of the classical heritage, to new centers of learning in the universities, to the use of reason to systematize the study of theology, to the development of a vernacular literature that appealed to both knights and townspeople, and to a dramatic increase in the number and size of churches.

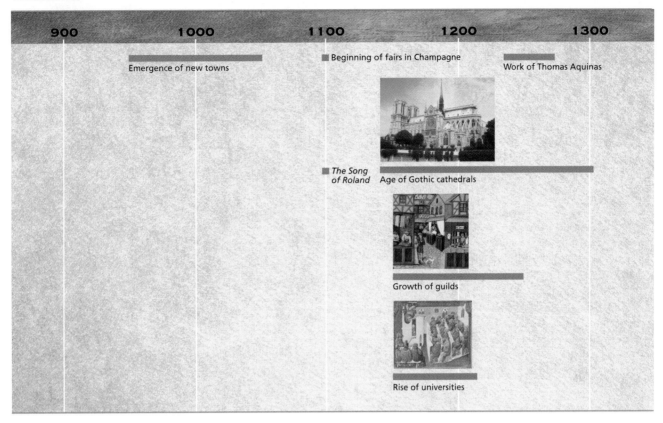

900   1000   1100   1200   1300

Emergence of new towns

Beginning of fairs in Champagne

Work of Thomas Aquinas

The Song of Roland   Age of Gothic cathedrals

Growth of guilds

Rise of universities

NOTES

1. Quoted in N. F. Cantor, ed., *The Medieval Reader* (New York, 1994), pp. 69–70.
2. Quoted in J. Gies and F. Gies, *Life in a Medieval Castle* (New York, 1974), p. 175.
3. Quoted in R. Delort, *Life in the Middle Ages,* trans. R. Allen (New York, 1972), p. 218.
4. Quoted in J. Gimpel, *The Medieval Machine* (Harmondsworth, England, 1977), p. 92.
5. Quoted in J. Mundy, *Europe in the High Middle Ages, 1150–1309* (New York, 1973), pp. 474–475.
6. Quoted in H. Waddell, *The Wandering Scholars* (New York, 1961), p. 222.
7. Quoted in J. W. Baldwin, *The Scholastic Cult of the Middle Ages, 1000–1300* (Lexington, Mass., 1971), p. 15.

SUGGESTIONS FOR FURTHER READING

For a good introduction to this period, see **W. C. Jordan, *Europe in the High Middle Ages*** (New York, 2003); **J. H. Mundy, *Europe in the High Middle Ages, 1150–1309,*** 3d ed. (New York, 1999); **M. Barber, *The Two Cities: Medieval Europe, 1050–1320*** (London, 1992); and **R. Bartlett, *The Making of Europe: Conquest, Colonization, and Cultural Change, 950–1350*** (Princeton, N.J., 1993). There is a good collection of essays on various facets of medieval history in **P. Linehan and J. L. Nelson,** eds., ***The Medieval World*** (London, 2001). On peasant life, see **R. Fossier, *Peasant Life in the Medieval West*** (New York, 1988).

Works on the function and activities of the nobility in the High Middle Ages include **S. Reynolds, *Kingdoms and Communities in Western Europe, 900–1300*** (Oxford, 1984); **R. W. Barber, *The Knight and Chivalry*** (Rochester, N.Y., 1995); and the classic work by **M. Bloch, *Feudal Society*** (London, 1961). Various aspects of the social history of the nobility can be found in **R. Barber** and **J. Barker, *Tournaments: Jousts, Chivalry, and Pageants in the Middle Ages*** (New York, 1989), on tournaments; **N. J. G. Pounds, *The Medieval Castle in England and Wales: A Social and Political History*** (New York, 1990); and **C. B. Bouchard, *Life and Society in the West: Antiquity and the Middle Ages*** (San Diego, Calif., 1988), ch. 6. On women, see **R. T. Morewedge,** ed., ***The Role of Women in the Middle Ages*** (Albany, N.Y., 1975), and **S. M. Stuard,** ed., ***Women in Medieval Society*** (Philadelphia, 1976).

On the revival of trade, see **R. S. Lopez, *The Commercial Revolution of the Middle Ages, 950–1350*** (Englewood Cliffs, N.J., 1971). Urban history is covered in **D. Nicholas, *The Growth of the Medieval City: From Late Antiquity to the Early Fourteenth Century*** (New York, 1997), and the classic work of **H. Pirenne, *Medieval Cities*** (Princeton, N.J., 1969). For a good collection of essays on urban culture, see **B. Hanawalt** and **K. I. Reyerson,** eds., ***City and Spectacle in Medieval Europe*** (Minneapolis, Minn., 1994).

A general work on medieval intellectual life is **M. L. Colish, *Medieval Foundations of the Western Intellectual Tradition, 400–1400*** (New Haven, Conn., 1997). See also the classic study by **F. Artz, *The Mind of the Middle Ages,*** 3d ed. (Chicago, 1980). The development of universities is covered in **S. Ferruolo, *The Origin of the University*** (Stanford, Calif., 1985); **A. B. Cobban, *The Medieval***

Universities (London, 1975); and the brief older work by **C. H. Haskins**, *The Rise of Universities* (Ithaca, N.Y., 1957). Various aspects of the intellectual and literary developments of the High Middle Ages are examined in **J. W. Baldwin**, *The Scholastic Culture of the Middle Ages, 1000–1300* (Lexington, Mass., 1971), and **H. Waddell**, *The Wandering Scholars* (New York, 1961). A good biography of Thomas Aquinas is **J. Weisheipl**, *Friar Thomas d'Aquino: His Life, His Thought and Work* (New York, 1974).

For a good introduction to the art and architecture of the Middle Ages, see **A. Shaver-Crandell**, *The Middle Ages,* in the Cambridge Introduction to Art Series (Cambridge, 1982). A good introduction to Romanesque style is **A. Petzold**, *Romanesque Art* (New York, 1995). On the Gothic movement, see **M. Camille**, *Gothic Art: Glorious Visions* (New York, 1996).

Thomson NOW! Enter *ThomsonNOW* using the access card that is available for *Western Civilization: A Brief History.* *ThomsonNOW* will help you understand this chapter with lesson plans generated for your needs. In addition, you can read the following documents, and many more, online:

Peter Abelard, *Story of My Misfortunes*
Thomas Aquinas, Part 1, Question 2, Article 3 of *Summa Theologica*

CHAPTER 10

THE RISE OF KINGDOMS AND THE GROWTH OF CHURCH POWER

CHAPTER OUTLINE AND FOCUS QUESTIONS

The Emergence and Growth of European Kingdoms, 1000–1300

▢ What steps did the rulers of England and France take during the High Middle Ages to reverse the decentralizing tendencies of fief-holding?

▢ What were the major developments in Spain, the Holy Roman Empire, and northern and eastern Europe during the High Middle Ages?

The Recovery and Reform of the Catholic Church

▢ What was at issue in the Investiture Controversy, and what effect did the controversy have on the church and on Germany?

Christianity and Medieval Civilization

▢ What were the characteristics of the papal monarchy and the new religious orders of the High Middle Ages, and what role did women play in the religious life of the period?

The Crusades

▢ What were the reasons for the Crusades, and who or what benefited the most from the experience of the Crusades?

CRITICAL THINKING

▢ Why did centralized kingdoms develop in some parts of Europe and not in others?

A medieval abbot and his monks

© British Library/HIP/Art Resource, NY

THE RECOVERY AND GROWTH of European civilization in the High Middle Ages also affected the state and the church. Both lords and vassals and the Catholic church recovered from the invasions and internal dissension of the Early Middle Ages. Although lords and vassals seemed forever mired in endless petty conflicts, some medieval kings began to exert a centralizing authority and inaugurated the process of developing new kinds of monarchical states. By the thirteenth century, European monarchs were solidifying their governmental institutions in pursuit of greater power.

The recovery of the Catholic church produced a reform movement that led to exalted claims of papal authority and subsequent conflict with state authorities. At the same time, vigorous papal leadership combined with new dimensions of religious life to make the Catholic church a forceful presence in every area of life. The role of the church in the new European civilization was quite evident in the career of a man named Samson, who became abbot or head of the great English abbey of Bury Saint Edmonds in 1182. According to Jocelyn of Brakeland, a monk who assisted him, Abbot Samson was a devout man who wore "undergarments of horsehair and a horsehair shirt." He loved virtue and "abhorred liars, drunkards and talkative folk." His primary concern was the spiritual well-being of his monastery, but he spent much of his time working on problems in the world beyond the abbey walls. Since the monastery had fallen into debt under his predecessors, Abbot Samson toiled tirelessly to recoup the abbey's fortunes by carefully supervising its manors. He also rounded up murderers to stand trial in Saint Edmunds and provided knights for the king's army. But his actions were not always tolerant or beneficial. He was instrumental in driving the Jews from the town of Saint Edmunds and was not above improving the abbey's possessions at the expense of his neighbors: "He built up the bank of the fish-pond at Babwell so high, for the service of a new mill, that by the keeping back the water there is not a man, rich or poor, but has lost his garden and his orchards." The abbot's worldly cares weighed heavily on him, but he had little choice if his abbey were to flourish and fulfill its spiritual and secular functions. But he did have regrets; as he remarked to Jocelyn: "If he could have returned to the circumstances he had enjoyed before he became a monk, he would never have become a monk or an abbot."[1] ◆

The Emergence and Growth of European Kingdoms, 1000–1300

The domination of society by the nobility reached its apex in the High Middle Ages. During the same period, however, kings began the process of extending their power in more effective ways. Out of these growing monarchies would eventually come the European states that dominated much of later European history.

Kings possessed some sources of power that other lords did not. Usually, kings had greater opportunities to increase their lands through war and marriage alliances and then could use their new acquisitions to reward their followers and bind powerful nobles to them. In the High Middle Ages, kings found ways to strengthen governmental institutions and consequently to extend their powers. The growth of cities, the revival of commerce, and the emergence of a money economy enabled monarchs to hire soldiers and officials and to rely less on their vassals.

England in the High Middle Ages

In 1066, an army of heavily armed knights under William of Normandy landed on the coast of England and soundly defeated King Harold and the Anglo-Saxon foot soldiers at the Battle of Hastings on October 14. William (1066–1087) was crowned king of England at Christmastime in London and began the process of combining Anglo-Saxon and Norman institutions. Many of the Norman knights were given parcels of land that they held as fiefs from the new English king. William made all nobles swear an oath of loyalty to him and insisted that all people owed loyalty to the king rather than to their lords.

Gradually, fusion between the victorious Normans and the defeated Anglo-Saxons created a new England. Although the Norman ruling class spoke French, the intermarriage of the Norman-French with Anglo-Saxon nobility gradually blended Anglo-Saxon and French into a new English language. The Normans also took over existing Anglo-Saxon institutions, such as the office of sheriff. William took a census and more fully developed the system of taxation and royal courts begun by the Anglo-Saxon kings of the tenth and eleventh centuries. All in all, William of Normandy created a strong, centralized monarchy.

The Norman conquest of England had other repercussions as well. Because the new king of England was still the duke of Normandy, he was both a king (of England) and at the same time a vassal to a king (of France), but a vassal who was now far more powerful than his lord. This connection with France kept England heavily involved in Continental affairs throughout the High Middle Ages.

Bridgeman-Giraudon/Art Resource, NY (Musée de la Tapisserie, Bayeux, France)

Norman Conquest of England. The Bayeux tapestry, which consists of woolen embroidery on a linen backing, was made by English needlewomen before 1082 for Bayeux Cathedral. It depicts scenes from the Norman invasion of England. This segment shows the Norman cavalry charging the shield wall of the Saxon infantry during the Battle of Hastings.

Henry II In the twelfth century, the power of the English monarchy was greatly enlarged during the reign of Henry II (1154–1189), the founder of the Plantagenet dynasty. The new king was particularly successful in strengthening the power of the royal courts. Henry expanded the number of criminal cases tried in the king's court and also devised ways of taking property cases from local courts to the royal courts. Henry's goals were clear: expanding the jurisdiction of royal courts extended the king's power and, of course, brought revenues into his coffers. Moreover, because the royal courts were now found throughout England, a body of **common law** (law that was common to the whole kingdom) began to replace the local law codes, which differed from place to place.

Henry was less successful at imposing royal control over the church. The king claimed the right to punish clergymen in church courts, but Thomas à Becket, archbishop of Canterbury and therefore the highest-ranking English cleric, claimed that only church courts could try clerics. Attempts at compromise failed, and the angry king publicly expressed the desire to be rid of Becket: "Who will free me of this priest?" he screamed. Four knights took the challenge, went to Canterbury, and murdered the archbishop in the cathedral. Met with public outrage, Henry was forced to allow the right of appeal from English church courts to the papal court.

King John and Magna Carta Many English nobles came to resent the continuing growth of the king's power and rose in rebellion during the reign of Henry's son, King John (1199–1216). At Runnymeade in 1215, John was forced to seal Magna Carta (the Great Charter). Magna Carta was, above all, a feudal document (see the box on p. 178). Feudal custom had always recognized that the relationship between king and vassals was based on mutual rights and obligations. Magna Carta gave written recognition to that fact and was used in subsequent years to strengthen the idea that the monarch's power was limited, not absolute.

Edward I and the Emergence of Parliament During the reign of Edward I (1272–1307), an institution of great importance in the development of representative government—the English Parliament—emerged. Originally the word *parliament* was applied to meetings of the king's Great Council in which the greater barons and chief prelates of the church met with the king's judges and principal advisers to deal with judicial affairs. But out of a need for money, Edward in 1295 invited two knights from every county and two residents ("burgesses") from each town to meet with the Great Council to consent to new taxes. This was the first Parliament.

The English Parliament, then, came to be composed of two knights from every county and two burgesses from every town as well as the barons and ecclesiastical lords. Eventually, barons and church lords formed the House of Lords; knights and burgesses, the House of Commons. The Parliaments of Edward I granted taxes, discussed politics, passed laws, and handled judicial business.

By the end of the thirteenth century, the law of the realm was being determined not by the king alone but by the king in consultation with representatives of various groups that constituted the community.

The Growth of the French Kingdom

In 843, the Carolingian Empire had been divided into three major sections. The west Frankish lands formed the core of the eventual kingdom of France. In 987, after the death of the last Carolingian king, the west Frankish nobles chose Hugh Capet as the new king, thus establishing the Capetian dynasty of French kings. Although they carried the title of kings, the Capetians had little real power. They controlled as the royal domain (the lands of the king) only the lands around Paris known as the Île-de-France. As kings of France, the Capetians were formally the overlords of the great lords of France, such as the dukes of Normandy, Brittany, Burgundy, and Aquitaine (see Map 10.1). In reality, however, many of the dukes were considerably more powerful than the Capetian kings. It would take the Capetian dynasty hundreds of years to create a truly centralized monarchical authority in France.

The reign of King Philip II Augustus (1180–1223) was an important turning point. Philip II waged war against the Plantagenet rulers of England, who also ruled the French territories of Normandy, Maine, Anjou, and Aquitaine, and was successful in gaining control of most of these territories. Through these conquests, Philip quadrupled the income of the French monarchy and greatly enlarged its power. To administer justice and collect royal revenues in his new territories, Philip appointed new royal officials, thus inaugurating a French royal bureaucracy.

Capetian rulers after Philip II continued to add lands to the royal domain. Although Philip had used military force, other kings used both purchase and marriage to achieve the same end. Much of the thirteenth century was dominated by Louis IX (1226–1270), whom many consider the greatest of the medieval French kings. A deeply religious man, he was later canonized as a saint by the church, an unusual action. Louis was known for his attempts to bring justice to his people and ensure their rights. Sharing in the religious sentiments of his age, Louis played a major role in two of the later Crusades, but both were failures, and he met his death during an invasion of North Africa.

Philip IV and the Estates-General One of Louis's successors, Philip IV the Fair (1285–1314), was particularly effective in strengthening the French monarchy. The machinery of government became even more specialized. French kings going back to the early Capetians had possessed a household staff for running their affairs. Over time, however, this household staff was enlarged and divided into three groups to form three major branches of royal administration: a council for advice, a chamber

Magna Carta

After the dismal failure of King John to reconquer Normandy from the French king, some of the English barons rebelled against their king. At Runnymeade in 1215, King John agreed to seal Magna Carta, the Great Charter of liberties regulating the relationship between the king and his vassals. What made Magna Carta an important historical document was its more general clauses defining rights and liberties. These were later interpreted in broader terms to make them applicable to all the English people.

Magna Carta

John, by the Grace of God, king of England, lord of Ireland, duke of Normandy and Aquitaine, count of Anjou, to the archbishops, bishops, abbots, earls, barons, justiciars, foresters, sheriffs, reeves, servants, and all bailiffs and his faithful people greeting.

1. In the first place we have granted to God, and by this our present charter confirmed, for us and our heirs forever, that the English church shall be free, and shall hold its rights entire and its liberties uninjured.... We have granted moreover to all free men of our kingdom for us and our heirs forever all the liberties written below, to be had and holden by themselves and their heirs from us and our heirs.

2. If any of our earls or barons, or others holding from us in chief by military service shall have died, and when he had died his heir shall be of full age and owe relief, he shall have his inheritance by the ancient relief; that is to say, the heir or heirs of an earl for the whole barony of an earl a hundred pounds; the heir or heirs of a baron for a whole barony a hundred pounds; the heir or heirs of a knight, for a whole knight's fee, a hundred shillings at most; and who owes less let him give less according to the ancient custom of fiefs.

3. If moreover the heir of any one of such shall be under age, and shall be in wardship, when he comes of age he shall have his inheritance without relief and without a fine....

12. No scutage or aid shall be imposed in our kingdom except by the common council of our kingdom, except for the ransoming of our body, for the making of our oldest son a knight, and for once marrying our oldest daughter, and for these purposes it shall be only a reasonable aid....

13. And the city of London shall have all its ancient liberties and free customs, as well by land as by water. Moreover, we will and grant that all other cities and boroughs and villages and ports shall have all their liberties and free customs.

14. And for holding a common council of the kingdom concerning the assessment of an aid otherwise than in the three cases mentioned above, or concerning the assessment of a scutage we shall cause to be summoned the archbishops, bishops, abbots, earls, and greater barons by our letters under seal; and besides we shall cause to be summoned generally, by our sheriffs and bailiffs all those who hold from us in chief, for a certain day, that is at the end of forty days at least, and for a certain place; and in all the letters of that summons, we will express the cause of the summons, and when the summons has thus been given the business shall proceed on the appointed day, on the advice of those who shall be present, even if not all of those who were summoned have come....

39. No free man shall be taken or imprisoned or dispossessed, or outlawed, or banished, or in any way destroyed, nor will we go upon him, nor send upon him, except by the legal judgment of his peers or by the law of the land....

60. Moreover, all those customs and franchises mentioned above which we have conceded in our kingdom, and which are to be fulfilled, as far as pertains to us, in respect to our men; all men of our kingdom as well as clergy as laymen, shall observe as far as pertains to them, in respect to their men.

What are the major principles of Magna Carta as seen in this excerpt? Why has Magna Carta been considered such an important historical document?

---

of accounts for finances, and a *parlement* or royal court. By the beginning of the fourteenth century, the Capetians had established firm foundations for a royal bureaucracy.

Philip IV also brought a French parliament into being by summoning representatives of the three estates, or classes—the clergy (First Estate), the nobles (Second Estate), and the townspeople (Third Estate)—to meet with him. They did so in 1302, inaugurating the Estates-General, the first French parliament, although it had little real power. By the end of the thirteenth century, France was the largest, wealthiest, and best-governed monarchical state in Europe.

Christian Reconquest: The Spanish Kingdoms

Much of Spain had been part of the Islamic world since the eighth century. Muslim Spain had flourished in the Early Middle Ages. Córdoba became a major urban center with a population exceeding 300,000 people. Agriculture prospered, and Spain became known as well for excellent leather, wool, silk, and paper. Beginning in the tenth century, however, the most noticeable feature of Spanish history was the beginning of a Christian reconquest that lasted until the final expulsion of the Muslims at the end of the fifteenth century. The **Reconquista,** as the Spaniards

MAP 10.1 **England and France in the High Middle Ages: (*left*) England and Its French Holdings; (*right*) Growth of the French State.** King Philip II Augustus of France greatly expanded the power of the Capetian royal family through his victories over the Plantagenet monarchy of England, which enabled Philip to gain control over much of north-central France. ❓ How might the existence of the English Channel have made it more difficult for England to rule its French possessions? 🔖 **View an animated version of this map or related maps at** http://thomsonedu.com/history/spielvogel

called it, became over a period of time a sacred mission to many of the Christian rulers and inhabitants of the peninsula.

By the eleventh century, a number of small Christian kingdoms in northern Spain took the offensive against the Muslims. Rodrigo Díaz de Vivar, known as El Cid, was the most famous military adventurer of the time. Unlike the Christian warriors of France, El Cid fought under either Christian or Muslim rulers. He carved out his own kingdom of Valencia in 1094 but failed to create a dynasty when it was reconquered by the Muslims after his death.

By the end of the twelfth century, the northern half of Spain had been consolidated into the Christian kingdoms of Castile, Navarre, Aragon, and Portugal, which had emerged by 1179 as a separate kingdom (see Map 10.2).

The southern half of Spain remained under the control of the Muslims.

In the thirteenth century, Christian rulers took the offensive again in the reconquest of Muslim territory. Aragon and Castile had become the two strongest Spanish kingdoms, and Portugal had reached its modern boundaries. All three states made significant conquests of Muslim territory. Castile subdued most of Andalusia in the south, down to the Atlantic and the Mediterranean; at the same time, Aragon conquered Valencia. The crucial battle occurred in 1212 at Las Navas de Tolosa. Alfonso VIII of Castile (1155–1214) had amassed an army of sixty thousand and crushed the Muslim forces, leading to Christian victories over the next forty years. By the mid-thirteenth century, the Muslims remained only in the kingdom of Granada, along the southeastern edge of the Iberian peninsula.

The Spanish kingdoms followed no consistent policy in the treatment of the conquered Muslim population. Muslim farmers continued to work the land but were forced to pay very high rents in Aragon. In Castile, King Alfonso X (1252–1284), who called himself the "King of Three Religions," encouraged the continued development of a cosmopolitan culture shared by Christians, Jews, and Muslims.

The Lands of the Holy Roman Empire: Germany and Italy

In the tenth century, the powerful dukes of Saxony became kings of the lands of the eastern Frankish kingdom (or Germany, as it came to be known). The best known of the Saxon kings of Germany was Otto I (936–973), who intervened in Italian politics and for his efforts was crowned emperor of the Romans by the pope in 962, reviving a title that had not been used since the time of Charlemagne. Otto's creation of a new "Roman Empire" in the hands of the eastern Franks (or Germans, as they came to be called) added a tremendous burden to the kings of Germany, who now took on the onerous task of ruling Italy as well.

In the eleventh century, German kings created a strong monarchy and a powerful empire by leading armies into Italy. To strengthen their power, German kings had come to rely on their ability to control the church and select bishops and abbots, whom they could then use as royal administrators. But the struggle between church and state during the reign of Henry IV (1056–1106) weakened the king's ability to use church officials in this way. The German kings also tried to bolster their power by using their position as emperors to exploit the resources of Italy. But this tended to backfire; many a German king lost armies in Italy in pursuit of a dream of empire, and no German dynasty demonstrates this better than the Hohenstaufens.

Frederick I Both Frederick I (1152–1190) and Frederick II (1212–1250), the two most famous members of the Hohenstaufen dynasty, tried to create a new kind of empire. Previous German kings had focused on building a strong German kingdom, to which Italy might be added as an appendage (see Map 10.3). Frederick I, known as Barbarossa (Redbeard) to the Italians, however, planned to get his chief revenues from Italy as the center of a "holy empire," as he called it (hence the name Holy Roman Empire). But his attempt to conquer northern Italy ran into severe difficulties. The pope opposed him, fearful that the emperor wanted to incorporate Rome and the Papal States into his empire. The cities of northern Italy, which had become used to their freedom, were also not willing to be Frederick's subjects. An alliance of these northern Italian cities, with the support of the papacy, defeated the forces of Emperor Frederick at Legnano in 1176.

Frederick II Frederick II was the most brilliant of the Hohenstaufen rulers. King of Sicily in 1198, king of Germany in 1212, and crowned emperor in 1220, Frederick II was a truly remarkable man who awed his contemporaries. Frederick had been raised in Sicily, with its diverse peoples, languages, and religions, and his court brought together a brilliant array of lawyers, poets, artists, and scientists. His main goal was to establish a strong centralized state in Italy dominated by his kingdom in Sicily. Frederick's major task was to gain control of northern Italy. In reaching to extend his power in Italy, he became involved in a deadly struggle with the popes, who realized that a single ruler of northern and southern Italy meant the end of papal secular power in central Italy. The northern Italian cities were also unwilling to give up their

MAP 10.2 **Christian Reconquests in the Western Mediterranean.** Muslims seized most of Spain in the eighth century, near the end of the period of rapid Islamic expansion. In the eleventh century, small Christian kingdoms in the north began the *Reconquista*, finally conquering the last Moors near the end of the fifteenth century. ❓ How can you explain the roughly north-to-south conquest of the Muslim lands in Spain? View an animated version of this map or related maps at http://thomsonedu.com/history/spielvogel

MAP 10.3 **The Holy Roman Empire in the Twelfth Century.** The Hohenstaufen rulers Frederick I and Frederick II sought to expand the Holy Roman Empire to include all of Italy. Frederick II had only fleeting success: after his death, several independent city-states arose in northern Italy, while at home, German nobles had virtually free reign within their domains. **?** Why did the territorial conquests of the Holy Roman Empire cause alarm in the papacy? **View an animated version of this map or related maps at** http://thomsonedu.com/history/spielvogel

freedom. Frederick waged a bitter struggle in northern Italy, winning many battles but ultimately losing the war.

Frederick's preoccupation with the creation of an empire in Italy left Germany in confusion and chaos until 1273, when the major German princes, serving as electors, chose an insignificant German noble, Rudolf of Habsburg, as the new German king. In choosing a weak king, the princes were ensuring that the German monarchy would remain impotent and incapable of reestablishing a centralized monarchical state. The failure of the Hohenstaufens had led to a situation where his exalted majesty, the German king and Holy Roman Emperor, had no real power over either Germany or Italy. Unlike France, England, and even Spain, neither Germany nor Italy created a unified national monarchy in the Middle Ages. Both became geographical designations for loose confederations of hundreds of petty states under the vague direction of king or emperor. In fact, neither Germany nor Italy would become united until the nineteenth century.

Following the death of Frederick II, Italy fell into political confusion. While the papacy remained in control of much of central Italy, the defeat of imperial power left the cities and towns of northern Italy independent of any other authority. Gradually, the larger ones began to emerge as strong city-states. Florence assumed the leadership of Tuscany, and Milan, under the guidance of the Visconti family, took control of the Lombard region.

With its great commercial wealth, the republic of Venice dominated the northeastern part of the peninsula.

New Kingdoms in Eastern Europe

In eastern Europe, Hungary, which had been a Christian state since 1000, remained relatively stable throughout the High Middle Ages, but the history of Poland and Russia was far more turbulent. In the thirteenth century, eastern Europe was beset by two groups of invaders, the Teutonic Knights from the west and the Mongols from the east.

In the eleventh century, a Polish kingdom existed as a separate state, but with no natural frontiers (see Map 10.4). Consequently, German settlers encroached on its territory on a regular basis, leading to considerable intermarriage between Slavs and Germans. During the thirteenth century, relations between the Germans and the Slavs of eastern Europe worsened due to the aggression of the Teutonic Knights. The Teutonic Knights had been founded near the end of the twelfth century to protect the Christian Holy Land. In the early thirteenth century, however, these Christian knights found greater opportunity to the east of Germany, where they attacked the pagan Slavs. East Prussia was given to the military order in 1226, and by the end of the thirteenth century, Prussia had become German and Christian as the pagan Slavs were forced to convert.

The Coronation of Frederick II. Shown here is the coronation of Frederick II of Germany as Holy Roman Emperor by Pope Honorius II in Rome on November 22, 1220. The pope agreed to do so after Frederick promised to lead a Crusade to the Holy Land, a promise that he took years to fulfill. This scene is taken from a fifteenth-century French manuscript on the monarchs of Europe.

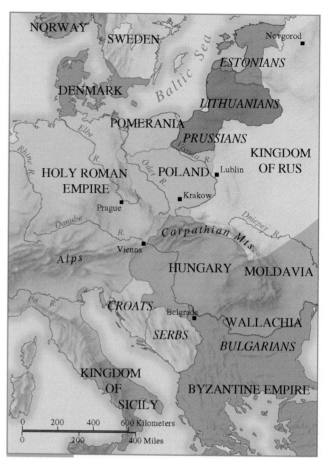

MAP 10.4 **Northern and Eastern Europe.**
Acceptance of Christianity gave many northern and eastern European kingdoms greater control over their subjects. Warfare was common in the region: dynastic struggles occurred in Scandinavia, and the Teutonic Knights, based in East Prussia, attacked the pagan Slavs. ❓ Which areas of northern and eastern Europe had large Slavic populations? (Look back at Map 8.4)

🔷 **View an animated version of this map or related maps at** http://thomsonedu.com/history/spielvogel

Central and eastern Europe had periodically been subject to invasions from fierce Asiatic nomads, including the Huns, Avars, Bulgars, and Magyars. In the thirteenth century, the Mongols exploded on the scene, causing far more disruption than earlier invaders.

Impact of the Mongol Empire

The Mongols rose to power in Asia with stunning speed. They were a pastoral people in the region of modern-day Outer Mongolia organized loosely in clans and tribes, often warring with each other. This changed when one leader, Temuchin, unified the Mongol tribes and gained the title of Genghis Khan (c. 1162–1227), which means "universal ruler." From that time on, Genghis Khan created a powerful military force and devoted himself to fighting. "Man's highest joy," Genghis Khan remarked, "is in victory: to conquer one's enemies, to pursue them, to deprive them of their possessions, to make their beloved weep, to ride on their horses, and to embrace their wives and daughters."[2] Genghis Khan was succeeded by equally competent sons and grandsons.

In the thirteenth century, the Mongols advanced eastward, eventually conquering China and Korea. One of Genghis Khan's grandsons, Khubilai Khan, completed the conquest of China and established a new Chinese dynasty of rulers known as the Yuan. In 1279, Khubilai Khan moved the capital of China northward to Khanbaliq ("city of the Khan"), which would later be known by the Chinese name Beijing.

The Mongol Empire

The Mongols also moved westward against the Islamic empire. Persia fell by 1233, and by 1258 they had conquered Baghdad and destroyed the Abbasid caliphate. Beginning in the 1230s, the Mongols had moved into Europe. They conquered Russia, advanced into Poland and Hungary, and destroyed a force of Poles and Teutonic Knights in Silesia in 1241. At that point, the Mongol hordes turned back because of internal fighting; western and southern Europe escaped their wrath. Overall, the Mongols had little impact in Europe, although their occupation of Russia had some residual effect.

The Development of Russia

The Kiev Rus state, which had become formally Christian in 987, prospered considerably afterward, reaching its high point in the first half of the eleventh century. Kievan society was dominated by a noble class of landowners known as the **boyars**. Kievan merchants maintained regular trade with Scandinavia to the north and the Islamic and Byzantine worlds to the south. But destructive civil wars and new invasions by Asiatic nomads caused the principality of Kiev to collapse, and the sack of Kiev by north Russian princes in 1169 brought an inglorious end to the first Russian state.

The fundamental civilizing and unifying force of early Russia was the Christian church. The Russian church imitated the liturgy and organization of the Byzantine Empire, whose Eastern Orthodox priests had converted the Kievan Rus to Christianity at the end of the tenth century. The Russian church became known for its rigid religious orthodoxy. Although Christianity provided a common bond between Russian and European civilization, Russia's religious development guaranteed an even closer affinity between Russian and Byzantine civilization.

In the thirteenth century, the Mongols conquered Russia and cut it off even more from western Europe. The Mongols were not numerous enough to settle the vast Russian lands but were content to rule directly an area along the lower Volga and north of the Caspian and Black Seas to Kiev and rule indirectly elsewhere. In the latter territories, Russian princes were required to pay tribute to the Mongol overlords.

One Russian prince soon emerged as more powerful than the others. Alexander Nevsky (c. 1220–1263), prince of Novgorod, defeated a German invading army in northwestern Russia in 1242. His cooperation with the Mongols won him their favor. The khan, leader of the western part of the Mongol empire, rewarded Alexander Nevsky with the title of grand-prince, enabling his descendants to become the princes of Moscow and eventually leaders of all Russia.

The Recovery and Reform of the Catholic Church

In the Early Middle Ages, the Catholic church had played a leading role in converting and civilizing first the Germanic invaders and later the Vikings and Magyars. Although

CHRONOLOGY	Growth of the European Kingdoms
England	
Battle of Hastings	1066
William the Conqueror	1066–1087
Henry II, first of the Plantagenet dynasty	1154–1189
Murder of Thomas à Becket	1170
John	1199–1216
Magna Carta	1215
Edward I	1272–1307
The "greater Parliaments"	1295, 1297
France	
Hugh Capet, French king	987
Philip II Augustus	1180–1223
Louis IX	1226–1270
Philip IV	1285–1314
First Estates-General	1302
Spain	
El Cid in Valencia	1094–1099
Alfonso VIII of Castile	1155–1214
Establishment of Portugal	1179
Alfonso X of Castile	1252–1284
Germany, The Holy Roman Empire, and Italy	
Otto I	936–973
Henry IV	1056–1106
Frederick I Barbarossa	1152–1190
Lombard League defeats Frederick at Legnano	1176
Frederick II	1212–1250
Election of Rudolf of Habsburg as king of Germany	1273
Eastern Europe	
Alexander Nevsky, prince of Novgorod	c. 1220–1263
East Prussia given to the Teutonic Knights	1226
Mongol conquest of Russia	1230s

highly successful, this effort brought challenges that undermined the spiritual life of the church itself.

The Problems of Decline

Since the eighth century, the popes had reigned supreme over the affairs of the Catholic church. They had also come to exercise control over the territories in central Italy known as the Papal States; this kept popes involved in political matters, often at the expense of their spiritual obligations. At the same time, the church became increasingly entangled in the evolving lord-vassal relationships.

High officials of the church, such as bishops and abbots, came to hold their offices as fiefs from nobles. As vassals, they were obliged to carry out the usual duties, including military service. Of course, lords assumed the right to choose their vassals, even when those vassals included bishops and abbots. Because lords often selected their vassals from other noble families for political reasons, these bishops and abbots were often worldly figures who cared little about their spiritual responsibilities.

The monastic ideal had also suffered during the Early Middle Ages. Benedictine monasteries had sometimes been exemplary centers of Christian living and learning, but the invasions of Vikings, Magyars, and Muslims wreaked havoc with many monastic establishments. Discipline declined, and with it the monastic reputation for learning and holiness. At the same time, a growing number of monasteries fell under the control of local lords, as did much of the church. A number of people believed that the time for reform had come.

The Cluniac Reform Movement

Reform of the Catholic church began in Burgundy in eastern France in 910 when Duke William of Aquitaine founded the abbey of Cluny. The monastery began with a renewed dedication to the highest spiritual ideals of the Benedictine rule and was fortunate in possessing a series of abbots in the tenth century who maintained these ideals. Cluny was deliberately kept independent from secular control. As Duke William stipulated in his original charter, "It has pleased us also to insert in this document that, from this day, those same monks there congregated shall be subject neither to our yoke, nor to that of our relatives, nor to the sway of the royal might, nor to that of any earthly power."[3]

The Cluniac reform movement sparked an enthusiastic response, first in France and eventually in all of western and central Europe. New monasteries were founded on Cluniac ideals, and existing monasteries rededicated themselves by adopting the Cluniac program. The movement also began to reach beyond monasticism and into the papacy itself, which was in dire need of help.

Reform of the Papacy

By the eleventh century, church leaders realized the need to free the church from the interference of lords in the appointment of church officials. This issue of **lay investiture,** the practice by which secular rulers both chose and invested their nominees to church offices with the symbols of their office, was dramatically taken up by the greatest of the reform popes of the eleventh century, Gregory VII (1073–1085).

Elected pope in 1073, Gregory was convinced that he had been chosen by God to reform the church. In pursuit of those aims, Gregory claimed that he, as pope, was God's "vicar on earth" and that the pope's authority extended over all Christians, including rulers. Gregory sought the

elimination of lay investiture. Only then could the church regain its freedom, by which Gregory meant the right to appoint its own clergy and run its own affairs. If rulers did not accept these "divine" commands, they could be deposed by the pope in his capacity as the vicar of Christ.

Gregory VII soon found himself in conflict with King Henry IV (1056–1106) of Germany over these claims. For many years, German kings had appointed high-ranking clerics, especially bishops, as their vassals in order to use them as administrators. Without them, the king could not hope to maintain his own power vis-à-vis the powerful German nobles. In 1075, Pope Gregory issued a decree forbidding important clerics from receiving their investiture from lay leaders: "We decree that no one of the clergy shall receive the investiture with a bishopric or abbey or church from the hand of an emperor or king or of any lay person."[4] Henry had no intention of obeying a decree that challenged the very heart of his administration.

The struggle between Henry IV and Gregory VII, which is known as the Investiture Controversy, was one of the great conflicts between church and state in the High Middle Ages. It dragged on until 1122, when a new German king and a new pope achieved a compromise in the Concordat of Worms. Under this agreement, a bishop in Germany was first elected by church officials. After election, the nominee paid homage to the king as his lord, who in turn invested him with the symbols of temporal office. A representative of the pope then invested the new bishop with the symbols of his spiritual office.

Christianity and Medieval Civilization

Christianity was an integral part of the fabric of medieval European society and the consciousness of Europe. Papal directives affected the actions of kings and princes alike, while Christian teaching and practices touched the economic, social, intellectual, cultural, and daily lives of all Europeans.

Growth of the Papal Monarchy

The popes of the twelfth century did not abandon the reform ideals of Gregory VII, but they were less dogmatic and more inclined to consolidate their power and build a strong administrative system. By the twelfth century, the Catholic church possessed a clearly organized hierarchical structure. The pope and **papal curia** (staffed by high church officials known as cardinals, the pope's major advisers and administrators) were at the center of the administrative structure. Below them were the bishops, since all of Christendom was divided into dioceses under their direction. Archbishops were in principle more powerful than the bishops, but at this time they were unable to exercise any real control over the internal affairs of the bishops' dioceses.

In the thirteenth century, the Catholic church reached the height of its political, intellectual, and secular power. The papal monarchy extended its sway over both ecclesiastical and temporal affairs, as was especially evident during the papacy of Pope Innocent III (1198–1216). At the beginning of his pontificate, in a letter to a priest, Innocent made a clear statement of his views on papal supremacy:

> As God, the creator of the universe, set two great lights in the firmament of heaven, the greater light to rule the day, and the lesser light to rule the night so He set two great dignities in the firmament of the universal church, . . . the greater to rule the day, that is, souls, and the lesser to rule the night, that is, bodies. These dignities are the papal authority and the royal power. And just as the moon gets her light from the sun, and is inferior to the sun . . . so the royal power gets the splendor of its dignity from the papal authority.[5]

Innocent's actions were those of a man who believed that he, as pope, was the supreme judge of European affairs. He forced King Philip Augustus of France to take back his wife and queen after Philip had tried to have the marriage annulled. The pope intervened in German affairs and installed his candidate as emperor. He compelled King John of England to accept the papal choice for the position of archbishop of Canterbury. To achieve his political ends, Innocent did not hesitate to use the spiritual weapons at his command, especially the **interdict**, which forbade priests to dispense the **sacraments** of the church in the hope that the people, deprived of the comforts of religion, would exert pressure against their ruler. Pope Innocent's interdict was so effective that it caused Philip to restore his wife to her rightful place as queen of France.

© Scala/Art Resource, NY

Pope Innocent III. Innocent III was an active and powerful pope during the High Middle Ages. He approved the creation of the Franciscan and Dominican religious orders and inaugurated the Fourth Crusade.

New Religious Orders and Spiritual Ideals

In the second half of the eleventh century and the first half of the twelfth, a wave of religious enthusiasm seized Europe, leading to a spectacular growth in the number of monasteries and the emergence of new monastic orders. Most important was the Cistercian order, founded in 1098 by a group of monks dissatisfied with the lack of strict discipline at their Benedictine monastery. Cistercian monasticism spread rapidly from southern France into the rest of Europe.

The Cistercians were strict. They ate a simple diet and possessed only a single robe each. All decorations were eliminated from their churches and monastic buildings. More time for prayer and manual labor was provided by shortening the number of hours spent at religious services. The Cistercians played a major role in developing a new, activist spiritual model for twelfth-century Europe. A Benedictine monk often spent hours in prayer to honor God. The Cistercian ideal had a different emphasis: "Arise, soldier of Christ, arise! Get up off the ground and return to the battle from which you have fled! Fight more boldly after your flight, and triumph in glory!"[6] These were the words of Saint Bernard of Clairvaux (1090–1153), who more than any other person embodied the new spiritual ideal of Cistercian monasticism (see the box on p. 186).

Women in Religious Orders Women were active participants in the spiritual movements of the age. The number of women joining religious houses increased perceptibly with the spread of the new orders of the twelfth century. In the High Middle Ages, most nuns were from the ranks of the landed aristocracy. Convents were convenient for families unable or unwilling to find husbands for their daughters and for aristocratic women who did not wish to marry. Female intellectuals found them a haven for their activities. Most of the learned women of the Middle Ages, especially in Germany, were nuns. One of the most distinguished was Hildegard of Bingen (1098–1179), who became abbess of a convent at Disibodenberg in western Germany.

Hildegard shared in the religious enthusiasm of the twelfth century. Soon after becoming abbess, she began to write an account of the mystical visions she had experienced for years. "A great flash of light from heaven pierced my brain and . . . in that instant my mind was imbued with the meaning of the sacred books,"[7] she wrote in a description typical of the world's mystical literature. Eventually she produced three books based on her visions. Hildegard gained considerable renown as a mystic and prophet, and popes, emperors, kings, dukes, and bishops eagerly sought her advice.

Living the Gospel Life In the thirteenth century, two new religious orders emerged that had a profound impact on the lives of ordinary people. The friars were particularly active in the cities, where, by their example, they strove to provide a more personal religious experience.

A MIRACLE OF SAINT BERNARD

Saint Bernard of Clairvaux has been called the most widely respected holy man of the twelfth century. He was an outstanding preacher, wholly dedicated to the service of God. His reputation reportedly influenced many young men to join the Cistercian order. He also inspired a myriad of stories dealing with his miracles.

A Miracle of Saint Bernard

A certain monk, departing from his monastery...threw off his habit, and returned to the world at the persuasion of the Devil. And he took a certain parish living; for he was a priest. Because sin is punished with sin, the deserter from his Order lapsed into the vice of lechery. He took a concubine to live with him, as in fact is done by many, and by her he had children.

But as God is merciful and does not wish anyone to perish, it happened that many years after, the blessed abbot [Saint Bernard] was passing through the village in which this same monk was living, and went to stay at his house. The renegade monk recognized him, and received him very reverently, and waited on him devoutly...but as yet the abbot did not recognize him.

On the morrow, the holy man said Matins and prepared to be off. But as he could not speak to the priest, since he had got up and gone to the church for Matins, he said to the priest's son "Go, give this message to your master." Now the boy had been born dumb. He obeyed the command and feeling in himself the power of him who had given it, he ran to his father and uttered the words of the Holy Father clearly and exactly. His father, on hearing his son's voice for the first time, wept for joy, and made him repeat the same words...and he asked what the abbot had done to him. "He did nothing to me," said the boy, "except to say 'Go and say this to your father.'"

At so evident a miracle the priest repented, and hastened after the holy man and fell at his feet saying, "My Lord and Father, I was your monk so-and-so, and at such-and-such a time I ran away from your monastery. I ask your Paternity to allow me to return with you to the monastery, for in your coming God has visited my heart." The saint replied unto him, "Wait for me here, and I will come back quickly when I have done my business, and I will take you with me." But the priest, fearing death (which he had not done before), answered, "Lord, I am afraid of dying before then." But the saint replied, "Know this for certain, that if you die in this condition, and in this resolve, you will find yourself a monk before God."

The saint [eventually] returned and heard that the priest had recently died and been buried. He ordered the tomb to be opened. And when they asked him what he wanted to do, he said, "I want to see if he is lying as a monk or a clerk in his tomb." "As a clerk," they said; "we buried him in his secular habit." But when they had dug up the earth, they found that he was not in the clothes in which they had buried him; but he appeared in all points, tonsure and habit, as a monk. And they all praised God.

What two miracles occur in this excerpt from the life of Saint Bernard? What does this document reveal about popular religious practices during the Middle Ages?

Archives Charmet/The Bridgeman Art Library International

A Group of Nuns. Although still viewed by the medieval church as inferior to men, women were as susceptible to the spiritual fervor of the twelfth century as men, and female monasticism grew accordingly. This manuscript illustration shows at left a group of nuns welcoming a novice (dressed in white) to their order. At the right a nun receives a sick person on a stretcher for the order's hospital care.

Like their founder, Saint Francis of Assisi (1182–1226), the Franciscan friars lived among the people, preaching repentance and aiding the poor. Their calls for a return to the simplicity and poverty of the early church, reinforced by their own example, were especially effective and made them very popular.

The Dominicans arose out of the desire of a Spanish priest, Dominic de Guzmán (1170–1221), to defend church teachings from heresy. The spiritual revival of the High Middle Ages had also led to the emergence of heretical movements, which became especially widespread in southern France. Unlike Francis, Dominic was an intellectual who was appalled by the growth of heresy within the church. He believed that a new religious order of men who lived lives of poverty but were learned and capable of preaching effectively would best be able to attack heresy.

Popular Religion in the High Middle Ages

We have witnessed the actions of popes, bishops, and monks. But what of ordinary clergy and laypeople? What were their religious hopes and fears? What were their spiritual aspirations?

The sacraments of the Catholic church ensured that the church was an integral part of people's lives, from birth to death. There were (and still are) seven sacraments, administered only by the clergy. Sacraments, such as baptism and the **Eucharist** (the Lord's Supper), were viewed as outward symbols of an inward grace (grace was God's freely given gift that enabled humans to be saved) and were considered imperative for a Christian's salvation. Therefore, the clergy were seen to have a key role in the attainment of salvation.

Other church practices were also important to ordinary people. Saints, it was believed, were men and women who, through their holiness, had achieved a special position in heaven, enabling them to act as intercessors before God. The saints' ability to protect poor souls enabled them to take on great importance at the popular level. Jesus' apostles were recognized throughout Europe as saints, but there were also numerous local saints who had special significance. New cults developed rapidly, particularly in the intense religious atmosphere of the eleventh and twelfth centuries. The English introduced Saint Nicholas, the patron saint of children, who remains instantly recognizable today through his identification with Santa Claus.

Of all the saints, the Virgin Mary occupied the foremost position in the High Middle Ages. Mary was viewed as the most important mediator with her son Jesus, the judge of all sinners. Moreover, from the eleventh century on, a fascination with Mary as Jesus' human mother became more evident. A sign of Mary's importance was the growing number of churches all over Europe that were dedicated to her in the twelfth and thirteenth centuries.

Emphasis on the role of the saints was closely tied to the use of **relics**, which also increased noticeably in the High Middle Ages. Relics were usually the bones of saints or objects intimately connected to saints that were considered worthy of veneration by the faithful. A twelfth-century English monk began his description of the abbey's relics by saying, "There is kept there a thing more precious than gold,... the right arm of St. Oswald.... This we have seen with our own eyes and have kissed, and have handled with our own hands.... There are kept here also part of his ribs and of the soil on which he fell."[8] The monk went on to list additional relics possessed by the abbey, which purported to include two pieces of Jesus' swaddling clothes, pieces of Jesus' manger, and part of the five loaves of bread with which Jesus fed five thousand people. Because the holiness of the saint was considered to be inherent in his relics, these objects were believed to be capable of healing people or producing other miracles.

Voices of Protest and Intolerance

The desire for more personal and deeper religious experience, which characterized the spiritual revival of the High Middle Ages, also led people in directions hostile to the institutional church. From the twelfth century on, heresy, or the holding of religious doctrines different from the orthodox teachings of the church as determined by church authorities, became a serious problem for the Catholic church. The best-known heresy of the twelfth and thirteenth centuries was Catharism. The Cathars (from the Greek word for "pure") were also called Albigensians, after the city of Albi, one of their strongholds in southern France. They believed in a dualist system in which good and evil were separate and distinct. The things of the spirit were good because they were created by God, the source of light; the things of the world were evil because they were created by Satan, the prince of darkness. Humans, too, were enmeshed in dualism. Their souls, which were good, were trapped in material bodies, which were evil. According to the Cathars, the Catholic church, itself a materialistic institution, had nothing to do with God and was essentially evil. There was no need to follow its teachings or recognize its authority. The Cathar movement gained valuable support from important nobles in southern France and northern Italy.

The spread of heresy in southern France alarmed the church authorities. Pope Innocent III appealed to the nobles of northern France for a **Crusade** (a military campaign in defense of Christianity) against the heretics. The Crusade against the Albigensians, which began in the summer of 1209 and lasted for almost two decades, was a bloody fight. Thousands of heretics (and innocents) were slaughtered, including entire populations of some towns. In Béziers, for example, seven thousand men, women, and children were massacred when they took refuge in the local church.

Southern France was devastated, but Catharism remained, which caused the Catholic church to devise a regular method for discovering and dealing with heretics. This led to the emergence of the Holy Office, as the papal Inquisition was called, a formal court whose job it was to

© British Library/Bridgeman Art Library

Expulsion of Albigensian Heretics. In 1209, Pope Innocent III authorized a Crusade against the heretical Albigensians. In this medieval illustration, French knights are shown expelling Albigensian heretics from the town of Carcassonne near Albi, an Albigensian stronghold in southern France.

CHRONOLOGY	The Catholic Church in the High Middle Ages	
Foundation of abbey of Cluny		910
Pope Gregory VII		1073–1085
Decree against lay investiture		1075
Pope Urban II		1088–1099
Founding of Cistercians		1098
Pope Innocent III		1198–1216
Start of Crusade against the Albigensians		1209
Fourth Lateran Council		1215

ferret out and try heretics. Anyone accused of heresy who refused to confess was considered guilty and was turned over to the secular authorities for execution. To the Christians of the thirteenth century, who believed that there was only one path to salvation, heresy was a crime against God and against humanity, and force was justified to save souls from damnation. The fanaticism and fear unleashed in the struggle against heretics were also used against others, especially the Jews.

Persecution of the Jews

The Jews were the only religious minority in medieval Europe that was allowed to practice a non-Christian religion. But the religious enthusiasm of the High Middle Ages produced an outburst of intolerance against the supposed enemies of Christianity. After Crusades were launched against the Muslims starting in 1096, European Christians took up the search for enemies at home, persecuting Jews in France and the Rhineland. Jews in Speyer, Worms, Mainz, and Cologne were all set upon by bands of Christian crusaders.

In the thirteenth century, in the supercharged atmosphere of fear created by the struggle with the heretics, Jews were persecuted more and more (see the box on p. 189). Friars urged action against these "murderers of Christ," contending that the Jews, having turned Jesus over to the Roman authorities, were responsible for his death, and organized the public burning of Jewish books. The Fourth Lateran Council in 1215 decreed that Jews must wear distinguishing marks, such as ribbons, yellow badges,

and special veils and cloaks, to differentiate themselves from Christians. The same council encouraged the development of Jewish ghettos, neighborhoods built behind walled enclosures to isolate Jews from Christians. The persecution and demonization of Jews stimulated a tradition of anti-Semitism that proved to be one of Christian Europe's most insidious contributions to the Western heritage.

European kings, who had portrayed themselves as protectors of the Jews, had so fleeced the Jewish communities of their money by the end of the thirteenth century that they no longer had reason to resist the mob fury. Edward I expelled all Jews from England in 1290. The French followed suit in 1306. As the policy of expulsion spread into central Europe, most northern European Jews were driven into Poland.

Intolerance and Homosexuality

The climate of intolerance that characterized thirteenth-century attitudes toward Muslims, heretics, and Jews was also evident toward homosexuals. Although the church had condemned homosexuality in the Early Middle Ages, it had not been overly concerned with homosexual behavior, an attitude also prevalent in the secular world. By the thirteenth century, these tolerant attitudes had altered drastically. Some historians connect this change to the century's climate of fear and intolerance against any group that deviated from the standards of the majority. A favorite approach of the critics was to identify homosexuals with other detested groups. Homosexuality was portrayed as a regular practice of Muslims and such notorious heretics as the Albigensians. Between 1250 and 1300, what had been tolerated in most of Europe became a criminal act deserving of death.

The legislation against homosexuality commonly referred to it as a "sin against nature." This is precisely the argument developed by Thomas Aquinas (see Chapter 9), who formed Catholic opinion on the subject for centuries to come. In his *Summa Theologica*, Aquinas argued that because the purpose of sex was procreation, it could only legitimately take place in ways that did not exclude this possibility. Hence homosexuality (like all other sexual

The development of new religious sensibilities in the High Middle Ages also had a negative side—the turning of Christians against their supposed enemies. Although the Crusades provide the most obvious example, Christians also turned on the "murderers of Christ," the Jews. As a result, Jews suffered increased persecution. These three documents show different sides of the picture. The first is Canon 68 of the decrees of the Fourth Lateran Council called by Pope Innocent III in 1215. The decree specifies the need for special dress, one of the ways Christians tried to separate Jews from their community. The second excerpt is a chronicler's account of the most absurd charge levied against the Jews—that they were guilty of the ritual murder of Christian children to obtain Christian blood for the Passover service. This charge led to the murder of many Jews. The third document, taken from a list of regulations issued by the city of Avignon, France, illustrates the contempt Christian society held for the Jews.

Canon 68

In some provinces a difference in dress distinguishes the Jews or Saracens [Muslims] from the Christians, but in certain others such a confusion has grown up that they cannot be distinguished by any difference. Thus it happens at times that through error Christians have relations with the women of Jews or Saracens, and Jews or Saracens with Christian women. Therefore, that they may not, under pretext of error of this sort, excuse themselves in the future for the excesses of such prohibited intercourse, we decree that such Jews and Saracens of both sexes in every Christian province and at all times shall be marked off in the eyes of the public from other peoples through the character of their dress....

Moreover, during the last three days before Easter and especially on Good Friday, they shall not go forth in public at all, for the reason that some of them on these very days, as we hear, do not blush to go forth better dressed and are not afraid to mock the Christians who maintain the memory of the most holy Passion by wearing signs of mourning.

The Jews and Ritual Murder of Christian Children

[The eight-year-old-boy] Harold, who is buried in the Church of St. Peter the Apostle, at Gloucester . . . is said to have been carried away secretly by Jews, in the opinion of many, on Feb. 21, and by them hidden till March 16. On that night, on the sixth of the preceding feast, the Jews of all England coming together as if to circumcise a certain boy, pretend deceitfully that they are about to celebrate the feast [Passover] appointed by law in such case, and deceiving the citizens of Gloucester with the fraud, they tortured the lad placed before them with immense tortures. It is true no Christian was present, or saw or heard the deed, nor have we found that anything was betrayed by any Jew. But a little while after when the whole convent of monks of Gloucester and almost all the citizens of that city, and innumerable persons coming to the spectacle, saw the wounds of the dead body, scars of fire, the thorns fixed on his head, and liquid wax poured into the eyes and face, and touched it with the diligent examination of their hands, those tortures were believed or guessed to have been inflicted on him in that manner. It was clear that they had made him a glorious martyr to Christ, being slain without sin, and having bound his feet with his own girdle, threw him into the river Severn.

The Regulations of Avignon, 1243

Likewise, we declare that Jews or whores shall not dare to touch with their hands either bread or fruit put out for sale, and that if they should do this they must buy what they have touched.

What do these documents reveal about Christian attitudes toward the Jews?

---

practices that could not result in pregnancy) was "contrary to nature" and a deviation from the natural order established by God. This argument and laws prohibiting homosexual activity on pain of death remained the norm in Europe until the twentieth century.

The Crusades

Another manifestation of the religious enthusiasm that seized Europe in the High Middle Ages was the series of Crusades mounted against the Muslims. These campaigns gave the revived papacy of the High Middle Ages yet another opportunity to demonstrate its influence over European society. The Crusades were a curious mix of God and warfare, two of the chief concerns of the Middle Ages.

Background to the Crusades

Although European civilization developed in relative isolation, it had never entirely lost contact with the lands and empires to the east. At the end of the eleventh century, that contact increased, in part because developments in the Islamic and Byzantine worlds prompted the first major attempt of the new European civilization to expand beyond Europe proper.

Islam and the Seljuk Turks By the mid-tenth century, the Islamic empire led by the Abbasid caliphate in Baghdad was in the process of disintegration. A Shi'ite dynasty known as the Fatimids managed to conquer Egypt and establish the new city of Cairo as their capital. In establishing a Shi'ite caliphate, they became rivals to the

Sunni caliphate of Baghdad, exacerbating the division in the Islamic world. Nevertheless, the Fatimid dynasty prospered and eventually surpassed the Abbasid caliphate as the dynamic center of the Islamic world. The Fatimids created a strong army by using nonnative peoples as mercenaries. One of these peoples, the Seljuk Turks, soon posed a threat to the Fatimids themselves.

The Seljuk Turks were a nomadic people from Central Asia who had been converted to Islam and flourished as military mercenaries for the Abbasid caliphate. Moving gradually into Persia and Armenia, they grew in number until by the eleventh century they were able to take over the eastern provinces of the Abbasid empire. In 1055, a Turkish leader captured Baghdad and assumed command of the Abbasid empire with the title of **sultan** ("holder of power"). By the second half of the eleventh century, the Seljuk Turks were exerting military pressure on Egypt and the Byzantine Empire. When the Byzantine emperor foolishly challenged the Turks, the latter routed the Byzantine army at Manzikert in 1071. In dire straits, the Byzantines turned to the west for help, setting in motion the papal pleas that led to the Crusades. To understand the complexities of the situation, however, we need to look first at the Byzantine Empire.

The Byzantine Empire The Macedonian dynasty of the tenth and eleventh centuries had restored much of the power of the Byzantine Empire; its incompetent successors, however, reversed most of the gains. After the Macedonian dynasty was extinguished in 1056, the empire was beset by internal struggles for power between ambitious military leaders and aristocratic families who attempted to buy the support of the great landowners of Anatolia by allowing them greater control over their peasants.

The growing division between the Catholic church of the west and the Eastern Orthodox church of the Byzantine Empire also weakened the Byzantine state. The Eastern Orthodox church was unwilling to accept the pope's claim that he was the sole head of the church. This issue reached a climax when Pope Leo IX and the Patriarch Michael Cerularius, head of the Byzantine church, formally excommunicated each other in 1054, initiating a schism between the two great branches of Christianity that has not been healed to this day.

The Byzantine Empire faced external threats to its security as well. The greatest challenge came from the Seljuk Turks who had moved into Asia Minor, the heartland of the empire and its main source of food and manpower. After defeating Byzantine forces in 1071, the Turks advanced into Anatolia, where many peasants, already disgusted by their exploitation at the hands of Byzantine landowners, readily accepted Turkish control.

Another dynasty, however, soon breathed new life into the Byzantine Empire. The Comneni, under Alexius I Comnenus (1081–1118), were victorious on the Greek Adriatic coast against the Normans, defeated the Pechenegs in the Balkans, and stopped the Turks in Anatolia. Lacking the resources to undertake additional campaigns

against the Turks, Emperor Alexius I turned to the west for military assistance. It was the positive response of the west to the emperor's request that led to the Crusades.

The Early Crusades

The Crusades were conceived as a holy war against the infidel or unbelievers. The immediate impetus for the Crusades came when the Byzantine emperor Alexius I asked Pope Urban II (1088–1099) for help against the Seljuk Turks. The pope saw a golden opportunity to provide papal leadership for a great cause: to rally the warriors of Europe for the liberation of Jerusalem and the Holy Land from the Muslim infidel. At the Council of Clermont in southern France near the end of 1095, Urban challenged Christians to take up their weapons against the infidel and join in a holy war to recover the Holy Land. The pope promised remission of sins: "All who die by the way, whether by land or by sea, or in battle against the pagans, shall have immediate remission of sins. This I grant them through the power of God with which I am invested."[9]

The warriors of western Europe, particularly France, formed the first crusading armies. The knights who made up this first serious crusading host were motivated by religious fervor, but there were other attractions as well. Some sought adventure and welcomed a legitimate opportunity to pursue their favorite pastime—fighting. Others saw an opportunity to gain territory, riches, status, possibly a title, and even salvation—had the pope not offered a full remission of sins for those who participated in these "armed pilgrimages"? From the perspective of the pope and European monarchs, the Crusades offered a way to rid Europe of contentious young nobles who disturbed the peace and wasted lives and energy fighting each other. And merchants in many Italian cities relished the prospect of new trading opportunities in Muslim lands.

In the First Crusade, begun in 1096, three organized bands of noble warriors, most of them French, made their way to the east (see Map 10.5). This first crusading army probably numbered several thousand cavalry and as many as ten thousand foot soldiers. After the capture of Antioch in 1098, much of the crusading host proceeded down the coast of Palestine, evading the garrisoned coastal cities, and reached Jerusalem in June 1099. After a five-week siege, the Holy City was taken amid a horrible massacre of the inhabitants, men, women, and children (see the box on p. 192).

After further conquest of Palestinian lands, the crusaders ignored the wishes of the Byzantine emperor (who foolishly believed the crusaders were working on his behalf) and organized four Crusader States (Edessa, Antioch, Tripoli, and Jerusalem). Because the Crusader States were surrounded by Muslim enemies, they grew increasingly dependent on the Italian commercial cities for supplies from Europe. Some Italian cities, such as Genoa, Pisa, and especially Venice, became rich and powerful in the process.

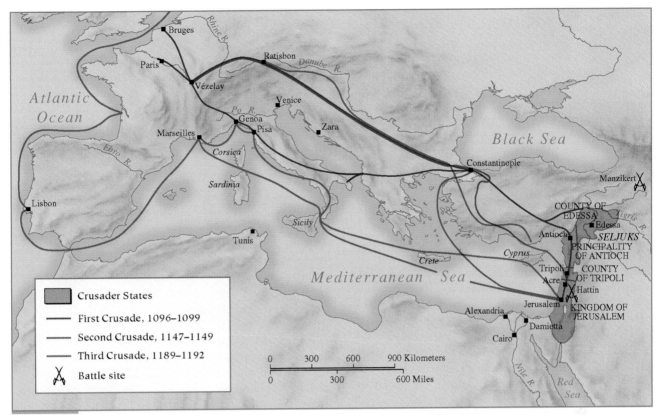

MAP 10.5 **The Early Crusades.** Pope Urban II launched the Crusades to recapture the Holy Land from the "enemies of God," a call met with great enthusiasm in Europe. The fighters of the First Crusade massacred the inhabitants of Jerusalem and established four Crusader States. ❓ In the Third Crusade, which countries sent crusaders by land and which by sea, and why would they choose these methods of travel? 🌀 **View an animated version of this map or related maps at** http://thomsonedu.com/history/spielvogel

But it was not easy for the Crusader States to maintain themselves in the east. Already by the 1120s, the Muslims had begun to strike back. In 1144, Edessa became the first of the four Latin states to be recaptured. Its fall led to renewed calls for another Crusade, especially from the monastic firebrand Saint Bernard of Clairvaux, who exclaimed, "Now, on account of our sins, the sacrilegious enemies of the cross have begun to show their faces. . . . What are you doing, you servants of the cross? Will you throw to the dogs that which is most holy? Will you cast pearls before swine?"[10] Bernard aimed his message at knights and even managed to enlist two powerful rulers, King Louis VII of France and Emperor Conrad III of Germany. Their Second Crusade, however, proved a total failure.

The Third Crusade was a reaction to the fall of the Holy City of Jerusalem in 1187 to the Muslim forces under Saladin. Now all of Christendom was ablaze with calls for a new Crusade in the east. Three major monarchs agreed to lead new crusading forces in person: Emperor Frederick Barbarossa of Germany (1152–1190), Richard I the Lionhearted of England (1189–1199), and Philip II Augustus, king of France (1180–1223). Some of the crusaders finally arrived in the east by 1189 only to encounter problems. Frederick Barbarossa drowned while

swimming in a local river, and his army quickly fell apart. The English and French arrived by sea and met with success against the coastal cities, where they had the support of their fleets, but when they moved inland, they failed miserably. Eventually, after Philip went home, Richard negotiated a settlement whereby Saladin agreed to allow Christian pilgrims free access to Jerusalem.

The Crusades of the Thirteenth Century

After the death of Saladin in 1193, Pope Innocent III initiated a Fourth Crusade. On its way to the east, the crusading army became involved in a dispute over the succession to the Byzantine throne. The Venetian leaders of the Fourth Crusade saw an opportunity to neutralize their greatest commercial competitor, the Byzantine Empire. Diverted to Constantinople, the crusaders sacked that great capital city in 1204 and declared the new Latin Empire of Constantinople. Not until 1261 did a Byzantine army recapture Constantinople. The Byzantine Empire had been saved, but it was no longer a great Mediterranean power. The restored empire now consisted only of the city of Constantinople and its surrounding territory along with some lands in Asia Minor. Though reduced in size, the empire limped along for another 190

The Siege of Jerusalem: Christian and Muslim Perspectives

During the First Crusade, Christian knights laid siege to Jerusalem in June 1099. The first excerpt is taken from an account by Fulcher of Chartres, who accompanied the crusaders to the Holy Land. The second selection is by a Muslim writer, Ibn al-Athir, whose account of the First Crusade can be found in his history of the Muslim world.

Fulcher of Chartres, *Chronicle of the First Crusade*

Then the Franks entered the city magnificently at the noonday hour on Friday, the day of the week when Christ redeemed the whole world on the cross. With trumpets sounding and with everything in an uproar, exclaiming: "Help, God!" they vigorously pushed into the city, and straightway raised the banner on the top of the wall. All the heathen, completely terrified, changed their boldness to swift flight through the narrow streets of the quarters. The more quickly they fled, the more quickly they put to flight.

Count Raymond and his men, who were bravely assailing the city in another section, did not perceive this until they saw the Saracens [Muslims] jumping from the top of the wall. Seeing this, they joyfully ran to the city as quickly as they could, and helped the others pursue and kill the wicked enemy.

Then some, both Arabs and Ethiopians, fled into the Tower of David; others shut themselves in the Temple of the Lord and of Solomon, where in the halls a very great attack was made on them. Nowhere was there a place where the Saracens could escape swordsmen.

On the top of Solomon's Temple, to which they had climbed in fleeing, many were shot to death with arrows and cast down headlong from the roof. Within this Temple, about ten thousand were beheaded. If you had been there, your feet would have been stained up to the ankles with the blood of the slain. What more shall I tell? Not one of them was allowed to live. They did not spare the women and children.

Account of Ibn al-Athir

In fact Jerusalem was taken from the north on the morning of Friday 22 Sha'ban 492/15 July 1099. The population was put to the sword by the Franks, who pillaged the area for a week. A band of Muslims barricaded themselves into the Oratory of David and fought on for several days. They were granted their lives in return for surrendering. The Franks honored their word, and the group left by night for Ascalon. In the Masjid al-Aqsa the Franks slaughtered more than 70,000 people, among them a large number of Imams and Muslim scholars, devout and ascetic men who had left their homelands to live lives of pious seclusion in the Holy Place. The Franks stripped the Dome of the Rock of more than forty silver candelabra, each of them weighing 3,600 drams, and a great silver lamp weighing forty-four Syrian pounds, as well as a hundred and fifty smaller candelabra and more than twenty gold ones, and a great deal more booty. Refugees from Syria reached Baghdad in Ramadan, among them the qadi Abu sa'd al-Harawi. They told the Caliph's ministers a story that wrung their hearts and brought tears to their eyes. On Friday they went to the Cathedral Mosque and begged for help, weeping so that their hearers wept with them as they described the sufferings of the Muslims in that Holy City: the men killed, the women and children taken prisoner, the homes pillaged. Because of the terrible hardships they had suffered, they were allowed to break the fast.

How do these two accounts differ? What was the fate of the Muslims in Jerusalem?

---

years until its weakened condition finally enabled the Ottoman Turks to conquer it in 1453.

Despite the failures, the crusading ideal was not yet completely lost. In Germany in 1212, a youth known as Nicholas of Cologne announced that God had inspired him to lead a "Children's Crusade" to the Holy Land. Thousands of young people joined Nicholas and made their way down the Rhine and across the Alps to Italy, where the pope told them to go home. Most tried to do so. At about the same time, a group of about twenty thousand French children, also inspired by the desire to free the Holy Land from the Muslims, made their way to Marseilles, where two shipowners agreed to transport them to the Holy Land. Seven ships packed with hymn-singing youths soon left the port. Two of the ships sank in a storm near Sardinia; the other five sailed to North Africa, where the children were sold into slavery. Four more Crusades of adult warriors over the next half century were no more successful.

Effects of the Crusades

Whether the Crusades had much effect on European civilization is debatable. The crusaders made little long-term impact on the east, where the only visible remnants of their conquests were their castles. There may have been some broadening of perspective that comes from the exchange between two cultures, but the interaction of Christian Europe with the Muslim world was actually both more intense and more meaningful in Spain and Sicily than in the Holy Land.

Did the Crusades help stabilize European society by removing large numbers of young warriors who would have fought each other in Europe? Some historians think so and believe that western monarchs established their control more easily as a result. There is no doubt that the Italian seaports, especially Genoa, Pisa, and Venice, benefited economically from the Crusades, but even without them, Italian merchants would have pursued new trade contacts with the eastern world.

Pope Urban II's call for a Crusade at Clermont	1095
First Crusade	1096–1099
Fall of Edessa	1144
Second Crusade	1147–1149
Saladin's conquest of Jerusalem	1187
Third Crusade	1189–1192
Fourth Crusade—sack of Constantinople	1204
Latin Empire of Constantinople	1204–1261
Children's Crusade	1212
Fifth Crusade	1219–1221
Frederick II occupies Jerusalem (Sixth Crusade)	1228
First Crusade of Louis IX (Seventh Crusade)	1248–1254
Second Crusade of Louis IX (Eighth Crusade)	1270
Surrender of Acre and end of Christian presence in the Holy Land	1291

The Crusades did have unfortunate side effects that would afflict European society for generations. The first widespread attacks on the Jews occurred during the Crusades. Some Christians argued that to undertake holy wars against infidel Muslims while the "murderers of Christ" ran free at home was unthinkable. The massacre of Jews became a regular feature of medieval European life.

The First Crusade. Recruited from the noble class of western Europe, the first crusading army reached Constantinople by 1097. By 1098, the crusaders had taken Antioch. Working down of coast of Palestine, they captured Jerusalem in 1099. Along the way, the crusaders had an encounter with Muslim forces at Ascalon, as seen in this illustration from a glass painting on the Abbey of St. Denis in France.

CONCLUSION

The period from 1000 to 1300 was a dynamic time in the development of Western civilization. The nobles, whose warlike attitudes were rationalized by labeling themselves the defenders of Christian society, continued to dominate the medieval world politically, economically, and socially. But kings gradually began to expand their powers. Although the popes sometimes treated rulers condescendingly, by the thirteenth century, the monarchs were developing the machinery of government that would enable them to challenge exalted claims of papal power and assume political authority in Europe. The actions of these medieval monarchs laid the foundation for the European kingdoms that in one form or another have dominated the European political scene ever since.

The Catholic church shared in the challenge of new growth by reforming itself and striking out on a path toward greater papal power, both within the church and over European society. The High Middle Ages witnessed a spiritual renewal that led to numerous and even divergent paths: revived papal leadership, the development of centralized administrative machinery that buttressed papal authority, and new dimensions to the religious life of the clergy and laity. At the same time, this spiritual renewal also gave rise to the crusading "holy warrior" who killed for God.

The religious enthusiasm of the twelfth century continued well into the thirteenth as new orders of friars gave witness to spiritual growth and passion, but underneath lay seeds of discontent and change. Dissent from church teaching and practices grew, leading to a climate of fear and intolerance as the church responded with inquisitorial procedures to enforce conformity to its teachings. At the same time, papal claims of supremacy over secular authorities were increasingly challenged by the rising power of monarchical authorities, who, because of the growth of cities, the revival of trade, and the emergence of a money economy, were now able to hire soldiers and officials to carry out their wishes.

The High Middle Ages of the eleventh, twelfth, and thirteenth centuries had been a period of great innovation, evident in significant economic, social, political, religious, intellectual, and cultural changes. And yet by the end of the thirteenth century, certain tensions had begun to creep into European society. As we shall see in the next chapter, these tensions would soon bring a torrent of troubles.

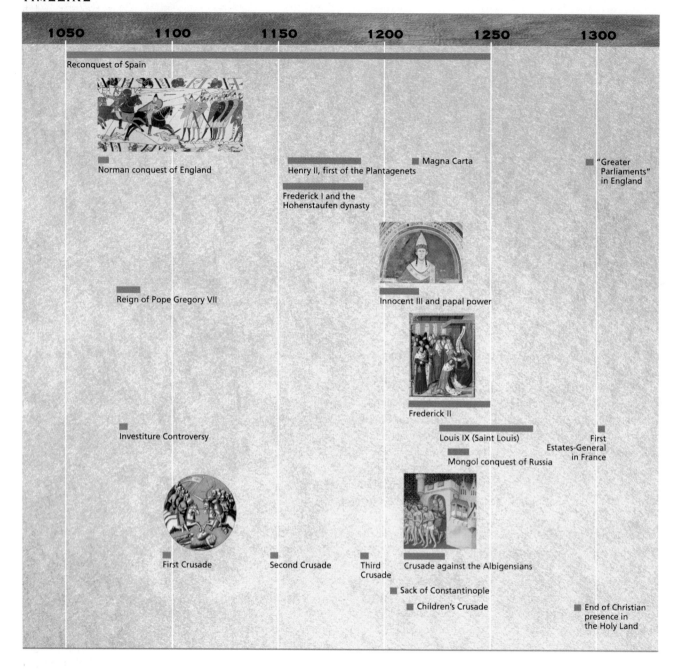

1050	1100	1150	1200	1250	1300

Reconquest of Spain

Norman conquest of England

Henry II, first of the Plantagenets

Frederick I and the Hohenstaufen dynasty

■ Magna Carta

■ "Greater Parliaments" in England

Reign of Pope Gregory VII

Innocent III and papal power

Frederick II

Investiture Controversy

Louis IX (Saint Louis)

Mongol conquest of Russia

First Estates-General in France

First Crusade

Second Crusade

Third Crusade

Crusade against the Albigensians

■ Sack of Constantinople

■ Children's Crusade

■ End of Christian presence in the Holy Land

NOTES

1. Quoted in N. F. Cantor, ed., *The Medieval Reader* (New York, 1994), pp. 42–47.
2. Quoted in J. K. Fairbank, E. O. Reischauer, and A. M. Craig, *East Asia: Tradition and Transformation* (Boston, 1973), p. 164.
3. E. F. Henderson, ed., *Selected Historical Documents of the Middle Ages* (London, 1892), p. 332.
4. Ibid., p. 365.
5. O. J. Thatcher and E. H. McNeal, eds., *A Source Book for Medieval History* (New York, 1905), p. 208.
6. Quoted in R. H. C. Davis, *A History of Medieval Europe from Constantine to Saint Louis*, 2d ed. (New York, 1988), p. 252.
7. Hildegard of Bingen, *The Book of Divine Works* (Santa Fe, N. M., 1987), 1:1.
8. Quoted in R. Brooke and C. N. L. Brooke, *Popular Religion in the Middle Ages* (London, 1984), p. 19.
9. Thatcher and McNeal, *Source Book for Medieval History*, p. 517.
10. Quoted in H. E. Mayer, *The Crusades*, trans. J. Gillingham (New York, 1972), pp. 99–100.

SUGGESTIONS FOR FURTHER READING

Works on the different medieval states are numerous. On England, see **R. Frame, *The Political Development of the British Isles, 1100–1400*** (Oxford, 1990). On France, see **J. Dunbabin, *France in the Making*,**

843–1180 (Oxford, 1985), and **E. M. Hallam, *Capetian France, 987–1328*** (London, 1980), a well-done general account. On Spain, see **B. F. Reilly, *The Medieval Spains*** (Cambridge, 1993), and **M. R. Menocal, *The Ornament of the World*** (Boston, 2002). On Germany, see **A. Haverkamp, *Medieval Germany*** (Oxford, 1988); **H. Fuhrmann, *Germany in the High Middle Ages, c. 1050–1250*** (Cambridge, 1986), an excellent account; and **B. Arnold, *Princes and Territories in Medieval Germany*** (Cambridge, 1991). On Italy, see **P. Jones, *The Italian City-State: From Commune to Signoria*** (Oxford, 1997). On eastern Europe, see **N. Davies, *God's Playground: A History of Poland*** (Oxford, 1981); **J. Fennell, *The Crisis of Medieval Russia, 1200–1304*** (New York, 1983); and the books listed for Chapter 8.

For specialized studies in the political history of the thirteenth century, see **D. Abulafia, *Frederick II: A Medieval Emperor*** (London, 1987); **M. W. Labarge, *St. Louis: The Life of Louis IX of France*** (London, 1968); and **C. J. Halperin, *Russia and the Golden Horde: The Mongol Impact on Medieval Russian History*** (Bloomington, Ind., 1987).

For a good survey of religion in medieval Europe, see **B. Hamilton, *Religion in the Medieval West*** (London, 1986). On Europe during the time of the Investiture Controversy, see **U.-R. Blumenthal, *The Investiture Controversy*** (Philadelphia, 1988). For a general survey of church life, see **R. W. Southern, *Western Society and the Church in the Middle Ages,*** rev. ed. (New York, 1990).

On the papacy in the High Middle Ages, see the general surveys by **C. Morris, *The Papal Monarchy*** (Oxford, 1989), and **I. S. Robinson, *The Papacy*** (Cambridge, 1990). The papacy of Innocent III is covered in **J. E. Sayers, *Innocent III, Leader of Europe, 1198–1216*** (New York, 1994).

Good works on monasticism include **B. Bolton, *The Medieval Reformation*** (London, 1983), and **C. H. Lawrence, *Medieval Monasticism*** (London, 1984), a good general account. On the impact of the Franciscans and Dominicans, see **C. H. Lawrence, *The Friars: The Impact of the Early Mendicant Movement on Western Society*** (New York, 1994). On Saint Francis, see **A. House, *Francis of Assisi: A Revolutionary Life*** (London, 2001). For a good introduction to popular religion in the eleventh and twelfth centuries, see **R. Brooke** and **C. N. L. Brooke, *Popular Religion in the Middle Ages*** (London, 1984).

On dissent and heresy, see **M. Lambert, *Medieval Heresy,*** 2d ed. (New York, 1992), and **J. Strayer, *The Albigensian Crusades,*** 2d ed. (New York, 1992). On the Inquisition, see **B. Hamilton, *The Medieval Inquisition*** (New York, 1981). The persecution of Jews in the thirteenth century can be examined in **J. Cohen, *The Friars and the Jews*** (Oxford, 1985). The basic study on intolerance and homosexuality is **J. Boswell, *Christianity, Social Tolerance, and Homosexuality*** (Chicago, 1980).

Two good general surveys of the Crusades are **H. E. Mayer, *The Crusades,*** 2d ed. (New York, 1988), and **J. Riley-Smith, *The Crusades: A Short History*** (New Haven, Conn., 1987). Also see **J. Riley-Smith, ed., *The Oxford Illustrated History of the Crusades*** (New York, 1995), and **A. Konstam, *Historical Atlas of the Crusades*** (New York, 2002). On the First Crusade, see **T. Asbridge, *The First Crusade: A New History*** (New York, 2003). The disastrous Fourth Crusade is examined in **J. Godfrey, *1204: The Unholy Crusade*** (Oxford, 1980). On the later Crusades, see **N. Housley, *The Later Crusades, 1274–1580*** (New York, 1992).

Thomson NOW! Enter *ThomsonNOW* using the access card that is available for *Western Civilization: A Brief History.* *ThomsonNOW* will help you understand this chapter with lesson plans generated for your needs. In addition, you can read the following documents, and many more, online:

Song of Roland
John of Salisbury, Book 5 of *Policraticus*

WESTERN CIVILIZATION RESOURCES

Visit the Web site for *Western Civilization: A Brief History* for resources specific to this book:
   http://www.thomsonedu.com/history/spielvogel
For a variety of tools to help you succeed in this course, visit the Western Civilization Resource Center at
   http://history.wadsworth.com/spielvogel
Included are quizzes, images, documents, interactive simulations, maps and timelines, movie explorations, and a wealth of other sources.

THE LATER MIDDLE AGES: CRISIS AND DISINTEGRATION IN THE FOURTEENTH CENTURY

CHAPTER OUTLINE AND FOCUS QUESTIONS

A Time of Troubles: Black Death and Social Crisis

☐ What was the Black Death, and what was its impact on European society?

War and Political Instability

☐ What major problems did European states face in the fourteenth century?

The Decline of the Church

☐ How and why did the authority and prestige of the papacy decline in the fourteenth century?

Cultural and Society in an Age of Adversity

☐ What were the major developments in art and literature in the fourteenth century?

☐ How did the adversities of the fourteenth century affect urban life and medical practices?

CRITICAL THINKING

☐ To what extent were climate and disease the key factors in producing economic, social, and political changes in the fourteenth century?

Mass burial of plague victims

Snark/Art Resource, NY (Bibliotheque Royale Albert I, Brussels)

AS A RESULT of their conquests in the thirteenth and fourteenth centuries, the Mongols created a vast empire stretching from Russia in the west to China in the east. Mongol rule brought stability to the Eurasian trade routes; increased trade brought prosperity but also avenues for the spread of flea-infested rats that carried bubonic plague to both East Asia and Europe. In the mid-fourteenth century, one of the most destructive natural disasters in history erupted—the Black Death. One contemporary observer named Henry Knighton, a canon of Saint Mary-of-the-Meadow Abbey in Leicester, England, was simply overwhelmed by the magnitude of the catastrophe. Knighton began his account of the great plague with these words: "In this year [1348] and in the following one there was a general mortality of people throughout the whole world." Few were left untouched; the plague struck even isolated monasteries: "At Montpellier, there remained out of a hundred and forty friars only seven." Knighton was also stunned by the economic and social consequences of the Black Death. Prices dropped: "And the price of everything was cheap, because of the fear of death; there were very few who took any care for their wealth, or for anything else." Meanwhile, laborers were scarce, so their wages increased: "In the following autumn, one could not hire a reaper at a lower wage than eight pence with food, or a mower at less than twelve pence with food. Because of this, much grain rotted in the fields for lack of harvesting." So many people died that some towns were deserted and some villages disappeared altogether: "Many small villages and hamlets were completely deserted; there was not one house left in them, but all those who had lived in them were dead." Some people thought the end of the world was at hand.

Plague was not the only disaster in the fourteenth century, however. Signs of disintegration were everywhere: famine, economic depression, war, social upheaval, a rise in crime and violence, and a decline in the power of the universal Catholic church. Periods of disintegration, however, are often fertile grounds for change and new developments. Out of the dissolution of medieval civilization came a rebirth of culture that has come to be known as the Renaissance.◆

A Time of Troubles: Black Death and Social Crisis

For much of the thirteenth century, Europe had experienced good harvests and an expanding population. By century's end, however, a succession of disastrous changes had begun.

For one thing, there were noticeable changes in weather patterns as Europe entered a "little ice age." Shortened growing seasons and disastrous weather conditions, including heavy storms and constant rain, led to widespread famine and hunger. The great famine of 1315–1317 in northern Europe began an all-too-familiar pattern, as is evident in this scene described by a contemporary chronicler:

> We saw a larger number of both sexes, not only from nearby places but from as much as five leagues away, barefooted and maybe even, except for women, in a completely nude state, together with their priests coming in procession at the Church of the Holy Martyrs, their bones bulging out, devoutly carrying bodies of saints and other relics to be adorned hoping to get relief.[1]

Some historians have pointed out that famine could have led to chronic malnutrition, which in turn contributed to increased infant mortality, lower birthrates, and higher susceptibility to disease because malnourished people are less able to resist infection. This, they argue, helps explain the virulence of the great plague known as the Black Death.

The Black Death

The **Black Death** of the mid-fourteenth century was the most devastating natural disaster in European history, ravaging the population and causing economic, social, political, and cultural upheaval. Contemporary chroniclers lamented how parents abandoned their children; one

related the words: "Oh father, why have you abandoned me? . . . Mother, where have you gone?"[2] People were horrified by an evil force they could not understand and by the subsequent breakdown of all normal human relations.

Bubonic plague, the most common form of plague at the time, was spread by black rats infested with fleas who were host to the deadly bacterium *Yersinia pestis*. Symptoms of bubonic plague included high fever, aching joints, swelling of the lymph nodes, and dark blotches caused by bleeding beneath the skin. Bubonic plague was actually the least toxic form of plague but nevertheless killed 50 to 60 percent of its victims. In pneumonic plague, the bacterial infection spread to the lungs, resulting in severe coughing, bloody sputum, and the relatively easy spread of the bacillus from human to human by coughing.

Spread of the Plague The Black Death was the first major epidemic disease to strike Europe in seven centuries, an absence that helps explain medieval Europe's remarkable population growth. Having disappeared from Europe and the Middle East in the Middle Ages, bubonic plague continued to haunt parts of southwestern China, especially isolated rural territories. The arrival of Mongol troops in this area in the mid-thirteenth century became the means for the spread of the plague as flea-infested rats accompanied the Mongols into central and northwestern China and Central Asia. From there, trading caravans brought the plague to Caffa on the Black Sea in 1346.

The plague reached Europe in October 1347 when Genoese merchants brought it from Caffa to the island of Sicily off the coast of southern Italy. It quickly spread to southern Italy and southern France and Spain by the end of 1347 (see Map 11.1). Diffusion of the Black Death followed commercial trade routes. In 1348, the plague spread through France and the Low Countries and into Germany. By the end of that year, it had moved to England, ravaging it in 1349. By the end of 1349, the plague had reached Scandinavia. Eastern Europe and Russia were affected by 1351, although mortality rates were never as high there as they were in western and central Europe.

Mortality figures for the Black Death were incredibly high. Italy was especially hard hit. Its crowded cities suffered losses of 50 to 60 percent (see the box on p. 199). In northern France, farming villages suffered mortality rates of 30 percent, and cities such as Rouen experienced losses as high as 40 percent. In England and Germany, entire villages disappeared. In Germany, of approximately 170,000 inhabited locations, only 130,000 were left by the end of the fourteenth century.

It has been estimated that the European population declined by 25 to 50 percent between 1347 and 1351. If we accept the recent scholarly assessment of a European population of 75 million in the early fourteenth century, this means a death toll of 19 to 38 million people in four years. And the plague did not end in 1351. There were major outbreaks again in 1361–1362 and 1369 and then regular recurrences during the remainder of the fourteenth century

MAP 11.1 **Spread of the Black Death.** The plague entered Europe in Sicily in 1347 and within three years had killed between one-quarter and one-half of the population. Outbreaks continued into the early eighteenth century, and it took Europe two hundred years to return to the population level it had before the Black Death. ❓ Is there a general pattern between distance from Sicily and the elapsed time before a region was infected with the plague? 🌐 **View an animated version of this map or related maps at** http://thomsonedu.com/history/spielvogel

and all of the fifteenth century. The European population did not start to recover until the end of the fifteenth century; not until the mid-sixteenth century did Europe return to thirteenth-century population levels.

Life and Death: Reactions to the Plague Attempts to explain the Black Death and mitigate its harshness led to extreme sorts of behavior. Many people believed that the plague had either been sent by God as a punishment for humans' sins or been caused by the devil. Some resorted to extreme asceticism to cleanse themselves of sin and gain God's forgiveness. Such was the flagellant movement, which became popular in 1348, especially in Germany. Groups of flagellants, both men and women, wandered from town to town, flogging each other with whips to win the forgiveness of a God whom they felt had sent the

plague to punish humans for their sinful ways. One contemporary chronicler described a flagellant procession:

> The penitents went about, coming first out of Germany. They were men who did public penance and scourged themselves with whips of hard knotted leather with little iron spikes. Some made themselves bleed very badly between the shoulder blades and some foolish women had cloths ready to catch the blood and smear it on their eyes, saying it was miraculous blood. While they were doing penance, they sang very mournful songs about the nativity and the passion of Our Lord. The object of this penance was to put a stop to the mortality, for in that time . . . at least a third of all the people in the world died.[3]

The flagellants attracted attention and caused mass hysteria wherever they went. The Catholic church, however, became alarmed when flagellant groups began to kill Jews and attack the clergy who opposed them. Pope

THE BLACK DEATH

The Black Death was the most terrifying natural calamity of the Middle Ages. It has been estimated that 25 to 50 percent of the population died as the plague spread throughout Europe between 1347 and 1351. This contemporary description of the great plague in Florence is taken from the preface to the *Decameron* by the fourteenth-century Italian writer Giovanni Boccaccio.

Giovanni Boccaccio, *Decameron*

In the year of Our Lord 1348 the deadly plague broke out in the great city of Florence, most beautiful of Italian cities. Whether through the operation of the heavenly bodies or because of our own iniquities which the just wrath of God sought to correct, the plague had arisen in the East some years before, causing the death of countless human beings. It spread without stop from one place to another, until, unfortunately, it swept over the West. Neither knowledge nor human foresight availed against it, though the city was cleansed of much filth by chosen officers in charge and sick persons were forbidden to enter it, while advice was broadcast for the preservation of health. Nor did humble supplications serve. Not once but many times they were ordained in the form of processions and other ways for the propitiation of God by the faithful, but, in spite of everything, toward the spring of the year the plague began to show its ravages....

It did not manifest itself as in the East, where if a man bled at the nose he had certain warning of inevitable death. At the onset of the disease both men and women were afflicted by a sort of swelling in the groin or under the armpits which sometimes attained the size of a common apple or egg. Some of these swellings were larger and some smaller, and were commonly called boils. From these two starting points the boils began in a little while to spread and appear generally all over the body. Afterwards, the manifestation of the disease changed into black or livid spots on the arms, thighs, and the whole person. In many these blotches were large and far apart, in others small and closely clustered. Like the boils, which had been and continued to be a certain indication of coming death, these blotches had the same meaning for everyone on whom they appeared.

Neither the advice of physicians nor the virtue of any medicine seemed to help or avail in the cure of these diseases. Indeed,...not only did few recover, but on the contrary almost everyone died within three days of the appearance of the signs—some sooner, some later.... The virulence of the plague was all the greater in that it was communicated by the sick to the well by contact, not unlike fire when dry or fatty things are brought near it. But the evil was still worse. Not only did conversation and familiarity with the diseased spread the malady and even cause death, but the mere touch of the clothes or any other object the sick had touched or used, seemed to spread the pestilence....

More wretched still were the circumstances of the common people and, for a great part, of the middle class, for, confined to their homes either by hope of safety or by poverty, and restricted to their own sections, they fell sick daily by thousands. There, devoid of help or care, they died almost without redemption. A great many breathed their last in the public streets, day and night; a large number perished in their homes, and it was only by the stench of their decaying bodies that they proclaimed their death to their neighbors. Everywhere the city was teeming with corpses....

So many bodies were brought to the churches every day that the consecrated ground did not suffice to hold them, particularly according to the ancient custom of giving each corpse its individual place. Huge trenches were dug in the crowded churchyards and the new dead were piled in them, layer upon layer, like merchandise in the hold of a ship. A little earth covered the corpses of each row, and the procedure continued until the trench was filled to the top.

According to Boccaccio, what was the cause of the plague, and what impact did it have on Florence and its inhabitants?

Clement VI condemned the flagellants in October 1349 and urged the public authorities to crush them. By the end of 1350, most of the flagellant movements had been destroyed.

An outbreak of virulent **anti-Semitism** also accompanied the Black Death. Jews were accused of causing the plague by poisoning town wells. Although Jews were persecuted in Spain, the worst **pogroms** against this helpless minority were carried out in Germany; more than sixty major Jewish communities in Germany had been exterminated by 1351. Many Jews fled eastward to Russia and especially to Poland, where the king offered them protection. Eastern Europe became home to large Jewish communities.

The prevalence of death because of the plague and its recurrences affected people in profound ways. Some survivors apparently came to treat life as something cheap and passing. Violence and violent death appeared to be more common after the plague than before. Post-plague Europe also demonstrated a morbid preoccupation with death. In their sermons, priests reminded parishioners that each night's sleep might be their last. Tombstones were decorated with macabre scenes of naked corpses in various stages of decomposition with snakes entwined in their bones and their innards filled with worms.

Economic Dislocation and Social Upheaval

The population collapse of the fourteenth century had dire economic and social consequences. Economic distress

The Flagellants. Reactions to the plague were extreme at times. Believing that asceticism could atone for humanity's sins and win God's forgiveness, flagellants wandered from town to town flogging themselves and each other with whips, as in this illustration.

brought social upheaval. Both peasants and noble landlords were affected. A serious labor shortage caused a dramatic rise in the price of labor. At Cuxham manor in England, for example, a farm laborer who had received 2 shillings a week in 1347 was paid 7 in 1349 and almost 11 by 1350. At the same time, the decline in population depressed the demand for agricultural produce, resulting in falling prices for output. Because landlords were having to pay more for labor at the same time that their income from rents was declining, they began to encounter economic hardship and lower standards of living. In England, aristocratic incomes dropped more than 20 percent between 1347 and 1353.

Landed aristocrats responded by seeking to lower the wage rate. The English Parliament passed the Statute of Laborers (1351), which attempted to limit wages to preplague levels and to forbid the mobility of peasants as well. Although such laws proved largely unworkable, they did keep wages from rising as high as they might have in a free market. Overall, the position of noble landlords continued to deteriorate during the late fourteenth and early fifteenth centuries. At the same time, the position of peasants improved, though not uniformly throughout Europe.

The decline in the number of peasants after the Black Death accelerated the process of converting labor services to rents, freeing peasants from the obligations of servile tenure and weakening the system of manorialism. But there were limits to how much the peasants could advance. They faced the same economic hurdles as the lords, while the latter also attempted to impose wage restrictions and

reinstate old forms of labor service. New governmental taxes also hurt. Peasant complaints became widespread and soon gave rise to rural revolts.

Peasant Revolts   In 1358, a peasant revolt known as the *Jacquerie* broke out in northern France. The destruction of normal order by the Black Death and the subsequent economic dislocation were important factors in causing the revolt, but the ravages created by the Hundred Years' War (see "War and Political Instability" later in this chapter) also affected the French peasantry. Both the French and English forces followed a deliberate policy of laying waste to peasants' lands while bands of mercenaries lived off the land by taking peasants' produce as well.

Peasant anger was also exacerbated by growing class tensions. Many aristocrats looked on peasants with utter contempt. One French aristocrat said, "Should peasants eat meat? Rather should they chew grass on the heath with the horned cattle and go naked on all fours." The peasants reciprocated this contempt for their so-called social superiors.

The outburst of peasant anger led to savage confrontations. Castles were burned and nobles murdered. Such atrocities did not go unanswered, however. The *Jacquerie* failed when the privileged classes closed ranks, savagely massacred the rebels, and ended the revolt.

The English Peasants' Revolt of 1381 was the most prominent of all. It was a product not of desperation but of rising expectations. After the Black Death, the condition of the English peasants had improved as they enjoyed greater freedom and higher wages or lower rents. Aristocratic landlords had fought back with legislation to depress wages and an attempt to reimpose old feudal dues. The most immediate cause of the revolt, however, was the monarchy's attempt to raise revenues by imposing a poll tax, a flat charge on each adult member of the population. Peasants in eastern England, the wealthiest part of the country, refused to pay the tax and expelled the collectors forcibly from their villages.

This action produced a widespread rebellion of both peasants and townspeople led by a well-to-do peasant called Wat Tyler and a preacher named John Ball. The latter preached an effective message against the noble class, as recounted by the chronicler Froissart:

> Good people, things cannot go right in England and never will, until goods are held in common and there are no more peasants and gentlefolk, but we are all one and the same. In what way are those whom we call lords greater masters than ourselves? How have they deserved it? Why do they hold us in bondage? If we all spring from a single father and mother, Adam and Eve, how can they claim or prove that they are lords more than us, except by making us produce and grow the wealth which they spend.[4]

The revolt was initially successful as the rebels burned down the manor houses of aristocrats, lawyers, and government officers and murdered several important officials, including the archbishop of Canterbury. After the peasants marched on London, the young King Richard II

Peasant Rebellion. The fourteenth century witnessed a number of revolts of the peasantry against noble landowners. Although the revolts often met with initial success, they were soon crushed. This fifteenth-century illustration shows nobles during the French *Jacquerie* of 1358 massacring the rebels in the town of Meaux, in northern France.

(1377–1399) promised to grant the rebels' demands if they returned to their homes. They accepted the king's word and dispersed, but the king reneged and, with the assistance of the aristocrats, arrested hundreds of the rebels. The poll tax was eliminated, however.

Revolts in the Cities   Revolts also erupted in the cities. Commercial and industrial activity suffered almost immediately from the Black Death. Florence's woolen industry, one of the giants, produced 70,000 to 80,000 pieces of cloth in 1338; in 1378, it was yielding only 24,000 pieces. Bourgeois merchants and manufacturers responded to a decline in trade and production by attempts to restrict competition and resist the demands of the lower classes.

In urban areas, where capitalist industrialists paid low wages and managed to prevent workers from forming organizations to help themselves, industrial revolts broke out throughout Europe. Most famous was the revolt of Florence's wool workers, the *ciompi*, in 1378. In the 1370s, the woolen industry was depressed, and wool workers saw their real wages decline when the coinage in which they were paid was debased. Their revolt won them some concessions from the municipal government, including the right to form guilds and be represented in the government. But their newly won rights were short-lived. A counterrevolution by government authorities brought an end to *ciompi* participation in the government by 1382.

Although the peasant and urban revolts sometimes resulted in short-term gains for the participants, the uprisings were relatively easily crushed and their gains quickly lost. Accustomed to ruling, the established classes easily combined and quashed dissent. Nevertheless, the rural and urban revolts of the fourteenth century ushered in an age of social conflict that characterized much of later European history.

War and Political Instability

Famine, plague, economic turmoil, social upheaval, and violence were not the only problems of the fourteenth century. War and political instability must also be added to the list. And of all the struggles of the period, the most famous and the most violent was the Hundred Years' War.

The Hundred Years' War

In the thirteenth century, the English king still held one small possession in France, known as the duchy of Gascony. As duke of Gascony, the English king pledged loyalty as a vassal to the French king. But when King Philip VI of France seized Gascony in 1337, the duke of Gascony—King Edward III of England—declared war on Philip. The attack on Gascony was a convenient excuse; Edward had already laid claim to the throne of France after the senior branch of the Capetian dynasty had become extinct in 1328 and a cousin of the Capetians, the duke of Valois, had become king as Philip VI.

The war began in a burst of knightly enthusiasm. Trained to be warriors, knights viewed the clash of battle as the ultimate opportunity to demonstrate their fighting abilities. But this struggle would change the nature of warfare, for as it dragged on, the outcomes of battles were increasingly determined not by knights but by peasant foot soldiers. The French army of 1337, with its heavily armed noble cavalry, resembled its twelfth- and thirteenth-century forebears. Considering themselves the fighting elite, the noble cavalry looked with contempt on foot soldiers and crossbowmen because they were peasants or other social inferiors. The English army, however, had evolved differently and had included peasants as paid foot soldiers. Armed with pikes, many of these foot soldiers had also adopted the longbow, invented by the Welsh. The longbow had greater striking power, longer range, and more rapid speed of fire than the crossbow. Although the English also used heavily armed cavalry, they relied even more on large numbers of foot soldiers.

Course of the War   Edward III's early campaigns in France were indecisive and achieved little. In 1346, Edward was forced to fight at Crécy, just south of Flanders. The larger French army followed no battle plan but simply attacked the English lines in a disorderly fashion. The arrows of the English archers decimated the French cavalry. As the chronicler Froissart described it, "The English continued to shoot into the thickest part of the crowd, wasting none of their arrows. They impaled or wounded horses and riders, who fell to the ground in great distress, unable to get up again without the help of several men."[5] It was a stunning victory for the English.

The Battle of Crécy was not decisive, however. The English simply did not possess the resources to subjugate all France, and hostilities continued intermittently for another fifty years until a twenty-year truce was negotiated in 1396, seemingly bringing an end to this protracted series of struggles between the French and English.

In 1415, however, the English king, Henry V (1413–1422), renewed the war at a time when the French were enduring a civil war as the dukes of Burgundy and Orléans competed to control the weak French king, Charles VI. In the summer of 1413, Paris exploded with bloody encounters. Taking advantage of the chaos, Henry V invaded France in 1415. At the Battle of Agincourt (1415), the French suffered a disastrous defeat, and fifteen hundred French nobles died when the heavy, armor-plated French knights attempted to attack across a field turned to mud by heavy rain. Altogether, French losses were six thousand dead; the English lost only three hundred men. Henry went on to reconquer Normandy and forge an alliance with the duke of Burgundy, making the English masters of northern France (see Map 11.2).

The seemingly hopeless French cause fell into the hands of Charles the dauphin (heir to the throne), the son of Charles VI. The dauphin governed the southern two-thirds of French lands from Bourges. Charles was weak and timid and was unable to rally the French against the English, who in 1428 had turned south and were besieging the city of Orléans to gain access to the valley of the Loire. The French monarch was saved, quite unexpectedly, by a French peasant woman.

Joan of Arc   Joan of Arc was born in 1412 to well-to-do peasants in the village of Domrémy in Champagne. Deeply religious, Joan experienced visions and came to believe

Joan of Arc.   Pictured here in a suit of armor, Joan of Arc is holding aloft a banner that shows Jesus and two angels. This portrait dates from the late fifteenth century; there are no portraits of Joan made from life.

that her favorite saints had commanded her to free France and have the dauphin crowned king. In February 1429, Joan made her way to the dauphin's court, where her sincerity and simplicity persuaded Charles to allow her to accompany a French army to Orléans. Apparently inspired by the faith of the peasant girl, the French armies found new confidence in themselves and liberated Orléans, changing the course of the war. Within a few weeks, the entire Loire valley had been freed of the English. Joan had brought the war to a decisive turning point.

But she did not live to see the war concluded. Captured by the Burgundian allies of the English in 1430, Joan was turned over first to the English and then to the Inquisition on charges of witchcraft (see the box on p. 204). In the fifteenth century, spiritual visions were thought to be inspired either by God or the devil. Because Joan dressed in men's clothing, it was relatively easy to convince others that she was in league with the "prince of darkness." She was condemned to death as a heretic and burned at the stake in 1431. To the end, as the flames rose up around her, she declared "that her voices came from God and had not deceived her." Twenty-five years later, a new ecclesiastical court exonerated her of these charges,

France in the Mid-Fourteenth Century

— Boundary of kingdom of France, 1360

······ Lands held by Edward III of England on accession, 1327

→ Route taken by Edward III, 1346–1347

→ Route taken by Edward, Black Prince, 1355–1357

✗ Site and date of important battle

▮ Lands ceded to Edward III of England

▮ Domain of king of France, 1360

▮ Lands held by relatives of the king of France

▮ Other territories held by the king of France

France in the Early Fifteenth Century

— Boundary of kingdom of France, 1429

······ Boundary of lands left to England, 1377

— Route taken by Henry V, 1415–1416

— Route taken by Joan of Arc, 1429–1431

✗ Site and date of important battle

▮ Lands held by Henry VI of England, 1429

▮ Lands held by Charles VII of France

▮ Lands held by the duke of Burgundy

▮ Burgundian lands recognizing Henry VI

MAP 11.2 The Hundred Years' War. This long, exhausting struggle began in 1337 and dragged on until 1453. The English initially gained substantial French territory, but in the later phases of the war, France turned the tide, eventually expelling the English from all Continental lands except the port of Calais. ❓ What gains had the English made by 1429, and how do they correlate to proximity to England and the ocean? 🌐 **View an animated version of this map or related maps at** http://thomsonedu.com/history/spielvogel

and five centuries later, in 1920, she was made a saint of the Roman Catholic church. Joan of Arc's accomplishments proved decisive.

End of the War Although the war dragged on for another two decades, defeats of English armies in Normandy and Aquitaine led to French victory. Important to the French success was the use of the cannon, a new weapon made possible by the invention of gunpowder. The Chinese had invented gunpowder in the eleventh century and devised a simple cannon by the thirteenth. The Mongols greatly improved this technology, developing more accurate cannons and cannonballs; both

spread to the Middle East by the thirteenth century and to Europe by the fourteenth.

The death of England's best commanders and the instability of the English government under King Henry VI (1422–1461) also contributed to England's defeat. By 1453, the only part of France that was left in England's hands was the coastal town of Calais, which remained English for another century.

Political Instability

The fourteenth century was a period of adversity for the internal political stability of European governments.

THE TRIAL OF JOAN OF ARC

Feared by the English and Burgundians, Joan of Arc was put on trial on charges of witchcraft and heresy after her capture. She was condemned for heresy and burned at the stake on May 30, 1431. This excerpt is taken from the records of Joan's trial, which presented a dramatic confrontation between the judges, trained in the complexities of legal questioning, and a nineteen-year-old woman who relied only on the "voices" of saints who gave her advice. In this selection, Joan describes what these voices told her to do.

The Trial of Joan of Arc

Afterward, she declared that at the age of thirteen she had a voice from God to help her and guide her. And the first time she was much afraid. And this voice came toward noon, in summer, in her father's garden.... She heard the voice on her right, in the direction of the church; and she seldom heard it without a light. This light came from the same side as the voice, and generally there was a great light....

Asked what instruction this voice gave her for the salvation of her soul: she said it taught her to be good and to go to church often.... She said that the voice told her to come, and she could no longer stay where she was; and the voice told her again that she should raise the siege of the city of Orléans. She said moreover that the voice told her that she, Joan, should go to Robert de Baudricourt, in the town of Vaucouleurs of which he was captain, and he would provide an escort for her. And the said Joan answered that she was a poor maid, knowing nothing of riding or fighting. She said she went to an uncle of hers, and told him she wanted to stay with him for some time; and she stayed there about eight days. And she told her uncle she must go to the said town of Vaucouleurs, and so her uncle took her.

Then she said that when she reached Vaucouleurs she easily recognized Robert de Baudricourt, although she had never seen him before; and she knew him through her voice, for the voice had told her it was he.... The said Robert twice refused to hear her and repulsed her; the third time he listened to her and gave her an escort. And the voice had told her that it would be so.

How would you explain Joan's "voices"? How would you defend Joan against her judges?

Although government bureaucracies grew ever larger, at the same time the question of who should control the bureaucracies led to internal conflict and instability. Like the lord and serf relationship, the lord and vassal relationship based on land and military service was being replaced by a contract based on money. Especially after the Black Death, money payments called **scutage** were increasingly substituted for military service. Monarchs welcomed this development because they could now hire professional soldiers, who tended to be more reliable anyway. As lord and vassal relationships became less personal and less important, new relationships based on political advantage began to be formed, creating new avenues for political influence—and for corruption as well. Especially noticeable, as the landed aristocrats suffered declining rents and social uncertainties with the new relationships, was the formation of factions of nobles who looked for opportunities to advance their power and wealth at the expense of other noble factions and of their monarchs. Others went to the royal courts, offering to serve the kings.

The kings had their own problems, however. By the mid-fifteenth century, reigning monarchs in many European countries were not the direct descendants of those ruling in 1300. The founders of these new dynasties had to struggle for position as factions of nobles vied to gain material advantages for themselves. At the end of the fourteenth century and beginning of the fifteenth, there were two claimants to the throne of France, and two aristocratic factions fought for control of England; in Germany, three princes struggled to be recognized as emperor.

Fourteenth-century monarchs, whether of old or new dynasties, faced financial problems as well. The shift to the use of mercenary soldiers left monarchs perennially short of cash. Traditional revenues, especially rents from property, increasingly proved insufficient to meet their needs. Monarchs attempted to generate new sources of revenues, especially through taxes, which often meant going through parliaments. This opened the door for parliamentary bodies to gain more power by asking for favors first. Although unsuccessful in most cases, the active role of parliaments added another element of uncertainty and confusion to fourteenth-century politics. Turning now to a survey of western and central European states, we can see how these disruptive factors worked.

Western Europe: England and France

In the fourteenth century, the lengthy reign of Edward III (1327–1377) was important for the evolution of English political institutions. Parliament increased in prominence and developed its basic structure and functions during Edward's reign. Due to his constant need for money to fight the Hundred Years' War, Edward came to rely on Parliament to levy new taxes. In return for regular grants, Edward made several concessions, including a commitment to levy no direct tax without Parliament's consent and to allow committees of Parliament to examine the

Outbreak of hostilities	1337
Battle of Crécy	1346
Truce	1396
War renewed by Henry V	1415
Battle of Agincourt	1415
French recovery under Joan of Arc	1429–1431
End of the war	1453

government accounts to ensure that the money was being spent properly. By the end of Edward's reign, Parliament had become an important component of the English governmental system.

During this same period, Parliament began to assume the organizational structure it has retained to this day. The Great Council of barons became the House of Lords and evolved into a body composed of the chief bishops and abbots of the realm and aristocratic peers whose position in Parliament was hereditary. The representatives of the shires and boroughs, who were considered less important than the lay and ecclesiastical lords, held collective meetings to decide policy and soon came to be regarded as the House of Commons. Together, the House of Lords and the House of Commons constituted Parliament. Although the House of Commons did little beyond approving measures proposed by the Lords, during Edward's reign the Commons did begin the practice of drawing up petitions, which, if accepted by the Lords and king, became law.

After Edward III's death, England began to experience the internal instability of aristocratic factionalism that was racking other European countries. After Richard II was deposed in 1399 and killed, the leader of the revolt of the barons, Henry of Lancaster, was made king. Although Henry IV (1399–1413) proved to be a competent ruler, factions of nobles rose to take advantage of the situation. England would soon be embroiled in a devastating series of civil wars known as the War of the Roses.

The Hundred Years' War left France prostrate. Depopulation, desolate farmlands, ruined commerce, and independent and unruly nobles made it difficult for the kings to assert their authority throughout the fourteenth century. The insanity of King Charles VI (1380–1422) especially opened the door to rival factions of French nobles aspiring to power and wealth. The dukes of Burgundy and Orléans competed to control Charles and the French monarchy. Their struggles created chaos for the French government and the French people. Many nobles supported the Orléanist faction; Paris and other towns favored the Burgundians. By the beginning of the fifteenth century, France seemed hopelessly mired in civil war.

The German Monarchy

England and France had developed strong national monarchies in the High Middle Ages. By the end of the fourteenth century, they seemed in danger of disintegrating due to dynastic problems and the pressures generated by the Hundred Years' War. In contrast, the Holy Roman Empire, whose core consisted of the lands of Germany, had already begun to fall apart in the High Middle Ages. Northern Italy, which the German emperors had tried to include in their medieval empire, had been free from any real imperial control since the end of the Hohenstaufen dynasty in the thirteenth century. In Germany itself, the failure of the Hohenstaufens ended any chance of centralized monarchical authority, and Germany became a land of hundreds of states that varied in size and power. These included princely states, such as the duchies of Bavaria and Saxony; free imperial city-states (self-governing cities directly under the control of the Holy Roman Emperor rather than a German territorial prince), such as Nuremberg; modest territories of petty imperial knights; and ecclesiastical states, such as the archbishopric of Cologne. In the ecclesiastical states, a high church official, such as a bishop, archbishop, or abbot, served in a dual capacity as an administrative official of the Catholic church and secular lord over the territories of the state. Although all of the rulers of these different states had some obligations to the German king and Holy Roman Emperor, more and more they acted independently.

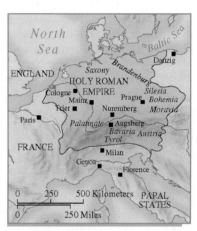

The Holy Roman Empire in the Fourteenth Century

Because of its unique pattern of development in the High Middle Ages, the German monarchy had become established on an elective rather than hereditary basis. This principle of election was standardized in 1356 by the Golden Bull issued by Emperor Charles IV (1346–1378). This document stated that four lay princes and three ecclesiastical rulers would serve as electors with the legal power to elect the "king of the Romans and future emperor, to be ruler of the world and of the Christian people." "King of the Romans" was the official title of the German king; after his imperial coronation, he would also have the title of emperor.

In the fourteenth century, the electoral principle further ensured that kings of Germany were generally weak. Their ability to exercise effective power depended on the extent of their own family possessions. At the beginning of the fifteenth century, three emperors claimed the throne. Although the dispute was quickly settled, Germany entered the fifteenth century in a condition that verged on anarchy. Princes fought princes and leagues of cities. The emperors were virtually powerless to control any of them.

The States of Italy

By the fourteenth century, Italy, too, had failed to develop a centralized monarchical state. Papal opposition to the rule of the Hohenstaufen emperors in the thirteenth century had virtually guaranteed that. Moreover, southern Italy was divided into the kingdom of Naples, ruled by the house of Anjou, and Sicily, whose kings came from the Spanish house of Aragon. The center of the peninsula remained under the rather shaky control of the papacy. Lack of centralized authority had enabled numerous city-states in northern and central Italy to remain independent of any political authority.

In the course of the fourteenth century, two general tendencies can be discerned in Italy: the replacement of republican governments by tyrants and the expansion of the larger city-states at the expense of the less powerful ones. Nearly all the cities of northern Italy began their existence as free communes with republican governments. But in the fourteenth century, intense internal strife led city-states to resort to temporary expedients, allowing rule by one man with dictatorial powers. Limited rule, however, soon became long-term despotism, as tyrants proved willing to use force to maintain power. Eventually, such tyrants tried to legitimize their power by purchasing titles from the emperor (still nominally ruler of northern Italy as Holy Roman Emperor). In this fashion, the Visconti became the dukes of Milan and the d'Este the dukes of Ferrara.

The States of Italy in the Fourteenth Century

The other change of great significance was the development of regional entities as the larger states expanded at the expense of the smaller ones. By the beginning of the fifteenth century, three major states came to dominate northern Italy. In the fertile Po valley, where the chief trade routes from Italian coastal cities to the Alpine passes crossed, Milan was one of the richest city-states in Italy. Politically, it was also one of the most agitated until members of the Visconti family established themselves as hereditary dukes of Milan and extended their power over all of Lombardy. The republic of Florence dominated the region of Tuscany. In the course of the fourteenth century, a small but wealthy merchant oligarchy established control of the Florentine government, led the Florentines in a series of successful wars against their neighbors, and established Florence as a major territorial state in northern Italy. The other major northern Italian state was the maritime republic of Venice, which had grown rich from commercial activity in the eastern Mediterranean and northern Europe. Venice remained a stable political entity governed by a small oligarchy of merchant-aristocrats who had become extremely wealthy through their trading activities. Venice's commercial empire brought in enormous revenues and gave it the status of an international power. At the end of the fourteenth century, Venice embarked on the conquest of a territorial state in northern Italy to protect its food supply and its overland trade routes.

The Decline of the Church

The papacy of the Roman Catholic church reached the height of its power in the thirteenth century. Theories of papal supremacy included a doctrine of "fullness of power" as the spiritual head of Christendom and claims to universal temporal authority over all secular rulers. But the growing secular monarchies of Europe presented a challenge to papal claims of temporal supremacy that led the papacy into a conflict with these territorial states that it was unable to win. Papal defeat in turn led to other crises that brought into question and undermined not only the pope's temporal authority over all Christendom but his spiritual authority as well.

Boniface VIII and the Conflict with the State

The struggle between the papacy and the secular monarchies began during the pontificate of Pope Boniface VIII (1294–1303). One major issue appeared to be at stake between the pope and King Philip IV (1285–1314) of France. Looking for a source of new revenues, Philip expressed the right to tax the French clergy. Boniface VIII claimed that the clergy of any state could not pay taxes to their secular ruler without the pope's consent. Underlying this issue, however, was a basic conflict between the claims of the papacy to universal authority over both church and state, which necessitated complete control over the clergy, and the claims of the king that all subjects, including the clergy, were under the jurisdiction of the crown and subject to the king's authority on matters of taxation and justice. In short, the fundamental issue was the universal sovereignty of the papacy versus the royal sovereignty of the monarch.

Boniface VIII asserted his position in a series of papal bulls or letters, the most important of which was *Unam Sanctam*, issued in 1302. It was the strongest statement ever made by a pope on the supremacy of the spiritual authority over the temporal authority (see the box on

Pope Boniface VIII. The conflict between church and state in the Middle Ages reached its height in the struggle between Pope Boniface VIII and Philip IV of France. This fourteenth-century miniature depicts Boniface VIII presiding over a gathering of cardinals.

p. 208). When it became apparent that the pope had decided to act on his principles by excommunicating Philip IV of France, the latter sent a small contingent of French forces to capture Boniface and bring him back to France for trial. The pope was captured in Anagni, although Italian nobles from the surrounding countryside rescued him. The shock of this experience, however, soon led to the pope's death. Philip's strong-arm tactics had produced a clear victory for the national monarchy over the papacy, since no later pope dared renew the extravagant claims of Boniface VIII. To ensure his position and avoid any future papal threat, Philip IV brought enough pressure on the college of cardinals to achieve the election of a Frenchman, Clement V (1305–1314), as pope. Using the excuse of turbulence in the city of Rome, the new pope took up residence in Avignon, on the east bank of the Rhône River. Although Avignon was located in the Holy Roman Empire and was not a French possession, it lay just across the river from the possessions of King Philip IV and was French in culture.

The Papacy at Avignon (1305–1378)

The residency of the popes in Avignon for most of the fourteenth century led to a decline in papal prestige and growing antipapal sentiment. The city of Rome was the traditional capital of the universal church. The pope was the bishop of Rome, and his position was based on being the successor to the apostle Peter, the first bishop of Rome. It was unseemly that the head of the Catholic church should reside outside of Rome. In the 1330s, the popes began to construct a stately palace in Avignon, a clear indication that they intended to stay for some time.

Other factors also led to a decline in papal prestige during the Avignonese residency. Many contemporaries believed that the popes at Avignon were captives of the French monarchy. Although questionable, since Avignon did not belong to the French monarchy, it was easy to

believe in view of Avignon's proximity to French lands. Moreover, during the seventy-three years of the Avignonese papacy, of the 134 new cardinals created by the popes, 113 of them were French. At the same time, the popes attempted to find new sources of revenue to compensate for their loss of revenue from the Papal States and began to impose new taxes on the clergy. Furthermore, the splendor in which the pope and cardinals were living in Avignon led to a highly vocal criticism of both clergy and papacy in the fourteenth century. Avignon had become a powerful symbol of abuses within the church, and many people began to call for the pope's return to Rome. One of the most prominent calls came from Catherine of Siena (c. 1347–1380), whose saintly demeanor and claims of visions from God led the city of Florence to send her on a mission to Pope Gregory XI (1370–1378) in Avignon. She told the pope, "Because God has given you authority and because you have accepted it, you ought to use your virtue and power; if you do not wish to use it, it might be better for you to resign what you have accepted; it would give more honor to God and health to your soul."[6]

Avignon

The Great Schism

Catherine of Siena's admonition seemed to be heeded in 1377, when at long last Pope Gregory XI, perceiving the disastrous decline in papal prestige, returned to Rome. He died soon afterward, however, the following spring. When the college of cardinals met in conclave to elect a new pope, the citizens of Rome, fearful that the French majority would choose another Frenchman who would

Boniface VIII's Defense of Papal Supremacy

*O*ne of the most remarkable documents of the fourteenth century was the exaggerated statement of papal supremacy issued by Pope Boniface VIII in 1302 in the heat of his conflict with the French king Philip IV. Ironically, this strongest statement ever made of papal supremacy was issued at a time when the rising power of the secular monarchies made it increasingly difficult for the premises to be accepted. Not long after issuing it, Boniface was taken prisoner by the French. Although freed by his fellow Italians, the humiliation of his defeat led to his death a short time later.

Pope Boniface VIII, *Unam Sanctam*

We are compelled, our faith urging us, to believe and to hold—and we do firmly believe and simply confess–that there is one holy catholic and apostolic church, outside of which there is neither salvation nor remission of sins.... In this church there is one Lord, one faith and one baptism.... Therefore, of this one and only church there is one body and one head ... Christ, namely, and the vicar of Christ, St. Peter, and the successor of Peter. For the Lord himself said to Peter, feed my sheep....

We are told by the word of the gospel that in this His fold there are two swords—a spiritual, namely, and a temporal.... Both swords, the spiritual and the material, therefore, are in the power of the church; the one, indeed, to be wielded for the church, the other by the church; the one by the hand of the priest, the other by the hand of kings and knights, but at the will and sufferance of the priest. One sword, moreover, ought to be under the other, and the temporal authority to be subjected to the spiritual....

Therefore if the earthly power err it shall be judged by the spiritual power; but if the lesser spiritual power err, by the greater. But if the greatest, it can be judged by God alone, not by man, the apostle bearing witness. A spiritual man judges all things, but he himself is judged by no one. This authority, moreover, even though it is given to man and exercised through man, is not human but rather divine, being given by divine lips to Peter and founded on a rock for him and his successors through Christ himself whom he has confessed; the Lord himself saying to Peter: "Whatsoever you shall bind, etc." Whoever, therefore, resists this power thus ordained by God, resists the ordination of God....

Indeed, we declare, announce and define, that it is altogether necessary to salvation for every human creature to be subject to the Roman pontiff.

What claims does Boniface VIII make in Unam Sanctam? *To what extent are these claims a logical continuation of the development of the papacy in the Middle Ages? If you were a monarch, why would you object to this papal bull?*

---

return the papacy to Avignon, threatened that the cardinals would not leave Rome alive unless a Roman or an Italian were elected pope. Indeed, the guards of the conclave warned the cardinals that they "ran the risk of being torn in pieces" if they did not choose an Italian. The terrified cardinals duly elected the Italian archbishop of Bari, who was subsequently crowned as Pope Urban VI (1378–1389) on Easter Sunday.

Following his election, Urban VI made clear his plans to reform the papal curia and even to swamp the college of cardinals with enough new Italian cardinals to eliminate the French majority. After many of the cardinals (the French ones) withdrew from Rome in late summer and were finally free of the Roman mob, they issued a manifesto, saying that they had been coerced by the mob and that Urban's election was therefore null and void. The dissenting cardinals thereupon chose one of their number, a Frenchman, who took the title of Clement VII and promptly returned to Avignon. Since Urban remained in Rome, there were now two popes, initiating what has been called the **Great Schism** of the church.

Europe's loyalties soon became divided: France, Spain, Scotland, and southern Italy supported Clement, while England, Germany, Scandinavia, and most of Italy supported Urban. These divisions generally followed political lines. Because the French supported the Avignonese, so

did their allies; their enemies, particularly England and its allies, supported the Roman pope.

The Great Schism badly damaged the faith of Christian believers. The pope was widely believed to be the leader of Christendom and, as Boniface VIII had pointed out, held the keys to the kingdom of heaven. Since both lines of popes denounced the other as the Antichrist, such a spectacle could not help but undermine the institution that had become the very foundation of the church. The Great Schism introduced uncertainty into the daily lives of ordinary Christians.

The Conciliar Movement

As dissatisfaction with the papacy grew, so did the calls for a revolutionary approach to solving the church's institutional problems. Final authority in spiritual matters must reside not with the popes, reformers claimed, but with a general church council representing all members. The Great Schism led large numbers of serious churchmen to take up the theory of **conciliarism** in the belief that only a general council of the church could end the schism and bring reform to the church in its "head and members." In desperation, a group of cardinals from both lines of popes finally heeded these theoretical formulations and convened a general council. This Council of

Pope Boniface VIII	1294–1303
Unam Sanctam	1302
Papacy at Avignon	1305–1378
Pope Gregory XI's return to Rome	1377
Start of the Great Schism	1378
Pope Urban VI	1378–1389
Failure of Council of Pisa to end schism	1409
Council of Constance	1414–1418
End of schism; election of Martin V	1417

Pisa, which met in 1409, deposed the two rival popes and elected a new one. The council's action proved disastrous when the two deposed popes refused to step down. There were now three popes, and the church seemed more hopelessly divided than ever.

Leadership in convening a new council now passed to the Holy Roman Emperor, Sigismund. As a result of his efforts, a new ecumenical church council met at Constance from 1414 to 1418. It had three major objectives: to end the schism, to eradicate heresy, and to reform the church in "head and members." The ending of the schism proved to be the Council of Constance's easiest task. After the three competing popes either resigned or were deposed, a new conclave elected a Roman cardinal, a member of a prominent Roman family, as Pope Martin V (1417–1431). The council was much less successful in dealing with the problems of heresy and reform.

Culture and Society in an Age of Adversity

In the midst of disaster, the fourteenth century proved creative in its own way. The rapid growth of vernacular literature and new inventions made an impact on European life at the same time that the effects of plague were felt in many areas of medieval towns and cities.

The Development of Vernacular Literature

Although Latin remained the language of the church liturgy and the official documents of both church and state, the fourteenth century witnessed a surge in literature written in vernacular languages, especially in Italy. By the late fifteenth century, vernacular literary forms had become so celebrated that they could compete with and would eventually replace works in Latin.

Dante Alighieri (1265–1321) came from an old Florentine noble family that had fallen on hard times. His masterpiece in the Italian vernacular was the *Divine Comedy*, written between 1313 and 1321. Cast in a typical medieval framework, the *Divine Comedy* is basically the story of the soul's progression to salvation, a fundamental medieval preoccupation. The lengthy poem was divided into three major sections corresponding to the realms of the afterworld: hell, purgatory, and heaven or paradise. In the "Inferno" (see the box on p. 210), Dante is led by his guide, the classical author Virgil, who is a symbol of human reason. But Virgil (or reason) can only lead the poet so far on his journey. At the end of "Purgatory," Beatrice (the true love of Dante's life), who represents revelation—which alone can explain the mysteries of heaven—becomes his guide into "Paradise." Here Beatrice presents Dante to Saint Bernard, a symbol of mystical contemplation. The saint turns Dante over to the Virgin Mary, since grace is necessary to achieve the final step of entering the presence of God, where one beholds "the love that moves the sun and the other stars."[7]

Geoffrey Chaucer (c. 1340–1400) brought a new level of sophistication to the English vernacular language in his famous work *The Canterbury Tales*. His beauty of expression and clear, forceful language were important in transforming his East Midland dialect into the chief ancestor of the modern English language. *The Canterbury Tales* is a collection of stories told by a group of twenty-nine pilgrims journeying from Southwark to the tomb of Saint Thomas at Canterbury. This format gave Chaucer the chance to portray an entire range of English society, from highborn to lowborn. The stories these pilgrims told to while away the time on the journey were just as varied as the storytellers themselves: knightly romances, fairy tales, saints' lives, sophisticated satires, and crude anecdotes.

One of the extraordinary vernacular writers of the age was Christine de Pizan (c. 1364–1430). Thanks to her father's position at the court of Charles V of France, she received a good education. Her husband died when she was only twenty-five (they had been married for ten years), leaving her with little income and three small children and her mother to support. Christine took the unusual step of becoming a writer to earn her living. Her poems were soon in demand, and by 1400 she had achieved financial security.

Christine de Pizan is best known, however, for her French prose works written in defense of women. In *The Book of the City of Ladies*, written in 1404, she denounced the many male writers who had argued that women by their very nature were prone to evil, unable to learn, and easily swayed and consequently needed to be controlled by men. With the help of Reason, Righteousness, and Justice, who appear to her in a vision, Christine refutes these antifeminist attacks. Women, she argues, are not evil by nature and could learn as well as men if they were permitted to attend the same schools: "Should I also tell you whether a woman's nature is clever and quick enough to learn speculative sciences as well as to discover them, and likewise the manual arts. I assure you that women are equally well-suited and skilled to carry them out and to put them to sophisticated use once they have learned them."[8] She ends the book by encouraging women to defend themselves against the attacks of men, who are incapable of understanding women.

DANTE'S VISION OF HELL

The *Divine Comedy* of Dante Alighieri is regarded as one of the greatest literary works of all time. Many people consider it the supreme summary of medieval thought. It combines allegory with a remarkable amount of contemporary history. Indeed, forty-three of the seventy-nine people consigned to hell in the "Inferno" were Florentines. This excerpt is taken from canto 18 of the "Inferno," in which Dante and Virgil visit the eighth circle of hell, which is divided into ten trenches containing those who had committed malicious frauds upon their fellow human beings.

Dante, "Inferno," *Divine Comedy*

We had already come to where the walk
crosses the second bank, from which it lifts
another arch, spanning from rock to rock.

Here we heard people whine in the next chasm,
and knock and thump themselves with open palms,
and blubber through their snouts as if in a spasm.

Steaming from that pit, a vapor rose
over the banks, crusting them with a slime
that sickened my eyes and hammered at my nose.

That chasm sinks so deep we could not sight
its bottom anywhere until we climbed
along the rock arch to its greatest height.

Once there, I peered down; and I saw long lines
of people in a river of excrement
that seemed the overflow of the world's latrines.

I saw among the felons of that pit
one wraith who might or might not have been tonsured—
one could not tell, he was so smeared with shit.

He bellowed: "You there, why do you stare at me
more than at all the others in this stew?"
And I to him: "Because if memory

serves me, I knew you when your hair was dry.
You are Alessio Interminelli da Lucca.
That's why I pick you from this filthy fry."

And he then, beating himself on his clown's head:
"Down to this have the flatteries I sold
the living sunk me here among the dead."

And my Guide prompted then: "Lean forward a bit
and look beyond him, there—do you see that one
scratching herself with dungy nails, the strumpet

who fidgets to her feet, then to a crouch?
It is the whore Thaïs who told her lover
when he sent to ask her, 'Do you thank me much?'

'Much? Nay, past all believing!' And with this
Let us turn from the sight of this abyss."

How does Dante's vision of hell reflect medieval religious thought? Why were there Florentines in hell?

Art and the Black Death

The fourteenth century produced an artistic outburst in new directions as well as a large body of morbid work influenced by the Black Death and the recurrence of the plague. The city of Florence witnessed the first dramatic break with medieval tradition in the work of Giotto (1266–1337), often considered a forerunner of Italian Renaissance painting. Although he worked throughout Italy, Giotto's most famous works were done in Padua and Florence. Coming out of the formal Byzantine school, Giotto transcended it with a new kind of realism, a desire to imitate nature that Renaissance artists later identified as the basic component of Classical art. Giotto's figures were solid and rounded, and placed realistically in relationship to each other and their background, they provided a sense of three-dimensional depth. The expressive faces and physically realistic bodies gave his sacred figures human qualities with which spectators could identify.

The Black Death had a visible impact on art. For one thing, it wiped out entire guilds of artists. At the same time, survivors, including the newly rich who patronized artists, were no longer so optimistic as before. Some were more guilty about enjoying life and more concerned about gaining salvation. Postplague art began to concentrate on pain and death. A fairly large number of artistic works came to be based on the *ars moriendi*, the art of dying.

Changes in Urban Life

One immediate by-product of the Black Death was a greater regulation of urban activities. Authorities tried to keep cities cleaner by enacting new ordinances against waste products in the streets. Viewed as unhealthy places, bathhouses were closed down, leading to a noticeable decline in cleanliness.

The effects of plague were also felt in other areas of medieval urban life. The basic unit of the late medieval urban environment was the nuclear family of husband, wife, and children. Especially in wealthier families, there might also be servants, apprentices, and other relatives, including widowed mothers and the husband's illegitimate children.

Before the Black Death, late marriages were common for urban couples. It was not unusual for husbands to be in their late thirties or forties and wives in their early

Giotto, *Lamentation*. The work of Giotto marked the first clear innovation in fourteenth-century painting, making him a forerunner of the early Renaissance. This fresco was part of a series done on the walls of the Arena chapel in Padua begun in 1305. Giotto painted thirty-eight scenes on three levels: the lives of Mary, the mother of Jesus, and her parents (top panel); the life and work of Jesus (middle panel); and his passion, crucifixion, and resurrection (bottom panel). Shown here from the bottom panel is the lamentation. A group of Jesus' followers, including his mother and Mary Magdalene, mourn over the body of Jesus before it is placed in its tomb. The solidity of Giotto's human figures gives them a three-dimensional quality. He also captured the grief and despair felt by the mourners.

twenties. The expense of beginning a household probably necessitated the delay in marriage. But the situation changed dramatically after the plague, reflecting new economic opportunities for the survivors and a reluctance to postpone living in the presence of so much death. The economic difficulties of the fourteenth century also had a tendency to strengthen the development of gender roles and to set new limits on employment opportunities for women. Based on the authority of Aristotle, Thomas Aquinas and other thirteenth-century scholastic theologians had advanced the belief that according to the natural order, men were active and domineering while women were passive and submissive. As more and more lawyers, doctors, and priests, who had been trained in universities where these notions were taught, entered society, these ideas of man's and woman's different natures became widely acceptable. Increasingly, women were expected to forgo any active functions in society and remain subject to direction from males. A fourteenth-century Parisian provost commented on glass cutters that "no master's widow who keeps working at his craft after her husband's death may take on apprentices, for the men of the craft do not believe that a woman can master it well enough to teach a child to master it, for the craft is a very delicate one."[9] Although this statement suggests that some women were in fact running businesses, it also reveals that they were viewed as incapable of undertaking all of men's activities. Based on a pattern of gender, Europeans created a division of labor roles between men and women that continued until the Industrial Revolution of the eighteenth and nineteenth centuries.

Inventions and New Patterns

Despite its problems, the fourteenth century witnessed a continuation of the technological innovations that had characterized the High Middle Ages. The most extraordinary of these inventions, and one that had a major impact on European cities, was the clock. The mechanical clock was invented at the end of the thirteenth century but not perfected until the fourteenth. The time-telling clock was actually a by-product of a larger astronomical clock. The best-designed one was constructed by Giovanni di Dondi in the mid-fourteenth century. Dondi's clock contained the signs of the zodiac but also struck on the hour. Because clocks were expensive, they were usually installed only in the towers of churches or municipal buildings. The first clock striking equal hours was in a church in Milan; in 1335, a chronicler described it as "a wonderful clock, with a very large clapper which strikes a bell twenty-four hours of the day and night and thus at the first hour of the night gives one sound, at the second two strikes...and so distinguishes one hour from another, which is of greatest use to men of every degree."[10]

Clocks introduced a wholly new conception of time into the lives of Europeans; they revolutionized how people thought about and used time. Throughout most of the Middle Ages, time was determined by natural rhythms (daybreak and nightfall) or church bells that were rung at more or less regular three-hour intervals, corresponding to the ecclesiastical offices of the church. Clocks made it possible to plan one's day and organize one's activities around the regular striking of bells. This brought a new regularity into the lives of workers and merchants, defining urban existence and enabling merchants and bankers to see the value of time in a new way.

Invented earlier by the Chinese, gunpowder also made its appearance in the West in the fourteenth century. The use of gunpowder eventually brought drastic changes to European warfare. Its primary use was in cannons, although early cannons were prone to blow up, making them as dangerous to the people firing them as to the enemy. Even as late as 1460, an attack on a castle using the "Lion," an enormous Flemish cannon, proved disastrous for the Scottish king James II when the "Lion" blew up, killing the king and a number of his retainers. Continued improvement in the construction of cannons, however, soon made them extremely valuable in reducing both castles and city walls.

Entertainment in the Middle Ages. Medieval people engaged in a variety of activities to be entertained. City dwellers enjoyed feast days and holidays, when minstrels and jugglers amused people with their arts and tricks. Castle life had its courtly feasts, featuring tournaments accompanied by banquets, music, and dancing. Games were popular at all levels of society; castle dwellers played backgammon, checkers, and chess. The illustration at the top, from a fifteenth-century fresco, shows a group of ladies and gentlemen playing cards.

Like children in all ages, medieval children joined with other children in playing a variety of games. A number of medieval writers on children saw play as a basic symbol of childhood itself. In this series of illustrations from medieval manuscripts, we see children engaged in riding hobbyhorses (undoubtedly popular in a society dependent on horses), catching butterflies and playing with a spinning top, and playing a game of blind man's bluff.

CONCLUSION

European civilization developed many of its fundamental features in the eleventh, twelfth, and thirteenth centuries. Territorial states, parliaments, capitalist trade and industry, banks, cities, and vernacular literatures were all products of that fertile period. During the same time, the Catholic church under the direction of the papacy reached its apogee. European society in the fourteenth century, however, was challenged by an overwhelming number of crises. Devastating plague, decline in trade and industry, bank failures, peasant revolts pitting lower classes against the upper classes, seemingly constant warfare, aristocratic factional conflict that undermined political stability, the absence of the popes from Rome, and even the spectacle of two popes condemning each other as the Antichrist all seemed to overpower Europeans in this "calamitous century." Not surprisingly, much of the art of the period depicted the Four Horsemen of the Apocalypse described in the New Testament book of Revelation: Death, Famine,

Pestilence, and War. To some people, no doubt, the last days of the world seemed to be at hand.

The new European society, however, proved remarkably resilient. Periods of crisis usually give rise to new ideas and new practices. Intellectuals of the period saw themselves as standing on the threshold of a new age and a rebirth of the best features of classical civilization, an era widely referred to as the Renaissance.

TIMELINE

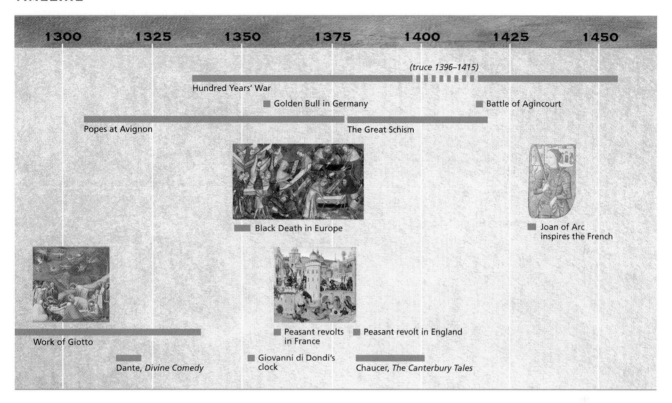

NOTES

1. Quoted in H. S. Lucas, "The Great European Famine of 1315, 1316, and 1317," *Speculum* 5 (1930): 359.
2. Quoted in D. Herlihy, *The Black Death and the Transformation of the West,* ed. S. K. Cohn Jr. (Cambridge, Mass., 1997), p. 9.
3. J. Froissart, *Chronicles,* ed. and trans. G. Brereton (Harmondsworth, England, 1968), p. 111.
4. Ibid. p. 212.
5. Ibid. p. 89.
6. Quoted in R. Coogan, *Babylon on the Rhône: A Translation of Letters by Dante, Petrarch, and Catherine of Siena* (Washington, D.C., 1983), p. 115.
7. Dante, *Divine Comedy,* trans. D. Sayers (New York, 1962), "Paradise," canto 33, line 145.
8. Christine de Pizan, *The Book of the City of Ladies,* trans. E. J. Richards (New York, 1982), pp. 83–84.
9. Quoted in S. Stuard, "Dominion of Gender: Women's Fortunes in the High Middle Ages," in R. Bridenthal, C. Koonz, and S. Stuard, eds., *Becoming Visible: Women in European History,* 2d ed. (Boston, 1987), p. 169.
10. Quoted in J. Gimpel, *The Medieval Machine* (New York, 1976), p. 168.

SUGGESTIONS FOR FURTHER READING

For a general introduction to the fourteenth century, see **D. P. Waley, Later Medieval Europe,** 2d ed. (London, 1985), and **G. Holmes, Europe: Hierarchy and Revolt, 1320–1450** (New York, 1975).

On the Black Death, see **P. Ziegler, The Black Death** (New York, 1969); **D. Herlihy, The Black Death and the Transformation of the West,** ed. **S. K. Cohn Jr.** (Cambridge, Mass., 1997); and the well-written popular history by **J. Kelly, The Great Mortality** (New York, 2005).

Good accounts of the Hundred Years' War include **A. Curry, The Hundred Years' War** (New York, 1993), and **R. H. Neillands, The Hundred Years' War** (New York, 1990). On Joan of Arc, see **M. Warner, Joan of Arc: The Image of Female Heroism** (New York, 1981). On the political history of the period, see **B. Guenée, States and Rulers in Later Medieval Europe,** trans. **J. Vale** (Oxford, 1985).

A good general study of the church in the fourteenth century can be found in **F. P. Oakley**, *The Western Church in the Later Middle Ages* (Ithaca, N.Y., 1980). See also **J. H. Lynch**, *The Medieval Church: A Brief History* (New York, 1992). On the Avignonese papacy, see **Y. Renouard**, *The Avignon Papacy, 1305–1403* (London, 1970). On late medieval religious practices, see **R. N. Swanson**, *Religion and Devotion in Europe, c. 1215–1515* (Cambridge, 1995).

A classic work on the life and thought of the Late Middle Ages is **J. Huizinga**, *The Autumn of the Middle Ages,* trans. **R. J. Payton and U. Mammitzsch** (Chicago, 1996). On the impact of the plague on culture, see the brilliant study by **M. Meiss**, *Painting in Florence and Siena After the Black Death* (New York, 1964). On Dante, see **J. Freccero**, *Dante and the Poetics of Conversion* (Cambridge, Mass., 1986). On Chaucer, see **G. Kane**, *Chaucer* (New York, 1984). The best work on Christine de Pizan is by **C. C. Willard**, *Christine de Pizan: Her Life and Works* (New York, 1984).

A wealth of material on everyday life is provided in the second volume of *A History of Private Life*, ed. **G. Duby**, *Revelations of the Medieval World* (Cambridge, Mass., 1988). On women in the Later Middle Ages, see **S. Shahar**, *The Fourth Estate: A History of Women in the Middle Ages,* trans. **C. Galai** (London, 1983), and **D. Herlihy**, *Women, Family, and Society: Historical Essays, 1978–1991* (Providence, R.I., 1995). Poor people are discussed in **M. Mollat**, *The Poor in the Middle Ages* (New Haven, Conn., 1986). The importance of inventions is discussed in **J. Gimpel**, *The Medieval Machine* (New York, 1976). Another valuable discussion of medieval technology can be found in **J. Le Goff**, *Time, Work, and Culture in the Middle Ages* (Chicago, 1980).

Thomson NOW! Enter *ThomsonNOW* using the access card that is available for *Western Civilization: A Brief History*. *ThomsonNOW* will help you understand this chapter with lesson plans generated for your needs. In addition, you can read the following documents, and many more, online:

Jean Froissart, *The Battle of Crécy, The Burghers of Calais, and The Battle of Poitiers*

WESTERN CIVILIZATION RESOURCES

Visit the Web site for *Western Civilization: A Brief History* for resources specific to this book:

http://www.thomsonedu.com/history/spielvogel

For a variety of tools to help you succeed in this course, visit the Western Civilization Resource Center at

http://history.wadsworth.com/spielvogel

Included are quizzes, images, documents, interactive simulations, maps and timelines, movie explorations, and a wealth of other sources.

12

RECOVERY AND REBIRTH: THE RENAISSANCE

Michelangelo's Creation of Adam *on the Sistine Chapel ceiling*

© Vatican Museums and Galleries, Vatican City, Vatican State/Bridgeman Art Library

*W*ERE THE FOURTEENTH and fifteenth centuries a continuation of the Middle Ages or the beginning of a new era? The answer is that both positions are true. Although the disintegrative patterns of the fourteenth century continued into the fifteenth, at the same time there were elements of recovery that made the fifteenth century a period of significant political, economic, artistic, and intellectual change. The humanists or intellectuals of the age considered their period (from the mid-fourteenth to the mid-sixteenth century) an age of rebirth, believing that they had restored arts and letters to new glory after they had been "neglected" or "dead" for centuries. The humanists also saw their age as one of accomplished individuals who dominated the landscape of their time. Michelangelo, the great Italian artist of the early sixteenth century, and Pope Julius II, the "warrior pope," were two such titans. The artist's temperament and the pope's temper led to many lengthy and often loud quarrels between the two. Among other commissions, the pope had hired Michelangelo to paint the ceiling of the Sistine Chapel in Rome, a daunting task for a man long accustomed to being a sculptor. Michelangelo undertook the project but refused for a long time to allow anyone, including the pope, to see his work. Julius grew anxious, pestering Michelangelo on a regular basis about when the ceiling would be finished. Exasperated by the pope's requests, Michelangelo once replied, according to Giorgio Vasari, his contemporary biographer, that the ceiling would be completed "when it satisfies me as an artist." The pope responded, "And we want you to satisfy us and finish it soon," and then threatened that if Michelangelo did not "finish the ceiling quickly [the pope] would have him thrown down from the scaffolding." Fearing the pope's anger, Michelangelo "lost no time in doing all that was wanted" and quickly completed the ceiling, one of the great masterpieces of Western art.

The humanists' view of their age as a rebirth of the classical civilization of the Greeks and Romans ultimately led historians to use the French word *Renaissance* to identify this age. Although recent historians have emphasized the many elements of continuity between the Middle Ages and the Renaissance, the latter age was also distinguished by its own unique characteristics.◆

Meaning and Characteristics of the Italian Renaissance

Renaissance means "rebirth." Many people who lived in Italy between 1350 and 1550 believed that they were witnessing a rebirth of antiquity or Greco-Roman civilization, marking a new age. To them, the thousand or so years between the end of the Roman Empire and their own era was a middle period (the "Middle Ages"), characterized by darkness because of its lack of classical culture. Historians of the nineteenth century later used similar terminology to describe this period in Italy. The Swiss historian and art critic Jacob Burckhardt created the modern concept of the **Renaissance** in his celebrated work *Civilization of the Renaissance in Italy*, published in 1860. He portrayed Italy in the fourteenth and fifteenth centuries as the birthplace of the modern world and saw the revival of antiquity, the "perfecting of the individual," and secularism ("worldliness of the Italians") as its distinguishing features. Burckhardt established the framework for all modern interpretations of the period. Although contemporary scholars do not believe that the Renaissance represents a sudden or dramatic cultural break with the Middle Ages (as Burckhardt argued)—there was, after all, much continuity between the two periods in economic, political, and social life—the Renaissance can still be viewed as a distinct period of European history that manifested itself first in Italy and then spread to the rest of Europe. What, then, are the characteristics of the Italian Renaissance?

Renaissance Italy was largely an urban society. The city-states, especially those of northern Italy, became the centers of Italian political, economic, and social life. In this new urban society, a secular spirit emerged as increasing wealth created new possibilities for the enjoyment of worldly things (see the box on p. 217).

Above all, the Renaissance was an age of recovery from the "calamitous fourteenth century." Italy and the rest of Europe began a slow process of recuperation from the effects of the Black Death, political disorder, and economic recession. Recovery was accompanied by a rediscovery of the culture of classical antiquity. Increasingly aware of their own historical past, Italian intellectuals became intensely interested in the Greco-Roman culture of the ancient Mediterranean world. This revival of classical antiquity (the Middle Ages had in fact preserved much of ancient Latin culture) affected politics and art and led to new attempts to reconcile the pagan philosophy of antiquity with Christian thought, as well as new ways of viewing human beings.

A revived emphasis on individual ability became characteristic of the Italian Renaissance. As the fifteenth-century Florentine architect Leon Battista Alberti expressed it, "Men can do all things if they will."[1] A high regard for human dignity and worth and a realization of individual potentiality created a new social ideal of the well-rounded personality or universal person (*l'uomo universale*) who was capable of achievements in many areas of life.

These general features of the Italian Renaissance were not characteristic of all Italians but were primarily the preserve of the wealthy upper classes, who constituted a small percentage of the total population. The achievements of the Italian Renaissance were thus the product of an elite, rather than a mass, movement. Nevertheless, indirectly it did have some impact on ordinary people, especially in the cities, where so many of the intellectual and artistic accomplishments of the period were most apparent.

The Making of Renaissance Society

After the severe economic reversals and social upheavals of the second half of the fourteenth century, the European economy gradually recovered during the fifteenth century as manufacturing and trade increased in volume.

Economic Recovery

By the fourteenth century, Italian merchants were carrying on a flourishing commerce throughout the Mediterranean and had also expanded their lines of trade north along the Atlantic seaboard. The great galleys of the Venetian Flanders Fleet maintained a direct sea route from Venice to England and the Netherlands, where Italian merchants came into contact with the increasingly powerful Hanseatic League of merchants. Hard hit by the plague, the Italians lost their commercial preeminence while the Hanseatic League continued to prosper.

Expansion of Trade   As early as the thirteenth century, a number of north German coastal towns had formed a commercial and military league known as the Hansa or Hanseatic League. By 1500, more than eighty cities belonged to the League, which established settlements and commercial bases in northern Europe and England. For

A RENAISSANCE BANQUET

As in Greek and Roman society, the Renaissance banquet was an occasion for good food, interesting conversation, music, and dancing. In Renaissance society, it was also a symbol of status and an opportunity to impress people with the power and wealth of one's family. Banquets were held to celebrate public and religious festivals, official visits, anniversaries, and weddings. The following menu lists the foods served at a grand banquet given by Pope Pius V in the sixteenth century.

A Sixteenth-Century Banquet

First Course: Cold Delicacies from the Sideboard

Pieces of marzipan and marzipan balls
Neapolitan spice cakes
Malaga wine and Pisan biscuits
Fresh grapes
Prosciutto cooked in wine, served with capers and grape pulp
Salted pork tongues cooked in wine, sliced
Spit-roasted songbirds, cold, with their tongues sliced over them
Sweet mustard

Second Course: Hot Foods from the Kitchen, Roasts

Fried veal sweetbreads and liver
Spit-roasted skylarks with lemon sauce
Spit-roasted quails with sliced eggplants
Stuffed spit-roasted pigeons with capers sprinkled over them
Spit-roasted rabbits, with sauce and crushed pine nuts
Partridges larded and spit-roasted, served with lemon
Heavily seasoned poultry with lemon slices
Slices of veal, spit-roasted with a sauce made from the juices
Leg of goat spit-roasted with a sauce made from the juices
Soup of almond paste, with the flesh of three pigeons to each serving

Third Course: Hot Foods from the Kitchen, Boiled Meats and Stews

Stuffed fat geese, boiled Lombard style and covered with sliced almonds
Stuffed breast of veal, boiled, garnished with flowers
Very young calf, boiled, garnished with parsley
Almonds in garlic sauce
Turkish-style rice with milk, sprinkled with cinnamon
Stewed pigeons with mortadella sausage and whole onions
Cabbage soup with sausages
Poultry pie, two chickens to each pie
Fricasseed breast of goat dressed with fried onions
Pies filled with custard cream
Boiled calves' feet with cheese and egg

Fourth Course: Delicacies from the Sideboard

Bean tarts
Quince pastries
Pear tarts, the pears wrapped in marzipan
Parmesan cheese and Riviera cheese
Fresh almonds on vine leaves
Chestnuts roasted over the coals and served with salt and pepper
Milk curds
Ring-shaped cakes
Wafers made from ground grain

What kinds of people would be present at a banquet where the foods listed on this menu would be served?

---

almost two hundred years, the Hansa had a monopoly on northern European trade in timber, fish, grain, metals, honey, and wines. Its southern outlet in Flanders, the city of Bruges, became the economic crossroads of Europe in the fourteenth century because it served as the meeting place between Hanseatic merchants and the Flanders Fleet of Venice. In the fifteenth century, however, the Hanseatic League proved increasingly unable to compete with the developing larger territorial states.

Overall, trade recovered dramatically from the economic contraction of the fourteenth century. The Italians and especially the Venetians continued to maintain a wealthy commercial empire. Not until the sixteenth century, when overseas discoveries gave new importance to the states facing the Atlantic, did the petty Italian city-states begin to suffer from the competitive advantages of the ever-growing and more powerful national territorial states.

Industries Old and New The economic depression of the fourteenth century also affected patterns of manufacturing. The woolen industries of Flanders and the northern Italian cities had been particularly devastated. By the beginning of the fifteenth century, however, the Florentine woolen industry began to recover. At the same time, the Italian cities began to develop and expand luxury industries, including lace and silk, glassware, and handworked items in metal and precious stones.

Other new industries, especially printing, mining, and metallurgy, began to rival the textile industry in importance in the fifteenth century. New machinery and techniques for digging deeper mines and for separating metals from ore and purifying them were developed, and **entrepreneurs** quickly developed large mining operations to produce copper, iron, and silver. Especially valuable were the rich mineral deposits in central Europe. Expanding iron production and new skills in metalworking in turn contributed to the development of firearms that were more effective than the crude weapons of the fourteenth century.

Banking and the Medici   The city of Florence regained its preeminence in banking in the fifteenth century, due primarily to the Medici family. In its best days (in the fifteenth century), the house of Medici was the greatest banking house in Europe, with branches in Venice, Milan, Rome, Avignon, Bruges, London, and Lyons. Moreover, the family had controlling interests in industrial enterprises for wool, silk, and the mining of alum, which was used to dye textiles. Despite its great success, the Medici bank suffered a sudden decline at the end of the fifteenth century due to poor leadership and a series of bad loans, especially to rulers. In 1494, when the French expelled the Medici from Florence and confiscated their property, the entire financial edifice collapsed.

Social Changes in the Renaissance

The Renaissance inherited its social structure from the Middle Ages. Society remained fundamentally divided into three **estates:** the First Estate, the clergy, whose preeminence was grounded in the belief that people should be guided to spiritual ends; the Second Estate, the nobility, whose privileges were based on the principle that the nobles provided security and justice for society; and the Third Estate, the peasants and inhabitants of the towns and cities. This social order experienced certain adaptations in the Renaissance, which we can see by examining the Second and Third Estates (the clergy will be examined in Chapter 13).

The Nobility   Throughout much of Europe, the landholding nobles faced declining real incomes during the greater part of the fourteenth and fifteenth centuries. But many members of the old nobility survived, and new blood infused its ranks. A reconstruction of the aristocracy was well under way by 1500. As a result of this reconstruction, the nobles, old and new, who constituted between 2 and 3 percent of the population in most countries, managed to dominate society as they had done in the Middle Ages, serving as military officers and holding important political posts as well as advising the king.

By 1500, the noble or aristocrat was expected to evince certain ideals. These ideals were best expressed in *The Book of the Courtier* by the Italian Baldassare Castiglione (1478–1529). Published in 1528, Castiglione's work soon became popular throughout Europe, and it remained a basic handbook for European aristocrats well into the twentieth century.

In his book, Castiglione described the three basic attributes of the perfect courtier. First, nobles should possess fundamental native endowments, such as impeccable character, grace, talents, and noble birth. The perfect courtier must also cultivate certain achievements. Primarily, he should participate in military and bodily exercises because the principal profession of a courtier was arms. But unlike the medieval knight, the Renaissance courtier was also expected to have a classical education and adorn his life with the arts by playing a musical instrument, drawing, and painting. In Castiglione's hands, the Renaissance ideal of the well-developed personality became a social ideal of the aristocracy. Finally, the aristocrat was expected to follow a certain standard of conduct. Nobles were to make a good impression; while being modest, they should not hide their accomplishments but show them with grace.

What was the purpose of these courtly standards? Castiglione said:

> I think that the aim of the perfect Courtier . . . is so to win for himself, by means of the accomplishments ascribed to him by these gentlemen, the favor and mind of the prince whom he serves that he may be able to tell him, and always will tell him, the truth about everything he needs to know, without fear or risk of displeasing him; and that when he sees the mind of his prince inclined to a wrong action, he may dare to oppose him . . . so as to dissuade him of every evil intent and bring him to the path of virtue.[2]

The aim of the perfect noble, then, was to serve his prince in an effective and honest way. Nobles would adhere to these principles for hundreds of years while they continued to dominate European life socially and politically.

Peasants and Townspeople   Peasants made up the overwhelming mass of the Third Estate, and except in the highly urbanized areas of northern Italy and Flanders, they continued to constitute as much as 85 to 90 percent of the total European population. The most noticeable trend produced by the economic crisis of the fourteenth century was the decline of the manorial system and the continuing elimination of serfdom. The contraction of the peasantry after the Black Death simply accelerated the process of converting servile labor dues into rents paid in money. By the end of the fifteenth century, primarily in western Europe, serfdom was declining, and more and more peasants were becoming legally free.

The remainder of the Third Estate centered around the inhabitants of towns and cities, originally the merchants and artisans who formed the bourgeoisie. The Renaissance town or city of the fifteenth century actually possessed a multitude of townspeople widely separated socially and economically.

At the top of urban society were the patricians, whose wealth from capitalistic enterprises in trade, industry, and banking enabled them to dominate their urban communities economically, socially, and politically. Below them were the petty burghers, the shopkeepers, artisans, guildmasters, and guildsmen who were largely concerned with providing goods and services for local consumption. Below these two groups were the propertyless workers earning pitiful wages and the unemployed, living squalid and miserable lives; these people constituted as much as 30 to 40 percent of the urban population. Everywhere in Europe in the late fourteenth and fifteenth centuries, urban poverty had increased dramatically. One rich merchant of Florence wrote:

MARRIAGE NEGOTIATIONS

Marriages were so important in maintaining families in Renaissance Italy that much energy was put into arranging them. Parents made the choices for their children, most often for considerations that had little to do with the modern notion of love. This selection is taken from the letters of a Florentine matron of the illustrious Strozzi family to her son Filippo in Naples. The family's considerations were complicated by the fact that the son was in exile.

Alessandra Strozzi to Her Son Filippo in Naples

[April 20, 1464]...Concerning the matter of a wife [for Filippo], it appears to me that if Francesco di Messer Tanagli wishes to give his daughter, that it would be a fine marriage....Now I will speak with Marco [Parenti, Alessandra's son-in-law], to see if there are other prospects that would be better, and if there are none, then we will learn if he wishes to give her [in marriage]....Francesco Tanagli has a good reputation, and he has held office, not the highest, but still he has been in office. You may ask: "Why should he give her to someone in exile?" There are three reasons. First, there aren't many young men of good family who have both virtue and property. Secondly, she has only a small dowry, 1,000 florins, which is the dowry of an artisan [although not a small sum, either—senior officials in the government bureaucracy earned 300 florins a year]....Third, I believe that he will give her away, because he has a large family and he will need help to settle them....

[July 26, 1465]...Francesco is a good friend of Marco and he trusts him. On [Saint] Jacopo's day, he spoke to him discreetly and persuasively, saying that for several months he had heard that we were interested in the girl and...that when we had made up our minds, she will come to us willingly. [He said that] you were a worthy man, and that his family had always made good marriages, but that he had only a small dowry to give her, and so he would prefer to send her outside of Florence to someone of worth, rather than to give her to someone here, from among those who were available, with little money....We have information that she is affable and competent. She is responsible for a large family (there are twelve children, six boys and six girls), and the mother is always pregnant and isn't very competent....

[August 31, 1465]...I have recently received some very favorable information [about the Tanagli girl] from two individuals....They are in agreement that whoever gets her will be content....Concerning her beauty, they told me what I had already seen, that she is attractive and well-proportioned. Her face is long, but I couldn't look directly into her face, since she appeared to be aware that I was examining her...and so she turned away from me like the wind....She reads quite well...and she can dance and sing....

So yesterday I sent for Marco and told him what I had learned. And we talked about the matter for a while, and decided that he should say something to the father and give him a little hope, but not so much that we couldn't withdraw, and find out from him the amount of the dowry....May God help us to choose what will contribute to our tranquility and to the consolation of us all.

[September 13, 1465]...Marco came to me and said that he had met with Francesco Tanagli, who had spoken very coldly, so that I understand that he had changed his mind....

[Filippo Strozzi eventually married Fiametta di Donato Adimari in 1466.]

What were the most important considerations in marriage negotiations? Why were they so important?

Those that are lazy and indolent in a way that does harm to the city, and who can offer no just reason for their condition, should either be forced to work or expelled from the Commune. The city would thus rid itself of that most harmful part of the poorest class....If the lowest order of society earn enough food to keep them going from day to day, then they have enough.[3]

But even this large group was not at the bottom of the social scale; beneath it stood a significantly large group of slaves, especially in the cities of Italy.

Family and Marriage in Renaissance Italy

The family bond was a source of great security in the urban world of Renaissance Italy. To maintain the family, careful attention was given to marriages that were arranged by parents, often to strengthen business or family ties. Details were worked out well in advance, sometimes when children were only five or six, and reinforced by a legally binding marriage contract (see the box above). The important aspect of the contract was the size of the dowry, a sum of money presented by the wife's family upon marriage. The dowry could involve large sums of money and was expected of all families.

The father-husband was the center of the Italian family. He gave it his name, was responsible for it in all legal matters, managed all finances (his wife had no share in his wealth), and made the crucial decisions in his children's lives. A father's authority over his children was absolute until he died or formally freed his children. The age of emancipation varied from early teens to late twenties.

The wife managed the household, a position that gave women a certain degree of autonomy in their daily lives. Most wives, however, also knew that their primary function was to bear children. Upper-class wives were frequently pregnant; Alessandra Strozzi of Florence, for example, who had been married at the age of sixteen, bore eight children in ten years.

Wedding Banquet. Parents arranged marriages in Renaissance Italy to strengthen business or family ties. A legally binding marriage contract was considered a necessary part of the marital arrangements. So was a wedding feast. This painting by Botticelli shows the wedding banquet in Florence that celebrated the marriage of Nastagio degli Onesti and the daughter of Paulo Traversaro.

For women in the Renaissance, childbirth was a fearful occasion. Not only was it painful, but it could be deadly; possibly as many as 10 percent of mothers died in childbirth. In his memoirs, the Florentine merchant Gregorio Dati recalled that three of his four wives died in childbirth. His third wife, after delivering eleven children in fifteen years, "died in childbirth after lengthy suffering, which she bore with remarkable strength and patience."[4] Nor did the tragedies end with childbirth. Surviving mothers often faced the death of their children. In Florence in the fifteenth century, for example, almost half of the children born to merchant families died before the age of twenty. Given these mortality rates, many upper-class families sought to have as many children as possible in order to ensure a surviving male heir to the family fortune. This concern is evident in the Florentine humanist Leon Battista Alberti's treatise *On the Family*, when one of the characters remarks, "How many families do we see today in decadence and ruin! . . . Of all these families not only the magnificence and greatness but the very men, not only the men but the very names are shrunk away and gone. Their memory . . . is wiped out and obliterated."[5]

The Italian States in the Renaissance

By the fifteenth century, five major powers dominated the Italian peninsula: the duchy of Milan, Venice, Florence, the Papal States, and the kingdom of Naples (see Map 12.1). Northern Italy was divided between Milan and Venice. After the death of the last Visconti ruler of Milan in 1447, Francesco Sforza, one of the leading *condottieri* (a *condottiere* was the leader of a mercenary band) of the time, turned on his Milanese employers, conquered the city, and became its new duke. Both the Visconti and Sforza rulers worked to create a highly centralized territorial

state. They were especially successful in devising systems of taxation that generated enormous revenues for the government. The maritime republic of Venice remained an extremely stable political entity governed by a small oligarchy of merchant-aristocrats. Its commercial empire brought in enormous revenues and gave it the status of an international power.

The republic of Florence dominated the region of Tuscany. In 1434, Cosimo de'Medici (1434–1464) took control of the ruling oligarchy. Although the wealthy Medici family maintained republican forms of government for appearance's sake, it ran the government from behind the scenes. Through lavish patronage and careful courting of political allies, Cosimo and later his grandson Lorenzo the Magnificent (1469–1492) were successful in dominating the city at a time when Florence was the center of the cultural Renaissance.

The Papal States lay in central Italy. Nominally under the control of the popes, papal residence in Avignon and the Great Schism had enabled individual cities and territories, such as Urbino and Ferrara, to become independent of papal authority. The popes of the fifteenth century directed much of their energy toward reestablishing their control over the Papal States. The kingdom of Naples, which encompassed most of southern Italy and usually the island of Sicily, remained a backward monarchy that shared little in the cultural glories of the Renaissance.

A number of independent city-states under the control of powerful ruling families also became brilliant centers of Renaissance culture in the fifteenth century. Perhaps most famous was Urbino, ruled by the Montefeltro dynasty. Federigo da Montefeltro, who ruled Urbino from 1444 to 1482, received a classical education. He had also learned the skills of fighting, since the Montefeltro family compensated for the poverty of Urbino by hiring themselves out as *condottieri*. Federigo was not only a good ruler but also a rather unusual *condottiere* by fifteenth-century standards.

Although not a brilliant general, he was reliable and honest. At the same time, Duke Federigo was one of the greatest patrons of Renaissance culture. Under his direction, Urbino became a well-known cultural and intellectual center.

A noticeable feature of these smaller Italian courts was the important role played by women. The most famous of the Italian ruling women was Isabella d'Este (1474–1539), daughter of the duke of Ferrara, who married Francesco Gonzaga, marquis of Mantua. Their court was another important center of art and learning in the Renaissance. Educated at the brilliant court of Ferrara, Isabella was known for her intelligence and political wisdom. Called the "first lady of the world," she attracted artists and intellectuals to the Mantuan court and was responsible for amassing one of the finest libraries in all of Italy. Her numerous letters to friends, family, princes, and artists all over Europe disclose her political acumen as well as a good sense of humor. Both before and after the death of her husband Francesco, she effectively ruled Mantua.

The growth of powerful monarchical states led to trouble for the Italians and brought an end to the independence of the Italian states. Attracted by the riches of Italy, the French king Charles VIII (1483–1498) led an army of thirty thousand men into Italy in 1494 and occupied the kingdom of Naples. Other Italian states turned for help to the Spanish, who gladly complied. For the next thirty years, the French and Spanish competed to dominate Italy, which was merely a pawn for the two great powers, a convenient arena for fighting battles. The terrible sack of Rome in 1527 by the armies of the Spanish king Charles I brought a temporary end to the Italian wars. From then on, the Spaniards dominated Italy; the Renaissance in Italy was at an end.

Machiavelli and the New Statecraft

No one gave better expression to the Renaissance preoccupation with political power than Niccolò Machiavelli (1469–1527). Although he ably served as a diplomat for Florence, he was eventually forced into exile. Embittered by this and compelled by the great love of his life—politics—he wrote *The Prince*, one of the most influential works on political power in the Western world.

Machiavelli's major concerns in *The Prince* were the acquisition, maintenance, and expansion of political power as the means to restore and maintain order in his time. In the Middle Ages, many political theorists stressed the ethical side of a prince's activity—how a ruler ought to behave based on Christian moral principles. Machiavelli bluntly contradicted this approach:

My hope is to write a book that will be useful, at least to those who read it intelligently, and so I thought it sensible to go straight to a discussion of how things are in real life and not waste time with a discussion of an imaginary world . . . for the gap between how people actually behave and how they ought to behave is so great that anyone who ignores everyday reality in order to live up to an ideal will soon discover he had been taught how to destroy himself, not how to preserve himself.[6]

Duchy of Milan	
Viscontis	1311–1447
Sforzas	1450–1494
Florence	
Cosimo de'Medici	1434–1464
Lorenzo de'Medici	1469–1492
Beginning of Italian wars—French invasion of Italy	1494
Sack of Rome	1527

Machiavelli considered his approach far more realistic than that of his medieval forebears.

From Machiavelli's point of view, a prince's attitude toward power must be based on an understanding of human nature, which he perceived as basically self-centered. He said, "Of men one can, in general, say this: They are ungrateful, fickle, deceptive and deceiving, avoiders of danger, eager to gain." Political activity, therefore, could not be restricted by moral considerations. The prince acts on behalf of the state and for the sake of the state must be willing to let his conscience sleep. As Machiavelli put it:

Niccolò Machiavelli. In *The Prince*, Machiavelli gave concrete expression to the Renaissance preoccupation with political power. This slender volume remains one of the most famous Western treatises on politics. Machiavelli is seen here in a portrait by Santi di Tito.

You need to understand this: A ruler, and particularly a ruler who is new to power, cannot conform to all those rules that men who are thought good are expected to respect, for he is often obliged, in order to hold on to power, to break his word, to be uncharitable, inhumane, and irreligious. So he must be mentally prepared to act as circumstances and changes in fortune require. As I have said, he should do what is right if he can; but he must be prepared to do wrong if necessary.[7]

In Cesare Borgia, the son of Pope Alexander VI (popes were supposed to be celibate), who used ruthless measures to achieve his goal of carving out a new state in central Italy, Machiavelli found a good example of the new Italian ruler. As he said, "So anyone who decides that the policy to follow when one has newly acquired power is to destroy one's enemies, to secure some allies, to win wars, whether by force or by fraud, to make oneself both loved and feared by one's subjects,... cannot hope to find, in the recent past, a better model to imitate than Cesare Borgia."[8] Machiavelli was among the first to abandon morality as the basis for the analysis of political activity (see the box on p. 223).

The Intellectual Renaissance in Italy

Individualism and **secularism**—two characteristics of the Italian Renaissance—were most noticeable in the intellectual and artistic realms. Italian culture had matured by the fourteenth century. For the next two centuries, Italy was the cultural leader of Europe. This new Italian culture was primarily the product of a relatively wealthy, urban lay society. The most important literary movement associated with the Renaissance is **humanism.**

Italian Renaissance Humanism

Renaissance humanism was an intellectual movement based on the study of the classical literary works of Greece and Rome. Humanists studied the liberal arts—grammar, rhetoric, poetry, moral philosophy or ethics, and history—all based on the writings of ancient Greek and Roman authors. These are the subjects we call the humanities.

Petrarch (1304–1374), often called the father of Italian Renaissance humanism, did more than any other individual in the fourteenth century to foster development of the movement. Petrarch sought to find forgotten Latin manuscripts and set in motion a search of monastic libraries throughout Europe. In his preoccupation with the classics and their secular content, Petrarch doubted at times whether he was sufficiently attentive to spiritual ideals. His qualms, however, did not prevent him from inaugurating the humanist emphasis on the use of pure classical Latin, making it fashionable for humanists to use Cicero as a model for prose and Virgil for poetry. Petrarch said, "Christ is my God; Cicero is the prince of the language."

MACHIAVELLI: "IS IT BETTER TO BE LOVED THAN FEARED?"

In 1513, Niccolò Machiavelli wrote a short treatise on political power that, justly or unjustly, has given him a reputation as a political opportunist. In this passage from Chapter 17 of *The Prince*, Machiavelli analyzes whether it is better for a ruler to be loved than feared.

Machiavelli, *The Prince*

This leads us to a question that is in dispute: Is it better to be loved than feared, or vice versa? My reply is one ought to be both loved and feared; but, since it is difficult to accomplish both at the same time, I maintain it is much safer to be feared than loved, if you have to do without one of the two. For of men one can, in general, say this: They are ungrateful, fickle, deceptive and deceiving, avoiders of danger, eager to gain. As long as you serve their interests, they are devoted to you. They promise you their blood, their possessions, their lives, and their children, as I said before, so long as you seem to have no need of them. But as soon as you need help, they turn against you. Any ruler who relies simply on their promises and makes no other preparations, will be destroyed. For you will find that those whose support you buy, who do not rally to you because they admire your strength of character and nobility of soul, these are people you pay for, but they are never yours, and in the end you cannot get the benefit of your investment. Men are less nervous of offending someone who makes himself lovable, than someone who makes himself frightening. For love attaches men by ties of obligation, which, since men are wicked, they break whenever their interests are at stake. But fear restrains men because they are afraid of punishment, and this fear never leaves them. Still, a ruler should make himself feared in such a way that, if he does not inspire love, at least he does not provoke hatred. For it is perfectly possible to be feared and not hated. You will only be hated if you seize the property or the women of your subjects and citizens. Whenever you have to kill someone, make sure that you have a suitable excuse and an obvious reason; but, above all else, keep your hands off other people's property; for men are quicker to forget the death of their father than the loss of their inheritance. Moreover, there are always reasons why you might want to seize people's property; and he who begins to live by plundering others will always find an excuse for seizing other people's possessions; but there are fewer reasons for killing people, and one killing need not lead to another.

When a ruler is at the head of his army and has a vast number of soldiers under his command, then it is absolutely essential to be prepared to be thought cruel; for it is impossible to keep an army united and ready for action without acquiring a reputation for cruelty.

Why does Machiavelli think it is better for a ruler to be loved than feared? How do his theories make his politics modern, and how do they differ from medieval and Roman notions of good rulership?

In Florence, the humanist movement took a new direction at the beginning of the fifteenth century when it became closely tied to Florentine civic spirit and pride, giving rise to what has been labeled **civic humanism**. Fourteenth-century humanists such as Petrarch had described the intellectual life as one of solitude. They rejected family and a life of action in the community. In the busy civic world of Florence, however, intellectuals began to take a new view of their role as intellectuals. The classical Roman statesman and intellectual Cicero became their model. Leonardo Bruni (1370–1444), a humanist, Florentine patriot, and chancellor of the city, wrote a biography of Cicero titled the *New Cicero*, in which he waxed enthusiastic about the fusion of political action and literary creation in Cicero's life. From Bruni's time on, Cicero served as the inspiration for the Renaissance ideal that it was the duty of an intellectual to live an active life for one's state. An individual only "grows to maturity—both intellectually and morally—through participation" in the life of the state. Civic humanism reflected the values of the urban society of the Italian Renaissance. Humanists came to believe that their study of the humanities should be put to the service of the state. It is no accident that humanists served the state as chancellors, councilors, and advisers.

Also evident in the humanism of the first half of the fifteenth century was a growing interest in classical Greek civilization. Bruni was one of the first Italian humanists to gain a thorough knowledge of Greek. He became an enthusiastic pupil of the Byzantine scholar Manuel Chrysoloras, who taught in Florence from 1396 to 1400. Humanists eagerly perused the works of Plato as well as Greek poets, dramatists, historians, and orators, such as Thucydides, Euripides, and Sophocles, all of whom had been neglected by the scholastics of the High Middle Ages.

Humanism and Philosophy In the second half of the fifteenth century, a dramatic upsurge of interest in the works of Plato occurred. Cosimo de'Medici, the de facto ruler of Florence, encouraged this development by commissioning a translation of Plato's dialogues by Marsilio Ficino (1433–1499), who dedicated his life to the translation of Plato and the exposition of the Platonic philosophy known as **Neoplatonism.**

In two major works, Ficino undertook the synthesis of Christianity and Platonism into a single system. His Neoplatonism was based on two primary ideas, the Neoplatonic hierarchy of substances and a theory of spiritual love. The former postulated a hierarchy of substances, or great chain of being, from the lowest form of physical matter (plants) to the purest spirit (God), in which humans occupied a central or middle position. They were the link between the material world (through the body) and the spiritual world (through the soul), and their highest duty was to ascend toward that union with God that was the true end of human existence. Ficino's theory of spiritual or Platonic love maintained that just as all people are bound together in their common humanity by love, so too are all parts of the universe held together by bonds of sympathetic love.

Renaissance Hermeticism **Hermeticism** was another product of the Florentine intellectual environment of the late fifteenth century. At the request of Cosimo de' Medici, Ficino translated into Latin a Greek work titled *Corpus Hermeticum*. The Hermetic manuscripts offered Renaissance intellectuals a new view of humankind. They believed that humans had been created as divine beings endowed with divine creative power but had freely chosen to enter the material world (nature). Humans could recover their divinity, however, through a regenerative experience or purification of the soul. Thus regenerated, they became true sages or magi, as the Renaissance called them, who had knowledge of God and of truth. In regaining their original divinity, they reacquired an intimate knowledge of nature and the ability to employ the powers of nature for beneficial purposes.

In Italy, the most prominent magi in the late fifteenth century were Ficino and his friend and pupil Giovanni Pico della Mirandola (1463–1494). Pico produced one of the most famous treatises of the Renaissance, *Oration on the Dignity of Man*. Pico combed diligently through the writings of many philosophers of different backgrounds for the common "nuggets of universal truth" that he believed were all part of God's revelation to humanity. In the *Oration*, Pico offered a ringing statement of unlimited human potential: "To him it is granted to have whatever he chooses, to be whatever he wills."[9] Like Ficino, Pico took an avid interest in Hermetic philosophy, accepting it as the "science of the Divine," which "embraces the deepest contemplation of the most secret things, and at last the knowledge of all nature."[10]

Education in the Renaissance

The humanist movement had a profound effect on education. Renaissance humanists believed that human beings could be dramatically changed by education, and as a result, they wrote treatises on education and opened schools based on their ideas. At the core of humanist schools were the "liberal studies." Humanists believed that the "liberal studies" (what we call the liberal arts) were the key to true freedom, enabling individuals to reach their full potential. The liberal studies included history, moral philosophy, eloquence (rhetoric), letters (grammar and logic), poetry, mathematics, astronomy, and music. The purpose of a liberal education was thus to produce individuals who followed a path of virtue and wisdom and possessed the rhetorical skills by which they could persuade others to do the same. Following the Greek precept of a sound mind in a sound body, humanist educators also stressed physical education. Pupils were taught the skills of javelin throwing, archery, and dancing and encouraged to run, wrestle, hunt, and swim.

The purpose of these humanist schools was to educate an elite, the ruling classes of their communities. Largely absent from such schools were females. The few female students who did attend humanist schools studied the classics and were encouraged to know some history and to ride, dance, sing, play the lute, and appreciate poetry. But they were told not to learn mathematics and rhetoric. Religion and morals were thought to hold first place in the education of Christian ladies and help prepare them for their roles as mothers and wives.

Nevertheless, some women in Italy who were educated in the humanist fashion went on to establish their own literary careers. Isotta Nogarola, born to a noble family in Verona, mastered Latin and wrote numerous letters and treatises that brought her praise from male Italian intellectuals. Laura Cereta was educated in Latin by her father, a physician from Brescia. Laura defended the ability of women to pursue scholarly pursuits (see the box on p. 225).

Humanist education was thought to be a practical preparation for life. Its aim was the creation not of a great scholar but of a complete citizen. As one humanist said, "Not everyone is obliged to excel in philosophy, medicine, or the law, nor are all equally favored by nature; but all are destined to live in society and to practice virtue."[11] Humanist schools provided the model for the basic education of the European ruling classes until the twentieth century.

The Impact of Printing

The Renaissance period witnessed the development of printing, one of the most important technological innovations of Western civilization. The art of printing had an immediate impact on European intellectual life and thought. Printing from hand-carved wooden blocks had been done in the West since the twelfth century and in China even before that. What was new to Europe in the fifteenth century was repeatable printing with movable metal type. The development of printing from movable type was a gradual process that culminated between 1445 and 1450; Johannes Gutenberg of Mainz played an important role in bringing the process to completion. Gutenberg's Bible, completed in 1455 or 1456, was the first true book in the West produced with movable type.

The new printing capability spread rapidly throughout Europe in the second half of the fifteenth century. By 1500, there were more than a thousand printers in Europe who had published almost forty thousand titles (between eight and ten million copies). Probably 50 percent of these books were religious—Bibles, books of devotion, and sermons. Next in importance were the Latin and Greek classics,

A WOMAN'S DEFENSE OF LEARNING

As a young woman, Laura Cereta was proud of her learning but condemned by a male world that found it unseemly for women to be scholars. One monk said to her father, "She gives herself to things unworthy of her—namely, the classics." Before being silenced, Laura Cereta wrote a series of letters, including one to a male critic who had argued that her work was so good it could not have been written by a woman.

Laura Cereta, *Defense of the Liberal Instruction of Women*

My ears are wearied by your carping. You brashly and publicly not merely wonder but indeed lament that I am said to possess as fine a mind as nature ever bestowed upon the most learned man. You seem to think that so learned a woman has scarcely before been seen in the world. You are wrong on both counts....

I would have been silent....But I cannot tolerate your having attacked my entire sex. For this reason my thirsty soul seeks revenge, my sleeping pen is aroused to literary struggle, raging anger stirs mental passions long chained by silence. With just cause I am moved to demonstrate how great a reputation for learning and virtue women have won by their inborn excellence, manifested in every age as knowledge....

Only the question of the rarity of outstanding women remains to be addressed. The explanation is clear: women have been able by nature to be exceptional, but have chosen lesser goals. For some women are concerned with parting their hair correctly, adorning themselves with lovely dresses, or decorating their fingers with pearls and other gems. Others delight in mouthing carefully composed phrases, indulging in dancing, or managing spoiled puppies. Still others wish to gaze at lavish banquet tables, to rest in sleep, or, standing at mirrors, to smear their lovely faces. But those in whom a deeper integrity yearns for virtue, restrain from the start their youthful souls, reflect on higher things, harden the body with sobriety and trials, and curb their tongues, open their ears, compose their thoughts in wakeful hours, their minds in contemplation, to letters bonded to righteousness. For knowledge is not given as a gift, but [is gained] with diligence. The free mind, not shirking effort, always soars zealously toward the good, and the desire to know grows ever more wide and deep. It is because of no special holiness, therefore, that we [women] are rewarded by God the Giver with the gift of exceptional talent. Nature has generously lavished its gifts upon all people, opening to all the doors of choice through which reason sends envoys to the will, from which they learn and convey its desires. The will must choose to exercise the gift of reason....

I have been praised too much; showing your contempt for women, you pretend that I alone am admirable because of the good fortune of my intellect....Do you suppose, O most contemptible man on earth, that I think myself sprung [like Athena] from the head of Jove? I am a school girl, possessed of the sleeping embers of an ordinary mind. Indeed I am too hurt, and my mind, offended, too swayed by passions, sighs, tormenting itself, conscious of the obligation to defend my sex. For absolutely everything—that which is within us and that which is without—is made weak by association with my sex.

What was Laura Cereta's attitude toward the man who had criticized her for her intellect? Why were Renaissance women not taken seriously in their desire for educational opportunities?

---

medieval grammars, legal handbooks, works on philosophy, and an ever-growing number of popular romances.

Printing became one of the largest industries in Europe, and its effects were soon felt in many areas of European life. The printing of books encouraged the development of scholarly research and the desire to attain knowledge. Moreover, printing facilitated cooperation among scholars and helped produce standardized and definitive texts. Printing also stimulated the development of an ever-expanding lay reading public, a development that had an enormous impact on European society. Indeed, the new religious ideas of the Reformation would never have spread as rapidly as they did in the sixteenth century without the printing press.

The Artistic Renaissance

Leonardo da Vinci, one of the great Italian Renaissance artists, once explained, "The painter will produce pictures of small merit if he takes for his standard the pictures of others, but if he will study from natural objects he will bear good fruit.... Those who take for their standard any one but nature...weary themselves in vain."[12] Renaissance artists considered the imitation of nature their primary goal. Their search for naturalism became an end in itself: to persuade onlookers of the reality of the object or event they were portraying. At the same time, the new artistic standards reflected a new attitude of mind as well, one in which human beings became the focus of attention, the "center and measure of all things," as one artist proclaimed.

Early Renaissance Art

The frescoes by Masaccio (1401–1428) in the Brancacci chapel in Florence have long been regarded as the first masterpieces of Early Renaissance art. In his use of monumental figures, the demonstration of a more realistic relationship

Masaccio, *Tribute Money*. With the frescoes of Masaccio, regarded by many as the first great works of Early Renaissance art, a new realistic style of painting was born. *Tribute Money* was one of a series of frescoes that Masaccio painted in the Brancacci Chapel of the Church of Santa Maria del Carmine in Florence. In *Tribute Money*, Masaccio illustrated the biblical story of Jesus' confrontation by a tax collector at the entrance to the town of Capernaum (seen at center). Jesus sent Peter to collect a coin from the mouth of a fish from Lake Galilee (seen at left); Peter then paid the tax collector (seen at right). In illustrating this story from the Bible, Masaccio used a rational system of perspective to create a realistic relationship between the figures and their background; the figures themselves are realistic. As one Renaissance observer said, "The works made before Masaccio's day can be said to be painted, while his are living, real, and natural."

between figures and landscape, and the visual representation of the laws of perspective, a new realistic style of painting was born. Onlookers became aware of a world of reality that appeared to be a continuation of their own world.

This new or Renaissance style was absorbed and modified by other Florentine painters in the fifteenth century. Especially important was the development of an experimental trend that took two directions. One emphasized the mathematical side of painting, the working out of the laws of perspective and the organization of outdoor space and light by geometry and perspective. The other aspect of the experimental trend involved the investigation of movement and anatomical structure. Indeed, the realistic portrayal of the human nude became one of the foremost preoccupations of Italian Renaissance art. The fifteenth century, then, was a period of experimentation and technical mastery.

The revolutionary achievements of Florentine painters in the fifteenth century were matched by equally stunning advances in sculpture and architecture. Donato di Donatello (1386–1466) spent time in Rome, studying and copying the statues of antiquity. His subsequent work in Florence reveals how well he had mastered the essence of what he saw. Among his numerous works was a statue of David that was the first known life-size freestanding bronze nude in European art since antiquity. Like Donatello's other statues, *David* radiated a simplicity and strength that reflected the dignity of humanity.

Filippo Brunelleschi (1377–1446) was a friend of Donatello's who accompanied him to Rome. Brunelleschi drew much inspiration from the architectural monuments of Roman antiquity, and when he returned to Florence, the Medici commissioned him to design the church of San Lorenzo. Inspired by Roman models, Brunelleschi created a church interior very different from that of the great medieval cathedrals. San Lorenzo's Classical columns, rounded arches, and coffered ceiling created an environment that did not overwhelm the worshiper, materially or psychologically, as Gothic cathedrals did; instead, it comforted in that it was a space created to fit human, not divine, measurements.

The Artistic High Renaissance

By the end of the fifteenth century, Italian painters, sculptors, and architects had created a new artistic environment. Many artists had mastered the new techniques for a scientific observation of the world around them and were now ready to move into individualistic forms of creative expression. This final stage of Renaissance art, which flourished between 1480 and 1520, is called the High Renaissance. The High Renaissance was marked by the increasing importance of Rome as a new cultural center.

The High Renaissance was dominated by the work of three artistic giants: Leonardo da Vinci (1452–1519), Raphael (1483–1520), and Michelangelo (1475–1564).

Filippo Brunelleschi, Interior of San Lorenzo. Cosimo de' Medici contributed massive amounts of money to the rebuilding of the Church of San Lorenzo. As seen in this view of the nave and choir of the church, Brunelleschi's architectural designs were based on the basilica plan borrowed by early Christians from pagan Rome. San Lorenzo's simplicity, evident in its rows of slender Corinthian columns, created a human-centered space.

Donatello, *David*. Donatello's *David* first stood in the courtyard of the Medici Palace. On its base was an inscription praising Florentine heroism and virtue, leading art historians to assume that the statue was meant to commemorate the victory of Florence over Milan in 1428. David's pose and appearance are reminiscent of the nude statues of antiquity.

Leonardo represents a transitional figure in the shift to High Renaissance principles. He stressed the need to advance beyond such realism and initiated the High Renaissance's preoccupation with the idealization of nature, or the attempt to generalize from realistic portrayal to an ideal form. Leonardo's *Last Supper,* painted in Milan, is a brilliant summary of fifteenth-century trends in its organization of space and use of perspective to depict subjects three dimensionally. But it is also more. The figure of Philip is idealized, and there are profound psychological dimensions to the work. Jesus' words—"One of you shall betray me"—are experienced directly as each of the apostles reveals his personality and his relationship to the Savior. Through gestures and movement, Leonardo hoped to reveal a person's inner life.

Raphael blossomed as a painter at an early age; at twenty-five, he was already regarded as one of Italy's best painters. Raphael was acclaimed for his numerous madonnas (portraits of the Virgin Mary), in which he attempted to achieve an ideal of beauty far surpassing human standards. He is well known for his frescoes in the Vatican Palace; his *School of Athens* reveals a world of balance, harmony, and order—the underlying principles of the art of classical Greece and Rome.

Michelangelo, an accomplished painter, sculptor, and architect, was another giant of the High Renaissance. Fiercely driven by his desire to create, he worked with great passion and energy on a remarkable number of projects. Michelangelo was influenced by Neoplatonism, especially evident in his figures on the ceiling of the Sistine Chapel in Rome. In 1508, Pope Julius II had called Michelangelo to Rome and commissioned him to decorate the chapel ceiling. This colossal project was not completed until 1512. Michelangelo attempted to tell the story of the Fall of Man by depicting nine scenes from the biblical book of Genesis. In his *Creation of Adam* (reproduced at the start of this chapter), the well-proportioned figure of Adam awaits the divine spark. Adam, like the other muscular figures on the ceiling, reveals an ideal type of human being with perfect proportions. In good Neoplatonic fashion, the beauty of these figures is meant to be a reflection of divine beauty; the more beautiful the body, the more God-like the figure.

Leonardo da Vinci, *The Last Supper.*   Leonardo da Vinci was the impetus behind the High Renaissance concern for the idealization of nature, moving from a realistic portrayal of the human figure to an idealized form. Evident in Leonardo's *Last Supper* is his effort to depict a person's character and inner nature by the use of gesture and movement. Unfortunately, Leonardo used an experimental technique in this fresco, which soon led to its physical deterioration.

Raphael, *School of Athens.*   Raphael arrived in Rome in 1508 and began to paint a series of frescoes commissioned by Pope Julius II for the papal apartments at the Vatican. In *School of Athens*, painted in 1510 or 1511, Raphael created an imaginary gathering of ancient philosophers. In the center stand Plato and Aristotle. At the left is Pythagoras, showing his system of proportions on a slate. At the right is Ptolemy, holding a celestial globe.

Michelangelo, *David*. This statue of David exalts the beauty of the human body and is a fitting symbol of the Italian Renaissance's affirmation of human power. Completed in 1504, *David* was moved by Florentine authorities to a special location in front of the Palazzo Vecchio, the seat of the Florentine government.

Jan van Eyck, *Giovanni Arnolfini and His Bride*. Northern painters took great care in depicting each object and became masters at rendering details. This emphasis on a realistic portrayal is clearly evident in this oil painting, said to be a portrait of Giovanni Arnolfini, an Italian merchant who had settled in Bruges, and his wife, Giovanna Cenami.

Another manifestation of Michelangelo's search for ideal beauty was his *David*, a colossal marble statue commissioned by the Florentine government in 1501 and completed in 1504. Michelangelo maintained that the form of a statue already resided in the uncarved piece of stone: "I only take away the surplus; the statue is already there."[13] Out of a piece of marble that had remained unused for fifty years, Michelangelo created a 14-foot-high figure, the largest sculpture in Italy since Roman times. An awe-inspiring hero, Michelangelo's *David* proudly proclaims the beauty of the human body and the glory of human beings.

The Northern Artistic Renaissance

In trying to provide an exact portrayal of their world, the artists of the north (especially the Low Countries) and Italy took different approaches. In Italy, the human form became the primary vehicle of expression as Italian artists sought to master the technical skills that allowed them to portray humans in realistic settings. The large wall spaces of Italian churches had given rise to the art of fresco painting, but in the north, the prevalence of Gothic cathedrals with their stained-glass windows resulted in more emphasis on illuminated manuscripts and wooden panel painting for altarpieces. The space available in these works was limited, and great care was required to depict each object, leading northern painters to become masters at rendering details.

The most influential northern school of art in the fifteenth century was centered in Flanders. Jan van Eyck (c. 1380–1441) was among the first to use oil paint, a medium that enabled the artist to use a varied range of colors and make changes to create fine details. In the famous *Giovanni Arnolfini and His Bride*, van Eyck's attention to detail is staggering in the precise portraits, a glittering chandelier, and a mirror reflecting the objects in the room. Although each detail was rendered as observed, it is evident that van Eyck's comprehension of perspective was still uncertain. His work is truly indicative of northern Renaissance painters, who, in their effort to imitate nature, did so not by mastery of the laws of perspective and proportion but by empirical observation of visual reality and the accurate portrayal of details. Moreover, northern painters placed great emphasis on the emotional intensity of religious feeling and created great works of devotional art, especially in their altarpieces. By the end of the fifteenth century, however, artists from the north began to study in Italy and were visually influenced by what artists were doing there.

One northern artist of this later period who was greatly influenced by the Italians was Albrecht Dürer (1471–1528) from Nuremberg. Dürer made two trips to Italy and absorbed most of what the Italians could teach, as is evident in his mastery of the laws of perspective and Renaissance theories of proportion. He wrote detailed treatises on both subjects. At the same time, as in his famous *Adoration of the Magi*, Dürer did not reject the use of minute details characteristic of northern artists. He did try, however, to integrate those details more harmoniously into his works and, like the Italian artists of the High Renaissance, tried to achieve a standard of ideal beauty by a careful examination of the human form.

The European State in the Renaissance

In the first half of the fifteenth century, European states continued the disintegrative patterns of the previous century. In the second half of the century, however, recovery set in, and attempts were made to reestablish the centralized power of monarchical governments. To characterize the results, some historians have used the label "Renaissance states"; others have spoken of the "new monarchies," especially those of France, England, and Spain at the end of the fifteenth century. Whereas monarchs succeeded to varying degrees at extending their political authority in western Europe, rulers in central and eastern Europe were often weak and unable to impose their will.

The Renaissance State in Western Europe

Although the Hundred Years' War (1337–1453; see Chapter 11) had made it difficult for French kings to assert their authority, the war had also developed a strong degree of French national feeling toward a common enemy that the kings could use to reestablish monarchical power. The process of developing a French territorial state was greatly advanced by King Louis XI (1461–1483), known as the Spider because of his devious ways. Louis strengthened the use of the *taille*—an annual direct tax, usually on land or property—as a tax imposed by royal authority, giving him a regular and reliable source of income. Louis repressed the French nobility and brought

Albrecht Dürer, *Adoration of the Magi*. By the end of the fifteenth century, northern artists began studying in Italy and adopting many of the techniques used by Italian painters. As is evident in this painting, which was the central panel for an altarpiece done for Frederick the Wise in 1504, Albrecht Dürer masterfully incorporated the laws of perspective and the ideals of proportion into his works. At the same time, he did not abandon the preoccupation with detail typical of northern artists.

the provinces of Anjou, Maine, Bar, and Provence under royal control.

England The Hundred Years' War also strongly affected the other protagonist in that conflict, England. The cost of the war in its final years and the losses in manpower strained the English economy. Moreover, the end of the war brought even greater domestic turmoil to England when the War of the Roses broke out in the 1450s. This civil war pitted the ducal house of Lancaster, whose symbol was a red rose, against the ducal house of York, whose symbol was a white rose. Many aristocratic families of England were drawn into the conflict. Finally, in 1485, Henry Tudor, duke of Richmond, defeated the last Yorkist king, Richard III (1483–1485), at Bosworth Field and established a new dynasty.

As the first Tudor king, Henry VII (1485–1509) worked to reduce internal dissension and establish a strong monarchical government. The new king was particularly successful in obtaining sufficient income from the traditional financial resources of the English monarch, such as the crown lands, judicial fees and fines, and customs duties. By using diplomacy to avoid wars, which are always expensive, the king avoided having to call Parliament on any regular basis to grant him funds. By not overburdening the landed gentry and middle class with taxes, Henry won their favor, and they provided much support for his monarchy. Henry's policies gave England

MAP 12.2 **Europe in the Second Half of the Fifteenth Century.** By the second half of the fifteenth century, states in western Europe, particularly France, Spain, and England, had begun the process of modern state building. With varying success, they reined in the power of the church and nobles, increased the ability to levy taxes, and established effective government bureaucracies. **?** What aspects of Europe's political boundaries help explain why France and the Holy Roman Empire were often at war with each other? 🌐 **View an animated version of this map or related maps at** http://thomsonedu.com/history/spielvogel

a stable and prosperous government and enhanced the status of the monarchy.

Spain Spain, too, experienced the growth of a strong national monarchy by the end of the fifteenth century. During the Middle Ages, several independent Christian kingdoms had emerged in the course of the long reconquest of the Iberian peninsula from the Muslims (see Map 12.2). Aragon and Castile were the strongest Spanish kingdoms; in the west was the independent monarchy of Portugal; in the north, the small kingdom of Navarre; and in the south, the Muslim kingdom of Granada.

A major step toward the unification of Spain was taken with the marriage of Isabella of Castile (1474–1504) and Ferdinand of Aragon (1479–1516) in 1469. This was a dynastic union of two rulers, not a political union. Both kingdoms maintained their own parliaments (Cortes), courts, laws, coinage, speech, customs, and political organs.

Nevertheless, the two rulers worked to strengthen royal control of government, especially in Castile. The royal council, which was supposed to supervise local administration and oversee the implementation of government policies, was stripped of aristocrats and filled primarily with middle-class lawyers. Trained in the principles of Roman law, these officials operated on the belief that the monarchy embodied the power of the state.

Ferdinand and Isabella reorganized the military forces of Spain, seeking to replace the undisciplined feudal levies they had inherited with a more professional royal army. The development of a strong infantry force as the heart of the new Spanish army made it the best in Europe by the sixteenth century, and Spain emerged as an important power in European affairs.

Ferdinand and Isabella also pursued a policy of strict religious uniformity. Spain possessed two large religious minorities, Jews and Muslims, both of whom had been largely tolerated in medieval Spain. Increased persecution in the fourteenth century, however, led the majority of Spanish Jews to convert to Christianity. But complaints about the sincerity of these Jewish converts prompted Ferdinand and Isabella to ask the pope to introduce the Inquisition into Spain in 1478. Under royal control, the Inquisition worked with cruel efficiency to guarantee the orthodoxy of the converts but had no authority over practicing Jews. Consequently, in 1492, flush with the success of the conquest of Muslim Granada, Ferdinand and Isabella took the drastic step of expelling all professed Jews from Spain. It is estimated that 150,000 out of possibly 200,000 Jews fled. Muslims, too, were then "encouraged" to convert to Christianity, and in 1502, Isabella issued a decree expelling all professed Muslims from her kingdom. To a very large degree, the "most Catholic" monarchs had achieved their goal of absolute religious orthodoxy as a basic ingredient of the Spanish state. To be Spanish was to be Catholic, a policy of uniformity enforced by the Inquisition.

Central Europe: The Holy Roman Empire

After 1438, the position of Holy Roman Emperor was in the hands of the Habsburg dynasty. Having gradually acquired a number of possessions along the Danube, known collectively as Austria, the house of Habsburg had become one of the wealthiest landholders in the empire and by the mid-fifteenth century began to play an important role in European affairs. Much of the Habsburg success in the fifteenth century was due not to military victories but to a well-executed policy of dynastic marriages.

Much was expected of the flamboyant Maximilian I (1493–1519) when he became emperor. Through the Reichstag, the imperial diet or parliament, Maximilian attempted to centralize the administration by creating new institutions common to the entire empire. Opposition from the German princes doomed these efforts, however. Maximilian's only real success lay in his marriage alliances, which led to a grandson, Charles V, inheriting the traditional lands of the Habsburg, Burgundian, and Spanish monarchical lines at the beginning of the sixteenth century, making him the leading monarch of his age (see Chapter 13).

The Struggle for Strong Monarchy in Eastern Europe

In eastern Europe, rulers struggled to achieve the centralization of their territorial states but faced serious obstacles. Although the population was mostly Slavic, there were islands of other ethnic groups that caused difficulties. Religious differences also troubled the area, as Roman Catholics, Greek Orthodox Christians, and pagans confronted each other.

Much of Polish history revolved around a bitter struggle between the crown and the landed nobility until the end of the fifteenth century, when the preoccupation of the Polish monarchy with problems in Bohemia and Hungary as well as war with the Russians and Turks enabled the aristocrats to reestablish their power. Through their control of the Sejm or national parliament, the magnates reduced the peasantry to serfdom by 1511 and established the right to elect their kings. The Polish kings proved unable to establish a strong royal authority.

Since the conversion of Hungary to Roman Catholicism by German missionaries, its history had been closely tied to that of central and western Europe. The church became a large and prosperous institution. Wealthy bishops, along with great territorial lords, became powerful, independent political figures. For a brief while, Hungary developed into an important European state, the dominant power in eastern Europe. King Matthias Corvinus (1458–1490) broke the power of the wealthy lords and created a well-organized central administration. After his death, Hungary returned to weak rule, however, and the work of Corvinus was largely undone.

Since the thirteenth century, Russia had been under the domination of the Mongols. Gradually, the princes of Moscow rose to prominence by using their close relationship to the Mongol khans to increase their wealth and expand their possessions. In the reign of the great prince Ivan III (1462–1505), a new Russian state was born. Ivan III annexed other Russian principalities and took advantage of dissension among the Mongols to throw off their yoke by 1480.

The Ottoman Turks and the End of the Byzantine Empire

Eastern Europe was increasingly threatened by the steadily advancing Ottoman Turks. The Byzantine Empire had served as a buffer between the Muslim Middle East and the Latin West for centuries, but it was severely weakened by the sack of Constantinople in 1204 and its occupation by the West. Although the Paleologus dynasty (1260–1453) had tried to reestablish Byzantine power in the Balkans, the threat from the Turks finally doomed the long-lasting empire.

Beginning in northeastern Asia Minor in the thirteenth century, the Ottoman Turks spread rapidly, seizing the lands of the Seljuk Turks and the Byzantine Empire. In 1345, they bypassed Constantinople and moved into the Balkans. Under Sultan Murad, Ottoman forces moved through Bulgaria and into the lands of the Serbians, who provided a strong center of opposition under King Lazar. But in 1389, at the Battle of Kosovo, Ottoman forces defeated the Serbs; both King Lazar and Sultan Murad perished in the battle. Kosovo became a battlefield long revered and remembered by the Serbs. Not until 1480 were Bosnia, Albania, and the rest of Serbia added to the Ottoman Empire in the Balkans.

In the meantime, in 1453, the Ottomans also completed the demise of the Byzantine Empire. With eighty thousand troops ranged against only seven thousand defenders, Sultan Mehmet II laid siege to Constantinople. In their attack on the city, the Turks made use of massive cannons with 26-foot barrels that could launch stone balls weighing up to 1,200 pounds each. Finally, the walls were breached; the Byzantine emperor died in the final battle. Mehmet II, standing before the palace of the emperor, paused to reflect on the passing nature of human glory.

After consolidating their power, the Turks prepared to exert renewed pressure on the West, both in the Mediterranean and up the Danube valley toward Vienna. By the end of the fifteenth century, they were threatening Hungary, Austria, Bohemia, and Poland.

The Church in the Renaissance

As a result of the efforts of the Council of Constance, the Great Schism of the Catholic church had finally been brought to an end in 1417. Ending the schism proved to be the council's easiest task; it was much less successful in dealing with the problems of heresy and reform.

The Problems of Heresy and Reform

Heresy was not a new problem, and in the thirteenth century, the church had developed inquisitorial machinery to deal with it. But two widespread movements in the fourteenth and early fifteenth centuries—Lollardy and Hussitism—posed new threats to the church.

Wyclif and Lollardy   English Lollardy was a product of the Oxford theologian John Wyclif (c. 1328–1384), whose disgust with clerical corruption led him to a far-ranging attack on papal authority and medieval Christian beliefs and practices. Wyclif alleged that there was no basis in Scripture for papal claims of temporal authority and advocated that the popes be stripped of their authority and their property. Believing that the Bible should be a Christian's sole authority, Wyclif urged that it be made available in the vernacular languages so that every Christian could read it. Rejecting all practices not mentioned in Scripture, Wyclif condemned pilgrimages and the veneration of saints. Wyclif attracted a number of followers who came to be known as Lollards.

Hus and the Hussites   A marriage between the royal families of England and Bohemia enabled Lollard ideas to spread to Bohemia, where they reinforced the ideas of a group of Czech reformers led by the chancellor of the university at Prague, John Hus (1374–1415). In his call for reform, Hus urged the elimination of the worldliness and corruption of the clergy and attacked the excessive power of the papacy within the Catholic church. Hus's objections fell on receptive ears, for the Catholic church, as one of the largest landowners in Bohemia, was already widely criticized. Moreover, many clergymen were German, and the native Czechs' strong resentment of the Germans who dominated Bohemia also contributed to Hus's movement.

The Council of Constance attempted to deal with the growing problem of heresy by summoning Hus to the council. Granted safe conduct by Emperor Sigismund, Hus went in the hope of a free hearing of his ideas. Instead he was arrested, condemned as a heretic, and burned at the stake in 1415. This action turned the unrest in Bohemia into revolutionary upheaval, and the resulting Hussite wars racked the Holy Roman Empire until a truce was arranged in 1436.

Reform of the Church   The reform of the church was even less successful than the attempt to eradicate heresy. The Council of Constance passed two reform decrees. One stated that a general council of the church received its authority from God; hence every Christian, including the pope, was subject to its authority. The other decree provided for the regular holding of general councils to ensure that church reform would continue. Decrees alone, however, proved insufficient to reform the church. Councils could issue decrees, but popes had to execute them, and popes would not cooperate with councils that diminished their absolute authority. Beginning already in 1417, successive popes worked steadfastly for the next thirty years to defeat the conciliar movement (see Chapter 11).

By the mid-fifteenth century, the popes had reasserted their supremacy over the Catholic church. No longer, however, did they have any possibility of asserting supremacy over temporal governments as the medieval papacy had. Although the papal monarchy had been maintained, it had lost much moral prestige. In the fifteenth century, the Renaissance papacy contributed to an even further decline in the moral leadership of the popes.

The Renaissance Papacy

The Renaissance papacy refers to the line of popes from the end of the Great Schism in 1417 to the beginning of the Reformation in the early sixteenth century. The primary concern of the papacy is governing the Catholic church as its spiritual leader. But as heads of the church, popes had temporal preoccupations as well, and the story of the Renaissance papacy is really an account of how the latter came to overshadow the popes' spiritual functions.

The manner in which Renaissance popes pursued their interests in the Papal States and Italian politics, especially their use of intrigue and even bloodshed, seemed shocking. Of all the Renaissance popes, Julius II (1503–1513) was most involved in war and politics. The fiery "warrior pope" personally led armies against his enemies, much to the disgust of pious Christians, who viewed the pope as a spiritual leader. As one intellectual wrote at the beginning of the sixteenth century: "How, O bishop standing in the room of the Apostles [the pope], dare you teach the people the things that pertain to war?"

To further their territorial aims in the Papal States, the popes needed loyal servants. Because they were not hereditary monarchs, popes could not build dynasties over several generations and came to rely on the practice of **nepotism** to promote their families' interests. Pope Sixtus IV (1471–1484), for example, made five of his nephews (the word *nepotism* is in fact derived from the Greek *nepos,* meaning "nephew") cardinals and gave them an abundance of church offices to build up their finances. The infamous Borgia pope, Alexander VI (1492–1503), known for his debauchery and sensuality, raised one son, one nephew, and the brother of one mistress to the cardinalate. Alexander scandalized the church by encouraging his son Cesare to carve a state out of the territories of the Papal States in central Italy.

The Renaissance popes were great patrons of Renaissance culture, and their efforts made Rome a cultural leader at the beginning of the sixteenth century. The warrior pope Julius II endeavored to add to the splendor of his pontificate by tearing down an old church and beginning construction of what was to be the greatest building in Christendom, Saint Peter's basilica. Julius's successor, Leo X (1513–1521), was also a patron of Renaissance culture. A member of the Medici family, he

A Renaissance Pope: Leo X. The Renaissance popes allowed secular concerns to overshadow their spiritual duties. Shown here is the Medici pope Leo X. Raphael portrays the pope as a collector of books, looking up after examining an illuminated manuscript with a magnifying glass. At the left is the pope's cousin Guilio, a cardinal. Standing behind the pope is Luigi de'Rossi, another relative who had also been made a cardinal.

was made a cardinal at the age of thirteen and acquired a refined taste in art, manners, and social life among the Florentine elite. He became pope at the age of thirty-seven, supposedly remarking to the Venetian ambassador, "Let us enjoy the papacy, since God has given it to us." Raphael was commissioned to do paintings, and the construction of Saint Peter's was accelerated as Rome became the literary and artistic center of the Renaissance.

CONCLUSION

The Renaissance was a period of transition that witnessed a continuation of the economic, political, and social trends that had begun in the High Middle Ages. It was also a movement in which intellectuals and artists proclaimed a new vision of humankind and raised fundamental questions about the value and importance of the individual. Of course, intellectuals and artists wrote and painted for the upper classes, and the brilliant intellectual, cultural, and artistic accomplishments of the Renaissance were really products of and for the elite. The ideas of the Renaissance did not have a broad base among the masses of the people. As Lorenzo the Magnificent, ruler of Florence, once commented, "Only men of noble birth can obtain perfection. The poor, who work with their hands and have no time to cultivate their minds, are incapable of it."

The Renaissance did, however, raise new questions about medieval traditions. In criticizing current religious practices, the humanists raised fundamental issues about the Catholic church, which was still an influential institution. As we shall see in the next chapter, the intellectual revolution of the fifteenth century gave way to a religious renaissance that touched the lives of people, including the masses, in new and profound ways. After the Reformation, Europe would never again be the unified Christian commonwealth it once believed it was.

TIMELINE

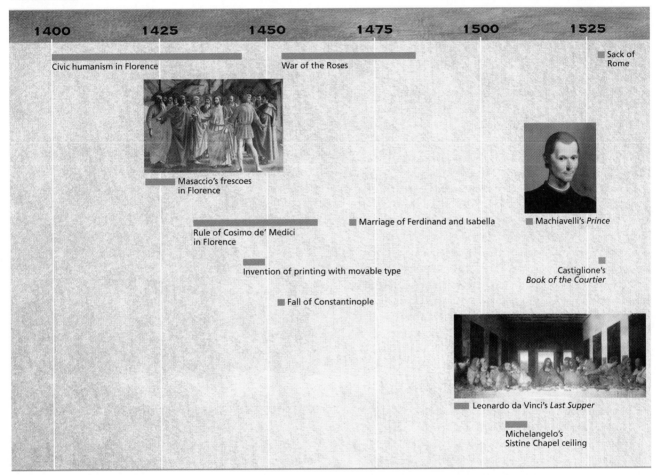

| | 1400 | 1425 | 1450 | 1475 | 1500 | 1525 |

Civic humanism in Florence

War of the Roses

Sack of Rome

Masaccio's frescoes in Florence

Rule of Cosimo de' Medici in Florence

Marriage of Ferdinand and Isabella

Machiavelli's *Prince*

Invention of printing with movable type

Castiglione's *Book of the Courtier*

Fall of Constantinople

Leonardo da Vinci's *Last Supper*

Michelangelo's Sistine Chapel ceiling

NOTES

1. Quoted in J. Burckhardt, *The Civilization of the Renaissance in Italy*, trans. S. G. C. Middlemore (London, 1960), p. 81.
2. B. Castiglione, *The Book of the Courtier*, trans. C. S. Singleton (Garden City, N.Y., 1959), pp. 288–289.
3. Quoted in D. L. Jensen, *Renaissance Europe* (Lexington, Mass., 1981), p. 94.
4. G. Brucker, ed., *Two Memoirs of Renaissance Florence* (New York, 1967), p. 132.
5. Quoted in M. L. King, *Women of the Renaissance* (Chicago, 1991), p. 3.
6. N. Machiavelli, *The Prince*, trans. D. Wootton (Indianapolis, 1995), p. 48.
7. Ibid., p. 55.
8. Ibid., p. 27.
9. G. Pico della Mirandola, *Oration on the Dignity of Man*, in E. Cassirer, P. O. Kristeller, and J. H. Randall Jr., eds., *The Renaissance Philosophy of Man* (Chicago, 1948), p. 225.
10. Ibid., pp. 247–249.
11. Quoted in I. Origo, *The Light of the Past* (New York, 1959), p. 136.
12. Quoted in E. G. Holt, ed., *A Documentary History of Art* (Garden City, N.Y., 1959), vol. 1, p. 286.
13. Quoted in R. M. Letts, *The Cambridge Introduction to Art: The Renaissance* (Cambridge, 1981), p. 86.

SUGGESTIONS FOR FURTHER READING

The classic study of the Italian Renaissance is **J. Burckhardt,** *The Civilization of the Renaissance in Italy*, trans. S.G.C. Middlemore (London, 1960), first published in 1860. General works on the Renaissance in Europe include **D. L. Jensen,** *Renaissance Europe* (Lexington, Mass., 1981); **P. Burke,** *The European Renaissance: Centres and Peripheries* (Oxford, 1998); **J. Hale,** *The Civilization of Europe in the Renaissance* (New York, 1994); and the classic work by **M. P. Gilmore,** *The World of Humanism, 1453–1517* (New York, 1962). Although many of its interpretations are outdated, **W. Ferguson,** *Europe in Transition, 1300–1520* (Boston, 1962), contains a wealth of information. The brief study by **P. Burke,** *The Renaissance,* 2d ed. (New York, 1997), is a good summary of modern literature on the Renaissance. For beautifully illustrated introductions to the Renaissance, see **G. Holmes,** *Renaissance* (New York, 1996), and **M. Aston, ed.,** *The Panorama of the Renaissance* (New York, 1996).

Brief but basic works on Renaissance economic matters are **H. A. Miskimin,** *The Economy of Early Renaissance Europe, 1300–1460* (New York, 1975) and *The Economy of Later Renaissance Europe, 1460–1600* (New York, 1978). For a reinterpretation of economic matters, see **L. Jardine,** *Worldly Goods* (New York, 1996). On family and marriage, see **D. Herlihy,** *The Family in Renaissance Italy* (Saint Louis, Mo., 1974), and **C. Klapisch-Zuber,** *Women, Family, and Ritual in Renaissance Italy* (Chicago, 1985). On women, see **M. L. King,** *Women of the Renaissance* (Chicago, 1991), and **N. Z. Davis and A. Farge, eds.,** *A History of Women: Renaissance and Enlightenment Paradoxes* (Cambridge, Mass., 1993).

The best overall study of the Italian city-states is **L. Martines,** *Power and Imagination: City-States in Renaissance Italy* (New York, 1979); **D. Hay and J. Law,** *Italy in the Age of the Renaissance* (London, 1989), is also a good survey. There is an enormous literature on Renaissance Florence. The best introduction is **G. Brucker,** *Florence: The Golden Age, 1138–1737* (Berkeley, Calif., 1988). Machiavelli's life can be examined in **Q. Skinner,** *Machiavelli* (Oxford, 1981).

Brief introductions to Renaissance humanism can be found in **D. R. Kelley,** *Renaissance Humanism* (Boston, 1991); **C. G. Nauert Jr.,** *Humanism and the Culture of Renaissance Europe* (Cambridge, 1995); and **F. B. Artz,** *Renaissance Humanism, 1300–1550* (Oberlin, Ohio, 1966). The impact of printing is exhaustively examined in **E. Eisenstein,** *The Printing Press as an Agent of Change,* 2 vols. (New York, 1978).

For brief introductions to Renaissance art, see **R. M. Letts,** *The Cambridge Introduction to Art: The Renaissance* (Cambridge, 1981), and **B. Cole** and **A. Gealt,** *Art of the Western World* (New York, 1989), ch. 6–8. Good surveys of Renaissance art include **F. Hartt,** *History of Italian Renaissance Art,* 4th ed. (Englewood Cliffs, N.J., 1994);

S. Elliott, *Italian Renaissance Painting,* 2d ed. (London, 1993); **R. Turner,** *Renaissance Florence: The Invention of a New Art* (New York, 1997); **P. F. Brown,** *Art and Life in Renaissance Venice* (Upper Saddle River, N.J., 1997); and **L. Murray,** *The High Renaissance* (New York, 1967). For a lively account of the painting of the Sistine Chapel ceiling, see **R. King,** *Michelangelo and the Pope's Ceiling* (New York, 2002).

For a general work on the political development of Europe in the Renaissance, see **J. H. Shennan,** *The Origins of the Modern European State, 1450–1725* (London, 1974). On France, see **R. J. Knecht,** *The Rise and Fall of Renaissance France, 1483–1610,* 2d ed. (Oxford, 2001). Early Renaissance England is examined in **J. R. Lander,** *Crown and Nobility, 1450–1509* (London, 1976). Good coverage of Renaissance Spain can be found in **J. N. Hillgarth,** *The Spanish Kingdoms, 1250–1516,* vol. 2, *Castilian Hegemony, 1410–1516* (New York, 1978). Two good works on eastern Europe include **P. W. Knoll,** *The Rise of the Polish Monarchy* (Chicago, 1972), and **C. A. Macartney,** *Hungary: A Short History* (Edinburgh, 1962). On the Ottomans and their expansion, see **H. Inalcik,** *The Ottoman Empire: The Classical Age, 1300–1600* (London, 1973).

Aspects of the Renaissance papacy can be examined in **E. Lee,** *Sixtus IV and Men of Letters* (Rome, 1978), and **M. Mallett,** *The Borgias* (New York, 1969). On Rome, see especially **P. Partner,** *Renaissance Rome, 1500–1559: A Portrait of a Society* (Berkeley, Calif., 1976).

Thomson NOW! Enter *ThomsonNOW* using the access card that is available for *Western Civilization: A Brief History.* *ThomsonNOW* will help you understand this chapter with lesson plans generated for your needs. In addition, you can read the following documents, and many more, online:

> Giovanni Villani, selections from Books 8 and 9 of *Chronicle*
> Two Tractates from Vittorino da Feltre and other Humanist Educators
> Giorgio Vasari, Excerpts from *Life of Michelangelo* and *Life of da Vinci*

WESTERN CIVILIZATION RESOURCES

Visit the Web site for *Western Civilization: A Brief History* for resources specific to this book:

http://www.thomsonedu.com/history/spielvogel

For a variety of tools to help you succeed in this course, visit the Western Civilization Resource Center at

http://history.wadsworth.com/spielvogel

Included are quizzes, images, documents, interactive simulations, maps and timelines, movie explorations, and a wealth of other sources.

13

REFORMATION AND RELIGIOUS WARFARE IN THE SIXTEENTH CENTURY

CHAPTER OUTLINE AND FOCUS QUESTIONS

Prelude to Reformation

☐ Who were the Christian humanists, and how did they differ from the Protestant reformers?

Martin Luther and the Reformation in Germany

☐ What were Martin Luther's main disagreements with the Roman Catholic church, and why did the movement he began spread so quickly across Europe?

The Spread of the Protestant Reformation

☐ What were the chief tenets of Zwinglianism, Anabaptism, Anglicanism, and Calvinism?

The Social Impact of the Protestant Reformation

☐ What impact did the Protestant Reformation have on the society of the sixteenth century?

The Catholic Reformation

☐ What measures did the Roman Catholic church take to reform itself and to combat Protestantism in the sixteenth century?

Politics and the Wars of Religion in the Sixteenth Century

☐ What role did religion play in the European wars of the sixteenth century?

CRITICAL THINKING

☐ What were the main tenets of the major Protestant groups, and how did they differ from each other and from Catholicism? What were the results of these differences?

A sixteenth-century engraving of Martin Luther in front of Charles V at the Diet of Worms

Bibliotheque Nationale, Paris/The Bridgeman Art Library

*O*N APRIL 18, 1520, a lowly monk stood before the emperor and princes of the Holy Roman Empire in the city of Worms. He had been called before this august gathering to answer charges of heresy, charges that could threaten his very life. The monk was confronted with a pile of his books and asked if he wished to defend them all or reject a part. Courageously, Martin Luther defended them all and asked to be shown where any part was in error on the basis of "Scripture and plain reason." The emperor was outraged by Luther's response and made his own position clear the next day: "Not only I, but you of this noble German nation, would be forever disgraced if by our negligence not only heresy but the very suspicion of heresy were to survive. After having heard yesterday the obstinate defense of Luther, I regret that I have so long delayed in proceeding against him and his false teaching. I will have no more to do with him." Luther's appearance at Worms set the stage for a serious challenge to the authority of the Catholic church. This was by no means the first crisis in the church's fifteen-hundred-year history, but its consequences were more far-reaching than anyone at Worms in 1520 could have imagined.

Throughout the Middle Ages, the Catholic church continued to assert its primacy of position. It had overcome defiance of its temporal authority by emperors while challenges to its doctrines had been crushed by the Inquisition and combated by new religious orders that carried its message of salvation to all the towns and villages of medieval Europe. The growth of the papacy had paralleled the growth of the church, but by the end of the Middle Ages, challenges to papal authority from the rising power of monarchical states had resulted in a loss of papal temporal authority. An even greater threat to papal authority and church unity arose in the sixteenth century when the unity of Christendom was shattered by the Reformation.

The movement begun by Martin Luther when he made his dramatic stand quickly spread across Europe, a clear indication of dissatisfaction with Catholic practices. Within a short time, new religious practices, doctrines, and organizations, including Zwinglianism, Calvinism, Anabaptism, and Anglicanism, were attracting adherents all over Europe. Seemingly helpless to stop the new Protestant churches, the Catholic church too underwent a religious renaissance and managed to revive its fortunes by the mid-sixteenth century. All too soon, the religious divisions between Protestants and Catholics became instrumental in triggering a series of religious wars that dominated the history of western Europe in the second half of the sixteenth century.◆

Prelude to Reformation

Martin Luther's reform movement was not the first in sixteenth-century Europe. During the second half of the fifteenth century, the new classical learning that was part of Italian Renaissance humanism spread to northern Europe and spawned a movement called **Christian** or **northern Renaissance humanism**, whose major goal was the reform of Christendom.

Christian or Northern Renaissance Humanism

The most important characteristic of northern Renaissance humanism was its reform program. Convinced of the ability of human beings to reason and improve themselves, the northern humanists thought that through education in the sources of classical, and especially Christian, antiquity, they could instill a true inner piety or an inward religious feeling that would bring about a reform of the church and society. For this reason, Christian humanists supported schools, brought out new editions of the classics, and prepared new editions of the Bible and writings of such church fathers as Augustine, Ambrose, and Jerome. In the preface to his edition of the Greek New Testament, the famous humanist Erasmus wrote:

> Indeed, I disagree very much with those who are unwilling that Holy Scripture, translated into the vulgar tongue, be read by the uneducated, as if Christ taught such intricate doctrines that they could scarcely be understood by very few theologians, or as if the strength of the Christian religion consisted in men's ignorance of it. . . . I would that even the lowliest women read the Gospels and the Pauline Epistles. And I would that they were translated into all languages so that they could be read and understood not only by Scots and Irish but also by Turks and Saracens [Arabs].[1]

Like later intellectuals, Christian humanists believed that to change society, they must first change the human beings who compose it.

Erasmus The most influential of all the Christian humanists was the Dutch-born scholar Desiderius Erasmus (1466–1536). After withdrawing from a monastery, he wandered to France, England, Italy, Germany, and Switzerland, conversing everywhere in the classical Latin that might be called his mother tongue. The *Handbook of the Christian Knight,* published in 1503, reflected his preoccupation with religion. He called his conception of religion "the philosophy of Christ," by which he meant that Christianity should be a guiding philosophy for the direction of daily life rather than the system of dogmatic beliefs and practices that the medieval church seemed to stress. In other words, he emphasized inner piety and deemphasized the external forms of religion (such as the sacraments, pilgrimages, fasts, veneration of saints, and relics). To return to the simplicity of the early church, people needed to understand the original meaning of the Scriptures and early church fathers.

To Erasmus, the reform of the church meant spreading an understanding of the philosophy of Jesus, providing enlightened education in the sources of early Christianity, and making commonsense criticism of the abuses in the church. This critical approach is especially evident in *The Praise of Folly,* written in 1511, in which Erasmus was able to engage in a humorous yet effective criticism of the most corrupt practices of his own society. He was especially harsh on the abuses within the ranks of the clergy:

> Many of [the monks] work so hard at protocol and at traditional fastidiousness that they think one heaven hardly a suitable reward for their labors; never recalling, however, that the time will come when Christ will demand a reckoning of that which he had prescribed, namely charity, and that he will hold their deeds of little account. One monk will then exhibit his belly filled with every kind of fish; another will profess a knowledge of over a hundred hymns. Still another will reveal a countless number of fasts that he has made, and will account for his large belly by explaining that his fasts have always been broken by a single large meal.[2]

Erasmus' program did not achieve the reform of the church that he so desired. His moderation and his emphasis on education were quickly overwhelmed by the passions of the Reformation. Undoubtedly, though, his work helped prepare the way for the Reformation; as contemporaries proclaimed, "Erasmus laid the egg that Luther hatched." Yet Erasmus eventually disapproved of

Erasmus. Desiderius Erasmus was the most influential of the northern Renaissance humanists. He sought to restore Christianity to the early simplicity found in the teachings of Jesus. This portrait of Erasmus was painted in 1523 by Hans Holbein the Younger, who had formed a friendship with the great humanist while they were in Basel.

Luther and the Protestant reformers. He had no intention of destroying the unity of the medieval Christian church; instead, his whole program was based on reform within the church.

Church and Religion on the Eve of the Reformation

Corruption in the Catholic church was another factor that spurred people to want reform. No doubt the failure of the Renaissance popes to provide spiritual leadership had affected the spiritual life of all Christendom. The papal court's preoccupation with finances had an especially strong impact on the clergy. So did the economic changes of the fourteenth and fifteenth centuries. The highest positions among the clergy were increasingly held by either nobles or wealthy members of the bourgeoisie. Moreover, to increase their revenues, high church officials (such as bishops, archbishops, and cardinals) took over more than one church office. This **pluralism** (the holding of multiple church offices) begat absenteeism: church officeholders ignored their duties and hired underlings

who were sometimes not appropriately qualified. Complaints about the ignorance and ineptness of parish priests became widespread in the fifteenth century.

While the leaders of the church were failing to meet their responsibilities, ordinary people were clamoring for meaningful religious expression and certainty of salvation. As a result, the salvation process became almost mechanical. As more and more people sought salvation through the veneration of relics, collections of such objects grew. Frederick the Wise, elector of Saxony and Luther's prince, had amassed over five thousand relics to which were attached **indulgences** (remissions of the penalties for sin) that could reduce one's time in purgatory by nearly two million years. Other people sought salvation in the popular mystical movement known as the Modern Devotion. The Modern Devotion downplayed religious dogma and stressed the need to follow the teachings of Jesus. Thomas à Kempis, author of *The Imitation of Christ,* wrote that "truly, at the day of judgment we shall not be examined by what we have read, but what we have done; not how well we have spoken, but how religiously we have lived."

What is striking about the revival of religious piety in the fifteenth century was its adherence to the orthodox beliefs and practices of the Catholic church. The agitation for certainty of salvation and spiritual peace was done within the framework of the "holy mother Church." But as the devout experienced the clergy's inability to live up to their expectations, disillusionment grew. The intensification of religious feeling, especially in the second half of the fifteenth century, resonated little among the worldly-wise clergy, and this divergence may explain the tremendous and immediate impact of Luther's ideas.

Martin Luther and the Reformation in Germany

The Protestant Reformation began with a typical medieval question: What must I do to be saved? Martin Luther, a deeply religious man, found an answer that did not fit within the traditional teachings of the late medieval church. Ultimately, he split with that church, destroying the religious unity of western Christendom.

The Early Luther

Martin Luther was born in Germany on November 10, 1483. His father wanted him to become a lawyer, so Luther enrolled at the University of Erfurt. In 1505, after becoming a master in the liberal arts, the young man began to study law. But Luther was not content, not in small part due to his long-standing religious inclinations. That summer, while returning to Erfurt after a brief visit home, he was caught in a ferocious thunderstorm and vowed that if he survived unscathed, he would become a monk. He then entered the monastic order of the

Augustinian Hermits in Erfurt, much to his father's disgust. In the monastery, Luther focused on his major concern, the assurance of salvation. The traditional beliefs and practices of the church seemed unable to relieve his obsession with this question. Luther threw himself into his monastic routine with a vengeance:

> I was indeed a good monk and kept my order so strictly that I could say that if ever a monk could get to heaven through monastic discipline, I was that monk. . . . And yet my conscience would not give me certainty, but I always doubted and said, "You didn't do that right. You weren't contrite enough. You left that out of your confession." The more I tried to remedy an uncertain, weak and troubled conscience with human traditions, the more I daily found it more uncertain, weaker and more troubled.[3]

Despite his herculean efforts, Luther achieved no certainty of salvation.

To help overcome his difficulties, his superiors recommended that he study theology. Luther received his doctorate in 1512 and then became a professor in the theological faculty at the University of Wittenberg, lecturing on the Bible. Sometime between 1513 and 1516, through his study of the Bible, he arrived at an answer to his problem.

Catholic doctrine had emphasized that both faith and good works were required of a Christian to achieve personal salvation. In Luther's eyes, human beings, weak and powerless in the sight of an almighty God, could never do enough good works to merit salvation. Through his study of the Bible, especially his work on Paul's Epistle to the Romans, Luther rediscovered another way of viewing this problem. To Luther, humans are saved not through their good works but through faith in the promises of God, made possible by the sacrifice of Jesus on the cross. The doctrine of salvation or justification by grace through faith alone became the primary doctrine of the Protestant Reformation (**justification** is the act by which a person is made deserving of salvation). Because Luther had arrived at this doctrine from his study of the Bible, the Bible became for him, as for all other Protestants, the chief guide to religious truth. Justification by faith and the Bible as the sole authority in religious affairs were the twin pillars of the Protestant Reformation.

The Indulgence Controversy   Luther did not see himself as either an innovator or a heretic, but his involvement in the indulgence controversy propelled him into an open confrontation with church officials and forced him to see the theological implications of justification by faith alone. Luther was greatly distressed by the widespread selling of indulgences, certain that people were guaranteeing their eternal damnation by relying on these pieces of paper to assure themselves of salvation. Johann Tetzel, a rambunctious Dominican, hawked the indulgences with the slogan "As soon as the coin in the coffer [money box] rings, the soul from purgatory springs."

Greatly angered, Luther issued a stunning indictment of the abuses in the sale of indulgences, known as the Ninety-Five Theses (see the box on p. 241). It is doubtful that Luther intended to break with the church over the issue of indulgences. If the pope had clarified the use of indulgences, as Luther wished, Luther would probably have been satisfied. But Pope Leo X did not take the issue seriously and is even reported to have said that Luther was simply "some drunken German who will amend his ways when he sobers up." A German translation of the Ninety-Five Theses was quickly printed in thousands of copies and received sympathetically in a Germany that had a long tradition of dissatisfaction with papal policies and power.

The Quickening Rebellion   In three pamphlets published in 1520, Luther moved toward a more definite break with the Catholic church. *Address to the Nobility of the German Nation* was a political tract written in German in which Luther called on the German princes to overthrow the papacy in Germany and establish a reformed German church. *The Babylonian Captivity of the Church* attacked the sacramental system as the means by which the pope and church had held the real meaning of the Gospel captive for a thousand years. He called for the reform of monasticism and for the clergy to marry. While virginity is good, Luther argued, marriage is better, and freedom of choice is best. *On the Freedom of a Christian Man* was a short treatise on the doctrine of salvation. It is faith alone, not good works, that justifies, frees, and brings salvation through Jesus. Being saved and freed by his faith in Jesus, however, does not free the Christian from doing good works. Rather he performs good works out of gratitude to God: "Good works do not make a good man, but a good man does good works."[4]

Unable to accept Luther's forcefully worded dissent from traditional Catholic teachings, the church excommunicated him in January 1521. He was also summoned to appear before the imperial diet (Reichstag) of the Holy Roman Empire in Worms, convened by the newly elected Emperor Charles V (1519–1556). Expected to recant the heretical doctrines he had espoused, Luther refused and made the famous reply that became the battle cry of the Reformation:

> Since then Your Majesty and your lordships desire a simple reply, I will answer without horns and without teeth. Unless I am convicted by Scripture and plain reason—I do not accept the authority of popes and councils, for they have contradicted each other—my conscience is captive to the Word of God. I cannot and I will not recant anything, for to go against conscience is neither right nor safe. Here I stand, I cannot do otherwise. God help me. Amen.[5]

The young Emperor Charles was outraged at Luther's audacity and gave his opinion that "a single friar who goes counter to all Christianity for a thousand years must be wrong." By the Edict of Worms, Martin Luther was made an outlaw within the empire. His works were to be

LUTHER AND THE NINETY-FIVE THESES

To most historians, the publication of Luther's Ninety-Five Theses marks the beginning of the Reformation. To Luther, they were simply a response to what he considered the blatant abuse of Johann Tetzel's selling of indulgences. Although written in Latin, the theses were soon translated into German and disseminated widely across Germany.

Martin Luther, *Selections from the Ninety-Five Theses*

5. The Pope has neither the will nor the power to remit any penalties beyond those he has imposed either at his own discretion or by canon law.

21. Hence those preachers of Indulgences are wrong when they say that a man is absolved and saved from every penalty by the Pope's Indulgences.

27. It is mere human talk to preach that the soul flies out [of purgatory] immediately the money clinks in the collection-box.

28. It is certainly possible that when the money clinks in the collection-box greed and avarice can increase; but the intercession of the Church depends on the will of God alone.

50. Christians should be taught that, if the Pope knew the exactions of the preachers of Indulgences, he would rather have the basilica of St. Peter reduced to ashes than built with the skin, flesh and bones of his sheep.

81. This wanton preaching of pardons makes it difficult even for learned men to redeem respect due to the Pope from the slanders or at least the shrewd questionings of the laity.

82. For example: "Why does not the Pope empty purgatory for the sake of most holy love and the supreme need of souls? This would be the most righteous of reasons, if he can redeem innumerable souls for sordid money with which to build a basilica, the most trivial of reasons."

86. Again: "Since the Pope's wealth is larger than that of the crassest Crassi of our time, why does he not build this one basilica of St. Peter with his own money, rather than with that of the faithful poor?"

90. To suppress these most conscientious questionings of the laity by authority only, instead of refuting them by reason, is to expose the Church and the Pope to the ridicule of their enemies, and to make Christian people unhappy.

94. Christians should be exhorted to seek earnestly to follow Christ, their Head, through penalties, deaths, and hells.

95. And let them thus be more confident of entering heaven through many tribulations rather than through a false assurance of peace.

What are the major ideas of Luther's Ninety-Five Theses? Why did they have such a strong appeal in Germany?

---

burned and Luther himself captured and delivered to the emperor.

The Development of Lutheranism

Between 1521 and 1525, Luther's religious movement became a revolution. Lutheranism had much appeal and spread rapidly. The preaching of evangelical sermons, based on a return to the original message of the Bible, found favor throughout Germany. Also useful to the spread of the Reformation were pamphlets illustrated with vivid woodcuts portraying the pope as a hideous Antichrist and titled with catchy phrases such as "I Wonder Why There Is No Money in the Land" (which, of course, was an attack on papal greed).

Luther was able to gain the support of his prince, the elector of Saxony, as well as other German rulers among the more than three hundred states that made up the Holy Roman Empire. Lutheranism spread to both princely and ecclesiastical states in northern and central Germany as well as to two-thirds of the free imperial cities, especially those of southern Germany, where prosperous burghers, for both religious and secular reasons, became committed to Luther's cause. At its outset, the Reformation in Germany was largely an urban phenomenon.

A series of crises in the mid-1520s made it apparent, however, that spreading the word of God was not as easy as Luther had originally envisioned—the usual plight of most reformers. Luther experienced dissent within his own ranks in Wittenberg as well as defection from many Christian humanists who feared that Luther's movement threatened the unity of Christendom. The Peasants' War constituted Luther's greatest challenge, however. In June 1524, peasants in Germany rose in revolt against their lords and looked to Luther for support. But Luther, who knew how much his reformation of the church depended on the full support of the German princes and magistrates, supported the rulers. To Luther, the state and its rulers were ordained by God and given the authority to maintain the peace and order necessary for the spread of the Gospel. It was the duty of princes to suppress all revolt. By May 1525, the German princes had ruthlessly suppressed the peasant hordes. By this time, Luther found himself ever more dependent on state authorities for the growth and maintenance of his reformed church.

Church and State

Justification by faith was the starting point for most of Protestantism's major doctrines. Since Luther downplayed

Woodcut: Luther Versus the Pope. In the 1520s, after Luther's return to Wittenberg, his teachings began to spread rapidly, ending ultimately in a reform movement supported by state authorities. Pamphlets containing picturesque woodcuts were important in the spread of Luther's ideas. In the woodcut shown here, the crucified Jesus attends Luther's service on the left, while on the right the pope is at a table selling indulgences.

the role of good works in salvation, the sacraments also had to be redefined. No longer were they merit-earning works; they were now divinely established signs signifying the promise of salvation. Luther kept only two of the Catholic church's seven sacraments: baptism and the Lord's Supper. Baptism signified rebirth through grace. Regarding the Lord's Supper or the Eucharist, Luther denied the Catholic doctrine of **transubstantiation,** which taught that the substance of the bread and wine consumed in the rite is miraculously transformed into the body and blood of Jesus. Yet he continued to insist on the real presence of Jesus' body and blood in the bread and wine given as a testament to God's forgiveness of sin.

Luther took an active role in establishing a reformed church. Since the Catholic ecclesiastical hierarchy had been scrapped, Luther came to rely increasingly on the princes or state authorities to organize and guide the new Lutheran reformed churches. The Lutheran churches in Germany (and later in Scandinavia) quickly became territorial or state churches in which the state supervised and disciplined church members. As part of the development of these state-dominated churches, Luther also instituted new religious services to replace the Mass. These featured a worship service consisting of a German liturgy that focused on Bible reading, preaching the word of God, and song. Following his own denunciation of clerical celibacy, Luther married a former nun, Katherina von Bora, in 1525. His union provided a model of married and family life for the new Protestant minister.

Germany and the Reformation: Religion and Politics

From its very beginning, the fate of Luther's movement was closely tied to political affairs. In 1519, Charles I, king of Spain and the grandson of the Emperor Maximilian, was elected Holy Roman Emperor as Charles V (1519–1556). Charles V ruled over an immense empire, consisting of Spain and its overseas possessions, the traditional Austrian Habsburg lands, Bohemia, Hungary, the Low Countries, and the kingdom of Naples in southern Italy (see Map 13.1). The extent of his possessions was reflected in the languages he used: "I speak Spanish to God, Italian to women, French to men, and German to my horse." Politically, Charles wanted to maintain his

MAP 13.1 **The Empire of Charles V.** Charles V spent much of his reign fighting wars in Italy, against France and the Ottoman Empire, and within the borders of the Holy Roman Empire. He failed in his main goal to secure Europe for Catholicism: the 1555 Peace of Augsburg recognized the equality of Catholicism and Lutheranism and let each German prince choose his realm's religion. **?** Why would France feel threatened by the empire of Charles V? **View an animated version of this map or related maps at** http://thomsonedu.com/history/spielvogel

dynasty's control over his enormous empire; religiously, he hoped to preserve the unity of the Catholic faith throughout his empire. Despite his strengths, Charles spent a lifetime in futile pursuit of his goals. Four major problems—the French, the papacy, the Turks, and Germany's internal situation—cost him both his dream and his health.

The chief political concern of Charles V was his rivalry with the Valois king of France, Francis I (1515–1547). Encircled by the possessions of the Habsburg empire, Francis became embroiled in conflict with Charles over disputed territories in southern France, the Netherlands, the Rhineland, northern Spain, and Italy. These conflicts, known as the Habsburg-Valois Wars,

were fought intermittently for more than two decades (1521–1544).

At the same time, Charles faced opposition from Pope Clement VII (1523–1534), who, guided by political considerations, joined the side of Francis I. The advance of the Ottoman Turks into the eastern part of Charles's empire forced the emperor to divert forces there as well. Under Suleiman the Magnificent (1520–1566), the Ottoman Turks overran most of Hungary, moved into Austria, and advanced as far as Vienna, where they were finally repulsed in 1529.

Finally, the internal political situation in the Holy Roman Empire was also not in Charles's favor. Germany was a land of several hundred territorial states—princely

Charles V. Charles V sought to create religious unity throughout his vast empire by keeping all his subjects within the bounds of the Catholic church. Due to his conflict with Francis I as well as his difficulties with the Turks, the papacy, and the German princes, Charles was never able to check the spread of Lutheranism. This is a portrait of Charles V by the Venetian painter Titian.

states, ecclesiastical principalities, and free imperial cities. Although all owed loyalty to the emperor, Germany's medieval development had enabled these states to become quite independent of imperial authority. They had no desire to have a strong emperor. By the time Charles V was able to bring military forces to Germany in 1546, Lutheranism had become well established and the Lutheran princes were well organized. Unable to impose his will on Germany, Charles was forced to negotiate a truce. An end to religious warfare in Germany came in 1555 with the Peace of Augsburg, which marked an important turning point in the history of the Reformation. The division of Christianity was formally acknowledged, with Lutheranism granted equal legal standing with Catholicism. Moreover, the peace settlement accepted the right of each German ruler to determine the religion of his subjects. Charles's hope for a united empire had been completely dashed, and the ideal of medieval Christian unity was irretrievably lost. The rapid proliferation of new Protestant groups served to underscore the new reality.

The Spread of the Protestant Reformation

For both Catholics and Protestant reformers, Luther's heresy also raised the question of how to determine what constituted the correct interpretation of the Bible. The inability to agree on this issue led not only to theological confrontations but also to bloody warfare because each Christian group was unwilling to admit that it could be wrong.

The Zwinglian Reformation

In the sixteenth century, the Swiss Confederation was a loose association of thirteen self-governing states called cantons. Theoretically part of the Holy Roman Empire, they had become virtually independent in 1499. The six forest cantons were democratic republics, while the seven urban cantons, which included Zürich, Bern, and Basel, were governed primarily by city councils controlled by narrow oligarchies of wealthy citizens.

Zwingli's Zürich

Ulrich Zwingli (1484–1531) was ordained a priest in 1506 and accepted an appointment as a cathedral priest in the Great Minster of Zürich in 1518. Zwingli's preaching of the Gospel caused such unrest that the city council in 1523 held a public disputation or debate in the town hall. Zwingli's party was accorded the victory, and the council declared that "Mayor, Council and Great Council of Zürich, in order to do away with disturbance and discord, have upon due deliberation and consultation decided and resolved that Master Zwingli should continue as heretofore to proclaim the Gospel and the pure sacred Scriptures."[6] Over the next two years, evangelical reforms were promulgated in Zürich by a city council strongly influenced by Zwingli. Relics and images were abolished; all paintings and decorations were removed from the churches and replaced by whitewashed walls. The Mass was replaced by a new liturgy consisting of Scripture reading, prayer, and sermons. Monasticism, pilgrimages, the veneration of saints, clerical celibacy, and the pope's authority were all abolished as remnants of papal Christianity.

A Reformation Debate: The Marburg Colloquy

Debates played a crucial role in the Reformation period. They were a primary instrument in introducing the Reformation into innumerable cities as well as a means of resolving differences among the like-minded Protestant groups. This selection contains an excerpt from the vivacious and often brutal debate between Luther and Zwingli over the sacrament of the Lord's Supper, held at Marburg in 1529. The two protagonists failed to reach agreement.

The Marburg Colloquy, 1529

HESSIAN CHANCELLOR FEIGE: My gracious prince and lord [Landgrave Philip of Hesse] has summoned you for the express and urgent purpose of settling the dispute over the sacrament of the Lord's Supper. . . . And let everyone on both sides present his arguments in a spirit of moderation, as becomes such matters. . . . Now then, Doctor Luther, you may proceed.

LUTHER: Noble prince, gracious lord! Undoubtedly the colloquy is well intentioned. . . . Although I have no intention of changing my mind, which is firmly made up, I will nevertheless present the grounds of my belief and show where the others are in error. . . . Your basic contentions are these: In the last analysis you wish to prove that a body cannot be in two places at once, and you produce arguments about the unlimited body which are based on natural reason. I do not question how Christ can be God and man and how the two natures can be joined. For God is more powerful than all our ideas, and we must submit to his word.

Prove that Christ's body is not there where the Scripture says, "This is my body!" Rational proofs I will not listen to. . . . God is beyond all mathematics and the words of God are to be revered and carried out in awe. It is God who commands, "Take, eat, this is my body." I request, therefore, valid scriptural proof to the contrary.

Luther writes on the table in chalk, "This is my body," and covers the words with a velvet cloth.

OECOLAMPADIUS [leader of the reform movement in Basel and a Zwinglian partisan]: The sixth chapter of John clarifies the other scriptural passages. Christ is not speaking there about a local presence. "The flesh is of no avail," he says [John 6:63]. It is not my intention to employ rational, or geometrical, arguments—neither am I denying the power of God—but as long as I have the complete faith I will speak from that. For Christ is risen; he sits at the right hand of God; and so he cannot be present in the bread. Our view is neither new nor sacrilegious, but is based on faith and Scripture. . . .

ZWINGLI: I insist that the words of the Lord's Supper must be figurative. This is ever apparent, and even required by the article of faith: "taken up into heaven, seated at the right hand of the Father." Otherwise, it would be absurd to look for him in the Lord's Supper at the same time that Christ is telling us that he is in heaven. One and the same body cannot possibly be in different places. . . . I stand by this passage in the sixth chapter of John, verse 63, and shall not be shaken from it. You'll have to sing another tune.

LUTHER: You're being obnoxious.

ZWINGLI: (*excitedly*) Don't you believe that Christ was attempting in John 6 to help those who did not understand?

LUTHER: You're trying to dominate things! You insist on passing judgment! Leave that to someone else! . . . It is your point that must be proved, not mine. But let us stop this sort of thing. It serves no purpose.

ZWINGLI: It certainly does! It is for you to prove that the passage in John 6 speaks of a physical repast.

LUTHER: You express yourself poorly and make about as much progress as a cane standing in a corner. You're going nowhere.

ZWINGLI: No, no, no! This is the passage that will break your neck!

LUTHER: Don't be so sure of yourself. Necks don't break this way. You're in Hesse, not Switzerland. . . .

Based on this example, why do you think Reformation debates led to further hostility rather than compromise and unity?

As his movement began to spread to other cities in Switzerland, Zwingli sought an alliance with Martin Luther and the German reformers. Protestant political leaders attempted to promote an alliance of the Swiss and German reformed churches by persuading the leaders of both groups to attend a colloquy (conference) at Marburg to resolve their differences. Although both the German and Swiss reformers realized the need for unity to defend against the opposition of Catholic authorities, they were unable to agree on the interpretation of the Lord's Supper (see the box above). Zwingli believed that the scriptural words "This is my body" and "This is my blood" should be taken symbolically, not literally. To Zwingli, the Lord's Supper was only a meal of remembrance, and he refused to accept Luther's insistence on the real presence of the body and blood of Jesus. The Marburg Colloquy produced no agreement.

In October 1531, war erupted between the Swiss Protestant and Catholic cantons. Zürich's army was routed, and Zwingli was found wounded on the battlefield. His enemies killed him, cut up his body, burned it, and scattered the ashes. This Swiss civil war of 1531 provided an early indication of what religious passions would lead to in the sixteenth century. Unable to find peaceful ways to agree on the meaning of the Gospel, the disciples of Christianity resorted to violence and decision by force. When informed of Zwingli's death, Martin Luther, who had not forgotten the confrontation at Marburg, is supposed to have remarked that Zwingli "got what he deserved."

The Radical Reformation: The Anabaptists

Although many reformers were ready to allow the state to play an important, if not dominant, role in church affairs, some people rejected this kind of magisterial reformation and favored a far more radical reform movement. Collectively called the Anabaptists, these radicals were actually members of a large variety of groups who had certain characteristics in common.

To the Anabaptists, the true Christian church was a voluntary association of believers who had undergone spiritual rebirth and had then been baptized into the church. Anabaptists advocated adult rather than infant baptism. No one, they believed, should be forced to accept the truth of the Bible. They also tried to return literally to the practices and spirit of early Christianity. Adhering to the accounts of early Christian communities in the New Testament, they followed a strict sort of democracy in which all believers were considered equal. Each church chose its own minister, who might be any member of the community because all Christians were considered priests (though women were often excluded). Those chosen as ministers had the duty to lead services, which were very simple and contained nothing not found in the early church. Like early Christians, Anabaptists, who called themselves "Christians" or "Saints," accepted that they would have to suffer for their faith. Anabaptists rejected theological speculation in favor of simple Christian living according to what they believed was the pure word of God. The Lord's Supper was interpreted as a remembrance, a meal of fellowship celebrated in the evening in private houses according to Jesus' example.

Unlike the Catholics and other Protestants, most Anabaptists believed in the complete separation of church and state. Not only was government to be excluded from the realm of religion, but it was not even supposed to exercise political jurisdiction over true Christians. Human law had no power over those whom God had saved. Anabaptists refused to hold political office or bear arms because many took the commandment "Thou shall not kill" literally, although some Anabaptist groups did resort to violence. Their political beliefs as much as their religious beliefs caused the Anabaptists to be regarded as dangerous radicals who threatened the fabric of sixteenth-century society. Indeed, the chief thing Protestants and Catholics could agree on was the need to stamp out the Anabaptists.

One early group of Anabaptists known as the Swiss Brethren arose in Zürich. Their ideas frightened Zwingli, and they were soon expelled from the city. As their teachings spread through southern Germany, the Austrian Habsburg lands, and Switzerland, Anabaptists suffered ruthless persecution, especially after the Peasants' War of 1524–1525, when the upper classes resorted to repression. Virtually eliminated in Germany, Anabaptist survivors emerged in Moravia, Poland, and the Netherlands.

Menno Simons (1496–1561) was the most responsible for rejuvenating Dutch Anabaptism. A popular leader, Menno dedicated his life to the spread of a peaceful, evangelical Anabaptism that stressed separation from the world in order to live a truly Jesus-like life. The Mennonites, as his followers were called, spread from the Netherlands into northwestern Germany and eventually into Poland and Lithuania as well as the New World. Remnant communities of both Mennonites and Amish, who are also descended from the Anabaptists, can still be found in the United States and Canada today.

The Reformation in England

The English Reformation was initiated by King Henry VIII (1509–1547), who wanted to divorce his first wife, Catherine of Aragon, because she had failed to produce a male heir. Furthermore, Henry had fallen in love with Anne Boleyn, a lady-in-waiting to Queen Catherine. Anne's discontent with being merely the king's mistress and the king's desire to have a legitimate male heir made their marriage imperative, but the king's first marriage stood in the way.

Normally, church authorities might have been willing to grant the king an annulment of his marriage, but Pope Clement VII was dependent on the Holy Roman Emperor, Charles V, who happened to be Catherine's nephew. Impatient with the pope's inaction, Henry sought to obtain an annulment of his marriage in England's own ecclesiastical courts. As archbishop of Canterbury and head of the highest ecclesiastical court in England, Thomas Cranmer held official hearings on the king's case and ruled in May 1533 that the king's marriage to Catherine was "null and absolutely void." He then validated Henry's secret marriage to Anne, who had become pregnant. At the beginning of June, Anne was crowned queen. Three months later, a child was born. Much to the king's disappointment, the baby was a girl, the future Queen Elizabeth.

In 1534, at Henry's request, Parliament moved to finalize the Church of England's break with Rome. The Act of Supremacy of 1534 declared that the king was "taken, accepted, and reputed the only supreme head on earth of the Church of England," a position that gave him control of doctrine, clerical appointments, and discipline.

Although Henry VIII had broken with the papacy, little changed in matters of doctrine, theology, and ceremony. Some of his supporters, such as Archbishop Cranmer, sought a religious reformation as well as an administrative one, but Henry was unyielding. When

Henry died in 1547, he was succeeded by his son, the underage and sickly Edward VI (1547–1553). During Edward's reign, Cranmer and others inclined toward Protestant doctrines were able to move the Church of England (also known as the Anglican church) in more of a Protestant direction. New acts of Parliament instituted the right of the clergy to marry, the elimination of religious images, and the creation of a revised Protestant liturgy that was elaborated in a new prayer book known as the Book of Common Prayer. These rapid changes in doctrine and liturgy aroused much opposition and prepared the way for the reaction that occurred when Mary, Henry's first daughter by Catherine of Aragon, came to the throne.

Mary (1553–1558) was a Catholic who intended to restore England to Roman Catholicism. But her restoration of Catholicism aroused much opposition. There was widespread antipathy to Mary's unfortunate marriage to Philip II, the son of Charles V and future king of Spain. Philip was strongly disliked in England, and Mary's foreign policy of alliance with Spain simply aroused further hostility. The burning of more than three hundred Protestant heretics aroused further ire against "Bloody Mary." As a result of her policies, Mary managed to achieve the opposite of what she had intended: England was more Protestant by the end of her reign than it had been at the beginning.

John Calvin and the Development of Calvinism

Of the second generation of Protestant reformers, one stands out as the premier systematic theologian and organizer of the Protestant movement—John Calvin (1509–1564). Calvin was educated in his native France, but after his conversion to Protestantism, he was forced to flee to the safety of Switzerland. In 1536, he published the first edition of the *Institutes of the Christian Religion,* a masterful synthesis of Protestant thought that immediately secured Calvin's reputation as one of the new leaders of Protestantism.

Calvin's Ideas   On most important doctrines, Calvin stood very close to Luther. He adhered to the doctrine of justification by faith alone to explain how humans achieved salvation. But Calvin also placed much emphasis on the absolute sovereignty of God or the "power, grace, and glory of God." One of the ideas derived from his emphasis on the absolute sovereignty of God— **predestination**—gave a unique cast to Calvin's teachings. This "eternal decree," as Calvin called it, meant that God had predestined some people to be saved (the elect) and others to be damned (the reprobate). According to Calvin, "He has once for all determined, both whom he would admit to salvation, and whom he would condemn to destruction."[7] Although Calvin stressed that there could be no absolute certainty of salvation, some of his followers did not always make this distinction. The

John Calvin.   After a conversion experience, John Calvin abandoned his life as a humanist and became a reformer. In 1536, Calvin began working to reform the city of Geneva, where he remained until his death in 1564. This sixteenth-century portrait of Calvin pictures him near the end of his life.

practical psychological effect of predestination was to give some later Calvinists an unshakable conviction that they were doing God's work on earth. Thus Calvinism became a dynamic and activist faith. It is no accident that Calvinism became the militant international form of Protestantism.

To Calvin, the church was a divine institution responsible for preaching the word of God and administering the sacraments. Calvin kept the same two sacraments as other Protestant reformers, baptism and the Lord's Supper. Calvin believed in the real presence of Jesus in the sacrament of the Lord's Supper, but only in a spiritual sense. Jesus' body is at the right hand of God and thus cannot be in the sacrament, but to the believer, Jesus is spiritually present in the Lord's Supper.

In 1536, Calvin began working to reform the city of Geneva. He established a church government that used both clergy and laymen in the service of the church. The Consistory, a special body for enforcing moral discipline,

Calvin's Geneva

was set up as a court to oversee the moral life and doctrinal purity of Genevans. The Consistory had the right to punish people who deviated from the church's teachings and moral principles.

Calvin's success in Geneva enabled the city to become a vibrant center of Protestantism. John Knox, the Calvinist reformer of Scotland, called Geneva "the most perfect school of Christ on earth." Following Calvin's lead, missionaries trained in Geneva were sent to all parts of Europe. Calvinism became established in France, the Netherlands, Scotland, and central and eastern Europe. By the mid-sixteenth century, Calvinism had replaced Lutheranism as the militant international form of Protestantism, and Calvin's Geneva stood as the fortress of the Reformation.

The Social Impact of the Protestant Reformation

Because Christianity was such an integral part of European life, it was inevitable that the Reformation would have an impact on the family and popular religious practices.

The Family

For centuries, Catholicism had praised the family and sanctified its existence by making marriage a sacrament. But the Catholic church's high regard for abstinence from sex as the surest way to holiness made the celibate state of the clergy preferable to marriage. Nevertheless, because not all men could remain chaste, marriage offered the best means to control sexual urges and give them a purpose, the procreation of children. To some extent, this attitude persisted among the Protestant reformers; Luther, for example, argued that sex in marriage allowed one to "make use of this sex in order to avoid sin," and Calvin advised that every man should "abstain from marriage only so long as he is fit to observe celibacy." If "his power to tame lust fails him," then he must marry.

But the Reformation did bring some change to the conception of the family. Both Catholic and Protestant clergy preached sermons advocating a more positive side to family relationships. The Protestants were especially important in developing this new view of the family. Because Protestantism had eliminated any idea of special holiness for celibacy, abolishing both monasticism and a

celibate clergy, the family could be placed at the center of human life, and a new stress on "mutual love between man and wife" could be extolled. But were doctrine and reality the same? For more radical religious groups, at times they were. One Anabaptist wrote to his wife before his execution: "My faithful helper, my loyal friend. I praise God that he gave you to me, you who have sustained me in all my trial."[8] But more often reality reflected the traditional roles of husband as the ruler and wife as the obedient servant whose chief duty was to please her husband. Luther stated it clearly:

> The rule remains with the husband, and the wife is compelled to obey him by God's command. He rules the home and the state, wages war, defends his possessions, tills the soil, builds, plants, etc. The woman on the other hand is like a nail driven into the wall . . . so the wife should stay at home and look after the affairs of the household, as one who has been deprived of the ability of administering those affairs that are outside and that concern the state. She does not go beyond her most personal duties.[9]

Obedience to her husband was not a woman's only role; her other important duty was to bear children. To Calvin and Luther, this function of women was part of the divine plan. God punishes women for the sins of Eve by the burdens of procreation and feeding and nurturing their children, but "it is a gladsome punishment if you consider the hope of eternal life and the honor of motherhood which had been left to her."[10] Although the Protestant reformers sanctified this role of woman as mother and wife, viewing it as a holy vocation, Protestantism also left few alternatives for women. Because monasticism had been destroyed, that career avenue was no longer available; for most Protestant women, family life was their only destiny. At the same time, by emphasizing the father as "ruler" and hence the center of household religion, Protestantism even removed the woman from her traditional role as controller of religion in the home. Overall, the Protestant Reformation did not noticeably transform women's subordinate place in society.

Religious Practices and Popular Culture

The attacks of Protestant reformers on the Catholic church led to radical changes in religious practices. The Protestant Reformation abolished or severely curtailed such customary practices as indulgences, the veneration of relics and saints, pilgrimages, monasticism, and clerical celibacy. The elimination of saints put an end to the numerous celebrations of religious holy days and changed a community's sense of time. Thus in Protestant communities, religious ceremonies and imagery, such as processions and statues, tended to be replaced with individual private prayer, family worship, and collective prayer and worship at the same time each week on Sunday.

In addition to abolishing saints' days and religious carnivals, some Protestant reformers even tried to eliminate customary forms of entertainment. Puritans (as

English Calvinists were known), for example, attempted to ban drinking in taverns, dramatic performances, and dancing. Dutch Calvinists denounced the tradition of giving small presents to children on the feast of Saint Nicholas in December. Many of these Protestant attacks on popular culture were unsuccessful, however. The importance of taverns in English social life made it impossible to eradicate them, and celebrations at Christmastime persisted in the Dutch Netherlands.

The Catholic Reformation

By the mid-sixteenth century, Lutheranism had become established in Germany and Scandinavia and Calvinism in parts of Switzerland, France, the Netherlands, and eastern Europe (see Map 13.2). In England, the split from Rome had resulted in the creation of a national church. The situation in Europe did not look particularly favorable for the Roman Catholic church. But even at the beginning of the sixteenth century, constructive, positive forces were at work for reform within the Catholic church, and in a few decades, these efforts were being directed by a revived and reformed papacy, giving rise to a Catholic Reformation. Historians focus on three chief pillars of the Catholic Reformation: the development of the Jesuits, the creation of a reformed and revived papacy, and the Council of Trent.

The Society of Jesus

The Society of Jesus, members of which are known as Jesuits, was founded by a Spanish nobleman, Ignatius of

MAP 13.2 **Catholics and Protestants in Europe by 1560.** The Reformation continued to evolve beyond the basic split of the Lutherans from the Catholics. Several Protestant sects broke away from the teachings of Martin Luther, each with a separate creed and different ways of worship. In England, Henry VIII broke with the Catholic church for political and dynastic reasons. ❓ Which areas of Europe were solidly Catholic, which were solidly Lutheran, and which were neither? 🌐 **View an animated version of this map or related maps at** http://thomsonedu.com/history/spielvogel

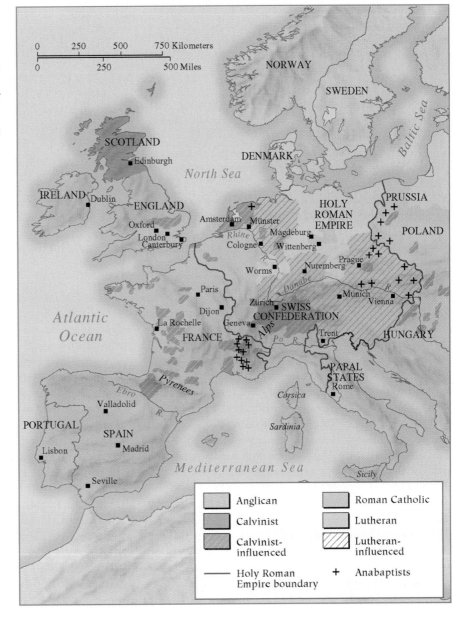

LOYOLA AND OBEDIENCE TO "OUR HOLY MOTHER, THE HIERARCHICAL CHURCH"

In his *Spiritual Exercises*, Ignatius of Loyola developed a systematic program for "the conquest of self and the regulation of one's life" for service to the hierarchical Catholic church. Ignatius' supreme goal was the commitment of the Christian to active service in the Church of Christ (the Catholic church). In the final section of *The Spiritual Exercises*, Loyola explained the nature of that commitment in a series of "rules for thinking with the church."

Ignatius of Loyola, "Rules for Thinking with the Church"

The following rules should be observed to foster the true attitude of mind we ought to have in the Church militant.

1. We must put aside all judgment of our own, and keep the mind ever ready and prompt to obey in all things the true Spouse of Jesus Christ, our holy Mother, the hierarchical Church.

2. We should praise sacramental confession, the yearly reception of the Most Blessed Sacrament [the Lord's Supper], and praise more highly monthly reception, and still more weekly Communion. . . .

3. We ought to praise the frequent hearing of Mass, the singing of hymns, psalmody, and long prayers whether in the church or outside. . . .

4. We must praise highly religious life, virginity, and continency; and matrimony ought not be praised as much as any of these. . . .

6. We should show our esteem for the relics of the saints by venerating them and praying to the saints. We should praise visits to the Station Churches, pilgrimages,

indulgences, jubilees, the lighting of candles in churches. . . .

8. We ought to praise not only the building and adornment of churches, but also images and veneration of them according to the subject they represent.

9. Finally, we must praise all the commandments of the Church, and be on the alert to find reasons to defend them, and by no means in order to criticize them.

10. We should be more ready to approve and praise the orders, recommendations, and way of acting of our superiors than to find fault with them. Though some of the orders, etc., may not have been praiseworthy, yet to speak against them, either when preaching in public or in speaking before the people, would rather be the cause of murmuring and scandal than of profit. As a consequence, the people would become angry with their superiors, whether secular or spiritual. But while it does harm in the absence of our superiors to speak evil of them before the people, it may be profitable to discuss their bad conduct with those who can apply a remedy.

13. If we wish to proceed securely in all things, we must hold fast to the following principle: What seems to me white, I will believe black if the hierarchical Church so defines. For I must be convinced that in Christ our Lord, the bridegroom, and in His spouse the Church, only one Spirit holds sway, which governs and rules for the salvation of souls.

What are the fundamental assumptions that inform Loyola's rules for thinking with the church? What do these assumptions tell you about the nature of the Catholic reform movement?

Loyola (1491–1556), whose injuries in battle cut short his military career. Loyola experienced a spiritual torment similar to Luther's, but unlike Luther, he resolved his problems not by a new doctrine but by a decision to submit to the will of the church. Unable to be a real soldier, he vowed to be a soldier of God. Over a period of twelve years, Loyola prepared for his lifework by prayer, pilgrimages, going to school, and working out a spiritual program in his brief but powerful book, *The Spiritual Exercises*. This was a training manual for spiritual development emphasizing exercises by which the human will could be strengthened and made to follow the will of God as manifested through his instrument, the Catholic church (see the box above).

Loyola gathered together a small group of individuals who were recognized as a religious order by a papal bull in 1540. The new order was grounded on the principles of absolute obedience to the papacy, a strict hierarchical order for the society, the use of education to achieve its

goals, and a dedication to engage in "conflict for God." Executive leadership was put in the hands of a general, who nominated all important positions in the order and was to be revered as the absolute head of the order. Loyola served as the first general of the order until his death in 1556. A special vow of absolute obedience to the pope made the Jesuits an important instrument for papal policy.

The Jesuits were active on behalf of the Catholic faith. They established well-disciplined schools, believing that the thorough education of young people was crucial to combat the advance of Protestantism. Another prominent Jesuit activity was the propagation of the Catholic faith among non-Christians. Francis Xavier (1506–1552), one of the original members of the Society of Jesus, carried the message of Catholic Christianity to the East. After converting tens of thousands in India, he traveled to Malacca and the Moluccas before reaching Japan in 1549. He spoke highly of the Japanese: "They are a people of excellent

Ignatius of Loyola. The Jesuits became the most important new religious order of the Catholic Reformation. Shown here in a sixteenth-century painting by an unknown artist is Ignatius of Loyola, founder of the Society of Jesus. Loyola is seen kneeling before Pope Paul III, who officially recognized the Jesuits in 1540.

morals—good in general and not malicious."[11] Thousands of Japanese, especially in the southernmost islands, became Christians. In 1552, Xavier set out for China but died of fever before he reached the mainland.

Although conversion efforts in Japan proved short-lived, Jesuit activity in China, especially that of the Italian Matteo Ricci (1552–1610), was more long-lasting. Recognizing the Chinese pride in their own culture, the Jesuits attempted to draw parallels between Christian and Confucian concepts and to show the similarities between Christian morality and Confucian ethics. For their part, the missionaries were impressed with many aspects of Chinese civilization, and reports of their experiences heightened European curiosity about this great society on the other side of the world.

The Jesuits were also determined to carry the Catholic banner and fight Protestantism. Jesuit missionaries succeeded in restoring Catholicism to parts of Germany and eastern Europe. Poland was largely won back for the Catholic church through Jesuit efforts.

A Revived Papacy

A reformed papacy was another important factor in the development of the Catholic Reformation. The pontificate of Pope Paul III (1534–1549) proved significant. Raised in the lap of luxury, Paul III continued Renaissance papal practices by appointing his nephews as cardinals, involving himself in politics, and patronizing arts and letters on a lavish scale. Nevertheless, he perceived the need for change and expressed it decisively. Advocates of reform,

such as Gasparo Contarini and Gian Pietro Caraffa, were made cardinals. In 1535, Paul took the audacious step of appointing a commission to study the church's condition. The Reform Commission's report in 1537 blamed the church's problems on the corrupt policies of popes and cardinals. It was also Paul III who formally recognized the Jesuits and began the Council of Trent.

A decisive turning point in the direction of the Catholic Reformation and the nature of papal reform came in the 1540s. In 1541, a colloquy had been held at Regensburg in a final attempt to settle the religious division peacefully. Here Catholic moderates, such as Cardinal Contarini, who favored concessions to Protestants in the hope of restoring Christian unity, reached a compromise with Protestant moderates on a number of doctrinal issues. When Contarini returned to Rome with these proposals, Cardinal Caraffa and other hard-liners, who regarded all compromise with Protestant innovations as heresy, accused him of selling out to the heretics. It soon became apparent that the conservative reformers were in the ascendancy when Caraffa was able to persuade Paul III to establish the Roman Inquisition or Holy Office in 1542 to ferret out doctrinal errors. There was to be no compromise with Protestantism.

When Cardinal Caraffa was chosen pope as Paul IV (1555–1559), he so increased the power of the Inquisition that even liberal cardinals were silenced. This "first true pope of the Catholic Counter-Reformation," as he has been called, also created the Index of Forbidden Books, a list of books that Catholics were not allowed to read. It included all the works of Protestant theologians.

Any hope of restoring Christian unity by compromise was fading fast. The activities of the Council of Trent, the third major pillar of the Catholic Reformation, made compromise virtually impossible.

The Council of Trent

In March 1545, a group of cardinals, archbishops, bishops, abbots, and theologians met in the city of Trent on the border between Germany and Italy and initiated the Council of Trent, which met intermittently from 1545 to 1563 in three major sessions. Moderate Catholic reformers hoped that compromises would be made in formulating doctrinal definitions that would encourage Protestants to return to the church. Conservatives, however, favored an uncompromising restatement of Catholic doctrines in strict opposition to Protestant positions. The latter group won, although not without a struggle.

The final doctrinal decrees of the Council of Trent reaffirmed traditional Catholic teachings in opposition to Protestant beliefs. Scripture and tradition were affirmed as equal authorities in religious matters; only the church could interpret Scripture. Both faith and good works were declared necessary for salvation. The seven sacraments, the Catholic doctrine of transubstantiation (rejected by the Protestant reformers), and clerical celibacy were all upheld. Belief in purgatory and in the efficacy of indulgences was strengthened, although the hawking of indulgences was prohibited.

After the Council of Trent, the Roman Catholic church possessed a clear body of doctrine and a unified church under the acknowledged supremacy of the popes who had triumphed over bishops and councils. The Roman Catholic church had become one Christian denomination among many with an organizational framework and doctrinal pattern that would not be significantly altered until the Second Vatican Council four hundred years later. With a new spirit of confidence, the Catholic church entered a militant phase, as well prepared as the Calvinists to do battle for the Lord. An era of religious warfare was about to unfold.

Politics and the Wars of Religion in the Sixteenth Century

By the middle of the sixteenth century, Calvinism and Catholicism had become militant religions dedicated to spreading the word of God as they interpreted it. Although this religious struggle for the minds and hearts of Europeans is at the core of the religious wars of the sixteenth century, economic, social, and political forces also played important roles in these conflicts. Of the sixteenth-century religious wars, none were more momentous or more shattering than the French civil wars known as the French Wars of Religion.

The French Wars of Religion (1562–1598)

Religion was the engine that drove the French civil wars of the sixteenth century. The growth of Calvinism led to persecution by the French kings but did little to stop the spread of Calvinism. **Huguenots,** as the French Calvinists were called, came from all layers of society: artisans and shopkeepers hurt by rising prices and a rigid guild system, merchants and lawyers in provincial towns whose local privileges were tenuous, and members of the nobility. Possibly 40 to 50 percent of the French nobility became Huguenots, including the house of Bourbon, which stood next to the Valois dynasty in the royal line of succession and ruled the southern French kingdom of Navarre. The conversion of so many nobles made the Huguenots a potentially dangerous political threat to monarchical power. Though the Calvinists constituted only about 7 percent of the population, they were a strong-willed and well-organized minority.

The Catholic majority greatly outnumbered the Calvinist minority. The Valois monarchy was staunchly Catholic, and its control of the Catholic church gave it little incentive to look favorably on Protestantism. At the same time, an extreme Catholic party—known as the Ultra-Catholics—favored strict opposition to the Huguenots and were led by the Guise family. They received support abroad from the papacy and Jesuits who favored their uncompromising Catholic position.

But religion was not the only factor that contributed to the French civil wars. Towns and provinces, which had long resisted the growing power of monarchical centralization, were only too willing to join a revolt against the monarchy. This was also true of the nobility, and the fact that so many of them were Calvinists created an important base of opposition to the crown. The French Wars of Religion, then, presented a major constitutional crisis for France and temporarily halted the development of the French centralized state. The claim to a person's loyalties by the ruling dynasty was temporarily superseded by loyalty to one's religious beliefs. For thirty years, battles raged in France between Catholic and Calvinist parties, who obviously considered the unity of France less important than religious truth. But there also emerged in France a group known as the *politiques* who placed politics before religion and believed that no religious truth was worth the ravages of civil war. The *politiques* ultimately prevailed, but not until both sides had become exhausted by bloodshed.

Finally, in 1589, Henry of Navarre, the political leader of the Huguenots and a member of the Bourbon dynasty, succeeded to the throne as Henry IV (1589–1610). Realizing, however, that he would never be accepted by Catholic France, Henry took the logical way out and converted to Catholicism. With his coronation in 1594, the Wars of Religion came to an end. The Edict of Nantes in 1598 solved the religious problem by acknowledging Catholicism as the official religion of France while guaranteeing the Huguenots the right to worship and to enjoy all political privileges, including the holding of public offices.

Philip II and Militant Catholicism

The greatest advocate of militant Catholicism in the second half of the sixteenth century was King Philip II of Spain (1556–1598), the son and heir of Charles V. Philip's reign ushered in an age of Spanish greatness, both politically and culturally. Philip's first major goal was to consolidate and secure the lands he had inherited from his father. These included Spain, the Netherlands, and possessions in Italy and the New World. For Philip, this meant strict conformity to Catholicism and the establishment of strong monarchical authority. Establishing this authority was not an easy task because Philip had inherited a governmental structure in which each of the various states and territories of his empire stood in an individual relationship to the king.

Crucial to an understanding of Philip II is the importance of Catholicism to the Spanish people and their ruler. Driven by a heritage of crusading fervor, the Spanish had little difficulty seeing themselves as a nation divinely chosen to save Catholic Christianity from the Protestant heretics. Philip II, the "Most Catholic King," became the champion of Catholicism throughout Europe, a role that led him to spectacular victories and equally spectacular defeats. Spain's leadership of a "holy league" against Turkish encroachments in the Mediterranean resulted in a stunning victory over the Turkish fleet in the Battle of Lepanto in 1571. But Philip's attempt to crush the revolt in the Netherlands and his tortured policy with England's Queen Elizabeth led to his greatest misfortunes.

Revolt of the Netherlands

As one of the richest parts of Philip's empire, the Spanish Netherlands was of great importance to the "Most Catholic King." Philip's attempt to strengthen his control in the Netherlands, which consisted of seventeen provinces (modern Netherlands, Belgium, and Luxembourg), soon led to a revolt. The nobles, who stood to lose the most politically if their jealously guarded privileges and freedoms were weakened, strongly opposed Philip's efforts. Resentment against Philip was also aroused by his use of taxes collected in the Netherlands to further Spanish interests. Finally, religion became a major catalyst for rebellion when Philip attempted to crush Calvinism. Violence erupted in 1566 when Calvinists—many of them nobles—began to smash statues and stained-glass windows in Catholic churches. Philip responded by sending the duke of Alva with ten thousand veteran Spanish and Italian troops to crush the rebellion.

But the revolt became organized, especially in the seven northern provinces, where the Dutch, under the

CHRONOLOGY	Wars of Religion in the Sixteenth Century	
The French Wars of Religion		1562–1598
Coronation of Henry IV		1594
Edict of Nantes		1598
Outbreak of revolt in the Netherlands		1566
Battle of Lepanto		1571
Spanish armada		1588
Twelve-year truce (Spain and the Netherlands)		1609
Independence of the United Provinces		1648

leadership of William of Nassau, the prince of Orange, offered growing resistance. The struggle dragged on for decades until 1609, when a twelve-year truce ended the war, virtually recognizing the independence of the northern provinces. These seven northern provinces, which began to call themselves the United Provinces of the Netherlands in 1581, soon emerged as the Dutch Republic, although the Spanish did not formally recognize them as independent until 1648. The ten southern provinces remained a Spanish possession.

The Netherlands

The England of Elizabeth

After the death of Queen Mary in 1558, her half-sister Elizabeth, the daughter of Henry VIII and Anne Boleyn, ascended the throne of England. During Elizabeth's reign, England rose to prominence as the relatively small island kingdom became the leader of the Protestant nations of Europe and laid the foundations for a world empire.

Intelligent, cautious, and self-confident, Elizabeth moved quickly to solve the difficult religious problem she inherited from her half-sister. Elizabeth's religious policy was based on moderation and compromise (see the box on p. 254). The Catholic laws of Mary's reign were repealed, and the new Act of Supremacy designated Elizabeth as "the only supreme governor" of both church and state. The church service used during the reign of Edward VI was revised to make it more acceptable to Catholics. The Church of England under Elizabeth was basically Protestant, but of a moderate sort that kept most people satisfied.

Caution, moderation, and expediency also dictated Elizabeth's foreign policy. Fearful of other countries' motives, Elizabeth realized that war could be disastrous for her island kingdom and her own rule. While encouraging

Queen Elizabeth Addresses Parliament (1601)

Queen Elizabeth I ruled England from 1558 to 1603 with a consummate skill that contemporaries considered unusual in a woman. Though shrewd and paternalistic, Elizabeth, like other sixteenth-century monarchs, depended for her power on the favor of her people. This selection is taken from her speech to Parliament in 1601, when she had been forced to retreat on the issue of monopolies after vehement protest by members of Parliament. Although the speech was designed to make peace with Parliament, some historians also feel that it was a sincere expression of the rapport that existed between the queen and her subjects.

Queen Elizabeth I, "The Golden Speech"

I do assure you there is no prince that loves his subjects better, or whose love can countervail our love. There is no jewel, be it of never so rich a price, which I set before this jewel: I mean your love. For I do esteem it more than any treasure of riches. . . . And, though God has raised me high, yet this I count the glory of my crown, that I have reigned with your loves. This makes me that I do not so much rejoice that God has made me to be a Queen, as to be a Queen over so thankful a people. . . .

Of myself I must say this: I never was any greedy, scraping grasper, nor a strait, fast-holding Prince, nor yet a waster. My heart was never set on any worldly goods, but only for my subjects' good. What you bestow on me, I will not hoard it up, but receive it to bestow on you again. Yea, mine own properties I account yours, to be expended for your good. . . .

I have ever used to set the Last-Judgment Day before mine eyes, and so to rule as I shall be judged to answer before a higher judge, to whose judgment seat I do appeal, that never thought was cherished in my heart that tended not unto my people's good. And now, if my kingly bounties have been abused, and my grants turned to the hurt of my people, contrary to my will and meaning, and if any in authority under me neglected or perverted what I have committed to them, I hope God will not lay their [crimes] and offenses to my charge; who, though there were danger in repealing our grants, yet what danger would I not rather incur for your good, than I would suffer them still to continue?

There will never Queen sit in my seat with more zeal to my country, care for my subjects, and that will sooner with willingness venture her life for your good and safety, than myself. For it is my desire to live nor reign no longer than my life and reign shall be for your good. And though you have had and may have many princes more mighty and wise sitting in this seat, yet you never had nor shall have any that will be more careful and loving.

What are the arguments that Elizabeth makes in her speech to Parliament? How does this speech reveal Elizabeth's intelligence as a ruler?

English piracy and providing clandestine aid to French Huguenots and Dutch Calvinists to weaken France and Spain, Elizabeth pretended complete aloofness and avoided alliances that would force her into war with any major power. Gradually, however, Elizabeth was drawn into conflict with Spain. After years of resisting the idea of invading England as too impractical, Philip II of Spain was finally persuaded to do so by advisers who assured him that the people of England would rise against their queen when the Spaniards arrived. A successful invasion of England would mean the overthrow of heresy and the return of England to Catholicism, surely an act in accordance with the will of God. Philip therefore ordered preparations for an armada (fleet of warships) to spearhead the invasion of England in 1588.

The armada proved a disaster. The Spanish fleet that finally set sail had neither the ships nor the troops that Philip had planned to send. A conversation between a papal emissary and an officer of the Spanish fleet before the armada departed reveals the fundamental flaw:

"And if you meet the English armada in the Channel, do you expect to win the battle?"

"Of course," replied the Spaniard.

"How can you be so sure?" [asked the emissary.]

"It's very simple. It is well known that we fight in God's cause. So, when we meet the English, God will surely arrange matters so that we can grapple and board them, either by sending some strange streak of weather, or, more likely, just by depriving the English of their wits. If we can come to close quarters, Spanish valor and Spanish steel (and the great masses of soldiers we shall have on board) will make our victory certain. But unless God helps us by a miracle the English, who have faster and handier ships than ours, and many more long-range guns, and who know their advantage just as well as we do, will never close with us at all, but stand aloof and knock us to pieces with their culverins, without our being able to do them any serious hurt. So," concluded the captain, and one fancies a grim smile, "we are sailing against England in the confident hope of a miracle."[12]

The hoped-for miracle never materialized. The Spanish fleet, battered by a number of encounters with the

Procession of Queen Elizabeth I. Intelligent and learned, Elizabeth was familiar with Latin and Greek and spoke several European languages. Served by able administrators, she ruled for nearly forty-five years and generally avoided open military action against any major power. Her participation in the revolt of the Netherlands, however, brought England into conflict with Spain. This picture, painted near the end of her reign, shows the queen on a ceremonial procession.

English, sailed back to Spain by a northward route around Scotland and Ireland along which it was further battered by storms. Although the English and Spanish would continue their war for another sixteen years, the defeat of the Spanish armada guaranteed for the time being that England would remain a Protestant country. Although Spain made up for its losses within a year and a half, the defeat was a psychological blow to the Spaniards.

TIMELINE

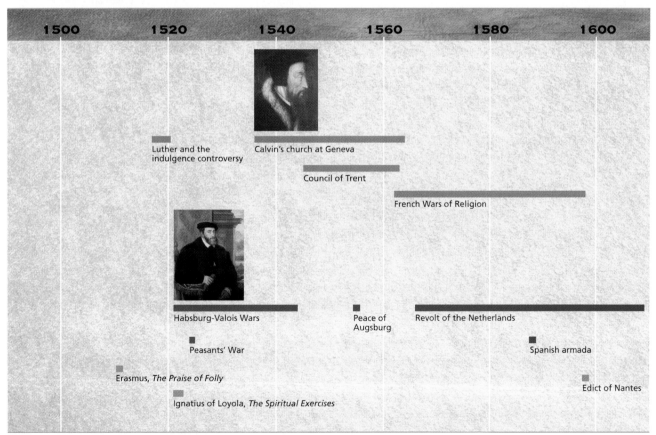

| 1500 | 1520 | 1540 | 1560 | 1580 | 1600 |

Luther and the indulgence controversy

Calvin's church at Geneva

Council of Trent

French Wars of Religion

Habsburg-Valois Wars

Peace of Augsburg

Revolt of the Netherlands

Peasants' War

Spanish armada

Erasmus, *The Praise of Folly*

Edict of Nantes

Ignatius of Loyola, *The Spiritual Exercises*

When the Augustinian monk Martin Luther burst onto the scene with a series of theses on indulgences, few people suspected that his observations would eventually split all of Europe along religious lines. But the yearning for reform of the church and meaningful religious experience caused a seemingly simple dispute to escalate into a powerful movement.

Although Luther felt that his revival of Christianity based on his interpretation of the Bible should be acceptable to all, others soon appeared who also read the Bible but interpreted it in different ways. Protestantism fragmented into different sects, which, though united in their dislike of Catholicism, were themselves divided over the interpretation of the sacraments and religious practices. As reform ideas spread, religion and politics became ever more intertwined.

By 1555, Lutheranism had lost much of its momentum; its energy was largely replaced by the new Protestant form of Calvinism, which had a clarity of doctrine and a fervor that made it attractive to a whole new generation of Europeans. Although Calvinism's militancy enabled it to expand across Europe, Catholicism was also experiencing its own revival and emerged as a militant faith, prepared to do combat for the souls of the faithful. An age of religious passion was followed by an age of religious warfare.

That people who were disciples of the Apostle of Peace would kill each other–often in brutal and painful fashion–aroused skepticism about Christianity itself. As one German writer put it, "Lutheran, popish, and Calvinistic, we've got all these beliefs here; but there is some doubt about where Christianity has got."[13] It is surely no accident that the search for a stable, secular order of politics and for order in the universe through natural laws soon came to play important roles. Before we look at this search for order in the seventeenth century, however, we need first to look at the adventures that plunged Europe into its new role in the world.

NOTES

1. D. Erasmus, *The Paraclesis,* in J. Olin, ed., *Christian Humanism and the Reformation: Selected Writings of Erasmus,* 3d ed. (New York, 1987), p. 101.

2. J. P. Dolan, ed., *The Essential Erasmus* (New York, 1964), p. 149.

3. Quoted in A. E. McGrath, *Reformation Thought: An Introduction* (Oxford, 1988), p. 72.

4. Quoted in E. G. Rupp and B. Drewery, eds., *Martin Luther* (New York, 1970), p. 50.

5. Quoted in R. Bainton, *Here I Stand: A Life of Martin Luther* (New York, 1950), p. 144.

6. Quoted in D. L. Jensen, *Reformation Europe* (Lexington, Mass., 1981), p. 83.

7. J. Calvin, *Institutes of the Christian Religion,* trans. J. Allen (Philadelphia, 1936), vol. 1, p. 228; vol. 2, p. 181.

8. Quoted in R. Bainton, *Women of the Reformation in Germany and Italy* (Boston, 1971), p. 154.

9. Quoted in B. S. Anderson and J. P. Zinsser, *A History of Their Own: Women in Europe from Prehistory to the Present* (New York, 1988), vol. 1, p. 259.

10. Quoted in J. A. Phillips, *Eve: The History of an Idea* (New York, 1984), p. 105.

11. Quoted in J. O'Malley, *The First Jesuits* (Cambridge, Mass., 1993), p. 76.

12. Quoted in G. Mattingly, *The Armada* (Boston, 1959), pp. 216–217.

13. Quoted in T. Schieder, *Handbuch der Europäischen Geschichte* (Stuttgart, 1979), vol. 3, p. 579.

SUGGESTIONS FOR FURTHER READING

Basic surveys of the Reformation period include **H. J. Grimm, *The Reformation Era, 1500–1650,*** 2d ed. (New York, 1973); **C. Lindberg,** *The European Reformations* (Cambridge, Mass., 1996); **D. L. Jensen, *Reformation Europe*** (Lexington, Mass., 1981); **G. R. Elton *Reformation Europe, 1517–1559*** (Cleveland, Ohio, 1963); **J. D. Tracy, *Europe's Reformations, 1450–1650*** (Oxford, 1999); **D. MacCulloch, *The Reformation*** (New York, 2003); and **E. Cameron, *The European Reformation*** (New York, 1991). The significance of the Protestant Reformation is examined in **S. Ozment, *Protestants: The Birth of a Revolution*** (New York, 1992). A brief but very useful introduction to the theology of the Reformation can be found in **A. McGrath, *Reformation Thought: An Introduction,*** 3d rev. ed. (Oxford, 1999).

The development of humanism outside Italy is examined in **C. G. Nauert Jr., *Humanism and the Culture of Renaissance Europe*** (Cambridge, 1995). On Erasmus, see **J. McConica, *Erasmus*** (Oxford, 1991).

The classic account of Martin Luther's life is **R. Bainton, *Here I Stand: A Life of Martin Luther*** (New York, 1950). More recent works include **H. A. Oberman, *Luther*** (New York, 1992), and **J. M. Kittelson, *Luther the Reformer: The Story of the Man and His Career*** (Minneapolis, 1986). See also the brief biography by **M. Marty, *Martin Luther*** (New York, 2004). On the Peasants' War, see especially **P. Blickle, *The Revolution of 1525: The German Peasants' War from a New Perspective*** (Baltimore, 1981). On the role of Charles V, see **W. Maltby, *The Reign of Charles V*** (New York, 2002).

The best account of Ulrich Zwingli is **G. R. Potter, *Zwingli*** (Cambridge, 1976), although **W. P. Stephens's *Zwingli*** (Oxford, 1994) is an important study of the man's ideas. The most comprehensive account of the various groups and individuals who are called Anabaptists is **G. H. Williams, *The Radical Reformation,*** 2d ed. (Kirksville, Mo., 1992).

Two worthwhile surveys of the English Reformation are **A. G. Dickens, *The English Reformation,*** 2d ed. (New York, 1989), and **G. R. Elton, *Reform and Reformation: England, 1509–1558*** (Cambridge, Mass., 1977). On John Calvin, see **A. McGrath, *A Life of John Calvin: A Study in the Shaping of Western Culture*** (Cambridge,

Mass., 1990), and **W. J. Bouwsma,** *John Calvin* (New York, 1988). On the impact of the Reformation on the family, see **J. F. Harrington,** *Reordering Marriage and Society in Reformation Germany* (New York, 1995). **M. E. Wiesner's** *Working Women in Renaissance Germany* (New Brunswick, N.J., 1986) covers primarily the sixteenth century.

Good introductions to the Catholic Reformation can be found in **M. R. O'Connell,** *The Counter-Reformation, 1559–1610* (New York, 1974), and **R. P. Hsia,** *The World of Catholic Renewal, 1540–1770* (Cambridge, 1998). For new perspectives, see **R. Bireley,** *The Refashioning of Catholicism, 1450–1700* (Washington, D.C., 1999), and **J. O'Malley,** *Trent and All That: Renaming Catholicism in the Early Modern Era* (Cambridge, Mass., 2002). On Loyola, see **P. Caravan,** *Ignatius Loyola: A Biography of the Founder of the Jesuits* (San Francisco, 1990). **J. O'Malley,** *The First Jesuits* (Cambridge, Mass., 1995), offers a clear discussion of the founding of the Jesuits.

For good introductions to the French Wars of Religion, see **M. P. Holt,** *The French Wars of Religion, 1562–1629* (Cambridge, 1995), and **R. J. Knecht,** *The French Wars of Religion, 1559–1598,* 2d ed. (New York, 1996). A good history of Spain in the sixteenth century is **J. Lynch,** *Spain, 1516–1598: From Nation-State to World Empire* (Cambridge, Mass., 1994). On Philip II, see **G. Parker,** *Philip II,* 3d ed. (Chicago, 1995). Elizabeth's reign can be examined in two good biographies: **C. Haigh,** *Elizabeth I,* 2d ed. (New York, 1998), and **W. T. MacCaffrey,** *Elizabeth I* (London, 1993). The classic work on the Spanish armada is the beautifully written book *The Armada* by **G. Mattingly** (Boston, 1959).

Thomson NOW! Enter *ThomsonNOW* using the access card that is available for *Western Civilization: A Brief History.* *ThomsonNOW* will help you understand this chapter with lesson plans generated for your needs. In addition, you can read the following documents, and many more, online:

Martin Luther, *Letter to the German Nobility, On Christian Liberty* and *Twelve Articles*
John Calvin, *Institutes of the Christian Religion*
Pope Paul III, Canons on Justification
King Henry IV, Edict of Nantes

WESTERN CIVILIZATION RESOURCES

Visit the Web site for *Western Civilization: A Brief History* for resources specific to this book:

http://www.thomsonedu.com/history/spielvogel

For a variety of tools to help you succeed in this course, visit the Western Civilization Resource Center at

http://history.wadsworth.com/spielvogel

Included are quizzes, images, documents, interactive simulations, maps and timelines, movie explorations, and a wealth of other sources.

EUROPE AND THE WORLD: NEW ENCOUNTERS, 1500–1800

A late-sixteenth-century map of the Americas featuring Columbus, Vespucci, Magellan, and Pizarro

Knud Petersen/Bildarchiv Preussischer Kulturbesitz/Art Resource, NY (Staatliche Museen zu Berlin)

WHILE MANY EUROPEANS were occupied with the problems of dynastic expansion and religious reform, others were taking voyages that propelled Europeans far beyond the medieval walls in which they had been enclosed for almost a thousand years. One of these adventurers was the Portuguese explorer Ferdinand Magellan. Convinced that he could find a sea passage to Asia through America, Magellan persuaded the king of Spain to finance an exploratory voyage. On August 10, 1519, Magellan set sail on the Atlantic with five ships and a Spanish crew of 277 men. After a stormy and difficult crossing of the ocean, Magellan's fleet moved down the coast of South America, searching for the strait that would take him through. His Spanish ship captains thought he was crazy: "The fool is obsessed with his search for a strait," one remarked. "On the flame of his ambition he will crucify us all." At last, in October 1520, he found it, passing through a narrow waterway (later named the Strait of Magellan) and emerging into an unknown ocean that he called the Pacific Sea. Magellan reckoned that it would then be a short distance to the Spice Islands of the East, but he was badly mistaken. Week after week, he and his crew sailed on across the Pacific as their food supplies dwindled. According to one account, "When their last biscuit had gone, they scraped the maggots out of the casks, mashed them and served them as gruel. They made cakes out of sawdust soaked with the urine of rats—the rats themselves, as delicacies, had long since been hunted to extinction." At last they reached the Philippines (named after King Philip II of Spain), where Magellan met his death at the hands of the natives. Although only one of his original fleet of five ships survived and returned to Spain, Magellan is still remembered as the first person to circumnavigate the world.

At the beginning of the sixteenth century, European adventurers like Magellan had begun launching small fleets into the vast reaches of the Atlantic Ocean. They were hardly aware that they were beginning a new era, not only for Europe, but for the peoples of Asia, Africa, and the Americas as well. Nevertheless, the voyages of these Europeans marked the beginning of a process that led to radical changes in the political, economic, and cultural life of the entire world.

Between 1500 and 1800, European power engulfed the globe. In the Americas, Europeans established colonies that spread their laws, religions, and cultures. In the island regions of Southeast Asia, Europeans firmly implanted their rule. In Africa and other parts of Asia, their trading activities dramatically affected the lifeways of the local peoples.◆

On the Brink of a New World

Never has the dynamic and at times ruthless energy of Western civilization been more apparent than during its sixteenth-century expansion into the rest of the world. By then the Atlantic seaboard had become the center of a commercial activity that raised Portugal and Spain and later the Dutch Republic, England, and France to prominence. Global expansion was a crucial factor in Europe's transition from the agrarian economy of the Middle Ages to a commercial and industrial capitalistic system that survives to this day. Expansion also led Europeans into new and lasting contacts with non-European peoples that inaugurated a new interactive age of world history in the sixteenth century.

The Motives for Expansion

Europeans had long been attracted to lands outside of Europe. Indeed, a large body of fantasy literature about "other worlds" blossomed in the Middle Ages. In *The Travels of John Mandeville* in the fourteenth century, the author spoke of lands (which he had never seen) filled with precious stones and gold. Other lands were more frightening, "where the folk be great giants of twenty-eight foot long, or thirty foot long. . . . And they eat more gladly man's flesh than any other flesh," as well as lands farther north full of "cruel and evil women. And they have precious stones in their eyes. And they be of that kind that if they behold any

man with wrath they slay him at once with the beholding."[1] Other writers spoke of mysterious Christian kingdoms: the magical kingdom of Prester John in Africa and a Christian community in southern India that was supposedly founded by Thomas, the apostle of Jesus.

Although Muslim control of Central Asia cut Europe off from the countries farther east, the Mongol conquests in the thirteenth century had reopened the doors. The most famous medieval travelers to the East were the Polos of Venice. Niccolò and Maffeo, merchants from Venice, accompanied by Niccolò's son Marco, undertook the lengthy journey to the court of the great Mongol ruler Khubilai Khan (1259–1294) in 1271. An account of Marco's experiences, the *Travels*, proved to be the most informative of all the descriptions of Asia by medieval European travelers. Others followed the Polos, but in the fourteenth century, the conquests of the Ottoman Turks and then the breakup of the Mongol Empire reduced Western traffic to the East. With the closing of the overland routes, a number of people in Europe became interested in the possibility of reaching Asia by sea to gain access to the spices and other precious resources of the region. Christopher Columbus had a copy of Marco Polo's *Travels* in his possession when he began to envision his epoch-making voyage across the Atlantic Ocean.

An economic motive thus loomed large in Renaissance European expansion. Merchants, adventurers, and government officials had high hopes of finding precious metals and new areas of trade. Many European explorers and conquerors did not hesitate to express their desire for material gain. One Spanish conquistador explained that he and his kind went to the New World to "serve God and His Majesty, to give light to those who were in darkness, and to grow rich, as all men desire to do."[2]

This statement expresses another major reason for the overseas voyages—religious zeal. Hernán Cortés, the conqueror of Mexico, asked his Spanish rulers if it was not their duty to ensure that the native Mexicans "are introduced into and instructed in their holy Catholic faith."[3] Spiritual and secular affairs were closely intertwined in the sixteenth century. No doubt grandeur and glory, as well as plain intellectual curiosity and the spirit of adventure, also played some role in the European expansion.

The Means for Expansion

If "God, glory, and gold" were the motives, what made the voyages possible? First of all, the expansion of Europe was connected to the growth of centralized monarchies during the Renaissance. By the second half of the fifteenth century, European monarchies had increased both their authority and their resources and were in a position to turn their energies beyond their borders. At the same time, by the end of the fifteenth century, European states had achieved a level of wealth and technology that enabled them to undertake a regular series of voyages beyond Europe. Europeans had developed remarkably seaworthy ships and reliable navigational aids, such as the compass and astrolabe (an instrument used to determine the position of heavenly bodies).

One of the most important world maps available to Europeans at the end of the fifteenth century was that of Ptolemy, an astronomer of the second century A.D. Ptolemy's work, the *Geography*, had been known to Arab geographers as early as the eighth century, but it was not until the fifteenth century that a Latin translation was made. Printed editions of Ptolemy's *Geography*, which contained his world map, became available in 1477. Ptolemy's map showed the world as spherical with three major landmasses—Europe, Asia, and Africa—and only two oceans. In addition to showing the oceans as considerably smaller than the landmasses, Ptolemy had also dramatically underestimated the circumference of the earth, which led Columbus and other adventurers to believe that it would be feasible to sail west from Europe to Asia.

New Horizons: The Portuguese and Spanish Empires

Portugal took the lead in the European age of expansion when it began to explore the coast of Africa under the sponsorship of Prince Henry the Navigator (1394–1460). His motives were a blend of seeking a Christian kingdom as an ally against the Muslims, acquiring trade opportunities for Portugal, and extending Christianity.

The Development of a Portuguese Maritime Empire

In 1419, Portuguese fleets began probing southward along the western coast of Africa. After Prince Henry's death in 1460, exploration slowed, but Portuguese ships gradually crept down the African coast until Bartholomeu Dias finally rounded the Cape of Good Hope at the southern tip of Africa in 1488 (see Map 14.1). Ten years later, a fleet under the command of Vasco da Gama rounded the cape and stopped at several ports controlled by Muslim merchants along the coast of East Africa. Da Gama's fleet then crossed the Arabian Sea and reached the port of Calicut on the southwestern coast of India on May 18, 1498. Upon his arrival, da Gama announced to his surprised hosts that he had come in search of "Christians and spices." He did not find the first, but he did find the second. Although he lost two ships en route, da Gama's remaining vessels returned to Europe with their holds filled with ginger and cinnamon, a cargo that earned the investors a profit of several thousand percent. Da Gama's successful voyage marked the beginning of an all-water trade route to India. By 1501, annual Portuguese fleets to India were making serious inroads into the Mediterranean trade of the Venetians and Turks.

Under the direction of officials known as viceroys, Portugal now created an overseas empire. Most important of the viceroys was Alfonso d'Albuquerque (c. 1462–1515), a tough nobleman who took the lead in establishing a ring of commercial-military bases centered at Goa, just north of the Malabar Coast of India. The Portuguese also reached beyond India by taking the island of Macao at the mouth of the Pearl River in China. The Portuguese empire remained a limited one of enclaves or trading posts on the coasts of India and China. The Portuguese did not have the power, the people, or the desire to colonize the Asian regions.

Why were the Portuguese so successful? Basically, it was a matter of guns and seamanship. By the end of the

Ptolemy's World Map. Contained in the Latin translation of Ptolemy's *Geography* was this world map, which did not become available to Europeans until the late 1400s. Scholars quickly accepted it as the most accurate map of its time. The twelve "wind-faces," meant to show wind currents around the earth, were a fifteenth-century addition to the ancient map.

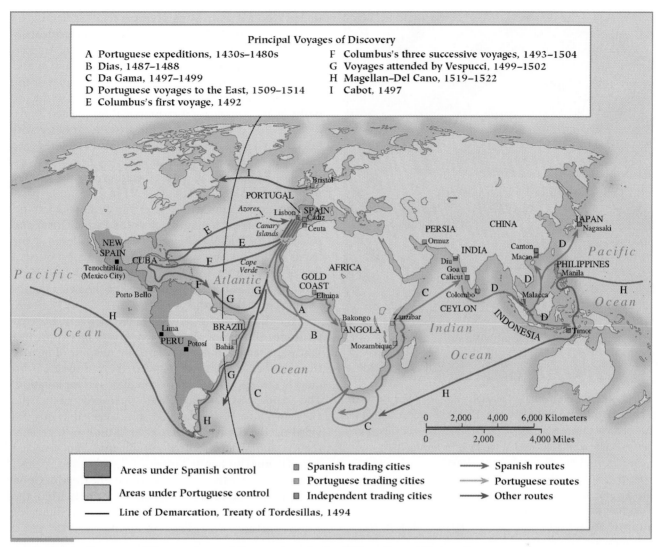

Principal Voyages of Discovery

A Portuguese expeditions, 1430s–1480s
B Dias, 1487–1488
C Da Gama, 1497–1499
D Portuguese voyages to the East, 1509–1514
E Columbus's first voyage, 1492

F Columbus's three successive voyages, 1493–1504
G Voyages attended by Vespucci, 1499–1502
H Magellan–Del Cano, 1519–1522
I Cabot, 1497

Areas under Spanish control
Areas under Portuguese control
Line of Demarcation, Treaty of Tordesillas, 1494

Spanish trading cities
Portuguese trading cities
Independent trading cities

Spanish routes
Portuguese routes
Other routes

MAP 14.1   European Discoveries and Possessions in the Fifteenth and Sixteenth Centuries.   Desire for wealth was the main motivation of the early explorers, although spreading Christianity was also an important factor. Portugal under Prince Henry the Navigator initiated the first voyages in the early fifteenth century; Spain's explorations began at the century's end. ❓ Which regions of the globe were primarily explored by Portugal, and which were the main focus of Spain's voyages? 🌐 **View an animated version of this map or related maps at** http://thomsonedu.com/history/spielvogel

sixteenth century, Portuguese fleets were heavily armed and able not only to intimidate but also to inflict severe defeats if necessary on local naval and land forces. The Portuguese did not possess a monopoly on the use of firearms and explosives, but their effective use of naval technology, heavy guns, and tactics gave them military superiority over lightly armed rivals that they were able to exploit until the arrival of other European forces—the English, Dutch, and French—in the seventeenth century.

Voyages to the New World

While the Portuguese were seeking access to the spice trade of the Indies by sailing eastward through the Indian Ocean, the Spanish were attempting to reach the same destination by sailing westward across the Atlantic. Although the Spanish came to overseas discovery and exploration after the initial efforts of Henry the Navigator, their greater resources enabled them to establish a far grander overseas empire quite different from that of the Portuguese.

An important figure in the history of Spanish exploration was an Italian known as Christopher Columbus (1451–1506). Europeans were aware that the world was round but had little understanding of its circumference or the size of the continent of Asia. Convinced that the earth was smaller and Asia larger than people thought, Columbus believed that Asia could be reached by sailing directly west instead of traveling around Africa. Rebuffed by the Portuguese, he persuaded Queen Isabella of Spain to finance his exploratory expedition.

Christopher Columbus. Columbus was an Italian explorer who worked for the queen of Spain. He has become a symbol for two entirely different perspectives. To some, he was a great and heroic explorer who discovered the New World; to others, especially in Latin America, he was responsible for beginning a process of invasion that led to the destruction of an entire way of life. Because Columbus was never painted in his lifetime, the numerous portraits of him are mostly fanciful rather than accurate. The portrait shown here was probably done by the Italian painter Ridolfo Ghirlandaio.

With three ships, the *Santa María*, the *Niña*, and the *Pinta*, and a crew of ninety men, Columbus set sail on August 3, 1492. On October 12, he reached the Bahamas and then went on to explore the coastline of Cuba and the northern shores of Hispaniola (present-day Haiti and the Dominican Republic). Columbus believed that he had reached Asia, and in his reports to Queen Isabella and King Ferdinand upon his return to Spain, he assured them not only that he would eventually find gold but also that they had a golden opportunity to convert the natives—whom Columbus persisted in calling "Indians"—to Christianity. In three subsequent voyages (1493, 1498, 1502), Columbus sought in vain to find a route to the Asian mainland. In his four voyages, Columbus landed on all the major islands of the Caribbean and the mainland of Central America, still convinced that he had reached the Indies in Asia.

Although Columbus clung to his belief until his death, other explorers soon realized that he had discovered a new frontier altogether. State-sponsored explorers joined the race to the New World. A Venetian seaman, John Cabot, explored the New England coastline of the Americas

under a license from King Henry VII of England. The continent of South America was discovered accidentally by the Portuguese sea captain Pedro Cabral in 1500. Amerigo Vespucci, a Florentine, accompanied several voyages and wrote a series of letters describing the geography of the New World. The publication of these letters led to the use of the name "America" (after Amerigo) for the new lands.

The first two decades of the sixteenth century witnessed numerous overseas voyages that explored the eastern coasts of both North and South America. Perhaps the most dramatic of all these expeditions was the journey of Ferdinand Magellan (1480–1521) in 1519. After passing through the strait named after him at the southern tip of South America, he sailed across the Pacific Ocean and reached the Philippines, where he met his death at the hands of the natives. Although only one of his original fleet of five ships survived and returned to Spain, Magellan's name is still associated with the first known circumnavigation of the earth.

The Europeans referred to the newly discovered territories as the New World, even though they contained flourishing civilizations populated by millions of people. But America was indeed new to the Europeans, who quickly saw opportunities for conquest and exploitation. The Spanish, in particular, were interested because the 1494 Treaty of Tordesillas had somewhat arbitrarily divided up the newly discovered world into separate Portuguese and Spanish spheres of influence, and it turned out that most of South America fell within the Spanish sphere. Hereafter the route east around the Cape of Good Hope was to be reserved for the Portuguese while the route across the Atlantic (except for the eastern hump of South America) was assigned to Spain.

The Spanish Empire in the New World

The Spanish **conquistadors** were hardy individuals motivated by a typical sixteenth-century blend of glory, greed, and religious zeal. Although authorized by the Castilian crown, these groups were financed and outfitted privately, not by the government. Their superior weapons, organizational skills, and determination brought the conquistadors incredible success. They also benefited from rivalries among the native peoples and the decimation of the native peoples by European diseases.

Early Civilizations in Mesoamerica   Before the Spaniards arrived in the New World, Mesoamerica (modern Mexico and Central America) had already hosted a number of flourishing civilizations. Beginning around A.D. 300, a people known as the Maya had developed on the Yucatán peninsula one of the most sophisticated civilizations in the Americas. The Maya built splendid temples and pyramids, were accomplished artists, and devised a sophisticated calendar, as accurate as any in existence in the world at that time. The Maya were an agrarian people who cleared the dense rain forests, farmed, and created a

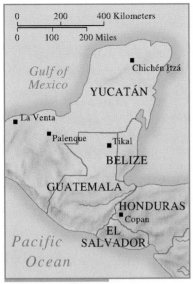
Lands of the Maya

patchwork of city-states. Mayan civilization came to include much of Central America and southern Mexico. For a number of reasons, Mayan civilization began to decline around 800 and collapsed within a century.

Sometime during the early twelfth century A.D., a people known as the Aztecs began a long migration that brought them to the Valley of Mexico. They established their capital at Tenochtitlán, on an island in the middle of Lake Texcoco (now the location of Mexico City). For the next hundred years, the Aztecs built their city, constructing temples, other public buildings, houses, and causeways of stone across Lake Texcoco to the north, south, and west, linking the many islands to the mainland.

The Aztecs were outstanding warriors, and while they were building their capital city, they also set out to bring the surrounding area under their control. By the early fifteenth century, they had become the leading city-state in the lake region. During the remainder of that century, the Aztecs consolidated their rule over much of what is modern Mexico, from the Atlantic to the Pacific Oceans and as far south as the Guatemalan border. The new kingdom was not a centralized state but a collection of semi-independent territories governed by local lords.

The Spanish Conquest of the Aztec Empire In 1519, a Spanish expedition under the command of Hernán Cortés (1485–1547) landed at Veracruz, on the Gulf of Mexico. He marched to the city of Tenochtitlán (see the box on p. 264) at the head of a small contingent of troops (550 soldiers and 16 horses); as he went, he made alliances with city-states that had tired of the oppressive rule of the Aztecs. Especially important was Tlaxcala, a state that the Aztecs had not been able to conquer. In November, Cortés arrived at Tenochtitlán, where he received a friendly welcome from the Aztec monarch Moctezuma (often called Montezuma). At first, Moctezuma believed that

his visitor was a representative of Quetzalcoatl, the god who had departed from his homeland centuries before and had promised that he would return.

But the Spaniards quickly wore out their welcome. The took Moctezuma hostage and proceeded to pillage the city. In the fall of 1520, one year after Cortés had arrived, the local population revolted and drove the invaders from the city. Many of the Spaniards were killed, but the Aztecs soon experienced new disasters. As one Aztec related, "At about the time that the Spaniards had fled from Mexico, there came a great sickness, a pestilence, the smallpox." With no natural immunity to the diseases of Europeans, many Aztecs fell sick and died. Meanwhile, Cortés received fresh soldiers from his new allies; the state of Tlaxcala alone provided fifty thousand warriors. After four months, the city capitulated. And then the destruction began. The pyramids, temples, and palaces were leveled, and the stones were used to build Spanish government buildings and churches. The rivers and canals were filled in. The mighty Aztec Empire on mainland Mexico was no more. Between 1531 and 1550, the Spanish gained control of northern Mexico.

The Inca and the Spanish In the late fourteenth century, the Inca were a small community in the area of Cuzco, a city located at an altitude of 10,000 feet in the mountains of southern Peru. In the 1440s, however, under the leadership of their powerful ruler Pachakuti,

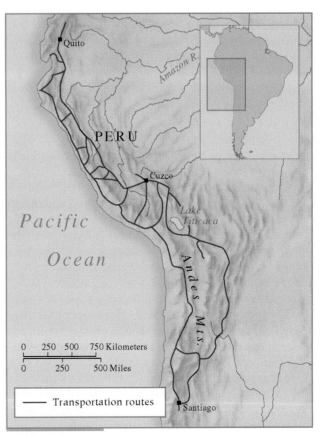
Lands of the Inca

The Aztec Empire

THE SPANISH CONQUISTADOR: CORTÉS AND THE CONQUEST OF MEXICO

*H*ernán Cortés was a minor Spanish nobleman who came to the New World in 1504 to seek his fortune. Contrary to his superior's orders, Cortés waged an independent campaign of conquest and overthrew the Aztec empire of Mexico (1519–1521). Cortés wrote a series of five reports to Emperor Charles V to justify his action. The second report includes a description of Tenochtitlán, the capital of the Aztec Empire. The Spanish conquistador and his men were obviously impressed by this city, awesome in its architecture yet built by people who lacked European technology, such as wheeled vehicles and tools of hard metal.

Cortés's Description of Tenochtitlán

The great city Tenochtitlán is built in the midst of this salt lake, and it is two leagues [about 6 miles] from the heart of the city to any point on the mainland. Four causeways lead to it, all made by hand and some twelve feet wide. The city itself is as large as Seville or Córdoba. The principal streets are very broad and straight, the majority of them being of beaten earth, but a few and at least half the smaller thoroughfares are waterways along which they pass in their canoes. Moreover, even the principal streets have openings at regular distances so that the water can freely pass from one to another, and these openings which are very broad are spanned by great bridges of huge beams, very stoutly put together, so firm indeed that over many of them ten horsemen can ride at once....

The city has many open squares in which markets are continuously held and the general business of buying and selling proceeds. One square in particular is twice as big as that of Salamanca and completely surrounded by arcades where there are daily more than sixty thousand folk buying and selling. Every kind of merchandise such as may be met with in every land is for sale there, whether of food and victuals, or ornaments of gold and silver, or lead, brass, copper, tin, precious stones, bones, shells, snails and feathers; limestone for building is likewise sold there, stone both rough and polished, bricks burnt and unburnt, wood of all kinds and in all stages of preparation....There is a street of herb-sellers where there are all manner of roots and medicinal plants that are found in the land. There are houses as it were of apothecaries where they sell medicines made from these herbs, both for drinking and for use as ointments and salves....

Finally, to avoid [excess] in telling all the wonders of this city, I will simply say that the manner of living among the people is very similar to that in Spain, and considering that this is a barbarous nation shut off from a knowledge of the true God or communication with enlightened nations, one may well marvel at the orderliness and good government which is everywhere maintained.

The actual service of Moctezuma and those things which call for admiration by the greatness and state would take so long to describe that I assure your Majesty I do not know where to begin with any hope of ending. For as I have already said, what could there be more astonishing than that a barbarous monarch such as he should have reproductions made in gold, silver, precious stones, and feathers of all things to be found in his land, and so perfectly reproduced that there is no goldsmith or silversmith in the world who could better them.

_____

What does Cortés focus on in his description of this Aztec city? Why do you think he felt justified in overthrowing the Aztec Empire?

---

the Inca launched a campaign of conquest that eventually brought the entire region under their control.

Pachakuti created a highly centralized state. The capital of Cuzco was transformed from a city of mud and thatch into an imposing city of stone. Under Pachakuti and his immediate successors, Topa Inca and Huayna Inca (the word *Inca* means "ruler"), the boundaries of the Inca Empire were extended as far as Ecuador, central Chile, and the edge of the Amazon basin. The empire included perhaps twelve million people.

The Inca were great builders. One major project was a system of 24,800 miles of roads that extended from the border of modern-day Colombia to a point south of modern-day Santiago, Chile. Two major roadways extended in a north-south direction, one through the Andes Mountains and the other along the coast, with connecting routes between them. Various types of bridges, including some of the finest examples of suspension bridges in premodern times, were built over ravines and waterways.

The Inca Empire was still flourishing when the first Spanish expeditions arrived in the area. In December 1530, Francisco Pizarro (c. 1475–1541) landed on the Pacific coast of South America with a band of about 180 men, but like Cortés, he had steel weapons, gunpowder, and horses, none of which were familiar to his hosts. Pizarro was also lucky because the Inca Empire had already succumbed to an epidemic of smallpox. Like the Aztecs, the Inca had no immunities to European diseases, and all too soon, smallpox was devastating entire villages. In another stroke of good fortune for Pizarro, even the Incan emperor was a victim. Upon the emperor's death, two sons claimed the throne, leading to a civil war. Pizarro took advantage of the situation by seizing Atahualpa, whose forces had just defeated his brother's. Armed only with stones, arrows, and light spears, Incan soldiers provided little challenge to the charging horses of the Spanish, let alone their guns and cannons. After executing Atahualpa, Pizarro and his soldiers, aided by their Incan allies, marched

The Portuguese and Spanish Empires in the Sixteenth Century

Bartholomeu Dias sails around the tip of Africa	1488
Voyages of Columbus	1492–1502
Treaty of Tordesillas	1494
Vasco da Gama lands at Calicut in India	1498
Portuguese ships land in southern China	1514
Magellan's voyage around the world	1519–1522
Spanish conquest of Mexico	1519–1522
Pizarro's conquest of the Inca	1530–1535

on Cuzco and captured the Incan capital. By 1535, Pizarro had established a capital at Lima for a new colony of the Spanish Empire.

Administration of the Spanish Empire Spanish policy toward the native peoples of the New World was a combination of confusion, misguided paternalism, and cruel exploitation. Whereas the conquistadors made decisions based on expediency and their own interests, Queen Isabella declared the natives to be subjects of Castile and instituted the Spanish *encomienda,* a system that permitted the conquering Spaniards to collect tribute from the natives and use them as laborers. In return, the holders of an *encomienda* were supposed to protect the Indians, pay them wages, and supervise their spiritual needs. In practice, this meant that the settlers were free to implement the paternalistic system of the government as they pleased. Three thousand miles from Spain, Spanish settlers largely ignored their government and brutally used the Indians to pursue their own economic interests. Indians were put to work on plantations and in the lucrative gold and silver mines. Forced labor, starvation, and especially disease took a fearful toll of Indian lives. The natives were ravaged by the smallpox, measles, and typhus that came with the explorers and the conquistadors—perhaps 30 to 40 percent of them died. Hispaniola was badly devastated: of an initial population of 100,000 when Columbus arrived in 1493, only 300 natives survived by 1570.

In the New World, the Spanish developed an administrative system based on viceroys. Spanish possessions were initially divided into two major administrative units: New Spain (Mexico, Central America, and the Caribbean islands), with its center at Mexico City, and Peru (western South America), governed by a viceroy in Lima. Each viceroy served as the king's chief civil and military officer.

By papal agreement, the Catholic monarchs of Spain were given extensive rights over ecclesiastical affairs in the New World. They could appoint all bishops and clergy, build churches, collect fees, and supervise the affairs of the various religious orders that sought to Christianize the heathen. Catholic missionaries—especially the Dominicans, Franciscans, and Jesuits—fanned out across the Spanish Empire, where they converted and baptized hundreds of thousands of Indians in the early years of the conquest. Soon after the missionaries came the establishment of dioceses, parishes, cathedrals, schools, and hospitals—all the trappings of civilized European society.

New Rivals on the World Stage

Portugal and Spain had been the first Atlantic nations to take advantage of the Age of Exploration, starting in the late fifteenth century, and both had become great colonial powers. In the seventeenth century, however, their European neighbors to the north—first the Dutch and then the French and British—moved to replace the Portuguese and Spanish and create their own colonial empires. The new rivals and their rivalry soon had an impact on much of the rest of the world—in Africa, Asia, and the Americas.

Africa: The Slave Trade

Although the primary objective of the Portuguese in sailing around Africa was to find a sea route to the Spice Islands, they soon discovered that profits could be made in Africa itself. So did other Europeans who also realized the financial benefits of trade in slaves.

Of course, traffic in slaves was not new, and at first, the Portuguese simply replaced European slaves with African ones. During the second half of the fifteenth century, about a thousand slaves were taken to Portugal each year. Most wound up serving as domestic servants for affluent families in Europe. But the discovery of the Americas in the 1490s and the planting of sugarcane in South America and on the islands of the Caribbean changed the situation drastically.

Cane sugar had first been introduced to Europeans from the Middle East during the Crusades. During the sixteenth century, sugarcane plantations were set up along the eastern coast of Brazil and on several islands in the Caribbean. Because the growing of cane sugar demands both skill and large quantities of labor, the new plantations required more workers than could be provided by the small native population in the New World, decimated by diseases imported from the Old World. Since the climate and soil of much of West Africa were not conducive to the cultivation of sugar, African slaves began to be shipped to Brazil and the Caribbean to work on the plantations. The first were sent from Portugal, but in 1518, a Spanish ship carried the first boatload of African slaves directly from Africa to the New World.

Growth in the Slave Trade During the next two centuries, the trade in slaves grew dramatically and became part of the **triangular trade** that characterized the new Atlantic economy connecting Europe, Africa, and the American continents (see Map 14.2). European merchant ships (primarily those of Britain, France, Spain, Portugal, and the Dutch Republic) carried European manufactured

MAP 14.2 **Triangular Trade in the Atlantic Economy.** As the trade in slaves grew, it became a part of the triangular trade route that characterized the Atlantic economy, involving the exchange of goods and slaves between the western coast of Europe, the slave depots on the African coast, and the ports of North and South America. **?** What were the important source regions for slaves, and where were most of the slaves taken? View an animated version of this map or related maps at http://thomsonedu.com/history/spielvogel

goods, such as guns, gin, and cloth, to Africa, where they were traded for cargoes of slaves. The slaves were then shipped to the Americas and sold. European merchants then bought tobacco, molasses, sugar, rum, coffee, and raw cotton and shipped them back to Europe to be sold in European markets.

An estimated 275,000 enslaved Africans were exported to other countries during the sixteenth century, with two thousand going annually to the Americas alone. In the seventeenth century, the total climbed to over a million and jumped to six million in the eighteenth century, when the trade spread from West and Central Africa to East Africa. Altogether as many as ten million African slaves were transported to the Americas between the early sixteenth and nineteenth centuries.

One reason for the astonishing numbers of slaves, of course, was the high death rate. The arduous journey of slaves from Africa to the Americas became known as the **Middle Passage,** the middle leg of the triangular trade route. African slaves were closely packed into cargo ships,

The Sale of Slaves. The slave trade was one of the most profitable commercial enterprises of the eighteenth century. This painting shows a Western slave merchant negotiating with a local African leader over slaves at Gorée, Senegal, in West Africa in the late eighteenth century.

300 to 450 per ship, and chained in holds without sanitary facilities or enough space to stand up; there they remained during the voyage to America, which took at least 100 days (see the box on p. 268). Mortality rates averaged 10 percent; longer journeys due to storms or adverse winds resulted in even higher death rates. The Africans who survived the journey were subject to high death rates from diseases to which they had little or no immunity.

Before the coming of Europeans in the fifteenth century, most slaves in Africa were prisoners of war. When Europeans first began to take part in the slave trade, they bought slaves from local African merchants at slave markets in return for gold, guns, or other European goods such as textiles or copper or iron utensils.

Local slave traders originally obtained their supply from regions nearby, but as demand increased, they had to move farther inland to find their victims. In a few cases, local rulers became concerned about the impact of the slave trade on the well-being of their societies. In a letter to the king of Portugal in 1526, King Affonso of Congo (Bakongo) complained, "So great, Sire, is the corruption and licentiousness that our country is being completely depopulated."[4] Protests from Africans were generally ignored by Europeans as well as by other Africans.

Effects of the Slave Trade   The effects of the slave trade varied from area to area. Of course, it had tragic effects on the lives of the slaves and their families. There was also an economic price as the importation of cheap manufactured goods from Europe undermined local cottage industries and forced countless families into poverty. The slave trade also led to the depopulation of some areas and deprived many African communities of their youngest and strongest men and women.

The political effects of the slave trade were devastating. The need to maintain a constant supply of slaves led to increased warfare and violence as African chiefs and their followers, armed with guns acquired from the proceeds of the trade in slaves, increased their raids and wars on neighboring peoples. A few Europeans lamented what they were doing to traditional African societies. One Dutch slave trader remarked, "From us they have learned strife, quarrelling, drunkenness, trickery, theft, unbridled desire for what is not one's own, misdeeds unknown to them before, and the accursed lust for gold."[5] But the slave trade continued unabated.

Despite a rising chorus of humanitarian sentiments from European intellectuals, the use of black slaves remained largely acceptable to Western society. Europeans continued to view blacks as inferior beings fit primarily for slave labor. Not until the Society of Friends, known as the Quakers, began to criticize slavery in the 1770s and exclude from their church any member adhering to slave trafficking did European sentiment against slavery begin to build. Even then, it was not until the radical stage of the French Revolution in the 1790s that the French abolished slavery. The British followed suit in 1807. Despite the elimination of the African source, slavery continued in the newly formed United States until the 1860s.

The West in Southeast Asia

Portugal's efforts to dominate the trade of Southeast Asia were never totally successful. The Portuguese lacked both the numbers and the wealth to overcome local resistance and colonize the Asian regions. Portugal's empire was simply too large and Portugal too small to maintain it. By the end of the sixteenth century, new European rivals had entered the fray.

One of them was Spain. The Spanish had established themselves in the region when Magellan had landed in the Philippines. Although he was killed there, the Spanish were able to gain control over the Philippines, which eventually became a major Spanish base in the trade across the Pacific. Spanish ships carried silk and other luxury goods to Mexico in return for silver from the mines of Mexico.

The primary threat to the Portuguese Empire in Southeast Asia, however, came with the arrival of the Dutch and the English, who were better financed than the Portuguese. The shift in power began in the early seventeenth century when the Dutch seized a Portuguese fort in the Moluccas and then gradually pushed the Portuguese out of the spice trade. During the next fifty years, the Dutch occupied most of the Portuguese coastal forts along the trade routes throughout the Indian Ocean, including the island of Ceylon (today's Sri Lanka) and Malacca. The aggressive Dutch drove the English traders out of the spice market as well.

The Dutch also began to consolidate their political and military control over the entire area. On the island of Java, where they had established a fort at Batavia (modern Jakarta) in 1619, the Dutch found that it was necessary to bring the inland regions under their control to protect their position. On Java and the neighboring island of Sumatra, the Dutch East India Company established pepper plantations, which soon became the source of massive profits for Dutch merchants in Amsterdam. By the end of the eighteenth century, the Dutch had

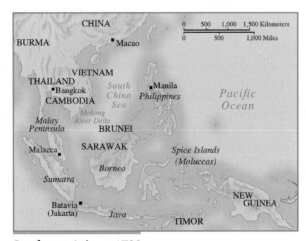

Southeast Asia, c. 1700

THE ATLANTIC SLAVE TRADE

One of the most odious practices of early modern Western society was the Atlantic slave trade, which reached its height in the eighteenth century. Blacks were transported in densely packed cargo ships from the western coast of Africa to the Americas to work as slaves in the plantation economy. This excerpt presents a criticism of the slave trade from an anonymous French writer.

Diary of a Citizen

As soon as the ships have lowered their anchors off the coast of Guinea, the price at which the captains have decided to buy the captives is announced to the Negroes who buy prisoners from various princes and sell them to Europeans. Presents are sent to the sovereign who rules over that particular part of the coast, and permission to trade is given. Immediately the slaves are brought by inhuman brokers like so many victims dragged to a sacrifice. White men who covet that portion of the human race receive them in a little house they have erected on the shore, where they have entrenched themselves with two pieces of cannon and twenty guards. As soon as the bargain is concluded, the Negro is put in chains and led aboard the vessel, where he meets his fellow sufferers....

The vessel sets sail for the Antilles, and the Negroes are chained in a hold of the ship, a kind of lugubrious prison where the light of day does not penetrate, but into which the air is introduced by means of a pump. Twice a day some disgusting food is distributed to them. Their consuming sorrow and the sad state to which they are reduced would make them commit suicide if they were not deprived of all the means for an attempt upon their lives. Without any kind of clothing it would be difficult to conceal from the watchful eyes of the sailors in charge any instrument apt to alleviate their despair. The fear of a revolt, such as sometimes happens on the voyage from Guinea, is the basis of a common concern and produces as many guards as there are men in the crew. The slightest noise or a secret conversation among two Negroes is punished with utmost severity. All in all, the voyage is made in a continuous state of alarm on the part of the white men, who fear a revolt, and in a cruel state of uncertainty on the part of the Negroes, who do not know the fate awaiting them.

When the vessel arrives at a port in the Antilles, they are taken to a warehouse where they are displayed, like any merchandise, to the eyes of buyers. The plantation owner pays according to the age, strength, and health of the Negro he is buying. He has him taken to his plantation, and there he is delivered to an overseer who then and there becomes his tormentor. In order to domesticate him, the Negro is granted a few days of rest in his new place, but soon he is given a hoe and a sickle and made to join a work gang. Then he ceases to wonder about his fate; he understands that only labor is demanded of him. But he does not know yet how excessive this labor will be. As a matter of fact, his work begins at dawn and does not end before nightfall; it is interrupted for only two hours at dinnertime. The food a full-grown Negro is given each week consists of two pounds of salt beef or cod and two pots of tapioca meal.

What does this account reveal about the nature of slave trade practices and white attitudes toward blacks in the eighteenth century?

---

succeeded in bringing almost the entire Indonesian archipelago under their control.

The arrival of the Europeans had less impact on mainland Southeast Asia, where strong monarchies in Burma, Siam (modern Thailand), and Vietnam resisted foreign encroachment. In the sixteenth century, the Portuguese established limited trade relations with several mainland states, including Siam, Burma, Vietnam, and the remnants of the old Angkor kingdom in Cambodia. By the early seventeenth century, other nations had followed and had begun to compete actively for trade and missionary privileges. In general, however, these states were able to unite and drive the Europeans out.

In Vietnam, the arrival of Western merchants and missionaries coincided with a period of internal conflict among ruling groups in the country. After their arrival in the mid-seventeenth century, the European powers began to take sides in local politics, with the Portuguese and the Dutch supporting rival factions. The Europeans also set up trading posts for their merchants, but by the end of the seventeenth century, when it became clear that economic opportunities were limited, most of them were abandoned. French missionaries attempted to remain, but their efforts were blocked by the authorities, who viewed converts to Catholicism as a threat to the prestige of the Vietnamese emperor (see the box on p. 270).

The French and British in India

When a Portuguese fleet arrived at the port of Calicut in the spring of 1498, the Indian subcontinent was divided into a number of Hindu and Muslim kingdoms. But it was on the verge of a new era of unity that would be brought about by a foreign dynasty called the Mughals. The founders of the Mughal Empire were not natives of India but came from the mountainous region north of the Ganges River valley. The founder of the dynasty, Babur, had an illustrious background. His father was descended from the great Asian conqueror Tamerlane; his mother, from the Mongol conqueror Genghis Khan. It was

Europe in Asia. As Europeans began to move into parts of Asia, they reproduced many of the physical surroundings of their homeland in the port cities they built there. This is evident in comparing these two scenes. Below is a seventeenth-century view of Batavia, which the Dutch built as their headquarters on the northern coast of Java in 1619. The scene at the right is from a sixteenth-century engraving of Amsterdam. This Dutch city had become the financial and commercial capital of Europe. It was also the chief port for the ships of the Dutch East India Company, which brought the spices of the East to Europe.

Akbar, Babur's grandson, however, who brought Mughal rule to most of India, creating the greatest Indian empire since the Mauryan dynasty nearly two thousand years earlier.

The Impact of the Western Powers As we have seen, the first Europeans to arrive in India were the Portuguese. At first, Portugal dominated regional trade in the Indian Ocean, but at the end of the sixteenth century, the British and the Dutch arrived on the scene. Soon both powers were competing with Portugal, and with each other, for trading privileges in the region.

During the first half of the seventeenth century, the British presence in India steadily increased. By 1650, British trading posts had been established at Surat (a thriving port along the northwestern coast of India), Fort William (later the great city of Calcutta) near the Bay of Bengal, and Madras on the southeastern coast. From Madras, British ships carried Indian-made cotton goods to the East Indies, where they were bartered for spices, which were shipped back to Britain.

British success in India attracted rivals, including the Dutch and the French. The Dutch abandoned their interests

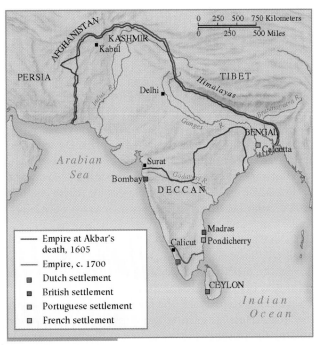

The Mughal Empire

WEST MEETS EAST: AN EXCHANGE OF ROYAL LETTERS

*E*conomic gain was not the only motivation of Western rulers who wished to establish a European presence in the East. In 1681, King Louis XIV of France wrote a letter to the king of Tonkin (the Trinh family head, then acting as viceroy to the Vietnamese emperor) asking permission for Christian missionaries to proselytize in Vietnam. The king of Tonkin politely declined the request.

A Letter to the King of Tonkin

Most high, most excellent, most mighty and most magnanimous Prince, our very dear and good friend, may it please God to increase your greatness with a happy end!

We hear from our subjects who were in your Realm what protection you accorded them. We appreciate this all the more since we have for you all the esteem that one can have for a prince as illustrious through his military valor as he is commendable for the justice which he exercises in his Realm....Since the war which we have had for several years, in which all of Europe had banded together against us, prevented our vessels from going to the Indies, at the present time, when we are at peace after having gained many victories and expanded our Realm through the conquest of several important places, we have immediately given orders to the Royal Company to establish itself in your kingdom as soon as possible....We have given orders to have brought to you some presents which we believe might be agreeable to you. But the one thing in the world which we desire most, both for you and for your Realm, would be to obtain for your subjects who have already embraced the law of the only true God of heaven and earth, the freedom to profess it, since this law is the highest, the noblest, the most sacred and especially the most suitable to have kings reign absolutely over the people.

We are even quite convinced that, if you knew the truths and the maxims which it teaches, you would give first of all to your subjects the glorious example of embracing it. We wish you this incomparable blessing together with a long and happy reign, and we pray God that it may please Him to augment your greatness with the happiest of endings.

Written at Saint-Germain-en-Laye, the 10th day of January; 1681.

Your very dear and good friend,
Louis

Answer from the King of Tonkin to Louis XIV

The King of Tonkin sends to the King of France a letter to express to him his best sentiments....Your communication, which comes from a country which is a thousand leagues away, and which proceeds from the heart as a testimony of your sincerity, merits repeated consideration and infinite praise. Politeness toward strangers is nothing unusual in our country. There is not a stranger who is not well received by us. How then could we refuse a man from France, which is the most celebrated among the kingdoms of the world and which for love of us wishes to frequent us and bring us merchandise? These feelings of fidelity and justice are truly worthy to be applauded. As regards your wish that we should cooperate in propagating your religion, we do not dare to permit it, for there is an ancient custom, introduced by edicts, which formally forbids it. Now, edicts are promulgated only to be carried out faithfully; without fidelity nothing is stable. How could we disdain a well-established custom to satisfy a private friendship?...This then is my letter. We send you herewith a modest gift which we offer you with a glad heart.

This letter was written at the beginning of winter and on a beautiful day.

What are the underlying beliefs and approaches of these two rulers? How are they alike? How are they different?

---

to concentrate on the spice trade in the middle of the seventeenth century, but the French were more persistent and established their own forts on the east coast. For a brief period, the French competed successfully with the British, even capturing the British fort at Madras.

But the British were saved by the military genius of Sir Robert Clive (1725–1774), an aggressive British empire-builder who became the chief representative of the East India Company in India. Eventually, the French were restricted to the fort at Pondicherry and a handful of small territories on the southeastern coast.

In the meantime, Clive began to consolidate British control in Bengal, where the local ruler had attacked Fort William and imprisoned the local British population in the "Black Hole of Calcutta" (an underground prison for holding the prisoners, many of whom died in captivity). In 1757, a small British force numbering about three thousand defeated a Mughal-led army more than ten times its size in the Battle of Plassey. As part of the spoils of victory, the British East India Company received from the now-decrepit Mughal court the authority to collect taxes from lands in the area surrounding Calcutta. During the Seven Years' War (1756–1763), the British forced the French to withdraw completely from India (see Chapter 18).

China

In 1514, a Portuguese fleet dropped anchor off the coast of China. At the time, the Chinese thought little of the event. China appeared to be at the height of its power as the most magnificent civilization on the face of the earth. Its empire stretched from the steppes of Central Asia to the China Sea, from the Gobi Desert to the tropical rain forests of Southeast Asia. From the lofty perspective of the imperial throne in Beijing, the Europeans could only be seen as an unusual form of barbarian. To the Chinese ruler, the rulers of all other countries were simply "younger brothers" of the Chinese emperor, who was viewed as the Son of Heaven.

By the time the Portuguese fleet arrived off the coast of China, the Ming dynasty, which ruled from 1369 to 1644, had already begun a new era of greatness in Chinese history. Under a series of strong rulers, China extended its rule into Mongolia and Central Asia. The Ming even briefly reconquered Vietnam. Along the northern frontier, they strengthened the Great Wall and made peace with the nomadic tribesmen who had troubled China for centuries.

But the days of the Ming dynasty were numbered. After a period of prosperity and growth, the Ming gradually began to decline. During the late sixteenth century, a series of weak rulers led to a period of government corruption. As always, internal problems went hand in hand with unrest along the northern frontier. The Ming had tried to come to terms with the frontier tribes by making alliances with them. One of the alliances was with the Manchus, who lived northeast of the Great Wall in the area known today as Manchuria. In 1644, the Manchus overthrew the last Ming emperor and declared the creation of a new dynasty with the reign title of the Qing (Ch'ing, "Pure"). The Qing were blessed with a series of strong early rulers who pacified the country, corrected the most serious social and economic ills, and restored peace and prosperity. Two Qing monarchs, Kangxi and Qianlong, ruled China for well over a century, from the middle of the seventeenth century to the end of the eighteenth. They were responsible for much of the greatness of Manchu China.

The Qing Empire

Western Inroads Although China was at the height of its power and glory in the mid-eighteenth century, the first signs of the internal decay of the Manchu dynasty were beginning to appear. Unfortunately for China, the decline of the Qing dynasty occurred just as Europe was increasing pressure for more trade. The first conflict had come from the north, where Russian traders sought skins and furs. Formal diplomatic relations between China and Russia were established in 1689 and provided for regular trade between the two countries.

Dealing with the foreigners who arrived by sea was more difficult. By the end of the seventeenth century, the

English had replaced the Portuguese as the dominant force in European trade. Operating through the East India Company, which served as both a trading unit and the administrator of English territories in Asia, the English established their first trading post at Canton in 1699. Over the next decades, trade with China, notably the export of tea and silk to England, increased rapidly. To limit contacts between Europeans and Chinese, the Qing government confined all European traders to a small island just outside the city walls of Canton and permitted them to reside there only from October through March.

By the end of the eighteenth century, some British traders had begun to demand access to other cities along the Chinese coast and insist that the country be opened to British manufactured goods. In 1793, a British mission under Lord Macartney visited Beijing to press for liberalization of trade restrictions. But Emperor Qianlong expressed no interest in British products. The Chinese would later pay for their rejection of the British request (see Chapter 24).

Japan

At the end of the fifteenth century, Japan was at a point of near anarchy, but in the course of the sixteenth century, a number of powerful individuals achieved the unification of Japan. One of them, Tokugawa Ieyasu (1543–1616), took the title of *shogun* ("general") in 1603, an act that initiated the most powerful and longest-lasting of all the Japanese shogunates. The Tokugawa rulers completed the restoration of central authority and remained in power until 1868.

Opening to the West Portuguese traders had landed on the islands of Japan in 1543, and in a few years, Portuguese ships began stopping at Japanese ports on a regular basis to take part in the regional trade between Japan, China, and Southeast Asia. The first Jesuit missionary, Francis Xavier, arrived in 1549 and had some success in converting the local population to Christianity.

Initially, the visitors were welcomed. The curious Japanese were fascinated by tobacco, clocks, eyeglasses, and other European goods, and local nobles were interested in purchasing all types of European weapons and armaments. Japanese rulers found the new firearms especially helpful in defeating their enemies and unifying the islands.

The success of Catholic missionaries, however, created a strong reaction against the presence of Westerners. When missionaries began to interfere in local politics, Tokugawa Ieyasu, newly come to power, expelled them all and sanctioned the persecution of Japanese Christians.

European merchants were the next to go. The government closed the two major foreign trading posts on the island of Hirado and at Nagasaki. Only a small Dutch community in Nagasaki was allowed to remain in Japan. The Dutch, unlike the Spanish and Portuguese, had not allowed missionary activities to interfere with their trade

Arrival of the Portuguese at Nagasaki. Portuguese traders landed accidentally in Japan in 1543. In a few years, they arrived regularly, taking part in a regional trade network between Japan, China, and Southeast Asia. In these panels, done in black lacquer and gold leaf, we see a late-sixteenth-century Japanese interpretation of the first Portuguese landing at Nagasaki.

interests. But the conditions for staying were strict. Dutch ships were allowed to dock at Nagasaki harbor once a year and could remain for only two to three months.

The Americas

In the sixteenth century, Spain and Portugal had established large colonial empires in the Americas. Portugal continued to profit from its empire in Brazil. The Spanish also maintained an enormous South American empire, but Spain's importance as a commercial power declined rapidly in the seventeenth century because of a drop in the output of the silver mines and the poverty of the Spanish monarchy. By the start of the seventeenth century, both Portugal and Spain found themselves facing new challenges to their American empires from the Dutch, British, and French, who increasingly sought to create their own colonial empires in the New World.

The West Indies Both the French and British colonial empires in the New World included large parts of the West Indies. The British held Barbados, Jamaica, and Bermuda, and the French possessed Saint-Domingue, Martinique, and Guadeloupe. On these tropical islands, both the British and the French had developed plantation

economies, worked by African slaves, that produced tobacco, cotton, coffee, and sugar, all products increasingly in demand in Europe.

The "sugar factories," as the sugar plantations in the Caribbean were called, played an especially prominent role. By the 1780s, Jamaica, one of Britain's most important colonies, was producing 50,000 tons of sugar annually with the slave labor of 200,000 blacks. The French colony of Saint-Domingue (later known as Haiti) had 500,000 slaves working on three thousand plantations at the same time. This colony produced 100,000 tons of sugar a year, but at the expense of a high death rate from the brutal treatment of the slaves.

British North America The Dutch were among the first to establish settlements on the North American continent after Henry Hudson, an English explorer hired by the Dutch, discovered in 1609 the river that bears his name. Within a few years, the Dutch had established the mainland colony of New Netherlands, which stretched from the mouth of the Hudson River as far north as Albany, New York. After 1650, competition from the English and French and years of warfare with those rivals led to the decline of the Dutch commercial empire. In 1664, the English

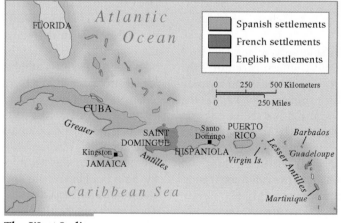

The West Indies

seized the colony of New Netherlands and renamed it New York.

In the meantime, the British had begun to establish their own colonies in North America. The first permanent English settlement in America was Jamestown, founded in 1607 in modern Virginia. It barely survived, making it clear that the colonizing of American lands was not necessarily conducive to quick profits. But the desire to practice one's own religion, combined with economic interests, could lead to successful colonization, as the Massachusetts Bay Company demonstrated. The Massachusetts colony had four thousand settlers in its early years but by 1660 had swelled to forty thousand. By the end of the seventeenth century, the English had established control over most of the eastern seaboard of the present United States.

British North America came to consist of thirteen colonies. They were thickly populated, containing about 1.5 million people by 1750, and prosperous. Ostensibly run by the British Board of Trade, the Royal Council, and Parliament, these thirteen colonies had legislatures that tended to act independently. Merchants in such port cities as Boston, Philadelphia, New York, and Charleston resented and resisted regulation from the British government.

French North America   The French also established a colonial empire in North America. In 1663, Canada was made the property of the French crown and administered by a French governor like a French province.

French North America was run autocratically as a vast trading area, where valuable furs, leather, fish, and timber were acquired. However, the inability of the French government to get people to emigrate to its Canadian possessions left them thinly populated. By 1750, there were about fifteen thousand French Canadians, most of whom were hunters, trappers, missionaries, and explorers. The French failed to provide adequate men or money, allowing their Continental wars to take precedence over the conquest of the North American continent.

Toward a World Economy

During the High Middle Ages, Europeans had engaged in a commercial revolution that created new opportunities for townspeople in a basically agrarian economy. Although this commercial thrust was slowed by the crises of the fourteenth century, Europe's discovery of the world outside in the fifteenth century led to an even greater burst of commercial activity and the inception of a world market.

Economic Conditions in the Sixteenth Century

Inflation was a major economic problem in the sixteenth and early seventeenth centuries. This so-called **price revolution** was a Europe-wide phenomenon, although different areas were affected at different times. Foodstuffs were most subject to price increases. But wages failed to keep up with price increases. Wage earners, especially agricultural laborers and salaried workers in urban areas, saw their standard of living drop. At the same time, landed aristocrats, who could raise rents, managed to prosper. Commercial and industrial entrepreneurs also benefited from the price revolution because of rising prices, expanding markets, and relatively cheaper labor costs. Some historians regard this profit inflation as a valuable stimulus to investment and the growth of capitalism, laying the groundwork for the economic expansion and prosperity of the sixteenth century. Governments were likewise affected by inflation. They borrowed heavily from bankers and imposed new tax burdens on their subjects, often stirring additional discontent.

The Growth of Commercial Capitalism

The flourishing European trade of the sixteenth century revolved around three major areas: the Mediterranean in the south, the Low Countries and the Baltic region in the north, and central Europe, whose inland trade depended on the Rhine and Danube Rivers. As overseas trade expanded, however, the Atlantic seaboard began to play a more important role, linking all three trading areas together and making Europe into a more integrated market that was all the more vulnerable to price shifts.

The commercial expansion of the sixteenth and seventeenth centuries was made easier by new forms of commercial organization, especially the **joint-stock company.** Individuals bought shares in a company and received dividends on their investment while a board of directors ran the company and made the important business decisions. The return on investments could be spectacular. During its first ten years, investors received 30 percent on their money from the Dutch East India Company, which opened the Spice Islands and Southeast Asia to Dutch activity. The joint-stock company made it easier to raise large amounts of capital for world trading ventures.

Traditional family banking firms were no longer able to supply the numerous services needed for the commercial capitalism of the seventeenth century, and new institutions arose to take their place. In 1609, the city of Amsterdam created the Bank of Amsterdam as both a deposit and a transfer institution and the Amsterdam Bourse, or Exchange, where the trading of stocks replaced the exchange of goods. By the first half of the seventeenth century, the Amsterdam Exchange had emerged as the hub of the European business world, just as Amsterdam had replaced Antwerp as the greatest commercial and banking center of Europe.

Despite the growth of commercial capitalism, most of the European economy still depended on an agricultural system that had experienced few changes since the thirteenth century. At least 80 percent of Europeans still worked on the land. Almost all of the peasants of western Europe were free of serfdom, although many still owed a variety of feudal dues to the nobility. Despite the expanding markets and rising prices, European peasants saw little or no improvement in their lot as they faced increased rents and fees and higher taxes imposed by the state.

Mercantilism

Mercantilism is the name historians use to identify a set of economic tendencies that came to dominate economic practices in the seventeenth century. Fundamental to mercantilism was the belief that the total volume of trade was unchangeable. Since one nation could expand its trade and hence its prosperity only at the expense of others, to mercantilists, economic activity was war carried on by peaceful means.

According to the mercantilists, the prosperity of a nation depended on a plentiful supply of bullion, or gold and silver. For this reason, it was desirable to achieve a favorable balance of trade in which goods exported were of greater value than those imported, promoting an influx of gold and silver payments that would increase the quantity of bullion. Furthermore, to encourage exports, governments should stimulate and protect export industries and trade by granting trade monopolies, encouraging investment in new industries through subsidies, importing foreign artisans, and improving transportation systems by building roads, bridges, and canals. By placing high tariffs on foreign goods, they could be kept out of the country and prevented from competing with domestic industries. Colonies were also deemed valuable as sources of raw materials and markets for finished goods.

Mercantilism focused on the role of the state, believing that state intervention in some aspects of the economy was desirable for the sake of the national good. Government regulations to ensure the superiority of export goods, the construction of roads and canals, and the granting of subsidies to create trade companies were all predicated on government involvement in economic affairs.

Overseas Trade and Colonies: Movement Toward Globalization

Mercantilist theory on the role of colonies was matched in practice by Europe's overseas expansion. With the development of colonies and trading posts in the Americas and the East, Europeans embarked on an adventure in international commerce in the seventeenth century. Although some historians speak of a nascent world economy, we should remember that local, regional, and intra-European trade still predominated. About one-tenth of English and Dutch exports were shipped across the Atlantic; slightly more went to the East. What made the transoceanic trade rewarding, however, was not the volume but the value of its goods. Dutch, English, and French merchants were bringing back products that were still consumed largely by the wealthy but were beginning to make their way into the lives of artisans and merchants. Pepper and spices from the Indies, West Indian and Brazilian sugar, and Asian coffee and tea were becoming more readily available to European consumers.

Trade within Europe remained strong throughout the eighteenth century, although this trade increased only slightly while overseas trade boomed. From 1716 to 1789, total French exports quadrupled; intra-European trade, which constituted 75 percent of these exports in 1716, accounted for only 50 percent of the total in 1789. This increase in overseas trade has led some historians to proclaim the emergence of a truly global economy in the eighteenth century. Trade patterns now interlocked Europe, Africa, the East, and the Americas.

The Impact of European Expansion

Between 1500 and 1800, the Atlantic nations of Europe moved into all parts of the world. The first had been Spain and Portugal, the two great colonial powers of the sixteenth century, followed by the Dutch, who built their colonial empire in the seventeenth century as Portugal and Spain declined. The Dutch were soon challenged by the British and French, who outstripped the others in the eighteenth century while becoming involved in a bitter rivalry. By the end of the eighteenth century, it appeared that Great Britain would become the great European imperial power. European expansion made a great impact on both the conquerors and the conquered.

The Conquered

The native American civilizations, which had their own unique qualities and a degree of sophistication not much appreciated by Europeans, were virtually destroyed. In addition to enormous losses of population from European diseases, ancient social and political structures were ripped up and replaced by European institutions, religion, language, and culture. In Africa, European involvement in the slave trade had devastating effects, especially in coastal areas. The Portuguese trading posts in the East had little impact on native Asian civilizations, although Dutch control of the Indonesian archipelago was more intrusive. China and Japan were still little affected by Westerners, although India was subject to ever-growing British encroachment.

In Central and South America, a new civilization arose that we have come to call Latin America. It was a multiracial society. Spanish and Portuguese settlers who arrived in the Western Hemisphere were few in number compared to the native Indians; many of the newcomers were males who not only used female natives for their sexual pleasure but married them as well. Already by 1501, Spanish rulers had authorized intermarriage between Europeans and native American Indians, whose offspring became known as mestizos. Another group of people brought to Latin America were the Africans. Over a period of three centuries, possibly as many as eight million slaves were brought to Spanish and Portuguese America to work the plantations. Africans also contributed to Latin America's multiracial character. Mulattoes—the offspring of Africans and whites—joined mestizos and descendants of whites, Africans, and native Indians to produce a unique society in Latin America. Unlike Europe or British North America, Latin America developed a multihued society with less rigid attitudes about race.

The ecology of conquered areas was also affected by the European presence. Europeans brought horses and cattle to the Americas. Horses revolutionized the life of the Plains Indians. Europeans brought new crops, such as wheat and cane sugar, to be cultivated on large plantations by native or imported slave labor. In their trips to other parts of the world, Europeans also carried New World plants with them. Thus Europeans introduced sweet potatoes and maize (Indian corn) to Africa in the sixteenth century.

Catholic Missionaries Although there were some Protestant missionaries in the world outside Europe, Catholic missionaries were far more active in spreading Christianity. From the beginning of their conquest of the New World, Spanish and Portuguese rulers were determined to Christianize the native peoples. This policy gave the Catholic church an important role to play in the New World, one that added considerably to church power. Catholic missionaries—especially the Dominicans, Franciscans, and Jesuits—fanned out to different parts of the Spanish Empire.

To facilitate their efforts, missionaries brought Indians together into villages, where the natives could be converted, taught trades, and encouraged to grow crops. These missions enabled the missionaries to control the lives of the Indians and helped ensure that they would remain docile members of the empire (see the box on p. 276). Basically, missions benefited the missionaries more than the Indians. In frontier districts such as California and Texas, missions also served as military barriers to foreign encroachment.

The Catholic church constructed hospitals, orphanages, and schools. Monastic schools instructed Indian students in the rudiments of reading, writing, and arithmetic. The Catholic church also provided outlets for women other than marriage. Nunneries were places of prayer and quiet contemplation, but women in religious orders, many of them of aristocratic background, often lived well and worked outside their establishments by running schools and hospitals. Indeed, one of these nuns, Sor Juana Inés de la Cruz (1651–1695), was one of seventeenth-century Latin America's best-known literary figures. She wrote poetry and prose and urged that women be educated.

Christian missionaries had also made the long voyage to China on European merchant ships. The Jesuits were among the most active and the most effective. Many of the early Jesuit missionaries to China were highly educated men who were familiar with European philosophical and scientific developments. They brought along clocks and various other instruments that impressed Chinese officials and made them more open to Western ideas.

The Jesuits used this openness to promote Christianity. To make it easier for the Chinese to accept Christianity, the Jesuits pointed to similarities between Christian morality and Confucian ethics. The efforts of the Christian missionaries reached their height in the early eighteenth century. Several hundred Chinese officials became Catholics, as did an estimated 300,000 ordinary Chinese. But ultimately the Christian effort was undermined by squabbling among the religious orders themselves. To make it easier for the Chinese to convert, the Jesuits had allowed the new Catholics to continue the practice of ancestor worship. Jealous Dominicans and Franciscans complained to the pope, who condemned the practice. Soon Chinese authorities began to suppress Christian activities throughout China.

The Jesuits also had some success in Japan, where they converted a number of local nobles. By the end of the sixteenth century, thousands of Japanese on the southernmost islands of Kyushu and Shikoku had become Christians. But the Jesuit practice of destroying local idols and shrines and turning some temples into Christian schools or churches caused a severe reaction. When a new group of Spanish Franciscans continued the same policies, the government ordered the execution of nine missionaries and a number of their Japanese converts.

The Conquerors

For some Europeans, expansion abroad brought hopes for land, riches, and social advancement. One Spaniard commented in 1572 that many "poor young men" left Spain for Mexico, where they might hope to acquire landed estates and call themselves "gentlemen." Although some wives accompanied their husbands abroad, many ordinary European women found new opportunities for marriage in the New World because of the lack of white women. Indeed, as one commentator bluntly put it, even "a whore, if handsome, [can] make a wife for some rich planter."[6] In the violence-prone world of early Spanish America, a number of women also found themselves rich after their husbands were killed unexpectedly. In one area of Central America, women owned about 25 percent of the landed estates by 1700.

THE MISSION

In 1609, two Jesuit priests embarked on a missionary calling with the Guaraní Indians in eastern Paraguay. Eventually, the Jesuits established more than thirty missions in the region. This description of a Jesuit mission in Paraguay was written by Félix de Azara, a Spanish soldier and scientist.

Félix de Azara, *Description and History of Paraguay and Rio de la Plata*

Having spoken of the towns founded by the Jesuit fathers, and of the manner in which they were founded, I shall discuss the government which they established in them...In each town resided two priests, a curate and a subcurate, who had certain assigned functions. The subcurate was charged with all the spiritual tasks, and the curate with every kind of temporal responsibility....

The curate allowed no one to work for personal gain; he compelled everyone, without distinction of age or sex, to work for the community, and he himself saw to it that all were equally fed and dressed. For this purpose the curates placed in storehouses all the fruits of agriculture and the products of industry, selling in the Spanish towns their surplus of cotton, cloth, tobacco, vegetables, skins, and wood, transporting them in their own boats down the nearest rivers, and returning with implements and whatever else was required.

From the foregoing one may infer that the curate disposed of the surplus funds of the Indian towns, and that no Indian could aspire to own private property. This deprived them of any incentive to use reason or talent, since the most industrious, able, and worthy person had the same food, clothing, and pleasures as the most wicked, dull, and indolent. It also follows that although this form of government was well designed to enrich the communities it also caused the Indian to work at a languid pace, since the wealth of his community was of no concern to him.

It must be said that although the Jesuit fathers were supreme in all respects, they employed their authority with a mildness and a restraint that command admiration. They supplied everyone with abundant food and clothing. They compelled the men to work only half a day, and did not drive them to produce more. Even their labor was given a festive air, for they went in procession to the fields, to the sound of music...and the music did not cease until they had returned in the same way they had set out. They gave them many holidays, dances, and tournaments, dressing the actors and the members of the municipal councils in gold or silver tissue and the most costly European garments, but they permitted the women to act only as spectators.

They likewise forbade the women to sew; this occupation was restricted to the musicians, sacristans, and acolytes. But they made them spin cotton; and the cloth that the Indians wove, after satisfying their own needs, they sold together with the surplus cotton in the Spanish towns, as they did with the tobacco, vegetables, wood, and skins. The curate and his companion, or subcurate, had their own plain dwellings, and they never left them except to take the air in the great enclosed yard of their college. They never walked through the streets of the town or entered the house of any Indian or let themselves be seen by any woman—or indeed, by any man, except for those indispensable few through whom they issued their orders.

How were the missions organized to enable missionaries to control many aspects of the Indian's lives? Why was this deemed necessary?

European expansion also had other economic effects on the conquerors. Wherever they went in the New World, Europeans sought to find sources of gold and silver. One Aztec commented that the Spanish conquerors "longed and lusted for gold. Their bodies swelled with greed, and their hunger was ravenous; they hungered like pigs for that gold."[7] Rich silver deposits were found and exploited in Mexico and southern Peru (modern Bolivia). When the mines at Potosí in Peru were opened in 1545, the value of precious metals imported into Europe quadrupled. Between 1503 and 1650, nearly 18,000 tons of silver and more than 200 tons of gold entered the port of Seville, setting off a price revolution in the Spanish economy.

But gold and silver were only two of the products that became part of the exchange between the New World and the Old. Historians refer to the reciprocal importation and exportation of plants and animals between Europe and the Americas as the **Columbian Exchange.** While Europeans were bringing horses, cattle, and wheat to the New World, they were taking new agricultural products such as potatoes, chocolate, corn, tomatoes, and tobacco back to Europe. Potatoes became especially popular as a basic dietary staple in some areas of Europe. High in carbohydrates and rich in vitamins A and C, potatoes could be easily stored for winter use and soon enabled more people to survive on smaller plots of land. This improvement in nutrition was soon reflected in a rapid increase in population.

The European lifestyle was greatly affected by new products from abroad. In addition to new foods, new drinks also appeared in Europe. Chocolate, which had been brought to Spain from Aztec Mexico, became a common drink by 1700. The first coffee and tea houses opened in London in the 1650s and spread rapidly to other parts of Europe. In the eighteenth century, a craze for Chinese furniture and porcelain spread among the upper classes. Chinese ideas would also make an impact on intellectual attitudes (see Chapter 17).

A Seventeenth-Century World Map. This beautiful map was prepared in 1630 by Henricus Hondius. The portraits in the corners are of Caesar, the Roman statesman; Ptolemy, the second-century astronomer; Mercator, the Flemish cartographer whose map projection Hondius followed; and Hondius himself. Comparing this map to the one of Ptolemy on page 260, you can see how much Europeans had learned about the shape of the world by the seventeenth century.

European expansion, which was in part a product of European rivalries, also deepened those rivalries and increased the tensions among European states. Bitter conflicts arose over the cargoes coming from the New World and Asia. The Anglo-Dutch trade wars and the British-French rivalry over India and North America became part of a new pattern of worldwide warfare in the eighteenth century (see Chapter 18). Bitter rivalries also led to state-sponsored piracy in which governments authorized private captains to attack enemy shipping and keep part of the proceeds for themselves.

In the course of their expansion, Europeans also came to have a new view of the world. When the travels began in the fifteenth century, Europeans were dependent on maps that were often fanciful and inaccurate. Their explorations helped them create new maps that gave a more realistic portrayal of the world, as well as new techniques called map projections that allowed them to represent the round surface of a sphere on a flat piece of paper. The most famous of these is the Mercator projection, the work of a Flemish cartographer, Gerardus Mercator (1512–1594). Mercator's is what mapmakers call a conformal projection, which tries to show the true shape of landmasses, but only of a limited area. On the Mercator projection, the shapes of lands near the equator are quite accurate, but the farther away from the equator they lie, the more exaggerated their size becomes. Nevertheless, the Mercator projection was valuable to ship captains. Every straight line on a Mercator projection is a line of true direction, whether north, south, east, or west. For four centuries, ship captains were very grateful to Mercator.

The psychological impact of colonization on the colonizers is awkward to evaluate but hard to deny. Europeans were initially startled by the discovery of new peoples in the Americas. Some deemed them inhuman and thus fit to be exploited for labor. Others, however, found them to be refreshingly natural and not yet touched by European corruption. But even most members of the latter group believed that the Indians should be converted—if not forcefully, at least peacefully—to Christianity. Overall, the relatively easy European success in dominating native peoples (in Africa and America) reinforced Christian Europe's belief in the inherent superiority of European civilization and religion. The Scientific Revolution of the seventeenth century (see Chapter 16), the Enlightenment of the eighteenth (see Chapter 17), and the imperialism of the nineteenth (see Chapter 24) would all bolster this Eurocentric perspective, which has pervaded Western civilization's relationship with the rest of the world.

CONCLUSION

At the end of the fifteenth century, Europeans sailed out into the world in all directions. Beginning with the handful of Portuguese ships that ventured southward along the West African coast in the mid-fifteenth century, the process accelerated with the epochal voyages of Christopher Columbus to the Americas and Vasco da Gama to the Indian Ocean in the 1490s. Soon a number of other European states had joined in the adventure, and by the end of the eighteenth century, they had created a global trade network dominated by Western ships and Western power.

In less than three hundred years, the European Age of Exploration changed the shape of the world. In some areas, such as the Americas and the Spice Islands, it led to the destruction of indigenous civilizations and the establishment of European colonies. In others, as in Africa, India, and mainland Southeast Asia, it left native regimes intact but had a strong impact on local societies and regional trade patterns.

At the time, many European observers viewed the process in a favorable light. It not only expanded wealth through world trade and exchanged crops and discoveries between the Old World and the New, they believed, but it also introduced "heathen peoples" to the message of Jesus Christ. The conquest of the Americas and expansion into the rest of the world brought out most of the worst and some of the best aspects of European civilization. The greedy plundering of resources and the brutal repression and enslavement were hardly balanced by attempts to create new institutions, convert the natives to Christianity, and foster the rights of the indigenous peoples. In any case, Europeans had begun to change the face of the world and increasingly saw their culture, with its religion, languages, and technology, as a coherent force to be exported to all corners of the earth.

TIMELINE

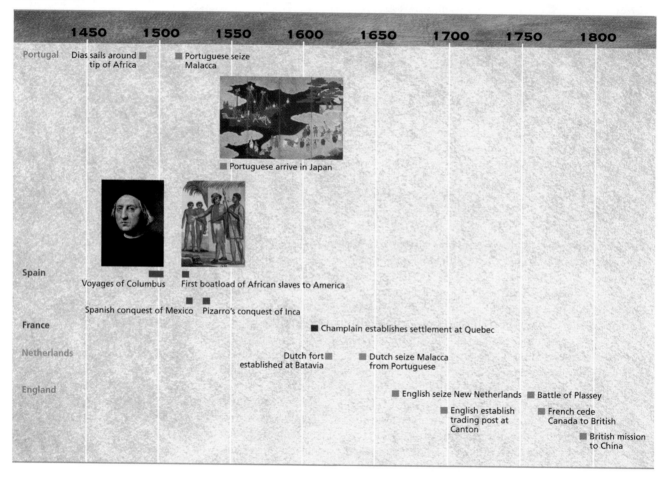

NOTES

1. Quoted in J. R. Hale, *Renaissance Exploration* (New York, 1968), p. 32.
2. Quoted in J. H. Parry, *The Age of Reconnaissance: Discovery, Exploration, and Settlement, 1450 to 1640* (New York, 1963), p. 33.
3. Quoted in R. B. Reed, "The Expansion of Europe," in R. De Molen, ed., *The Meaning of the Renaissance and Reformation* (Boston, 1974), p. 308.
4. Quoted in B. Davidson, *Africa in History: Themes and Outlines*, rev. ed. (New York, 1991), p. 213.
5. Quoted in ibid., p. 198
6. Quoted in G.V. Scammell, *The First Imperial Age: European Overseas Expansion, c. 1400–1715* (London, 1989), p. 62.
7. M. Leon-Portilla, ed., *The Broken Spears: The Aztec Account of the Conquest of Mexico* (Boston, 1969), p. 51.

SUGGESTIONS FOR FURTHER READING

The best general accounts of European discovery and expansion are **G. V. Scammell**, *The First Imperial Age: European Overseas Expansion, c. 1400–1715* (London, 1989); **J. H. Parry**, *The Age of Reconnaissance: Discovery, Exploration, and Settlement, 1450 to 1650* (New York, 1963); and **B. Penrose**, *Travel and Discovery in the Renaissance, 1420–1620* (New York, 1962). On the medieval background to European expansion, see **J.R.S. Phillips**, *The Medieval Expansion of Europe* (New York, 1988). On European perceptions of the world outside Europe, see **M. Campbell**, *The Witness and the Other World: Exotic European Travel Writing, 400–1600* (Ithaca, N.Y., 1991). On the technological aspects, see **R. C. Smith**, *Vanguard of Empire: Ships of Exploration in the Age of Columbus* (Oxford, 1993).

On Portuguese expansion, see **S. Subrahmanyam**, *The Portuguese Empire in Asia, 1500–1700: A Political and Economic History* (New York, 1993). On Columbus, see **F. Fernandez-Armesto**, *Columbus* (New York, 1991), and **W. D. Phillips and C. R. Phillips**, *The Worlds of Christopher Columbus* (Cambridge, 1992). On the Spanish Empire in the New World, see **J. H. Parry**, *The Spanish Seaborne Empire* (New York, 1966). For a theoretical discussion of violence and gender in America, see **R. Trexler**, *Sex and Conquest: Gendered Violence, Political Order, and the European Conquest of the Americas* (Ithaca, N.Y., 1995). On the conquistadors, see the beautifully illustrated work by **M. Wood**, *Conquistadors* (Berkeley, Calif., 2000). On the destructive nature of the Spanish conquest of the Americas, see **D. E. Standard**, *American Holocaust: Columbus and the Conquest of the New World* (New York, 1993). For a revisionist view of the Spanish conquest of the Americas, see **M. Restall**, *Seven Myths of the Spanish Conquest* (Oxford, 2003).

The subject of mercantile empires and worldwide trade is covered in **J. D. Tracy**, *The Rise of Merchant Empires: Long-Distance Trade in the Early Modern World, 1350–1750* (Cambridge, 1990), and **T. Benjamin, T. Hall**, and **D. Rutherford**, eds., *The Atlantic World in the Age of Empire* (New York, 2001). See also **A. Pagden**, *Lords of All the Worlds: Ideologies of Empire in Spain, Britain and France, c. 1500–c. 1850* (New Haven, Conn., 1995). On the African slave trade, see **H. Thomas**, *The Slave Trade: The Story of the Atlantic Slave Trade, 1440–1870* (New York, 1997), and the collection of articles in **D. Northrup**, ed., *The Atlantic Slave Trade* (Lexington, Mass., 1994). The effects of European trade in Southeast Asia are discussed in **A. Reid**, *Southeast Asia in the Age of Commerce, 1450–1680* (New Haven, Conn., 1989). See also **K. N. Chaudhuri**, *Trade and Civilization in the Indian Ocean: An Economic History from the Rise of Islam to 1750* (Cambridge, 1985).

On the economic dimensions of expansion, there are the three volumes by **F. Braudel**, *Civilization and Capitalism in the 15th to 18th Century: The Structures of Everyday Life* (London, 1981), *The Wheels of Commerce* (London, 1982), and *The Perspective of the World* (London, 1984). On mercantilism, see **L. Magnusson**, *Mercantilism: The Shaping of an Economic Language* (New York, 1994). On the concept of a world economy, see **A. K. Smith**, *Creating a World Economy: Merchant Capital, Colonialism, and World Trade, 1400–1825* (Boulder, Colo., 1991).

The impact of expansion on European consciousness is explored in **A. Pagden**, *European Encounters with the New World: From Renaissance to Romanticism* (New Haven, Conn., 1993). The human and ecological effects of the interaction of New World and Old World cultures are examined thoughtfully in **A. W. Crosby**, *The Columbian Exchange: Biological and Cultural Consequences of 1492* (Westport, Conn., 1972) and *Ecological Imperialism: The Biological Expansion of Europe* (New York, 1986). For a general view of the interaction of cultures, see **J. Diamond**, *Guns, Germs, and Steel* (New York, 1997). The native American female experience with the European encounter is presented in **R. Gutierrez**, *When Jesus Came the Corn Mother Went Away: Marriage, Sexuality, and Power in New Mexico, 1500–1846* (Stanford, Calif., 1991).

Thomson NOW! Enter *ThomsonNOW* using the access card that is available for *Western Civilization: A Brief History*. *ThomsonNOW* will help you understand this chapter with lesson plans generated for your needs. In addition, you can read the following documents, and many more, online:

> Marco Polo, Prologue to *Travels*
> Prince Henry the Navigator, *Chronicle of the Discovery and Conquest of Guinea*, chapters 7–9
> Nicolò Conti (as told to Bracciolini), *Travels of Nicolò Conti in the East*
> Francesco Pegolotti, *Cathay and the Way Thither*

WESTERN CIVILIZATION RESOURCES

Visit the Web site for *Western Civilization: A Brief History* for resources specific to this book:

http://www.thomsonedu.com/history/spielvogel

For a variety of tools to help you succeed in this course, visit the Western Civilization Resource Center at

http://history.wadsworth.com/spielvogel

Included are quizzes, images, documents, interactive simulations, maps and timelines, movie explorations, and a wealth of other sources.

15

STATE BUILDING AND THE SEARCH FOR ORDER IN THE SEVENTEENTH CENTURY

CHAPTER OUTLINE AND FOCUS QUESTIONS

Social Crises, War, and Rebellions

☐ What economic, social, and political crises did Europe experience in the first half of the seventeenth century?

The Practice of Absolutism: Western Europe

☐ What was absolutism in theory, and how did its actual practice in France measure up against the theory?

Absolutism in Central and Eastern Europe

☐ What developments enabled Brandenburg-Prussia, Austria, and Russia to emerge as major powers in the seventeenth century?

Limited Monarchy: The Dutch Republic and England

☐ What were the main issues in the struggle between king and Parliament in seventeenth-century England, and how were they resolved?

The Flourishing of European Culture

☐ What were the main features of art and literature in the sixteenth and seventeenth centuries?

CRITICAL THINKING

☐ How did the artistic and literary achievements of this era reflect the political and economic developments of the period?

Hyacinth Rigaud's portrait of Louis XIV captures the king's sense of royal grandeur

*B*Y THE END of the sixteenth century, Europe was beginning to experience some decline in religious passions and a growing secularization that affected both the political and intellectual worlds (the intellectual effect will be discussed in Chapter 16). Some historians like to speak of the seventeenth century as a turning point in the evolution of the modern state system in Europe. The ideal of a united Christian Europe gave way to the practical realities of a system of secular entities in which matters of state took precedence over the salvation of subjects' souls. By the seventeenth century, the credibility of Christianity had been so weakened through religious wars that more and more Europeans came to think of politics in secular terms.

One of the responses to the religious wars and other crises of the time was a yearning for order. As the internal social and political rebellions and revolts died down, it became apparent that the privileged classes of society—the aristocrats—remained in control, although important differences in political forms existed in the various states. In many places, the extension of monarchical power was viewed as a stabilizing force. This development, which historians have called absolutism or absolute monarchy, was most evident in France during the flamboyant reign of Louis XIV, widely

Hervé Lewandowski/Réunion des Musées Nationaux/Art Resource, NY (Louvre, Paris)

regarded as the perfect embodiment of an absolute monarch. In his memoirs, the duc de Saint-Simon, who had firsthand experience of French court life, said that Louis was "the very figure of a hero, so imbued with a natural but most imposing majesty that it appeared even in his most insignificant gestures and movements." The king's natural grace gave him a special charm as well: "He was as dignified and majestic in his dressing gown as when dressed in robes of state, or on horseback at the head of his troops." His life was orderly: "Nothing could be regulated with greater exactitude than were his days and hours." His self-control was impeccable: "He did not lose control of himself ten times in his whole life, and then only with inferior persons." But even absolute monarchs had imperfections, and Saint-Simon had the courage to point them out: "Louis XIV's vanity was without limit or restraint," which led to his "distaste for all merit, intelligence, education, and, most of all, for all independence of character and sentiment in others," as well as his "mistakes of judgment in matters of importance."

But absolutism was not the only response to the search for order in the seventeenth century. Other states, such as England, reacted differently to domestic crisis, and another very different system emerged where monarchs were limited by the power of their representative assemblies. Absolute and limited monarchy were the two poles of seventeenth-century state building.✦

Social Crises, War, and Rebellions

The inflation-fueled prosperity of the sixteenth century showed signs of slackening in the seventeenth. Economic contraction was evident in some parts of Europe by the 1620s. In the 1630s and 1640s, as imports of silver from the Americas declined, economic recession intensified, especially in the Mediterranean area. Italy, the industrial and financial center of Europe in the Renaissance, was becoming an economic backwater. Spain's economy was also seriously failing by the 1640s.

Population trends of the sixteenth and seventeenth centuries also testify to Europe's worsening conditions. The sixteenth century was a period of expanding population, possibly related to a warmer climate and increased food supplies. It has been estimated that the population of Europe increased from 60 million in 1500 to 85 million by 1600, the first major recovery since the devastation of the Black Death in the mid-fourteenth century. However, records also indicate a leveling off of the population by 1620 and even a decline by 1650, especially in central and southern parts of the Continent. Europe's longtime adversaries—war, famine, and plague—continued to affect population levels, and another "little ice age" midway through the sixteenth century, when average temperatures fell, affected harvests and gave rise to famines. These problems created social tensions that came to a boil in the witchcraft craze.

The Witchcraft Craze

Hysteria over witchcraft affected the lives of many Europeans in the sixteenth and seventeenth centuries. Witchcraft trials were held in England, Scotland, Switzerland, Germany, some parts of France and the Low Countries, and even New England in America.

Witchcraft was not a new phenomenon. Its practice had been part of traditional village culture for centuries, but it came to be viewed as both sinister and dangerous when the medieval church began to connect witches to the activities of the devil, thereby transforming witchcraft into a heresy that had to be extirpated. After the creation of the Inquisition in the thirteenth century, people were accused of a variety of witchcraft practices and, following the biblical injunction "Thou shalt not suffer a witch to live," were turned over to secular authorities for burning at the stake or, in England, hanging.

The Spread of Witchcraft What distinguished witchcraft in the sixteenth and seventeenth centuries from these previous developments was the increased number of trials and executions of presumed witches. Perhaps more than a hundred thousand people were prosecuted throughout Europe on charges of witchcraft. Although larger cities were affected first, the trials spread to smaller towns and rural areas as the hysteria persisted well into the seventeenth century (see the box on p. 282).

The accused witches usually confessed to a number of practices, most often after intense torture. Many said that they had sworn allegiance to the devil and attended sabbats, nocturnal gatherings where they feasted, danced, and even copulated with the devil in sexual orgies. More common, however, were admissions of using evil incantations and special ointments and powders to wreak havoc on neighbors by killing their livestock, injuring their children, or raising storms to destroy their crops.

A number of contributing factors have been suggested to explain why the witchcraft frenzy became so widespread in the sixteenth and seventeenth centuries. Religious uncertainties clearly played some part. Many witchcraft trials occurred in areas where Protestantism had been recently victorious or in regions, such as southwestern Germany, where controversies between Protestants and Catholics still raged. As religious passions became inflamed, accusations of being in league with the devil became common on both sides. Recently, however, historians have emphasized the importance of social conditions, especially the problems of a society in turmoil, in explaining the witchcraft hysteria. At a time when the old communal values that stressed working together for the good of the community were disintegrating, property owners became more fearful of the growing numbers of poor among them and transformed them psychologically into agents of the devil. Old women were particularly susceptible to suspicion. When problems arose—and there were many in this crisis-laden period—these people were the most likely scapegoats.

A Witchcraft Trial in France

Persecutions for witchcraft reached their high point in the sixteenth and seventeenth centuries when tens of thousands of people were brought to trial. In this excerpt from the minutes of a trial in France in 1652, we can see why the accused witch stood little chance of exonerating herself.

The Trial of Suzanne Gaudry

28 May, 1652 . . . . Interrogation of Suzanne Gaudry, prisoner at the court of Rieux. . . . [During interrogations on May 28 and May 29, the prisoner confessed to a number of activities involving the devil.]

Deliberation of the Court—June 3, 1652

The undersigned advocates of the Court have seen these interrogations and answers. They say that the afore-mentioned Suzanne Gaudry confesses that she is a witch, that she had given herself to the devil, that she had re-nounced God, Lent, and baptism, that she has been marked on the shoulder, that she has cohabited with the devil and that she has been to the dances, confessing only to have cast a spell upon and caused to die a beast of Philippe Cornié. . . .

Third Interrogation—June 27

The prisoner being led into the chamber, she was examined to know if things were not as she had said and confessed at the beginning of her imprisonment.

—Answers no, and that what she has said was done so by force.

Pressed to say the truth, that otherwise she would be subjected to torture, having pointed out to her that her aunt was burned for this same subject.

—Answers that she is not a witch. . . .

She was placed in the hands of the officer in charge of torture, throwing herself on her knees, struggling to cry, uttering several exclamations, without being able, never-theless, to shed a tear. Saying at every moment that she is not a witch.

The Torture

On this same day, being at the place of torture.

This prisoner, before being strapped down, was admon-ished to maintain herself in her first confessions and to re-nounce her lover.

—Says that she denies everything she has said, and that she has no lover. Feeling herself being strapped down, says

that she is not a witch, while struggling to cry . . . and upon being asked why she confessed to being one, said that she was forced to say it.

Told that she was not forced, that on the contrary she declared herself to be a witch without any threat.

—Says that she confessed it and that she is not a witch, and being a little stretched [on the rack] screams ceaselessly that she is not a witch. . . .

Asked if she did not confess that she had been a witch for twenty-six years.

—Says that she said it, that she retracts it, crying that she is not a witch.

Asked if she did not make Philippe Cornié's horse die, as she confessed.

—Answers no, crying Jesus-Maria, that she is not a witch.

The mark having been probed by the officer, in the presence of Doctor Bouchain, it was adjudged by the afore-said doctor and officer truly to be the mark of the devil.

Being more tightly stretched upon the torture-rack, urged to maintain her confessions.

—Said that it was true that she is a witch and that she would maintain what she had said.

Asked how long she has been in subjugation to the devil.

—Answers that it was twenty years ago that the devil appeared to her, being in her lodgings in the form of a man dressed in a little cow-hide and black breeches. . . .

Verdict

July 9, 1652. In the light of the interrogations, answers and investigations made into the charge against Suzanne Gaudry, . . . seeing by her own confessions that she is said to have made a pact with the devil, received the mark from him, . . . and that following this, she had renounced God, Lent, and baptism and had let herself be known carnally by him, in which she received satisfaction. Also, seeing that she is said to have been a part of nocturnal carols and dances.

For expiation of which the advice of the undersigned is that the office of Rieux can legitimately condemn the aforesaid Suzanne Gaudry to death, tying her to a gallows, and strangling her to death, then burning her body and burying it here in the environs of the woods.

Why were women, particularly older women, especially vulnerable to accusations of witchcraft? What "proofs" are offered here that Suzanne Gaudry had consorted with the devil? What does this account tell us about the spread of witchcraft persecutions in the seventeenth century?

That women should be the chief victims of witchcraft trials was hardly accidental. Nicholas Rémy, a witchcraft judge in France in the 1590s, found it "not unreasonable that this scum of humanity, i.e., witches, should be drawn chiefly from the feminine sex."[1] To another judge, it came as no surprise that witches would confess to sexual ex-periences with Satan: "The Devil uses them so, because he knows that women love carnal pleasures, and he means to bind them to his allegiance by such agreeable provocations."[2] Of course, not only witch hunters held such low estimates of women. Most theologians, lawyers, and philosophers in early modern Europe maintained a belief in the natural inferiority of women, making it seem plausible that women would be more susceptible to witchcraft.

Decline By the mid-seventeenth century, the witchcraft hysteria began to subside. The destruction of the religious wars had at least forced people to accept a grudging toleration, tempering religious passions. Moreover, as governments began to stabilize after the period of crisis, fewer magistrates were willing to accept the unsettling and divisive conditions generated by the trials of witches. Finally, by the turn of the eighteenth century, more and more people were questioning their old attitudes toward religion and found it contrary to reason to believe in a world haunted by evil spirits.

The Thirty Years' War

Although many Europeans responded to the upheavals of the second half of the sixteenth century with a desire for peace and order, the first fifty years of the seventeenth century continued to be plagued by crises. A devastating war that affected much of Europe and rebellions seemingly everywhere protracted an atmosphere of disorder and violence.

Religion, especially the struggle between militant Catholicism and militant Calvinism, played an important role in the outbreak of the Thirty Years' War (1618–1648), often called the "last of the religious wars." As the war progressed, however, it became increasingly clear that secular, dynastic-nationalist considerations were far more important.

The Thirty Years' War began in the Germanic lands of the Holy Roman Empire as a struggle between Catholic forces, led by the Habsburg Holy Roman Emperors, and Protestant—primarily Calvinist—nobles in Bohemia who rebelled against Habsburg authority. What began as a struggle over religious issues soon became a wider conflict determined by political motivations as both minor and major European powers—Denmark, Sweden, France, and Spain—made the war a Europe-wide struggle (see Map 15.1). The struggle for European leadership between the Bourbon dynasty of France and the Habsburg dynasties of Spain and the Holy Roman Empire was an especially important factor. Nevertheless, most of the battles were fought on German soil, with devastating results for the German people.

The war in Germany was officially ended by the Peace of Westphalia in 1648, which ensured that all German states, including the Calvinist ones, were free to determine their own religion. The major contenders gained new territories, and one of them, France, emerged as the dominant nation in Europe. The more than three hundred states that made up the Holy Roman Empire were virtually recognized as independent, since each received the power to conduct its own foreign policy. The Habsburg emperor had been reduced to a figurehead. The Peace of Westphalia also made it clear that religion and politics were now separate in the Holy Roman Empire. Political motives became the guiding forces in public affairs as religion moved closer to becoming primarily a matter of personal conviction and individual choice.

The economic and social effects of the Thirty Years' War on Germany are still debated. An older view pictured a ruined German economy and a decline in German population from 21 to 13 million between 1600 and 1650, but more recent opinions have estimated that Germany's population grew from 16 to 17 million while a redistribution of economic activity rather than an overall decline took place. Both views contain some truth. Some areas of Germany were completely devastated while others remained relatively untouched and even experienced economic growth.

Rebellions

Before, during, and after the Thirty Years' War, a series of rebellions and civil wars stemming from the discontent of both nobles and commoners rocked the domestic stability of many European governments. To strengthen their power, monarchs attempted to extend their authority at the expense of traditional powerful elements who resisted the rulers' efforts. At the same time, to fight their battles, governments increased taxes and caused such hardships that common people also rose in opposition.

Between 1590 and 1640, peasant and lower-class revolts occurred in central and southern France, Austria, and Hungary. Portugal and Catalonia rebelled against the Spanish government in 1640. Russia, too, was rocked by urban uprisings in 1641, 1645, and 1648. Nobles rebelled in France from 1648 to 1652 to halt the growth of royal power. The northern states of Sweden, Denmark, and the United Provinces were also not immune from upheavals involving clergy, nobles, and mercantile groups. Even relatively stable Switzerland had a peasant rebellion in 1656. The most famous and widest-ranging struggle, however, was the civil war and rebellion in England, commonly known as the English Revolution (discussed later in this chapter).

The Practice of Absolutism: Western Europe

Absolute monarchy or **absolutism** meant that the sovereign power or ultimate authority in the state rested in the hands of a king who claimed to rule by divine right—that kings received their power from God and were responsible to no one (including parliaments) except God. But what did sovereignty mean? The late-sixteenth-century political theorist Jean Bodin believed that sovereign power consisted of the authority to make laws, tax, mete out justice, control the state's administrative system,

MAP 15.1 **The Thirty Years' War.** The conflict began in the German states as Europe's major powers backed either the northern Protestant Union or the southern Catholic League. As the war progressed, religion receded in importance, replaced by a dynastic struggle between the French Bourbons and the Spanish and Austrian Habsburgs. ❓ Compare this map with Map 13.2. Which countries engaged in the war were predominantly Protestant, which were predominantly Catholic, and which were mixed? 🌐 **View an animated version of this map or related maps at** http://thomsonedu.com/history/spielvogel

and determine foreign policy. These powers made a ruler sovereign.

France: Foundations of Absolutism

France during the reign of Louis XIV (1643–1715) has traditionally been regarded as the best example of the practice of absolute monarchy in the seventeenth century. French culture, language, and manners reached into all levels of European society. French diplomacy and wars shaped the political affairs of western and central Europe. Of course, the stability of Louis's reign was magnified by the instability that had preceded it.

The fifty years of French history before Louis XIV came to power were a time in which royal and ministerial governments struggled to avoid the breakdown of the

state. The situation was especially complicated by the fact that in 1610 and 1643, when Louis XIII and Louis XIV, respectively, succeeded to the throne, they were only boys, leaving the government dependent on royal ministers. Two especially competent ministers played crucial roles in maintaining monarchical authority.

Cardinal Richelieu, Louis XIII's chief minister from 1624 to 1642, initiated policies that eventually strengthened the power of the monarchy. By eliminating the political and military rights of the Huguenots while preserving their religious ones, Richelieu transformed the Huguenots into more reliable subjects. Richelieu acted more cautiously in "humbling the pride of the great men," the important French nobility. He understood the influential role played by the nobles in the French state. The dangerous ones were those who asserted their territorial independence when they were excluded from participating in the central government. Proceeding slowly but determinedly, Richelieu developed an efficient network of spies to uncover noble plots and then crushed the conspiracies and executed the conspirators, thereby eliminating a major threat to royal authority.

When Louis XIV succeeded to the throne in 1643 at the age of four, Cardinal Mazarin, the trained successor of Cardinal Richelieu, dominated the government. An Italian who had come to France as a papal legate and then became naturalized, Mazarin attempted to carry on Richelieu's policies. The most important event during Mazarin's rule was the Fronde, a revolt led primarily by nobles who wished to curb the centralized administrative power being built up at the expense of the provincial nobility. The Fronde was crushed by 1652, and with its end, a vast number of French people concluded that the best hope for stability in France lay in the crown. When Mazarin died in 1661, the greatest of the seventeenth-century monarchs, Louis XIV, took over supreme power.

The Reign of Louis XIV (1643–1715)

The day after Cardinal Mazarin's death, Louis XIV, at the age of twenty-three, expressed his determination to be a real king and the sole ruler of France:

> Up to this moment I have been pleased to entrust the government of my affairs to the late Cardinal. It is now time that I govern them myself. You [secretaries and ministers of state] will assist me with your counsels when I ask for them. I request and order you to seal no orders except by my command. . . . I order you not to sign anything, not even a passport . . . without my command; to render account to me personally each day and to favor no one.[3]

His mother, who was well aware of Louis's proclivity for fun and games and getting into the beds of the maids in the royal palace, laughed aloud at these words. But Louis was quite serious.

Louis proved willing to pay the price of being a strong ruler. He established a conscientious routine from which he seldom deviated. Eager for glory (in the French sense of achieving what was expected of a person who held an important position), Louis created a grand and majestic spectacle at the court of Versailles. Consequently, Louis and his court came to set the standard for monarchies and aristocracies all over Europe.

Although Louis may have believed in the theory of absolute monarchy and consciously fostered the myth of himself as the Sun King, the source of light for all of his people, historians are quick to point out that the realities fell far short of the aspirations. Despite the centralizing efforts of Cardinals Richelieu and Mazarin, seventeenth-century France still possessed a bewildering system of overlapping authorities. Provinces had their own regional courts, their own local Estates, their own sets of laws. Members of the high nobility, with their huge estates, and clients among the lesser nobility still exercised much authority. Both towns and provinces possessed privileges and powers seemingly from time immemorial that they would not easily relinquish.

Administration of the Government One of the keys to Louis's power was that he was able to restructure the central policy-making machinery of government because it was part of his own court and household. The royal court located at Versailles was an elaborate structure that served three purposes simultaneously: it was the personal household of the king, the location of central governmental machinery, and the place where powerful subjects came to find favors and offices for themselves and their clients, as well as the main arena where rival aristocratic factions jostled for power. The greatest danger to Louis's personal rule came from the very high nobles and "princes of the blood" (royal princes) who considered it their natural function to assert the policy-making role of royal ministers. Louis eliminated this threat by removing them from the royal council, the chief administrative body of the king and overseer of the central machinery of government, and enticing them to his court, where he could keep them preoccupied with court life and out of politics. In place of the high nobility and royal princes, Louis relied for his ministers on other nobles. His ministers were expected to be subservient; said Louis, "I had no intention of sharing my authority with them."

Louis's domination of his ministers and secretaries gave him control of the central policy-making machinery of government and thus authority over the traditional areas of monarchical power: the formulation of foreign policy, the making of war and peace, the assertion of the secular power of the crown against any religious authority, and the ability to levy taxes to fulfill these functions. However, Louis had considerably less success with the internal administration of the kingdom. The traditional groups and institutions of French society—the nobles, officials, town councils, guilds, and representative Estates in some provinces—were simply too powerful for the king to control. As a result, the actual governing of the provinces and the people was accomplished largely by careful bribery of important people to ensure that the king's policies were carried out.

Religious Policy The maintenance of religious harmony had long been considered an area of monarchical power. The desire to keep it led Louis to pursue an anti-Protestant policy, aimed at converting the Huguenots to Catholicism. In October 1685, Louis issued the Edict of Fontainebleau. In addition to revoking the Edict of Nantes, the new edict provided for the destruction of the Huguenots' churches and the closing of their schools.

Financial Issues The cost of building palaces, maintaining his court, and pursuing his wars made finances a crucial issue for Louis XIV. He was most fortunate in

The Palace of Versailles as Depicted in an Eighteenth-Century Engraving.
Louis XIV spent untold sums of money on the construction of a new royal residence at Versailles.
The enormous palace (it was more than a quarter of a mile long) also housed the members of the
king's government and served as home for thousands of French nobles. As the largest royal
residence in Europe, Versailles impressed foreigners and became a source of envy for other rulers.

having the services of Jean-Baptiste Colbert (1619–1683) as controller-general of finances. Colbert was an avid practitioner of mercantilism. To decrease the need for imports and increase exports, he founded new luxury industries and granted special privileges, including tax exemptions, loans, and subsidies, to individuals who established new industries. To improve communications and the transportation of goods internally, he built roads and canals. To decrease imports directly, Colbert raised tariffs on foreign manufactured goods and created a merchant marine to carry French goods.

The Wars of Louis XIV Both the increase in royal power that Louis pursued and his desire for military glory led the king to develop a professional army numbering 100,000 men in peacetime and 400,000 in time of war. Louis made war an almost incessant activity of his reign. To achieve the prestige and military glory befitting the Sun King as well as to ensure the domination of his Bourbon dynasty over European affairs, Louis waged four wars between 1667 and 1713. His ambitions roused much of Europe to form coalitions to prevent destruction of the European balance of power that Bourbon hegemony would cause. Although Louis added some territory to France's northeastern frontier and established a member of his own Bourbon dynasty on the throne of Spain, he also left France impoverished and surrounded by enemies.

The Decline of Spain

At the beginning of the seventeenth century, Spain possessed the most populous empire in the world, controlling

France	
Louis XIII	1610–1643
Cardinal Richelieu as chief minister	1624–1642
Ministry of Cardinal Mazarin	1642–1661
Fronde	1648–1652
Louis XIV	1643–1715
Edict of Fontainebleau	1685
Spain	
Philip III	1598–1621
Philip IV	1621–1665

almost all of South America and a number of settlements in Asia and Africa. To most Europeans, Spain still seemed the greatest power of the age, but the reality was quite different. The treasury was empty; Philip II went bankrupt in 1596 from excessive expenditures on war, and his successor did the same in 1607 by spending a fortune on his court. The armed forces were obsolescent, the government was inefficient, and the commercial class was weak in the midst of a suppressed peasantry, a luxury-loving class of nobles, and an oversupply of priests and monks.

During the reign of Philip III (1598–1621), many of Spain's weaknesses became all too apparent. Interested only in court luxury or miracle-working relics, Philip III allowed his first minister, the greedy duke of Lerma, to run the country. The aristocratic Lerma's primary interest was accumulating power and wealth for himself and his family. As important offices were filled with his relatives, crucial problems went unsolved.

At first, the reign of Philip IV (1621–1665) seemed to offer hope for a revival of Spain's energies, especially in the capable hands of his chief minister, Gaspar de Guzman, the count of Olivares. This clever, dedicated, and power-hungry statesman worked to revive the interests of the monarchy. A flurry of domestic reform decrees, aimed at curtailing the power of the church and the landed aristocracy, was soon followed by a political reform program whose purpose was to further centralize the government of all Spain and its possessions in monarchical hands. All of these efforts met with little real success, however, because both the number (estimated at one-fifth of the population) and power of the Spanish aristocrats made them too strong to curtail in any significant fashion.

At the same time, most of the efforts of Olivares and Philip were undermined by their desire to pursue Spain's imperial glory and by a series of internal revolts. Spain's involvement in the Thirty Years' War led to a series of frightfully expensive military campaigns that provoked internal revolts and years of civil war. Unfortunately for Spain, the campaigns also failed to produce victory. As

Olivares wrote to King Philip IV, "God wants us to make peace; for He is depriving us visibly and absolutely of all the means of war."[4]

The defeats in Europe and the internal revolts of the 1640s ended any illusions about Spain's greatness. The actual extent of its economic difficulties is still debated, but there is no question about its foreign losses. Dutch independence was formally recognized by the Peace of Westphalia in 1648, and the Peace of the Pyrenees with France in 1659 meant the surrender of some border regions to France.

Absolutism in Central and Eastern Europe

During the seventeenth century, a development of great importance for the modern Western world took place in central and eastern Europe, the appearance of three new powers: Prussia, Austria, and Russia.

The German States

The Peace of Westphalia, which officially ended the Thirty Years' War in 1648, left each of the more than three hundred German states comprising the Holy Roman Empire virtually autonomous and sovereign. Of these states, two emerged in the seventeenth and eighteenth centuries as great European powers.

The Rise of Brandenburg-Prussia The development of Brandenburg as a state was largely the story of the Hohenzollern dynasty. By the seventeenth century, the dominions of the house of Hohenzollern, now called Brandenburg-Prussia, consisted of three disconnected masses in western, central, and eastern Germany (see Map 15.2).

The foundation for the Prussian state was laid by Frederick William the Great Elector (1640–1688). Realizing that Brandenburg-Prussia was a small, open territory with no natural frontiers for defense, Frederick William built an army of forty thousand men, making it the fourth largest in Europe. To sustain the army, Frederick William established the General War Commissariat to levy taxes to support the army and oversee its growth. The Commissariat soon evolved into an agency for civil government as well. Directly responsible to the elector, the new bureaucratic machine became his chief instrument to govern the state. Many of its officials were members of the Prussian landed aristocracy, the Junkers, who also served as officers in the all-important army.

Frederick William was succeeded by his son Frederick III (1688–1713), who made one significant contribution to the development of Prussia. In return for his commitment to aid the Holy Roman Emperor in a war against Spain, he received the title of King-in-Prussia in

MAP 15.2 **The Growth of Brandenberg-Prussia.** Frederick William the Great Elector laid the foundation for a powerful state when he increased the size and efficiency of the army, raised taxes and created an efficient bureaucracy to collect them, and gained the support of the landed aristocracy. Later rulers added more territory. **?** Why was the acquisition of Pomerania and West Prussia important for the continued rise in power of Brandenburg-Prussia? **View an animated version of this map or related maps at** http://thomsonedu.com/history/spielvogel

1701. Elector Frederick III was transformed into King Frederick I, and Brandenburg-Prussia became simply Prussia. In the eighteenth century, Prussia emerged as a great power on the European stage.

The Emergence of Austria

The Austrian Habsburgs had long played a significant role in European politics as Holy Roman Emperors. By the end of the Thirty Years' War, the Habsburg hopes of forging an empire in Germany had been dashed. In the seventeenth century, the house of Austria assembled a new empire in eastern and southeastern Europe.

The nucleus of the new Austrian Empire remained the traditional Austrian hereditary possessions: Lower and Upper Austria, Carinthia, Carniola, Styria, and Tyrol (see Map 15.3). To these had been added the kingdom of Bohemia and parts of northwestern Hungary in the sixteenth century. In the seventeenth century, Leopold I (1658–1705) encouraged the eastward movement of the Austrian Empire, but he was sorely challenged by the revival of Ottoman power. The Ottomans eventually pushed westward and laid siege to Vienna in 1683. A European army, led by the Austrians, counterattacked and decisively defeated the Ottomans in 1687. Austria took control of Hungary, Transylvania, Croatia, and Slovenia, thus establishing an Austrian Empire in southeastern Europe. By the beginning of the eighteenth century, the house of Austria had acquired an empire of considerable size.

Yet Austria never became a highly centralized, absolutist state, primarily because it contained so many different national groups. The empire remained a collection of territories held together by a personal union. The Habsburg emperor was archduke of Austria, king of Bohemia, and king of Hungary. Each of these areas, however, had its own laws, Estates-General, and political life.

Russia: From Fledgling Principality to Major Power

A new Russian state had emerged in the fifteenth century under the leadership of the principality of Moscow and its grand dukes. In the sixteenth century, Ivan IV the Terrible (1533–1584) was the first ruler to take the title of tsar (the Russian word for "Caesar"). Ivan expanded the territories of Russia eastward and also extended the autocracy of the tsar by crushing the power of the Russian nobility, known as the boyars. Ivan's dynasty came to an end in 1598 and was followed by a resurgence of aristocratic power in a period of anarchy known as the Time of Troubles. It did not end until the Zemsky Sobor, or national assembly, chose Michael Romanov in 1613 as the new tsar, beginning a dynasty that lasted until 1917.

In the seventeenth century, Muscovite society was highly stratified. At the top was the tsar, who claimed to be a divinely ordained autocratic ruler. Russian society was dominated by an upper class of landed aristocrats who, in the course of the seventeenth century, managed to bind their peasants to the land. Townspeople were also controlled. Many merchants were not allowed to move from their cities without government permission or to sell their businesses to anyone outside their class. In the seventeenth century, merchant and peasant revolts as well as a schism in the Russian Orthodox church created very unsettled conditions. In the midst of these political and religious upheavals, Russia was experiencing more frequent contacts with the West, and Western ideas were beginning to penetrate a few Russian circles. At the end of the seventeenth century, Peter the Great noticeably accelerated this westernizing process.

The Reign of Peter the Great (1689–1725) Peter the Great was an unusual character. A strong man towering

MAP 15.3 **The Growth of the Austrian Empire.** The Habsburgs had hoped to establish an empire of Germans, but the results of the Thirty Years' War crushed that dream. So Austria expanded to the east and the south, primarily at the expense of the Ottoman Empire, and also gained the Spanish Netherlands and former Spanish territories in Italy. [?] In which areas did the Austrian Empire have access to the Mediterranean Sea, and why would that potentially be important? [icon] **View an animated version of this map or related maps at** http://thomsonedu.com/history/ spielvogel

6 feet 9 inches tall, Peter enjoyed low humor—belching contests and crude jokes—and vicious punishments—flogging, impalings, and roastings (see the box on p. 290). He got a firsthand view of the West when he made a trip there in 1697–1698 and returned home determined to Europeanize Russia. He was especially eager to borrow European technology, convinced it would give him the military muscle he needed to make Russia a great power.

As could be expected, one of his first priorities was the reorganization of the armed forces. Employing both Russians and Europeans as officers, he conscripted peasants for twenty-five-year stints of service to build a standing army of 210,000 men. Peter has also been given credit for forming the first Russian navy.

Peter reorganized the central government, partly along Western lines. To impose the rule of the central government more effectively throughout the land, he divided Russia into eight provinces and later, in 1719, into fifty. Although he hoped to create a "police state," by which he meant a well-ordered community governed in accordance with law, few of his bureaucrats shared his concept of honest service and duty to the state. Peter hoped for a sense of civic duty, but his own forceful personality created an atmosphere of fear that prevented it.

Peter also sought to gain state control of the Russian Orthodox church. In 1721, he abolished the position of patriarch and created a body called the Holy Synod to make decisions for the church. At its head stood a **procurator**, a layman who represented the interests of the tsar and assured Peter of effective domination of the church.

Immediately upon returning from his trip to the West in 1698, Peter began to introduce Western customs, practices, and manners into Russia. He ordered the preparation of the first Russian book of etiquette to teach Western manners. Among other things, it pointed out that it was not polite to spit on the floor or scratch oneself at dinner. Because Westerners did not wear beards or the traditional long-skirted coat, Russian beards had to be shaved and coats shortened, a reform Peter personally enforced at court by shaving off his nobles' beards and cutting their coats at the knees with his own hands. Outside the court, the edicts were enforced by barbers and tailors planted at town gates with orders to cut the beards and cloaks of all who entered or left.

One group of Russians benefited greatly from Peter's cultural reforms—women. Having watched women mixing freely with men in Western courts, Peter shattered the

PETER THE GREAT DEALS WITH A REBELLION

*D*uring his first visit to the West in 1697–1698, Peter received word that the Streltsy, an elite military unit stationed in Moscow, had revolted against his authority. Peter hurried home and crushed the revolt in a very savage fashion. This selection is taken from an Austrian account of how Peter dealt with the rebels.

Peter and the Streltsy

How sharp was the pain, how great the indignation, to which the tsar's Majesty was mightily moved, when he knew of the rebellion of the Streltsy, betraying openly a mind panting for vengeance! He was still tarrying at Vienna, quite full of the desire of setting out for Italy; but, fervid as was his curiosity of rambling abroad, it was, nevertheless, speedily extinguished on the announcement of the troubles that had broken out in the bowels of his realm. Going immediately to Lefort . . . , he thus indignantly broke out: "Tell me, Francis, how I can reach Moscow by the shortest way, in a brief space, so that I may wreak vengeance on this great perfidy of my people, with punishments worthy of their abominable crime. Not one of them shall escape with impunity. Around my royal city, which, with their impious efforts, they planned to destroy, I will have gibbets and gallows set upon the walls and ramparts, and each and every one of them will I put to a direful death." Nor did he long delay the plan for his justly excited wrath; he took the quick post, as his ambassador suggested, and in four weeks' time he had got over about three hundred miles without accident, and arrived the 4th of September, 1698,–a monarch for the well deposed, but an avenger for the wicked.

His first anxiety after his arrival was about the rebellion—in what it consisted, what the insurgents meant, who dared to instigate such a crime. And as nobody could answer accurately upon all points, and some pleaded their own ignorance, others the obstinacy of the Streltsy, he began to have suspicions of everybody's loyalty. . . . No day, holy or profane, were the inquisitors idle; every day was deemed fit and lawful for torturing. There was as many scourges as there were accused, and every inquisitor was a butcher. . . . The whole month of October was spent on lacerating the backs of culprits with the knout and with flames; no day were those that were left alive exempt from scourging or scorching; or else they were broken upon the wheel, or driven to the gibbet, or slain with the ax. . . .

To prove to all people how holy and inviolable are those walls of the city which the Streltsy rashly meditated scaling in a sudden assault, beams were run out from all the embrasures in the walls near the gates, in each of which two rebels were hanged. This day beheld about two hundred and fifty die that death. There are few cities fortified with as many palisades as Moscow has given gibbets to her guardian Streltsy.

How did Peter the Great deal with the revolt of the Streltsy? What does his approach to this problem tell us about the tsar?

---

seclusion of upper-class Russian women and demanded that they remove the traditional veils that covered their faces. Peter also decreed that social gatherings be held three times a week in the large houses of Saint Petersburg where men and women could mix for conversation, card games, and dancing, which Peter had learned in the West. The tsar also now insisted that women could marry of their own free will.

The object of Peter's domestic reforms was to make Russia into a great state and military power. His primary goal was to "open a window to the West," which required an ice-free port easily accessible to Europe. This could be achieved only on the Baltic, but at that time the Baltic coast was controlled by Sweden, the most important power in northern Europe. Desirous of these lands, Peter attacked Sweden in the summer of 1700, believing that its young king, Charles XII, could easily be defeated. Charles, however, proved to be a brilliant general and, with a well-disciplined force of only eight thousand men, routed the Russian army of forty thousand at the Battle of Narva (1700). The Great Northern War (1701–1721) soon ensued.

Peter fought back. He reorganized his army along Western lines and at the Battle of Poltava in July 1709 decisively defeated Charles's army. Although the war dragged on for another twelve years, the Peace of Nystadt in 1721 gave formal recognition to what Peter had already achieved: the acquisition of Estonia, Livonia, and Karelia (see Map 15.4). Sweden became a second-rate power, and Russia was now the great European state Peter had envisioned. Already in 1703, Peter had begun the construction of a new city on the Baltic, Saint Petersburg, his window to the West and a symbol that Russia was looking toward Europe. Peter realized his dream: by the time of his death in 1725, Russia had become a great military power and an important actor on the European stage.

The Ottoman Empire

After their conquest of Constantinople in 1453, the Ottoman Turks tried but failed to complete their conquest of the Balkans, where they had been established since the fourteenth century (see Map 15.3). The reign of Sultan Suleiman I the Magnificent (1520–1566), however, brought the Ottomans back to Europe's attention. Advancing up the Danube, the Ottomans seized Belgrade in

MAP 15.4 Russia: From Principality to Nation-State. Russia had swelled in size since its emergence in the fifteenth century. However, Peter the Great modernized the country, instituting bureaucratic and taxation reforms and building up the military. He won territory on the Baltic from Sweden, giving Russia a port at Saint Petersburg. **?** Why would the westward expansion of Russia during Peter's reign affect the international balance of power in Europe?

View an animated version of this map or related maps at http://thomsonedu.com/history/spielvogel

1521 and Hungary by 1526, although their attempts to conquer Vienna in 1529 were repulsed. At the same time, the Ottomans extended their power into the western Mediterranean, threatening to turn it into an Ottoman lake until a large Ottoman fleet was destroyed by the Spanish at Lepanto (in modern-day Greece) in 1571. Despite the defeat, the Ottomans continued to hold nominal control over the southern shores along the Mediterranean.

Although Europeans frequently spoke of new Christian crusades against the "infidel" Ottomans, by the beginning of the seventeenth century, their empire was being treated like any other European power by European rulers seeking alliances and trade concessions. In the first half of the century, the Ottoman Empire was a "sleeping giant." Occupied by domestic bloodletting and severely threatened by a challenge from Persia, the Ottomans were content with the status quo in eastern Europe. But under a new line of grand viziers in the second half of the seventeenth century, the Ottoman Empire again took the offensive. By 1683, the Ottomans had marched through the Hungarian plain and laid siege to Vienna. Repulsed by a mixed army of Austrians, Poles, Bavarians, and Saxons, the Ottomans retreated and were pushed out of Hungary by a new European coalition. Although they retained the core of their empire, the Ottoman Turks would never again be a threat to Europe.

The Limits of Absolutism

In recent decades, historical studies of local institutions have challenged the traditional picture of absolute monarchs. It is misleading to think that these rulers actually controlled the lives of their subjects. In 1700, government for most people still meant the local institutions that affected their lives: local courts, local tax collectors, and local organizers of armed forces. Kings and ministers might determine policies and issue guidelines, but they still had to function through local agents and had no guarantee that their wishes would be carried out. A mass of urban and provincial privileges, liberties, and exemptions (including from taxation) and a whole host of corporate bodies and interest groups—provincial and national Estates, clerical officials, officeholders who had bought or inherited their positions, and provincial nobles—limited what monarchs could achieve. The most successful rulers were not those who tried to destroy the old system but rather those like Louis XIV who knew how to use the old system to their advantage. Above all other considerations stood the landholding nobility. Everywhere in the seventeenth century, the landed aristocracy played an important role in the European monarchical system. As military officers, judges, officeholders, and landowners in control of vast, untaxed estates, their power remained immense. In some places, their strength even put severe limits on how effectively monarchs could rule.

Limited Monarchy: The Dutch Republic and England

Almost everywhere in Europe in the seventeenth century, kings and their ministers were in control of central governments. But not all European states followed the pattern of absolute monarchy. In western Europe, two great states—the Dutch Republic and England—successfully resisted the power of hereditary monarchs.

The Golden Age of the Dutch Republic

The seventeenth century has often been called the golden age of the Dutch Republic as the United Provinces held center stage as one of Europe's great powers. Like France and England, the United Provinces was an Atlantic power, underlining the importance of that shift of political and economic power in the seventeenth century from the Mediterranean Sea to the countries on the Atlantic seaboard. As a result of the sixteenth-century revolt of the Netherlands, the seven northern provinces, which began to call themselves the United Provinces of the Netherlands in 1581, became the core of the modern Dutch state. The new state was officially recognized by the Peace of Westphalia in 1648.

With independence came internal dissension. There were two chief centers of political power in the new state. Each province had an official known as a stadholder who was responsible for leading the army and maintaining order. Beginning with William of Orange and his heirs, the house of Orange occupied the stadholderate in most provinces and favored the development of a centralized government with themselves as hereditary monarchs. The States General, an assembly of representatives from every province, opposed the Orangist ambitions and advocated a decentralized or republican form of government. For much of the seventeenth century, the republican forces were in control. But in 1672, burdened with war against both France and England, the United Provinces allowed William III (1672–1702) of the house of Orange to establish a monarchical regime. However, his death in 1702 without direct heirs enabled the republican forces to gain control once more. The Dutch Republic would not be seriously threatened again by the monarchical forces.

Underlying Dutch prominence in the seventeenth century was its economic prosperity, fueled by the role of the Dutch as carriers of European trade. But war proved disastrous to the Dutch Republic. Wars with France and England placed heavy burdens on Dutch finances and manpower. English shipping began to challenge what had been Dutch commercial supremacy, and by 1715, the Dutch were experiencing a serious economic decline.

England and the Emergence of Constitutional Monarchy

One of the most prominent examples of resistance to absolute monarchy came in seventeenth-century England, where king and Parliament struggled to determine the role each should play in governing the nation.

Revolution and Civil War With the death of Queen Elizabeth in 1603, the Tudor dynasty became extinct, and the Stuart line of rulers was inaugurated with the accession to the throne of Elizabeth's cousin, King James VI of Scotland, who became James I (1603–1625) of England. James espoused the divine right of kings, a viewpoint that alienated Parliament, which had grown accustomed under the Tudors to act on the premise that monarch and Parliament together ruled England as a "balanced polity." Parliament expressed its displeasure with James's claims by refusing his requests for additional monies he needed to meet the increased cost of government. Parliament's power of the purse proved to be its trump card in its relationship with the king.

Some members of Parliament were also alienated by James's religious policy. The **Puritans**—Protestants within the Anglican church inspired by Calvinist theology—wanted James to eliminate the episcopal system of church organization used in the Church of England (in which the

Cleanliness Is Next to Godliness. During the Golden Age of the Dutch Republic, Dutch burghers held to very strict standards of cleanliness. Household manuals, such as *The Experienced and Knowledgeable Hollands Householder*, provided detailed outlines of the cleaning tasks that should be performed each day of the week. This emphasis on cleanliness is evident in this work by Pieter de Hooch, who specialized in painting pictures of Dutch interiors. In *The Mother*, de Hooch portrays a tranquil scene of a mother with her infant and small daughter. The spotless, polished floors reflect the sunlight streaming in through the open door. The rooms are both clean and in good order.

bishop or *episcopos* played the major administrative role) in favor of a Presbyterian model (used in Scotland and patterned after Calvin's church organization in Geneva, where ministers and elders—also called presbyters—played an important governing role). James refused because he realized that the Anglican church, with its bishops appointed by the crown, was a major supporter of monarchical authority. But the Puritans were not easily cowed and added to the rising chorus of opposition to the king. Many of England's **gentry,** mostly well-to-do landowners below the level of the nobility, had become Puritans, and these Puritan gentry formed an important and substantial part of the House of Commons, the lower house of Parliament. It was not wise to alienate them.

The conflict that began during the reign of James came to a head during the reign of his son, Charles I (1625–1649). In 1628, Parliament passed a petition of right that the king was supposed to accept before being granted any tax revenues. This petition prohibited levying taxes without Parliament's consent, arbitrary imprisonment, the quartering of soldiers in private houses, and the declaration of martial law in peacetime. Although he initially accepted it, Charles later reneged on the agreement because of its limitations on royal power. In 1629,

Charles decided that because he could not work with Parliament, he would not summon it to meet. From 1629 to 1640, Charles pursued a course of "personal rule," which forced him to find ways to collect taxes without Parliament's cooperation. These expedients aroused opposition from middle-class merchants and landed gentry who believed that the king was attempting to tax without Parliament's consent.

The king's religious policy also proved disastrous. His attempt to impose more ritual on the Anglican church struck the Puritans as a return to Catholic popery. Charles's efforts to force them to conform to his religious policies infuriated the Puritans, thousands of whom abandoned England for the "howling wildernesses" of America.

Grievances mounted until England finally slipped into a civil war (1642–1648) that was won by the parliamentary forces. Most important to Parliament's success was the creation of the New Model Army, one of whose leaders was Oliver Cromwell, the only real military genius of the war. The New Model Army was composed primarily of more extreme Puritans known as the Independents, who, in typical Calvinist fashion, believed they were doing battle for the Lord. As Cromwell wrote in one of his military reports, "Sir, this is none other but the hand of God; and to Him alone belongs the glory."

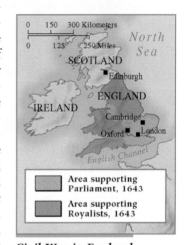

Civil War in England

Between 1648 and 1660, England faced a trying situation. After the execution of Charles I on January 30, 1649, Parliament abolished the monarchy and the House of Lords and proclaimed England a republic or commonwealth. But Cromwell and his army, unable to work effectively with Parliament, dispersed it by force. As the members of Parliament departed in April 1653, Cromwell shouted after them, "It's you that have forced me to do this, for I have sought the Lord night and day that He would slay me rather than put upon me the doing of this work." With the certainty of one who is convinced he is right, Cromwell had destroyed both king and Parliament.

Finally, Cromwell dissolved Parliament and divided the country into eleven regions, each ruled by a major general who served virtually as a military governor. Unable to establish a constitutional basis for a working government, Cromwell had resorted to military force to maintain the rule of the Independents.

Oliver Cromwell died in 1658. After floundering for eighteen months, the military establishment decided that arbitrary rule by the army was no longer feasible and reestablished the monarchy in the person of Charles II

Oliver Cromwell. Oliver Cromwell was a dedicated Puritan who formed the New Model Army and defeated the forces supporting King Charles I. Unable to work with Parliament, he came to rely on military force to rule England. Cromwell is pictured here in 1649, on the eve of his military campaign in Ireland.

(1660–1685), the son of Charles I. The restoration of the Stuart monarchy ended England's time of troubles, but it was not long before yet another constitutional crisis arose.

Restoration and a Glorious Revolution Charles was sympathetic to and perhaps even inclined to Catholicism. Moreover, Charles's brother James, heir to the throne, did not hide the fact that he was a Catholic. Parliament's suspicions were therefore aroused in 1672 when Charles took the audacious step of issuing a declaration of indulgence that suspended the laws that Parliament had passed against Catholics and Puritans after the restoration of the Anglican church as the official church of England. Parliament would have none of it and induced the king to suspend the declaration. Propelled by strong anti-Catholic sentiment, Parliament then passed the Test Act of 1673, specifying that only Anglicans could hold military and civil offices.

The accession of James II (1685–1688) to the crown virtually guaranteed a new constitutional crisis for England. An open and devout Catholic, his attempt to further Catholic interests made religion once more a primary cause of conflict between king and Parliament. In 1687, James issued a declaration of indulgence that suspended all laws that excluded Catholics and Puritans from office. Parliamentary outcries against James's policies stopped short of rebellion because members knew that he was an old man and his successors were his Protestant daughters Mary and Anne, born to his first wife. But on June 10, 1688, a son was born to James II's second wife, also a Catholic. Suddenly the specter of a Catholic hereditary monarchy loomed large. A group of prominent English noblemen invited the Dutch chief executive, William of Orange, husband of James's daughter Mary, to invade England. William and Mary raised an army and invaded England while James, his wife, and their infant son fled to France. With almost no bloodshed, England had undergone its "Glorious Revolution," not over the issue of whether there would be monarchy but rather over who would be monarch.

In January 1689, Parliament offered the throne to William and Mary, who accepted it along with the provisions of a bill of rights (see the box on p. 295). The Bill of Rights affirmed Parliament's right to make laws and levy taxes and made it impossible for kings to oppose or do without Parliament by stipulating that standing armies could be raised only with the consent of Parliament. The rights of citizens to petition the sovereign, keep arms,

THE BILL OF RIGHTS

In 1688, the English experienced yet another revolution, a bloodless one in which the Stuart king James II was replaced by Mary, James's daughter, and her husband, William of Orange. After William and Mary had assumed power, Parliament passed a bill of rights that specified the rights of Parliament and laid the foundation for a constitutional monarchy.

The Bill of Rights

Whereas the said late King James II having abdicated the government, and the throne being thereby vacant, his Highness the prince of Orange (whom it has pleased Almighty God to make the glorious instrument of delivering this kingdom from popery and arbitrary power) did (by the device of the lords spiritual and temporal, and diverse principal persons of the Commons) cause letters to be written to the lords spiritual and temporal, being Protestants, and other letters to the several counties, cities, universities, boroughs, and Cinque Ports, for the choosing of such persons to represent them, as were of right to be sent to parliament, to meet and sit at Westminster upon the two and twentieth day of January, in this year 1689, in order to such an establishment as that their religion, laws, and liberties might not again be in danger of being subverted; upon which letters elections have been accordingly made.

And thereupon the said lords spiritual and temporal and Commons, pursuant to their respective letters and elections, being now assembled in a full and free representation of this nation, taking into their most serious consideration the best means for attaining the ends aforesaid, do in the first place (as their ancestors in like case have usually done), for the vindication and assertion of their ancient rights and liberties, declare:

1. That the pretended power of suspending laws, or the execution of laws, by regal authority, without consent of parliament is illegal.
2. That the pretended power of dispensing with the laws, or the execution of law by regal authority, as it has been assumed and exercised of late, is illegal.
3. That the commission for erecting the late court of commissioners for ecclesiastical causes, and all other commissions and courts of like nature, are illegal and pernicious.
4. That levying money for or to the use of the crown by pretense of prerogative, without grant of parliament, for longer time or in other manner than the same is or shall be granted, is illegal.
5. That it is the right of the subjects to petition the king, and all commitments and prosecutions for such petitioning are illegal.
6. That the raising or keeping a standing army within the kingdom in time of peace, unless it be with consent of parliament, is against law.
7. That the subjects which are Protestants may have arms for their defense suitable to their conditions, and as allowed by law.
8. That election of members of parliament ought to be free.
9. That the freedom of speech, and debates or proceedings in parliament, ought not to be impeached or questioned in any court or place out of parliament.
10. That excessive bail ought not to be required, nor excessive fines imposed, nor cruel and unusual punishments inflicted.
11. That jurors ought to be duly impaneled and returned, and jurors which pass upon men in trials for high treason ought to be freeholders.
12. That all grants and promises of fines and forfeitures of particular persons before conviction are illegal and void.
13. And that for redress of all grievances, and for the amending, strengthening, and preserving of the laws, parliament ought to be held frequently.

How did the Bill of Rights lay the foundation for a constitutional monarchy in England?

have a jury trial, and not be subject to excessive bail were also confirmed. The Bill of Rights helped fashion a system of government based on the rule of law and a freely elected Parliament, thus laying the foundation for a constitutional monarchy.

The Bill of Rights did not settle the religious questions that had played such a large role in England's troubles in the seventeenth century. The Toleration Act of 1689 granted Puritan dissenters the right of free public worship (Catholics were still excluded). Although the Toleration Act did not mean complete religious freedom and equality, it marked a departure in English history in that few people would ever again be persecuted for religious reasons.

Many historians have viewed the Glorious Revolution as the end of the seventeenth-century struggle between king and Parliament. By deposing one king and establishing another, Parliament had destroyed the divine-right theory of kingship (William was, after all, king by grace of Parliament, not God) and confirmed its right to participate in the government. Parliament did not have complete control of the government, but it now had an unquestioned right to participate in affairs of state. During the next century, it would gradually prove to be the real authority in the English system of constitutional monarchy.

Responses to Revolution   The English revolutions of the seventeenth century prompted very different responses from two English political thinkers, Thomas Hobbes and John Locke. Thomas Hobbes (1588–1679), who lived during the English Civil War, was alarmed by the revolutionary upheavals in his contemporary England. His name has since been associated with the state's claim to absolute authority over its subjects, which he elaborated in his major treatise on political thought known as the *Leviathan,* published in 1651.

Hobbes claimed that in the state of nature, before society was organized, human life was "solitary, poor, nasty, brutish, and short." Humans were guided by animalistic instincts and a ruthless struggle for self-preservation. To save themselves from destroying each other (the "war of every man against every man"), people contracted to form a commonwealth, which Hobbes called "that great Leviathan (or rather, to speak more reverently, that mortal god) to which we owe our peace and defense." This commonwealth placed its collective power in the hands of a sovereign authority, preferably a single ruler, who served as executor, legislator, and judge. This absolute ruler possessed unlimited power. In Hobbes's view, subjects may not rebel; if they do, they must be suppressed.

John Locke (1632–1704), author of a political work called *Two Treatises of Government,* viewed the exercise of political power quite differently from Hobbes and argued against the absolute rule of one man. Like Hobbes, Locke began with the state of nature before human existence became organized socially. But unlike Hobbes, Locke believed that humans lived then in a state of equality and freedom rather than a state of war. In this state of nature, humans had certain inalienable natural rights—to life, liberty, and property. Like Hobbes, Locke did not believe that all was well in the state of nature, and people found it difficult to protect these rights. So they mutually agreed to establish a government to ensure the protection of their rights. This agreement established mutual obligations: government would protect the rights of people, and the people would act reasonably toward their government. But if a government broke this agreement—if a king, for example, failed to live up to his obligation to protect the people's rights or claimed absolute authority and made laws without the consent of the community—the people might form a new government. For Locke, however, the community of people was primarily the landholding aristocracy who were represented in Parliament, not the landless masses. Locke was hardly an advocate of political democracy, but his ideas proved important to both the Americans and the French in the eighteenth century and were used to support demands for constitutional government, the rule of law, and the protection of rights.

The Flourishing of European Culture

In the midst of religious wars and the growth of absolutism, European culture continued to flourish. The era was blessed with a number of prominent artists and writers.

The Changing Faces of Art

After the Renaissance, European art passed through a number of stylistic stages. The artistic Renaissance came to an end when a new movement called Mannerism emerged in Italy in the 1520s and 1530s.

Mannerism   The Reformation had brought a revival of religious values accompanied by much political turmoil. Especially in Italy, the worldly enthusiasm of the Renaissance gave way to anxiety, uncertainty, suffering, and a yearning for spiritual experience. **Mannerism** reflected this environment in its deliberate attempt to break down the High Renaissance principles of balance, harmony, and moderation. Italian Mannerist painters deliberately distorted the rules of proportion by portraying elongated figures that conveyed a sense of suffering and a strong emotional atmosphere filled with anxiety and confusion.

The Baroque   Mannerism was eventually replaced by a new movement—the **Baroque**—that dominated the artistic world for another century and a half. The Baroque began in Italy in the last quarter of the sixteenth century and spread to the rest of Europe. Baroque artists sought to harmonize the classical traditions of Renaissance art with the intense religious feelings fostered by the revival of religion in the Reformation. Although Protestants were also affected, the Baroque was most wholeheartedly embraced by the Catholic reform movement, as is evident at the Catholic courts, especially those of the Habsburgs in Madrid, Prague, Vienna, and Brussels. Eventually, the Baroque style spread to all of Europe and Latin America.

In large part, Baroque art and architecture reflected the search for power that was characteristic of much of the seventeenth century. Baroque churches and palaces featured richly ornamented facades, sweeping staircases, and an overall splendor intended to impress people. Kings and princes wanted their subjects—as well as other kings and princes—to be in awe of their power. The Catholic church, which commissioned many new churches, wanted people to see the triumphant power of the Catholic faith.

Baroque painting was known for its use of dramatic effects to heighten emotional intensity. This style was especially evident in the works of the Flemish painter Peter Paul Rubens (1577–1640), a prolific artist and an important figure in the spread of the Baroque from Italy to other parts of Europe. In his artistic masterpieces,

Peter Paul Rubens, *The Landing of Marie de'Medici at Marseilles.* The Fleming Peter Paul Rubens played a key role in spreading the Baroque style from Italy to other parts of Europe. In *The Landing of Marie de'Medici at Marseilles*, Rubens made a dramatic use of light and color, bodies in motion, and luxurious nudes to heighten the emotional intensity of the scene. This was one of a cycle of twenty-one paintings dedicated to the queen mother of France.

Artemisia Gentileschi, *Judith Beheading Holofernes.* Artemisia Gentileschi painted a series of pictures portraying scenes from the lives of courageous Old Testament women. In this painting, a determined Judith, armed with her victim's sword, struggles to saw off the head of Holofernes. Gentileschi realistically and dramatically shows the gruesome nature of Judith's act.

bodies in vigorous motion, fleshy nudes, a dramatic use of light and shadow, and rich, sensuous pigments convey intense emotions. The restless forms and sense of movement blend into a dynamic unity.

Perhaps the greatest figure of the Baroque was the Italian architect and sculptor Gian Lorenzo Bernini (1598–1680), who completed Saint Peter's Basilica and designed the vast colonnade enclosing the piazza in front of it. Action, exuberance, profusion, and dramatic effects mark his work in the interior of Saint Peter's, where Bernini's *Throne of Saint Peter* hovers in midair, held by the hands of the four great doctors of the Catholic church.

Less well known than the male artists who dominated the seventeenth-century art world in Italy but prominent in her own right was Artemisia Gentileschi (1593–1653). Born in Rome, she studied painting under her father's direction. In 1616, she moved to Florence

and began a successful career as a painter. At the age of twenty-three, she became the first woman to be elected to the Florentine Academy of Design. Although she was known internationally in her day as a portrait painter, her fame now rests on a series of pictures of heroines from the Old Testament, including Judith, Esther, and Bathsheba. Most famous is her *Judith Beheading Holofernes,* a dramatic rendering of the biblical scene in which Judith slays the Assyrian general Holofernes in order to save her besieged town from the Assyrian army.

French Classicism and Dutch Realism In the second half of the seventeenth century, France replaced Italy as the cultural leader of Europe. Rejecting the Baroque style as showy and overly passionate, the French remained committed to the classical values of the High Renaissance. French late classicism, with its emphasis on clarity,

Rembrandt van Rijn, *Syndics of the Cloth Guild*.   The Dutch experienced a golden age of painting during the seventeenth century. The burghers and patricians of Dutch urban society commissioned works of art, and these quite naturally reflected the burghers' interests, as this painting by Rembrandt illustrates.

simplicity, balance, and harmony of design, was, however, a rather austere version of the High Renaissance style. Its triumph reflected the shift in seventeenth-century French society from chaos to order. While rejecting the emotionalism and high drama of the Baroque, French classicism continued the Baroque's conception of grandeur in the portrayal of noble subjects, especially those from classical antiquity.

The supremacy of Dutch commerce in the seventeenth century was paralleled by a brilliant flowering of Dutch painting. Wealthy patricians and burghers of Dutch urban society commissioned works of art for their guild halls, town halls, and private dwellings. Following the wishes of these patrons, Dutch painters became primarily interested in the realistic portrayal of secular, everyday life.

The finest exemplar of the golden age of Dutch painting was Rembrandt van Rijn (1606–1669). Although Rembrandt shared the Dutch predilection for realistic portraits, he became more introspective as he grew older. He refused to follow his contemporaries, whose pictures were largely secular in subject matter; half of his paintings focused on scenes from biblical tales. Because the traditional Protestant hostility toward religious

pictures had discouraged artistic expression, Rembrandt stands out as the one great Protestant painter of the seventeenth century.

A Wondrous Age of Theater

In both England and Spain, writing for the stage reached new heights between 1580 and 1640. The golden age of English literature is often called the Elizabethan era because much of this English cultural flowering occurred during the reign of Queen Elizabeth. Elizabethan literature exhibits the exuberance and pride associated with English exploits at the time. Of all the forms of Elizabethan literature, none expressed the energy and intellectual versatility of the era better than drama. And of all the dramatists, none is more famous than William Shakespeare (1564–1614).

William Shakespeare   Shakespeare was the son of a prosperous glove maker from Stratford-upon-Avon. When he appeared in London in 1592, Elizabethans were already addicted to the stage. In Greater London, as many as six theaters were open six afternoons a week. London

WILLIAM SHAKESPEARE: IN PRAISE OF ENGLAND

William Shakespeare is one of the most famous playwrights of the Western world. He was a universal genius, outclassing all others in his psychological insights, depth of characterization, imaginative skills, and versatility. His historical plays reflected the patriotic enthusiasm of the English in the Elizabethan era, as this excerpt from *Richard II* illustrates.

William Shakespeare, *Richard II*

This royal throne of kings, this sceptered isle,
This earth of majesty, this seat of Mars,
This other Eden, demi-Paradise,
This fortress built by Nature for herself
Against infection and the hand of war,
This happy breed of men, this little world,
This precious stone set in the silver sea,
Which serves it in the office of a wall
Or as a moat defensive to a house
Against the envy of less happier lands—
This blessed plot, this earth, this realm, this England,
This nurse, this teeming womb of royal kings,
Feared by their breed and famous by their birth,

Renowned for their deeds as far from home,
For Christian service and true chivalry,
As is the sepulcher in stubborn Jewry [the Holy
   Sepulcher in Jerusalem]
Of the world's ransom, blessed Mary's Son—
This land of such dear souls, this dear dear land,
Dear for her reputation through the world,
Is now leased out, I die pronouncing it,
Like a tenement or pelting farm.
England, bound in with the triumphant sea,
Whose rocky shore beats back the envious siege
Of watery Neptune, is now bound in with shame,
With inky blots and rotten parchment bonds.
That England, what was wont to conquer others,
Hath made a shameful conquest of itself.
Ah, would the scandal vanish with my life,
How happy then were my ensuing death!

Why is William Shakespeare aptly described as not merely a playwright but a "complete man of the theater"? Which countries might Shakespeare have meant to suggest by the phrase "the envy of less happier lands"?

---

theaters ranged from the Globe, which was a circular unroofed structure holding three thousand spectators, to the Blackfriars, which was roofed and held only five hundred. In the former, the admission charge of only a penny or two enabled even the lower classes to attend, while the higher prices charged in the latter attracted the well-to-do. Elizabethan audiences varied greatly, consisting as they did of nobles, lawyers, merchants, and even vagabonds—putting pressure on playwrights to create works that pleased all.

Shakespeare was a "complete man of the theater." Although best known for writing plays, he was also an actor and a shareholder in the chief performing company of the time, the Lord Chamberlain's Company, which played in theaters as diverse as the Globe and the Blackfriars. Shakespeare has long been recognized as a universal genius. He was a master of the English language, but this technical proficiency was matched by an incredible insight into human psychology. In both tragedies and comedies, Shakespeare exhibited a remarkable understanding of the human condition (see the box above).

Spain's Golden Century The theater was one of the most creative forms of expression during Spain's golden century. The first professional theaters founded in Seville and Madrid in the 1570s were run by actors' companies, as in England. Soon a public playhouse could be found in every large town, including Mexico City in the New World. Touring companies brought the latest Spanish plays to all parts of the Spanish Empire.

Beginning in the 1580s, the agenda for playwrights was set by Lope de Vega (1562–1635). Like Shakespeare, he was from a middle-class background. He was an incredibly prolific writer; almost one-third of his fifteen hundred plays survive. They have been characterized as witty, charming, action-packed, and realistic. Lope de Vega made no apologies for the fact that he wrote his plays to please his audiences. In a treatise on drama written in 1609, he stated that the foremost duty of the playwright was to satisfy public demand. He remarked that if anyone thought he had written his plays for fame, "undeceive him and tell him that I wrote them for money."

French Drama As the great age of theater in England and Spain was drawing to a close around 1630, a new dramatic era began to dawn in France that lasted into the 1680s. Unlike Shakespeare in England and Lope de Vega in Spain, French playwrights wrote more for an elite audience and were forced to depend on royal patronage. Louis XIV used theater as he did art and architecture—to attract attention to his monarchy. French dramatists cultivated a classical style that emphasized the clever, polished, and correct over the emotional and imaginative. Many of the French works of this period derived their themes and plots from Greek and Roman sources.

Jean-Baptiste Molière (1622–1673) enjoyed the favor of the French court and benefited from the patronage of the Sun King. He wrote, produced, and acted in a series of comedies that often satirized the religious and social world of his time. In *The Misanthrope*, he mocked the corruption of court society, while in *Tartuffe*, he ridiculed religious hypocrisy. Molière's satires, however, sometimes got him into trouble. The Paris clergy did not find *Tartuffe* funny and had it banned for five years. Only the protection of Louis XIV saved Molière from more severe harassment.

TIMELINE

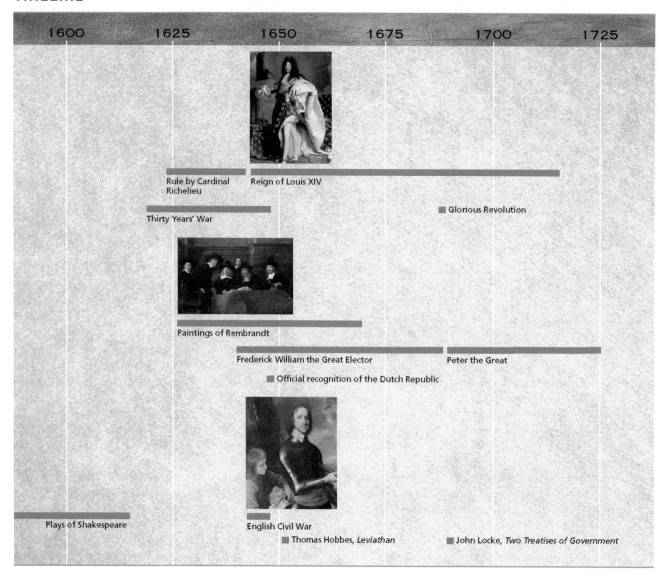

| 1600 | 1625 | 1650 | 1675 | 1700 | 1725 |

Rule by Cardinal Richelieu

Reign of Louis XIV

Thirty Years' War

Glorious Revolution

Paintings of Rembrandt

Frederick William the Great Elector

Peter the Great

Official recognition of the Dutch Republic

Plays of Shakespeare

English Civil War

Thomas Hobbes, *Leviathan*

John Locke, *Two Treatises of Government*

CONCLUSION

To many historians, the seventeenth century has assumed extraordinary proportions. The divisive effects of the Reformation had been assimilated, and the concept of a united Christendom, held as an ideal since the Middle Ages, had been irrevocably destroyed by the religious wars, making possible the emergence of a system of nation-states in which power politics took on increasing significance. The growth of political thought focusing on the secular origins of state power reflected the changes that were going on in seventeenth-century society.

Within those states, there slowly emerged some of the machinery that made possible a growing centralization of power. In those states called absolutist, strong monarchs with the assistance of their aristocracies took the lead in providing the leadership for greater centralization. But in England, where the landed aristocracy gained power at the expense of the monarchs, the foundations were laid for a constitutional government in which Parliament provided the focus for the institutions of centralized power. In all the major European states, a growing concern for power and dynastic expansion led to larger armies and greater conflict. War remained an endemic feature of Western civilization.

But the search for order and harmony continued, evident in art and literature. At the same time, religious preoccupations and values were losing ground to secular considerations. The seventeenth century was a period of transition toward the more secular spirit that has characterized modern Western civilization ever since. No stronger foundation for this spirit could be found than in the new view of the universe that was ushered in by the Scientific Revolution of the seventeenth century, and it is to that story that we now turn.

NOTES

1. Quoted in J. Klaits, *Servants of Satan: The Age of the Witch Hunts* (Bloomington, Ind., 1985), p. 68.
2. Quoted in ibid., p. 68.
3. Quoted in J. B. Wolf, *Louis XIV* (New York, 1968), p. 134.
4. Quoted in J. H. Elliot, *Imperial Spain, 1469–1716* (New York, 1963), p. 306.

SUGGESTIONS FOR FURTHER READING

For general works on the seventeenth century, see **D. H. Pennington, *Europe in the Seventeenth Century*,** 2d ed. (New York, 1989); **T. Munck, *Seventeenth-Century Europe, 1598–1700*** (London, 1990); and **R. S. Dunn, *The Age of Religious Wars, 1559–1715*,** 2d ed. (New York, 1979).

The story of the witchcraft craze can be examined in **J. Klaits, *Servants of Satan: The Age of the Witch Hunts*** (Bloomington, Ind., 1985); **J. B. Russell, *A History of Witchcraft*** (London, 1980); and **B. P. Levack, *The Witch-Hunt in Early Modern Europe*** (London, 1987).

The classic study on the Thirty Years' War is **C. V. Wedgwood, *The Thirty Years' War*** (Garden City, N.Y., 1961), but it needs to be supplemented by the more recent works by **G. Parker, ed., *The Thirty Years' War*,** 2d ed. (London, 1997); **R. G. Asch, *The Thirty Years' War: The Holy Roman Empire and Europe, 1618–1648*** (New York, 1997); and the brief study by **S. J. Lee, *The Thirty Years' War*** (London, 1991).

For a succinct account of seventeenth-century French history, see **J. B. Collins, *The State in Early Modern France*** (Cambridge, 1995). A solid and very readable biography of Louis XIV is **J. B. Wolf, *Louis XIV*** (New York, 1968), but also see **A. Levi, *Louis XIV*** (New York, 2004). A good general work on seventeenth-century Spanish history is **J. Lynch, *Spain Under the Habsburgs*,** 2d ed. (New York, 1981).

On the German states, see **P. H. Wilson, *The Holy Roman Empire, 1495–1806*** (New York, 1999), and **M. Hughes, *Early Modern Germany, 1477–1806*** (Philadelphia, 1992). On the creation of Austria, see **C. Ingrao, *The Habsburg Monarchy, 1618–1815*** (Cambridge, 1994), and **P. S. Fichtner, *The Habsburg Monarchy,***

1490–1848 (New York, 2003). On Austria and Prussia, see **P. H. Wilson, *Absolutism in Central Europe*** (New York, 2000). On Frederick William the Great Elector, see **D. McKay, *The Great Elector*** (Essex, 2001).

On Russian history before Peter the Great, see the classic work by **V. O. Klyuchevsky, *A Course in Russian History: The Seventeenth Century*** (Chicago, 1968). Works on Peter the Great include **L. Hughes, *Russia in the Age of Peter the Great*** (New Haven, Conn., 1998), and **M. S. Anderson, *Peter the Great,*** 2d ed. (New York, 1995).

Good general works on the period of the English Revolution include **M. A. Kishlansky, *A Monarchy Transformed*** (London, 1996); **G. E. Aylmer, *Rebellion or Revolution? England, 1640–1660*** (New York, 1986); and **A. Hughes, *The Causes of the English Civil War*** (New York, 1991). On Oliver Cromwell, see **R. Howell Jr., *Cromwell*** (Boston, 1977), and **P. Gaunt, *Oliver Cromwell*** (Cambridge, Mass., 1996). For a general survey of the post-Cromwellian era, see **T. Harris, *Politics Under the Late Stuarts*** (London, 1993). On Charles II, see the scholarly biography by **R. Hutton, *Charles II*** (Oxford, 1989). Locke's political ideas are examined in **J. H. Franklin, *John Locke and the Theory of Sovereignty*** (London, 1978). On Thomas Hobbes, see **D. D. Raphael, *Hobbes*** (London, 1977).

On the United Provinces, **J. Israel, *The Dutch Republic: Its Rise, Greatness, and Fall*** (New York, 1995), is a valuable but lengthy study. Of much value is **S. Schama, *The Embarrassment of Riches: An Interpretation of Dutch Culture in the Golden Age*** (New York, 1987).

A brief, readable guide to Mannerism is **L. Murray, *The Late Renaissance and Mannerism*** (New York, 1967). For a general survey of Baroque culture, see **M. Mainstone and L. Mainstone, *The Cambridge Introduction to Art: The Seventeenth Century*** (Cambridge, 1981), and **J. S. Held, *Seventeenth and Eighteenth Century Art: Baroque Painting, Sculpture, Architecture*** (New York, 1971). The literature on Shakespeare is enormous. For a biography, see **A. L. Rowse, *The Life of Shakespeare*** (New York, 1963). French theater and literature are examined in **A. Adam, *Grandeur and Illusion: French Literature and Society, 1600–1715, trans.* J. Tint** (New York, 1972). For an examination of French and Dutch art, see **A. Merot, *French Painting in the Seventeenth Century*** (New Haven, Conn., 1995), and **S. Slive, *Dutch Painting, 1600–1800*** (New Haven, Conn., 1993).

Thomson NOW! Enter *ThomsonNOW* using the access card that is available for *Western Civilization: A Brief History*. *ThomsonNOW* will help you understand this chapter with lesson plans generated for your needs. In addition, you can read the following documents, and many more, online:

John Locke, *An Essay Concerning Human Understanding*
King Frederick William, Welcoming the Huguenots to Prussia
John Milton, *The Tenure of Kings and Magistrates*
Jean Rousset de Missy, describing Russians in Western dress

WESTERN CIVILIZATION RESOURCES

Visit the Web site for *Western Civilization: A Brief History* for resources specific to this book:

http://www.thomsonedu.com/history/spielvogel

For a variety of tools to help you succeed in this course, visit the Western Civilization Resource Center at

http://history.wadsworth.com/spielvogel

Included are quizzes, images, documents, interactive simulations, maps and timelines, movie explorations, and a wealth of other sources.

TOWARD A NEW HEAVEN AND A NEW EARTH: THE SCIENTIFIC REVOLUTION AND THE EMERGENCE OF MODERN SCIENCE

CHAPTER OUTLINE AND FOCUS QUESTIONS

Background to the Scientific Revolution

☐ What developments during the Middle Ages and the Renaissance contributed to the Scientific Revolution of the sixteenth century?

Toward a New Heaven: A Revolution in Astronomy

☐ What did Copernicus, Kepler, Galileo, and Newton contribute to a new vision of the universe, and how did it differ from the Ptolemaic conception of the universe?

Advances in Medicine and Chemistry

☐ What did Paracelsus, Vesalius, and Harvey contribute to a scientific view of medicine?

Women in the Origins of Modern Science

☐ What role did women play in the Scientific Revolution?

Toward a New Earth: Descartes, Rationalism, and a New View of Humankind

☐ Why is Descartes considered the "founder of modern rationalism"?

The Spread of Scientific Knowledge

☐ How were the ideas of the Scientific Revolution spread, and what impact did they have on society and religion?

CRITICAL THINKING

☐ In what ways were the intellectual, political, social, and religious developments of the seventeenth century related?

The trial of Galileo

Erich Lessing/Art Resource, NY

*I*N ADDITION TO POLITICAL, economic, and social crises, the seventeenth century witnessed an intellectual one. The Scientific Revolution questioned and ultimately challenged conceptions and beliefs about the nature of the external world and reality that had crystallized into a rather strict orthodoxy by the Later Middle Ages. Derived from the works of ancient Greeks and Romans and grounded in Christian thought, the medieval worldview had become almost overpowering. But the breakdown of Christian unity during the Reformation and the subsequent religious wars had created an environment in which Europeans became more comfortable with challenging both the ecclesiastical and political powers that be. Should it surprise us that a challenge to intellectual authority soon followed?

The Scientific Revolution taught Europeans to view the universe and their place in it in a new way. The shift from an earth-centered to a sun-centered cosmos had an emotional as well as intellectual effect on those who understood it. Thus the Scientific Revolution, popularized in the eighteenth-century Enlightenment, stands as the major force in the transition to the largely secular, rational, and materialistic perspective that has defined the modern Western mentality in modern times.

The transition to a new worldview, however, was far from easy. In the seventeenth century, the Italian scientist Galileo, an outspoken advocate of the new worldview, found that his ideas were strongly opposed by the authorities of the Catholic church. Galileo's position was clear: "I hold the sun to be situated motionless in the center of the revolution of the celestial bodies, while the earth rotates on its axis and revolves about the sun." Moreover, "nothing physical that sense-experience sets before our eyes...ought to be called in question (much less condemned) upon the testimony of biblical passages." But the church had a different view, and in 1633, Galileo, now sixty-eight and in ill health, was called before the dreaded Inquisition in Rome. He was kept waiting for two months before he was tried and found guilty of heresy and disobedience. Completely shattered by the experience, he denounced his errors: "With a sincere heart and unfeigned faith I curse and detest the said errors and heresies contrary to the Holy Church." Legend holds that when he left the trial rooms, Galileo muttered to himself: "And yet it does move!" In any case, Galileo had been silenced, but his writings remained, and they began to spread through Europe. The actions of the Inquisition had failed to stop the spread of the new ideas of the Scientific Revolution.

In one sense, the Scientific Revolution was not a revolution. It was not characterized by the explosive change and rapid overthrow of traditional authority that we normally associate with the word *revolution*. The Scientific Revolution did overturn centuries of authority, but only in a gradual and piecemeal fashion. Nevertheless, its results were truly revolutionary. The Scientific Revolution was a key factor in setting Western civilization on its modern secular and material path.✦

Background to the Scientific Revolution

To say that the **Scientific Revolution** brought about a dissolution of the medieval worldview is not to say that the Middle Ages was a period of scientific ignorance. Many educated Europeans took an intense interest in the world around them, regarding it as "God's handiwork" and therefore an appropriate subject for study. Late medieval scholastic philosophers had advanced mathematical and physical thinking in many ways, but the subjection of these thinkers to a strict theological framework and their unquestioning reliance on a few ancient authorities, especially Aristotle and Galen, limited where they could go. Many "natural philosophers," as medieval scientists were known, preferred refined logical analysis to systematic observations of the natural world. A number of changes and advances in the fifteenth and sixteenth centuries may have played a major role in helping "natural philosophers" abandon their old views and develop new ones.

Ancient Authors and Renaissance Artists

The Renaissance humanists mastered both Greek and Latin and made works by Ptolemy and Archimedes as well as Plato newly available. These writings made it clear that even the unquestioned authorities of the Middle Ages, Aristotle and Galen, had been contradicted by other thinkers. The desire to discover which school of thought was correct stimulated new scientific work that sometimes led to a complete rejection of the classical authorities.

Renaissance artists have also been credited with having an impact on scientific study. Their desire to imitate nature led them to rely on a close observation of nature. Their accurate renderings of rocks, plants, animals, and human anatomy established new standards for the study of natural phenomena. At the same time, the "scientific" study of the problems of perspective and correct anatomical proportions led to new insights. "No painter," one Renaissance artist declared, "can paint well without a thorough knowledge of geometry."[1]

Technological Innovations and Mathematics

Technical problems, such as calculating the tonnage of ships accurately, also served to stimulate scientific activity because they required careful observation and accurate measurements. Then, too, the invention of new instruments and machines, such as the telescope and microscope, often made new scientific discoveries possible. The printing press played a crucial role in spreading innovative ideas quickly and easily.

Mathematics, so fundamental to the scientific achievements of the sixteenth and seventeenth centuries, was promoted in the Renaissance by the rediscovery of the works of ancient mathematicians and the influence of Plato, who had emphasized the importance of mathematics in explaining the universe. Applauded as the key to navigation, military science, and geography, mathematics was also regarded as the key to understanding the nature of things. According to Leonardo da Vinci, since God eternally geometrizes, nature is inherently mathematical: "Proportion is not only found in numbers and measurements but also in sounds, weights, times, positions, and in whatsoever power there may be."[2] Copernicus, Kepler, Galileo, and Newton were all great mathematicians who believed that the secrets of nature were written in the language of mathematics.

Renaissance Magic

Another factor in the Scientific Revolution may have been magic. Renaissance magic was the preserve of the intellectual elite of Europe. By the end of the sixteenth century, Hermetic magic (see Chapter 12) had become fused with alchemical thought into a single intellectual framework. This tradition believed that the world was a living embodiment of divinity. Humans, who it was believed also had that spark of divinity within, could use magic, especially mathematical magic, to understand and dominate

ON THE REVOLUTIONS OF THE HEAVENLY SPHERES

Nicolaus Copernicus began a revolution in astronomy when he argued that the sun and not the earth was at the center of the universe. Expecting controversy and scorn, Copernicus hesitated to publish the work in which he put forth his heliocentric theory. He finally relented, however, and managed to see a copy of it just before he died.

Nicolaus Copernicus, *On the Revolutions of the Heavenly Spheres*

For a long time, then, I reflected on this confusion in the astronomical traditions concerning the derivation of the motions of the universe's spheres. I began to be annoyed that the movements of the world machine, created for our sake by the best and most systematic Artisan of all, were not understood with greater certainty by the philosophers, who otherwise examined so precisely the most insignificant trifles of this world. For this reason I undertook the task of re-reading the works of all the philosophers which I could obtain to learn whether anyone had ever proposed other motions of the universe's spheres than those expounded by the teachers of astronomy in the schools. And in fact first I found in Cicero that Hicetas supposed the earth to move. Later I also discovered in Plutarch that certain others were of this opinion. I have decided to set his words down here, so that they may be available to everybody:

> Some think that the earth remains at rest. But Philolaus the Pythagorean believes that, like the sun and moon, it revolves around the fire in an oblique circle. Heraclides of Pontus and Ecphantus the Pythagorean make the earth move, not in a progressive motion, but like a wheel in a rotation from the west to east about its own center.

Therefore, having obtained the opportunity from these sources, I too began to consider the mobility of the earth. And even though the idea seemed absurd, nevertheless I know that others before me had been granted the freedom to imagine any circles whatever for the purpose of explaining the heavenly phenomena. Hence I thought that I too would be readily permitted to ascertain whether explanations sounder than those of my predecessors could be found for the revolution of the celestial spheres on the assumption of some motion of the earth.

Having thus assumed the motions which I ascribe to the earth later on in the volume, by long and intense study I finally found that if the motions of the other planets are correlated with the orbiting of the earth, and are computed for the revolution of each planet, not only do their phenomena follow therefrom but also the order and size of all the planets and spheres, and heaven itself is so linked together that in no portion of it can anything be shifted without disrupting the remaining parts and the universe as a whole....

Hence I feel no shame in asserting that this whole region engirdled by the moon, and the center of the earth, traverse this grand circle amid the rest of the planets in an annual revolution around the sun. Near the sun is the center of the universe. Moreover, since the sun remains stationary, whatever appears as a motion of the sun is really due rather to the motion of the earth.

What major new ideas did Copernicus discuss in this excerpt? What was the source of these ideas?

---

the world of nature or employ the powers of nature for beneficial purposes. Was it Hermeticism, then, that inaugurated the shift in consciousness that made the Scientific Revolution possible, since the desire to control and dominate the natural world was a crucial motivating force in the Scientific Revolution? Scholars debate the issue, but histories of the Scientific Revolution frequently overlook the fact that the great names we associate with the revolution in cosmology—Copernicus, Kepler, Galileo, and Newton—all had a serious interest in Hermetic ideas and the fields of astrology and alchemy. The mention of these names also reminds us of one final consideration in the origins of the Scientific Revolution: it resulted largely from the work of a handful of great intellectuals.

Toward a New Heaven: A Revolution in Astronomy

The cosmological views of the Later Middle Ages had been built on a synthesis of the ideas of Aristotle, Ptolemy (the greatest astronomer of antiquity, who lived in the second century A.D.), and Christian theology. In the resulting Ptolemaic or **geocentric conception**, the universe was seen as a series of concentric spheres with a fixed or motionless earth as its center. Composed of material substance, the earth was imperfect and constantly changing. The spheres that surrounded the earth were made of a crystalline, transparent substance and moved in circular orbits around the earth. Circular movement, according to Aristotle, was the most "perfect" kind of motion and hence appropriate for the "perfect" heavenly bodies thought to consist of a nonmaterial, incorruptible "quintessence." These heavenly bodies, pure orbs of light, were embedded in the moving, concentric spheres, which in 1500 numbered ten. Working outward from the earth, eight spheres contained the moon, Mercury, Venus, the sun, Mars, Jupiter, Saturn, and the fixed stars. The ninth sphere imparted to the eighth sphere of the fixed stars its motion, while the tenth sphere was frequently described as the prime mover that moved itself and imparted motion to the other spheres. Beyond the tenth sphere was the

Medieval Conception of the Universe. As this sixteenth-century illustration shows, the medieval cosmological view placed the earth at the center of the universe, surrounded by a series of concentric spheres. The earth was imperfect and constantly changing, whereas the heavenly bodies that surrounded it were perfect and incorruptible. Beyond the tenth and final sphere was heaven, where God and all the saved souls were located. (The circles read, from the center outward: 1. Moon, 2. Mercury, 3. Venus, 4. Sun, 5. Mars, 6. Jupiter, 7. Saturn, 8. Firmament (of the Stars), 9. Crystalline Sphere, 10. Prime Mover; and around the outside, Empyrean Heaven—Home of God and All the Elect, that is, saved souls.)

Empyrean Heaven—the location of God and all the saved souls. This Christianized Ptolemaic universe, then, was finite. It had a fixed outer boundary in harmony with Christian thought and expectations. God and the saved souls were at one end of the universe, humans at the center. Humans had been given power over the earth, but their real purpose was to achieve salvation.

Copernicus

Shortly before his death, Nicolaus Copernicus (1473–1543), who had studied mathematics and astronomy first at Krakow in his native Poland and later at the Italian universities of Bologna and Padua, published his famous book *On the Revolutions of the Heavenly Spheres.* Copernicus was not an accomplished observational astronomer and relied for his data on the records of his predecessors. But he was a mathematician who felt that Ptolemy's geocentric system was too complicated and failed to accord with the observed motions of the heavenly bodies (see the box on p. 305). Copernicus hoped that his **heliocentric** (sun-centered) **conception** would offer a more accurate explanation.

Copernicus argued that the universe consisted of eight spheres with the sun motionless at the center and the sphere of the fixed stars at rest in the eighth sphere. The planets revolved around the sun in the order of Mercury, Venus, the earth, Mars, Jupiter, and Saturn. The moon, however, revolved around the earth. Moreover, according to Copernicus, what appeared to be the movement of the sun and the fixed stars around the earth was really

explained by the daily rotation of the earth on its axis and the journey of the earth around the sun each year.

The heliocentric theory had little immediate impact; most people were not yet ready to accept Copernicus' thinking. But doubts about the Ptolemaic system were growing. The next step in destroying the geocentric conception and supporting the Copernican system was taken by the German scientist Johannes Kepler.

Kepler

The work of Johannes Kepler (1571–1630) illustrates the narrow line that often separated magic and science in the early Scientific Revolution. An avid astrologer, Kepler possessed a keen interest in Hermetic thought and mathematical magic. In a book written in 1596, he elaborated on his theory that the universe was constructed on the basis of geometric figures, such as the pyramid and the cube. Believing that the harmony of the human soul (a divine attribute) was mirrored in the numerical relationships existing between the planets, he focused much of his attention on discovering the "music of the spheres." Kepler was also a brilliant mathematician and astronomer who took a post as imperial mathematician to Emperor Rudolf II. Using the detailed astronomical data of his predecessor, Kepler derived laws of planetary motion that confirmed the heliocentric theory. In his first law, he contradicted Copernicus by showing that the orbits of the planets around the sun were not circular but elliptical, with the sun at one focus of the ellipse rather than at the center.

The Copernican System. The Copernican system was presented in *On the Revolutions of the Heavenly Spheres*, published shortly before Copernicus' death. As shown in this illustration from the first edition of the book, Copernicus maintained that the sun was the center of the universe and that the planets, including the earth, revolved around it. Moreover, the earth rotated daily on its axis. (The circles read, from the center outward: 1. Sun; 2. Mercury, orbit of 80 days; 3. Venus; 4. Earth, with the moon, orbit of one year; 5. Mars, orbit of 2 years; 6. Jupiter, orbit of 12 years; 7. Saturn, orbit of 30 years; 8. Immobile Sphere of the Fixed Stars.)

Kepler's work effectively eliminated the idea of uniform circular motion as well as the idea of crystalline spheres revolving in circular orbits. The basic structure of the traditional Ptolemaic system had been destroyed, and people had been freed to think in new ways of the paths of planets revolving around the sun. By the end of Kepler's life, the Ptolemaic system was rapidly losing ground to the new ideas. Important questions remained unanswered, however. What were the planets made of? And how does one explain motion in the universe? It was an Italian scientist who achieved the next important breakthrough to a new cosmology by answering the first question.

Galileo

Galileo Galilei (1564–1642) taught mathematics, first at Pisa and later at Padua, one of the most prestigious universities in Europe. Galileo was the first European to make systematic observations of the heavens by means of a telescope, thereby inaugurating a new age in astronomy. He had heard of a Flemish lens grinder who had created a "spyglass" that magnified objects seen at a distance and soon constructed his own. Instead of peering at terrestrial objects, Galileo turned his telescope to the skies and made a remarkable series of discoveries: mountains on the moon, four moons revolving around Jupiter, the phases of Venus, and sunspots. Galileo's observations seemed to destroy yet another aspect of the traditional cosmology in that the universe seemed to be composed of a material substance similar to that of earth rather than an ethereal or perfect and unchanging substance.

Galileo's revelations, published in *The Starry Messenger* in 1610, stunned his contemporaries and probably did more to make Europeans aware of the new picture of the universe than the mathematical theories of Copernicus and Kepler (see the box on p. 308). But his newfound acclaim brought Galileo the increasing scrutiny of the Catholic church. The Roman Inquisition (or Holy Office) of the church condemned Copernicanism and ordered Galileo to abandon the Copernican thesis. The Inquisition's report insisted that "the doctrine that the sun was the center of the world and immovable was false and absurd, formally heretical and contrary to Scripture, whereas the doctrine that the earth was not the center of the world but moved, and has further a daily motion, was philosophically false and absurd and theologically at least erroneous."[3] Thus the church attacked the Copernican system because it threatened not only Scripture but also the entire prevailing conception of the universe. The heavens were no longer a spiritual world but a world of matter. Humans were no longer at the center, and God was no longer in a specific place. All this the church found intolerable. In 1633, Galileo was found guilty of teaching the condemned Copernican system and was forced to recant his "errors".

The condemnation of Galileo by the Inquisition, coming at a time of economic decline, seriously undermined further scientific work in Italy, which had been at the forefront of scientific innovation. Leadership in science now passed to the northern countries, especially England, France, and the Dutch Netherlands. By the 1630s and 1640s, no reasonable astronomer could overlook that Galileo's discoveries combined with Kepler's mathematical

THE STARRY MESSENGER

The Italian Galileo Galilei was the first European to use a telescope to make systematic observations of the heavens. His observations, as reported in *The Starry Messenger* in 1610, stunned European intellectuals by revealing that the celestial bodies were not perfect and immutable, as had been believed, but were apparently composed of material substance similar to the earth. In this selection, Galileo describes how he devised a telescope and what he saw with it.

Galileo Galilei, *The Starry Messenger*

About ten months ago a report reached my ears that a certain Fleming had constructed a spyglass by means of which visible objects, though very distant from the eye of the observer, were distinctly seen as if nearby. Of this truly remarkable effect several experiences were related, to which some persons gave credence while others denied them. A few days later the report was confirmed to me in a letter from a noble Frenchman at Paris, Jacques Badovere, which caused me to apply myself whole-heartedly to inquire into the means by which I might arrive at the invention of a similar instrument. This I did shortly afterwards, my basis being the theory of refraction. First I prepared a tube of lead, at the ends of which I fitted two glass lenses, both plane on one side while on the other side one was spherically convex and the other concave. Then placing my eye near the concave lens I perceived objects satisfactorily large and near, for they appeared three times closer and nine times larger than when seen with the naked eye alone. Next I constructed another one, more accurate, which represented objects as enlarged more than sixty times. Finally, sparing neither labor nor expense, I succeeded in constructing for myself so excellent an instrument that objects seen by means of it appeared nearly one thousand times larger and over thirty times closer than when regarded without natural vision.

It would be superfluous to enumerate the number and importance of the advantages of such an instrument at sea as well as on land. But forsaking terrestrial observations, I turned to celestial ones, and first I saw the moon from as near at hand as if it were scarcely two terrestrial radii. After that I observed often with wondering delight both the planets and the fixed stars, and since I saw these latter to be very crowded, I began to seek (and eventually found) a method by which I might measure their distances apart....

Now let us review the observations made during the past two months, once more inviting the attention of all who are eager for true philosophy to the first steps of such important contemplations. Let us speak first of that surface of the moon which faces us. For greater clarity I distinguish two parts of this surface, a lighter and a darker; the lighter part seems to surround and to pervade the whole hemisphere, while the darker part discolors the moon's surface like a kind of cloud, and makes it appear covered with spots....From observation of these spots repeated many times I have been led to the opinion and conviction that the surface of the moon is not smooth, uniform, and precisely spherical as a great number of philosophers believe it (and the other heavenly bodies) to be, but is uneven, rough, and full of cavities and prominences, being not unlike the face of the earth, relieved by chains of mountains and deep valleys.

What was the significance of Galileo's invention? What impressions did he receive of the moon?

---

laws had made nonsense of the Ptolemaic-Aristotelian world system and clearly established the reasonableness of the Copernican model. Nevertheless, the problem of explaining motion in the universe and tying together the ideas of Copernicus, Galileo, and Kepler had not yet been solved. This would be the work of an Englishman who has long been considered the greatest genius of the Scientific Revolution.

Newton

Born in the English village of Woolsthorpe, Isaac Newton (1642–1727) showed little promise until he attended Cambridge University. In 1669, he accepted a chair of mathematics at the university. During an intense period of creativity from 1684 to 1686, he wrote his major work, *Mathematical Principles of Natural Philosophy*, known simply as the *Principia*, from the first word of its Latin title. In this work, Newton spelled out the mathematical proofs demonstrating his universal law of gravitation.

Newton's work was the culmination of the theories of Copernicus, Kepler, and Galileo. While each had undermined some part of the Ptolemaic-Aristotelian cosmology, no one until Newton had pieced together a coherent synthesis for a new cosmology.

In the first book of the *Principia*, Newton defined the basic concepts of mechanics by elaborating the three laws of motion: every object continues in a state of rest or uniform motion in a straight line unless deflected by a force, the rate of change of motion of an object is proportional to the force acting on it, and to every action there is always an equal and opposite reaction. In book three, Newton applied his theories of mechanics to the problems of astronomy by demonstrating that these three laws of motion govern the planetary bodies as well as terrestrial objects. Integral to his whole argument was the universal law of gravitation to explain why the planetary bodies did not go off in straight lines but continued in elliptical orbits about the sun. In mathematical terms, Newton explained that every object in the universe was

Isaac Newton. Pictured here is a portrait of Isaac Newton by Godfrey Kneller. With a single law of universal gravitation, Newton was able to explain all motion in the universe. His great synthesis of the work of his predecessors created a new picture of the universe as a great machine operating according to natural laws.

attracted to every other object with a force (gravity) that is directly proportional to the product of their masses and inversely proportional to the square of the distances between them.

The implications of Newton's universal law of gravitation were enormous, even if it took another century before they were widely recognized. Newton had demonstrated that one universal law, mathematically proved, could explain all motion in the universe. At the same time, the Newtonian synthesis created a new cosmology in which the world was seen largely in mechanistic terms. The universe was one huge, regulated, and uniform machine that operated according to natural laws in absolute time, space, and motion. Although Newton believed that God was "everywhere present" and acted as the force that moved all bodies on the basis of the laws he had discovered, later generations dropped his spiritual assumptions. Newton's world-machine, conceived as operating absolutely in space, time, and motion, dominated the modern worldview until the twentieth century, when the Einsteinian revolution based on a concept of relativity superseded the Newtonian mechanistic concept.

Newton's ideas were soon accepted in England but were resisted on the Continent, and it took much of the eighteenth century before they were generally accepted everywhere in Europe. They were also reinforced by developments in other fields, especially medicine.

Advances in Medicine and Chemistry

Although the Scientific Revolution of the sixteenth and seventeenth centuries is associated primarily with the dramatic changes in astronomy and mechanics that precipitated a new perception of the universe, a third field that had been dominated by Greek thought in the Later Middle Ages, medicine, also experienced a transformation. Late medieval medicine was dominated by the teachings of the Greek physician Galen, who had lived in the second century A.D.

Galen's influence on the medieval medical world was pervasive in anatomy, physiology, and disease. Galen had relied on animal, rather than human, dissection to arrive at a picture of human anatomy that was quite inaccurate in many instances. Even when Europeans began to practice human dissection in the Later Middle Ages, instruction in anatomy still relied on Galen. While a professor read a text of Galen, an assistant dissected a cadaver for illustrative purposes. Physiology, or the functioning of the body, was also dominated by Galenic hypotheses, including the belief that there were two separate blood systems, one controlling muscular activities and containing bright red blood moving upward and downward through the arteries, the other governing the digestive functions and containing dark red blood that ebbed and flowed in the veins.

Vesalius

Two major figures are associated with the changes in medicine in the sixteenth and seventeenth centuries: Andreas Vesalius and William Harvey. The new anatomy of the sixteenth century was the work of the Belgian Andreas Vesalius (1514–1564). After receiving a doctorate in medicine at the University of Padua in 1536, Vesalius accepted a position there as professor of surgery. In 1543, he published his masterpiece, *On the Fabric of the Human Body*. This book was based on his Paduan lectures, in which he deviated from traditional practice by personally dissecting a body to illustrate what he was discussing. Vesalius' anatomical treatise presented a careful examination of the individual organs and general structure of the human body. The book would not have been feasible without the artistic advances of the Renaissance and the technical developments in the art of printing. Together, these advances made possible the creation of illustrations superior to any hitherto produced.

Vesalius' hands-on approach to teaching anatomy enabled him to overthrow some of Galen's most glaring errors. He did not hesitate, for example, to correct Galen's assertion that the great blood vessels originated from the liver since his own observations made it clear that they came from the heart. Nevertheless, Vesalius still clung to a number of Galen's erroneous assertions, including the Greek physician's ideas on the ebb and flow of two kinds of blood in the veins and arteries. It was not until William Harvey's work on the circulation of the blood that this Galenic misperception was corrected.

Harvey

The Englishman William Harvey (1578–1657) attended Cambridge University and later Padua, where he earned a doctorate in medicine in 1602. His reputation rests on his book *On the Motion of the Heart and Blood*, published in 1628. Although questions had been raised in the sixteenth century about Galen's physiological principles, no major challenge to his system had emerged. Harvey's work, based on meticulous observations and experiments, led him to reject the ancient Greek's contentions. Harvey demonstrated that the heart was the beginning point of the circulation of blood in the body, that the same blood flows in both veins and arteries, and that the blood makes a complete circuit as it passes through the body. Although Harvey's work dealt a severe blow to Galen's theories, his ideas did not begin to achieve general recognition until the 1660s,when the capillaries, which explained how the blood passed from the arteries to the veins, were discovered. Harvey's theory of the circulation of the blood laid the foundation for modern physiology.

Chemistry

In the seventeenth and eighteenth centuries, a science of chemistry emerged. Robert Boyle (1627–1691) was one of the first scientists to conduct controlled experiments. His pioneering work on the properties of gases led to Boyle's Law, which states that the volume of a gas varies with the pressure exerted on it. Boyle also rejected the medieval belief that all matter consisted of the same components in favor of the view that matter is composed of atoms, which he called "little particles of all shapes and sizes" and which in various combinations formed the chemical elements. In the eighteenth century, the Frenchman Antoine Lavoisier (1743–1794) invented a system for naming the chemical elements, much of which is still used today. He is regarded by many historians as the founder of modern chemistry.

Women in the Origins of Modern Science

During the Middle Ages, except for members of religious orders, women who sought a life of learning were severely hampered by the traditional attitude that a woman's proper role was as a daughter, wife, and mother. But in the late fourteenth and early fifteenth centuries, new opportunities for elite women emerged as enthusiasm for the new secular learning called humanism encouraged Europe's privileged and learned men to encourage women to read and study

classical and Christian texts. The ideal of a humanist education for some of the daughters of Europe's elite persisted into the seventeenth century.

Margaret Cavendish

Much as they were drawn to humanism, women were also attracted to the Scientific Revolution. Unlike females educated formally in humanist schools, women interested in science had to obtain a largely informal education. European nobles had the leisure and resources that gave them easy access to the world of learning. This door was also open to noblewomen, who could participate in the informal scientific networks of their fathers and brothers.

One of the most prominent female scientists of the seventeenth century, Margaret Cavendish (1623–1673), came from an aristocratic background. Cavendish was not a popularizer of science for women but a participant in the crucial scientific debates of her time. Despite her achievement, however, she was excluded from membership in the

F. Scriven, sc.

Margaret Cavendish. Shown in this portrait is Margaret Cavendish, the duchess of Newcastle. Her husband, thirty years her senior, encouraged her to pursue her literary interests. In addition to scientific works, she wrote plays, an autobiography, and a biography of her husband titled *The Life of the Thrice Noble, High and Puissant Prince William Cavendish, Duke, Marquess and Earl of Newcastle*. The autobiography and biography led one male literary critic to call her "a mad, conceited and ridiculous woman."

Copernicus, *On the Revolutions of the Heavenly Spheres*	1543
Vesalius, *On the Fabric of the Human Body*	1543
Galileo, *The Starry Messenger*	1610
Harvey, *On the Motion of the Heart and Blood*	1628
Cavendish, *Grounds of Natural Philosophy*	1668
Newton, *Principia*	1687

Royal Society (see "The Spread of Scientific Knowledge" later in this chapter), although she was once allowed to attend a meeting. She wrote a number of works on scientific matters, including *Observations upon Experimental Philosophy* and *Grounds of Natural Philosophy*. In these works, she did not hesitate to attack what she considered the defects of the rationalist and empiricist approaches to scientific knowledge and was especially critical of the growing belief that humans through science were the masters of nature: "We have no power at all over natural causes and effects . . . for man is but a small part . . . His powers are but particular actions of Nature, and he cannot have a supreme and absolute power."[4]

As an aristocrat, Cavendish, the duchess of Newcastle, was a good example of the women in France and England who worked in science. Women interested in science who lived in Germany came from a different background. There the tradition of female participation in craft production enabled some women to become involved in observational science, especially astronomy. Between 1650 and 1710, one in every seven German astronomers was a woman.

Maria Winkelmann

The most famous of the female astronomers in Germany was Maria Winkelmann (1670–1720). She was educated by her father and uncle and received advanced training from a local self-taught astronomer. When she married Gottfried Kirch, Germany's foremost astronomer, she became his assistant at the astronomical observatory operated in Berlin by the Academy of Science. She made some original contributions, including a hitherto undiscovered comet, as her husband related:

> Early in the morning (about 2:00 A.M.) the sky was clear and starry. Some nights before, I had observed a variable star, and my wife (as I slept) wanted to find and see it for herself. In so doing, she found a comet in the sky. At which time she woke me, and I found that it was indeed a comet. . . . I was surprised that I had not seen it the night before.[5]

When her husband died in 1710, she applied for a position as assistant astronomer, for which she was highly qualified. As a woman, with no university degree, she was denied the post by the Berlin Academy, which feared that it would establish a precedent if it hired a woman ("mouths would gape").

Winkelmann's difficulties with the Berlin Academy reflect the obstacles women faced in being accepted in scientific work, which was considered a male preserve. Although there were no formal statutes excluding women from membership in the new scientific societies, no woman was invited to join either the Royal Society of England or the French Academy of Sciences until the twentieth century. All of these female scientists were exceptional women because a life devoted to any kind of scholarship was still viewed as at odds with the domestic duties women were expected to perform.

Debates on the Nature of Women

The nature and value of women had been the subject of an ongoing, centuries-long debate. Male opinions in the debate were largely a carryover from medieval times and were not favorable. Women were portrayed as inherently base, prone to vice, easily swayed, and "sexually insatiable." Hence men needed to control them. Learned women were viewed as having overcome female liabilities to become like men. One man in praise of a woman scholar remarked that her writings were so good that you "would hardly believe they were done by a woman at all."

In the seventeenth century, women joined this debate by arguing against the distorted images of women held by men. They argued that women also had rational minds and could grow from education. Further, since most women were pious, chaste, and temperate, there was no need for male authority over them. These female defenders of women emphasized education as the key to women's ability to move into the world. How, then, did the Scientific Revolution affect this debate over the nature of women? As an era of intellectual revolution in which traditional authorities were being overthrown, we might expect significant change in men's views of women. But by and large, instead of becoming an instrument for liberation, science was used to find new support for the old, traditional views about a woman's "true place" in the scheme of things. New views were used to perpetrate old stereotypes about women.

An important project in the new anatomy of the sixteenth and seventeenth centuries was the attempt to illustrate the human body and skeleton. For Vesalius, the portrayal of physical differences between males and females was limited to external bodily form (the outlines of the body) and the sexual organs. Vesalius saw no difference in skeletons and portrayed them as the same for men or women. It was not until the eighteenth century, in fact, that a new anatomy finally prevailed. Drawings of female skeletons between 1730 and 1790 varied, but females tended to have a larger pelvic area, and in some instances, female skulls were portrayed as smaller than those of males. Eighteenth-century studies on the anatomy and physiology of sexual differences provided "scientific evidence" to

THE "NATURAL" INFERIORITY OF WOMEN

Despite the shattering of old views and the emergence of a new worldview in the Scientific Revolution of the seventeenth century, attitudes toward women remained tied to traditional perspectives. In this selection, the philosopher Benedict de Spinoza argues for the "natural" inferiority of women to men.

Benedict de Spinoza, *A Political Treatise*

But, perhaps, someone will ask, whether women are under men's authority by nature or institution. For if it has been by mere institution, then we had no reason compelling us to exclude women from government. But if we consult experience itself, we shall find that the origin of it is in their weakness. For there has never been a case of men and women reigning together, but wherever on the earth men are found, there we see that men rule, and women are ruled, and that on this plan, both sexes live in harmony. But on the other hand, the Amazons, who are reported to have held rule of old, did not suffer men to stop in their country, but reared only their female children, killing males to whom they gave birth. But if by nature women were equal to men, and were equally distinguished by force of character and ability, in which human power and therefore human right chiefly consist; surely among nations so many and different some would be found, where both sexes rule alike, and others, where men are ruled by women, and so brought up, that they can make less use of their abilities. And since this is nowhere the case, one may assert with perfect propriety, that women have not by nature equal right with men: but that they necessarily give way to men, and that thus it cannot happen, that both sexes should rule alike, much less that men should be ruled by women. But if we further reflect upon human passions, how men, in fact, generally love women merely from the passion of lust, and esteem their cleverness and wisdom in proportion to the excellence of their beauty, and also how very ill-disposed men are to suffer the women they love to show any sort of favor to others, and other facts of this kind, we shall easily see that men and women cannot rule alike without greater hurt to peace.

What arguments did Spinoza use to support the idea of female inferiority? What was the effect of this line of reasoning on the roles women could play?

reaffirm the traditional inferiority of women. The larger pelvic area "proved" that women were meant to be childbearers, and men's larger skull "demonstrated" the superiority of the male mind. Male-dominated science had been used to "prove" male social dominance.

Overall, the Scientific Revolution reaffirmed traditional ideas about women's nature. Male scientists used the new science to spread the view that women were inferior by nature, subordinate to men, and suited by nature to play a domestic role as nurturing mothers. The widespread distribution of books—written primarily by men, of course—ensured the continuation of these ideas (see the box above). Jean de La Bruyère, the seventeenth-century French moralist, was typical when he remarked that an educated woman was like a collector's item "which one shows to the curious, but which has no use at all, any more than a carousel horse."[6]

Toward a New Earth: Descartes, Rationalism, and a New View of Humankind

The fundamentally new conception of the universe contained in the cosmological revolution of the sixteenth and seventeenth centuries inevitably had an impact on the Western view of humankind. Nowhere is this more evident than in the work of the Frenchman René Descartes (1596–1650), an extremely important figure in Western history. Descartes began by reflecting the doubt and uncertainty that seemed pervasive in the confusion of the seventeenth century and ended with a philosophy that dominated Western thought until the twentieth century.

The starting point for Descartes' new system was doubt, as he explained at the beginning of his most famous work, *Discourse on Method*, written in 1637:

> From my childhood I have been familiar with letters; and as I was given to believe that by their means a clear and assured knowledge can be acquired of all that is useful in life, I was extremely eager for instruction in them. As soon, however, as I had completed the course of study, at the close of which it is customary to be admitted into the order of the learned, I entirely changed my opinion. For I found myself entangled in so many doubts and errors that, as it seemed to me, the endeavor to instruct myself had served only to disclose to me more and more of my ignorance.[7]

Descartes decided to set aside all that he had learned and begin again. One fact seemed beyond doubt—his own existence:

> But I immediately became aware that while I was thus disposed to think that all was false, it was absolutely necessary that I who thus thought should be something; and noting that this truth *I think, therefore I am*, was so steadfast and so assured that the suppositions of the skeptics, to whatever extreme they might all be carried, could not avail to shake it, I concluded that I might without scruple accept it as being the first principle of the philosophy I was seeking.[8]

With this emphasis on the mind, Descartes asserted that he would accept only things that his reason said were true.

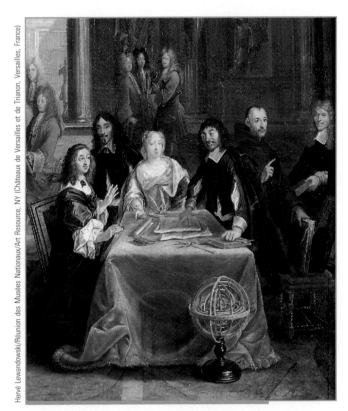

Descartes with Queen Christina of Sweden. René Descartes was one of the primary figures in the Scientific Revolution. Claiming to use reason as his sole guide to truth, Descartes posited a sharp distinction between mind and matter. He is shown here, standing to the right of Queen Christina of Sweden. The queen had a deep interest in philosophy and invited Descartes to her court.

From his first postulate, Descartes deduced an additional principle, the separation of mind and matter. Descartes argued that since "the mind cannot be doubted but the body and material world can, the two must be radically different." From this came an absolute dualism between mind and matter, or what has also been called **Cartesian dualism**. Using mind or human reason, the path to certain knowledge, and its best instrument, mathematics, humans can understand the material world because it is pure mechanism, a machine that is governed by its own physical laws because it was created by God—the great geometrician.

Descartes' conclusions about the nature of the universe and human beings had important implications. His separation of mind and matter allowed scientists to view matter as dead or inert, as something that was totally separate from themselves and could be investigated independently by reason. The split between mind and body led Westerners to equate their identity with mind and reason rather than with the whole organism. Descartes has rightly been called the father of modern **rationalism**. The radical Cartesian split between mind and matter, and between mind and body, had devastating implications

not only for traditional religious views of the universe but also for how Westerners viewed themselves.

The Spread of Scientific Knowledge

During the seventeenth century, scientific learning and investigation began to increase dramatically. Major universities in Europe established new chairs of science, especially in medicine. Royal and princely patronage of individual scientists became an international phenomenon. Of greater importance to the work of science, however, was the creation of a scientific method and new learned societies that enabled the new scientists to communicate their ideas to each other and to disseminate them to a wider, literate public.

The Scientific Method

In the course of the Scientific Revolution, attention was paid to the problem of establishing the proper means to examine and understand the physical realm. This creation of a **scientific method** was crucial to the evolution of science in the modern world. Curiously enough, it was an Englishman with few scientific credentials who attempted to put forth a new method of acquiring knowledge that made an impact on English scientists in the seventeenth century and other European scientists in the eighteenth century. Francis Bacon (1561–1626), a lawyer and lord chancellor, rejected Copernicus and Kepler and misunderstood Galileo. And yet in his unfinished work *The Great Instauration* (*The Great Restoration*), he called for his contemporaries "to commence a total reconstruction of sciences, arts, and all human knowledge, raised upon the proper foundations." Bacon did not doubt humans' ability to know the natural world, but he believed that they had proceeded incorrectly: "The entire fabric of human reason which we employ in the inquisition of nature is badly put together and built up, and like some magnificent structure without foundation."[9]

Bacon's new foundation—a correct scientific method— was to be built on inductive principles. Rather than beginning with assumed first principles from which logical conclusions could be deduced, he urged scientists to proceed from the particular to the general. From carefully organized experiments and systematic, thorough observations, correct generalizations could be developed. Bacon was clear about what he believed his method could accomplish. His concern was more for practical than for pure science. He stated that "the true and lawful goal of the sciences is none other than this: that human life be endowed with new discoveries and power." He wanted science to contribute to the "mechanical arts" by creating devices that would benefit industry, agriculture, and trade. Bacon was prophetic when he said that "I am laboring to lay the foundation, not of any sect or doctrine, but of human utility and power." And how would this "human power" be used? To "conquer nature in action."[10] The control and domination of nature became a central proposition of modern science and the technology that accompanied it. Only in the twentieth century did some scientists ask whether this assumption might not be at the heart of the modern ecological crisis.

René Descartes proposed a different approach to scientific methodology by emphasizing deduction and mathematical logic. Descartes believed that one could start with self-evident truths, comparable to geometrical axioms, and deduce more complex conclusions. His emphasis on deduction and mathematical order complemented Bacon's stress on experiment and induction. It was Newton who synthesized them into a single scientific methodology by uniting Bacon's empiricism with Descartes' rationalism. This scientific method began with systematic observations and experiments, which were used to arrive at general concepts. New deductions derived from these general concepts could then be tested and verified by precise experiments.

The Scientific Societies

The first of the scientific societies appeared in Italy, but those of England and France were ultimately of more significance. The English Royal Society evolved out of informal gatherings of scientists at London and Oxford in the 1640s, although it did not receive a formal charter from King Charles II until 1662. The French Royal Academy of Sciences also arose out of informal scientific meetings in Paris during the 1650s. In 1666, Louis XIV bestowed formal recognition on the group. The French Academy received abundant state support and remained under government control; its members were appointed and paid salaries by the state. In contrast, the Royal Society of England received little government encouragement, and its fellows simply co-opted new members.

Early on, both the English and French scientific societies formally emphasized the practical value of scientific research. The Royal Society created a committee to investigate technological improvements for industry; the French Academy collected tools and machines. This concern with the practical benefits of science proved short-lived, however, as both societies came to focus their primary interest on theoretical work in mechanics and astronomy. The construction of observatories at Paris in 1667 and at Greenwich, England, in 1675 greatly facilitated research in astronomy by both groups. While both the English and French societies made useful contributions to scientific knowledge in the second half of the seventeenth century, their true significance arose from their example that science should proceed along the lines of a cooperative venture.

Science and Society

The importance of science in the history of modern Western civilization is usually taken for granted. But how did science become such an integral part of Western culture in the seventeenth and early eighteenth centuries? One cannot simply assert that people perceived that science was a rationally superior system. An important social factor, however, might help explain the relatively rapid acceptance of the new science.

Louis XIV and Colbert Visit the Academy of Sciences. In the seventeenth century, individual scientists received royal and princely patronage, and a number of learned societies were established. In France, Louis XIV, urged on by his minister Colbert, gave formal recognition to the French Academy in 1666. In this painting by Henri Testelin, Louis XIV is shown seated, surrounded by Colbert and members of the French Royal Academy of Sciences.

It has been argued that the literate mercantile and propertied elites of Europe were attracted to new science because it offered new ways to exploit resources for profit. Some of the early scientists made it easier for these groups to accept the new ideas by demonstrating how the ideas could be applied directly to specific industrial and technological needs. Galileo, for example, consciously sought an alliance between science and the material interests of the educated elite when he assured his listeners that the science of mechanics would be quite useful "when it becomes necessary to build bridges or other structures over water, something occurring mainly in affairs of great importance." At the same time, Galileo stressed that science was fit for the "minds of the wise" and not for "the shallow minds of the common people." This made science part of the high culture of Europe's wealthy elites at a time when that culture was being increasingly separated from the popular culture of the lower classes.

Science and Religion

In Galileo's struggle with the Holy Office of the Catholic church, we see the beginning of the conflict between science and religion that has marked the history of modern Western civilization. Since time immemorial, theology had seemed to be the queen of the sciences. It was natural that the churches would continue to believe that religion was the final measure of everything. The emerging scientists, however, tried to draw lines between the knowledge of religion and the knowledge of "natural philosophy" or nature. Galileo had clearly felt that it was unnecessary to pit science against religion when he wrote that

> in discussions of physical problems we ought to begin not from the authority of scriptural passages, but from sense-experiences and necessary demonstrations; for the holy Bible and the phenomena of nature proceed alike from the divine word, the former as the dictate of the Holy Ghost and the latter as the observant executrix of God's commands. It is necessary for the Bible, in order to be accommodated to the understanding of every man, to speak many things which appear to differ from the absolute truth so far as the bare meaning of the words is concerned. But Nature, on the other hand, is inexorable and immutable; she never transgresses the laws imposed upon her, or cares a whit whether her abstruse reasons and methods of operation are understandable to men.[11]

To Galileo, it made little sense for the church to determine the nature of physical reality on the basis of biblical texts that were subject to radically divergent interpretations. The church, however, decided otherwise in Galileo's case and lent its great authority to one scientific theory, the Ptolemaic-Aristotelian cosmology, no doubt because it fit so well with its own philosophical views of reality. But the church's decision had tremendous consequences. For educated individuals, it established a dichotomy between scientific investigations and religious beliefs. As the scientific beliefs triumphed, it became almost inevitable that religious beliefs would suffer, leading to a growing secularization in European intellectual life.

Many seventeenth-century intellectuals were both religious and scientific and believed that the implications of this split would be tragic. Some believed that the split was largely unnecessary, while others felt the need to combine God, humans, and a mechanistic universe into a new philosophical synthesis.

Pascal Blaise Pascal (1623–1662) was a French scientist who sought to keep science and religion united. An accomplished scientist and a brilliant mathematician, Pascal excelled at both the practical (he invented a calculating machine) and the abstract (he devised a theory of probability and did work on conic sections). After a profound mystical vision on the night of November 23, 1654, which assured him that God cared for the human soul, he devoted the rest of his life to religious matters. He planned to write an "apology for the Christian religion" but died before he could do so. He did leave a set of notes for the larger work, however, which in published form became known as the *Pensées*, or *Thoughts*.

In the *Pensées*, Pascal tried to convert rationalists to Christianity by appealing to both their reason and their emotions. Humans were, he argued, frail creatures, often deceived by their senses, misled by reason, and battered by their emotions. And yet they were beings whose very nature involved thinking: "Man is but a reed, the weakest in nature; but he is a thinking reed."[12]

Pascal was determined to show that the Christian religion was not contrary to reason: "If we violate the principles of reason, our religion will be absurd, and it will be laughed at."[13] To a Christian, a human being was both fallen and at the same time God's special creation. But it was not necessary to emphasize one at the expense of the other—to view humans as only rational or only hopeless. Pascal even had an answer for skeptics in his famous wager: God is a reasonable bet; it is worthwhile to assume that God exists. If he does, we win all; if he does not, we lose nothing.

Despite his own background as a scientist and mathematician, Pascal refused to rely on the scientist's world of order and rationality to attract people to God: "If we submit everything to reason, there will be no mystery and no supernatural element in our religion." In the new cosmology of the seventeenth century, "finite man," Pascal believed, was lost in the new infinite world, a realization that frightened him: "The eternal silence of those infinite spaces strikes me with terror" (see the box on p. 316). The world of nature, then, could never reveal God: "Because they have failed to contemplate these infinites, men have rashly plunged into the examination of nature, as though they bore some proportion to her. . . . Their assumption is as infinite as their object." A Christian could only rely on a God who through Jesus cared for human beings. In the final analysis, after providing reasonable arguments for Christianity, Pascal came to rest on faith. Reason, he believed, could take people only so far: "The heart has its reasons of which the reason knows nothing." As a Christian, faith was the final step: "The heart feels God, not the reason. This is what constitutes faith: God experienced by the heart, not by the reason."[14]

PASCAL: "WHAT IS A MAN IN THE INFINITE?"

*P*erhaps no intellectual in the seventeenth century gave greater expression to the uncertainties generated by the cosmological revolution than Blaise Pascal. Himself a scientist, Pascal's mystical vision of God's presence caused him to pursue religious truths with a passion. His work, the *Pensées,* consisted of notes for a larger, unfinished work justifying the Christian religion. In this selection, Pascal presents his musings on the human place in an infinite world.

Blaise Pascal, *Pensées*

Let man then contemplate the whole of nature in her full and exalted majesty. Let him turn his eyes from the lowly objects which surround him. Let him gaze on that brilliant light set like an eternal lamp to illumine the Universe; let the earth seem to him a dot compared with the vast orbit described by the sun, and let him wonder at the fact that this vast orbit itself is no more than a very small dot compared with that described by the stars in their revolutions around the firmament. But if our vision stops here, let the imagination pass on; it will exhaust its powers of thinking long before nature ceases to supply it with material for thought. All this visible world is no more than an imperceptible speck in nature's ample bosom. No idea approaches it. We may extend our conceptions beyond all imaginable space; yet produce only atoms in comparison with the reality of things.

It is an infinite sphere, the center of which is everywhere, the circumference nowhere. In short, it is the greatest perceptible mark of God's almighty power that our imagination should lose itself in that thought.

Returning to himself, let man consider what he is compared with all existence; let him think of himself as lost in his remote corner of nature; and from this little dungeon in which he finds himself lodged—I mean the Universe—let him learn to set a true value on the earth, its kingdoms, and cities, and upon himself. What is a man in the infinite? . . .

For, after all, what is a man in nature? A nothing in comparison with the infinite, an absolute in comparison with nothing, a central point between nothing and all. Infinitely far from understanding these extremes, the end of things and their beginning are hopelessly hidden from him in an impenetrable secret. He is equally incapable of seeing the nothingness from which he came, and the infinite in which he is engulfed. What else then will he perceive but some appearance of the middle of things, in an eternal despair of knowing either their principle or their purpose? All things emerge from nothing and are borne onward to infinity. Who can follow this marvelous process? The Author of these wonders understands them. None but He can.

Why did Pascal question whether human beings could achieve scientific certainty? What is the significance of Pascal's thoughts for modern science?

CONCLUSION

The Scientific Revolution marked a major turning point in modern Western civilization as the Western world overthrew the medieval, Ptolemaic-Aristotelian worldview and arrived at a new conception of the universe with the sun at the center, the planets as material bodies revolving around the sun in elliptical orbits, and an infinite rather than finite world. With the changes in the conception of heaven came changes in the conception of earth. The work of Bacon and Descartes left Europeans with the separation of mind and matter and the belief that they could understand and dominate the world of nature using reason alone. The development of a scientific method furthered the work of scientists, and the creation of scientific societies and learned journals spread their results. Although traditional churches stubbornly resisted the new ideas and a few intellectuals pointed to some inherent flaws, nothing was able to halt the replacement of the traditional ways of thinking by new ways that marked a more fundamental

break with the past than that represented by the breakup of Christian unity in the Reformation.

The Scientific Revolution forced Europeans to change their conception of themselves. At first, some were appalled and even frightened by its implications. Formerly, humans on earth had been at the center of the universe. Now the earth was only a tiny planet revolving around a sun that was itself only a speck in a boundless universe. Most people remained optimistic despite the apparent blow to human dignity. After all, had Newton not demonstrated that the universe was a great machine governed by natural laws? Newton had found one—the universal law of gravitation. Could others not find other laws? Were there not natural laws governing every aspect of human endeavor that could be found by the new scientific method? Thus the Scientific Revolution leads us logically to the Enlightenment of the eighteenth century.

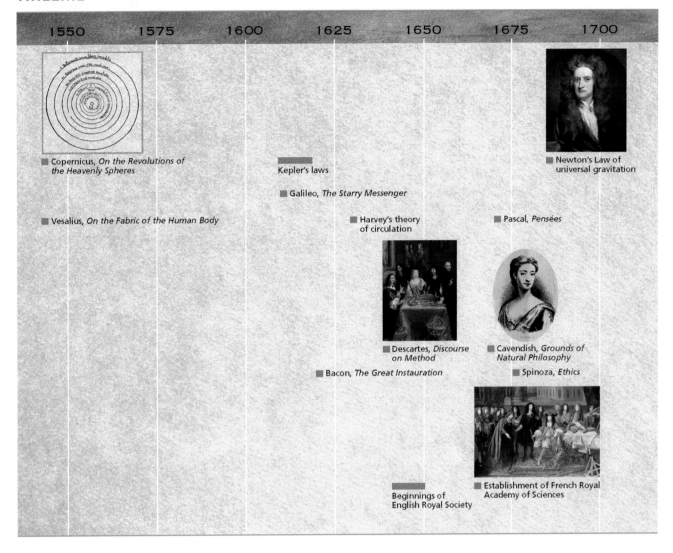

1550	1575	1600	1625	1650	1675	1700

■ Copernicus, *On the Revolutions of the Heavenly Spheres*

■ Kepler's laws

■ Newton's Law of universal gravitation

■ Galileo, *The Starry Messenger*

■ Vesalius, *On the Fabric of the Human Body*

■ Harvey's theory of circulation

■ Pascal, *Pensées*

■ Descartes, *Discourse on Method*

■ Cavendish, *Grounds of Natural Philosophy*

■ Bacon, *The Great Instauration*

■ Spinoza, *Ethics*

■ Beginnings of English Royal Society

■ Establishment of French Royal Academy of Sciences

NOTES

1. Quoted in A. G. R. Smith, *Science and Society in the Sixteenth and Seventeenth Centuries* (London, 1972), p. 59.
2. Quoted in E. MacCurdy, *The Notebooks of Leonardo da Vinci* (London, 1948), vol. 1, p. 634.
3. Quoted in J. H. Randall, *The Making of the Modern Mind* (Boston, 1926), p. 234.
4. Quoted in L. Schiebinger, *The Mind Has No Sex? Women in the Origins of Modern Science* (Cambridge, Mass., 1989), pp. 52–53.
5. Quoted in ibid. p. 85.
6. Quoted in P. Stock, *Better than Rubies: A History of Women's Education* (New York, 1978), p. 16.
7. R. Descartes, *Philosophical Writings*, ed. and trans. N. K. Smith (New York, 1958), p. 95.
8. Ibid. pp. 118–119.
9. F. Bacon, *The Great Instauration*, trans. J. Weinberger (Arlington Heights, Ill., 1989), pp. 2, 8.
10. Ibid. pp. 2, 16, 21.
11. S. Drake, ed. and trans., *Discoveries and Opinions of Galileo* (New York, 1957), p. 182.
12. B. Pascal, *Pensées*, trans. J. M. Cohen (Harmondsworth, England, 1961), p. 100.
13. Ibid. p. 31.
14. Ibid. pp. 52–53, 164, 165.

SUGGESTIONS FOR FURTHER READING

Three general surveys of the Scientific Revolution are **A. G. R. Smith, *Science and Society in the Sixteenth and Seventeenth Centuries*** (London, 1972); **J. R. Jacob, *The Scientific Revolution: Aspirations and Achievements, 1500–1700*** (Atlantic Highlands, N.J., 1998); and **J. Henry, *The Scientific Revolution and the Origins of Modern Science*** (New York, 1997). For a revisionist perspective, see. **S. Shapin, *The Scientific Revolution*** (Chicago, 1996). On the relationship of magic to science, see the pioneering works by **F. Yates, *Giordano Bruno and the Hermetic Tradition*** (New York, 1964) and ***The Rosicrucian Enlightenment*** (London, 1975). On the importance of mathematics, see **P. Dear, *Discipline and Experience: The Mathematical Way in the Scientific Revolution*** (Chicago, 1995).

The major figures of the revolution in astronomy are examined in **E. Rosen,** *Copernicus and the Scientific Revolution* (New York, 1984); **M. Sharratt,** *Galileo: Decisive Innovator* (Oxford, 1994); **S. Drake,** *Galileo, Pioneer Scientist* (Toronto, 1990); **M. Casper,** *Johannes Kepler,* trans. **C. D. Hellman** (London, 1959), the standard biography; and **R. S. Westfall,** *The Life of Isaac Newton* (New York, 1993). On Newton's relationship to alchemy, see **M. White,** *Isaac Newton: The Last Sorcerer* (Reading, Mass., 1997).

The standard biography of Vesalius is **C. D. O'Malley,** *Andreas Vesalius of Brussels, 1514–1564* (Berkeley, Calif., 1964). The work of Harvey is discussed in **G. Whitteridge,** *William Harvey and the Circulation of the Blood* (London, 1971).

The importance of Francis Bacon in the early development of science is underscored in **P. Zagorin,** *Francis Bacon* (Princeton, N.J., 1998). A good introduction to the work of Descartes can be found in **G. Radis-Lewis,** *Descartes: A Biography* (Ithaca, N.Y., 1998). The standard biography of Spinoza in English is **S. Hampshire,** *Spinoza* (New York, 1961).

For histories of the scientific academies, see **R. Hahn,** *The Anatomy of a Scientific Institution: The Paris Academy of Sciences, 1666–1803* (Berkeley, Calif., 1971), and **M. Purver,** *The Royal Society, Concept and Creation* (London, 1967).

On the subject of women and early modern science, see the comprehensive and highly informative work by L. Schiebinger, *The Mind Has No Sex? Women in the Origins of Modern Science* (Cambridge, Mass., 1989). See also **C. Merchant,** *The Death of Nature: Women, Ecology, and the Scientific Revolution*

(San Francisco, 1980). The social and political context for the triumph of science in the seventeenth and eighteenth centuries is examined in **M. Jacobs,** *The Cultural Meaning of the Scientific Revolution* (New York, 1988) and *The Newtonians and the English Revolution, 1689–1720* (Ithaca, N.Y., 1976).

Thomson NOW! Enter *ThomsonNOW* using the access card that is available for *Western Civilization: A Brief History.* *ThomsonNOW* will help you understand this chapter with lesson plans generated for your needs. In addition, you can read the following documents, and many more, online:

William Harvey, excerpts from *On the Motion of the Heart*
Isaac Newton, excerpts from *Principia*
René Descartes, excerpts from *Discourse on Method*
Blaise Pascal, exerpts from *Pensées*

WESTERN CIVILIZATION RESOURCES

Visit the Web site for *Western Civilization: A Brief History* for resources specific to this book:

http://www.thomsonedu.com/history/spielvogel

For a variety of tools to help you succeed in this course, visit the Western Civilization Resource Center at

http://history.wadsworth.com/spielvogel

Included are quizzes, images, documents, interactive simulations, maps and timelines, movie explorations, and a wealth of other sources.

THE EIGHTEENTH CENTURY:
AN AGE OF ENLIGHTENMENT

CHAPTER OUTLINE
AND FOCUS QUESTIONS

The Enlightenment

▢ Who were the leading figures of the Enlightenment, and what were their main contributions?

▢ In what type of social environment did the philosophes thrive, and what role did women play in that environment?

Culture and Society in the Enlightenment

▢ What innovations in art, music, and literature occurred in the eighteenth century?

▢ How did popular culture differ from high culture in the eighteenth century?

Religion and the Churches

▢ How did popular religion differ from institutional religion in the eighteenth century?

CRITICAL THINKING

▢ What is the relationship between the Scientific Revolution and the Enlightenment?

*The Parisian salon of Madame Geoffrin
(third figure from the right in the first row)*

D. Arnaudet/Réunion des Musées Nationaux/Art Resource, NY
(Châteaux de Malmaison et Bois-Preau, Rueil-Malmaison, France)

*T*HE EARTH-SHATTERING WORK of the "natural philosophers" in the Scientific Revolution had affected only a relatively small number of Europe's educated elite. In the eighteenth century, this changed dramatically as a group of intellectuals known as the philosophes popularized the ideas of the Scientific Revolution and used them to undertake a dramatic examination of all aspects of life. In Paris, the cultural capital of Europe, women took the lead in bringing together groups of men and women to discuss the new ideas of the philosophes. At her fashionable home in the Rue Saint-Honoré, Marie-Thérèse de Geoffrin, the wife of a wealthy merchant, held sway over gatherings that became the talk of France and even Europe. Distinguished foreigners, including a future king of Sweden and a future king of Poland, competed to receive invitations. When Madame Geoffrin made a visit to Vienna, she was so well received that she exclaimed, "I am better known here than a couple of yards from my own house!" Madame Geoffrin was an amiable but firm hostess who allowed wide-ranging discussions as long as they remained in good taste. When she found that artists and philosophers did not mix particularly well (the artists were high-strung and the philosophers talked too much), she set up separate meetings: artists were invited on Mondays, philosophers on Wednesdays. These gatherings were but one of many avenues for the spread of the ideas of the philosophes. And those ideas had such a widespread impact on their society that historians ever since have called the eighteenth century the Age of Enlightenment.

For most of the philosophes, "enlightenment" included the rejection of traditional Christianity. The religious wars and intolerance of the sixteenth and seventeenth centuries had left intellectuals so disgusted with religious fanaticism that they were open to the new ideas of the Scientific Revolution. Whereas the great scientists of the seventeenth century believed that their work exalted God, the intellectuals of the eighteenth century read the same conclusions a different way and increasingly turned their backs on Christian orthodoxy. Consequently, European intellectual life in the eighteenth century was marked by the emergence of the secularization that has characterized the modern Western mentality ever since. Ironically, at the same time that reason and materialism were beginning to replace faith and worship, a great outburst of religious sensibility manifested itself in music and art. Clearly, the growing secularization of the eighteenth century had not yet captured the hearts and minds of all Europeans.◆

The Enlightenment

In 1784, the German philosopher Immanuel Kant defined the **Enlightenment** as "man's leaving his self-caused immaturity." Whereas earlier periods had been handicapped by the inability to "use one's intelligence without the guidance of another," Kant proclaimed as the motto of the Enlightenment: "Dare to know! Have the courage to use your own intelligence!" The eighteenth-century Enlightenment was a movement of intellectuals who dared to know. They were greatly impressed with the accomplishments of the Scientific Revolution, and when they used the word *reason*—one of their favorite words— they were advocating the application of the scientific method to an understanding of every aspect of life. All institutions and all systems of thought were subject to the rational, scientific way of thinking if people would only free themselves from the shackles of past, worthless traditions, especially religious ones. If Isaac Newton could discover the natural laws regulating the world of nature, they too, using reason, could find the laws that governed human society. This belief in turn led them to hope that they could make progress toward a better society than the one they had inherited. *Reason, natural law, hope, progress*—these were buzzwords in the heady atmosphere of the eighteenth century.

The Paths to Enlightenment

Although the intellectuals of the eighteenth century were much influenced by the scientific ideas of the seventeenth century, they did not always acquire this knowledge directly from the original sources. After all, Newton's *Principia* was not an easy book to read or comprehend. Scientific ideas were spread to ever-widening circles of educated Europeans not so much by scientists themselves as by popularizers. Especially important as the direct link between the Scientific Revolution of the seventeenth century and the intellectuals of the eighteenth was Bernard de Fontenelle (1657–1757). In his *Plurality of Worlds,* he used the form of an intimate conversation between a lady aristocrat and her lover to present a

The Popularization of Science in the Enlightenment. During the Enlightenment, the ideas of the Scientific Revolution were spread and popularized in a variety of ways. Scientific societies funded by royal and princely patronage were especially valuable in providing outlets for the spread of new scientific ideas. This illustration shows the German prince Frederick Christian visiting his Academy of Sciences in 1739. Note the many instruments of the new science around the rooms—human skeletons, globes, microscopes, telescopes, and orreries, mechanical models of the solar system.

detailed account of the new mechanistic universe. Scores of the educated elite of Europe learned the new cosmology in this lighthearted fashion.

A New Skepticism

Although the Reformation had attempted to restore religion as the central focus of people's lives, it was perhaps inevitable that the dogmatic controversies, religious intolerance, and religious warfare engendered by it would open the door to the questioning of religious truths and values. The overthrow of medieval cosmology and the advent of scientific ideas and rational explanations in the seventeenth century likewise affected the belief of educated men and women in the traditional teachings of Christianity. **Skepticism** about religion and a growing secularization of thought were important factors in the emergence of the Enlightenment.

The Impact of Travel Literature

Skepticism about both Christianity and European culture was nourished by travel reports. In the course of the seventeenth century, traders, missionaries, medical practitioners, and explorers began to publish an increasing number of travel books that gave accounts of many different cultures. Then, too, the new geographical adventures of the eighteenth century, especially the discovery in the Pacific of Tahiti, New Zealand, and Australia by the British explorer James Cook, aroused much enthusiasm. Educated Europeans responded to these accounts of far-off lands in different ways.

For some intellectuals, the existence of exotic peoples, such as the natives of Tahiti, presented an image of a "natural man" who was far happier than many Europeans. Denis Diderot, one of the important figures of the Enlightenment, wrote:

> The life of savages is so simple, and our societies are such complicated machines! The Tahitian is close to the origin of the world, while the European is closer to its old age. . . . They understand nothing about our manners or our laws, and they are bound to see in them nothing but shackles disguised in a hundred different ways. Those shackles could only provoke the indignation and scorn of creatures in whom the most profound feeling is a love of liberty.[1]

To Diderot, the noble primitives of Tahiti were honest and simple people unencumbered by the inequality, religious hypocrisy, sexual repression, and vices of European society. The idea of the "noble savage" would play an important role in the political work of some philosophes.

The travel literature of the seventeenth and eighteenth centuries also led to the realization that there were highly developed civilizations with different customs in other parts of the world. One German university professor praised the Confucian morality of China as superior to the intolerant attitudes of Christianity. Some European intellectuals began to evaluate their own civilization relative to others. What had once seemed universal truths and practices grounded in reason now appeared to be mere matters of custom.

The Legacy of Locke and Newton

A final source of inspiration for the Enlightenment came primarily from Isaac Newton and John Locke. Newton was frequently singled out for praise as the "greatest and rarest genius that ever rose for the ornament and instruction of the species." One English poet declared, "Nature and Nature's Laws lay hid in Night; God said, 'Let Newton be,' and all was Light." Enchanted by the grand design of the Newtonian world-machine, the intellectuals of the Enlightenment were convinced that by following Newton's rules of reasoning, they could discover the natural laws that governed politics, economics, justice, religion, and the arts.

John Locke's theory of knowledge had a great impact on eighteenth-century intellectuals. In his *Essay Concerning Human Understanding*, written in 1690, Locke denied Descartes' belief in innate ideas. Instead, argued Locke, every person was born with a *tabula rasa*, a blank mind:

> Let us then suppose the mind to be, as we say, white paper, void of all characters, without any ideas. How comes it to be furnished? Whence comes it by that vast store which the busy and boundless fancy of man has painted on it with an almost endless variety? Whence has it all the materials of reason and knowledge? To this I answer, in one word, from experience. . . . Our observation, employed either about external sensible objects or about the internal operations of our minds perceived and reflected on by ourselves, is that which supplies our understanding with all the materials of thinking.[2]

Our knowledge, then, is derived from our environment, not from heredity; from reason, not from faith. Locke's philosophy implied that people were molded by their environment, by the experiences that they received through their senses from their surrounding world. By changing the environment and subjecting people to proper influences, they could be changed and a new society created. And how should the environment be changed? Newton had already paved the way by showing how reason enabled enlightened people to discover the natural laws to which all institutions should conform. No wonder the philosophes were enamored of Newton and Locke. Taken together, their ideas seemed to offer the hope of a "brave new world" built on reason.

The Philosophes and Their Ideas

The intellectuals of the Enlightenment were known by the French term **philosophes**, although not all of them were French and few were actually philosophers. They were literary people, professors, journalists, statesmen, economists, political scientists, and above all, social reformers. They came from both the nobility and the middle class, and a few even stemmed from lower-middle-class origins. Although it was a truly international and cosmopolitan movement, the Enlightenment also enhanced the dominant role already being played by French culture; Paris

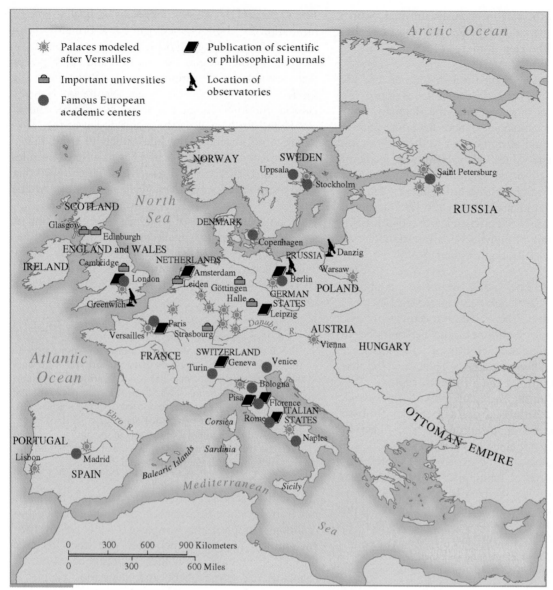

MAP 17.1 **The Enlightenment in Europe.** "Have the courage to use your own intelligence!" The words of the German Enlightenment philosopher Immanuel Kant (1724–1804) epitomize the role of the individual in using reason to understand all aspects of life—the natural world and the sphere of human nature, behavior, and institutions. **?** Which countries or regions were at the center of the Enlightenment, and what reasons could account for peripheral regions being less involved? ✦ **View an animated version of this map or related maps at** http://thomsonedu.com/history/spielvogel

was its recognized capital. Most of the leaders of the Enlightenment were French. The French philosophes in turn affected intellectuals elsewhere and started a movement that enveloped the entire Western world, including the British and Spanish colonies in America (see Map 17.1).

Although the philosophes faced different political circumstances depending on the country in which they lived, they shared common bonds as part of a truly international movement. Although they were called philosophers, what did philosophy mean to them? The role of philosophy was to change the world, not just to discuss it. To the philosophes, rationalism did not mean the creation of a grandiose system of thought to explain all things. Reason was scientific method, an appeal to facts and experience. A spirit of rational criticism was to be applied to everything, including religion and politics.

Although the philosophes constituted a kind of "family circle" bound together by common intellectual bonds, they often disagreed. Spanning almost a century, the Enlightenment evolved over time, with each succeeding generation becoming more radical as it built on the contributions of the previous one. A few people, however, dominated the landscape completely, and we might best begin our survey of the ideas of the philosophes by looking at the three French giants—Montesquieu, Voltaire, and Diderot.

Montesquieu and Political Thought Charles de Secondat, baron de Montesquieu (1689–1755), came from the French nobility. He received a classical education and then studied law. In his first work published in 1721, the *Persian Letters,* he used the format of two Persians supposedly traveling in western Europe and sending their impressions back home to enable him to criticize French institutions, especially the Catholic church and the French monarchy. Much of the program of the French Enlightenment is contained in this work: the attack on traditional religion, the advocacy of religious toleration, the denunciation of slavery, and the use of reason to liberate human beings from their prejudices.

His most famous work, *The Spirit of the Laws,* was published in 1748. This treatise was a comparative study of governments in which Montesquieu attempted to apply the scientific method to the social and political arena to ascertain the "natural laws" governing the social relationships of human beings. Montesquieu distinguished three basic kinds of governments: republics, suitable for small states and based on citizen involvement; monarchy, appropriate for middle-sized states and grounded in the ruling class's adherence to law; and despotism, apt for large empires and dependent on fear to inspire obedience. Montesquieu used England as an example of the second category, and it was his praise and analysis of England's constitution that led to his most far-reaching and lasting contribution to political thought—the importance of checks and balances created by means of a **separation of powers.** He believed that England's system, with its separate executive, legislative, and judicial powers that served to limit and control each other, provided the greatest freedom and security for a state. The translation of his work into English two years after publication ensured its being read by American philosophes who incorporated its principles into the American constitution (see Chapter 19).

Voltaire and the Enlightenment The greatest figure of the Enlightenment was François-Marie Arouet, known simply as Voltaire (1694–1778). Born to a prosperous middle-class family from Paris, Voltaire received a classical education typical of Jesuit schools. Although he studied law, he wished to be a writer and achieved his first success as a playwright. Voltaire was a prolific author and wrote an almost endless stream of pamphlets, novels, plays, letters, philosophical essays, and histories. His writings brought him both fame and wealth.

Although he touched on all of the themes of importance to the philosophes, Voltaire was especially well known for his criticism of traditional religion and his strong attachment to the ideal of religious toleration (see

the box on p. 324). He lent his prestige and skills as a polemicist to fight intolerance in France. In 1763, he penned his *Treatise on Toleration,* in which he argued that religious toleration had created no problems for England and Holland and reminded governments that "all men are brothers under God." As he grew older, Voltaire became ever more strident in his denunciations. "Crush the infamous thing," he thundered repeatedly—the infamous thing being religious fanaticism, intolerance, and superstition.

Throughout his life, Voltaire championed not only religious tolerance but also **deism,** a religious outlook shared by most other philosophes. Deism was built on the Newtonian world-machine, which conceived of the universe as a huge, regulated, and uniform machine that operated on impersonal natural laws. To the deists, reason dictated that such an elegant design of the universe implied the existence of a mechanic (God) who had created it and allowed it to run according to its natural laws. The universe was like a clock. God, the clockmaker, had created it, set it in motion, and allowed it to run without interference. To Voltaire and most other philosophes, God had no direct involvement in the world he had created. They rejected religious miracles and Jesus' resurrection, important elements of Christian belief, as contrary to the laws of nature. Jesus might be a "good

THE ATTACK ON RELIGIOUS INTOLERANCE

Although Voltaire's attacks on religion were in no way original, his lucid prose, biting satire, and clever wit caused his works to be widely read and all the more influential. These two selections present different sides of Voltaire's attack on religious intolerance. The first is from his straightforward treatise The Ignorant Philosopher, *and the second is from his only real literary masterpiece, the novel* Candide, *in which he uses humor to make the same fundamental point about religious intolerance.*

Voltaire, *The Ignorant Philosopher*

The contagion of fanaticism then still subsists. . . . The author of the *Treatise upon Toleration* has not mentioned the shocking executions wherein so many unhappy victims perished in the valleys of Piedmont. He has passed over in silence the massacre of six hundred inhabitants of Valtelina, men, women, and children, who were murdered by the Catholics in the month of September, 1620. I will not say it was with the consent and assistance of the archbishop of Milan, Charles Borome, who was made a saint. Some passionate writers have averred this fact, which I am very far from believing; but I say, there is scarce any city or borough in Europe, where blood has not been spilt for religious quarrels; I say, that the human species has been perceptibly diminished, because women and girls were massacred as well as men; I say, that Europe would have had a third larger population, if there had been no theological disputes. In fine, I say, that so far from forgetting these abominable times, we should frequently take a view of them, to inspire an eternal horror for them; and that it is for our age to make reparation by toleration, for this long collection of crimes, which has taken place through the want of toleration, during sixteen barbarous centuries.

Let it not then be said, that there are no traces left of that shocking fanaticism, of the want of toleration; they are still everywhere to be met with, even in those countries that are esteemed the most humane. The Lutheran and Calvinist preachers, were they masters, would, perhaps, be as little inclined to pity, as obdurate, as insolent as they upbraid their antagonists with being.

Voltaire, *Candide*

At last [Candide] approached a man who had just been addressing a big audience for a whole hour on the subject of charity. The orator peered at him and said:

"What is your business here? Do you support the Good Old Cause?"

"There is no effect without a cause," replied Candide modestly. "All things are necessarily connected and arranged for the best. It was my fate to be driven from Lady Cunégone's presence and made to run the gauntlet, and now I have to beg my bread until I can earn it. Things should not have happened otherwise."

"Do you believe that the Pope is Antichrist, my friend?" said the minister.

"I have never heard anyone say so," replied Candide; "but whether he is or he isn't, I want some food."

"You don't deserve to eat," said the other. "Be off with you, you villain, you wretch! Don't come near me again or you'll suffer for it."

The minister's wife looked out of the window at that moment, and seeing a man who was not sure that the Pope was Antichrist, emptied over his head a chamber pot, which shows to what lengths ladies are driven by religious zeal.

Compare the two approaches of Voltaire to the problem of religious intolerance. Do you think one is more effective? Why?

---

fellow," as Voltaire called him, but he was not divine as Christianity claimed.

Diderot and the *Encyclopedia* Denis Diderot (1713–1784), the son of a skilled craftsman from eastern France, decided to become a writer so that he could be free to study and read in many subjects and languages. One of his favorite topics was Christianity, which he condemned as fanatical and unreasonable. As he grew older, his literary attacks on Christianity grew more vicious. Of all religions, Christianity, he maintained, was the worst, "the most absurd and the most atrocious in its dogma." This progression reflected his own movement from deism to atheism, ending with a basic materialistic conception of life: "This world is only a mass of molecules."

Diderot's most famous contribution to the Enlightenment was the twenty-eight-volume *Encyclopedia, or Classified Dictionary of the Sciences, Arts, and Trades,* which he edited and referred to as the "great work of his life." Its purpose, he said, was to "change the general way of thinking." It did precisely that, becoming a major weapon of the philosophes' crusade against the old French society. The contributors included many philosophes, who expressed their major concerns. They attacked religious superstition and advocated toleration as well as a program for social, legal, and political improvements that would lead to a society that was more cosmopolitan, more tolerant, more humane, and more reasonable. In later editions, the price of the *Encyclopedia* was drastically reduced, dramatically increasing its sales and making it available to doctors, clergymen, teachers, lawyers, and even military officers. The ideas of the Enlightenment spread even further as a result.

Toward a New "Science of Man" The Enlightenment belief that Newton's scientific methods could be used to discover the natural laws underlying all areas of human life led to the emergence in the eighteenth century of what the philosophes called a "science of man" or what we would call the social sciences. In a number of areas, philosophes arrived at natural laws that they believed governed human actions.

The Physiocrats and Adam Smith have been regarded as founders of the modern discipline of economics. The leader of the Physiocrats was François Quesnay (1694–1774), a successful French court physician. Quesnay and the Physiocrats claimed they would discover the natural economic laws that governed human society. Their major "natural law" of economics was a repudiation of mercantilism, specifically its emphasis on a controlled economy for the benefit of the state. Instead the Physiocrats stressed that the existence of the natural economic forces of supply and demand made it imperative that individuals should be left free to pursue their own economic self-interest. In doing so, all of society would ultimately benefit. Consequently, they argued that the state should in no way interrupt the free play of natural economic forces by government regulation of the economy but rather just leave it alone, a doctrine that subsequently became known by the French term **laissez-faire** ("let it alone").

The clearest statement of *laissez-faire* was made by a Scottish philosopher, Adam Smith (1723–1790), in his *Inquiry into the Nature and Causes of the Wealth of Nations*, known simply as *The Wealth of Nations*, published in 1776. Like the Physiocrats, Smith believed that the state should not interfere in economic matters; indeed, he gave to government only three basic functions: to protect society from invasion (army), to defend individuals from injustice and oppression (police), and to keep up public works, such as roads and canals, that private individuals could not afford. Thus in Smith's view, the state should be a kind of "passive policeman" that remains out of the lives of individuals. In emphasizing the economic liberty of the individual, the Physiocrats and Adam Smith laid the foundation for what became known in the nineteenth century as **economic liberalism**.

The Later Enlightenment By the late 1760s, a new generation of philosophes who had grown up with the worldview of the Enlightenment began to move beyond their predecessors' beliefs. Baron Paul d'Holbach (1723–1789), a wealthy German aristocrat who settled in Paris, preached a doctrine of strict atheism and materialism. In his *System of Nature*, written in 1770, he argued that everything in the universe consisted of matter in motion. Human beings were simply machines; God was a product of the human mind and was unnecessary for leading a moral life. People needed only reason to live in this world. Holbach shocked almost all of his fellow philosophes with his uncompromising atheism. Most intellectuals remained more comfortable with deism and feared the effect of atheism on society.

No one was more critical of the work of his predecessors than Jean-Jacques Rousseau (1712–1778). Almost entirely self-educated, Rousseau spent a wandering existence as a youth, holding various jobs in France and Italy. Eventually he made his way to Paris, where he was introduced into the circles of the philosophes.

Rousseau's political beliefs were presented in two major works. In his *Discourse on the Origins of the Inequality of Mankind*, Rousseau argued that people had adopted laws and governors to protect their private property, but in the process, they had become enslaved by government. In his most celebrated treatise, *The Social Contract*, published in 1762, Rousseau tried to harmonize individual liberty with governmental authority (see the box on p. 326). The social contract was basically an agreement on the part of an entire society to be governed by its general will. If any individual wished to follow his own self-interest, he should be forced to abide by the general will. "This means nothing less than that he will be forced to be free," Rousseau said, because the general will represented a community's highest aspirations, what was best for the entire community. Thus liberty was achieved through being forced to follow what was best for all people because, he believed, what was best for all was best for each individual. To Rousseau, because everybody was responsible for framing the general will, the creation of laws could never be delegated to a parliamentary body:

> Thus the people's deputies are not and could not be its representatives; they are merely its agents; and they cannot decide anything finally. Any law which the people has not ratified in person is void; it is not law at all. The English people believes itself to be free; it is gravely mistaken; it is free only during the election of Members of Parliament; as soon as the Members are elected, the people is enslaved; it is nothing.[3]

This is an extreme, idealistic statement, but it is the ultimate statement of participatory democracy.

Another influential treatise by Rousseau also appeared in 1762. Titled *Émile*, it is one of the Enlightenment's most important works on education. Written in the form of a novel, the work was really a general treatise "on the education of the natural man." Rousseau's fundamental concern was that education should encourage rather than restrict children's natural instincts. Life's experiences had shown Rousseau the importance of the promptings of the heart, and what he sought was a balance between heart and mind, between sentiment and reason. This emphasis on heart and sentiment made him a precursor of the intellectual movement called **Romanticism** that dominated Europe at the beginning of the nineteenth century.

But Rousseau did not necessarily practice what he preached. His own children were sent to foundling homes, where many children died young. Rousseau also viewed women as "naturally" different from men: "to fulfill [a woman's] functions, an appropriate physical constitution is necessary to her. . . . She needs a soft sedentary life to suckle her babies. How much care and tenderness does she need to hold her family together?" In *Émile*, Sophie, who was Émile's intended wife, was

A SOCIAL CONTRACT

Although Jean-Jacques Rousseau was one of the French philosophes, he has also been called "the father of Romanticism." His political ideas have proved extremely controversial. While some political theorists have hailed him as the prophet of democracy, others have labeled him an apologist for totalitarianism. This selection is taken from one of his most famous books, *The Social Contract*.

Jean-Jacques Rousseau, *The Social Contract*

Book 1, Chapter 6: The Social Pact

"How to find a form of association which will defend the person and goods of each member with the collective force of all, and under which each individual, while uniting himself with the others, obeys no one but himself, and remains as free as before." This is the fundamental problem to which the social contract holds the solution. . . .

Book 1, Chapter 7: The Sovereign

Despite their common interest, subjects will not be bound by their commitment unless means are found to guarantee their fidelity.

For every individual as a man may have a private will contrary to, or different from, the general will that he has as a citizen. His private interest may he speak with a very different voice from that of the public interest; his absolute and naturally independent existence may make him regard what he owes to the common cause as a gratuitous contribution, the loss of which would be less painful for others than the payment is onerous for him; and fancying that the artificial person which constitutes the state is a mere rational entity, he might seek to enjoy the rights of a citizen without doing the duties of a subject. The growth of this kind of injustice would bring about the ruin of the body politic.

Hence, in order that the social pact shall not be an empty formula, it is tacitly implied in that commitment—which alone can give force to all others—that whoever refused to obey the general will shall be constrained to do so by the whole body, which means nothing other than that he shall be forced to be free; for this is the condition which, by giving each citizen to the nation, secures him against all personal dependence, it is the condition which shapes both the design and the working of the political machine, and which alone bestows justice on civil contracts—without it, such contracts would be absurd, tyrannical and liable to the grossest abuse.

What is Rousseau's concept of the social contract? What implications did it contain for political thought, especially in regard to the development of democratic ideals?

---

educated for her role as wife and mother by learning obedience and the nurturing skills that would enable her to provide loving care for her husband and children. Not everyone in the eighteenth century, however, agreed with Rousseau, making ideas of gender an important issue in the Enlightenment.

The "Woman Question" in the Enlightenment For centuries, men had dominated the debate about the nature and value of women. In general, many male intellectuals had argued that the base nature of women made them inferior to men and made male domination of women necessary (see Chapter 16). In the seventeenth and eighteenth centuries, many male thinkers reinforced this view by arguing that it was based on "natural" biological differences between men and women. Like Rousseau, they argued that the female constitution made women suitable only as mothers. Male writers, in particular, were critical of the attempts of some women in the Enlightenment to write on intellectual issues, arguing that women by nature were intellectually inferior to men. Nevertheless, there were some Enlightenment thinkers who offered more positive views of women. Diderot, for example, maintained that men and women were not all that different, and Voltaire asserted that "women are capable of all that men are" with regard to intellectual activity.

It was women thinkers, however, who added new perspectives to the "woman question" by making specific suggestions for improving the conditions of women. Mary Astell (1666–1731), daughter of a wealthy English coal merchant, argued in 1697 in *A Serious Proposal to the Ladies* that women needed to become better educated. Men, she believed, would resent her proposal, "but they must excuse me, if I be as partial to my own sex as they are to theirs, and think women as capable of learning as men are, and that it becomes them as well."[4]

The strongest statement for the rights of women in the eighteenth century was advanced by the English writer Mary Wollstonecraft (1759–1797), viewed by many as the founder of modern European feminism. In *Vindication of the Rights of Woman*, written in 1792, Wollstonecraft pointed out two contradictions in the views of women held by such Enlightenment thinkers as Rousseau. To argue that women must obey men, she said, was contrary to the beliefs of the same individuals that a system based on the arbitrary power of monarchs over their subjects or slave owners over their slaves was wrong. The subjection of women to men was equally wrong. In addition, she argued that the Enlightenment was based on an ideal of reason innate in all human beings. If women have reason, then they too are entitled to the same rights that men have. Women, Wollstonecraft declared, should have equal rights with men in education and in economic and political life as well (see the box on p. 328).

The Social Environment of the Philosophes

The social backgrounds of the philosophes varied considerably, from the aristocratic Montesquieu to the lower-middle-class Diderot and Rousseau. The Enlightenment was not the preserve of any one class, although obviously its greatest appeal was to the aristocracy and upper middle classes of the major cities. The common people, especially the peasants, were little affected by the Enlightenment.

Of great importance to the Enlightenment was the spread of its ideas to the literate elite of European society. Although the publication and sale of books and treatises were crucial to this process, the salon was also a factor. **Salons** came into being in the seventeenth century but rose to new heights in the eighteenth. These were elegant drawing rooms in the urban houses of the wealthy where philosophes and guests gathered to engage in witty, sparkling conversations that often centered on the ideas of the philosophes. In France's rigid hierarchical society, the salons were important in bringing together writers and artists with aristocrats, government officials, and wealthy members of the bourgeoisie.

As hostesses of the salons, women found themselves in a position to affect the decisions of kings, sway political opinion, and influence literary and artistic taste. Salons provided havens for people and views unwelcome in the royal court. When Diderot's *Encyclopedia* was suppressed by the French authorities, Marie-Thérèse de Geoffrin (1699–1777), a wealthy bourgeois widow whose father had been a valet, welcomed the encyclopedists to her salon and offered financial assistance to complete the work in secret. Madame Geoffrin was not without rivals, however. The marquise du Deffand (1697–1780) had abandoned her husband in the provinces and established herself in Paris, where her ornate drawing room attracted many of the Enlightenment's great figures, including Montesquieu and Voltaire.

Although the salons were run by women, the reputation of a salon depended on the stature of the males a hostess was able to attract. Despite this male domination, however, both French and foreign observers complained that females exerted undue influence in French political affairs. Though exaggerated, this perception led to the decline of salons during the French Revolution toward the end of the century.

The salon served an important role in making possible conversation and sociability between upper-class men and women as well as spreading the ideas of the Enlightenment. But other means of spreading Enlightenment ideas were also available. Coffeehouses, cafés, reading clubs, and public lending libraries established by the state were gathering places to exchange ideas. Secret societies also developed. The most famous was the Freemasons, established in London in 1717, France and Italy in 1726, and Prussia in 1744. It was no secret that the Freemasons were sympathetic to the ideas of the philosophes.

Culture and Society in the Enlightenment

The intellectual adventure fostered by the philosophes was accompanied by both traditional practices and important changes in eighteenth-century culture and society.

Innovations in Art, Music, and Literature

Although the Baroque and neoclassical styles that had dominated the seventeenth century continued into the eighteenth century, by the 1730s a new style known as **Rococo** began to affect decoration and architecture all over Europe. Unlike the Baroque, which stressed majesty, power, and movement, Rococo emphasized grace and gentle action. Rococo rejected strict geometrical patterns and favored curves; it liked to follow the wandering lines of natural objects, such as seashells and flowers. It made much use of interlaced designs colored in gold with delicate contours and graceful curves. Highly secular, its lightness and charm spoke of the pursuit of pleasure, happiness, and love.

Some of Rococo's appeal is evident in the work of Antoine Watteau (1684–1721), whose lyrical views of aristocratic life—refined, sensual, civilized, with gentlemen and ladies in elegant dress—revealed a world of upper-class pleasure and joy. Underneath that exterior, however, was an element of sadness as the artist revealed the fragility and transitory nature of pleasure, love, and life.

Another aspect of Rococo was that its decorative work could easily be used with Baroque architecture. The palace of Versailles had an enormous impact on Europe. "Keeping up with the Bourbons" became important as the Austrian emperor, the Swedish king, German princes, Italian princes, and even a Russian tsar built grandiose palaces. While imitating Versailles' size, they were modeled less after the French classical style of Versailles than

THE RIGHTS OF WOMEN

Mary Wollstonecraft responded to an unhappy childhood in a large family by seeking to lead an independent life. Few occupations were available for middle-class women in her day, but she survived by working as a teacher, chaperone, and governess to aristocratic children. All the while, she wrote and developed her ideas on the rights of women. This excerpt is taken from her *Vindication of the Rights of Woman*, written in 1792. This work led to her reputation as the foremost British feminist thinker of the eighteenth century.

Mary Wollstonecraft, *Vindication of the Rights of Woman*

It is a melancholy truth—yet such is the blessed effect of civilization—the most respectable women are the most oppressed; and, unless they have understandings far superior to the common run of understandings, taking in both sexes, they must, from being treated like contemptible beings, become contemptible. How many women thus waste life away the prey of discontent, who might have practiced as physicians, regulated a farm, managed a shop, and stood erect, supported by their own industry, instead of hanging their heads surcharged with the dew of sensibility, that consumes the beauty to which it at first gave luster. . . .

Proud of their weakness, however, [women] must always be protected, guarded from care, and all the rough toils that dignify the mind. If this be the fiat of fate, if they will make themselves insignificant and contemptible, sweetly to waste "life away," let them not expect to be valued when their beauty fades, for it is the fate of the fairest flowers to be admired and pulled to pieces by the careless hand that plucked them. In how many ways do I wish, from the purest benevolence, to impress this truth on my sex; yet I fear that they will not listen to a truth that dear-bought experience has brought home to many an agitated bosom, nor willingly resign the privileges of rank and sex for the privileges of humanity, to which those have no claim who do not discharge its duties. . . .

Would men but generously snap our chains, and be content with rational fellowship instead of slavish obedience, they would find us more observant daughters, more affectionate sisters, more faithful wives, and more reasonable mothers—in a word, better citizens. We should then love them with true affection, because we should learn to respect ourselves; and the peace of mind of a worthy man would not be interrupted by the idle vanity of his wife. . . .

What picture does the author paint of the women of her day? Why are they in such a deplorable state? How does Wollstonecraft suggest that both women and men are at fault for the "slavish" situation of women?

---

after the seventeenth-century Italian Baroque, as modified by a series of brilliant German and Austrian sculptor-architects. This Baroque-Rococo architectural style of the eighteenth century was used in both palaces and churches, and often the same architects designed both. This is evident in the work of one of the greatest architects of the eighteenth century, Balthasar Neumann (1687–1753).

Neumann's two masterpieces are the pilgrimage church of the Vierzehnheiligen (Fourteen Saints) in southern Germany and the palace known as the Residenz, the home of the Schönborn prince-bishop of Würzburg. Secular and spiritual become easily interchangeable as lavish and fanciful ornament, light, bright colors, and elaborate and rich detail greet the eye in both buildings.

The eighteenth century was one of the greatest in the history of European music. In the first half of the century, two composers—Handel and Bach—stand out as musical geniuses. Johann Sebastian Bach (1685–1750) came from a family of musicians. Bach served as organist and music director at a number of small German courts before becoming director of liturgical music at the church of Saint Thomas in Leipzig in 1723. There Bach composed his Mass in B Minor, his Saint Matthew's Passion, and the cantatas and motets that have established his reputation as one of the greatest composers of all time. Above all for Bach, music was a means to worship God; in his own words, his task in life was to make "well-ordered music in the honor of God."

The other great musical giant of the early eighteenth century, George Frederick Handel (1685–1759), was, like Bach, born in Saxony in Germany and in the same year. Unlike Bach, however, he was profoundly secular in temperament. After studying in Italy, where he began his career writing operas in the Italian manner, in 1712 he moved to England, where he spent most of his adult life trying to run an operatic company. Although patronized by the English royal court, Handel wrote music for large public audiences and was not adverse to writing ambitious, unusual-sounding pieces. The band for his Fireworks Music, for example, was supposed to be accompanied by 101 cannons. Although he wrote much secular music, ironically, the worldly Handel is probably best known for his religious creations. His *Messiah* has been called "one of those rare works that appeal immediately to everyone, and yet is indisputably a masterpiece of the highest order."[5]

Bach and Handel perfected the Baroque musical style, with its monumental and elaborate musical structures. Two geniuses of the second half of the eighteenth century—Haydn and Mozart—were innovators who wrote music called classical rather than Baroque. Their

Antoine Watteau, *Return from Cythera.* Antoine Watteau was one of the most gifted painters in eighteenth-century France. His portrayal of aristocratic life reveals a world of elegance, wealth, and pleasure. In this painting, which is considered his masterpiece, Watteau depicts a group of aristocratic lovers about to depart the island of Cythera, where they have paid homage to Venus, the goddess of love. Luxuriously dressed, they move from the woodlands to a golden barge that is waiting to take them from the island.

renown caused the musical center of Europe to shift from Italy to the Austrian Empire.

Franz Joseph Haydn (1732–1809) spent most of his adult life as musical director for wealthy Hungarian princes, the Esterhazy brothers. Haydn was incredibly prolific, composing 104 symphonies in addition to string quartets, concerti, songs, oratorios, and Masses. His visits to England in 1790 and 1794 introduced him to a world where musicians wrote for public concerts rather than for princely patrons. This "liberty," as he called it, induced him to write his two great oratorios, *The Creation* and *The Seasons,* both of which were dedicated to the common people.

Wolfgang Amadeus Mozart (1756–1791) was a child prodigy who gave his first harpsichord concert at six and wrote his first opera at twelve. He, too, sought a patron, but his discontent with the overly demanding archbishop of Salzburg forced him to

Vierzehnheiligen, Interior View. Pictured here is the interior of the Vierzehnheiligen, the pilgrimage church designed by Balthasar Neumann. As this illustration shows, the Baroque-Rococo style of architecture produced lavish buildings in which secular and spiritual elements became easily interchangeable. Elaborate detail, blazing light, rich colors, and opulent decoration were blended together to create a work of stunning beauty.

move to Vienna, where his failure to find a permanent patron made his life miserable. Nevertheless, he wrote music prolifically and passionately—string quartets, sonatas, symphonies, concerti, and operas—until he died at thirty-five, a debt-ridden pauper. *The Marriage of Figaro, The Magic Flute,* and *Don Giovanni* are three of the world's greatest operas. Mozart composed with an ease of melody and a blend of grace and precision that arguably no one has ever surpassed.

The eighteenth century was also decisive in the development of the novel. The modern novel grew out of the medieval romances and the picaresque stories of the sixteenth century. The English are credited with establishing the novel as the primary form of fiction writing. With no established rules, the novel was open to much experimentation.

The High Culture of the Eighteenth Century

Historians and cultural anthropologists have grown accustomed to distinguishing between a civilization's high culture and its popular culture. **High culture** usually means the literary and artistic world of the educated and wealthy ruling classes; **popular culture** refers to the written and unwritten lore of the masses, most of which is passed down orally. By the eighteenth century, European high culture consisted of a learned world of theologians, scientists, philosophers, intellectuals, poets, and dramatists, for whom Latin remained a living and truly international language. Their work was supported by a wealthy and literate lay group, the most important of whom were the landed aristocracy and the wealthier upper classes in the cities.

Especially notable in the eighteenth century was an expansion of both the reading public and publishing. One study revealed that French publishers were issuing about sixteen hundred titles yearly in the 1780s, up from three hundred titles in 1750. Though many of these titles were still aimed at small groups of the educated elite, some were also directed to the new reading public of the middle classes, which included women and urban artisans. The growth of publishing houses made it possible for authors to make money from their works and be less dependent on wealthy patrons.

An important aspect of the growth of publishing and reading in the eighteenth century was the development of magazines for the general public. Great Britain, an important center for the new magazines, saw 25 periodicals published in 1700, 103 in 1760, and 158 in 1780. Along with magazines came daily newspapers. The first was printed in London in 1702, but by 1780, thirty-seven other English towns had their own newspapers. Filled with news and special features, they were relatively cheap and were available free of charge in coffeehouses.

Popular Culture

Popular culture refers to the written and unwritten literature and the social activities and pursuits that are fundamental to the lives of most people in a society. The distinguishing characteristic of popular culture is its collective and public nature. Group activity was especially evident in the festival, a broad name used to cover a variety of celebrations: community festivals in Catholic Europe that celebrated the feast day of the local patron saint; annual festivals, such as Christmas and Easter, that go back to medieval Christianity; and Carnival, which was celebrated in Spain, Italy, France, Germany, and Austria. All of these festivals were special occasions on which people ate, drank, and celebrated to excess. In traditional societies, festival was a time for relaxation and enjoyment because much of the rest of the year was taken up with unrelieved work. As the poet Thomas Gray in 1739 said of Carnival in Turin: "This Carnival lasts only from Christmas to Lent; one half of the remaining part of the year is passed in remembering the last, the other in expecting the future Carnival."[6]

Carnival began around the start of the year and lasted until the first day of Lent, the forty-day period of fasting and purification leading up to Easter. Because people were expected to abstain from meat, sex, and most recreations during Lent, Carnival was a time of great indulgence. Hearty consumption of food, especially meat and other delicacies, and heavy drinking were the norm. Carnival was a time of intense sexual activity as well. Songs with double meanings could be sung publicly at this time of year, whereas at other times they would be considered offensive. A float of Florentine key makers, for example, sang this ditty to the ladies: "Our tools are fine, new and useful. / We always carry them with us. / They are good for anything. / If you want to touch them, you can." Finally, Carnival was a time of aggression, a time to release pent-up feelings. Most often this took the form of verbal aggression, since people were allowed to openly insult other people and even to criticize their social superiors and authorities.

The same sense of community evident in festival was also present in the chief gathering places of the common people, the local taverns or cabarets. Taverns functioned as a regular gathering place for neighborhood men to talk, play games, conduct small business matters, and of course drink. In some countries, the favorite drinks of poor people, such as gin in England and vodka in Russia, proved devastating as poor people regularly drank themselves into oblivion. Gin was cheap; the classic sign in English taverns, "Drunk for a penny, dead drunk for two pence," was literally true. In England, the consumption of gin rose from 2 million to 5 million gallons between 1714 and 1733 and declined only when complaints finally led to laws to restrict sales in the 1750s.

In the eighteenth century, the gulf between elite and poor grew ever wider. In 1500, popular culture was for everyone, including members of the aristocracy. But between 1500 and 1800, the nobility, clergy, and bourgeoisie gradually abandoned popular culture to the lower classes. By abandoning the popular festivals, the upper classes were also cutting themselves off from the popular

Popular Culture: Carnival.   Pictured here in a painting by Giovanni Signorini is a scene from
the celebration of Carnival on the Piazza Santa Croce in Florence, Italy. Carnival was a period
of festivities before Lent, celebrated in most Roman Catholic countries. Carnival became an
occasion for indulgence in food, drink, games, practical jokes, and merriment, all of which are
evident here.

worldview as well. Their new scientific outlook led them
to regard such things as witchcraft, faith healing, fortune-
telling, and prophecy as the beliefs of people, as one writer
said, "of the weakest judgment and reason, as women,
children, and ignorant and superstitious persons."

Crime and Punishment

By the eighteenth century, most European states had developed a hierarchy of courts to deal with crimes. Except
in England, judicial torture remained an important means
of obtaining evidence before a trial. Courts used the rack,
thumbscrews, and other instruments to obtain confessions in criminal cases. Punishments for crimes were
often cruel and even spectacular. Public executions were a
basic part of traditional punishment and were regarded as
a necessary means of deterring potential offenders in an
age when a state's police arm was too weak to ensure the
capture of criminals. Although nobles were executed by
simple beheading, lower-class criminals condemned to
death were tortured, broken on the wheel, or drawn
(eviscerated) and quartered. The death penalty was still
commonly used in property as well as criminal cases. By
1800, more than two hundred crimes were subject to the
death penalty in England. In addition to executions,

European states resorted to forced labor in mines, forts,
and navies. England also sent criminals as indentured
servants to colonies in the New World and, after the
American Revolution, to Australia.

Appalled by the unjust laws and brutal punishments
of their times, some philosophes had sought to create a
new approach to justice. The most notable effort was
made by the Italian philosophe Cesare Beccaria (1738–
1794). In his essay *On Crimes and Punishments,* written in
1764, Beccaria argued that punishments should serve only
as deterrents, not as exercises in brutality: "Such punishments . . . ought to be chosen as will make the strongest
and most lasting impressions on the minds of others, with
the least torment to the body of the criminal."[7] Beccaria
was also opposed to the use of capital punishment. It was
spectacular but failed to stop others from committing
crimes. Imprisonment, the deprivation of freedom, made
a far more lasting impression. Moreover, capital punishment was harmful to society because it set an example of
barbarism: "Is it not absurd, that the laws, which detest
and punish homicide, should, in order to prevent murder,
publicly commit murder themselves?"[8]

By the end of the eighteenth century, a growing sentiment against executions and torture led to a decline in
both corporal and capital punishment. A new type of

prison, in which criminals were placed in cells and subjected to discipline and regular work to rehabilitate them, began to replace the public spectacle of barbarous punishments.

Religion and the Churches

The music of Bach and the pilgrimage and monastic churches of southern Germany and Austria make us aware of a curious fact. While much of the great art and music of the time was religious, the thought of the time was antireligious as life became increasingly secularized and men of reason attacked the established churches. And yet most Europeans were still Christians. Even many of those most critical of the churches accepted that society could not function without religious faith.

The Institutional Church

In the eighteenth century, the established Catholic and Protestant churches were basically conservative institutions that upheld society's hierarchical structure, privileged classes, and traditions. Although churches experienced change because of new state policies, they did not sustain any dramatic internal changes. In both Catholic and Protestant countries, the parish church run by priest or pastor remained the center of religious practice. In addition to providing religious services, the parish church kept records of births, deaths, and marriages, provided charity for the poor, supervised whatever primary education there was, and cared for orphans.

Religious Populations of Eighteenth-Century Europe

Toleration and Religious Minorities

One of the chief battle cries of the philosophes had been a call for religious toleration. Out of political necessity, a certain level of tolerance of different creeds had occurred in the seventeenth century, but many rulers still found it difficult to accept. Even devout rulers continued to believe that there was only one path to salvation; it was the true duty of a ruler not to allow subjects to be condemned to hell by being heretics. Persecution of heretics continued; the last burning of a heretic took place in 1781.

The Jews remained the despised religious minority of Europe. The largest number of Jews (known as the Ashkenazic Jews) lived in eastern Europe. Except in relatively tolerant Poland, Jews were restricted in their movements, forbidden to own land or hold certain jobs, forced to pay burdensome special taxes, and subject to periodic outbursts of popular wrath. The resulting pogroms, in which Jewish communities were looted and massacred, made Jewish existence precarious and dependent on the favor of their territorial rulers.

John Wesley. In leading a deep spiritual revival in Britain, John Wesley founded a religious movement that came to be known as Methodism. He loved to preach to the masses, and this 1766 portrait by Nathaniel Hope shows him as he might have appeared before a crowd of people.

THE CONVERSION EXPERIENCE IN WESLEY'S METHODISM

*A*fter his own conversion experience, John Wesley traveled extensively to bring the "glad tidings" to other people. It has been estimated that he preached over forty thousand sermons, some of them to audiences numbering twenty thousand listeners. Wesley gave his message wherever people gathered—in the streets, hospitals, private houses, and even pubs. In this selection from his journal, Wesley describes how emotional and even violent conversion experiences could be.

The Works of the Reverend John Wesley

Sunday, May 20 [1759], being with Mr. B——ll at Everton, I was much fatigued, and did not rise: but Mr. B. did, and observed several fainting and crying out, while Mr. Berridge was preaching: afterwards at Church, I heard many cry out, especially children, whose agonies were amazing: one of the eldest, a girl of ten or twelve years old, was full in my view, in violent contortions of body, and weeping aloud, I think incessantly, during the whole service. . . . The Church was equally crowded in the afternoon, the windows being filled within and without, and even the outside of the pulpit to the very top; so that Mr. B. seemed almost stifled by their breath; yet feeble and sickly as he is, he was continually strengthened, and his voice, for the most part, distinguishable; in the midst of all the outcries. I believe there were present three times more men than women, a great part of whom came from far; thirty of them having set out at two in the morning, from a place thirteen miles off. The text was, *Having a form of godliness, but denying the power thereof.* When the power of religion began to be spoken of, the presence of God really filled the place: and while poor sinners felt the sentence of death in their souls, what sounds of distress did I hear! The greatest number of them who cried or fell, were men: but

some women, and several children, felt the power of the same almighty Spirit, and seemed just sinking into hell. This occasioned a mixture of several sounds; some shrieking, some roaring aloud. The most general was a loud breathing, like that of people half strangled and gasping for life: and indeed almost all the cries were like those of human creatures, dying in bitter anguish. Great numbers wept without any noise: others fell down as death: some sinking in silence; some with extreme noise and violent agitation. I stood on the pew-seat, as did a young man in the opposite pew, an able-bodied, fresh, healthy countryman: but in a moment, while he seemed to think of nothing less, down he dropped with a violence inconceivable. The adjoining pews seemed to shake with his fall: I heard afterwards the stamping of his feet; ready to break the boards, as he lay in strong convulsions, at the bottom of the pew. Among several that were struck down in the next pew, was a girl, who was as violently seized as he. . . . Among the children who felt the arrows of the Almighty, I saw a sturdy boy, about eight years old, who roared above his fellows, and seemed in his agony to struggle with the strength of a grown man. His face was as red as scarlet: and almost all on whom God laid his hand, turned either very red or almost black. . . .

The violent struggling of many in the above-mentioned churches, has broken several pews and benches. Yet it is common for people to remain unaffected there, and afterwards to drop down on their way home. Some have been found lying as dead on the road: others, in Mr. B.'s garden; not being able to walk from the Church to his house, though it is not two hundred yards. . . .

What was a conversion experience? What would you compare it to in today's world? Why?

Another major group was the Sephardic Jews who had been expelled from Spain in the fifteenth century. Although many had migrated to the Ottoman Empire, some had settled in cities such as Amsterdam, Venice, London, and Frankfurt, where they were relatively free to engage in the banking and commercial activities that Jews had conducted since the Middle Ages. The highly successful ones came to provide valuable services to rulers, especially in central Europe. But even these Jews were insecure because their religion set them apart from the Christian majority and served as a catalyst for social resentment.

Some Enlightenment thinkers in the eighteenth century favored a new acceptance of Jews. They argued that Jews and Muslims were human and deserved the full rights of citizenship despite their religion. Many philosophes denounced persecution of the Jews but made no attempt to hide their hostility and ridiculed Jewish customs. Diderot, for example, said that the Jews had "all the

defects peculiar to an ignorant and superstitious nation." Many Europeans favored assimilation of the Jews into the mainstream of society, but only through the conversion of Jews to Christianity. This, of course, was not acceptable to most Jews.

The Austrian emperor Joseph II (1780–1790) attempted to adopt a new policy toward the Jews, although it too was limited. It freed Jews from nuisance taxes and allowed them more freedom of movement and job opportunities, but they were still prohibited from owning land and worshiping in public. At the same time, Joseph encouraged Jews to learn German and to work toward greater assimilation into Austrian society.

Popular Religion in the Eighteenth Century

Despite the rise of skepticism and the intellectuals' belief in deism and natural religion, religious devotion remained strong in the eighteenth century. It is difficult to assess precisely the religiosity of Europe's Catholics. The Catholic parish church remained a center of life for the entire community. How many people went to church regularly cannot be known exactly, but 90 to 95 percent of Catholic populations did go to Mass on Easter Sunday, one of the church's most important celebrations.

After the initial century of religious fervor that gave rise to Protestantism in the sixteenth century, Protestant churches in the seventeenth century had settled down into established patterns controlled by state authorities and served by a well-educated clergy. Protestant churches became bureaucratized and bereft of religious enthusiasm. In Germany and England, where rationalism and deism had become influential and moved some theologians to a more "rational" Christianity, the desire of ordinary Protestant churchgoers for greater depths of religious experience led to new and dynamic religious movements.

One of the most famous movements—Methodism—was the work of John Wesley (1703–1791). An ordained Anglican minister, Wesley underwent a mystical experience in which "the gift of God's grace" assured him of

salvation and led him to become a missionary to the English people, bringing the "glad tidings" of salvation to all people, despite opposition from the Anglican church, which criticized this emotional mysticism or religious enthusiasm as superstitious nonsense. To Wesley, all could be saved by experiencing God and opening the doors to his grace.

In taking the Gospel to the people, Wesley preached to the masses in open fields, appealing especially to the lower classes neglected by the socially elitist Anglican church. He tried, he said, "to lower religion to the level of the lowest people's capacities." Wesley's charismatic preaching often provoked highly charged and even violent conversion experiences (see the box on p. 333). Afterward, converts were organized into so-called Methodist societies or chapels in which they could aid each other in doing the good works that Wesley considered a component of salvation. Although Wesley sought to keep Methodism within the Anglican church, after his death it became a separate and independent sect. Methodism represented an important revival of Christianity and proved that the need for spiritual experience had not been extinguished by the eighteenth-century search for reason.

TIMELINE

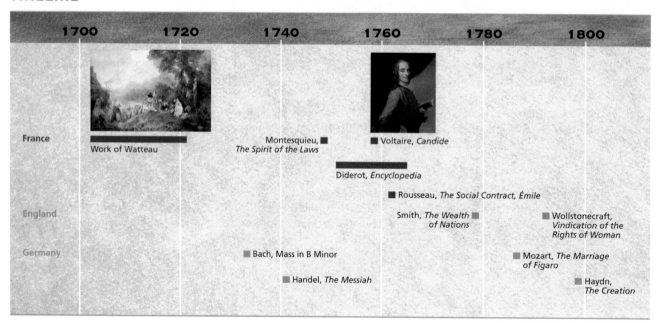

	1700	1720	1740	1760	1780	1800
France	Work of Watteau		Montesquieu, ■ *The Spirit of the Laws*	■ Voltaire, *Candide*		
				Diderot, *Encyclopedia*		
				■ Rousseau, *The Social Contract, Émile*		
England				Smith, *The Wealth* ■ *of Nations*	■ Wollstonecraft, *Vindication of the Rights of Woman*	
Germany			■ Bach, *Mass in B Minor*		■ Mozart, *The Marriage of Figaro*	
			■ Handel, *The Messiah*		■ Haydn, *The Creation*	

CONCLUSION

The eighteenth was a century of change but also of tradition. Highly influenced by the new worldview ushered in by the Scientific Revolution and especially the ideas of Locke and Newton, the philosophes hoped that they could

create a new society by using reason to discover the natural laws that governed it. Like the Christian humanists of the fifteenth and sixteenth centuries, they believed that education could produce better human beings and a better human society. By attacking traditional religion as the enemy and creating the new "sciences of man" in economics, politics, and justice, the philosophes laid the foundation for a modern worldview based on rationalism and secularism.

But despite the secular thought and rational ideas that began to penetrate the minds of the elites, most people in eighteenth-century Europe still lived by seemingly eternal verities and practices—God, religious wor-

ship, and farming. The most brilliant architecture and music of the age were religious. And yet the forces of secularization were too strong to stop. In the midst of intellectual change, economic, political, and social transformations of great purport were taking shape and would lead to both political and industrial upheavals before the century's end. It is time now to examine the political, economic, and social traditions and changes of the century.

NOTES

1. Quoted in D. Outram, *The Enlightenment* (Cambridge, 1995), p. 67.
2. J. Locke, *An Essay Concerning Human Understanding* (New York, 1964), pp. 89–90.
3. J.-J. Rousseau, *The Social Contract*, trans. M. Cranston (Harmondsworth, England, 1968), p. 141.
4. M. Astell, *A Serious Proposal to the Ladies*, in M. Ferguson, ed., *First Feminists: British Women Writers, 1578–1799* (Bloomington, Ind., 1985), p. 190.
5. K. Clark, *Civilization* (New York, 1969), p. 231.
6. Quoted in P. Burke, *Popular Culture in Early Modern Europe* (New York, 1978), p. 179.
7. C. Beccaria, *An Essay on Crimes and Punishments*, trans. E. D. Ingraham (Philadelphia, 1819), pp. 59–60.
8. Ibid., p. 60.

SUGGESTIONS FOR FURTHER READING

Two sound, comprehensive surveys of eighteenth-century Europe are **I. Woloch**, *Eighteenth-Century Europe* (New York, 1982), and **M. S. Anderson**, *Europe in the Eighteenth Century*, 4th ed. (London, 2000).

Good introductions to the Enlightenment can be found in **U. Im Hof**, *The Enlightenment* (Oxford, 1994); **D. Goodman**, *The Republic of Letters: A Cultural History of the French Enlightenment* (Ithaca, N.Y., 1994); and **D. Outram**, *The Enlightenment* (Cambridge, 1995). A more detailed synthesis can be found in **P. Gay**, *The Enlightenment: An Interpretation*, 2 vols. (New York, 1966–69). On the social history of the Enlightenment, see **T. Munck**, *The Enlightenment: A Comparative Social History, 1721–1794* (London, 2000). For a short, popular survey on the French philosophes, see **F. Artz**, *The Enlightenment in France* (Kent, Ohio, 1968). Also of value are **E. J. Wilson and P. H. Reill**, *Encyclopedia of the Enlightenment* (New York, 1996), and **J. W. Yolton**, ed., *The Blackwell Companion to the Enlightenment* (Cambridge, Mass., 1995). Studies of the major Enlightenment intellectuals include **J. Sklar**, *Montesquieu* (Oxford, 1987); **R. Pearson**, *Voltaire Almighty* (New York, 2005); **P. N. Furbank**, *Diderot: A Critical Biography* (New York, 1992); and **L. Damrosch**, *Jean-Jacques Rousseau: Restless Genius* (Boston, 2005). On women in the eighteenth century, see **N. Z. Davis and A. Farge**, eds., *A History of Women: Renaissance and Enlightenment Paradoxes* (Cambridge, Mass., 1993); **C. Lougee**, *Le Paradis des Femmes: Women, Salons, and Social Stratification* (Princeton, N.J., 1976); and **O. Hufton**, *The Prospect Before Her: A History of Women in Western Europe, 1500–1800* (New York, 1998).

Two readable general surveys on the arts and literature are **M. Levy**, *Rococo to Revolution* (London, 1966), and **H. Honour**, *Neo-Classicism* (Harmondsworth, England, 1968). On the eighteenth-century novel, see **G. J. Barker-Benfield**, *The Culture of Sensibility: Sex and Society in the Eighteenth-Century English Novel* (Chicago, 1992). On the growth of literacy, see **R. A. Houston**, *Literacy in Early Modern Europe: Culture and Education, 1500–1800* (New York, 1988). Different facets of crime and punishment are examined in **M. Foucault**, *Discipline and Punish: The Birth of the Prison* (New York, 1977), and **J. Langbein**, *Torture and the Law of Proof* (Chicago, 1977).

Important studies on popular culture include **P. Burke**, *Popular Culture in Early Modern Europe* (New York, 1978), and **R. Darnton**, *The Great Cat Massacre and Other Episodes in French Cultural History* (New York, 1984).

A good introduction to the religious history of the eighteenth century can be found in **G. R. Cragg**, *The Church and the Age of Reason, 1648–1789* (London, 1966). The problem of religious toleration is examined in **J. I. Israel**, *European Jewry in the Age of Mercantilism, 1550–1750*, 2d ed. (New York, 1989). On John Wesley, see **H. Rack**, *Reasonable Enthusiast: John Wesley and the Rise of Methodism* (New York, 1989).

Thomson NOW! Enter ThomsonNOW using the access card that is available for *Western Civilization: A Brief History*. ThomsonNOW will help you understand this chapter with lesson plans generated for your needs. In addition, you can read the following documents, and many more, online:

Voltaire, entries from *Philosophical Dictionary*
Immanuel Kant, *What Is Enlightenment?*
Daniel Defoe, excerpts from *Life and Adventures of Robinson Crusoe*
Baron de Montesquieu, selected books from *The Spirit of Laws*
Mary Wollstonecraft, *A Vindication of the Rights of Woman*

WESTERN CIVILIZATION RESOURCES

Visit the Web site for *Western Civilization: A Brief History* for resources specific to this book:
http://www.thomsonedu.com/history/spielvogel
For a variety of tools to help you succeed in this course, visit the Western Civilization Resource Center at
http://history.wadsworth.com/spielvogel
Included are quizzes, images, documents, interactive simulations, maps and timelines, movie explorations, and a wealth of other sources.

CHAPTER
18

THE EIGHTEENTH CENTURY: EUROPEAN STATES, INTERNATIONAL WARS, AND SOCIAL CHANGE

Catherine the Great on horseback

Erich Lessing/Art Resource, NY (Musée des Beaux-Arts, Chartres, France)

ISTORIANS OFTEN DEFINE the eighteenth century as the years from 1715 to 1789. Politically, this makes sense because 1715 marks the end of the age of Louis XIV and 1789 was the year in which the French Revolution erupted. This period has often been portrayed as the final phase of Europe's old order, swept away by the violent upheaval and reordering of society associated with the French Revolution. Europe's old order, still largely agrarian, dominated by kings and landed aristocrats, and grounded in privileges for nobles, clergy, towns, and provinces, seemed to continue a basic pattern that had prevailed in Europe since medieval times. But new ideas and practices were beginning to emerge. Just as a new intellectual order based on rationalism and secularism was evolving from the Scientific Revolution and the Enlightenment, demographic, economic, and social patterns were beginning to change in ways that heralded the emergence of a modern new order.

The ideas of the Enlightenment seemed to proclaim a new political age as well. Catherine the Great, who ruled Russia from 1762 to 1796, wrote to Voltaire: "Since 1746 I have been under the greatest obligations to you. Before that period I read nothing but romances, but by chance your works fell into my hands, and ever since then I have never ceased to read them, and have no desire for books less well written than yours, or less instructive." The empress also invited Diderot to Russia and, when he arrived, urged him to speak frankly "as man to man." Diderot did, offering her advice for a far-ranging program of political and financial reform. But Catherine's apparent eagerness to make enlightened reforms was tempered by skepticism. She said of Diderot, "If I had believed him everything would have been turned upside down in my kingdom; legislation, administration, finance—all would have been turned topsy-turvy to make room for impractical theories." For Catherine, enlightened reform remained more a dream than a reality, and in the end, the waging of wars to gain more power was more important.

In the eighteenth century, the process of centralization that had characterized the growth of states since the Middle Ages continued as most European states enlarged their bureaucratic machinery and consolidated their governments in order to collect the revenues and build the armies they needed to compete militarily with the other European states. International competition continued to be the favorite pastime of eighteenth-century rulers. Within the European state system, the nations that would dominate Europe until World War I—Britain, France, Austria, Prussia, and Russia—emerged as the five great powers of Europe. Their rivalries led to major wars. In the midst of this state building and warmaking, dramatic demographic, economic, and social changes gave rise to a radical transformation in the way Europeans would raise food and produce goods.◆

The European States

Most European states in the eighteenth century were ruled by monarchs. Although the seventeenth-century justification for strong monarchy on the basis of divine right continued into the succeeding century, as the eighteenth century became increasingly secularized, divine-right assumptions were gradually superseded by influential utilitarian arguments. The Prussian king Frederick II expressed these well when he attempted to explain the services a monarch must provide for his people:

These services consisted in the maintenance of the laws; a strict execution of justice; an employment of his whole powers to prevent any corruption of manners; and defending the state against its enemies. It is the duty of this magistrate to pay attention to agriculture; it should be his care that provisions for the nation should be in abundance, and that commerce and industry should be encouraged. He is a perpetual sentinel, who must watch the acts and the conduct of the enemies of the state. . . . If he be the first general, the first minister of the realm, it is not that he should remain the shadow of authority, but that he should fulfill the duties of such titles. He is only the first servant of the state.[1]

This utilitarian argument was reinforced by the praises of the philosophes.

Enlightened Absolutism?

There is no doubt that Enlightenment thought had an impact on the political development of European states in the eighteenth century. Closely related to the Enlightenment idea of **natural laws** was the belief in **natural rights,** which were thought to be fundamental privileges that must not be withheld from any person. These natural rights included equality before the law, freedom of religious worship, freedom of speech and the press, and the rights to assemble, hold property, and seek happiness. The United States' Declaration of Independence in 1776 summarized the Enlightenment concept of natural rights in its opening paragraph: "We hold these truths to be self-evident, that all men are created equal, that they are endowed by their Creator with certain unalienable rights, that among these are Life, Liberty and the pursuit of Happiness."

But how were these natural rights to be established and preserved? In the opinion of most philosophes, people needed the direction provided by an enlightened ruler. What made rulers enlightened? They must allow religious toleration, freedom of speech and the press, and the rights of private property. They must foster the arts, sciences, and education. Above all, they must not be arbitrary in their rule; they must obey the laws and enforce them fairly for all subjects. Only strong monarchs seemed capable of overcoming vested interests and effecting the reforms society needed. Reforms, then, should come from above—from the rulers rather than from the people. Distrustful of the masses, the philosophes believed that absolute rulers, swayed by enlightened principles, were the best hope of reforming their societies.

The extent to which rulers actually did so is frequently discussed in the political history of Europe in the eighteenth century. Many historians once assumed that a new type of monarchy emerged in the late eighteenth century, which they called enlightened despotism or **enlightened absolutism.** Monarchs such as Frederick II of Prussia, Catherine the Great of Russia, and Joseph II of Austria supposedly followed the advice of the philosophes and ruled by enlightened principles, establishing a path to modern nationhood. Recent scholarship, however, has questioned the usefulness of the concept of enlightened absolutism. We can best determine the extent to which it can be applied by surveying the development of the European states and then making a judgment about the enlightened absolutism of the late eighteenth century.

The Atlantic Seaboard States

As a result of overseas voyages in the sixteenth century, the European economic axis began to shift from the Mediterranean to the Atlantic seaboard. In the seventeenth century, English and Dutch influence expanded as Spain's and Portugal's declined. By the eighteenth century, Dutch power had waned, and it fell to the English and French to build the commercial empires that ultimately fostered a true global economy.

The British House of Commons.
A sharing of power between king and Parliament characterized the British political system in the eighteenth century. Parliament was divided into the House of Lords and the House of Commons. This painting shows the House of Commons in session in 1793 during a debate over the possibility of war with France. William Pitt the Younger is addressing the chamber.

© National Portrait Gallery/SuperStock

France: The Problems of the French Monarchy In the eighteenth century, France experienced an economic revival as the Enlightenment gained strength. The French monarchy, however, was not overly influenced by the philosophes and resisted reforms even as the French aristocracy grew stronger.

Louis XIV had left France with enlarged territories, an enormous debt, an unhappy populace, and a five-year-old great-grandson as his successor. Louis XV (1715–1774) did not begin to rule in his own right until 1743. But Louis was both lazy and weak, and ministers and mistresses soon began to influence the king, control the affairs of state, and undermine the prestige of the monarchy. The loss of an empire in the Seven Years' War (discussed later in this chapter), accompanied by burdensome taxes, an ever-mounting public debt, more hungry people, and a frivolous court life at Versailles, forced even Louis to recognize the growing disgust with his monarchy.

The next king, Louis' twenty-year-old grandson, who became Louis XVI (1774–1792), knew little about the operations of the French government and lacked the energy to deal decisively with state affairs. His wife, Marie Antoinette, was a spoiled Austrian princess who devoted much of her time to court intrigues. As France's financial crises worsened, neither Louis nor his queen seemed able to fathom the depths of despair and discontent that soon led to violent revolution (see Chapter 19).

Great Britain: King and Parliament The success of the Glorious Revolution in England had prevented absolutism without clearly inaugurating constitutional monarchy. The eighteenth-century British political system was characterized by a sharing of power between king and Parliament, with Parliament gradually gaining the upper hand. (The United Kingdom of Great Britain came into existence in 1707 when the governments of England and

Scotland were united; the term *British* came to refer to both English and Scots.) The king chose ministers responsible to himself who set policy and guided Parliament; Parliament had the power to make laws, levy taxes, pass the budget, and indirectly influence the king's ministers. The eighteenth-century British Parliament was dominated by a landed aristocracy that historians usually divide into two groups: the peers, who sat for life in the House of Lords, and the landed gentry, who sat in the House of Commons and served as justices of the peace. The two groups had much in common: both were made up of landowners with similar economic interests, and they frequently intermarried.

The deputies to the House of Commons were chosen from the boroughs and counties but not by popular voting. Who was eligible to vote in the boroughs varied widely, enabling wealthy landed aristocrats to gain support by **patronage** and bribery; the result was a number of "pocket boroughs" controlled by a single person (hence "in his pocket"). The duke of Newcastle, for example, controlled the representatives from seven boroughs. It has been estimated that out of 405 borough deputies, 293 were chosen by fewer than 500 voters. This aristocratic control also extended to the county delegates, two from each of England's forty counties. Although all holders of property worth at least 40 shillings a year could vote, members of the leading landed gentry families were elected over and over again.

In 1714, a new dynasty—the Hanoverians—was established. When the last Stuart ruler, Queen Anne, died without an heir, the crown was offered to the Protestant rulers of the German state of Hanover. Because the first Hanoverian king, George I (1714–1727), did not speak English and neither he nor George II (1727–1760) had much familiarity with the British system, their chief ministers were allowed to handle Parliament. Many historians believe that this exercise of ministerial power was

France	
Louis XV	1715–1774
Louis XVI	1774–1792
Great Britain	
The Stuarts	
Anne	1702–1714
The Hanoverians	
George I	1714–1727
George II	1727–1760
Robert Walpole	1721–1742
William Pitt the Elder	1757–1761
George III	1760–1820
William Pitt the Younger	1783–1801

an important step in the development of the modern cabinet system in British government.

Robert Walpole served as prime minister from 1721 to 1742 and pursued a peaceful foreign policy to avoid new land taxes. But new forces were emerging in eighteenth-century England as growing trade and industry led an ever-increasing middle class to favor expansion of trade and world empire. The exponents of empire found a spokesperson in William Pitt the Elder, who became prime minister in 1757 and furthered imperial ambitions by acquiring Canada and India in the Seven Years' War.

Despite his successes, however, Pitt the Elder was dismissed in 1761 by the new king, George III (1760–1820), and replaced by the king's favorite, Lord Bute. However, discontent over the electoral system and the loss of the American colonies (see Chapter 19) brought public criticism of the king. In 1780, the House of Commons affirmed that "the influence of the crown has increased, is increasing, and ought to be diminished." King George III managed to avoid drastic change by appointing William Pitt the Younger (1759–1806), son of William Pitt the Elder, as prime minister in 1783. Supported by the merchants, industrial classes, and the king, Pitt managed to stay in power. George III, however, remained an uncertain supporter because of periodic bouts of insanity (he once mistook a tree in Windsor Park for the king of Prussia). Thanks to Pitt's successes, however, serious reform of the corrupt parliamentary system was avoided for another generation.

Absolutism in Central and Eastern Europe

Of the five major European powers, three were located in central and eastern Europe and came to play an increasingly important role in European international politics (see Map 18.1).

Prussia: Army and Bureaucracy Two able Prussian kings in the eighteenth century, Frederick William I and Frederick II the Great, further developed the two major institutions—the army and the bureaucracy—that were the backbone of Prussia. Frederick William I (1713–1740) promoted the evolution of Prussia's highly efficient civil bureaucracy by establishing the General Directory. It served as the chief administrative agent of the central government, supervising military, police, economic, and financial affairs. Frederick William strove to maintain a highly efficient bureaucracy of civil service workers. It had its own code in which the supreme values were obedience, honor, and service to the king as the highest duty. As Frederick William asserted, "One must serve the king with life and limb, with goods and chattels, with honor and conscience, and surrender everything except salvation. The latter is reserved for God. But everything else must be mine."[2] Close personal supervision of the bureaucracy became a hallmark of the eighteenth-century Prussian rulers.

Frederick William's other major concern was the army. By the end of his reign, it had grown from 45,000 to 83,000 men. Though the tenth-largest nation in physical size and thirteenth in population in Europe, Prussia had the fourth-largest army, after France, Russia, and Austria. The nobility or landed aristocracy known as Junkers, who owned large estates with many serfs, were the officers in the Prussian army. They too had a strong sense of service to the king or state. Prussian nobles believed in duty, obedience, and sacrifice. At the same time, because of its size and its reputation as one of the best armies in Europe, the Prussian army was the most important institution in the state.

Frederick the Great (1740–1786) was one of the best-educated and most cultured monarchs in the eighteenth century. He was well versed in Enlightenment thought and even invited Voltaire to live at his court for several years. His intellectual interests were despised by his father, who forced his intelligent son to prepare for a career in rulership. A believer in the king as the "first servant of the state," Frederick became a conscientious ruler who made few innovations in administration. His diligence in overseeing its operation, however, made the Prussian bureaucracy well known for both efficiency and honesty.

For a time, Frederick seemed quite willing to follow the philosophes' suggestions for reform. He established a single code of laws for his territories that eliminated the use of torture except in treason and murder cases. He also granted a limited freedom of speech and the press as well as complete religious toleration—no difficult task since he had no strong religious convictions anyway. Although Frederick was well aware of the philosophes' condemnation of serfdom, he was too dependent on the Prussian nobility to interfere with it or with the hierarchical structure of Prussian society. In fact, Frederick was a social conservative who made Prussian society even more aristocratic than it had been before. Frederick reversed his father's policy of allowing commoners to have power in

MAP 18.1 **Europe in 1763.** By the middle of the eighteenth century, five major powers dominated Europe—Prussia, Austria, Russia, Britain, and France. Each sought to enhance its power both domestically, through a bureaucracy that collected taxes and ran the military, and internationally, by capturing territory or preventing other powers from capturing territory. ❓ Given the distribution of Prussian and Habsburg holdings, in what areas of Europe were they most likely to compete for land and power? 🌐 **View an animated version of this map or related maps at** http://thomsonedu.com/history/spielvogel

the civil service and reserved the higher positions in the bureaucracy for members of the nobility. The upper ranks of the bureaucracy came close to constituting a hereditary caste.

Like his predecessors, Frederick the Great took a great interest in military affairs and enlarged the Prussian army (to 200,000 men). Unlike his predecessors, he had no objection to using it. Frederick did not hesitate to take advantage of a succession crisis in the Habsburg monarchy to seize the Austrian province of Silesia for Prussia. This act aroused Austria's bitter hostility toward Prussia and embroiled Frederick in two major wars, the War of the Austrian Succession and the Seven Years' War. Although the latter war left his country exhausted, Frederick succeeded in keeping Silesia. After the wars, the first partition of Poland with Austria and Russia in 1772 won him the Polish territory between Prussia and Brandenburg and gave greater unity to the scattered lands of Prussia. By the end of his reign, Prussia was recognized as a great European power.

The Austrian Empire of the Habsburgs The Austrian Empire had become one of the great European states by the beginning of the eighteenth century. The city of Vienna, center of the Habsburg monarchy, was filled with magnificent palaces and churches built in the Baroque style and became the music capital of Europe. Yet the sprawling assemblage of nationalities, languages, religions, and cultures that was Austria made it difficult to provide common laws and administrative centralization for its people. Although Empress Maria Theresa (1740–1780) managed to make administrative reforms that helped centralize the Austrian Empire, these reforms were done for practical reasons—to strengthen the power of the Habsburg state—and were accompanied by an enlargement and modernization of the armed forces. Maria Theresa remained staunchly Catholic and conservative and was not open to the wider reform calls of the philosophes. But her successor was.

Joseph II (1780–1790) was determined to make changes; at the same time, he carried on his mother's

Lauros/Giraudon/The Bridgeman Art Library (Schloss Sanssouci, Potsdam, Germany)

Frederick II at Sans-Souci. Frederick II, known as Frederick the Great, was one of the most cultured and best-educated European monarchs. In this painting, he is shown (holding walking stick) visiting the building site of his residential retreat, Sans-Souci, at Potsdam, accompanied by the marquis of Argens.

chief goal of enhancing Habsburg power within the monarchy and Europe. Joseph was an earnest man who believed in the need to sweep away anything standing in the path of reason. As he expressed it, "I have made

Philosophy the lawmaker of my empire; her logical applications are going to transform Austria."

Joseph's reform program was far-reaching. He abolished serfdom and tried to give the peasants hereditary rights to their holdings. A new penal code was instituted that abrogated the death penalty and established the principle of equality of all before the law. Joseph introduced drastic religious reforms as well, including complete religious toleration and restrictions on the Catholic church. Altogether, Joseph II issued six thousand decrees and eleven thousand laws in his effort to transform his empire.

Joseph's reform program proved overwhelming for Austria, however. He alienated the nobility by freeing the serfs and alienated the church by his attacks on the monastic establishment. Even the serfs were unhappy, unable to comprehend the drastic changes inherent in Joseph's policies. His attempt to rationalize the administration of the empire by imposing German as the official bureaucratic language alienated the non-German nationalities. As Joseph complained, there were not enough people for the kind of bureaucracy he needed. His deep sense of failure is revealed in the epitaph he wrote for his gravestone: "Here lies Joseph II, who was unfortunate in everything that he undertook." His successors undid many of his reform efforts.

Russia Under Catherine the Great Peter the Great was followed by a series of six successors who were made and unmade by the palace guard. After the last of these six, Peter III, was murdered by a faction of nobles, his German wife emerged as autocrat of all the Russians (see the box on p. 342). Catherine II (1762–1796) was an intelligent woman who was familiar

Chateau de Versailles, Versailles, France/The Bridgeman Art Library International

Maria Theresa and Her Family. Maria Theresa governed the vast possessions of the Austrian Empire from 1740 to 1780. Of her ten surviving children, Joseph II (shown here in red standing to the left of his mother) succeeded her; Leopold became grand-duke of Tuscany and the ruler of Austria after Joseph's death; Ferdinand was made duke of Modena; and Marie Antoinette became the bride of King Louis XVI of France.

The Childhood of Catherine the Great

atherine the Great was the daughter of the prince and princess of Anhalt-Zerbst in central Germany. Catherine wrote an account of her early life in French, subsequently published as her Memoirs, in which she recounted a number of painful experiences.

Catherine the Great, *Memoirs*

I was born on April 21st, 1729 (forty-two years ago), at Stettin in Pomerania. I was told later that, a son having been more desired, my arrival as the first-born had given rise to some disappointment. My father, however, showed more satisfaction at the event than all the rest of the entourage. My mother almost died in bringing me into the world and it took her nineteen irksome weeks to recover....

My father, whom I saw very seldom, considered me to be an angel, my mother did not bother much about me. She had had, eighteen months after my birth, a son whom she passionately loved, whereas I was merely tolerated and often repulsed with violence and temper, not always with justice. I was aware of all this, but not always able to understand what I really felt about it.

At the age of seven I was suddenly seized with a violent cough. It was the custom that we should kneel every night and every morning to say our prayers. One night as I knelt and prayed I began to cough so violently that the strain caused me to fall on my left side, and I had such sharp pains in my chest that they almost took my breath away.

Finally, after much suffering, I was well enough to get up and it was discovered, as they started to put on my clothes, that I had in the meantime assumed the shape of the letter Z; my right shoulder was much higher than the left, the backbone running in a zigzag and the left side falling in. The women who attended me, also my mother's women, whom they consulted, decided to break the news to my father and my mother. The first step undertaken was to swear everybody to secrecy concerning my condition....[A specialist] was called in. This man, after examining me, ordered that every morning at six, a girl should come to me on an empty stomach and rub my shoulder and backbone with her saliva. Then he proceeded to fabricate a sort of frame, which I never removed day or night except when changing my underclothes, and every other day he came to examine me in the morning. Besides this he made me wear a large black ribbon which went under the neck, crossed the right shoulder round the right arm, and was fastened at the back. I do not know whether it was because of all these remedies or that I was not meant to become a cripple, but after eighteen months I began to show signs of straightening out. I was ten or eleven when I was at last allowed to discard this more cumbersome framework.

At the age of seven all my dolls and other toys were taken away, and I was told that I was now a big girl and therefore it was no longer suitable that I should have them. I had never liked dolls, and found a way of making a plaything out of anything, my hands, a handkerchief, all served that purpose. The trend of my life went on as before and this deprivation of toys must have been a mere question of etiquette, as no one interfered with me in my games.

I began to grow taller and the extreme ugliness with which I was afflicted was beginning to disappear when I went to visit the future King of Sweden, my uncle, then Bishop of Lübeck.

I do not know if I was actually ugly as a child, but I know that I was so often told that I was and that because of this I should try to acquire wit and other merits that until the age of fourteen or fifteen I was convinced that I was a regular ugly duckling and tried much more to acquire these other virtues than rely upon my face. It is true that I have seen a portrait of myself painted when I was ten, excessively ugly–if it was a good likeness, then I was not being deceived.

_____

What hardships did Catherine experience in her childhood? What do you think was the impact of these hardships on Catherine's later life?

---

with the works of the philosophes. She claimed that she wished to reform Russia along the lines of Enlightenment ideas, but she was always shrewd enough to realize that her success depended on the support of the palace guard and the gentry class from which it stemmed. She could not afford to alienate the Russian nobility.

Initially, Catherine seemed eager to pursue reform. She called for the election of an assembly in 1767 to debate the details of a new law code. In her *Instruction*, written as a guide to the deliberations, Catherine questioned the institution of serfdom, torture, and capital punishment and even advocated the principle of the equality of all people in the eyes of the law. But a year and a half of negotiation produced little real change.

In fact, Catherine's subsequent policies had the effect of strengthening the landholding class at the expense of all others, especially the Russian serfs. To reorganize local government, Catherine divided Russia into fifty provinces, each of which was in turn subdivided into districts ruled by officials chosen by the nobles. In this way, the local nobility became responsible for the day-to-day governing of Russia. Moreover, the gentry were now formed into corporate groups with special legal privileges, including the right to trial by peers and exemption from personal taxation and corporal punishment. The Charter of the Nobility formalized these rights in 1785.

Catherine's policy of favoring the landed nobility led to even worse conditions for the Russian peasants and

Pugachev's Rebellion

provoked a rebellion. Led by an illiterate Cossack, Emelyan Pugachev, the rebellion spread across southern Russia. But the insurrection soon faltered, and Pugachev was captured, tortured, and executed. Catherine responded to the failed revolt with even harsher measures against the peasantry. All rural reform was halted, and serfdom was expanded into new parts of the empire.

Catherine proved a worthy successor to Peter the Great by expanding Russia's territory westward into Poland and southward to the Black Sea. Russia gained land to the south by defeating the Ottoman Turks. In the Treaty of Kuchuk-Kainarji in 1774, the Russians also gained the privilege of protecting Greek Orthodox Christians in the Ottoman Empire. Russian expansion westward came at the expense of neighboring Poland. In the three partitions of Poland in 1772, 1793, and 1795, Russia gained about 50 percent of Polish territory; Austria and Prussia took the rest.

Enlightened Absolutism Revisited

Of the three major rulers most closely associated traditionally with enlightened absolutism—Joseph II, Frederick II, and Catherine the Great—only Joseph sought truly radical changes based on Enlightenment ideas. Both Frederick and Catherine liked to be cast as disciples of the Enlightenment, expressed interest in enlightened reforms, and even attempted some. But the policies of neither seemed seriously affected by Enlightenment thought. Necessities of state and maintenance of the existing system took precedence over reform. Indeed, many historians maintain that Joseph, Frederick, and Catherine were all guided primarily by a concern for the power and well-being of their states and that their policies were not all that different from those of their predecessors. In the final analysis, state power was used to build armies and wage wars to gain even more power. Nevertheless, in their desire to forge stronger state systems, these rulers did pursue such enlightened ideas as legal reform, religious toleration, and the extension of education, since these served to create more satisfied subjects and strengthened the state in significant ways.

It would be foolish, however, to overlook the fact that political and social realities limited the ability of enlightened rulers to make reforms. Everywhere in Europe, the hereditary aristocracy was still the most powerful class in society. Enlightened reforms were often limited to changes in the administrative and judicial systems that did not seriously undermine the powerful interests of the European nobility. Although aristocrats might join the populace in

CHRONOLOGY	Central and Eastern Europe in the Eighteenth Century
Prussia	
Frederick William I	1713–1740
Frederick II the Great	1740–1786
Austrian Empire	
Maria Theresa	1740–1780
Joseph II	1780–1790
Russia	
Peter III	1762
Catherine II the Great	1762–1796
Pugachev's rebellion	1773–1775
Charter of the Nobility	1785
Poland	
First partition	1772
Second partition	1793
Third partition	1795

opposing monarchical extension of centralizing power, as the chief beneficiaries of a system based on traditional rights and privileges for their class, they were certainly not willing to support a political ideology that trumpeted the principle of equal rights for all.

Wars and Diplomacy

The philosophes condemned war as a foolish waste of life and resources in stupid quarrels of no value to humankind. Despite their words, the rivalry among states that led to costly struggles remained unchanged in the European world of the eighteenth century. Europe consisted of a number of self-governing states guided by the self-interest of the ruler. And as Frederick the Great of Prussia said, "The fundamental rule of governments is the principle of extending their territories."

International rivalry and the continuing centralization of the European states were closely related. The need for taxes to support large armies and navies created its own imperative for more efficient and effective control of power in the hands of bureaucrats who could collect taxes and organize states for the task of winning wars. At the same time, the development of large standing armies ensured that political disputes would periodically be resolved by armed conflict rather than diplomacy. Between 1715 and 1740, it had seemed that Europe preferred peace. But in 1740, a major conflict erupted over the succession to the Austrian throne.

After the death of the Habsburg emperor Charles VI (1711–1740), King Frederick II of Prussia took advantage of the succession of Maria Theresa to the throne of Austria by invading Austrian Silesia. The vulnerability of Maria Theresa encouraged France to enter the war against its traditional enemy, Austria; in turn, Maria Theresa made an alliance with Great Britain, which feared French hegemony over Continental affairs. All too quickly, the Austrian succession had set off a worldwide conflagration. The War of the Austrian Succession (1740–1748) was fought not only in Europe, where Prussia seized Silesia and France occupied the Austrian Netherlands, but also in the East, where France took Madras in India from the British, and in North America, where the British captured the French fortress of Louisbourg at the entrance to the Saint Lawrence River. By 1748, all parties were exhausted and agreed to a peace that guaranteed the return of all occupied territories except for Silesia to their original owners. Prussia's refusal to return Silesia guaranteed another war, at least between the two hostile central European powers of Prussia and Austria.

The Seven Years' War (1756–1763)

Maria Theresa refused to accept the loss of Silesia and prepared for its return by rebuilding her army while working diplomatically to separate Prussia from its chief ally, France. In 1756, Austria achieved what was soon labeled a diplomatic revolution. French-Austrian rivalry had been a fact of European diplomacy since the late sixteenth century. But two new rivalries made this old one seem superfluous: Britain and France over colonial empires and Austria and Prussia over Silesia. France abandoned Prussia and allied with Austria. Russia, which saw Prussia as a major hindrance to Russian goals in central Europe, joined the new alliance. In turn, Great Britain allied with Prussia. This diplomatic revolution of 1756 now led to another worldwide war.

There were three major areas of conflict: Europe, India, and North America (see Map 18.2). Europe witnessed the clash of the two major alliances: the British and Prussians against the Austrians, Russians, and French. With his superb army and military prowess, Frederick the Great of Prussia was able for some time to dominate the Austrian, French, and Russian armies. Eventually, however, Frederick's forces were gradually worn down and

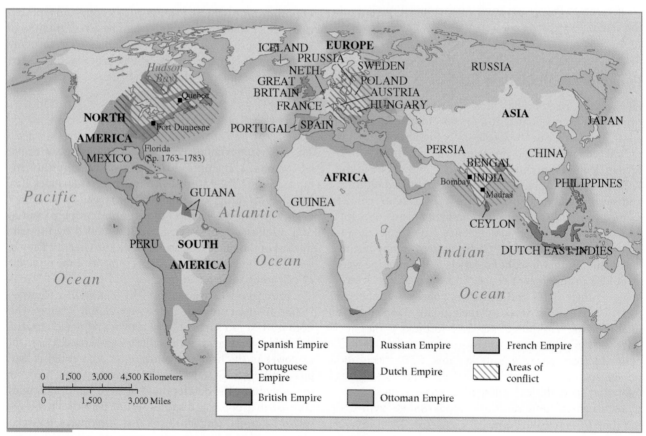

MAP 18.2 Battlefields of the Seven Years' War. A major struggle between the five great powers, the Seven Years' War was truly a worldwide conflict. In central Europe, Prussia survived against the combined forces of France, Austria, and Russia, while Britain emerged victorious against France in the struggle for empire, gaining control of French North America and India. **?** Why were naval strength and ability important in the conflict between Britain and France? **View an animated version of this map or related maps at** http://thomsonedu.com/history/spielvogel

faced defeat until a new Russian tsar, Peter III, withdrew Russia's troops from the conflict. His withdrawal guaranteed a stalemate and resuscitated the desire for peace. The European conflict was ended by the Peace of Hubertusburg in 1763. All occupied territories were returned, with the exception that Austria officially recognized Prussia's permanent control of Silesia.

The Anglo-French struggle in the rest of the world had more decisive results. Known as the Great War for Empire, it was fought in India and North America. The French had returned Madras to Britain after the War of the Austrian Succession, but jockeying for power continued as the French and British supported opposing native Indian princes. The British under Robert Clive (1725–1774) ultimately won out, not because they had better forces but because they were more persistent (see the box on p. 346). By the Treaty of Paris in 1763, the French withdrew and left India to the British.

By far the greatest conflicts of the Seven Years' War took place in North America (where the war was known as the French and Indian War). There were two primary areas of contention. One consisted of the waterways of the Gulf of Saint Lawrence, protected by the fortress of Louisbourg and by forts near the Great Lakes and Lake Champlain that protected French Quebec and French

traders. The other was the unsettled Ohio River valley. As the French moved south from the Great Lakes and north from their forts on the Mississippi, they began to establish forts from the Appalachians to the Mississippi River. To British settlers in the thirteen colonies to the east, this French activity threatened to cut off a vast area of the continent from British exploitation.

Despite initial French successes, British fortunes were revived by the efforts of William Pitt the Elder, who was convinced that the destruction of the French colonial empire was a prerequisite for the survival of Britain's own colonial empire. Accordingly, Pitt decided to make a minimal effort in Europe while concentrating resources, especially the British navy, on the war in the colonies. Although French troops were greater in number, the ability of the French to use them in the New World was contingent on naval support. The defeat of French fleets in major naval battles in 1759 gave the British an advantage because the French could no longer easily reinforce their garrisons. A series of British victories soon followed. On the night of September 13, 1759, British forces led by General James Wolfe scaled the heights outside Quebec and defeated the French under General Louis-Joseph Montcalm on the Plains of Abraham. Both generals died in the battle. The British went on to seize

Robert Clive in India. Robert Clive was the leader of the army of the British East India Company. He had been commanded to fight the ruler of Bengal in order to gain trading privileges. After the Battle of Plassey in 1757, Clive and the East India Company took control of Bengal. In this painting by Edward Penny, Clive is shown receiving a grant of money for his injured soldiers from the local nabob or governor of Bengal.

BRITISH VICTORY IN INDIA

The success of the British in defeating the French in India was due to Robert Clive, who, in this excerpt from one of his letters, describes his famous victory at Plassey, north of Calcutta, on June 23, 1757. This battle demonstrated the inability of native Indian soldiers to compete with Europeans and signified the beginning of British control in Bengal. Clive claimed to have a thousand Europeans, two thousand sepoys (local soldiers), and eight cannons available for this battle.

Robert Clive's Account of His Victory at Plassey

At daybreak we discovered the [governor's] army moving toward us, consisting, as we since found, of about fifteen thousand horse and thirty-five thousand foot, with upwards of forty pieces of cannon. They approached apace, and by six began to attack with a number of heavy cannon, supported by the whole army, and continued to play on us very briskly for several hours, during which our situation was of the utmost service to us, being lodged in a large grove with good mud banks. To succeed in an attempt on their cannon was next to impossible, as they were planted in a manner round us and at considerable distances from each other. We therefore remained quiet in our post, in expectation of a successful attack upon their camp at night. About noon the enemy drew off their artillery and retired to their camp....

On finding them make no great effort to dislodge us, we proceeded to take possession of one or two more eminences lying very near an angle of their camp, from whence, and an adjacent eminence in their possession, they kept a smart fire of musketry upon us. They made several attempts to bring out their cannon, but our advanced fieldpieces played so warmly and so well upon them that they were always driven back. Their horse exposing themselves a good deal on this occasion, many of them were killed, and among the rest four or five officers of the first distinction; by which the whole army being visibly dispirited and thrown into some confusion, we were encouraged to storm both the eminence and the angle of their camp, which were carried at the same instant, with little or no loss; though the latter was defended (exclusively of blacks) by forty French and two pieces of cannon; and the former by a large body of blacks, both horse and foot. On this a general rout ensued, and we pursued the enemy six miles, passing upwards of forty pieces of cannon they had abandoned, with an infinite number of carts and carriages filled with baggage of all kinds.... It is computed there are killed of the enemy about five hundred. Our loss amounted to only twenty-two killed and fifty wounded, and those chiefly blacks.

How does Robert Clive explain the success of his troops in the battle at Plassey? What is the significance of his victory?

Montreal, the Great Lakes area, and the Ohio valley. The French were forced to make peace. By the Treaty of Paris, they ceded Canada and the lands east of the Mississippi to England. Their ally Spain transferred Spanish Florida to British control; in return, the French gave their Louisiana territory to the Spanish. By 1763, Great Britain had become the world's greatest colonial power.

Economic Expansion and Social Change

The eighteenth century witnessed the beginning of economic changes in Europe that ultimately had a strong impact on the rest of the world. Rapid population growth, an agricultural revolution, industrialization, and an increase in worldwide trade characterized these new economic patterns.

Population and Food

Europe's population began to grow around 1750 and continued a slow but steady rise, with some regional variations. It has been estimated that the total European population was around 120 million in 1700, expanded to 140 million by 1750, and grew to 190 million by 1790;

thus the growth rate in the second half of the century was double that of the first half. These increases occurred during the same time that several million Europeans were going abroad as colonists. A falling death rate was perhaps the most important cause of population growth. More plentiful food and better transportation of available food supplies led to some improvement in diet and relief from devastating famines. Also of great significance in lowering death rates was the disappearance of bubonic plague.

More food was in part a result of improvements in agricultural practices and methods in the eighteenth century, especially in Britain, parts of France, and the Low Countries. Eighteenth-century agriculture was characterized by increases in food production that can be attributed to four interrelated factors: more farmland, healthier and more abundant livestock, increased yields per acre, and an improved climate.

Climatologists believe that the "little ice age" of the seventeenth century abated in the eighteenth, especially evident in the moderate summers that provided more ideal growing conditions. The amount of land under cultivation was increased by abandoning the old open-field system, in which part of the land was left to lie fallow to renew it. New crops, such as alfalfa and clover, which stored nitrogen in their roots, restored the soil's fertility and also provided winter fodder for livestock, enabling landlords to maintain an ever-larger number of animals. The more numerous livestock made available more animal manure, which was used to fertilize fields and produce better yields per acre. Also important to the increased yields was the spread of new vegetables, including two important American crops, the potato and maize (Indian corn). Although they were not grown in quantity until after 1700, they had been brought to Europe from America in the sixteenth century and were part of the Columbian exchange—the reciprocal exchange of plants and animals between Europe and America. The potato became a staple in Germany, the Low Countries, and especially Ireland, where repression by British landlords forced large numbers of poor peasants to survive on small pieces of marginal land. The potato took relatively little effort to produce in large quantities. High in carbohydrates and calories and rich in vitamins A and C, it could be easily stored for winter use.

In the eighteenth century, the English were the leaders in adopting the new techniques that have been characterized as an **agricultural revolution**. This early modernization of English agriculture with its noticeable increase in productivity made possible the feeding of an expanding population.

Family, Marriage, and Birthrate Patterns

The family, rather than the individual, was still at the heart of Europe's social organization. For the most part, people still thought of the family in traditional terms, as a patriarchal institution with the husband dominating his wife and children. The upper classes in particular were still concerned for the family as a "house," an association whose collective interests were more important than those of its individual members. Parents (especially fathers) still generally selected marriage partners for their children, based on the interests of the family (see the box on p. 348). One French noble responded to his son's inquiry about his upcoming marriage, "Mind your own business."

In most of Europe, newly married couples established their own households independent of their parents. This nuclear family, which had its beginning in the Middle Ages, had become a common pattern, especially in northwestern Europe. To save up what they needed to establish their own households, both men and women (outside the aristocracy) married quite late; the average age for men in northwestern Europe was between twenty-seven and twenty-eight; for women, between twenty-five and twenty-seven.

Late marriages imposed limits on the birthrate; in fact, they might be viewed as a natural form of birth control. For married couples, the first child usually appeared within one year of marriage, and additional children came at intervals of two or three years, producing an average of five births per family. It would appear, then, that the birthrate had the potential of causing a significant increase in population. This possibility was restricted, however, because 40 to 60 percent of European women of childbearing age (between fifteen and forty-four) were not married at any given time. Moreover, by the end of the eighteenth century, especially among the upper classes in France and Britain, birth control techniques were being used to limit the number of children. Figures for the French aristocracy indicate that the average number of children declined from six in the period between 1650 and 1700 to three between 1700 and 1750 and to two between 1750 and 1780. These figures are even more significant when one considers that aristocrats married at younger ages than the rest of the population. Coitus interruptus remained the most commonly used form of birth control.

New Methods of Finance

A decline in the supply of gold and silver in the seventeenth century had created a chronic shortage of money that undermined the efforts of governments to meet their needs. The establishment of new public and private banks and the acceptance of paper notes made possible an expansion of credit in the eighteenth century.

Perhaps the best example of this process can be observed in England, where the Bank of England was founded in 1694. Unlike other banks accustomed to receiving deposits and exchanging foreign currencies, the Bank of England also made loans. In return for lending money to the government, the bank was allowed to issue paper "banknotes" backed by its credit. These soon became negotiable and provided a paper substitute for gold and silver currency.

European Industry

The most important product of European industry in the eighteenth century was textiles, most of which were still produced by traditional methods. In cities that were textile centers, master artisans used time-worn methods to turn out finished goods in their guild workshops. But textile production was shifting to the countryside in parts of Europe by the eighteenth century. Industrial production in the countryside was done by the so-called putting-out or domestic system, in which a merchant-capitalist entrepreneur bought the raw materials, mostly wool and flax, and "put them out" to rural workers, who spun the raw material into yarn and then wove it into cloth on simple looms. Capitalist entrepreneurs sold the finished product, made a profit, and used the profit to manufacture more. This system became known as the **cottage industry** because spinners and weavers did their work at home, in their own cottages. The cottage industry was truly a family enterprise—women and children could spin while men wove on the looms, enabling rural people to supplement their pitiful wages as agricultural laborers. The cottage system spread to many areas of rural Europe in the eighteenth century. But in the second half of the century, significant

MARITAL ARRANGEMENTS

*I*n the eighteenth century, upper-class parents continued to choose marriage partners for their children. This practice and the turmoil it could cause are evident in this selection from *The Rivals*, a play written in 1775 by Richard Sheridan. Sheridan was an Irish playwright who quit writing plays to pursue a political career. In this scene from *The Rivals*, a father, Sir Anthony Absolute, informs his son, Captain Jack Absolute, of the arrangements he has made for his son's marriage. Jack, in love with another woman, is dumbfounded by his father's proposal.

Richard Sheridan, *The Rivals*

ABSOLUTE: Now, Jack, I am sensible that the income of your commission, and what I have hitherto allowed you, is but a small pittance for a lad of your spirit.

CAPTAIN JACK: Sir, you are very good.

ABSOLUTE: And it is my wish, while yet I live, to have my boy make some figure in the world. I have resolved, therefore, to fix you at once in a noble independence.

CAPTAIN JACK: Sir, your kindness overpowers me–such generosity makes the gratitude of reason more lively than the sensations even of filial affection.

ABSOLUTE: I am so glad you are so sensible of my attention–and you shall be master of a large estate in a few weeks.

CAPTAIN JACK: Let my future life, sir, speak my gratitude; I cannot express the sense I have of your munificence. –Yet, sir, I presume you would not wish me to quit the army?

ABSOLUTE: Oh, that shall be as your wife chooses.

CAPTAIN JACK: My wife, sir!

ABSOLUTE: Ay, ay, settle that between you–settle that between you.

CAPTAIN JACK: A wife, sir, did you say?

ABSOLUTE: Ay, a wife–why, did I not mention her before?

CAPTAIN JACK: Not a word of her, sir.

ABSOLUTE: Odd, so! I mus'n't forget her though. –Yes, Jack, the independence I was talking of is by marriage–the fortune is saddled with a wife–but I suppose that makes no difference.

CAPTAIN JACK: Sir! Sir! You amaze me!

ABSOLUTE: Why, what the devil's the matter with you, fool? Just now you were all gratitude and duty.

CAPTAIN JACK: I was, sir–you talked of independence and a fortune, but not a word of a wife!

ABSOLUTE: Why–what difference does that make? Odds life, sir! If you had an estate, you must take it with the live stock on it, as it stands!

CAPTAIN JACK: If my happiness is to be the price, I must beg leave to decline the purchase. Pray, sir, who is the lady?

ABSOLUTE: What's that to you, sir? Come, give me your promise to love, and to marry her directly.

CAPTAIN JACK: Sure, sir, this is not very reasonable.... You must excuse me, sir, if I tell you, once for all, that in this point I cannot obey you....

ABSOLUTE: Sir, I won't hear a word–not one word! . . .

CAPTAIN JACK: What, sir, promise to link myself to some mass of ugliness!

ABSOLUTE: Zounds! Sirrah! The lady shall be as ugly as I choose: she shall have a hump on each shoulder; she shall be as crooked as the crescent; her one eye shall roll like the bull's in Cox's Museum; she shall have a skin like a mummy, and the beard of a Jew–she shall be all this, sirrah! Yet I will make you ogle her all day, and sit up all night to write sonnets on her beauty.

What point is Sheridan making about upper-class marriages in the eighteenth century? What social, political, and economic considerations were significant in eighteenth-century marriages?

---

changes began to occur that would soon revolutionize industrial production (see Chapter 20).

The Social Order of the Eighteenth Century

The pattern of Europe's social organization, first established in the Middle Ages, continued well into the eighteenth century. Social status was still largely determined not by wealth and economic standing but by the division into the traditional "orders" or "estates" determined by heredity. This divinely sanctioned division of society into traditional orders was supported by Christian teaching, which emphasized the need to fulfill the responsibilities of one's estate. Although Enlightenment intellectuals attacked these traditional distinctions, they did not die easily. In the Prussian law code of 1794, marriage between noble males and middle-class females was forbidden without a government dispensation. Even without government regulation, however, different social groups remained easily distinguished everywhere in Europe by the distinctive, traditional clothes they wore.

Nevertheless, some forces of change were at work in this tradition-bound society. The ideas of the Enlightenment made headway as reformers argued that the idea of an unchanging social order based on privilege was hostile to the progress of society. However, not until the revolutionary upheavals at the end of the eighteenth century did the old order finally begin to disintegrate.

Cottage Industry. One important source of textile production in the eighteenth century was the cottage industry, truly a family enterprise. Shown here is a family at work producing knitwear. It was customary in the cottage industry for women to spin and wind the yarn and for men to weave the yarn into cloth on looms.

The Peasants

Because society was still mostly rural in the eighteenth century, the peasantry constituted the largest social group, making up as much as 85 percent of Europe's population. There were rather wide differences, however, between peasants from area to area. The most important distinction, at least legally, was between the free peasant and the serf. Peasants in Britain, northern Italy, the Low Countries, Spain, most of France, and some areas of western Germany shared freedom despite numerous regional and local differences. Legally free peasants, however, were not exempt from burdens. Some free peasants in Andalusia in Spain, southern Italy, Sicily, and Portugal lived in a poverty more desperate than that of many serfs in Russia and eastern Germany. In France, 40 percent of free peasants owned little or no land by 1789.

Small peasant proprietors or tenant farmers in western Europe were also not free from compulsory services. Most owed **tithes,** often one-third of their crops. Although tithes were intended for parish priests, in France only 10 percent of the priests received them. Instead they wound up in the hands of wealthy townspeople and aristocratic landowners. Moreover, in addition to giving up their crops, some peasants owed a variety of dues and fees. Local aristocrats claimed hunting rights on peasant land and had monopolies over the flour mills, community ovens, and wine and oil presses needed by the peasants. Hunting rights, dues, fees, and tithes were all deeply resented.

The local villages in which they dwelt remained the centers of peasants' social lives. Villages, especially in western Europe, maintained public order; provided poor relief, a village church, and sometimes a schoolmaster; collected taxes for the central government; maintained roads and bridges; and established common procedures for sowing, plowing, and harvesting crops. But villages were often dominated by richer peasants and proved highly resistant to innovations, such as new agricultural practices.

The Nobility

The nobles, who constituted only 2 to 3 percent of the European population, played a dominating role in society. Being born a noble automatically guaranteed a place at the top of the social order, with all of the attendant special privileges and rights. The legal privileges of the nobility included judgment by their peers, immunity from severe punishment, and exemption from many forms of taxation. Especially in central and eastern Europe, the rights of landlords over their serfs were overwhelming.

Nobles also played important roles in military and government affairs. Since medieval times, landed aristocrats had functioned as military officers. Although commoners occasionally became officers, nobles were still considered the most natural and hence the best officers. The eighteenth-century nobility also played a significant role in the administrative machinery of state. In some countries, such as Prussia, the entire bureaucracy reflected aristocratic values. Moreover, in most of Europe, the landholding nobles controlled much of the life of their local districts.

Although the nobles clung to their privileged status and struggled to keep others out, almost everywhere the possession of money made it possible to enter the ranks of the nobility. Rights of nobility were frequently attached to certain lands, so purchasing the lands made one a noble; the acquisition of government offices also often conferred noble status.

The Aristocratic Way of Life. The eighteenth-century country house in Britain fulfilled the desire of aristocrats for both elegance and privacy. The painting above by Richard Wilson shows a typical English country house of the eighteenth century surrounded by a simple and serene landscape. Thomas Gainsborough's *Conversation in the Park,* shown at right, captures the relaxed life of two aristocrats in the park of their country estate.

The Inhabitants of Towns and Cities

Townspeople were still a distinct minority of the total population except in the Dutch Republic, Britain, and parts of Italy. At the end of the eighteenth century, about one-sixth of the French population lived in towns of two thousand inhabitants or more. The biggest city in Europe was London, with one million inhabitants; Paris numbered between 550,000 and 600,000. Altogether, Europe had at least twenty cities in twelve countries with populations over 100,000, including Naples, Lisbon, Moscow, Saint Petersburg, Vienna, Amsterdam, Berlin, Rome, and Madrid.

Although in every country urban dwellers were vastly outnumbered by rural inhabitants, towns played an important role in Western culture. The contrasts between the city, with its education, culture, and material consumption, and the surrounding, often poverty-stricken countryside were striking, as evidenced by this British traveler's account of Russia's Saint Petersburg in 1741:

> The country about Petersburg has full as wild and desert a look as any in the Indies; you need not go above 200 paces out of the town to find yourself in a wild wood of firs, and such a low, marshy, boggy country that you would think God when he created the rest of the world for the use of mankind had created this for an inaccessible retreat for all sorts of wild beasts.[3]

Peasants often resented the prosperity of towns and their exploitation of the countryside to serve urban interests. Palermo in Sicily consumed one-third of the island's food production while paying only one-tenth of the taxes.

Towns lived off the countryside not by buying their goods and crops but by using tithes, rents, and feudal dues to acquire peasant produce.

Many cities in western and even central Europe had a long tradition of patrician oligarchies that continued to control their communities by dominating town and city councils. Despite their highly visible role, patricians constituted only a small minority of the urban population. Just below the patricians stood an upper crust of the middle classes: nonnoble officeholders, financiers and bankers, merchants, wealthy **rentiers** who lived off their investments, and important professionals, including lawyers. Another large urban group was the petty bourgeoisie or lower middle class, made up of master artisans, shopkeepers, and small traders. Below them were the laborers or working classes. Much urban industry was still done in small guild workshops by masters, journeymen, and apprentices. Urban communities also had a large group of unskilled workers who served as servants, maids, and cooks at pitifully low wages.

Despite an end to the ravages of plague, eighteenth-century cities still experienced high death rates, especially among children, because of unsanitary living conditions, polluted water, and a lack of sewage facilities. One observer compared the stench of Hamburg to an open sewer that could be smelled for miles around. Overcrowding also exacerbated urban problems as cities continued to absorb rural immigrants. But cities proved no paradise for them, for unskilled workers found few employment opportunities. The result was a serious problem of poverty in the eighteenth century (see the box on p. 351).

POVERTY IN FRANCE

*U*nlike the British, who had a system of public-supported poor relief, the French responded to poverty with ad hoc policies when conditions became acute. This selection is taken from an **intendant's** report to the controller-general at Paris describing his suggestions for a program to relieve the grain shortages expected for the winter months.

M. de la Bourdonnaye, Intendant of Bordeaux, to the Controller-General, September 30, 1708

Having searched for the means of helping the people of Agen in this cruel situation and having conferred with His Eminence, the Bishop, it seems to us that three things are absolutely necessary if the people are not to starve during the winter.

Most of the inhabitants do not have seed to plant their fields. However, we decided that we would be going too far if we furnished it, because those who have seed would also apply [for more]. Moreover, we are persuaded that all the inhabitants will make strenuous efforts to find some seed, since they have every reason to expect prices to remain high next year....

But this project will come to nothing if the collectors of the taille continue to be as strict in the exercise of their functions as they have been of late and continue to employ troops [to force collection]. Those inhabitants who have seed grain would sell it to be freed from an oppressive garrison, while those who must buy seed, since they have none left from their harvest and have scraped together a little money for this purchase, would prefer to give up that money [for taxes] when put under police constraint. To avoid this, I feel it is absolutely necessary that you order the receivers-general to reduce their operations during this winter, at least with respect to the poor....

We are planning to import wheat for this region from Languedoc and Quercy, and we are confident that there will

be enough. But there are two things to be feared: one is the greed of the merchants. When they see that general misery has put them in control of prices, they will raise them to the point where the calamity is almost as great as if there were no provisions at all. The other fear is that the artisans and the lowest classes, when they find themselves at the mercy of the merchants, will cause disorders and riots. As a protective measure, it would seem wise to establish two small storehouses.... Ten thousand ecus [30,000 livres] would be sufficient for each....

A third point demanding our attention is the support of beggars among the poor, as well as of those who have no other resources than their wages. Since there will be very little work, these people will soon be reduced to starvation. We should establish public workshops to provide work as was done in 1693 and 1694. I should choose the most useful kind of work, located where there are the greatest number of poor. In this manner, we should rid ourselves of those who do not want to work and assure the others a moderate subsistence. For these workshops, we would need about 40,000 livres, or altogether 100,000 livres. The receiver-general of the taille of Agen could advance this sum. The 60,000 livres for the storehouses he would get back very soon. I shall await your orders on all of the above.

Marginal Comments by the Controller-General

Operations for the collection of the taille are to be suspended. The two storehouses are to be established; great care must be taken to put them to good use. The interest on the advances will be paid by the king. His Majesty has agreed to the establishment of the public workshops for the able-bodied poor and is willing to spend up to 40,000 livres on them this winter.

What does this document reveal about the nature of poverty in France in the eighteenth century?

CONCLUSION

Everywhere in Europe at the beginning of the eighteenth century, the old order remained strong. Nobles, clerics, towns, and provinces all had privileges, some medieval in origin, others the result of the attempt of monarchies in the sixteenth and seventeenth centuries to gain financial support from their subjects. Everywhere in the eighteenth century, monarchs sought to enlarge their bureaucracies to raise taxes to support the new large standing armies that had originated in the seventeenth century. The existence of these armies made wars more likely. The existence of five great powers, two of them (France and Britain) in conflict in the East and the New World, initiated a new scale of strife; the Seven Years' War could legitimately be viewed as the first world war. The wars altered some boundaries on the

European continent but were perhaps more significant for the victories that marked the emergence of Great Britain as the world's greatest naval and colonial power. Everywhere in Europe, increased demands for taxes to support these conflicts led to attacks on the privileged orders and a desire for change not met by the ruling monarchs.

At the same time, sustained population growth, dramatic changes in finance, trade, and industry, and the growth of poverty created tensions that undermined the traditional foundations of the old order. The inability of that old order to deal meaningfully with these changes led to a revolutionary outburst at the end of the eighteenth century that marked the beginning of the end for that old order.

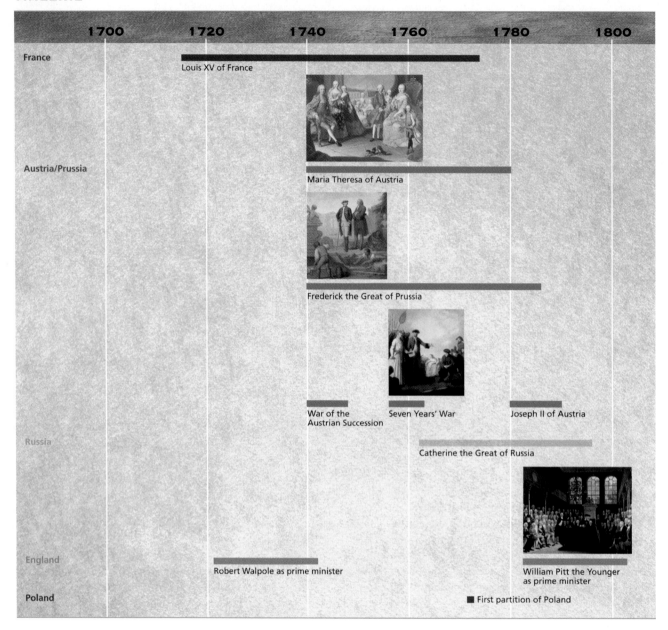

	1700	1720	1740	1760	1780	1800
France						

Louis XV of France

Maria Theresa of Austria

Frederick the Great of Prussia

Austria/Prussia

War of the Austrian Succession   Seven Years' War   Joseph II of Austria

Russia

Catherine the Great of Russia

England

Robert Walpole as prime minister

William Pitt the Younger as prime minister

Poland

■ First partition of Poland

NOTES

1. Frederick II, *Forms of Government*, in E. Weber, *The Western Tradition* (Lexington, Mass., 1972), pp. 538, 544.
2. Quoted in R. A. Dorwart, *The Administrative Reforms of Frederick William I of Prussia* (Cambridge, Mass., 1953), p. 36.
3. I. Vinogradoff, "Russian Missions to London, 1711–1789: Further Extracts from the Cottrell Papers," *Oxford Slavonic Papers*, New Series (1982), 15:76.

SUGGESTIONS FOR FURTHER READING

For a good introduction to the political history of the eighteenth century, see the relevant chapters in the general works by **Woloch** and **Anderson** listed in Chapter 17. See also **O. Hufton**, *Europe: Privilege and Protest, 1730–1789*, 2d ed. (London, 2000), and **W. Doyle**, *The Old European Order, 1500–1800* (New York, 1996). On enlightened absolutism, see **H. M. Scott, ed.,** *Enlightened Absolutism: Reform and Reformers in Later Eighteenth-Century Europe* (Ann Arbor, Mich., 1990). Good studies of individual states include **J. B. Owen**, *The Eighteenth Century, 1714–1815* (London, 1975), on England; **P. R. Campbell**, *The Ancien Régime in France* (Oxford, 1988); **C. W. Ingrao**, *The Habsburg Monarchy*, 2d ed. (Cambridge, 2000); **J. Gagliardo**, *Germany Under the Old Regime* (London, 1991); **H. W. Koch**, *A History of Prussia* (London, 1978); and **P. Dukes**, *The Making of Russian Absolutism, 1613–1801*, 2d ed. (London, 1990). Good biographies of some of Europe's monarchs include **R. Asprey**, *Frederick the Great: The Magnificent Enigma* (New York, 1986); **I. De Madariaga**, *Catherine the Great: A Short History* (New Haven,

Conn., 1990); **T. C. W. Blanning**, *Joseph II* (New York, 1994); and **J. Brooke**, *King George III* (London, 1972).

The warfare of this period is examined in **M. S. Anderson**, *War and Society in Europe of the Old Regime, 1615–1789* (New York, 1988). **R. S. Browning**, *The War of Austrian Succession* (London, 1995), is illuminating.

A good introduction to European population can be found in **M. W. Flinn**, *The European Demographic System, 1500–1820* (Brighton, England, 1981). One of the best works on family and marriage patterns is **L. Stone**, *The Family, Sex, and Marriage in England, 1500–1800* (New York, 1977).

A different perspective on economic history can be found in **F. Braudel**, *Capitalism and Material Life, 1400–1800* (New York, 1973). Eighteenth-century cottage industry and the beginnings of industrialization are examined in the early chapters of **D. Landes**, *The Unbound Prometheus: Technological Change and Industrial Development in Western Europe from 1750 to the Present* (New York, 1969), and in **M. Berg**, *The Age of Manufactures: Industry, Innovation, and Work in Britain, 1700–1820* (Oxford, 1985).

On the European nobility, see **J. Dewald**, *The European Nobility, 1400–1800* (Cambridge, 1996), and **H. M. Scott**, *The European Nobility in the Seventeenth and Eighteenth Centuries* (London, 1995). On the peasantry, see **J. Blum**, *The End of the Old Order in Rural Europe* (Princeton, N.J., 1978), and **R. Evans, ed.**, *The German Peasantry* (New York, 1986). On European cities, see **J. de Vries**, *European Urbanization, 1500–1800* (Cambridge, Mass., 1984). On the lower urban classes, see **J. Kaplow**, *The Names of Kings: The Parisian Laboring Poor in the Eighteenth Century* (New York, 1972), and **B. Hill**, *Servants: English Domestics in the Eighteenth Century* (New York, 1996). There is no better work on the problem of poverty than **O. Hufton**, *The Poor of Eighteenth-Century France* (Oxford, 1974).

Thomson NOW! Enter *ThomsonNOW* using the access card that is available for *Western Civilization: A Brief History*. *ThomsonNOW* will help you understand this chapter with lesson plans generated for your needs. In addition, you can read the following documents, and many more, online:

> Peace of Westphalia
> Jean Bodin, excerpts from *The Six Books of a Commonweale*

WESTERN CIVILIZATION RESOURCES

Visit the Web site for *Western Civilization: A Brief History* for resources specific to this book:

http://www.thomsonedu.com/history/spielvogel

For a variety of tools to help you succeed in this course, visit the Western Civilization Resource Center at

http://history.wadsworth.com/spielvogel

Included are quizzes, images, documents, interactive simulations, maps and timelines, movie explorations, and a wealth of other sources.

CHAPTER

19

A REVOLUTION IN POLITICS: THE ERA OF THE FRENCH REVOLUTION AND NAPOLEON

CHAPTER OUTLINE AND FOCUS QUESTIONS

The Beginning of the Revolutionary Era: The American Revolution

▢ What were the causes and results of the American Revolution, and what impact did it have on Europe?

Background to the French Revolution

▢ What were the long-range and immediate causes of the French Revolution?

The French Revolution

▢ What were the main events of the French Revolution between 1789 and 1799?

▢ What role did each of the following play in the French Revolution: lawyers, peasants, women, the clergy, the Jacobins, the sans-culottes, the French Revolutionary Army, and the Committee of Public Safety?

The Age of Napoleon

▢ Which aspects of the French Revolution did Napoleon preserve, and which did he destroy?

CRITICAL THINKING

▢ In what ways were the American Revolution, the French Revolution, and the seventeenth-century English revolutions alike? In what ways were they different?

The storming of the Bastille

Réunion des Musées Nationaux/Art Resource, NY (Châteaux de Versailles et de Trianon, Versailles, France)

𝒪N THE MORNING of July 14, 1789, a Parisian mob of some eight thousand people in search of weapons streamed toward the Bastille, a royal armory filled with arms and ammunition. The Bastille was also a state prison, and although it now contained only seven prisoners, in the eyes of these angry Parisians it was a glaring symbol of the government's despotic policies. The armory was defended by the marquis de Launay and a small garrison of 114 men. The attack began in earnest in the early afternoon, and after three hours of fighting, de Launay and the garrison surrendered. Angered by the loss of ninety-eight of their members, the victorious mob beat de Launay to death, cut off his head, and carried it aloft in triumph through the streets of Paris. When King Louis XVI was informed of the fall of the Bastille by the duc de La Rochefoucauld-Liancourt, he exclaimed, "Why, this is a revolt." "No, Sire," replied the duke, "it is a revolution."

Historians have long held that the modern history of Europe began with two significant transformations—the French Revolution and the Industrial Revolution (on the latter, see Chapter 20). Accordingly, the French Revolution has been portrayed as the major turning point in European political and social history when the institutions of the "old regime" were destroyed and a new order was created based on individual rights, representative institutions, and a concept of loyalty to the nation rather than the monarch. This perspective has certain limitations, however.

France was only one of a number of places in the Western world where the assumptions of the old order were challenged. Although some historians have used the phrase "democratic revolution" to refer to the upheavals of the late eighteenth and nineteenth centuries, it is probably more appropriate to speak not of a democratic movement but of a liberal movement to extend political rights and power to the bourgeoisie "possessing capital," people not of the aristocracy who were literate and had become wealthy through capitalist enterprises in trade, industry, and finance. The years preceding and accompanying the French Revolution included attempts at reform and revolt in the North American colonies, Britain, the Dutch Republic, some Swiss cities, and the Austrian Netherlands. The success of the American and French Revolutions makes them the center of attention for this chapter.

Not all of the decadent privileges that characterized the old European regime were destroyed in 1789, however. The revolutionary upheaval of the era, especially in France, did create new liberal and national political ideals, summarized in the French revolutionary slogan, "Liberty, Equality, Fraternity," that transformed France and were then spread to other European countries through the conquests of Napoleon.◆

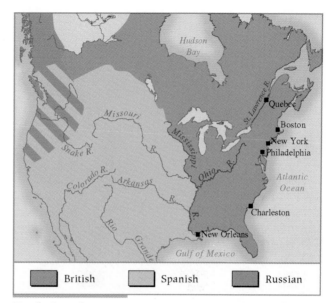

North America, 1763

The Beginning of the Revolutionary Era: The American Revolution

At the end of the Seven Years' War in 1763, Great Britain had become the world's greatest colonial power. In North America, Britain controlled Canada and the lands east of the Mississippi. After the Seven Years' War, British policy makers sought to obtain new revenues from the thirteen American colonies to pay for British army expenses in defending the colonists. An attempt to levy new taxes by the Stamp Act in 1765 led to riots and the law's quick repeal.

The Americans and the British had different conceptions of empire. The British envisioned a single empire with Parliament as the supreme authority throughout. Only Parliament could make laws for all the people in the empire, including the American colonists. The Americans, in contrast, had their own representative assemblies. They believed that neither the king nor Parliament had any right to interfere in their internal affairs and that no tax could be levied without the consent of the people or their chosen representatives.

Crisis followed crisis in the 1770s until 1776, when the colonists decided to declare their independence from the British Empire. On July 4, 1776, the Second Continental Congress released a declaration written by

Thomas Jefferson. A stirring political document, the Declaration of Independence affirmed the Enlightenment's natural rights of "life, liberty, and the pursuit of happiness" and declared the colonies to be "free and independent states absolved from all allegiance to the British crown." The war for American independence had begun—not with a gun but with a page of parchment.

The War for Independence

The war against Great Britain was a huge gamble. Britain was a strong European military power with enormous financial resources. The Second Continental Congress had authorized the formation of the Continental Army under George Washington as commander in chief. Washington, who had had political experience in Virginia and military experience in the French and Indian War, was a good choice for the job. As a southerner, he brought balance to an effort that to that point had been led by New Englanders. Nevertheless, compared to the British forces, the Continental Army consisted of undisciplined amateurs whose terms of service were usually very brief.

Complicating the war effort were the internal divisions within the colonies. Fought for independence, the Revolutionary War was also a civil war, pitting family members and neighbors against one another. The Loyalists, 15 to 30 percent of the population, questioned whether British policies justified the rebellion.

Since probably half of the people living in the colonies were apathetic at the start of the struggle, the Patriots, like the Loyalists, constituted a minority of the population. The Patriots, however, managed to win over many of the uncommitted, either by persuasion or by force. There were rich Patriots as well; Washington owned an estate with 15,000 acres and 150 slaves. But the rich Patriots joined an extensive coalition that included

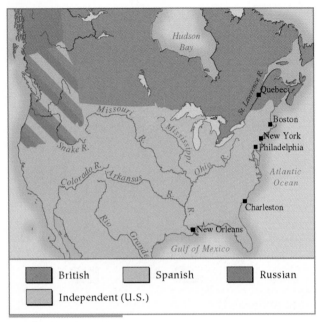

North America, 1783

farmers and artisans. The wide social spectrum in this coalition had an impact on representative governments in the states after the war. The right to vote was often broadened; Pennsylvania, for example, dropped all property qualifications for voting.

Of great importance to the colonists' cause was the assistance provided by foreign countries that were eager to gain revenge for earlier defeats at the hands of the British. The French supplied arms and money to the rebels from the beginning of the war, and French officers and soldiers also served in the Continental Army. When the British army of General Cornwallis was forced to surrender to a combined American and French army and French fleet under Washington at Yorktown in 1781, the British government decided to call it quits. The Treaty of Paris, signed in 1783, recognized the independence of the American colonies and granted the Americans control of the territory from the Appalachians to the Mississippi River.

Forming a New Nation

The thirteen American colonies had gained their independence as the United States of America, but a fear of concentrated power and concern for their own interests caused them to have little enthusiasm for establishing a united nation with a strong central government. The Articles of Confederation, ratified in 1781, gave most power to the states and little to the central government. But that arrangement proved unworkable, and movement for reform soon arose. In the summer of 1787, fifty-five delegates attended a convention in Philadelphia to revise the Articles of Confederation. The convention's delegates—wealthy, politically experienced, and well educated—rejected revision and decided to devise a new constitution.

The proposed constitution created a central government distinct from and superior to the governments of the individual states. The national government was given the power to levy taxes, raise a national army, regulate domestic and foreign trade, and create a national currency. The central or federal government was divided into three branches, each with some power to check the functioning of the others. A president would serve as the chief executive, with the power to execute laws, veto the legislature's acts, supervise foreign affairs, and direct military forces. Legislative power was vested in the second branch of government, a bicameral legislature composed of the Senate, elected by the state legislatures, and the House of Representatives, elected directly by the people. The Supreme Court and other courts "as deemed necessary" by Congress served as the third branch of government. They would enforce the Constitution as the "supreme law of the land."

The United States Constitution was approved by the states—by a slim margin—in 1788. Important to its success was the promise to add to it a "bill of rights" as the new government's first piece of business. Accordingly, in March 1789, the new Congress proposed twelve amendments to the Constitution; the ten that were ratified by the states have been known ever since as the Bill of Rights. These guaranteed freedom of religion, speech, the press, petition, and assembly, as well as the right to bear arms, be protected against unreasonable searches and arrests, trial by jury, due process of law, and the protection of property rights. Many of these rights were derived from the natural rights philosophy of the eighteenth-century philosophes, which was popular among the American colonists. Many European intellectuals saw the American Revolution as the embodiment of the Enlightenment's political dreams. And when French officers who had fought in the American War for Independence returned to France, they did so with ideas of individual liberties and notions of republicanism and popular sovereignty that would soon play a role in the early stages of the French Revolution.

Background to the French Revolution

Although we associate events like the French Revolution with sudden changes, such events involve long-range problems as well as immediate precipitating forces. The causes of the French Revolution must be sought in a multifaceted examination of French society and its problems in the late eighteenth century.

Social Structure of the Old Regime

The long-range or indirect causes of the French Revolution must first be sought in the condition of French society. Before the Revolution, French society was grounded in the idea of privilege or an inequality of rights. The population of 27 million was divided, as it had been since the Middle Ages, into legal categories known as the three orders or estates.

The First Estate The First Estate consisted of the clergy and numbered about 130,000 people. The church owned approximately 10 percent of the land. Clergy were exempt from the taille, France's chief tax, although the church had agreed to pay a "voluntary" contribution every five years to the state. Clergy were also radically divided: the higher clergy, stemming from aristocratic families, shared the interests of the nobility, while the parish priests were often poor commoners.

The Second Estate The Second Estate was the nobility, composed of no more than 350,000 people who nevertheless owned perhaps 30 percent of the land. The nobility had continued to play an important and even crucial role in French society in the eighteenth century, holding many of the leading positions in the government, the military, the law courts, and the higher church offices. The French nobility was also divided. The "nobility of the robe" derived its status from officeholding, a pathway that had often enabled commoners to attain noble rank. These nobles now dominated the royal law courts and important administrative offices. The "nobility of the sword" claimed to be descended from the original medieval nobility. As a group, the nobles sought to expand their privileges at the expense of the monarchy—to defend liberty by resisting the arbitrary actions of monarchy, as some nobles asserted—and to maintain their monopolistic control over positions in the military, church, and government. Moreover, the possession of privileges remained a hallmark of the nobility. Common to all nobles were tax exemptions, especially from the taille.

The Third Estate The Third Estate, the commoners of French society, constituted the overwhelming majority of the population. They were divided by vast differences in occupation, level of education, and wealth. The peasants, who alone made up 75 to 80 percent of the total population, were by far the largest segment of the Third Estate. They owned about 35 to 40 percent of the land, although these holdings varied from area to area and more than half the peasants had little or no land on which to support themselves. Serfdom no longer existed on any large scale in France, but French peasants still had obligations to their local landlords that they deeply resented. These "relics of feudalism," survivals from an earlier age, included the payment of fees for the use of village facilities, such as the flour mill, community oven, and winepress, as well as tithes to the clergy.

Another part of the Third Estate consisted of skilled artisans, shopkeepers, and other wage earners in the cities. Although the eighteenth century had been a period of rapid urban growth, 90 percent of French towns had fewer than ten thousand inhabitants, and only nine cities had more than fifty thousand. In the eighteenth century, consumer prices rose faster than wages, with the result that these urban groups experienced a decline in purchasing power. In Paris, for example, income lagged behind food prices and well behind a 140 percent rise in rents for working people in skilled and unskilled trades. The economic discontent of this segment of the Third Estate—and often simply the struggle for survival—led the common people to play an important role in the French Revolution, especially in the city of Paris.

About 8 percent, or 2.3 million people, constituted the bourgeoisie or middle class, who owned about 20 to 25 percent of the land. This group included merchants, bankers, and industrialists who controlled the resources of trade, finance, and manufacturing and benefited from the economic prosperity after 1730. The bourgeoisie also included professional people—lawyers, holders of public offices, doctors, and writers. Many members of the bourgeoisie sought security and status through the purchase of land. They had their own set of grievances because they were often excluded from the social and political privileges monopolized by nobles. At the same time, remarkable similarities existed at the upper levels of society between the wealthier bourgeoisie and the nobility. It was still possible for wealthy middle-class individuals to enter the ranks of the nobility by obtaining public offices and entering the nobility of the robe. During this century, 6,500 new noble families were created in this way. Moreover, the new and critical ideas of the Enlightenment proved attractive to aristocrats and bourgeoisie alike. Members of both groups shared a common world of liberal political thought. Both aristocratic and bourgeois elites, long accustomed to a new socioeconomic reality based on wealth and economic achievement, were increasingly frustrated by a monarchical system resting on privileges and on an old and rigid social order based on the concept of estates. The opposition of these elites to the **old order** ultimately led them to take drastic action against the monarchical regime, although they soon split over the problem of how far to proceed in eliminating traditional privileges. In a real sense, the revolution had its origins in political grievances.

Other Problems Facing the French Monarchy

The inability of the French monarchy to deal with new social realities was exacerbated by specific problems in the 1780s. Although France had enjoyed fifty years of growth overall, periodic economic crises still occurred. Bad harvests in 1787 and 1788 and an incipient manufacturing depression resulted in food shortages, rising prices for food and other necessities, and unemployment in the cities. The number of poor, estimated by some analysts at almost one-third of the population, reached crisis proportions on the eve of the revolution.

The immediate cause of the French Revolution was the near collapse of government finances. French governmental expenditures continued to grow due to costly wars and royal extravagance. On the verge of a complete financial collapse, the government of Louis XVI was finally forced to call a meeting of the Estates-General, the French parliamentary body that had not met since 1614.

The French Revolution

In summoning the Estates-General, the government was merely looking for a way to solve the immediate financial crisis. The monarchy had no wish for a major reform of the government, nor did the delegates who arrived at Versailles come with plans for the revolutionary changes that ultimately emerged. Yet over the next years, through the interplay of the deputies meeting in various legislative assemblies, the common people in the streets of Paris and other cities, and the peasants in the countryside, much of the old regime would be destroyed, and Europe would have a new model for political and social change.

From Estates-General to National Assembly

The Estates-General consisted of representatives from the three orders of French society. In the elections for the Estates-General, the government had ruled that the Third Estate should get double representation (it did, after all, constitute 97 percent of the population). Consequently, while both the First Estate (the clergy) and the Second Estate (the nobility) had about three hundred delegates each, the commoners had almost six hundred representatives. Two-thirds of the latter were people with legal training, and three-fourths were from towns with over two thousand inhabitants, giving the Third Estate a particularly strong legal and urban representation. Most members of the Third Estate advocated a regular constitutional government that would abolish the fiscal privileges of the church and nobility as the major way to regenerate France.

The Estates-General opened at Versailles on May 5, 1789. It was divided from the start over the question of whether voting should be by order or by head (one vote per delegate). Traditionally, each order would vote separately; each would have veto power over the other two, thus guaranteeing aristocratic control over reforms. But the Third Estate was opposed to this approach and pushed its demands for voting by head. Since it

had double representation, with the assistance of liberal nobles and clerics, it could turn the three estates into a single-chamber legislature that would reform France in its own way. Most delegates still desired to make changes within a framework of respect for the authority of the king; revival or reform did not mean the overthrow of traditional institutions. But when the First Estate declared in favor of voting by order, the Third Estate felt compelled to respond in a significant fashion. On June 17, 1789, the Third Estate voted to constitute itself a "national assembly" and decided to draw up a constitution. Three days later, on June 20, the deputies of the Third Estate arrived at their meeting place only to find the door locked; thereupon they moved to a nearby indoor tennis court and swore (in what became known as the Tennis Court Oath) that they would continue to meet until they had produced a French constitution. These actions of June 17 and June 20 constitute the first step in the French Revolution, since the Third Estate had no legal right to act as the National Assembly. This bold move, largely the work of the lawyers of the Third Estate, was soon in jeopardy, however, as the king sided with the First Estate and threatened to dissolve the Estates-General. Louis XVI now prepared to use force.

The common people, however, in a series of urban and rural uprisings in the summer of 1789, saved the Third Estate from the king's attempt to stop the revolution. The most famous of the urban risings was the fall of the Bastille (see the box on p. 359). Parisians organized a popular force and on July 14 attacked the Bastille, a royal armory. But the Bastille had also been a state prison, and

The Tennis Court Oath. Finding themselves locked out of their regular meeting place on June 20, 1789, the deputies of the Third Estate met instead in the nearby tennis courts of the Jeu de Paume and committed themselves to continue to meet until they established a new constitution for France. In this painting, the neoclassicist Jacques-Louis David presents a dramatic rendering of the Tennis Court Oath.

THE FALL OF THE BASTILLE

*O*n July 14, 1789, Parisian crowds in search of weapons attacked and captured the royal armory known as the Bastille. It had also been a state prison, and its fall marked the triumph of "liberty" over despotism. This intervention of the Parisian populace saved the Third Estate from Louis XVI's attempted counterrevolution.

A Parisian Newspaper Account of the Fall of the Bastille

First, the people tried to enter this fortress by the Rue St.-Antoine, this fortress, which no one has ever penetrated against the wishes of this frightful despotism and where the monster still resided. The treacherous governor had put out a flag of peace. So a confident advance was made; a detachment of French Guards, with perhaps five to six thousand armed bourgeois, penetrated the Bastille's outer courtyards, but as soon as some six hundred persons had passed over the first drawbridge, the bridge was raised and artillery fire mowed down several French Guards and some soldiers; the cannon fired on the town, and the people took fright; a large number of individuals were killed or wounded; but then they rallied and took shelter from the fire. . . . Meanwhile, they tried to locate some cannon; they attacked from the water's edge through the gardens of the arsenal, and from there made an orderly siege; they advanced from various directions, beneath a ceaseless round of fire. It was a terrible scene. . . . The fighting grew steadily more intense; the citizens had become hardened to the fire; from all directions they clambered onto the roofs or broke into the rooms; as soon as an enemy appeared among the turrets on the tower, he was fixed in the sights of a hundred guns and mown down in an instant; meanwhile cannon fire was hurriedly directed against the second drawbridge, which it pierced, breaking the chains; in vain did the cannon on the tower reply, for most people were sheltered from it; the fury was at its height; people bravely faced death and every danger; women, in their eagerness, helped us to the utmost; even the children, after the discharge of fire from the fortress, ran here and there picking up the bullets and shot; [and so the Bastille fell and the governor, De Launey, was captured]. . . . Serene and blessed liberty, for the first time, has at last been introduced into this abode of horrors, this frightful refuge of monstrous despotism and its crimes.

Meanwhile, they get ready to march; they leave amidst an enormous crowd; the applause, the outbursts of joy, the insults, the oaths hurled at the treacherous prisoners of war; everything is confused; cries of vengeance and of pleasure issue from every heart; the conquerors, glorious and covered in honor, carry their arms and the spoils of the conquered, the flags of victory, the militia mingling with the soldiers of the fatherland, the victory laurels offered them from every side, all this created a frightening and splendid spectacle. On arriving at the square, the people, anxious to avenge themselves, allowed neither De Launey nor the other officers to reach the place of trial; they seized them from the hands of their conquerors, and trampled them underfoot one after the other. De Launey was struck by a thousand blows, his head was cut off and hoisted on the end of a pike with blood streaming down all sides. . . . This glorious day must amaze our enemies, and finally usher in for us the triumph of justice and liberty. In the evening, there were celebrations.

Why did the fall of the Bastille come to mark the triumph of French "liberty" over despotism?

though it now contained only seven prisoners (five forgers and two insane people), its fall quickly became a popular symbol of the common people's triumph over despotism. Paris was abandoned to the insurgents, and Louis XVI was soon informed that the royal troops were unreliable. Louis' acceptance of that reality signaled the collapse of royal authority; the king could no longer enforce his will. The fall of the Bastille had saved the National Assembly.

At the same time, independent of what was going on in Paris, popular revolts broke out in numerous cities. The collapse of royal authority in the cities was paralleled by peasant insurrections in the countryside. A growing resentment of the entire landholding system, with its fees and obligations, created the conditions for a popular uprising. The fall of the Bastille and the king's apparent capitulation to the demands of the Third Estate now encouraged peasants to take matters into their own hands. In July and August, peasant rebellions occurred throughout France. The agrarian revolts served as a backdrop to the Great Fear, a vast panic that spread like wildfire through France between July 20 and August 6. Fear of invasion by foreign troops, aided by a supposed aristocratic plot, encouraged the formation of more citizens' militias and permanent committees. The greatest impact of the agrarian revolts and Great Fear was on the National Assembly meeting in Versailles.

Destruction of the Old Regime

One of the first acts of the National Assembly was to destroy the relics of feudalism or aristocratic privileges. On the night of August 4, 1789, the National Assembly in an astonishing session voted to abolish seigneurial rights as well as the fiscal privileges of nobles, clergy, towns, and provinces. On August 26, the assembly provided the ideological foundation for its actions and an educational device for the nation by adopting the Declaration of the Rights of Man and the Citizen (see the box on p. 360). This charter of basic liberties began with a ringing

DECLARATION OF THE RIGHTS OF MAN AND THE CITIZEN

*O*ne of the important documents of the French Revolution, the Declaration of the Rights of Man and the Citizen, was adopted in August 1789 by the National Assembly. The declaration affirmed that "men are born and remain free and equal in rights," that governments must protect these natural rights, and that political power is derived from the people.

Declaration of the Rights of Man and the Citizen

The representatives of the French people, organized as a national assembly, considering that ignorance, neglect, and scorn of the rights of man are the sole causes of public misfortunes and of corruption of governments, have resolved to display in a solemn declaration the natural, inalienable, and sacred rights of man, so that this declaration, constantly in the presence of all members of society, will continually remind them of their rights and their duties. . . . Consequently, the National Assembly recognizes and declares, in the presence and under the auspices of the Supreme Being, the following rights of man and citizen:

1. Men are born and remain free and equal in rights; social distinctions can be established only for the common benefit.
2. The aim of every political association is the conservation of the natural and imprescriptible rights of man; these rights are liberty, property, security, and resistance to oppression.
3. The source of all sovereignty is located in essence in the nation; no body, no individual can exercise authority which does not emanate from it expressly.
4. Liberty consists in being able to do anything that does not harm another person. . . .
6. The law is the expression of the general will; all citizens have the right to concur personally or through their representatives in its formation; it must be the same for all, whether it protects or punishes. All citizens being equal in its eyes are equally admissible to all honors, positions, and public employments, according to their capabilities and without other distinctions than those of their virtues and talents.
7. No man can be accused, arrested, or detained except in cases determined by the law, and according to the forms which it has prescribed. . . .
10. No one may be disturbed because of his opinions, even religious, provided that their public demonstration does not disturb the public order established by law.
11. The free communication of thoughts and opinions is one of the most precious rights of man: every citizen can therefore freely speak, write, and print. . . .
12. The guaranteeing of the rights of man and citizen necessitates a public force; this force is therefore instituted for the advantage of all, and not for the private use of those to whom it is entrusted. . . .
14. Citizens have the right to determine for themselves or through their representatives the need for taxation of the public, to consent to it freely, to investigate its use, and to determine its rate, basis, collection, and duration.
15. Society has the right to demand an accounting of his administration from every public agent.
16. Any society in which guarantees of rights are not assured nor the separation of powers determined has no constitution.
17. Property being an inviolable and sacred right, no one may be deprived of it unless public necessity, legally determined, clearly requires such action, and then only on condition of a just and prior indemnity.

What "natural rights" does this document proclaim? To what extent was the document influenced by the writings of the philosophes?

---

affirmation of "the natural and imprescriptible rights of man" to "liberty, property, security and resistance to oppression." It went on to affirm the destruction of aristocratic privileges by proclaiming an end to exemptions from taxation, freedom and equal rights for all men, and access to public office based on talent. The monarchy was restricted, and all citizens were to have the right to take part in the legislative process. Freedom of speech and the press were coupled with the outlawing of arbitrary arrests.

The Declaration also raised another important issue. Did the proclamation's ideal of equal rights for all men also include women? Many deputies insisted that it did, at least in terms of civil liberties, provided that, as one said, "women do not aspire to exercise political rights and functions." Olympe de Gouges, a playwright and pamphleteer, refused to accept this exclusion of women from political rights. Echoing the words of the official declaration, she penned a Declaration of the Rights of Woman and the Female Citizen, in which she insisted that women should have all the same rights as men. The National Assembly ignored her demands.

In the meantime, Louis XVI had remained inactive at Versailles. He did refuse, however, to promulgate the decrees on the abolition of feudalism and the Declaration of Rights, but an unexpected turn of events soon forced the king to change his mind. On October 5, thousands of Parisian women, described by one eyewitness as "detachments of women coming up from every direction, armed with broomsticks, lances, pitchforks, swords, pistols and muskets," marched to Versailles, 12 miles away, and insisted that the royal family return to Paris. On October 6, the king complied. As a goodwill gesture, he brought along wagonloads of flour from the palace stores. All were escorted by women armed with pikes (some of which held the severed heads of the king's guards), singing, "We are bringing back the baker, the baker's wife, and the baker's boy" (the king, queen, and their son). The king now accepted the National Assembly's decrees and was virtually a prisoner in Paris.

Because the Catholic church was viewed as an important pillar of the old order, it soon felt the impact of reform. Most of the lands of the church were confiscated, and the church was also secularized. In July 1790, the Civil Constitution of the Clergy was put into effect. Both bishops and priests of the Catholic church were to be elected by the people and paid by the state. All clergy were also required to swear an oath of allegiance to the Civil Constitution. Only 54 percent of the French parish clergy took the oath, and the majority of bishops refused. The Catholic church, still an important institution in the life of the French people, now became an enemy of the Revolution.

A New Constitution By 1791, the National Assembly had completed a new constitution that established a limited constitutional monarchy. There was still a monarch (now called "king of the French"), but he enjoyed few powers not subject to review by the new Legislative Assembly. The Legislative Assembly, in which sovereign power was vested, was to sit for two years and consist of 745 representatives chosen by an indirect system of election that preserved power in the hands of the more affluent members of society. Only active citizens (men over the age of twenty-five paying taxes equivalent in value to three days' unskilled labor) could vote for electors (men paying taxes equal in value to ten days' labor). This relatively small group of fifty thousand electors then chose the deputies. To qualify as a deputy, one had to pay taxes equal in value to fifty-four days' labor.

Opposition From Within By 1791, a revolutionary consensus that was largely the work of the wealthier members of the bourgeoisie had moved France into a drastic reordering of the old regime. By mid-1791, however, this consensus faced growing opposition from clerics angered by the Civil Constitution of the Clergy, lower classes hurt by a rise in the cost of living, peasants angry that dues had still not been abandoned, and political clubs like the Jacobins who offered more radical solutions to France's problems. In addition, by mid-1791, the government was still facing severe financial difficulties due to massive tax evasion. Despite all of their problems, however, the bourgeois politicians in charge remained relatively unified on the basis of their trust in the king. But Louis XVI disastrously undercut them. Upset with the whole turn of revolutionary events, he attempted to flee France in June 1791 and almost succeeded before

being recognized, captured, and brought back to Paris. In this unsettled situation, with a discredited and seemingly disloyal monarch, the new Legislative Assembly held its first session in October 1791. France's relations with the rest of Europe soon led to Louis' downfall.

Opposition from Abroad Over a period of time, some Europeans had become concerned about the French example and feared that revolution would spread to their countries. On August 27, 1791, Emperor Leopold II of Austria and King Frederick William II of Prussia invited other European monarchs to use force to reestablish monarchical authority in France. Insulted by this threat, the Legislative Assembly declared war on Austria on April 20, 1792.

The French fared badly in the initial fighting, and loud recriminations were soon heard in Paris. A frantic search for scapegoats began; as one observer noted, "Everywhere you hear the cry that the king is betraying us, the generals are betraying us, that nobody is to be trusted; . . . that Paris will be taken in six weeks by the Austrians. . . . We are on a volcano ready to spout flames."[1] Defeats in war coupled with economic shortages in the spring reinvigorated popular groups that had been dormant since the previous summer and led to renewed political demonstrations, especially against the king. Radical Parisian political groups, declaring themselves an insurrectionary "commune," organized a mob attack on the royal palace and Legislative Assembly in August 1792, took the king captive, and forced the assembly to suspend the monarchy and call for a national convention, chosen on the basis of universal male suffrage, to decide on the future form of government. The French Revolution was about to enter a more radical stage as power passed from the assembly to the new Paris Commune, composed of many who proudly called themselves the *sans-culottes,* ordinary patriots without fine clothes. Although it has become customary to equate the more radical sans-culottes with working people or the poor, many were merchants and better-off artisans who were often the elite of their neighborhoods.

The Radical Revolution

In September 1792, the newly elected National Convention began its sessions. Although it was called to draft a new constitution, it also acted as the sovereign ruling body of France. Socially, the composition of the National Convention was similar to its predecessors. Dominated by lawyers, professionals, and property owners, two-thirds of its deputies were under forty-five, and almost all had had political experience as a result of the revolution. Almost all were also intensely distrustful of the king and his activities. It was therefore no surprise that the Convention's first major step on September 21 was to abolish the monarchy and establish a republic. At the beginning of 1793, the Convention passed a decree condemning Louis XVI to death. With his execution on January 21,

1793, the destruction of the old regime was complete. There could be no turning back. But the dispatch of the king produced new challenges by creating new enemies for the revolution both at home and abroad while strengthening groups that were already opposed to it.

In Paris, the local government, the Commune, led by the newly appointed minister of justice, Georges Danton, favored drastic change and put constant pressure on the Convention, pushing it to ever more radical positions. Moreover, the National Convention still did not rule all of France. Peasants in the west and inhabitants of France's major provincial cities refused to accept the authority of the Convention. Domestic turmoil was paralleled by a foreign crisis. By the time the king was executed, most of Europe—an informal coalition of Austria, Prussia, Spain, Portugal, Britain, the Dutch Republic, and Russia—had aligned against France, and by late spring some members of the coalition were poised to invade France in an effort to destroy the revolutionaries and reestablish the old regime.

To meet these crises, the Convention gave broad powers to an executive committee of twelve known as the Committee of Public Safety, which came to be dominated by Maximilien Robespierre, the leader of the Jacobins. For a twelve-month period, this committee gave the country the leadership it needed to weather the domestic and foreign crises of 1793.

A Nation in Arms   To meet the foreign crisis and save the republic from its foreign enemies, the Committee of Public Safety decreed a universal mobilization of the nation on August 23, 1793:

> Young men will fight, young men are called to conquer. Married men will forge arms, transport military baggage and guns and prepare food supplies. Women, who at long last are to take their rightful place in the revolution and follow their true destiny, will forget their futile tasks: their delicate hands will work at making clothes for soldiers; they will make tents and they will extend their tender care to shelters where the defenders of the [nation] will receive the help that their wounds require. Children will make lint of old cloth. It is for them that we are fighting: children, those beings destined to gather all the fruits of the revolution, will raise their pure hands toward the skies. And old men, performing their missions again, as of yore, will be guided to the public squares of the cities where they will kindle the courage of young warriors and preach the doctrines of hate for kings and the unity of the Republic.[2]

In less than a year, the French revolutionary government had raised an army of 650,000; by September 1794, it numbered 1,169,000. The Republic's army—a **nation in arms**—was the largest ever seen in European history. It pushed the allies back across the Rhine and even conquered the Austrian Netherlands to the north (see Map 19.1).

Historians have focused on the importance of the French revolutionary army as an important step in the creation of modern **nationalism.** Previously, wars had been fought between governments or ruling dynasties by relatively small armies of professional soldiers. The new French army, however, was the creation of a "people's" government; its wars were now "people's" wars. The entire nation was to be involved in the war. But when dynastic wars became people's wars, warfare increased in ferocity and lack of restraint. Although innocent civilians had suffered in the earlier struggles, now the carnage became appalling at times. The wars of the French revolutionary era opened the door to the total war of the modern world.

The Committee of Public Safety and the Reign of Terror   To meet the domestic crisis, the National Convention and the Committee of Public Safety established the Reign of Terror. Revolutionary courts were organized to protect the republic from its internal enemies (see the box on p. 364). In the course of nine months, sixteen thousand people were officially killed under the blade of the guillotine, a revolutionary device for the quick and efficient separation of heads from bodies. But the true number of the Terror's victims was probably closer to fifty thousand. The bulk of the Terror's executions took

Execution of the King.   At the beginning of 1793, the National Convention sentenced the king to death, and Louis XVI was duly executed on January 21. As seen in this engraving by Carnavalet, the execution of the king was accomplished using a favorite revolutionary device, the guillotine.

Citizens Enlisting in the New French Army.
To save the fledgling French republic from its foreign enemies, the National Convention created a new revolutionary army of unprecedented size. In this painting, citizens joyfully hasten to sign up at recruitment tables set up in the streets. Officials are distributing coins to those who have enrolled.

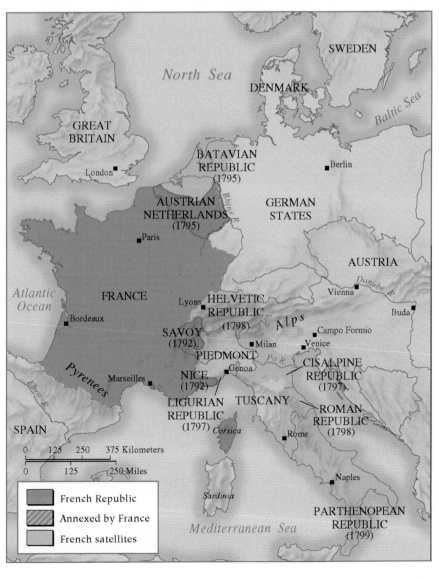

MAP 19.1 **French Expansion During the Revolutionary Wars, 1792–1799.** The conservative rulers of Europe, appalled at the republican character of the French Revolution, took up arms to restore the power of the Bourbon monarchy. The French responded with a people's army, the largest ever seen, which pushed the invaders out of France, annexed the Austrian Netherlands and some Italian territory, and created a number of French satellite states. **?** Why would Austria desire cooperation from the German states if it wanted to wage war on France?

View an animated version of this map or related maps at http://thomsonedu.com/history/spielvogel

JUSTICE IN THE REIGN OF TERROR

*T*he Reign of Terror created a repressive environment in which courts often acted quickly to condemn traitors to the revolutionary cause. In this account, an English visitor describes the court, the procession to the scene of execution, and the final execution procedure.

J. G. Milligen, *The Revolutionary Tribunal*

In the center of the hall, under a statue of Justice, holding scales in one hand, and a sword in the other, sat Dumas, the President, with the other judges. Under them were seated the public accuser, Fourquier-Tinville, and his scribes. . . . To the right were benches on which the accused were placed in several rows, and *gendarmes* with carbines and fixed bayonets by their sides. To the left was the jury.

Never can I forget the mournful appearance of these funereal processions to the place of execution. The march was opened by a detachment of mounted *gendarmes*—the carts followed; they were the same carts as those that are used in Paris for carrying wood; four boards were placed across them for seats, and on each board sat two, and sometimes three victims; their hands were tied behind their backs, and the constant jolting of the cart made them nod their heads up and down, to the great amusement of the spectators. On the front of the cart stood Samson, the executioner, or one of his sons or assistants; *gendarmes* on foot marched by the side; then followed a hackney, in which was the reporting clerk, whose duty it was to witness the execution, and then return to the public accuser's office to report the execution of what they called the law.

The process of execution was also a sad and heart-rending spectacle. In the middle of the Place de la Revolution was erected a guillotine, in front of a colossal statue of Liberty, represented seated on a rock, a cap on her head, a spear in her hand, the other reposing on a shield. On one side of the scaffold were drawn out a sufficient number of carts, with large baskets painted red, to receive the heads and bodies of the victims. Those bearing the condemned moved on slowly to the foot of the guillotine; the culprits were led out in turn, and if necessary, supported by two of the executioner's assistants, but their assistance was rarely required. Most of these unfortunates ascended the scaffold with a determined step—many of them looked up firmly on the menacing instrument of death, beholding for the last time the rays of the glorious sun, beaming on the polished axe: and I have seen some young men actually dance a few steps before they went up to be strapped to the perpendicular plane, which was then tilted to a horizontal plane in a moment, and ran on the grooves until the neck was secured and closed in by a moving board, when the head passed through what was called, in derision, "the republican toilet seat"; the weighty knife was then dropped with a heavy fall; and, with incredible dexterity and rapidity, two executioners tossed the body into the basket, while another threw the head after it.

How were the condemned taken to the executioner? How did this serve to inflame the crowds? How were people executed? Why?

---

place in places that had been in open rebellion against the authority of the National Convention. The Terror demonstrated no class prejudice. Estimates are that the nobles constituted 8 percent of its victims; the middle classes, 25; the clergy, 6; and the peasant and laboring classes, 61. To the Committee of Public Safety, this bloodletting was only a temporary expedient. After the wars and domestic emergencies were over, there would arise a "republic of virtue" in which the Declaration of the Rights of Man and the Citizen would be fully established.

Military force in the form of revolutionary armies was used to bring recalcitrant cities and districts back under the control of the National Convention. Because Lyons was France's second city after Paris and had defied the National Convention during a time when the republic was in peril, the Committee of Public Safety decided to make an example of it. By April 1794, a total of 1,880 citizens of Lyons had been executed. When guillotining proved too slow, cannon fire and grapeshot were used to blow condemned men into open graves. A German observed:

Whole ranges of houses, always the most handsome, burnt. The churches, convents, and all the dwellings of the former patricians were in ruins. When I came to the guillotine, the blood of those who had been executed a few hours beforehand was still running in the street. . . . I said to a group of sans-culottes that it would be decent to clear away all this human blood. Why should it be cleared? one of them said to me. It's the blood of aristocrats and rebels. The dogs should lick it up.[3]

In western France, revolutionary armies were also brutal in defeating the rebel armies. The commander of the revolutionary army ordered that no quarter be given: "The road to Laval is strewn with corpses. Women, priests, monks, children, all have been put to death. I have spared nobody." Perhaps the most notorious act of violence occurred in Nantes, where victims were executed by sinking them in barges in the Loire River.

The "Republic of Virtue" Along with the Terror, the Committee of Public Safety took other steps both to control France and to create a new republican order and new republican citizens. By spring 1793, it was sending "representatives on mission" as agents of the central government to all parts of France to implement the laws dealing with the wartime emergency. The committee also attempted to provide some economic controls by the Law of the General Maximum, which established price limits on goods declared of first necessity, ranging from food and drink to fuel and clothing. The controls failed to work very well because the government lacked the machinery to enforce it.

In its attempts to create a new order, the National Convention also pursued a policy of de-Christianization. A new calendar was instituted in which years would no longer be numbered from the birth of Jesus but from September 22, 1792, the first day of the French Republic. The new calendar also eliminated Sundays and church holidays. The word *saint* was removed from street names, churches were pillaged and closed by revolutionary armies, and priests were encouraged to marry. In Paris, the cathedral of Notre-Dame was designated a "temple of reason"; in November 1793, a public ceremony dedicated to the worship of Reason was held in the former cathedral in which patriotic maidens adorned in white dresses paraded where the high altar had once stood.

Equality and Slavery Early in the French Revolution, the desire for equality led to a discussion of what to do about slavery. A club called Friends of the Blacks advocated the abolition of slavery, which was achieved in France in September 1791. However, French planters in the West Indies, who profited greatly from the use of slaves on their sugar plantations, opposed the abolition of slavery in the French colonies. When the National Convention came to power, the issue was revisited, and on February 4, 1794, guided by ideals of equality, the government abolished slavery in the colonies.

In one French colony, slaves had already rebelled for their freedom. In 1791, black slaves in the French sugar colony of Saint-Domingue (the western third of the island of Hispaniola), inspired by the ideals of the revolution occurring in France, revolted against French plantation owners, killing the owners and their families and burning their buildings. White planters retaliated with equal brutality. One wealthy French settler reported, "How can we stay in a country where slaves have raised their hands against their masters?"

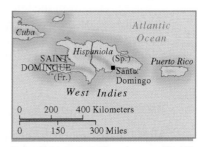

Revolt in Saint-Domingue (Haiti)

Eventually, leadership of the revolt was taken over by Toussaint L'Ouverture (1746–1803), the son of African slaves, who seized control of all of Hispaniola by 1801. Although Napoleon (see "The Age of Napoleon" below) had accepted the revolutionary ideal of equality, he did not deny the reports that the massacres of white planters by slaves demonstrated the savage nature of blacks. In 1802, he reinstated slavery in the French West Indian colonies and sent an army that captured L'Ouverture, who died in a French dungeon within a year. But the French soldiers, weakened by disease, soon succumbed to the slave forces. On January 1, 1804, the western part of Hispaniola, now called Haiti, announced its freedom and became the first independent state in Latin America. Despite Napoleon's efforts to the contrary, one of the French revolutionary ideals had triumphed abroad.

The Decline of the Committee of Public Safety Maintaining the revolutionary ideals in France, however, proved not to be easy. By the summer of 1794, the French had been successful on the battlefield against their foreign foes. The military successes meant that the Terror no longer served much purpose. But the Terror continued because Robespierre, now its dominant figure, had become obsessed with purifying the body politic of all corruption. Many deputies in the National Convention feared, however, that they were not safe while Robespierre was free to act. An anti-Robespierre coalition in the National Convention gathered enough votes to condemn him. Robespierre was guillotined on July 28, 1794, beginning a reaction that brought an end to this radical stage of the French Revolution.

Women Patriots. Women played a variety of roles in the events of the French Revolution. This picture shows a women's patriotic club discussing the decrees of the National Convention, an indication that some women had become highly politicized by the upheavals of the revolution.

The National Convention and its Committee of Public Safety had accomplished a great deal. By creating a nation in arms, they preserved the French Revolution and prevented it from being destroyed by its foreign enemies, who, if they had succeeded, would have reestablished the old monarchical order. Domestically, the revolution had also been saved from the forces of counterrevolution. The committee's tactics, however, provided an example for the use of violence in domestic politics that has continued to bedevil the Western world to this day.

Reaction and the Directory

After the execution of Robespierre, revolutionary fervor began to give way to the Thermidorean Reaction, named after the month of Thermidor on the new French calendar. The Terror began to abate. The National Convention curtailed the power of the Committee of Public Safety, shut down the Jacobin club, and attempted to provide better protection for its deputies against the Parisian mobs. Churches were allowed to reopen for public worship. Economic regulation was dropped in favor of laissez-faire policies, another clear indication that moderate forces were again gaining control of the revolution. In addition, a new constitution was adopted in August 1795 that reflected this more conservative republicanism and a desire for a stability that did not sacrifice the ideals of 1789.

To avoid the dangers of another single legislative assembly, the Constitution of 1795 established a national legislative assembly consisting of two chambers: a lower house, known as the Council of 500, which initiated legislation, and an upper house, the Council of Elders, which accepted or rejected the proposed laws. The 750 members of the two legislative bodies were chosen by electors who had to be owners or renters of property worth between 100 and 200 days' labor, a requirement that limited their number to thirty thousand. The Council of Elders elected five directors from a list presented by the Council of 500 to act as the executive committee or Directory.

The period of the Directory was an era of stagnation, corruption, and graft, a materialistic reaction to the suffering and sacrifices that had been demanded in the Reign of Terror and the Republic of Virtue. Speculators made fortunes in property by taking advantage of the republic's severe monetary problems. At the same time, the government of the Directory faced political enemies from both ends of the political spectrum. On the right, royalists who dreamed of restoring the monarchy continued their agitation. On the left, Jacobin hopes of power were revived by continuing economic problems. Battered by the left and right, unable to find a definitive solution to the country's economic problems, and still carrying on the wars inherited from the Committee of Public Safety, the Directory increasingly relied on the military to maintain its power. This led to a coup d'état

CHRONOLOGY   **The French Revolution**

National Assembly (Constituent Assembly)	1789–1791
Meeting of Estates-General	May 5, 1789
Formation of National Assembly	June 17, 1789
Tennis Court Oath	June 20, 1789
Fall of the Bastille	July 14, 1789
Great Fear	Summer 1789
Abolition of feudalism	August 4, 1789
Declaration of the Rights of Man and the Citizen	August 26, 1789
Women's march to Versailles; king's return to Paris	October 5-6, 1789
Civil Constitution of the Clergy	July 12, 1790
Flight of the king	June 1791
Legislative Assembly	1791–1792
French declaration of war on Austria	April 20, 1792
Attack on the royal palace	August 1792
National Convention	1792–1795
Abolition of the monarchy	September 21, 1792
Execution of the king	January 21, 1793
Universal mobilization of the nation	August 23, 1793
Execution of Robespierre	July 28, 1794
Directory	1795–1799
Constitution of 1795	August 22, 1795

in 1799 in which the successful and popular military general Napoleon Bonaparte was able to seize power.

The Age of Napoleon

Napoleon dominated both French and European history from 1799 to 1815. In a sense, Napoleon brought the revolution to an end, but he was also its product; he even called himself the "son of the revolution." The French Revolution had made possible his rise first in the military and then to supreme power in France. Even beyond this, Napoleon had once said, "I am the Revolution," and he never ceased to remind the French that they owed to him the preservation of all that was beneficial in the revolutionary program.

The Rise of Napoleon

Napoleon Bonaparte was born in 1769 in Corsica, a few months after France had annexed the island. The son of a lawyer whose family stemmed from the Florentine nobility, the young Napoleon obtained a royal scholarship to study at a military school in France. When the revolution broke out in 1789, Napoleon was a lieutenant, but the revolution and the European war that followed broadened his sights and presented him with new opportunities.

Napoleon rose quickly through the ranks. In 1794, when he was only twenty-five, the Committee of Public Safety promoted him to the rank of brigadier general. Two years later, he was made commander of the French armies in Italy (see the box above), where he won a series of stunning victories and dictated peace to the Austrians in 1797. Throughout his Italian campaigns, Napoleon won the confidence of his men by his energy, charm, and ability to comprehend complex issues quickly and make decisions rapidly. These qualities, combined with his keen intelligence, ease with words, and supreme confidence in himself, enabled him throughout the rest of his life to influence people and win their firm support. He returned to France as a conquering hero. After a disastrous expedition to Egypt in 1799, Napoleon returned to Paris, where he participated in the coup d'état that ultimately led to his virtual dictatorship of France. He was only thirty years old at the time.

With the coup of 1799, a new form of the republic was proclaimed in which, as first consul, Napoleon directly controlled the entire executive authority of government. He had overwhelming influence over the legislature, appointed members of the administrative bureaucracy, controlled the army, and conducted foreign affairs. In 1802, Napoleon was made consul for life and in 1804 returned France to monarchy when he crowned himself Emperor Napoleon I. The revolutionary era that had begun with an attempt to limit arbitrary government had ended with a government far more autocratic than the monarchy of the old regime.

The Domestic Policies of Emperor Napoleon

Napoleon once claimed that he had preserved the gains of the revolution for the French people. The ideal of republican liberty had, of course, been destroyed by Napoleon's thinly disguised autocracy. But were revolutionary ideals maintained in other ways? An examination of his domestic policies will enable us to judge the accuracy of Napoleon's assertion.

Napoleon and the Catholic Church   In 1801, Napoleon established peace with the oldest and most implacable enemy of the revolution, the Catholic church. Both sides gained from the Concordat that Napoleon arranged with the pope. Napoleon agreed to recognize Catholicism as the religion of a majority of the French people. Although the Catholic church was permitted to hold processions again and reopen the seminaries, the pope agreed not to raise the question of the church lands confiscated in the revolution. As a result of the Concordat, the Catholic church was no longer an enemy of the French government. At the same time, the agreement reassured those who had acquired church lands during the revolution that they would not be stripped of them, an assurance that obviously made them supporters of the Napoleonic regime.

A New Code of Laws   Napoleon's most famous domestic achievement was his codification of the laws. Before the revolution, France did not have a single set of laws but

The Coronation of Napoleon. In 1804, Napoleon restored monarchy to France when he crowned himself emperor. In the coronation scene painted by Jacques-Louis David, Napoleon is shown crowning his wife, the empress Josephine, while the pope looks on. Shown seated in the box in the background is Napoleon's mother, even though she was in fact not present at the ceremony.

rather a conglomeration of three hundred legal systems. During the revolution, efforts were made to codify the laws for the entire nation, but it remained for Napoleon to oversee the project and bring the work to completion in seven codes, of which the most important was the Civil Code (or *Code Napoléon*). This preserved most of the revolutionary gains by recognizing the principle of the equality of all citizens before the law, the right of the individual to choose a profession, religious toleration, and the abolition of serfdom and feudalism. Property rights continued to be carefully protected, and the interests of employers were safeguarded by outlawing trade unions and strikes. The Civil Code clearly reflected the revolutionary aspirations for a uniform legal system, legal equality, and protection of property and individuals.

But the rights of some people were strictly curtailed by the Civil Code. During the radical phase of the French Revolution, new laws had made divorce an easy process for both husbands and wives, restricted the rights of fathers over their children (they could no longer have their children put in prison arbitrarily), and allowed all children (including daughters) to inherit property equally. Napoleon's Civil Code undid most of this legislation. The control of fathers over their families was restored. Divorce was still allowed but was made more difficult for women to obtain. A wife caught in adultery, for example, could be divorced by her husband and even imprisoned. A husband, however, could be accused of adultery only if he moved his mistress into his home. Women were now "less equal than men" in other ways as well. When they

married, their property passed into the control of their husbands. In lawsuits, they were treated as minors, and their testimony was regarded as less reliable than that of men.

The French Bureaucracy Napoleon also worked on rationalizing the bureaucratic structure of France by developing a powerful, centralized administrative machine. Administrative centralization required a bureaucracy of capable officials, and Napoleon worked hard to develop one. Early on, the regime showed its preference for experts and cared little whether that expertise had been acquired in royal or revolutionary bureaucracies. Promotion, in civil as well as military offices, was to be based not on rank or birth but on demonstrated abilities. This was, of course, what many bourgeois had wanted before the revolution. Napoleon, however, also created a new aristocracy based on merit in the state service. Napoleon created 3,263 nobles between 1808 and 1814; nearly 60 percent were military officers; the remainder came from the upper ranks of the civil service and other state and local officials. Socially, only 22 percent of Napoleon's aristocracy came from the nobility of the old regime; almost 60 percent were bourgeois in origin.

Napoleon's Growing Despotism In his domestic policies, then, Napoleon both destroyed and preserved aspects of the revolution. Although equality was preserved in the law code and the opening of careers to talent, the creation of a new aristocracy, the strong protection accorded to property rights, and the use of conscription for the military make it clear that much equality had been lost. Liberty had been replaced by an initially benevolent despotism that grew increasingly arbitrary. Napoleon shut down sixty of France's seventy-three newspapers and insisted that all manuscripts be subjected to government scrutiny before they were published. Even the mail was opened by government police.

One prominent writer, Germaine de Stael (1766–1817), refused to accept Napoleon's growing despotism. Educated in Enlightenment ideas, she set up a salon in Paris that was a prominent intellectual center by 1800. She wrote novels and political works that denounced Napoleon's rule as tyrannical. Napoleon banned her books in France and exiled her to the German states, where she continued to write, although not without considerable homesickness for France. "The universe is in France," she once wrote; "outside it there is nothing." After the overthrow of Napoleon, Germaine de Stael returned to her beloved Paris, where she died two years later.

Napoleon's Empire and the European Response

When Napoleon became first consul in 1799, France was at war with a second European coalition of Russia, Great Britain, and Austria. Napoleon realized the need for a pause and achieved a peace treaty in 1802 that left France with new frontiers and a number of client territories from the North Sea to the Adriatic. But the peace did not last because the British and French both regarded it as temporary and had little intention of adhering to its terms.

In 1803, war was renewed with Britain, which was soon joined by Austria and Russia in the Third Coalition. At the Battle of Ulm in southern Germany in 1805, Napoleon crushed an Austrian army of fifty thousand men. Proceeding eastward from Ulm, Napoleon attacked Austrian and Russian forces gathered at Austerlitz and devastated the combined armies. Austria sued for peace, and Tsar Alexander I took his remaining forces back to Russia.

At first, Prussia had refused to join the Third Coalition, but after Napoleon began to reorganize the German states, Prussia reversed course. Acting quickly, Napoleon crushed Prussian forces at Jena and Auerstadt in October 1806 and then moved on to defeat the Russians, who had decided to reenter the fray, at Eylau and Friedland in June 1807. Napoleon's Grand Army had defeated the Continental members of the coalition, giving him the opportunity to create a new European order.

Napoleon's Grand Empire The Grand Empire was composed of three major parts: the French empire, dependent states, and allied states (see Map 19.2). The French empire, the inner core of the Grand Empire, consisted of an enlarged France extending to the Rhine in the east and including the western half of Italy north of Rome. Dependent states were kingdoms under the rule of Napoleon's relatives; these included Spain, the United Provinces, the kingdom of Italy, the Swiss Republic, the Grand Duchy of Warsaw, and the Confederation of the Rhine, the latter a union of all German states except Austria and Prussia. Allied states were those defeated by Napoleon and forced to join his struggle against Britain; they included Prussia, Austria, and Russia. Although the structure of the Grand Empire varied outside its inner core, Napoleon considered himself leader of the whole.

Within his empire, Napoleon sought acceptance everywhere of certain revolutionary principles, including legal equality, religious toleration, and economic freedom. As he explained to his brother Jerome after naming him king of the new German state of Westphalia:

> What the peoples of Germany desire most impatiently is that talented commoners should have the same right to your esteem and to public employments as the nobles, that any trace of serfdom and of an intermediate hierarchy between the sovereign and the lowest class of the people should be completely abolished. The benefits of the *Code Napoléon*, the publicity of judicial procedure, the creation of juries must be so many distinguishing marks of your monarchy. . . . What nation would wish to return under the arbitrary Prussian government once it had tasted the benefits of a wise and liberal administration? The peoples of Germany, the peoples of France, of Italy, of Spain all desire equality and liberal ideas. I have guided the affairs of Europe for many years now, and I have had occasion to convince myself that the buzzing of the privileged classes is contrary to the general opinion. Be a constitutional king.[4]

In the inner core and dependent states of his Grand Empire, Napoleon tried to destroy the old order. Nobility and clergy everywhere in these states lost their special privileges. He decreed equality of opportunity with offices open to talent, equality before the law, and religious toleration. This spread of French revolutionary principles was an important factor in the development of liberal traditions in these countries.

The Problem of Great Britain Like Hitler 130 years later, Napoleon hoped that his Grand Empire would last for centuries; like Hitler's empire, it collapsed almost as rapidly as it had been formed. Two major reasons help explain this: the survival of Great Britain and the force of nationalism. Britain's survival was due primarily to its sea power. As long as Britain ruled the waves, it was almost invulnerable to military attack. Although Napoleon contemplated an invasion of Britain and even collected ships for it, he could not overcome the British navy's decisive defeat of a combined French-Spanish fleet at Trafalgar in 1805. Napoleon then turned to his Continental System to defeat Britain. Put into effect between 1806 and 1808, it attempted to prevent British goods from reaching the European continent in order to weaken Britain economically and destroy its capacity to wage war. But the Continental System failed. Allied states resented

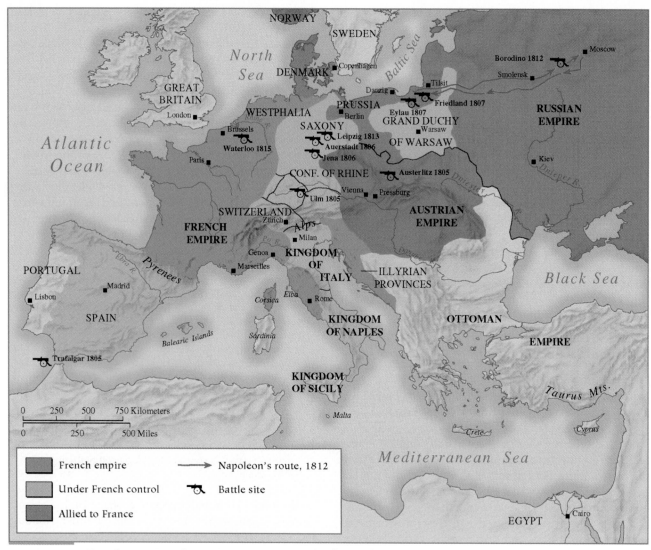

MAP 19.2 Napoleon's Grand Empire in 1810. Napoleon's Grand Army won a series of victories against Britain, Austria, Prussia, and Russia that gave the French emperor full or partial control over much of Europe by 1807. ❓ On the Continent, what is the overall relationship between distance from France and degree of French control, and how can you account for this?

▲ **View an animated version of this map or related maps at** http://thomsonedu.com/history/spielvogel

the ever-tightening French economic hegemony; some began to cheat and others to resist, thereby opening the door to British collaboration. New markets in the Levant (Middle East) and in Latin America also provided compensation for the British. Indeed, in 1809 and 1810, British overseas exports reached near-record highs.

Nationalism The second important factor in the failure of Napoleon was nationalism. This political creed had arisen during the French Revolution in the French people's emphasis on brotherhood (*fraternité*) and solidarity against other peoples. Nationalism involved the unique cultural identity of a people based on common language, religion, and national symbols. The spirit of French nationalism had made possible the mass armies of the

revolutionary and Napoleonic eras. But Napoleon's extending of the principles of the French Revolution beyond France inadvertently spread nationalism as well. The French aroused nationalism in two ways: by making themselves hated oppressors, and thus arousing the patriotism of others in opposition to French nationalism, and by showing the people of Europe what nationalism was and what a nation in arms could do. The lesson was not lost on other peoples and rulers. A Spanish uprising against Napoleon's rule, aided by British support, kept a French force of 200,000 pinned down for years.

The Fall of Napoleon The beginning of Napoleon's downfall came in 1812 with the invasion of Russia. The latter's defection from the Continental System left

Napoleon with little choice. Although aware of the risks of invading such a large country, he also knew that if the Russians were allowed to challenge the Continental System unopposed, others would soon follow suit. In June 1812, a Grand Army of more than 600,000 men entered Russia. Napoleon's hopes for victory depended on quickly meeting and defeating the Russian armies, but the Russian forces refused to give battle and retreated across hundreds of miles while torching their own villages and countryside to prevent Napoleon's army from finding food and shelter. When the Russians did stop to fight at Borodino, Napoleon's forces won an indecisive and costly victory. When the remaining troops of the Grand Army arrived in Moscow, they found the city ablaze. Lacking food and supplies, Napoleon abandoned Moscow late in October and made the "Great Retreat" across Russia in terrible winter conditions. Only one-fifth of the original army managed to straggle back to Poland in January 1813. This military disaster then led to a war of liberation all over Europe, culminating in Napoleon's defeat in April 1814.

The vanquished emperor of the French was allowed to play ruler on the island of Elba, off the coast of Tuscany, while the Bourbon monarchy was restored to France in the person of Louis XVIII, brother of the executed king. But the new king had little support, and Napoleon, bored on Elba, slipped back into France. When troops were sent to capture him, Napoleon opened his coat and addressed them: "Soldiers of the fifth regiment, I am your Emperor. . . . If there is a man among you would kill his Emperor, here I am!" No one fired a shot. Shouting *"Vive l'Empereur! Vive l'Empereur,"* the

troops went over to his side, and Napoleon entered Paris in triumph on March 20, 1815.

The powers who had defeated him pledged once more to fight this person, whom they called the "enemy and disturber of the tranquillity of the world." Having decided to strike first at his enemies, Napoleon raised yet another army and moved to attack the nearest allied forces stationed in Belgium. At Waterloo on June 18, Napoleon met a combined English and Prussian army under the duke of Wellington and suffered a bloody defeat. This time the victorious Allies exiled him to Saint Helena, a small and forsaken island in the South Atlantic, where he died in 1821. Only Napoleon's memory would continue to haunt French political life.

Erich Lessing/Art Resource, NY (Museo del Prado, Madrid)

Francisco Goya, *The Third of May 1808.* After Napoleon imposed his brother Joseph on Spain as its king, the Spanish people revolted against his authority, and a series of riots broke out in Madrid. This painting by Francisco Goya shows the French response—a deliberate execution of Spanish citizens to frighten people into submission. Goya portrays the French troops as a firing squad, killing people (including a monk) reacting in terror. The peasant in the middle throws out his arms in a gesture reminiscent of crucifixion. Goya painted many scenes in Napoleonic Spain depicting the horrors of war.

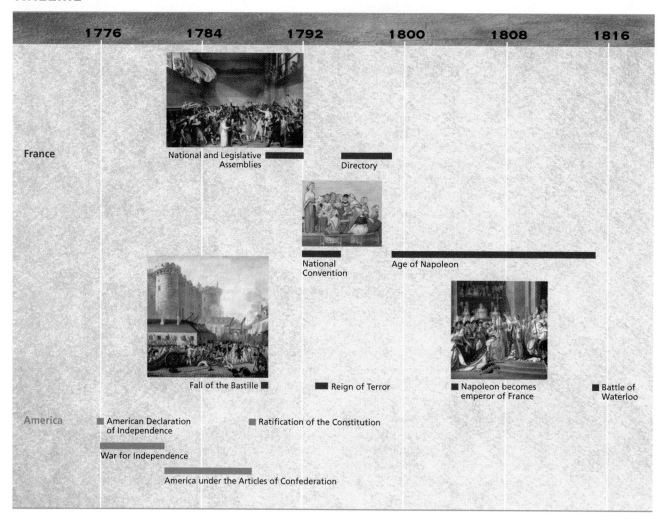

| 1776 | 1784 | 1792 | 1800 | 1808 | 1816 |

France

National and Legislative Assemblies

Directory

National Convention

Age of Napoleon

Fall of the Bastille ■

■ Reign of Terror

■ Napoleon becomes emperor of France

■ Battle of Waterloo

America

■ American Declaration of Independence

■ Ratification of the Constitution

War for Independence

America under the Articles of Confederation

CONCLUSION

The late eighteenth century was a time of dramatic political transformation. Revolutionary upheavals, beginning in North America and continuing in France, produced movements for political liberty and equality. The documents promulgated by these revolutions, the Declaration of Independence and the Declaration of the Rights of Man and the Citizen, embodied the fundamental ideas of the Enlightenment and set forth a liberal political agenda based on a belief in popular sovereignty–the people as the source of political power–and the principles of liberty and equality. Liberty, frequently limited in practice, meant, in theory, freedom from arbitrary power as well as the freedom to think, write, and worship as one chose. Equality meant equality in rights and the equality of opportunity based on talent rather than birth. In practice, equality remained limited; those who owned property had greater opportunities for voting and officeholding, and there was no equality between men and women.

The French Revolution established a modern revolutionary concept. No one had foreseen or consciously planned the upheaval that began in 1789, but thereafter revolutionaries knew that the proper mobilization of the masses could succeed in overthrowing unwanted governments. For these people, the French Revolution became a symbol of hope; for those who feared such changes, it became a symbol of dread. The French Revolution became the classical political and social model for revolution. At the same time, the liberal and national political ideals fostered by the revolution and spread through Europe by Napoleon dominated the political landscape of the nineteenth and early twentieth centuries. A new European era had begun.

NOTES

1. Quoted in W. Doyle, *The Oxford History of the French Revolution* (Oxford, 1989), p. 184.
2. Quoted in L. Gershoy, *The Era of the French Revolution* (Princeton, N.J., 1957), p. 157.
3. Quoted in Doyle, *Oxford History*, p. 254.
4. Quoted in J. C. Herold, ed., *The Mind of Napoleon* (New York, 1955), pp. 74–75.

SUGGESTIONS FOR FURTHER READING

A well-written introduction to the French Revolution can be found in **W. Doyle, *The Oxford History of the French Revolution*** (Oxford, 1989). On the entire revolutionary and Napoleonic eras, see **O. Connelly, *The French Revolution and Napoleonic Era***, 3d ed. (Fort Worth, Tex., 2000), and **D. M. G. Sutherland, *France, 1789–1815: Revolution and Counter-Revolution*** (New York, 1986). Two brief works are **A. Forrest, *The French Revolution*** (Oxford, 1995), and **J. M. Roberts, *The French Revolution***, 2d ed. (New York, 1997). More comprehensive are **S. F. Scott and B. Rothaus, eds., *Historical Dictionary of the French Revolution***, 2 vols. (Westport, Conn., 1985); **F. Furet and M. Ozouf, *A Critical Dictionary of the French Revolution*,** trans. A. Goldhammer (Cambridge, Mass., 1989); and **O. Connelly et al., *Historical Dictionary of Napoleonic France, 1799–1815*** (Westport, Conn., 1985).

The origins of the French Revolution are examined in **W. Doyle, *Origins of the French Revolution*** (Oxford, 1988). See also **R. Chartier, *The Cultural Origins of the French Revolution*** (Durham, N.C., 1991). On the early years of the Revolution, see **N. Hampson, *Prelude to Terror*** (Oxford, 1988); **T. Tackett, *Becoming a Revolutionary*** (Princeton, N.J., 1996), on the deputies to the National Assembly; and **J. Markoff, *The Abolition of Feudalism: Peasants, Lords, and Legislators in the French Revolution*** (University Park, Pa., 1996). For interesting insight into Louis XVI and French society, see **T. Tackett, *When the King Took Flight*** (Cambridge, Mass., 2003). Important works on the radical stage of the French Revolution include **D. Andress, *The Terror*** (New York, 2005); **R. R. Palmer, *Twelve Who Ruled*** (New York, 1965); and **R. Cobb, *The People's Armies*** (London, 1987). For a biography of Robespierre, one of the leading figures of this period, see **N. Hampson, *The Life and Opinions of Maximilien Robespierre*** (London, 1974). The importance of the revolutionary wars in the radical stage of the Revolution is underscored in **T. C. W. Blanning, *The French Revolutionary Wars, 1787–1802*** (New York, 1996). On the Directory, see **M. Lyons, *France Under the Directory*** (Cambridge, 1975).

On the role of women in revolutionary France, see **O. J. Hufton, *Women and the Limits of Citizenship in the French Revolution*** (Toronto, 1992); **J. Landes, *Women and the Public Sphere in the Age of the French Revolution*** (Ithaca, N.Y., 1988); and the essays in **G. Fraisse and M. Perrot, eds., *A History of Women in the West*,** vol. 4 (Cambridge, Mass., 1993).

On Napoleon, see **S. Englund, *Napoleon: A Political Life*** (New York, 2004); **G. J. Ellis, *Napoleon*** (New York, 1997); **M. Lyons, *Napoleon Bonaparte and the Legacy of the French Revolution*** (New York, 1994); and the massive biographies by **F. J. McLynn, *Napoleon: A Biography*** (London, 1997), and **A. Schom, *Napoleon Bonaparte*** (New York, 1997). On Napoleon's wars, see **S. J. Woolf, *Napoleon's Integration of Europe*** (New York, 1991).

A history of the revolutionary era in America can be found in **R. Middlekauff, *The Glorious Cause: The American Revolution, 1763–1789*** (New York, 1982), and **C. Bonwick, *The American Revolution*** (Charlottesville, Va., 1991). The importance of ideology is treated in **G. Wood, *The Radicalism of the American Revolution*** (New York, 1992).

Thomson NOW! Enter *ThomsonNOW* using the access card that is available for *Western Civilization: A Brief History*. *ThomsonNOW* will help you understand this chapter with lesson plans generated for your needs. In addition, you can read the following documents, and many more, online:

Edmund Burke, *Reflections on the Revolution in France*
Thomas Paine, *Common Sense*
King George III, letter on loss of colonies
James Madison, selected *Federalist Papers*

WESTERN CIVILIZATION RESOURCES

Visit the Web site for *Western Civilization: A Brief History* for resources specific to this book:

http://www.thomsonedu.com/history/spielvogel

For a variety of tools to help you succeed in this course, visit the Western Civilization Resource Center at

http://history.wadsworth.com/spielvogel

Included are quizzes, images, documents, interactive simulations, maps and timelines, movie explorations, and a wealth of other sources.

CHAPTER
20

THE INDUSTRIAL REVOLUTION
AND ITS IMPACT ON EUROPEAN SOCIETY

Power looms in an English textile factory

© British Library, London/HIP/Art Resource, NY

CHAPTER OUTLINE
AND FOCUS QUESTIONS

The Industrial Revolution in Great Britain

▢ What conditions and developments coalesced in Great Britain to bring about the first Industrial Revolution?

▢ What were the basic features of the new industrial system created by the Industrial Revolution?

The Spread of Industrialization

▢ How did the Industrial Revolution spread from Great Britain to the Continent and the United States, and how did industrialization in those areas differ from British industrialization?

The Social Impact of the Industrial Revolution

▢ What effects did the Industrial Revolution have on urban life, social classes, and standards of living?

▢ What were working conditions like in the early decades of the Industrial Revolution, and what efforts were made to improve them?

CRITICAL THINKING

▢ What role did government play in the industrial development of the Western world?

*T*HE FRENCH REVOLUTION dramatically altered the political structure of France; the Napoleonic conquests then spread many of the revolutionary principles to other parts of Europe. At the same time, during the late eighteenth and early nineteenth centuries, another revolution—an industrial one—was transforming the economic and social structure of Europe, although somewhat less radically and rapidly.

The Industrial Revolution initiated a quantum leap in industrial production. New sources of energy and power, especially coal and steam, replaced wind and water to run laborsaving machines that dramatically decreased the use of human and animal labor and at the same time increased productivity. In turn, power machinery called for new ways of organizing human labor to maximize the benefits and profits from the new machines; factories replaced workshops and home workrooms. Many early factories were dreadful places with difficult working conditions. Reformers, appalled at these conditions, were especially critical of the treatment of married women. One reported, "We have repeatedly seen married females, in the last stage of pregnancy, slaving from morning to night beside these never-tiring machines, and

374

when . . . they were obliged to sit down to take a moment's ease, and being seen by the manager, were fined for the offense." But some factories were well run. William Cobbett described one in Manchester in 1830: "In this room, which is lighted in the most convenient and beautiful manner, there were five hundred pairs of looms at work, and five hundred persons attending those looms; and, owing to the goodness of the masters, the whole looking healthy and well-dressed."

During the Industrial Revolution, Europe experienced a shift from a traditional, labor-intensive economy based on farming and handicrafts to a more capital-intensive economy based on manufacturing by machines, specialized labor, and industrial factories. Although the Industrial Revolution took decades to spread, it was truly revolutionary in the way it fundamentally changed Europeans, their society, and their relationship to other peoples. The development of large factories encouraged mass movements of people from the countryside to urban areas where impersonal coexistence replaced the traditional intimacy of rural life. Higher levels of productivity led to a search for new sources of raw materials, new consumption patterns, and a revolution in transportation that allowed raw materials and finished products to be moved quickly around the world. The rise of a wealthy industrial middle class and a huge industrial working class (or proletariat) substantially transformed traditional social relationships.✦

The Industrial Revolution in Great Britain

Historians generally agree that the Industrial Revolution began in Britain in the second half of the eighteenth century. By 1850, industry had made Great Britain the wealthiest country in the world, and the revolution had spread to the European continent and the New World.

Origins of the Industrial Revolution

A number of factors or conditions coalesced in Britain to produce the Industrial Revolution. One of these was the agricultural revolution of the eighteenth century, which led to a significant increase in food production. British agriculture could now feed more people at lower prices with less labor; even ordinary British families did not have to use most of their income to buy food, giving them the potential to purchase manufactured goods. At the same time, a rapid growth of population in the second half of the eighteenth century provided a substantial pool of labor for the new factories of the emerging British industry.

Britain had a ready supply of **capital** for investment in the new industrial machines and the factories that were needed to house them. In addition to profits from trade and the cottage industry, Britain had an effective central bank and well-developed, flexible credit facilities. Many early factory owners were merchants and entrepreneurs who had profited from the eighteenth-century cottage industry. But capital is only part of the story; Britain had a fair number of individuals who were interested in making profits if the opportunity presented itself (see the box on p. 376). The British were a people, as one historian has said, "fascinated by wealth and commerce, collectively and individually." No doubt the English revolutions of the seventeenth century had helped create an environment in Britain, unlike that of the absolutist states on the Continent, where political power rested in the hands of a progressive group of people who favored innovation in economic matters.

Britain was richly supplied with the important mineral resources, such as coal and iron ore, needed in the manufacturing process. Britain was also a small country, and the relatively short distances made transportation unproblematic. In addition to nature's provision of abundant rivers, from the mid-seventeenth century onward, both private and public investment poured into the construction of new roads, bridges, and waterways. By 1780, roads, rivers, and canals linked the major industrial centers of the North, the Midlands, London, and the Atlantic.

Finally, a supply of markets gave British industrialists a ready outlet for their manufactured goods. British exports quadrupled from 1660 to 1760. In the course of its eighteenth-century wars and conquests, Great Britain had developed a vast colonial empire at the expense of its leading Continental rivals, the Dutch Republic and France. Britain also possessed a well-developed merchant marine that was able to transport goods to any place in the world. A crucial factor in Britain's successful industrialization was the ability to cheaply produce the articles that were most in demand abroad. And the best markets abroad were not in Europe, where countries protected their own incipient industries, but in the Americas, Africa, and the East, where people wanted sturdy, inexpensive clothes rather than costly, highly finished luxury items. Britain's machine-produced textile industry fulfilled that demand. Nor should we overlook the British domestic market. Britain had the highest standard of living in Europe and a rapidly growing population. This demand from both domestic and foreign markets and the inability of the old system to fulfill it led entrepreneurs to seek and accept the new methods of manufacturing that a series of inventions provided. Thus was the Industrial Revolution born.

Technological Changes and New Forms of Industrial Organization

In the 1770s and 1780s, the cotton textile industry took the first major revolutionary step by inventing the modern factory.

The Cotton Industry   Already in the eighteenth century, Great Britain had surged ahead in the production of cheap cotton goods using traditional cottage industry methods. The development of the flying shuttle had sped the process

THE TRAITS OF THE BRITISH INDUSTRIAL ENTREPRENEUR

*R*ichard Arkwright (1732–1792), inventor of a spinning frame and founder of cotton factories, was a good example of the successful entrepreneur in the early Industrial Revolution in Britain. In this selection, Edward Baines, who wrote *The History of the Cotton Manufacture in Great Britain* in 1835, discusses the traits that explain the success of Arkwright and presumably other British entrepreneurs.

Edward Baines, *The History of the Cotton Manufacture in Great Britain*

Richard Arkwright rose by the force of his natural talents from a very humble condition in society. He was born at Preston on the 23rd of December, 1732, of poor parents: being the youngest of thirteen children, his parents could only afford to give him an education of the humblest kind, and he was scarcely able to write. He was brought up to the trade of a barber at Kirkham and Preston, and established himself in that business at Bolton in the year 1760. Having become possessed of a chemical process for dyeing human hair, which in that day (when wigs were universal) was of considerable value, he traveled about collecting hair, and again disposing of it when dyed. In 1761, he married a wife from Leigh, and the connections he thus formed in that town are supposed to have afterwards brought him acquainted with Highs's experiments in making spinning machines. He himself manifested a strong bent for experiments in mathematics, which he is stated to have followed with so much devotedness as to have neglected his business and injured his circumstances. His natural disposition was ardent, enterprising, and stubbornly persevering: his mind was as coarse as it was bold and active, and his manners were rough and unpleasing....

The most marked traits in the character of Arkwright were his wonderful ardour, energy, and perseverance. He commonly laboured in his multifarious concerns from five o'clock in the morning till nine at night; and when considerably more than fifty years of age,—feeling that the defects of his education placed him under great difficulty and inconvenience in conducting his correspondence, and in the general management of his business,—he encroached upon his sleep, in order to gain an hour each day to learn English grammar, and another hour to improve his writing and orthography [spelling]! He was impatient of whatever interfered with his favorite pursuits; and the fact is too strikingly characteristic not to be mentioned, that he separated from his wife not many years after their marriage, because she, convinced that he would starve his family [because of the impractical nature of his schemes], broke some of his experimental models of machinery. Arkwright was a severe economist of time; and, that he might not waste a moment, he generally traveled with four horses, and at a very rapid speed. His concerns in Derbyshire, Lancashire, and Scotland were so extensive and numerous, as to [show] at once his astonishing power of transacting business and his all grasping spirit. In many of these he had partners, but he generally managed in such a way, that, whoever lost, he himself was a gainer.

As seen in the life of Richard Arkwright, what traits did Edward Baines think were crucial to be a successful entrepreneur?

---

of weaving on a loom and enabled weavers to double their output. This led to shortages of yarn, however, until James Hargreaves's spinning jenny, perfected by 1768, allowed spinners to produce yarn in greater quantities. Edmund Cartwright's power loom, invented in 1787, allowed the weaving of cloth to catch up with the spinning of yarn and presented new opportunities to entrepreneurs. It was much more efficient to bring workers to the machines and organize their labor collectively in factories located next to rivers and streams, the sources of power for many of these early machines, than to leave the workers dispersed in their cottages. The concentration of labor in the new factories also brought the laborers and their families to live in the new towns that rapidly grew up around the factories.

The Steam Engine What pushed the cotton industry to even greater heights of productivity was the invention of the steam engine, which revolutionized the production of cotton goods and allowed the factory system to spread to other areas of production, thereby creating whole new industries. The steam engine secured the triumph of the Industrial Revolution.

In the 1760s, a Scottish engineer, James Watt (1736–1819), created an engine powered by steam that could pump water from mines three times as quickly as previous engines. In 1782, Watt enlarged the possibilities of the steam engine when he developed a rotary engine that could turn a shaft and thus drive machinery. Steam power could now be applied to spinning and weaving cotton, and before long, cotton mills using steam engines were multiplying across Britain. Because steam engines were fired by coal, they did not need to be located near rivers; entrepreneurs now had greater flexibility in their choice of location.

The new boost given to cotton textile production by technological changes became readily apparent. In 1760, Britain had imported 2.5 million pounds of raw cotton, which was farmed out to cottage industries. In 1787, the British imported 22 million pounds of cotton; most of it was spun on machines, some powered by water in large mills. By 1840, fully 366 million pounds of cotton—now

Britain's most important product in value—were imported. By this time, most cotton industry employees worked in factories. The cheapest labor in India could not compete in quality or quantity with Britain. British cotton goods sold everywhere in the world. And in Britain itself, cheap cotton cloth made it possible for millions of poor people to wear undergarments, long a luxury of the rich, who could afford expensive linen cloth. Cotton clothing was tough, comfortable, cheap, and easily washable.

The steam engine proved indispensable. Unlike horses, the steam engine was a tireless source of power and depended for fuel on a substance—coal—that seemed unlimited in quantity. The popular saying that "steam is an Englishman" had real significance by 1850. The success of the steam engine led to a need for more coal and an expansion in coal production; between 1815 and 1850, the output of coal quadrupled. In turn, new processes using coal furthered the development of the iron industry.

The Iron Industry The British iron industry was radically transformed during the Industrial Revolution. Britain had large resources of iron ore, but at the beginning of the eighteenth century, the basic process for producing iron had altered little since the Middle Ages and still depended heavily on charcoal. In the early eighteenth century, new methods of smelting iron ore to produce cast iron were devised using coke derived from coal. Still, a better quality of iron was not attained until the 1780s, when Henry Cort developed a system called puddling, in which coke was used to burn away impurities in pig iron to produce an iron of high quality. A boom then ensued in the British iron industry. In 1740, Britain produced 17,000 tons of iron; by the 1840s, over 2 million tons; and by 1852, almost 3 million tons, more than the rest of the world combined.

A Revolution in Transportation The high-quality wrought iron produced by the Cort process encouraged the use of machinery in other industries, most noticeably in such new means of transportation as steamboats and railroads. In 1804, Richard Trevithick pioneered the first steam-powered locomotive on an industrial rail line in southern Wales. It pulled 10 tons of ore and seventy people at 5 miles per hour. Better locomotives soon followed. The engines built by George Stephenson and his son proved superior, and it was in their workshops in Newcastle-upon-Tyne that the locomotives for the first modern railways in Britain were built. George Stephenson's *Rocket* was used on the first public railway line, which opened in 1830, extending 32 miles from Liverpool to Manchester. *Rocket* sped along at 16 miles per hour. Within twenty years, locomotives had reached 50 miles per hour, an incredible speed to contemporary passengers. During the same period, new companies were formed to build additional railroads as the infant industry proved successful not only technically but also financially. In 1840, Britain had almost 2,000 miles of railroads; ten years later, 6,000 miles of track crisscrossed the country (see Map 20.1).

The railroad contributed significantly to the maturing of the Industrial Revolution. The railroad's demands for coal and iron furthered the growth of those industries. Railway construction created new job opportunities, especially for farm laborers and peasants who had long been accustomed to finding work outside their local villages. Perhaps most important, the availability of a cheaper and faster means of transportation had a domino effect on the growth of the industrial economy. By lowering the price of goods, fast transportation caused markets to grow, and this increased demand necessitated more factories and more machinery, thereby reinforcing the self-sustaining nature of the Industrial Revolution. This dynamism marked a fundamental break with the traditional European economy. The great productivity of the Industrial Revolution enabled entrepreneurs to reinvest their profits in new capital equipment, further expanding the productive capacity of

Railroad Line from Liverpool to Manchester. The railroad line from Liverpool to Manchester, first opened in 1830, relied on steam locomotives. As is evident in this illustration, carrying passengers was the railroad's main business. First-class passengers rode in covered cars, second-and third-class passengers in open cars.

sense of power over nature not felt before in Western civilization.

The Industrial Factory Another visible symbol of the Industrial Revolution was the factory, which became the chief means of organizing labor for the new machines. From its beginning, the factory system demanded a new type of discipline from its employees. Factory owners could not afford to let their expensive machinery stand idle. Workers were forced to work regular hours and in shifts to keep the machines producing at a steady pace for maximum output. This required a massive adjustment on the part of early factory laborers.

Preindustrial workers were not accustomed to a "timed" format. Agricultural laborers had always kept irregular hours; hectic work at harvest time might be followed by days or weeks of inactivity. Even in the burgeoning cottage industry of the eighteenth century, weavers and spinners who worked at home might fulfill their weekly quotas by working around the clock for two or three days and then proceeding at a leisurely pace until the next week's demands forced another work spurt.

Factory owners therefore faced a formidable task. They had to create a system of time-work discipline in which employees became accustomed to working regular, unvarying hours during which they performed a set number of tasks over and over again as efficiently as possible. One early industrialist said that his aim was "to make such machines of the men as cannot err." Such work, of course, tended to be repetitive and boring, and factory owners resorted to tough methods to accomplish their goals. Factory regulations were minute and detailed (see the box on p. 380). Adult workers were fined for a wide variety of minor infractions, such as being a few minutes late for work, and dismissed for more serious misdeeds, especially intoxication. Drunkenness was viewed as particularly offensive because it set a bad example for younger workers and also courted disaster around dangerous machinery. Employers found that dismissals and fines worked well for adult employees; in a time when great population growth had produced large masses of unskilled labor, dismissal could be disastrous. Children were less likely to understand the implications of dismissal, so they were sometimes disciplined more directly— by beating. In one crucial sense, the early industrialists proved successful in their efforts. As the nineteenth century progressed, the second and third generations of workers came to view a regular workweek as a natural way of life. That attitude sustained Britain's incredible economic growth in that century.

The Great Exhibition: Britain in 1851

In 1851, the British organized the world's first industrial fair. It was housed at Kensington in London in the Crystal Palace, an enormous structure made entirely of glass and iron, a tribute to British engineering skills. Covering 19 acres, the Crystal Palace contained 100,000

MAP 20.1 **The Industrial Revolution in Britain by 1850.** The Industrial Revolution began in the mid-1700s. Increased food production, rapid population growth, higher incomes, plentiful capital, solid banking and financial institutions, an abundance of mineral resources, and easy transport all furthered the process, making Britain the world's wealthiest country by 1850. ❓ How well does the railroad system connect important British industrial areas? 🔊 **View an animated version of this map or related maps at** http://thomsonedu.com/history/spielvogel

the economy. Continuous, self-sustaining economic growth came to be seen as a fundamental characteristic of the new industrial economy.

The railroad was the perfect symbol of this aspect of the Industrial Revolution. The ability to transport goods and people at dramatic speeds also provided visible confirmation of a new sense of power. When railway builders penetrated mountains with tunnels and spanned chasms with breathtaking bridges, contemporaries experienced a

A British Textile Factory. The development of the factory changed the relationship between workers and employers as workers were encouraged to adjust to a new system of discipline that forced them to work regular hours under close supervision. This 1851 illustration shows women working in a British textile factory.

exhibits that showed the wide variety of products created by the Industrial Revolution. Six million people visited the fair in six months. The Great Exhibition displayed Britain's wealth to the world; it was a gigantic symbol of British success. Even trees were brought inside the Crystal Palace as a visible symbol of how the Industrial Revolution had achieved human domination over nature.

By the year of the Great Exhibition, Great Britain had become the world's first and richest industrial nation. Britain was the "workshop, banker, and trader of the world." It produced one-half of the world's coal and manufactured goods; its cotton industry alone in 1851 was equal in size to the industries of all other European countries combined. No doubt Britain's certainty about its mission in the world in the nineteenth century was grounded in its incredible material success.

The Spread of Industrialization

Industrialization spread from Great Britain to the Continental countries of Europe and America at different times and speeds during the nineteenth century. First to be industrialized on the Continent were Belgium, France, and the German states, and in North America, the young

United States. Not until after 1850 did the Industrial Revolution spread to the rest of Europe and other parts of the world.

Industrialization on the Continent

Industrialization on the Continent faced numerous hurdles, and as it proceeded in earnest after 1815, it did so along lines that were somewhat different from Britain's. Lack of technical knowledge was initially a major obstacle to industrialization. But the Continental countries had an advantage here: they could simply borrow British techniques and practices. Of course, the British tried to prevent that. Until 1825, British artisans were prohibited from leaving the country; until 1842, the export of important machinery and machine parts was forbidden. Nevertheless, the British were not able to control this situation by legislation. Already by 1825, there were at least two thousand skilled British mechanics on the Continent, and British equipment was being sold abroad, legally or illegally.

Gradually, the Continent achieved technological independence as local people learned all the skills their British teachers had to offer. By the 1840s, a new generation of skilled mechanics from Belgium and France

DISCIPLINE IN THE NEW FACTORIES

orkers in the new factories of the Industrial Revolution had been accustomed to a lifestyle free of overseers. Unlike the cottages, where workers spun thread and wove cloth in their own rhythm and time, the factories demanded a new, rigorous discipline geared to the requirements of the machines. This selection is taken from a set of rules for a factory in Berlin in 1844. They were typical of company rules everywhere the factory system had been established.

The Foundry and Engineering Works of the Royal Overseas Trading Company, Factory Rules

In every large works, and in the co-ordination of any large number of workmen, good order and harmony must be looked upon as the fundamentals of success, and therefore the following rules shall be strictly observed.

1. The normal working day begins at all seasons at 6 A.M. precisely and ends, after the usual break of half an hour for breakfast, an hour for dinner and half an hour for tea, at 7 P.M., and it shall be strictly observed. . . .

   Workers arriving 2 minutes late shall lose half an hour's wages; whoever is more than 2 minutes late may not start work until after the next break; or at least shall lose his wages until then. Any disputes about the correct time shall be settled by the clock mounted above the gatekeeper's lodge. . . .

3. No workman, whether employed by time or piece, may leave before the end of the working day, without having first received permission from the overseer and having given his name to the gatekeeper. Omission of these two actions shall lead to a fine of ten silver groschen [pennies] payable to the sick fund.

4. Repeated irregular arrival at work shall lead to dismissal. This shall also apply to those who are found idling by an official or overseer, and refused to obey their order to resume work. . . .

6. No worker may leave his place of work otherwise than for reasons connected with his work.

7. All conversation with fellow-workers is prohibited; if any worker requires information about his work, he must turn to the overseer, or to the particular fellow-worker designated for the purpose.

8. Smoking in the workshops or in the yard is prohibited during working hours; anyone caught smoking shall be fined five silver groschen for the sick fund for every such offense. . . .

10. Natural functions must be performed at the appropriate places, and whoever is found soiling walls, fences, squares, etc., and similarly, whoever is found washing his face and hands in the workshop and not in the places assigned for the purpose, shall be fined five silver groschen for the sick fund. . . .

12. It goes without saying that all overseers and officials of the firm shall be obeyed without question, and shall be treated with due deference. Disobedience will be punished by dismissal.

13. Immediate dismissal shall also be the fate of anyone found drunk in any of the workshops. . . .

14. Every workman is obliged to report to his superiors any acts of dishonesty or embezzlement on the part of his fellow workmen. If he omits to do so, and it is shown after subsequent discovery of a misdemeanor that he knew about it at the time, he shall be liable to be taken to court as an accessory after the fact and the wage due to him shall be retained as punishment.

What impact did factories have on the lives of workers? To what extent have such rules determined much of modern industrial life?

---

was spreading their knowledge to the east and south. More important, however, Continental countries, especially France and the German states, began to establish a wide range of technical schools to train engineers and mechanics.

That government played an important role in this brings us to a second difference between British and Continental industrialization. Governments in most of the Continental countries were accustomed to playing a significant role in economic affairs. Furthering the development of industrialization was a logical extension of that attitude. Hence governments provided for the costs of technical education, awarded grants to inventors and foreign entrepreneurs, exempted foreign industrial equipment from import duties, and in some places even financed factories. Of equal if not greater importance in the long run, governments actively bore much of the cost of building roads and canals, deepening and widening river channels, and constructing railroads. By 1850, a network of iron rails had spread across Europe, although only Germany and Belgium had largely completed their systems by that time.

Centers of Continental Industrialization

As noted earlier, the Industrial Revolution on the Continent occurred in three major centers between 1815 and 1850—Belgium, France, and the German states (see Map 20.2). Cotton played an important role, although it was not as significant as heavy industry. The development of cotton manufacturing on the Continent and Britain differed in two significant ways. Unlike Britain, where cotton manufacturing was mostly centered in Lancashire (in northwestern England) and

The Great Exhibition of 1851. The Great Exhibition of 1851 was a symbol of the success of Great Britain, which had become the world's first industrial nation and its richest. Over 100,000 exhibits were housed in the Crystal Palace, a giant structure of cast iron and glass. The first illustration shows the front of the palace and some of its numerous visitors. The second shows the opening day ceremonies. Queen Victoria is seen at the center with her family, surrounded by visitors from all over the world. Note the large tree inside the building, providing a visible symbol of how the Industrial Revolution had supposedly achieved human domination over nature.

the Glasgow area of Scotland, cotton mills in France, Germany, and to a lesser degree Belgium were dispersed through many regions. Noticeable, too, was the mixture of old and new. The old techniques of the cottage system, such as the use of hand looms, held on much longer. In the French district of Normandy, for example, in 1849, eighty-three mills were still driven by hand or animal power.

MAP 20.2 The Industrialization of Europe by 1850. Great Britain was Europe's first industrialized country; however, by the middle of the nineteenth century, several regions on the Continent had made significant advances in industrialization, especially in Belgium, France, and the German states. ❓ What reasons could explain why coal mining and iron industries are densely clustered in manufacturing and industrial areas? 🌐 **View an animated version of this map or related maps at** http://thomsonedu.com/history/spielvogel

Heavy industry on the Continent before 1850 was likewise a mixture of old and new. The adoption of new techniques, such as coke-smelted iron and puddling furnaces, coincided with the expansion of old-type charcoal blast furnaces. Before 1850, Germany lagged significantly behind both Belgium and France in heavy industry, and most German iron manufacturing remained based on old techniques. Not until the 1840s was coke-blast iron produced in the Rhineland. At that time, no one had yet realized the treasure of coal buried in the Ruhr valley. A German official wrote in 1852 that "it is clearly not to be expected that Germany will ever be able to reach the level of production of coal and iron currently attained in England. This is implicit in our far more limited resource endowment." Little did he realize that

although the industrial development of Continental Europe was about a generation behind Britain at mid-century, after 1850 an incredibly rapid growth in Continental industry would demonstrate that Britain was not, after all, destined to remain the world's greatest industrial nation.

The Industrial Revolution in the United States

In 1800, the United States was an agrarian society. There were no cities with populations of more than 100,000, and six out of every seven American workers were farmers. By 1860, however, the population had grown from 5 to 30 million people, larger than Great Britain. Almost half of them lived west of the Appalachian Mountains. The number of states had more than doubled, from sixteen to thirty-four, and nine American cities had populations of more than 100,000. Only 50 percent of American workers were farmers. In those sixty years, the United States was transformed from a farm-centered society of small communities to an industrializing, urbanizing nation.

The initial application of machinery to production was accomplished, as in Continental Europe, by borrowing from Great Britain. A British immigrant, Samuel Slater, established the first textile factory using water-powered spinning machines in Rhode Island in 1790. By 1813, factories with power looms copied from British versions were being established. Soon thereafter, however, Americans began to equal or surpass British technical inventions. The Harpers Ferry arsenal, for example, built muskets with interchangeable parts. Because all the individual parts of a musket were identical (for example, all triggers were the same), the final product could be put together quickly and easily; this enabled Americans to avoid the more costly system in which skilled craftspeople fitted together individual parts made separately. The so-called American system reduced costs and revolutionized production by saving labor, important to a society that had few skilled artisans.

Unlike Britain, the United States was a large country. The lack of a good system of internal transportation seemed to limit American economic development by making the transport of goods prohibitively expensive. This was gradually remedied, however. Thousands of miles of roads and canals were built linking east and west. The steamboat facilitated transportation on the Great Lakes, Atlantic coastal waters, and rivers. It was especially important to the Mississippi River valley; by 1860, a thousand steamboats plied the Mississippi (see the box on p. 384). Most important of all in the development of an American transportation system was the railroad. Beginning with 100 miles in 1830, by 1860 there were more than 27,000 miles of railroad track covering the United States. This transportation revolution turned the United States into a single massive market for the manufactured goods of the Northeast, the early center of American industrialization.

Labor for the growing number of factories in this area came primarily from rural New England. The United States did not possess a large number of craftspeople, but it did have a rapidly expanding farm population; its size in the Northeast soon outstripped the available farmland. While some of this excess population, especially men, went west, others, mostly women, found work in the new textile and shoe factories of New England. Indeed, women made up more than 80 percent of the labor force in the large textile factories. In Massachusetts mill towns, company boarding houses provided rooms for large numbers of young women who worked for several years before marriage. Outside Massachusetts, factory owners sought entire families including children to work in their mills; one mill owner ran this advertisement in a newspaper in Utica, New York: "Wanted: A few sober and industrious families of at least five children each, over the age of eight years, are wanted at the Cotton Factory in Whitestown. Widows with large families would do well to attend this notice." When a decline in rural births threatened to dry up this labor pool in the 1830s and 1840s, European immigrants, especially poor and unskilled Irish, English, Scottish, and Welsh, appeared in large numbers to replace American women and children in the factories.

By 1860, the United States was well on its way to being an industrial nation. In the Northeast, the most industrialized section of the country, per capita income was 40 percent higher than the national average. Diets, it has been argued, were better and more varied; machine-made clothing was more abundant. Nevertheless, despite a growing belief in a myth of social mobility based on equality of economic opportunity, the reality was that the richest 10 percent of the population in the cities held 70 to 80 percent of the wealth, compared to 50 percent in 1800. Nevertheless, American historians generally argue that while the rich got richer, the poor, as a result of experiencing an increase in their purchasing power, did not get poorer.

Limiting the Spread of Industrialization

Before 1870, the industrialization that had developed in western and central Europe and the United States did not extend in any significant way to the rest of the world. Even in eastern Europe, industrialization lagged far behind. Russia, for example, remained largely rural and agricultural with an autocratic regime that kept the peasants in serfdom. There was not much of a middle class, and the tsarist regime, fearful of change, preferred to import industrial goods in return for the export of raw materials, such as grain and timber. Russia would not have an Industrial Revolution until the end of the nineteenth century.

The Example of India   In other parts of the world where they had established control, newly industrialized European states pursued a deliberate policy of preventing the growth of mechanized industry. A good example is India. In the eighteenth century, India had become one of the world's greatest exporters of cotton cloth produced by hand labor. In the first half of the nineteenth century, much of India fell under the control of the British East India Company (see Chapter 24). With British control came inexpensive British factory-produced textiles, and soon thousands of Indian spinners and handloom weavers were unemployed. British policy encouraged Indians to export their raw materials while buying British-made goods. Although modest industrial factories for making textiles and jute (used in making rope) were opened in India in the 1850s, a lack of local capital and the advantages given to British imports limited the growth of new manufacturing operations. India, then, provides an excellent example of how some of the rapidly industrializing nations of Europe worked to deliberately thwart the spread of the Industrial Revolution to their colonial dominions.

"S-T-E-A-M-BOAT A-COMIN'!"

Steamboats and railroads were crucial elements in a transportation revolution that enabled industrialists to expand markets by shipping goods cheaply and efficiently. At the same time, these marvels of technology aroused a sense of power and excitement that was an important aspect of the triumph of industrialization. The American writer Mark Twain captured this sense of excitement in this selection from *Life on the Mississippi.*

Mark Twain, *Life on the Mississippi*

After all these years I can picture that old time to myself now, just as it was then: the white town drowsing in the sunshine of a summer's morning; the streets empty, or pretty nearly so; one or two clerks sitting in front of the Water street stores, with their splint-bottomed chairs tilted back against the walls, chins on breasts, hats slouched over their faces, asleep; . . . two or three lonely little freight piles scattered about the "levee"; a pile of "skids" on the slope of the stone-paved wharf, and the fragrant town drunkard asleep in the shadow of them; . . . the great Mississippi, the majestic, the magnificent Mississippi, rolling its mile-wide along, shining in the sun; the dense forest away on the other side; the "point" above the town, and the "point" below, bounding the river glimpse and turning it into a sort of sea, and withal a very still and brilliant and lonely one. Presently a film of dark smoke appears above on those remote "points"; instantly a negro drayman, famous for his quick eye and prodigious voice, lifts up to cry, "S-t-e-a-m-boat a-comin'!" and the scene changes! The town drunkard stirs, the clerks wake up, a furious clatter of drays follows, every house and store pours out a human contribution, and all in a twinkling the dead town [Hannibal, Missouri] is alive and moving. Drays, carts, men, boys, all go hurrying from many quarters to a common center, the wharf. Assembled there, the people fasten their eyes upon the coming boat as upon a wonder they are seeing for the first time. And the boat is rather a handsome sight, too. She is long and sharp and trim and pretty; she has two tall, fancy-topped chimneys, with a gilded device of some kind swung between them; a fanciful pilot-house, all glass and "ginger bread," perched on top of the "texas" deck behind them; the paddle-boxes are gorgeous with a picture or with gilded rays above the boat's name; the boiler deck, the hurricane deck, and the texas deck are fenced and ornamented with clean white railings; there is a flag gallantly flying from the jack-staff; the furnace doors are open and the fires glaring bravely; the upper decks are black with passengers; the captain stands by the big bell, calm, imposing, the envy of all; great volumes of the blackest smoke are rolling and tumbling out of the chimneys—a husbanded grandeur created with a bit of pitch pine just before arriving at a town; the crew are grouped on the forecastle; the broad stage is run far out over the port bow, and an envied deck-hand stands picturesquely on the end of it with a coil of rope in his hand; the pent steam is screaming through the gauge-cocks; the captain lifts his hand, a bell rings, the wheels stop; then they turn back, churning the water to foam, and the steam is at rest. Then such a scramble as there is to get aboard, and to get ashore, and to take in freight and discharge freight, all at one and the same time; and such a yelling and cursing as the mates facilitate it all with! Ten minutes later the steamer is under way again, with no flag on the jack-staff and no black smoke issuing from the chimneys. After ten more minutes the town is dead again, and the town drunkard asleep by the skids once more.

In what ways does Twain's passage illustrate the impact of the transportation revolution on daily life in the United States?

The Social Impact of the Industrial Revolution

The Industrial Revolution transfigured the social life of Europe and the world. Although much of Europe remained bound by its traditional ways, the social impact of the Industrial Revolution was already being felt in the first half of the nineteenth century, and future avenues of growth were becoming apparent. Vast changes in the number of people and where they lived were already dramatically evident.

Population Growth

Population increases had begun in the eighteenth century, but they became dramatic in the nineteenth century. In 1750, the total European population stood at an estimated 140 million; by 1800, it had increased to 187 million and by 1850 to 266 million, almost twice its 1750 level. The key to the expansion of population was the decline in death rates evident throughout Europe. Two major factors explain this decline: fewer premature deaths and better nutrition. The number of deaths from famines, epidemics, and war dropped substantially. Major epidemic diseases in particular, such as plague and smallpox, became less common, although small-scale epidemics did occur. The ordinary death rate also declined as a general increase in the food supply, already evident in the agricultural revolution of Britain in the late eighteenth century, spread to more areas. More food enabled a greater number of people to be better fed and therefore more resistant to disease. Famine largely disappeared from western Europe, although there were dramatic exceptions in isolated areas where overpopulation magnified the problem of rural poverty. In Ireland, it produced the century's great catastrophe.

The Great Hunger Ireland was one of the most oppressed areas in western Europe. The predominantly Catholic peasant population rented land from mostly absentee British Protestant landlords whose primary concern was collecting their rents. Irish peasants lived in mud hovels in desperate poverty. The cultivation of the potato, a nutritious and relatively easy crop to grow that produced three times as much food per acre as grain, gave Irish peasants a basic staple that enabled them to survive and even expand in numbers. Between 1781 and 1845, the Irish population doubled from four to eight million. Probably half of this population depended on the potato for survival. In the summer of 1845, the potato crop in Ireland was struck by a fungus that turned the potato black. The resulting Great Famine decimated the Irish population between 1845 and 1851. More than one million inhabitants died of starvation and disease, and almost two million more emigrated to the United States and Britain. Of all the European nations, only Ireland lost population in the nineteenth century.

The flight of so many Irish to America reminds us that the traditional safety valve for overpopulation has always been emigration. Between 1821 and 1850, the number of emigrants from Europe averaged about 110,000 a year. Most of these emigrants came from places like Ireland and southern Germany, where peasant life had been reduced to a marginal existence. More often than emigration, however, the rural masses sought a solution to their poverty by moving to towns and cities within their own countries to find work. It should not astonish us then that the first half of the nineteenth century was a period of rapid urbanization.

The Growth of Cities

Cities and towns grew dramatically in the first half of the nineteenth century, a phenomenon related to industrialization. Cities had traditionally been centers for princely courts, government and military offices, churches, and commerce. By 1850, especially in Great Britain and Belgium, they were rapidly becoming places for manufacturing and industry. With the steam engine, entrepreneurs could locate their manufacturing plants in urban centers where they had ready access to transportation facilities and influxes of people from the countryside looking for work.

In 1800, Great Britain had one major city, London, with a population of one million and six cities that were home to 50,000 to 100,000 people. Fifty years later, London's population had swelled to 2,363,000, and there were nine cities with populations over 100,000 and eighteen with populations between 50,000 and 100,000. More than 50 percent of the British population now lived in towns and cities. Urban populations also grew on the Continent, but less dramatically.

Urban Living Conditions in the Early Industrial Era The dramatic growth of cities in the first half of the nineteenth century produced miserable living conditions for many of the inhabitants. Of course, this had been true for centuries in European cities, but the rapid urbanization associated with the Industrial Revolution intensified the problems and made these wretched conditions all the more apparent. Wealthy, middle-class inhabitants, as usual, insulated themselves as best they could, often living in suburbs or the outer ring of the city where they could have individual houses and gardens. In the inner ring of the city stood the small row houses, some with gardens, of the artisans and lower middle class. Finally, located in the center of most industrial towns were the row houses of the industrial workers. This report on working-class housing in the British city of Birmingham in 1843 gives an idea of the general conditions they faced:

> The courts [of working-class row houses] are extremely numerous;...a very large portion of the poorer classes of the

© Oxford Science Archive, Oxford, UK/HIP/Art Resource, NY

A New Industrial Town. Cities and towns grew dramatically in Britain in the first half of the nineteenth century, largely as a result of industrialization. Pictured here is Saltaire, a model textile factory and town founded near Bradford by Titus Salt in 1851. To facilitate the transportation of goods, the town was built on the Leeds and Liverpool canals.

inhabitants reside in them. . . . The courts vary in the number of the houses which they contain, from four to twenty, and most of these houses are three stories high, and built, as it is termed, back to back. There is a wash-house, an ash-pit, and a privy at the end, or on one side of the court, and not unfrequently one or more pigsties and heaps of manure. Generally speaking, the privies in the old courts are in a most filthy condition. Many which we have inspected were in a state which renders it impossible for us to conceive how they could be used; they were without doors and overflowing with filth.[1]

Rooms were not large and were frequently overcrowded, as this government report of 1838 revealed: "I entered several of the tenements. In one of them, on the ground floor, I found six persons occupying a very small room, two in bed, ill with fever. In the room above this were two more persons in one bed, ill with fever." Another report said, "There were 63 families where there were at least five persons to one bed; and there were some in which even six were packed in one bed, lying at the top and bottom—children and adults."[2]

Sanitary conditions in these towns were appalling. Due to the lack of municipal direction, city streets were often used as sewers and open drains: "In the centre of this street is a gutter, into which potato parings, the refuse of animal and vegetable matters of all kinds, the dirty water from the washing of clothes and of the houses, are all poured, and there they stagnate and putrefy."[3] Unable to deal with human excrement, cities in the new industrial era smelled horrible and were extraordinarily unhealthy. Towns and cities were fundamentally death traps. As deaths outnumbered births in most large cities in the first half of the nineteenth century, only a constant flow of people from rural areas kept them alive and growing.

Urban Reformers To many of the well-to-do middle classes, this situation presented a clear danger to society. Were not these masses of workers, sunk in crime, filth, disease, and immorality, a potential threat to their own well-being? Might not the masses be organized and used by unscrupulous demagogues to overthrow the established order? Some observers, however, wondered if the workers could be held responsible for their fate. One of the best of a new breed of urban reformers was Edwin Chadwick (1800–1890). Chadwick became obsessed with eliminating the poverty and squalor of the metropolitan areas. As secretary of the Poor Law Commission, he initiated a passionate search for detailed facts about the living conditions of the working classes. After three years of investigation, Chadwick summarized the results in his *Report on the Condition of the Labouring Population of Great Britain,* published in 1842. In it he concluded that "the various forms of epidemic, endemic, and other disease" were directly caused by the "atmospheric impurities produced by decomposing animal and vegetable substances, by damp and filth, and close overcrowded dwellings [prevailing] amongst the population in every

part of the kingdom." Such conditions, he argued, could be eliminated. As to the means, "The primary and most important measures, and at the same time the most practicable, and within the recognized province of public administration, are drainage, the removal of all refuse of habitations, streets, and roads, and the improvement of the supplies of water."[4] In other words, Chadwick was advocating a system of modern sanitary reforms consisting of efficient sewers and a supply of piped water. Six years after his report and largely due to his efforts, Britain's first Public Health Act created the National Board of Health, which was empowered to form local boards that would establish modern sanitary systems.

New Social Classes: The Industrial Middle Class

The rise of industrial capitalism added a new group to the middle class. The bourgeoisie or middle class was not new; it had existed since the emergence of cities in the Middle Ages. Originally, the bourgeois was a burgher or town dweller—a merchant, official, artisan, lawyer, or man of letters—who enjoyed a special set of rights from the charter of his town. As wealthy townspeople bought land, the term *bourgeois* came to include people involved in commerce, industry, and banking as well as professionals, such as lawyers, teachers, and physicians, and government officials at varying levels. At the lower end of the economic scale were master craftspeople and shopkeepers.

Lest we make the industrial middle class too much of an abstraction, we need to look at who the new industrial entrepreneurs actually were. These were the people who constructed the factories, purchased the machines, and figured out where the markets were. Their qualities included resourcefulness, single-mindedness, resolution, initiative, vision, ambition, and often greed. As Jedediah Strutt, a cotton manufacturer said, "Getting of money . . . is the main business of the life of men." But this was not an easy task. The early industrial entrepreneurs were called on to superintend an enormous array of functions that are handled today by teams of managers; they raised capital, determined markets, set company objectives, organized the factory and its labor, and trained supervisors who could act for them. The opportunities for making money were great, but the risks were also tremendous.

By 1850, in Britain at least, the kind of traditional entrepreneurship that had fueled the Industrial Revolution was declining and being replaced by a new business aristocracy. This new generation of entrepreneurs stemmed from the professional and industrial middle classes, especially as sons inherited successful businesses established by their fathers. Increasingly, the new industrial entrepreneurs—the bankers and owners of factories and mines—came to amass much wealth and play an important role alongside the traditional landed elites of their societies. The Industrial Revolution began at a time when the agrarian world was still largely dominated by landed elites. As members of the new bourgeoisie bought great estates and acquired social respectability, they also sought political power, and in the course of the nineteenth century, their wealthiest members would merge with those old elites.

New Social Classes: Workers in the Industrial Age

At the same time that the members of the industrial middle class were seeking to reduce the barriers between themselves and the landed elite, they were also trying to separate themselves from the laboring classes below them. The working class was actually a mixture of groups in the first half of the nineteenth century. Factory workers would eventually form an industrial proletariat, but they did not yet constitute a majority of the working class in any major city, even in Britain. According to the 1851 census in Britain, while there were 1.8 million agricultural laborers and 1 million domestic servants, there were only 811,000 workers in the cotton and woolen industries, and one-third of these were still working in small workshops or in their own homes.

Working Conditions for the Industrial Working Class

Workers in the new industrial factories faced wretched working conditions. Unquestionably, in the early decades of the Industrial Revolution, "places of work," as early factories were called, were dreadful. Work hours ranged from twelve to sixteen hours a day, six days a week, with a half hour for lunch and dinner. There was no security of employment and no minimum wage. The worst conditions were endured by workers in the cotton mills, where temperatures were especially debilitating. One report noted that "in the cotton-spinning work, these creatures are kept, fourteen hours in each day, locked up, summer and winter, in a heat of from eighty to eighty-four degrees." Mills were also dirty, dusty, and unhealthy:

Not only is there not a breath of sweet air in these truly infernal scenes, but . . . there is the abominable and pernicious stink of the gas to assist in the murderous effects of the heat. In addition to the noxious effluvia of the gas, mixed with the steam, there are the dust, and what is called cotton-flyings or fuz, which the unfortunate creatures have to inhale; and . . . the notorious fact is that well constituted men are rendered old and past labour at forty years of age, and that children are rendered decrepit and deformed, and thousands upon thousands of them slaughtered by consumptions [wasting away of body tissues, especially the lungs], before they arrive at the age of sixteen.[5]

Conditions in the coal mines were also harsh. The introduction of steam power in the coal mines meant only that steam-powered engines mechanically lifted coal to the top. Inside the mines, men still bore the burden of digging the coal out while horses, mules, women, and children hauled coal carts on rails to the lift. Dangers abounded in coal mines; cave-ins, explosions, and gas fumes (called "bad air") were a way of life. The cramped conditions—tunnels often did not exceed 3 or 4 feet in height—and constant dampness in the mines resulted in deformed bodies and ruined lungs.

Both children and women were employed in large numbers in early factories and mines. Children had been an important part of the family economy in preindustrial times, working in the fields or carding and spinning wool at home with the growth of the cottage industry. In the Industrial Revolution, however, child labor was exploited more than ever and in a considerably more systematic fashion (see the box on p. 388). The owners of cotton factories appreciated certain features of child labor. Children had an especially delicate touch as spinners of cotton. Their smaller size made it easier for them to crawl under machines to gather loose cotton. Moreover, children were more easily accustomed to factory work. Above all, children represented a cheap supply of labor. In 1821, half the British population was under twenty years of age. Hence children made up a particularly abundant supply of labor, and they were paid only one-sixth to one-third of what a man was paid. In the cotton factories in 1838, children under eighteen made up 29 percent of the workforce; children as young as seven worked twelve to fifteen hours per day, six days a week, in the cotton mills.

Woman in the Mines. Women and children were often employed in the early factories and mines of the nineteenth century. As is evident in this illustration of a woman dragging a cart loaded with coal behind her, they often worked under very trying conditions.

© CORBIS

CHILD LABOR: DISCIPLINE IN THE TEXTILE MILLS

*C*hild labor was not new, but in the early Industrial Revolution it was exploited more systematically. These selections are taken from the Report of Sadler's Committee, which was commissioned in 1832 to inquire into the condition of child factory workers.

How They Kept the Children Awake

It is a very frequent thing at Mr. Marshall's [at Shrewsbury] where the least children were employed (for there were plenty working at six years of age), for Mr. Horseman to start the mill earlier in the morning than he formerly did; and provided a child should be drowsy, the overlooker walks round the room with a stick in his hand, and he touches that child on the shoulder, and says, "Come here." In a corner of the room there is an iron cistern; it is filled with water; he takes this boy, and takes him up by the legs, and dips him over head in the cistern, and sends him to work for the remainder of the day....

What means were taken to keep the children to their work?—Sometimes they would tap them over the head, or nip them over the nose, or give them a pinch of snuff, or throw water in their faces, or pull them off where they were, and job them about to keep them waking.

The Sadistic Overlooker

Samuel Downe, age 29, factory worker living near Leeds; at the age of about ten began work at Mr. Marshall's mills at Shrewsbury, where the customary hours when work was brisk were generally 5 A.M. to 8 P.M., sometimes from 5:30 A.M. to 8 or 9:

What means were taken to keep the children awake and vigilant, especially at the termination of such a day's labor as you have described?—There was generally a blow or a box, or a tap with a strap, or sometimes the hand.

Have you yourself been strapped?—Yes, most severely, till I could not bear to sit upon a chair without having pillows, and through that I left. I was strapped both on my own legs, and then I was put upon a man's back, and then strapped and buckled with two straps to an iron pillar, and flogged, and all by one overlooker; after that he took a piece of tow, and twisted it in the shape of a cord, and put it in my mouth, and tied it behind my head.

He gagged you?—Yes; and then he ordered me to run round a part of the machinery where he was overlooker, and he stood at one end, and every time I came there he struck me with a stick, which I believe was an ash plant, and which he generally carried in his hand, and sometimes he hit me, and sometimes he did not; and one of the men in the room came and begged me off, and that he let me go, and not beat me any more, and consequently he did.

You have been beaten with extraordinary severity?—Yes, I was beaten so that I had not power to cry at all, or hardly speak at one time.

What age were you at that time?—Between 10 and 11.

What kind of working conditions did children face in the mills during the early Industrial Revolution? Why were they beaten?

By 1830, women and children made up two-thirds of the cotton industry's labor. However, as the number of children employed declined under the Factory Act of 1833, their places were taken by women, who came to dominate the labor forces of the early factories. Women made up 50 percent of the labor force in textile (cotton and woolen) factories before 1870. They were mostly unskilled labor and were paid half or less of what men received. Excessive working hours for women were outlawed in 1844, but only in textile factories and mines; not until 1867 were they outlawed in craft workshops.

The employment of children and women in large part represents a continuation of a preindustrial kinship pattern. The cottage industry had always involved the efforts of the entire family, and it seemed perfectly natural to continue this pattern. Men migrating from the countryside to industrial towns and cities took their wives and children with them into the factory or into the mines. Of 136 employees in Robert Peel's factory at Bury in 1801, 95 came from twenty-six families. The impetus for this family work often came from the family itself. The factory owner Jedediah Strutt was opposed to employing children under ten but was forced by parents to take children as young as seven.

The employment of large numbers of women in factories did not produce a significant transformation in female working patterns, as was once assumed. Studies of urban households in France and Britain, for example, have revealed that throughout the nineteenth century, traditional types of female labor still predominated in the women's work world. In 1851, fully 40 percent of the working women in Britain were employed as domestic servants. In France, the largest group of female workers, 40 percent, worked in agriculture. Only 20 percent of female workers labored in Britain's factories, and only 10 percent in France. Regional and local studies have also indicated that most of them were single women. Few married women worked outside the home.

The laws that limited the work hours of children and women also began to break up the traditional kinship pattern of work and led to a new pattern based on a separation of work and home. Men were expected to shoulder the primary work obligations while women assumed daily control of the family and performed low-paying jobs such as laundry work that could be done in the home. Domestic industry made it possible for women to continue their contributions to family survival.

Efforts at Change: The Workers

Before long, workers in Great Britain began to look to the formation of labor organizations to gain decent wages and working conditions. Despite government opposition, new associations known as **trade unions** were formed by skilled workers in a number of new industries, including the cotton spinners, ironworkers, coal miners, and shipwrights. These unions served two purposes. One was to preserve their own workers' positions by limiting entry into their trade; another was to gain benefits from the employers. These early trade unions had limited goals. They favored a working-class struggle against employers, but only to win improvements for the members of their own trades. The largest and most successful was the Amalgamated Society of Engineers, formed in 1850. Its provision of generous unemployment benefits in return for a small weekly payment was precisely the kind of practical gains these trade unions sought.

Luddites Trade unionism was not the only type of collective action by workers in the early decades of the Industrial Revolution. The Luddites were skilled craftsmen in the Midlands and northern England who in 1812 physically attacked the machines that they believed threatened their livelihoods. Their actions failed to stop the industrial mechanization of Britain, but the inability of twelve thousand troops to track down the culprits provides stunning evidence of the local support they enjoyed.

Chartism A more meaningful expression of the attempts of British workers to improve their condition developed in the movement known as Chartism. Its aim was to achieve political democracy. It took its name from the People's Charter, a document drawn up in 1838 by the London Working Men's Association. The charter demanded universal male suffrage, payment for members of Parliament, the elimination of property qualifications for members of Parliament, and annual sessions of Parliament.

Two national petitions incorporating these demands gained millions of signatures and were presented to Parliament in 1839 and 1842. Chartism attempted to encourage change through peaceful, constitutional means, although there was an underlying threat of force, as is evident in the Chartist slogan, "Peacefully if we can, forcibly if we must." In 1842, Chartist activists organized a general strike on behalf of their goals, but it had little success.

Despite the pressures exerted by Chartists, both national petitions were rejected by the members of Parliament, who were not at all ready for political democracy. As one member said, universal suffrage would be "fatal to all the purposes for which government exists" and was "utterly incompatible with the very existence of civilization." After 1848, Chartism as a movement had largely played itself out. It had never really posed a serious threat to the British establishment, but it had not been a total failure either. Its true significance stemmed from its ability to arouse and organize millions of working-class men and women, to give them a sense of working-class consciousness that they had not really possessed before. The political education of working people was important to the ultimate acceptance of the goals expressed in the People's Charter.

Efforts at Change: Reformers and Government

Efforts to improve the worst conditions of the industrial factory system also came from outside the ranks of the working classes. Reform-minded individuals, be they factory owners who felt twinges of conscience or social reformers in Parliament, campaigned against the evils of the industrial factory, especially condemning the abuse of children. Their efforts eventually met with success, especially in the reform-minded decades of the 1830s and 1840s.

A Trade Union Membership Card. Skilled workers in a number of new industries formed trade unions in an attempt to gain higher wages, better working conditions, and special benefits. The scenes at the bottom of this membership card for the Associated Shipwright's Society illustrate some of the medical and social benefits it provided for its members.

The Factory Act of 1833 stipulated that children between nine and thirteen could work only eight hours a day; those between thirteen and eighteen, twelve hours. Another piece of legislation in 1833 required that children between nine and thirteen have at least two hours of elementary education during the working day. In 1847, the Ten Hours Act reduced the workday for children between thirteen and eighteen to ten hours. Women were also now included in the ten-hour limitation. In 1842, the Coal Mines Act eliminated the employment of boys under ten and all women in mines. Eventually, men too would benefit from the move to restrict factory hours.

TIMELINE

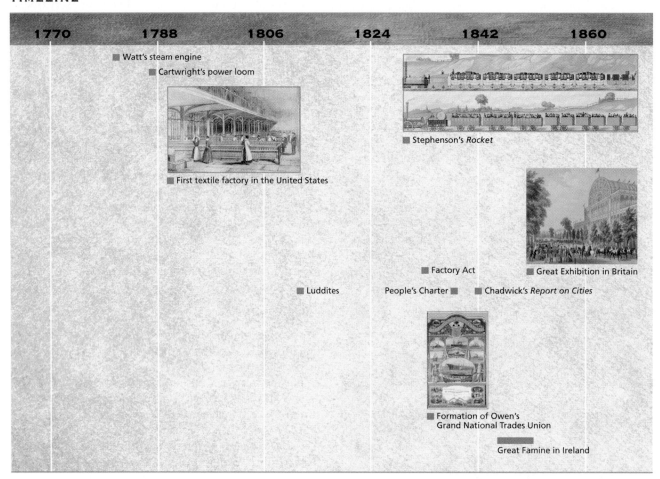

1770   1788   1806   1824   1842   1860

■ Watt's steam engine
■ Cartwright's power loom

■ First textile factory in the United States

■ Stephenson's *Rocket*

■ Factory Act   ■ Great Exhibition in Britain

■ Luddites   People's Charter ■   ■ Chadwick's *Report on Cities*

■ Formation of Owen's
Grand National Trades Union

Great Famine in Ireland

CONCLUSION

The Industrial Revolution became one of the major forces of change in the nineteenth century as it led Western civilization into the industrial era that has characterized the modern world. Beginning in Britain, its spread to the Continent and the new American nation ensured its growth and domination of the Western world.

The Industrial Revolution seemed to prove to Europeans the underlying assumption of the Scientific Revolution of the seventeenth century—that human beings were capable of dominating nature. By rationally manipulating the material environment for human benefit, people could create new levels of material prosperity and produce machines not dreamed of in their wildest imaginings. Lost in the excitement of the Industrial Revolution were the voices that pointed to the dehumanization of the workforce and the alienation from one's work, one's associates, oneself, and the natural world.

The Industrial Revolution also transformed the social world of Europe. The rise of an industrial proletariat produced a whole new force for change. The development of a wealthy industrial middle class presented a challenge to the long-term hegemony of landed wealth. Though that wealth had been threatened by the fortunes of commerce, it had never been overturned. But the new bourgeoisie was more demanding. How, in some places, this new industrial bourgeoisie came to play a larger role in the affairs of state will become evident in the next chapter.

NOTES

1. Quoted in E. R. Pike, *Human Documents of the Industrial Revolution in Britain* (London, 1966), p. 320.
2. Ibid., pp. 314, 343.
3. Ibid., p. 315.
4. Ibid., pp. 343–344.
5. Ibid., pp. 60–61.

SUGGESTIONS FOR FURTHER READING

The well-written work by **D. Landes, *The Unbound Prometheus: Technological Change and Industrial Development in Western Europe from 1750 to the Present*** (Cambridge, 1969), is a good introduction to the Industrial Revolution. Interesting collections of essays can be found in **P. Mathias and J. A. Davis, eds., *The First Industrial Revolutions*** (Oxford, 1989), and **M. Teich and R. Porter, eds., *The Industrial Revolution in National Context: Europe and the USA*** (Cambridge, 1996). See also **D. Fisher, *The Industrial Revolution*** (New York, 1992). For a broader perspective, see **P. Stearns, *The Industrial Revolution in World History*** (Boulder, Colo., 1993). On the Industrial Revolution in Britain, see **K. Morgan, *The Birth of Industrial Britain: Economic Change, 1750–1850*** (London, 1999); **P. Mathias, *The First Industrial Nation: An Economic History of Britain, 1700–1914*,** 2d ed. (New York, 1983); and **R. Brown, *Society and Economy in Modern Britain, 1700–1850*** (London, 1991). On the spread of industrialization to the Continent, see **T. Kemp, *Industrialization in Nineteenth-Century Europe*,** 2d ed. (London, 1985).

Given the importance of Great Britain in the Industrial Revolution, a number of books are available that place it in a broader context. See **E. J. Evans, *The Forging of the Modern State: Early Industrial Britain, 1783–1870*** (London, 1983), and **P. K. O'Brien and R. Quinault, eds., *The Industrial Revolution and British Society*** (New York, 1993).

The early industrialization of the United States is examined in **B. Hindle and S. Lubar, *Engines of Change: The American Industrial Revolution, 1790–1860*** (Washington, D.C., 1986). On the economic ties between Great Britain and the United States, see **D. Jeremy, *Transatlantic Industrial Revolution: The Diffusion of Textile Technology Between Britain and America, 1790–1830*** (Cambridge, Mass., 1981).

A general discussion of population growth in Europe can be found in **T. McKeown, *The Modern Rise of Population*** (London,

1976). For an examination of urban growth, see the classic work of **A. F. Weber, *The Growth of Cities in the Nineteenth Century: A Study in Statistics*** (Ithaca, N.Y., 1963); **A. R. Sutcliffe, *Towards the Planned City: Germany, Britain, the United States and France, 1780–1914*** (Oxford, 1981); and **L. D. Schwarz, *London in the Age of Industrialization*** (New York, 1992). **C. Kinealy, *A Death-Dealing Famine: The Great Hunger in Ireland*** (Chicago, 1997), is a good account of the great Irish tragedy. Many of the works cited here have much information on the social impact of the Industrial Revolution, but additional material is available in **F. Crouzet, *The First Industrialists: The Problems of Origins*** (Cambridge, 1985), on British entrepreneurs; **J. Merriman, *The Margins of City Life*** (New York, 1991), on French cities; **P. Pilbeam, *The Middle Classes in Europe, 1789–1914*** (Basingstoke, England, 1990); and **T. Koditschek, *Class Formation and Urban Industrial Society*** (New York, 1990). **M. J. Maynes, *Taking the Hard Road*** (Chapel Hill, N.C., 1995), offers a glimpse into the lives of workers. A classic work on female labor patterns is **L. A. Tilly** and **J. W. Scott, *Women, Work, and Family*** (New York, 1978). See also **J. Lown, *Women and Industrialization: Gender at Work in Nineteenth-Century England*** (Minneapolis, Minn., 1990), and **L. L. Frader,** "Doing Capitalism's Work: Women in the Western European Industrial Economy," in **R. Bridenthal, S. M. Stuard, and M. E. Wiesner, eds., *Becoming Visible*,** 3d ed. (Boston, 1998).

Thomson NOW! Enter *ThomsonNOW* using the access card that is available for *Western Civilization: A Brief History*. *ThomsonNOW* will help you understand this chapter with lesson plans generated for your needs. In addition, you can read the following documents, and many more, online:

Adam Smith, selected chapters from *The Wealth of Nations*
Charles Dickens, excerpts from *Hard Times*
Alexis de Tocqueville, excerpts from *Democracy in America*

WESTERN CIVILIZATION RESOURCES

Visit the Web site for *Western Civilization: A Brief History* for resources specific to this book:

http://www.thomsonedu.com/history/spielvogel

For a variety of tools to help you succeed in this course, visit the Western Civilization Resource Center at

http://history.wadsworth.com/spielvogel

Included are quizzes, images, documents, interactive simulations, maps and timelines, movie explorations, and a wealth of other sources.

21

REACTION, REVOLUTION, AND ROMANTICISM, 1815–1850

CHAPTER OUTLINE AND FOCUS QUESTIONS

The Conservative Order, 1815–1830

☐ What were the goals of the Congress of Vienna and the Concert of Europe, and how successful were they in achieving those goals?

The Ideologies of Change

☐ What were the main tenets of conservatism, liberalism, nationalism, and utopian socialism, and what role did each ideology play in Europe in the first half of the nineteenth century?

Revolution and Reform, 1830–1850

☐ What forces for change were present in France and Great Britain between 1830 and 1848, and how did each nation respond?

☐ What were the causes of the revolutions of 1848, and why did they fail?

Culture in an Age of Reaction and Revolution: The Mood of Romanticism

☐ What were the characteristics of Romanticism, and how were they reflected in literature, art, and music?

CRITICAL THINKING

☐ In what ways were intellectual and artistic developments of the first half of the nineteenth century related to the political and social forces of the age?

A meeting of the Congress of Vienna

Scala/Art Resource, NY (Museo del Risorgimento, Milan)

*I*N SEPTEMBER 1814, hundreds of foreigners began to converge on Vienna, the capital city of the Austrian Empire. Many were members of European royalty–kings, princes, archdukes, and their wives–accompanied by their diplomatic advisers and scores of servants. Their congenial host was the Austrian emperor Francis I, who never tired of regaling Vienna's guests with concerts, glittering balls, sumptuous feasts, and hunting parties. One participant re-membered, "Eating, fireworks, public illuminations. For eight or ten days, I haven't been able to work at all. What a life!" Of course, not every waking hour was spent in pleasure during this gathering of notables, known to history as the Congress of Vienna. These people were also representatives of all the states that had fought Napoleon, and their real business was to arrange a final peace settlement after almost a decade of war. On June 8, 1815, they completed their task.

The forces of upheaval unleashed during the French revolutionary and Napoleonic wars were temporarily quieted in 1815 as rulers sought to restore stability by reestablishing much of the old order to a Europe weary of war. Kings, landed aristocrats, and bureaucratic elites regained their control over domestic governments, while internationally the forces of conservatism tried to maintain the new status quo; some states even used military force to intervene in the internal affairs of other countries in their desire to crush revolutions.

But the Western world had been changed, and it would not readily go back to the old system. New ideologies, especially liberalism and nationalism, both products of the revolutionary upheaval initiated in France, had become too powerful to be contained. Not content with the status quo, the forces of change gave rise first to the revolts and revolutions that periodically shook Europe in the 1820s and 1830s and then to the widespread revolutions of 1848. Some of the revolutions and revolutionaries were successful; most were not. Although the old order usually appeared to have prevailed, by 1850 it was apparent that its days were numbered. This perception was reinforced by the changes wrought by the Industrial Revolution. Together the forces unleashed by the French Revolution and the Industrial Revolution made it impossible to turn back. Nevertheless, although these two revolutions initiated what historians like to call the modern European world, remnants of the old persisted in the midst of the new.♦

The Conservative Order, 1815–1830

After the defeat of Napoleon, European rulers moved to restore the old order. This was the goal of the great powers—Great Britain, Austria, Prussia, and Russia—when they met at the Congress of Vienna in September 1814 to arrange a final peace settlement. The leader of the congress was the Austrian foreign minister, Prince Klemens von Metternich (1773–1859), who claimed that he was guided at Vienna by the **principle of legitimacy**. To keep peace and stability in Europe, he said it was necessary to restore the legitimate monarchs who would preserve traditional institutions. This had already been done in France by restoring the Bourbon monarchy.

In fact, however, the principle of legitimacy was largely ignored elsewhere. At the Congress of Vienna, the great powers all grabbed land to add to their states. They believed that they were forming a new **balance of power** that would keep any one country from dominating Europe. For example, to balance Russian gains, Prussia and Austria had been strengthened (see Map 21.1). According to Metternich, this arrangement had clearly avoided a great danger: "Prussia and Austria are completing their systems of defence; united, the two monarchies form an unconquerable barrier against the enterprises of any conquering prince who might perhaps once again occupy the throne of France or that of Russia."[1]

Conservative Domination

The peace arrangements of 1815 were the beginning of a conservative reaction determined to contain the liberal and nationalist forces unleashed by the French Revolution. Metternich and his kind were representatives of the **ideology** known as **conservatism** (see the box on p. 395). As a modern political philosophy, conservatism dates from 1790 when Edmund Burke wrote *Reflections on the Revolution in France* in reaction to the French Revolution, especially its radical republican and democratic ideas.

Metternich and the Congress of Vienna.
Prince Klemens von Metternich, the foreign minister of Austria, played a major role at the Congress of Vienna as the chief exponent of the principle of legitimacy. This painting by Engelbert Seibertz shows a group of the statesmen who participated in the discussions at Vienna. From left to right, they are Talleyrand, the French representative; Montgelas, the Bavarian minister; Hardenberg, the Prussian minister; Metternich, who appears to be the focus of attention in the group; and von Gentz, a German political theorist.

MAP 21.1 **Europe After the Congress of Vienna, 1815.** The Congress of Vienna imposed order on Europe based on the principles of monarchical government and a balance of power. Monarchs were restored in France, Spain, and other states recently under Napoleon's control, and much territory changed hands, often at the expense of small and weak states. ❓ How did Europe's major powers manipulate territory to decrease the probability that France could again threaten the Continent's stability? ◀ **View an animated version of this map or related maps at** http://thomsonedu.com/history/spielvogel

Burke maintained that society was a contract, but "the state ought not to be considered as nothing better than a partnership agreement in a trade of pepper and coffee, to be taken up for a temporary interest and to be dissolved by the fancy of the parties."[2] No one generation has the right to destroy this partnership; each generation has the duty to preserve and transmit it to the next. Burke advised against the violent overthrow of a government by revolution, but he did not reject the possibility of change. Sudden change was unacceptable, but that did not eliminate gradual or evolutionary improvements.

Most conservatives favored obedience to political authority, believed that organized religion was crucial to social order, hated revolutionary upheavals, and were unwilling to accept either the liberal demands for civil liberties and representative governments or the nationalistic aspirations generated by the French revolutionary era. The community took precedence over individual rights. After 1815, the political philosophy of conservatism was supported by hereditary monarchs, government bureaucracies, landowning aristocracies, and revived churches, Protestant and Catholic alike. The conservative forces seemed dominant both internationally and domestically after 1815.

The Concert of Europe One method used by the great powers to maintain the new status quo they had constructed was the Concert of Europe, according to which Great Britain, Russia, Prussia, and Austria (and later France) agreed to meet periodically in conferences to discuss their common interests and examine measures that "will be judged most salutary . . . for the maintenance of peace in Europe."

Eventually, the five great powers formed the Quintuple Alliance and adopted a **principle of intervention** that was based on the right of the great powers to send armies into countries where revolutions were occurring to restore legitimate monarchs to their thrones. Britain refused to agree to the principle, arguing that it had never been the intention of the alliance to interfere in the internal affairs of other states. Ignoring the British response, Austria, Prussia, Russia, and France used military intervention to defeat revolutionary movements in Spain and Italy and to restore legitimate (and conservative) monarchs to their thrones. This success for the policy of intervention came at a price, however. The Concert of Europe had broken down when the British rejected Metternich's principle of intervention and ultimately prevented the Continental

THE VOICE OF CONSERVATISM: METTERNICH OF AUSTRIA

There was no greater symbol of conservatism in the first half of the nineteenth century than Prince Klemens von Metternich of Austria. Metternich played a crucial role at the Congress of Vienna and worked tirelessly for thirty years to repress the "revolutionary seed," as he called it, that had been spread to Europe by the "military despotism of Bonaparte."

Klemens von Metternich, *Memoirs*

We are convinced that society can no longer be saved without strong and vigorous resolutions on the part of the Governments still free in their opinions and actions.

We are also convinced that this may be, if the Governments face the truth, if they free themselves from all illusion, if they join their ranks and take their stand on a line of correct, unambiguous, and frankly announced principles.

By this course the monarchs will fulfill the duties imposed upon them by Him who, by entrusting them with power, has charged them to watch over the maintenance of justice, and the rights of all, to avoid the paths of error, and tread firmly in the way of truth....

If the same elements of destruction which are now throwing society into convulsions have existed in all ages—for every age has seen immoral and ambitious men, hypocrites, men of heated imaginations, wrong motives, and wild projects—yet ours, by the single fact of the liberty of the press, possesses more than any preceding age the means of contact, seduction, and attraction whereby to act on these different classes of men.

We are certainly not alone in questioning if society can exist with the liberty of the press, a scourge unknown to the world before the latter half of the seventeenth century, and restrained until the end of the eighteenth, with scarcely any expectations but England—a part of Europe separated from the continent by the sea, as well as by her language and by her peculiar manners.

The first principle to be followed by the monarchs, united as they are by the coincidence of their desires and opinions, should be that of maintaining the stability of political institutions against the disorganized excitement which has taken possession of men's minds; the immutability of principles against the madness of their interpretation; and respect for laws actually in force against a desire for their destruction....

The first and greatest concern for the immense majority of every nation is the stability of the laws, and their uninterrupted action—never their change. Therefore, let the Governments govern, let them maintain the groundwork of their institutions, both ancient and modern; for if it is at all times dangerous to touch them, it certainly would not now, in the general confusion, be wise to do so....

Let them maintain religious principles in all their purity, and not allow the faith to be attacked and morality interpreted according to the social contract or the visions of foolish sectarians.

Let them suppress Secret Societies, that gangrene of society....

To every great State determined to survive the storm there still remain many chances of salvation, and a strong union between the States on the principles we have announced will overcome the storm itself.

Based on Metternich's discussion, how would you define conservatism? What experience conditioned Metternich's ideas? Based on this selection, what policies do you think Metternich would have wanted his government to pursue?

---

powers from intervening in the revolutions in Latin America.

The Revolt of Latin America Whereas much of North America had been freed of European domination in the eighteenth century by the American Revolution, Latin America remained in the hands of the Spanish and Portuguese. However, when the Bourbon monarchy of Spain was toppled by Napoleon Bonaparte, Spanish authority in its colonial empire was weakened. By 1810, the disintegration of royal power in Argentina had led to that nation's independence. In Venezuela, a bitter struggle for independence was led by Simón Bolívar, hailed as "the Liberator." His forces freed Colombia in 1819 and Venezuela in 1821. A second liberator was José de San Martín, who freed Chile in 1817 and then in 1821 moved on to Lima, Peru, the center of Spanish authority. He was soon joined by Bolívar, who assumed the task of crushing the last significant Spanish army in 1824. Mexico and the Central American provinces also achieved their freedom, and by 1825, after Portugal had recognized the independence of Brazil, almost all of Latin America had been freed of colonial domination (see Map 21.2).

Although political independence brought economic independence, old patterns were quickly reestablished. Instead of Spain and Portugal, Great Britain now dominated the Latin American economy. British merchants moved in in large numbers, while British investors poured in funds, especially in the mining industry. Old trade patterns soon reemerged. Because Latin America served as a source of raw materials and foodstuffs for the industrializing nations of Europe and the United States, exports—especially wheat, tobacco, wool, sugar, coffee, and hides—to the North Atlantic countries increased noticeably. At the same time, finished consumer goods, especially textiles, were imported in increasing quantities,

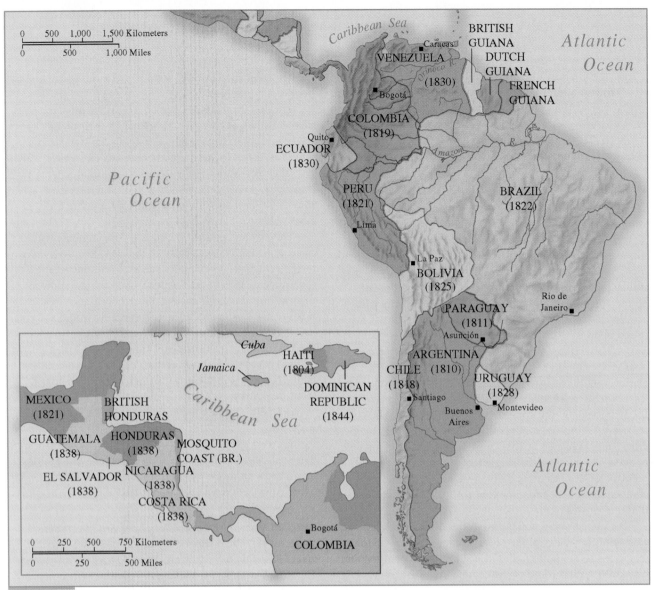

MAP 21.2 **Latin America in the First Half of the Nineteenth Century.** Latin American colonies took advantage of Spain's weakness during the Napoleonic wars to fight for independence, beginning with Argentina in 1810 and spreading throughout the region over the next decade with the help of leaders like Simón Bolívar and José de San Martín. ❓ How many South American countries are sources of rivers that feed the Amazon, and roughly what percentage of the continent is contained within the Amazon's watershed? 🌐 **View an animated version of this map or related maps at** http://thomsonedu.com/history/spielvogel

causing a decline in industrial production in Latin America. As in India, the emphasis on exporting raw materials and importing finished products ensured the ongoing domination of the Latin American economy by foreigners.

The Greek Revolt The principle of intervention proved to be a double-edged sword. Designed to prevent revolution, it could also be used to support revolution if the great powers found it in their interests to do so. In 1821, the Greeks revolted against their Ottoman Turkish masters. Although subject to Muslim control for four hundred

years, they had been allowed to maintain their language and their Greek Orthodox faith. A revival of Greek national sentiment at the beginning of the nineteenth century added to the growing desire for liberation. The Greek revolt was soon transformed into a noble cause by an outpouring of European sentiment for the Greeks' struggle. In 1827, a combined British and French fleet went to Greece and defeated a large Ottoman armada. A year later, Russia declared war on the Ottoman Empire and invaded its European provinces of Moldavia and Wallachia. By the Treaty of Adrianople in 1829, which ended the Russian-Turkish war, the Russians

The Balkans by 1830

received a protectorate over the two provinces. By the same treaty, the Ottoman Empire agreed to allow Russia, France, and Britain to decide the fate of Greece. In 1830, the three powers declared Greece an independent kingdom, and two years later, a new royal dynasty was established. The revolution in Greece had been successful only because the great powers themselves supported it. The conservative domination was still largely intact.

Conservatives in the European States

Between 1815 and 1830, the conservative domination of Europe evident in the Concert of Europe was also apparent in domestic affairs as conservative governments throughout Europe worked to preserve the old order.

Great Britain   In 1815, Great Britain was governed by the aristocratic landowning classes that controlled both houses of Parliament. Within Parliament, there were two political factions, the Tories and the Whigs. Both were still dominated by members of the landed classes, although the Whigs were beginning to gain support from the new industrial middle class. Tory ministers largely ran the government until 1830 and had little desire to change the existing political and electoral system.

Restoration in France   In 1814, the Bourbon family was restored to the throne of France in the person of Louis XVIII (1814–1824). Louis understood the need to accept some of the changes brought to France by the revolution and Napoleon. He accepted Napoleon's Civil Code, with its recognition of the principle of equality before the law. The property rights of individuals who had purchased confiscated lands during the revolution were also preserved. In 1824, Louis died and was succeeded by his brother, who became Charles X (1824–1830). Charles's attempt to restore the old regime as far as possible led to public outrage. By 1830, France was on the brink of another revolution.

The Italian States   The Congress of Vienna had established nine states in Italy, including the kingdom of Sardinia in the north, ruled by the house of Savoy; the kingdom of the Two Sicilies (Naples and Sicily); the Papal States; a handful of small duchies ruled by relatives of the Austrian emperor; and the important northern

provinces of Lombardy and Venetia, which were now part of the Austrian Empire. Italy was largely under Austria's thumb, and all the states had extremely reactionary governments eager to smother any liberal or nationalist sentiment.

Repression in Central Europe   After 1815, the forces of repression were particularly successful in central Europe. The Habsburg empire and its chief agent, Prince Klemens von Metternich, played an

Italy, 1815

important role. Metternich boasted, "You see in me the chief Minister of Police in Europe. I keep an eye on everything. My contacts are such that nothing escapes me."[3] Metternich's spies were everywhere, searching for evidence of liberal or nationalist plots. Metternich worried too much in 1815. Although both liberalism and nationalism emerged in the German states and the Austrian Empire, they were initially weak as central Europe tended to remain under the domination of aristocratic landowning classes and autocratic, centralized monarchies.

The Vienna settlement in 1815 had recognized the existence of thirty-eight sovereign states (called the Germanic Confederation) in what had once been the Holy Roman Empire. Austria and Prussia were the two major powers; the other, smaller states varied considerably in size. The confederation had little real power. It had no true executive, and its only central organ was the federal diet, which needed the consent of all member states to take action.

The Austrian Empire was a multinational state, a collection of different peoples under the Habsburg emperor, who provided a common bond. The empire contained people of eleven ethnicities, including Germans, Czechs, Slovaks, Magyars (Hungarians), Romanians, Slovenes, Poles, Serbs, and Italians. The Germans, accounting for only a quarter of the population, were economically the most advanced and played a leading role in governing Austria. Although these national groups began to favor the belief that each national group had the right to its own system of government, Metternich managed to repress the nationalist forces and hold the empire together.

Russia: Autocracy of the Tsars   At the beginning of the nineteenth century, Russia was overwhelmingly rural, agricultural, and autocratic. The Russian tsar was still regarded as a divine-right monarch. Alexander I (1801–1825) had been raised in the ideas of the Enlightenment and initially seemed willing to make reforms. He relaxed

Private Collection/The Bridgeman Art Library International

Portrait of Nicholas I. Tsar Nicholas I was a reactionary ruler who sought to prevent rebellion in Russia by strengthening the government bureaucracy, increasing censorship, and suppressing individual freedom by the use of political police. One of his enemies remarked about his facial characteristics: "The sharply retreating forehead and the lower jaw were expressive of iron will and feeble intelligence."

censorship, freed political prisoners, and reformed the educational system. But after the defeat of Napoleon, Alexander became a reactionary, and his government reverted to strict and arbitrary censorship. His brother Nicholas I (1825–1855), who succeeded him, became a strict reactionary after a military revolt at the beginning of his reign. Nicholas strengthened both the bureaucracy and the secret police to maintain order. There would be no revolutions in Russia during the rest of his reign; if he could help it, there would be none in Europe either. Contemporaries called him the Policeman of Europe because of his willingness to use Russian troops to crush uprisings.

The Ideologies of Change

Although conservative forces were in the ascendancy from 1815 to 1830, powerful movements for change were also at work. These depended on ideas embodied in a series of political philosophies or ideologies that came into their own in the first half of the nineteenth century.

Liberalism

One of these ideologies was **liberalism**, which owed much to the Enlightenment of the eighteenth century and the American and French Revolutions at the end of that century. It was based on the belief that people should be as free from restraint as possible. This opinion is evident in both economic and political liberalism.

Economic Liberalism Also called classical economics, economic liberalism has as its primary tenet the concept of laissez-faire, the belief that the state should not interrupt the free play of natural economic forces, especially supply and demand. Government should not interfere with the economic liberty of the individual and should restrict itself to only three primary functions: defense of the country, police protection of individuals, and the construction and maintenance of public works too expensive for individuals to undertake.

Political Liberalism Politically, liberals came to hold a common set of beliefs. Chief among them was the protection of civil liberties or the basic rights of all people, which included equality before the law; freedom of assembly, speech, and the press; and freedom from arbitrary arrest. All of these freedoms should be guaranteed by a written document, such as the American Bill of Rights. In addition to religious toleration for all, most liberals advocated separation of church and state. The right of peaceful opposition to the government in and out of parliament and the making of laws by a representative assembly (legislature) elected by qualified voters constituted two other liberal demands. Many liberals believed, then, in a constitutional monarchy or constitutional state with limits on the powers of government in order to prevent despotism and in written constitutions that would also help guarantee these rights.

Many liberals also advocated **ministerial responsibility**, a system in which ministers of the king were responsible to the legislature rather than to the king, giving the legislative branch a check on the power of the executive. Liberals in the first half of the nineteenth century also believed in a limited suffrage. While all people were entitled to equal civil rights, they should not have equal political rights. The right to vote and hold office would be open only to men who met certain property qualifications. As a political philosophy, liberalism was tied to middle-class and especially industrial middle-class men who favored the extension of voting rights so that they could share power with the landowning classes. They had little desire to let the lower classes share that power. Liberals were not democrats.

One of the most prominent advocates of liberalism in the nineteenth century was the English philosopher John Stuart Mill (1806–1873). *On Liberty,* his most famous work, published in 1859, has long been regarded as a classic statement on the liberty of the individual (see the box on p. 399). Mill argued for an "absolute freedom of opinion and sentiment on all subjects" that needed to be

THE VOICE OF LIBERALISM: JOHN STUART MILL ON LIBERTY

*J*ohn Stuart Mill was one of Britain's most famous philosophers of liberalism. Mill's *On Liberty* is viewed as a classic statement of the liberal belief in the unfettered freedom of the individual. In this excerpt, Mill defends freedom of opinion from both government and the coercion of the majority.

John Stuart Mill, *On Liberty*

The object of this Essay is to assert one very simple principle, as entitled to govern absolutely the dealings of society with the individual in the way of compulsion and control, whether the means used be physical force in the form of legal penalties, or the moral coercion of public opinion. That principle is, that the sole end for which mankind are warranted, individually or collectively, interfering with the liberty of action of any of their number, is self-protection. That the only purpose for which power can be rightfully exercised over any members of a civilized community, against his will, is to prevent harm to others. His own good, either physical or moral, is not a sufficient warrant.... These are good reasons for remonstrating with him, or reasoning with him, or persuading him, or entreating him, but not for compelling him, or visiting him with any evil in case he do otherwise....

Society can and does execute its own mandates: and if it issues wrong mandates instead of right, or any mandates at all in things with which it ought not to meddle, it practices a social tyranny more formidable than many kinds of political oppression, since, though not usually upheld by such extreme penalties, it leaves fewer means of escape, penetrating more deeply into the details of life, and enslaving the soul itself. Protection, therefore, against the tyranny of the magistrate is not enough: there needs protection also against the tyranny of prevailing opinion and feeling, against the tendency of society to impose, by other means than civil penalties, its own ideas and practices as rules of conduct on those who dissent from them....

But there is a sphere of action in which society, as distinguished from the individual has, if any, only an indirect interest; comprehending all that portion of a person's life and conduct which affects only himself, or if it also affects others, only with their free, voluntary and undeceived consent and participation.... This then is the appropriate region of human liberty. It comprises, first, the inward domain of consciousness; demanding liberty of conscience in the most comprehensive sense; liberty of thought and feeling; absolute freedom of opinion and sentiment on all subjects, practical or speculative, scientific, moral, or theological....

Let us suppose, therefore, that the government is entirely at one with the people, and never thinks of exerting any power of coercion unless in agreement with what it conceives to be their voice. But I deny the right of the people to exercise such coercion, either by themselves or by their government. The power itself is illegitimate. The best government has no more title to it than the worst. It is as noxious, or more noxious, when exerted in accordance with public opinion, than when in opposition to it. If all mankind minus one were of one opinion, and only one person were of the contrary opinion, mankind would be no more justified in silencing that one person, than he, if he had the power, would be justified in silencing mankind.... The peculiar evil of silencing the expression of an opinion is, that it is robbing the human race; posterity as well as the existing generation; those who dissent from the opinion, still more than those who hold it. If the opinion is right, they are deprived of the opportunity of exchanging error for truth: if wrong, they lose, what is almost as great a benefit, the clearer perception and livelier impression of truth, produced by its collision with error.

Based on the principles outlined here, how would you define liberalism? How do Mill's ideas fit into the concept of democracy?

---

protected from both government censorship and the tyranny of the majority.

Mill was also instrumental in expanding the meaning of liberalism by becoming an enthusiastic supporter of women's rights. When his attempt to include women in the voting reform bill of 1867 failed, Mill published an essay titled *On the Subjection of Women*, which he had written earlier with his wife, Harriet Taylor. He argued that "the legal subordination of one sex to the other" was wrong. Differences between women and men, he claimed, were due not to different natures but simply to social practices. With equal education, women could achieve as much as men. *On the Subjection of Women* would become an important work in the nineteenth-century movement for women's rights.

Nationalism

Nationalism was an even more powerful ideology for change in the nineteenth century. Nationalism arose out of an awareness of being part of a community that has common institutions, traditions, language, and customs. This community is called a nation, and the primary political loyalty of individuals would be to the nation. Nationalism did not become a popular force for change until the French Revolution. From then on, nationalists came to believe that each nationality should have its own government. Thus a divided people such as the Germans wanted national unity in a German nation-state with one central government. Subject peoples, such as the Hungarians, wanted the right to establish their own

MAP 21.3 **The Distribution of Languages in Nineteenth-Century Europe.**
Numerous languages were spoken in Europe. People who used the same language often had a
shared history and culture, which laid the seeds for growing nationalism in the nineteenth century.
Such nationalism eventually led to unification for Germany and Italy but spelled trouble for the
polyglot Habsburg empire. ❓ Look at the distribution of Germanic, Latin, and Slavic languages.
What patterns emerge, and how can you explain them? 🔊 **View an animated version of this map or**
related maps at http://thomsonedu.com/history/spielvogel

autonomy, rather than be subject to a German minority
in a multinational empire.

Nationalism threatened to upset the existing political
order, both internationally and nationally (see Map 21.3).
This meant that nationalism was fundamentally radical.
A united Germany or united Italy would upset the balance of power established in 1815. By the same token, an
independent Hungarian state would mean the breakup of
the Austrian Empire. Because many European states were

multinational, conservatives tried hard to repress the
radical threat of nationalism.

At the same time, in the first half of the nineteenth
century, nationalism and liberalism became strong allies.
Most liberals believed that freedom could be realized only
by peoples who ruled themselves. One British liberal said,
"It is in general a necessary condition of free institutions
that the boundaries of government should coincide in
the main with those of nationalities." Many nationalists

believed that once each people obtained its own state, all nations could be linked into a broader community of all humanity.

Early Socialism

In the first half of the nineteenth century, the pitiful conditions found in the slums, mines, and factories of the Industrial Revolution gave rise to another ideology for change known as **socialism**. The term eventually became associated with a Marxist analysis of human society (see Chapter 22), but early socialism was largely the product of political theorists or intellectuals who wanted to introduce equality into social conditions and believed that human cooperation was superior to the competition that characterized early industrial capitalism. To later Marxists, such ideas were impractical dreams, and they contemptuously labeled the theorists **utopian socialists**. The term has endured to this day.

The utopian socialists were against private property and the competitive spirit of early industrial capitalism. By eliminating these things and creating new systems of social organization, they thought, a better environment for humanity could be achieved. One prominent utopian socialist was Robert Owen (1771–1858), a British cotton manufacturer who believed that humans would reveal their true natural goodness if they lived in a cooperative environment. At New Lanark in Scotland, he was successful in transforming a squalid factory town into a flourishing, healthy community. But when he attempted to create a self-contained cooperative community at New Harmony, Indiana, in the United States in the 1820s, internal bickering within the community eventually destroyed his dream.

With their plans for the reconstruction of society, utopian socialists attracted a number of woman supporters who believed that only a reordering of society would help women. One of Owen's disciples, a wealthy woman named Frances Wright, bought slaves in order to set up a model community at Nashoba, Tennessee. The community failed, but Wright continued to work for women's rights.

Revolution and Reform, 1830–1850

Beginning in 1830, the forces of change began to break through the conservative domination of Europe, more successfully in some places than in others.

The Revolutions of 1830

In France, the attempt of the ultraroyalists under the Bourbon monarch Charles X (1824–1830) to restore the old regime as far as possible led to a revolt by liberals in 1830 known as the July Revolution. Barricades went up in Paris as a provisional government led by a group of moderate, propertied liberals was hastily formed and appealed to Louis-Philippe, a cousin of Charles X, to become the constitutional king of France. Charles X fled to Britain; a new monarchy had been born.

Louis-Philippe (1830–1848) was soon called the bourgeois monarch because political support for his rule came from the upper middle class. Louis-Philippe even dressed like a member of the middle class, in business suits and hats. Constitutional changes that favored the interests of

The Revolution of 1830. In 1830, the forces of change began to undo the conservative domination of Europe. In France, the reactionary Charles X was overthrown and replaced by the constitutional monarch Louis-Philippe, a liberal and former revolutionary soldier. In this painting by Gustave Wappers, Louis-Philippe is seen riding to the Hôtel de Ville, the city hall, preceded by a man holding the French revolutionary tricolor flag, which had not been seen in France since 1815.

the upper bourgeoisie were instituted. Financial qualifications for voting were reduced yet remained sufficiently high that the number of voters only increased from 100,000 to barely 200,000, continuing to guarantee that only the wealthiest people would vote. To the upper middle class, the bourgeois monarchy represented the stopping place for political progress.

Supporters of liberalism played a primary role in the revolution in France, but nationalism was the crucial force in three other revolutionary outbursts in 1830. In an effort to create a stronger, larger state on France's northern border, the Congress of Vienna had added the area once known as the Austrian Netherlands (modern-day Belgium) to the Dutch Republic. The merger of Catholic Belgium into the Protestant Dutch Republic never sat well with the Belgians, however, and in 1830, they rose up against the Dutch and succeeded in convincing the major European powers to accept their independence. The revolutionary scenarios in Poland and Italy were much less successful. Russian forces crushed the attempt of Poles to liberate themselves from foreign domination, and Metternich sent Austrian troops to crush revolts in three Italian states.

The successful July Revolution in France served to catalyze change in Britain. The Industrial Revolution had led to an expanding group of industrial leaders who objected to the corrupt British electoral system, which excluded them from political power. The Whigs, though also members of the landed classes, realized that concessions to reform were superior to revolution; the demands of the wealthy industrial middle class could no longer be ignored. In 1832, Parliament passed a reform bill that increased the numbers of male voters, primarily benefiting the upper middle class; the lower middle class, artisans, and industrial workers still had no vote. Nevertheless, a significant step had been taken. The "monied, manufacturing, and educated elite" had been joined to the landed interest in ruling Britain. As a result of reforms, Britain would be immune to the revolutionary disturbances of 1848.

The Revolutions of 1848

Despite the successful revolutions in France, Belgium, and Greece, the conservative order remained in control of much of Europe. But liberalism and nationalism continued to grow. In 1848, these forces of change erupted once more. Yet again, revolution in France provided the spark for other countries, and soon most of central and southern Europe was ablaze with revolutionary fires. Tsar Nicholas I of Russia lamented to Queen Victoria in April 1848, "What remains standing in Europe? Great Britain and Russia."

Another French Revolution A severe industrial and agricultural depression beginning in 1846 brought great hardship in France to the lower middle class, workers, and peasants. Scandals, graft, and corruption were rife,

and the government's persistent refusal to extend the suffrage angered the disfranchised members of the middle class. As Louis-Philippe's government continued to refuse to make changes, opposition grew and finally overthrew the monarchy on February 24, 1848. A group of moderate and radical republicans established a provisional government and called for the election by universal male suffrage of a "constituent assembly" that would draw up a new constitution.

The provisional government also established national workshops, which were supposed to be cooperative factories run by the workers. In fact, the workshops came to provide jobs for unemployed workers, consisting primarily of leaf raking and ditch digging. The cost of the program became increasingly burdensome to the government.

The result was a growing split between the moderate republicans, who had the support of most of France, and the radical republicans, whose main support came from the Parisian working class. From March to June, the number of unemployed enrolled in the national workshops rose from 10,000 to almost 120,000, emptying the treasury and frightening the moderates, who responded by closing the workshops on June 23. The workers refused to accept this decision and poured into the streets. Four days of bitter and bloody fighting by government forces crushed the working-class revolt. Thousands were killed, and four thousand prisoners were deported to the French colony of Algeria in northern Africa.

The new constitution, ratified in November, established a republic (the Second Republic) with a one-house legislature with 750 members elected by universal male suffrage for three years and a president, also elected by universal male suffrage, for four years. In the elections for the presidency held in December 1848, Charles Louis Napoleon Bonaparte, the nephew of the famous French ruler, won a resounding victory.

Revolution in the Germanic States News of the revolution in Paris in February 1848 led to upheavals in central Europe as well (see the box on p. 403). Revolutionary cries for change caused many German rulers to promise constitutions, a free press, jury trials, and other liberal reforms. Concessions to appease the revolutionaries were also made in Prussia. King Frederick William IV (1840–1861) agreed to abolish censorship, establish a new constitution, and work for a united Germany. This last promise had its counterpart throughout all the German states as governments allowed elections by universal male suffrage for deputies to an all-German parliament. Its purpose was to fulfill a liberal and nationalist dream—the preparation of a constitution for a new united Germany.

But the Frankfurt Assembly, as the parliament was called, failed to achieve its goals. Although some members spoke of using force, they had no real means of compelling the German rulers to accept the constitution they had drawn up. The attempt of the German liberals at Frankfurt to create a German state had failed.

Revolutionary Excitement: Carl Schurz and the Revolution of 1848 in Germany

The excitement with which German liberals and nationalists received the news of the February Revolution in France and their own expectations for Germany are well captured in this selection from the *Reminiscences* of Carl Schurz (1829–1906). Schurz made his way to the United States after the failure of the German revolution and eventually became a U.S. senator.

Carl Schurz, *Reminiscences*

One morning, toward the end of February, 1848, I sat quietly in my attic-chamber, working hard at my tragedy of "Ulrich von Hutten" [a sixteenth-century German knight], when suddenly a friend rushed breathlessly into the room, exclaiming: "What, you sitting here! Do you not know what has happened?"

"No, what?"

"The French have driven away Louis Philippe and proclaimed the republic."

I threw down my pen—and that was the end of "Ulrich von Hutten." I never touched the manuscript again. We tore down the stairs, into the street, to the market-square, the accustomed meeting-place for all the student societies after their midday dinner. Although it was still forenoon, the market was already crowded with young men talking excitedly. There was no shouting, no noise, only agitated conversation. What did we want there? This probably no one knew. But since the French had driven away Louis Philippe and proclaimed the republic, something of course must happen here, too.... We were dominated by a vague feeling as if a great outbreak of elemental forces had begun, as if an earthquake was impending of which we had felt the first shock, and we instinctively crowded together....

The next morning there were the usual lectures to be attended. But how profitless! The voice of the professor sounded like a monotonous drone coming from far away. What he had to say did not seem to concern us. The pen that should have taken notes remained idle. At last we closed with a sigh the notebook and went away, impelled by a feeling that now we had something more important to do—to devote ourselves to the affairs of the fatherland. And this we did by seeking as quickly as possible again the company of our friends, in order to discuss what had happened and what was to come. In these conversations, excited as they were, certain ideas and catchwords worked themselves to the surface, which expressed more or less the feelings of the people. Now had arrived in Germany the day for the establishment of "German Unity," and the founding of a great, powerful national German Empire. In the first line the convocation of a national parliament. Then the demands for civil rights and liberties, free speech, free press, the right of free assembly, equality before the law, a freely elected representation of the people with legislative power, responsibility of ministers, self-government of the communes, the right of the people to carry arms, the formation of a civic guard with elective officers, and so on—in short, that which was called a "constitutional form of government on a broad democratic basis." Republican ideas were at first only sparingly expressed. But the word *democracy* was soon on all tongues, and many, too, thought it a matter of course that if the princes should try to withhold from the people the rights and liberties demanded, force would take the place of mere petition. Of course the regeneration of the fatherland must, if possible, be accomplished by peaceable means....Like many of my friends, I was dominated by the feeling that at last the great opportunity had arrived for giving to the German people the liberty which was their birthright and to the German fatherland its unity and greatness, and that it was now the first duty of every German to do and to sacrifice everything for this sacred object.

Why was Carl Schurz so excited when he heard the news about the revolution in France? Do you think his being a university student helps explain his reaction? Why or why not?

Upheaval in the Austrian Empire   The Austrian Empire also had its social, political, and nationalist grievances and needed only the news of the revolution in Paris to encourage it to erupt in flames in March 1848. The Hungarian liberals under Louis Kossuth agitated for "commonwealth" status; they were willing to keep the Habsburg monarch but wanted their own legislature. In March, demonstrations in Buda, Prague, and Vienna led to Metternich's dismissal, and the archsymbol of the conservative order fled abroad. In Vienna, revolutionary forces, carefully guided by the educated and propertied classes, took control of the capital and insisted that a constituent assembly be summoned to draw up a liberal constitution. Hungary was granted its wish for its own legislature, a separate national army, and control over foreign policy and budget. In Bohemia, the Czechs began to demand their own government as well.

Although Emperor Ferdinand I (1835–1848) and Austrian officials had made concessions to appease the revolutionaries, they awaited an opportunity to reestablish their firm control. As in the German states, they were increasingly encouraged by the divisions between radical and moderate revolutionaries and played on the middle-class fear of a working-class social revolution. Their first success came in June 1848 when Austrian military forces under General Alfred Windischgrätz ruthlessly suppressed

Austrian Students in the Revolutionary Civil Guard. In 1848, revolutionary fervor swept through Europe and toppled governments in France, central Europe, and Italy. In the Austrian Empire, students joined the revolutionary civil guard in taking control of Vienna and forcing the Austrian emperor to call a constituent assembly to draft a liberal constitution.

the Czech rebels in Prague. By the end of October, radical rebels had been crushed in Vienna. In December, the feeble-minded Ferdinand agreed to abdicate in favor of his nephew, Francis Joseph I (1848–1916), who worked vigorously to restore the imperial government in Hungary. The Austrian armies, however, were unable to defeat Kossuth's forces, and it was only through the intervention of Nicholas I, who sent a Russian army of 140,000 men to aid the Austrians, that the Hungarian revolution was finally crushed in 1849. The revolutions in the Austrian Empire had also failed.

Revolts in the Italian States The failure of revolutionary uprisings in Italy in 1830 and 1831 had encouraged the Italian movement for unification to take a new direction. The leadership of Italy's resurgence passed into the hands of Giuseppe Mazzini (1805–1872), a dedicated Italian nationalist who founded an organization known as Young Italy in 1831. This group set as its goal the creation of a united Italian republic. In *The Duties of Man*, Mazzini urged Italians to dedicate their lives to the Italian nation: "O my Brother! Love your country. Our Country is our home." A number of Italian women also took up Mazzini's call. Especially notable was Cristina Belgioioso (1808–1871), a wealthy aristocrat who worked to bring about Italian unification. Pursued by the Austrian authorities, she fled to Paris and started a newspaper to espouse the Italian cause.

The dreams of Mazzini and Belgioioso seemed on the verge of fulfillment when a number of Italian states rose in revolt in 1848. Beginning in Sicily, rebellions spread northward as ruler after ruler granted a constitution to his people. Citizens in Lombardy and Venetia also rebelled

against their Austrian overlords. The Venetians declared a republic in Venice. The king of the northern Italian state of Piedmont, Charles Albert (1831–1849), took up the call and assumed the leadership for a war of liberation from Austrian domination. His invasion of Lombardy proved unsuccessful, however, and by 1849 the Austrians had reestablished complete control over Lombardy and Venetia. Counterrevolutionary forces also prevailed throughout Italy as Italian rulers managed to recover power on their own. Only Piedmont was able to keep its liberal constitution.

The Failures of 1848 Throughout Europe in 1848, popular revolts had initiated revolutionary upheavals that had prodded the formation of liberal constitutions and liberal governments. But the failure of the revolutionaries to stay united soon led to the reestablishment of the old regimes. In 1848, nationalities everywhere had also revolted in pursuit of self-government. But again, frightfully little was achieved because divisions among nationalities proved utterly disastrous. Though the Hungarians demanded autonomy from the Austrians, at the same time they refused the same to their minorities—the Slovenes, Croats, and Serbs. Instead of joining together against the old empire, minorities fought each other.

The Maturing of the United States

The American Constitution, ratified in 1789, committed the United States to two of the major forces of the first half of the nineteenth century, liberalism and nationalism. Initially, this constitutional commitment to national unity was challenged by divisions over the power of the

Great Britain

Reform Act	1832

France

Louis XVIII	1814–1824
Charles X	1824–1830
July Revolution	1830
Louis-Philippe	1830–1848
Abdication of Louis-Philippe; formation of provisional government	1848 (February 22–24)
June Days: workers' revolt in Paris	1848 (June)
Establishment of Second Republic	1848 (November)
Election of Louis Napoleon as French president	1848 (December)

Low Countries

Union of Netherlands and Belgium	1815
Belgian revolt and independence	1830

German States

Germanic Confederation	1815
Frederick William IV of Prussia	1840–1861
Revolution in Germany	1848
Frankfurt Assembly	1848–1849

Austrian Empire

Emperor Ferdinand I	1835–1848
Revolt in Austrian Empire; dismissal of Metternich	1848 (March)
Suppression of Czech rebels	1848 (June)
Suppression of Viennese rebels	1848 (October)
Francis Joseph I	1848–1916
Defeat of Hungarians with help of Russian troops	1849

Italian States

King Charles Albert of Piedmont	1831–1849
Revolutions in Italy	1848
Attack on Austria	1848
Restoration of Austrian control in Lombardy and Venetia	1849

Russia

Tsar Alexander I	1801–1825
Tsar Nicholas I	1825–1855
Suppression of Polish revolt	1831

Madison (1751–1836), feared centralization and its consequences for popular liberties. These divisions were intensified by European rivalries because the Federalists were pro-British and the Republicans pro-French. The successful conclusion of the War of 1812 against the British brought an end to the Federalists, who had opposed the war, while the surge of national feeling generated by the war served to heal the nation's divisions.

Another strong force for national unity came from the Supreme Court while John Marshall (1755–1835) was chief justice from 1801 to 1835. Marshall made the Supreme Court into an important national institution by asserting the right of the Court to overrule an act of Congress if the Court found it to be in violation of the Constitution. Under Marshall, the Supreme Court contributed further to establishing the supremacy of the national government by curbing the actions of state courts and legislatures.

The election of Andrew Jackson (1767–1845) as president in 1828 opened a new era in American politics. Jacksonian democracy introduced a mass democratic politics. The electorate was expanded by dropping traditional property qualifications; by the 1830s, suffrage had been extended to almost all adult white males.

Culture in an Age of Reaction and Revolution: The Mood of Romanticism

At the end of the eighteenth century, a new intellectual movement known as Romanticism emerged to challenge the Enlightenment's preoccupation with reason in discovering truth. The Romantics tried to balance the use of reason by stressing the importance of feeling, emotion, and imagination as sources of knowing. As one German Romantic put it, "It was my heart that counseled me to do it, and my heart cannot err."

The Characteristics of Romanticism

Romantic writers emphasized emotion, sentiment, and inner feelings in their works. An important model for Romantics was the tragic figure in *The Sorrows of Young Werther*, a novel by the great German writer Johann Wolfgang von Goethe (1749–1832), who later rejected Romanticism in favor of classicism. Werther was a Romantic figure who sought freedom as the source of personal fulfillment. Misunderstood and rejected by society, he continued to believe in his own worth through his inner feelings, but his deep love for a girl who did not love him finally led him to commit suicide. After Goethe's *Sorrows of Young Werther*, numerous novels and plays appeared whose plots revolved around young maidens tragically carried off at an early age (twenty-three was most common) by disease (usually tuberculosis, at that time a protracted disease that was usually fatal) to the sorrow and sadness of their male lovers.

federal government vis-à-vis the individual states. Bitter conflict erupted between the Federalists and the Republicans. Led by Alexander Hamilton (1757–1804), the Federalists favored a financial program that would establish a strong central government. The Republicans, guided by Thomas Jefferson (1743–1826) and James

GOTHIC LITERATURE: EDGAR ALLAN POE

American writers and poets made significant contributions to the movement of Romanticism. Although Edgar Allan Poe was influenced by the German Romantic school of mystery and horror, many literary historians give him the credit for pioneering the modern short story. This selection from the conclusion of "The Fall of the House of Usher" gives a sense of the nature of so-called Gothic literature.

Edgar Allan Poe, "The Fall of the House of Usher"

No sooner had these syllables passed my lips, than—as if a shield of brass had indeed, at the moment, fallen heavily upon a floor of silver—I became aware of a distinct, hollow, metallic, and clangorous, yet apparently muffled, reverberation. Completely unnerved, I leaped to my feet; but the measured rocking movement of Usher was undisturbed. I rushed to the chair in which he sat. His eyes were bent fixedly before him, and throughout his whole countenance there reigned a stony rigidity. But, as I placed my hand upon his shoulder, there came a strong shudder over his whole person; a sickly smile quivered about his lips and I saw that he spoke in a low, hurried, and gibbering murmur, as if unconscious of my presence. Bending closely over him, I at length drank in the hideous import of his words.

"Not hear it?—yes, I hear it, and *have* heard it. Long-long-long-many minutes, many hours, many days, have I heard it—yet I dared not—oh, pity me, miserable wretch that I am!—I dared not—I *dared* not speak! *We have put her living in the tomb!* Said I not that my senses were acute? I *now* tell you

that I heard her first feeble movements in the hollow coffin. I heard them—many, many days ago—yet I dared not—I *dared not speak!* And now—to-night—...the rending of her coffin, and the grating of the iron hinges of her prison, and her struggles within the coppered archway of the vault! Oh whither shall I fly? Will she not be here anon? Is she not hurrying to upbraid me for my haste? Have I not heard her footstep on the stair? Do I not distinguish that heavy and horrible beating of her heart? MADMAN!"—here he sprang furiously to his feet, and shrieked out his syllables, as if in the effort he were giving up his soul—"MADMAN! I TELL YOU THAT SHE NOW STANDS WITHOUT THE DOOR!"

As if in the superhuman energy of his utterance there had been found the potency of a spell, the huge antique panels to which the speaker pointed threw slowly back, upon the instant, their ponderous and ebony jaws. It was the work of the rushing gust—but then without those doors there DID stand the lofty and enshrouded figure of the lady Madeline of Usher. There was blood upon her white robes, and the evidence of some bitter struggle upon every portion of her emaciated frame. For a moment she remained trembling and reeling to and fro upon the threshold, then, with a low moaning cry, fell heavily inward upon the person of her brother, and in her violent and now final death-agonies, bore him to the floor a corpse, and a victim to the terrors he had anticipated.

What characteristics of Romanticism are revealed in Poe's tale?

Another important characteristic of Romanticism was individualism, an interest in the unique traits of each person. The Romantics' desire to follow their inner drives led them to rebel against middle-class conventions. Long hair, beards, and outrageous clothes served to reinforce the individualism that young Romantics were trying to express.

Many Romantics possessed a passionate interest in the past. In Germany, brothers Jacob and Wilhelm Grimm collected and published local fairy tales, as Hans Christian Andersen did in Denmark. The revival of Gothic architecture left European countrysides adorned with pseudo-medieval castles and cities bedecked with grandiose neo-Gothic cathedrals, city halls, parliamentary buildings, and even railway stations. Literature, too, reflected this historical consciousness. The novels of Walter Scott (1771–1832) became European best-sellers in the first half of the nineteenth century. *Ivanhoe*, in which Scott tried to evoke the clash between Saxon and Norman knights in medieval England, became one of his most popular works.

To the historical-mindedness of the Romantics could be added an attraction to the bizarre and unusual. In an

exaggerated form, this preoccupation gave rise to so-called **Gothic literature** (see the box above), chillingly evident in short stories of horror by the American Edgar Allan Poe (1808–1849) and in *Frankenstein* by Mary Wollstonecraft Shelley (1797–1851). Shelley's novel was the story of a mad scientist who brings into being a humanlike monster who goes berserk. Some Romantics even sought the unusual in their own lives by experimenting with cocaine, opium, and hashish to achieve altered states of consciousness.

Romantic Poets and the Love of Nature

To the Romantics, poetry ranked above all other literary forms because they believed it was the direct expression of one's soul. The Romantic poets were viewed as seers who could reveal the invisible world to others. Their sense of drama made some of them the most colorful figures of their era, living intense but short lives. Percy Bysshe Shelley (1792–1822), expelled from school for advocating atheism, set out to reform the world. His *Prometheus Unbound*, completed in 1820, is a portrait of the revolt of human beings against the laws and customs that oppress them. He drowned in a storm in the Mediterranean. Lord Byron (1788–1824) dramatized himself as the melancholy Romantic hero that he had described in his own work, *Childe Harold's Pilgrimage*. He participated in the movement for Greek independence and died in Greece fighting the Ottomans.

Romantic poetry gave full expression to one of the most important characteristics of Romanticism: love of nature, especially evident in the works of William Wordsworth (1770–1850). His experience of nature was almost mystical as he claimed to receive "authentic tidings of invisible things":

> *One impulse from a vernal wood*
> *May teach you more of man,*
> *Of Moral Evil and of good,*
> *Than all the sages can.[4]*

To Wordsworth, nature contained a mysterious force that the poet could perceive and learn from. Nature served as a mirror into which humans could look to learn about themselves. Nature was, in fact, alive and sacred:

> *To every natural form, rock, fruit or flower,*
> *Even the loose stones that cover the high-way,*
> *I gave a moral life, I saw them feel,*
> *Or link'd them to some feeling: the great mass*
> *Lay bedded in a quickening soul, and all*
> *That I beheld, respired with inward meaning.[5]*

Other Romantics carried this worship of nature further into **pantheism** by identifying the great force in nature with God. As the German Romantic poet Friedrich Novalis said, "Anyone seeking God will find him anywhere."

Romanticism in Art

Like the literary arts, the visual arts were also deeply affected by Romanticism. To Romantic artists, all artistic expression was a reflection of the artist's inner feelings; a painting should mirror the artist's vision of the world and be the instrument of his own imagination. Moreover, Romantic artists deliberately rejected the principles of classicism. Beauty was not a timeless thing; its expression depended on one's culture and one's age. The Romantics abandoned classical restraint for warmth, emotion, and movement.

The early life experiences of the German painter Caspar David Friedrich (1774–1840) left him with a life-long preoccupation with God and nature. Friedrich painted landscapes, but with an interest that transcended the mere presentation of natural details. His portrayal of mountains shrouded in mist, gnarled trees bathed in moonlight, and the stark ruins of monasteries all conveyed a feeling of mystery and mysticism. For Friedrich, nature was a manifestation of divine life, as is evident in *Man and Woman Gazing at the Moon*. To Friedrich, the artistic process depended on the use of an unrestricted imagination that could only be achieved through inner vision. He advised artists: "Shut your physical eye and look first at your picture with your spiritual eye, then bring to the light of day what you have seen in the darkness."

Eugène Delacroix (1798–1863) was one of the most famous French exponents of the Romantic school of painting. Delacroix's paintings exhibited a fascination with the exotic and a passion for color, exemplified by *Death of Sardanapalus*. In Delacroix, theatricality and movement combined with a daring color palette. Many of his works reflect his belief that "a painting should be a feast to the eye."

Joerg P. Anders/Bildarchiv Preussischer Kulturbesitz/Art Resource, NY (Staatliche Museen zu Berlin)

Caspar David Friedrich, *Man and Woman Gazing at the Moon.* The German artist Caspar David Friedrich sought to express in painting his own mystical view of nature. "The divine is everywhere," he once wrote, "even in a grain of sand." In this painting, two solitary wanderers are shown from the back gazing at the moon. Overwhelmed by the all-pervasive presence of nature, the two figures express the human longing for infinity.

Eugéne Delacroix, *Death of Sardanapalus.* Delacroix's *Death of Sardanapalus* was based on Lord Byron's verse account of the decadent Assyrian king's dramatic last moments. Besieged by enemy troops and with little hope of survival, Sardanapalus orders that his harem women and prize horses go to their death with him. At the right, a guard stabs one of the women as the king looks on.

Romanticism in Music

To many Romantics, music was the most Romantic of the arts because it enabled the composer to probe deeply into human emotions. Music historians have called the eighteenth century an age of classicism and the nineteenth the era of Romanticism. One of the greatest composers of all time, Ludwig van Beethoven, served as a bridge between the two.

Beethoven (1770–1827) was born in Bonn, Germany, but soon made his way to Vienna, then the musical capital of Europe. During his first major period of composing, from 1792 to 1802, his work was still largely within the classical framework of the eighteenth century, and the influences of Mozart and Haydn were paramount. But with the composition of the Third Symphony (1804), the *Eroica*, originally intended for Napoleon, Beethoven broke through to Romanticism in his use of uncontrolled rhythms to create dramatic struggle and uplifted resolutions. E.T.A. Hoffman, a contemporary composer and writer, said, "Beethoven's music opens the flood gates of fear, of terror, of horror, of pain, and arouses that longing for the eternal which is the essence of Romanticism. He is thus a pure Romantic composer."[6] Beethoven went on to write a vast quantity of works, but in the midst of this productivity and growing fame, he was more and more burdened by his growing deafness. One of the most moving pieces of music of all time, the chorale finale of his Ninth Symphony, was composed when Beethoven was totally deaf.

CONCLUSION

In 1815, a conservative order was reestablished throughout Europe, and the cooperation of the great powers, embodied in the Concert of Europe, tried to ensure its durability. But the revolutionary waves of the 1820s and early 1830s made it clear that the ideologies of liberalism and nationalism, unleashed by the French Revolution and now reinforced by the spread of the Industrial Revolution, were still alive and active. They faced enormous difficulties, however, as failed revolutions in Poland, Russia, Italy, and Germany all testify.

At the same time, reform legislation in Britain and successful revolutions in Greece, France, and Belgium demonstrated the continuing strength of these forces of change. In 1848, they erupted once more all across Europe. And once more they failed. But all was not lost. Both liberalism and nationalism would succeed in the second half of the nineteenth century, but in ways not foreseen by the idealistic liberals and nationalists, who were utterly convinced that their time had come when they manned the barricades in 1848.

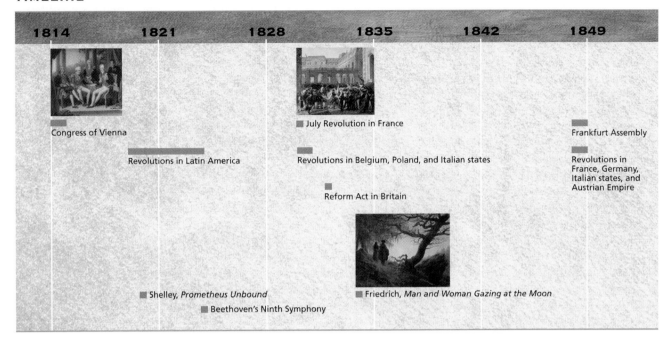

1814　　　　1821　　　　1828　　　　1835　　　　1842　　　　1849

Congress of Vienna

July Revolution in France

Revolutions in Latin America

Revolutions in Belgium, Poland, and Italian states

Frankfurt Assembly

Revolutions in France, Germany, Italian states, and Austrian Empire

Reform Act in Britain

Shelley, *Prometheus Unbound*

Beethoven's Ninth Symphony

Friedrich, *Man and Woman Gazing at the Moon*

NOTES

1. Quoted in M. S. Anderson, *The Ascendancy of Europe 1815–1914*, 2d ed. (London, 1985), p. 1.
2. Quoted in P. Viereck, *Conservatism* (Princeton, N.J., 1956), p. 27.
3. Quoted in G. de Berthier de Sauvigny, *Metternich and His Times* (London, 1962), p. 105.
4. W. Wordsworth, "The Tables Turned," *Poems of Wordsworth*, ed. M. Arnold (London, 1963), p. 138.
5. W. Wordsworth, *The Prelude* (Harmondsworth, England, 1971), p. 109.
6. Quoted in S. Prawer, ed., *The Romantic Period in Germany* (London, 1970), p. 285.

SUGGESTIONS FOR FURTHER READING

For a good survey of the entire nineteenth century, see **R. Gildea, Barricades and Borders: Europe, 1800–1914**, 2d ed. (Oxford, 1996), in the Short Oxford History of the Modern World series. Also valuable is **M. S. Anderson, The Ascendancy of Europe, 1815–1914**, 2d ed. (London, 1985). For surveys of the period covered in this chapter, see **M. Broers, Europe After Napoleon: Revolution, Reaction, and Romanticism, 1814–1848** (New York, 1996), and **C. Breunig, The Age of Revolution and Reaction, 1789–1850**, 2d ed. (New York, 1979). There are also some useful books on individual countries that cover more than the subject of this chapter. These include **R. Magraw, France, 1815–1914: The Bourgeois Century** (London, 1983); **D. Saunders, Russia in the Age of Reaction and Reform, 1801–1881** (London, 1992); **J. J. Sheehan, German History, 1770–1866** (New York, 1989); **A. Sked, The Decline and Fall of the Habsburg Empire, 1815–1918** (London, 1989); and **N. McCord, British History, 1815–1906** (New York, 1991).

On the peace settlement of 1814–1815, see **T. Chapman, The Congress of Vienna** (London, 1998). A concise summary of the international events of the entire nineteenth century can be found in **R. Bullen and F. R. Bridge, The Great Powers and the European States System, 1815–1914** (London, 1980). See also **N. Rich, Great Power Diplomacy, 1814–1914** (New York, 1992). On the man whose conservative policies dominated this era, see the brief but good biography by **A. Palmer, Metternich** (New York, 1972). On the revolutions in Europe in 1830, see **C. Church, Europe in 1830: Revolution and Political Change** (Chapel Hill, N.C., 1983). The Greek revolt is examined in detail in **D. Dakin, The Greek Struggle for Independence, 1821–33** (Berkeley, Calif., 1973).

The best introduction to the revolutions of 1848 is **J. Sperber, The European Revolutions, 1848–1851** (New York, 1994). Good accounts of the revolutions in individual countries include **G. Duveau, 1848: The Making of a Revolution** (New York, 1967); **R. J. Rath, The Viennese Revolution of 1848** (Austin, Tex., 1957); **I. Déak, The Lawful Revolution: Louis Kossuth and the Hungarians, 1848–49** (New York, 1979); **R. Stadelmann, Social and Political History of the German 1848 Revolution** (Athens, Ohio, 1975); and **P. Ginsborg, Daniele Manin and the Venetian Revolution of 1848–49** (New York, 1979). On Mazzini, see **D. M. Smith, Mazzini** (New Haven, Conn., 1994).

Good introductions to the major ideologies of the first half of the nineteenth century, including both analysis and readings from the major figures, can be found in **H. Kohn, Nationalism** (Princeton, N.J., 1955); **J. S. Schapiro, Liberalism: Its Meaning and History** (Princeton, N.J., 1958); and **P. Viereck, Conservatism** (Princeton, N.J., 1956). For a more detailed examination of liberalism, see **J. Gray, Liberalism** (Minneapolis, Minn., 1995). On the ideas of the Romantics, see **M. Cranston, The Romantic Movement** (Oxford, 1994). An excellent collection of writings by Romantics is **J. B. Halsted, ed., Romanticism** (New York, 1969). On Wordsworth and English Romanticism, see **S. Hebron, William Wordsworth** (New York, 2000). For an introduction to the arts, see **W. Vaughan, Romanticism and Art** (New York, 1994).

Enter *ThomsonNOW* using the access card that is available for *Western Civilization: A Brief History.* *ThomsonNOW* will help you understand this chapter with lesson plans generated for your needs. In addition, you can read the following documents, and many more, online:

James Monroe, the Monroe Doctrine
Klemens von Metternich, excerpts from *Memoirs*
Louis Napoleon, campaign address

WESTERN CIVILIZATION RESOURCES

Visit the Web site for *Western Civilization: A Brief History* for resources specific to this book:

http://www.thomsonedu.com/history/spielvogel

For a variety of tools to help you succeed in this course, visit the Western Civilization Resource Center at

http://history.wadsworth.com/spielvogel

Included are quizzes, images, documents, interactive simulations, maps and timelines, movie explorations, and a wealth of other sources.

AN AGE OF NATIONALISM
AND REALISM, 1850–1871

Proclamation of the German Empire in the Hall of Mirrors in the palace of Versailles

Bildarchiv Preussischer Kulturbesitz/Art Resource, NY (Bismarck Museum, Friedrichsruh, Germany)

$\mathcal{A}$CROSS THE CONTINENT, the revolutions of 1848 had failed. The forces of liberalism and nationalism appeared to have been decisively defeated as authoritarian governments reestablished control almost everywhere in Europe by 1850. And yet within twenty-five years, many of the goals sought by the liberals and nationalists during the first half of the century seemed to have been achieved. National unity became a reality in Italy and Germany, and many European states were governed by constitutional monarchies, even though the constitutional-parliamentary features were frequently facades.

All the same, these goals were not achieved by liberal nationalist leaders but by a new generation of conservative leaders who were proud of being practitioners of *Realpolitik,* the "politics of reality." One reaction to the failure of the revolutions of 1848 had been a new toughness of mind in which people prided themselves on being realistic in their handling of power. The new conservative leaders used armies and power politics to achieve their foreign policy goals. And they did not hesitate to manipulate liberal means to achieve conservative ends at home. Nationalism had failed as a revolutionary movement in 1848–1849, but in the ensuing decades, these new leaders found a variety of ways to pursue nation building. One of the most successful was the Prussian Otto von Bismarck, who used both astute diplomacy and war to achieve the unification of Germany. On January 18, 1871, Bismarck and six hundred German princes, nobles, and generals filled the Hall of Mirrors in the palace of Versailles, 12 miles outside the city of Paris. The Prussian army had defeated the French, and the assembled notables were gathered for the proclamation of the Prussian king as the new emperor of a united German state. When the words "Long live His Imperial Majesty, the Emperor William!" rang out, the assembled guests took up the cry. One participant wrote, "A thundering cheer, repeated at least six times, thrilled through the room while the flags and standards waved over the head of the new emperor of Germany." European rulers who feared the power of the new German state were not so cheerful. "The balance of power has been entirely destroyed," declared the British prime minister.◆

The France of Napoleon III

After 1850, a new generation of conservative leaders came to power in Europe. Foremost among them was Napoleon III (1852–1870) of France, who taught his contemporaries how authoritarian governments could use liberal and nationalistic forces to bolster their own power. It was a lesson others quickly learned.

Louis Napoleon: Toward the Second Empire

Even after his election as the president of the French Republic, many of his contemporaries dismissed "Napoleon the Small" as a nonentity whose success was due only to his name. But Louis Napoleon was a clever politician who was especially astute at understanding the popular forces of his day. After his election, he was at least clear about his desire to have personal power. He wrote, "I shall never submit to any attempt to influence me. . . . I follow only the promptings of my mind and heart. . . . Nothing, nothing shall trouble the clear vision of my judgment or the strength of my resolution."[1]

Louis Napoleon was a patient man. For three years, he persevered in winning the support of the French people, and when the National Assembly rejected his wish to be allowed to stand for reelection, Louis used troops to seize control of the government on December 1, 1851. After restoring universal male suffrage, Napoleon asked the French people to restore the empire. Ninety-seven percent responded affirmatively, and on December 2, 1852, Louis Napoleon assumed the title of Napoleon III (the first Napoleon had abdicated in favor of his son, Napoleon II, on April 6, 1814). The Second Empire had begun.

The Second Napoleonic Empire

The government of Napoleon III was clearly authoritarian in a Bonapartist sense. As chief of state, Napoleon III controlled the armed forces, police, and civil service. Only he could introduce legislation and declare war. The Legislative Corps gave an appearance of representative government since its members were elected by universal male suffrage to six-year terms. But they could neither initiate legislation nor affect the budget.

The first five years of Napoleon III's reign were a spectacular success as he reaped the benefits of worldwide economic prosperity as well as some of his own economic policies. Napoleon believed in using the resources of government to stimulate the national economy and took many steps to expand industrial growth. Government subsidies were used to foster the construction of railroads, harbors, roads, and canals. The major French railway lines were completed during Napoleon's reign,

Emperor Napoleon III. On December 2, 1852, Louis Napoleon took the title of Napoleon III and then proceeded to create an authoritarian monarchy. As opposition to his policies intensified in the 1860s, Napoleon III began to liberalize his government. However, a disastrous military defeat at the hands of Prussia in 1870–1871 brought the collapse of his regime.

and industrial expansion was evident in the tripling of iron production. Napoleon III also undertook a vast reconstruction of the city of Paris. The medieval Paris of narrow streets and old city walls was replaced by a modern Paris of broad boulevards, spacious buildings, public squares, an underground sewage system, a new public water supply, and gaslights. The new Paris served a military as well as an aesthetic purpose. Broad streets made it more difficult for would-be insurrectionists to throw up barricades and easier for troops to move rapidly through the city to put down revolts.

In the 1860s, as opposition to some of his policies began to mount, Napoleon III liberalized his regime. He reached out to the working class by legalizing trade unions and granting them the right to strike. He also began to open up the political process. The Legislative Corps was permitted more say in affairs of state, including debate over the budget. Liberalization policies did serve initially to strengthen the hand of the government. In a plebiscite in May 1870 on whether to accept a new constitution that might have inaugurated a parliamentary regime, the French people gave Napoleon another resounding victory. This triumph was short-lived, however. Foreign policy failures led to growing criticism, and war with Prussia in 1870 turned out to be the death blow for Napoleon III's regime. Napoleon was ousted, and the Third Republic was proclaimed.

Foreign Policy: The Mexican Adventure

Napoleon III had considerably less success in his foreign policy, especially in his imperialistic adventure in Mexico. Seeking to dominate Mexican markets for French goods, the emperor sent French troops to Mexico in 1861 to join British and Spanish forces in protecting their interests in the midst of the upheaval caused by a struggle between liberal and conservative Mexican factions. Although the British and Spanish withdrew their troops after order had been restored, French forces remained, and in 1864, Napoleon III installed Archduke Maximilian of Austria, his handpicked choice, as the new emperor of Mexico. When the French troops were needed in Europe, Maximilian became an emperor without an army. He surrendered to liberal Mexican forces in May 1867 and was executed in June. His execution was a blow to the prestige of the French emperor.

Foreign Policy: The Crimean War

Napoleon III's participation in the Crimean War (1854–1856) was more rewarding. As heir to the Napoleonic empire, Napoleon III was motivated by the desire to free France from the restrictions of the peace settlements of 1814–1815 and to make France the chief arbiter of Europe.

The Ottoman Empire The Crimean War was yet another attempt to answer the Eastern Question: Who would be the chief beneficiaries of the disintegration of the Ottoman Empire? In the seventeenth century, the Ottoman Empire had control of southeastern Europe but in 1699 had lost Hungary, Transylvania, Croatia, and Slovenia to the expanding Austrian Empire. The Russian Empire to its north also encroached on the Ottoman Empire by seizing the Crimea in 1783 and Bessarabia in 1812.

By the beginning of the nineteenth century, the Ottoman Empire had entered a fresh period of decline. Nationalist revolts led to the creation of an independent Serbia in 1817 and a free Greece in 1830. The Russians had gained a protectorate over the Danubian provinces of Moldavia and Wallachia in 1829.

War in the Crimea As Ottoman authority over the outlying territories in southeastern Europe waned, European governments began to take an active interest in

The Crimean War

the empire's apparent demise. Russia's proximity to the Ottoman Empire naturally gave it special opportunities to enlarge its sphere of influence. In 1853, the Russians demanded the right to protect Christian shrines in Palestine, a privilege that had already been extended to the French. When the Ottomans refused, the Russians invaded Ottoman Moldavia and Wallachia. Failure to resolve the dispute by negotiations led the Turks to declare war on Russia on October 4, 1853. The following year, on March 28, Great Britain and France, fearful of Russian gains at the expense of the disintegrating Ottoman Empire, declared war on Russia.

The Crimean War was poorly planned and poorly fought. Britain and France decided to attack Russia's Crimean peninsula in the Black Sea. After a long siege and at a terrible cost in lives for both sides, the main Russian fortress of Sevastopol fell in September 1855, and the Russians soon sued for peace. By the Treaty of Paris, signed in March 1856, Russia was forced to give up Bessarabia and accept the neutrality of the Black Sea. In addition, Moldavia and Wallachia were placed under the protection of all five great powers.

The Crimean War proved costly to both sides. More than 250,000 soldiers died in the war, 60 percent of the deaths coming from disease (especially cholera). Even more would have died on the British side had it not been for the efforts of the nurse Florence Nightingale (1820–1910). Her insistence on strict sanitary conditions saved

Florence Nightingale. Florence Nightingale is shown caring for wounded soldiers at the British military hospital at Scutari in Turkey. After a British journalist, W. H. Russell, issued a scathing denunciation of the quality of medical care afforded to wounded British soldiers, the British government allowed Nightingale to take a group of nurses to the Crimean warfront. Through her efforts in the Crimean War, Nightingale helped make nursing an admirable profession for middle-class women.

many lives and helped make nursing a profession of trained, middle-class women.

The Crimean War broke up long-standing European power relationships and effectively destroyed the Concert of Europe. Austria and Russia, the two chief powers maintaining the status quo in the first half of the nineteenth century, were now enemies because of Austria's unwillingness to support Russia in the war. Russia, defeated, humiliated, and weakened by the obvious failure of its armies, withdrew from European affairs for the next two decades to set its house in order. Great Britain, disillusioned by its role in the war, also pulled back from Continental affairs. Austria, paying the price for its neutrality, was now without friends among the great powers. Not until the 1870s were new combinations formed to replace those that had disappeared, and in the meantime the European international situation remained fluid. It was this new situation that made the unification of Italy and Germany possible.

National Unification: Italy and Germany

The breakdown of the Concert of Europe opened the way for the Italians and the Germans to establish national states. Their successful unification transformed the power structure of the Continent. Well into the twentieth century, Europe and the world would still be dealing with the consequences.

The Unification of Italy

In 1850, Austria was still the dominant power on the Italian peninsula. After the failure of the revolution of 1848–1849, a growing number of advocates for Italian unification focused on the northern Italian state of Piedmont as their best hope to achieve their goal. The royal house of Savoy ruled the kingdom of Piedmont, which also included the island of Sardinia (see Map 22.1). The little state seemed unlikely to supply the needed leadership to unify Italy, however, until King Victor Emmanuel II (1849–1878) selected Count Camillo di Cavour (1810–1861) as his prime minister in 1852.

The Leadership of Cavour Cavour was a consummate politician with the ability to persuade others of the rightness of his own convictions. As prime minister, he pursued a policy of economic expansion that increased government revenues and enabled him to pour money into equipping a large army. Cavour, however, had no illusions about Piedmont's military strength and was well aware that he could not challenge Austria directly. Consequently, he made an alliance in 1858 with the French emperor Louis Napoleon and then provoked the Austrians into invading Piedmont in 1859. In the initial stages of fighting, the Austrians were defeated in two major battles by mostly French armies. A peace settlement gave the French Nice and Savoy, which they had been promised for making the alliance, and awarded Lombardy to Cavour and the Piedmontese. More important, however, Cavour's success caused nationalists in the northern Italian states of Parma, Modena, and Tuscany to overthrow their governments and join their states to Piedmont.

The Efforts of Garibaldi Meanwhile, in southern Italy, a new leader of Italian unification had come to the fore. Giuseppe Garibaldi (1807–1882), a dedicated Italian patriot, raised an army of a thousand Red Shirts, as his volunteers were called because of their distinctive dress, and landed in Sicily, where a revolt had broken out against the Bourbon king of the Two Sicilies. By the end of July 1860, most of Sicily had been pacified under Garibaldi's control. In August, Garibaldi and his forces crossed over to the mainland and began a victorious march up the Italian peninsula. Naples and the Two Sicilies fell in early September. Ever the patriot, Garibaldi chose to turn over his conquests to Cavour's Piedmontese forces. On March 17, 1861, the new kingdom of Italy was proclaimed under a centralized government subordinated to the control of Piedmont and King Victor Emmanuel II of the house of Savoy. Worn out by his efforts, Cavour died three months later.

Despite the proclamation of the new kingdom, unification was not yet complete because Venetia in the north was still held by Austria and Rome remained under papal control, supported by French troops. To attack either one meant war with a major European state, which the Italian army was not prepared to handle. It was the Prussian army that indirectly completed the task of Italian unification. In the Austro-Prussian War of 1866, the new Italian state became an ally of Prussia. Although the Italian army was defeated by the Austrians, Prussia's victory left the Italians with Venetia. In 1870, the Franco-

Prussian War resulted in the withdrawal of French troops from Rome. The Italian army then annexed the city on September 20, 1870, and Rome became the new capital of the united Italian state.

The Unification of Germany

After the failure of the Frankfurt Assembly to achieve German unification in 1848–1849, German nationalists focused on Austria and Prussia as the only two states powerful enough to unify Germany. But Austria, a large multinational empire, feared the creation of a strong

CHRONOLOGY   **The Unification of Italy**

Victor Emmanuel II	1849–1878
Count Cavour as prime minister of Piedmont	1852
Austrian War	1859
Plebiscites in the northern Italian states	1860
Garibaldi's invasion of the Two Sicilies	1860
Kingdom of Italy is proclaimed	1861
Italy's annexation of Venetia	1866
Italy's annexation of Rome	1870

MAP 22.1   The Unification of Italy. Piedmont under the able guidance of Count Camillo di Cavour provided the nucleus for Italian unification. Alliances with France and Prussia, combined with the military actions of republican nationalists like Giuseppe Garibaldi, led to complete unification in 1870. ❓ Of the countries displayed on this map, which would likely, taking geographical and population-size factors into account, pose the greatest military threat to the new Italian state? 🖥 **View an animated version of this map or related maps at** http://thomsonedu.com/history/spielvogel

German state in central Europe, and more and more Germans began to look to Prussia for leadership in the cause of German unification.

Bismarck

In the 1860s, King William I (1861–1888) attempted to enlarge and strengthen the Prussian army. When the Prussian legislature refused to levy new taxes for the proposed military changes in March 1862, William appointed a new prime minister, Count Otto von Bismarck (1815–1898). Bismarck ignored the legislative opposition to the military reforms, arguing that "Germany does not look to Prussia's liberalism but to her power. . . . Not by speeches and majorities will the great questions of the day be decided—that was the mistake of 1848–1849—but by iron and blood."[2] Bismarck went ahead, collected the taxes, and reorganized the army anyway. From 1862 to 1866, Bismarck governed Prussia by simply ignoring parliament. Unwilling to revolt, parliament did nothing. In the meantime, opposition to his domestic policy determined Bismarck on an active foreign policy, which led to war and German unification.

Because Bismarck succeeded in guiding Prussia's unification of Germany, it is often assumed that he had determined on a course of action that led precisely to that goal. That is hardly the case. Bismarck was an opportunist. He was not a political gambler but rather a moderate who waged war only when all other diplomatic alternatives had been exhausted and when he was reasonably sure that all the military and diplomatic advantages were on his side. Bismarck has often been portrayed as the ultimate realist, the foremost nineteenth-century practitioner of **Realpolitik**. He was also quite open about his strong dislike of anyone who opposed him. He said one morning to his wife, "I could not sleep the whole night; I hated throughout the whole night."

The Danish War (1864)

Bismarck's first war was against Denmark, fought over the duchies of Schleswig and Holstein. Bismarck persuaded the Austrians to join Prussia in declaring war on Denmark on February 1, 1864. The Danes were quickly defeated and surrendered Schleswig and Holstein to the victors (see Map 22.2). Austria and Prussia then agreed to divide the administration of the two duchies; Prussia took Schleswig while Austria administered Holstein. But Bismarck used the joint administration of the two duchies to create friction with the Austrians and goad them into a war on June 14, 1866.

The Austro-Prussian War (1866)

Many Europeans expected a quick Austrian victory, but they overlooked the effectiveness of the Prussian military reforms of the 1860s. The Prussian breech-loading needle gun had a much faster rate of fire than the Austrian muzzle-loader, and a superior network of railroads enabled the Prussians to mass troops quickly. At Königgrätz (Sadowa) on July 3, the Austrian army was defeated. Austria was now excluded from German affairs, and the German states north of the Main River were organized into a north German confederation controlled by Prussia. The south German states, largely Catholic, remained independent but were coerced into signing military agreements with Prussia.

The Franco-Prussian War (1870–1871)

Bismarck and William I had achieved a major goal by 1866. Prussia now dominated all of northern Germany, and Austria had been excluded from any significant role in German affairs. Nevertheless, unsettled business led to new international complications and further change. Bismarck realized that France would never be content with a strong German state to its east because of the potential threat to French security. At the same time, after a series of setbacks, Napoleon III, the French ruler, needed a diplomatic triumph to offset his serious domestic problems. The French were not happy with the turn of events in Germany and looked for opportunities to humiliate the Prussians.

In 1870, Prussia and France became embroiled in a dispute over the candidacy of a relative of the Prussian king for the throne of Spain. Bismarck manipulated the misunderstandings between the French and Prussians to goad the French into declaring war on Prussia on July 15, 1870 (see the box on p. 418). The French proved no match for the better-led and better-organized Prussian forces. The south German states honored their military alliances with Prussia and joined the war effort against the French. The Prussian armies advanced into France, and at Sedan, on September 2, 1870, an entire French army and Napoleon III himself were captured. Paris finally capitulated on January 28, 1871, and an official peace treaty was signed in May. France had to pay an indemnity of 5 billion francs (about $1 billion) and give up the provinces of Alsace and Lorraine to the new German state, a loss that angered the French and left them burning for revenge.

Even before the war had ended, the south German states had agreed to enter the North German Confederation. On January 18, 1871, in the Hall of Mirrors in Louis XIV's palace at Versailles, William I, with Bismarck standing at the foot of the throne, was proclaimed kaiser or emperor of the Second German Empire (the first was the medieval Holy Roman Empire). German unity had been achieved by the Prussian monarchy and the Prussian army. In a real sense, Germany had been merged into Prussia, not Prussia into Germany. German liberals also rejoiced. They had dreamed of unity and freedom, but the achievement of unity now seemed much more important. One old liberal proclaimed:

> I cannot shake off the impression of this hour. I am no devotee of Mars; I feel more attached to the goddess of beauty and the mother of graces than to the powerful god of war, but the trophies of war exercise a magic charm even upon the child of peace. One's view is involuntarily chained and one's spirit goes along with the boundless row of men who acclaim the god of the moment—success.[3]

The Prussian leadership of German unification meant the triumph of authoritarian, militaristic values over liberal,

King William I of Prussia	1861–1888
Bismarck as minister-president of Prussia	1862
Danish War	1864
Austro-Prussian War	1866
Battle of Königgrätz	1866 (July 3)
Franco-Prussian War	1870–1871
Battle of Sedan	1870 (September 2)
Fall of Paris	1871 (January 28)
German Empire proclaimed	1871 (January 18)

constitutional sentiments in the development of the new German state. With its industrial resources and military might, the new state had become the strongest power on the Continent. A new European balance of power was at hand.

Nation Building and Reform: The National State in Mid-Century

While European affairs were dominated by the unification of Italy and Germany, other states in the Western world were also undergoing transformations (see Map 22.3). War, civil war, and changing political alignments served as catalysts for domestic reforms.

MAP 22.2   The Unification of Germany.   Count Otto von Bismarck, the Prussian prime minister, skillfully combined domestic policies with wars with Denmark, Austria, and France to achieve the creation of the German Empire in 1871. ❓ From the Prussian perspective of increasing its military power and ability to rule all parts of its lands, which was more important, formation of the North German Confederation or absorption of the South German Confederation?

🔊 View an animated version of this map or related maps at http://thomsonedu.com/history/spielvogel

BISMARCK "GOADS" FRANCE INTO WAR

*A*fter his meeting with the French ambassador at Ems, King William I of Prussia sent a telegram to Bismarck with a report of their discussions. By editing the telegram from King William before releasing it to the press, Bismarck made it sound as if the Prussian king had treated the ambassador in a demeaning fashion. Six days later, France declared war on Prussia.

The Abeken [Privy Councillor] Text, Ems, July 13, 1870

To the Federal Chancellor, Count Bismarck. His Majesty the King writes to me:

"M. Benedetti intercepted me on the Promenade in order to demand of me most insistently that I should authorize him to telegraph immediately to Paris that I shall obligate myself for all future time never again to give my approval to the candidacy of the Hohenzollerns should it be renewed. I refused to agree to this, the last time somewhat severely, informing him that one dare not and cannot assume such obligations *à tout jamais* [forever]. Naturally, I informed him that I had received no news as yet, and since he had been informed earlier than I by way of Paris and Madrid, he could easily understand why my government was once again out of the matter."

Since then His Majesty has received a dispatch from the Prince [father of the Hohenzollern candidate for the Spanish throne]. As His Majesty has informed Count Benedetti that he was expecting news from the Prince, His Majesty himself, in view of the above-mentioned demand and in consonance with the advice of Count Eulenburg and myself, decided not to receive the French envoy again but to inform him through an adjutant that His Majesty had now received from the Prince confirmation of the news which Benedetti had already received from Paris, and that he had nothing further to say to the Ambassador. His Majesty leaves it to the judgment of Your Excellency whether or not to communicate at once the new demand by Benedetti and its rejection to our ambassadors and to the press.

Bismarck's Edited Version

After the reports of the renunciation by the hereditary Prince of Hohenzollern had been officially transmitted by the Royal Government of Spain to the Imperial Government of France, the French Ambassador presented to His Majesty the King at Ems the demand to authorize him to telegraph to Paris that His Majesty the King would obligate himself for all future time never again to give his approval to the candidacy of the Hohenzollerns should it be renewed.

His Majesty the King thereupon refused to receive the French envoy again and informed him through an adjutant that His Majesty had nothing further to say to the Ambassador.

What did Bismarck do to the Ems telegram? What does this affair tell us about Bismarck's motives?

The Austrian Empire: Toward a Dual Monarchy

After crushing the revolutions of 1848–1849, the Habsburgs restored centralized, autocratic government to their empire. But failure in war led to severe internal consequences for Austria. Defeat at the hands of the Prussians in 1866 forced the Austrians to deal with the fiercely nationalistic Hungarians. The result was the negotiated *Ausgleich*, or Compromise, of 1867, which created the Dual Monarchy of Austria-Hungary. Each part of the empire now had its constitution, its own bicameral legislature, its own governmental machinery for domestic affairs, and its own capital (Vienna for Austria and Buda, which soon merged with the city of Pest to become Budapest, for Hungary). Holding the two states together were a single monarch (Francis Joseph was emperor of Austria and king of Hungary) and a common army, foreign policy, and system of finances. In domestic affairs, the Hungarians had become an independent nation. The *Ausgleich* did not, however, satisfy the other nationalities that made up the multinational Austro-Hungarian Empire (see Map 22.4). The Dual Monarchy simply enabled the German-speaking Austrians and Hungarian Magyars to dominate the minorities, especially the Slavs, in their respective states. As the Hungarian nationalist Louis Kossuth remarked, "Dualism is the alliance of the conservative, reactionary and any apparently liberal elements in Hungary with those of the Austrian Germans who despise liberty, for the oppression of the other nationalities and races."[4]

Imperial Russia

The defeat in the Crimean War in 1856 at the hands of the British and French revealed the blatant deficiencies behind the facade of absolute power and made it clear even to staunch conservatives that Russia was falling hopelessly behind the western European powers. Tsar Alexander II (1855–1881) turned his energies to a serious overhaul of the Russian system.

Serfdom was the most burdensome problem in tsarist Russia. The continuing subjugation of millions of peasants to the land and their landlords was an obviously corrupt and failing system. On March 3, 1861, Alexander issued his emancipation edict (see the box on p. 421). Peasants could now own property, marry as they chose, and bring suits in the law courts. Nevertheless, the benefits of emancipation were limited. The government provided land for the peasants by purchasing it from the

MAP 22.3 **Europe in 1871.** By 1871, most of the small states of Europe had been absorbed into larger ones, leaving the major powers uncomfortably rubbing shoulders with one another. Meanwhile, the power equation was shifting: the German Empire increased in power while Austria-Hungary and the Ottoman Empire declined. ❓ Of the great powers, which had the greatest overall exposure to the others in terms of shared borders and sea access? 🌐 **View an animated version of this map or related maps at** http://thomsonedu.com/history/spielvogel

landlords, but the landowners often chose to keep the best parcels. The Russian peasants soon found that they had inadequate amounts of good arable land to support themselves, a situation that worsened as the peasant population increased rapidly in the second half of the nineteenth century.

Nor were the peasants completely free. The state compensated the landowners for the land given to the peasants, but the peasants, in turn, were expected to repay the state in long-term installments. To ensure that the payments were made, peasants were subjected to the authority of their *mir*, or village commune, which was collectively responsible for the land payments to the government. In a very real sense, then, the village commune, not the individual peasants, owned the land the

peasants were purchasing. And since the village communes were responsible for the payments, they were reluctant to allow peasants to leave their land. Emancipation, then, led not to a free, landowning peasantry along the Western model but to an unhappy, land-starved peasantry that largely followed the old ways of farming.

Alexander II also attempted other reforms. In 1864, he instituted a system of **zemstvos**, or local assemblies, that provided a moderate degree of self-government. Zemstvos were given limited power to provide public services, such as education, famine relief, and road and bridge maintenance. They could levy taxes for these services, but their efforts were frequently disrupted by bureaucrats who feared any hint of self-government. The legal reforms of 1864, which created a regular system of

MAP 22.4 **Ethnic Groups in the Dual Monarchy, 1867.** Nationalism continued to be a problem in the Austrian Empire after suppression of the 1848–1849 revolutions. Military defeats led Emperor Francis Joseph to create the Dual Monarchy, giving Hungary power over its domestic affairs. However, the demands of other ethnic minorities went largely unmet. ❓ Which ethnic group was most widely dispersed throughout the Dual Monarchy? 🖱 **View an animated version of this map or related maps at** http://thomsonedu.com/history/spielvogel

Emancipation of the Serfs.
On March 3, 1961, Tsar Alexander II issued an edict emancipating the Russian serfs. This illustration shows at left the emperor making his proclamation while at the right serfs express their gratitude to the tsar.

EMANCIPATION: SERFS AND SLAVES

Although overall their histories have been quite different, Russia and the United States shared a common feature in the 1860s. They were the only states in the Western world that still had large enslaved populations (the Russian serfs were virtually slaves). The leaders of both countries issued emancipation proclamations within two years of each other. The first excerpt is taken from Tsar Alexander II's Imperial Decree of March 3, 1861, which freed the Russian serfs. The second excerpt is from Abraham Lincoln's Emancipation Proclamation, issued on January 1, 1863.

The Imperial Decree, March 3, 1861

By the grace of God, we, Alexander II, Emperor and Autocrat of all the Russias, King of Poland, Grand Duke of Finland, etc., to all our faithful subjects, make known:

Called by Divine Providence and by the sacred right of inheritance to the throne of our ancestors, we took a vow in our innermost heart to respond to the mission which is intrusted to us as to surround with our affection and our Imperial solicitude all our faithful subjects of every rank and of every condition, from the warrior, who nobly bears arms for the defense of the country to the humble artisan devoted to the works of industry; from the official in the career of the high offices of the State to the laborer whose plow furrows the soil. . . .

We thus came to the conviction that the work of a serious improvement of the condition of the peasants was a sacred inheritance bequeathed to us by our ancestors, a mission which, in the course of events, Divine providence called upon us to fulfill. . . .

In virtue of the new dispositions above mentioned, the peasants attached to the soil will be invested within a term fixed by the law with all the rights of free cultivators. . . .

At the same time, they are granted the right of purchasing their close, and, with the consent of the proprietors, they may acquire in full property the arable lands and other appurtenances which are allotted to them as a permanent holding. By the acquisition in full property of the quantity of land fixed, the peasants are free from their obligations toward the proprietors for land thus purchased, and they enter definitely into the condition of free peasants—landholders.

The Emancipation Proclamation, January 1, 1863

Now therefore, I, Abraham Lincoln, President of the United States, by virtue of the power in me vested as Commander-in-Chief of the Army and Navy of the United States in time of actual armed rebellion against the authority and government of the United States, and as a fit and necessary war measure for suppressing such rebellion, do, on this 1st day of January, A.D. 1863, and in accordance with my purpose to do so, . . . order and designate as the States and parts of States wherein the people thereof, respectively, are this day in rebellion against the United States the following, to wit:

Arkansas, Texas, Louisiana, . . . Mississippi, Alabama, Florida, Georgia, South Carolina, North Carolina, and Virginia. . . .

And by virtue of the power for the purpose aforesaid, I do order and declare that all persons held as slaves within said designated States and parts of States are, and henceforward shall be free; and that the Executive Government of the United States, including the military and naval authorities thereof, will recognize and maintain the freedom of said persons.

What changes did Tsar Alexander's emancipation of the serfs initiate in Russia? What effect did Lincoln's Emancipation Proclamation have on the southern "armed rebellion"? What reason does each leader give for his actions?

local and provincial courts and a judicial code that accepted the principle of equality before the law, proved successful, however.

Even the autocratic tsar was unable to control the forces he unleashed by his reform program. Reformers wanted more and rapid change; conservatives opposed what they perceived as the tsar's attempts to undermine the basic institutions of Russian society. By 1870, Russia was witnessing increasing levels of dissatisfaction. When one group of radicals assassinated Alexander II in 1881, his son and successor, Alexander III (1881–1894), turned against reform and returned to the traditional methods of repression.

Great Britain: The Victorian Age

Like Russia, Britain was not troubled by revolutionary disturbances during 1848, although for quite different reasons. The Reform Act of 1832 had opened the door to political representation for the industrial middle class, and in the 1860s, Britain's liberal parliamentary system demonstrated once again its ability to make both social and political reforms that kept the country stable and prosperous.

One of the reasons for Britain's stability was its continuing economic growth. After 1850, middle-class prosperity was at last coupled with some improvements for the working classes. Real wages for laborers increased more than 25 percent between 1850 and 1870. The British feeling of national pride was well reflected in Queen Victoria, whose reign from 1837 to 1901 was the longest in English history. Victoria had nine children and, when she died at age eighty-one, thirty-seven great-grandchildren. Her sense of duty and moral respectability reflected the attitudes of her age, which has ever since been known as the Victorian Age.

Politically, this was an era of uneasy stability as the aristocratic and upper-middle-class representatives who dominated Parliament blurred party lines by their internal strife and shifting positions. One important issue was the extension of voting rights. The Tory (Conservative Party) leader in Parliament, Benjamin Disraeli (1804–1881), became a supporter of voting reform, primarily because he thought he could win over the newly enfranchised groups to his party. The Reform Act of 1867 was an important step toward the democratization of Britain. By lowering the monetary requirements for voting (taxes paid or income earned), it enfranchised many male urban workers. The number of voters increased from about one million to slightly over two million. Although Disraeli believed this would benefit the Conservatives, industrial workers helped produce a huge Liberal victory in 1868.

The United States: Slavery and War

By the mid-nineteenth century, American national unity was increasingly threatened by the issue of slavery. Like the North, the South had grown dramatically in population during the first half of the nineteenth century. But its development was quite different. Its cotton economy and social structure were based on the exploitation of enslaved black Africans and their descendants. The importance of cotton is evident from production figures. In 1810, the South produced a raw cotton crop of 178,000 bales worth $10 million. By 1860, it was generating 4.5 million bales of cotton with a value of $249 million. Ninety-three percent of southern cotton in 1850 was produced by a slave population that had grown dramatically in fifty years. Although new slave imports had been barred in 1808, there were four million African American slaves in the South by 1860, four times the number in 1800. The cotton economy and plantation-based slavery were intimately related, and the attempt to maintain them in the first half of the nineteenth century led the South to become increasingly defensive, monolithic, and isolated. At the same time, the growth of an abolitionist movement in the North challenged the southern order and created an "emotional chain reaction" that led to civil war.

As polarization over the issue of slavery intensified, compromise became less feasible. When Abraham Lincoln, the man who had said in a speech in Illinois in 1858 that "this government cannot endure permanently half slave and half free," was elected president in November 1860, the die was cast. Lincoln carried only 2 of the 1,109 counties in the South; the Republicans were not even on the ballot in ten southern states. On December 20, 1860, a South Carolina convention voted to repeal ratification of the Constitution of the United States. In February 1861, six more southern states did the same, and a rival nation—the Confederate States of America—was formed. In March, fighting erupted between North and South.

CHRONOLOGY The National State

France	
Louis Napoleon's election as president	1848
Creation of the Second Empire	1852
Emperor Napoleon III	1852–1870
"Authoritarian empire"	1852–1860
Crimean War	1854–1856
"Liberal empire"	1860–1870
Austrian Empire	
Ausgleich: Dual Monarchy	1867
Russia	
Tsar Alexander II	1855–1881
Emancipation edict	1861 (March 3)
Creation of zemstvos and legal reforms	1864
Great Britain	
Queen Victoria	1837–1901
Reform Act	1867
United States	
Election of Lincoln and secession of South Carolina	1860
Outbreak of Civil War	1861
Surrender of Lee	1865 (April 9)
Canada	
Formation of Dominion of Canada	1867

The Civil War The American Civil War (1861–1865) was an extraordinarily bloody struggle. More than 600,000 soldiers died, either in battle or from deadly infectious diseases spawned by filthy camp conditions. Over a period of four years, the Union states of the North mobilized their superior assets and gradually wore down the Confederate forces of the South. As the war dragged on, it had the effect of radicalizing public opinion in the North. What began as a war to save the Union became a war against slavery. On January 1, 1863, Lincoln's Emancipation Proclamation made most of the nation's slaves "forever free" (see the box on p. 421). An increasingly effective Union blockade of the South combined with a shortage of fighting men made the Confederate cause desperate by the end of 1864. The final push of Union troops under General Ulysses S. Grant forced General Robert E. Lee's Confederate army to surrender on April 9, 1865. Although problems lay ahead, the Union victory confirmed that the United States would be "one nation, indivisible."

The Emergence of a Canadian Nation

Nation building was also taking place to the north of the United States. By the Treaty of Paris in 1763, Canada—or New France, as it was called—passed into the hands of the

British. By 1800, most Canadians favored more autonomy, although the colonists disagreed on the form this autonomy should take. Upper Canada (now Ontario) was predominantly English-speaking, while Lower Canada (now Quebec) was dominated by French Canadians. Increased immigration to Canada after 1815 also fueled the desire for self-government.

In 1837, a number of Canadian groups rose in rebellion against British authority. Rebels in Lower Canada demanded separation from Britain, creation of a republic, universal male suffrage, and freedom of the press. Although the rebellions were crushed by the following year, the British government now began to seek ways to satisfy some of the Canadian demands. The American Civil War proved to be a turning point. Fearful of U.S. designs on Canada during the war and eager to reduce the costs of maintaining the colonies, the British government finally capitulated to Canadian demands. In 1867, Parliament established the Canadian nation—the Dominion of Canada—with its own constitution. Canada now possessed a parliamentary system and ruled itself, although foreign affairs still remained under the control of the British government.

Industrialization and the Marxist Response

Between 1850 and 1871, Continental industrialization came of age. The innovations of the British Industrial Revolution—mechanized factory production, the use of coal, the steam engine, and the transportation revolution—all became regular features of economic expansion. Although marred periodically by economic depression (1857–1858) or recession (1866–1867), this was an age of considerable economic prosperity, particularly evident in the growth of domestic and foreign markets.

Before 1870, capitalist factory owners remained largely free to hire labor on their own terms based on market forces. Although workers formed trade unions as organizations that would fight for improved working conditions and reasonable wages, they tended to represent only a small part of the industrial working class and proved largely ineffective. Real change for the industrial proletariat would come only with the development of socialist parties and socialist trade unions. These emerged after 1870, but the theory that made them possible had already been developed by mid-century in the work of Karl Marx.

Marx and Marxism

The beginnings of **Marxism** can be traced to the 1848 publication of a short treatise titled *The Communist Manifesto,* written by two Germans, Karl Marx (1818–1883) and Friedrich Engels (1820–1895). It became one of the most influential political treatises in modern European history.

© Bettmann/CORBIS

Karl Marx. Karl Marx was a radical journalist who joined with Friedrich Engels to write *The Communist Manifesto*, which proclaimed the ideas of a revolutionary socialism. After the failure of the 1848 revolution in Germany, Marx fled to Britain, where he continued to write and became involved in the work of the first International Working Men's Association.

Marx and Engels began their treatise with the statement that "the history of all hitherto existing society is the history of class struggles." Throughout history, oppressed and oppressor have "stood in constant opposition to one another." In an earlier struggle, the feudal classes of the Middle Ages were forced to accede to the emerging middle class or bourgeoisie. As the bourgeoisie took control in turn, its ideas became the dominant views of the era, and government became its instrument. Marx and Engels declared, "The executive of the modern State is but a committee for managing the common affairs of the whole bourgeoisie."[5] In other words, the government of the state reflected and defended the interests of the industrial middle class and its allies.

Although bourgeois society had emerged victorious out of the ruins of feudal society, Marx and Engels insisted that it had not triumphed completely. Now once again the bourgeois were antagonists in an emerging class struggle, but this time they faced the **proletariat**, or the industrial working class. The struggle would be fierce; in fact, Marx and Engels predicted that the workers would

THE CLASSLESS SOCIETY

In The Communist Manifesto, Karl Marx and Friedrich Engels projected the creation of a classless society as the end product of the struggle between the bourgeoisie and the proletariat. In this selection, they discuss the steps by which that classless society would be reached.

Karl Marx and Friedrich Engels, *The Communist Manifesto*

We have seen above, that the first step in the revolution by the working class, is to raise the proletariat to the position of ruling class. . . . The proletariat will use its political supremacy to wrest, by degrees, all capital from the bourgeoisie, to centralize all instruments of production in the hands of the State, i.e., of the proletariat organized as the ruling class; and to increase the total of productive forces as rapidly as possible.

Of course, in the beginning, this cannot be effected except by means of despotic inroads on the rights of property, and on the conditions of bourgeois production; by means of measures, therefore, which . . . necessitate further inroads upon the old social order, and are unavoidable as a means of entirely revolutionizing the mode of production.

These measures will of course be different in different countries.

Nevertheless, in the most advanced countries, the following will be pretty generally applicable:

1. Abolition of property in land and application of all rents of land to public purposes.
2. A heavy progressive or graduated income tax.
3. Abolition of all right of inheritance. . . .
5. Centralization of credit in the hands of the State, by means of a national bank with State capital and an exclusive monopoly.
6. Centralization of the means of communication and transport in the hands of the State.
7. Extension of factories and instruments of production owned by the State. . . .
8. Equal liability of all to labor. Establishment of industrial armies, especially for agriculture.
9. Combination of agriculture with manufacturing industries; gradual abolition of the distinction between town and country, by a more equable distribution of the population over the country.
10. Free education for all children in public schools. Abolition of children's factory labor in its present form. . . .

When, in the course of development, class distinctions have disappeared, and all production has been concentrated in the whole nation, the public power will lose its political character. Political power, properly so called, is merely the organized power of one class for oppressing another. If the proletariat during its contest with the bourgeoisie is compelled, by the force of circumstances, to organize itself as a class, if, by means of a revolution, it makes itself the ruling class, and, as such, sweeps away by force the old conditions of production, then it will, along with these conditions, have swept away the conditions for the existence of class antagonisms and of classes generally, and will thereby have abolished its own supremacy as a class.

In place of the old bourgeois society, with its classes and class antagonisms, we shall have an association, in which the free development of each is the condition for the free development of all.

How did Marx and Engels define the proletariat? The bourgeoisie? Why did Marxists come to believe that this distinction was paramount for understanding history? What steps did Marx and Engels believe would lead to a classless society?

---

eventually overthrow their bourgeois masters. After their victory, the proletariat would form a dictatorship to reorganize the means of production. Then a classless society would emerge, and the state—itself an instrument of the bourgeoisie—would wither away, since it no longer represented the interests of a particular class. Class struggles would be over (see the box above). Marx believed that the emergence of a classless society would lead to progress in science, technology, and industry and to greater wealth for all.

After the failure of the revolutions of 1848, Marx went to London, where he spent the rest of his life. He continued his writing on political economy, especially his famous work *Das Kapital* (*Capital*), but his own preoccupation with organizing the working-class movement kept Marx from ever finishing the book. In *The Communist Manifesto,* Marx had defined the communists as "the most advanced and resolute section of the working-class parties of every country." Their advantage was their ability to understand "the line of march, the conditions, and the ultimate general results of the proletarian movement."[6] Marx saw his role in this light and participated enthusiastically in the activities of the International Working Men's Association. Formed in 1864 by British and French trade unionists, this "First International" served as an umbrella organization for working-class interests. Marx was the dominant personality on the organization's General Council and devoted much time to its activities. Internal dissension, however, soon crippled the organization, and it failed in 1872. Although it would be revived in 1889, the fate of socialism by that time was in the hands of national socialist parties.

Science and Culture in an Age of Realism

Between 1850 and 1870, two major intellectual developments were evident: the growth of scientific knowledge, with its rapidly increasing impact on the Western worldview, and the shift from Romanticism, with its emphasis on the inner world of reality, to Realism, with its focus on the outer, material world.

A New Age of Science

By the mid-nineteenth century, science was having an ever-greater impact on European life. The Scientific Revolution of the sixteenth and seventeenth centuries had fundamentally transformed the Western worldview and fostered a modern, rational approach to the study of the natural world. Even in the eighteenth century, however, these intellectual developments had remained the preserve of an educated elite and resulted in few practical benefits. Moreover, the technical advances of the early Industrial Revolution had depended little on pure science and much more on the practical experiments of technologically oriented amateur inventors. Advances in industrial technology, however, fed an interest in basic scientific research, which from the 1830s on resulted in a rash of basic scientific discoveries that were soon transformed into technological improvements that affected all Europeans.

The development of the steam engine was important in encouraging scientists to work out its theoretical foundations, a preoccupation that led to the study of thermodynamics, the science of the relationship between heat and mechanical energy. The laws of thermodynamics were at the core of nineteenth-century physics. In biology, the Frenchman Louis Pasteur (1822–1895) postulated the germ theory of disease, which had enormous practical applications in the development of modern, scientific medical practices. In chemistry, the Russian Dmitri Mendeleyev (1834–1907) in the 1860s classified all the material elements then known on the basis of their atomic weights and provided the systematic foundation for the periodic law. The Briton Michael Faraday (1791–1867) discovered the phenomenon of electromagnetic induction and put together a primitive generator that laid the groundwork for the use of electricity, although economically efficient generators were not built until the 1870s.

The steadily increasing and often dramatic material benefits generated by science and technology led Europeans to a growing faith in the benefits of science. The popularity of scientific and technological achievements produced a widespread acceptance of the scientific method, based on observation, experiment, and logical analysis, as the only path to objective truth and objective reality. This, in turn, undermined the faith of many people in religious revelation and truth. It is no accident that the nineteenth century was an age of increasing secularization, particularly evident in the growth of

materialism, the belief that everything mental, spiritual, or ideal was simply a result of physical forces. Truth was to be found in the concrete material existence of human beings, not, as the Romantics imagined, in revelations gained by feeling or intuitive flashes. The importance of materialism was strikingly evident in the most important scientific event of the nineteenth century, the development of the theory of **organic evolution** according to **natural selection**. On the theories of Charles Darwin could be built a picture of humans as material beings that were simply part of the natural world.

Charles Darwin and the Theory of Organic Evolution

In 1859, Charles Darwin (1809–1882) published his celebrated book *On the Origin of Species by Means of Natural Selection.* The basic idea of this book was that all plants and animals had evolved over a long period of time from earlier and simpler forms of life, a principle known as organic evolution. Darwin was important in explaining how this natural process worked. In every species, he argued, "many more individuals of each species are born than can possibly survive." This results in a "struggle for existence": "As more individuals are produced than can possibly survive, there must in every case be a struggle for existence, either one individual with another of the same species, or with the individuals of distinct species, or with the physical conditions of life." Those who succeeded in this struggle for existence had adapted better to their environment, a process made possible by the appearance of "variants." Chance variations that occurred in the process of inheritance enabled some organisms to be more adaptable to the environment than others, a process that Darwin called natural selection: "Owing to this struggle [for existence], variations, however slight . . . , if they be in any degree profitable to the individuals of a species, in their infinitely complex relations to other organic beings and to their physical conditions of life, will tend to the preservation of such individuals, and will generally be inherited by the offspring."[7] Those that were naturally selected for survival ("survival of the fit") survived. The unfit did not and became extinct. The fit who survived, in turn, propagated and passed on the variations that enabled them to survive until, from Darwin's point of view, a separate species emerged.

In *On the Origin of Species,* Darwin discussed plant and animal species only. He was not concerned with human beings and only later applied his theory of natural selection to humans. In *The Descent of Man,* published in 1871, he argued for the animal origins of human beings: "Man is the co-descendant with other mammals of a common progenitor." Humans were not an exception to the rule governing other species.

Darwin's ideas were highly controversial at first. Some people fretted that Darwin's theory made human beings ordinary products of nature rather than unique beings. Others were disturbed by the implications of life

REALISM: CHARLES DICKENS AND AN IMAGE OF HELL ON EARTH

*C*harles Dickens was one of Britain's greatest novelists. While he realistically portrayed the material, social, and psychological milieu of his time, an element of Romanticism still pervaded his novels. This is evident in this selection from *The Old Curiosity Shop,* in which his description of the English mill town of Birmingham takes on the imagery of Dante's Hell.

Charles Dickens, *The Old Curiosity Shop*

A long suburb of red brick houses,—some with patches of garden ground, where coal-dust and factory smoke darkened the shrinking leaves, and coarse rank flowers; and where the struggling vegetation sickened and sank under the hot breath of kiln and furnace, making them by its presence seem yet more blighting and unwholesome than in the town itself,—a long, flat, straggling suburb passed, they came by slow degrees upon a cheerless region, where not a blade of grass was seen to grow; where not a bud put forth its promise in the spring; where nothing green could live but on the surface of the stagnant pools, which here and there lay idly sweltering by the black roadside.

Advancing more and more into the shadow of this mournful place, its dark depressing influence stole upon their spirits, and filled them with a dismal gloom. On every side, and as far as the eye could see into the heavy distance, tall chimneys, crowding on each other, and presenting that endless repetition of the same dull, ugly form, which is the horror of oppressive dreams, poured out their plague of smoke, obscured the light, and made foul the melancholy air. On mounds of ashes by the wayside, sheltered only by a few rough boards, or rotten pent-house roofs, strange engines spun and writhed like tortured creatures; clanking their iron chains, shrieking in their rapid whirl from time to time as though in torment unendurable, and making the ground tremble with their agonies. Dismantled houses here and there appeared, tottering to the earth, propped up by fragments of others that had fallen down, unroofed, windowless, blackened, desolate, but yet inhabited. Men, women, children, wan in their looks and ragged in attire, tended the engines, fed their tributary fires, begged upon the road, or scowled half-naked from the doorless houses. Then came more of the wrathful monsters, whose like they almost seemed to be in their wildness and their untamed air, screeching and turning to the right and left, with the same interminable perspective of brick towers, never ceasing in their black vomit, blasting all things living or inanimate, shutting out the face of day, and closing in on all these horrors with a dense dark cloud.

But night-time in this dreadful spot!—night, when the smoke was changed to fire; when every chimney spurted up its flame; and places, that had been dark vaults all day, now shone red-hot, with figures moving to and fro within their blazing jaws, and calling to one another with hoarse cries—night, when the noise of every strange machine was aggravated by the darkness; when the people near them looked wilder and more savage; when bands of unemployed laborers paraded in the roads, or clustered by torchlight round their leaders, who told them in stern language of their wrongs, and urged them on by frightful cries and threats; when maddened men, armed with sword and firebrand, spurning the tears and prayers of women who would restrain them, rushed forth on errands of terror and destruction, to work no ruin half so surely as their own—night, when carts came rumbling by, filled with rude coffins (for contagious disease and death had been busy with the living crops); or when orphans cried, and distracted women shrieked and followed in their wake. . . .

What image of Birmingham do you get from this selection by Dickens? Why is it so powerful? What does it reveal about Dickens himself?

---

as a struggle for survival, of "nature red in tooth and claw." Was there a place in the Darwinian world for moral values? For those who believed in a rational order in the world, Darwin's theory seemed to eliminate purpose and design from the universe. Gradually, however, Darwin's theory was accepted by scientists and other intellectuals. In the process of accepting Darwin's ideas, some people even tried to apply them to society, yet another example of science's increasing prestige.

Realism in Literature

The belief that the world should be viewed realistically, frequently expressed after 1850, was closely related to the materialistic outlook. The term **Realism** was first employed in 1850 to describe a new style of painting and soon spread to literature.

The literary Realists of the mid-nineteenth century were distinguished by their deliberate rejection of Romanticism. The literary Realists wanted to deal with ordinary characters from actual life rather than Romantic heroes in unusual settings. They also sought to avoid flowery and sentimental language by using careful observation and accurate description, an approach that led them to eschew poetry in favor of prose and the novel. Realists often combined their interest in everyday life with a searching examination of social questions.

The leading novelist of the 1850s and 1860s, the Frenchman Gustave Flaubert (1821–1880), perfected the Realist novel. His *Madame Bovary* (1857) was a

Gustave Courbet, *The Stonebreakers*. Realism, largely developed by French painters, aimed at a lifelike portrayal of the daily activities of ordinary people. Gustave Courbet was the most famous of the Realist artists. As is evident in *The Stonebreakers*, he sought to portray things as they really appear. He shows an old road builder and his young assistant in their tattered clothes, engrossed in their dreary work of breaking stones to construct a road.

straightforward description of barren and sordid provincial life in France. Emma Bovary, a woman of some vitality, is trapped in a marriage to a drab provincial doctor. Impelled by the images of romantic love she has read about in novels, she seeks the same thing for herself in adulterous affairs. Unfulfilled, she is ultimately driven to suicide, unrepentant to the end for her lifestyle. Flaubert's contempt for bourgeois society was evident in his portrayal of middle-class hypocrisy and smugness.

William Thackeray (1811–1863) wrote the prototypical Realist novel in Britain: *Vanity Fair*, published in 1848. Subtitled *A Novel Without a Hero*, the book deliberately flaunted Romantic conventions. A novel, Thackeray said, should "convey as strongly as possible the sentiment of reality as opposed to a tragedy or poem, which may be heroical." Perhaps the greatest of the Victorian novelists was Charles Dickens (1812–1870), whose realistic novels focusing on the lower and middle classes in Britain's early industrial age became extraordinarily popular. His descriptions of the urban poor and the brutalization of human life were vividly realistic (see the box on p. 426).

Realism in Art

In art, Realism became dominant after 1850, although Romanticism was by no means dead. Among the most important characteristics of Realism are a desire to depict

Jean-François Millet, *The Gleaners*. Jean-François Millet, another prominent French Realist painter, took a special interest in the daily activities of French peasants, although he tended to transform his peasants into heroic figures who dominated their environment. In *The Gleaners*, for example, the three peasant women who are engaged in the backbreaking work of gathering grain left after the harvest still appear as powerful figures, symbolizing the union of humans with the earth.

the everyday life of ordinary people, whether peasants, workers, or prostitutes; an attempt at photographic realism; and an interest in the natural environment. The French became leaders in Realist painting.

Gustave Courbet (1819–1877) was the most famous artist of the Realist school. In fact, the term *Realism* was first applied to one of his paintings. Courbet reveled in a straightforward portrayal of everyday life. His subjects were factory workers, peasants, and the wives of saloon keepers. "I have never seen either angels or goddesses, so I am not interested in painting them," he exclaimed. One of his famous works, *The Stonebreakers*, painted in 1849, shows two men engaged in the exhausting work of breaking stones to build a road. This representation of

human misery was a scandal to those who objected to his "cult of ugliness." To Courbet, no subject was too ordinary, too harsh, or too ugly.

Jean-François Millet (1814–1875) was preoccupied with scenes from rural life, especially peasants laboring in the fields, although his Realism still contained an element of Romantic sentimentality. In *The Gleaners*, Millet's most famous work, three peasant women gather grain in a field, a centuries-old practice that for Millet showed the symbiotic relationship between humans and nature. Millet made landscapes and country life important subjects for French artists, but he too was criticized by his contemporaries for crude subject matter and unorthodox technique.

TIMELINE

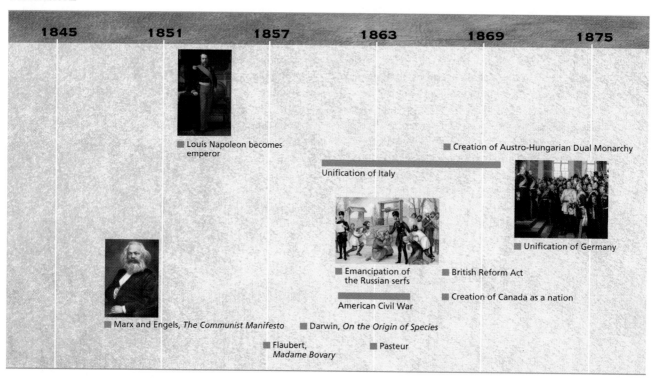

1845   1851   1857   1863   1869   1875

- Louis Napoleon becomes emperor
- Creation of Austro-Hungarian Dual Monarchy
- Unification of Italy
- Unification of Germany
- Emancipation of the Russian serfs
- British Reform Act
- Creation of Canada as a nation
- American Civil War
- Marx and Engels, *The Communist Manifesto*
- Darwin, *On the Origin of Species*
- Flaubert, *Madame Bovary*
- Pasteur

CONCLUSION

Between 1850 and 1871, the national state became the focus of people's loyalty. Wars, both foreign and civil, were fought to create unified nation-states. Political nationalism had emerged during the French revolutionary era and had become a powerful force of change during the first half of the nineteenth century, but its triumph came only after 1850. Tied initially to middle-class liberals, by the end of the nineteenth century it would have great appeal to the broad masses as well. In 1871, however, the political transformations stimulated

by the force for nationalism were incomplete. Large minorities, especially in the polyglot empires controlled by the Austrians, Ottoman Turks, and Russians, had not achieved the goal of their own national states. Moreover, the nationalism that had triumphed by 1871 was no longer the nationalism that had been closely identified with liberalism. Liberal nationalists had believed that unified nation-states would preserve individual rights and lead to a greater community of peoples. Rather than unifying people, however, the loud and chauvinistic nationalism of the late nineteenth century divided them as the new national states became embroiled in bitter competition after 1871.

Europeans, however, were hardly aware of nationalism's dangers in 1871. The spread of industrialization and the wealth of scientific and technological achievements were sources of optimism. After the revolutionary and military upheavals of the mid-century decades, many Europeans believed that they stood on the verge of a new age of progress.

NOTES

1. Quoted in J. F. McMillan, *Napoleon III* (New York, 1991), p. 37.
2. L. L. Snyder, ed., *Documents of German History* (New Brunswick, N.J., 1958), p. 202.
3. Quoted in O. Pflanze, *Bismarck and the Development of Germany: The Period of Unification, 1815–1871* (Princeton, N.J., 1963), p. 327.
4. Quoted in G. Szabad, *Hungarian Political Trends Between the Revolution and the Compromise, 1849–1867* (Budapest, 1977), p. 163.
5. K. Marx and F. Engels, *The Communist Manifesto* (Harmondsworth, England, 1967), pp. 79, 81, 82.
6. Ibid., p. 95.
7. C. Darwin, *On the Origin of Species* (New York, 1872), vol. 1, pp. 77, 79.

SUGGESTIONS FOR FURTHER READING

Three general surveys of the mid-century decades are **N. Rich, *The Age of Nationalism and Reform, 1850–1890,*** 2d ed. (New York, 1979); **E. Hobsbawm, *The Age of Capital, 1845–1875*** (London, 1975); and **J.A.S. Grenville, *Europe Reshaped, 1848–1878*** (London, 1976). In addition to the books listed for individual countries in Chapter 21 that also cover the material of this chapter, see **G. Craig, *Germany, 1866–1945*** (Oxford, 1981); the two detailed volumes of **T. Zeldin, *France, 1848–1945*** (Oxford, 1973–1977); **A. J. May, *The Habsburg Monarchy, 1867–1914*** (Cambridge, Mass., 1951); and **D. Read, *England, 1868–1914*** (London, 1979).

For a good introduction to the French Second Empire, see **A. Plessis, *The Rise and Fall of the Second Empire, 1852–1871,*** trans. **J. Mandelbaum** (New York, 1985). Napoleon's role can be examined in **J. F. McMillan, *Napoleon III*** (New York, 1991). The Crimean War and its impact are examined in **P. W. Schroeder, *Austria, Great Britain, and the Crimean War: The Destruction of the European Concert*** (Ithaca, N.Y., 1972), and **N. Rich, *Why the Crimean War?*** (Hanover, N.H., 1985).

The unification of Italy can be examined in **F. Coppa, *The Origins of the Italian Wars of Independence*** (New York, 1992); **D. M. Smith, *Cavour*** (London, 1985); and **H. Hearder, *Cavour*** (New York, 1994). The unification of Germany can be pursued first in **W. Carr, *The Origins of the Wars of German Unification*** (New York, 1991), and two good biographies of Bismarck, **E. Crankshaw, *Bismarck*** (New York, 1981), and **E. Feuchtwanger, *Bismarck*** (London, 2002). See also the brief study by **B. Waller, *Bismarck,***

2d ed. (Oxford, 1997). On the Franco-Prussian War, see **G. Wawro, *The Franco-Prussian War*** (Cambridge, 2003).

On the emancipation of the Russian serfs, see **D. Field, *The End of Serfdom: Nobility and Bureaucracy in Russia, 1855–1861*** (Cambridge, 1976). On Disraeli, see **I. Machlin, *Disraeli*** (London, 1995). A good one-volume survey of the Civil War can be found in **P. J. Parish, *The American Civil War*** (New York, 1975).

In addition to the general works on economic development listed in Chapters 20 and 21, some specialized works on this period are worthwhile. These include **W. O. Henderson, *The Rise of German Industrial Power, 1834–1914*** (Berkeley, Calif., 1975), and **F. Crouzet, *The Victorian Economy*** (London, 1982). On Marx, the standard work is **D. McLellan, *Karl Marx: His Life and Thought*** (New York, 1975), but it can be supplemented by the interesting and comprehensive work by **L. Kolakowski, *Main Currents of Marxism,*** 3 vols. (Oxford, 1978).

For an introduction to the intellectual changes of the nineteenth century, see **O. Chadwick, *The Secularization of the European Mind in the Nineteenth Century*** (Cambridge, 1975). A detailed biography of Darwin is **J. Bowlby, *Charles Darwin: A Biography*** (London, 1990). On Realism, **J. Malpas, *Realism*** (Cambridge, 1997), is a good introduction.

Thomson NOW! Enter *ThomsonNOW* using the access card that is available for *Western Civilization: A Brief History.* *ThomsonNOW* will help you understand this chapter with lesson plans generated for your needs. In addition, you can read the following documents, and many more, online:

> Charles Darwin, *On the Origin of Species*
> Otto von Bismarck, *Memoirs*
> Abraham Lincoln and Stephen Douglas debates
> The Emancipation of the Russian Serfs
> Karl Marx and Friedrich Engels, *The Communist Manifesto*

WESTERN CIVILIZATION RESOURCES

Visit the Web site for *Western Civilization: A Brief History* for resources specific to this book:

http://www.thomsonedu.com/history/spielvogel

For a variety of tools to help you succeed in this course, visit the Western Civilization Resource Center at

http://history.wadsworth.com/spielvogel

Included are quizzes, images, documents, interactive simulations, maps and timelines, movie explorations, and a wealth of other sources.

23

MASS SOCIETY IN AN "AGE OF PROGRESS," 1871–1894

CHAPTER OUTLINE
AND FOCUS QUESTIONS

The Growth of Industrial Prosperity

☐ What was the Second Industrial Revolution, and what effects did it have on European economic and social life?

☐ What roles did socialist parties and trade unions play in improving conditions for the working classes?

The Emergence of a Mass Society

☐ What is a mass society, and what were its main characteristics?

☐ What role were women expected to play in society and family life in the latter part of the nineteenth century, and how closely did patterns of family life correspond to this ideal?

The National State

☐ What general political trends were evident in the nations of western Europe in the last decades of the nineteenth century, and how did these trends differ from the policies pursued in Germany, Austria-Hungary, and Russia?

CRITICAL THINKING

☐ What was the relationship between economic, social, and political developments between 1871 and 1894?

Swimmers gather in front of concession stands at Coney Island

𝓘N THE LATE nineteenth century, Europe was enjoying a dynamic age of material prosperity. Bringing new industries, new sources of energy, and new goods, a second Industrial Revolution transformed the human environment, dazzled Europeans, and led them to believe that their material progress was human progress. Scientific and technological achievements, many naively believed, would improve the human condition and solve all problems. The doctrine of progress became an article of great faith.

The new urban and industrial environment resulting from the rapid economic changes of the nineteenth century led to the emergence of a mass society. With it came improvements for the lower classes, who benefited from the extension of voting rights, a better standard of living, and free education. It also brought mass leisure. New work patterns established the "weekend" as a distinct time of recreation and fun, while new forms of mass transportation—railroads and streetcars—enabled even workers to make brief excursions to amusement parks. Coney Island was only 8 miles from central New York City; Blackpool in England was a short train ride from nearby industrial towns. With their Ferris wheels and other daring rides that threw young men and women together, amusement parks offered a whole new world of entertainment. Thanks to the railroad, seaside resorts, once the preserve of the wealthy, became accessible to more people for weekend visits, much to the disgust of one upper-class regular who described the new "day-trippers": "They swarm upon the beach, wandering listlessly about with apparently no other aim than to get a mouthful of fresh air." Entrepreneurs in resort areas, however, welcomed the masses of new visitors and built piers laden with food, drink, and entertainment to serve them.

The coming of mass society also created new roles for the governments of European nation-states, which now fostered national loyalty, formed vast armies by conscription, and took more responsibility for public health and housing measures in their cities. By 1871, the national state had become the focus of Europeans' lives. Within many of these nation-states, the growth of the middle class had led to the triumph of liberal practices: constitutional governments, parliaments, and principles of equality. The period after 1871 also witnessed the growth of political democracy as the right to vote was extended to all adult males; women, though, would still have to fight for their political rights. With political democracy came a new mass politics and a new mass press. Both would become standard features of the twentieth century.◆

The Growth of Industrial Prosperity

At the heart of Europeans' belief in progress after 1871 was the stunning material growth produced by what historians have called the Second Industrial Revolution. The original Industrial Revolution had given rise to textiles, railroads, iron, and coal. In the second revolution, steel, chemicals, electricity, and petroleum led the way to new industrial frontiers.

New Products

The first major change in industrial development after 1870 was the substitution of steel for iron. New methods of rolling and shaping steel made it useful in the construction of lighter, smaller, and faster machines and engines, as well as railways, ships, and armaments. In 1860, Great Britain, France, Germany, and Belgium produced 125,000 tons of steel; by 1913, the total was 32 million tons. By 1910, German steel production was double that of Great Britain, and both had been surpassed by the United States in 1890.

Electricity was a major new form of energy that proved to be of great value because it could be easily converted into other forms of energy, such as heat, light, and motion, and moved relatively effortlessly through wires. The first commercially practical generators of electrical current were developed in the 1870s. By 1910, hydroelectric

Courtesy private collection

An Age of Progress. Between 1871 and 1914, the Second Industrial Revolution led many Europeans to believe that they were living in an age of progress when most human problems would be solved by scientific achievements. This illustration is taken from a special issue of the *Illustrated London News* celebrating the Diamond Jubilee of Queen Victoria in 1897. On the left are scenes from 1837, when Victoria came to the British throne; on the right are scenes from 1897. The vivid contrast underscored the magazine's conclusion: "The most striking . . . evidence of progress during the reign is the ever increasing speed which the discoveries of physical science have forced into everyday life. Steam and electricity have conquered time and space to a greater extent during the last sixty years than all the preceding six hundred years witnessed."

power stations and coal-fired steam-generating plants enabled entire districts to be tied in to a single power distribution system that provided a common source of power for homes, shops, and industrial enterprises.

Electricity spawned spectacular new products. The invention of the lightbulb by the American Thomas Edison and the Briton Joseph Swan opened homes and cities to illumination by electric lights. A revolution in communications was fostered when Alexander Graham Bell invented the telephone in 1876 and Guglielmo Marconi sent the first radio waves across the Atlantic in 1901. Although most electricity was initially used for lighting, it was eventually put to use in transportation. By the 1880s, streetcars and subways had appeared in major European cities. Electricity also transformed the factory. Conveyor belts, cranes, machines, and machine tools could all be powered by electricity and located anywhere. Thanks to electricity, all countries could now enter the industrial age.

The development of the internal combustion engine had a similar effect. The processing of oil and gasoline made possible the widespread use of the internal combustion engine as a source of power in transportation. An oil-fired engine was made in 1897, and by 1902, the Hamburg-Amerika Line had switched from coal to oil on its new ocean liners. By the end of the nineteenth century, some naval fleets had been converted to oil burners as well.

The internal combustion engine gave rise to the automobile and the airplane. In 1900, world production stood at 9,000 cars; by 1906, Americans had overtaken the initial lead of the French. It was an American, Henry Ford, who revolutionized the car industry with the mass production of the affordable Model T. By 1916, Ford's factories were turning out 735,000 cars a year. In the meantime, air transportation began with the Zeppelin airship in 1900. In 1903, at Kitty Hawk, North Carolina, the Wright brothers, Orville and Wilbur, made the first flight in a fixed-wing plane powered by a gasoline engine. It took World War I to stimulate the aircraft industry, however, and the first regular passenger air service was not established until 1919.

New Markets

The growth of industrial production depended on the development of markets for the sale of manufactured goods. After 1870, the best foreign markets were already heavily saturated, forcing Europeans to take a renewed look at their domestic markets. Between 1850 and 1900, real wages increased by two-thirds in Britain and by one-third in Germany. As the prices of both food and manufactured goods declined due to lower transportation costs, Europeans could spend more on consumer products. Businesses soon perceived the value of using new techniques of mass marketing to sell the consumer goods made possible by the development of the steel and electrical industries. Bringing together a vast array of new products in one place, they created the department store (see the box on p. 433). The desire to own sewing machines, clocks, bicycles, electric lights, and typewriters created a new consumer ethic that rapidly became a crucial part of the modern economy.

Meanwhile, increased competition for foreign markets and the growing importance of domestic demand led to a reaction against the free trade that had characterized much of the European economy between 1820 and 1870. To many industrial and political leaders, protective **tariffs** guaranteed domestic markets for the products of their own industries. By the 1870s, Europeans were returning to tariff protection. At the same time, **cartels** were being formed to decrease competition internally. In a cartel, independent enterprises worked together to control prices and fix production quotas, thereby restraining the kind of competition that led to reduced prices.

The formation of cartels was paralleled by a move toward ever-larger factories, especially in the iron and steel, machine, heavy electrical equipment, and chemical industries. This growth in the size of industrial plants led to pressure for greater efficiency in factory production at the same time that competition led to demands for greater economy. The result was a desire to streamline or rationalize production as much as possible. The development of precision tools enabled manufacturers to produce interchangeable parts, which in turn led to the creation of the assembly line for production. First used in the United States for small arms and clocks, the assembly line had moved to Europe by 1850. In the second half of the nineteenth century, it was primarily used in manufacturing nonmilitary goods, such as sewing machines, typewriters, bicycles, and finally automobiles.

New Patterns in an Industrial Economy

The Second Industrial Revolution played a role in the emergence of basic economic patterns that have characterized much of modern European economic life. Although the period after 1871 has been characterized as an age of material prosperity, recessions and crises were still very much a part of economic life. From 1873 to 1895, Europeans experienced a series of economic crises. Prices, especially those of agricultural products, fell dramatically. After 1895, however, until World War I, Europe overall experienced an economic boom and achieved a level of prosperity that encouraged people later to look back to that era as *la belle époque*—a golden age in European civilization.

After 1870, Germany replaced Great Britain as the industrial leader of Europe. Already in the 1890s, Germany's superiority was evident in new areas of manufacturing, such as organic chemicals and electrical equipment, and was increasingly apparent in its ever-greater share of worldwide trade. But the struggle for economic (and political) supremacy between Great Britain and Germany should not cause us to overlook the other great polarization of the age. By 1900, Europe was divided into two economic zones. Great Britain, Belgium, France, the Netherlands, Germany, the western part of the Austro-Hungarian Empire, and northern Italy constituted an advanced industrialized core that had a high standard of living, decent systems of transportation, and relatively healthy and educated populations (see Map 23.1). The backward and little industrialized areas to the south and east, consisting of southern Italy, most of Austria-Hungary, Spain, Portugal, the Balkan kingdoms, and Russia, were still largely agricultural and relegated by the industrial countries to the function of providing food and raw materials. The presence of Romanian oil, Greek olive oil, and Serbian pigs and prunes in western Europe served as reminders of an economic division of Europe that continued well into the twentieth century.

THE DEPARTMENT STORE AND THE BEGINNINGS OF MASS CONSUMERISM

*D*omestic markets were especially important for the sale of the goods being turned out by Europe's increasing number of industrial plants. New techniques of mass marketing arose to encourage people to purchase the new consumer goods. The Parisians pioneered in the development of the department store, and this selection is taken from a contemporary's account of the growth of these stores in the French capital city.

E. Lavasseur, *"On Parisian Department Stores,"* 1907

It was in the reign of Louis-Philippe that department stores for fashion goods and dresses, extending to material and other clothing, began to be distinguished. The type was already one of the notable developments of the Second Empire; it became one of the most important ones of the Third Republic. These stores have increased in number and several of them have become extremely large. Combining in their different departments all articles of clothing, toilet articles, furniture and many other ranges of goods, it is their special object so to combine all commodities as to attract and satisfy customers who will find conveniently together an assortment of a mass of articles corresponding to all their various needs. They attract customers by permanent display, by free entry into the shops, by periodic exhibitions, by special sales, by fixed prices, and by their ability to deliver the goods purchased to customers' homes, in Paris and to the provinces. Turning themselves into direct intermediaries between the producer and the consumer, even producing sometimes some of their articles in their own workshops, buying at lowest prices because of their large orders and because they are in a position to profit from bargains, working with large sums, and selling to most of their customers for cash only, they can transmit these benefits in lowered selling prices. They can even decide to sell at a loss, as an advertisement or to get rid of out-of-date fashions. Taking 5–6 percent on 100 million [francs] brings them in more than 20 percent would bring to a firm doing a turnover of 50,000 francs.

The success of these department stores is only possible thanks to the volume of their business and this volume needs considerable capital and a very large turnover. Now capital, having become abundant, is freely combined nowadays in large enterprises, although French capital has the reputation of being more wary of the risks of industry than of State or railway securities. On the other hand, the large urban agglomerations, the ease with which goods can be transported by the railways, the diffusion of some comforts to strata below the middle classes, have all favored these developments.

As example we may cite some figures relating to these stores. . . . *Le Louvre,* dating to the time of the extension of the rue de Rivoli under the Second Empire, did in 1893 a business of 120 million at a profit of 6.4 percent. *Le Bon-Marché,* which was a small shop when Mr. Boucicaut entered it in 1852, already did a business of 20 million at the end of the Empire. During the republic its new buildings were erected; Mme. Boucicaut turned it by her will into a kind of cooperative society, with shares and an ingenious organization; turnover reached 150 million in 1893, leaving a profit of 5 percent. . . .

According to the tax records of 1891, these stores in Paris, numbering 12, employed 1,708 persons and were rated on their site values at 2,159,000 francs; the largest had then 542 employees. These same stores had, in 1901, 9,784 employees; one of them over 2,000 and another over 1,600; their site value has doubled (4,089,000 francs).

Did the invention of department stores respond to or create the new "consumer ethic" in industrialized societies? What was this new turn-of-the-century ethic? According to Lavasseur, what were the positive effects of department stores on Parisian society?

The Spread of Industrialization After 1870, industrialization began to spread beyond western and central Europe and North America. Especially noticeable was its rapid development in Japan and Russia (see Chapter 24). In Japan, the imperial government took the lead in promoting industry. The government financed industries, built railroads, brought foreign experts to train Japanese employees in new industrial techniques, and instituted a universal educational system based on applied science. By the end of the nineteenth century, Japan had developed key industries in tea, silk, armaments, and shipbuilding. Workers for these industries came from the large number of people who had abandoned their farms due to severe hardships in the countryside and had fled to the cities, where they provided an abundant source of cheap labor.

As in Europe during the early decades of the Industrial Revolution, workers toiled for long hours in the coal mines and textile mills, often under horrendous conditions. Reportedly, coal miners employed on a small island in Nagasaki harbor worked naked in temperatures up to 130 degrees Fahrenheit. If they tried to escape, they were shot.

A World Economy The economic developments of the late nineteenth century, combined with the transportation revolution that saw the growth of marine transport and railroads, also fostered a true world economy. By 1900, Europeans were importing beef and wool from Argentina and Australia, coffee from Brazil, nitrates from Chile, iron ore from Algeria, and sugar from Java. European capital was also invested abroad to develop

Railroad development
— Lines completed by 1848
— Area of main railroad completed by 1870
— Other major lines

▲ Steel
◆ Engineering
⬮ Chemicals
■ Electrical industry

⛏ Low-grade coal
⛏ High-grade coal
⚒ Iron ore deposits
⬛ Petroleum deposits

○ Oil production

Industrial concentration:
□ Cities
▨ Areas

MAP 23.1 The Industrial Regions of Europe at the End of the Nineteenth Century. By the end of the nineteenth century, the Second Industrial Revolution—in steelmaking, electricity, petroleum, and chemicals—had spurred substantial economic growth and prosperity in western and central Europe; it also sparked economic and political competition between Great Britain and Germany. ❓ Look back at Map 20.2. What parts of Europe not industrialized in 1850 had become industrialized in the ensuing decades? 🖱 **View an animated version of this map or related maps at** http://thomsonedu.com/history/spielvogel

railways, mines, electrical power plants, and banks. Of course, foreign countries also provided markets for the surplus manufactured goods of Europe. With its capital, industries, and military might, Europe dominated the world economy by the end of the nineteenth century.

Women and Work: New Job Opportunities

The Second Industrial Revolution had an enormous impact on the position of women in the labor market. During the course of the nineteenth century, considerable controversy erupted over a woman's "right to work." Working-class organizations tended to reinforce the underlying ideal of domesticity: women should remain at home to bear and nurture children and should not be allowed in the industrial workforce. Working-class men argued that keeping women out of industrial work would ensure the moral and physical well-being of families. In reality, keeping women out of the industrial workforce simply made it easier to exploit them when they needed income to supplement their husbands' wages or to support their families when their husbands were unemployed.

The desperate need to work at times forced women to do marginal work at home or piecework in sweatshops.

After 1870, however, new job opportunities for women became available. The development of larger industrial plants and the expansion of government services created a large number of service or white-collar jobs. The increased demand for white-collar workers at relatively low wages coupled with a shortage of male workers led employers to hire women. Big businesses and retail shops needed clerks, typists, secretaries, file clerks, and sales clerks. The expansion of government services created opportunities for women to be secretaries and telephone operators and to take jobs in health and social services. Compulsory education necessitated more teachers, and the development of modern hospital services opened the way for an increase in nurses.

Many of the new white-collar jobs were far from exciting. Their work was routine and, except for teaching and nursing, required few skills beyond basic literacy. Although there was little hope for advancement, these jobs had distinct advantages for the daughters of the middle classes and especially the upward-aspiring working classes. For some middle-class women, the new jobs offered freedom from the domestic patterns expected of them. Moreover, because middle-class women did not receive an education comparable to men's, they were limited in the careers they could pursue. Thus they found it easier to fill the jobs at the lower end of middle-class occupations, such as teaching and civil service jobs, especially in the postal service. Most of the new white-collar jobs, however, were filled by working-class females who saw their opportunity to escape from the physical labor of the lower-class world.

Organizing the Working Classes

In the first half of the nineteenth century, many workers had formed trade unions that had functioned primarily as mutual aid societies (see Chapter 20). In return for a small weekly payment, benefits were provided to assist unemployed workers. In the late nineteenth century, the desire to improve their working and living conditions led many industrial workers to form political parties and labor unions, often based on the ideas of Karl Marx (see Chapter 22). One of the most important of the working-class or socialist parties was formed in Germany in 1875.

Socialist Parties Under the direction of its two Marxist leaders, Wilhelm Liebknecht and August Bebel, the German Social Democratic Party (SPD) espoused revolutionary Marxist rhetoric while organizing itself as a mass political party competing in elections for the Reichstag, the German parliament. Once in the Reichstag, SPD delegates worked to enact legislation to improve the condition of the working class. As Bebel explained, "Pure negation would not be accepted by the voters. The masses demand that something should be done for today irrespective of what will happen on the morrow."[1] Despite government efforts to

"Proletarians of the World, Unite." To improve their working and living conditions, many industrial workers, inspired by the ideas of Karl Marx, joined working-class or socialist parties. Pictured here is a socialist-sponsored poster that proclaims in German the closing words of *The Communist Manifesto:* "Proletarians of the World, Unite!" At the top of the posters are the slogans of the French Revolution: equality, liberty, fraternity (brotherhood).

destroy it, the SPD continued to grow. In 1890, it received 1.5 million votes and thirty-five seats in the Reichstag. When it got 4 million votes in the 1912 elections, it became the largest single party in Germany.

Socialist parties also emerged in other European states, although none proved as successful as the German Social Democrats. As the socialist parties gained adherents, agitation for an international organization that would strengthen their position against international capitalism grew. In 1889, leaders of the various socialist parties formed the Second International, which was organized as a loose association of national groups. Though the Second International took some coordinated actions—for example, it proclaimed May 1 an international labor day (May Day), to be marked by strikes and mass labor demonstrations—differences of opinion often wreaked havoc at the congresses of the organization. Two issues proved particularly divisive: nationalism and revisionism.

Despite the belief of Karl Marx and Friedrich Engels that "the working men have no country," in truth socialist parties varied from country to country and focused on national concerns and issues. Thus nationalism remained a much more powerful force than socialism.

Evolutionary Socialism Marxist parties also divided over the issue of **revisionism**, also known as **evolutionary socialism**. Some Marxists believed in a pure Marxism that accepted the imminent collapse of capitalism and the need for socialist ownership of the means of production. But others rejected the revolutionary approach and argued in a revisionist direction that the workers must continue to organize in mass political parties and even work together with the other progressive elements in a nation to gain reform. With the extension of the right to vote, workers were in a better position than ever to achieve their aims through democratic channels. As the most prominent revisionist, Eduard Bernstein (1850–1932), argued in his book *Evolutionary Socialism*, evolution by democratic means, not revolution, would achieve the desired goal of socialism. Many socialist parties, including the German Social Democrats, while spouting revolutionary slogans, followed Bernstein's gradualist approach.

Trade Unions Workers also formed trade unions to improve their working conditions. Attempts to organize the workers did not come until after unions had won the right to strike in the 1870s. Strikes proved necessary to achieve the workers' goals. A walkout by female workers in the match industry in 1888 and by dockworkers in London the following year led to the establishment of trade union organizations for both groups. By 1900, two million workers were enrolled in British trade unions, and by the outbreak of World War I in 1914, the number had risen to between three and four million, although this was still less than one-fifth of the total workforce. By 1914, its three million members made the German trade union movement the largest in Europe after Great Britain's.

The Emergence of a Mass Society

The new patterns of industrial production, mass consumption, and working-class organization that we identify with the Second Industrial Revolution were only one aspect of the new **mass society** that emerged in Europe after 1871. A larger and vastly improved urban environment, new patterns of social structure, gender issues, mass education, and mass leisure were also important features of Europe's mass society.

Population Growth

The European population increased dramatically between 1850 and 1910, rising from 270 million to more than

TABLE 23.1 European Populations, 1851–1911

	1851	1881	1911
England and Wales	17,928,000	25,974,000	36,070,000
Scotland	2,889,000	3,736,000	4,761,000
Ireland	6,552,000	5,175,000	4,390,000
France	35,783,000	37,406,000	39,192,000
Germany	33,413,000	45,234,000	64,926,000
Belgium	4,530,000	5,520,000	7,424,000
Netherlands	3,309,000	4,013,000	5,858,000
Denmark	1,415,000	1,969,000	2,757,000
Norway	1,490,000	1,819,000	2,392,000
Sweden	3,471,000	4,169,000	5,522,000
Spain	15,455,000	16,622,000	19,927,000
Portugal	3,844,000	4,551,000	5,958,000
Italy	24,351,000	28,460,000	34,671,000
Switzerland	2,393,000	2,846,000	3,753,000
Austria	17,535,000	22,144,000	28,572,000
Hungary	18,192,000	15,739,000	20,886,000
Russia	68,500,000	97,700,000	160,700,000
Romania	N.A.	4,600,000	7,000,000
Bulgaria	N.A.	2,800,000	4,338,000
Greece	N.A.	1,679,000	2,632,000
Serbia	N.A.	1,700,000	2,912,000

Source: B. R. Mitchell, *European Historical Statistics, 1750–1970* (New York, 1975).

460 million (see Table 23.1). After 1880, a noticeable decline in death rates largely explains the increase. Although the causes of this decline have been debated, two major factors—medical discoveries and environmental conditions—stand out. Some historians have stressed the importance of developments in medical science. Smallpox vaccinations, for example, were compulsory in many European countries by the mid-1850s. More important were improvements in the urban environment in the second half of the nineteenth century that greatly decreased fatalities from such infectious diseases as diarrhea, dysentery, typhoid fever, and cholera, which had been spread through contaminated water supplies and improper elimination of sewage. Improved nutrition also made a significant difference in the health of the population. The increase in agricultural productivity combined with improvements in transportation facilitated the shipment of food supplies from areas of surplus to regions with poor harvests.

Emigration

Although agricultural and industrial prosperity supported an increase in population, it could not do so indefinitely, especially in areas that had little industrialization and severe overpopulation. Some of the excess labor from underdeveloped areas migrated to the industrial regions of Europe (see Map 23.2). By 1913, more than 400,000 Poles were working in the heavily industrialized Ruhr region

1820

Inhabitants per square mile

<20   20–50   50–100   100+

1900

MAP 23.2 **Population Growth in Europe, 1820–1900.** European population increased steadily throughout the nineteenth century. Advances in medical science, hygiene, nutrition, living conditions, and standards of living help account for the population increase, even though emigration to the United States, South America, and other regions reduced the total growth numbers. **?** Which regions experienced the greatest population growth between 1820 and 1900, and how can you account for this? **◆** View an animated version of this map or related maps at http://thomsonedu.com/history/spielvogel

Transformation of the Urban Environment

One of the most important consequences of industrialization and the population explosion of the nineteenth century was urbanization. In 1800, city dwellers constituted 40 percent of the population in Britain, 25 percent in France and Germany, and only 10 percent in eastern Europe. By 1914, urban inhabitants had increased to 80 percent of the population in Britain, 45 percent in France, 60 percent in Germany, and 30 percent in eastern Europe. The size of cities also expanded dramatically, especially in industrialized countries. Between 1800 and 1900, London's population grew from 960,000 to 6.5 million and Berlin's from 172,000 to 2.7 million.

Urban populations grew faster than the general population primarily because of the vast migration from rural areas to cities. People were driven from the countryside to the city by sheer economic necessity—unemployment, land hunger, and physical want. Urban centers offered something positive as well, usually ample opportunities for employment in factories and later in service trades and professions. But cities also grew faster in the second half of the nineteenth century because health and living conditions in them were improving.

of western Germany. But a booming American economy and cheap shipping fares after 1898 led to substantial emigration from southern and eastern Europe to America. In 1880, about half a million people left Europe each year on average; between 1906 and 1910, annual departures increased to 1.3 million, many of them from southern and eastern Europe.

Improving Living Conditions In the 1840s, a number of urban reformers, such as Edwin Chadwick in England and Rudolf Virchow and Solomon Neumann in Germany, had pointed to filthy living conditions as the primary cause of epidemic diseases and urged sanitary reforms to correct the problem. Soon legislative acts created boards of health that brought governmental action to bear on

The Emigrant Ship. In this painting done in 1880, C. J. Staniland presented a sentimental image of the scene faced by the tens of millions of Europeans who migrated to other parts of the world, especially the United States, Canada, and Latin America. Shown in the painting are people boarding a ship, saying farewell to family members and loved ones they might never see again. Ships were often crowded, making conditions uncomfortable during the journey.

public health issues. Urban medical officers and building inspectors were authorized to inspect dwellings for public health hazards. New building regulations made it more difficult for private contractors to build shoddy housing. The Public Health Act of 1875 in Britain, for example, required that all new buildings have running water and an internal drainage system. For the first time in Western history, the role of municipal governments had been expanded to include detailed regulations for the improvement of the living conditions of urban dwellers.

Essential to the public health of the modern European city was the ability to bring clean water into the city and to expel sewage from it. The problem of fresh water was solved by a system of dams and reservoirs that stored the water and aqueducts and tunnels that carried it from the countryside to the city and into individual dwellings. By the second half of the nineteenth century, regular private baths became accessible to many people as gas heaters in the 1860s and later electric heaters made hot baths possible. The treatment of sewage was also improved by building mammoth underground pipes that carried raw sewage far from the city for disposal. Unfortunately, in many places the new underground sewers simply continued to discharge their raw sewage into what soon became highly polluted lakes and rivers. Nevertheless, the development of pure water and sewage systems dramatically improved the public health of European cities by 1914.

Housing Needs Middle-class reformers who denounced the unsanitary living conditions of the working classes also focused on their housing needs. Overcrowded, disease-ridden slums were viewed as dangerous not only to physical health but also to the political and moral health of the entire nation. Victor Huber, the foremost early German housing reformer, wrote in 1861, "Certainly it would not be too much to say that the home is the communal embodiment of family life. Thus the purity of the dwelling is almost as important for the family as is the cleanliness of the body for the individual."[2] To Huber,

good housing was a prerequisite for a satisfying family life, one of the "stabilising elements of society."

Early efforts to attack the housing problem emphasized the middle-class, liberal belief in the efficacy of private enterprise. Reformers such as Huber believed that the construction of model dwellings renting at a reasonable price would force other private landlords to elevate their housing standards. A fine example of this approach was the work of Octavia Hill (see the box on p. 439). With the financial assistance of a friend, she rehabilitated some old dwellings and constructed new ones to create housing for 3,500 tenants.

As the number and size of cities continued to mushroom, governments by the 1880s came to the conclusion—reluctantly—that private enterprise could not solve the housing crisis. In 1890, a British housing act empowered local town councils to construct cheap housing for the working classes. London and Liverpool were the first communities to take advantage of their new powers. Similar activity had been set in motion in Germany by 1900. Everywhere, however, these lukewarm measures failed to do much to meet the real housing needs of the working classes. In housing as in so many other areas of life in the late nineteenth and early twentieth centuries, the liberal principle that the government that governs least governs best had simply proved untrue. More and more, governments were stepping into areas of activity that they would have never touched earlier.

The Social Structure of a Mass Society

At the top of European society stood a wealthy elite, constituting only 5 percent of the population but controlling 30 to 40 percent of its wealth. In the course of the nineteenth century, aristocrats coalesced with the most successful industrialists, bankers, and merchants (the wealthy upper middle class) to form this new elite. The growth of big business had produced this group of wealthy plutocrats, while aristocrats, whose income from

THE HOUSING VENTURE OF OCTAVIA HILL

*O*ctavia Hill was a practical-minded British housing reformer who believed that workers and their families were entitled to happy homes. At the same time, she was convinced that the poor needed guidance and encouragement, not charity. In this selection, she describes her housing venture.

Octavia Hill, "Homes of the London Poor, 1875"

About four years ago I was put in possession of three houses in one of the worst courts of Marylebone. Six other houses were bought subsequently. All were crowded with inmates.

The first thing to be done was to put them in decent tenantable order. The set last purchased was a row of cottages facing a bit of desolate ground, occupied with wretched, dilapidated cow-sheds, manure heaps, old timber, and rubbish of every description. The houses were in a most deplorable condition—the plaster was dropping from the walls; on one staircase a pail was placed to catch the rain that fell through the roof. All the staircases were perfectly dark; the banisters were gone, having been burnt as firewood by tenants. The grates, with large holes in them, were falling forward into the rooms. The washhouse, full of lumber belonging to the landlord, was locked up; thus the inhabitants had to wash clothes, as well as to cook, eat and sleep, in their small rooms. The dustbin [trash bin], standing in the front part of the houses, was accessible to the whole neighbourhood, and boys often dragged from it quantities of unseemly objects and spread them over the court. The state of the drainage was in keeping with everything else. The pavement of the back-yard was all broken up, and great puddles stood in it, so that the damp crept up the outer walls. . . .

As soon as I entered into possession, each family had an opportunity of doing better: those who would not pay, or who led clearly immoral lives, were ejected. The rooms they vacated were cleansed; the tenants who showed signs of improvement moved into them, and thus, in turn, an opportunity was obtained for having each room distempered

[painted] and papered. The drains were put in order, a large slate cistern was fixed, the washhouse was cleared of its lumber, and thrown open on stated days to each tenant in turn. The roof, the plaster, the woodwork were repaired; the staircase walls were distempered; new grates were fixed; the layers of paper and rag (black with age) were torn from the windows, and glass put in; out of 192 panes only eight were found unbroken. The yard and footpath were paved.

The rooms, as a rule, were re-let at the same prices at which they had been let before; but tenants with large families were counselled to take two rooms, and for these much less was charged than if let singly: this plan I continue to pursue. In-coming tenants are not allowed to take a decidedly insufficient quantity of room, and no sub-letting is permitted. . . .

The pecuniary result has been very satisfactory. Five percent has been paid on all the capital invested. A fund for the repayment of capital is accumulating. A liberal allowance has been made for repairs. . . .

My tenants are mostly of a class far below that of mechanics. They are, indeed, of the very poor. And yet, although the gifts they have received have been next to nothing, none of the families who have passed under my care during the whole four years have continued in what is called "distress," except such as have been unwilling to exert themselves. Those who will not exert the necessary self-control cannot avail themselves of the means of livelihood held out to them. But, for those who are willing, some small assistance in the form of work has, from time to time, been provided—not much, but sufficient to keep them from want or despair.

Did Octavia Hill's housing venture generate financial returns on her initial investment? What benefits did her tenants receive in turn? What feelings and beliefs about the lower classes are evident in Hill's account?

---

landed estates declined, invested in railway shares, public utilities, government bonds, and even businesses.

The Upper Classes Increasingly, aristocrats and plutocrats fused as the wealthy upper middle class purchased landed estates to join the aristocrats in the pleasures of country living while the aristocrats bought lavish town houses for part-time urban life. Common bonds were also forged when the sons of wealthy middle-class families were admitted to the elite schools dominated by the children of the aristocracy. This educated elite, whether aristocratic or middle-class in background, assumed leadership roles in government bureaucracies and military hierarchies. Marriage also served to unite the two groups. Daughters of tycoons acquired titles, and aristocratic heirs

gained new sources of cash. Wealthy American heiresses were in special demand. When Consuelo Vanderbilt married the duke of Marlborough, the new duchess brought £2 million (approximately $10 million) to her husband.

The Middle Classes The middle classes consisted of a variety of groups. Below the upper middle class was a level that included such traditional groups as professionals in law, medicine, and the civil service as well as moderately well-to-do industrialists and merchants. The industrial expansion of the nineteenth century also added new groups to this segment of the middle class. These included business managers and new professionals, such as the engineers, architects, accountants, and chemists who formed professional associations as the symbols of their newfound importance. A lower middle class of small shopkeepers, traders, manufacturers, and prosperous peasants provided goods and services for the classes above them.

Standing between the lower middle class and the lower classes were new groups of white-collar workers who were the product of the Second Industrial Revolution. They were the traveling salespeople, bookkeepers, bank tellers, telephone operators, department store clerks, and secretaries. Although largely propertyless and often paid only marginally more than skilled laborers, these white-collar workers were often committed to middle-class ideals and optimistic about improving their status.

The individuals in the moderately prosperous and successful middle classes shared a common lifestyle, and their values came to dominate much of later nineteenth-century society. Members of the middle classes were especially active in preaching their worldview to their children and to the upper and lower classes of their society. This was especially evident in Victorian Britain, often considered a model of middle-class society. The European middle classes embraced and promulgated the importance of progress and science. They believed in hard work, which they viewed as the primary human good, open to everyone and guaranteed to have positive results. They were also regular churchgoers who believed in the good conduct associated with traditional Christian morality. The middle classes were concerned with propriety, the right way of doing things. This concern gave rise to an endless succession of books aimed at the middle-class market with such titles as *The Habits of Good Society* and *Don't: A Manual of Mistakes and Improprieties More or Less Prevalent in Conduct and Speech.*

The Lower Classes Below the middle classes on the social scale were the working classes of European society, who made up almost 80 percent of the population. Many of the members of these classes were landholding peasants, farm laborers, and sharecroppers, especially in eastern Europe. The urban working class consisted of many different groups, including skilled artisans in such trades as cabinetmaking and printing and semiskilled laborers such as carpenters and many factory workers, who earned wages that were about two-thirds of those of highly skilled workers. At the bottom of the urban working class were the unskilled laborers. They were the largest group of workers and included day laborers and large numbers of domestic servants. One out of every seven employed persons in Great Britain in 1900 was a domestic servant. Most of these were women.

Urban workers did experience a real betterment in the material conditions of their lives after 1871. For one thing, urban improvements meant better living conditions. A rise in real wages, accompanied by a decline in many consumer costs, especially in the 1880s and 1890s, made it possible for workers to afford more than just food and housing. Workers' budgets now provided money for more clothes and even leisure at the same time that strikes and labor agitation were providing shorter (ten-hour) workdays and Saturday afternoons off.

The "Woman Question": The Role of Women

The "woman question" was the term used to identify the debate over the role of women in society. In the nineteenth century, women remained legally inferior, economically dependent, and largely defined by family and household roles. Many women still aspired to the ideal of femininity popularized by writers and poets. Alfred Lord Tennyson's poem *The Princess* expressed it well:

> *Man for the field and woman for the hearth:*
> *Man for the sword and for the needle she:*
> *Man with the head and woman with the heart:*
> *Man to command and woman to obey;*
> *All else confusion.*

This traditional characterization of the sexes, based on gender-defined social roles, was elevated to the status of universal male and female attributes in the nineteenth century, due largely to the impact of the Industrial Revolution on the family. As the chief family wage earners, men worked outside the home while women were left with the care of the family, for which they were paid nothing. Of course, the ideal did not always match reality, especially for the lower classes, where the need for supplemental income drove women to do "sweated" work.

Throughout most of the nineteenth century, marriage was viewed as the only honorable and available career for most women. While the middle classes glorified the ideal of domesticity (see the box on p. 441), for most women marriage was a matter of economic necessity. The lack of meaningful work and the lower wages paid to women made it difficult for single women to earn a living. Most women chose to marry, which was reflected in the increase in marriage rates and a decline in illegitimacy rates in the course of the nineteenth century.

Birthrates also dropped significantly at this time. A very important factor in the evolution of the modern family was the decline in the number of offspring born to the average woman. The change was not necessarily due to new technological products. Although the invention of vulcanized rubber in the 1840s made possible the production of condoms and diaphragms, they were not widely used as contraceptive devices until the era of World War I. Some historians maintain that the change in attitude that led parents to deliberately limit the number of offspring was more important than the method used. While some historians attribute increased birth control to more widespread use of coitus interruptus, or male withdrawal before ejaculation, others have emphasized the ability of women to restrict family size through abortion and even infanticide or abandonment. That a change in attitude occurred was apparent in the emergence of a movement to increase awareness of birth control methods.

ADVICE TO WOMEN: BE DEPENDENT

Industrialization had a strong impact on middle-class women as gender-based social roles became the norm. Men worked outside the home to support the family while women provided for the needs of their children and husband at home. In this selection, one woman gives advice to middle-class women on their proper role and behavior.

Elizabeth Poole Sanford, *Woman in Her Social and Domestic Character*

The changes wrought by Time are many. It influences the opinions of men as familiarity does their feelings; it has a tendency to do away with superstition, and to reduce every thing to its real worth.

It is thus that the sentiment for woman has undergone a change. The romantic passion which once almost deified her is on the decline; and it is by intrinsic qualities that she must now inspire respect. She is no longer the queen of song and the star of chivalry. But if there is less of enthusiasm entertained for her, the sentiment is more rational, and, perhaps, equally sincere; for it is in relation to happiness that she is chiefly appreciated.

And in this respect it is, we must confess, that she is most useful and most important. Domestic life is the chief source of her influence; and the greatest debt society can owe to her is domestic comfort; for happiness is almost an element of virtue; and nothing conduces more to improve the character of men than domestic peace. A woman may make a man's home delightful, and may thus increase his motives for virtuous exertion. She may refine and tranquilize his mind,— may turn away his anger or allay his grief. Her smile may be the happy influence to gladden his heart, and to disperse the cloud that gathers on his brow. And in proportion to her endeavors to make those around her happy, she will be esteemed and loved. She will secure by her excellence that interest and that regard which she might formerly claim as the privilege of her sex, and will really merit the deference which was then conceded to her as a matter of course. . . .

Perhaps one of the first secrets of her influence is adaptation to the tastes, and sympathy in the feelings, of those around her. This holds true in lesser as well as in graver points. It is in the former, indeed, that the absence of interest in a companion is frequently most disappointing. Where want of congeniality impairs domestic comfort, the fault is generally chargeable on the female side. It is for woman, not for man, to make the sacrifice, especially in indifferent matters. She must, in a certain degree, be plastic herself if she would mould others. . . .

Nothing is so likely to conciliate the affections of the other sex as a feeling that woman looks to them for support and guidance. In proportion as men are themselves superior, they are accessible to this appeal. On the contrary, they never feel interested in one who seems disposed rather to offer than to ask assistance. There is, indeed, something unfeminine in independence. It is contrary to nature, and therefore it offends. We do not like to see a woman affecting tremors, but still less do we like to see her acting the amazon. A really sensible woman feels her dependence. She does what she can; but she is conscious of inferiority, and therefore grateful for support. She knows that she is the weaker vessel, and that as such she should receive honor. In this view, her weakness is an attraction, not a blemish.

In everything, therefore, that women attempt, they should show their consciousness of dependence. If they are learners, let them evince a teachable spirit; if they give an opinion, let them do it in an unassuming manner. There is something so unpleasant in female self-sufficiency that it not unfrequently deters instead of persuading, and prevents the adoption of advice which the judgment even approves.

―――――――――

According to Elizabeth Sanford, what is the proper role of women? What forces in late-nineteenth-century European society merged to shape Sanford's understanding of "proper" gender roles?

Europe's first birth control clinic, founded by Dr. Aletta Jacob, opened in Amsterdam in 1882.

The Middle-Class Family The family was the central institution of middle-class life. Men provided the family income, while women focused on household and child care. The use of domestic servants in many middle-class homes, made possible by an abundant supply of cheap labor, reduced the amount of time middle-class women had to spend on household chores. At the same time, by reducing the number of children in the family, mothers could devote more time to child care and domestic leisure.

The middle-class family fostered an ideal of togetherness. The Victorians codified the family Christmas, with its yule log, Christmas tree, songs, and exchange of gifts.

In the United States, Fourth of July celebrations changed from drunken revels to family picnics by the 1850s. The education of middle-class females in domestic crafts, singing, and piano playing prepared them for their function of providing a proper environment for home recreation.

The Working-Class Family Women in working-class families were more accustomed to hard work. Daughters in working-class families were expected to work until they married; even after marriage, they often did piece-work at home to support the family. For the children of the working class, childhood was over by the age of nine or ten when they became apprentices or were employed in odd jobs.

A Middle-Class Family.
Nineteenth-century middle-class moralists considered the family the pillar of a healthy society, and family togetherness was an important ideal. This painting by William P. Frith, titled *Many Happy Returns of the Day*, shows a family birthday celebration for a little girl in which grandparents, parents, and children take part. The servant at the left holds presents for the little girl.

Between 1890 and 1914, however, family patterns among the working class began to change. High-paying jobs in heavy industry and improvements in the standard of living made it possible for working-class families to depend on the income of husbands and the wages of grown children. By the early twentieth century, some working-class mothers could afford to stay at home, following the pattern of middle-class women. At the same time, new consumer products, such as sewing machines, clocks, bicycles, and cast-iron stoves, created a new mass consumer society whose focus was on higher levels of consumption.

These working-class families also followed the middle classes in limiting the size of their families. Children began to be viewed as dependents rather than wage earners as child labor laws and compulsory education took children out of the workforce and into schools. Improvements in public health as well as advances in medicine and a better diet resulted in a decline in infant mortality rates for the lower classes and made it easier for working-class families to choose to have fewer children. At the same time, strikes and labor agitation led to laws that reduced work hours to ten per day by 1900 and eliminated work on Saturday afternoons, which enabled working-class parents to devote more attention to their children and develop deeper emotional ties with them.

Education in the Mass Society

Mass education was a product of the mass society of the late nineteenth century. Being "educated" in the early nineteenth century meant attending a secondary school or possibly even a university. Secondary schools mostly emphasized a classical education based on the study of Greek and Latin. Secondary and university education was primarily for the elite, the sons of government officials, nobles, or the wealthier members of the middle classes. After 1850, secondary education was

expanded as more middle-class families sought employment in public service and the professions or entry into elite scientific and technical schools.

Universal Elementary Education In the decades after 1870, the functions of the state were extended to include the development of mass education in state-run systems. Between 1870 and 1914, most Western governments began to offer at least primary education to both boys and girls between the ages of six and twelve. States also assumed responsibility for the quality of teachers by establishing teacher-training schools. By 1900, many European states, especially in northern and western Europe, were providing state-financed primary schools, salaried and trained teachers, and free, compulsory mass elementary education.

Why did European states make this commitment to mass education? Liberals believed that education was important to personal and social improvement and sought in Catholic countries to supplant Catholic education with moral and civic training based on secular values. Even conservatives were attracted to mass education as a means of improving the quality of military recruits and training people in social discipline. In 1875, a German military journal stated, "We in Germany consider education to be one of the principal ways of promoting the strength of the nation and above all military strength."[3]

Another incentive for mass education came from industrialization. In the early Industrial Revolution, unskilled labor was sufficient to meet factory needs, but the new firms of the Second Industrial Revolution demanded skilled labor. Both boys and girls with an elementary education had new possibilities of jobs beyond their villages or small towns, including white-collar jobs in railway and subway stations, post offices, banking and shipping firms, teaching, and nursing. To industrialists, then, mass education furnished the trained workers they needed.

Nevertheless, the chief motive for mass education was political. The expansion of voting rights necessitated a more educated electorate. Even more important, mass compulsory education instilled patriotism and nationalized the masses, providing an opportunity for even greater national integration. As people lost their ties to local regions and even to religion, nationalism supplied a new faith. The use of a single common language created greater national unity than loyalty to a ruler ever did.

A nation's motives for universal elementary education largely determined what was taught in the schools. Obviously, indoctrination in national values took on great importance. At the core of the academic curriculum were reading, writing, arithmetic, national history (especially geared to a patriotic view), geography, literature, and some singing and drawing. The education of boys and girls varied, however. Where possible, the sexes were separated. Girls did less math and no science but concentrated on such domestic skills as sewing, washing, ironing, and cooking, all prerequisites for providing a good home for husband and children. Boys were taught some practical skills, such as carpentry, and even some military drill. Most of the elementary schools also inculcated the middle-class virtues of hard work, thrift, sobriety, cleanliness, and respect for the family. For most students, elementary education led to apprenticeship and a job.

Female Teachers   The development of compulsory elementary education created a demand for teachers, and most of them were female. In the United States, for example, females constituted two-thirds of all teachers by the 1880s. Many men viewed the teaching of children as an extension of women's "natural role" as nurturers of children. Moreover, females were paid lower salaries, in itself a considerable incentive for governments to encourage the establishment of teacher-training institutes for women. The first colleges for women were teacher-training schools; not until the beginning of the twentieth century were women permitted to enter the male-dominated universities. In France, 3 percent of university students in 1902 were women; by 1914, their number had increased to 10 percent of the total.

Literacy and Mass Newspaper   The most immediate result of mass education was an increase in literacy. In Germany, Great Britain, France, and the Scandinavian countries, adult illiteracy was virtually eliminated by 1900. Where there was less schooling, the story is very different. Adult illiteracy rates were 79 percent in Serbia, 78 percent in Romania, and 79 percent in Russia. All of these countries had made only a minimal investment in mass education.

With the dramatic increase in literacy after 1871 came the rise of mass newspapers, such as the *Evening News* (1881) and *Daily Mail* (1896) in London, which sold millions of copies a day. These newspapers were written in an easily understood style and tended to be extremely sensational. Unlike eighteenth-century newspapers, which were full of serious editorials and lengthy political analysis, these tabloids provided lurid details of crimes, jingoistic diatribes, gossip, and sports news. There were other forms of cheap literature as well. Specialty magazines, such as the *Family Herald* for the entire family, and women's magazines began to appear in the 1860s. Pulp fiction for adults included the extremely popular westerns with their innumerable variations on conflicts between cowboys and Indians. Literature for the masses was but one feature of the new mass culture; another was the emergence of new forms of **mass leisure**.

A Women's College.   Women were largely excluded from male-dominated universities before 1900. Consequently, the demand of women for higher education led to the establishment of women's colleges, most of which were primarily teacher-training schools. This photograph shows female medical students dissecting cadavers in anatomy class at the Women's Medical College of Philadelphia, Pennsylvania.

Mass Leisure

In the preindustrial centuries, play or leisure activities had been closely connected to work patterns based on the seasonal or daily cycles typical of the life of peasants and artisans. The process of industrialization in the nineteenth century had an enormous impact on that traditional pattern. The factory imposed new work patterns that were determined by the rhythms of machines and clocks and removed work time completely from the family environment of farms and workshops. Work and leisure became opposites as leisure came to be defined as what people did for fun when they were not at work. In fact, the new leisure hours created by the industrial system—evening hours after work, weekends, and later a week or two in the summer—largely determined the contours of the new mass leisure.

New technology also determined mass leisure pursuits. The new technology created novel experiences for leisure, such as the Ferris wheel at amusement parks, and the mechanized urban transportation systems of the 1880s meant that even the working classes were no longer dependent on neighborhood bars but could make their way to athletic games, amusement parks, and dance halls. Railroads could take people to the beaches on weekends.

The upper and middle classes had created the first market for tourism, but as wages increased and workers were given paid vacations, tourism became another form of mass leisure. Thomas Cook (1808–1892) was a British pioneer of mass tourism. Secretary to a British temperance group, Cook had been responsible for organizing a railroad trip to temperance gatherings in 1841. This experience led him to offer trips on a regular basis after he found that he could make substantial profits by renting special trains, lowering prices, and increasing the number of passengers.

By the late nineteenth century, team sports had also developed into yet another focus of mass leisure. Unlike the old rural games, however, they were no longer chaotic and spontaneous activities but became strictly organized with sets of rules and officials to enforce them. These rules were the products of organized athletic groups, such as the English Football Association (1863) and the American Bowling Congress (1895).

The new team sports rapidly became professionalized. In Britain, soccer had its Football Association in 1863 and rugby its Rugby Football Union in 1871. In the United States, the first national association to recognize professional baseball players was formed in 1863. By 1900, the National League and American League had a complete monopoly over professional baseball. The development of urban transportation systems made possible the construction of stadiums where thousands could attend, making mass spectator sports a big business.

Standardized forms of amusement drew mass audiences. Although some theorists argued that the new amusements were important for improving people, they served primarily to provide entertainment and distract people from the realities of their work lives. The new mass leisure also represented a significant change from earlier forms of popular culture. Festivals and fairs had been based on active and spontaneous community participation, whereas the new forms of mass leisure were businesses, standardized for largely passive mass audiences and organized to make profits.

The National State

Within the major European states, considerable progress was made in achieving such liberal practices as constitutions and parliaments, but it was largely in western Europe that **mass politics** became a reality. Reforms encouraged the expansion of political democracy through voting rights for men and the creation of mass political parties. At the same time, however, these latter developments were strongly resisted in parts of Europe where the old political forces remained strong.

Western Europe: The Growth of Political Democracy

In general, parliamentary government was most firmly rooted in the western European states. Both Britain and France saw an expansion of the right to vote, but liberal reforms proved less successful in Italy.

Reform in Britain By 1871, Great Britain had a functioning two-party parliamentary system, and the growth of political democracy became one of the preoccupations of British politics. Its cause was pushed along by the expansion of suffrage. Much advanced by the Reform Act of 1867 (see Chapter 22), the right to vote was further extended during the second ministry of William Gladstone (1880–1885) with the passage of the Reform Act of 1884. It gave the vote to all men who paid regular rents or taxes, thus largely enfranchising agricultural workers, a group previously excluded. The following year, the Redistribution Act eliminated historic boroughs and counties and established constituencies with approximately equal populations and one representative each. The payment of salaries to members of the House of Commons beginning in 1911 further democratized that institution by opening the door to people other than the wealthy. The British system of gradual reform through parliamentary institutions had become the way of British political life.

The Third Republic in France The defeat of France by the Prussian army in 1870 brought the downfall of Louis Napoleon's Second Empire. In new elections based on universal male suffrage, the French people rejected the republicans and overwhelmingly favored the monarchists, who won two-thirds of the seats in the new National Assembly. In response, on March 26, 1871, radical republicans formed an independent republican government in Paris known as the Commune.

But the National Assembly refused to give up its power and decided to crush the renegade Commune. Vicious

A LEADER OF THE PARIS COMMUNE

*L*ouise Michel became active among revolutionary groups in Paris in 1870 and emerged the following year as a leader of the Paris Commune. Arrested and exiled to New Caledonia, she was allowed to return to France in 1880, where she became a heroic figure among radical groups. Later she spent three years in prison for anarchism and much of the time thereafter in England in self-imposed exile. In her memoirs, Louise Michel discussed what happened when the National Assembly sent troops on March 18, 1871, to seize cannons that had been moved earlier to the hills of Montmartre. She also reflected on her activities in the Commune.

Louise Michel, *Memoirs*

Learning that the Versailles soldiers [troops of the National Assembly] were trying to seize the cannon, men and women of Montmartre swarmed up the Butte in a surprise maneuver. Those people who were climbing believed they would die, but they were prepared to pay the price.

The Butte of Montmartre was bathed in the first light of day, through which things were glimpsed as if they were hidden behind a thin veil of water. Gradually the crowd increased. The other districts of Paris, hearing of the events taking place on the Butte of Montmartre, came to our assistance.

The women of Paris covered the cannon with their bodies. When their officers ordered the soldiers to fire, the men refused. The same army that would be used to crush Paris two months later decided now that it did not want to be an accomplice of the reaction. They gave up their attempt to seize the cannon from the National Guard. They understood that the people were defending the Republic by defending the arms that the royalists and imperialists would have turned on Paris in agreement with the Prussians. When we had won our victory, I looked around and noticed my poor mother, who had followed me to the Butte of Montmartre, believing that I was going to die.

On this day, the eighteenth of March, the people awakened. If they had not, it would have been the triumph of some king; instead it was a triumph of the people. The eighteenth of March could have belonged to the allies of kings, or to foreigners, or to the people. It was the people's. . . .

During the entire time of the Commune, I only spent one night at my poor mother's. I never really went to bed during that time. I just napped a little whenever there was nothing better to do, and many other people lived the same way. Everybody who wanted deliverance gave himself totally to the cause. . . . During the Commune I went unhurt except for a bullet that grazed my wrist, although my hat was literally riddled with bullet holes.

What does this account from the memoirs of the Parisian feminist Louise Michel tell you about new opportunities for political involvement available to female and male residents of European capital cities during the late nineteenth century?

---

fighting broke out in April. Many working-class men and women stepped forth to defend the Commune. At first, women's activities were the traditional ones: caring for the wounded soldiers and feeding the troops. Gradually, however, women expanded their activities to include taking care of weapons, working as scouts, and even setting up their own fighting brigades. Louise Michel (1830–1905), a schoolteacher, emerged as one of the leaders of the Paris Commune (see the box above). She proved tireless in forming committees for the defense of the Commune.

All of these efforts were in vain, however. In the last week of May, government troops massacred thousands of the Commune's defenders. Estimates are that twenty thousand were shot; another ten thousand (including Louise Michel) were shipped to the French penal colony of New Caledonia, in the South Pacific. The brutal repression of the Commune bequeathed a legacy of hatred that continued to plague French politics for decades. The harsh punishment of women who participated in antigovernment activities also served to discourage any future action by working-class women to improve their conditions.

Although a majority of the members of the monarchist-dominated National Assembly wished to restore a monarchy in France, inability to agree on who should be king caused the monarchists to miss their opportunity and led in 1875 to an improvised constitution that established a republican form of government as the least divisive compromise. This constitution established a **bicameral legislature** with an upper house, the Senate, elected indirectly and a lower house, the Chamber of Deputies, chosen by universal male suffrage; a president, selected by the legislature for a term of seven years, served as executive of the government. The Constitution of 1875, intended only as a stopgap measure, solidified the republic—the Third Republic—which lasted sixty-five years. New elections in 1876 and 1877 strengthened the hands of the republicans, who managed by 1879 to institute ministerial responsibility and establish the power of the Chamber of Deputies. The prime minister or premier and his ministers were now responsible not to the president but to the Chamber of Deputies.

Italy By 1870, Italy had emerged as a geographically united state with pretensions to great power status. Its internal weaknesses, however, gave that claim a particularly hollow ring. One Italian leader said after unification, "We have made Italy; now we must make Italians." But many Italians continued to put loyalty to their families, towns, and regions above their loyalty to the new state.

Sectional differences—a poverty-stricken south and an industrializing north—also weakened any sense of unity, and most of the Italian leaders were northerners who treated southern Italians with contempt. The Catholic church, which had lost control of the Papal States as a result of unification, even refused to accept the existence of the new state. Chronic turmoil between workers and industrialists undermined the social fabric. And few Italians felt empowered in the new Italy: only 2.5 percent of the people could vote for the legislative body. In 1882, the number was increased, but only to 10 percent. The Italian government was unable to deal effectively with these problems because of extensive corruption among government officials and a lack of stability resulting from ever-changing government coalitions. The granting of universal male suffrage in 1912 did little to correct the corruption and weak government. Even the Italians' pretensions to great power status came up empty when Italy became the first modern European nation to be defeated in battle by an African state, Ethiopia.

Central and Eastern Europe: Persistence of the Old Order

Germany, Austria-Hungary, and Russia pursued political policies that were quite different from those of the western European nations. Germany and Austria-Hungary had the trappings of parliamentary government, including legislative bodies and elections by universal male suffrage, but authoritarian forces, especially powerful monarchies and conservative social groups, remained strong. In eastern Europe, especially Russia, the old system of autocracy was barely touched by the winds of change.

Germany   The constitution of the new imperial Germany begun by Bismarck in 1871 provided for a federal system with a bicameral legislature. The lower house of the German parliament, the Reichstag, was elected on the basis of universal male suffrage, but it did not have ministerial responsibility. Ministers of government, the most important of which was the chancellor, were responsible not to the parliament but to the emperor. The emperor also commanded the armed forces and controlled foreign policy and internal administration. Although the creation of a parliament elected by universal male suffrage presented opportunities for the growth of a real political democracy, it failed to develop in Germany before World War I. The army and Bismarck were two major reasons why it did not.

The German (largely Prussian) army viewed itself as the defender of monarchy and aristocracy and sought to escape control by the Reichstag by operating under a general staff responsible only to the emperor. Prussian military tradition was strong, and military officers took steps to ensure the loyalty of their subordinates to the emperor.

The policies of Bismarck, who served as chancellor of the new German state until 1890, often prevented the growth of more democratic institutions. At first, Bismarck worked with the liberals, especially in launching an attack on the

Catholic church, the so-called *Kulturkampf* or "struggle for civilization." Like Bismarck, middle-class liberals distrusted Catholic loyalty to the new Germany. But Bismarck's tactics proved counterproductive, and Bismarck soon abandoned the attack on Catholicism by making an abrupt shift in policy.

In 1878, Bismarck abandoned the liberals and, alarmed by the growth of the Social Democratic Party, began to go after the socialists. He genuinely believed that the socialists' antinationalistic, anticapitalistic, and antimonarchical stance represented a danger to the empire. So Bismarck got the parliament to pass a law that limited socialist meetings and publications while still allowing socialist candidates to run for the Reichstag. Bismarck also attempted to woo workers away from socialism by enacting social welfare legislation. Between 1883 and 1889, the Reichstag passed laws that provided sickness, accident, and disability benefits as well as old-age pensions, financed by compulsory contributions from workers, employers, and the state. Bismarck's **social security** system was the most progressive the world had yet seen. Nevertheless, both the repressive and the social welfare measures failed to stop the growth of socialism. In his frustration, Bismarck planned still more antisocialist measures in 1890, but before he could carry them out, the new emperor, William II (1888–1918), eager to pursue his own policies, cashiered the aged chancellor.

Bismarck and William II. In 1890, Bismarck sought to undertake new repressive measures against the Social Democrats. Disagreeing with this policy, Emperor William II forced him to resign. This political cartoon shows William II reclining on a throne made of artillery and cannonballs and holding a doll labeled "socialism." Bismarck bids farewell while Germany, personified as a woman, looks on with grave concern.

Austria-Hungary After the creation of the Dual Monarchy of Austria-Hungary in 1867, the Austrian part received a constitution that established a parliamentary system with the principle of ministerial responsibility. But Emperor Francis Joseph (1848–1916) largely ignored ministerial responsibility and proceeded to personally appoint and dismiss his ministers and rule by decree when parliament was not in session.

The problem of the minorities continued to trouble the empire. The ethnic Germans, who made up only one-third of Austria's population, governed Austria but felt increasingly threatened by the Czechs, Poles, and other Slavic groups within the empire.

What held the Austro-Hungarian Empire together was a combination of forces. Francis Joseph, the emperor, was one unifying factor. Although strongly anti-Hungarian, the cautious emperor made an effort to take a position above national differences. Loyalty to the Catholic church also helped keep such national groups as Czechs, Slovaks, and Poles loyal to the Catholic Habsburg dynasty. Finally, although dominated by German-speaking officials, the large imperial bureaucracy served as a unifying force for the empire.

Russia In Russia, the government made no concession whatever to liberal and democratic reforms, eliminating altogether any possibility of a mass politics. The assassination of Alexander II in 1881 convinced his son and successor, Alexander III (1881–1894), that reform had been a mistake, and he quickly instituted what he said were "exceptional measures." The powers of the secret police were expanded. Advocates of constitutional monarchy and social reform, along with revolutionary groups, were persecuted. Entire districts of Russia were placed under martial law if the government suspected the inhabitants of treason. The powers of the zemstvos, created by the reforms of Alexander II, were sharply curtailed.

Alexander also pursued a radical Russification program of the numerous nationalities that made up the Russian Empire. Russians themselves constituted only 40 percent of the population, which did not stop the tsar from banning the use of all languages except Russian in schools. The policy of Russification served primarily to anger national groups and create new sources of opposition to tsarist policies.

When Alexander III died, his weak son and successor, Nicholas II (1894–1917), began his rule with his father's conviction that the absolute power of the tsars should be preserved: "I shall maintain the principle of autocracy just as firmly and unflinchingly as did my unforgettable father."[4] But conditions were changing, especially with the spread of industrialization, and the tsar's approach was not realistic in view of the new circumstances he faced.

CHRONOLOGY The National States, 1871–1894

Great Britain	
Second ministry of William Gladstone	1880–1885
Reform Act	1884
Redistribution Act	1885
France	
Paris Commune	1871 (March–May)
Republican constitution (Third Republic)	1875
Germany	
Bismarck as chancellor	1871–1890
Antisocialist law	1878
Social welfare legislation	1883–1889
Austria-Hungary	
Emperor Francis Joseph	1848–1916
Imperial Russia	
Tsar Alexander III	1881–1894

CONCLUSION

The Second Industrial Revolution helped create a material prosperity that led Europeans to believe they had ushered in a new "age of progress." A major feature of this age was the emergence of a mass society. The lower classes in particular benefited from the right to vote, a higher standard of living, and new schools that provided them with an education. New forms of mass transportation, combined with new work patterns, enabled large numbers of people to enjoy weekend excursions to amusement parks and seaside resorts and to participate in new mass leisure activities.

By 1871, the national state had become the focus of people's lives. Liberal and democratic reforms brought new possibilities for greater participation in the political process, although women were still largely excluded from political rights. After 1871, the national state also began to expand its functions beyond all previous limits. Fearful of the growth of socialism and trade unions, governments attempted to appease the working masses by adopting such social insurance measures as protection against accidents, illness, and old age. These social welfare measures were narrow in scope and limited in benefits, but they signaled a new direction for state action to benefit the mass of its citizens. The enactment of public health and housing measures, designed to curb the worst ills of urban living, was yet another indication of how state power could be used to benefit the people.

This extension of state functions took place in an atmosphere of increased national loyalty. After 1871, nation-states increasingly sought to solidify the social order and win the active loyalty and support of their citizens by deliberately cultivating national feelings. Yet this policy contained potentially great dangers. As we shall see in the next chapter, nations had discovered once again that imperialistic adventures and military successes could arouse nationalistic passions and smother domestic political unrest. But they also found that nationalistic feelings could lead to intense international rivalries that made war almost inevitable.

TIMELINE

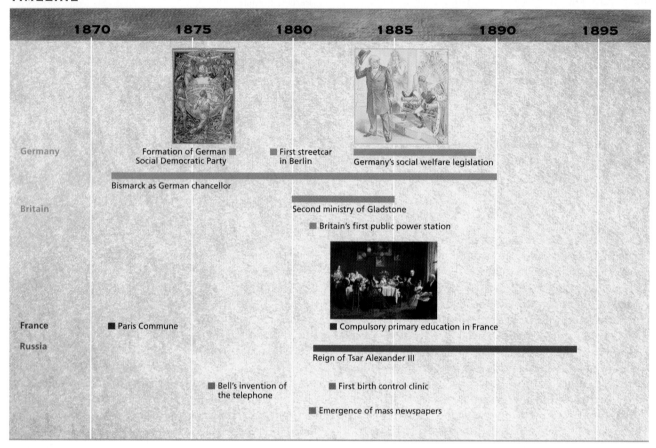

NOTES

1. Quoted in W. L. Guttsman, *The German Social Democratic Party, 1875–1933* (London, 1981), p. 63.
2. Quoted in N. Bullock and J. Read, *The Movement for Housing Reform in Germany and France, 1840–1914* (Cambridge, 1985), p. 42.
3. Quoted in R. Gildea, *Barricades and Borders: Europe, 1800–1914*, 2d ed. (Oxford, 1996), pp. 240–241.
4. Quoted in S. Galai, *The Liberation Movement in Russia, 1900–1905* (Cambridge, 1973), p. 26.

SUGGESTIONS FOR FURTHER READING

In addition to the general works on the nineteenth century and individual European countries cited in Chapters 21 and 22, two more specialized works on the subject matter of this chapter are available in **N. Stone**, *Europe Transformed, 1878–1919* (London, 1983), and **F. Gilbert**, *The End of the European Era, 1890 to the Present*, 4th ed. (New York, 1991).

The subject of the Second Industrial Revolution is well covered in **D. Landes**, *The Unbound Prometheus,* cited in Chapter 20. For a fundamental survey of European industrialization, see **A. S. Milward** and **S. B. Saul**, *The Development of the Economies of Continental Europe, 1850–1914* (Cambridge, Mass., 1977). For an introduction to the development of mass consumerism in Britain, see **W. H. Fraser**, *The Coming of the Mass Market, 1850–1914* (Hamden, Conn., 1981). The impact of the new technology on European thought is imaginatively discussed in **S. Kern**, *The Culture of Time and Space, 1880–1918* (Cambridge, Mass., 1983).

For an introduction to international socialism, see **A. Lindemann**, *A History of European Socialism* (New Haven, Conn., 1983), and **L. Derfler**, *Socialism Since Marx: A Century of the European Left* (New York, 1973). On the emergence of German social democracy, see **W. L. Guttsman**, *The German Social Democratic Party, 1875–1933* (London, 1981).

Demographic problems are examined in **T. McKeown**, *The Modern Rise of Population* (New York, 1976). On European emigration, see **L. P. Moch**, *Moving Europeans: Migration in Western Europe Since 1650* (Bloomington, Ind., 1993). For a good introduction to housing reform on the Continent, see **N. Bullock and J. Read**, *The Movement for Housing Reform in Germany and France, 1840–1914* (Cambridge, 1985).

An interesting work on aristocratic life is **D. Cannadine**, *The Decline and Fall of the British Aristocracy* (New Haven, Conn., 1990). On the middle classes, see **P. Pilbeam**, *The Middle Classes in Europe, 1789–1914* (Basingstoke, England, 1990). On the working classes, see **L. Berlanstein**, *The Working People of Paris, 1871–1914* (Baltimore, 1984), and **R. Magraw**, *A History of the French Working Class* (Cambridge, Mass., 1992).

There are good overviews of women's experiences in the nineteenth century in **B. G. Smith**, *Changing Lives: Women in European History Since 1700* (Lexington, Mass., 1989), and **M. J. Boxer and J. H. Quataert, eds.**, *Connecting Spheres: Women in the Western World, 1500 to the Present* (New York, 1987). Important studies of women include **M. J. Peterson**, *Family, Love, and Work in the Lives of Victorian Gentlewomen* (Bloomington, Ind., 1989); **B. G. Smith**, *Ladies of the Leisure Class: The Bourgeoises of Northern France in the Nineteenth Century* (Princeton, N.J., 1981); **P. Robertson**, *An Experience of Women: Pattern and Change in Nineteenth-Century Europe* (Philadelphia, 1982); and **B. Franzoi**, *At the Very Least She Pays the Rent: Women and German Industrialization, 1871–1914* (Westport, Conn., 1985). For a new perspective on domestic life, see **J. Flanders**, *Inside the Victorian Home: A Portrait of Domestic Life in Victorian England* (New York, 2004).

On various aspects of education, see **M. J. Maynes**, *Schooling in Western Europe: A Social History* (Albany, N.Y., 1985). A concise and well-presented survey of leisure patterns is **G. Cross**, *A Social History of Leisure Since 1600* (State College, Pa., 1990).

The domestic politics of the period can be examined in the general works on individual countries listed in Chapters 21 and 22. There are also specialized works on aspects of each country's history. On Britain, see **D. Read**, *The Age of Urban Democracy: England, 1868–1914* (New York, 1994). For a detailed examination of French history during the Third Republic, see **J. M. Mayeur and M. Reberioux**, *The Third Republic from Its Origins to the Great War, 1871–1914* (Cambridge, 1984). On Italy, see **C. Seton-Watson**, *Italy from Liberalism to Fascism* (London, 1967). On Germany, see **W. J. Mommsen**, *Imperial Germany, 1867–1918* (New York, 1995), and **E. Feuchtwanger**, *Imperial Germany, 1850–1918* (London, 2001). On aspects of Russian history, see **H. Rogger**, *Russia in the Age of Modernization and Revolution, 1881–1917* (London, 1983).

Thomson **NOW!** Enter *ThomsonNOW* using the access card that is available for *Western Civilization: A Brief History*. *ThomsonNOW* will help you understand this chapter with lesson plans generated for your needs. In addition, you can read the following documents, and many more, online:

Ethel Snowden, selected chapters from *The Feminist Movement*
Oliver Wendell Holmes, "Dissent in *Lochner* v. *New York*"
Theodore Roosevelt, speeches

WESTERN CIVILIZATION RESOURCES

Visit the Web site for *Western Civilization: A Brief History* for resources specific to this book:

http://www.thomsonedu.com/history/spielvogel

For a variety of tools to help you succeed in this course, visit the Western Civilization Resource Center at

http://history.wadsworth.com/spielvogel

Included are quizzes, images, documents, interactive simulations, maps and timelines, movie explorations, and a wealth of other sources.

24

AN AGE OF MODERNITY, ANXIETY, AND IMPERIALISM, 1894–1914

CHAPTER OUTLINE AND FOCUS QUESTIONS

Toward the Modern Consciousness: Intellectual and Cultural Developments

☐ What developments in science, intellectual affairs, and the arts in the late nineteenth and early twentieth centuries "opened the way to a modern consciousness," and how did this consciousness differ from earlier worldviews?

Politics: New Directions and New Uncertainties

☐ What difficulties did women, Jews, and the working classes face in the late nineteenth and early twentieth centuries, and how successful were they in achieving their goals?

☐ What political problems did Great Britain, France, Austria-Hungary, Germany, and Russia face between 1894 and 1914, and how did they solve them?

The New Imperialism

☐ What were the causes of the new imperialism that emerged after 1880, and what effects did the European quest for colonies have on Africa and Asia?

International Rivalry and the Coming of War

☐ What issues lay behind the international crises that Europe faced in the late nineteenth and early twentieth centuries?

CRITICAL THINKING

☐ What is the connection between the new imperialism of the late nineteenth century and the underlying causes for World War I?

Police stop Emmeline Pankhurst and her two daughters from entering Buckingham Palace to present a petition to the king

© Bettmann/CORBIS

*M*ANY EUROPEANS after 1894 continued to believe they lived in an era of material and human progress. For some, however, progress entailed much struggle. Emmeline Pankhurst, who became the leader of the women's suffrage movement in Britain, said that her determination to fight for women's rights stemmed from a childhood memory: "My father bent over me, shielding the candle flame with his big hand, and I heard him say, somewhat sadly, 'What a pity she wasn't born a lad.'" Eventually, Emmeline Pankhurst and her daughters marched and fought for women's right to vote. The struggle was often violent: "They came in bruised, hatless, faces scratched, eyes swollen, noses bleeding," one of the Pankhurst daughters recalled. Arrested and jailed in 1908, Pankhurst informed her judges, "If you had the power to send us to prison, not for six months, but for six years, or for our lives, the Government must not think they could stop this agitation. It would go on!" It did go on, and women in Britain did eventually receive the right to vote; to some, this was yet another confirmation of Europe's progress.

But the period after 1894 was not just a time of progress; it was also a time of great tension as imperialist adventures, international rivalries, and cultural uncertainties disturbed the apparent calm. After 1880, Europeans engaged in a great race for colonies around the world. This competition for lands abroad greatly intensified existing antagonisms among European states.

Ultimately, Europeans proved incapable of finding constructive ways to cope with their international rivalries. The development of two large alliance systems—the Triple Alliance and the Triple Entente—may have helped preserve peace for a time, but eventually the alliances made it easier for the European nations to be drawn into the catastrophic carnage of World War I.

The cultural life of Europe in the decades before 1914 reflects similar dynamic tensions. The advent of mass education produced better-informed citizens but also made it easier for governments to stir up the masses by nationalistic appeals through the new mass journalism. At the same time, despite the appearance of progress, European philosophers, writers, and artists were advancing cultural expressions that questioned traditional ideas and values and undermined public confidence. Leading up to 1914, many intellectuals had a sense of unease about the direction in which society was heading and a feeling of imminent catastrophe. They proved remarkably prophetic.◆

Toward the Modern Consciousness: Intellectual and Cultural Developments

Before 1914, most Westerners continued to believe in the values and ideals that had been generated by the Scientific Revolution and the Enlightenment. The ability of human beings to improve themselves and achieve a better society seemed well demonstrated by the rising standard of living, urban improvements, and mass education. Such products of modern technology as electric lights, phonographs, and automobiles reinforced the popular prestige of science and the belief in the ability of the human mind to comprehend the universe. Near the end of the nineteenth century, however, a dramatic transformation in the realm of ideas and culture challenged many of these assumptions. A new view of the physical universe, alternative views of human nature, and radically innovative forms of literary and artistic expression shattered old beliefs and opened the way to a modern consciousness. Although the real impact of many of these ideas was not felt until after World War I, they provoked a sense of confusion and anxiety before 1914 that would become even more pronounced after the war.

Developments in the Sciences: A New Physics

Science was one of the chief pillars supporting the optimistic and rationalistic view of the world that many Westerners shared in the nineteenth century. Supposedly based on hard facts and cold reason, science offered a certainty of belief in the orderliness of nature that was comforting to many people for whom traditional religious beliefs no longer had much meaning. Many naively believed that the application of already known scientific laws would give humanity a complete understanding of the physical world and an accurate picture of reality. The new physics dramatically altered that perspective.

Throughout much of the nineteenth century, Westerners adhered to the mechanical conception of the universe postulated by the classical physics of Isaac Newton. In this perspective, the universe was viewed as a giant machine in which time, space, and matter were objective realities that existed independent of the individuals observing them. Matter was thought to be composed of indivisible, solid material bodies called atoms.

These views were first seriously questioned at the end of the nineteenth century. The French scientist Marie Curie (1867–1934) and her husband Pierre (1859–1906) discovered that an element called radium gave off rays of radiation that apparently came from within the atom

Marie Curie. Marie Curie was born in Warsaw, Poland, but studied at the University of Paris, where she received degrees in both physics and mathematics. She was the first woman to win two Nobel Prizes, one in 1903 in physics and another in chemistry in 1911. She is shown here in her Paris laboratory in 1921. She died of leukemia, a result of her laboratory work with radioactivity.

itself. Atoms were not simply hard, material bodies but small worlds containing such subatomic particles as electrons and protons that behaved in a seemingly random and inexplicable fashion.

Building on this work, in 1900 a Berlin physicist, Max Planck (1858–1947), rejected the belief that a heated body radiates energy in a steady stream but maintained instead that energy is radiated discontinuously, in irregular packets of energy that he called "quanta." The quantum theory raised fundamental questions about the subatomic realm of the atom. By 1900, the old view of atoms as the basic building blocks of the material world was being seriously questioned.

The Work of Einstein Albert Einstein (1879–1955), a German-born patent officer working in Switzerland, pushed these new theories into new terrain. In 1905, Einstein published a paper titled "The Electro-Dynamics of Moving Bodies" that contained his special theory of relativity. According to **relativity theory,** space and time are not absolute but relative to the observer, and both are interwoven into what Einstein called a four-dimensional space-time continuum. Neither space nor time had an existence independent of human experience. As Einstein later explained simply to a journalist, "It was formerly believed that if all material things disappeared out of the universe, time and space would be left. According to the relativity theory, however, time and space disappear together with the things."[1] Moreover, Einstein concluded that matter was nothing but another form of energy. His epochal formula $E = mc^2$—each particle of matter is equivalent to its mass times the square of the velocity of light—was the key to explaining the vast energies contained within the atom. It led to the atomic age.

Toward a New Understanding of the Irrational: Nietzsche

Intellectually, the decades before 1914 witnessed a combination of contradictory developments. Thanks to the influence of science, confidence in human reason and progress still remained a dominant thread. At the same time, however, a small group of intellectuals attacked the idea of optimistic progress, dethroned reason, and glorified the irrational.

Friedrich Nietzsche (1844–1900) was one of the intellectuals who glorified the irrational. According to Nietzsche, Western bourgeois society was decadent and incapable of any real cultural creativity, primarily because of its excessive emphasis on the rational faculty at the expense of emotions, passions, and instincts. Reason, claimed Nietzsche, actually played little role in human life because humans were at the mercy of irrational life forces.

How, then, could Western society be renewed? First, said Nietzsche, one must recognize that "God is dead." Europeans had killed God, he said, and it was no longer possible to believe in some kind of cosmic order. Eliminating

God and hence Christian morality had liberated human beings and made it possible to create a higher kind of being Nietzsche called the superman: "I teach you the Superman. Man is something that is to be surpassed."[2] Superior intellectuals must free themselves from the ordinary thinking of the masses, create their own values, and lead the masses. Nietzsche rejected and condemned political democracy, social reform, and universal suffrage.

Sigmund Freud and Psychoanalysis

At the end of the nineteenth and beginning of the twentieth centuries, the Viennese doctor Sigmund Freud (1856–1939) put forth a series of theories that undermined optimism about the rational nature of the human mind. Freud's thought, like the new physics, added to the uncertainties of the age. His major ideas were published in 1900 in *The Interpretation of Dreams*, which contained the basic foundation of what came to be known as **psychoanalysis.**

According to Freud, human behavior was strongly determined by the unconscious, by earlier experiences and inner forces of which people were largely unaware. Why did some experiences whose influence persisted in controlling an individual's life remain unconscious? According to Freud, the answer was repression (see the box on p. 453), a process by which unsettling experiences were blotted from conscious awareness but still continued to influence behavior because they had become part of the unconscious. To explain how repression worked, Freud elaborated an intricate theory of the inner life of human beings.

According to Freud, a human being's inner life was a battleground of three contending forces: the id, the ego, and the superego. The id was the center of unconscious drives and was ruled by what Freud termed the pleasure principle. As creatures of desire, human beings directed their energy toward pleasure and away from pain. The id contained all kinds of lustful drives and desires and crude appetites and impulses. The ego was the seat of reason and hence the coordinator of the inner life. It was governed by the reality principle. Although humans were dominated by the pleasure principle, a true pursuit of pleasure was not feasible. The reality principle meant that people rejected pleasure so that they might live together in society. The superego was the locus of conscience and represented the inhibitions and moral values that society in general and parents in particular imposed on people. The superego served to force the ego to curb the unsatisfactory drives of the id.

The human being was thus a battleground among id, ego, and superego. Ego and superego exerted restraining influences on the unconscious id and repressed or kept out of consciousness what they wanted to. Repression began in childhood, and psychoanalysis was accomplished through a dialogue between psychotherapist and patient in which the therapist probed deeply into memory in order to retrace the chain of repression all the way

FREUD AND THE CONCEPT OF REPRESSION

reud's psychoanalytical theories resulted from his attempt to understand the world of the unconscious. This excerpt is taken from a lecture given in 1909 in which Freud describes how he arrived at his theory of the role of repression.

Sigmund Freud, *Five Lectures on Psychoanalysis*

I did not abandon it [his technique of encouraging patients to reveal forgotten experiences], however, before the observations I made during my use of it afforded me decisive evidence. I found confirmation of the fact that the forgotten memories were not lost. They were in the patient's possession and were ready to emerge in association to what was still known by him; but there was some force that prevented them from becoming conscious and compelled them to remain unconscious. The existence of this force could be assumed with certainty, since one became aware of an effort corresponding to it if, in opposition to it, one tried to introduce the unconscious memories into the patient's consciousness. The force which was maintaining the pathological condition became apparent in the form of resistance on the part of the patient.

It was on this idea of resistance, then, that I based my view of the course of physical events in hysteria. In order to effect a recovery, it had proved necessary to remove these resistances. Starting out from the mechanism of cure, it now became possible to construct quite definite ideas of the origin of the illness. The same forces which, in the form of resistance, were now offering opposition to the forgotten material's being made conscious, must formerly have

brought about the forgetting and must have pushed the pathogenic experiences in question out of consciousness. I gave the name of "repression" to this hypothetical process, and I considered that it was proved by the undeniable existence of resistance.

The further question could then be raised as to what these forces were and what the determinants were of the repression in which we now recognized the pathogenic mechanism of hysteria. A comparative study of the pathogenic situations which we had come to know through the cathartic procedure made it possible to answer this question. All these experiences had involved the emergence of a wishful impulse which was in sharp contrast to the subject's other wishes and which proved incompatible with the ethical and aesthetic standards of his personality. There had been a short conflict, and the end of this internal struggle was that the idea which had appeared before consciousness as the vehicle of this irreconcilable wish fell a victim to repression, was pushed out of consciousness with all its attached memories, and was forgotten. Thus the incompatibility of the wish in question with the patient's ego was the motive for the repression; the subject's ethical and other standards were the repressing forces. An acceptance of the incompatible wishful impulse or a prolongation of the conflict would have produced a high degree of unpleasure; this unpleasure was avoided by means of repression, which was thus revealed as one of the devices serving to protect the mental personality.

According to Freud, how did he discover the existence of repression? What function does repression perform?

---

back to its childhood origins. By making the conscious mind aware of the unconscious and its repressed contents, the patient's psychic conflict was resolved.

The Impact of Darwin: Social Darwinism and Racism

In the second half of the nineteenth century, scientific theories were sometimes wrongly applied to achieve other ends. The application of Darwin's principle of organic evolution to the social order came to be known as **social Darwinism**. Using Darwin's terminology, social Darwinists argued that societies were organisms that evolved through time from a struggle with their environment. Progress came from the "struggle for survival," as the "fit"—the strong—advanced while the weak declined.

Darwin's ideas were also applied to human society in an even more radical way by rabid nationalists and racists. In their pursuit of national greatness, extreme nationalists argued that nations, too, were engaged in a "struggle for existence" in which only the fittest survived.

The German general Friedrich von Bernhardi argued in 1907 that "war is a biological necessity of the first importance, a regulative element in the life of mankind which cannot be dispensed with, since without it an unhealthy development will follow, which excludes every advancement of the race, and therefore all real civilization. 'War is the father of all things.'"[3] Numerous nationalist organizations preached the same doctrine as Bernhardi.

Racism, too, was dramatically revived and strengthened by new biological arguments. Perhaps nowhere was the combination of extreme nationalism and racism more evident and more dangerous than in Germany. One of the chief propagandists for German racism at the turn of the twentieth century was Houston Stewart Chamberlain (1855–1927), a Briton who became a German citizen. His book, *The Foundations of the Nineteenth Century*, published in 1899, made a special impact on Germany. Modern-day Germans, according to Chamberlain, were the only pure successors of the Aryans, who were portrayed as the true and original creators of Western culture. The Aryan race, under German leadership, must be prepared to fight for Western civilization and save it from the destructive assaults of such "lower" races as Jews, Negroes, and Orientals. Increasingly, Jews were singled out as the racial enemy who wanted to destroy the Aryan race (see "Jews in the European Nation-State" later in this chapter).

The Culture of Modernity

The revolution in physics and psychology was paralleled by a revolution in literature and the arts. Before 1914, writers and artists were rebelling against the traditional literary and artistic styles that had dominated European cultural life since the Renaissance. The changes that they produced have since been called **Modernism.**

Naturalism and Symbolism in Literature Throughout much of the late nineteenth century, literature was dominated by Naturalism. Naturalists accepted the material world as real and felt that literature should be realistic. By addressing social problems, writers could contribute to an objective understanding of the world. Although Naturalism was a continuation of Realism, it lacked the underlying note of liberal optimism about people and society that had been prevalent in the 1850s. The Naturalists often portrayed characters caught in the grip of forces beyond their control.

The novels of the French writer Émile Zola (1840–1902) provide a good example of Naturalism. Against a backdrop of the urban slums and coalfields of northern France, Zola showed how alcoholism and different environments affected people's lives. He had read Darwin's *Origin of Species* and had been impressed by its emphasis on the struggle for survival and the importance of environment and heredity. These themes were central to his *Rougon-Macquart,* a twenty-volume series of novels on the "natural and social history of a family." Zola maintained that the artist must analyze and dissect life as a biologist would a living organism. He said, "I have simply done on living bodies the work of analysis which surgeons perform on corpses."

At the turn of the century, a new group of writers, known as the Symbolists, reacted against Realism. Primarily interested in writing poetry, the Symbolists believed that objective knowledge of the world was impossible. The external world was not real but only a collection of symbols that reflected the true reality of the individual human mind. Art, they believed, should function for its own sake instead of serving, criticizing, or seeking to understand society. In the works of two of the symbolist poets, William Butler Yeats and Rainer Maria Rilke, poetry ceased to be part of popular culture because only through a knowledge of the poet's personal language could one hope to understand what the poet was saying.

Modernism in the Arts Since the Renaissance, artists had largely tried to represent reality as accurately as possible. By the late nineteenth century, however, artists were seeking new forms of expression. The preamble to modern painting can be found in **Impressionism,** a movement that originated in France in the 1870s when a group of artists rejected the studios and museums and went out into the countryside to paint nature directly. Camille Pissarro (1830–1903), one of Impressionism's founders, expressed what they sought:

> Precise drawing is dry and hampers the impression of the whole, it destroys all sensations. Do not define too closely the outlines of things; it is the brush stroke of the right value and color which should produce the drawing.... Work at the same time upon sky, water, branches, ground, keeping everything going on an equal basis and unceasingly rework until you have got it.... Don't proceed according to rules and principles, but paint what you observe and feel. Paint generously and unhesitatingly, for it is best not to lose the first impression.[4]

Impressionists like Pissarro sought to put into painting their impressions of the changing effects of light on objects in nature.

An important Impressionist painter was Berthe Morisot (1841–1895), whose dedication to the new style of painting won her the disfavor of the traditional French academic artists. Morisot believed that women had a special vision that was, she said, "more delicate than that of men." Her special touch is evident in *Young Girl by the Window,* in which she makes use of lighter colors and flowing brushstrokes. Near the end of her life, she lamented the refusal of men to take her work seriously: "I don't think there has ever been a man who treated a woman as an equal, and that's all I would have asked, for I know I'm worth as much as they."[5]

By the 1880s, a new movement known as **Postimpressionism** arose in France and soon spread to other European countries. Postimpressionism retained the Impressionist emphasis on light and color but carried it even further by paying more attention to structure and form. Postimpressionists sought to use both color and line to express inner feelings and produce a personal statement of reality rather than an imitation of objects. Impressionist paintings had retained a sense of realism, but the Postimpressionists shifted from objective reality to subjective reality and in so doing began to withdraw from the artist's traditional task of depicting the external world. The works of the Postimpressionists were the real forerunners of modern art.

A famous Postimpressionist was the tortured and tragic figure Vincent van Gogh (1853–1890). For van Gogh, art was a spiritual experience. He was especially interested in color and believed that it could act as its own form of language. Van Gogh maintained that artists should paint what they feel.

By the beginning of the twentieth century, the belief that the task of art was to "represent reality" had lost much of its meaning. By that time, the new psychology and the new physics had made it evident that many people were not sure what constituted reality anyway.

Erich Lessing/Art Resource, NY (Musée Fabre, Montpellier, France)

Berthe Morisot, *Young Girl by the Window*. Berthe Morisot came from a wealthy French family that settled in Paris when she was seven. The first female Impressionist painter, she developed her own unique style. Her gentle colors and strong use of pastels are especially evident in *Young Girl by the Window*, painted in 1878. Many of her paintings focus on women and domestic scenes.

Then, too, the development of photography gave artists another reason to reject visual realism. Invented in the 1830s, photography became popular and widespread after George Eastman created the first Kodak camera for the mass market in 1888. What was the point of an artist doing what the camera did better? Unlike the camera, which could only mirror reality, artists could *create* reality. In modern art, as in literature, individual consciousness became the source of meaning.

As the twentieth century began, one of the most important figures in modern art was just beginning his career. Pablo Picasso (1881–1973) was from Spain but settled in Paris in 1904. Picasso was extremely flexible and painted in a remarkable variety of styles. He was instrumental in the development of a new style called **Cubism** that used geometric designs as visual stimuli to re-create reality in the viewer's mind.

The modern artist's flight from "visual reality" reached a high point in 1910 with the beginning of **abstract painting.** Vasily Kandinsky (1866–1944), a Russian who worked in Germany, was one of its originators. As is evident in his *Painting with White Border*, Kandinsky sought to avoid representation altogether. He believed that art should speak directly to the soul. To do so, it must avoid any reference to visual reality and concentrate on color.

At the start of the twentieth century, developments in music paralleled those in painting. Expressionism in music was a Russian creation, the product of the composer Igor Stravinsky (1882–1971) and the Ballet Russe, the dancing company of Sergei Diaghilev (1872–1929). Together they revolutionized the world of music with Stravinsky's ballet *The Rite of Spring*. At the premiere on May 29, 1913, the pulsating rhythms, sharp dissonances, and unusual dancing overwhelmed the Paris audience and caused a riot at the theater.

Politics: New Directions and New Uncertainties

The uncertainties in European intellectual and cultural life were paralleled by growing anxieties in European political life. The seemingly steady progress in the growth of liberal principles and **political democracy** after 1871 soon slowed or even ceased altogether after 1894. The new mass politics had opened the door to changes that many nineteenth-century liberals found unacceptable, and liberals themselves were forced to move in new directions. The appearance of a new right-wing politics based on racism added an ugly note to the existing anxieties. With their newfound voting rights, workers elected socialists who demanded new reforms when they took their places in legislative bodies. Women, too, made new demands, insisting on the right to vote and using new tactics to gain it. In central and eastern Europe, tensions grew as authoritarian governments refused to meet the demands of reformers. And outside Europe, a new giant appeared in the Western world as the United States emerged as a great industrial power with immense potential.

The Movement for Women's Rights

In the 1830s, a number of women in the United States and Europe, who worked together in several reform movements, argued for the right of women to divorce and own property. These early efforts, however, were not

Vincent van Gogh, _The Starry Night_.   The Dutch painter Vincent van Gogh was a major figure among the Postimpressionists. His originality and power of expression made a strong impact on his artistic successors. In _The Starry Night_, painted in 1889, van Gogh's subjective vision was given full play as the dynamic swirling forms of the heavens above overwhelmed the village below. The heavens seem alive with a mysterious spiritual force. Van Gogh painted this work in an asylum one year before he committed suicide.

particularly successful. For example, women did not gain the right to their own property until 1870 in Britain, 1900 in Germany, and 1907 in France.

New Professions   Custody and property rights were only a beginning for the women's movement, however. Some middle- and upper-middle-class women gained access to higher education while others sought entry into occupations dominated by men. The first field to open was teaching. Since medical training was largely closed to women, they sought alternatives in the development of nursing. One nursing pioneer was Amalie Sieveking (1794–1859), who founded the Female Association for the Care of the Poor and Sick in Hamburg, Germany. As she explained, "To me, at least as important were the

benefits which [work with the poor] seemed to promise for those of my sisters who would join me in such a work of charity. The higher interests of my sex were close to my heart."[6] Sieveking's work was followed by the more famous British nurse Florence Nightingale (1820–1910), whose efforts during the Crimean War, like those of Clara Barton (1821–1912) in the American Civil War, transformed nursing into a profession of trained, middle-class "women in white."

The Right to Vote   By the 1840s and 1850s, the movement for women's rights had entered the political arena with the call for equal political rights. Many feminists believed that the right to vote was the key to all other reforms to improve the position of women.

Vasily Kandinsky, *Square with White Border.* One of the originators of abstract painting was the Russian Vasily Kandinsky, who sought to eliminate representation altogether by focusing on color and avoiding any resemblance to visual reality. In *Square with White Border*, Kandinsky used color "to send light into the darkness of men's hearts." He believed that color, like music, could fulfill a spiritual goal of appealing directly to the human senses.

Suffragists had one basic aim: women's full citizenship in the nation-state. The British women's movement was the most vocal and most active in Europe. Emmeline Pankhurst (1858–1928) and her daughters, Christabel and Sylvia, founded the Women's Social and Political Union, which enrolled mostly middle- and upper-class women, in 1903. Pankhurst's organization realized the value of the media and used unusual publicity stunts to call attention to its demands. Derisively labeled "suffragettes" by male politicians, they pelted government officials with eggs, chained themselves to lampposts, smashed the windows of department stores on fashionable shopping streets, burned railroad cars, and went on hunger strikes in jail.

Although demands for women's rights were heard throughout Europe and the United States before World War I, only in Finland, Norway, and a few American states did women actually receive the right to vote. It would take the dramatic upheaval of World War I before male-dominated governments capitulated on this basic issue.

Women reformers also took on issues besides suffrage. In many countries, women supported peace movements. Bertha von Suttner (1843–1914) became head of the Austrian Peace Society and protested against the growing arms race of the 1890s. Her novel *Lay Down Your Arms* became a best-seller and brought her the Nobel Peace Prize in 1905. Lower-class women also took up the cause of peace. A group of women workers marched in Vienna in 1911 and demanded, "We want an end to armaments, to the means of murder, and we want these millions to be spent on the needs of the people."[7]

The New Woman Bertha von Suttner was but one example of the "new women" who were becoming more prominent at the turn of the twentieth century. These women rejected traditional feminine roles (see the box on p. 459). Although some of them supported political ideologies, such as socialism, that flew in the face of the ruling classes, others simply sought new freedom outside the household and new roles other than those of wives and mothers.

Maria Montessori (1870–1952) was a good example of the "new woman." Breaking with tradition, she attended medical school at the University of Rome and in 1896 became the first Italian woman to receive a medical degree. Three years later, she began a lecture tour in Italy on the subject of the "new woman," whom she characterized as a woman who followed a rational, scientific perspective. In keeping with this ideal, Montessori put her medical background to work in a school for mentally retarded children. She devised new teaching materials that enabled these children to read and write and became convinced, as she later wrote, "that similar methods applied to normal students would develop or set free their personality in a marvelous and surprising way." Subsequently, she established a system of childhood education based on natural and spontaneous activities in which students learned at their own pace. By the 1930s, hundreds of Montessori schools had been established in Europe and the United States. As a professional woman and a woman who chose to have a child without being married, Montessori also embodied some of the freedoms of the "new woman."

Jews in the European Nation-State

Near the end of the nineteenth century, a revival of racism combined with extreme nationalism to produce a new right-wing politics directed against the Jews. Anti-Semitism had a long history in Europe, but as a result of the ideals of the Enlightenment and the French Revolution, Jews had been granted legal equality in many European countries during the nineteenth century, and

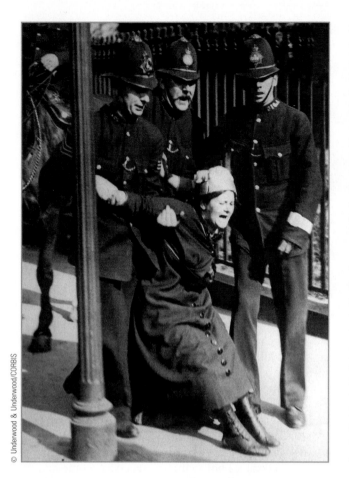

many Jews left the ghetto and became assimilated into the cultures around them. Jews became successful bankers, lawyers, scientists, scholars, journalists, and stage performers. In 1880, for example, Jews made up 10 percent of the population of the city of Vienna but 39 percent of its medical students and 23 percent of its law students.

These achievements represent only one side of the picture, however. In Germany and Austria during the 1880s and 1890s, conservatives founded right-wing anti-Semitic parties that used anti-Semitism to win the votes of traditional lower-middle-class groups who felt threatened by the economic forces of the times. However, the worst treatment of Jews at the turn of the century

Struggle for the Right to Vote. For many feminists, the right to vote came to represent the key to other reforms that would benefit women. In Britain, suffragists attracted attention to their cause by unusual publicity stunts. The photograph at left shows London policemen arresting a suffragette outside Buckingham Palace where women had chained themselves to the railings. Below is a photo of Emily Davison throwing herself under the king's horse at the Epsom Derby horse race. Shortly before her sacrificial action, she had written, "The glorious and indomitable Spirit of Liberty has but one further penalty within its power, the surrender of life itself, the supreme consummation of sacrifice."

ADVICE TO WOMEN: BE INDEPENDENT

Although a majority of women probably followed the nineteenth-century middle-class ideal of women as keepers of the household and nurturers of husband and children, an increasing number of women fought for women's rights. This selection is taken from act 3 of Henrik Ibsen's play *A Doll's House* (1879), in which Nora Helmer declares her independence from her husband's control.

Henrik Ibsen, *A Doll's House*

NORA: *(Pause)* Does anything strike you as we sit here?

HELMER: What should strike me?

NORA: We've been married eight years; does it not strike you that this is the first time we two, you and I, man and wife, have talked together seriously?

HELMER: Seriously? What do you mean, *seriously?*

NORA: For eight whole years, and more—ever since the day we first met—we have never exchanged one serious word about serious things....

HELMER: Why, my dearest Nora, what have you to do with serious things?

NORA: There we have it! You have never understood me. I've had great injustice done to me, Torvald; first by father, then by you.

HELMER: What! Your father *and* me? We, who have loved you more than all the world!

NORA: *(Shaking her head)* You have never loved me. You just found it amusing to think you were in love with me.

HELMER: Nora! What a thing to say!

NORA: Yes, it's true, Torvald. When I was living at home with father, he told me his opinions and mine were the same. If I had different opinions, I said nothing about them, because he would not have liked it. He used to call me his doll-child and played with me as I played with my dolls. Then I came to live in your house.

HELMER: What a way to speak of our marriage!

NORA: *(Undisturbed)* I mean that I passed from father's hands into yours. You arranged everything to your taste and I got the same tastes as you; or pretended to—I don't know which—both, perhaps; sometimes one, sometimes the other....You and father have done me a great wrong. It is your fault that my life has come to naught.

HELMER: Why, Nora, how unreasonable and ungrateful! Haven't you been happy here?

NORA: No, never. I thought I was, but I never was.

HELMER: Not—not happy!...

NORA: I must stand quite alone if I am ever to know myself and my surroundings; so I cannot stay with you.

HELMER: Nora! Nora!

NORA: I am going at once. I daresay [my friend] Christina will take me in for tonight....

HELMER: This is madness!

NORA: Tomorrow I shall go home—I mean to what was my home. It will be easier for me to find a job there....

HELMER: Forsake your home, your husband, your children! And you don't consider what the world will say.

NORA: I can't pay attention to that. I only know that I must do it.

HELMER: This is monstrous! Can you forsake your holiest duties?

NORA: What do you consider my holiest duties?

HELMER: Need I tell you that? Your duties to your husband and children.

NORA: I have other duties equally sacred.

HELMER: Impossible! What do you mean?

NORA: My duties toward myself.

HELMER: Before all else you are a wife and a mother.

NORA: That I no longer believe. Before all else I believe I am a human being just as much as you are—or at least that I should try to become one. I know that most people agree with you, Torvald, and that they say so in books. But I can no longer be satisfied with what most people say and what is in books. I must think things out for myself and try to get clear about them.

In Ibsen's play, what challenges does Nora Helmer make to the prevailing view of the proper role and behavior of wives? Why is her husband so shocked? Why did Ibsen title this play A Doll's House?

---

occurred in eastern Europe, where 72 percent of the world Jewish population lived. Russian Jews were admitted to secondary schools and universities only under a quota system and were forced to live in certain regions of the country. Persecutions and pogroms were widespread. Hundreds of thousands of Jews decided to emigrate.

Many went to the United States, although some (perhaps 25,000 in all) moved to Palestine, the biblical homeland of the Jews, which soon became the focus of a Jewish nationalist movement called **Zionism.**

A key figure in the growth of Zionism was Theodor Herzl (1860–1904). In 1896, he published a book called *The Jewish State* in which he advocated that "the Jews who wish it will have their state." Settlement in Palestine was difficult, however, because it was then part of the Ottoman Empire, which was opposed to Jewish immigration. Despite the problems, however, the First Zionist Congress, which met in Switzerland in 1897, proclaimed as its aim the creation of a "home in

Palestine

Palestine secured by public law" for the Jewish people. Although about a thousand Jews migrated to Palestine in 1900 and three thousand more each year after that, the Zionist dream remained a dream on the eve of World War I.

The Transformation of Liberalism: Great Britain

In dealing with the problems created by the new mass politics, liberal governments often followed policies that undermined the basic tenets of liberalism. This was certainly true in Great Britain, where the demands of the working-class movement caused Liberals to move away from their ideals. Liberals were forced to adopt significant social reforms due to the pressure of two new working-class organizations: trade unions and the Labour Party.

Frustrated by the government failure to enact social reform, trade unions began to advocate more radical change of the economic system, calling for "collective ownership and control over production, distribution and exchange." At the same time, a movement for laborers emerged among a group of intellectuals known as the Fabian Socialists. Neither the Fabian Socialists nor the British trade unions were Marxist. They did not advocate class struggle and revolution but rather evolution toward a socialist state by democratic means. In 1900, representatives of the trade unions and Fabian Socialists coalesced to form the Labour Party. By 1906, they had managed to elect twenty-nine members to the House of Commons.

The Liberals, who led the government from 1906 to 1914, perceived that they would have to enact a program of social welfare or lose the support of the workers. Under the leadership of David Lloyd George (1863–1945), the Liberals abandoned the classical principles of laissez-faire and voted for a series of social reforms. The National Insurance Act of 1911 provided benefits for workers in case of sickness and unemployment, to be paid for by compulsory contributions from workers, employers, and the state. Additional legislation provided a small pension for retirees over seventy and compensation for workers injured in accidents on the job. Though the benefits of the program and tax increases were both modest, they were the first hesitant steps toward the future British welfare state.

In the effort to achieve social reform, Lloyd George was also forced to confront the power of the House of Lords. Composed of hereditary aristocrats, the House of Lords took a strong stance against Lloyd George's effort to pay for social reform measures by taxes, however modest, on the wealthy. The prime minister pushed through a law in 1911 that restricted the ability of the House of Lords to impede legislation enacted by the House of Commons. After 1911, the House of Lords became largely a debating society.

France: Travails of the Third Republic

In the 1890s, the fragile Third Republic experienced a crisis that was an outgrowth of the renewed anti-Semitism in Europe in the late nineteenth century. Alfred Dreyfus, a Jew, was a captain on the French general staff who was found guilty by a secret military court early in 1895 of selling army secrets and condemned to life imprisonment. Evidence soon emerged that pointed to his innocence. Another officer, a Catholic aristocrat, was more obviously the traitor, but the army, a stronghold of aristocratic and Catholic officers, refused a new trial. Some right-wing journalists even used the case to push their own anti-Semitic views. Republic leaders, however, insisted on a new trial after a wave of immense public outrage. Although the new trial failed to set aside the guilty verdict, the government pardoned Dreyfus in 1899, and in 1906 he was finally fully exonerated.

One result of the Dreyfus affair was a change in government. Moderate republicans lost control to radical republicans who were determined to make greater progress toward a more democratic society by breaking the power of the Republic's enemies, especially the army and the Catholic church. The army was purged of all high-ranking officers who had antirepublican reputations. Moreover, church and state were officially separated in 1905, and during the next two years, the government seized church property and began to pay clerical salaries. These changes ended the political threat from the right to the Third Republic, which by now commanded the loyalty of most French people.

Growing Tensions in Germany

The new imperial Germany begun by Bismarck continued as an "authoritarian, conservative, military-bureaucratic power state" during the reign of Emperor William II (1888–1918). By 1914, Germany had become the strongest military and industrial power on the Continent. More than 50 percent of German workers had jobs in industry, while only 30 percent of the workforce was still in agriculture. Urban centers had mushroomed in number and size. These rapid changes in William's Germany helped produce a society torn between modernization and traditionalism.

With the expansion of industry and cities came demands for more political participation and growing sentiment for reforms that would produce greater democratization. Conservative forces, especially the land-owning nobility and representatives of heavy industry, two of the powerful ruling groups in Germany, tried to block it by supporting William II's activist foreign policy of finding Germany's "place in the sun." Expansionism, they believed, would divert people from further democratization.

The tensions in German society created by the conflict between modernization and traditionalism were also manifested in a new, radicalized, right-wing politics. A number of pressure groups arose to support nationalistic goals. Such groups as the Pan-German League stressed strong German nationalism and advocated imperialism as a tool to overcome social divisions and unite all classes.

They were also anti-Semitic and denounced Jews as the destroyers of national community.

Austria-Hungary: The Problem of the Nationalities

At the beginning of the 1890s, Austria-Hungary remained troubled by the problem of its numerous nationalities (see Chapter 23). The granting of universal male suffrage in 1907 served only to exacerbate the problem when nationalities that had played no role in the government now agitated in the parliament for autonomy. This led prime ministers after 1900 to ignore the parliament and rely increasingly on imperial emergency decrees to govern. Parliament itself became a bizarre forum in which, in the words of one incredulous observer, "about a score of men, all decently clad, were seated or standing, each at his little desk. Some made an infernal noise violently opening and shutting the lids of their desks. Others emitted a blaring sound from little toy trumpets; . . . still others beat snare drums."[8]

The threat the nationalities posed to the position of the dominant German minority in Austria also produced a backlash in the form of virulent German nationalism. As Austria industrialized in the 1870s and 1880s, two working-class parties came into existence, both strongly influenced by nationalism. The Social Democrats, although a Marxist party, supported the Austrian government, fearful that the autonomy of the different nationalities would hinder industrial development and prevent improvements for workers. Even more nationalistic, however, were the Christian Socialists, who combined agitation for workers with virulent anti-Semitism.

Industrialization and Revolution in Imperial Russia

Although industrialization came late to Russia, it progressed rapidly after 1890, especially with the assistance of foreign investment capital. By 1900, Russia had become the fourth-largest producer of steel, behind the United States, Germany, and Great Britain. With industrialization came factories, an industrial working class, and the development of socialist parties, although repression in Russia soon forced these parties to go underground and become revolutionary. The Marxist Social Democratic Party, for example, held its first congress in Minsk in 1898, but the arrest of its leaders caused the next one to be held in Brussels in 1903, attended by Russian émigrés. The Social Revolutionaries worked to overthrow the tsarist autocracy and establish peasant socialism. Having no other outlet for opposition to the regime, they advocated political terrorism, attempting to assassinate government officials and members of the ruling dynasty. The growing opposition to the tsarist regime finally exploded into revolution in 1905.

The defeat of the Russians by the Japanese in 1904–1905 encouraged antigovernment groups to rebel against

CHRONOLOGY Politics, 1894–1914	
Reign of Emperor William II	1888–1918
Reign of Tsar Nicholas II	1894–1917
Dreyfus affair in France	1895–1899
Theodor Herzl, *The Jewish State*	1896
First congress of Social Democratic Party in Russia	1898
Beginning of the Progressive era in the United States	1900
Formation of Labour Party in Britain	1900
Pankhursts establish Women's Social and Political Union	1903
Russo-Japanese War	1904–1905
Revolution in Russia	1905
National Insurance Act in Britain	1911

the tsarist regime. After a general strike in October 1905, the government capitulated. Nicholas II granted civil liberties and agreed to create a legislative assembly, the Duma, elected directly by a broad franchise. But real constitutional monarchy proved short-lived. Already by 1907, the tsar had curtailed the power of the Duma, and he fell back on the army and bureaucracy to rule Russia.

The Rise of the United States

Between 1860 and World War I, the United States made the shift from an agrarian to a mighty industrial nation. American heavy industry stood unchallenged in 1900. In that year, the Carnegie Steel Company alone produced more steel than Great Britain's entire steel industry. Industrialization also led to urbanization. While established cities, such as New York, Philadelphia, and Boston, grew even larger, other moderate-size cities, such as Pittsburgh, grew by leaps and bounds because of industrialization. Whereas 20 percent of Americans lived in cities in 1860, more than 40 percent did in 1900.

By 1900, the United States had become the world's richest nation and greatest industrial power. Yet serious questions remained about the quality of American life. In 1890, the richest 9 percent of Americans owned an incredible 71 percent of all the wealth. Labor unrest over unsafe working conditions, strict work discipline, and periodical cycles of devastating unemployment led workers to organize. By the turn of the century, one national organization, the American Federation of Labor, emerged as labor's dominant voice. In 1900, however, it included only 8.4 percent of the American industrial labor force.

During the so-called Progressive era after 1900, a wave of reform swept across the United States. The Meat Inspection Act and the Pure Food and Drug Act provided for a limited degree of federal regulation of corrupt industrial practices. The presidency of Woodrow Wilson

(1913–1921) witnessed the imposition of a graduated federal income tax and the establishment of the Federal Reserve System, which permitted the federal government to play a role in important economic decisions formerly made by bankers. Like European states, the United States was moving slowly into policies that extended the functions of the state.

The Growth of Canada

Canada faced problems of national unity at the end of the nineteenth century. In 1870, the Dominion of Canada had four provinces: Quebec, Ontario, Nova Scotia, and New Brunswick. With the addition of the provinces of Manitoba and British Columbia in 1871, the Dominion of Canada stretched from the Atlantic to the Pacific.

Canada, 1871

Real unity was difficult to achieve, however, because of the distrust between the English-speaking majority and the French-speaking Canadians living primarily in Quebec. Wilfred Laurier, who became the first French Canadian prime minister in 1896, was able to reconcile the two groups. During his administration, industrialization boomed, especially in the production of textiles, furniture, and railway equipment. Hundreds of thousands of immigrants, especially from Europe, also flowed into Canada. Many settled on lands in the west, thus helping populate Canada's vast territories.

The New Imperialism

Beginning in the 1880s, European states engaged in an intense scramble for overseas territory. This **new imperialism**, as some have called it, led Europeans to carve up Asia and Africa. What triggered the mad scramble for colonies?

Causes of the New Imperialism

The existence of competitive nation-states after 1870 was undoubtedly a major determinant in the outbreak of the new imperialism. As European affairs grew tense, competition led European states to acquire colonies abroad to provide ports and coaling stations for their navies. Great Britain also often expanded into new regions not for economic reasons but to keep the French, Germans, or Russians from setting up bases that could harm British interests. Colonies were also a source of international prestige. Once the dash for colonies began, failure to enter the race was perceived as a sign of weakness, totally unacceptable to an aspiring great power. As a British foreign minister wrote, "When I left the Foreign Office in 1880, nobody thought about Africa. When I returned to it in 1885, the nations of Europe were almost quarreling with each other as to the various portions of Africa which they should obtain."[9] Late-nineteenth-century imperialism was thus closely tied to nationalism.

It was also tied to social Darwinism and racism. Social Darwinists believed that in the struggle between nations, the fit are victorious and survive. Superior races must dominate inferior races by military force to show how strong and virile they are. As one Englishman wrote, "To the development of the White Man, the Black Man and the Yellow must ever remain inferior, and as the former raised itself higher and yet higher, so did these latter seem to shrink out of humanity and appear nearer and nearer to the brutes."[10]

Some Europeans gave a more religious or humanitarian justification for imperialism by arguing that they had a "moral responsibility" to civilize "ignorant" peoples. This notion of the "white man's burden" (see the box on p. 463) helped at least the more idealistic individuals rationalize imperialism in their own minds. One British official declared that the British Empire was, "under Providence, the greatest instrument for good that the world has seen." Thousands of Catholic and Protestant missionaries went abroad to seek converts to their faith. Nevertheless, the belief among Europeans that the superiority of their civilization obliged them to impose it on supposedly primitive nonwhites, even if the primitives suffered or died in the process, was yet another manifestation of racism.

Some historians have emphasized an economic motivation for imperialism. There was a great demand for natural resources and products not found in Western countries, such as rubber, oil, and tin. Instead of trading for these products, European investors advocated direct control of the areas where they originated. The large surpluses of capital that were being accumulated by bankers and industrialists often encouraged them to seek higher rates of profit in underdeveloped areas. All of these factors combined to form an **economic imperialism** whereby European finance dominated the economic activity of a large part of the world.

The Creation of Empires

Whatever the reasons for the new imperialism, it had a dramatic effect on Africa and Asia as European powers competed for control of the two continents.

The Scramble for Africa Europeans controlled relatively little of the African continent before 1880. During the Napoleonic wars, the British had established themselves in southern Africa by taking control of Cape Town, originally founded by the Dutch. After the wars, the British encouraged settlers to come to what they called the Cape Colony. British policies disgusted the Boers or

WHITE MAN'S BURDEN, BLACK MAN'S BURDEN

*O*ne of the justifications for European imperialism was the notion that superior white peoples had the moral responsibility to raise ignorant native peoples to a higher level of civilization. The British poet Rudyard Kipling (1865–1936) captured this notion in his poem "The White Man's Burden."

The Western justification of imperialism that was based on a sense of moral responsibility, evident in Kipling's poem, was often hypocritical. Edward Morel, a British journalist who spent time in the Congo, pointed out the destructive effects of Western imperialism on Africans in his book *The Black Man's Burden*.

Rudyard Kipling, "The White Man's Burden"

Take up the White Man's burden—
Send forth the best ye breed—
Go bind your sons to exile
to serve your captives' needs;
To wait in heavy harness,
On fluttered folk and wild—
Your new-caught sullen peoples,
Half-devil and half-child....

Take up the White Man's burden—
The savage wars of peace—
Fill full the mouth of Famine
And bid the sickness cease;
And when your goal is nearest
The end for others sought,
Watch sloth and heathen Folly
Bring all your hopes to nought....

Take up the White Man's burden—
And reap his old reward:
The blame of those ye better,
The hate of those ye guard—

The cry of hosts ye humour
(Ah, slowly) toward the light—
"Why brought ye us from bondage,
Our loved Egyptian night?"

Edward Morel, *The Black Man's Burden*

It is [the Africans] who carry the "black man's burden." They have not withered away before the white man's occupation. Indeed... Africa has ultimately absorbed within itself every Caucasian and, for that matter, every Semitic invader, too. In hewing out for himself a fixed abode in Africa, the white man has massacred the African in heaps. The African has survived, and it is well for the white settlers that he has....

What the partial occupation of his soil by the white man has failed to do; what the mapping out of European political "spheres of influence" has failed to do; what the Maxim [machine gun] and the rifle, the slave gang, labor in the bowels of the earth and the lash, have failed to do; what imported measles, smallpox and syphilis have failed to do; whatever the overseas slave trade failed to do; the power of modern capitalistic exploitation, assisted by modern engines of destruction, may yet succeed in accomplishing.

For from the evils of the latter, scientifically applied and enforced, there is no escape for the African. Its destructive effects are not spasmodic: they are permanent. In its permanence resides its fatal consequences. It kills not the body merely, but the soul. It breaks the spirit. It attacks the African at every turn, from every point of vantage. It wrecks his polity, uproots him from the land, invades his family life, destroys his natural pursuits and occupations, claims his whole time, enslaves him in his own home....

According to Kipling, why should Western nations take up the "white man's burden"? What was the "black man's burden," in the eyes of Edward Morel?

Afrikaners, as the descendants of the Dutch colonists were called, and led them in 1835 to migrate north on the Great Trek to the region between the Orange and Vaal rivers (later known as the Orange Free State) and north of the Vaal River (the Transvaal). Hostilities between the British and the Boers continued.

In the 1880s, British policy in southern Africa was largely determined by Cecil Rhodes (1853–1902). Rhodes founded diamond and gold mining companies that enabled him to gain control of a territory north of the Transvaal that he named Rhodesia after himself. Rhodes was a great champion of British expansion. He said once, "If there be a God, I think what he would like me to do is to paint as much of Africa British red as possible." His imperialist ambitions led to his downfall in 1896, however, when the British government forced him to resign as prime minister of Rhodesia after he conspired to

overthrow the neighboring Boer government without British approval. Although the British government had hoped to avoid war with the Boers, it could not stop extremists on both sides from precipitating such action. The Boer War dragged on from 1899 to 1902, when the Boers were overwhelmed by the larger British army. British policy toward the defeated Boers was remarkably conciliatory. Transvaal and the Orange Free State had representative governments by 1907, and in 1910, the Union of South Africa was formed. Like Canada, Australia, and New Zealand, it became a self-governing dominion within the British Empire.

Before 1880, the only other European settlements in Africa had been established by the French and the Portuguese. The Portuguese had held on to their settlements in Angola on the west coast and Mozambique on the east coast. The French had started the conquest of Algeria in

Muslim North Africa in 1830, although it was not until 1879 that French civilian rule was established there. The next year, 1880, the European scramble for possession of Africa began in earnest. By 1900, the French had added the huge area of French West Africa and Tunis.

The British took an active interest in Egypt after the Suez Canal was opened by the French in 1869. Believing the canal their lifeline to India, the British sought to control the canal area. They landed an expeditionary force in 1882 and soon established a protectorate over Egypt. From there, the British moved south into the Sudan and seized it after narrowly averting a war with France. Not to be outdone, Italy joined in the imperialist scramble. A humiliating defeat in Ethiopia in 1896 only led the Italians to try again in 1911 by invading and seizing Ottoman Tripoli, which they renamed Libya.

Central Africa was also added to the list of European colonies. Popular interest in the forbiddingly dense tropical jungles of Central Africa was first aroused in the 1860s and 1870s by explorers such as the Scottish missionary David Livingstone and the British-American journalist Henry M. Stanley. But the real driving force for the colonization of Central Africa was King Leopold II (1865–1909) of Belgium, who had rushed enthusiastically into pursuit of empire in Africa: "To open to civilization," he said, "the only part of our globe where it has not yet penetrated, to pierce the darkness which envelops whole populations, is a crusade, if I may say so, a crusade worthy of this century of progress." Profit, however, was far more important to Leopold than progress. In 1876, Leopold engaged Stanley to establish Belgian settlements in the Congo.

Between 1884 and 1900, most of the rest of Africa was carved up by the European powers. Germany also entered the ranks of the imperialist powers at this time. Initially, Bismarck had downplayed the significance of colonies, but as domestic political pressures for a German empire increased, Bismarck became a political convert to colonialism. As he expressed it, "All this colonial business is a sham, but we need it for the elections." The Germans established colonies in South West Africa, Cameroons, Togoland, and East Africa.

By 1914, Britain, France, Germany, Belgium, Spain, and Portugal had divided Africa (see Map 24.1). Only Liberia, founded by emancipated American slaves, and Ethiopia remained free states. Despite the humanitarian rationalizations about the "white man's burden," Africa had been conquered by European states determined to create colonial empires. Any peoples who dared to resist (with the exception of the Ethiopians, who defeated the Italians) were simply devastated by the superior military force of the Europeans.

Imperialism in Asia   Although Asia had been open to Western influence since the sixteenth century, not much of its immense territory had fallen under direct European control. The Dutch were established in the East Indies and the Spanish in the Philippines, while the French and Portuguese had trading posts on the Indian coast.

CHRONOLOGY The New Imperialism: Africa	
Opening of the Suez Canal	1869
Leopold II of Belgium's settlements in the Congo	1876
French conquest of Algeria	1879
British expeditionary force in Egypt	1882
Defeat of Italians by Ethiopians	1896
Boer War	1899–1902
Union of South Africa	1910
Italian seizure of Tripoli	1911
French protectorate over Morocco	1912

It was not until the explorations of Australia by Captain James Cook between 1768 and 1771 that Britain took an active interest in the East. The availability of land for grazing sheep and the discovery of gold led to an influx of free settlers, who slaughtered many of the indigenous inhabitants. In 1850, the British government had granted the various Australian colonies virtually complete self-government, and on January 1, 1901, all the colonies were unified into the Commonwealth of Australia. Nearby New Zealand, which the British had declared a colony in 1840, was granted dominion status in 1907.

A private trading company known as the British East India Company had been responsible for subjugating much of India. In 1858, however, after a revolt of the sepoys (Indian troops) of the East India Company's army had been crushed, the British Parliament transferred the company's powers directly to the government in London. In 1876, the title of empress of India was bestowed on Queen Victoria; Indians were now her colonial subjects.

Russian expansion in Asia was a logical outgrowth of its traditional territorial aggrandizement. Gradually, Russian settlers moved into cold and forbidding Siberia. They also moved south, attracted by the crumbling Ottoman Empire. By 1830, the Russians had established control over the entire northern coast of the Black Sea and then pressed on into Central Asia. These advances brought the Russians to the borders of Persia and Afghanistan, where the British also had interests because of their desire to protect their holdings in India. In 1907, the Russians and British agreed to make Afghanistan a buffer state between Russian Turkestan and British India and divide Persia into two spheres of influence. Halted by the British in their expansion to the south, the Russians moved east in Asia. The Russians' occupation of Manchuria and their attempt to move into Korea brought war with Japan. After losing the Russo-Japanese War in 1905, the Russians agreed to a Japanese protectorate in Korea; their Asian expansion was brought to a temporary halt (see Map 24.2).

The thrust of imperialism after 1880 led Westerners to move into new areas of Asia hitherto largely free of Western influence. By the nineteenth century, the ruling

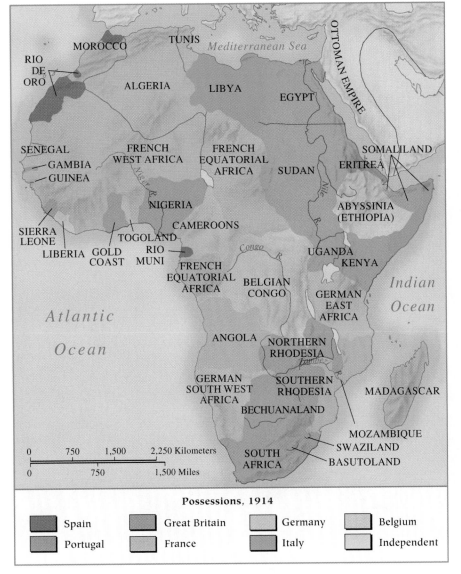

MAP 24.1 **Africa in 1914.**
The rush to acquire colonies by Europe's major powers was motivated by a combination of factors: ports and fueling stations for navies, enhancement of international prestige, outlets for nationalist feelings, expression of social Darwinism, and a desire to "civilize" non-Europeans.
❓ Of the two countries with the largest amount of territory in Africa, which one had colonies that were the most geographically concentrated, and what could be the benefits of this? 🔊 **View an animated version of this map or related maps at** http://thomsonedu.com/history/spielvogel

In the 1880s, the French extended "protection" over Cambodia, Annam, Tonkin, and Laos and organized them into the Union of French Indo-China. Only Siam (Thailand) remained free as a buffer state because of British-French rivalry.

The Pacific was also the scene of great power struggles and witnessed the entry of the United States onto the imperialist stage. Soon after Americans had made Hawaii's Pearl Harbor into a naval station in 1887, American settlers gained control of the sugar industry on the islands. When Hawaiian natives tried to reassert their authority, the U.S. Marines were brought in to "protect" American lives. Hawaii was annexed by the United States in 1898 during the era of American nationalistic fervor generated by the Spanish-American War. The American defeat of Spain encouraged Americans to extend their empire by acquiring Cuba, Puerto Rico, Guam, and the Philippine Islands. Although the Filipinos hoped for independence, the Americans refused to grant it. As President McKinley said, the United States had the duty "to educate the Filipinos and uplift and Christianize them," a remarkable statement in view of the fact that most of them had been Roman Catholics for centuries. It took three years and sixty thousand troops to pacify the Philippines and establish American control.

Responses to Imperialism

When Europeans imposed their culture on peoples they considered inferior, how did the conquered peoples respond? Initial attempts to expel the foreigners only led to devastating defeats at the hands of Westerners, whose

Manchu dynasty of the Chinese empire was showing signs of decline. In 1842, the British had obtained (through war) the island of Hong Kong and rights to trade in a number of Chinese cities. Other Western nations soon rushed in to gain similar trading privileges. Britain, France, Germany, Russia, the United States, and Japan established spheres of influence and long-term leases on Chinese territory.

Japan avoided Western intrusion until 1853–1854, when American naval forces under Commodore Matthew Perry forced the Japanese to grant the United States trading and diplomatic privileges. Japan, however, managed to avoid China's fate. By absorbing and adopting Western military and industrial methods, the Japanese developed a modern commercial and industrial system as well as a powerful military state. They established their own sphere of influence in China, and five years after they defeated the Russians in 1905, the Japanese formally annexed Korea.

In Southeast Asia, Britain established control over Burma (modern Myanmar) and the Malay States while France played an active role in subjugating Indochina.

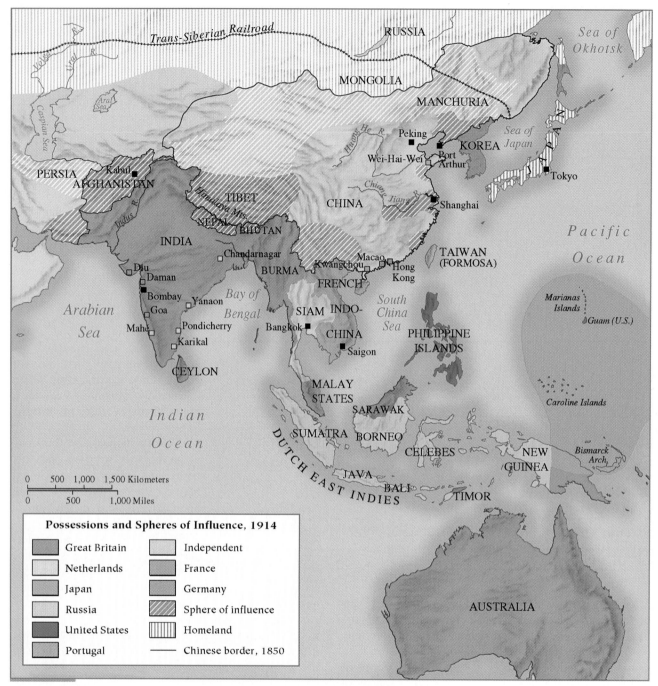

MAP 24.2 **Asia in 1914.** Asia became an important arena of international competition in the nineteenth and early twentieth centuries. Beset by economic stagnation and an inability to modernize, a weak China was unable to withstand the demands of the United States, European powers, and a westernizing Japan. Britain, France, Russia, Japan, and the United States had direct or indirect control of nearly all of Asia by 1914. ❓ Why would both Russia and Japan covet Manchuria? View an animated version of this map or related maps at http://thomsonedu.com/history/ spielvogel

industrial technology gave them far superior weapons of war. Most of the indigenous peoples, accustomed to rule by small elites, simply accepted their new governors, making the imposition of Western rule relatively easy. The conquered peoples subsequently adjusted to the rule of foreigners in different ways. Some sought to maintain their cultural traditions, but others believed that adoption of Western ways would enable them to reform their societies and eventually challenge Western rule. Most people probably stood somewhere between the two extremes. Four examples illustrate different approaches to adjusting to foreign rule.

foreigners occurred in the Boxer Rebellion in 1900–1901. "Boxers" was the popular name given to Chinese who belonged to a secret organization called the Society of Harmonious Fists, whose aim was to push the foreigners out of China. The Boxers murdered foreign missionaries, Chinese who had converted to Christianity, railroad workers, foreign businessmen, and even the German envoy to Beijing. Response to the killings was immediate and overwhelming. An allied army consisting of British, French, German, Russian, American, and Japanese troops attacked Beijing, restored order, and demanded more concessions from the Chinese government. The imperial government was so weakened that the forces of the revolutionary leader Sun Yat-sen (1866–1925), who adopted a program of "nationalism, democracy, and socialism," overthrew the Manchu dynasty in 1912. The new Republic of China remained weak and ineffective, and China's travails were far from over.

Africa   By the beginning of the twentieth century, a new class of African leaders had emerged. Educated in colonial schools and some even in the West, they were the first generation of Africans to know a great deal about the West and to write in the language of their colonial masters. Although this "new class" admired Western culture and even disliked the ways of their own countries, many came to resent the foreigners and their arrogant contempt for colonial peoples. Equally vexing was the fact that the economic prosperity of the West was never brought to the colonies. To many Africans, colonialism meant the loss of their farmlands or terrible jobs on plantations or in sweatshops and factories run by foreigners.

Although middle-class Africans did not suffer to the extent that poor peasants or workers on plantations did, they too had complaints. They usually qualified only for menial jobs in the government or business. Segregated clubs, schools, and churches were set up as more European officials brought their wives and began to raise families. Europeans also had a habit of addressing natives by their first names or calling an adult male "boy."

Such conditions led many members of the new urban educated class to harbor mixed feelings toward their colonial masters and the civilization they represented. They were willing to admit the superiority of many aspects of Western culture but fervently felt that they should be allowed to assert their own nationality and determine their own cultural destiny. Out of this mixture of hopes and resentments emerged the first stirrings of modern nationalism in Africa. During the first quarter of the twentieth century, in colonial societies across Africa, educated native peoples began to organize political parties and movements seeking the end of foreign rule.

China   The humiliation of China by the Western powers led to much antiforeign violence, but the Westerners used this lawlessness as an excuse to extort further concessions from the Chinese. A major outburst of violence against

Japan   In the late 1850s and early 1860s, it looked as if Japan would follow China's fate and be carved up into spheres of influence by aggressive Western powers. A remarkably rapid transformation, however, produced a very different result. Before 1868, the shogun, a powerful hereditary military governor assisted by a warrior nobility known as the samurai, exercised real power in Japan. The emperor's functions had become primarily religious. After the shogun's concessions to the Western nations, antiforeign sentiment led to a samurai revolt in 1867 and the restoration of the emperor as the rightful head of the government. The new emperor was the astute, dynamic, young Mutsuhito (1867–1912), who called his reign the Meiji ("enlightened government"). The new leaders who controlled the emperor now inaugurated a remarkable transformation of Japan that has since been known as the Meiji Restoration.

Recognizing the obvious military and industrial superiority of the West, the new leaders decided to modernize Japan by absorbing and adopting Western methods. Thousands of young Japanese were sent abroad to receive Western educations, especially in the social and natural sciences. A German-style army and a British-style navy were established. The Japanese copied the industrial and financial methods of the United States and developed a modern commercial and industrial system. A highly centralized administrative system copied from the French replaced the old system. Initially, the Japanese adopted the French principles of social and legal equality, but by 1890, they had created a political system that was democratic in form but authoritarian in practice. In imitating the West, Japan also developed a powerful military state.

India   The British government had been in control of India since the mid-nineteenth century. Under Parliament's supervision, a small group of British civil servants directed the affairs of India's almost 300 million people.

The West and Japan. In their attempt to modernize, the Japanese absorbed and adopted Western methods. They were also influenced by Western culture as Western fashions became the rage in elite circles. Baseball was even imported from the United States. This painting shows Western-style stone houses in Tokyo and streets filled with people dressed in a variety of styles.

The British brought order to a society that had been divided by civil wars for some time and created a relatively honest and efficient government. They also brought Western technology—railroads, banks, mines, industry, medical knowledge, and hospitals. The British introduced Western-style secondary schools and colleges where the Indian upper and middle classes and professional classes were educated so that they could serve as trained subordinates in the government and the army.

But the Indian people paid a high price for the peace and stability brought by British rule. Due to population growth in the nineteenth century, extreme poverty was a way of life for most Indians; almost two-thirds of the population suffered from malnutrition in 1901. British industrialization brought little improvement for the masses. British manufactured goods destroyed local industries, and Indian wealth was used to pay British officials and the large army. The system of education served only elite, upper-class Indians, and it was conducted only

in the rulers' English language, meaning that 90 percent of the population remained illiterate. Even for the Indians who benefited the most from their Western educations, British rule was degrading. The best jobs and the best housing were reserved for Britons. Despite their education, the Indians were never considered equals of the British, whose racial attitudes were made quite clear by Lord Kitchener, one of Britain's foremost military commanders in India, when he said, "It is this consciousness of the inherent superiority of the European which has won for us India. However well educated and clever a native may be, and however brave he may prove himself, I believe that no rank we can bestow on him would cause him to be considered an equal of the British officer."[11] Such smug racial attitudes made it difficult for British rule, no matter how beneficent, ever to be ultimately accepted and led to the rise of an Indian nationalist movement. By 1883, when the Indian National Congress was formed, moderate, educated Indians were beginning to seek self-government. By 1919, in response to British violence and British insensitivity, Indians were demanding complete independence.

Results of the New Imperialism

By 1900, almost all the societies of Africa and Asia were either under full colonial rule or, as in the case of China and the Ottoman Empire, at a point of virtual collapse. Only a handful of states, such as Japan in East Asia, Thailand in Southeast Asia, Afghanistan and Persia in the Middle East, and mountainous Ethiopia in East Africa, managed to escape internal disintegration or subjection to colonial rule. For the most part, the exceptions were the result of good fortune rather than design. Thailand escaped subjugation primarily because officials in Britain and France found it more convenient to transform the country into a buffer state than to fight over it. Ethiopia and Afghanistan survived due to their remote location and mountainous terrain. Only Japan managed to avoid the common fate through a concerted strategy of political and economic reform. With the coming of imperialism, a global economy was finally established, and the domination of Western civilization over the cultures of Africa and Asia appeared to be complete. At the same time, the competition for lands abroad exacerbated the rivalry among European states.

International Rivalry and the Coming of War

Before 1914, Europeans had experienced almost fifty years of peace. There had been wars (including wars of conquest in the non-Western world), but none had involved the great powers. A series of crises occurred that might easily have led to general war. One reason they did not is that until 1890, Bismarck of Germany exercised a restraining influence on the Europeans.

Bismarck knew that the emergence of a unified Germany in 1871 had upset the balance of power established at Vienna in 1815. Fearing a possible anti-German alliance between France, Russia, and possibly even Austria, Bismarck made a defensive alliance with Austria in 1879. In 1882, this German-Austrian alliance was enlarged with the entrance of Italy. The Triple Alliance of 1882 committed Germany, Austria-Hungary, and Italy to support the existing political order while providing a defense against France. At the same time, Bismarck maintained a separate treaty with Russia, hoping to prevent a French-Russian alliance that would threaten Germany with the possibility of a two-front war. The Bismarckian system of alliances, geared to preserving peace and the status quo, had worked, but in 1890, Emperor William II dismissed Bismarck and began to chart a new direction for Germany's foreign policy.

New Directions and New Crises

Emperor William II embarked on an activist foreign policy dedicated to enhancing German power by finding, as he put it, Germany's rightful "place in the sun." One of his changes in Bismarck's foreign policy was to drop the treaty with Russia, which he viewed as being at odds with Germany's alliance with Austria. The ending of the alliance achieved what Bismarck had feared: it brought France and Russia together. Republican France leapt at the chance to draw closer to tsarist Russia, and in 1894, the two powers concluded a military alliance.

During the next ten years, German policies abroad caused the British to draw closer to France (see the box on p. 470). By 1907, a loose confederation of Great Britain, France, and Russia—known as the Triple Entente—stood opposed to the Triple Alliance of Germany, Austria-Hungary, and Italy. Europe was divided into two opposing camps that became more and more inflexible and unwilling to compromise. When the members of the two alliances became involved in a new series of crises between 1908 and 1913 over control of the remnants of the Ottoman Empire in the Balkans (see Map 24.3), the stage was set for World War I.

Crises in the Balkans, 1908–1913

The Bosnian Crisis of 1908–1909 initiated a chain of events that eventually spun out of control. Since 1878, Bosnia and Herzegovina had been under the protection of Austria, but in 1908, Austria took the drastic step of annexing these two Slavic-speaking territories. Serbia became outraged at this action because it dashed the Serbs' hopes of creating a large Serbian kingdom that would include most of the southern Slavs. But this possibility was why the Austrians had annexed Bosnia and Herzegovina. A large Serbia would be a threat to the unity of their empire

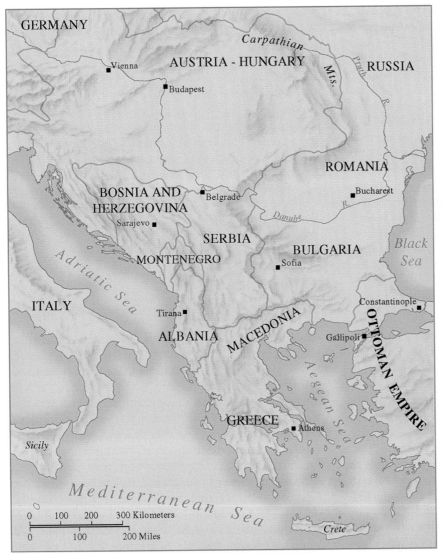

MAP 24.3 **The Balkans in 1913.** The First Balkan War (1912) liberated most of the region from Ottoman control; the Second Balkan War (1913) increased the size of Greece and Serbia at Bulgaria's expense. Russia supported the ambitions of fellow Slavs in Serbia, who sought to rule a large Slavic kingdom in the Balkans. Austria and its ally Germany opposed Serbia's ambitions. **?** What territories had the Ottomans lost by the end of 1913?

View an animated version of this map or related maps at http://thomsonedu.com/history/spielvogel

THE EMPEROR'S "BIG MOUTH"

Emperor William II's world policy engendered considerable ill will and unrest among other European states, especially Britain. Moreover, the emperor had the unfortunate tendency to stir up trouble by his often tactless public remarks. In this 1908 interview, for example, William II intended to strengthen Germany's ties with Britain. His words had just the opposite effect and raised a storm of protest in both Britain and Germany.

Daily Telegraph Interview, October 28, 1908

As I have said, his Majesty honoured me with a long conversation, and spoke with impulsive and unusual frankness. "You English," he said, "are mad, mad, mad as March hares. What has come over you that you are so completely given over to suspicions quite unworthy of a great nation? What more can I do than I have done? I declared with all the emphasis at my command, in my speech at Guildhall, that my heart is set upon peace, and that it is one of my dearest wishes to live on the best of terms with England. Have I ever been false to my word? Falsehood and prevarication are alien to my nature. My actions ought to speak for themselves, but you listen not to them but to those who misinterpret and distort them. That is a personal insult which I feel and resent. To be forever misjudged, to have my repeated offers of friendship weighed and scrutinized with jealous, mistrustful eyes, taxes my patience severely. I have said time after time that I am a friend of England, and your Press—or, at least, a considerable section of it—bids the people of England to refuse my proffered hand, and insinuates that the other holds a dagger. How can I convince a nation against its will?

"I repeat," continued his Majesty, "that I am a friend of England, but you make things difficult for me. My task is not of the easiest. The prevailing sentiment among large sections of the middle and lower classes of my own people is not friendly to England. I am, therefore, so to speak, in a minority in my own land, but it is a minority of the best elements as it is in England with respect to Germany. That is another reason why I resent your refusal to accept my pledged word that I am the friend of England. I strive without ceasing to improve relations, and you retort that I am your arch-enemy. You make it hard for me. Why is it? . . .

"But, you will say, what of the German Navy? Surely, that is a menace to England! Against whom but England are my squadrons being prepared? If England is not in the minds of those Germans who are bent on creating a powerful fleet, why is Germany asked to consent to such new and heavy burdens of taxation? My answer is clear. Germany is a young and growing Empire. She has a world-wide commerce, which is rapidly expanding, and to which the legitimate ambition of patriotic Germans refuses to assign any bounds. Germany must have a powerful fleet to protect that commerce, and her manifold interests in even the most distant seas. She expects those interests to go on growing, and she must be able to champion them manfully in any quarter of the globe. Germany looks ahead. Her horizons stretch far away. She must be prepared for any eventualities in the Far East. Who can foresee what may take place in the Pacific in the days to come, days not so distant as some believe, but days, at any rate, for which all European Powers with Far Eastern interests ought steadily to prepare? Look at the accomplished rise of Japan; think of the possible national awakening of China; and then judge of the vast problems of the Pacific. Only those Powers which have great navies will be listened to with respect, when the future of the Pacific comes to be solved; and, if for that reason only, Germany must have a powerful fleet. It may even be that England herself will be glad that Germany has a fleet when they speak together on the same side in the great debates of the future."

What did William II mean to say? What did he actually say? What does this interview with William II reveal about the emperor's attitudes and character?

---

with its large Slavic population. The Russians, as protectors of their fellow Slavs and with their own desire to increase their authority in the Balkans, supported the Serbs and opposed the Austrian action. Backed by the Russians, the Serbs prepared for war against Austria. At this point, William II intervened and demanded that the Russians accept Austria's annexation of Bosnia and Herzegovina or face war with Germany. Weakened from their defeat in the Russo-Japanese War in 1904–1905, the Russians backed down. Humiliated, they vowed revenge.

European attention returned to the Balkans in 1912 when Serbia, Bulgaria, Montenegro, and Greece organized the Balkan League and defeated the Ottomans in the First Balkan War. When the victorious allies were unable to agree on how to divide the conquered Ottoman territory, the Second Balkan War erupted in 1913. Greece, Serbia, Romania, and the Ottoman Empire attacked and defeated Bulgaria. As a result, Bulgaria obtained only a small part of Macedonia, and most of the rest was divided between Serbia and Greece. Yet Serbia's aspirations remained unfulfilled. The two Balkan wars left the inhabitants embittered and created more tensions among the great powers.

One of Serbia's major ambitions had been to acquire Albanian territory that would give it a port on the Adriatic. At the London Conference, arranged by Austria at the end of the two Balkan wars, the Austrians had blocked Serbia's wishes by creating an independent

Albania. The Germans, as Austrian allies, had supported this move. In their frustration, Serbian nationalists increasingly portrayed the Austrians as monsters who were keeping the Serbs from becoming a great nation. As Serbia's chief supporters, the Russians were also upset by the turn of events in the Balkans. A feeling had grown among Russian leaders that they could not back down again in the event of a confrontation with Austria or Germany in the Balkans.

Austria-Hungary had achieved another of its aims, but it was still convinced that Serbia was a mortal threat to its empire and must at some point be crushed. Meanwhile, the French and Russian governments renewed their alliance and promised each other that they would not back down at the next crisis. Britain drew closer to France. By the beginning of 1914, two armed camps viewed each other with suspicion. The European "age of progress" was about to come to an inglorious and bloody end.

CONCLUSION

What many Europeans liked to call their "age of progress" in the decades before 1914 was also an era of anxiety. Frenzied imperialist expansion had created vast European empires and spheres of influence around the globe. This feverish competition for colonies, however, had markedly increased the existing antagonisms among the European states. At the same time, the Western treatment of non-Western peoples as racial inferiors impelled educated, non-Western elites in these colonies to found movements for national independence. Before these movements could succeed, however, the power that Europeans had achieved through their mass armies and technological superiority had to be weakened. The Europeans inadvertently accomplished this task for their colonial subjects by demolishing their own civilization on the battlegrounds of Europe in World War I and World War II.

The cultural revolutions before 1914 had also produced anxiety and a crisis of confidence in European civilization. A brilliant minority of intellectuals had created a modern consciousness that questioned most Europeans' optimistic faith in reason, the rational structure of nature, and the certainty of progress. The devastating experiences of World War I turned this culture of uncertainty into a way of life after 1918.

TIMELINE

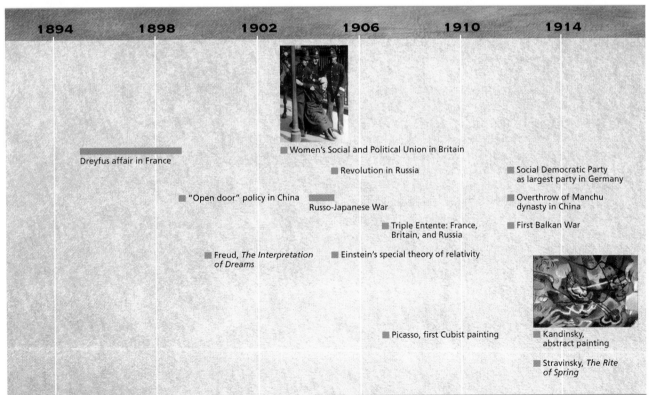

1894   1898   1902   1906   1910   1914

Dreyfus affair in France

Women's Social and Political Union in Britain

Revolution in Russia

Social Democratic Party as largest party in Germany

"Open door" policy in China

Russo-Japanese War

Overthrow of Manchu dynasty in China

Triple Entente: France, Britain, and Russia

First Balkan War

Freud, *The Interpretation of Dreams*

Einstein's special theory of relativity

Picasso, first Cubist painting

Kandinsky, abstract painting

Stravinsky, *The Rite of Spring*

NOTES

1. Quoted in A.E.E. McKenzie, *The Major Achievements of Science* (New York, 1960), vol. 1, p. 310.
2. F. Nietzsche, *Thus Spake Zarathustra,* in *The Philosophy of Nietzsche* (New York, 1954), p. 6.
3. F. von Bernhardi, *Germany and the Next War,* trans. A. H. Powles (New York, 1914), pp. 18–19.
4. Quoted in J. Rewald, *History of Impressionism* (New York, 1961), pp. 456–458.
5. Quoted in A. Higonnet, *Berthe Morisot's Images of Women* (Cambridge, Mass., 1992), p. 19.
6. Quoted in C. M. Prelinger, "Prelude to Consciousness: Amalie Sieveking and the Female Association for the Care of the Poor and the Sick," in J. C. Fout, ed., *German Women in the Nineteenth Century: A Social History* (New York, 1984), p. 119.
7. Quoted in B. Smith, *Changing Lives: Women in European History Since 1700* (Lexington, Mass., 1989), p. 379.
8. Quoted in J. Merriman, *A History of Modern Europe* (New York, 1996), p. 953.
9. Quoted in Ibid., p. 965.
10. Quoted in J. Ellis, *The Social History of the Machine Gun* (New York, 1975), p. 80.
11. Quoted in K. M. Panikkar, *Asia and Western Dominance* (London, 1959), p. 116.

SUGGESTIONS FOR FURTHER READING

A well-regarded study of Freud is **P. Gay, *Freud: A Life for Our Time*** (New York, 1988). Also see **J. Neu, ed., *The Cambridge Companion to Freud*** (New York, 1991). Nietzsche is examined in **R. C. Holub, *Friedrich Nietzsche*** (New York, 1995). Very valuable on modern art are **M. Powell-Jones, *Impressionism*** (London, 1994); **G. Crepaldi, *The Impressionists*** (New York, 2002); **B. Denvir, *Post-Impressionism*** (New York, 1992); and **T. Parsons, *Post-Impressionism: The Rise of Modern Art*** (London, 1992). On literature, see **R. Pascal, *From Naturalism to Expressionism: German Literature and Society, 1880–1918*** (New York, 1973).

The rise of feminism is examined in **J. Rendall, *The Origins of Modern Feminism: Women in Britain, France and the United States*** (London, 1985). The subject of modern anti-Semitism is covered in **J. Katz, *From Prejudice to Destruction*** (Cambridge, Mass., 1980), and **A. S. Lindemann, *Esau's Tears: Modern Anti-Semitism and the Rise of the Jews*** (New York, 1997). European racism is analyzed in **G. L. Mosse, *Toward the Final Solution*** (New York, 1980). Anti-Semitism in France is the subject of **E. Cahm, *The Dreyfus Affair in French Society and Politics*** (New York, 1996). The problems of Jews in Russia are examined in **J. Frankel, *Prophecy and Politics: Socialism, Nationalism and the Russian Jews, 1862–1917***

(Cambridge, 1981). On Theodor Herzl, see **J. Kornberg, *Theodor Herzl: From Assimilation to Zionism*** (Bloomington, Ind., 1993). There are good introductions to the political world of William II's Germany in **T. A. Kohut, *Wilhelm II and the Germans: A Study in Leadership*** (New York, 1991), and **C. Clark, *Kaiser Wilhelm II*** (London, 2000). On Russia, see **A. Ascher, *The Revolution of 1905: Russia in Disarray,*** 2 vols. (Stanford, Calif., 1988–1992).

For broad perspectives on imperialism, see **T. Smith, *The Pattern of Imperialism*** (Cambridge, 1981); **M. W. Doyle, *Empires*** (Ithaca, N.Y., 1986); and **P. Darby, *Three Faces of Imperialism: British and American Approaches to Asia and Africa, 1870–1970*** (New Haven, Conn., 1987). Various aspects of imperialism are covered in **A. Burton, *Burdens of History: British Feminists, Indian Women, and Imperial Culture, 1865–1915*** (Chapel Hill, N.C., 1994); **M. Strobel, *European Women and the Second British Empire*** (Bloomington, Ind., 1991); **P. J. Marshall, ed., *The Cambridge Illustrated History of the British Empire*** (Cambridge, 1996); and **T. Pakhenham, *The Scramble for Africa*** (New York, 1991).

Two fundamental works on the diplomatic history of the period are **W. L. Langer, *European Alliances and Alignments,*** 2d ed. (New York, 1966), and ***The Diplomacy of Imperialism,*** 2d ed. (New York, 1965). Also valuable is the masterful study by **P. Kennedy, *The Rise of Anglo-German Antagonism, 1860–1914*** (London, 1982).

Thomson NOW! Enter *ThomsonNOW* using the access card that is available for *Western Civilization: A Brief History.* *ThomsonNOW* will help you understand this chapter with lesson plans generated for your needs. In addition, you can read the following documents, and many more, online:

King Leopold II of Belgium, letter to the minister of the Congo
Henry Morton Stanley, "How I Found Livingstone"
Sigmund Freud, excerpts from *The Interpretation of Dreams*
Friedrich Nietzsche, selected chapters from *Thus Spake Zarathustra*
Georges Sorel, "The Proletarian Strike"

WESTERN CIVILIZATION RESOURCES

Visit the Web site for *Western Civilization: A Brief History* for resources specific to this book:

http://www.thomsonedu.com/history/spielvogel

For a variety of tools to help you succeed in this course, visit the Western Civilization Resource Center at

http://history.wadsworth.com/spielvogel

Included are quizzes, images, documents, interactive simulations, maps and timelines, movie explorations, and a wealth of other sources.

25

THE BEGINNING OF THE TWENTIETH-CENTURY CRISIS: WAR AND REVOLUTION

CHAPTER OUTLINE AND FOCUS QUESTIONS

The Road to World War I

◻ What were the long-range and immediate causes of World War I?

The Great War

◻ What did the belligerents expect at the beginning of World War I, and why did the course of the war turn out to be so different from their expectations?

◻ How did World War I affect the belligerents' governmental and political institutions, economic affairs, and social life?

War and Revolution

◻ What were the causes of the Russian Revolution of 1917, and why did the Bolsheviks prevail in the civil war and gain control of Russia?

The Peace Settlement

◻ What were the objectives of the chief participants at the Paris Peace Conference of 1919, and how closely did the final settlement reflect these objectives?

CRITICAL THINKING

◻ Nationalism was the driving force behind the post–World War I reshaping of the European continent. What conclusions can you draw about the impact this change had on the political and social structure of Europe?

British troops in the trenches wait for the signal to attack

© Private Collection/Archives Charmet/Bridgeman Art Library

*O*N JULY 1, 1916, British and French infantry forces attacked German defensive lines along a 25-mile front near the Somme River in France. Each soldier carried almost 70 pounds of equipment, making it "impossible to move much quicker than a slow walk." German machine guns soon opened fire: "We were able to see our comrades move forward in an attempt to cross No-Man's Land, only to be mown down like meadow grass," recalled one British soldier. "I felt sick at the sight of this carnage and remember weeping."[1] In one day, more than 21,000 British soldiers died. After six months of fighting, the British had advanced 5 miles; one million British, French, and German soldiers had been killed or wounded.

Philip Gibbs, an English war correspondent, described what he saw in the German trenches that the British forces overran: "Victory!...Some of the German dead were young boys, too young to be killed for old men's crimes, and others might have been old or young. One could not tell because they had no faces, and were just masses of raw flesh in rags of uniforms. Legs and arms lay separate without any bodies thereabout."[2]

World War I (1914–1918) was the defining event of the twentieth century. It devastated the prewar economic, social, and political order of Europe, and its uncertain outcome prepared the way for an even more destructive war. Overwhelmed by the size of its battles, the extent of its casualties, and its effects on all facets of life, contemporaries referred to it simply as the "Great War."

The Great War was all the more disturbing to Europeans because it came after what many considered an age of progress. There had been international crises before 1914, but somehow Europeans had managed to avoid serious and prolonged military confrontations. Material prosperity and a fervid belief in scientific and technological progress had convinced many people that the world was on the verge of creating the utopia that humans had dreamed of for centuries. The historian Arnold Toynbee expressed what the pre–World War I era had meant to his generation: "[We had expected] that life throughout the World would become more rational, more humane, and more democratic and that, slowly, but surely, political democracy would produce greater social justice. We had also expected that the progress of science and technology would make mankind richer, and that this increasing wealth would gradually spread from a minority to a majority. We had expected that all this would happen peacefully. In fact we thought that mankind's course was set for an earthly paradise."[3]

After 1918, it was no longer possible to maintain naive illusions about the progress of Western civilization. As World War I was followed by the destructiveness of World War II and the mass murder machines of totalitarian regimes, it became all too apparent that instead of a utopia, European civilization had become a nightmare. The Great War resulted not only in great loss of life and property but also in the annihilation of one of the basic intellectual precepts on which Western civilization had been thought to have been founded—the belief in progress. World War I and the revolutions it spawned can properly be seen as the first stage in the crisis of the twentieth century.◆

The Road to World War I

On June 28, 1914, the heir to the Austrian throne, Archduke Francis Ferdinand, was assassinated in the Bosnian city of Sarajevo. Although this event precipitated the confrontation between Austria and Serbia that led to World War I, there were also long-range, underlying forces that were propelling Europeans toward armed conflict.

Nationalism and Internal Dissent

In the first half of the nineteenth century, liberals had maintained that the organization of European states along national lines would lead to a peaceful Europe based on a sense of international fraternity. They were very wrong. The system of nation-states that had emerged in Europe in the second half of the nineteenth century

led not to cooperation but to competition. Rivalries over colonial and commercial interests intensified during an era of frenzied imperialist expansion while the division of Europe's great powers into two loose alliances (Germany, Austria, and Italy versus France, Great Britain, and Russia; see Map 25.1) only added to the tensions. The series of crises that tested these alliances in the 1900s and early 1910s had left European states with the belief that their allies were important and that their security depended on supporting those allies, even when they took foolish risks.

The growth of nationalism in the nineteenth century had yet another serious consequence. Not all ethnic groups had achieved the goal of nationhood. Slavic minorities in the Balkans and the polyglot Habsburg empire, for example, still dreamed of creating their own national states. So did the Irish in the British Empire and the Poles in the Russian Empire.

National aspirations, however, were not the only source of internal strife at the beginning of the twentieth century. Socialist labor movements had grown more powerful and were increasingly inclined to use strikes, even violent ones, to achieve their goals. Some conservative leaders, alarmed at the increase in labor strife and class division, even feared that European nations were on the verge of revolution. Did these statesmen opt for war in 1914 because they believed that "prosecuting an active foreign policy," as one leader expressed it, would smother "internal troubles"? Some historians have argued that the desire to suppress internal disorder may have encouraged some leaders to take the plunge into war in 1914.

Militarism

The growth of large mass armies after 1900 not only heightened the existing tensions in Europe but also made it inevitable that if war did come, it would be enormously destructive. **Conscription** had been established as a regular practice in most Western countries before 1914 (the United States and Britain were major exceptions). European military machines had doubled in size between 1890 and 1914. With its 1.3 million men, the Russian army had grown to be the largest, while the French and Germans were not far behind with 900,000 each. The British, Italian, and Austrian armies numbered between 250,000 and 500,000 soldiers each.

Militarism, however, involved more than just large armies. As armies grew, so did the influence of military leaders, who drew up vast and complex plans for quickly mobilizing millions of men and enormous quantities of supplies in the event of war. Fearful that changes in these plans would cause chaos in the armed forces, military leaders insisted that their plans could not be altered. In the crises during the summer of 1914, the generals' lack of flexibility forced European political leaders to make decisions for military instead of political reasons.

MAP 25.1 **Europe in 1914.** By 1914, two alliances dominated Europe: the Triple Entente of Britain, France, and Russia and the Triple Alliance of Germany, Austria-Hungary, and Italy. Russia sought to bolster fellow Slavs in Serbia, whereas Austria-Hungary was intent on increasing its power in the Balkans and thwarting Serbia's ambitions. Thus the Balkans became the flash point for World War I. ❓ Which nonaligned nations were positioned between the two alliances? 🐭 **View an animated version of this map or related maps at** http://thomsonedu.com/history/spielvogel

The Outbreak of War: The Summer of 1914

Militarism, nationalism, and the desire to stifle internal dissent may all have played a role in the coming of World War I, but the decisions made by European leaders in the summer of 1914 directly precipitated the conflict. It was another crisis in the Balkans that forced this predicament on European statesmen.

Another Crisis in the Balkans States in southeastern Europe had struggled to free themselves of Ottoman rule for more than a century. But the rivalry between Austria-Hungary and Russia for domination of these new states created serious tensions in the region. By 1914, Serbia, supported by Russia, was determined to create a large, independent Slavic state in the Balkans, whereas Austria, which had its own Slavic minorities to contend with, was equally set on preventing that possibility. Many Europeans perceived the inherent dangers in this combination of Serbian ambition bolstered by Russian opposition to Austria and Austria's conviction that Serbia's success would mean the end of its empire. The British ambassador to Vienna wrote in 1913:

Serbia will some day set Europe by the ears, and bring about a universal war on the Continent. . . . I cannot tell you how exasperated people are getting here at the continual worry which that little country causes to Austria under encouragement from Russia. . . . It will be lucky if Europe succeeds in avoiding war as

a result of the present crisis. The next time a Serbian crisis arises . . . , I feel sure that Austria-Hungary will refuse to admit of any Russian interference in the dispute and that she will proceed to settle her differences with her little neighbor by herself.[4]

It was against this backdrop of mutual distrust and hatred that the events of the summer of 1914 played out.

The Assassination of Francis Ferdinand The assassination of the Austrian archduke Francis Ferdinand and his wife, Sophia, on June 28, 1914, was carried out by a Bosnian activist who worked for the Black Hand, a Serbian terrorist organization dedicated to the creation of a pan-Slavic kingdom. Although the Austrian government did not know whether the Serbian government had been directly involved in the archduke's assassination, it saw an opportunity to "render Serbia innocuous once and for all by a display of force," as the Austrian foreign minister put it. Fearful of Russian intervention on Serbia's behalf, Austrian leaders sought the backing of their German allies. Emperor William II and his chancellor gave their assurance that Austria-Hungary could rely on Germany's "full support," even if "matters went to the length of a war between Austria-Hungary and Russia."

Declarations of War Strengthened by German support, Austrian leaders issued an ultimatum to Serbia on July 23 in which they made such extreme demands that Serbia had little choice but to reject some of them in order to preserve its sovereignty. Austria then declared war on Serbia on July 28. Still smarting from its humiliation in the Bosnian crisis of 1908, Russia was determined to support Serbia's cause. On July 28, Tsar Nicholas II ordered partial **mobilization** of the Russian army against Austria. At this point, the Russian General Staff informed the tsar that its mobilization plans were based on a war against both Germany and Austria simultaneously. They could not execute partial mobilization without creating chaos in the army. Consequently, the Russian government ordered full mobilization of the Russian army on July 29, knowing that the Germans would consider this an act of war against them. Germany responded to Russian mobilization with its own ultimatum that the Russians must halt their mobilization within twelve hours. When the Russians ignored it, Germany declared war on Russia on August 1.

At this stage of the conflict, German war plans determined whether or not France would become involved in the war. Under the guidance of General Alfred von Schlieffen, chief of staff from 1891 to 1905, the German General Staff had devised a military plan based on the assumption of a two-front war with France and Russia, since the two powers had formed a military alliance in 1894. The Schlieffen plan called for a minimal troop deployment against Russia while most of the German army would rapidly invade western France by way of neutral Belgium. After the planned quick defeat of the French, the German army expected to redeploy to the east against Russia. Under the Schlieffen plan, Germany could not mobilize its troops solely against Russia and therefore declared war on France on August 3 after issuing an ultimatum to Belgium on August 2 demanding the right of German troops to pass through Belgian territory. On August 4, Great Britain declared war on Germany, officially over this violation of Belgian neutrality but in fact over the British desire to maintain world power. As one British diplomat argued, if Germany and Austria won the war, "what would be the position of a friendless England?" By August 4, all the great powers of Europe were at war.

The Schlieffen Plan

The Great War

Before 1914, many political leaders had become convinced that war involved so many political and economic risks that it was not worth fighting. Others had believed

CHRONOLOGY	The Road to World War I	
		1914
Assassination of Archduke Francis Ferdinand		June 28
Austria's ultimatum to Serbia		July 23
Austria's declaration of war on Serbia		July 28
Russian mobilization		July 29
German ultimatum to Russia		July 31
German declaration of war on Russia		August 1
German declaration of war on France		August 3
Invasion of Belgium by German troops		August 4
British declaration of war on Germany		August 4

that "rational" diplomats could control any situation and prevent the outbreak of war. At the beginning of August 1914, both of these prewar illusions were shattered, but the new illusions that replaced them soon proved to be equally foolish.

1914–1915: Illusions and Stalemate

Europeans went to war in 1914 with remarkable enthusiasm. Government propaganda had been successful in stirring up national antagonisms before the war. Now in August 1914, the urgent pleas of governments for defense against aggressors fell on receptive ears in every belligerent nation. Most people seemed genuinely convinced that their nation's cause was just. A new set of illusions also fed the enthusiasm for war. Almost everyone in August 1914 believed that the war would be over in a few weeks. People were reminded that all European wars since 1815 had in fact ended in a matter of weeks, ignoring the American Civil War (1861–1865), which was the true prototype for a "modern" war. Both the soldiers who exuberantly boarded the trains for the war front in August 1914 and the jubilant citizens who bombarded them with flowers when they departed believed that the warriors would be home by Christmas.

German hopes for a quick end to the war rested on a military gamble. The Schlieffen plan had called for the German army to make a vast encircling movement through Belgium into northern France that would sweep around Paris and encircle most of the French army. But the German advance was halted only 20 miles east of Paris at the first Battle of the Marne (September 6–10; see Map 25.2). The war quickly turned into a stalemate—neither the Germans nor the French could dislodge each other from the trenches they had begun to dig for shelter. Two lines of trenches soon extended from the English Channel to the frontiers of Switzerland. The Western Front had become bogged down in **trench warfare** that kept both sides immobilized in virtually the same positions for four years.

Courtesy of Librairie Larousse, Paris

The Excitement of War. World War I was greeted with incredible enthusiasm. Each of the major belligerents was convinced of the rightness of its cause. Everywhere in Europe, jubilant civilians sent their troops off to war with joyous fervor as is evident in the photograph at right, showing French troops marching off to war. The photograph below shows a group of German soldiers marching off to battle with civilian support. The belief that the soldiers would be home by Christmas proved to be a pathetic illusion.

Three Lions/Getty Images

The Austrians, Germany's allies, fared less well initially. They had been defeated by the Russians in Galicia and thrown out of Serbia as well. To make matters worse, the Italians broke their alliance with the Germans and Austrians and entered the war on the Allied side by attacking Austria in May 1915. By this time, the Germans had come to the aid of the Austrians. A German-Austrian army defeated and routed the Russian army in Galicia and pushed the Russians back 300 miles into their own territory. Russian casualties stood at 2.5 million killed, captured, or wounded; the Russians had almost been knocked out of the war. Buoyed by their success, the Germans and Austrians, joined by the Bulgarians in September 1915, attacked and eliminated Serbia from the war.

1916–1917: The Great Slaughter

The successes in the east enabled the Germans to move back to the offensive in the west. The early trenches dug

In contrast to the west, the war in the east was marked by much more mobility, although the cost in lives was equally enormous. At the beginning of the war, the Russian army moved into eastern Germany but was decisively defeated at the Battles of Tannenberg on August 26–30 and the Masurian Lakes on September 15 (see Map 25.3). The Russians were no longer a threat to German territory.

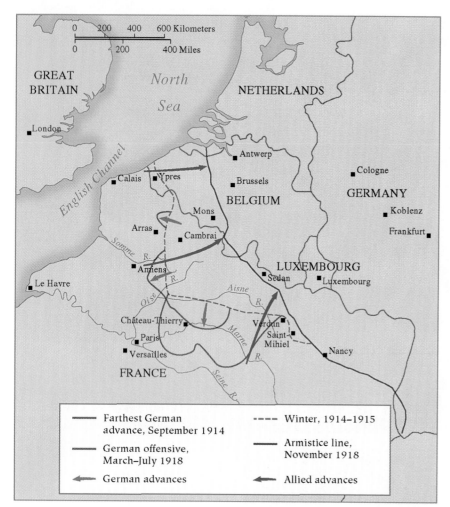

MAP 25.2 **The Western Front, 1914–1918.** The Western Front was the site of massive carnage: millions of soldiers died in offensives and counteroffensives as they moved battle lines a few miles at a time in France and Belgium from 1914 to 1917. Soldiers in the trenches were often surrounded by the rotting bodies of dead comrades. ❓ What is the approximate distance between the armistice line near Sedan and the closest approach of the Germans to Paris? 🔊 **View an animated version of this map or related maps at** http://thomsonedu.com/history/spielvogel

Warfare in the trenches of the Western Front produced unimaginable horrors (see the box on p. 480). Battlefields were hellish landscapes of barbed wire, shell holes, mud, and injured and dying men. The introduction of poison gas in 1915 produced new forms of injuries, as one British writer described:

> I wish those people who write so glibly about this being a holy war could see a case of mustard gas . . . could see the poor things burnt and blistered all over with great mustard-coloured suppurating blisters with blind eyes all sticky . . . and stuck together, and always fighting for breath, with voices a mere whisper, saying that their throats are closing and they know they will choke.[5]

Soldiers in the trenches also lived with the persistent presence of death. Because combat went on for months, soldiers had to carry on in the midst of countless bodies of dead men or the remains of men dismembered by artillery barrages. Many soldiers remembered the stench of decomposing bodies and the swarms of rats that grew fat in the trenches.

The Widening of the War

As another response to the stalemate on the Western Front, both sides sought to gain new allies who might provide a winning advantage. The Ottoman Empire had already come into the war on Germany's side in August 1914. Russia, Great Britain, and France declared war on the Ottoman Empire in November. Although the Allies attempted to open a Balkan front by landing forces at Gallipoli, southwest of Constantinople, in April 1915, the entry of Bulgaria into the war on the side of the Central Powers (as Germany, Austria-Hungary, and the Ottoman Empire were called) and a disastrous campaign at Gallipoli caused them to withdraw. The Italians, as noted, also entered the war on the Allied side after France and Britain

in 1914 had by now become elaborate systems of defense. Both lines of trenches were protected by barbed-wire entanglements 3 to 5 feet high and 30 yards wide, concrete machine-gun nests, and mortar batteries, supported farther back by heavy artillery. Troops lived in holes in the ground, separated from each other by a "no-man's land."

The unexpected development of trench warfare baffled military leaders, who had been trained to fight wars of movement and maneuver. Periodically, the high command on either side would order an offensive that would begin with an artillery barrage to flatten the enemy's barbed wire and leave the enemy in a state of shock. After "softening up" the enemy in this fashion, a mass of soldiers would climb out of their trenches with fixed bayonets and hope to work their way toward the enemy trenches. The attacks rarely worked, since the machine gun put hordes of men advancing unprotected across open fields at a severe disadvantage. In 1916 and 1917, millions of young men were killed in the search for the elusive breakthrough. In ten months at Verdun, 700,000 men lost their lives over a few miles of terrain. At the Battle of the Somme, the British suffered 57,000 casualties, including 21,000 dead, on the first day of the battle, the heaviest one-day loss in World War I.

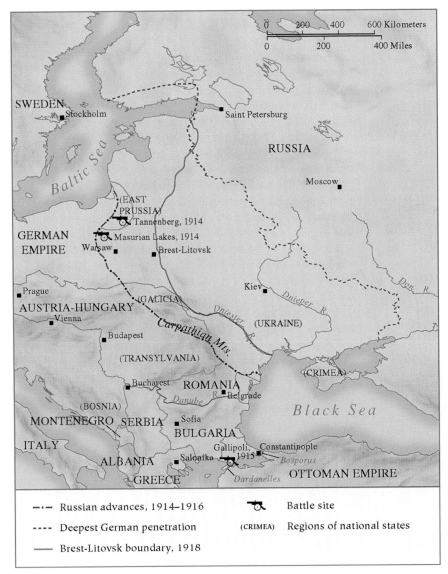

MAP 25.3 **The Eastern Front, 1914–1918.** Russia made early gains but then was pushed far back into its own territory by the German army. After the Bolsheviks seized power, they negotiated the Treaty of Brest-Litovsk, which extracted Russia from the war at the cost of substantial Russian territory (see Map 25.4). ❓ What is the approximate average distance between the farthest advances of Russia into Germany and the farthest advances of Germany into Russia? 🐭 **View an animated version of this map or related maps at** http://thomsonedu.com/history/spielvogel

Map legend:

- · — Russian advances, 1914–1916
- - - - Deepest German penetration
- —— Brest-Litovsk boundary, 1918

⚔ Battle site

(CRIMEA) Regions of national states

promised to further their acquisition of Austrian territory. In the long run, however, Italian military incompetence forced the Allies to come to the assistance of Italy.

A Global Conflict The war that originated in Europe rapidly became a worldwide conflict. In the Middle East, a British officer who came to be known as Lawrence of Arabia (1888–1935) incited Arab princes to revolt against their Ottoman overlords in 1917. In 1918, British forces from Egypt destroyed the rest of the Ottoman Empire in the Middle East. For their Middle East campaigns, the British mobilized forces from India, Australia, and New Zealand.

The Allies also took advantage of Germany's preoccupations in Europe and lack of naval strength to seize German colonies in Africa and Asia. In the battles in Africa, Allied governments drew on mainly African soldiers, but some states, especially France, also recruited African troops to fight in Europe. The French drafted more than 170,000 West African soldiers, many of whom fought in the trenches on the Western

Impact of the Machine Gun. Trench warfare on the Western Front stymied military leaders, who expected to fight a war based on movement and maneuver. Their efforts to advance by sending masses of men against enemy lines was the height of folly in view of the machine gun. Soldiers advancing across open land made magnificent targets.

THE BEGINNING OF THE TWENTIETH-CENTURY CRISIS: WAR AND REVOLUTION   **479**

THE REALITY OF WAR: TRENCH WARFARE

The romantic illusions about the excitement and adventure of war that filled the minds of so many young men who marched off to battle quickly disintegrated after a short time in the trenches on the Western Front. This description of trench warfare is taken from the most famous novel that emerged from World War I, Erich Maria Remarque's *All Quiet on the Western Front,* written in 1929. Remarque had fought in the trenches in France.

Erich Maria Remarque, *All Quiet on the Western Front*

We wake up in the middle of the night. The earth booms. Heavy fire is falling on us. We crouch into corners. We distinguish shells of every calibre.

Each man lays hold of his things and looks again every minute to reassure himself that they are still there. The dug-out heaves, the night roars and flashes. We look at each other in the momentary flashes of light, and with pale faces and pressed lips shake our heads.

Every man is aware of the heavy shells tearing down the parapet, rooting up the embankment and demolishing the upper layers of concrete.... Already by morning a few of the recruits are green and vomiting. They are too inexperienced....

The bombardment does not diminish. It is falling in the rear too. As far as one can see it spouts fountains of mud and iron. A wide belt is being raked.

The attack does not come, but the bombardment continues. Slowly we become mute. Hardly a man speaks. We cannot make ourselves understood.

Our trench is almost gone. At many places it is only eighteen inches high, it is broken by holes, and craters, and mountains of earth. A shell lands square in front of our post. At once it is dark. We are buried and must dig ourselves out....

Towards morning, while it is still dark, there is some excitement. Through the entrance rushes in a swarm of fleeing rats that try to storm the walls. Torches light up the confusion. Everyone yells and curses and slaughters. The madness and despair of many hours unloads itself in this outburst. Faces are distorted, arms strike out, the beasts scream; we just stop in time to avoid attacking one another....

Suddenly it howls and flashes terrifically, the dugout cracks in all its joints under a direct hit, fortunately only a light one that the concrete blocks are able to withstand. It rings metallically, the walls reel, rifles, helmets, earth, mud, and dust fly everywhere. Sulphur fumes pour in.... The recruit starts to rave again and two others follow suit. One jumps up and rushes out, we have trouble with the other two. I start after the one who escapes and wonder whether to shoot him in the leg—then it shrieks again, I fling myself down and when I stand up the wall of the trench is plastered with smoking splinters, lumps of flesh, and bits of uniform. I scramble back.

The first recruit seems actually to have gone insane. He butts his head against the wall like a goat. We must try tonight to take him to the rear. Meanwhile we bind him, but so that in case of attack he can be released.

Suddenly the nearer explosions cease. The shelling continues but it has lifted and falls behind us, our trench is free. We seize the hand-grenades, pitch them out in front of the dug-out and jump after them. The bombardment has stopped and a heavy barrage now falls behind us. The attack has come.

No one would believe that in this howling waste there could still be men; but steel helmets now appear on all sides out of the trench, and fifty yards from us a machine-gun is already in position and barking.

The wire-entanglements are torn to pieces. Yet they offer some obstacle. We see the storm-troops coming. Our artillery opens fire. Machine-guns rattle, rifles crack. The charge works its way across. Haie and Kropp begin with the hand-grenades. They throw as fast as they can, others pass them, the handles with the strings already pulled. Haie throws seventy-five yards, Kropp sixty, it has been measured, the distance is important. The enemy as they run cannot do much before they are within forty yards.

We recognize the distorted faces, the smooth helmets: they are French. They have already suffered heavily when they reach the remnants of the barbed-wire entanglements. A whole line has gone down before our machine-guns; then we have a lot of stoppages and they come nearer.

I see one of them, his face upturned, fall into a wire cradle. His body collapses, his hands remain suspended as though he were praying. Then his body drops clean away and only his hands with the stumps of his arms, shot off, now hang in the wire.

What is causing the "madness and despair" Remarque describes in the trenches? Why does the recruit in this scene apparently go insane?

front. About 80,000 Africans were killed or injured in Europe. They were often at a distinct disadvantage due to the unfamiliar terrain and climate.

Hundreds of thousands of Africans were also used for labor, especially for carrying supplies and building roads and bridges. In East Africa, both sides drafted African laborers as carriers for their armies. Disease and starvation caused by neglect led to the death of more than 100,000 of these laborers.

In East Asia and the Pacific, Japan joined the Allies on August 23, 1914, primarily to seize control of German territories in China and the Pacific. New Zealand and Australia quickly joined the Japanese in conquering the German-held parts of New Guinea.

The Horrors of War. The slaughter of millions of men in the trenches of World War I created unimaginable horrors for the participants. For the sake of survival, many soldiers learned to harden themselves against the stench of decomposing bodies and the sight of bodies horribly dismembered by artillery barrages.

Entry of the United States Most important to the Allied cause was the entry of the United States into the war. At first, the United States tried to remain neutral in the Great War, but it found neutrality difficult to maintain as the war dragged on. The immediate spur to American involvement grew out of the naval conflict between Germany and Great Britain. Britain used its superior naval power to maximum effect by throwing up a naval blockade of Germany. Germany retaliated by imposing a counterblockade enforced by unrestricted submarine warfare. Strong American protests over the German sinking of passenger liners, especially the British ship *Lusitania* on May 7, 1915, in which more than one hundred Americans lost their lives, forced the German government to suspend unrestricted submarine warfare in September 1915 to avoid further antagonizing the Americans.

In January 1917, however, eager to break the deadlock in the war, the Germans decided to gamble by returning to unrestricted submarine warfare. German naval officers convinced Emperor William II that use of the submarines could starve the British into submission within five months, before the Americans could act. The return to unrestricted submarine warfare brought the United States into the war on April 6, 1917. Although American troops did not arrive in large numbers in Europe until 1918, the entry of the United States into the war in 1917 gave the Allied Powers a psychological boost when they needed it. The year 1917 was not a good year for them. Allied offensives on the Western Front were

French African Troops. The French drafted more than 170,000 West African soldiers to fight in Europe. Shown here are some French African troops who fought in France on the Western Front. The French also drafted African soldiers from their North African colonies and Madagascar.

disastrously defeated. The Italian armies were smashed in October, and in November 1917 the Bolshevik revolution in Russia (see "The Russian Revolution" later in this chapter) led to Russia's withdrawal from the war. The cause of the Central Powers looked favorable, although war weariness in the Ottoman Empire, Bulgaria, Austria-Hungary, and Germany was beginning to take its toll. The home front was rapidly becoming a cause for as much concern as the war front.

The Home Front: The Impact of Total War

The prolongation of World War I made it a **total war** that affected the lives of all citizens, however remote they might be from the battlefields. The need to organize masses of men and matériel for years of combat (Germany alone had 5.5 million men in active units in 1916) led to increased centralization of government powers, economic regimentation, and manipulation of public opinion to keep the war effort going.

Political Centralization and Economic Regimentation
Because the war was expected to be short, little thought had been given to economic problems and long-term wartime needs. Governments had to respond quickly, however, when the war machines failed to achieve their knockout blows and made ever-greater demands for men and matériel. The extension of government power was a logical outgrowth of these needs. Most European countries had already devised some system of mass conscription or military draft. It was now carried to unprecedented heights as countries mobilized millions of young men for that elusive breakthrough to victory. Even countries that continued to rely on volunteers (Great Britain had the largest volunteer army in modern history—one million men—in 1914 and 1915) were forced to resort to conscription, especially to ensure that skilled laborers did not enlist but remained in factories that were important to the production of munitions. In 1916, despite widespread resistance to this extension of government power, compulsory military service was introduced in Great Britain.

Throughout Europe, wartime governments expanded their powers over their economies. Free market capitalistic systems were temporarily shelved as governments experimented with price, wage, and rent controls, the rationing of food supplies and materials, the regulation of imports and exports, the **nationalization** of transportation systems and industries, and compulsory labor employment. In effect, to mobilize the entire resources of their nations for the war effort, European nations had moved toward planned economies directed by government agencies. Under total war mobilization, the distinction between soldiers at war and civilians at home was narrowed. In the view of political leaders, all citizens constituted a national army dedicated to victory. As the American president Woodrow Wilson expressed it, the men and women "who remain to till the soil and man the factories are no less a part of the army than the men beneath the battle flags."

Public Order and Public Opinion
As the Great War dragged on and both casualties and privations worsened, internal dissatisfaction replaced the patriotic enthusiasm that had marked the early stages of the conflict. By 1916, there were numerous signs that civilian morale was beginning to crack. War governments, however, fought back against the growing opposition to the war. Authoritarian regimes, such as those of Germany, Russia, and Austria-Hungary, had always relied on force to subdue their populations. Under the pressures of the war, however, even parliamentary regimes resorted to an expansion of police powers to stifle internal dissent. At the very beginning of the war, the British Parliament passed the Defence of the Realm Act (DORA), which allowed the public authorities to arrest dissenters as traitors. The act was later extended to authorize public officials to censor newspapers by deleting objectional material and even to suspend newspaper publication. In France, government authorities had initially been lenient about public opposition to the war. But when Georges Clemenceau became premier near the end of 1917, the lenient French policies came to an end, and basic civil liberties were suppressed for the duration of the war. The editor of an antiwar newspaper was even executed on a charge of treason.

Wartime governments made active use of propaganda to arouse enthusiasm for the war. At the beginning, public officials needed to do little to achieve this goal. The British and French, for example, exaggerated German atrocities in Belgium and found that their citizens were only too willing to believe these accounts. But as the war progressed and morale sagged, governments were forced to devise new techniques for reviving flagging enthusiasm. In one British recruiting poster, for example, a small daughter asked her father, "Daddy, what did YOU do in the Great War?" while her younger brother played with toy soldiers and cannons.

The Social Impact of Total War
Total war had a significant impact on European society, most visibly by bringing an end to unemployment. The withdrawal of millions of men from the labor market to fight, combined with the heightened demand for wartime products, led to jobs for everyone able to work.

World War I also created new roles for women. With so many men off fighting at the front, women were called on to take over jobs and responsibilities that had not been available to them before. They were now employed in jobs that had earlier been considered "beyond the capacity of women," including such occupations as chimney sweeps, truck drivers, farm laborers, and factory workers in heavy industry (see the box on p. 484). Thirty-eight percent of the workers in the Krupp Armaments works in Germany in 1918 were women.

While male workers expressed concern that the employment of females at lower wages would depress their

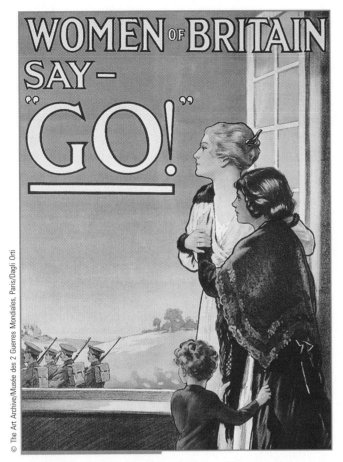

© The Art Archive/Musée des 2 Guerres Mondiales, Paris/Dagli Orti

British Recruiting Poster. As the conflict persisted month after month, governments resorted to active propaganda campaigns to generate enthusiasm for the war. In this British recruiting poster, the government tried to pressure men into volunteering for military service. By 1916, the British were forced to adopt compulsory military service.

own wages, women began to demand equal pay. The French government passed a law in July 1915 that established a minimum wage for women homeworkers in textiles, an industry that had grown dramatically because of the need for military uniforms. Later in 1917, the government decreed that men and women should receive equal rates for piecework. Despite the noticeable increase in women's wages that resulted from government regulations, women's industrial wages still were not equal to men's wages by the end of the war.

Even worse, women had achieved little real security about their place in the workforce. Both men and women seemed to think that many of the new jobs for women were only temporary, an expectation quite evident in the British poem "War Girls," written in 1916:

> *There's the girl who clips your ticket for the train,*
> *And the girl who speeds the lift from floor to floor,*
> *There's the girl who does a milk-round in the rain,*
> *And the girl who calls for orders at your door.*
> *Strong, sensible, and fit,*

> *They're out to show their grit,*
> *And tackle jobs with energy and knack.*
> *No longer caged and penned up,*
> *They're going to keep their end up*
> *Till the khaki soldier boys come marching back.*[6]

At the end of the war, governments moved quickly to remove women from the jobs they had encouraged them to take earlier. By 1919, there were 650,000 unemployed women in Britain, and wages for women who were still employed had been lowered. The work benefits for women from World War I seemed to be short-lived.

Nevertheless, in some countries, the role played by women in the wartime economies did have a positive impact on women's crusade for social and political emancipation. The most obvious gain was the right to vote, given to women in Germany and Austria immediately after the war (Britain had done the same in January 1918). The Nineteenth Amendment to the Constitution gave women in the United States the right to vote in 1920. Contemporary media, however, tended to focus on the more noticeable, yet in some ways more superficial, social emancipation of upper- and middle-class women. In ever-larger numbers, these young women took jobs, had their own apartments, and flaunted their new independence by smoking in public and wearing shorter dresses, cosmetics, and boyish hairstyles.

War and Revolution

By 1917, total war was creating serious domestic turmoil in all of the European belligerent states. Only one, however, experienced the kind of complete collapse in 1917 that others were predicting might happen throughout Europe. Out of Russia's collapse came the Russian Revolution.

The Russian Revolution

Tsar Nicholas II was an autocratic ruler who relied on the army and bureaucracy to prop up his regime. Russia was unprepared both militarily and technologically for the total war of World War I. Competent military leadership was lacking, and Russian industry was unable to produce the weapons needed for the army. Ill-led and ill-armed, Russian armies suffered incredible losses. Between 1914 and 1916, two million soldiers had been killed and another four to six million had been wounded or captured.

In the meantime, Tsar Nicholas II was increasingly insulated from events by his German-born wife, Alexandra, a well-educated woman who had fallen under the influence of Rasputin, a Siberian peasant whom the tsarina regarded as a holy man because he alone seemed able to stop the bleeding of her hemophiliac son, Alexis. Rasputin's influence made him an important

WOMEN IN THE FACTORIES

During World War I, women were called on to assume new job responsibilities, including factory work. In this selection, Naomi Loughnan, a young, upper-middle-class woman, describes the experiences in a munitions plant that considerably broadened her perspective on life.

Naomi Loughnan, "Munition Work"

We little thought when we first put on our overalls and caps and enlisted in the Munition Army how much more inspiring our life was to be than we had dared to hope. Though we munition workers sacrifice our ease we gain a life worth living. Our long days are filled with interest, and with the zest of doing work for our country in the grand cause of Freedom. As we handle the weapons of war we are learning great lessons of life. In the busy, noisy workshops we come face to face with every kind of class, and each one of these classes has something to learn from the others....

Engineering mankind is possessed of the unshakable opinion that no woman can have the mechanical sense. If one of us asks humbly why such and such an alteration is not made to prevent this or that drawback to a machine, she is told, with a superior smile, that a man has worked her machine before her for years, and that therefore if there were any improvement possible it would have been made. As long as we do exactly what we are told and do not attempt to use our brains, we give entire satisfaction, and are treated as nice, good children. Any swerving from the easy path prepared for us by our males arouses the most scathing contempt in their manly bosoms.... Women have, however, proved that their entry into the munition world has

increased the output. Employers who forget things personal in their patriotic desire for large results are enthusiastic over the success of women in the shops. But their workmen have to be handled with the utmost tenderness and caution lest they should actually imagine it was being suggested that women could do their work equally well, given equal conditions of training–at least where muscle is not the driving force....

The coming of the mixed classes of women into the factory is slowly but surely having an educative effect upon the men. "Language" is almost unconsciously becoming subdued. There are fiery exceptions who make our hair stand up on end under our close-fitting caps, but a sharp rebuke or a look of horror will often straighten out the most savage.... It is grievous to hear the girls also swearing and using disgusting language. Shoulder to shoulder with the children of the slums, the upper classes are having their eyes opened at last to the awful conditions among which their sisters have dwelt. Foul language, immorality, and many other evils are but the natural outcome of overcrowding and bitter poverty.... Sometimes disgust will overcome us, but we are learning with painful clarity that the fault is not theirs whose actions disgust us, but must be placed to the discredit of those other classes who have allowed the continued existence of conditions which generate the things from which we shrink appalled.

The two groups Naomi Loughnan observes in this passage are men and lower-class women. What has she learned about these groups while working in the munitions factory? What did she learn about herself?

---

power behind the throne, and he did not hesitate to interfere in government affairs. As the leadership at the top stumbled its way through a series of military and economic disasters, the middle class, aristocrats, peasants, soldiers, and workers grew more and more disenchanted with the tsarist regime. Even conservative aristocrats who supported the monarchy felt the need to do something to reverse the deteriorating situation. For a start, they assassinated Rasputin in December 1916. By then it was too late to save the monarchy, and its fall came quickly.

The March Revolution At the beginning of March 1917, a series of strikes broke out in the capital city of Petrograd (the renamed Saint Petersburg). Here the actions of working-class women helped change the course of Russian history. Weeks earlier, the government had introduced bread rationing in the city after the price of bread skyrocketed. Many of the women who stood in the lines waiting for bread were also factory workers who put in twelve-hour days. The Russian government had be-

come aware of the volatile situation in the capital from a police report:

> Mothers of families, exhausted by endless standing in line at stores, distraught over their half-starving and sick children, are today perhaps closer to revolution than [the liberal opposition leaders] and of course they are a great deal more dangerous because they are the combustible material for which only a single spark is needed to burst into flame.[7]

On March 8, about ten thousand Petrograd women marched through the city chanting "Peace and Bread" and "Down with Autocracy." Soon the women were joined by other workers, and together they called for a general strike that succeeded in shutting down all the factories in the city on March 10. Nicholas ordered the troops to disperse the crowds by shooting them if necessary, but soon significant numbers of the soldiers joined the demonstrators. The Duma, the legislative body that the tsar had tried to dissolve, met anyway and on March 12 declared that it was assuming governmental responsibility. It established a provisional government on March 15; the tsar abdicated the same day.

In just one week, the tsarist regime had fallen apart. Although no particular group had been responsible for the outburst, the moderate Constitutional Democrats were responsible for establishing the provisional government. They represented primarily a middle-class and liberal aristocratic minority. Their program consisted of a liberal agenda that included working toward a parliamentary democracy and passing reforms that provided universal suffrage, civil equality, and an eight-hour workday.

The Provisional Government also faced another authority, the **soviets**, or councils of workers' and soldiers' deputies. Soviets sprang up spontaneously in cities, factory towns, army units, and rural areas. The soviets represented the more radical interests of the lower classes and were largely composed of socialists of different kinds. One group, the Bolsheviks, came to play a crucial role.

The Bolshevik Revolution The **Bolsheviks** were a small faction of Marxist Social Democrats who had come under the leadership of Vladimir Ulianov, known to the world as V. I. Lenin (1870–1924). Arrested for his revolutionary activity, Lenin was shipped to Siberia. After his release, he chose to go into exile in Switzerland and eventually assumed the leadership of the Bolshevik wing of the Russian Social Democratic Party. Under Lenin's direction, the Bolsheviks became a party dedicated to a violent revolution that would destroy the capitalist system. He believed that a "vanguard" of activists must form

a small party of well-disciplined professional revolutionaries to accomplish the task. Lenin spent most of the years between 1900 and 1917 in Switzerland. When the provisional government was formed in March 1917, he believed that an opportunity for the Bolsheviks to seize power had come. Shortly thereafter, with the connivance of the German High Command, who hoped to create disorder in Russia, Lenin was shipped to Russia in a "sealed train" by way of Finland.

Lenin's arrival opened a new stage of the Russian Revolution. Lenin maintained that the soviets of soldiers, workers, and peasants were ready-made instruments of power. The Bolsheviks must work toward gaining control of these groups and then use them to overthrow the provisional government. At the same time, the Bolsheviks articulated the discontent and aspirations of the people, promising an end to the war, redistribution of all land to the peasants, the transfer of factories and industries from capitalists to committees of workers, and the relegation of government power from the provisional government to the soviets. Three simple slogans summed up the Bolshevik program: "Peace, Land, Bread," "Worker Control of Production," and "All Power to the Soviets."

By the end of October, the Bolsheviks had achieved a slight majority in the Petrograd and Moscow soviets. The number of party members had also grown from 50,000 to 240,000. With Leon Trotsky (1877–1940), a fervid revolutionary, as chairman of the Petrograd soviet, the Bolsheviks were in a position to seize power in the name of the soviets. During the night of November 6, pro-soviet and pro-Bolshevik forces took control of Petrograd

Lenin and Trotsky. V. I. Lenin and Leon Trotsky were important figures in the success of the Bolsheviks in seizing power in Russia. On the left, Lenin is seen addressing a rally in Moscow in 1917. On the right, Trotsky, who became commissar of war in the new regime, is shown haranguing his troops.

SOLDIER AND PEASANT VOICES

In 1917, Russia experienced a cataclysmic upheaval as two revolutions overthrew the tsarist regime and then the provisional government that replaced it. Peasants, workers, and soldiers poured out their thoughts and feelings on these events, some of them supporting the Bolsheviks and others denouncing the Bolsheviks for betraying their socialist revolution. These selections are taken from two letters, the first from a soldier and the second from a peasant. Both are addressed to Bolshevik leaders.

Letter from a Soldier in Leningrad to Lenin, January 6, 1918

Bastard! What the hell are you doing? How long are you going to keep on degrading the Russian people? After all, it's because of you they killed the former minister ... and so many other innocent victims. Because of you, they might kill even other former ministers belonging to the [Socialist Revolutionary] party because you call them counter-revolutionaries and even monarchists.... And you, you Bolshevik gang leader hired either by Nicholas II or by Wilhelm II, are waging this pogrom propaganda against men who may have done time with you in exile.

Scoundrel! A curse on you from the politically conscious Russian proletariat, the conscious ones and not the kind who are following you—that is, the Red Guards, the tally clerks, who, when they are called to military service, all hide at the factories and now are killing . . . practically their own father, the way the soldiers did in 1905 when they killed their own, or the way the police and gendarmes did in [1917]. That's who they're more like. They're not pursuing the ideas of socialism because they don't understand them (if they did they wouldn't act this way) but because they get paid a good salary both at the factory and in the Red Guards. But not all the workers are like that—there are very politically aware ones—and the soldiers—again not all of them—are like that but only former policemen, constables, gendarmes and the very very ignorant ones who under the old regime ... couldn't tell their right foot from their left and they are pursuing not the ideas of socialism that you advocate but to be able to lie on their cots in the barracks and do absolutely nothing not even be asked to sweep the floor, which is already piled with several inches of filth. And so the entire proletariat of Russia is following you, by count fewer than are against you, but they are only physically or rather technically stronger than the majority, and that is what you're abusing when you disbanded the Constituent Assembly the way Nicholas II disbanded the Duma. You point out that counterrevolutionaries gathered there. You lie, scoundrel, there wasn't a single counterrevolutionary and if there was then it was you, the Bolsheviks, which you proved by your actions when you encroached on the gains of the revolution: you are shutting down newspapers, even socialist ones, arresting socialists, committing violence and deceiving the people; you promised loads but did none of it.

Letter from a Peasant to the Bolshevik Leaders, January 10, 1918

To you! Rulers, plunderers, rapists, destroyers, usurpers, oppressors of Mother Russia, citizens Lenin, Trotsky, Uritsky, Zinoviev, Spiridonova, Antonov, Lunacharsky, Krylenko, and Co. [leaders of the Bolshevik party]:

Allow me to ask you how long you are going to go on degrading Russia's millions, its tormented and exhausted people. Instead of peace, you signed an armistice with the enemy, and this gave our opponent a painful advantage, and you declared war on Russia. You moved the troops you had tricked to the Russian-Russian front and started a fratricidal war. Your mercenary Red Guards are looting, murdering, and raping everywhere they go. A fire has consumed all our dear Mother Russia. Rail transport is idle, as are the plants and factories; the entire population has woken up to find itself in the most pathetic situation, without bread or kerosene or any of the other essentials, unclothed and unshod in unheated houses. In short: hungry and cold.... You have strangled the entire press, and freedom with it, you have wiped out the best freedom fighters, you have destroyed all Russia. Think it over, you butchers, you hirelings of the Kaiser [William II]. Isn't your turn about up, too? For all you are doing, we, politically aware Great Russians, are sending you butchers, you hirelings of the Kaiser, our curse. May you be damned, you accursed one, you bloodthirsty butchers, you hirelings of the Kaiser—don't think you're in the clear, because the Russian people will sober up and that will be the end of you. I'm writing in red ink to show that you are bloodthirsty....

What arguments do both of the writers of these letters use against Lenin and the Bolsheviks? Why do they feel so betrayed by the Bolsheviks?

under the immensely popular slogan "All Power to the Soviets." The provisional government collapsed with little bloodshed. The following night, the all-Russian Congress of Soviets, representing local soviets from all over the country, affirmed the transfer of power. At the second session, the night of November 8, Lenin announced the new Soviet government, the Council of People's Commissars, with himself as its head.

But the Bolsheviks, soon renamed the Communists, still had a long way to go (see the box above). Lenin had promised peace, and that, he realized, was not easy to deliver because of the humiliating losses of Russian territory that it would entail. There was no real choice, however. On March 3, 1918, Lenin signed the Treaty of Brest-Litovsk with Germany and gave up eastern Poland, the Ukraine, Finland, and the Baltic provinces. To his critics, Lenin argued that it made no difference since the spread of socialist revolution throughout Europe would make the treaty largely irrelevant. In any case, he had promised peace to the Russian people; but real peace did not come because the country soon sank into civil war.

Civil War   There was great opposition to the new Bolshevik or Communist regime, not only from groups loyal to the tsar but also from bourgeois and aristocratic liberals and anti-Leninist socialists. In addition, thousands of Allied troops were eventually sent to different parts of Russia in the hope of bringing Russia back into the war.

Between 1918 and 1921, the Bolshevik (or Red) Army was forced to fight on many fronts. The first serious threat to the Bolsheviks came from Siberia, where a White (anti-Bolshevik) force attacked westward and advanced almost to the Volga River before being stopped. Attacks also came from the Ukrainians in the southeast and from the Baltic regions. In mid-1919, White forces swept through the Ukraine and advanced almost to Moscow. At one point toward the end of 1919, three separate White armies seemed to be closing in on the Bolsheviks but were eventually pushed back. By 1920, the major White forces had been defeated and the Ukraine had been retaken. The next year, the Communist regime regained control over the independent nationalist governments in the Caucasus: Georgia, Russian Armenia, and Azerbaijan.

The royal family was yet another victim of the civil war. After the tsar had abdicated, he, his wife, and their five children had been taken into captivity. They were moved in August 1917 to Tobolsk in Siberia and in April 1918 to Ekaterinburg, a mining town in the Urals. On the night of July 16, members of the local soviet murdered the tsar and his family and burned their bodies in a nearby mine shaft.

How had Lenin and the Bolsheviks triumphed over what seemed at one time to be overwhelming forces? For one thing, the Red Army became a well-disciplined and formidable fighting force, due largely to the organizational genius of Leon Trotsky. As commissar of war, Trotsky reinstated the draft and insisted on rigid discipline; soldiers who deserted or refused to obey orders were summarily executed.

The disunity of the anti-Communist forces seriously weakened their efforts. Political differences created distrust among the Whites and prevented them from cooperating effectively with each other. Some Whites insisted on restoring the tsarist regime, while others understood that only a more liberal and democratic program had any chance of success. It was difficult enough to achieve military cooperation; political differences made it virtually impossible. The lack of a common goal on the part of the Whites was paralleled by a clear sense of purpose on the part of the Communists. Inspired by their vision of a new socialist order, the Communists had the advantage of possessing the determination that comes from revolutionary fervor and strong convictions.

CHRONOLOGY The Russian Revolution	
	1916
Murder of Rasputin	December
	1917
March of women in Petrograd	March 8
General strike in Petrograd	March 10
Establishment of the provisional government	March 15
Abdication of the tsar	March 15
Formation of the Petrograd soviet	March
Arrival of Lenin in Russia	April 3
Bolshevik majority in the Petrograd soviet	October
Bolshevik overthrow of the provisional government	November 6–7
	1918
Treaty of Brest-Litovsk	March 3
Civil war	1918–1921

The Communists also succeeded in translating their revolutionary faith into practical instruments of power. A policy of **war communism**, for example, was used to ensure regular supplies for the Red Army. War communism included the nationalization of banks and most industries, the forcible requisition of grain from peasants, and the centralization of state administration under Bolshevik control. Another Bolshevik instrument was "revolutionary terror." Although the old tsarist secret police had been abolished, a new Red secret police—known as the Cheka—replaced it. The Red Terror instituted by the Cheka aimed at nothing less than the destruction of all opponents of the new regime.

Finally, the intervention of foreign armies enabled the Communists to appeal to the powerful force of Russian patriotism. Although the Allied Powers had intervened initially in Russia to encourage the Russians to remain in the war, the end of the war on November 11, 1918, had made that purpose inconsequential. Nevertheless, Allied troops remained, and even more were sent because Allied countries did not hide their anti-Bolshevik feelings. At one point, more than 100,000 foreign troops, mostly Japanese, British, French, and American, were stationed on Russian soil. These forces rarely engaged in pitched battles, however, nor did they pursue a common strategy, although they did give material assistance to anti-Bolshevik forces. This intervention by the Allies enabled the Communist government to appeal to patriotic Russians to fight the attempts of foreigners to control their country.

By 1921, the Communists had succeeded in retaining control of Russia. In the course of the civil war, the Bolshevik regime had also transformed Russia into a bureaucratically centralized state dominated by a single party. It was also a state that was largely hostile to the

Allied Powers, who had sought to assist the Bolsheviks' enemies in the civil war.

The Last Year of the War

For Germany, the withdrawal of the Russians from the war in March 1918 offered renewed hope for a favorable end to the war. The victory over Russia persuaded Erich Ludendorff, who guided German military operations, and most German leaders to make one final military gamble—a grand offensive in the west to break the military stalemate. The German attack was launched in March and lasted into July, but an Allied counterattack, supported by the arrival of 140,000 fresh American troops, defeated the Germans at the Second Battle of the Marne on July 18. Ludendorff's gamble had failed. With the arrival of two million more American troops on the Continent, Allied forces began making a steady advance toward Germany.

On September 29, 1918, General Ludendorff informed German leaders that the war was lost and demanded that the government sue for peace at once. When German officials discovered that the Allies were unwilling to make peace with the autocratic imperial government, they instituted reforms to set up a liberal government. But these constitutional reforms came too late for the exhausted and angry German people. On November 3, naval units in Kiel mutinied, and within days, councils of workers and soldiers were forming throughout northern Germany and taking over the supervision of civilian and military administrations. William II capitulated to public pressure and abdicated on November 9, and the Socialists under Friedrich Ebert announced the establishment of a republic. Two days later, on November 11, 1918, the new German government agreed to an armistice. The war was over.

The Casualties of the War World War I devastated European civilization. Between 8 and 9 million soldiers died on the battlefields; another 22 million were wounded. Many of those who survived later died from war injuries or suffered the loss of arms or legs or other forms of mutilation. The birthrate in many European countries declined noticeably as a result of the death or maiming of so many young men. World War I also created a "lost generation" of war veterans who had become accustomed to violence and who would form the postwar bands of fighters who supported Mussolini and Hitler in their bids for power (see Chapter 26).

Nor did the killing affect only soldiers. Untold numbers of civilians died from war, civil war, or starvation. In 1915, after an Armenian uprising against the Ottoman government, the government retaliated with fury by killing Armenian men and expelling women and children. Within seven months, 600,000 Armenians had been killed, and 500,000 had been deported. Of the latter, 400,000 died while marching through the deserts and swamps of Syria and Iraq. By September 1915, an estimated one million Armenians were dead, the victims of **genocide.**

CHRONOLOGY World War I

1914	
Battle of Tannenberg	August 26–30
First Battle of the Marne	September 6–10
Battle of the Masurian Lakes	September 15
Russian, British, and French declaration of war on the Ottoman Empire	November
1915	
Start of Battle of Gallipoli	April 25
Italian declaration of war on Austria-Hungary	May 23
Entry of Bulgaria into the war	September
1916	
Battle of Verdun	February 21–December 18
1917	
German resumption of unrestricted submarine warfare	January
U.S. entry in the war	April 6
1918	
Last German offensive	March 21–July 18
Second Battle of the Marne	July 18
Allied counteroffensive	July 18–November 10
Armistice between Allies and Germany	November 11
1919	
Start of Paris Peace Conference	January 18
Peace of Versailles	June 28

The Peace Settlement

In January 1919, the delegations of twenty-seven victorious Allied nations gathered in Paris to conclude a final settlement of the Great War. Over the years, the reasons for fighting World War I had been transformed from selfish national interests to idealistic principles. No one expressed the latter better than United States President Woodrow Wilson. Wilson's proposals for a truly just and lasting peace included "open covenants of peace, openly arrived at" instead of secret diplomacy; the reduction of national armaments to a "point consistent with domestic safety"; and the self-determination of people so that "all well-defined national aspirations shall be accorded the utmost satisfaction." Wilson characterized World War I as a people's war waged against "absolutism and militarism," two scourges of liberty that could be eliminated only by creating democratic governments and a "general association of nations" that would guarantee the "political independence and territorial integrity to great and small states alike" (see the box on p. 489). As the spokesman for a new world

TWO VOICES OF PEACEMAKING:
WOODROW WILSON AND GEORGES CLEMENCEAU

*W*hen the Allied Powers met at Paris in January 1919, it soon became apparent that the victors had different opinions on the kind of peace they expected. The first excerpt is from a speech by Woodrow Wilson in which the American president presented his idealistic goals for a peace based on justice and reconciliation. The French wanted revenge and security. In the second selection, from Georges Clemenceau's *Grandeur and Misery of Victory,* the French premier revealed his fundamental dislike and distrust of Germany.

Woodrow Wilson, May 26, 1917

We are fighting for the liberty, the self-government, and the undictated development of all peoples, and every feature of the settlement that concludes this war must be conceived and executed for that purpose. Wrongs must first be righted and then adequate safeguards must be created to prevent their being committed again....

No people must be forced under sovereignty under which it does not wish to live. No territory must change hands except for the purpose of securing those who inhabit it a fair chance of life and liberty. No indemnities must be insisted on except those that constitute payment for manifest wrongs done. No readjustments of power must be made except such as will tend to secure the future peace of the world and the future welfare and happiness of its peoples.

And then the free peoples of the world must draw together in some common covenant, some genuine and practical cooperation that will in effect combine their force to secure peace and justice in the dealings of nations with one another.

Georges Clemenceau, *Grandeur and Misery of Victory*

War and peace, with their strong contrasts, alternate against a common background. For the catastrophe of 1914 the Germans are responsible. Only a professional liar would deny this. . . .

I have sometimes penetrated into the sacred cave of the Germanic cult, which is, as every one knows, the *Bierhaus* [beer hall]. A great aisle of massive humanity where there accumulate, amid the fumes of tobacco and beer, the popular rumblings of a nationalism upheld by the sonorous brasses blaring to the heavens the supreme voice of Germany, *Deutschland über alles! Germany above everything!* Men, women, and children, all petrified in reverence before the divine stoneware pot, brows furrowed with irrepressible power, eyes lost in a dream of infinity, mouths twisted by the intensity of willpower, drink in long draughts the celestial hope of vague expectations. These only remain to be realized presently when the chief marked out by Destiny shall have given the word. There you have the ultimate framework of an old but childish race.

How did the peacemaking aims of Wilson and Clemenceau differ? How did their different views affect the deliberations of the Paris Peace Conference and the nature of the final peace settlement?

order based on democracy and international cooperation, Wilson was enthusiastically cheered by many Europeans when he arrived in Europe for the peace conference.

Wilson soon found, however, that other states at the Paris Peace Conference were guided by considerably more pragmatic motives. The secret treaties and agreements that had been made before the war could not be totally ignored, even if they did conflict with the principle of **self-determination** enunciated by Wilson. National interests also complicated the deliberations of the Paris Peace Conference. David Lloyd George, prime minister of Great Britain, had won a decisive electoral victory in December 1918 on a platform of making the Germans pay for this dreadful war.

France's approach to peace was determined primarily by considerations of national security. To Georges Clemenceau, the feisty premier of France who had led his country to victory, the French people had borne the brunt of German aggression. They deserved revenge and security against future German aggression. Clemenceau wanted a demilitarized Germany, vast German reparations to pay for the costs of the war, and a separate Rhineland as a buffer state between France and Germany.

The most important decisions at the Paris Peace Conference were made by Wilson, Clemenceau, and Lloyd George. Italy was considered one of the so-called Big Four powers but played a much less important role than the other three countries. Germany, of course, was not invited to attend, and Russia could not do so because of its civil war.

In view of the many conflicting demands at Versailles, it was inevitable that the Big Three would quarrel. Wilson was determined to create a "league of nations" to prevent future wars. Clemenceau and Lloyd George were equally determined to punish Germany. In the end, only compromise made it possible to achieve a peace settlement. On January 25, 1919, the conference adopted the principle of a league of nations and Wilson agreed to make compromises on territorial arrangements. Clemenceau also compromised to obtain some guarantees for French security. He renounced France's desire for a separate Rhineland and instead accepted a defensive alliance with Great Britain and the United States. Both states pledged to help France if it were attacked by Germany.

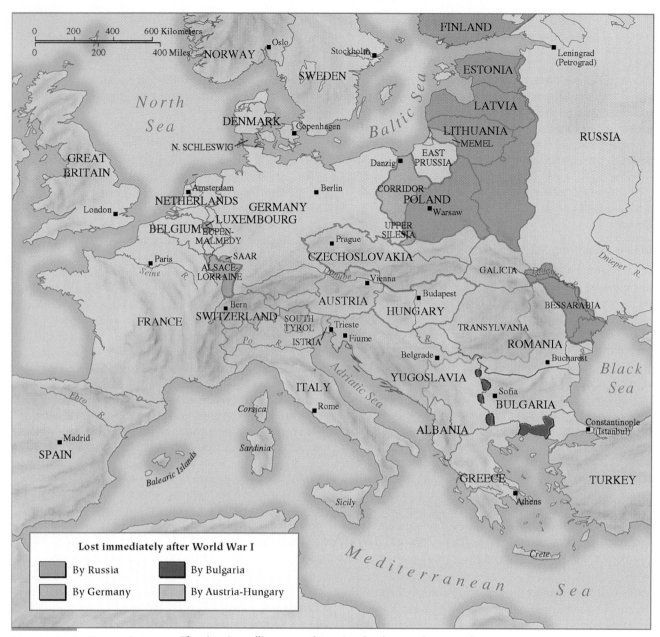

Lost immediately after World War I	
By Russia	By Bulgaria
By Germany	By Austria-Hungary

MAP 25.4 **Europe in 1919.** The victorious allies met to determine the shape and nature of postwar Europe. At the urging of U.S. President Woodrow Wilson, many nationalist aspirations of former imperial subjects were realized with the creation of several new countries from the prewar territory of Austria-Hungary, Germany, and Russia. **?** What new countries emerged, and what countries gained territory when Austria-Hungary was dismembered? **View an animated version of this map or related maps at** http://thomsonedu.com/history/spielvogel

The Treaty of Versailles

The final peace settlement of Paris consisted of five separate treaties with the defeated nations—Germany, Austria and Hungary (now separate nations), Bulgaria, and Turkey. The Treaty of Versailles with Germany, signed on June 28, 1919, was by far the most important one. The Germans considered it a harsh peace and were particularly unhappy with Article 231, the so-called **War Guilt Clause**, which declared Germany (and Austria) responsible for

starting the war and ordered Germany to pay **reparations** for all the damage the Allied governments and their people suffered as a result of the war.

The military and territorial provisions of the treaty also rankled Germans, although they were by no means as harsh as the Germans claimed. Germany had to reduce its army to 100,000 men, cut back its navy, and eliminate its air force. German territorial losses included the cession of Alsace and Lorraine to France and sections of Prussia to the new Polish state (see Map 25.4). German land west and as far as 30 miles east of the Rhine was established as a demilitarized zone and stripped of all armaments or fortifications to serve as a barrier to any future German military moves westward against France. Outraged by the "dictated peace," the new German government complained but accepted the treaty.

The Other Peace Treaties

The separate peace treaties made with the other Central Powers (Austria, Hungary, Bulgaria, and the Ottoman Empire) extensively redrew the map of eastern Europe. Many of these changes merely ratified what the war had already accomplished. Both the German and Russian Empires lost considerable territory in eastern Europe, and the Austro-Hungarian Empire disappeared altogether. New nation-states emerged from the lands of these three empires: Finland, Latvia, Estonia, Lithuania, Poland, Czechoslovakia, Austria, and Hungary. Territorial rearrangements were also made in the Balkans. Romania acquired additional lands from Russia, Hungary, and Bulgaria. Serbia formed the nucleus of a new southern Slav state, the kingdom of the Serbs, Croats, and Slovenes (renamed Yugoslavia in 1929).

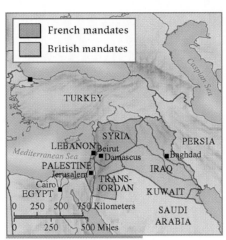

The Middle East in 1919

Although the Paris Peace Conference was supposedly guided by the principle of self-determination, the mixtures of peoples in eastern Europe made it impossible to draw boundaries along neat ethnic lines. As a result of compromises, virtually every eastern European state was left with a minorities problem that could lead to future conflicts. Germans in Poland; Hungarians, Poles, and Germans in Czechoslovakia; and Serbs, Croats, Slovenes, Macedonians, and Albanians in Yugoslavia all became sources of later conflict.

Yet another centuries-old empire—the Ottoman Empire—was dismembered by the peace settlement after the war. To gain Arab support against the Ottomans during the war, the Allies had promised to recognize the independence of Arab states in the Middle Eastern lands of the Ottoman Empire. But the imperialist habits of Europeans died hard. After the war, France took control of Lebanon and Syria while Britain received Iraq and Palestine. Officially, these acquisitions were called **mandates**, meaning that the lands were to be officially administered on behalf of the newly formed League of Nations. The system of mandates could not hide the fact that the principle of national self-determination at the Paris Peace Conference was largely for Europeans.

Successful enforcement of the peace necessitated the active involvement of its principal architects, especially in helping the new German state set up a peaceful and democratic republic. The failure of the U.S. Senate to ratify the Treaty of Versailles, however, meant that the United States never joined the League of Nations. In addition, the Senate also rejected Wilson's defensive alliance with Great Britain and France. Already by the end of 1919, the United States was pursuing policies intended to limit its direct involvement in future European wars.

This retreat had dire consequences. American withdrawal from the defensive alliance with Britain and France led Britain to withdraw as well. By removing itself from European affairs, the United States forced France to stand alone facing its old enemy, leading the embittered nation to take strong actions against Germany that only intensified German resentment. By the end of 1919, it appeared that the peace was already beginning to unravel.

CONCLUSION

World War I shattered the liberal and rational assumptions of late-nineteenth- and early-twentieth-century Europe. The incredible destruction and the death of almost ten million people undermined the whole idea of progress. New propaganda techniques had manipulated entire populations into sustaining their involvement in a meaningless slaughter.

World War I was a total war and involved a mobilization of resources and populations and increased government centralization of power over the lives of its citizens. Civil liberties, such as freedom of the press, of speech, of assembly, and of movement, were circumscribed in the name of national security. Governments' need to plan the production and distribution of goods and to ration consumer goods restricted economic freedom. Although the late nineteenth and early twentieth centuries had

witnessed the extension of government authority into such areas as mass education, social welfare legislation, and mass conscription, World War I made the practice of strong central authority a way of life.

Finally, World War I ended the age of European hegemony over world affairs. In 1917, the Russian Revolution laid the foundation for a new world power, and the United States entered the war. The termination of the European age was not evident to all, however, for it was clouded by two developments—American isolationism and the withdrawal of the Russian Communists from world affairs while they nurtured their own socialist system. Although these developments were only temporary, they created a political vacuum in Europe that was filled all too soon by a resurgence of German power.

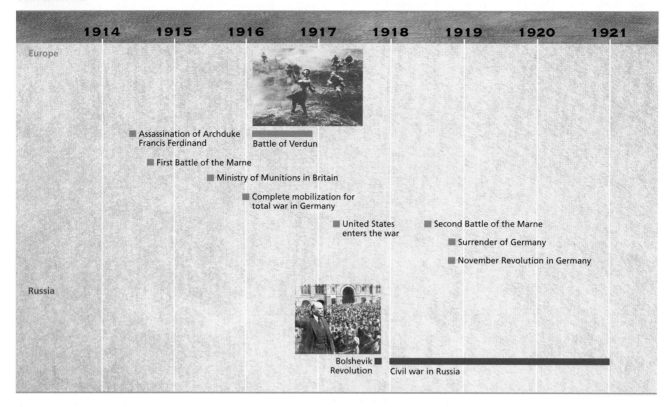

	1914	1915	1916	1917	1918	1919	1920	1921

Europe

■ Assassination of Archduke Francis Ferdinand

Battle of Verdun

■ First Battle of the Marne

■ Ministry of Munitions in Britain

■ Complete mobilization for total war in Germany

■ United States enters the war

■ Second Battle of the Marne

■ Surrender of Germany

■ November Revolution in Germany

Russia

Bolshevik ■ Revolution

Civil war in Russia

NOTES

1. M. Gilbert, *The First World War: A Complete History* (New York, 1994), p. 259.
2. Quoted in ibid., p. 264.
3. A. Toynbee, *Surviving the Future* (New York, 1971), pp. 106-107.
4. Quoted in J. Remak, "1914—The Third Balkan War: Origins Reconsidered," *Journal of Modern History,* 43 (1971): 364–365.
5. Quoted in J. M. Winter, *The Experience of World War I* (New York, 1989), p. 142.
6. Quoted in C. W. Reilly, ed., *Scars upon My Heart: Women's Poetry and Verse of the First World War* (London, 1981), p. 90.
7. Quoted in W. M. Mandel, *Soviet Women* (Garden City, N.Y., 1975), p. 43.

SUGGESTIONS FOR FURTHER READING

The historical literature on the causes of World War I is enormous. Good starting points are **J. Joll, *The Origins of the First World War,*** 2d ed. (London, 1992), and **J. Remak, *The Origins of World War I, 1871–1914,*** 2d ed. (Fort Worth, Tex., 1995). On the role of militarism, see **D. Hermann, *The Arming of Europe and the Making of the First World War*** (New York, 1997). On the events leading to war, see **D. Fromkin, *Europe's Last Summer: Who Started the Great War in 1914?*** (New York, 2004).

The best brief account of World War I is **H. Strachan, *The First World War*** (New York, 2003). Strachan has also completed the first volume of a massive three-volume study, ***First World War: To Arms*** (New York, 2003). Two additional accounts of World War I are **M. Gilbert, *The First World War*** (New York, 1994), and the lavishly illustrated book by **J. M. Winter, *The Experience of World War I*** (New York, 1989). See also **M. S. Neiberg, *Fighting the Great War: A Global History*** (Cambridge, Mass., 2005), and **J. Keegan, *An Illustrated History of the First World War*** (New York, 2001). For a different interpretation, see **D. Stevenson, *Cataclysm: The First World War as Political Tragedy*** (New York, 2004).

On the role of women in World War I, see **G. Braybon, *Women Workers in the First World War: The British Experience*** (London, 1981); **J. M. Winter and R. M. Wall, eds., *The Upheaval of War: Family, Work and Welfare in Europe, 1914–1918*** (Cambridge, 1988); **G. Braybon and P. Summerfield, *Women's Experiences in Two World Wars*** (London, 1987); and **M. R. Higonnet, J. Jensen, S. Michel, and M. C. Weitz, *Behind the Lines: Gender and the Two World Wars*** (New Haven, Conn., 1987).

A good introduction to the Russian Revolution can be found in **R. A. Wade, *The Russian Revolution, 1917*** (Cambridge, 2000), and **S. Fitzpatrick, *The Russian Revolution, 1917–1932,*** 2d ed. (New York, 1994). See also **R. Pipes, *The Russian Revolution*** (New York, 1990). For a study that puts the Russian Revolution into the context of World War I, see **P. Holquist, *Making War, Forging Revolution*** (Cambridge, Mass., 2002). Reliable analysis as well as a good collection of the thoughts and experiences of ordinary Russian people in 1917 can be found in **M. D. Steinberg, *Voices of Revolution, 1917***

(New Haven, Conn., 2001). On Lenin, see **R. Service, *Lenin: A Biography*** (Cambridge, Mass., 2000). A comprehensive study of the Russian civil war is **W. B. Lincoln, *Red Victory: A History of the Russian Civil War*** (New York, 1989).

The role of war aims in shaping the peace settlement is examined in **V. H. Rothwell, *British War Aims and Peace Diplomacy, 1914–1918*** (Oxford, 1971), and **D. R. Stevenson, *French War Aims Against Germany, 1914–1919*** (New York, 1982).

World War I and the Russian Revolution are also well covered in a good general survey of European history in the twentieth century, **R. Paxton, *Europe in the Twentieth Century,*** 2d ed. (New York, 1985).

Thomson NOW! Enter *ThomsonNOW* using the access card that is available for *Western Civilization: A Brief History.* *ThomsonNOW* will help you understand this chapter with lesson plans generated for your needs. In addition, you can read the following documents, and many more, online:

Entente Cordiale (*Declaration of Understanding*)
Siegfried Sassoon, poems "Attack" and "Dreamers"
Treaty of Versailles

WESTERN CIVILIZATION RESOURCES

THE FUTILE SEARCH FOR STABILITY: EUROPE BETWEEN THE WARS, 1919–1939

© Bettmann/CORBIS

Men are served in a soup line in Berlin in 1930

ONLY TWENTY YEARS after the Treaty of Versailles, Europeans were again at war. And yet in the 1920s, many people assumed that they were about to enter a new era of world peace, economic growth, and political democracy. In all of these areas, the optimistic hopes of the 1920s failed to be realized. After 1919, most people wanted peace but were unsure about how to maintain it. The League of Nations, conceived as a new instrument to provide for collective security, failed to work well. New treaties that renounced the use of war looked good on paper but had no means of enforcement. Virtually everyone favored disarmament, but few could agree on how to achieve it.

Europe faced severe economic challenges after World War I. The European economy did not begin to recover from the war until 1922, and even then it was beset by financial problems left over from the war and, most devastating of all, the severe depression that began at the end of 1929. The Great Depression brought untold misery to millions of people. Begging for food on the streets became widespread, especially when soup kitchens were unable to keep up with the demand. Larger and larger numbers of people were homeless and moved from place to place looking for work and shelter.

In the United States, the homeless set up shantytowns they named "Hoovervilles" after the American president, Herbert Hoover. In their misery, some people saw but one solution, as one unemployed person expressed it: "Today, when I am experiencing this for the first time, I think that I should prefer to do away with myself, to take gas, to jump into the river, or leap from some high place.... Would I really come to such a decision? I do not know. Animals die, plants wither, but men always go on living." Social unrest spread rapidly, and some unemployed staged hunger marches to get attention. In democratic countries, more and more people began to listen to and vote for radical voices calling for extreme measures.

According to Woodrow Wilson, World War I had been fought to make the world safe for democracy, and for a while after 1919, political democracy seemed well established. But hope soon faded as authoritarian regimes spread into Italy and Germany and across eastern Europe.◆

An Uncertain Peace: The Search for Security

United States President Woodrow Wilson had recognized that the peace treaties ending World War I contained unwise provisions that could serve as new causes for conflicts, and he had placed his hopes for ensuring the future in the League of Nations. The League, however, was not particularly good at maintaining the peace. The failure of the United States to join the League and the subsequent American retreat into isolationism undermined the League's effectiveness from the very start. Moreover, the League's sole weapon for halting aggression was economic sanctions.

The French Policy of Coercion, 1919–1924

The weakness of the League of Nations and the failure of both the United States and Great Britain to honor their promises to form defensive military alliances with France left France embittered and alone. France's search for security between 1919 and 1924 was founded primarily on a strict enforcement of the Treaty of Versailles. This tough policy toward Germany began with the issue of reparations, the payments that the Germans were to make to compensate for the "damage done to the civilian population of the Allied and Associated Powers and to their property," as the treaty asserted. In April 1921, the Allied Reparations Commission settled on a sum of 132 billion marks ($33 billion) for German reparations, payable in annual installments of 2.5 billion (gold) marks. The new German republic made its first payment in 1921, but by the following year, facing financial problems, it announced that it was unable to pay more. Outraged by what it considered Germany's violation of the peace settlement, the French government sent troops to occupy the Ruhr valley, Germany's chief industrial and mining center. Because the Germans would not pay reparations, the French would collect reparations in kind by operating and using the Ruhr mines and factories.

Both Germany and France suffered from the French occupation of the Ruhr. The German government adopted a policy of passive resistance that was largely financed by printing more paper money, but this only intensified the inflationary pressures that had already appeared in Germany by the end of the war. The German mark soon became worthless. In 1914, a dollar bought 4.2 marks; by the end of November 1923, a single dollar bought an incredible 4.2 trillion marks. Germany faced total economic collapse. The formation of new governments in both Great Britain and France opened the door to conciliatory approaches to Germany and the reparations problem. At the same time, a new German government led by Gustav Stresemann (1878–1929) ended the policy of passive resistance and committed Germany to seek a new settlement of the reparations question.

The Hopeful Years, 1924–1929

In August 1924, an international commission produced a new plan for reparations. Named the Dawes plan after the American banker who chaired the commission, it reduced reparations and stabilized Germany's payments on the basis of its ability to pay. The Dawes plan also granted an initial $200 million loan for German recovery, which opened the door to heavy American investments in Europe that helped create a glimmer of European prosperity between 1924 and 1929.

With prosperity came a new spate of European diplomacy. A spirit of cooperation was fostered by Stresemann, the foreign minister of Germany, and his French counterpart, Aristide Briand (1862–1932), who concluded the Treaty of Locarno in 1925. This guaranteed Germany's new western borders with France and Belgium. Although Germany's new eastern borders with Poland were conspicuously absent from the agreement, the Locarno pact was viewed by many as the beginning of a new era of European peace. On the day after the pact was concluded, the headlines in the *New York Times* ran "France and Germany Ban War Forever," and the *London Times* declared, "Peace at Last."[1]

The spirit of Locarno was based on little real substance, however. Germany lacked the military power to alter its western borders even if it wanted to. And the issue of disarmament soon proved that even the spirit of Locarno could not bring nations to cut back on their weapons. The League of Nations had suggested the "reduction of national armaments to the lowest point consistent with national safety." Germany, of course, had been disarmed with the expectation that other states would do likewise. Numerous disarmament conferences, however, failed to achieve anything substantial as states proved unwilling to trust their security to anyone but their own military forces.

The Great Depression

Two factors played a major role in the coming of the Great Depression: a downturn in domestic economies and an international financial crisis precipitated by the collapse of the American stock market in 1929. In the mid-1920s, prices for agricultural goods were beginning to decline rapidly due to overproduction of basic commodities, such as wheat, and an increase in the use of oil and hydroelectricity led to a slump in the coal industry. In addition to these domestic economic troubles, much of the European prosperity between 1924 and 1929 had been built on American bank loans to Germany. In 1928 and 1929, American investors began to pull money out of Germany in order to invest in the booming New York stock market. The crash of the stock market in October 1929 led panicky American investors to withdraw even more of their funds from Germany and other European markets. The withdrawal of funds seriously weakened the banks of Germany and other central European states. The Credit-Anstalt, Vienna's most prestigious bank, collapsed on May 31, 1931. By that time, trade was slowing down, industrialists were cutting back production, and unemployment was increasing as the ripple effects of international bank failures had a devastating impact on domestic economies.

Economic depression was not a new phenomenon in European history, but the depth of the economic downturn after 1929 fully justifies calling it the Great Depression. During 1932, the worst year of the depression, 25 percent of the British and 40 percent of the German labor force was out of work. The unemployed and homeless filled the streets of the cities throughout the industrialized countries (see the box on p. 497).

The economic crisis also had unexpected social repercussions. Women were often able to secure low-paying jobs as servants, housecleaners, or laundresses while many men remained unemployed, either begging on the streets or remaining at home to do household tasks. This reversal of traditional gender roles caused resentment on the part of many unemployed men, opening them to the shrill cries of demagogues with simple solutions to the economic crisis. High unemployment rates among young males often led them to join gangs that gathered in parks or other public places, spreading fear among local residents.

Governments seemed powerless to deal with the crisis. The classical liberal remedy for depression, a deflationary policy of balanced budgets, which involved cutting costs by lowering wages and raising tariffs to exclude other countries' goods from home markets, served only to worsen the economic crisis and create even greater mass discontent. This in turn led to serious political repercussions. Increased government activity in the economy was one reaction, even in countries like the United States that had a strong laissez-faire tradition. Another effect was a renewed interest in Marxist doctrines since Marx had predicted that capitalism would destroy itself through overproduction. Communism took on new popularity, especially among workers and intellectuals. Finally, the Great Depression increased the attractiveness of simplistic solutions, especially from a new authoritarian movement known as **fascism**. Everywhere, democracy seemed on the defensive in the 1930s.

The Democratic States

After World War I, Great Britain went through a period of serious economic difficulties. During the war, Britain had lost many of the markets for its industrial products, especially to the United States and Japan. The postwar decline of such staple industries as coal, steel, and textiles led to a rise in unemployment, which reached the two million mark in 1921. But Britain soon rebounded and from 1925 to 1929 experienced renewed prosperity.

The Great Depression: Unemployed in Paris. The Great Depression devastated the European economy and had serious political repercussions. Because of its more balanced economy, France did not feel the effects of the depression as quickly as other European countries. By 1931, however, even France was experiencing lines of unemployed people at free-food centers. This one in the Rue Reumur gave out free hot soup in the mornings from 11 to 12 and in the evenings from 6 to 7.

THE GREAT DEPRESSION: UNEMPLOYED AND HOMELESS IN GERMANY

In 1932, Germany had six million unemployed workers, many of them wandering aimlessly through the country, begging for food and seeking shelter in city lodgings for the homeless. The Great Depression was an important factor in the rise to power of Adolf Hitler and the Nazis. This selection presents a description of unemployed homeless in 1932.

Heinrich Hauser, "With Germany's Unemployed"

An almost unbroken chain of homeless men extends the whole length of the great Hamburg-Berlin highway....All the highways in Germany over which I have traveled this year presented the same aspect....

Most of the hikers paid no attention to me. They walked separately or in small groups, with their eyes on the ground. And they had the queer, stumbling gait of barefooted people, for their shoes were slung over their shoulders....[Most of them were] unskilled young people, for the most part, who had been unable to find a place for themselves in any city or town in Germany, and who had never had a job and never expected to have one. There was something else that had never been seen before—whole families that had piled all their goods into baby carriages and wheelbarrows that they were pushing along as they plodded forward in dumb despair. It was a whole nation on the march.

I saw them—and this was the strongest impression that the year 1932 left with me—I saw them, gathered into groups of fifty or a hundred men, attacking fields of potatoes. I saw them digging up the potatoes and throwing them into sacks while the farmer who owned the field watched them in despair and the local policeman looked on gloomily from the distance. I saw them staggering toward the lights of the city as night fell, with their sacks on their backs. What did it remind me of? Of the War, of the worst periods of starvation in 1917 and 1918, but even then people paid for the potatoes....

I know what it is to be a tramp. I know what cold and hunger are....But there are two things that I have only recently experienced—begging and spending the night in a municipal lodging house.

I entered the huge Berlin municipal lodging house in a northern quarter of the city....

Distribution of spoons, distribution of enameled-ware bowls with the words "Property of the City of Berlin" written on their sides. Then the meal itself. A big kettle is carried. Men with yellow smocks have brought it in and men with yellow smocks ladle out the food. These men, too, are homeless and they have been expressly picked by the establishment and given free food and lodging and a little pocket money in exchange for their work about the house.

Where have I seen this kind of food distribution before? In a prison that I once helped to guard in the winter of 1919 during the German civil war. There was the same hunger then, the same trembling, anxious expectation of rations. Now the men are standing in a long row, dressed in their plain nightshirts that reach to the ground, and the noise of their shuffling feet is like the noise of big wild animals walking up and down the stone floor of their cages before feeding time. The men lean far over the kettle so that the warm steam from the food envelops them and they hold out their bowls as if begging and whisper to the attendant, "Give me a real helping. Give me a little more." A piece of bread is handed out with every bowl.

My next recollection is sitting at a table in another room on a crowded bench that is like a seat in a fourth-class railway carriage. Hundreds of hungry mouths make an enormous noise eating their food. The men sit bent over their food like animals who feel that someone is going to take it away from them. They hold their bowl with their left arm part way around it, so that nobody can take it away, and they also protect it with their other elbow and with their head and mouth, while they move the spoon as fast as they can between their mouth and the bowl.

Why did Hauser compare the scene he describes from 1932 with the years of 1917 and 1918? Why does he compare the hungry men with animals?

But Britain was not immune to the effects of the Great Depression. The Labour Party, now the largest party in Britain, failed to solve the nation's economic problems and fell from power in 1931. A national government (a coalition of Liberals and Conservatives) claimed credit for bringing Britain out of the worst stages of the depression, primarily by using the traditional policies of balanced budgets and protective tariffs. British politicians largely ignored the new ideas of a Cambridge economist, John Maynard Keynes (1883–1946), who published _A General Theory of Employment, Interest, and Money_ in 1936. He condemned the traditional view that in a free economy, depressions should be left to work themselves out. Instead, Keynes argued that unemployment stemmed not from overproduction but from a decline in demand and that demand could be increased by public works, financed, if necessary, through deficit spending to stimulate production.

After the defeat of Germany, France had become the strongest power on the European continent. Its greatest need was to rebuild the devastated areas of northern and eastern France. But no French government seemed capable of solving France's financial problems between 1921 and 1926. Like other European countries, though, France did experience a period of relative prosperity between 1926 and 1929. By 1932, France began to feel the full effects of the Great Depression, and economic instability soon had political repercussions. During a nineteen-month period in 1932 and 1933, six different cabinets were formed as France faced political chaos. Finally, in 1936, fearful that rightists intended to seize power, a coalition of leftist parties—Communists, Socialists, and Radicals—formed a Popular Front government.

Although the Popular Front succeeded in initiating a program for workers that established the right of collective bargaining, a forty-hour workweek, two-week paid vacations, and minimum wages, its policies failed to solve the problems of the depression. By 1938, the French were experiencing a serious decline of confidence in their political system that left them unprepared to deal with their aggressive enemy to the east, Nazi Germany.

After Germany, no Western nation was more affected by the Great Depression than the United States. By the end of 1932, industrial production had fallen to 50 percent of what it had been in 1929. Soon there were fifteen million unemployed. Under these circumstances, the Democrat Franklin Delano Roosevelt (1882–1945) won the 1932 presidential election by a landslide. He and his advisers pursued a policy of active government intervention in the economy that came to be known as the New Deal, which included a stepped-up program of public works, such as the Works Progress Administration (WPA), established in 1935. This government organization put between two and three million people to work building bridges, roads, post offices, and airports. The Roosevelt administration was also responsible for social legislation that launched the American welfare state. In 1935, the Social Security Act created a system of old-age pensions and unemployment insurance.

No doubt the New Deal provided some social reform measures that perhaps averted the possibility of social revolution in the United States. It did not, however, solve the unemployment problems of the Great Depression. In May 1937, during what was considered a period of full recovery, American unemployment still stood at seven million; by the following year, it had increased to eleven million. Only World War II and the subsequent growth of armament-related industries brought American workers back to full employment.

European States and the World: The Colonial Empires

World War I and the Great Depression had an impact on Europe's colonial empires. Despite the war, the Allied nations had managed to keep their colonial empires intact. Great Britain and France had even added to their empires by dividing up many of Germany's colonial possessions and taking control of large parts of the Middle East through a system of mandates. Although Europe had emerged from World War I relatively intact, its political and social foundations and its self-confidence had been severely undermined. In Asia and Africa, a rising tide of unrest against European political domination began to emerge and led to movements for change.

The Middle East   For the countries of the Middle East, the period between the two world wars was a time of transition. With the fall of the Ottoman and Persian Empires, new modernizing regimes emerged in Turkey and Iran. A fiercely independent government was established in Saudi Arabia in 1932. Iraq, too, gained its independence from Britain in the same year. Elsewhere in the Middle East, European influence remained strong: the British maintained their mandates in Jordan and Palestine, the French in Syria and Lebanon.

Although Britain and France had made plans to divide up Ottoman territories in the Middle East, Colonel Mustafa Kemal led Turkish forces in creating the new republic of Turkey in 1923. Kemal wanted to modernize Turkey along Western lines. The trappings of a democratic system were put in place, although the new president did not tolerate opposition. Kemal, who adopted the surname Atatürk ("Father Turk"), made Turkey a secular republic and broke the power of the Islamic religion. By and large, the Turkish republic was the product of Atatürk's determined efforts to use nationalism and Western ways to create a modern Turkish nation from the Ottoman remnants in Asia Minor.

India   By the time of World War I, the Indian people had already begun to refer to Mohandas Gandhi as India's "Great Soul," or Mahatma. Gandhi (1869–1948) spearheaded a movement based on nonviolent resistance, whose aim was to force the British to improve the lot of the poor and grant independence to India. When the British tried to suppress Indian calls for independence, Gandhi called on his followers to follow a peaceful policy of civil disobedience by refusing to obey British regulations. Although the British resisted Gandhi's movement, in 1935 they granted India internal self-government. Independence, however, would have to wait until after World War II.

Africa   Black Africans who fought in World War I in the armies of the British and the French hoped for independence after the war. As one newspaper in the Gold Coast put it, if African volunteers who fought on European battlefields were "good enough to fight and die in the Empire's cause, they were good enough to have a share in the government of their countries." This feeling was shared by many. The peace settlement after World War I, then, turned out to be a great disappointment. Germany was stripped of its African colonies, but they were awarded to the British and the French.

After World War I, Africans became more active politically. Africans who had fought in World War I had learned new ideas in the West about freedom and nationalism. Even in Africa itself, missionary schools had often taught their African pupils ideas about liberty and equality. As more Africans became aware of the enormous gulf between Western ideals and practices, they decided to seek reform. Independence remained but a dream. Although the colonial powers responded to protest movements with force, they also began to make some reforms in the hope of satisfying indigenous peoples. Reforms, however, were too few and too late, and by the 1930s, an increasing number of African leaders were calling for independence. The clearest calls came from a new generation of young African leaders who had been educated in Europe and the United States.

Retreat from Democracy: The Authoritarian and Totalitarian States

By 1939, only two major states in Europe, France and Great Britain, remained democratic. Italy and Germany had succumbed to the political movement called fascism, while the Soviet Union, under Stalin, had moved toward a repressive **totalitarian state.** A host of other European nations, especially in eastern Europe, adopted authoritarian structures of various kinds.

The dictatorial regimes between the wars assumed both old and new forms. Dictatorship was not new, but the modern totalitarian state was. The totalitarian regimes, best exemplified by Stalinist Russia and Nazi Germany, greatly extended the functions and powers of the central state. The modern totalitarian state expected the active commitment of citizens to the regime's goals. They used modern mass **propaganda** techniques and high-speed communication media to conquer the minds and hearts of their subjects. The total state sought to control not only the economic, political, and social aspects of life but the intellectual and cultural aspects as well.

The modern totalitarian state was to be led by a single leader and a single party. It ruthlessly rejected the liberal ideal of limited government power and constitutional guarantees of individual freedoms. Indeed, individual freedom was to be subordinated to the collective will of the masses, organized and determined for them by their leader. Modern technology also gave total states unprecedented police controls to enforce their wishes on their subjects.

Fascist Italy

In the early 1920s, Benito Mussolini burst onto the Italian scene with the first fascist movement in Europe. Mussolini (1883–1945) began his political career as a socialist, but in 1919, he established a new political group, the *Fascio di Combattimento*, or League of Combat. It received little attention in the elections of 1919, but political stalemate in Italy's parliamentary system and strong nationalist sentiment gave Mussolini and the Fascists the opportunity to rise to power.

The new parliament elected in November quickly proved incapable of governing Italy. The three major parties were unable to form an effective governmental coalition, and the Socialists, now the largest party, spoke theoretically of the need for revolution and alarmed conservatives, who quickly associated them with Bolsheviks

(Communists) in Russia. Thousands of industrial and agricultural strikes in 1919 and 1920 created a climate of class warfare and continual violence. In 1920 and 1921, bands of armed Fascists called **squadristi** were formed and turned loose in attacks on socialist offices and newspapers. Strikes by trade unionists and socialist workers and peasant leagues were broken up by force. Mussolini's Fascist movement began to gain support from middle-class industrialists fearful of working-class agitation and large landowners who objected to the agricultural strikes. Mussolini also perceived that Italians were angry over the failure of Italy to receive more territorial acquisitions after World War I. By 1922, the movement began to mushroom as Mussolini's nationalist rhetoric and the middle-class fear of socialism, Communist revolution, and disorder made the Fascists seem attractive. On October 29, 1922, after Mussolini and the Fascists threatened to march on Rome if they were not given power, King Victor Emmanuel III (1900–1946) capitulated and made Mussolini prime minister of Italy.

Mussolini and the Italian Fascist State By 1926, Mussolini had established his Fascist dictatorship. Press laws gave the government the right to suspend any publications that fostered disrespect for the Catholic church, the monarchy, or the state. The prime minister was made "head of government," with the power to legislate by decree. A police law empowered the police to arrest and confine anybody for political or nonpolitical crimes without due process of law. In 1926, all antifascist parties were outlawed, and a secret police force, known as the OVRA, was established. By the end of 1926, Mussolini ruled Italy as *Il Duce,* "the leader."

Mussolini conceived of the Fascist state as totalitarian: "Fascism is totalitarian, and the Fascist State, the synthesis and unity of all values, interprets, develops and gives strength to the whole life of the people."[2] Mussolini did try to create a police state, but police activities in Italy were never as repressive, efficient, or savage as those of Nazi Germany. Likewise, the Italian Fascists' attempt to exercise control over all forms of mass media, including newspapers, radio, and cinema, in order to use propaganda as an instrument to integrate the masses into the state failed to achieve its major goals. Most commonly, Fascist propaganda was disseminated through simple slogans, such as "Mussolini is always right," plastered on walls all over Italy.

Mussolini and the Fascists also attempted to mold Italians into a single-minded community by developing Fascist organizations. Because the secondary schools maintained considerable freedom from Fascist control, the regime relied more and more on the activities of youth organizations, known as the Young Fascists, to indoctrinate the young people of the nation in Fascist ideals. By 1939, nearly seven million children and young adults of both sexes—two-thirds of the population between eight and eighteen—were enrolled in some kind of Fascist youth group. Activities for these groups included Saturday afternoon marching drills and calisthenics, seaside

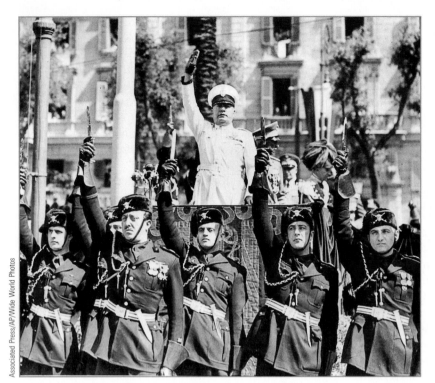

Mussolini–The Iron *Duce*. One of Mussolini's favorite images of himself was that of the iron *Duce*—the strong leader who is always right. Consequently, he was often seen in military-style uniforms and military poses. This photograph shows Mussolini in one of his numerous uniforms with his Black Shirt bodyguards giving the Fascist salute.

and mountain summer camps, and contests. Beginning in the 1930s, all male groups were given military exercises to develop discipline and provide training for war. Results were mixed. Italian teenagers, who liked neither military training nor routine discipline of any kind, simply refused to attend Fascist youth group meetings on a regular basis.

The Fascists portrayed the family as the pillar of the state and women as the basic foundation of the family. "Woman into the home" became the Fascist slogan. Women were to be homemakers and baby producers, "their natural and fundamental mission in life," according to Mussolini, who viewed population growth as an indicator of national strength. Employment outside the home distracted women from reproduction. "It forms an independence and consequent physical and moral habits contrary to child bearing."[3] A practical consideration also underlay the Fascist attitude toward women: eliminating women from the job market reduced male unemployment figures in the depression economy of the 1930s.

Despite the instruments of repression, the use of propaganda, and the creation of numerous Fascist organizations, Mussolini never achieved the degree of totalitarian control accomplished in Hitler's Germany or Stalin's Soviet Union. Mussolini and the Fascist party never really destroyed the old power structure. Some institutions, including the armed forces and the monarchy, were never absorbed into the Fascist state and managed to maintain their independence. Mussolini had boasted that he would help workers and peasants, but instead he generally allied himself with the interests of industrialists and large landowners at the expense of the lower classes.

Even more indicative of Mussolini's compromise with the traditional institutions of Italy was his attempt to gain the support of the Catholic church. In the Lateran Accords of February 1929, Mussolini's regime recognized the sovereign independence of a small enclave of 109 acres in Rome, known as Vatican City, which had remained in the church's possession since the unification of Italy in 1870; in return, the papacy recognized the Italian state. The Lateran Accords also guaranteed the church a large grant of money and recognized Catholicism as the "sole religion of the state." In return, the Catholic church urged Italians to support the Fascist regime.

In all areas of Italian life under Mussolini and the Fascists, there was a dichotomy between Fascist ideals and practice. The Italian Fascists promised much but actually delivered considerably less, and they were soon overshadowed by a much more powerful fascist movement to the north.

Hitler and Nazi Germany

In 1923, a small rightist party known as the Nazis, led by an obscure Austrian rabble-rouser named Adolf Hitler, tried to seize power in southern Germany. Although the attempt failed, Hitler and the Nazis achieved sudden national prominence. Within ten years, they had taken over complete power.

Weimar Germany After Germany's defeat in World War I, a German democratic state known as the Weimar Republic was established. From its beginnings, the Weimar

Creation of *Fascio di Combattimento*	1919
Squadristi violence	1920–1921
Mussolini as prime minister	1922 (October 29)
Establishment of Fascist dictatorship	1925–1926
Lateran Accords with Catholic church	1929

Republic was plagued by problems. The republic had no truly outstanding political leaders. In 1925, Paul von Hindenburg (1847–1934), a World War I military hero, was elected president. Hindenburg was a traditional military man, monarchist in sentiment, who at heart was not in favor of the republic. The young republic also suffered politically from attempted uprisings and attacks from both the left and right.

The Weimar Republic also faced serious economic difficulties. As Germany experienced runaway inflation in 1922 and 1923, middle-class Germans and others who lived on fixed incomes watched their monthly stipends become worthless and their savings evaporate. These economic losses increasingly pushed the middle class toward rightist parties that were hostile to the republic. To make matters worse, after a short recovery between 1924 and 1929, the Great Depression hit Germany hard. Unemployment increased to nearly 4.4 million people by December 1930. The depression fanned social discontent and fear and paved the way for extremist parties. The political, economic, and social problems of the Weimar Republic provided an environment in which Hitler and the Nazis were able to seize power.

Rise of the Nazis   Born in 1889, Adolf Hitler was the son of an Austrian customs official. He was a total failure in secondary school and eventually made his way to Vienna to become an artist. In Vienna, Hitler established the basic ideas of an ideology from which he never deviated for the rest of his life. At the core of Hitler's ideas was racism, especially anti-Semitism. Hitler had also become an extreme German nationalist who had learned from the mass politics of Vienna how political parties could make effective use of propaganda and terror. Finally, in his Viennese years, Hitler came to a firm belief in the need for struggle, which he saw as the "granite foundation of the world."

At the end of World War I, after four years of service on the Western Front, Hitler went to Munich and decided to enter politics. He joined the obscure German Workers' Party, one of a number of right-wing extreme nationalist parties in Munich. By the summer of 1921, Hitler had assumed control of the party, which he renamed the National Socialist German Workers' Party (NSDAP), or Nazi Party for short. His idea was that the party's name would distinguish the Nazis from the socialist parties while gaining support from both working-class and nationalist circles. Hitler worked assiduously to develop the party into a mass political movement with flags, badges, uniforms, its own newspaper, and its own police force or party militia known as the SA, the *Sturmabteilung*, or Storm Troops. The SA was used to defend the party in meeting halls and break up the meetings of other parties. Hitler's own oratorical skills were largely responsible for attracting an increasing number of followers. By 1923, the party had grown from its early hundreds into a membership of 55,000, with 15,000 SA members.

Overconfident, Hitler staged an armed uprising against the government in Munich in November 1923. The so-called Beer Hall Putsch was quickly crushed, and Hitler was sentenced to prison. During his brief stay in jail, Hitler wrote *Mein Kampf* (My Struggle), an autobiographical account of his movement and its underlying ideology. Extreme German nationalism, virulent anti-Semitism, and vicious anticommunism are linked by a social Darwinian theory of struggle that stresses the right of superior nations to **Lebensraum** (living space) through expansion and the right of "superior" individuals to secure authoritarian leadership over the masses.

The Nazi Seizure of Power   During his imprisonment, Hitler also came to the realization that the Nazis would have to acquire power by constitutional means, not by overthrowing the Weimar Republic. This implied the formation of a mass political party that would actively compete for votes with the other political parties. After his release from prison, Hitler reorganized the Nazi Party on a regional basis and expanded it to all parts of Germany. By 1929, the Nazis had a national party organization whose membership grew from 27,000 in 1925 to 178,000 by the end of 1929. Especially noticeable was the youthfulness of the regional, district, and branch leaders of the Nazi organization. Many were under thirty and were fiercely committed to Hitler because he gave them the kind of active politics they sought. Rather than democratic debate, they wanted brawls in beer halls, enthusiastic speeches, and comradeship in the building of a new Germany. One new, young Nazi member expressed his excitement about the party:

> For me this was the start of a completely new life. There was only one thing in the world for me and that was service in the movement. All my thoughts were centred on the movement. I could talk only politics. I was no longer aware of anything else. At the time I was a promising athlete; I was very keen on sport, and it was going to be my career. But I had to give this up too. My only interest was agitation and propaganda.[4]

Such youthful enthusiasm gave the Nazi movement an aura of a "young man's movement" and a sense of dynamism that the other parties could not match.

By 1932, the Nazi Party had 800,000 members and had become the largest party in the Reichstag. No doubt Germany's economic difficulties were a crucial factor in the Nazi rise to power. Unemployment increased dramatically, from 4.4 million at the start of 1931 to 6 million by the winter of 1932. The economic and psychological impact of the Great Depression made extremist parties more attractive. The Nazis were especially effective in developing modern electioneering techniques. In their campaigns, party members pitched their themes to the needs and fears of different social groups. But even as they were making blatant appeals to class interests, the Nazis were denouncing conflicts of interest and maintaining that they stood above classes and parties. Hitler, in particular, claimed to transcend all differences and promised to create a new Germany free of class differences and party infighting. His appeal to national pride, national honor, and traditional militarism struck chords of emotion in his listeners.

Increasingly, the right-wing elites of Germany—the industrial magnates, landed aristocrats, military establishment, and higher bureaucrats—began to see Hitler as the man who had the mass support to establish an authoritarian regime that would save Germany and their privileged positions from a Communist takeover. Under pressure, President Hindenburg agreed to allow Hitler to become chancellor (on January 30, 1933) and form a new government.

Within two months, Hitler had laid the foundations for the Nazis' complete control of Germany. The day after a fire broke out in the Reichstag building (February 27), supposedly set by the Communists, Hitler convinced President Hindenburg to issue a decree that gave the government emergency powers. It suspended all basic rights of citizens for the duration of the emergency, thus enabling the Nazis to arrest and imprison anyone without redress. The final step in Hitler's "legal seizure" of power came on March 23 when a two-thirds majority of the Reichstag passed the Enabling Act, which empowered the government to dispense with constitutional forms for four years while it issued laws that would deal with the country's problems. In effect, Hitler became a dictator appointed by parliament.

With their new source of power, the Nazis acted quickly to enforce *Gleichschaltung*, the coordination of all institutions under Nazi control. The civil service was purged of Jews and democratic elements, concentration camps were established for opponents of the new regime, the autonomy of the federal states was eliminated, trade unions were dissolved, and all political parties except the Nazis were abolished. By the end of the summer of 1933, within seven months of being appointed chancellor, Hitler and the Nazis had established the foundations for a totalitarian state. When Hindenburg died on August 2, 1934, the office of president was abolished, and Hitler became the sole ruler of Germany. Public officials and soldiers were all required to take a personal oath of loyalty to Hitler as the "*Führer* [leader] of the German Reich and people."

The Nazi State, 1933–1939 Having demolished the parliamentary republic, Hitler now felt that the real task was at hand: to develop the "total state." Hitler's aims had not been simply power for power's sake; he had larger ideological goals. The development of an "Aryan" racial state that would dominate Europe and possibly the world for generations to come required a movement in which the German people would be actively involved, not passively cowed by force. Hitler stated:

> We must develop organizations in which an individual's entire life can take place. Then every activity and every need of every individual will be regulated by the collectivity represented by the party. There is no longer any arbitrary will, there are no longer any free realms in which the individual belongs to himself. . . . The time of personal happiness is over.[5]

The Nazis pursued the creation of this total state in a variety of ways. Mass demonstrations and spectacles were employed to integrate the German nation into a collective fellowship and to mobilize it as an instrument for Hitler's policies (see the box on p. 503). These mass demonstrations, especially the Nuremberg party rallies that were held every September, combined the symbolism of a

The Nazi Mass Spectacle. Hitler and the Nazis made clever use of mass spectacles to rally the German people behind the Nazi regime. These mass demonstrations evoked intense enthusiasm, as is evident in this photograph of Hitler arriving at the Bückeberg near Hamelin for the Harvest Festival in 1937. Almost one million people were present for the celebration.

PROPAGANDA AND MASS MEETINGS IN NAZI GERMANY

Propaganda and mass rallies were two of the instruments that Hitler used to prepare the German people for the tasks he set before them. In the first selection, taken from a speech to a crowd at Nuremberg, Hitler describes the kind of mystical bond he hoped to create through his mass rallies. In the second excerpt, a Hamburg schoolteacher provides her impression of a Hitler rally.

Adolf Hitler, Speech at the Nuremberg Party Rally, 1936

Do we not feel once again in this hour the miracle that brought us together? Once you heard the voice of a man, and it struck deep into your hearts; it awakened you, and you followed this voice. Year after year you went after it, though him who had spoken you never even saw. You heard only a voice, and you followed it. When we meet each other here, the wonder of our coming together fills us all. Not everyone of you sees me, and I do not see everyone of you. But I feel you, and you feel me. It is the belief in our people that has made us small men great, that has made us poor men rich, that has made brave and courageous men out of us wavering, spiritless, timid folk; this belief made us see our road when we were astray; it joined us together into one whole! . . . You come, that . . . you may, once in a while, gain the feeling that now we are together; we are with him and he with us, and we are now Germany!

A Teacher's Impression of a Hitler Rally

The April sun shone hot like in summer and turned everything into a picture of gay expectation. There was immaculate order and discipline, although the police left the whole square to the stewards and stood on the sidelines. Nobody spoke of "Hitler," always just "the Führer," "the Führer says," "the Führer wants," and what he said and wanted seemed right and good. The hours passed, the sun shone, expectations rose. In the background, at the edge of the track there were columns of carriers like ammunition carriers. . . . Aeroplanes above us. Testing of the loudspeakers, buzzing of the cine-cameras. It was nearly 3 P.M. "The Führer is coming!" A ripple went through the crowds. Around the speaker's platform one could see hands raised in the Hitler salute. A speaker opened the meeting, abused the "system," nobody listened to him. A second speaker welcomed Hitler and made way for the man who had drawn 120,000 people of all classes and ages. There stood Hitler in a simple black coat and looked over the crowd, waiting—a forest of swastika pennants swished up, the jubilation of this moment was given vent in a roaring salute. Main theme: Out of parties shall grow a nation, the German nation. He censured the "system" ("I want to know what there is left to be ruined in this state!"). "On the way here Socialists confronted me with a poster, 'Turn back, Adolf Hitler.' Thirteen years ago I was a simple unknown soldier. I went my way. I never turned back. Nor shall I turn back now." Otherwise he made no personal attacks, nor any promises, vague or definite. His voice was hoarse after all his speaking during the previous days. When the speech was over, there was roaring enthusiasm and applause. Hitler saluted, gave his thanks, the Horst Wessel song sounded out across the course. Hitler was helped into his coat. Then he went.—How many look up to him with touching faith! as their helper, their savior, their deliverer from unbearable distress—to him who rescues the Prussian prince, the scholar, the clergyman, the farmer, the worker, the unemployed, who rescues them from the parties back into the nation.

In Hitler's view, what do mass meetings accomplish for his movement? How do mass rallies further the development of nationalism?

religious service with the merriment of a popular amusement. They had great appeal and usually evoked mass enthusiasm and excitement.

Some features of the state apparatus of Hitler's total state seem contradictory. One usually thinks of Nazi Germany as having an all-powerful government that maintained absolute control and order. In truth, Nazi Germany was the scene of almost constant personal and institutional conflict, which resulted in administrative chaos. Incessant struggle characterized relationships within the party, within the state, and between party and state. By fostering rivalry within the party and between party and state, Hitler became the ultimate decision maker.

Hitler and the Nazis also established control in the economic sphere. Although the regime pursued the use of public works projects and "pump-priming" grants to private construction firms to foster employment and end the depression, there is little doubt that rearmament was a far more important contributor to solving the unemployment problem. Unemployment dropped to 2.6 million in 1934 and less than half a million in 1937. The regime claimed full credit for solving Germany's economic woes, an important factor that led many Germans to accept the new regime, despite its excesses.

For those who needed coercion, the Nazi total state had its instruments of terror and repression. Especially important was the *Schutzstaffel*, or SS. Originally created as Hitler's personal bodyguard, the SS, under the direction of Heinrich Himmler (1900–1945), came to control all of the regular and secret police forces. Himmler and the SS functioned on the basis of two principles: terror and ideology. Terror included repression and murder: secret police, criminal police, concentration camps, and later execution squads and death camps for the extermination of the Jews. For Himmler, the primary goal of the SS was to ensure the dominance of the Aryan master race.

Other institutions, such as the Catholic and Protestant churches, primary and secondary schools, and universities, were also brought under the control of the Nazi total state. Nazi professional organizations and leagues were formed for civil servants, teachers, women, farmers, doctors, and lawyers. Because the early indoctrination of youth would create the foundation for a strong totalitarian state for the future, youth organizations, the *Hitler Jugend* (Hitler Youth) and its female counterpart, the *Bund Deutscher Mädel* (League of German Maidens), were given special attention. The oath required of Hitler Youth members demonstrates the degree of dedication expected of youth in the Nazi state: "In the presence of this blood banner, which represents our Führer, I swear to devote all my energies and my strength to the savior of our country, Adolf Hitler. I am willing and ready to give up my life for him, so help me God."

Women played a crucial role in the Aryan racial state as bearers of the children who would bring about the triumph of the Aryan race. To the Nazis, the differences between men and women were quite natural. Men were warriors and political leaders, while women were destined to be wives and mothers. Motherhood was also exalted in an annual ceremony on August 12, Hitler's mother's birthday, when Hitler awarded the German Mother's Cross to a select group of German mothers. Those with four children received a bronze cross, those with six a silver cross, and those with eight or more a gold cross.

Nazi ideas determined employment opportunities for women. The Nazis hoped to drive women out of heavy industry or other jobs that might hinder women from bearing healthy children, as well as certain professions, including university teaching, law, and medicine, which were considered inappropriate for women, especially married women. The Nazis encouraged women to pursue professional occupations that had direct practical application, such as social work and nursing. In addition to restrictive legislation against females, the Nazi regime pushed its campaign against working women with such poster slogans as "Get hold of pots and pans and broom and sooner you will find a groom!"

The Nazi total state was intended to be an Aryan racial state. From its beginning, the Nazi Party embraced Hitler's strong anti-Semitic beliefs. Once in power, the Nazis translated these ideas into anti-Semitic policies. In September 1935, the Nazis announced new racial laws at the annual party rally in Nuremberg. These "Nuremberg laws" excluded German Jews from German citizenship, forbade marriages and extramarital relations between Jews and German citizens, and essentially separated Jews from the Germans politically, socially, and legally. They were the natural extension of Hitler's professed superiority of the pure Aryan race.

Another considerably more violent phase of anti-Jewish activity took place in 1938 and 1939; it was initiated on November 9–10, 1938, the infamous *Kristallnacht*, or Night of Shattered Glass. The assassination of a low-

CHRONOLOGY Nazi Germany	
Hitler as Munich politician	1919–1923
Beer Hall Putsch	1923 (November)
Election of Hindenburg as president	1925
Hitler as chancellor	1933 (January 30)
Reichstag fire	1933 (February 27)
Enabling Act	1933 (March 23)
Death of Hindenburg; Hitler as sole ruler	1934 (August 2)
Nuremberg laws	1935
Kristallnacht	1938 (November 9–10)

ranking secretary in the German embassy in Paris by a Polish Jew became the excuse for a Nazi-led destructive rampage against the Jews in Germany in which synagogues were burned, seven thousand Jewish businesses were destroyed, and at least one hundred Jews were killed. Moreover, thirty thousand Jewish males were rounded up and sent to concentration camps. Further drastic steps followed: Jews were barred from all public buildings and prohibited from owning, managing, or working in any retail store. Finally, under the direction of the SS, Jews were encouraged to "emigrate from Germany." After the outbreak of World War II, the policy of emigration was replaced by a more gruesome one.

The Soviet Union

Another kind of totalitarianism took shape in the Soviet Union. The civil war in Russia had taken an enormous toll of life. Drought, which caused a great famine between 1920 and 1922, claimed as many as five million lives. Industrial collapse paralleled the agricultural disaster. By 1921, industrial output was only 20 percent of its 1913 level. Russia was exhausted. As Leon Trotsky said, "The collapse of the productive forces surpassed anything of the kind that history had ever seen. The country, and the government with it, were at the very edge of the abyss."[6]

Lenin's Policies In March 1921, Lenin pulled Russia back from the abyss by establishing his **New Economic Policy** (NEP), a modified version of the old capitalist system. Peasants were now allowed to sell their produce openly, and retail stores and small industries that employed fewer than twenty employees could now operate under private ownership; heavy industry, banking, and mines remained in the hands of the government. In 1922, Lenin and the Communists merged Russia with several smaller adjacent states to form the Union of Soviet Socialist Republics, known by its initials as the USSR and commonly called the Soviet Union. Already by that year, a revived market and a good harvest had brought the famine to an end; Soviet agriculture climbed to 75 percent of its prewar level. Industry, especially state-owned heavy industry, fared less well and continued to stagnate. Overall, the NEP had saved the Soviet Union from complete economic disaster even though Lenin and other leading Communists intended it to be only a temporary, tactical retreat from the goals of communism.

In the meantime, Lenin and the Communists were strengthening their one-party authoritarian state. The number of bureaucrats increased dramatically and soon constituted a new elite with the best jobs, food, and dwellings. Even Lenin pronounced warnings about the widening power of the bureaucracy that he had helped create.

The Struggle for Power   Lenin's death in 1924 provoked a struggle for power among the seven members of the Politburo, the institution that had become the leading organ of the party. The Politburo was severely divided over the future direction of the Soviet Union. The Left, led by Leon Trotsky, wanted to end the NEP and launch the Soviet Union on the path of rapid industrialization. This group also believed that survival of the revolutionary vision depended on spreading communism abroad. The Right rejected the cause of world revolution and wanted instead to concentrate on constructing a socialist state at home.

These ideological divisions were underscored by an intense personal rivalry between Leon Trotsky and Joseph Stalin. In 1924, Trotsky held the post of commissar of war and was the leading spokesman for the Left in the Politburo. Joseph Stalin (1879–1953) was content to hold the dull bureaucratic job of party general secretary. But Stalin was a good organizer, and the other members of the Politburo soon found that the position of party secretary was really the most important in the party hierarchy. Stalin used his post as party general secretary to gain control of the Communist Party. Trotsky was expelled from the party in 1927. By 1929, Stalin had succeeded in eliminating the old Bolsheviks of the revolutionary era from the Politburo and establishing a dictatorship so powerful that the Russian tsars of old would have been envious.

The Stalin Era, 1929–1939   Stalin made a significant shift in economic policy in 1928 when he launched his first five-year plan. Its real goal was nothing less than the transformation of the Soviet Union from an agricultural country into an industrial state virtually overnight. Instead of consumer goods, the first five-year plan emphasized maximum production of capital goods and armaments and succeeded in quadrupling the production of heavy machinery and doubling oil production. Between 1928 and 1937, during the first two five-year plans, steel production increased from 4 to 18 million tons per year and hard coal output went from 36 to 128 million tons.

The social and political costs of industrialization were enormous. While the industrial labor force increased by millions between 1932 and 1940, total investment in housing actually declined after 1929, with the result that

CHRONOLOGY	The Soviet Union
New Economic Policy begins in Russia	1921
Formation of the Soviet Union	1922
Death of Lenin	1924
Trotsky's expulsion from the Communist Party	1927
First five-year plan	1928–1932
Start of Stalin's dictatorship	1929
Second five-year plan	1933–1937
Stalin's purges	1936–1938

millions of workers and their families lived in pitiful conditions. Real wages in industry also declined by 43 percent between 1928 and 1940, and strict laws limited workers' freedom of movement. To inspire and pacify the workers, government propaganda stressed the need for sacrifice to build the new socialist state.

Rapid industrialization was accompanied by an equally rapid collectivization of agriculture. Stalin believed that the capital needs for industrial growth could be gained by creating agricultural surpluses through eliminating private farms and pushing people into **collective farms** (see the box on p. 506). By eliminating private property, a Communist ideal would also be achieved.

By 1930, some 10 million peasant households had been collectivized; by 1934, the Soviet Union's 26 million family farms had been reorganized into 250,000 collective units. This was done at tremendous cost, since Stalin did not hesitate to starve the peasants, especially in the Ukraine, to gain their compliance with the policy of collectivization. Stalin himself is supposed to have told Winston Churchill during World War II that ten million peasants died in the artificially created famines of 1932 and 1933. The only concession Stalin made to the peasants was to allow each farmworker to have one tiny, privately owned garden plot.

Stalin's program of rapid industrialization entailed additional costs as well. To achieve his goals, Stalin strengthened his control over the party. Bureaucrats who resisted were sent to forced-labor camps in Siberia. Stalin's desire for sole control of decision making also led to purges of the old Bolsheviks, army officers, diplomats, union officials, party members, intellectuals, and numerous ordinary citizens. Estimates are that between 1936 and 1938, eight million Soviets were arrested; millions were sent to Siberian labor camps, from which they never returned.

Troubled by a rapidly declining birthrate, Stalin also reversed much of the permissive social legislation of the early 1920s. Advocating complete equality of rights for women, the Communists had made divorce and abortion easy to obtain while also encouraging women to work outside the home. After Stalin came to power, the family was praised as a miniature collective in which parents were responsible for inculcating values of duty, discipline,

THE FORMATION OF COLLECTIVE FARMS

*A*ccompanying the rapid industrialization of the Soviet Union was the collectivization of agriculture, a feat that involved nothing less than transforming Russia's 26 million family farms into 250,000 collective farms (*kolkhozes*). This selection provides a firsthand account of how the process worked.

Max Belov, *The History of a Collective Farm*

General collectivization in our village was brought about in the following manner: Two representatives of the [Communist] Party arrived in the village. All the inhabitants were summoned by the ringing of the church bell to a meeting at which the policy of general collectivization was announced. ...The upshot was that although the meeting lasted two days, from the viewpoint of the Party representatives nothing was accomplished.

After this setback the Party representatives divided the village into two sections and worked each one separately. Two more officials were sent to reinforce the first two. A meeting of our section of the village was held in a stable which had previously belonged to a kulak [wealthy farmer]. The meeting dragged on until dark. Suddenly someone threw a brick at the lamp, and in the dark the peasants began to beat the Party representatives who jumped out the window and escaped from the village barely alive. The following day seven people were arrested. The militia was called in and stayed in the village until the peasants, realizing their helplessness, calmed down....

By the end of 1930 there were two kolkhozes in our village. Though at first these collectives embraced at most only 70 percent of the peasant households, in the months that followed they gradually absorbed more and more of them.

In these kolkhozes the great bulk of the land was held and worked communally, but each peasant household owned a house of some sort, a small plot of ground and perhaps some livestock. All the members of the kolkhoz were required to work on the kolkhoz a certain number of days each month; the rest of the time they were allowed to work on their own holdings. They derived their income partly from what they grew on their garden strips and partly from their work in the kolkhoz.

When the harvest was over, and after the farm had met its obligations to the state and to various special funds (for instance, seed, etc.) and had sold on the market whatever undesignated produce was left, the remaining produce and the farm's monetary income were divided among the kolkhoz members according to the number of "labor days" each one had contributed to the farm's work....It was in 1930 that the kolkhoz members first received their portions out of the "communal kettle." After they had received their earnings, at the rate of 1 kilogram of grain and 55 kopecks per labor day, one of them remarked, "You will live, but you will be very, very thin."

In the spring of 1931 a tractor worked the fields of the kolkhoz for the first time. The tractor was "capable of plowing every kind of hard soil and virgin soil," as Party representatives told us at the meeting in celebration of its arrival. The peasants did not then know that these "steel horses" would carry away a good part of the harvest in return for their work....

By late 1932 more than 80 percent of the peasant households....had been collectivized....That year the peasants harvested a good crop and had hopes that the calculations would work out to their advantage and would help strengthen them economically. These hopes were in vain. The kolkhoz workers received only 200 grams of flour per labor day for the first half of the year; the remaining grain, including the seed fund, was taken by the government. The peasants were told that industrialization of the country, then in full swing, demanded grain and sacrifices from them.

What was the purpose of collectivizing Soviet agriculture? According to Belov, why did the peasants of his village assault the Party representatives? What was the result of their protest?

---

and hard work. Abortion was outlawed, and divorced fathers who did not support their children were fined heavily. The regime now praised motherhood and urged women to have large families as a patriotic duty. But by this time, many Soviet women worked in factories and spent many additional hours in line waiting to purchase increasingly scarce consumer goods. There was no dramatic increase in the birthrate.

Authoritarian States

A number of other states in Europe were not totalitarian but did have conservative authoritarian governments. These states adopted some of the trappings of totalitarian states, especially wide police powers, but their greatest concern was not the creation of a mass movement aimed at the establishment of a new kind of society but rather the defense of the existing social order. Consequently, the **authoritarian states** tended to limit the participation of the masses and were content with passive obedience rather than active involvement in the goals of the regime.

Eastern Europe   Nowhere had the map of Europe been more drastically altered by World War I than in eastern Europe. The new states of Austria, Poland, Czechoslovakia, and the kingdom of the Serbs, Croats, and Slovenes (Yugoslavia) adopted parliamentary systems, while the preexisting kingdoms of Romania and Bulgaria gained

Stalin at His Desk. Terror played an important role in the authoritarian system established by Joseph Stalin. In this photograph, Stalin is shown at his desk, possibly signing what might be a death warrant. As the terror increased in the late 1930s, Stalin signed such lists every day.

Eastern Europe in the 1920s

new parliamentary constitutions in 1920. Greece became a republic in 1924. Hungary's government was parliamentary in form but was controlled by its landed aristocrats. At the beginning of the 1920s, political democracy seemed well established, but almost everywhere in eastern Europe, parliamentary governments soon gave way to authoritarian regimes.

Several problems helped create this situation. Eastern European states had little tradition of liberalism or parliamentary politics and no substantial middle class to support them. Then, too, these states were primarily agrarian. Much of the land was still dominated by large landowners who feared the growth of peasant parties with schemes for land redistribution. Ethnic conflicts also threatened to tear these countries apart. Fearful of land reform, agrarian upheaval, and ethnic conflict, powerful landowners and the churches looked to authoritarian governments to maintain the old system. In eastern Europe, only Czechoslovakia, with its substantial middle class, liberal tradition, and strong industrial base, managed to maintain political democracy.

Franco's Spain Elsewhere on the Continent, the failure of political democracy was particularly dramatic in Spain. Led by General Francisco Franco (1892–1975), Spanish military forces revolted against the democratic govern-

ment in 1936 and launched a brutal and bloody civil war that lasted three years. Foreign intervention complicated the Spanish Civil War. Franco's forces were aided by arms, money, and men from the fascist regimes of Italy and Germany while the government was assisted by forty thousand foreign volunteers and trucks, planes, tanks, and military advisers from the Soviet Union. After Franco's forces captured Madrid on March 28, 1939, the Spanish Civil War finally came to an end. Franco soon established a dictatorship that favored large landowners, businessmen, and the Catholic clergy—yet another traditional, conservative, authoritarian regime.

The Expansion of Mass Culture and Mass Leisure

The decade was known as the Roaring Twenties for the exuberance of its popular culture. Berlin, the capital of Germany, became the entertainment center of Europe with its theaters, cabarets, cinemas, and jazz clubs. The Roaring Twenties was especially known for its dance crazes. People danced in clubs and dance halls, at home, and in the streets, doing the Charleston, the Bunny Hug, and a variety of other dances. An American singer and dancer, Josephine Baker (1906–1975), became especially well known in Europe, appearing at European clubs featuring American "Negro" jazz music. One critic said, "She dances for hours without the slightest trace of tiredness." She became a symbol of the popular "flapper," the unconventional and lively young woman of the 1920s.

So popular was jazz, a musical form that had originated with African American musicians in the United States, that the 1920s also became known as the Jazz Age.

Admired for its improvisations and forceful rhythms, jazz spread throughout the Western world as King Oliver, Bix Beiderbecke, Jelly Roll Morton, and others wrote and played some of the greatest jazz music of the time.

Radio and Movies

A series of technological inventions in the late nineteenth century had prepared the way for a revolution in mass communications. Especially important was Marconi's discovery of "wireless" radio waves. But it was not until June 16, 1920, that a radio broadcast (of a concert by soprano Nellie Melba from London) for a mass audience was attempted. Permanent broadcasting facilities were then constructed in the United States, Europe, and Japan during 1921 and 1922, and mass production of radios (receiving sets) also began. In 1926, when the British Broadcasting Corporation (BBC) was made into a public corporation, there were 2.2 million radios in Great Britain. By the end of the 1930s, there were 9 million. The technical foundation for motion pictures had already been developed in the 1890s when short movies were produced as novelties for music halls. Shortly before World War I, full-length features, such as the Italian film *Quo Vadis* and the American film *Birth of a Nation,* became available and made it apparent that cinema had become a new form of mass entertainment.

The increased size of mass audiences and the ability of radio and cinema to provide an immediate experience added new dimensions to mass culture. Favorite film actors and actresses became stars whose lives then became subject to public adoration and scrutiny. Sensuous actresses such as Marlene Dietrich, whose appearance in the early sound film *The Blue Angel* catapulted her to fame, projected new images of women's sexuality.

Of course, mass culture could also be used for political purposes. Film, for example, had propaganda potential, a possibility not lost on Joseph Goebbels (1897–1945), the propaganda minister of Nazi Germany. Believing that film constituted one of the "most modern and scientific means of influencing the masses," Goebbels created a special film section in his Propaganda Ministry and encouraged the production of both documentaries and popular feature films that carried the Nazi message. *The Triumph of the Will,* a prime example, was a documentary of the 1934 Nuremberg party rally that forcefully conveyed the power of Nazism to viewers.

Mass Leisure

Mass leisure activities had developed at the turn of the century, but new work patterns after World War I dramatically expanded the amount of free time available to take advantage of them. By 1920, the eight-hour day had become the norm for many office and factory workers in northern and western Europe.

Professional sporting events for mass audiences became an important aspect of mass leisure. Attendance at association football (soccer) games soared, and the inauguration of the World Cup contest in 1930 intensified the nationalistic rivalries that came to surround mass sporting events. Increased attendance also made the 1920s and 1930s a great era of stadium building. The Germans built a stadium in Berlin for the 1936 Olympics that seated 140,000 people.

Travel opportunities also added new dimensions to mass leisure activities. The military use of aircraft during World War I helped improve planes and make civilian air travel a reality. The first regular international mail service began in 1919, and regular passenger service soon followed. Although air travel remained the preserve of the wealthy or the adventurous, trains, buses, and private cars made excursions to beaches or holiday resorts more popular and possible for the less wealthy.

Mass leisure provided totalitarian regimes with new ways to control their populations. The Nazi regime created a program known as *Kraft durch Freude* (Strength Through Joy) to coordinate the free time of the working class by offering a variety of activities, including concerts, operas, films, guided tours, and sporting events. Especially popular were the inexpensive vacations, essentially modern package tours. These could be cruises to Scandinavia or the Mediterranean or, more likely for workers, shorter trips to various sites in Germany. Essentially, *Kraft durch Freude* enabled the German government to supervise recreational activities. In doing so, the state imposed new rules and regulations on previously spontaneous activities, thus breaking down old group solidarities and allowing these groups to be guided by the goals of the state.

Cultural and Intellectual Trends in the Interwar Years

The artistic and intellectual innovations of the pre–World War I period, which many Europeans found shocking, had been the preserve primarily of a small group of avant-garde artists and intellectuals. In the 1920s and 1930s, these adventurous approaches became more widespread. What made the prewar avant-garde culture so much more acceptable in the 1920s and the 1930s? Perhaps most important was the impact of World War I.

Four years of devastating war left many Europeans with a profound sense of despair and disillusionment. To many people, the experiences of World War I seemed to confirm the prewar avant-garde belief that human beings were really violent and irrational animals who were incapable of creating a sane and rational world. The Great Depression, as well as the growth of fascist movements based on violence and the degradation of individual rights, only added to the uncertainties generated by World War I.

Political and economic uncertainties were paralleled by social insecurities. World War I had served to break down many traditional middle-class attitudes, especially toward sexuality. In the 1920s, women's physical appearance changed dramatically. Short skirts, short hair, the use of cosmetics once thought suitable only for prostitutes, and the new practice of suntanning gave women a radically different image. This change in physical appearance, which exposed more of a woman's body than ever before, was also accompanied by frank discussions of sexual matters. In 1926, the Dutch physician Theodor van de Velde published *Ideal Marriage: Its Physiology and Technique*, which described female and male anatomy, discussed birth control techniques, and glorified sexual pleasure in marriage. Translated into a number of languages, it became an international best-seller. New ideas on sexuality and birth control were also spread to the working classes by family planning clinics, such as those of Margaret Sanger in the United States and Marie Stopes in Britain.

Nightmares and New Visions: Art and Music

Uncertainty also pervaded the cultural and intellectual achievements of the interwar years. Postwar artistic trends were largely a working out of the implications of prewar developments. Abstract painting, for example, became ever more popular as many pioneering artists of the early twentieth century matured between the two world wars. In addition, prewar fascination with the absurd and the unconscious contents of the mind seemed even more appropriate after the nightmarish landscapes of World War I battlefronts. This gave rise to both the Dada movement and Surrealism.

Dadaism   **Dadaism** attempted to enshrine the purposelessness of life. Tristan Tzara, a Romanian French poet and one of the founders of Dadaism, expressed the Dadaist contempt for the Western tradition in a lecture in 1922: "The acts of life have no beginning or end. Everything happens in a completely idiotic way. . . . Like everything in life, Dada is useless."[7] Revolted by the insanity of life, the Dadaists tried to give it expression by creating anti-art. In the hands of Hannah Höch (1889–1978), however, Dada became an instrument to comment on women's roles in the new mass culture.

Surrealism   More important as an artistic movement was **Surrealism**, which sought a reality beyond the material, sensible world and found it in the unconscious through the portrayal of fantasies, dreams, or nightmares. Employing logic to portray the illogical, the Surrealists created disturbing and evocative images. The Spaniard Salvador Dalí (1904–1989) became the high priest of Surrealism and in his mature phase became a master of representational Surrealism. In *The Persistence of Memory*, Dalí portrayed recognizable objects divorced from their normal context. By placing these objects into unrecognizable relationships, Dalí created a disturbing world in which the irrational had become tangible.

Functionalism in Architecture   The move to **functionalism** in modern architecture also became more

Hannah Höch, *Cut with the Kitchen Knife Dada Through the Last Weimar Beer Belly Cultural Epoch of Germany*.   Hannah Höch, a prominent figure in the postwar Dada movement, used photomontage to create images that reflected on women's issues. In *Cut with the Kitchen Knife*, she combined pictures of German political leaders with sports stars, Dada artists, and scenes from urban life. One major theme emerged: the confrontation between the anti-Dada world of German political leaders and the Dada world of revolutionary ideals. Höch associated women with Dada and the new world.

widespread in the 1920s and 1930s. First conceived near the end of the nineteenth century, functionalism meant that buildings should be useful, fulfilling the purpose for which they were constructed. Art and engineering were to be unified, and all unnecessary ornamentation was to be stripped away. Especially important in the spread of functionalism was the Bauhaus school, founded in 1919 at Weimar, Germany, by the Berlin architect Walter Gropius. The Bauhaus teaching staff consisted of architects, artists, and designers who worked together to combine the study of fine arts (painting and sculpture) with the applied arts (printing, weaving, and furniture making).

Art in Nazi Germany   The postwar acceptance of modern art forms was by no means universal. Many traditionalists denounced what they considered degeneracy and decadence in the arts. This was especially evident in the totalitarian state of Nazi Germany. In the

Salvador Dalí, *The Persistence of Memory, 1931*. Surrealism was an important artistic movement between the wars. Influenced by the theories of Freudian psychology, Surrealists sought to reveal the world of the unconscious, or the "greater reality" that they believed existed beyond the world of physical appearances. As is evident in this painting, Salvador Dalí sought to portray the world of dreams by painting recognizable objects in unrecognizable relationships.

1920s, Weimar Germany was one of the chief European centers for modern arts and sciences. Hitler and the Nazis rejected modern art as "degenerate" or "Jewish" art. In 1937, Hitler said, "The people regarded this art as the outcome of an impudent and unashamed arrogance or of a simply shocking lack of skill;...these achievements which might have been produced by untalented children of from eight to ten years old could never be valued as an expression of our own times or of the German future."[8] Hitler and the Nazis believed that they had laid the foundation for a new and genuine German art, which would glorify the strong, the healthy, and the heroic—mirroring the supposed attributes of the Aryan race.

A New Style in Music   At the beginning of the twentieth century, a revolution in music parallel to the revolution in art had begun with the work of Igor Stravinsky. But Stravinksy still wrote music in a definite key. The Viennese composer Arnold Schönberg (1874–1951) began to experiment with a radically new style by creating musical pieces devoid of tonality, a system that he called atonal music.

The Search for the Unconscious in Literature

The interest in the unconscious evident in Surrealism was also apparent in the development of new literary techniques that emerged in the 1920s. One of its most apparent manifestations was a "stream of consciousness" technique in which the writer presented an interior monologue or a report of the innermost thoughts of each character. The most famous example of this genre was written by the Irish exile James Joyce (1882–1941). His *Ulysses,* published in 1922, told the story of one day in the life of ordinary people in Dublin by following the flow of their inner thoughts.

The German writer Hermann Hesse (1877–1962) dealt with the unconscious in a different way. His novels reflected the influence of new psychological theories and Eastern religions and focused on, among other things, the spiritual loneliness of modern human beings in a mechanized urban society. *Demian* was a psychoanalytical study of incest, and *Steppenwolf* mirrored the psychological confusion of modern existence. Hesse's novels had a large impact on German youth in the 1920s (see the box on p. 511). He won the Nobel Prize for literature in 1946.

The Unconscious in Psychology

The growing concern with the unconscious also led to greater popular interest in psychology. The full impact of Sigmund Freud's thought was not felt until after World War I. The 1920s witnessed a worldwide acceptance of his ideas. Freudian terms such as *unconscious, repression, id,* and *ego* entered the popular vocabulary. Popularization of Freud's ideas led to the widespread misconception that an uninhibited sex life was necessary for mental health. Psychoanalysis developed into a major profession, especially in the United States, but Freud's ideas did not go unchallenged, even by his own pupils. One of the most prominent challenges came from Carl Jung.

A disciple of Freud, Carl Jung (1875–1961) came to believe that Freud's theories were too narrow and based on Freud's own personal biases. Jung's study of dreams—his own and others—led him to diverge sharply from Freud. Whereas for Freud the unconscious was the seat of repressed desires or appetites, for Jung it was an opening to deep spiritual needs and ever-greater vistas for humans.

Jung viewed the unconscious as twofold: a "personal unconscious" and a deeper "collective unconscious." The

HESSE AND THE UNCONSCIOUS

The novels of Hermann Hesse made a strong impact on young people, first in Germany in the 1920s and then in the United States in the 1960s after they had been translated into English. Many of these young people shared Hesse's fascination with the unconscious and his dislike of modern industrial civilization. This excerpt from *Demian* spoke directly to many of them.

Hermann Hesse, *Demian*

The following spring I was to leave the preparatory school and enter a university. I was still undecided, however, as to where and what I was to study. I had grown a thin mustache, I was a full-grown man, and yet I was completely helpless and without a goal in life. Only one thing was certain: the voice within me, the dream image. I felt the duty to follow this voice blindly wherever it might lead me. But it was difficult and each day I rebelled against it anew. Perhaps I was mad, as I thought at moments; perhaps I was not like other men? But I was able to do the same things the others did; with a little effort and industry I could read Plato, was able to solve problems in trigonometry or follow a chemical analysis. There was only one thing I could not do: wrest the dark secret goal from myself and keep it before me as others did who knew exactly what they wanted to be—professors, lawyers, doctors, artists, however long this would take them and whatever difficulties and advantages this decision would bear in its wake. This I could not do. Perhaps I would become something similar, but how was I to know? Perhaps I would have to continue my search for years on end and would not become anything, and would not reach a goal. Perhaps I would reach this goal but it would turn out to be an evil, dangerous, horrible one?

I wanted only to try to live in accord with the promptings which came from my true self. Why was that so very difficult?

How does Hesse's interest in the unconscious appear in this excerpt? Why was a dislike of mechanized society particularly intense after World War I?

collective unconscious was the repository of memories that all human beings share and consisted of archetypes, mental forms or images that appear in dreams. The archetypes are common to all people and have a special energy that gives rise to myths, religions, and philosophies. To Jung, the mind was only in part personal or individual because the origin of the archetypes was buried so far in the past that they seemed to have no human source. Their function was to bring the original mind of humans into a new, higher state of consciousness.

The "Heroic Age of Physics"

The prewar revolution in physics initiated by Max Planck and Albert Einstein continued in the interwar period. In fact, Ernest Rutherford (1871–1937), one of the physicists responsible for demonstrating that the atom could be split, dubbed the 1920s the "heroic age of physics."

The new picture of the universe that was unfolding continued to undermine the old scientific certainties of classical physics. Classical physics had rested on the fundamental belief that all phenomena could be predicted if they could be completely understood; thus the weather could be predicted if we knew everything about the wind, sun, and water. In 1927, the German physicist Werner Heisenberg (1901–1976) upset this belief when he posited the **uncertainty principle.** In essence, Heisenberg suggested that no one could determine the path of an electron because the very act of observing the electron by illuminating it with light affected the electron's location. The uncertainty principle was more than an explanation for the path of an electron, however; it was a new worldview. Heisenberg shattered confidence in predictability and dared to propose that uncertainty was at the root of all the physical laws.

CONCLUSION

The devastation wrought by World War I dashed the liberal optimism of the prewar era. Yet many people in the 1920s still hoped that the progress of Western civilization, so seemingly evident before 1914, could somehow be restored. These hopes proved largely unfounded as plans for economic reconstruction gave way to inflation and to an even more devastating economic depression at the end of the 1920s. Likewise, confidence in political democracy was soon shattered by the rise of authoritarian governments that not only restricted individual freedoms but, in the cases of Italy, Germany, and the Soviet Union, sought even greater control over the lives of their subjects in order to manipulate and guide them to achieve the goals of their totalitarian regimes. For many people, despite the loss of personal freedom, these mass movements at least offered some sense of security in a world that seemed fraught with uncertainties.

These uncertainties grew even greater as Europeans, after a brief twenty-year interlude, again plunged into war, this time on a scale even more horrendous than that of World War I. The twentieth-century crisis begun in 1914 seemed only to be worsening in 1939.

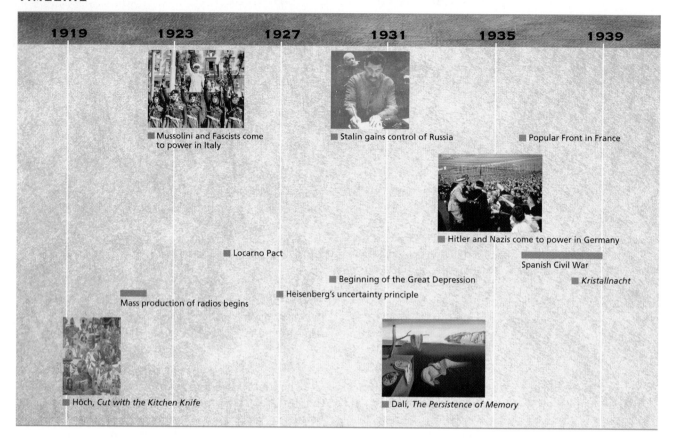

1919	1923	1927	1931	1935	1939

■ Mussolini and Fascists come to power in Italy

■ Stalin gains control of Russia

■ Popular Front in France

■ Hitler and Nazis come to power in Germany

■ Locarno Pact

Spanish Civil War

■ Beginning of the Great Depression

■ Kristallnacht

■ Heisenberg's uncertainty principle

Mass production of radios begins

■ Höch, *Cut with the Kitchen Knife*

■ Dalí, *The Persistence of Memory*

NOTES

1. R. Paxton, *Europe in the Twentieth Century*, 2d ed. (San Diego, Calif., 1985), p. 237.
2. B. Mussolini, "The Doctrine of Fascism," in A. Lyttleton, ed., *Italian Fascisms from Pareto to Gentile* (London, 1973), p. 42.
3. Quoted in A. De Grand, "Women Under Italian Fascism," *Historical Journal*, 19 (1976): 958–959.
4. Quoted in J. Noakes and G. Pridham, eds., *Nazism, 1919–1945* (Exeter, England, 1983), vol. 1, pp. 50–51.
5. Quoted in J. Fest, *Hitler*, trans. R. Winston and C. Winston (New York, 1974), p. 418.
6. I. Howe, ed., *The Basic Writings of Trotsky* (London, 1963), p. 162.
7. T. Tzara, "Lecture on Dada," in R. Motherwell, ed., *The Dada Painters and Poets* (New York, 1951), p. 52.
8. N. H. Baynes, ed., *The Speeches of Adolf Hitler, 1922–1939* (Oxford, 1942), vol. 1, p. 591.

SUGGESTIONS FOR FURTHER READING

For a general introduction to the interwar period, see **M. Kitchen, *Europe Between the Wars: A Political History*** (London, 1988), and the general survey by **R. Paxton, *Europe in the Twentieth Century*,** 2d ed. (New York, 1985). The best study on the problem of reparations is **M. Trachtenberg, *Reparations in World Politics*** (New York, 1980), which paints a positive view of French policies. On the Great Depression, see **C. P. Kindleberger, *The World in Depression, 1929–39,*** rev. ed. (Berkeley, Calif., 1986).

The best biographies of Mussolini are **D. Mack Smith, *Mussolini*** (New York, 1982), and **R.J.B. Bosworth, *Mussolini*** (London, 2002). Two brief but excellent surveys of Fascist Italy are **A. Cassels, *Fascist Italy,*** 2d ed. (Arlington Heights, Ill., 1985), and **J. Whittam, *Fascist Italy*** (New York, 1995).

On the Weimar Republic, see **P. Bookbinder, *Weimar Germany*** (New York, 1996), and **R. Henig, *The Weimar Republic, 1919–1933*** (New York, 1998). Two brief but sound surveys of Nazi Germany are **J. J. Spielvogel, *Hitler and Nazi Germany: A History,*** 5th ed. (Upper Saddle River, N.J., 2005), and **J. Dülffer, *Nazi Germany, 1933–1945*** (New York, 1996). A more detailed examination can be found in **K. P. Fischer, *Nazi Germany: A New History*** (New York, 1995). On the rise of the Nazis to power, see **R. J. Evans, *The Coming of the Third Reich*** (New York, 2004). On the Nazis in power, see **R. J. Evans, *The Third Reich in Power*** (New York, 2005). The best biographies of Hitler are **A. Bullock, *Hitler: A Study in Tyranny*** (New York, 1964); **J. Fest, *Hitler,*** trans. R. Winston and C. Winston (New York, 1974); and **I. Kershaw, *Hitler, 1889–1936: Hubris*** (New York, 1999), and **_Hitler: Nemesis_** (New York, 2000). Two works that examine the enormous literature on Hitler are **J. Lukacs, *The Hitler of History*** (New York, 1997), and **R. Rosenbaum, *Explaining Hitler*** (New York, 1998).

On women, see **C. Koonz**, *Mothers in the Fatherland: Women, the Family, and Nazi Politics* (New York, 1987). The Hitler Youth is examined in **M. Kater, Hitler Youth** (Cambridge, Mass., 2004). The books on the Holocaust cited in Chapter 27 contain background information on Nazi anti-Jewish policies between 1933 and 1939.

For a general study of other fascist movements, see **S. Payne**, *A History of Fascism* (Madison, Wis., 1996), and **R. O. Paxton,** *The Anatomy of Fascism* (New York, 2004). Starting points for the study of eastern Europe are **J. Rothschild,** *East Central Europe Between the Two World Wars* (New York, 1974), and **B. Jelavich,** *History of the Balkans, vol. 2: The Twentieth Century* (New York, 1983). On Franco, see **J.W.D. Trythall,** *El Caudillo: A Political Biography* (New York, 1970).

The collectivization of agriculture in the Soviet Union is examined in **S. Fitzpatrick,** *Stalin's Peasants: Resistance and Survival in the Russian Village After Collectivization* (New York, 1995); industrialization is covered in **H. Kuromiya,** *Stalin's Industrial Revolution: Politics and Workers, 1928–1932* (New York, 1988). On Stalin, see **R. H. McNeal,** *Stalin: Man and Ruler* (New York, 1988); **R. Tucker,** *Stalin in Power: The Revolution from Above, 1928–1941* (New York, 1990); **S. S. Montefiore,** *Stalin: The Court of the Red Tsar* (New York, 2004); and **R. W. Thurston,** *Life and Terror in Stalin's Russia* (New Haven, Conn., 1996).

The use of cinema for propaganda purposes is well examined in **D. Welch,** *Propaganda and the German Cinema* (New York, 1985).

Gender issues are discussed in **S. Pedersen,** *Family, Dependence, and the Origins of the Welfare State: Britain and France, 1914–1945* (New York, 1994), and **M. L. Roberts,** *Civilization Without Sexes: Reconstructing Gender in Postwar France, 1917–1927* (Chicago, 1994). For a study of Carl Jung, see **G. Wehr,** *Jung: A Biography* (New York, 1987).

Thomson NOW! Enter *ThomsonNOW* using the access card that is available for *Western Civilization: A Brief History.* *ThomsonNOW* will help you understand this chapter with lesson plans generated for your needs. In addition, you can read the following documents, and many more, online:

Adolf Hitler, speech

WESTERN CIVILIZATION RESOURCES

Visit the Web site for *Western Civilization: A Brief History* for resources specific to this book:

http://www.thomsonedu.com/history/spielvogel

For a variety of tools to help you succeed in this course, visit the Western Civilization Resource Center at

http://history.wadsworth.com/spielvogel

Included are quizzes, images, documents, interactive simulations, maps and timelines, movie explorations, and a wealth of other sources.

27

THE DEEPENING EUROPEAN CRISIS: WORLD WAR II

CHAPTER OUTLINE AND FOCUS QUESTIONS

Prelude to War

☐ What were Hitler's foreign policy goals, and what steps did he take to achieve them between 1933 and 1939?

The Course of World War II

☐ What were the main events of World War II in Europe and in Asia, and why were the Allies ultimately victorious?

The New Order

☐ What was the Holocaust, and what role did it play in Nazi policy?

The Home Front

☐ What were conditions like on the home front for Japan and the major Western nations involved in World War II?

Aftermath: Emergence of the Cold War

☐ How did the Allies' visions of postwar Europe differ, and how did these differences contribute to the emergence of the Cold War?

CRITICAL THINKING

☐ What was the relationship between World War I and World War II, and what were the differences in the way the wars were fought?

Adolf Hitler salutes military leaders and soldiers during a military rally

Time Life Pictures/Getty Images

$\mathcal{O}$N FEBRUARY 3, 1933, only four days after he had been appointed chancellor of Germany, Adolf Hitler met secretly with Germany's leading generals. He revealed to them his desire to remove the "cancer of democracy," create a new authoritarian leadership, and forge a new domestic unity. All Germans would need to realize that "only a struggle can save us and that everything else must be subordinated to this idea." Youth especially must be trained and their will strengthened "to fight with all means." Because Germany's living space was too small for its people, above all, Hitler said, Germany must rearm and prepare for "the conquest of new living space in the east and its ruthless Germanization." Even before he had consolidated his power, Adolf Hitler had a clear vision of his goals, and their implementation meant another European war. World War II was clearly Hitler's war. Although other countries may have helped make the war possible by not resisting Hitler's Germany earlier, Nazi Germany's actions made World War II inevitable.

This chapter focuses on the European theater of war, but both European and American armies were involved in fighting around the world. World War II was actually two major conflicts, one provoked by the ambitions of Germany in Europe and the other by the ambitions of Japan in Asia. By 1941, with the United States drawn into both, the two had merged into a single global conflict.

Although World War I has been described as a total war, World War II was even more so and was fought on a scale unheard of in history. Almost everyone in the warring countries was involved in one way or another: as soldiers; as workers in wartime industries; as ordinary citizens subject to invading armies, military occupation, or bombing raids; as refugees; or as victims of mass extermination. The world had never witnessed such widespread intentional death and destruction.◆

Prelude to War

Only twenty years after the "war to end war," the world plunged back into the nightmare of total war. The efforts at collective security in the 1920s—the League of Nations, the attempts at disarmament, the pacts and treaties—all proved meaningless in light of the growth of Nazi Germany and its deliberate scrapping of the postwar settlement in the 1930s.

The "Diplomatic Revolution," 1933–1937

World War II in Europe began in the mind of Adolf Hitler, who believed that only the "Aryans" were capable of building a great civilization. But the Germans, in his view the purest Aryans, were threatened from the east by a large mass of inferior peoples, the Slavs, who had learned to use German weapons and technology. Germany needed more land to support a larger population and be a great power. Already in the 1920s, in the second volume of *Mein Kampf*, Hitler had indicated where a National Socialist regime would find this land: "And so we National Socialists . . . take up where we broke off six hundred years ago. We stop the endless German movement to the south and west, and turn our gaze toward the land in the east. . . . If we speak of soil in Europe today, we can primarily have in mind only Russia and her vassal border states."[1] Once it had been conquered, the land of Russia could be resettled by German peasants while the Slavic population could be used as slave labor to build the Aryan racial state that would dominate Europe for a thousand years. Hitler was unequivocal: Germany must prepare for its inevitable war with the Soviet Union.

When Hitler became chancellor of Germany on January 30, 1933, Germany's situation in Europe seemed weak. The Treaty of Versailles had created a demilitarized zone on Germany's western border that would allow the French to move into the heavily industrialized parts of Germany in the event of war. To Germany's east, the smaller states, such as Poland and Czechoslovakia, had defensive treaties with France. The Versailles treaty had also limited Germany's army to 100,000 troops with no air force and limited naval forces.

Posing as a man of peace in his public speeches, Hitler emphasized that Germany wished only to revise the unfair provisions of Versailles by peaceful means and achieve Germany's rightful place among the European states. On March 9, 1935, Hitler announced the creation of a new air force and one week later the introduction of a military draft that would expand Germany's army from 100,000 to 550,000 troops. Hitler's unilateral repudiation of the Versailles treaty brought a swift reaction as France, Great Britain, and Italy condemned Germany's action and warned against future aggressive steps. But nothing concrete was done.◆

On March 7, 1936, buoyed by his conviction that the Western democracies had no intention of using force to maintain the Treaty of Versailles, Hitler sent German troops into the demilitarized Rhineland. According to the Versailles treaty, the French had the right to use force against any violation of the demilitarized Rhineland. But France would not act without British support, and the British viewed the occupation of German territory by German troops as a reasonable action by a dissatisfied power. The *London Times* noted that the Germans were only "going into their own back garden."

Meanwhile, Hitler gained new allies. In October 1935, Benito Mussolini had committed Fascist Italy to imperial expansion by invading Ethiopia. Angered by French and British opposition to his invasion, Mussolini welcomed Hitler's support and began to draw closer to the German dictator he had once called a buffoon. In October 1936, Mussolini and Hitler concluded an agreement that recognized their common political and economic interests, and one month later, Mussolini referred publicly to the new Rome-Berlin Axis. Also in November, Germany and Japan (the rising military power in the East), concluded the Anti-Comintern Pact and agreed to maintain a common front against communism. By the beginning of 1937, Hitler and Nazi Germany had achieved a "diplomatic revolution" in Europe. The Treaty of Versailles had been virtually scrapped, and Germany was once again a "world power," Hitler proclaimed.

The Path to War in Europe, 1938–1939

By the beginning of 1938, Hitler was convinced that neither the French nor the British would provide much opposition to his plans and decided to move on Austria. By threatening Austria with invasion, Hitler coerced the Austrian chancellor into putting Austrian Nazis in charge of the government. The new government promptly invited German troops to enter Austria and assist in maintaining law and order. One day later, on March 13, 1938, after his triumphal return to his native land, Hitler formally annexed Austria to Germany. Great Britain's swift acknowledgment of Hitler's action only increased the German dictator's contempt for Western weakness.

Hitler Arrives in Vienna. By threatening to invade Austria, Adolf Hitler forced the Austrian government to capitulate to his wishes. Austria was annexed to Germany. Shown here is Hitler's triumphal arrival in Vienna on March 13, 1938. Seated in the car to Hitler's right is Arthur Seyss-Inquart, Hitler's new handpicked governor of Austria.

Czechoslovakia The annexation of Austria improved Germany's strategic position in central Europe and put Germany in position for Hitler's next objective—the destruction of Czechoslovakia (see Map 27.1). This goal might have seemed unrealistic since democratic Czechoslovakia was quite prepared to defend itself and was well supported by pacts with France and the Soviet Union. Nevertheless, Hitler believed that France and Britain would not use force to defend Czechoslovakia.

He was right again. When on September 15, 1938, Hitler demanded the cession to Germany of the Sudetenland, the mountainous northwestern border area of Czechoslovakia that was home to 3.5 million ethnic Germans, and expressed his willingness to risk "world war" to achieve his objective, the British, French, Germans, and Italians—at a hastily arranged conference at Munich—reached an agreement that essentially met all of Hitler's demands. German troops were allowed to occupy the Sudetenland as the Czechs, abandoned by their Western allies, stood by helplessly. The Munich Conference was the high point of Western **appeasement** of Hitler. When Neville Chamberlain, the British prime minister, returned to England from Munich, he boasted that the Munich agreement meant "peace in our times." Hitler had promised Chamberlain that he had made his last demand. Like many German politicians, Chamberlain had believed Hitler's assurances (see the box on p. 518).

In fact, Munich confirmed Hitler's perception that the Western democracies were weak and would not fight. Increasingly, Hitler was convinced of his own infallibility, and he had by no means been appeased at Munich. In March 1939, Hitler occupied the Czech lands (Bohemia and Moravia) while the Slovaks, with Hitler's encouragement, declared their independence of the Czechs and became a puppet state (Slovakia) of Nazi Germany. On the evening of March 15, 1939, Hitler triumphantly declared in Prague that he would be known as the greatest German of them all.

Poland At last, the Western states reacted to Hitler's threat. Hitler's naked aggression made clear that his promises were utterly worthless. When Hitler began to demand the return to Germany of Danzig (which had been made a free city by the Treaty of Versailles to serve as a seaport for Poland), Britain recognized the danger and offered to protect Poland in the event of war. At the same time, both France and Britain realized that only the Soviet Union was powerful enough to help contain Nazi aggression and began political and military negotiations with Joseph Stalin and the Soviets. The West's distrust of Soviet communism, however, made an alliance unlikely.

Meanwhile, Hitler pressed on in the belief that the West would not really fight over Poland. To preclude an alliance between the West and the Soviet Union, which would create the danger of a two-front war, Hitler, ever the opportunist, negotiated his own nonaggression pact with Stalin and shocked the world with its announcement on August 23, 1939. The treaty with the Soviet Union gave Hitler the freedom to attack Poland. He told his generals, "Now Poland is in the position in which I wanted her. . . . I am only afraid that at the last moment some swine or other will yet submit to me a plan for mediation."[2] He need not have worried. On September 1, German forces invaded Poland; two days later, Britain and France declared war on Germany. Europe was again at war.

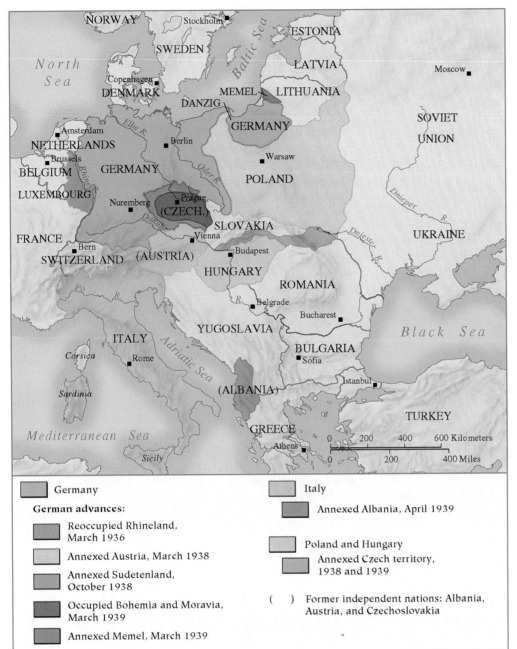

MAP 27.1 **Changes in Central Europe, 1936–1939.** Hitler's main objectives in the late 1930s were the reoccupation of the Rhineland, incorporation into a greater Germany of lands that contained German people (Austria and the Sudetenland), and the acquisition of *Lebensraum* (living space) in eastern Europe for the expansion of the German people. ❓ What aspects of Czechoslovakia's location would have made it difficult for France and Britain to come directly to its aid in 1938? 🔊 **View an animated version of this map or related maps at** http://thomsonedu.com/history/spielvogel

The Path to War in Asia

The war in Asia arose from the ambitions of Japan, whose rise to the status of world power had been swift. Economic crises in the 1930s had stifled the growth of democracy and allowed right-wing militant elements connected with the government and the armed forces to control Japanese politics and push a program of expansion. In September 1931, Japanese soldiers had seized Manchuria, an area of northeastern China that had natural resources Japan needed. During the next several years, Japan consolidated its hold on Manchuria, which it renamed Manchukuo, and then began to expand its control in North China. As Japan moved steadily southward, popular protests in Chinese cities

against Japanese aggression intensified. In July 1937, a clash between Chinese and Japanese forces broke out at Marco Polo bridge, south of Beijing, and hostilities spread. The Japanese advanced up the Yangtze valley and seized the Chinese capital of Nanjing, raping and killing thousands of innocent civilians in the process. But the Chinese Nationalist leader Chiang Kai-shek refused to capitulate and moved his government upriver to Hankou. Japanese strategists had hoped to force Chiang to join a Japanese-dominated new order in East Asia, consisting of Japan, Manchuria, and China. This aim was part of a larger plan to seize Soviet Siberia with its rich resources and create a new order for Asia, in which Japan would guide its Asian neighbors on the path to development and prosperity.

THE MUNICH CONFERENCE

At the Munich Conference, the leaders of France and Great Britain capitulated to Hitler's demands on Czechoslovakia. While the British prime minister, Neville Chamberlain, defended his actions at Munich as necessary for peace, another British statesman, Winston Churchill, characterized the settlement at Munich as "a disaster of the first magnitude."

Winston Churchill, Speech to the House of Commons, October 5, 1938

I will begin by saying what everybody would like to ignore or forget but which must nevertheless be stated, namely, that we have sustained a total and unmitigated defeat, and that France has suffered even more than we have.... The utmost my right honorable Friend the Prime Minister...has been able to gain for Czechoslovakia and in the matters which were in dispute has been that the German dictator, instead of snatching his victuals from the table, has been content to have them served to him course by course.... And I will say this, that I believe the Czechs, left to themselves and told they were going to get no help from the Western Powers, would have been able to make better terms than they have got....

We are in the presence of a disaster of the first magnitude which has befallen Great Britain and France. Do not let us blind ourselves to that....

And do not suppose that this is the end. This is only the beginning of the reckoning. This is only the first sip, the first foretaste of a bitter cup which will be proffered to us year by year unless by a supreme recovery of moral health and martial vigor, we arise again and take our stand for freedom as in the olden time.

Neville Chamberlain, Speech to the House of Commons, October 6, 1938

That is my answer to those who say that we should have told Germany weeks ago that, if her army crossed the border of Czechoslovakia, we should be at war with her. We had no treaty obligations and no legal obligations to Czechoslovakia.... When we were convinced, as we became convinced, that nothing any longer would keep the Sudetenland within the Czechoslovakian State, we urged the Czech Government as strongly as we could to agree to the cession of territory, and to agree promptly.... It was a hard decision for anyone who loved his country to take, but to accuse us of having by that advice betrayed the Czechoslovakian State is simply preposterous. What we did was to save her from annihilation and give her a chance of new life as a new State, which involves the loss of territory and fortifications, but may perhaps enable her to enjoy in the future and develop a national existence under a neutrality and security comparable to that which we see in Switzerland today. Therefore, I think the Government deserve the approval of this House for their conduct of affairs in this recent crisis which has saved Czechoslovakia from destruction and Europe from Armageddon.

What were the opposing views of Churchill and Chamberlain on the Munich Conference? With whom do you agree? Why?

During the late 1930s, Japan began to cooperate with Nazi Germany on the assumption that the two countries would ultimately launch a joint attack on the Soviet Union and divide up its resources between them. But when Germany surprised the world by signing a nonaggression pact with the Soviets in August 1939, Japanese strategists were compelled to reevaluate their long-term objectives. Japan was not strong enough to defeat the Soviet Union alone, so the Japanese began to shift their gaze southward to the vast resources of Southeast Asia—the oil of the Dutch East Indies, the rubber and tin of Malaya, and the rice of Burma and Indochina.

A move southward, of course, would risk war with the European colonial powers, especially Britain and France, as well as with the other rising power in the Pacific, the United States. When the Japanese occupied Indochina in July 1941, the Americans responded by cutting off sales of vital scrap iron and oil to Japan. Japan's military leaders decided to preempt any further American response by attacking the American naval fleet in the Pacific.

The Course of World War II

Unleashing a *Blitzkrieg*, or "lightning war," Hitler stunned Europe with the speed and efficiency of the German attack. Armored columns or panzer divisions (a panzer division was a strike force of about three hundred tanks, with accompanying troops and supplies) supported by airplanes broke quickly through Polish lines and encircled the bewildered Polish troops. Regular infantry units then moved in to hold the newly conquered territory. Soon after, Soviet military forces attacked eastern Poland. Within four weeks, Poland had surrendered. On September 28, 1939, Germany and the Soviet Union officially divided Poland between them.

Victory and Stalemate

Although Hitler's hopes to avoid warfare with the West were dashed when France and Britain declared war on September 3, he was confident that he could control the situation. After a winter of waiting (called the "phony war"), Hitler resumed the fight on April 9, 1940, with

Japan seizes Manchuria	September 1931
Hitler becomes chancellor	January 30, 1933
Hitler announces military conscription	March 16, 1935
Mussolini invades Ethiopia	October 1935
Hitler occupies demilitarized Rhineland	March 7, 1936
Rome-Berlin Axis	October 1936
Anti-Comintern Pact (Japan and Germany)	November 1936
Japan invades China	1937
Germany annexes Austria	March 13, 1938
Munich Conference: Germany occupies Sudetenland	September 29, 1938
Germany occupies the rest of Czechoslovakia	March 1939
German-Soviet Nonaggression Pact	August 23, 1939
Germany invades Poland	September 1, 1939
Britain and France declare war on Germany	September 3, 1939

another *Blitzkrieg*, this time against Denmark and Norway. One month later, on May 10, the Germans launched their attack on the Netherlands, Belgium, and France. The main assault through Luxembourg and the Ardennes forest was completely unexpected by the French and British forces. German panzer divisions broke through the weak French defensive positions there and raced across northern France, splitting the Allied armies and trapping French troops and the entire British army on the beaches of Dunkirk. Only by heroic efforts did the British succeed in achieving an evacuation of 330,000 Allied (mostly British) troops. The French surrendered on June 22. German armies occupied about three-fifths of France while the French hero of World War I, Marshal Henri Pétain (1856–1951), established an authoritarian regime (known as Vichy France) over the remainder. Germany was now in control of western and central Europe, but Britain had still not been defeated.

The Problem of Britain   As Hitler realized, an amphibious invasion of Britain would be possible only if Germany gained control of the air. At the beginning of August 1940, the *Luftwaffe* (the German air force) launched a major offensive against British air and naval bases, harbors, communication centers, and war industries. Led by the stubbornly determined Winston Churchill, now prime minister of Britain, the British fought back doggedly, supported by an effective radar system that gave them early warning of German attacks. Nevertheless, the British air force suffered critical losses by the end of August and was probably saved by Hitler's change of strategy. In September, in retaliation for a British attack on Berlin, Hitler ordered a shift from military targets to massive bombing of British cities to break British morale. The British rebuilt their air strength quickly and were soon inflicting major losses on *Luftwaffe* bombers. By the end of September, Germany had lost the Battle of Britain, and the invasion of Britain had to be postponed.

At this point, Hitler pursued the possibility of a Mediterranean strategy, which would involve capturing Egypt and the Suez Canal and closing the Mediterranean to British ships, thereby shutting off Britain's supply of oil. Hitler's commitment to the Mediterranean was never wholehearted, however. His initial plan was to let the Italians defeat the British in North Africa, but this strategy failed when the British routed the Italian army. Although Hitler then sent German troops to the North African theater of war, his primary concern lay elsewhere; he had already reached the decision to fulfill his lifelong obsession with the acquisition of territory in the east.

Invasion of the Soviet Union   Although he had no desire for a two-front war, Hitler became convinced that Britain was remaining in the war only because it expected Russian support. If Russia were smashed, Britain's last hope would be eliminated. Moreover, Hitler had convinced himself that the Soviet Union, with its Jewish-Bolshevik leadership and a pitiful army, could be defeated quickly and decisively. Although the invasion of the Soviet Union was scheduled for spring 1941, the attack was delayed because of problems in the Balkans. Hitler had already obtained the political cooperation of Hungary, Bulgaria, and Romania, but Mussolini's disastrous invasion of Greece in October 1940 exposed Hitler's southern flank to British air bases in Greece. To secure his Balkan flank, German troops seized both Yugoslavia and Greece in April. Now reassured, Hitler turned to the east and invaded the Soviet Union on June 22, 1941, in the belief that the Russians could still be decisively defeated before winter arrived.

The massive attack stretched out along an 1,800-mile front (see Map 27.2). German troops advanced rapidly, capturing two million Russian soldiers. By November, one German army group had swept through the Ukraine while a second was besieging Leningrad; a third approached within 25 miles of Moscow, the Russian capital. An early winter and unexpected Russian resistance, however, brought a halt to the German advance. For the first time in the war, German armies had been stopped. A counterattack in December 1941 by the Soviet army, which Hitler assumed had been exhausted by Nazi victories, came as an ominous sign for the Germans. By then, another of Hitler's decisions—the declaration of war on the United States—had probably made Hitler's defeat inevitable and again turned a European conflict into a global war.

The War in Asia

On December 7, 1941, Japanese carrier-based aircraft attacked the United States naval base at Pearl Harbor in

MAP 27.2 **World War II in Europe and North Africa.** With its fast and effective military, Germany quickly overwhelmed much of western Europe. However, Hitler overestimated his country's capabilities and underestimated those of his foes. By late 1942, his invasion of the Soviet Union was failing, and the United States had become a major factor in the war. The Allies successfully invaded Italy in 1943 and France in 1944. ❓ Which countries were neutral, and how did geography help make their neutrality an option? 🖳 **View an animated version of this map or related maps at** http://thomsonedu.com/history/spielvogel

the Hawaiian Islands. The same day, other units launched additional assaults on the Philippines and began advancing toward the British colony of Malaya. Shortly after, Japanese forces invaded the Dutch East Indies and occupied a number of islands in the Pacific Ocean (see Map 27.3). In some cases, as on the Bataan peninsula and the island of Corregidor in the Philippines, resistance was fierce, but by the spring of 1942, almost all of Southeast Asia and much of the western Pacific had fallen into Japanese hands. Tokyo declared the creation of the Greater East Asia Co-Prosperity Sphere, encompassing the entire region under Japanese tutelage, and announced

its intention to liberate the colonial areas of Southeast Asia from Western colonial rule. For the moment, however, Japan needed the resources of the region for its war machine and placed the countries under its rule on a wartime basis.

Japanese leaders had hoped that their strike at American bases would destroy the United States Pacific Fleet and persuade the Roosevelt administration to accept Japanese domination of the Pacific. The American people, in the eyes of Japanese leaders, had been made soft by material indulgence. But Tokyo had miscalculated. The attack on Pearl Harbor galvanized American opinion and

German Troops in the Soviet Union. At first, the German attack on the Soviet Union was enormously successful, leading one German general to remark in his diary: "It is probably no overstatement to say that the Russian campaign has been won in the space of two weeks." This picture shows German panzer troops jumping from their armored troop carriers to attack Red Army snipers who had taken refuge in a farmhouse.

won broad support for Roosevelt's war policy. The United States now joined with European nations and Nationalist China in a combined effort to defeat Japan and bring to an end its hegemony in the Pacific.

The Turning Point of the War, 1942–1943

The entry of the United States into the war created a coalition (the Grand Alliance) that ultimately defeated the Axis powers (Germany, Italy, Japan). Nevertheless, the three major Allies—Britain, the United States, and the Soviet Union—had to overcome mutual suspicions before they could operate as an effective team. Two factors aided that process. First, Hitler's declaration of war on the United States made it easier for the United States to accept the British and Russian contention that the defeat of Germany should be the Americans' first priority. For that reason, the United States increased the quantity of trucks, planes, and other arms that it sent to the British and the Soviets. Also important to the alliance was the tacit agreement of the three chief Allies to stress military operations while ignoring political differences. At the beginning of 1943, the Allies agreed to fight until the Axis powers surrendered unconditionally. This principle of **unconditional surrender** had the effect of cementing the Grand Alliance by making it nearly impossible for Hitler to divide his foes.

Defeat was far from Hitler's mind at the beginning of 1942, however. As Japanese forces advanced into Southeast Asia and the Pacific, Hitler and his European allies continued the war in Europe against Britain and the Soviet Union. Until the fall of 1942, it appeared that the Germans might still prevail on the battlefield. Reinforcements in North Africa enabled the Afrika Korps under General Erwin Rommel to break through the British defenses in Egypt and advance toward Alexandria.

In the spring of 1942, a renewed German offensive in Russia led to the capture of the entire Crimea, causing Hitler to boast in August 1942:

> As the next step, we are going to advance south of the Caucasus and then help the rebels in Iran and Iraq against the English. Another thrust will be directed along the Caspian Sea toward Afghanistan and India. Then the English will run out of oil. In two years we'll be on the borders of India. Twenty to thirty elite German divisions will do. Then the British Empire will collapse.[3]

But this would be Hitler's last optimistic outburst. By the fall of 1942, the war had turned against the Germans.

In North Africa, British forces had stopped Rommel's troops at El Alamein in the summer of 1942 and then forced them back across the desert. In November 1942, British and American forces invaded French North Africa and forced the German and Italian troops to surrender in May 1943. On the Eastern Front, the turning point of the war occurred at Stalingrad. After the capture of the Crimea, Hitler's generals wanted him to concentrate on the Caucasus and its oil fields, but Hitler decided that Stalingrad, a major industrial center on the Volga, should be taken first. Between November 1942 and February 1943, German troops were stopped, then encircled, and finally forced to surrender on February 2, 1943 (see the box on p. 523). The entire German Sixth Army of 300,000 men was lost. By February 1943, German forces in Russia were back to their positions of June 1942.

The tide of battle in the East also turned dramatically in 1942. In the Battle of the Coral Sea on May 7–8, 1942, American naval forces stopped the Japanese advance and temporarily relieved Australia of the threat of invasion. On June 4, at the Battle of Midway Island, American planes destroyed all four of the attacking Japanese aircraft carriers and established American naval superiority in the

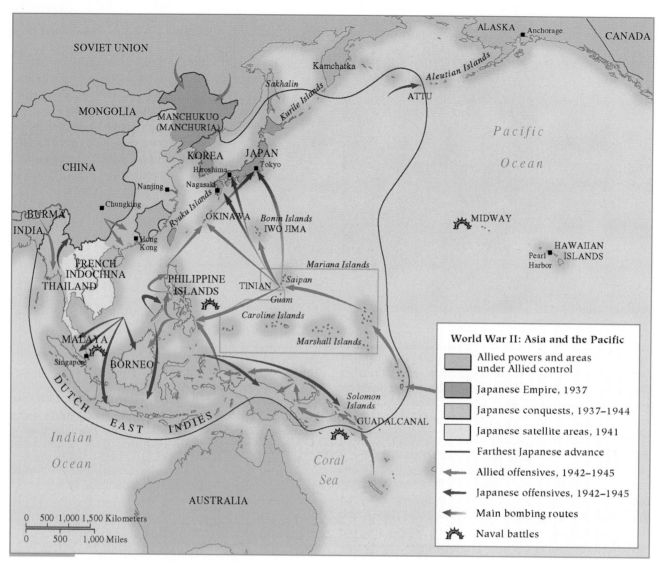

MAP 27.3 **World War II in Asia and the Pacific.** In 1937, Japan invaded northern China, beginning its effort to create a "Greater East Asia Co-Prosperity Sphere." Further expansion induced America to end iron and oil sales to Japan. Deciding that war with the United States was inevitable, Japan engineered a surprise attack on Pearl Harbor. ❓ Why was control of the islands in the western Pacific of great importance both to the Japanese and to the Allies? 🖱 **View an animated version of this map or related maps at** http://thomsonedu.com/history/spielvogel

Pacific. After a series of bitter engagements in the waters of the Solomon Islands from August to November, Japanese fortunes began to fade.

The Last Years of the War

By the beginning of 1943, the tide of battle had turned against Germany, Italy, and Japan. After the Axis forces had surrendered in Tunisia on May 13, 1943, the Allies crossed the Mediterranean and carried the war to Italy. After taking Sicily, Allied troops began the invasion of mainland Italy in September. In the meantime, after the ouster and arrest of Benito Mussolini, a new Italian government offered to surrender to Allied forces. But

Mussolini was liberated by the Germans in a daring raid and then set up as the head of a puppet German state in northern Italy while German troops moved in and occupied much of Italy. The new defensive lines established by the Germans in the hills south of Rome were so effective that the Allied advance up the Italian peninsula was a painstaking affair accompanied by heavy casualties. Rome did not fall to the Allies until June 4, 1944. By that time, the Italian war had assumed a secondary role anyway as the Allies opened their long-awaited "second front" in western Europe.

Allied Advances in the West Since the autumn of 1943, the Allies had been planning a cross-channel invasion of

A German Soldier at Stalingrad

The Russian victory at Stalingrad was a major turning point in World War II. This excerpt comes from the diary of a German soldier who fought and died in the Battle of Stalingrad. His dreams of victory and a return home with medals were soon dashed by the realities of Russian resistance.

Diary of a German Soldier

Today, after we'd had a bath, the company commander told us that if our future operations are as successful, we'll soon reach the Volga, take Stalingrad and then the war will inevitably soon be over. Perhaps we'll be home by Christmas.

July 29. The company commander says the Russian troops are completely broken, and cannot hold out any longer. To reach the Volga and take Stalingrad is not so difficult for us. The Führer knows where the Russians' weak point is. Victory is not far away....

August 10. The Führer's orders were read out to us. He expects victory of us. We are all convinced that they can't stop us.

August 12. This morning outstanding soldiers were presented with decorations.... Will I really go back to Elsa without a decoration? I believe that for Stalingrad the Führer will decorate even me....

September 4. We are being sent northward along the front toward Stalingrad. We marched all night and by dawn had reached Voroponovo Station. We can already see the smoking town. It's a happy thought that the end of the war is getting nearer. That's what everyone is saying....

September 8. Two days of non-stop fighting. The Russians are defending themselves with insane stubbornness. Our regiment has lost many men....

September 16. Our battalion, plus tanks, is attacking the [grain storage] elevator, from which smoke is pouring—the grain in it is burning, the Russians seem to have set light to it themselves. Barbarism. The battalion is suffering heavy losses....

October 10. The Russians are so close to us that our planes cannot bomb them. We are preparing for a decisive attack. The Führer has ordered the whole of Stalingrad to be taken as rapidly as possible....

October 22. Our regiment has failed to break into the factory. We have lost many men; every time you move you have to jump over bodies....

November 10. A letter from Elsa today. Everyone expects us home for Christmas. In Germany everyone believes we already hold Stalingrad. How wrong they are. If they could only see what Stalingrad has done to our army....

November 21. The Russians have gone over to the offensive along the whole front. Fierce fighting is going on. So, there it is—the Volga, victory and soon home to our families! We shall obviously be seeing them next in the other world.

November 29. We are encircled. It was announced this morning that the Führer has said: "The army can trust me to do everything necessary to ensure supplies and rapidly break the encirclement."

December 3. We are on hunger rations and waiting for the rescue that the Führer promised....

December 14. Everybody is racked with hunger. Frozen potatoes are the best meal, but to get them out of the ice-covered ground under fire from Russian bullets is not so easy....

December 26. The horses have already been eaten. I would eat a cat; they say its meat is also tasty. The soldiers look like corpses or lunatics, looking for something to put in their mouths. They no longer take cover from Russian shells; they haven't the strength to walk, run away and hide. A curse on this war!

What does this soldier believe about the Führer? Why? What has been the source of his information? Why is the battle for Stalingrad considered a major turning point in World War II?

France from Britain. On June 6, 1944, under the direction of the American general Dwight D. Eisenhower (1890–1969), the Allies landed five assault divisions on the beaches of Normandy in history's greatest amphibious invasion. The Germans' initially indecisive response enabled the Allied forces to establish a beachhead. Within three months, they had landed two million men and a half-million vehicles that pushed inland and broke through German defensive lines.

After the breakout, Allied troops moved south and east and liberated Paris by the end of August. By March 1945, they had crossed the Rhine River and advanced farther into Germany. At the end of April, Allied forces in northern Germany moved toward the Elbe River, where they finally linked up with the Soviets.

Soviet Offensive in the East The Soviets had come a long way since the Battle of Stalingrad in 1943. In the summer of 1943, Hitler gambled on taking the offensive by making use of newly developed heavy tanks. German forces were soundly defeated by the Russians at the Battle of Kursk (July 5–12), the greatest tank battle of the war. Soviet forces now began a relentless advance westward. The Soviets had reoccupied the Ukraine by the end of 1943 and lifted the siege of Leningrad and moved into the Baltic States by the beginning of 1944. Advancing along a northern front, Soviet troops occupied Warsaw in January 1945 and entered Berlin in April. Meanwhile, Soviet troops swept along a southern front through Hungary, Romania, and Bulgaria.

In January 1945, Hitler had moved into a bunker 55 feet under Berlin to direct the final stages of the war. In his

Division of Poland by Germany and the Soviet Union	September 1939
Blitzkrieg against Denmark and Norway	April 1940
Blitzkrieg against Belgium, Netherlands, and France	May 1940
Churchill as British prime minister	May 10, 1940
Surrender of France	June 22, 1940
Battle of Britain	Fall 1940
Nazi seizure of Yugoslavia and Greece	April 1941
German invasion of the Soviet Union	June 22, 1941
Japanese attack on Pearl Harbor	December 7, 1941
Battle of the Coral Sea	May 7–8, 1942
Battle of Midway Island	June 4, 1942
Allied invasion of North Africa	November 1942
German surrender at Stalingrad	February 2, 1943
Surrender of Axis forces in North Africa	May 1943
Battle of Kursk	July 5–12, 1943
Invasion of mainland Italy	September 1943
Allied invasion of France	June 6, 1944
Hitler's suicide	April 30, 1945
Surrender of Germany	May 7, 1945
Atomic bomb dropped on Hiroshima	August 6, 1945
Surrender of Japan	August 14, 1945

last political testament, Hitler, consistent to the end in his rabid anti-Semitism, blamed the Jews for the war: "Above all I charge the leaders of the nation and those under them to scrupulous observance of the laws of race and to merciless opposition to the universal poisoner of all peoples, international Jewry."[4] Hitler committed suicide in his bunker on April 30, two days after Mussolini had been shot by partisan Italian forces. On May 7, German commanders surrendered. The war in Europe was over.

The war in Asia continued. Beginning in 1943, American forces had gone on the offensive and advanced, slowly at times, across the Pacific. The Americans took an increasing toll of enemy resources, especially at sea and in the air. When President Harry Truman (Roosevelt had died on April 12, 1945) and his advisers became convinced that American troops might suffer heavy casualties in an invasion of the Japanese homeland, they made the decision to drop the newly developed atomic bomb on Hiroshima and Nagasaki. The Japanese surrendered unconditionally on August 14. World War II—in which seventeen million men died in battle and perhaps eighteen million civilians perished as well (some estimates place total losses as high as fifty million)—was finally over.

The New Order

The initial victories of the Germans and the Japanese gave them the opportunity to create new orders in Europe and Asia. Although both countries presented positive images of these new orders for publicity purposes, in practice both followed policies of ruthless domination of their subject peoples.

The Nazi Empire

After the German victories in Europe between 1939 and 1941, Nazi propagandists painted glowing images of a new European order based on "equal chances" for all

Crossing the Rhine. After landing at Normandy, Allied forces liberated France and prepared to move into Germany. Makeshift bridges enabled the Allies to cross the Rhine in some areas and advance deeper into Germany. Units of the 7th United States Army of General Patch are shown here crossing the Rhine at Worms on a pontoon bridge constructed by battalions of engineers alongside the ruins of the old bridge.

National Archives (111-C-273)

nations and an integrated economic community. This was not Hitler's conception of a European New Order. He saw the Europe he had conquered simply as subject to German domination. Only the Germans, he once said, "can really organize Europe."

The Nazi empire stretched across continental Europe from the English Channel in the west to the outskirts of Moscow in the east. In no way was this empire organized systematically or governed efficiently. Nazi-occupied Europe was organized in one of two ways. Some areas, such as western Poland, were annexed and made into German provinces. Most of occupied Europe was administered by German military or civilian officials, combined with different degrees of indirect control from collaborationist regimes.

Racial considerations played an important role in how conquered peoples were treated in the **Nazi New Order.** German civil administrations were established in Norway, Denmark, and the Netherlands because the Nazis considered these populations Aryan, racially akin to the Germans and hence worthy of more lenient treatment. "Inferior" Latin peoples, such as the occupied French, were given military administrations. By 1943, however, as Nazi losses continued to mount, all the occupied territories of northern and western Europe were ruthlessly exploited for material goods and manpower for Germany's war needs.

Plans for an Aryan Racial Empire   Because the conquered lands in the east contained the living space for German expansion and were populated in Nazi eyes by racially inferior Slavic peoples, Nazi administration there was considerably more ruthless. Hitler's racial ideology and his plans for an Aryan racial empire were so important to him that he and the Nazis began to implement their racial program soon after the conquest of Poland. Heinrich Himmler, a strong believer in Nazi racial ideology and the leader of the SS, was put in charge of German resettlement plans in the east. Himmler's task was to evacuate the inferior Slavic peoples and replace them with Germans, a policy first applied to the new German provinces created from the lands of western Poland. One million Poles were uprooted and dumped in southern Poland. Hundreds of thousands of ethnic Germans (descendants of Germans who had migrated years earlier from Germany to different parts of southern and eastern Europe) were encouraged to colonize the designated areas in Poland. By 1942, two million ethnic Germans had been settled in Poland.

The invasion of the Soviet Union inflated Nazi visions of German colonization in the east. Hitler spoke to his intimate circle of a colossal project of social engineering after the war, in which Poles, Ukrainians, and Russians would become slave labor while German peasants settled on the abandoned lands and Germanized them. Nazis involved in this kind of planning were well aware of the human costs. Himmler told a gathering of SS officers that although the destruction of thirty million Slavs was a prerequisite for German plans in the east, "whether nations live in prosperity or starve to death interests me only insofar as we need them as slaves for our culture. Otherwise it is of no interest."[5]

Use of Foreign Workers   Labor shortages in Germany led to a policy of ruthless mobilization of foreign labor. In 1942, a special office was created to recruit labor for German farms and industries. By the summer of 1944, seven million foreign workers were laboring in Germany and constituted 20 percent of Germany's labor force. At the same time, another seven million workers were supplying forced labor in their own countries on farms, in industries, and even in military camps. Forced labor often proved counterproductive, however, because the brutal character of Germany's recruitment policies often led more and more people to resist the Nazi occupation forces.

The Holocaust

There was no more terrifying aspect of the Nazi New Order than the deliberate attempt to exterminate the Jews of Europe. Racial struggle was a key element in Hitler's ideology and meant to him a clearly defined conflict of opposites: the Aryans, creators of human cultural development, against the Jews, parasites who were trying to destroy the Aryans. By the beginning of 1939, Nazi policy focused on promoting the "emigration" of German Jews from Germany. Once the war began in September 1939, however, the so-called Jewish problem took on new dimensions. For a while, there was discussion of the Madagascar plan, which aspired to ship Jews en masse to the African island of Madagascar. When war contingencies made this plan impractical, an even more drastic policy was conceived.

The SS and the *Einsatzgruppen*   Heinrich Himmler and the SS organization shared Adolf Hitler's racial ideology. The SS was given responsibility for what the Nazis called their **Final Solution** to the Jewish problem, the annihilation of the Jews. Reinhard Heydrich (1904–1942), head of the SS's Security Service, was given administrative responsibility for the Final Solution. After the defeat of Poland, Heydrich ordered the special strike forces (*Einsatzgruppen*) that he had created to round up all Polish Jews and concentrate them in ghettos established in a number of Polish cities.

In June 1941, the *Einsatzgruppen* were given new responsibilities as mobile killing units. These SS death squads followed the regular army's advance into Russia. Their job was to round up Jews in their villages and execute and bury them in mass graves, often giant pits dug by the victims themselves before they were shot. Such regular killing produced morale problems among the SS executioners. During a visit to Minsk in the Soviet Union, purpose (see Map 27.4). The largest and most infamous was Auschwitz-Birkenau. Medical technicians chose Zyklon B (the commercial name for hydrogen cyanide) as the most effective gas for quickly killing large numbers of people in gas chambers designed to look like "shower rooms" to facilitate the cooperation of the victims. After gassing, the corpses would be burned in specially built crematoria.

By the spring of 1942, the death camps were in operation. Although initial priority was given to the elimination of the ghettos in Poland, by the summer of 1942, Jews were also being shipped from France, Belgium, and the Netherlands. Even as the Allies were making important advances in 1944, Jews were being shipped from Greece and Hungary. These shipments depended on the cooperation of Germany's Transport Ministry, and despite desperate military needs, the Final Solution had priority in using railroad cars for the transportation of Jews to death camps.

A harrowing experience awaited the Jews when they arrived at one of the six death camps. Rudolf Höss, commandant at Auschwitz-Birkenau, described it:

> We had two SS doctors on duty at Auschwitz to examine the incoming transports of prisoners. The prisoners would be marched by one of the doctors who would make spot decisions as they walked by. Those who were fit for work were sent into the camp. Others were sent immediately to the extermination plants. Children of tender years were invariably exterminated since by reason of their youth they were unable to work.... At Auschwitz we endeavored to fool the victims into thinking that they were to go through a delousing process. Of course, frequently they realized our true intentions and we sometimes had riots and difficulties due to that fact.[7]

About 30 percent of the arrivals at Auschwitz were sent to a labor camp; the remainder went to the gas chambers (see the box on p. 528). After they had been gassed, the bodies were burned in the crematoria. The victims' goods and even their bodies were used for economic gain. Women's hair was cut off, collected, and turned into mattresses or cloth. Some inmates were also subjected to cruel and painful "medical" experiments. The Germans killed between five and six million Jews, more than three million of them in the death camps. Virtually 90 percent of the Jewish populations of Poland, the Baltic countries, and Germany were exterminated. Overall, the **Holocaust** was responsible for the death of nearly two out of every three European Jews.

The Other Holocaust The Nazis were also responsible for the deliberate death by shooting, starvation, or overwork of at least another nine to ten million people. Because the Nazis also considered the Gypsies of Europe (like the Jews) a race containing alien blood, they were systematically rounded up for extermination. About 40 percent of Europe's one million Gypsies were killed in the death camps. The leading elements of the "subhuman" Slavic peoples—the clergy, intelligentsia, civil leaders, judges, and lawyers—were arrested and murdered.

The Holocaust: Activities of the *Einsatzgruppen.*
The activities of the mobile killing units known as the *Einsatzgruppen* were the first stage in the mass killings of the Holocaust. This picture shows the execution of a Jew by a member of one of these SS killing squads. Onlookers include members of the German Army, the German Labor Service, and even Hitler Youth. When it became apparent that this method of killing was inefficient, it was replaced by the death camps.

SS leader Himmler tried to build morale by pointing out that

> he would not like it if Germans did such a thing gladly. But their conscience was in no way impaired, for they were soldiers who had to carry out every order unconditionally. He alone had responsibility before God and Hitler for everything that was happening,... and he was acting from a deep understanding of the necessity for this operation.[6]

The Death Camps Although it has been estimated that as many as one million Jews were killed by the *Einsatzgruppen*, this approach to solving the Jewish problem was soon perceived as inadequate. Instead, the Nazis opted for the systematic annihilation of the European Jewish population in specially built death camps. The plan was simple. Jews from countries occupied by Germany or sympathetic to Germany would be rounded up, packed like cattle into freight trains, and shipped to Poland, where six extermination centers were built for this

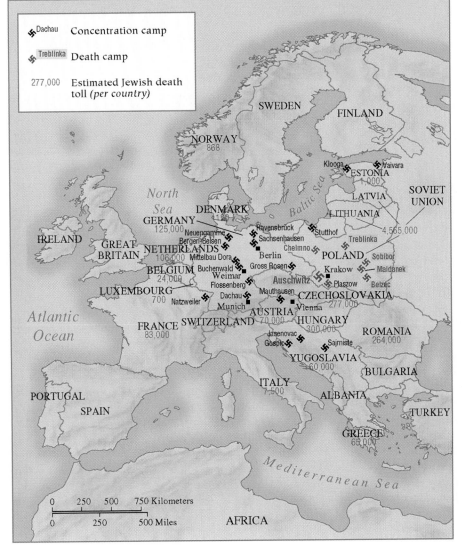

MAP 27.4 The Holocaust. Hitler used the fiction of the Aryan race, to which Germans supposedly belonged, to help radicalize the German people and justify his hatred of Jews. Hitler's "Final Solution" to the "Jewish problem" was mass execution of Europe's Jews in death camps. **?** Which region lost the largest number of Jews in the camps, and what helps explain this? **View an animated version of this map or related maps at** http://thomsonedu.com/history/spielvogel

Probably an additional four million Poles, Ukrainians, and White Russians lost their lives as slave laborers for Nazi Germany, and three to four million Soviet prisoners of war were killed in captivity. The Nazis also singled out homosexuals for persecution, and thousands lost their lives in concentration camps.

The New Order in Asia

Once Japan's takeover was completed, Japanese war policy in the occupied areas in Asia became essentially defensive, as Japan hoped to use its new possessions to meet its needs for raw materials, such as tin, oil, and rubber, as well as to serve as an outlet for Japanese manufactured goods. To provide a structure for the arrangement, Japanese leaders set up the Greater East Asia Co-Prosperity Sphere as a self-sufficient community designed to provide mutual benefits to the occupied areas and the home country.

The Japanese conquest of Southeast Asia had been accomplished under the slogan "Asia for the Asians."

Japanese officials in occupied territories promised that independent government would be established under Japanese tutelage. Such governments were eventually established in Burma, the Dutch East Indies, Vietnam, and the Philippines.

In fact, however, real power rested with Japanese military authorities in each territory, and the local Japanese military command was directly subordinated to the army general staff in Tokyo. The economic resources of the colonies were exploited for the benefit of the Japanese war machine, while natives were recruited to serve in local military units or were conscripted to work on public works projects. In some cases, the people living in the occupied areas were subjected to severe hardships.

Like German soldiers in occupied Europe, Japanese military forces often had little respect for the lives of their subject peoples. In their conquest of Nanjing, China, in 1937, Japanese soldiers had spent several days killing, raping, and looting. Almost 800,000 Koreans were sent overseas, most of them as forced laborers, to Japan. Tens of thousands of Korean women were forced to serve as "comfort women" (prostitutes) for Japanese troops. In construction projects to help their war effort, the Japanese also made extensive use of labor forces composed of both prisoners of war and local peoples. In building the Burma-Thailand railway in 1943, for example, the Japanese used 61,000 Australian, British, and Dutch prisoners of war and almost 300,000 workers from Burma, Malaya, Thailand, and the Dutch East Indies. An inadequate diet and appalling work conditions in an unhealthy climate led to the death of 12,000 Allied prisoners of war and 90,000 native workers by the time the railway was completed.

THE HOLOCAUST: THE CAMP COMMANDANT AND THE VICTIMS

The systematic annihilation of millions of men, women, and children in extermination camps makes the Holocaust one of the most horrifying events in history. The first document is taken from an account by Rudolf Höss, commandant of the extermination camp at Auschwitz-Birkenau. In the second document, a French doctor explains what happened to the victims at one of the crematoria described by Höss.

Commandant Höss Describes the Equipment

The two large crematoria, Nos. I and II, were built during the winter of 1942–43.... They each...could cremate c. 2,000 corpses within twenty-four hours.... Crematoria I and II both had underground undressing and gassing rooms which could be completely ventilated. The corpses were brought up to the ovens on the floor above by lift. The gas chambers could hold c. 3,000 people.

The firm of Topf had calculated that the two smaller crematoria, III and IV, would each be able to cremate 1,500 corpses within twenty-four hours. However, owing to the wartime shortage of materials, the builders were obliged to economize and so the undressing rooms and gassing rooms were built above ground and the ovens were of a less solid construction. But it soon became apparent that the flimsy construction of these two four-retort ovens was not up to the demands made on it. No. III ceased operating altogether after a short time and later was no longer used. No. IV had to be repeatedly shut down since after a short period in operation of 4–6 weeks, the ovens and chimneys had burnt out. The victims of the gassing were mainly burnt in pits behind crematorium IV.

The largest number of people gassed and cremated within twenty-four hours was somewhat over 9,000.

A French Doctor Describes the Victims

It is mid-day, when a long line of women, children, and old people enter the yard. The senior official in charge...climbs on a bench to tell them that they are going to have a bath and that afterward they will get a drink of hot coffee. They all undress in the yard.... The doors are opened and an indescribable jostling begins. The first people to enter the gas chamber begin to draw back. They sense the death which awaits them. The SS men put an end to this pushing and shoving with blows from their rifle butts beating the heads of the horrified women who are desperately hugging their children. The massive oak double doors are shut. For two endless minutes one can hear banging on the walls and screams which are no longer human. And then—not a sound. Five minutes later the doors are opened. The corpses, squashed together and distorted, fall out like a waterfall.... The bodies which are still warm pass through the hands of the hairdresser who cuts their hair and the dentist who pulls out their gold teeth.... One more transport has just been processed through No. IV crematorium.

What equipment does Höss describe? What process does the French doctor describe? Is there any sympathy for the victim in either account? Why or why not? How could such a horrifying process have been allowed to occur?

The Home Front

World War II was even more of a total war than World War I. Fighting was much more widespread and covered most of the globe. Economic mobilization was more extensive; so was the mobilization of women. The number of civilians killed was far higher: almost twenty million died as a result of bombing raids, mass extermination policies, and attacks by invading armies.

The Mobilization of Peoples

The home fronts of the major belligerents varied considerably, based on national circumstances.

The Soviet Union World War II had an enormous impact on the Soviet Union. Known to the Soviets as the Great Patriotic War, the German-Soviet war witnessed the greatest land battles in history as well as incredible ruthlessness. Two out of every five persons killed in World War II were Soviet citizens.

The Soviets' initial defeats led to drastic emergency mobilization measures that affected the civilian population. Leningrad, for example, spent nine hundred days under siege, during which its inhabitants were so desperate for food that they ate dogs, cats, and mice. As the German army made its rapid advance into Soviet territory, the factories in the western part of the Soviet Union were dismantled and shipped to the interior—to the Urals, western Siberia, and the Volga regions. Machines were placed on the bare ground, and walls went up around them as workers began factory operations.

Stalin called this widespread military, industrial, and economic mobilization a "battle of machines," and the Soviets won, producing 78,000 tanks and 98,000 artillery pieces. Fifty-five percent of Soviet national income went for war materials, compared to 15 percent in 1940. As a result of the emphasis on military goods, Soviet citizens experienced dire shortages of both food and housing.

Soviet women played a major role in the war effort. Women and girls worked in industries, mines, and railroads. Overall, the number of women working in industry increased almost 60 percent. Soviet women were also expected to dig antitank ditches and work as air-raid wardens. In addition, the Soviet Union was the only country in World War II to use women as combatants.

Soviet women functioned as snipers and also as crews in bomber squadrons. The female pilots who helped defeat the Germans at Stalingrad were known as the "night witches."

The United States   The home front in the United States was quite different from those of the other major belligerents, largely because the United States faced no threat of war on its own soil. Although the economy and labor force were slow to mobilize, eventually the United States became the arsenal of the Allied Powers, producing the military equipment they needed. During the high point of war production in the United States in November 1943, the country was constructing six ships a day and $6 billion worth of war-related goods a month.

The mobilization of the American economy caused social problems. The construction of new factories created boomtowns where thousands came to work but then faced a shortage of houses, health facilities, and schools. The dramatic expansion of small towns into large cities often brought a breakdown in traditional social mores, especially evident in the growth of teenage prostitution. Economic mobilization also led to a widespread movement of people, which in turn created new social tensions. Sixteen million men and women were enrolled in the military, and another sixteen million, mostly wives and sweethearts of the servicemen or workers looking for jobs, also relocated. More than one million blacks migrated from the rural South to the industrial cities of the North and West, looking for jobs in industry. The presence of blacks in areas where they had not lived before led to racial tensions and sometimes even racial riots. In Detroit in June 1943, white mobs roamed the streets attacking blacks.

Japanese Americans were treated even more shabbily. On the West Coast, 110,000 Japanese Americans, 65 percent of whom had been born in the United States, were removed to inland camps encircled by barbed wire and required to take loyalty oaths. Although public officials claimed this policy was necessary for security reasons, no similar treatment of German Americans or Italian Americans ever took place. The racism inherent in this treatment of Japanese Americans was evident when the California governor, Culbert Olson, said, "You know, when I look out at a group of Americans of German or Italian descent, I can tell whether they're loyal or not. I can tell how they think and even perhaps what they are thinking. But it is impossible for me to do this with inscrutable orientals, and particularly the Japanese."[8]

Germany   In August 1914, Germans had enthusiastically cheered their soldiers marching off to war. In September 1939, the streets were quiet. Many Germans were apathetic or, even worse for the Nazi regime, had a foreboding of disaster. Hitler was very aware of the importance of the home front. He believed that the collapse of the home front in World War I had caused Germany's defeat, and in his determination to avoid a repetition of that experience, he adopted economic policies that may have cost Germany the war.

To maintain the morale of the home front during the first two years of the war, Hitler refused to convert production from consumer goods to armaments. The *Blitzkrieg* allowed the Germans to win quick victories, after which they could plunder the food and raw materials of conquered countries in order to avoid diverting resources away from the civilian economy. After the German defeats on the Russian front and the American entry into the war, the economic situation changed. Early in 1942, Hitler finally ordered a massive increase in armaments production and the size of the army. Hitler's personal architect, Albert Speer, was made minister for armaments and munitions in 1942. By eliminating waste and rationalizing procedures, Speer was able to triple the production of armaments between 1942 and 1943 despite the intense Allied air raids. Speer's urgent plea for a total mobilization of resources for the war effort went unheeded, however. Hitler, fearful of civilian morale problems that would undermine the home front, refused any dramatic cuts in the production of consumer goods. A total mobilization of the economy was not implemented until July 1944, when schools, theaters, and cafés were closed and Speer was finally permitted to use all remaining resources for the production of a few basic military items. But by that time, it was too late to save Germany from defeat.

The war produced a reversal in Nazi attitudes toward women. Nazi resistance to female employment declined as the war progressed and more and more men were called up for military service. Nazi magazines now proclaimed, "We see the woman as the eternal mother of our people, but also as the working and fighting comrade of the man."[9] But the number of women working in industry, agriculture, commerce, and domestic service increased only slightly. The total number of employed women in September 1944 was 14.9 million, compared to 14.6 million in May 1939. Many women, especially those of the middle class, resisted regular employment, particularly in factories.

Japan   Wartime Japan was a highly mobilized society. To guarantee its control over all national resources, the government set up a planning board to control prices, wages, the utilization of labor, and the allocation of resources. Traditional habits of obedience and hierarchy, buttressed by the concept of imperial divinity, were emphasized to encourage citizens to sacrifice their resources, and sometimes their lives, for the national cause. Especially important was the code of *bushido*, or the way of the warrior, the old code of morality of the samurai, who had played a prominent military role in medieval and early modern Japanese history. The code of *bushido* was revived during the nationalistic fervor of the 1930s. Based on an ideal of loyalty and service, the code emphasized the obligation to honor and defend emperor, country, and family and to sacrifice one's life if one failed in this

THE BOMBING OF CIVILIANS

The home front became a battle front when civilian populations became the targets of mass bombing raids. Many people believed that mass bombing could effectively weaken the morale of the people and shorten the war. Rarely did it achieve its goal. In these selections, British, German, and Japanese civilians relate their experiences during bombing raids.

London, 1940

Early last evening, the noise was terrible. My husband and Mr. P. were trying to play chess in the kitchen. I was playing draughts with Kenneth in the cupboard.... Presently I heard a stifled voice: "Mummy! I don't know what's become of my glasses." "I should think they are tied up in my wool." My knitting had disappeared and wool seemed to be everywhere! We heard a whistle, a bang which shook the house, and an explosion.... Well, we straightened out, decided draughts and chess were no use under the circumstances, and waited for a lull so we could have a pot of tea.

Hamburg, 1943

As the many fires broke through the roofs of the burning buildings, a column of heated air rose more than two and a half miles high and one and a half miles in diameter.... This column was turbulent, and it was fed from its base by in-rushing cooler ground-surface air. One and one half miles from the fires this draught increased the wind velocity from eleven to thirty-three miles per hour. At the edge of the area the velocities must have been appreciably greater, as trees three feet in diameter were uprooted. In a short time the temperature reached ignition point for all combustibles, and the entire area was ablaze. In such fires complete burnout occurred; that is, no trace of combustible material remained, and only after two days were the areas cool enough to approach.

Hiroshima, August 6, 1945

I heard the airplane; I looked up at the sky, it was a sunny day, the sky was blue.... Then I saw something drop—and pow!—a big explosion knocked me down. Then I was unconscious—I don't know for how long. Then I was conscious but I couldn't see anything.... Then I see people moving away and I just follow them. It is not light like it was before, it is more like evening. I look around; houses are all flat!... I follow the people to the river. I couldn't hear anything, my ears are blocked up. I am thinking a bomb has dropped!... I didn't know my hands were burned, nor my face.... My eyes were swollen and felt closed up.

What common elements do you find in these three different descriptions of bombing raids? What effect did aerial bombing have on the nature of warfare?

---

sacred mission. The system culminated in the final years of the war, when young Japanese were encouraged to volunteer en masse to serve as pilots in the suicide missions (known as *kamikaze,* "divine wind") against U.S. battleships.

Women's rights, too, were to be sacrificed to the greater national cause. Already by 1937, Japanese women were being exhorted to fulfill their patriotic duty by bearing more children and by espousing the slogans of the Greater Japanese Women's Association. However, Japan was extremely reluctant to mobilize women on behalf of Japan's war effort. Female employment increased during the war, but only in areas where women traditionally worked, such as the textile industry and farming. Instead of using women to meet labor shortages, the Japanese government brought in Korean and Chinese laborers.

Civilians on the Front Line: The Bombing of Cities

Bombing was used in World War II in a variety of ways: against nonhuman military targets, against enemy troops, and against civilian populations. These last made World War II as devastating for civilians as for frontline soldiers (see the box above). A small number of bombing raids in the last year of World War I had given rise to the argument that the public outcry generated by the bombing of civilian populations would be an effective way to coerce governments into making peace. Consequently, European air forces began to develop long-range bombers in the 1930s.

Luftwaffe Attacks The first sustained use of civilian bombing contradicted this theory. Beginning in early September 1940, the German *Luftwaffe* subjected London and many other British cities and towns to nightly air raids, making the Blitz (as the British called the German air raids) a national experience. Londoners took the first heavy blows and set the standard for the rest of the British population by refusing to panic. But London morale was helped by the fact that German raids were widely scattered over a very large city. Smaller communities were more directly affected by the devastation. On November 14, 1940, for example, the *Luftwaffe* destroyed hundreds of shops and 100 acres of the city center of Coventry. Morale sank as wild rumors of heavy casualties spread in these communities but soon rebounded.

The Bombing of Germany The British failed to learn from their own experience, however, and soon embarked on the bombing of Germany. Churchill and his advisers believed that destroying German communities would break

The Destruction of Clydebank.
The bombing of an enemy's cities brought the war home to civilian populations. This picture shows a street in Clydebank, near Glasgow in Scotland, the day after the city was bombed by the Germans in March 1941. Only seven of the city's 12,000 houses were left undamaged; 35,000 of the 47,000 inhabitants became homeless overnight. Clydebank was the only city in Scotland to suffer severe bombing damage.

civilian morale and bring victory. Major bombing raids began in 1942 under the direction of Arthur Harris, the wartime leader of the British air force's Bomber Command, which was rearmed with four-engine heavy bombers capable of taking the war into the center of occupied Europe. On May 31, 1942, Cologne became the first German city to be subjected to an attack by one thousand bombers.

With the entry of the Americans into the war, bombing strategy changed. American planes flew daytime missions aimed at the precision bombing of transportation facilities and wartime industries, while the British Bomber Command continued nighttime saturation bombing of all German cities with populations over 100,000. Bombing raids added an element of terror to circumstances already made difficult by growing shortages of food, clothing, and fuel. Germans especially feared incendiary bombs, which set off firestorms that swept destructive paths through the cities. Four raids on Hamburg in August 1943 produced temperatures of 1,800 degrees Fahrenheit, obliterated half the city's buildings, and killed fifty thousand civilians. The ferocious bombing of Dresden on February 13–15, 1945, created a firestorm that may have killed as many as 100,000 inhabitants and refugees.

Germany suffered enormously from the Allied bombing raids. Millions of buildings were destroyed, and possibly half a million civilians died in the raids. Nevertheless, it is highly unlikely that Allied bombing sapped the morale of the German people. Instead, Germans, whether pro- or anti-Nazi, fought on stubbornly, often driven simply by a desire to live. Nor did the bombing destroy Germany's industrial capacity. The Allied Strategic Bombing survey revealed that the production of war materials actually increased between 1942 and 1944. Even in 1944 and 1945, Allied raids cut German production of armaments by only 7 percent.

The Bombing of Japan: The Atomic Bomb The bombing of civilians reached a horrific new level with the dropping of the first atomic bomb. Japan was especially vulnerable to air raids because its air force had been virtually destroyed in the course of the war and its crowded cities were built of flimsy materials. Attacks on Japanese cities by the new American B-29 Superfortresses, the biggest bombers of the war, had begun on November 24, 1944. By the summer of 1945, many of Japan's factories had been destroyed along with one-fourth of its dwellings. After the Japanese government decreed the mobilization of all people between the ages of thirteen and sixty into the People's Volunteer Corps, President Truman and his advisers feared that Japanese fanaticism might mean a million American casualties. This concern led them to drop the newly perfected atomic bomb on Hiroshima (August 6) and Nagasaki (August 9). The destruction was incredible. Of 76,000 buildings near the center of the explosion in Hiroshima, only 6,000 remained standing, and 140,000 of the city's 400,000 inhabitants had died by the end of 1945. Another 50,000 perished from the effects of radiation over the next five years.

Aftermath: Emergence of the Cold War

The total victory of the Allies in World War II was followed not by peace but by a new conflict known as the Cold War that dominated world politics until the end of the 1980s. The Cold War grew out of military, political, and ideological differences, especially between the Soviet Union and the United States, that became apparent during the last years of the war. Although Allied leaders were preoccupied primarily with ending the war, they

The Victorious Allied Leaders at Yalta. Even before World War II ended, the leaders of the Big Three of the Grand Alliance, Churchill, Roosevelt, and Stalin (shown from left to right), met in wartime conferences to plan the final assault on Germany and negotiate the outlines of the postwar settlement. At the Yalta meeting (February 5–11, 1945), the three leaders concentrated on postwar issues. The American president died two months later.

were also strongly motivated by differing and often conflicting visions of postwar Europe.

The Conference at Tehran

Stalin, Roosevelt, and Churchill, the leaders of the Big Three of the Grand Alliance, met at Tehran, the capital of Iran, in November 1943 to decide the future course of the war. Their major tactical decision concerned the final assault on Germany. Stalin and Roosevelt argued successfully for an American-British invasion of the Continent through France, which they scheduled for the spring of 1944. The acceptance of this plan had important consequences. It meant that Soviet and British-American forces would meet in defeated Germany along a north-south dividing line and that eastern Europe would most likely be liberated by Soviet forces. The Allies also agreed to an administrative partition of postwar Germany.

The Yalta Conference

By the time of the conference at Yalta, in the Soviet republic of the Ukraine, in February 1945, the defeat of Germany was a foregone conclusion. The Western powers, which had earlier believed that the Soviets were in a weak position, now faced the reality of eleven million Red Army soldiers taking possession of eastern and much of central Europe. Stalin was still operating under the notion of spheres of influence. He was deeply suspicious of the Western powers and desired a buffer to protect the Soviet Union from possible future Western aggression. At the same time, however, Stalin was eager to obtain economically important resources and strategic military positions. Roosevelt by this time was moving away from the notion of spheres of influence to the ideal of self-determination. He called for "the end of the system of unilateral action, exclusive alliances, and spheres of

influence." The Grand Alliance approved the Declaration on Liberated Europe. This was a pledge to assist liberated European nations in the creation of "democratic institutions of their own choice." Liberated countries were to hold free elections to determine their political systems.

At Yalta, Roosevelt sought Soviet military help against Japan. The atomic bomb was not yet assured, and American military planners feared the possible loss of as many as one million men in amphibious assaults on the Japanese home islands. Roosevelt therefore agreed to Stalin's price for military assistance against Japan: possession of Sakhalin and the Kurile Islands, as well as two warm-water ports and railroad rights in Manchuria.

The creation of the United Nations was a major American concern at Yalta. Roosevelt hoped to ensure the participation of the Big Three powers in a postwar international organization before difficult issues divided them into hostile camps. After a number of compromises, both Churchill and Stalin accepted Roosevelt's plans for a United Nations organization and set the first meeting for San Francisco in April 1945.

The issues of Germany and eastern Europe were treated less decisively. The Big Three reaffirmed that Germany must surrender unconditionally and created four occupation zones (see Map 27.5). German reparations were set at $20 billion. A compromise was also worked out in regard to Poland. Stalin agreed to free elections in the future to determine a new government. But the issue of free elections in eastern Europe caused a serious rift between the Soviets and the Americans. The principle was that eastern European governments would be freely elected, but they were also supposed to be pro-Soviet. This attempt to reconcile two irreconcilable goals was doomed to failure, as soon became evident at the next conference of the Big Three powers.

Even before the conference at Potsdam, near Berlin, took place in July 1945, Western relations with the Soviets were deteriorating rapidly. The Grand Alliance had been one of necessity in which disagreements had been subordinated to the pragmatic concerns of the war. The Allied powers' only common aim was the defeat of Nazism. Once this aim had all but been accomplished, the many differences that troubled East-West relations came to the surface. Each side committed acts that the other viewed as unbecoming of allies.

From the perspective of the Soviets, the United States' termination of lend-lease aid before the war was over and its failure to respond to a Soviet request for a $6 billion loan for reconstruction exposed the Western desire to keep the Soviet state weak. On the American side, the Soviet Union's failure to fulfill its Yalta pledge on the Declaration on Liberated Europe as applied to eastern Europe set a dangerous precedent. This was evident in Romania as early

as February 1945, when the Soviets engineered a coup and installed a new government under the Communist Petra Groza, known as the "Little Stalin." One month later, the Soviets sabotaged the Polish settlement by arresting West-leaning Polish leaders and their sympathizers and placing Soviet-backed Poles in power. To the Americans, the Soviets seemed to be asserting control of eastern European countries under puppet Communist regimes.

The Potsdam Conference

The Potsdam conference of July 1945 consequently began under a cloud of mistrust. Roosevelt had died on April 12 and had been succeeded as president by Harry Truman. During the conference, Truman received word that the

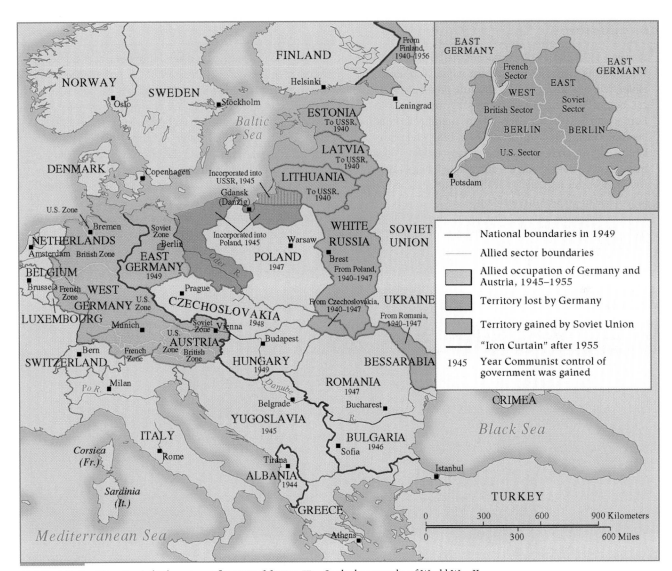

MAP 27.5 Territorial Changes After World War II.   In the last months of World War II, the Red Army occupied much of eastern Europe. Stalin sought pro-Soviet satellite states in the region as a buffer against future invasions from western Europe, whereas Britain and the United States wanted democratically elected governments. Soviet military control of the territory settled the question. ❓ Which country gained the most territory at the expense of Germany?

🌐 **View an animated version of this map or related maps at** http://thomsonedu.com/history/spielvogel

atomic bomb had been successfully tested. Some historians have argued that this knowledge resulted in Truman's stiffened resolve against the Soviets. Whatever the reasons, there was a new coldness in the relations between the Soviets and the Americans. At Potsdam, Truman demanded free elections throughout eastern Europe. Stalin responded, "A freely elected government in any of these East European countries would be anti-Soviet, and that we cannot allow."[10] After a bitterly fought and devastating war, Stalin sought absolute military security. To him, it could be gained only by the presence of Communist states in eastern Europe. Free elections might result in governments hostile to the Soviets. By the middle of 1945, only an invasion by Western forces could undo developments in eastern Europe, and after the world's most destructive conflict had ended, few people favored such a policy.

As the war slowly receded into the past, the reality of conflicting ideologies had come back into focus. Many people in the West interpreted Soviet policy as part of a worldwide Communist conspiracy. The Soviets viewed Western, especially American, policy as global capitalist expansionism or, in Leninist terms, economic imperialism. Vyacheslav Molotov, the Russian foreign minister, referred to the Americans as "insatiable imperialists" and "war-mongering groups of adventurers."[11] In March 1946, in a speech to an American audience, former British prime minister Winston Churchill declared that "an iron curtain" had "descended across the continent," dividing Germany and Europe into two hostile camps. Stalin branded Churchill's speech a "call to war with the Soviet Union." Only months after the world's most devastating conflict had ended, the world seemed once again bitterly divided.

CONCLUSION

Between 1933 and 1939, Europeans watched as Adolf Hitler rebuilt Germany into a great military power. For Hitler, military power was an absolute prerequisite for the creation of a German racial empire that would dominate Europe and the world for generations to come. If Hitler had been successful, the Nazi New Order, built on authoritarianism, racism, and brutal oppression, would have meant a triumph of barbarism and the end of freedom and equality, which, however imperfectly realized, had become important ideals in Western civilization.

The Nazis lost, but only after tremendous sacrifices and costs. Much of European civilization lay in ruins, and the old

Europe had disappeared forever. Europeans, accustomed to dominating the world at the start of the twentieth century, now watched helplessly at mid-century as the two new superpowers emerging from the two world wars took control of their destinies. Even before the last battles had been fought, the United States and the Soviet Union had arrived at different visions of the postwar world. No sooner had the war ended than their differences sparked a new and potentially even more devastating conflict known as the Cold War. Yet even though Europeans seemed mere pawns in the struggle between the two superpowers, they managed to stage a remarkable recovery of their own civilization.

TIMELINE

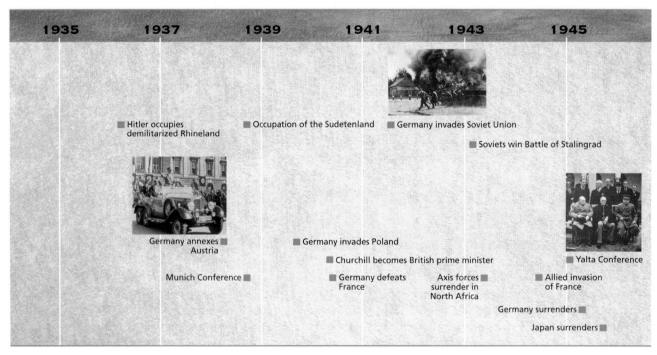

1935   1937   1939   1941   1943   1945

■ Hitler occupies demilitarized Rhineland   ■ Occupation of the Sudetenland   ■ Germany invades Soviet Union

■ Soviets win Battle of Stalingrad

Germany annexes ■ Austria   ■ Germany invades Poland   ■ Yalta Conference

■ Churchill becomes British prime minister

Munich Conference ■   ■ Germany defeats France   Axis forces ■ surrender in North Africa   ■ Allied invasion of France

Germany surrenders ■

Japan surrenders ■

NOTES

1. A. Hitler, *Mein Kampf*, trans. R. Manheim (Boston, 1971), p. 654.
2. *Documents on German Foreign Policy* (London, 1956), ser. D, vol. 7, p. 204.
3. Quoted in A. Speer, *Spandau*, trans. R. Winston and C. Winston (New York, 1976), p. 50.
4. Quoted in *Nazi Conspiracy and Aggression* (Washington, D.C., 1946), vol. 6, p. 262.
5. International Military Tribunal, *Trial of the Major War Criminals* (Nuremberg, 1947–1949), vol. 22, p. 480.
6. Quoted in R. Hilberg, *The Destruction of the European Jews*, rev. ed. (New York, 1985), vol. 1, pp. 332–333.
7. *Nazi Conspiracy and Aggression*, vol. 6, p. 789.
8. Quoted in J. Campbell, *The Experience of World War II* (New York, 1989), p. 170.
9. Quoted in C. Koonz, "Mothers in the Fatherland: Women in Nazi Germany," in R. Bridenthal and C. Koonz, eds., *Becoming Visible: Women in European History* (Boston, 1977), p. 466.
10. Quoted in N. Graebner, *Cold War Diplomacy, 1945–1960* (Princeton, N.J., 1962), p. 117.
11. Quoted in W. Loth, *The Division of the World, 1941–1955* (New York, 1988), p. 81.

SUGGESTIONS FOR FURTHER READING

An analysis of Germany's prewar foreign policy can be found in **G. Weinberg**, *The Foreign Policy of Hitler's Germany: Diplomatic Revolution in Europe, 1933–36* (Chicago, 1970), and *The Foreign Policy of Hitler's Germany: Starting World War II, 1937–1939* (Chicago, 1980). For a detailed account of the immediate events leading to World War II, see **D. C. Watt**, *How War Came: The Immediate Origins of the Second World War, 1938–1939* (New York, 1989).

Hitler's war aims and the importance of ideology to those aims are examined in **N. Rich**, *Hitler's War Aims*, vol. 1, *Ideology, the Nazi State, and the Course of Expansion* (New York, 1973), and vol. 2, *The Establishment of the New Order* (New York, 1974). On the origins of the war in the Pacific, see **A. Iriye**, *The Origins of the Second World War in Asia and the Pacific* (London, 1987). General works on World War II include the comprehensive volume by **G. Weinberg**, *A World at Arms: A Global History of World War II*, 2d ed. (Cambridge, 2005); **M. K. Dziewanowski**, *War at Any Price: World War II in Europe, 1939–1945*, 2d ed. (Englewood Cliffs, N.J., 1991); and **J. Campbell**, *The Experience of World War II* (New York, 1989). On Hitler as a military leader, see **R. Lewin**, *Hitler's Mistakes* (New York, 1986). On Hitler's attack on Poland, see **A. B. Rossino**, *Hitler Strikes Poland: Blitzkrieg, Ideology, and Atrocity* (Lawrence, Kans., 2003). The Eastern Front is covered in **O. Bartov**, *The Eastern Front, 1941–45: German Troops and the Barbarisation of Warfare* (London, 1986).

A standard work on the Nazi New Order in Russia is **A. Dallin**, *German Rule in Russia, 1941–1945*, rev. ed. (London, 1981). On Poland, see **J. T. Gross**, *Polish Society Under German Occupation* (Princeton, N.J., 1981). On foreign labor, see **E. Homze**, *Foreign Labor in Nazi Germany* (Princeton, N.J., 1967).

The best studies of the Holocaust include **R. Hilberg**, *The Destruction of the European Jews*, rev. ed., 3 vols. (New York, 1985); **L. Dawidowicz**, *The War Against the Jews* (New York, 1975); **L. Yahil**, *The Holocaust* (Oxford, 1990); and **M. Gilbert**, *The Holocaust: The History of the Jews of Europe During the Second World War* (New York, 1985). For brief studies, see **J. Fischel**, *The Holocaust* (Westport, Conn., 1998); **R. S. Botwinick**, *A History of the Holocaust* (Upper Saddle River, N.J., 1996); and **D. Dwork and R. J. van Pelt**, *Holocaust: A History* (New York, 2002). On the extermination camps, see **K. G. Feig**, *Hitler's Death Camps: The Sanity of Madness* (New York, 1981). On Auschwitz, see **S. Steinbacher**, *Auschwitz: A History* (New York, 2005). Other Nazi atrocities are examined in **R. C. Lukas**, *Forgotten Holocaust: The Poles Under German Occupation, 1939–44* (Lexington, Ky., 1986), and **B. Wytwycky**, *The Other Holocaust* (Washington, D.C., 1980).

General studies on the impact of total war include **J. Costello**, *Love, Sex and War: Changing Values, 1939–1945* (London, 1985); **P. Summerfield**, *Women Workers in the Second World War: Production and Patriarchy in Conflict* (London, 1984); and **M. R. Marrus**, *The Unwanted: European Refugees in the Twentieth Century* (New York, 1985). On the home front in Germany, see **E. R. Beck**, *Under the Bombs: The German Home Front, 1942–1945* (Lexington, Ky., 1986); **M. Kitchen**, *Nazi Germany at War* (New York, 1995); and **J. Stephenson**, *The Nazi Organisation of Women* (London, 1981). The Soviet Union during the war is examined in **M. Harrison**, *Soviet Planning in Peace and War, 1938–1945* (Cambridge, 1985). On the American home front, see the collection of essays in **K. P. O'Brien and L. H. Parsons**, *The Home-Front War: World War II and American Society* (Westport, Conn., 1995).

On the destruction of Germany by bombing raids, see **H. Rumpf**, *The Bombing of Germany* (London, 1963). The German bombing of Britain is covered in **T. Harrisson**, *Living Through the Blitz* (London, 1985). On Hiroshima, see **A. Chisholm**, *Faces of Hiroshima* (London, 1985).

On the emergence of the Cold War, see **W. Loth**, *The Division of the World, 1941–1955* (New York, 1988), and the more extensive list of references at the end of Chapter 28.

Thomson **NOW!** Enter *ThomsonNOW* using the access card that is available for *Western Civilization: A Brief History*. *ThomsonNOW* will help you understand this chapter with lesson plans generated for your needs. In addition, you can read the following documents, and many more, online:

Adolf Hitler, Proclamation to the German Nation
Winston Churchill, speeches
Charles de Gaulle, Tunis speech
Nuremberg Trials, excerpts

WESTERN CIVILIZATION RESOURCES

Visit the Web site for *Western Civilization: A Brief History* for resources specific to this book:

http://www.thomsonedu.com/history/spielvogel

For a variety of tools to help you succeed in this course, visit the Western Civilization Resource Center at

http://history.wadsworth.com/spielvogel

Included are quizzes, images, documents, interactive simulations, maps and timelines, movie explorations, and a wealth of other sources.

CHAPTER
28

COLD WAR AND A NEW WESTERN WORLD, 1945–1973

CHAPTER OUTLINE AND FOCUS QUESTIONS

Development of the Cold War

☐ What events between 1945 and 1949 heightened the tensions between the United States and the Soviet Union, and how and why did the Cold War become a global affair after 1949?

Recovery and Renewal in Europe

☐ What were the main developments in the Soviet Union and Eastern Europe between 1945 and 1970?

Europe and the World: Decolonization

☐ Why and how did the European colonies in Africa, the Middle East, and Asia gain independence between 1945 and 1973?

The United States and Canada: A New Era

☐ What were the main political developments in the nations of Western Europe and North America between 1945 and 1973?

Postwar Society and Culture in the Western World

☐ What major changes occurred in Western society and culture between 1945 and 1973?

CRITICAL THINKING

☐ What were the similarities and differences in the political, social, and economic history of Eastern Europe and Western Europe between 1945 and 1973?

Children play amid the ruins of Warsaw, Poland, at the end of World War II

Reginald Kenny/© Bettmann/CORBIS

THE END OF WORLD WAR II in Europe was met with great joy. One visitor to Moscow reported, "I looked out of the window [at 2 A.M.], almost everywhere there were lights in the window–people were staying awake. Everyone embraced everyone else, someone sobbed aloud." But after the victory parades and celebrations, Europeans awoke to a devastating realization: their civilization was in ruins. Some wondered if Europe would ever regain its former prosperity and importance. Winston Churchill wrote, "What is Europe now? A rubble heap, a charnel house, a breeding ground of pestilence and hate." There was ample reason for his pessimism. Almost forty million people (both soldiers and civilians) had been killed during the last six years. Massive air raids and artillery bombardments had reduced many of the great cities of Europe to heaps of rubble. An American general described Berlin: "Wherever we looked we saw desolation. It was like a city of the dead. Suffering and shock were visible in every face. Dead bodies still remained in canals and lakes and were being dug out from under bomb debris." Millions of Europeans faced starvation because grain harvests were only half of what they had been in 1939. Millions were also homeless. In the parts of the Soviet Union that had been occupied by the Germans, almost twenty-five million people were without homes. The destruction of bridges, roads, and railroads had left transportation systems paralyzed. Eleven million prisoners of war had to be returned to their native countries, and fifteen million Germans and Eastern Europeans were driven out of countries where they were no longer wanted. Yet despite the chaos, Europe was soon on the road to a remarkable recovery. Already by 1950, Europe's industrial and agricultural output was 30 percent above prewar levels.

World War II had also destroyed European supremacy in world affairs. After 1945, the colonial empires of the European nations rapidly disintegrated, and Europe's place in the world changed radically. As the Cold War conflict between the world's two superpowers—the United States and the Soviet Union—intensified, the European nations were divided into two armed camps dependent on one or the other of these two major powers. The United States and the Soviet Union, whose rivalry raised the specter of nuclear war, seemed to hold the survival of Europe and the world in their hands.♦

Development of the Cold War

Even before World War II had ended, the two major Allied powers—the United States and the Soviet Union—had begun to disagree on their vision for postwar Europe. Unity had been maintained during the war because of the urgent need to defeat the Axis powers, but once they were defeated, the differences between the Americans and Soviets again surged to the fore.

Confrontation of the Superpowers

Considerable historical debate has been waged about who was responsible for starting the Cold War. Both the United States and the Soviet Union took steps at the end of the war that were unwise or might have been avoided. Both nations, however, were working within a framework conditioned by the past. Ultimately, the rivalry between the two superpowers stemmed from their different historical perspectives and their irreconcilable political ambitions. Intense competition for political and military supremacy had long been a regular feature of Western civilization. The United States and the Soviet Union were the heirs of that European tradition of power politics, and it should not surprise us that two such different systems would seek to extend their way of life to the rest of the world. Because of its need to feel secure on its western border, the Soviet Union was not prepared to give up the advantages it had gained in Eastern Europe from Germany's defeat. But neither were American leaders willing to give up the power and prestige the United States had gained throughout the world. Suspicious of each other's motives, the two nations soon raised their mutual fears to a level of intense competition. Between 1945 and 1949, a number of events entangled the two in irreconcilable conflict.

Eastern Europe was the first area of disagreement. The United States and Great Britain had championed self-determination and democratic freedom for the liberated nations of Eastern Europe. Stalin, however, fearful that the Eastern European nations would return to traditional anti-Soviet attitudes if they were permitted free elections, opposed the West's plans. Having liberated Eastern Europe from the Nazis, the Red Army proceeded to install pro-Soviet governing regimes in Poland, Romania, Bulgaria, and Hungary. These pro-Soviet governments satisfied Stalin's desire for a buffer zone against the West, but the local populations and their sympathizers in the West regarded the regimes as an expansion of Stalin's empire.

The Truman Doctrine A civil war in Greece served as another arena for confrontation between the superpowers. The Communist People's Liberation Army and the anti-Communist forces supported by the British were fighting each other for control of Greece in 1946. President Harry Truman of the United States, alarmed by British weakness and the possibility of Soviet expansion into the eastern Mediterranean, responded with the **Truman Doctrine** (see the box on p. 538). Truman requested $400 million in economic and military aid for Greece and Turkey from the U.S. Congress. The Truman Doctrine said, in essence, that the United States would provide money to countries that claimed they were threatened by Communist expansion. If the Soviets were not stopped in Greece, the United States would have to face the spread of communism throughout the free world. As Dean Acheson, the American secretary of state, explained, "Like apples in a barrel infected by disease, the corruption of Greece would infect Iran and all the East . . . likewise Africa . . . Italy . . . France. . . . Not since Rome and Carthage has there been such a polarization of power on this earth."[1]

The proclamation of the Truman Doctrine was soon followed in June 1947 by the European Recovery Program, better known as the **Marshall Plan.** Intended to rebuild prosperity and stability, this program included $13 billion for the economic recovery of war-torn Europe. Underlying it was the belief that Communist aggression fed off economic turmoil. General George C. Marshall had noted in a speech at Harvard, "Our policy is not directed against any country or doctrine but against hunger, poverty, desperation, and chaos."[2] From the Soviet perspective, the Marshall Plan guaranteed "the American loans in return for the relinquishing by the European states of their economic and later also their political independence." To some scholars, the Marshall Plan encouraged Stalin to push for even greater control of Eastern Europe to safeguard Soviet interests.

Containment By 1947, the split in Europe between East and West had become a fact of life. At the end of World War II, the United States had favored a quick end to its commitments in Europe. But American fears of Soviet aims caused the United States to play an increasingly large role in Europe. In an important article in *Foreign*

THE TRUMAN DOCTRINE

*B*y 1947, the battle lines in the Cold War had been clearly drawn. This selection is taken from a speech by President Harry S Truman to the U.S. Congress in which he justified his request for aid to Greece and Turkey. Truman expressed the urgent need to contain the expansion of communism.

President Harry S Truman, Address to Congress, March 12, 1947

The peoples of a number of countries of the world have recently had totalitarian regimes forced upon them against their will. The Government of the United States has made frequent protests against coercion and intimidation, in violation of the Yalta agreement, in Poland, Romania, and Bulgaria. I must also state that in a number of other countries there have been similar developments.

At the present moment in world history nearly every nation must choose between alternative ways of life. The choice is too often not a free one.

One way of life is based upon the will of the majority, and is distinguished by free institutions, representative government, free elections, guarantees of individual liberty, freedom of speech and religion, and freedom from political oppression.

The second way of life is based upon the will of a minority forcibly imposed upon the majority. It relies upon terror and oppression, a controlled press and radio, fixed elections, and the suppression of personal freedoms.

I believe that it must be the policy of the United States to support free peoples who are resisting attempted subjugation by armed minorities or by outside pressures.

I believe that we must assist free people to work out their own destinies in their own way.

I believe that our help should be primarily through economic and financial aid which is essential to economic stability and orderly political processes. . . . I therefore ask the Congress for assistance to Greece and Turkey in the amount of $400,000,000.

_____

How did President Truman defend his request for aid to Greece and Turkey? Did this decision play a role in intensifying the Cold War? Why or why not?

Affairs in July 1947, George Kennan, a well-known American diplomat with much knowledge of Soviet affairs, advocated a policy of **containment** against further aggression by the Soviets. Kennan favored the "adroit and vigilant application of counterforce at a series of constantly shifting geographical and political points, corresponding to the shifts and manoeuvres of Soviet policy." By 1948, containment of the Soviet Union became formal American policy.

Contention over Germany The fate of Germany also became a source of heated contention between East and West. Besides the partitioning of Germany (and Berlin) into four occupied zones, the Allied powers had agreed on little else with regard to the conquered nation. The Soviets, hardest hit by the war, took reparations from Germany in the form of booty. The technology-starved Soviets dismantled and removed to Russia 380 factories from the western zones of Berlin before transferring their control to the Western powers. At the same time, the German Communist Party was reestablished under the control of Walter Ulbricht (1893–1973) and was soon in charge of the political reconstruction of the Soviet zone in eastern Germany.

At the same time, the British, French, and Americans gradually began to merge their zones economically and by February 1948 were making plans for the unification of these three western sections of Germany and the formal creation of a West German federal government. The Soviets responded with a blockade of West Berlin that allowed neither trucks nor trains to enter the three western zones of Berlin.

The Western powers faced a dilemma. Direct military confrontation seemed dangerous, and no one wished to risk World War III. Therefore, an attempt to break through the blockade with tanks and trucks was ruled out. The solution was the Berlin Air Lift. At its peak, 13,000 tons of supplies were flown daily to Berlin. The Soviets, also not wanting war, did not interfere and finally lifted the blockade in May 1949. The blockade of Berlin had severely increased tensions between the United States and the Soviet Union and resulted in the separation of Germany into two states. The Federal Republic of Germany, known as West Germany, was formally created in September 1949, and a month later, the separate German Democratic Republic was established in East Germany. Berlin remained a divided city and the source of much contention between East and West.

New Military Alliances The Soviet Union also detonated its first atomic bomb in 1949, and all too soon, both powers were involved in an escalating arms race that resulted in the construction of ever more destructive nuclear weapons. Soon the search for security took the form of **mutual deterrence,** the belief that an arsenal of nuclear weapons prevented war by ensuring that if one nation launched its nuclear weapons in a preemptive first strike, the other nation would still be able to respond and devastate the attacker. It was assumed that neither side would risk using the massive arsenals that had been assembled.

The Berlin Air Lift. The Berlin Air Lift enabled the United States to fly 13,000 tons of supplies daily to Berlin and thus break the Soviet land blockade of the city. In this photograph, residents of West Berlin watch an American plane arrive with supplies for the city.

The search for security in the uncertain atmosphere of the Cold War also led to the formation of military alliances. The North Atlantic Treaty Organization (**NATO**) was formed in April 1949 when Belgium, Luxembourg, the Netherlands, France, Britain, Italy, Denmark, Norway, Portugal, and Iceland signed a treaty with the United States and Canada. All the powers agreed to provide mutual assistance if any one of them was attacked. A few years later, West Germany, Greece, and Turkey joined NATO.

The Eastern European states soon followed suit. In 1955, Albania, Bulgaria, Czechoslovakia, East Germany, Hungary, Poland, Romania, and the Soviet Union organized a formal military alliance in the **Warsaw Pact.** Like so many times before, Europe was divided into hostile alliance systems.

Globalization of the Cold War

The Cold War soon spread from Europe to the rest of the world. The victory of the Chinese Communists in 1949 in the Chinese civil war brought a new Communist regime and intensified American fears about the spread of communism. Shortly thereafter, the Korean War turned the Cold War into a worldwide struggle, eventually leading to a system of military alliances around the world.

The Korean War Korea had been liberated from the Japanese in 1945 but soon split into two parts. The land north of the 38th parallel became the Democratic People's Republic of Korea (North Korea) and was supported by the Soviet Union. The Republic of Korea (South Korea) received aid from the United States. In 1950, probably with Stalin's approval, North Korean forces invaded South Korea. The Americans, seeing this as yet another example of Communist aggression and expansion, gained the support of the United Nations and intervened by sending American troops to turn back the invasion. When the American and South Korean forces pushed the North Koreans back toward the Chinese border, Chinese forces entered the fray and forced the American and South Korean troops to retreat back to South Korea. Believing that the Chinese were simply the puppets of Moscow, American policy makers created an image of communism as a monolithic force directed by the Soviet Union. After two more years of inconclusive fighting, an uneasy truce was reached in 1953, leaving Korea divided. To many Americans, the policy of containing communism had succeeded in Asia, just as it had earlier in Europe.

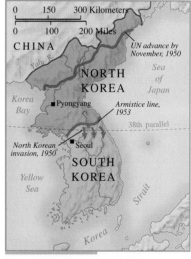

The Korean War

Escalation of the Cold War The Korean experience seemed to confirm American fears of communist expansion and reinforced American determination to contain Soviet power. In the mid-1950s, the administration of President Dwight D. Eisenhower (1890–1969) adopted a policy of massive retaliation, which advocated the full use of American nuclear bombs to counteract even a Soviet ground attack in Europe. Moreover, American military alliances were extended around the world. The Central Treaty Organization (CENTO) of Turkey, Iraq, Iran, Pakistan, Britain, and the United States was intended to prevent the Soviet Union from expanding at the expense of its southern neighbors. The United States, Britain, France, Pakistan, Thailand, the Philippines, Australia, and New Zealand formed the Southeast Asia Treaty Organization (SEATO). By the mid-1950s, the United States found itself allied militarily with forty-two states around the world.

Despite the continued escalation of the Cold War, hopes for a new era of peaceful coexistence also appeared. The death of Stalin in 1953 caused some people in the West to think that the new Soviet leadership might be more flexible in its policies. But this optimism proved premature. All talk of **rapprochement** between East and West temporarily ceased when the Soviet Union used its armed forces in 1956 to crush Hungary's attempt to assert its independence from Soviet control.

A crisis over Berlin also added to the tension in the late 1950s. In August 1957, the Soviet Union had launched its first intercontinental ballistic missile (ICBM) and, shortly after, *Sputnik I,* the first space satellite. Fueled by partisan political debate, fears of a "missile gap" between the United States and the Soviet Union seized the American public. Nikita Khrushchev (1894–1971), the new leader of the Soviet Union, attempted to take advantage of the American frenzy over missiles to solve the problem of West Berlin. Khrushchev had said that Berlin was like "the testicles of the West: every time I want to make the West scream, I squeeze on Berlin."[3] West Berlin had remained a "Western island" of prosperity in the midst of the relatively poverty-stricken East Germany. Many East Germans also managed to escape by fleeing to West Berlin.

In November 1958, Khrushchev announced that unless the West removed its forces from West Berlin within six months, he would turn over control of the access routes to Berlin to the East Germans. Unwilling to accept an ultimatum that would have abandoned West Berlin to the Communists, Eisenhower and the West stood firm, and Khrushchev eventually backed down. In 1961, the East German government built a wall separating West Berlin from East Berlin, and the Berlin issue faded.

It was revived when John F. Kennedy (1917–1963) became the U.S. president. During a summit meeting in Vienna in June 1961, Khrushchev threatened Kennedy with another six-month ultimatum over West Berlin. Kennedy left Vienna convinced of the need to deal firmly with the Soviet Union, and Khrushchev was forced once again to lift his six-month ultimatum. However, determined to achieve some foreign policy success, the Soviet leader soon embarked on an even more dangerous adventure in Cuba.

The Cuban Missile Crisis   The Cold War confrontation between the United States and the Soviet Union reached frightening levels during the Cuban Missile Crisis. In 1959, a left-wing revolutionary named Fidel Castro (b. 1927) had overthrown the Cuban dictator Fulgencio Batista and established a Soviet-supported totalitarian regime. In 1961, an American-supported attempt to invade via the Bay of Pigs and overthrow Castro's regime ended in utter failure. The next year, the Soviet Union decided to station nuclear missiles in Cuba. The United States was not prepared to allow nuclear weapons within such close striking distance of the American mainland, even though it had placed nuclear weapons in Turkey within easy range of the Soviet Union. Khrushchev was quick to point out that "your rockets are in Turkey. You are worried by Cuba . . . because it is 90 miles from the American coast. But Turkey is next to us."[4] When U.S. intelligence discovered that a Soviet fleet carrying missiles was heading to Cuba, President Kennedy decided to blockade Cuba and prevent the fleet from reaching its destination. This approach to the problem had the benefit of delaying confrontation and giving each side time to find a peaceful solution (see the box on p. 541). Khrushchev agreed to turn back the fleet if Kennedy pledged not to invade Cuba.

The intense feeling that the world might have been annihilated in a few days had a profound influence on both sides. A hotline communication system between Moscow and Washington was installed in 1963 to expedite rapid communication between the two superpowers in time of crisis. The same year, the two powers agreed to ban nuclear tests in the atmosphere, a step that served to lessen the tensions between the two nations.

The Vietnam War   By that time, the United States had also been drawn into a new confrontation that had an important impact on the Cold War—the Vietnam War. In 1964, under President Lyndon B. Johnson (1908–1973), increasing numbers of U.S. troops were sent to Vietnam to keep the Communist regime of the north from uniting the entire country under its control. Although nationalism played a powerful role in this conflict, the American policy makers saw it in terms of a **domino theory** concerning the spread of communism. If the Communists succeeded in Vietnam, the

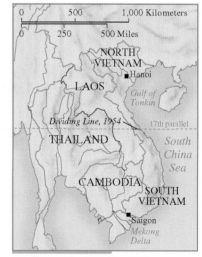

The Vietnam War

argument went, all the other countries in Asia freeing themselves from colonial domination would fall, like dominoes, to communism.

THE CUBAN MISSILE CRISIS: KHRUSHCHEV'S PERSPECTIVE

The Cuban Missile Crisis was one of the most sobering experiences of the Cold War. It led the two superpowers to seek new ways to lessen the tensions between them. This version of the events is taken from the memoirs of Nikita Khrushchev.

Khrushchev Remembers

I will explain what the Caribbean crisis of October 1962, was all about.... At the time that Fidel Castro led his revolution to victory and entered Havana with his troops, we had no idea what political course his regime would follow.... All the while the Americans had been watching Castro closely. At first they thought that the capitalist underpinnings of the Cuban economy would remain intact. So by the time Castro announced that he was going to put Cuba on the road toward Socialism, the Americans had already missed their chance to do any thing about it by simply exerting their influence: there were no longer any forces left which could be organized to fight on America's behalf in Cuba. That left only one alternative–invasion!...

After Castro's crushing victory over the counter-revolutionaries we intensified our military aid to Cuba.... We were sure that the Americans would never reconcile themselves to the existence of Castro's Cuba. They feared, as much as we hoped, that a Socialist Cuba might become a magnet that would attract other Latin American countries to Socialism.... It was clear to me that we might very well lose Cuba if we didn't take some decisive steps in her defense.... We had to think up some way of confronting America with more than words. We had to establish a tangible and effective deterrent to American interference in the Caribbean. But what exactly? The logical answer was missiles. We knew that American missiles were aimed against us in Turkey and Italy, to say nothing of West Germany.... My

thinking went like this: if we installed the missiles secretly and then if the United States discovered the missiles were there after they were already poised and ready to strike, the Americans would think twice before trying to liquidate our installations by military means.... I want to make one thing absolutely clear: when we put our ballistic missiles in Cuba we had no desire to start a war. On the contrary, our principal aim was only to deter America from starting a war....

President Kennedy issued an ultimatum, demanding that we remove our missiles and bombers from Cuba.... We sent the Americans a note saying that we agreed to remove our missiles and bombers on the condition that the President give us his assurance that there would be no invasion of Cuba by the forces of the United States or anybody else. Finally Kennedy gave in and agreed to make a statement giving us such an assurance.... It had been, to say the least, an interesting and challenging situation. The two most powerful nations of the world had been squared off against each other, each with its finger on the button. You'd have thought that war was inevitable. But both sides showed that if the desire to avoid war is strong enough, even the most pressing dispute can be solved by compromise. And a compromise over Cuba was indeed found. The episode ended in a triumph of common sense.... It was a great victory for us, though, that we had been able to extract from Kennedy a promise that neither America nor any of her allies would invade Cuba.... The Caribbean crisis was a triumph of Soviet foreign policy and a personal triumph in my own career as a statesman and as a member of the collective leadership. We achieved, I would say, a spectacular success without having to fire a single shot!

_____

Why, according to his memoirs, did Nikita Khrushchev decide to place missiles in Cuba? Why did he later agree to remove them?

Despite their massive superiority in equipment and firepower, U.S. forces failed to prevail over the persistence of the North Vietnamese. The mounting destruction and increasing brutality of the war, brought into American homes every evening on television, also turned American public opinion against U.S. participation in the war. In 1973, President Richard Nixon (1913–1994) reached an agreement with North Vietnam that allowed the United States to withdraw its forces. Within two years, Vietnam had been forcibly reunited by Communist armies from the North.

Despite the success of the North Vietnamese Communists, the domino theory proved unfounded. A noisy rupture between Communist China and the Soviet Union put an end to the idea of a monolithic communism directed by Moscow. Under President Nixon, U.S. relations with China were resumed. Above all, Vietnam helped

show the limitations of American power. By the end of the Vietnam War, a new era in American-Soviet relations, known as **détente,** had begun to emerge.

Recovery and Renewal in Europe

Within a few years after the defeat of Germany and Italy in World War II, economic revival brought renewed growth to European society, although major differences remained between Western and Eastern Europe.

The Soviet Union: From Stalin to Khrushchev

World War II devastated the Soviet Union. To create a new industrial base, Stalin returned to the method that

Truman Doctrine	1947
European Recovery Program (Marshall Plan)	1947
Berlin blockade	1948–1949
Communist victory in Chinese civil war	1949
Soviet Union's first atomic bomb	1949
Formation of North Atlantic Treaty Organization	1949
Korean War	1950–1953
Formation of Warsaw Pact	1955
Berlin Crisis	1958
Cuban Missile Crisis	1962
Vietnam War	1964–1973

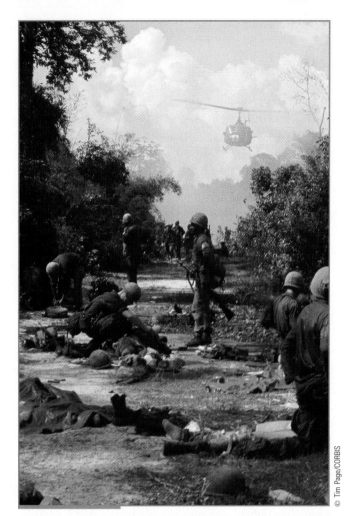

© Tim Page/CORBIS

The Vietnam War. Starting in 1964, U.S. troops fought against Vietcong guerrillas and North Vietnamese regular forces until they were withdrawn as a result of the Paris Agreement, reached in January 1973. Shown here are U.S. troops after a Vietcong attack. The helicopter that is arriving would soon remove the American wounded from the battlefield.

he had used in the 1930s—the acquisition of development capital from Soviet labor. Working hard for little pay, poor housing, and precious few consumer goods, Soviet laborers were expected to produce goods for export with little in return for themselves. The incoming capital from abroad could then be used to purchase machinery and Western technology. The loss of millions of men in the war meant that much of this tremendous workload fell on Soviet women. Almost 40 percent of heavy manual labor was performed by women.

Economic recovery in the Soviet Union was nothing less than spectacular. By 1947, Russian industrial production had attained prewar levels; three years later, it had surpassed them by 40 percent. New power plants, canals, and giant factories were built, while new industrial plants and oil fields were established in Siberia and Soviet Central Asia.

Stalin's Policies   Although Stalin's economic policy was successful in promoting growth in heavy industry, primarily for the benefit of the military, consumer goods were scarce. The development of thermonuclear weapons in 1953, MIG fighter planes from 1950 to 1953, and the first space satellite in 1957 may have elevated the Soviet state's reputation as a world power abroad, but domestically the Russian people were shortchanged. Heavy industry grew at a rate three times that of personal consumption. Moreover, the housing shortage was acute. A British military attaché in Moscow reported that "all houses, practically without exception, show lights from every window after dark. This seems to indicate that every room is both a living room by day and a bedroom by night. There is no place in overcrowded Moscow for the luxury of eating and sleeping in separate rooms."[5]

When World War II ended in 1945, Stalin had been in power for more than fifteen years. During that time, he had removed all opposition to his rule and remained the undisputed master of the Soviet Union. Stalin's morbid suspicions fueled the constantly increasing repression that was a characteristic of his regime. In 1946, the government decreed that all literary and scientific works must conform to the political needs of the state. Along with this anti-intellectual campaign came political terror. A new series of purges seemed imminent in 1953, but Stalin's death on March 5, 1953, prevented more bloodletting.

Khrushchev's Rule   A new collective leadership succeeded Stalin until Nikita Khrushchev emerged as the chief Soviet policy maker. Khrushchev had been responsible for ending the system of forced-labor camps, a regular feature of Stalinist Russia. At the Twentieth Congress of the Communist Party in 1956, Khrushchev condemned Stalin for his "administrative violence, mass repression, and terror."

Once in power, Khrushchev took steps to undo some of the worst features of Stalin's repressive regime. A certain degree of intellectual freedom was now permitted; Khrushchev said that "readers should be given the chance to make their own judgments" regarding the acceptability of controversial literature and that "police measures shouldn't be used."[6] In 1962, he allowed the publication of Alexander Solzhenitsyn's novel *A Day in the Life of Ivan Denisovich,* a grim portrayal of the horrors of Russia's forced-labor camps. Most important, Khrushchev extended the process of **destalinization** by reducing the powers of the secret police and closing some of the Siberian prison camps. Nevertheless, Khrushchev's revelations about Stalin at the Twentieth Congress caused turmoil in Communist ranks everywhere and encouraged a spirit of rebellion in Soviet satellite countries in Eastern Europe. Soviet troops reacted by crushing an uprising in Hungary in 1956, and Khrushchev and the Soviet leaders, fearful of further undermining the basic foundations of the regime, downplayed their campaign of destalinization.

Economically, Khrushchev tried to place more emphasis on light industry and consumer goods. Khrushchev's attempts to increase agricultural output by cultivating vast lands east of the Ural Mountains proved less successful and damaged his reputation within the Party. These failures, combined with increased military spending, hurt the Soviet economy. The industrial growth rate, which had soared in the early 1950s, now declined dramatically from 13 percent in 1953 to 7.5 percent in 1964.

Khrushchev's personality also did not endear him to the higher Soviet officials, who frowned at his tendency to crack jokes and play the clown. Foreign policy failures caused additional damage to Khrushchev's reputation among his colleagues. His rash plan to place missiles in Cuba was the final straw. While he was on vacation in 1964, a special meeting of the Soviet Politburo voted him out of office (because of "deteriorating health") and forced him into retirement. Although a group of leaders succeeded him, real power came into the hands of Leonid Brezhnev (1906–1982), the "trusted" supporter of Khrushchev who had engineered his downfall.

Eastern Europe: Behind the Iron Curtain

At the end of World War II, Soviet military forces remained in all the lands they had liberated from the Nazis in Eastern Europe and the Balkans except for Greece, Albania, and Yugoslavia. All of the occupied states came to be part of the Soviet sphere of influence and, after 1945, experienced similar political developments. Between 1945 and 1947, one-party Communist governments became firmly entrenched in East Germany, Bulgaria, Romania, Poland, and Hungary. In Czechoslovakia, where there was a strong tradition of democratic institutions, the Communists did not achieve their goals until 1948 when all other parties were dissolved and Klement Gottwald, the leader of the Communists, became the new president of Czechoslovakia.

Albania and Yugoslavia were notable exceptions to this progression of Soviet dominance in Eastern Europe. Both had had strong Communist resistance movements during the war, and in both countries, the Communist Party simply assumed power when the war ended. In Albania, local Communists established a rigidly Stalinist regime that grew increasingly independent of the Soviet Union.

In Yugoslavia, Josip Broz, known as Tito (1892–1980), leader of the Communist resistance movement, seemed to be a loyal Stalinist. After the war, however, he moved toward the establishment of an independent Communist state in Yugoslavia. In 1958, the Yugoslav party congress asserted that Yugoslav Communists would pursue a more decentralized economic and political system in which workers could manage themselves and local communes could exercise some political power.

Between 1948 and Stalin's death in 1953, the Eastern European satellite states followed a policy of **Stalinization.** They instituted Soviet-type five-year plans with an emphasis on heavy industry rather than consumer goods. They began to collectivize agriculture. They established the institutions of repression—secret police and military forces. But communism—a foreign product—had not developed deep roots among the peoples of Eastern Europe. Moreover, Soviet economic exploitation of Eastern Europe made living conditions harsh for most people.

1956: Upheaval in Eastern Europe After Stalin's death, many Eastern European states began to pursue a more nationalistically oriented course while the new Soviet leaders, including Khrushchev, interfered less in the internal affairs of their satellites. But in the late 1950s and 1960s, the Soviet Union also made it clear, particularly in Poland, Hungary, and Czechoslovakia, that it would not allow its Eastern European satellites to become independent of Soviet control.

In 1956, worker protests erupted in Poland. In response, the Polish Communist Party adopted a series of reforms in October and elected Wladyslaw Gomulka (1905–1982) as first secretary. Gomulka declared that Poland had the right to follow its own socialist path. Fearful of Soviet armed response, however, the Poles compromised. Poland pledged to remain loyal to the Warsaw Pact, and the Soviets agreed to allow Poland to follow its own path to socialism.

The developments in Poland in 1956 inspired national Communists in Hungary to seek the same kinds of reforms and independence. Intense debates eventually resulted in the ouster of the ruling Stalinist and the selection of Imre Nagy (1896–1958) as the new Hungarian leader. Internal dissent, however, was not directed simply against the Soviets but against communism in general, which was viewed as a creation of the Soviets, not the Hungarians. The Stalinist secret police had also bred much terror and hatred. This dissatisfaction, combined with economic difficulties, created a situation ripe for revolt. To quell the rising rebellion, Nagy declared Hungary a free nation on November 1, 1956. He promised free elections, and the mood of the country made it clear that this could mean the end of Communist rule in Hungary. But Khrushchev was in no position at home to allow a member of the Communist flock to leave.

SOVIET REPRESSION IN EASTERN EUROPE: HUNGARY, 1956

*D*evelopments in Poland in 1956 inspired the Communist leaders of Hungary to begin to remove their country from Soviet control. But there were limits to Khrushchev's tolerance, and he sent Soviet troops to crush Hungary's movement for independence. The first selection is a statement by the Soviet government justifying the use of Soviet troops; the second is a brief and tragic final statement from Imry Nagy, the Hungarian leader.

Statement of the Soviet Government, October 30, 1956

The Soviet Government regards it as indispensable to make a statement in connection with the events in Hungary.

The course of the events has shown that the working people of Hungary, who have achieved great progress on the basis of their people's democratic order, correctly raise the question of the necessity of eliminating serious short-comings in the field of economic building, the further raising of the material well-being of the population, and the struggle against bureaucratic excesses in the state apparatus.

However, this just and progressive movement of the working people was soon joined by forces of black reaction and counterrevolution, which are trying to take advantage of the discontent of part of the working people to undermine the foundations of the people's democratic order in Hungary and to restore the old landlord and capitalist order.

The Soviet Government and all the Soviet people deeply regret that the development of events in Hungary has led to bloodshed. On the request of the Hungarian People's Government the Soviet Government consented to the entry into Budapest of the Soviet Army units to assist the Hungarian People's Army and the Hungarian authorities to establish order in the town.

The Last Message of Imry Nagy, November 4, 1956

This fight is the fight for freedom by the Hungarian people against the Russian intervention, and it is possible that I shall only be able to stay at my post for one or two hours. The whole world will see how the Russian armed forces, contrary to all treaties and conventions, are crushing the resistance of the Hungarian people. They will also see how they are kidnapping the Prime Minister of a country which is a Member of the United Nations, taking him from the capital, and therefore it cannot be doubted at all that this is the most brutal form of intervention. I should like in these last moments to ask the leaders of the revolution, if they can, to leave the country. I ask that all that I have said in my broadcast, and what we have agreed on with the revolutionary leaders during meetings in Parliament, should be put in a memorandum, and the leaders should turn to all the peoples of the world for help and explain that today it is Hungary and tomorrow, or the day after tomorrow, it will be the turn of other countries because the imperialism of Moscow does not know borders, and is only trying to play for time.

Based on this selection, what was Soviet policy in the 1950s toward its Eastern European satellite states? Compare this policy to Soviet policy in Eastern Europe in the late 1980s (see Chapter 29). What impact did this change of policy have on Eastern Europe?

Just three days after Nagy's declaration, the Red Army attacked Budapest (see the box above). The Soviets reestablished control over the country while János Kádár (1912–1989), a reform-minded cabinet minister, replaced Nagy. By collaborating with the Soviet invaders, Kádár saved many of Nagy's economic reforms.

1968: "Prague Spring" The developments in Poland and Hungary in 1956 did not generate similar revolts in Czechoslovakia. The "Little Stalin," Antonin Novotny (1904–1975), placed in power in 1952 by Stalin himself, remained firmly in control. By the late 1960s, however, Novotny had alienated many members of his own party and was particularly resented by Czechoslovakia's writers, such as the playwright Vaclav Havel (b. 1936). A writers' rebellion late in 1967, in fact, led to Novotny's resignation. In January 1968, Alexander Dubček (1921–1992) was elected first secretary of the Communist Party and soon introduced a number of reforms, including freedom of speech and of the press, freedom to travel abroad, and a relaxation of secret police activities. Dubček hoped to create "communism with a human face." A period of euphoria erupted that came to be known as the "Prague Spring."

It proved short-lived. To forestall the spreading of this "spring fever," the Red Army invaded Czechoslovakia in August 1968 and crushed the reform movement. Gustav Husák (1913–1991), a committed nonreformist, replaced Dubček, abolished his reforms, and reestablished the old order.

Western Europe: The Revival of Democracy and the Economy

Thanks to the economic aid of the Marshall Plan, the countries of Western Europe recovered relatively rapidly from the devastation of World War II. Between 1947 and 1950, European countries received $9.4 billion to be used for new equipment and raw materials. By 1950, industrial output in Europe was 30 percent above prewar levels. And this economic recovery continued well into the 1950s and 1960s, both decades of dramatic economic growth and prosperity in Western Europe. Indeed, Western Europe experienced virtually full employment during these decades.

France: The Domination of de Gaulle The history of France for nearly a quarter century after the war was dominated by one man—Charles de Gaulle (1890–1970)—who possessed an unshakable faith that he had a historical mission to reestablish the greatness of the French nation. De Gaulle had played an important role in ensuring the establishment of a French provisional government after the war. The declaration of the Fourth Republic, with a return to a parliamentary system based on parties that de Gaulle considered weak, led him to withdraw from politics. Eventually, he formed the French Popular Movement, a decidedly rightist organization, which called for an even stronger presidency, a goal that de Gaulle finally achieved in 1958.

The fragile political stability of the Fourth Republic had been badly shaken by the Algerian crisis. The French army had suffered defeat in Indochina in 1954 and was determined to resist Algerian demands for independence. But a strong antiwar movement among French intellectuals and church leaders led to bitter divisions within France that opened the door to the possibility of civil war. The panic-stricken leaders of the Fourth Republic offered to let de Gaulle take over the government and revise the constitution.

In 1958, de Gaulle immediately drafted a new constitution for the Fifth Republic that greatly enhanced the power of the office of president, who now had the right to choose the prime minister, dissolve parliament, and supervise both defense and foreign policy. As the new president, de Gaulle sought to return France to the position of a great power. He believed that playing a pivotal role in the Cold War might enhance France's stature. For that reason, he pulled France out of the NATO high command. With an eye toward achieving the status of a world power, de Gaulle invested heavily in the nuclear arms race. France exploded its first nuclear bomb in 1960. Despite his successes, de Gaulle did not really achieve his ambitious goals of world power. Although his successors maintained that France was the "third nuclear power" after the United States and the Soviet Union, in truth France was too small for such global ambitions.

Although the cost of the nuclear program increased the defense budget, de Gaulle did not neglect the French economy. Economic decision making was centralized. Between 1958 and 1968, the French gross national product experienced an annual increase of 5.5 percent, greater than that of the United States. By the end of de Gaulle's era, France was a major industrial producer and exporter, particularly in such areas as automobiles and armaments. Nevertheless, problems remained. The expansion of traditional industries, such as coal, steel, and railroads, which had all been nationalized (put under government ownership), led to large government deficits. The cost of living increased faster than in the rest of Europe.

Soviet Invasion of Czechoslovakia, 1968. The attempt of Alexander Dubček, the new first secretary of the Communist Party, to liberalize Communist rule in Czechoslovakia failed when Soviet troops invaded and crushed the reform movement. This photograph shows a Czech youth climbing aboard a Russian tank during demonstrations near the Prague radio station on August 21.

© Bettmann/CORBIS

Increased dissatisfaction with the inability of de Gaulle's government to deal with these problems soon led to more violent action. In May 1968, a series of student protests, followed by a general strike by the labor unions, shook the government. Although de Gaulle managed to restore order, the events of May 1968 had seriously undermined the French people's respect for their aloof and imperious president. Tired and discouraged, de Gaulle resigned from office in April 1969 and died within a year.

West Germany: A Nation Reborn As a result of the pressures of the Cold War, the unification of the three western zones into the Federal Republic of Germany became a reality in 1949. Konrad Adenauer (1876–1967), the leader of the Christian Democratic Union (CDU) who served as chancellor from 1949 to 1963, became the "founding hero" of the Federal Republic. Adenauer sought respect for West Germany by cooperating with the United States and the other Western European nations. He was especially desirous of reconciliation with France—Germany's longtime enemy. The beginning of the Korean War in June 1950 had unexpected repercussions for West Germany. The fear that South Korea might fall to the Communist forces of the North led many Germans and Westerners to worry about the security of West Germany and led to calls for the rearmament of West Germany. Although many people, concerned about a revival of German militarism, condemned this proposal, Cold War tensions were decisive. West Germany rearmed in 1955 and became a member of NATO.

Adenauer's chancellorship is associated with the resurrection of the West German economy, often referred to as the "economic miracle." It was largely guided by the minister of finance, Ludwig Erhard. Although West Germany had only 75 percent of the population and 52 percent of the territory of prewar Germany, by 1955 the West German gross national product exceeded that of prewar Germany. Real wages doubled between 1950 and 1965 even though work hours were cut by 20 percent. Unemployment fell from 8 percent in 1950 to 0.4 percent in 1965. To maintain its economic expansion, West Germany even imported hundreds of thousands of **guest workers**, primarily from Italy, Spain, Greece, Turkey, and Yugoslavia.

Adenauer resigned in 1963, after fourteen years of firmly guiding West Germany through its postwar recovery. Adenauer had wanted no grand experimentation at home or abroad; he was content to give Germany time to regain its equilibrium. Ludwig Erhard succeeded Adenauer and largely continued his policies. But an economic downturn in the mid-1960s opened the door to the rise of the Social Democrats, which in 1969 became the leading party.

Great Britain: The Welfare State The end of World War II left Britain with massive economic problems. In elections held immediately after the war, the Labour Party overwhelmingly defeated Churchill's Conservatives. Labour had promised far-reaching reforms, particularly in the area of social welfare, and in a country with a tremendous shortage of consumer goods and housing, its platform was quite appealing. The new Labour government, with Clement Atlee (1883–1967) as prime minister, proceeded to enact reforms that created a modern **welfare state.**

The establishment of the British welfare state began with the nationalization of the Bank of England, the coal and steel industries, public transportation, and public utilities, such as electricity and gas. In the area of social welfare, the new government enacted the National Insurance Act and the National Health Service Act in 1946. The insurance act established a comprehensive social security program and nationalized medical insurance, thereby enabling the state to subsidize the unemployed, the sick, and the aged. The health act created a system of **socialized medicine** that forced doctors and dentists to work with state hospitals, although private practices could be maintained. This measure was especially costly for the state, but within a few years, 90 percent of medical professionals were participating. The British welfare state became the model for most European states after the war.

The cost of building a welfare state at home forced the British to reduce expenses abroad. This meant the dismantling of the British Empire and the reduction of military aid to such countries as Greece and Turkey. It was not a belief in the morality of self-determination but economic necessity that brought an end to the British Empire.

Continuing economic problems brought the Conservatives back into power from 1951 to 1964. Although they favored private enterprise, the Conservatives accepted the welfare state and even extended it when they undertook an ambitious construction program to improve British housing. Although the British economy had recovered from the war, it had done so at a slower rate than other European countries. Moreover, the slow rate of recovery masked a long-term economic decline caused by a variety of factors. The demands of British trade unions for wages that rose faster than productivity were a problem in the 1950s and 1960s. The unwillingness of the British to invest in modern industrial machinery and to adopt new methods also did not help. Underlying the immediate problems, however, was a deeper issue. As a result of World War II, Britain had lost much of its prewar revenues from abroad but was left with a burden of debt from its many international commitments. At the same time, with the rise of the United States and the Soviet Union, Britain's ability to play the role of a world power declined substantially.

Western Europe: The Move Toward Unity

As noted, the divisions created by the Cold War led the nations of Western Europe to form the North Atlantic Treaty Organization in 1949. But the destructiveness of two world wars caused many thoughtful Europeans to consider the need for some form of European unity beyond

Welfare state in Great Britain	1946
Konrad Adenauer as chancellor of West Germany	1949
Formation of European Coal and Steel Community	1951
West German entry into NATO	1955
Formation of European Economic Community (Common Market)	1957
Charles de Gaulle in power in France	1958
Erhard as chancellor of Germany	1963
Student protests in France	1968

the military. National feeling was still too powerful for European nations to give up their political sovereignty, so the desire for a sense of solidarity came to focus primarily on the economic arena.

In 1951, France, West Germany, the Benelux countries (Belgium, the Netherlands, and Luxembourg), and Italy formed the European Coal and Steel Community (ECSC). Its purpose was to create a common market for coal and steel products among the six nations by eliminating tariffs and other trade barriers. The success of the ECSC encouraged its members to proceed further, and in 1957 they signed the Treaty of Rome, which created the European Economic Community (EEC), also known as the Common Market. The EEC eliminated customs barriers for the six member nations and created a large free-trade area protected from the rest of the world by a common external tariff. By promoting free trade, the EEC also encouraged cooperation and standardization in many aspects of the six nations' economies. All the member nations benefited economically. With a total population of 165 million, the EEC became the world's largest exporter and purchaser of raw materials. Only the United States surpassed the EEC in steel production.

European Economic Community, 1957

Europe and the World: Decolonization

As noted in Chapter 26, movements for independence had begun in earnest in Africa and Asia in the years between the wars. After World War II, these movements gained momentum. The continued subjugation of peoples by colonial powers seemed at odds with the goals the Allies had pursued in overthrowing the repressive regimes of Germany, Italy, and Japan. Then, too, indigenous peoples everywhere took up the call for national self-determination and expressed their determination to fight for independence.

The ending of the colonial European empires, however, did not come easy. In 1941, Churchill had said, "I have not become His Majesty's Chief Minister in order to preside over the liquidation of the British Empire." And both Britain and France especially seemed reluctant to let go of their colonies but for a variety of reasons eventually gave in to the obvious: the days of empire were over.

The power of the European states had been destroyed by the exhaustive struggles of World War II. The greatest colonial empire builder, Great Britain, no longer had the energy or the wealth to maintain its colonial empire after the war. A rush of **decolonization** swept the world. Between 1947 and 1962, virtually every colony achieved independence and attained statehood. Although some colonial powers willingly relinquished their control, others had to be driven out by national wars of liberation. Decolonization was a difficult and even bitter process, but it created a new geopolitics as the long era of Western domination of non-Western states ended.

Africa: The Struggle for Independence

After World War II, Europeans reluctantly realized that colonial rule in Africa would have to come to an end, but little had been done to prepare Africans for self-rule. Political organizations that had been formed by Africans before the war to gain their rights became formal political parties with independence as their goal. In the Gold Coast, Kwame Nkrumah formed the Convention People's Party, the first African political party in sub-Saharan Africa. In the late 1940s, Jomo Kenyatta founded the Kenya African National Union, which focused on economic issues but also sought self-rule for Kenya.

In North Africa, the French granted full independence to Morocco and Tunisia in 1956 (see Map 28.1). Since Algeria was home to two million French settlers, however, France chose to retain its dominion there. But a group of Algerian nationalists organized the National Liberation Front (FLN) and in 1954 initiated a guerrilla war to free their homeland. The French people became so divided over this war that the French leader, Charles de Gaulle, accepted the inevitable and granted Algeria independence in 1962.

In areas such as South Africa, where the political system was dominated by European settlers, the transition to independence was more complicated. In South Africa, political activity by local blacks began with the formation in 1912 of the African National Congress (ANC), whose goal was to gain economic and political reforms within the framework of the existing system. The ANC's efforts, however, met with little success. At the same time, by the 1950s, South African whites were strengthening the laws separating whites and blacks, creating a

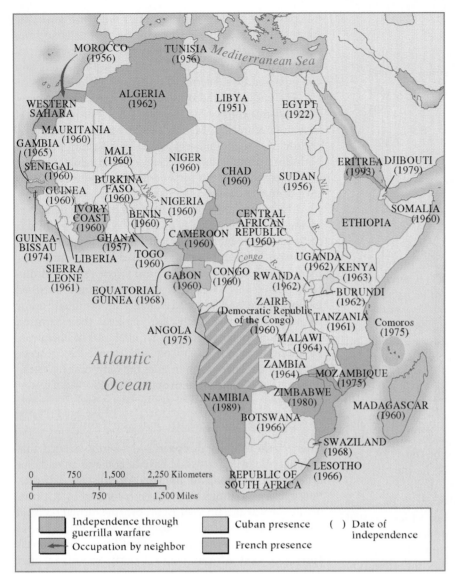

MAP 28.1 **Decolonization in Africa.** By the late 1950s, Britain and France had decided to grant independence to most of their African colonies, although France fought hard before relinquishing Algeria. Most of the new states had difficulty promoting economic growth and dealing with internal ethnic animosities. ❓ Of the countries that gained independence from 1975 onward, what is a significant characteristic shared by a majority of them? 🎧 **View an animated version of this map or related maps at** http://thomsonedu.com/history/spielvogel

Conflict in the Middle East

Although Turkey, Iran, Saudi Arabia, and Iraq had become independent states between the two world wars, the end of World War II led to the emergence of other independent states in the Middle East. Jordan, Syria, and Lebanon, all European mandates before the war, became independent (see Map 28.2). Sympathy for the idea of Arab unity led to the formation of the Arab League in 1945, but different points of view among its members prevented it from achieving anything of substance.

The one issue on which all Muslim states in the area could agree was the question of Palestine. As tensions between Jews and Arabs intensified in that mandate during the 1930s, the British reduced Jewish immigration into the area and firmly rejected Jewish proposals for an independent state in Palestine. The Zionists, who wanted Palestine as a home for Jews, were not to be denied, however. Many people had been shocked at the end of World War II when they learned of the Holocaust, and sympathy for the Jewish cause grew dramatically. As a result, the Zionists turned for support to the United States, and in March 1948, the Truman administration approved the concept of an independent Jewish state in Palestine. When a United Nations resolution divided Palestine into a Jewish state and an Arab state, the Jews in Palestine acted. On May 14, 1948, they proclaimed the state of Israel.

To its Arab neighbors, the new state was seen as a betrayal of the Palestinian people, 90 percent of whom were Muslim. Outraged at the lack of Western support

system of racial segregation in South Africa known as **apartheid.** When blacks demonstrated against the apartheid laws, the white government brutally repressed the demonstrators. After the arrest of Nelson Mandela, the ANC leader, in 1962, members of the ANC called for armed resistance to the white government.

When both the British and the French decided to let go of their colonial empires, most black African nations achieved their independence in the late 1950s and 1960s. The Gold Coast, now renamed Ghana and under the guidance of Kwame Nkrumah, was first in 1957. Nigeria, the Belgian Congo (renamed Zaire), Kenya, Tanganyika (later joined with Zanzibar and renamed Tanzania), and others soon followed. Seventeen new African nations emerged in 1960. Another eleven followed between 1961 and 1965. By the late 1960s, only parts of southern Africa and the Portuguese possessions of Mozambique and Angola remained under European rule. After a series of brutal guerrilla wars, the Portuguese finally gave up their colonies in the 1970s.

MAP 28.2 Decolonization in the Middle East. Under the control of the Ottoman Empire prior to World War I, much of the Middle East was ruled directly or indirectly by the British and French after the war. Britain, the main colonial power, granted independence to most of its holdings in the first years after World War II, although it did maintain control of small states in the Persian Gulf and Arabian Sea region until 1971.

❓ Which countries are major oil producers? 🌐 **View an animated version of this map or related maps at** http://thomsonedu.com/history/spielvogel

for Muslim interests in the area, several Arab countries invaded the new Jewish state. The invasion failed, but both sides remained bitter. The Arab states refused to recognize the existence of Israel.

The growing Arab hostility was a constant threat to the security of Israel. At a meeting of Arab leaders held in Jerusalem in 1964, the Egyptians took the lead in forming the Palestine Liberation Organization (PLO) to represent the interests of the Palestinians. The PLO believed that only the Palestinian peoples (and not Jewish immigrants from abroad) had the right to form a state in Palestine.

During the 1960s, the dispute between Israel and other states in the Middle East intensified. Fearing an imminent attack by Arab forces, especially those of Egypt, Israel launched preemptive air strikes against Egypt and several of its Arab neighbors on June 5, 1967. During the Six-Day War, as it came to be called, Israeli forces defeated the Egyptians, seized Jordanian territory on the West Bank of the Jordan River, and occupied all of Jerusalem (formerly divided between Israel and Jordan). Israel tripled the size of its territory. The new Israel aroused even more bitter hatred among the Arabs. Besides, another million Palestinians now lived inside Israel's new borders, most of them on the West Bank. Israel's victories secured

its existence, but the Arab-Israeli conflict remains unresolved to this day.

Asia: Nationalism and Communism

In Asia, the United States initiated the process of decolonization in 1946 when it granted independence to the Philippines (see Map 28.3). Britain soon followed suit with India. Over the years, Mohandas "Mahatma" Gandhi (1869–1948) and his civil disobedience movement had greatly furthered the drive for India's independence. But unable to resolve the conflict between the Hindu and Muslim populations within India, the British created two states, a mostly Hindu India and a predominantly Muslim Pakistan, in 1947. In 1948, Britain granted independence to Ceylon (modern Sri Lanka) and Burma (modern Myanmar). When the Dutch failed to reestablish control over the Dutch East Indies, Indonesia emerged as an independent nation in 1949. The French effort to remain in Indochina led to a bloody struggle with the Vietminh, Vietnamese nationalist guerrillas, led by Ho Chi Minh, the Communist and nationalist leader of the Vietnamese. After their defeat in 1954, the French granted independence to Laos and Cambodia, and Vietnam was temporarily divided in anticipation of elections in 1956 that would decide its fate. But the elections were never held, and the division of Vietnam into Communist and pro-Western regimes eventually led to the Vietnam War.

China Under Communism At the end of World War II, two Chinese governments existed side by side. The Nationalist government of Chiang Kai-shek (1887–1975), based in southern and central China, was supported by the Americans. The Communists, under the leadership of Mao Zedong (1893–1976), had built a strong base in North China. Their People's Liberation Army included nearly one million troops.

When efforts to form a coalition government in 1946 failed, full-scale war between the Nationalists and the Communists broke out. In the countryside, millions of peasants were attracted to the Communists by promises of land, and many joined Mao's army. By 1948, the People's Liberation Army had routed Chiang's government, and Chiang and two million of his followers fled to the island of Taiwan, off the coast of mainland China. On October 1, 1949, Mao mounted the rostrum of the Gate of Heavenly Peace in Beijing and made a victory statement to the thousands gathered in the square before him. The Chinese people have stood up, he said, and no one will be able to humiliate us again.

The newly victorious Communist Party, under the leadership of its chairman, Mao, had a long-term goal of building a socialist society. In 1955, the Chinese government collectivized all private farmland and nationalized most industry and commerce. Mao then embarked on a more radical program known as the Great Leap Forward in 1958. Existing collective farms, normally the size of the traditional village, were combined into vast

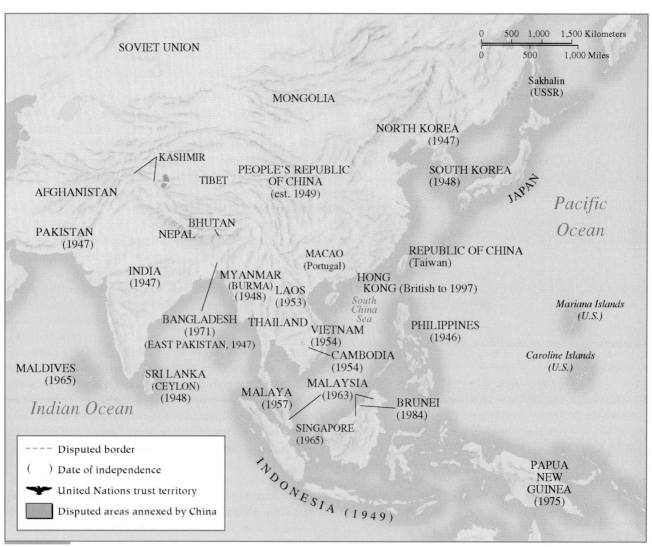

MAP 28.3 Decolonization in Asia. Britain and the United States facilitated relatively peaceful transitions to independence for their possessions in Asia. France fought hard to hold Indochina but left after major military defeats. Cold War tensions in Asia led to both the Korean War and the Vietnam War. ❓ The presence of what two neighboring countries helps explain why Korea has had difficulty maintaining complete independence throughout much of its history?

🌐 **View an animated version of this map or related maps at** http://thomsonedu.com/history/spielvogel

"people's communes," each containing more than thirty thousand people. Mao hoped this program would mobilize the people for a massive effort to speed up economic growth and reach the final stage of communism—the classless society—before the end of the twentieth century. But the Great Leap Forward proved to be a disaster.

Despite his failures, Mao was not yet ready to abandon his dream of a totally classless society. In 1966, he returned to the attack and unleashed the Red Guards, revolutionary units composed of unhappy Party members and discontented young people who were urged to take to the streets to cleanse Chinese society of impure elements guilty of taking the capitalist road. Mao launched China on a new forced march toward communism, the so-called Great Proletarian Cultural Revolution (literally, the Chinese name translates as "great revolution to create

a proletarian culture"). It lasted for ten years, from 1966 to 1976. Mao was convinced that only an atmosphere of constant revolutionary fervor could enable the Chinese to overcome the past and achieve the final stage of communism. Red Guards set out across the nation to eliminate the "four olds"—old ideas, old culture, old customs, and old habits. They destroyed temples, books written by foreigners, and jazz records.

Mao found, however, that it was not easy to maintain a constant mood of revolutionary enthusiasm. Key groups, including Party members, urban professionals, and many military officers, did not share Mao's desire for "permanent revolution." People began to turn against the movement, and in September 1976, when Mao died, a group of reformers seized power from the radicals and adopted a more practical approach to China's problems.

The United States and Canada: A New Era

At the end of World War II, the United States emerged as one of the world's two superpowers. As the Cold War with the Soviet Union intensified, the United States worked hard to prevent the spread of communism throughout the world. American domestic political life after 1945 was played out against a background of U.S. military power abroad.

American Politics and Society in the 1950s

Between 1945 and 1973, the ideals of Franklin Roosevelt's New Deal largely determined the patterns of American domestic politics. The New Deal had brought basic changes to American society. These included a dramatic increase in the role and power of the federal government, the rise of organized labor as a significant force in the economy and politics, the beginning of a welfare state, and a grudging realization of the need to deal fairly with the concerns of minorities.

The New Deal tradition in American politics was bolstered by the election of Democratic presidents—Harry Truman in 1948, John Kennedy in 1960, and Lyndon Johnson in 1964. Even the election of a Republican president, Dwight Eisenhower, in 1952 and 1956 did not change the basic direction of the New Deal. As Eisenhower stated, "Should any political party attempt to abolish Social Security and eliminate labor laws and farm programs, you would not hear of that party again in our political history."

The economic boom after World War II fueled confidence in the American way of life. A shortage of consumer goods during the war left Americans with both extra income and the desire to buy those goods after the war. Then, too, the growth of labor unions brought higher wages and gave more and more workers the ability to buy consumer goods. Between 1945 and 1973, real wages grew an average of 3 percent a year, the most prolonged advance in American history.

Prosperity was not the only characteristic of the early 1950s. Cold War confrontations abroad had repercussions at home. The takeover of China by Mao Zedong's Communist forces in 1949 and Communist North Korea's invasion of South Korea in 1950 led to a fear that Communists had infiltrated America. President Truman's attorney general warned that Communists "are everywhere—in factories, offices, butcher stores, on street corners, in private businesses. And each carried in himself the germ of death for society." The demagogic senator from Wisconsin, Joseph R. McCarthy, helped intensify a massive "Red Scare" with his exposés of supposed Communists in high government positions. McCarthy went too far when he attacked alleged "Communist conspirators" in the United States Army and was censured by Congress in 1954. Very quickly, his anti-Communist crusade came to an end.

An Age of Upheaval: America in the 1960s

Between 1960 and 1973, the United States experienced a period of upheaval that brought to the fore problems that had been glossed over in the 1950s. The 1960s began on a youthful and optimistic note. At age forty-three, John F. Kennedy became the youngest president in the history of the United States. His administration, focused primarily on foreign affairs, was cut short by an assassin's bullet on November 22, 1963. Kennedy's successor, Lyndon B. Johnson, who won a new term as president in a landslide in 1964, used his stunning mandate to pursue what he called the Great Society, heir to the welfare state first begun in the New Deal. Johnson's programs included health care for the elderly, a War on Poverty to be fought with food stamps and a Job Corps, a new Department of Housing and Urban Development to deal with the problems of the cities, and federal assistance for education.

The Civil Rights Movement Johnson's other domestic passion was equal rights for African Americans. The civil rights movement had its beginnings in 1954 when the United States Supreme Court took the dramatic step of striking down the practice of racial segregation in public schools. The eloquent Martin Luther King Jr. (1929–1968) became the leader of a growing movement for racial equality, and by the early 1960s, a number of groups, including King's Southern Christian Leadership Conference (SCLC), were organizing sit-ins and demonstrations across the South to end racial segregation. In August 1963, King led the March on Washington for Jobs and Freedom to dramatize black Americans' desire for freedom. This march and King's impassioned plea for racial equality had an electrifying effect on the American people.

President Johnson took up the cause of civil rights. As a result of his initiative, Congress passed the Civil Rights Act of 1964, which created the machinery to end segregation and discrimination in the workplace and all public places. A voting rights act the following year made it easier for nonwhites to vote in southern states. But laws alone could not guarantee the Great Society, and Johnson soon faced bitter social unrest, both from African Americans and from the burgeoning movement opposing the Vietnam War.

African Americans had officially had voting rights for many years, but local patterns of segregation led to higher unemployment rates for blacks than for whites and left blacks segregated in urban ghettos. In these ghettos, the calls for action by radical black leaders, such as Malcolm X of the Black Muslims, attracted more attention than the nonviolent appeals of Martin Luther King. In the summer of 1965, race riots broke out in the Watts district of Los Angeles. Thirty-four people died and over one thousand buildings were destroyed. Cleveland, San Francisco, Chicago, Newark, and Detroit exploded in the summers of 1966 and 1967. The riots led to a "white backlash" and a severe division of America.

Antiwar Protests Antiwar protests also divided the American people after President Johnson sent American troops to Vietnam. As the war progressed and a military draft ensued, protests escalated. Teach-ins, sit-ins, and the occupation of buildings at universities alternated with more radical demonstrations that led to violence. The killing of four student protesters at Kent State University in 1970 by the Ohio National Guard caused a furor, and the antiwar movement began to decline. By that time, however, antiwar demonstrations had worn down the willingness of many Americans to continue the war. The combination of antiwar demonstrations and ghetto riots in the cities also heightened the appeal of a call for "law and order," used by Richard Nixon, the Republican presidential candidate in 1968. Nixon's election set in motion a shift to the right in American politics.

The Development of Canada

Canada experienced many of the same developments that the United States did in the postwar years. For twenty-five years after World War II, a prosperous Canada set out on a new path of industrial development. Canada had always had a strong export economy based on its abundant natural resources. Now it developed electronic, aircraft, nuclear, and chemical engineering industries as well on a large scale. Much of the Canadian growth, however, was financed by capital from the United States, which led to American ownership of Canadian businesses. Although many Canadians welcomed the economic growth, others feared American economic domination of Canada.

Canadians also worried about playing a secondary role politically and militarily to its neighboring superpower. Canadians agreed to join the North Atlantic Treaty Organization in 1949 and even sent military forces to fight in Korea the following year. But to avoid subordination to the United States, Canada actively supported the United Nations. Nevertheless, concerns about the United States did not keep Canada from maintaining a special relationship with its southern neighbor. The North American Air Defense Command (NORAD), formed in 1957, was based on close cooperation between the air forces of the two countries for the defense of North America against missile attack.

After 1945, the Liberal Party continued to dominate Canadian politics until 1957, when John Diefenbaker (1895–1979) achieved a Conservative Party victory. But major economic problems returned the Liberals to power, and under Lester Pearson (1897–1972), they created Canada's welfare state by enacting a national social security system (the Canada Pension Plan) and a national health insurance program.

Postwar Society and Culture in the Western World

During the postwar era, Western society and culture witnessed remarkably rapid change. Computers, television, jet planes, contraceptive devices, and new surgical techniques all dramatically and quickly altered the pace and nature of human life. The rapid changes in postwar society, fueled by scientific advances and rapid economic growth, led many to view it as a new society.

The Structure of European Society

The structure of European society was altered after 1945. Especially noticeable were the changes in the middle class. Such traditional middle-class groups as businesspeople and professionals in law, medicine, and the universities were joined by a new group of managers and technicians as large companies and government agencies employed increasing numbers of white-collar supervisory and administrative personnel. Whether in Eastern or Western Europe, the new managers and experts were very much alike. Everywhere their positions depended on specialized knowledge acquired from some form of higher education. Because their positions usually depended on their skills, they took steps to ensure that their own children would be educated.

Changes also occurred among the traditional lower classes. Especially noticeable was the dramatic shift of people from rural to urban areas. The number of people engaged in agriculture declined drastically; by the 1950s, the number of farmers throughout most of Europe had dropped by 50 percent. Nor did the size of the industrial working class expand. In West Germany, industrial workers made up 48 percent of the labor force throughout the 1950s and 1960s. Thereafter, the number of industrial workers began to dwindle as the number of white-collar service employees increased. At the same time, a substantial increase in their real wages enabled the working classes to aspire to the consumption patterns of the middle class, leading to what some observers have called the "consumer society." Buying on the installment plan, introduced in the 1930s, became widespread beginning in the 1950s and gave workers a chance to imitate the middle class by buying such products as televisions, washing machines, refrigerators, vacuum cleaners, and stereos. But the most visible symbol of mass consumerism was the automobile. Before World War II, cars were reserved mostly for the European upper classes. In 1948, there were 5 million cars in all of Europe, but by 1957, the number had tripled. By the 1960s, there were almost 45 million cars.

Rising incomes, combined with shorter working hours, created an even greater market for mass leisure activities. Between 1900 and 1960, the workweek was reduced from sixty hours to about forty, and the number of paid holidays increased. All aspects of popular culture—music, sports, media—became commercialized and offered opportunities for leisure activities, including concerts, sporting events, and television viewing.

Another very visible symbol of mass leisure was the growth of tourism. Before World War II, mostly the upper and middle classes traveled for pleasure. After the war, the combination of more vacation time, increased prosperity, and the flexibility provided by package tours, with their lower rates and budget-priced rooms, enabled millions to expand their travel possibilities. By the mid-1960s, some 100 million tourists were crossing European boundaries each year.

Patterns New and Old: Women in the Postwar Western World

Despite their enormous contributions to the war effort, women at the end of World War II were removed from the workforce to provide jobs for the soldiers returning home. After the horrors and separations of the war, people seemed willing for a while to return to traditional family life. Female participation in the workforce declined, and birthrates began to rise, creating a "baby boom." This increase in the birthrate, however, did not last, and the size of families began to decline by the end of the 1950s. Largely responsible for this decline was the widespread practice of birth control. Invented in the nineteenth century, the condom was already in wide use, but the development in the 1960s of oral contraceptives, known as birth control pills (or simply "the pill") provided an effective means of birth control that quickly spread to all Western countries.

Women in the Workforce The trend toward smaller families contributed to the change in the nature of women's employment in both Europe and the United States as women spent considerably more years not involved in rearing children. The most important development was the increased number of married women in the workforce. At the beginning of the twentieth century, even working-class wives tended to stay at home if they could afford to do so. In the postwar period, this was no longer the case. In the United States, for example, in 1900, married women made up about 15 percent of the female labor force; by 1970, their number had increased to 62 percent. The percentage of married women in the female labor force in Sweden increased from 47 to 66 percent between 1963 and 1975.

But the increased number of women in the workforce did not change some old patterns. Working-class women in particular still earned salaries lower than those of men for equal work. In the 1960s, women earned only 60 percent of men's wages in Britain, 50 percent in France, and 63 percent in West Germany. In addition, women still tended to enter traditionally female jobs. Many European women also still faced the double burden of earning income on the one hand and raising a family and maintaining the household on the other.

In the Soviet Union and Eastern Europe, however, women did have greater opportunities in the workforce and even in the professions. In the Soviet Union, women comprised 51 percent of the labor force in 1980; by the mid-1980s, they constituted 50 percent of the engineers, 80 percent of the doctors, and 75 percent of the teachers and teachers' aides. But many of these were low-paying jobs; most female doctors, for example, worked in primary care and were paid less than skilled machinists. The chief administrators in hospitals and schools were still men.

Moreover, although women were part of the workforce, they were never freed of their traditional roles in the home. Most women confronted what came to be known as the double shift. After working eight hours at their jobs, they came home to face the housework and care of the children. They might spend two hours a day in long lines at a number of stores waiting to buy food and clothes. Because of the housing situation, they were forced to use kitchens that were shared by a number of families.

The Feminist Movement: The Quest for Liberation The participation of women in World Wars I and II helped them achieve one of the major aims of the nineteenth-century feminist movement—the right to vote. After World War I, many governments acknowledged the contributions of women to the war effort by granting them **suffrage,** although women in France and Italy did not obtain the vote until 1945. After World War II, European women tended to fall back into the traditional roles expected of them, but by the late 1960s, women began to assert their rights again. Along with the student upheavals of the late 1960s came renewed interest in **feminism,** or the women's liberation movement, as it was now known. Increasingly, women protested that the acquisition of political and legal equality had not brought true equality with men:

> We are economically oppressed: in jobs we do full work for half pay, in the home we do unpaid work full time. We are commercially exploited by advertisement, television and the press; legally we often have only the status of children. We are brought up to feel inadequate, educated to narrower horizons than men. This is our specific oppression as women. It is as women that we are, therefore, organizing.[7]

These were the words of a British Woman's Liberation Workshop in 1969.

Of great importance to the emergence of the postwar women's liberation movement was the work of Simone de Beauvoir (1908–1986). Born into a Catholic middle-class family and educated at the Sorbonne in Paris, she supported herself as a teacher and later as a writer. She maintained a lifelong relationship (but not marriage) with the existentialist writer Jean-Paul Sartre and became actively involved in political causes. De Beauvoir believed that she lived a "liberated" life for a twentieth-century European woman, but for all her freedom, she still came to perceive that as a woman she faced limits that men did not. In 1949, she published her highly influential work, *The Second Sex,* in which she argued that as a result of male-dominated societies, women had been defined by their differences from men and consequently received second-class status. De Beauvoir took an active role in the French women's movement of the 1970s, and her book was a major influence on the feminist movement on both sides of the Atlantic.

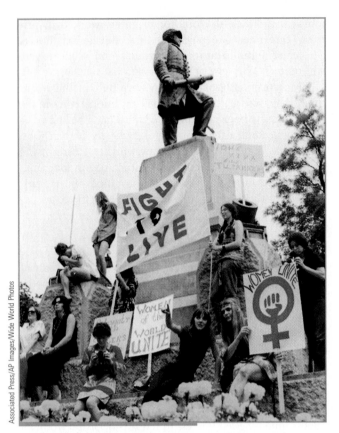

Women's Liberation Movement. In the late 1960s, as women began once again to assert their rights, a revived women's liberation movement emerged. Feminists in the movement maintained that women themselves must alter the conditions of their lives. During this women's liberation rally, some women climbed the statue of Admiral Farragut in Washington, D.C., to exhibit their signs.

The Permissive Society

The **permissive society** was yet another characterization of postwar Europe. World War I had opened the first significant crack in the rigid code of manners and morals of the nineteenth century. Subsequently, the 1920s had witnessed experimentation with drugs, the appearance of hard-core pornography, and a new sexual freedom (police in Berlin, for example, issued cards that permitted female and male homosexual prostitutes to practice their trade). But these indications of a new attitude appeared mostly in major cities and touched only small numbers of people. After World War II, changes in manners and morals were far more extensive and far more noticeable.

Sweden took the lead in the propagation of the so-called sexual revolution of the 1960s, but the rest of Europe and the United States soon followed. Sex education in the schools and the decriminalization of homosexuality were but two aspects of Sweden's liberal legislation. The introduction of the birth control pill, which became widely available by the mid-1960s, gave people more freedom in sexual behavior. Meanwhile, sexually explicit movies, plays, and books broke new ground in the treatment of once-hidden subjects.

The new standards were evident in the breakdown of the traditional family. Divorce rates increased dramatically, especially in the 1960s, and premarital and extramarital sexual experiences also rose substantially. A survey in the Netherlands in 1968 revealed that 78 percent of men and 86 percent of women had participated in extramarital sex. The appearance of *Playboy* magazine in the 1950s also added a new dimension to the sexual revolution for adult males. Along with photographs of nude women, *Playboy* offered well-written articles on various aspects of masculinity. *Playboy*'s message was clear: men were encouraged to seek sexual gratification outside of marriage.

The decade of the 1960s also saw the emergence of a drug culture. Marijuana was widely used among college and university students as a recreational drug. For young people more interested in mind expansion into higher levels of consciousness, Timothy Leary, who had done research at Harvard on the hallucinogenic effects of LSD (lysergic acid diethylamide), became the high priest of "psychedelic" experiences.

New attitudes toward sex and the use of drugs were only two manifestations of a growing youth movement in the 1960s that questioned authority and fostered rebellion against the older generation. Spurred on by the Vietnam War and a growing political consciousness, the youth rebellion became a youth protest movement by the second half of the 1960s (see the box on p. 556).

Education and Student Revolt

Before World War II, higher education had largely remained the preserve of Europe's wealthier classes. After the war, European states began to foster greater equality of opportunity in higher education by eliminating fees, and universities experienced an influx of students from the middle and lower classes. Enrollments grew dramatically: in France, 4.5 percent of young people went to a university in 1950. By 1965, the figure had increased to 14.5 percent.

But there were problems. Overcrowded classrooms, professors who paid little attention to students, administrators who acted in an authoritarian fashion, and an education that to many seemed irrelevant to the realities of the modern age led to an outburst of student revolts in the late 1960s. In part, these protests were an extension of the spontaneous disruptions in American universities in the mid-1960s, which were often sparked by student opposition to the Vietnam War. Perhaps the most famous student revolt occurred in France in 1968. It erupted at the University of Nanterre outside Paris but soon spread to the Sorbonne, the main campus of the University of Paris. French students demanded a greater voice in the administration of the university, took over buildings, and then expanded the scale of their protests by inviting workers to support them. Half of France's workforce went

The "Love-in." In the 1960s, a number of outdoor public festivals for young people combined music, drugs, and sex. Flamboyant dress, face painting, free-form dancing, and drugs were vital ingredients in creating an atmosphere dedicated to "love and peace." Shown here are dozens of hippies dancing around a decorated bus at a "love-in" during the Summer of Love, 1967.

on strike in May 1968. After the Gaullist government instituted a hefty wage hike, the workers returned to work and the police repressed the remaining student protesters.

The student protest movement reached its high point in 1968, although scattered incidents occurred into the early 1970s. There were several reasons for the student radicalism. Some students were genuinely motivated by the desire to reform the university. Others were protesting the Vietnam War, which they viewed as Western imperialism. They also attacked other aspects of Western society, such as its materialism, and expressed concern about becoming cogs in the large and impersonal bureaucratic jungles of the modern world. For many students, the calls for democratic decision making within the universities reflected their deeper concerns about the direction of Western society. Although student revolts fizzled out in the 1970s, the larger issues they raised revived in the 1990s.

Postwar Art

Following the war, the United States dominated the art world. New York City replaced Paris as the artistic center of the West. The Guggenheim Museum, the Museum of Modern Art, and the Whitney Museum of Modern Art, together with New York's numerous art galleries, promoted modern art and helped determine artistic tastes throughout much of the world. One of the styles that became synonymous with the emergence of the New York art scene was **Abstract Expressionism.**

Dubbed "action painting" by one critic, Abstract Expressionism was energetic and spontaneous, qualities evident in the enormous canvases of Jackson Pollock (1912–1956). In such works as *Lavender Mist* (1950), paint seems to explode, enveloping the viewer with emotion and movement. Pollock's swirling forms and seemingly chaotic patterns broke all conventions of form and structure. His drip paintings, with their total abstraction, were extremely influential with other artists, and he eventually became a celebrity. Inspired by Native American sand painters, Pollock painted with the canvas on the floor. He explained, "On the floor I am more at ease. I feel nearer, more a part of the painting, since this way I can walk around in, work from four sides and be literally *in* the painting. When I am in the painting, I am not aware of what I am doing. There is pure harmony."

The early 1960s saw the emergence of Pop Art, which took images of popular culture and transformed them into works of fine art. Andy Warhol (1930–1987), who began as an advertising illustrator, was the most famous of the Pop artists. Warhol adapted images from commercial art, such as Campbell's soup cans, and photographs of such celebrities as Marilyn Monroe.

Postwar Literature

In postwar literature the most significant new trend was called the Theater of the Absurd. Its most famous proponent was the Irishman Samuel Beckett (1906–1990), who lived in France. In Beckett's *Waiting for Godot* (1952), two men wait for the appearance of someone with whom they may or may not have an appointment. No background information on the two men is provided. During the course of the play, the men talk, but nothing seems to happen. The audience is never told if what they see in front of them is real or imagined. Unlike traditional

"THE TIMES THEY ARE A-CHANGIN'": THE MUSIC OF YOUTHFUL PROTEST

In the 1960s, song lyrics reflected the rebellious mood of many young people. Bob Dylan (b. 1941), a popular recording artist, expressed the feelings of the younger generation. His song "The Times They Are A-Changin'," released in 1964, has been called an "anthem for the protest movement."

Bob Dylan, "The Times They Are A-Changin' "

Come gather round people
Wherever you roam
And admit that the waters
Around you have grown
And accept it that soon
You'll be drenched to the bone
If your time to you
Is worth savin'
Then you better start swimmin'
Or you'll sink like a stone
For the times they are a-changin'

Come writers and critics
Who prophesize with your pen
And keep your eyes wide
The chance won't come again
And don't speak too soon
For the wheel's still in spin
And there's no tellin' who
That it's namin'
For the loser now
Will be later to win
For the times they are a-changin'

Come senators, congressmen
Please heed the call
Don't stand in the doorway

Don't block up the hall
For he that gets hurt
Will be he who has stalled
There's a battle outside
And it is ragin'
It'll soon shake your windows
And rattle your walls
For the times they are a-changin'

Come mothers and fathers
Throughout the land
And don't criticize
What you can't understand
Your sons and your daughters
Are beyond your command
Your old road is
Rapidly agin'
Please get out of the new one
If you can't lend your hand
For the times they are a-changin'

The line it is drawn
The curse it is cast
The slow one now
Will later be fast
As the present now
Will later be past
The order is
Rapidly fadin'
And the first one now
Will later be last
For the times they are a-changin'

What caused the student campus revolts of the 1960s? What and whom does Dylan identify in this song as the problem?

theater, suspense is maintained not by having the audience wonder "What is going to happen next?" but simply "What is happening now?"

The sense of meaninglessness that inspired the Theater of the Absurd also underscored the philosophy of **existentialism** of Albert Camus (1913–1960) and Jean-Paul Sartre (1905–1980). The central point of the existentialism of Sartre and Camus was the absence of God in the universe. Though the death of God was tragic, it meant that humans had no preordained destiny and were utterly alone in the universe, with no future and no hope. As Camus expressed it:

A world that can be explained even with bad reasons is a familiar world. But, on the other hand, in a universe suddenly divested of illusions and lights, man feels an alien, a stranger. His exile is without remedy since he is deprived of the memory of a lost home or the hope of a promised land. This divorce between man and his life, the actor and his setting, is properly the feeling of absurdity.[8]

According to Camus, then, the world was absurd and without meaning; humans, too, are without meaning and purpose. Reduced to despair and depression, humans have but one source of hope—themselves.

The Revival of Religion

Existentialism was one response to the despair generated by the apparent collapse of civilized values in the twentieth century. The revival of religion was another. Ever since the Enlightenment of the eighteenth century, Christianity and religion had been on the defensive. But a number of

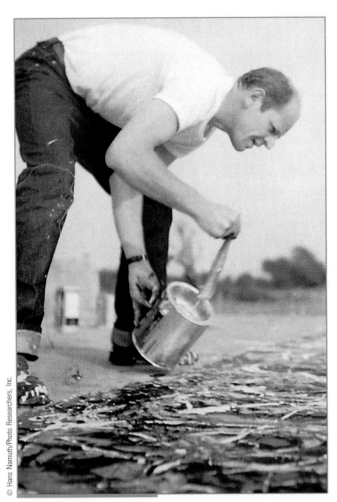

Jackson Pollock Painting. One of the best-known practitioners of Abstract Expressionism, which took over the artistic mainstream after World War II, was the American Jackson Pollock, who achieved his ideal of total abstraction in his drip paintings. He is shown here at work at his Long Island studio. Pollock found it easier to produce his large canvases, covered with exploding patterns of color, by laying them on the floor.

religious thinkers and leaders attempted to bring new life to Christianity in the twentieth century.

One expression of this religious revival was the attempt by the Protestant theologian Karl Barth (1886–1968) to infuse traditional Christian teachings with new life. In his numerous writings, Barth attempted to reinterpret the religious insights of the Reformation era for the modern world. To Barth, the sinful and hence imperfect nature of human beings meant that humans could know religious truth not through reason but only through the grace of God.

In the Catholic church, an attempt at religious renewal also came from a charismatic pope. Pope John XXIII (1881–1963) reigned as pope for only a short time (1958–1963) but sparked a dramatic revival of Catholicism when he summoned the twenty-first ecumenical

council of the Catholic church. Known as Vatican II, the council liberalized a number of Catholic practices. For example, the liturgy of the Mass, the central feature of Catholic worship, was now to be spoken in the vernacular, not in Latin.

The Explosion of Popular Culture

Since World War II, popular culture has played an increasingly important role in helping Western people define themselves. The history of popular culture is also the history of the economic system that supports it, for this system manufactures, distributes, and sells the images that people consume as popular culture. As popular culture and its economic support system became increasingly intertwined, industries of leisure emerged. As one historian of popular culture has argued, "Industrial societies turn the provision of leisure into a commercial activity, in which their citizens are sold entertainment, recreation, pleasure, and appearance as commodities that differ from the goods at the drugstore only in the way they are used."[9] Modern popular culture is therefore inextricably tied to the mass consumer society in which it emerged.

Popular Culture and the Americanization of the World The United States has been the most influential force in shaping popular culture in the West and, to a lesser degree, the rest of the world. Through movies, music, advertising, and television, the United States has spread its particular form of consumerism and the American dream to millions around the world. Already in 1923, the New York *Morning Post* noted that "the film is to America what the flag was once to Britain. By its means Uncle Sam may hope some day . . . to Americanize the world."[10] In movies, television, and music, the impact of American popular culture on the Western world was pervasive.

Motion pictures were the primary vehicle for the diffusion of American popular culture in the years immediately following the war, and they continued to dominate both European and American markets in the next decades. Although developed in the 1930s, television did not become readily available until the late 1940s. By 1954, there were 32 million sets in the United States as television became the centerpiece of middle-class life. In the 1960s, as television spread around the world, American networks sold their products in Europe and the Third World at extraordinarily low prices. The United States also dominated popular music. Jazz, blues, rhythm and blues, rap, hip-hop, and rock and roll have been by far the most popular music forms in the Western world—and much of the non-Western world—since the end of World War II. All of them originated in the United States, and all are rooted in African American musical innovations. As these forms spread to the rest of the world, they inspired local artists, who then transformed the music in their own ways.

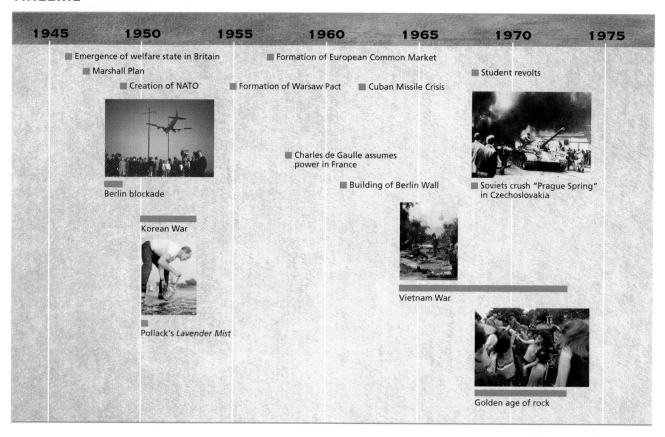

| 1945 | 1950 | 1955 | 1960 | 1965 | 1970 | 1975 |

■ Emergence of welfare state in Britain   ■ Formation of European Common Market

■ Marshall Plan   ■ Student revolts

■ Creation of NATO   ■ Formation of Warsaw Pact   ■ Cuban Missile Crisis

Berlin blockade

Korean War

Pollack's *Lavender Mist*

■ Charles de Gaulle assumes power in France

■ Building of Berlin Wall

■ Soviets crush "Prague Spring" in Czechoslovakia

Vietnam War

Golden age of rock

CONCLUSION

At the end of World War II, a new conflict erupted in the Western world as the two new superpowers, the United States and the Soviet Union, competed for political domination. Europeans, whether they wanted to or not, were forced to become supporters of one side or the other. But this ideological division also spread to the rest of the world as the United States fought in Korea and Vietnam to prevent the spread of communism, and the Soviet Union used its armies to prop up pro-Soviet regimes in Eastern Europe.

In addition to the Cold War conflict, the postwar era was characterized by decolonization. After World War II, the colonial empires of the European states were largely dissolved, and the liberated territories of Africa, Asia, and the Middle East emerged as sovereign states. By the late 1980s, the approximately 160 sovereign states of the world would become an emerging global community.

Western Europe also became a new community in the 1950s and 1960s. Although Western Europeans staged a remarkable economic recovery, their future still depended on relations between the two superpowers. At the same time, the student protests of the late 1960s caused many to rethink some of their basic assumptions. And yet, looking back, the student upheavals were not a turning point in the history of postwar Europe, as some people thought at the time. Student rebels would become middle-class professionals, and the vision of a revolutionary politics would remain mostly a memory.

NOTES

1. Quoted in J. M. Jones, The Fifteen Weeks (February 21–June 5, 1947), 2d ed. (New York, 1964), pp. 140–141.
2. Quoted in W. Laqueur, *Europe in Our Time* (New York, 1992), p. 111.
3. Quoted in W. I. Hitchcock, *The Struggle for Europe: The Turbulent History of a Divided Continent, 1945–2002* (New York, 2003), p. 215.
4. Quoted in P. Lane, *Europe Since 1945: An Introduction* (Totowa, N.J., 1985), p. 248.
5. R. Hilton, *Military Attaché in Moscow* (London, 1949), p. 41.
6. N. S. Khrushchev, *Khrushchev Remembers*, trans. S. Talbott (Boston, 1970), p. 77.
7. Quoted in M. Rowe et al., *Spare Rib Reader* (Harmondsworth, England, 1982), p. 574.
8. Quoted in H. Grosshans, *The Search for Modern Europe* (Boston, 1970), p. 421.
9. R. Maltby, ed. *Passing Parade: A History of Popular Culture in the Twentieth Century* (New York, 1989), p. 8.
10. Quoted in ibid., p. 11.

SUGGESTIONS FOR FURTHER READING

For well-written surveys on Europe since 1945, see **W. I. Hitchcock,** *The Struggle for Europe: The Turbulent History of a Divided Continent, 1945–2002* (New York, 2002); **T. Judt,** *Postwar: A History of Europe Since 1945* (New York, 2005); and **W. Laqueur,** *Europe in Our Time* (New York, 1992). On the Cold War, see **J. L. Gaddis,** *The Cold War: A New History* (New York, 2005), and **J. W. Langdon,** *A Hard and Bitter Peace: A Global History of the Cold War* (Englewood Cliffs, N.J., 1995). For an illustrated history, see **J. Isaacs and T. Downing,** *Cold War: An Illustrated History, 1945–1991* (Boston, 1998). For a study of Soviet foreign policy, see **J. L. Nogee,** *Soviet Foreign Policy Since World War I,* 4th ed. (New York, 1992). For a good introduction to the arms race, see **E. M. Bottome,** *The Balance of Terror: A Guide to the Arms Race,* rev. ed. (Boston, 1986). On decolonization after World War II, see **R. F. Betts,** *Decolonization* (London, 1998).

For a general view of Soviet society, see **D. K. Shipler,** *Russia: Broken Idols, Solemn Dreams* (New York, 1983). On the Khrushchev years, see **C. A. Linden,** *Khrushchev and the Soviet Leadership* (Baltimore, 1990). For a general study of the Soviet satellites in Eastern Europe, see **J. Rothschild,** *Return to Diversity: A Political History of East Central Europe Since World War II,* 2d ed. (New York, 1992). On the Soviet Union's actions against Czechoslovakia in 1968, see **J. Valenta,** *Intervention in Czechoslovakia in 1968* (Baltimore, 1991).

The rebuilding of postwar Europe is examined in **D. W. Ellwood,** *Rebuilding Europe: Western Europe, America, and Postwar Reconstruction* (London, 1992), and **M. Hogan,** *The Marshall Plan: America, Britain, and the Reconstruction of Western Europe, 1947–1952* (New York, 1987). On the building of common institutions in Western Europe, see **S. Henig,** *The Uniting of Europe: From Discord to Concord* (London, 1997). For surveys of West Germany, see **H. A. Turner,** *Germany from Partition to Reunification* (New Haven, Conn., 1992), and **T. G. Ash,** *In Europe's Name: Germany and the Enduring Balance* (New York, 1993). France under de Gaulle is examined in **J. Jackson,** *Charles de Gaulle* (London, 2003), and **D. J. Mahoney,** *De Gaulle: Statesmanship, Grandeur, and Modern Democracy* (Westport, Conn., 1996). On Britain, see **K. O. Morgan,** *The People's Peace: British History, 1945–1990* (Oxford, 1992).

The student revolts of the late 1960s are put into a broader context in **D. Caute,** *The Year of the Barricades: A Journey Through 1968* (New York, 1988). On the women's liberation movement, see **D. Bouchier,** *The Feminist Challenge: The Movement for Women's Liberation in Britain and the United States* (New York, 1983); **D. Meyer,** *Sex and Power: The Rise of Women in America, Russia, Sweden, and Italy* (Middletown, Conn., 1987); **T. Keefe,** *Simone de Beauvoir* (New York, 1998); and **C. Duchen,** *Women's Rights and Women's Lives in France, 1944–1968* (New York, 1994). More general works that include much information on the contemporary period are **B.G. Smith,** *Changing Lives: Women in European History Since 1700* (Lexington, Mass., 1989), and **F. Thebaud, ed.,** *A History of Women in the West, vol. 5, Toward a Cultural Identity in the Twentieth Century* (Cambridge, Mass., 1994).

On the sexual revolution, see **D. Allyn,** *Make Love, Not War: The Sexual Revolution—An Unfettered History* (New York, 2000). On the turbulent 1960s, see **A. Marwick,** *The Sixties: Social and Cultural Transformation in Britain, France, Italy, and the United States* (Oxford, 1999). A classic work on existentialism is **W. Barrett,** *Irrational Man* (Garden City, N.Y., 1962). On the arts, see **A. Marwick,** *Arts in the West Since 1945* (Oxford, 2002). An excellent survey of twentieth-century popular culture is **R. Maltby, ed.,** *Passing Parade: A History of Popular Culture in the Twentieth Century* (Oxford, 1989).

Thomson NOW! Enter *ThomsonNOW* using the access card that is available for *Western Civilization: A Brief History.* *ThomsonNOW* will help you understand this chapter with lesson plans generated for your needs. In addition, you can read the following documents, and many more, online:

Winston Churchill, The Sinews of Peace
McCarran International Security Act

WESTERN CIVILIZATION RESOURCES

Visit the Web site for *Western Civilization: A Brief History* for resources specific to this book:

http://www.thomsonedu.com/history/spielvogel

For a variety of tools to help you succeed in this course, visit the Western Civilization Resource Center at

http://history.wadsworth.com/spielvogel

Included are quizzes, images, documents, interactive simulations, maps and timelines, movie explorations, and a wealth of other sources.

29

THE CONTEMPORARY WESTERN WORLD SINCE 1973

CHAPTER OUTLINE AND FOCUS QUESTIONS

Toward a New Western Order

☐ What reforms did Gorbachev institute in the Soviet Union, and what role did he play in the Soviet Union's demise?

☐ What changes have occurred in Eastern Europe as a result of the revolutions of 1989?

After the Cold War: New World Order or Age of Terrorism?

☐ How and why did the Cold War end?

New Directions and New Problems in Western Society

☐ What are the major political and social developments in Western Europe and North America since 1973?

Western Culture Today

☐ What major cultural and intellectual trends have emerged since 1973?

CRITICAL THINKING

☐ What are the similarities and differences among major social, economic, and political developments in the first and second halves of the twentieth century?

Boris Yeltsin waves the Russian tricolor flag before a crowd of supporters

Czarek Sokolowski/© Associated Press/AP Images/Wide World Photos

*A*FTER MORE THAN two decades of the Cold War, Europeans had become accustomed to the division of Europe into West and East. Prosperous Western Europe, still allied with the United States, stood opposed to still-struggling Eastern Europe, which remained largely subject to the Soviet Union. The division of Germany symbolized a new order that seemed well established. Yet in another two decades, a revolutionary upheaval in the Soviet Union and Eastern Europe brought an end to the Cold War and to the division of postwar Europe. The Soviet Union itself ceased to exist. On August 19, 1991, a group of Soviet leaders who opposed reform arrested Mikhail Gorbachev, the president of the Soviet Union, and tried to seize control of the government.

Hundreds of thousands of Russians, led by Boris Yeltsin, poured into the streets of Moscow and Leningrad to resist the attempted coup. Some army units defected to Yeltsin's side, and within days, the rebels were forced to surrender. This failed attempt to seize power had unexpected results as Russia and a host of other Soviet constituent republics declared their independence. By the end of 1991, the Soviet Union—one of the largest empires in world history—had disappeared, and a new era of cooperation between the successor states in the old Soviet Union and the nations of the West had begun.

As the world adjusted to the transformation from Cold War to post–Cold War sensibilities, other changes shaped the Western outlook. The demographic face of European countries changed as massive numbers of immigrants created more ethnically diverse populations. New artistic and intellectual currents, the continued advance of science and technology, the coming to grips with environmental problems, the surge of the women's liberation movement—all spoke of a vibrant, ever-changing world. At the same time, a devastating terrorist attack on the World Trade Center in New York City and the Pentagon outside Washington, D.C., on September 11, 2001, made the Western world vividly aware of its vulnerability to international terrorism.◆

Toward a New Western Order

The decades after World War II brought economic recovery and renewed growth to Europe. Nevertheless, the political divisions between Western and Eastern Europe remained; so did the disparity in levels of prosperity. But in the late 1980s and early 1990s, the Soviet Union and its Eastern European satellite states underwent a revolutionary upheaval that dramatically altered the European landscape (see Map 29.1) and left many Europeans with both new hopes and new fears.

The Revolutionary Era in the Soviet Union

Between 1964 and 1982, significant change in the Soviet Union seemed highly unlikely. After the overthrow of Khrushchev in 1964, Leonid Brezhnev (1906–1982) had become head of both party and state. He was always optimistic yet reluctant to reform. The **Brezhnev Doctrine**—the right of the Soviet Union to intervene if socialism was threatened in another "socialist state"—became an article of faith and led to the use of Soviet troops in Czechoslovakia in 1968.

The Brezhnev Years   Brezhnev benefited from the more relaxed atmosphere associated with détente. The Soviets had reached a rough parity with the United States in nuclear arms and enjoyed a sense of external security that seemed to allow for a relaxation of authoritarian rule. The regime permitted more access to Western styles of

music, dress, and art, although political dissenters were still punished.

In his economic policies, Brezhnev continued to emphasize heavy industry. Overall industrial growth declined, although the Soviet production of iron, steel, coal, and cement surpassed that of the United States. Two problems bedeviled the Soviet economy. The government's insistence on strict central planning led to a huge, complex bureaucracy that discouraged efficiency and reduced productivity. Moreover, the Soviet system, based on guaranteed employment and a lack of incentives, bred apathy, complacency, absenteeism, and drunkenness. Agricultural problems added to Soviet economic woes. Bad harvests in the mid-1970s, caused by a series of droughts, heavy rains, and early frosts, forced the Soviet government to buy grain from the West, particularly the United States.

By the 1970s, party and state leaders—as well as leaders of the army and secret police (KGB)—had come to expect numerous advantages and material privileges. Brezhnev was unwilling to tamper with the party leadership and state bureaucracy, regardless of the inefficiency and corruption that the system encouraged. By 1980, the Soviet Union was seriously ailing. A declining economy, a rise in infant mortality rates, a dramatic surge in alcoholism, and a deterioration in working conditions all gave impetus to a decline in morale and a growing perception that the system was floundering. Within the party, a small group of reformers emerged who understood the real condition of the Soviet Union, including a young reforming leader, Mikhail Gorbachev (b. 1931).

The Gorbachev Era   After receiving his law degree in 1955, Mikhail Gorbachev returned to his native southern Russia, where he eventually became first secretary of the Communist Party in the city of Stavropol (he had joined the Party in 1952). In 1980, Gorbachev became a full member of the ruling Politburo and secretary of the Central Committee. In March 1985, he was elected general secretary of the Party and became the new leader of the Soviet Union.

Educated during the years of Khrushchev's reforms, Gorbachev seemed intent on taking those reforms to their logical conclusions. By the 1980s, Soviet economic problems were obvious. Rigid, centralized planning led to mismanagement and stifled innovation. Although the Soviets still excelled in space exploration, they fell behind the West in high technology, especially in the development and production of computers for private and public use. Most noticeable to the Soviet people was the decline in the standard of living. From the start, Gorbachev preached the need for radical reforms.

The cornerstone of Gorbachev's radical reforms was **perestroika**, or "restructuring" (see the box on p. 563). At first, he intended only a reordering of economic policy: the beginning of a market economy with limited free enterprise and some private property. However, Gorbachev soon perceived that in the Soviet system, the

MAP 29.1 **The New Europe.** The combination of an inefficient economy and high military spending had led to stagnation in the Soviet Union by the early 1980s. Mikhail Gorbachev came to power in 1985, unleashing political, economic, and nationalist forces that led to independence for the former Soviet republics and also for Eastern Europe. ❓ Compare this map with Map 27.5. What new countries had emerged by the beginning of the twenty-first century?

🐾 **View an animated version of this map or related maps at** http://thomsonedu.com/history/spielvogel

economic sphere was intimately tied to the social and political spheres. Any attempt to reform the economy without political or social reform would be doomed to failure. One of the most important instruments of *perestroika* was **glasnost**, or "openness." Soviet citizens and officials were encouraged to openly discuss the strengths and weaknesses of the Soviet Union. *Pravda* (Truth), the official newspaper of the Communist Party, began for the first time to include reports of official corruption, sloppy factory work, and protests against government policy.

Political reforms were equally revolutionary. At the Communist Party conference in 1988, Gorbachev called for the creation of a new Soviet parliament, the Congress of People's Deputies, whose members were to be chosen in competitive elections. It convened in 1989, the first meeting of a democratically elected legislative body in Russia since 1918. Early in 1990, Gorbachev legalized the formation of other political parties and struck out Article 6 of the Soviet constitution, which had guaranteed the "leading role" of the Communist Party. At the same time, Gorbachev attempted to consolidate his power by creating a new state presidency. Hitherto, the position of first

secretary of the Party was the most important post in the Soviet Union, but as the Communist Party became less closely associated with the state, the powers of this office diminished correspondingly. In March 1990, Gorbachev became the Soviet Union's first president.

One of Gorbachev's most serious problems stemmed from the very nature of the Soviet Union. The Union of Soviet Socialist Republics was a truly multiethnic country encompassing 15 constituent republics, 92 nationalities, and 112 recognized languages. Previously, the iron hand of the Communist Party, centered in Moscow, had kept a lid on the centuries-old ethnic tensions that had periodically erupted in the history of this region. As Gorbachev released this iron grip, tensions resurfaced, an unanticipated by-product of *glasnost*. Ethnic groups took advantage of the new openness to protest what they perceived to be ethnically motivated slights. As violence erupted, the Soviet Army, in disarray after a decade-long war in Afghanistan, had difficulty controlling the situation.

The late 1980s also witnessed the appearance of nationalist movements in the republics of the Soviet Union.

GORBACHEV AND PERESTROIKA

*A*fter assuming the leadership of the Soviet Union in 1985, Mikhail Gorbachev worked to liberalize and restructure the country. His policies opened the door to rapid changes in Eastern Europe and in Soviet-American relations at the end of the 1980s. In his book *Perestroika,* Gorbachev explained some of his "New Thinking."

Mikhail Gorbachev, *Perestroika*

The fundamental principle of the new political outlook is very simple: *nuclear war cannot be a means of achieving political, economic, ideological or any other goals.* This conclusion is truly revolutionary, for it means discarding the traditional notions of war and peace. It is the political function of war that has always been a justification for war, a "rational" explanation. Nuclear war is senseless; it is irrational. There would be neither winners nor losers in a global nuclear conflict: world Civilization would inevitably perish. . . .

But military technology has developed to such an extent that even a non-nuclear war would now be comparable with a nuclear war in its destructive effect. That is why it is logical to include in our category of nuclear wars this "variant" of an armed clash between major powers as well.

Thereby, an altogether different situation has emerged. A way of thinking and a way of acting, based on the use of force in world politics, have formed over centuries, even millennia. It seems they have taken root as something unshakable. Today, they have lost all reasonable grounds. . . . For the first time in history, basing international politics on moral and ethical norms that are common to all humankind, as well as humanizing interstate relations, has become a vital requirement. . . .

There is a great thirst for mutual understanding and mutual communication in the world. It is felt among politicians, [and] it is gaining momentum among the intelligentsia, representatives of culture, and the public at large. And if the Russian word *perestroika* has easily entered the international lexicon, this is due to more than just interest in what is going on in the Soviet Union. Now the whole world needs restructuring, i.e., progressive development, a fundamental change.

People feel this and understand this. They have to find their bearings, to understand the problems besetting mankind, to realize how they should live in the future. The restructuring is a must for a world overflowing with nuclear weapons; for a world ridden with serious economic and ecological problems; for a world laden with poverty, backwardness and disease; for a human race now facing the urgent need of ensuring its own survival.

We are all students, and our teacher is life and time. I believe that more and more people will come to realize that through RESTRUCTURING in the broad sense of the word, the integrity of the world will be enhanced. Having earned good marks from our main teacher—life—we shall enter the twenty-first century well prepared and sure that there will be further progress.

How revolutionary was Gorbachev's rejection of nuclear war? What impact did this idea of restructuring have on communism and the Soviet Union's ability to reform itself?

Many were motivated by ethnic concerns, with calls for sovereignty of the republics and independence from Russian-based rule centered in Moscow. These movements first sprang up in Georgia in late 1988 and then in Latvia, Estonia, Moldavia, Uzbekistan, Azerbaijan, and most dramatically, Lithuania. On March 11, 1990, the Lithuanian Supreme Council proclaimed Lithuania an independent nation.

The End of the Soviet Union In 1990 and 1991, Gorbachev struggled to deal with the problems unleashed by his reforms. On one hand, he tried to appease conservative forces who complained about the growing disorder within the Soviet Union. On the other hand, he tried to accommodate the liberal forces, especially those in the republics, who increasingly favored a new kind of decentralized Soviet federation. In particular, Gorbachev labored to cooperate more closely with Boris Yeltsin, who had been elected president of the Russian Republic in June 1991.

On August 19, 1991, a group of discontented rightists (conservative leaders of the traditional Soviet institutions—the army, government, KGB, and military industries) arrested Gorbachev and attempted to seize power. Gorbachev's unwillingness to work with the conspirators and the brave resistance in Moscow of Yeltsin and thousands of Russians who had grown accustomed to their new liberties caused the coup to disintegrate rapidly. The actions of these right-wing plotters, however, served to accelerate the very process they had hoped to stop—the disintegration of the Soviet Union.

Despite desperate pleas by Gorbachev, the republics soon moved for complete independence. Ukraine voted for independence on December 1, 1991, and a week later, the leaders of Russia, Ukraine, and Belarus announced that the Soviet Union had "ceased to exist." Gorbachev resigned on December 25, 1991, and turned over his responsibilities as commander in chief to Boris Yeltsin, the president of Russia. By the end of 1991, one of the largest empires in world history had come to an end, and a new era had begun in its lands.

Within Russia, a new power struggle soon ensued. Yeltsin was committed to introducing a free market economy as quickly as possible, but the transition was not easy. Economic hardships and social disarray, made worse by a dramatic rise in the activities of organized crime mobs, led increasing numbers of Russians to support both former Communists and hard-line nationalists, who criticized Russia's loss of prestige in world affairs. Yeltsin's brutal use of force against the Chechens, who wanted to secede from Russia and create their own state, also undermined his support. Despite the odds against him, however, Yeltsin won reelection as Russia's president in 1996, although his precarious health raised serious questions about his ability to govern.

The Putin Era   At the end of 1999, Yeltsin suddenly resigned and was replaced by Vladimir Putin, a former member of the KGB. Putin vowed to return the breakaway

Chechnya

state of Chechnya to Russian authority and to adopt a more assertive role in international affairs. Fighting in Chechnya continued throughout 2000, nearly reducing the republic's capital city of Grozny to ruins. In July 2001, Putin launched reforms, which included the unrestricted sale and purchase of land and tax cuts aimed at boosting economic growth and budget revenues. Although Russia soon experienced a growing economy, serious problems remained. The economy continued to rely on exports of natural gas, oil, and metals, all products whose prices can fluctuate wildly. Most disturbing was the large number of people—possibly 40 percent of the population—who still lived in poverty.

President Putin has attempted to deal with the chronic problems in Russian society by centralizing his control over the system and by silencing critics—notably in the Russian media. Although chastised by the West for these moves, many Russians today are distressed by the decline of social order and sympathize with Putin's efforts to restore a sense of pride and discipline in Russian society.

Eastern Europe: The Revolutions of 1989 and Collapse of the Communist Order

Stalin's postwar order had imposed Communist regimes throughout Eastern Europe, and few people believed that the new order could be undone. But discontent with their Soviet-style regimes always simmered beneath the surface of these satellite states, and after Mikhail Gorbachev made it clear that his government would not intervene militarily, their Communist regimes fell quickly in the revolutions of 1989.

Poland   Poland had achieved a certain stability in the 1960s, but economic problems continued. Edward Gierek, who came to power in 1971, attempted to solve these problems by borrowing heavily from the West. But in 1980, when he announced huge increases in food prices in an effort to pay off part of the Western debt, workers' protests erupted and led directly to the rise of the independent labor movement called Solidarity. Led by Lech Walesa, Solidarity gained the support of the workers, many intellectuals, and the Catholic church and was able to win a series of concessions. In 1988, new demonstrations led the Polish regime to agree to free parliamentary elections—the first free elections in Eastern Europe in forty years. The newly elected Solidarity coalition formed a new government, ending forty-five years of Communist rule in Poland. In December 1990, Walesa was chosen as the new Polish president. But rapid free market reforms led to severe unemployment and popular discontent, and in November 1995, Alexander Kwasniewski, a former Communist, defeated Walesa and became the new Polish president. However, he continued Poland's move toward an increasingly prosperous free market economy and was elected to a second term in 2000.

Hungary   In Hungary, too, the process of liberation from Communist rule had begun before 1989. Remaining in power for more than thirty years, the government of János Kádár enacted the most far-reaching economic reforms in Eastern Europe. In the early 1980s, Kádár legalized small private enterprises, such as shops and restaurants. Hungary moved slowly away from its strict adherence to Soviet dominance and even established fairly friendly relations with the West.

As the 1980s progressed, however, the economy sagged, and Kádár fell from power in 1988. By 1989, the Hungarian Communist government was aware of the growing dissatisfaction and began to undertake reforms. But they came too late as new political parties called for Hungary to become a democratic republic. In elections in March 1990, the Communists came in fourth, winning only 8.5 percent of the vote, a clear repudiation of communism. The Democratic Forum, a right-of-center, highly patriotic party, won the election and formed a new coalition government that committed Hungary to representative democracy and a free market economy. Since 1997, Hungary's economy has grown almost 5 percent a year, although inflation and budget deficits remain a problem.

Czechoslovakia   After Soviet troops had crushed the reform movement in Czechoslovakia in 1968, hard-line Communists under Gustav Husák purged the party and instituted a policy of massive repression to maintain their power. Only writers and other intellectuals provided any real opposition to the government, but they did not meet with success until the late 1980s. Government attempts to suppress mass demonstrations in Prague and other

VÁCLAV HAVEL: THE CALL FOR A NEW POLITICS

In attempting to deal with the world's problems, some European leaders have pointed to the need for a new perspective, especially a moral one, if people are to live in a sane world. These two excerpts are taken from speeches by Václav Havel, who was elected president of Czechoslovakia at the end of 1989. The first is from his inaugural address as president of Czechoslovakia on January 1, 1990; the second is from a speech given to the United States Congress.

Václav Havel, Address to the People of Czechoslovakia, January 1, 1990

But all this [the environmental devastation of the country by its Communist leaders] is still not the main problem. The worst thing is that we live in a contaminated moral environment. We fell morally ill because we became used to saying something different from what we thought. We learned not to believe in anything, to ignore each other, to care only about ourselves. Concepts such as love, friendship, compassion, humility, or forgiveness lost their depth and dimensions, and for many of us they represented only psychological peculiarities, or they resembled gone-astray greetings from ancients, a little ridiculous in the era of computers and spaceships. Only a few of us were able to cry out loud that the powers that be should not be all-powerful, and that special farms, which produce ecologically pure and top-quality food just for them, should send their produce to schools, children's homes and hospitals if our agriculture was unable to offer them to all. The previous regime—armed with its arrogant and intolerant ideology—reduced man to a force of production and nature to a tool of production. In this it attacked both their very substance and their mutual relationship. It reduced gifted and autonomous people, skillfully working in their own country, to nuts and bolts of some monstrously huge, noisy, and stinking machine, whose real meaning is not clear to anyone.

Václav Havel, Speech to the U.S. Congress, February 21, 1990

The salvation of this human world lies nowhere else than in the human heart, in the human power to reflect, in human meekness and in human responsibility.

Without a global revolution in the sphere of human consciousness, nothing will change for the better in the sphere of our being as humans, and the catastrophe toward which this world is headed—be it ecological, social, demographic or a general breakdown of civilization—will be unavoidable....

We are still a long way from that "family of man." In fact, we seem to be receding from the ideal rather than growing closer to it. Interests of all kinds—personal, selfish, state, nation, group, and if you like, company interests—still considerably outweigh genuinely common and global interests. We are still under the sway of the destructive and vain belief that man is the pinnacle of creation and not just a part of it and that therefore everything is permitted....

In other words, we still don't know how to put morality ahead of politics, science and economics. We are still incapable of understanding that the only genuine backbone of all our actions, if they are to be moral, is responsibility.

Responsibility to something higher than my family, my country, my company, my success—responsibility to the order of being where all our actions are indelibly recorded and where and only where they will be properly judged.

The interpreter or mediator between us and this higher authority is what is traditionally referred to as human conscience.

How different is Havel's view of politics from the views of mainstream politicians? What broader forces in modern European society do you believe shape Havel's thinking? How can Havel's view of our common humanity and responsibility to conscience help revitalize Western civilization?

Czechoslovakian cities in 1988 and 1989 only led to more and larger demonstrations. In December 1989, as demonstrations continued, the Communist government, lacking any real support, collapsed. President Husák resigned and at the end of December was replaced by Václav Havel, a dissident playwright who had played an important role in bringing the Communist government down. In January 1990, Havel declared amnesty for some thirty thousand political prisoners. He also set out on a goodwill visit to various Western countries in which he proved to be an eloquent spokesman for Czech democracy and a new order in Europe (see the box above).

Within Czechoslovakia, the shift to non-Communist rule was complicated by old problems, especially ethnic issues. Czechs and Slovaks disagreed over the makeup of the new state but were able to agree to a peaceful division of the country. On January 1, 1993, Czechoslovakia split into two nations, the Czech Republic and Slovakia. Havel was elected the first president of the new Czech Republic, which rapidly became one of Eastern Europe's most prosperous and politically stable countries. Slovakia, however, suffered from political instability and sluggish economic growth, with almost 20 percent unemployment by 2002.

Romania Czechoslovakia's revolutionary path was considerably less violent than Romania's. In 1965, leadership of the Communist government in Romania passed into the hands of Nicolae Ceauşescu, who with his wife, Elena, established a rigid and dictatorial regime. Ceauşescu ruled Romania with an iron grip, using the secret police—the Securitate—as his personal weapon against dissent.

Nevertheless, opposition to his regime grew as Ceaușescu rejected the reforms in Eastern Europe promoted by Gorbachev. A small incident became the spark that ignited long-suppressed flames of discontent. The ruthless crushing of a demonstration in Timisoara in December 1989 led to other mass demonstrations. After the dictator was booed at a mass rally on December 21, the army refused to support any more repression. Ceaușescu and his wife were captured on December 22 and tried and executed three days later. Leadership passed to the hastily formed National Salvation Front, which won elections in the spring of 1990. Although it has maintained democratic institutions, Romania has fallen prey to rampant political corruption and a weak economy. Recently, its annual rate of inflation reached 60 percent.

The Reunification of Germany

The existence of two Germanies was the most powerful symbol of divided postwar Europe. In the early 1950s, the ruling Communist government in East Germany, led by Walter Ulbricht (1893–1973) had consolidated its position and become a faithful Soviet satellite. Industry was nationalized and agriculture collectivized. A steady flight of East Germans—especially skilled laborers—to West Germany, primarily through the city of Berlin, led the East German government in 1961 to build the infamous Berlin Wall separating West from East Berlin. After building the wall, East Germany succeeded in developing the strongest economy among the Soviet Union's Eastern European satellites. In 1971, Ulbricht was succeeded by Erich Honecker (1912–1992), a party hard-liner who made use of the *Stasi,* the secret police, to rule with an iron fist for the next eighteen years.

In 1988, however, popular unrest, fueled in part by an economic slump as well as the ongoing oppressiveness of Honecker's regime, caused another mass exodus of East German refugees, followed by mass demonstrations against the regime in the summer and fall of 1989. Thousands gathered in the streets of Dresden, Berlin, and especially Leipzig. After more than half a million people flooded the streets of East Berlin on November 4, shouting, "The wall must go!" the German Communist government capitulated to popular pressure and on November 9 opened the entire border with the West. The Berlin Wall, long a symbol of the Cold War, became the site of massive celebrations as thousands of people used sledgehammers to tear it down. New political parties swiftly emerged, and on March 18, 1990, in East Germany's first free elections ever, the Christian Democrats won almost 50 percent of the vote. The Christian Democrats, like nearly all East Germans, favored political reunification with West Germany, which was achieved on October 3, 1990.

The Disintegration of Yugoslavia

From its beginning in 1918, Yugoslavia had been an artificial creation. After World War II, the dictatorial Marshal

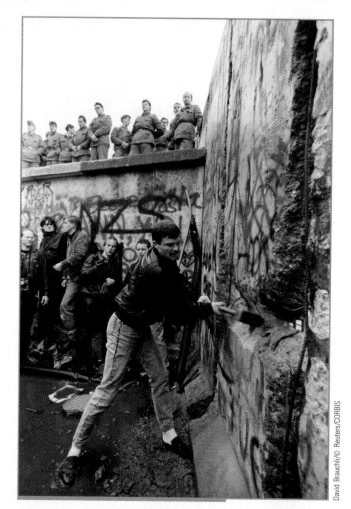

David Brauchli/© Reuters/CORBIS

And the Wall Came Tumbling Down. The Berlin Wall, long a symbol of Europe's Cold War divisions, became the site of massive celebrations after the East German government opened its border with the West. The activities included spontaneous acts of demolition as Germans used sledgehammers and crowbars to tear down parts of the wall. In this photograph, a demonstrator pounds away at the Berlin Wall as East German border guards observe from above.

Tito had managed to hold its six republics and two autonomous provinces together, but after his death in 1980, no strong leader emerged, and his responsibilities passed to a collective state presidency and the League of Communists of Yugoslavia. At the end of the 1980s, Yugoslavia was caught up in the reform movements sweeping Eastern Europe. The League of Communists collapsed, and new parties quickly formed.

In 1990, the republics of Slovenia, Croatia, Bosnia-Herzegovina, and Macedonia began to lobby for a new federal structure of Yugoslavia that would fulfill their separatist desires. Slobodan Milošević, who had become leader of the Serbian Communist Party in 1987 and had managed to stay in power by emphasizing his Serbian nationalism, rejected these efforts. He asserted that these republics could be independent only if new border arrangements were made to accommodate the Serb minorities in those republics who did not want to live outside the boundaries of a greater Serbian state. Serbs constituted 11.6 percent of Croatia's population and 32 percent of Bosnia-Herzegovina's in 1981.

After negotiations among the six republics failed, Slovenia and Croatia declared their independence in June 1991. Milošević's government sent the Yugoslavian army, which it controlled, into Slovenia, without success. In September 1991, it began a full assault against Croatia. Increasingly, the Yugoslavian army was becoming the Serbian army. Before a cease-fire was arranged, the Serbian forces had captured one-third of Croatia's territory in brutal and destructive fighting.

The War in Bosnia Early in 1992, the Serbs, who are Eastern Orthodox Christians, turned their guns on multireligious Bosnia-Herzegovina and by mid-1993 had seized 70 percent of Bosnia's territory. The Serbian policy of **ethnic cleansing**—killing or forcibly removing Bosnian Muslims from their lands—revived memories of Nazi atrocities in World War II. This account by one Muslim survivor from the town of Srebrenica is eerily reminiscent of the activities of the Nazi *Einsatzgruppen* (see Chapter 27):

> When the truck stopped, they told us to get off by groups of five. We immediately heard shooting next to the trucks.... About ten Serbs with automatic rifles told us to lie down on the ground face first. As we were getting down, they started to shoot, and I fell into a pile of corpses. I felt hot liquid running down my face. I realized that I was only grazed. As they continued to shoot more groups, I kept on squeezing myself in between dead bodies.[1]

Almost eight thousand men and boys were killed by the Serbian massacre at Srebrenica. Nevertheless, despite worldwide outrage, European governments failed to take a decisive and forceful stand against these Serbian activities. By 1995, some 250,000 Bosnians had been killed and two million others left homeless.

Then a sudden turn of events occurred. New offensives by mostly Muslim Bosnian government army forces and by the Croatian army regained considerable territory that had been lost to Serbian forces. Air strikes by NATO bombers, strongly advocated by U.S. President Bill Clinton, were launched in retaliation for Serb attacks on civilians and weakened the Serb military positions. A formal peace treaty was signed in Paris on December 14 that split Bosnia into a loose union of a Serb republic and a Muslim-Croat federation. NATO agreed to send a force of sixty thousand troops to monitor the frontier between the new political entities (see Map 29.2).

The War in Kosovo Peace in Bosnia, however, did not bring peace to all of the former Yugoslavia. A new war erupted in 1999 over Kosovo, which had been made an

MAP 29.2 The Lands of the Former Yugoslavia. By 1991, resurgent nationalism and the European independence wave overcame the forces that held Yugoslavia together. Independence declarations by Slovenia, Croatia, and Bosnia-Herzegovina brought war with the Serbian-dominated rump Yugoslavia of Slobodan Milošević. **?** What aspects of Slovenia's location help explain why its war of liberation was briefer and less bloody than others in the former Yugoslavia?

View an animated version of this map or related maps at http://thomsonedu.com/history/spielvogel

Era of Brezhnev	1964–1982
Rule of Ceaușescu in Romania	1965–1989
Honecker as leader of East Germany	1971
Emergence of Solidarity in Poland	1980
Gorbachev in power in the Soviet Union	1985
	1989
Collapse of Communist government in Czechoslovakia	December
Collapse of East German government	December
Execution of Ceaușescu in Romania	December 25
	1990
East German elections—victory of Christian Democrats	March 18
Reunification of Germany	October 3
Walesa as president of Poland	December
	1991
Yeltsin as president of Russia	June
Slovenia and Croatia declarations of independence	June
Attempted right-wing coup in the Soviet Union	August 19
Dissolution of the Soviet Union	December
	1993
Division of Czechoslovakia into Czech Republic and Slovakia	January 1
Havel as president of Czech Republic	February 2
	1995
Aleksander Kwasniewski as Polish president	November
Dayton Accords—end of war in Bosnia	December
Russian presidential elections	1996
War in Kosovo	1999
Putin as president of Russia	2000
Death of Milošević	2006

autonomous province within Yugoslavia by Tito in 1974. Kosovo's inhabitants were mainly ethnic Albanians. But the province was also home to a Serbian minority that asserted a historical claim to the territory, where Serbian forces in the fourteenth century had been defeated by the Ottoman Turks.

In 1989, Slobodan Milošević, the Yugoslav president, stripped Kosovo of its autonomous status and outlawed any official use of the Albanian language. In 1993, some groups of ethnic Albanians founded the Kosovo Liberation Army (KLA) and began a campaign against Serbian rule in Kosovo. When Serb forces began to massacre ethnic Albanians in an effort to crush the KLA, the United States and its NATO allies sought to arrange a settlement. After months of negotiations, the Kosovo

Albanians agreed to a peace plan that would have given the ethnic Albanians in Kosovo broad autonomy for a three-year interim period. When Milošević refused to sign the agreement, the United States and its NATO allies began a bombing campaign that forced the Yugoslavian government into compliance.

The Aftermath By 2000, the Serbian people had finally grown weary of the violence and in the fall elections ousted Milošević from power. The new Serbian government under Vojislav Kostunica moved quickly to cooperate with the international community and begin rebuilding the Serbian economy. On June 28, 2001, the Serbian government agreed to allow Milošević to be tried by an international tribunal for crimes against humanity for his ethnic cleansing policies throughout Yugoslavia's disintegration. He died in 2006 during that trial.

The fate of Bosnia and Kosovo has not yet been finally determined. Thirty thousand NATO troops remain in Bosnia, trying to keep the peace between the Serbs and the Muslim-Croat federation. More than thirty international organizations are at work rebuilding schools, roads, and sewers, but only the presence of NATO troops keeps old hatreds from erupting again.

In Kosovo, NATO military forces were brought in to maintain the uneasy peace, while United Nations officials worked to create democratic institutions and the European Union provided funds for rebuilding the region's infrastructure. These efforts are ongoing but made difficult by the festering hatred between Kosovo Albanians and the remaining Serbs.

The last political vestiges of Yugoslavia ceased to exist in 2004 when the Kostunica government officially renamed the truncated country Serbia and Montenegro. Two years later, Montenegrans voted in favor of independence. Thus by 2006, all six republics cobbled together to form Yugoslavia in 1918 were once again independent nations.

Western Europe: The Winds of Change

After two decades of incredible economic growth, Europe experienced severe economic recessions in the mid-1970s and early 1980s. Both inflation and unemployment rose dramatically. A substantial increase in the price of oil in 1973 was a major cause of the first downturn. Moreover, a worldwide recession had led to a decline in demand for European goods. The economies of the Western European states recovered in the course of the 1980s, although problems remained.

Germany Restored After the Adenauer era, West German voters moved politically from the center-right politics of the Christian Democrats to center-left politics, and in 1969, the Social Democrats became the leading party. The first Social Democratic chancellor was Willy Brandt (1913–1992). Brandt was especially successful with his "opening toward the east" (known as *Ostpolitik*), for which he received the Nobel Peace Prize in 1972.

In that year, Brandt made a treaty with East Germany that called for "good neighborly" relations, which soon led to greater cultural, personal, and economic contacts between West and East Germany.

Brandt's successor, Helmut Schmidt (b. 1918), was more of a technocrat than a reform-minded socialist and concentrated primarily on the economic problems largely brought about by high oil prices between 1973 and 1975. Schmidt was successful in eliminating a deficit of 10 billion marks in three years. In 1982, when the coalition of Schmidt's Social Democrats with the Free Democrats fell apart over the reduction of social welfare expenditures, the Free Democrats joined with the Christian Democratic Union of Helmut Kohl (b. 1930) to form a new government.

Kohl was a clever politician who benefited greatly from the reunification of the two Germanies, which made the new Germany, with its 79 million people, the leading power in Europe. But the excitement over reunification soon dissipated as problems arose. The realization set in that the revitalization of eastern Germany would take far more money than was originally thought, and Kohl's government was soon forced to raise taxes. Moreover, the virtual collapse of the economy in eastern Germany led to extremely high levels of unemployment and severe discontent. One response was a return to power for the Social Democrats under the leadership of Gerhard Schroeder (b. 1944) as a result of elections in 1998. But Schroeder had little success with Germany's economic woes, and as a result of elections in 2005, Angela Merkel (b. 1954), leader of the Christian Democrats, became the first female chancellor in German history.

Great Britain: Thatcher and Thatcherism Between 1964 and 1979, the Conservative and Labour Parties alternated in power. Neither could solve the problem of fighting between Catholics and Protestants in Northern Ireland. Violence increased as the Irish Republican Army (IRA) staged a series of dramatic terrorist acts in response to the suspension of Northern Ireland's parliament in 1972 and the establishment of direct rule by London. Nor was either party able to deal with Britain's ailing economy. Failure to modernize made British industry less and less competitive. Moreover, Britain was hampered by frequent labor strikes, many of them caused by conflicts between rival labor unions.

In 1979, the Conservatives returned to power under Margaret Thatcher (b. 1925), who became the first woman prime minister in British history (see the box on p. 570). Thatcher pledged to lower taxes, reduce government bureaucracy, limit social welfare, restrict union power, and end inflation. The "Iron Lady," as she was called, did break the power of the labor unions. Although she did not eliminate the basic components of the social welfare system, she did use austerity measures to control inflation. Thatcherism, as her economic policy was termed, improved the British economic situation, but at a price. The south of England, for example, prospered, but the old industrial areas of the Midlands and the north declined and were beset by high unemployment and poverty.

In foreign policy, Thatcher, like Ronald Reagan in the United States, took a hard-line approach against communism. She oversaw a large military buildup aimed at replacing older technology and reestablishing Britain as a world policeman. In 1982, when Argentina attempted to take control of the Falkland Islands (one of Britain's few remaining colonial outposts) 300 miles off its coast, the British successfully repelled the Argentines.

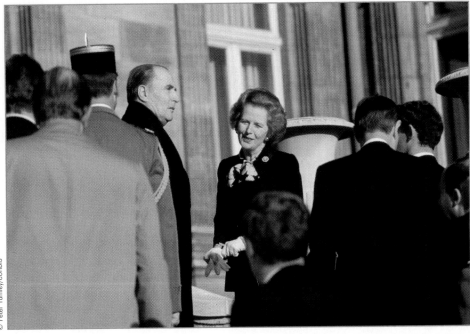

Margaret Thatcher. Great Britain's first female prime minister, Margaret Thatcher was a strong leader who dominated British politics in the 1980s. This picture of Thatcher was taken during a meeting with French president François Mitterrand in 1986.

MARGARET THATCHER: ENTERING A MAN'S WORLD

In this excerpt from her autobiography, Margaret Thatcher describes how she was interviewed by Conservative Party officials when they first considered her as a candidate for Parliament. Thatcher ran for Parliament for the first time in 1950; she lost but increased the Conservative vote total in the district by 50 percent over the previous election.

Margaret Thatcher, *The Path to Power*

And, as always with me, there was politics. I immediately joined the Conservative Association and threw myself into the usual round of Party activities. In particular, I thoroughly enjoyed what was called the "'39–'45" discussion group, where Conservatives of the war generation met to exchange views and argue about the political topics of the day....It was as a representative of the Oxford University Graduate Conservative Association (OUGCA) that I went to the Llandudno Conservative Party Conference in October 1948....

After one of the debates, I found myself engaged in one of those speculative conversations which young people have about their future prospects. An Oxford friend, John Grant, said he supposed that one day I would like to be a Member of Parliament. "Well, yes," I replied, "but there's not much hope of that. The chances of my being selected are just nil at the moment." I might have added that with no private income of my own there was no way I could have afforded to be an MP on the salary then available. I had not even tried to get on the Party's list of approved candidates.

Later in the day, John Grant happened to be sitting next to the Chairman of the Dartford Conservative Association, John Miller. The Association was in search of a candidate. I learned afterwards that the conversation went something

like this: "I understand that you're still looking for a candidate at Dartford?"

"That's right. Any suggestions?"

"Well, there's a young woman, Margaret Roberts, that you might look at. She's very good."

"Oh, but Dartford is a real industrial stronghold. I don't think a woman would do at all."

"Well, you know best of course. But why not just look at her?"

And they did. I was invited to have lunch with John Miller and his wife, Phee, and the Dartford Woman's Chairman, Mrs. Fletcher, on the Saturday on Llandudno Pier. Presumably, and in spite of any reservations about the suitability of a woman candidate for their seat, they liked what they saw. I certainly got on well with them....

I did not hear from Dartford until December, when I was asked to attend an interview at Palace Chambers, Bridge Street....I found myself short-listed, and was asked to go to Dartford itself for a further interview....As one of five would-be candidates, I had to give a fifteen-minute speech and answer questions for a further ten minutes.

It was the questions which were more likely to cause me trouble. There was a good deal of suspicion of woman candidates, particularly in what was regarded as a tough industrial seat like Dartford. This was quite definitely a man's world into which not just angels feared to tread....

The most reliable sign that a political occasion has gone well is that you have enjoyed it. I enjoyed that evening at Dartford, and the outcome justified my confidence. I was selected.

In this account, is Margaret Thatcher's being a woman more important to her or to others? Why would this disparity exist?

Thatcher dominated British politics in the 1980s. Only in 1990 did Labour's fortunes seem to revive when Thatcher's government attempted to replace local property taxes with a flat-rate tax that would enable the rich to pay the same rate as the poor. Thatcher's once remarkable popularity fell to all-time lows. At the end of November 1990, a revolt within her own party caused Thatcher to resign as prime minister and be replaced by John Major. His government, however, failed to please most Britons. In elections on May 1, 1997, the Labour Party won a landslide victory. The new prime minister, Tony Blair (b. 1953), was a moderate whose youthful energy immediately instilled a new vigor on the political scene. Blair was one of the major leaders in forming an international coalition against terrorism after the terrorist attacks on the United States in 2001. Four years later, his ongoing support of the U.S. war in Iraq when a majority of Britons opposed it caused his popularity to plummet.

Uncertainties in France The worsening of France's economic situation in the 1970s brought a shift to the left politically. By 1981, the Socialists had become the dominant party in the National Assembly, and the Socialist leader, François Mitterrand (1916–1995), was elected president. His first concern was with France's economic difficulties. In 1982, Mitterrand froze prices and wages in the hope of reducing the huge budget deficit and high inflation. He also passed a number of liberal measures to aid workers: an increased minimum wage, expanded social benefits, a thirty-nine-hour workweek, higher taxes for the rich, and nationalization of major banks. Mitterrand's administrative reforms included both centralization (nationalization of banks and industry) and decentralization (granting local governments greater powers).

The Socialist policies largely failed to work, however, and within three years, a decline in support for the

Socialists caused the Mitterrand government to turn portions of the economy back over to private enterprise. Economic improvements enabled Mitterrand to win a second seven-year term in the 1988 presidential election, but France's overall economic decline continued. In 1993, French unemployment stood at 10.6 percent, and in the elections in March of that year, the Socialists won only 28 percent of the vote while a coalition of conservative parties won 80 percent of the seats in the National Assembly. The move to the right was strengthened when the conservative mayor of Paris, Jacques Chirac (b. 1932), was elected president in 1995 and reelected in 2002. Chirac pursued a plan of sending illegal immigrants back to their home countries and in 2003 became an outspoken opponent of the U.S. invasion of Iraq.

The Unification of Europe

Western European states continued to pursue the postwar goal of integrating their economies. Beginning with six states in 1957, the European Economic Community expanded in 1973 when Great Britain, Ireland, and Denmark joined what its members now renamed the European Community (EC). Greece joined in 1981, followed by Spain and Portugal in 1986. In 1995, Austria, Finland, and Sweden also became members of the EC.

The European Union   The European Community was an economic union, not a political one. In the 1980s and 1990s, the EC moved toward even greater economic integration. The treaty on European Union, which went into effect on January 1, 1994, turned the European Community into the European Union, a true economic and monetary union of all EC members. By 2000, the EC contained 370 million people and constituted the world's largest single trading entity, transacting one-fourth of the

world's commerce. Another of its goals was achieved in 1999 with the introduction of a common currency, the euro. On January 1, 2002, the euro officially replaced twelve national currencies.

In addition to having a single internal market for those twelve members and a common currency, the EU also established a common agricultural policy, in which subsidies were provided to farmers to enable them to sell their goods competitively on the world market. The EU also provides aid to the European Union's poorest regions as well as subsidies for job training, education, and modernization. The end of national passports gave millions of Europeans greater flexibility in travel. The European Union has been less successful in setting common foreign policy goals, primarily because individual nations still regard foreign policy as a national priority and are reluctant to give up this power to a single overriding institution.

Toward a United Europe   At the start of the twenty-first century, the EU set a new goal: to incorporate into the union the states of eastern and southeastern Europe. Many of these states are considerably poorer than the current members, which raises the possibility that adding these nations might weaken the EU itself. To lessen the danger, EU members established a set of qualifications that focus on demonstrating a commitment both to market capitalism and to democracy, including not only the rule of law but also respect for minorities and human rights. In May 2004, the European Union took the plunge and added ten new members—Cyprus, the Czech Republic, Estonia, Hungary, Latvia, Lithuania, Malta, Poland, Slovakia, and Slovenia—thus enlarging the population of the EU to 455 million people (see Map 29.3).

The United States: Turmoil, Tranquility, and Terrorism

With the election of Richard Nixon as president in 1968, American politics made a shift to the right. Nixon ended U.S. involvement in Vietnam by gradually withdrawing American troops. Politically, he pursued a "southern strategy," carefully calculating that "law and order" issues and a slowdown in racial desegregation would appeal to southern whites. The South, which had once been a stronghold for the Democrats, began to form a new allegiance to the Republican Party.

As president, Nixon was paranoid about conspiracies and began to use illegal methods to gain intelligence on his political opponents. Nixon's zeal led to the Watergate scandal—an attempted bugging of Democratic National Headquarters, located in the Watergate complex in Washington, D.C. Although Nixon repeatedly lied to the American public about his involvement in the affair, secret tapes of his own conversations in the White House revealed the truth. On August 9, 1974, Nixon resigned the presidency rather than face impeachment and then trial by the Senate.

MAP 29.3 The European Union, 2004. Beginning in 1967 as the European Economic Community, also known as the Common Market, the union of European states seeking to integrate their economies gradually grew from six members to twenty-five in 2004. By 2002, the European Union had achieved two major goals—the creation of a single internal market and a common currency—although it has been less successful at working toward common political and foreign policy goals. ❓ What additional nations do you think will eventually join the European Union? 🐭 **View an animated version of this map or related maps at** http://thomsonedu.com/history/ spielvogel

Legend:
- 1967: France, West Germany, Belgium, Netherlands, Luxembourg, Italy
- 1973: Great Britain, Ireland, Denmark
- 1981: Greece
- 1986: Spain, Portugal
- 1995: Austria, Finland, Sweden
- 2004: Czech Republic, Estonia, Hungary, Latvia, Lithuania, Malta, Poland, Slovakia, Slovenia, and Cyprus

After Watergate, American domestic politics focused on economic issues. Vice President Gerald Ford (b. 1913) became president when Nixon resigned, only to lose in the 1976 election to the former governor of Georgia, Jimmy Carter (b. 1924). Both Ford and Carter faced severe economic problems. The period from 1973 to the mid-1980s was one of economic stagnation, which came to be known as **stagflation**—the simultaneous occurrence of high inflation and high unemployment. In part, the economic downturn stemmed from a dramatic rise in oil prices. An oil embargo and price increases by the Organization of Petroleum Exporting Countries (OPEC) in the aftermath of the Arab-Israeli war in 1973 quadrupled oil prices. Additional price hikes led oil prices to increase twentyfold by the end of the 1970s, encouraging inflationary tendencies throughout the entire economy.

By 1980, the Carter administration faced two devastating problems. High inflation and a noticeable decline in average weekly earnings were causing a drop in American living standards. At the same time, a crisis abroad had erupted when fifty-three Americans were taken hostage by the Iranian government of Ayatollah Khomeini. Carter's inability to gain the release of the American hostages led to perceptions at home that he was a weak president. His overwhelming loss to Ronald Reagan (1911–2004) in the election of 1980 brought forward the chief exponent of right-wing Republican policies and a new political order.

The Reagan Revolution, as it has been called, consisted of a number of new directions. Reversing decades of changes, Reagan cut back on the welfare state by decreasing spending on food stamps, school lunch programs, and job programs. At the same time, his administration fostered the largest peacetime military buildup in American history. Total federal spending rose from $631 billion in 1981 to over $1 trillion by 1986. But instead of raising taxes to pay for the new expenditures, which far outweighed the budget cuts in social areas, Reagan convinced Congress to trust in "supply-side economics." Massive tax cuts would supposedly stimulate rapid economic growth and produce new revenues. Much of the tax cut went to the wealthy. Reagan's policies seemed to work in the short run as the United States experienced an economic upturn that lasted until the end of the 1980s. The spending policies of the Reagan administration, however, also produced record government deficits, which loomed as an obstacle to long-term growth. In the 1970s, the total deficit was $420 billion. Between 1981 and 1987, Reagan budget deficits were three times that amount.

The inability of George H.W. Bush (b. 1924), Reagan's successor, to deal with the deficit problem, accompanied by an economic downturn, enabled a Democrat, Bill Clinton (b. 1946), to become president in November 1992. The new president was a southern Democrat who favored a number of the Republican policies of the 1980s. This was a clear indication that the Democratic victory had by no means halted the rightward drift in American politics. In fact, Clinton's reelection in 1996 was due in part to his adoption of Republican ideas and policies. Much of Clinton's second term, however, was overshadowed by charges of presidential misconduct stemming from the president's affair with Monica Lewinsky, a White House intern. After a bitter partisan struggle, the U.S. Senate acquitted the president on two articles of impeachment brought by the House of Representatives. But Clinton's problems helped the Republican candidate, George W. Bush (b. 1946), son of the first President Bush, to win the presidential election in 2000. Although Bush lost the popular vote to Al Gore, he narrowly won the electoral vote after a controversial victory in the state of Florida.

The first four years of Bush's administration were largely occupied with the war on terrorism and the U.S.-led war on Iraq. The Office of Homeland Security was established after the 2001 terrorist assaults to help protect the United States from future terrorist acts. At the same time, Bush pushed tax cuts through Congress that mainly favored the wealthy and helped produce record deficits reminiscent of the Reagan years. Environmentalists were especially disturbed by the Bush administration's efforts to weaken environmental laws and impose regulations to benefit American corporations. In November 2004, after a highly negative political campaign, Bush was narrowly elected to a second term. In 2005 and 2006, Bush's popularity plummeted drastically as discontent grew over the Iraq War and financial corruption in the Republican Party, as well as the administration's poor handling of relief efforts after Hurricane Katrina.

Contemporary Canada

In 1963, during a major economic recession, the Liberals had been returned to power in Canada. The most prominent Liberal government was that of Pierre Trudeau (1919–2000), who came to power in 1968. Although French Canadian in background, Trudeau was dedicated to Canada's federal union, and in 1968 his government passed the Official Languages Act, which allowed both English and French to be used in the federal civil service. Although Trudeau's government vigorously pushed an industrialization program, high inflation and Trudeau's efforts to impose the will of the federal government on the powerful provincial governments alienated voters. Economic recession in the early 1980s brought Brian Mulroney (b. 1939), leader of the Progressive Conservative party, to power in 1984. Mulroney's government sought greater privatization of Canada's state-run corporations and negotiated a free-trade agreement with the United States. Bitterly resented by many Canadians, the agreement cost Mulroney's government much of its popularity. In 1993, the ruling Conservatives were drastically defeated, and the Liberal leader, Jean Chrétien (b. 1934), became prime minister. Chrétien's conservative fiscal policies, combined with strong economic growth, enabled his government to have a budgetary surplus by the late 1990s and led to another Liberal victory in the elections of 1997. However, charges of widespread financial corruption in the government led to a Conservative win early in 2006, and Stephen Harper (b. 1959) became the new prime minister.

Mulroney's government had been unable to settle the ongoing crisis over the French-speaking province of Quebec. In the late 1960s, the Parti Québécois, headed by René Lévesque (1922–1987), ran on a platform of Quebec's secession from the Canadian union. To pursue their dream of separation, some underground separatist groups even resorted to terrorist bombings. In 1976, the Parti Québécois won Quebec's provincial elections and in 1980 called for a referendum that would enable the provincial government to negotiate Quebec's independence from the rest of Canada. Voters in Quebec narrowly rejected the plan in 1995, however, and debate over Quebec's status continues to divide Canada.

Quebec

After the Cold War: New World Order or Age of Terrorism?

By the 1970s, American-Soviet relations had entered the phase known as détente, marked by a reduction of tensions between the two superpowers. An appropriate symbol of détente was the Antiballistic Missile Treaty, signed in 1972, in which the two nations agreed to limit their antiballistic missile systems. The U.S. objective in pursuing the treaty was to make it unlikely that either superpower could win a nuclear exchange by launching a preemptive strike against the other. U.S. officials believed that a policy of "equivalence," in which there was a roughly equal power balance on each side, was the best way to avoid a nuclear confrontation.

In 1975, the Helsinki Agreements marked another effort to reduce tensions between the superpowers. Signed by the United States, Canada, and the European nations, these accords recognized all borders in Europe that had been established since the end of World War II, thereby acknowledging the Soviet sphere of influence in Eastern Europe. The Helsinki Agreements also committed the signatory powers to recognizing and protecting the human rights of their citizens.

This protection of human rights became one of the major foreign policy goals of the next American president, Jimmy Carter. Although hopes ran high for the continuation of détente, the Soviet invasion of Afghanistan in 1979, undertaken to restore a pro-Soviet regime, hardened relations between the United States and the Soviet Union. President Carter placed an embargo on the shipment of American grain to the Soviet Union.

The early administration of Ronald Reagan witnessed a return to the harsh rhetoric, if not all of the harsh practices, of the Cold War. Calling the Soviet Union an "evil empire," Reagan began a military buildup that stimulated a renewed arms race. By providing military support to the Afghan insurgents, the Reagan administration helped maintain a Vietnam-like war in Afghanistan that the Soviet Union could not win. Like the Vietnam War, the war in Afghanistan demonstrated that the power of a superpower was actually limited in the face of strong nationalist, guerrilla-type opposition.

The End of the Cold War

The accession of Mikhail Gorbachev to power in the Soviet Union in 1985 eventually brought a dramatic end to the Cold War. Gorbachev was willing to question many of the fundamental assumptions underlying Soviet foreign policy, and his "New Thinking," as it was called, opened the door to a series of stunning changes. For one, Gorbachev initiated a plan for arms limitation that led in 1987 to an agreement with the United States to eliminate intermediate-range nuclear weapons (the INF Treaty). Both sides had incentives to dampen the expensive arms race. Gorbachev hoped to make extensive economic and internal reforms, and the United States had serious deficit problems. During the Reagan years, the United States, originally a creditor nation, had become the world's biggest debtor nation. By 1990, both countries were aware that their large military budgets left insufficient funds for resolving their serious social problems.

The years 1989 and 1990 were a crucial period in the ending of the Cold War. The postwar settlements came unstuck as a mostly peaceful revolutionary upheaval swept through Eastern Europe. According to Gorbachev's new policy, the Soviet Union would no longer militarily support Communist governments that faced internal revolt. The unwillingness of the Soviet regime to use force to maintain the status quo opened the door to the overthrow of the Communist regimes. On October 3,

Reagan and Gorbachev. The willingness of Mikhail Gorbachev and Ronald Reagan to dampen the arms race was a significant factor in ending the Cold War confrontation between the United States and the Soviet Union. Reagan and Gorbachev are shown here standing before Saint Basil's Cathedral during Reagan's visit to Moscow in 1988.

1990, the reunification of Germany also destroyed one of the most prominent symbols of the Cold War era.

The Persian Gulf War provided the first major opportunity for testing the new relationship between the United States and the Soviet Union in the post–Cold War era. In early August 1990, Iraqi military forces occupied the small neighboring country of Kuwait in the northeastern corner of the Arabian peninsula at the head of the Persian Gulf. The Iraqi invasion sparked an international outcry and the assembling of an international force led by the United States that liberated Kuwait and destroyed a substantial part of Iraq's armed forces in the early months of 1991. Gorbachev and the Soviets played a minor role in the crisis and supported the American action.

By the end of 1991, the Soviet Union had disintegrated, making any renewal of the global rivalry between two competing superpowers impossible. Although the United States emerged as the world's leading military power by 1992, its role in the creation of the "New World

Order" that President George H.W. Bush advocated at the time of the Gulf War was not clear. After some hesitation, President Bill Clinton began to reassert American power in the world. In December 1995, the United States took the lead in bringing a negotiated end to the war in Bosnia, and in 1999, the United States and its NATO allies used a bombing campaign to force Yugoslavia to accept a settlement in Kosovo.

After al-Qaeda terrorists struck at the United States in September 2001, President George W. Bush declared war on terrorism, formed an international coalition led by the United States, and attacked the Taliban-led regime in Afghanistan that was providing a base of operations for Osama bin Laden's al-Qaeda terrorists (see the next section). The U.S.-led operation quickly overwhelmed the Taliban, but the attempt to build a new government has yet to achieve much success.

One year later, the Bush administration began to threaten to remove Saddam Hussein from power in Iraq. U.S. claims that Saddam possessed weapons of mass destruction and had close ties to al-Qaeda, however, were widely doubted by other member states at the United Nations, forcing the United States to attack Iraq with little world support. After a quick victory in March and April 2003, U.S. forces became bogged down in a guerrilla-type war that finally led the Bush administration to seek the help of the United Nations in forming a new Iraqi state. Election were held and a coalition government was formed, but the nation itself descending into civil war.

An Age of Terrorism?

Acts of terror by individuals and groups opposed to governments became a frightening aspect of modern Western society. In 1996, President Clinton called terrorism "the enemy of our generation," and after the end of Cold War, it indeed seemed as if terrorism had replaced communism as the West's number one enemy.

Already during the late 1970s and 1980s, concern about terrorism was often at the top of foreign policy agendas in the United States and many European countries. Bands of terrorists used assassination, indiscriminate bombings of civilians, the taking of hostages, and the hijacking of airplanes to draw attention to their demands or to destabilize governments in the hope of achieving their political goals. Terrorist acts garnered considerable media attention. When Palestinian terrorists kidnapped and killed eleven Israeli athletes at the Munich Olympic Games in 1972, hundreds of millions of people watched the drama unfold on television. Indeed, some observers believe that media exposure has been an important catalyst for some terrorist groups.

Motivations for terrorist acts varied considerably. Left-wing groups, such as the Baader-Meinhof gang (also known as the Red Army Faction) in Germany and the Red Brigades in Italy, consisted chiefly of affluent middle-class young people who denounced the injustices of capitalism and supported acts of "revolutionary terrorism" to bring

down the system. Right-wing terrorist groups, such as the New Order in Italy and the Charles Martel Club in France, used bombings to foment disorder and bring about authoritarian regimes. These groups received little or no public support, and authorities were able to crush them fairly quickly.

But terrorist acts also stemmed from militant nationalists who wished to create separatist states. Because they received considerable support from local populations sympathetic to their cause, these terrorist groups could maintain their activities over a long period of time. Most prominent was the Irish Republican Army, which resorted to vicious attacks against the ruling government and innocent civilians in Northern Ireland. Over a period of twenty years, IRA terrorists were responsible for the deaths of two thousand people in Northern Ireland; three-fourths of them were civilians.

Terrorist Attacks on the United States   One of the most destructive acts of terrorism occurred on September 11, 2001, in the United States. Four groups of terrorists hijacked four commercial jet airplanes in Boston, Newark, and Washington, D.C. The hijackers flew two of the airplanes directly into the towers of the World Trade Center in New York City, causing these buildings, as well as a number of surrounding buildings, to collapse. A third hijacked plane slammed into the Pentagon near Washington, D.C. The fourth plane, apparently headed for Washington, crashed instead in an isolated area of Pennsylvania, probably as the result of an attack on the hijackers by a group of heroic passengers. Three thousand people were killed, including everyone aboard the four airliners.

These coordinated acts of terror were carried out by hijackers connected to an international terrorist organization known as al-Qaeda, run by Osama bin Laden. A native of Saudi Arabia of Yemeni extraction, bin Laden used an inherited fortune to set up terrorist training camps in Afghanistan under the protection of the nation's militant fundamentalist Islamic rulers known as the Taliban.

U.S. president George W. Bush vowed to wage a lengthy war on terrorism and worked to create a coalition of nations around the world to assist in ridding the world of al-Qaeda and other terrorist groups. In October 2001, United States and NATO air forces began bombing Taliban-controlled command centers, airfields, and al-Qaeda hiding places in Afghanistan. On the ground, Afghan forces pushed the Taliban out of the capital city of Kabul and seized control of nearly all of the country by the end of November. A democratic multiethnic government was installed but continues to face problems from revived Taliban activity.

New Directions and New Problems in Western Society

Dramatic social developments have accompanied political and economic changes since 1973. New opportunities for women emerged while new problems for Western

Terrorist Attack on the World Trade Center in New York City. On September 11, 2001, hijackers flew two commercial jetliners into the twin towers of the World Trade Center. Shown at left are the two towers in the New York skyline before the attack. The middle picture shows the second of the two jetliners about to hit one of the towers while smoke billows from the site of the first attack. In the scene below, firefighters are making their way through what was left of the 110-story towers after they collapsed.

society arose with the advent of terrorism and a growing awareness of environmental dangers.

Transformation in Women's Lives

Parents need to average approximately 2.1 children to ensure the natural replacement of a country's population. In many European countries, the population stopped growing in the 1960s, and the trend has continued downward since then. Among the nations of the European Union, the average number of children per mother was 1.4. Spain's rate—1.15—was among the lowest in the world in 2002.

At the same time, the number of women in the workforce has continued to rise. In Britain, for example, the number of women in the labor force went from 32 percent to 44 percent between 1970 and 1990. Moreover, women have entered new employment areas. Greater access to universities and professional schools enabled women to take jobs in law, medicine, government, business, and education. In the Soviet Union, for example, about 70 percent of doctors and teachers were women. Nevertheless, economic inequality still often prevailed; women received lower wages than men for comparable work and received fewer opportunities to achieve management positions.

The Women's Movement Feminists in the women's liberation movement came to believe that women themselves must transform the fundamental conditions of their lives. They did so in a variety of ways. First, they formed numerous "consciousness-raising" groups to further awareness of women's issues. Women met to share their personal experiences and become aware of the many ways that male dominance affected their lives. This new consciousness helped many women become activists.

Women sought and gained a measure of control over their own bodies by seeking to overturn laws prohibiting contraception and abortion. Hundreds of thousands of European women worked to repeal those laws in the 1960s and 1970s and began to meet with success. A French law in 1968 permitted the sale of contraceptive devices, and in the 1970s French feminists worked to legalize abortion, an effort that succeeded in 1979. Even in Catholic countries, where the church remained strongly opposed to abortion, legislation allowing contraception and abortion was passed in the 1970s and 1980s.

As more women became activists, they also became involved in new issues. In the 1980s and 1990s, women faculty in universities concentrated on reforming cultural attitudes through the new academic field of women's studies. Courses in women's studies, which stressed the role and contributions of women in history, mushroomed in both American and European colleges and universities.

Other women began to try to affect the political environment by allying with the antinuclear movement. In 1981, a group of women protested American nuclear missiles in Britain by chaining themselves to the fence of an American military base. Thousands more joined in creating a peace camp around the military compound.

Enthusiasm ran high; one participant said, "I'll never forget that feeling. . . . It was for women; it was for peace; it was for the world."[2]

Some women joined the ecological movement. As one German writer who was concerned with environmental issues said, it is women "who must give birth to children, willingly or unwillingly, in this polluted world of ours." Women became especially prominent members of the Green Party in Germany (see next section), which supported environmental issues. One delegate was Petra Kelly (b. 1947), one of the founders of the German Green Party and a tireless campaigner for the preservation of the environment as well as human rights and equality.

Women in the West have also reached out to work with women from the rest of the world in international conferences to change the conditions of their lives. Between 1975 and 1995, the United Nations held conferences in Mexico City, Copenhagen, Nairobi, and Beijing. These meetings made clear the differences between women from Western and non-Western countries. Whereas women from Western countries spoke about political, economic, cultural, and sexual rights, women from developing countries in Latin America, Africa, and Asia focused on bringing an end to the violence, hunger, and disease that haunted their lives. Despite these differences, these meetings made it clear that women in both developed and developing nations were organizing to make all people aware of women's issues.

The Environment and the Green Movements

By the 1970s, serious ecological problems had become all too apparent. Air pollution, produced by nitrogen oxide and sulfur dioxide emissions from road vehicles, power plants, and industrial factories, was causing respiratory illnesses and having corrosive effects on buildings and monuments. Many rivers, lakes, and seas had become so polluted that they posed serious health risks. Dying forests and disappearing wildlife alarmed more and more people. A 1986 nuclear power disaster at Chernobyl in the Ukraine (at the time still part of the Soviet Union) released radiation that killed hundreds and made Europeans even more aware of potential environmental hazards. The opening of Eastern Europe after the revolutions of 1989 brought to the world's attention the incredible environmental destruction of that region caused by unfettered industrial pollution. By the beginning of the twenty-first century, an overwhelming number of scientists were warning that global warming could soon result in dire consequences for all peoples on the planet.

Environmental concerns forced the major political parties in Europe to advocate new regulations for the protection of the environment. Growing ecological awareness also gave rise to Green movements and political parties throughout Europe in the 1970s. Most started at the local level and then gradually expanded to include activities at the national level, where they became formally organized as political parties. Green Parties competed successfully in elections in Sweden, Austria, and Switzerland. Most visible was the Green Party in Germany, which was officially organized in 1979 and by 1987 had elected forty-two delegates to the West German parliament. In 1998, when the Green Party became a coalition partner with the Socialists under Gerhard Schroeder, one Green Party member, Joschka Fischer (b. 1948), became the nation's foreign minister.

Although the Green movements and parties have played an important role in making people aware of ecological problems, they have not replaced the traditional political parties, as some political analysts in the mid-1980s forecast. For one thing, the coalitions that made up the Greens found it difficult to agree on all issues and tended to splinter into cliques. Moreover, traditional political parties have co-opted the environmental issues of the Greens. By the 1990s, more and more European governments were beginning to sponsor projects to safeguard the environment and clean up the worst sources of pollution.

Western Culture Today

Intellectually and culturally, the Western world since 1973 has been notable for its diversity and innovation. New directions have led some observers to speak of a postmodern cultural world.

Postmodern Thought

The term *Postmodern* covers a variety of intellectual and artistic styles and ways of thinking prominent since the 1970s. In the broadest sense, **Postmodernism** rejects the modern Western belief in an objective truth and instead focuses on the relative nature of reality and knowledge.

While existentialism wrestled with notions of meaning and existence, a group of French philosophers in the 1960s attempted to understand how meaning and knowledge operate through the study of language and signs. **Poststructuralism,** or **deconstruction,** which was formulated by Jacques Derrida (1930–2004), believes that culture is created and can therefore be analyzed in a variety of ways, according to the manner in which people create their own meaning. Hence there is no fixed truth or universal meaning.

Michel Foucault (1926–1984) drew on Derrida to explore relationships of power. Believing that "power is exercised, rather than possessed," Foucault argued that the diffusion of power and oppression marks all relationships. For example, any act of teaching entails components of assertion and submission as the student adopts the ideas of the one in power. Therefore, all norms are culturally produced and entail some degree of power struggle.

Trends in Art and Literature

Beginning in the 1960s and continuing well into the 1980s, styles emerged that some have referred to as Postmodern. Postmodernism tends to move away from the futurism or cutting-edge qualities of Modernism. Instead it favors tradition, whether that means using earlier styles of painting or elevating traditional crafts to the level of fine art. Weavers, potters, glassmakers, metalsmiths, and furniture makers have gained respect as artists. Postmodern artists and architects frequently blur the distinction between the arts, creating works that include elements of film, performance, popular culture, sculpture, and architecture.

One Postmodern response to Modernism can be seen in a return to Realism in the arts, a movement called Photorealism. Some Photorealists paint or sculpt with such minute attention to detail that their paintings appear to be photographs and their sculptures living human beings. Their subjects are often ordinary individuals, stuck in ordinary lives, demonstrating the Postmodern emphasis on low culture and the commonplace rather than the ambitious nature of high art.

One of the best examples of a Postmodern artist who makes use of Expressionism (thus creating a style called Neo-Expressionism) is Anselm Kiefer. Born in Germany in 1945, Kiefer combines aspects of Abstract Expressionism, collage, and German Expressionism to create works that are stark and haunting. Another example of Neo-Expressionism can be seen in the work of Jean-Michel Basquiat (1960–1988). The son of Haitian and Puerto Rican immigrants, Basquiat first made his name as a graffiti artist in New York City and became an overnight success during the 1980s art market boom.

Postmodernism was also evident in literature. One center of Postmodernism was in central and eastern Europe, especially in the work of Milan Kundera (b. 1929) of Czechoslovakia. Kundera blended fantasy with realism, using fantasy to examine moral issues while remaining optimistic about the human condition. Indeed, in his first novel, *The Unbearable Lightness of Being*, published in 1984, Kundera does not despair because of the political repression that he so aptly describes in his native land but allows his characters to use love as a way to a better life. The human spirit can be diminished but not destroyed.

Varieties of Religious Life

Despite the revival of religion after World War II, church attendance in Europe and the United States declined dramatically in the 1960s and 1970s as a result of growing secular attitudes. Yet even though the numbers of regular churchgoers in established Protestant and Catholic churches continued to decline, the number of fundamentalist churches and churchgoers has been growing, especially in the United States.

Fundamentalism was originally a movement within Protestantism that arose early in the twentieth century. Its goal was to maintain a strict traditional interpretation of the Bible and the Christian faith, especially in opposition to the theory of Darwinian evolution and secularism. In the 1980s and 1990s, fundamentalists became involved in a struggle against so-called secular humanism, godless communism, legalized abortion, and homosexuality. Especially in the United States, fundamentalists organized politically to elect candidates who supported their views.

The Growth of Islam Fundamentalism, however, was not unique to Protestantism. In Islam, the term *fundamentalism* is used to refer to a return to traditional Islamic values, especially in opposition to a perceived weakening of moral values due to the corrupting influence of Western ideas and practices. After the Iranian Revolution of 1979, the term was also applied to militant Islamic movements, such as the Taliban in Afghanistan, who favored militant action against Western influence.

Despite wariness about Islamic radicalism in the aftermath of the

Jean-Michel Basquiat, *Self Portrait*, 1986. In his paintings, Basquiat combined Abstract Expressionist brushwork with the popular culture of urban life. He dabbled with hip-hop and included references to comic book characters, jazz musicians, and sports heroes in his work.

September 11, 2001, terrorist attacks on the United States, Islam is growing in both Europe and the United States, thanks primarily to the migration of people from Muslim countries. Muslim communities became established in France, Germany, Great Britain, Italy, and Spain, and during the 1980s and 1990s, they built mosques for religious worship and religious education.

Pope John Paul II Although changes have also occurred in the Catholic church, much of its history since 1973 has been dominated by the charismatic Pope John Paul II (1920–2005), who had been the archbishop of Krakow in Poland before his elevation to the papacy in 1978. Although he alienated a number of people by reasserting traditional Catholic teaching on such issues as birth control, women in the priesthood, and clerical celibacy, John Paul's numerous travels around the world helped strengthen the Catholic church throughout the non-Western world. John Paul was a powerful figure in reminding Europeans of their spiritual heritage and the need to temper the pursuit of materialism with spiritual concerns.

The World of Science and Technology

Many of the scientific and technological achievements since World War II have revolutionized people's lives. During the war, university scientists were recruited to work for their governments and develop new weapons and practical instruments of war. British physicists played a crucial role in the development of an improved radar system in 1940 that helped defeat the German air force in the Battle of Britain. German scientists designed self-propelled rockets and jet airplanes to keep hopes alive for a miraculous turnaround in the war. The computer, too, was a wartime creation. The British mathematician Alan Turing designed a primitive computer to assist British intelligence in breaking the secret codes of German ciphering machines. The most famous product of wartime scientific research was the atomic bomb, created by a team of American and European scientists under the guidance of the physicist J. Robert Oppenheimer. Obviously, most wartime devices were created for destructive purposes, but merely to mention computers and jet airplanes demonstrates that they could easily be adapted for peacetime uses.

The computer may yet prove to be the most revolutionary of all the technological inventions of the twentieth century. Early computers, which required thousands of vacuum tubes to function, were large and took up considerable space. The development of the transistor and then the silicon chip provided a revolutionary new approach to computers. In 1971, the invention of the microprocessor, a machine that combines the equivalent of thousands of transistors on a single, tiny silicon chip, opened the road for the development of the personal computer.

The computer is a new kind of machine whose chief function is to store and produce information, now considered a fundamental asset of our fast-paced civilization. By 2000, the personal computer had become a regular fixture in businesses, schools, and homes. The Internet—the world's largest computer network—provides billions of people around the world with quick access to immense quantities of information. Not only does the computer make a whole host of tasks much easier, but it has also become an important tool in virtually every area of modern life. Indeed, other tools and machines now depend for their functioning on computers. Many of the minute-by-minute decisions required to fly an airplane, for example, are done by a computer.

Despite the marvels that were produced by science and technology, the underlying assumption—that scientific knowledge gave human beings the ability to manipulate the environment for their benefit—was questioned by some in the 1960s and 1970s who believed that some technological advances had far-reaching side effects damaging to the environment. Chemical fertilizers, for example, that were touted for producing larger crops wreaked havoc with the ecological balance of streams, rivers, and woodlands. *Small Is Beautiful*, written by the British economist E. F. Schumacher (1911–1977), was a fundamental critique of the dangers of the new science and technology (see the box on p. 580). The threat of global warming and the dwindling of forests and lakes made environmentalism one of the important issues of the early twenty-first century.

Popular Culture: Image and Globalization

The introduction of the video music channel MTV in the early 1980s radically changed the music scene by making image as important as sound in the selling of records. Artists like Michael Jackson became stars in part by approaching the music video as an art form. Jackson's videos often were short films of elaborate staging and special effects set to music. Technological advances became prevalent in the music of the 1980s with the advent of the synthesizer, an electronic piano that produced computerized sounds. Some performers replaced ensembles of guitar, bass, and drums with synthesizers, creating a futuristic and manufactured sound.

Paralleling the rise of the music video was the emergence of rap or hip-hop. Developed in New York City in the late 1970s and early 1980s, rap combined rhymed lyrics with disco beats and turntable manipulations. Early rap groups like Public Enemy and Grandmaster Flash and the Furious Five instilled social commentaries into their songs, using the popularity of hip-hop to raise awareness about social conditions in American cities. By the 1990s, rappers like Dr. Dre and Snoop Doggy Dogg created "gangsta rap," an offshoot of rap with raw lyrics praising violence, drugs, and promiscuous sexuality.

In the 1990s, teen and preteen consumers steered the music industry back toward pop music, generating

SMALL IS BEAUTIFUL: THE LIMITS OF MODERN TECHNOLOGY

Although science and technology have produced an amazing array of achievements in the postwar world, some voices have been raised in criticism of their sometimes destructive aspects. In 1975, in his book *Small Is Beautiful,* the British economist E. F. Schumacher examined the effects modern industrial technology has had on the earth's resources.

E. F. Schumacher, *Small Is Beautiful*

Is it not evident that our current methods of production are already eating into the very substance of industrial man? To many people this is not at all evident. Now that we have solved the problem of production, they say, have we ever had it so good? Are we not better fed, better clothed, and better housed than ever before—and better educated? Of course we are: most, but by no means all, of us: in the rich countries. But this is not what I mean by "substance." The substance of man cannot be measured by Gross National Product. Perhaps it cannot be measured at all, except for certain symptoms of loss. However, this is not the place to go into the statistics of these symptoms, such as crime, drug addiction, vandalism, mental breakdown, rebellion, and so forth. Statistics never prove anything.

I started by saying that one of the most fateful errors of our age is the belief that the problem of production has been solved. This illusion, I suggested, is mainly due to our inability to recognize that the modern industrial system, with all its intellectual sophistication, consumes the very basis on which it has been erected. To use the language of the economist, it lives on irreplaceable capital which it cheerfully treats as income. I specified three categories of such capital: fossil fuels, the tolerance margins of nature, and the human substance. Even if some readers should refuse to accept all three parts of my argument, I suggest that any one of them suffices to make my case.

And what is my case? Simply that our most important task is to get off our present collision course. And who is there to tackle such a task? I think every one of us.... To talk about the future is useful only if it leads to action *now*. And what can we do *now*, while we are still in the position of "never having had it so good"? To say the least...we must thoroughly understand the problem and begin to see the possibility of evolving a new lifestyle, with new methods of production and new patterns of consumption: a life-style designed for permanence. To give only three preliminary examples: in agriculture and horticulture, we can interest ourselves in the perfection of production methods which are biologically sound, build up soil fertility, and produce health, beauty and permanence. Productivity will then look after itself. In industry, we can interest ourselves in the evolution of small-scale technology, relatively nonviolent technology, "technology with a human face," so that people have a chance to enjoy themselves while they are working, instead of working solely for their pay packet and hoping, usually forlornly, for enjoyment solely during their leisure time.

According to Schumacher, under what illusion are modern humans living? What three irreplaceable things does he suggest people are consuming without noticing? What is "technology with a human face"? How does the author suggest this might transform modern life?

---

millions of dollars of sales in the process. Many pop acts became successful as music turned away from gangsta rap. Instead, musicians and audiences favored the light-hearted music that made Ricky Martin and Britney Spears famous.

Film: Fantasy and Epics   The films, video games, and literature of the late 1990s made fantasy and historical epics internationally popular. The successful adaptation of the *Lord of the Rings* trilogy and the Harry Potter series indicated the manner in which mythology, magic, and medieval fantasies appeal to contemporary sensibilities. At the heart of these epic motion pictures was a mythical struggle between good and evil, governed by a moral sense of right and wrong, love and companionship. Yet these romanticized tales also portrayed non-Western cultures as Japanese anime and martial arts films increased in worldwide popularity. The computer animation and digitized special effects of these movies reflected the impact of computers on the film industry as it entered the digital age.

The Growth of Mass Sports   Sports have become a major product of both popular culture and the leisure industry. The development of satellite television and various electronic breakthroughs helped make sports a global phenomenon. Olympic Games could now be broadcast around the world from anywhere in the world. Sports became a cheap form of entertainment for the consumers, as fans did not have to leave their homes to enjoy athletic competitions.

As sports assumed a prominent position in the social life of the world, the pressures and rewards to not just compete but win intensified. Fueled by advertising endorsements, the scientific study of sport led to aerodynamic helmets for cyclists, skin-tight body suits for skiers and swimmers, and improved nutritional practices in all sports. Such technological advances, however, have increased the manner in which athletes might break the rules. From steroids to blood doping, some have used medical supplements to illegally enhance their conditioning. Mandatory drug testing in the Olympics, Tour de France, and World Cup attempts to level the playing field and avoid repercussions such as occurred when reports of steroid abuse prompted a governmental investigation of major league baseball.

Toward a Global Civilization?

Increasingly, people are becoming aware of the political and economic interdependence of the world's nations and the global nature of our contemporary problems. We are coming to understand that destructive forces unleashed in any part of the world soon affect all of it. Nuclear proliferation makes nuclear war an ever-present possibility; such a war would mean radioactive fallout for the entire planet. Smokestack pollution in one nation can produce acid rain in another. Oil spills and dumping of wastes in the ocean have an impact on the shores of many nations. The consumption of drugs in the world's wealthy nations affects the stability of both wealthy and less developed nations. As crises involving food, water, energy, and natural resources proliferate, solutions implemented by one nation often affect other nations. The new globalism includes the recognition that the challenges that seem to threaten human existence today are global. In reflecting on the terrorist crisis, Tony Blair, the British prime minister, said in October 2001, "We are realizing how fragile are our frontiers in the face of the world's new challenges. Today, conflicts rarely stay within national boundaries."

Courtesy of NASA

The Earth. For many people in the West, as in the rest of the world, the view of earth from outer space fostered an important image of global unity. The American astronaut Russell Schweickart wrote, "From where you see it, the thing is a whole, and it is so beautiful." In a similar reaction, Yuri Gagarin, a Soviet cosmonaut, remarked, "What strikes me, is not only the beauty of the continents . . . but their closeness to one another . . . their essential unity."

As the heirs of Western civilization have become aware that the problems humans face are global, not just national, they have responded to this challenge in different ways. One approach has been to develop grassroots social movements, including those devoted to the environment, women's and men's liberation, human potential, appropriate technologies, and nonviolence. "Think globally, act locally" is one slogan these groups use. Related to the emergence of these social movements is the growth of nongovernmental organizations (NGOs). According to one analyst, NGOs are an important instrument in the cultivation of global perspectives: "Since NGOs by definition are identified with interests that transcend national boundaries, we expect all NGOs to define problems in global terms, to take account of human interests and needs as they are found in all parts of the planet."[3] NGOs are often represented at the United Nations and include professional, business, and cooperative organizations; foundations; religious, peace, and disarmament groups; youth and women's organizations; environmental and human rights groups; and research institutes. The number of international NGOs increased from 176 in 1910 to 29,000 in 1995.

Yet hopes for global approaches to global problems have also been hindered by political, ethnic, and religious disputes. Pollution of the Rhine River by factories along its banks provokes angry disputes among European nations, and the United States and Canada have argued about the effects of acid rain on Canadian forests. The collapse of the Soviet Union and its satellite system between 1989 and 1991 seemed to provide an enormous boost to the potential for international cooperation on global issues, but it has had almost the opposite effect. The bloody conflict in the former Yugoslavia indicates the dangers in the rise of nationalist sentiment among various ethnic and religious groups in Eastern Europe. The widening gap between the wealthy nations in the Northern Hemisphere and the poor, developing nations in the Southern Hemisphere threatens global economic stability. Many conflicts begin with regional issues and then develop into international concerns. International terrorist groups seek to wreak havoc around the world.

Thus even as the world becomes more global in culture and interdependent in its mutual relations, centrifugal forces are still at work attempting to redefine the political, cultural, and ethnic ways in which the world is divided. Such efforts are often disruptive and can sometimes work against measures to enhance our human destiny.

Many lessons can be learned from the history of Western civilization, but one of them is especially clear. Lack of involvement in the affairs of one's society can lead to a sense of powerlessness. In an age that is often crisis-laden and chaotic, an understanding of our Western heritage and its lessons can be instrumental in helping us create new models for the future. For we are all creators of history, and the future of Western and indeed world civilization depends on us.

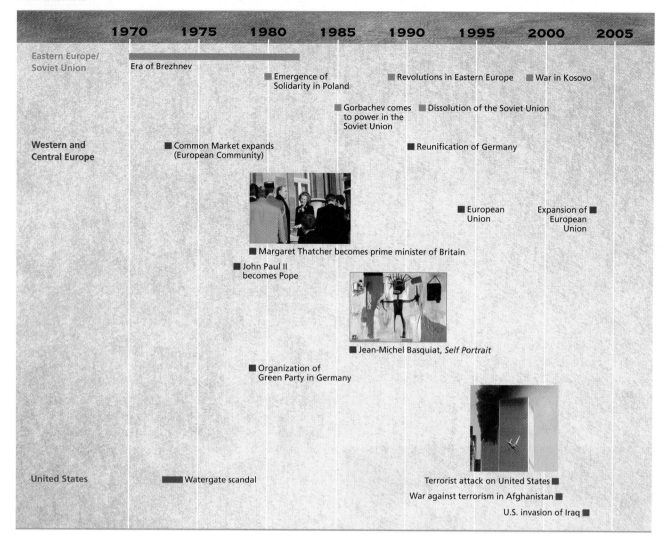

	1970	1975	1980	1985	1990	1995	2000	2005

Eastern Europe/Soviet Union

Era of Brezhnev

■ Emergence of Solidarity in Poland

■ Revolutions in Eastern Europe   ■ War in Kosovo

■ Gorbachev comes to power in the Soviet Union   ■ Dissolution of the Soviet Union

Western and Central Europe

■ Common Market expands (European Community)

■ Reunification of Germany

■ Margaret Thatcher becomes prime minister of Britain

■ John Paul II becomes Pope

■ European Union

Expansion of ■ European Union

■ Jean-Michel Basquiat, *Self Portrait*

■ Organization of Green Party in Germany

United States

Watergate scandal

Terrorist attack on United States ■

War against terrorism in Afghanistan ■

U.S. invasion of Iraq ■

NOTES

1. Quoted in W. I. Hitchcock, *The Struggle for Europe: The Turbulent History of a Divided Continent, 1945–2002* (New York, 2003), pp. 399–400.
2. Quoted in R. Bridenthal, "Women in the New Europe," in R. Bridenthal, S. M. Stuard, and M. E. Wiesner, eds., *Becoming Visible: Women in European History*, 3d ed. (Boston, 1998), pp. 564–565.
3. E. Boulding, *Women in the Twentieth Century World* (New York, 1977), p. 186.

SUGGESTIONS FOR FURTHER READING

For well-written surveys on Europe since 1973, see **W. I. Hitchcock**, *The Struggle for Europe: The Turbulent History of a Divided Continent, 1945–2002* (New York, 2003), and **T. Judt**, *Postwar: A History of Europe Since 1945* (New York, 2005).

Problems in the Soviet Union are analyzed in **A. Brown**, *The Gorbachev Factor* (New York, 1996); **G. Hosking**, *The Awakening of the Soviet Union* (London, 1990); and **M. McCauley**, *Gorbachev* (London, 2000). For a general study of the Soviet satellites in Eastern

Europe, see **G. Stokes**, *The Walls Came Tumbling Down: The Collapse of Communism in Eastern Europe* (Oxford, 1993). Additional studies on the recent history of these countries include **T. G. Ash**, *The Polish Revolution: Solidarity* (New York, 1984); **T. G. Ash**, *The Magic Lantern: The Revolution of '89 Witnessed in Warsaw, Budapest, Berlin, and Prague* (New York, 1990); **C. S. Maier**, *Dissolution: The Crisis of Communism and the End of East Germany* (Princeton, N.J., 1997); and **S. Ramet**, *Nationalism and Federalism in Yugoslavia* (Bloomington, Ind., 1992).

For general works on Western Europe and individual countries, see the works cited in Chapter 28. On the recent history of these countries, see **E. J. Evans**, *Thatcher and Thatcherism* (New York, 1997); **P. A. Hall**, *Governing the Economy: The Politics of State Intervention in Britain and France* (New York, 1986); **S. Baumann-Reynolds**, *François Mitterrand* (Westport, Conn., 1995); and **K. Jarausch**, *The Rush to German Unity* (New York, 1994).

For a general study of the Cold War, see **J. L. Gaddis**, *The Cold War: A New History* (New York, 2005). A detailed analysis of American-Soviet relations in the 1970s and 1980s is available in **R. Garthoff**, *Détente and Confrontation: American-Soviet Relations from Nixon to Reagan* (Washington, D.C., 1985). On terrorism, see **W. Laqueur**,

Terrorism, 2d ed. (New York, 1988), and **R. Rubenstein**, *Alchemists of Revolution: Terrorism in the Modern World* (London, 1987).

The changing role of women is examined in **C. Duchen**, *Feminism in France* (London, 1986). The problems of guest workers and immigrants are examined in **J. Miller**, *Foreign Workers in Western Europe* (London, 1981), and **S. Castles**, *Here for Good: Western Europe's New Ethnic Minorities* (London, 1984). On the development of the Green Parties, see **M. O'Neill**, *Green Parties and Political Change in Contemporary Europe* (Aldershot, England, 1997), and **D. Richardson and C. Rootes, eds.**, *The Green Challenge: The Development of the Green Parties in Europe* (London, 1995).

On Western thought, art, and literature since 1973, see **A. Marwick**, *The Arts in the West Since 1945* (New York, 2002). A physicist's view of science is contained in **J. Ziman**, *The Force of Knowledge: The Scientific Dimension of Society* (Cambridge, 1976). Sport is examined in **A. Guttmann**, *From Ritual to Record: The Nature of Modern Sports* (New York, 1978), and **R. Mandell**, *Sport: A Cultural History* (New York, 1984).

Thomson NOW! Enter *ThomsonNOW* using the access card that is available for *Western Civilization: A Brief History*. *ThomsonNOW* will help you understand this chapter with lesson plans generated for your needs. In addition, you can read the following documents, and many more, online:

Maatstricht Accords, excerpts
Brezhnev Doctrine

WESTERN CIVILIZATION RESOURCES

Visit the Web site for *Western Civilization: A Brief History* for resources specific to this book:

http://www.thomsonedu.com/history/spielvogel

For a variety of tools to help you succeed in this course, visit the Western Civilization Resource Center at

http://history.wadsworth.com/spielvogel

Included are quizzes, images, documents, interactive simulations, maps and timelines, movie explorations, and a wealth of other sources.

GLOSSARY

abbess head of a convent or monastery for women.

abbot head of a monastery.

absolutism a form of government in which the sovereign power or ultimate authority rested in the hands of a monarch who claimed to rule by divine right and was therefore responsible only to God.

Abstract Expressionism a post–World War II artistic movement that broke with all conventions of form and structure in favor of total abstraction.

abstract painting an artistic movement that developed early in the twentieth century in which artists focused on color to avoid any references to visual reality.

aediles Roman officials who supervised the public games and the grain supply of the city of Rome.

Agricultural (Neolithic) Revolution the shift from hunting animals and gathering plants for sustenance to producing food by systematic agriculture that occurred gradually between 10,000 and 4000 B.C. (the Neolithic or "New Stone" Age).

agricultural revolution the application of new agricultural techniques that allowed for a large increase in productivity in the eighteenth century.

anti-Semitism hostility toward or discrimination against Jews.

apartheid the system of racial segregation practiced in the Republic of South Africa until the 1990s, which involved political, legal, and economic discrimination against nonwhites.

appeasement the policy, followed by the European nations in the 1930s, of accepting Hitler's annexation of Austria and Czechoslovakia in the belief that meeting his demands would assure peace and stability.

Arianism a Christian heresy that taught that Jesus was inferior to God. Though condemned by the Council of Nicaea in 325, Arianism was adopted by many of the Germanic peoples who entered the Roman Empire over the next centuries.

aristocracy a class of hereditary nobility in medieval Europe; a warrior class who shared a distinctive lifestyle based on the institution of knighthood, although there were social divisions within the group based on extremes of wealth.

Ausgleich the "Compromise" of 1867 that created the dual monarchy of Austria-Hungary. Austria and Hungary each had its own capital, constitution, and legislative assembly but were united under one monarch.

authoritarian state a state that has a dictatorial government and some other trappings of a totalitarian state but does not demand that the masses be actively involved in the regime's goals as totalitarian states do.

balance of power a distribution of power among several states such that no single nation can dominate or interfere with the interests of another.

Baroque an artistic movement of the seventeenth century in Europe that used dramatic effects to arouse the emotions and reflected the search for power that was a large part of the seventeenth-century ethos.

bicameral legislature a legislature with two houses.

Black Death the outbreak of plague (mostly bubonic) in the mid-fourteenth century that killed from 25 to 50 percent of Europe's population.

Blitzkrieg "lightning war." A war conducted with great speed and force, as in Germany's advance at the beginning of World War II.

Bolsheviks a small faction of the Russian Social Democratic Party who were led by Lenin and dedicated to violent revolution; they seized power in Russia in 1917 and were subsequently renamed the Communists.

bourgeoisie (burghers) inhabitants (merchants and artisans) of boroughs and burghs (towns).

boyars the Russian nobility.

Brezhnev Doctrine the doctrine, enunciated by Leonid Brezhnev, that the Soviet Union had a right to intervene if socialism was threatened in another socialist state; used to justify moving Soviet troops into Czechoslovakia in 1968.

Bronze Age the period from around 3000 to 1200 B.C. It was characterized by the widespread use of bronze for making tools and weapons.

caliph the secular leader of the Islamic community.

capital material wealth used or available for use in the production of more wealth.

cartel a combination of independent commercial enterprises that work together to control prices and limit competition.

Cartesian dualism Descartes's principle of the separation of mind and matter (and mind and body) that enabled scientists to view matter as something separate from themselves that could be investigated by reason.

centuriate assembly the chief popular assembly of the Roman Republic. It passed laws and elected the chief magistrates.

chansons de geste a form of vernacular literature in the High Middle Ages that consisted of heroic epics focusing on the deeds of warriors.

chivalry the ideal of civilized behavior that emerged among the nobility in the eleventh and twelfth centuries under the influence of the church; a code of ethics knights were expected to uphold.

Christian (northern) humanism an intellectual movement in northern Europe in the late fifteenth and early sixteenth centuries that combined the interest in the classics of the Italian Renaissance with an interest in the sources of early Christianity, including the New Testament and the writings of the church fathers.

civic humanism an intellectual movement of the Italian Renaissance that saw Cicero, who was both an intellectual and a statesman, as the ideal and held that humanists should be involved in government and use their rhetorical training in the service of the state.

civilization a complex culture in which large numbers of humans share a variety of common elements, including cities; religious, political, military, and social structures; writing; and significant artistic and intellectual activity.

civil rights the basic rights of citizens, including equality before the law, freedom of speech and press, and freedom from arbitrary arrest.

Cold War the ideological conflict between the Soviet Union and the United States after World War II.

collective farms large farms created in the Soviet Union by Stalin by combining many small holdings into large farms worked by the peasants under government supervision.

Columbian Exchange the reciprocal importation and exportation of plants and animals between Europe and the Americas.

commercial capitalism beginning in the Middle Ages, an economic system in which people invested in trade and goods in order to make profits.

common law law common to the entire kingdom of England; imposed by the king's courts beginning in the twelfth century to replace the customary law used in county and feudal courts that varied from place to place.

conciliarism a movement in fourteenth- and fifteenth-century Europe that held that final authority in spiritual matters resided with a general church council, not the pope; it emerged in response to the Avignon papacy and the Great Schism and was used to justify the summoning of the Council of Constance (1414–1418).

condottieri leaders of bands of mercenary soldiers in Renaissance Italy who sold their services to the highest bidder.

conquistadors "conquerors." Leaders in the Spanish conquests in the Americas, especially Mexico and Peru, in the sixteenth century.

conscription a military draft.

conservatism an ideology based on tradition and social stability that favored the maintenance of established institutions, organized religion, and obedience to authority and resisted change, especially abrupt change.

consuls the chief executive officers of the Roman Republic. Two were chosen annually to administer the government and lead the army in battle.

containment a policy adopted by the United States in the Cold War. Its goal was to use whatever means, short of all-out war, to limit Soviet expansion.

cosmopolitanism the quality of being sophisticated and having wide international experience.

cottage industry a system of textile manufacturing in which spinners and weavers worked at home in their cottages using raw materials supplied to them by capitalist entrepreneurs.

council of the plebs a council only for plebeians. After 287 B.C., however, its resolutions were binding on all Romans.

Crusade in the Middle Ages, a military campaign in defense of Christendom.

Cubism an artistic style developed at the beginning of the twentieth century, especially by Pablo Picasso, that used geometric designs to re-create reality in the viewer's mind.

cuneiform "wedge-shaped." A system of writing developed by the Sumerians that consisted of wedge-shaped impressions made by a reed stylus on clay tablets.

Dadaism an artistic movement in the 1920s and 1930s by artists who were revolted by the senseless slaughter of World War I and used their "anti-art" to express contempt for the Western tradition.

decolonization the process of becoming free of colonial status and achieving statehood; it occurred in most of the world's colonies between 1947 and 1962.

deconstruction (poststructuralism) a system of thought, formulated by Jacques Derrida, that holds that culture is created in a variety of ways, according to the manner in which people create their own meaning. Hence there is no fixed truth or universal meaning.

deism belief in God as the creator of the universe who, after setting it in motion, ceased to have any direct involvement in it and allowed it to run according to its own natural laws.

demesne the part of a manor retained under the direct control of the lord and worked by the serfs as part of their labor services.

destalinization the policy of denouncing and undoing the most repressive aspects of Stalin's regime; begun by Nikita Khrushchev in 1956.

détente the relaxation of tension between the Soviet Union and the United States that occurred in the 1970s.

divination the practice of seeking to foretell future events by interpreting divine signs, which could appear in various forms, such as in entrails of animals, in patterns in smoke, or in dreams.

domino theory the belief that if the Communists succeeded in Vietnam, other countries in Southeast and East Asia would also fall (like dominoes) to communism; cited as a justification for the U.S. intervention in Vietnam.

economic imperialism the process in which banks and corporations from developed nations invest in underdeveloped regions and establish a major presence there in the hope of making high profits; not necessarily the same as colonial expansion in that businesses invest where they can make a profit, which may not be in their own nation's colonies.

economic liberalism the idea that government should not interfere in the workings of the economy.

Einsatzgruppen in Nazi Germany, special strike forces in the SS that played an important role in rounding up and killing Jews.

encomienda in Spanish America, a form of economic and social organization in which a Spaniard was given a royal grant that enabled the holder of the grant to collect tribute from the Indians and use them as laborers.

enlightened absolutism an absolute monarchy in which the ruler follows the principles of the Enlightenment by introducing reforms for the improvement of society, allowing freedom of speech and the press, permitting religious toleration, expanding education, and ruling in accordance with the laws.

Enlightenment an eighteenth-century intellectual movement, led by the philosophes, that stressed the application of reason and the scientific method to all aspects of life.

entrepreneur one who organizes, operates, and assumes the risk in a business venture in the expectation of making a profit.

Epicureanism a philosophy founded by Epicurus in the fourth century B.C. that taught that happiness (freedom from emotional turmoil) could be achieved through the pursuit of pleasure (intellectual rather than sensual pleasure).

equestrians a group of extremely wealthy men in the late Roman Republic who were effectively barred from high office but sought political power commensurate with their wealth; called equestrians because many had gotten their start as cavalry officers (*equites*).

estates *see* orders.

ethnic cleansing the policy of killing or forcibly removing people of another ethnic group; used by the Serbs against Bosnian Muslims in the 1990s.

Eucharist a Christian sacrament in which consecrated bread and wine are consumed in celebration of Jesus' Last Supper; also called the Lord's Supper or communion.

evolutionary socialism a socialist doctrine espoused by Eduard Bernstein who argued that socialists should stress cooperation and evolution to attain power by democratic means rather than by conflict and revolution.

existentialism a philosophical movement that arose after World War II that emphasized the meaninglessness of life, born of the desperation caused by two world wars.

fascism an ideology or movement that exalts the nation above the individual and calls for a centralized government with a dictatorial leader, economic and social regimentation, and forcible suppression of opposition; in particular, the ideology of Mussolini's Fascist regime in Italy.

feminism the belief in the social, political, and economic equality of the sexes; also, organized activity to advance women's rights.

fief a landed estate granted to a vassal in exchange for military services.

Five Pillars of Islam the core requirements of the faith, observation of which would lead to paradise: belief in Allah and his Prophet Muhammad; prescribed prayers; observation of Ramadan; pilgrimage to Mecca; and giving alms (charitable contributions) to the poor.

Final Solution the attempted physical extermination of the Jewish people by the Nazis during World War II.

free trade the unrestricted international exchange of goods with low or no tariffs.

functionalism the idea that the function of an object should determine its design and materials.

genocide the deliberate extermination of a people.

gentry well-to-do English landowners below the level of the nobility. They played an important role in the English Civil War of the seventeenth century.

geocentric conception the belief that the earth was at the center of the universe and that the sun and other celestial objects revolved around the earth.

glasnost "openness." Mikhail Gorbachev's policy of encouraging Soviet citizens to openly discuss the strengths and weaknesses of the Soviet Union.

good emperors the five emperors who ruled from 96 to 180 (Nerva, Trajan, Hadrian, Antoninus Pius, and Marcus Aurelius), a period of peace and prosperity for the Roman Empire.

Gothic a term used to describe the art and especially architecture of Europe in the twelfth, thirteenth, and fourteenth centuries.

Gothic literature a form of literature used by Romantics to emphasize the bizarre and unusual, especially evident in horror stories.

Great Schism the crisis in the late medieval church when there were first two and then three popes; ended by the Council of Constance (1414–1418).

guest workers foreign workers working temporarily in European countries.

guild an association of people with common interests and concerns, especially people working in the same craft. In medieval Europe, guilds came to control much of the production process and to restrict entry into various trades.

Hadith a collection of the sayings of the Prophet Muhammad, used to supplement the revelations contained in the Qur'an.

heliocentric conception the belief that the sun, not the earth, is at the center of the universe.

Hellenistic literally, "imitating the Greeks"; the era after the death of Alexander the Great when Greek culture spread into the Near East and blended with the culture of that region.

helots serfs in ancient Sparta who were permanently bound to the land that they worked for their Spartan masters.

heresy the holding of religious doctrines different from the official teachings of the church.

Hermeticism an intellectual movement beginning in the fifteenth century that taught that divinity is embodied in all aspects of nature; it included works on alchemy and magic as well as theology and philosophy. The tradition continued into the seventeenth century and influenced many of the leading figures of the Scientific Revolution.

hieroglyphics a pictorial system of writing used in ancient Egypt.

high culture the literary and artistic culture of the educated and wealthy ruling classes.

Holocaust the mass slaughter of European Jews by the Nazis during World War II.

hoplites heavily armed infantry soldiers in ancient Greece who entered battle in a phalanx formation.

Huguenots French Calvinists.

humanism an intellectual movement in Renaissance Italy based on the study of the Greek and Roman classics.

ideology a political philosophy such as conservatism or liberalism.

imperium In the Roman Republic, the right to command troops that belonged to the chief executive officers (consuls and praetors); a military commander was known as an *imperator*. In the Roman Empire, the title *imperator* (emperor) came to be used for the ruler.

Impressionism an artistic movement that originated in France in the 1870s. Impressionists sought to capture their impressions of the changing effects of light on objects in nature.

individualism emphasis on and interest in the unique traits of each person.

indulgence in Christian theology, the remission of part or all of the temporal punishment in purgatory due to sin; granted for charitable contributions and other good deeds. Indulgences became a regular practice of the Christian church in the High Middle Ages, and their abuse was instrumental in sparking Luther's reform movement in the sixteenth century.

inflation a sustained rise in the price level.

intendants royal officials in seventeenth-century France who were sent into the provinces to execute the orders of the central government.

interdict in the Catholic church, a censure by which a region or country is deprived of receiving the sacraments.

intervention, principle of the idea, after the Congress of Vienna, that the great powers of Europe had the right to send armies into countries experiencing revolution to restore legitimate monarchs to their thrones.

jihad "striving in the way of the Lord." In Islam, the attempt to achieve personal betterment, although it can also mean fair, defensive fighting to preserve one's life and one's faith.

joint-stock company a company or association that raises capital by selling shares to individuals who receive dividends on their investment while a board of directors runs the company.

justification the primary doctrine of the Protestant Reformation, teaching that humans are saved not through good works but by the grace of God, bestowed freely through the sacrifice of Jesus.

Kulturkampf "culture conflict." The name given to Bismarck's attack on the Catholic church in Germany, which has come to refer to conflict between church and state anywhere.

laissez-faire "let (them) do (as they please)." An economic doctrine that holds that an economy is best served when the government does not interfere but allows the economy to self-regulate according to the forces of supply and demand.

latifundia large landed estates in the Roman Empire (singular: *latifundium*).

lay investiture the practice in which someone other than a member of the clergy chose a bishop and invested him with the symbols of both his temporal office and his spiritual office; led to the Investiture Controversy, which was ended by compromise in the Concordat of Worms in 1122.

Lebensraum "living space." The doctrine, adopted by Hitler, that a nation's power depends on the amount of land it occupies; thus a nation must expand to be strong.

legitimacy, principle of the idea that after the Napoleonic wars, peace could best be reestablished in Europe by restoring legitimate monarchs who would preserve traditional institutions; guided Metternich at the Congress of Vienna.

liberal arts the seven areas of study that formed the basis of education in medieval and early modern Europe. Following Boethius and other late Roman authors, they consisted of grammar, rhetoric, and dialectic or logic (the *trivium*) and arithmetic, geometry, astronomy, and music (the *quadrivium*).

liberalism an ideology based on the belief that people should be as free from restraint as possible. Economic liberalism is the idea that the government should not interfere in the workings of the economy. Political liberalism is the idea that there should be restraints on the exercise of power so that people can enjoy basic civil rights in a constitutional state with a representative assembly.

mandates a system established after World War I whereby a nation officially administered a territory (mandate) on behalf of the League of Nations. Thus France administered Lebanon and Syria as mandates, and Britain administered Iraq and Palestine.

Mannerism a sixteenth-century artistic movement in Europe that deliberately broke down the High Renaissance principles of balance, harmony, and moderation.

manor an agricultural estate operated by a lord and worked by peasants who performed labor services and paid various rents and fees to the lord in exchange for protection and sustenance.

Marshall Plan the European Recovery Program, under which the United States provided financial aid to European countries to help them rebuild after World War II.

Marxism the political, economic, and social theories of Karl Marx, which included the idea that history is the story of class struggle and that ultimately the proletariat will overthrow the bourgeoisie and establish a dictatorship en route to a classless society.

mass education a state-run educational system, usually free and compulsory, that aims to ensure that all children in society have at least a basic education.

mass leisure forms of leisure that appeal to large numbers of people in a society, including the working classes; emerged at the end of the nineteenth century to provide workers with amusements after work and on weekends; used during the twentieth century by totalitarian states to control their populations.

mass politics a political order characterized by mass political parties and universal male and (eventually) female suffrage.

mass society a society in which the concerns of the majority—the lower classes—play a prominent role; characterized by extension of voting rights, an improved standard of living for the lower classes, and mass education.

materialism the belief that everything mental, spiritual, or ideal is an outgrowth of physical forces and that truth is found in concrete material existence, not through feeling or intuition.

mercantilism an economic theory that held that a nation's prosperity depended on its supply of gold and silver and that the total volume of trade is unchangeable; its adherents therefore advocated that the government play an active role in the economy by encouraging exports and discouraging imports, especially through the use of tariffs.

Middle Passage the journey of slaves from Africa to the Americas as the middle leg of the triangular trade.

militarism a policy of aggressive military preparedness; in particular, the large armies based on mass conscription and complex, inflexible plans for mobilization that most European nations had before World War I.

millenarianism the belief that the end of the world is at hand and the kingdom of God is about to be established on earth.

ministerial responsibility a tenet of nineteenth-century liberalism that held that ministers of the monarch should be responsible to the legislative assembly rather than to the monarch.

mir a peasant village commune in Russia.

mobilization the organization of troops and supplies for service in time of war.

Modernism the artistic and literary styles that emerged in the decades before 1914 as artists rebelled against traditional efforts to portray reality as accurately as possible (leading to Impressionism and Cubism) and writers explored new forms.

monasticism a movement that began in early Christianity whose purpose was to create communities of men and women who practiced a communal life dedicated to God as a moral example to the world around them.

monk a man who chooses to live a communal life divorced from the world in order to dedicate himself totally to the will of God.

monogamy the practice of being married to one person at a time.

monotheism the doctrine or belief that there is only one God.

mutual deterrence the belief that nuclear war could best be prevented if both the United States and the Soviet Union had sufficient nuclear weapons so that even if one nation launched a preemptive first strike, the other could respond and devastate the attacker.

mystery religions religions that involve initiation into secret rites that promise intense emotional involvement with spiritual forces and a greater chance of individual immortality.

nationalism a sense of national consciousness based on awareness of being part of a community—a "nation"—that has common institutions, traditions, language, and customs and that becomes the focus of the individual's primary political loyalty.

nationalization the process of converting a business or industry from private ownership to government control and ownership.

nation in arms the people's army raised by universal mobilization to repel the foreign enemies of the French Revolution.

NATO the North Atlantic Treaty Organization, a military alliance formed in 1949 in which the signatories (Belgium, Canada, Denmark, France, Great Britain, Iceland, Italy, Luxembourg, the Netherlands, Norway, Portugal, and the United States) agreed to provide mutual assistance if any one of them was attacked; later expanded to include other nations.

natural laws a body of laws or specific principles held to be derived from nature and binding on all human societies even in the absence of written laws governing such matters.

natural rights certain inalienable rights to which all people are entitled, including the right to life, liberty, and property; freedom of speech and religion; and equality before the law.

natural selection Darwin's idea that organisms that are most adaptable to their environment survive and pass on the variations that enabled them to survive, while less adaptable organisms become extinct; "survival of the fittest."

Nazi New Order the Nazis' plan for their conquered territories; it included the extermination of Jews and others considered inferior, ruthless exploitation of resources, German colonization in the east, and the use of Poles, Russians, and Ukrainians as slave labor.

Neoplatonism a revival of Platonic philosophy in the third century A.D., associated with Plotinus; a similar revival in the Italian Renaissance, associated with Marsilio Ficino, who attempted to synthesize Christianity and Platonism.

nepotism the appointment of family members to important political positions; derived from the regular appointment of nephews (Greek, *nepos*) by Renaissance popes.

New Economic Policy a modified version of the old capitalist system introduced in the Soviet Union by Lenin in 1921 to revive the economy after the ravages of the civil war and war communism.

new imperialism the revival of imperialism after 1880 in which European nations established colonies throughout much of Asia and Africa.

nobiles "nobles." The small group of families from both patrician and plebeian origins who produced most of the men who were elected to office in the late Roman Republic.

nuclear family a family group consisting only of a father, a mother, and one or more children.

nuns female religious monks.

old regime (old order) the political and social system of France in the eighteenth century before the Revolution.

oligarchy rule by a few.

optimates "best men." Aristocratic leaders in the late Roman Republic who generally came from senatorial families and wished to retain their oligarchical privileges.

orders (estates) the traditional tripartite division of European society based on heredity and quality rather than wealth or economic standing, first established in the Middle Ages and continuing into the eighteenth century; traditionally consisted of those who pray (the clergy), those who fight (the nobility), and those who work (all the rest).

organic evolution Darwin's principle that all plants and animals have evolved over a long period of time from earlier and simpler forms of life.

Paleolithic Age the period of human history when humans used simple stone tools (c. 2,500,000–10,000 B.C.).

pantheism a doctrine that equates God with the universe and all that is in it.

papal curia the administrative staff of the Catholic church, composed of cardinals who assist the pope in running the church.

paterfamilias the dominant male in a Roman family whose powers over his wife and children were theoretically unlimited, though they were sometimes circumvented in practice.

patricians great landowners who became the ruling class in the Roman Republic.

patronage the practice of awarding titles and making appointments to government and other positions to gain political support.

Pax Romana "Roman peace." A term used to refer to the stability and prosperity that Roman rule brought to the Mediterranean world and much of western Europe during the first and second centuries A.D.

perestroika "restructuring." A term applied to Mikhail Gorbachev's economic, political, and social reforms in the Soviet Union.

perioikoi in ancient Sparta, free inhabitants but not citizens who were required to pay taxes and perform military service.

permissive society a term applied to Western society after World War II to reflect the new sexual freedom and the emergence of a drug culture.

philosophes intellectuals of the eighteenth-century Enlightenment who believed in applying a spirit of rational criticism to all things, including religion and politics, and who focused on improving and enjoying this world, rather than on the afterlife.

plebeians the class of Roman citizens that included nonpatrician landowners, craftspeople, merchants, and small farmers in the Roman Republic. Their struggle for equal rights with the patricians dominated much of the Republic's history.

plebiscita laws passed by the council of the plebs.

pluralism the practice of holding several church offices simultaneously; a problem of the late medieval church.

pogroms organized massacres of Jews.

polis an ancient Greek city-state encompassing both an urban area and its surrounding countryside; a small but autonomous political unit where all major political and social activities were carried out centrally.

political democracy a form of government characterized by universal suffrage and mass political parties.

politiques a group who emerged during the French Wars of Religion in the sixteenth century, placed politics above religion, and believed that no religious truth was worth the ravages of civil war.

polytheism belief in or worship of more than one god.

popular culture as opposed to high culture, the unofficial written and unwritten culture of the masses, much of which was traditionally passed down orally and centered on public and group activities such as festivals. In the modern age, the term refers to the entertainment, recreation, and pleasures that people purchase as part of the mass consumer society.

populares "favoring the people." Aristocratic leaders in the late Roman Republic who tended to use the people's assemblies in an effort to break the stranglehold of the *nobiles* on political offices.

Post-Impressionism an artistic movement that began in France in the 1880s. Post-Impressionists sought to use color and line to express inner feelings and produce a personal statement of reality.

Postmodernism a term used to cover a variety of artistic and intellectual styles and ways of thinking prominent since the 1970s.

Poststructuralism *see* deconstruction

praetor a Roman executive official responsible for the administration of the law.

praetorian guard the military unit that served as the personal bodyguard of the Roman emperors.

predestination the belief, associated with Calvinism, that God, as a consequence of his foreknowledge of all events, has predetermined those who will be saved (the elect) and those who will be damned.

price revolution the dramatic rise in prices (inflation) that occurred throughout Europe in the sixteenth and early seventeenth centuries.

principate the form of government established by Augustus for the Roman Empire; it continued the constitutional forms of the Republic and consisted of the *princeps* ("first citizen") and the senate, although the *princeps* was clearly the dominant partner.

procurator the head of the Holy Synod, the chief decision-making body for the Russian Orthodox church.

proletariat the industrial working class. In Marxism, the class that will ultimately overthrow the bourgeoisie.

propaganda a program of distorted information put out by an organization or government to spread its policy, cause, or doctrine.

psychoanalysis a method developed by Sigmund Freud to resolve a patient's psychic conflict.

Puritans English Protestants inspired by Calvinist theology who wished to remove all traces of Catholicism from the Church of England.

quadrivium arithmetic, geometry, astronomy, and music; four of the seven liberal arts (the others made up the *trivium*) that formed the basis of medieval and early modern education.

quaestors Roman officials responsible for the administration of financial affairs.

Ramadan the holy month of Islam, during which believers fast from dawn to sunset; since the Islamic calendar is lunar, Ramadan migrates through the seasons

rapprochement the rebuilding of harmonious relations between nations.

rationalism a system of thought based on the belief that human reason and experience are the chief sources of knowledge.

Realism a nineteenth-century school of painting that emphasized the everyday life of ordinary people, depicted with photographic accuracy.

Realpolitik "politics of reality." Politics based on practical concerns rather than theory or ethics.

real wages, income, and prices wages, income, and prices that have been adjusted for inflation.

Reconquista in Spain, the reconquest of Muslim lands by Christian rulers and their armies.

relativity theory Einstein's theory that, among other things, (1) space and time are not absolute but are relative to the observer and interwoven into a four-dimensional space-time continuum and (2) matter is a form of energy ($E = mc^2$).

relics the bones of Christian saints or objects intimately associated with saints that were considered worthy of veneration.

Renaissance the "rebirth" of classical culture that occurred in Italy between c. 1350 and c. 1550; also, the earlier revivals of classical culture that occurred under Charlemagne and in the twelfth century.

rentier a person who lives on income from property and is not personally involved in its operation.

reparations payments made by a defeated nation after a war to compensate another nation for damage sustained as a result of the war; required from Germany after World War I.

revisionism a socialist doctrine that rejected Marx's emphasis on class struggle and revolution and argued instead that workers should work through political parties to bring about gradual change (*see also* evolutionary socialism).

revolutionary socialism a socialist doctrine that violent action was the only way to achieve the goals of socialism.

rhetoric the art of persuasive speaking; in the Middle Ages, one of the seven liberal arts.

risorgimento a movement in Italy in the nineteenth century aimed at the creation of a united Italian republic.

Rococo an eighteenth-century artistic movement that emphasized grace, gentility, lightness, and charm.

Romanesque a term used to describe the art and especially architecture of Europe in the eleventh and twelfth centuries.

Romanticism a nineteenth-century intellectual and artistic movement that rejected the emphasis on reason of the Enlightenment. Instead, Romantics stressed the importance of intuition, feeling, emotion, and imagination as sources of knowing.

sacraments rites considered imperative for a Christian's salvation. By the thirteenth century, these consisted of the Eucharist or Lord's Supper, baptism, marriage, penance, extreme unction, holy orders, and confirmation of children; Protestant reformers of the sixteenth century generally recognized only two—baptism and communion (the Lord's Supper).

salons gatherings of philosophes and other notables to discuss the ideas of the Enlightenment; so called from the elegant drawing rooms (salons) where they met.

sans-culottes "without breeches." The common people, who did not wear the fine clothes of the upper classes and played an important role in the radical phase of the French Revolution.

satrap a governor with both civil and military duties in the ancient Persian Empire, which was divided into satrapies, or provinces, each administered by a satrap.

scholasticism the philosophical and theological system of the medieval schools, which emphasized rigorous analysis of contradictory authorities; often used to try to reconcile faith and reason.

scientific method a method of seeking knowledge through inductive principles, using experiments and observations to develop generalizations.

Scientific Revolution the transition from the medieval worldview to a largely secular, rational, and materialistic perspective that began in the seventeenth century and was popularized in the eighteenth.

scriptoria writing rooms for the copying of manuscripts in medieval monasteries.

scutage in the fourteenth century, a money payment for military service that replaced the obligation of military service in the lord-vassal relationship.

secularization the process of becoming more concerned with material, worldly, temporal things and less with spiritual and religious things.

self-determination the doctrine that the people of a given territory or a particular nationality should have the right to determine their own government and political future.

senate the leading council of the Roman Republic; composed of about three hundred men (senators) who served for life and dominated much of the political life of the Republic.

separation of powers a doctrine enunciated by Montesquieu in the eighteenth century that separate executive, legislative, and judicial powers serve to limit and control each other.

Shari'a a law code, originally drawn up by Muslim scholars shortly after the death of Muhammad, that provides believers with a set of prescriptions to regulate their daily lives.

skepticism a doubtful or questioning attitude, especially about religion.

social Darwinism the application of Darwin's principle of organic evolution to the social order; led to the belief that progress comes from the struggle for survival as the fittest advance and the weak decline.

socialism an ideology that calls for collective or government ownership of the means of production and the distribution of goods.

socialized medicine health services for all citizens provided by government assistance.

social security government programs that provide social welfare measures such as old-age pensions and sickness, accident, and disability insurance.

Socratic method a form of teaching that uses a question-and-answer format to enable students to reach conclusions by using their own reasoning.

Sophists wandering scholars and professional teachers in ancient Greece who stressed the importance of rhetoric and tended toward skepticism and relativism.

soviets councils of workers' and soldiers' deputies formed throughout Russia in 1917 that played an important role in the Bolshevik Revolution.

squadristi in Italy in the 1920s, bands of armed Fascists used to create disorder by attacking Socialist offices and newspapers.

stagflation a combination of high inflation and high unemployment that was prevalent in the United States and elsewhere from 1973 to the mid-1980s.

Stalinization the adoption by Eastern European Communist countries of features of the economic, political, and military policies implemented by Stalin in the Soviet Union.

Stoicism a philosophy founded by Zeno in the fourth century B.C. that taught that happiness could be obtained by accepting one's lot and living in harmony with the will of God, thereby achieving inner peace.

subinfeudation the practice whereby a lord's greatest vassals subdivided their fiefs and had vassals of their own, who in turn subdivided their fiefs, and so on down to simple knights, whose fiefs were too small to subdivide.

suffrage the right to vote.

suffragists advocates of extending the right to vote to women.

sultan "holder of power." A title taken by Turkish leaders who took command of the Abbasid Empire in 1055.

Surrealism an artistic movement that arose between World War I and World War II. Surrealists portrayed recognizable objects in unrecognizable relationships in order to reveal the world of the unconscious.

syncretism the combining of different forms of belief or practice, as, for example, when two gods are regarded as different forms of the same underlying divine force and are fused together.

tariffs duties (taxes) imposed on imported goods, usually to raise revenue and to discourage imports and protect domestic industries.

three-field system in medieval agriculture, the practice of dividing the arable land into three fields so that one could lie fallow while the others were planted in winter grains and spring crops.

tithe a portion of one's harvest or income, paid by medieval peasants to the village church.

totalitarian state a state characterized by government control over all aspects of economic, social, political, cultural, and intellectual life, the subordination of the individual to the state, and insistence that the masses be actively involved in the regime's goals.

total war warfare in which all of a nation's resources, including civilians at home as well as soldiers in the field, are mobilized for the war effort.

trade union an association of workers in the same trade, formed to help members secure better wages, benefits, and working conditions.

transformism the theory that societies evolve gradually.

transubstantiation a doctrine of the Roman Catholic church that during the Eucharist, the substance of the bread and wine is miraculously transformed into the body and blood of Jesus.

trench warfare warfare in which the opposing forces attack and counterattack from a relatively permanent system of trenches protected by barbed wire; characteristic of World War I.

triangular trade a pattern of trade in early modern Europe that connected Europe, Africa, and the Americas in an Atlantic economy.

tribunes of the plebs beginning in 494 B.C., Roman officials who were given the power to protect plebeians against arrest by patrician magistrates.

trivium grammar, rhetoric, and dialectic or logic; three of the seven liberal arts (the others made up the *quadrivium*) that were the basis of medieval and early modern education.

Truman Doctrine the doctrine, enunciated by Harry Truman in 1947, that the United States would provide economic aid to countries that said they were threatened by Communist expansion.

tyrant in an ancient Greek *polis* (or an Italian city-state during the Renaissance), a ruler who came to power in an unconstitutional way and ruled without being subject to the law.

ultraroyalists in nineteenth-century France, a group of aristocrats who sought to return to a monarchical system dominated by a landed aristocracy and the Catholic church.

uncertainty principle a principle in quantum mechanics, posited by Heisenberg, that holds that one cannot determine the path of an electron because the very act of observing the electron would affect its location.

unconditional surrender complete, unqualified surrender of a belligerent nation.

umma the Muslim community, as a whole.

utopian socialists intellectuals and theorists in the early nineteenth century who favored equality in social and economic conditions and wished to replace private property and competition with collective ownership and cooperation.

vassalage the granting of a fief, or landed estate, in exchange for providing military services to the lord and fulfilling certain other obligations such as appearing at the lord's court when summoned and making a payment on the knighting of the lord's eldest son.

war communism Lenin's policy of nationalizing industrial and other facilities and requisitioning the peasants' produce during the civil war in Russia.

War Guilt Clause the clause in the Treaty of Versailles that declared that Germany (with Austria) was responsible for starting World War I and ordered Germany to pay reparations for the damage the Allies had suffered as a result of the war.

Warsaw Pact a military alliance, formed in 1955, in which Albania, Bulgaria, Czechoslovakia, East Germany, Hungary, Poland, Romania, and the Soviet Union agreed to provide mutual assistance.

welfare state a sociopolitical system in which the government assumes primary responsibility for the social welfare of its citizens by providing such things as social security, unemployment benefits, and health care.

wergeld "money for a man." In early Germanic law, a person's value in monetary terms, paid by a wrongdoer to the family of the person who had been injured or killed.

zemstvos local assemblies established in Russia in 1864 by Tsar Alexander II.

ziggurat a massive stepped tower on which a temple dedicated to the chief god or goddess of a Sumerian city was built.

Zionism an international movement that called for the establishment of a Jewish state or a refuge for Jews in Palestine.

Zoroastrianism a religion founded by the Persian Zoroaster in the seventh century B.C., characterized by worship of a supreme god, Ahuramazda, who represents the good against the evil spirit, identified as Ahriman.

PRONUNCIATION

Abbasid ah-BAH-sid *or* AB-uh-sid

Abd al-Rahman ub-duh-rahkh-MAHN

Abu al-Abbas uh-BOOL-uh-BUSS

Abu Bakr ah-bu-BAHK-ur

Adenauer, Konrad AD-uh-now-ur, KOHN-raht

aediles EE-dylz

Aeolians ee-OH-lee-unz

Aequi EE-kwy

Aeschylus ESS-kuh-luss

Aetius ay-EE-shuss

Afrikaners ah-fri-KAH-nurz

Agesilaus uh-jess-uh-LAY-uss

Agincourt AH-zhen-koor

Ahlwardt, Hermann AHL-vart, hay-uh-MAHN

Ahuramazda uh-HOOR-uh-MAHZ-duh

Aix-la-Chapelle ex-lah-shah-PEL

Akhenaten ah-kuh-NAH-tun

Akkadians uh-KAY-dee-unz

Alaric AL-uh-rik

Alberti, Leon Battista al-BAYR-tee, lay-OHN bah-TEESS-tah

Albigensians al-buh-JEN-see-unz

Albuquerque, Afonso de AL-buh-kur-kee, ah-FAHN-soh day

Alcibiades al-suh-BY-uh-deez

Alcuin AL-kwin

Alemanni al-uh-MAH-nee

al-Fatah al-FAH-tuh

al-Hakim al-hah-KEEM

Alia, Ramiz AH-lee-uh, rah-MEEZ

al-Khwarizmi al-KHWAR-iz-mee

Allah AH-lah

al-Ma'mun al-muh-MOON

al-Sadat, Anwar el-suh-DAHT, ahn-WAHR

Amenhotep ah-mun-HOH-tep

Andreotti, Giulio ahn-dray-AH-tee, JOOL-yoh

Andropov, Yuri ahn-DRAHP-awf, YOOR-ee

Anjou AHN-zhoo

Antigonid an-TIG-uh-nid

Antigonus Gonatus an-TIG-oh-nuss guh-NAH-tuss

Antiochus an-TY-uh-kuss

Antonescu, Ion an-tuh-NESS-koo, YON

Antoninus Pius an-tuh-NY-nuss PY-uss

apella uh-PEL-uh

Aphrodite af-roh-DY-tee

Apollonius ap-uh-LOH-nee-uss

appartement uh-par-tuh-MUNH

Aquinas, Thomas uh-KWY-nuss, TAHM-uss

Arafat, Yasir ah-ruh-FAHT, yah-SEER

aratrum uh-RAH-trum

Archimedes ahr-kuh-MEE-deez

Argonautica ahr-guh-NAWT-uh-kuh

Aristarchus ar-iss-TAR-kus

Aristophanes ar-iss-TAHF-uh-neez

Aristotle AR-iss-tot-ul

Arsinoë ahr-SIN-oh-ee

artium baccalarius ar-TEE-um bak-uh-LAR-ee-uss

artium magister ar-TEE-um muh-GISS-ter

Aryan AR-ee-un

Ashkenazic ash-kuh-NAH-zik

Ashurbanipal ah-shur-BAH-nuh-pahl

Ashurnasirpal ah-shur-NAH-zur-pahl

asiento ah-SYEN-toh

Asoka uh-SOH-kuh

assignat ah-see-NYAH

Assyrians uh-SEER-ee-unz

Astell, Mary AST-ul, MAYR-ee

Atahualpa ah-tuh-WAHL-puh

Attalid AT-uh-lid

audiencias ow-dee-en-SEE-uss

Auerstadt OW-urr-shtaht

augur AW-gurr

Augustine AW-guh-steen

Aurelian aw-REEL-yun

Auschwitz-Birkenau OWSH-vitz-BEER-kuh-now

Ausgleich OWSS-glykh

auspices AWSS-puh-sizz

Austerlitz AWSS-tur-litz

Australopithecines aw-stray-loh-PITH-uh-synz

Austrasia au-STRY-zhuh

Autun oh-TUNH

Avicenna av-i-SENN-uh

Avignon ah-veen-YONH

Azerbaijan az-ur-by-JAN

Baader-Meinhof BAH-durr-MYN-huff

Babeuf, Gracchus bah-BUFF, GRAK-uss

Bach, Johann Sebastian BAKH, yoh-HAHN suh-BASS-chun

Baden-Powell, Robert BAD-un-POW-ul

Bakunin, Michael buh-KOON-yun

Balboa, Vasco Nuñez de bal-BOH-uh, BAHS-koh NOON-yez day

Ballin, Albert BAH-leen, AHL-bayrt

Banque de Belgique BAHNK duh bel-ZHEEK

Barbarossa bar-buh-ROH-suh

Baroque buh-ROHK

Barth, Karl BAHRT, KAHRL

Bastille bass-STEEL

Batista, Fulgencio bah-TEES-tuh, ful-JEN-see-oh

Bauhaus BOW-howss

Bayle, Pierre BEL, PYAYR

Beauharnais, Josephine de boh-ar-NAY, zhoh-seff-FEEN duh

Beauvoir, Simone de boh-VWAR, see-MUHN duh

Bebel, August BAY-bul, ow-GOOST

Beccaria, Cesare buh-KAH-ree-uh, CHAY-zuh-ray

Bede BEED

Beguines bay-GEENZ

Beiderbecke, Bix BY-der-bek, BIKS

Beijing bay-ZHING

Belarus bel-uh-ROOSS

Belgioioso, Cristina bel-joh-YOH-soh, kriss-TEE-nuh

Belisarius bel-uh-SAH-ree-uss

benefice BEN-uh-fiss

Bergson, Henri BERG-son, ahnh-REE

Berlioz, Hector BAYR-lee-ohz, ek-TAWR

Berlusconi, Silvio bayr-loo-SKOH-nee, SEEL-vee-oh

Bernhardi, Friedrich von bayrn-HAR-dee, FREED-reekh fun

Bernini, Gian Lorenzo bur-NEE-nee, ZHAHN loh-RENT-zoh

Bernstein, Eduard BAYRN-shtyn, AY-doo-art

Bethman-Hollweg, Theobald von BET-mun-HOHL-vek, TAY-oh-bahlt fun

Blanc, Louis BLAHNH, LWEE

Blitzkrieg BLITZ-kreeg

Blum, Léon BLOOM, LAY-ohnh

Boccaccio, Giovanni boh-KAH-choh, joh-VAH-nee

Bodichon, Barbara boh-di-SHOHNH, bar-bah-RAH

Boer BOOR *or* BOR

Boethius boh-EE-thee-uss

Boleyn, Anne BUH-lin *or* buh-LIN, AN

Bolívar, Simón buh-LEE-var, see-MOHN

Bologna buh-LOHN-yuh

Bolsheviks BOHL-shuh-vikss

Bora, Katherina von BOH-rah, kat-uh-REE-nuh fun

Borgia, Cesare BOHR-zhuh, CHEZ-uh-ray

Bosnia BAHZ-nee-uh

Bossuet, Jacques baw-SWAY, ZHAHK

Botta, Giuseppe BOH-tah, joo-ZEP-pay

Botticelli, Sandro bot-i-CHEL-ee, SAHN-droh

Boulanger, Georges boo-lahnh-ZHAY, ZHORZH

boule BOO-lee

Bracciolini, Poggio braht-choh-LEE-nee, POH-djoh

Brahe, Tycho BRAH, TY-koh

Bramante, Donato brah-MAHN-tay, doh-NAH-toh

Brandt, Willy BRAHNT, VIL-ee

Brasidas BRASS-i-duss

Brest-Litovsk BREST-li-TUFFSK

Brétigny bray-tee-NYEE

Brezhnev, Leonid BREZH-neff, lee-oh-NYEET

Briand, Aristide bree-AHNH, ah-ruh-STEED

Broz, Josip BRAWZ, yaw-SEEP

Brumaire broo-MAYR

Brunelleschi, Filippo BROO-nuh-LESS-kee, fee-LEE-poh

Brüning, Heinrich BROO-ning, HYN-rikh

Bückeberg BOOK-uh-bayrk

Bulganin, Nicolai bool-GAN-yin, nyik-uh-LY

Bund Deutscher Mädel BOONT DOIT-chuh MAY-dul

Bundesrat BOON-duhs-raht

Burckhardt, Jacob BOORK-hart, YAK-ub

Burschenschaften BOOR-shun-shahf-tuhn

bushido BOO-shee-doh

Cabral, Pedro kuh-BRAL

cahiers de doléances ka-YAY duh doh-lay-AHNSS

Calais ka-LAY

Calas, Jean ka-LAH, ZHAHNH

Caligula kuh-LIG-yuh-luh

caliph KAY-liff

caliphate KAY-luh-fayt

Callicrates kuh-LIK-ruh-teez

Calonne, Charles de ka-LUN, SHAHRL duh

Cambyses kam-BY-seez

Camus, Albert ka-MOO, ahl-BAYR

Canaanites KAY-nuh-nytss

Capet, Hugh ka-PAY, YOO

Capetian kuh-PEE-shun

Caracalla kuh-RAK-uh-luh

Caraffa, Gian Pietro kuh-RAH-fuh, JAHN PYAY-troh

Caral kuh-RAHL

carbonari kar-buh-NAH-ree

Carolingian kar-uh-LIN-jun

carruca kuh-ROO-kuh

Carthage KAR-thij

Carthaginian kar-thuh-JIN-ee-un

Cartier, Jacques kar-TYAY, ZHAK

Cassiodorus kass-ee-uh-DOR-uss

Castiglione, Baldassare ka-steel-YOH-nay, bal-duh-SAH-ray

Castro, Fidel KASS-troh, fee-DEL

Çatal Hüyük chaht-ul hoo-YOOK

Catharism KA-thuh-riz-um

Catullus kuh-TUL-uss

Cavendish, Margaret KAV-un-dish, MAHR-guh-ret

Cavour, Camillo di kuh-VOOR, kuh-MEEL-oh dee

Ceauşescu, Nicolae chow-SHES-koo, nee-koh-LY

celibacy SEL-uh-buh-see

cenobitic sen-oh-BIT-ik

Cereta, Laura say-REE-tuh, LOW-ruh

Cézanne, Paul say-ZAHN, POHL

Chaeronea ker-uh-NEE-uh

Chaldean kal-DEE-un

Chandragupta Maurya chun-druh-GOOP-tuh MOWR-yuh

chanson de geste shahn-SAWNH duh ZHEST

Charlemagne SHAR-luh-mayn

Chateaubriand, François-René de shah-TOH-bree-AHNH, frahnh-SWAH-ruh-NAY duh

Chatelet, marquise du shat-LAY, mahr-KEEZ duh

Chauvet shoh-VAY

Cheka CHEK-uh

Chiang Kai-Shek CHANG ky-SHEK

Chirac, Jacques shee-RAK, ZHAHK

Chrétien, Jean kray-TYEN, ZHAHNH

Chrétien de Troyes kray-TYEN duh TRWAH

Chrysoloras, Manuel kriss-uh-LOHR-uss, MAN-yuh-wul

Cicero SIS-uh-roh

ciompi CHAHM-pee

Cistercians sis-TUR-shunz

Claudius KLAW-dee-uss

Cleisthenes KLYSS-thuh-neez

Clemenceau, Georges kluh-mahn-SOH, ZHORZH

Clovis KLOH-viss

Codreanu, Corneliu   kaw-dree-AH-noo, kor-NEL-yoo
Colbert, Jean-Baptiste   kohl-BAYR, ZHAHN bap-TEEST
Colonia Agrippinensis   kuh-LOH-nee-uh uh-grip-uh-NEN-suss
colonus   kuh-LOH-nuss
Columbanus   kah-lum-BAY-nuss
comitia centuriata   kuh-MISH-ee-uh sen-choo-ree-AH-tuh
Commodus   KAHM-uh-duss
Comnenus   kahm-NEE-nuss
Comte, Auguste   KOHNT, ow-GOOST
concilium plebis   kahn-SIL-ee-um PLEE-biss
Concordat of Worms   kun-KOR-dat uv WURMZ *or* VORMPS
Condorcet, Marie-Jean de   kohn-dor-SAY, muh-REE-ZHAHNH duh
condottieri   kahn-duh-TYAY-ree
consul   KAHN-sul
Contarini, Gasparo   kahn-tuh-REE-nee, GAHS-puh-roh
conversos   kohn-VAYR-sohz
Copernicus, Nicolaus   kuh-PURR-nuh-kuss, nee-koh-LOW-uss
Córdoba   KOR-duh-buh
Corinth   KOR-inth
Corpus Hermeticum   KOR-pus hur-MET-i-koom
Corpus Iuris Civilis   KOR-pus YOOR-iss SIV-i-liss
corregidores   kuhr-reg-uh-DOR-ayss
Cortés, Hernán   kor-TAYSS *or* kor-TEZ, hayr-NAHN
Corvinus, Matthias   kor-VY-nuss, muh-THY-uss
Courbet, Gustave   koor-BAY, goo-STAHV
Crassus   KRASS-uss
Crécy   kray-SEE
Crédit Mobilier   kray-DEE moh-bee-LYAY
Croatia   kroh-AY-shuh
Croesus   KREE-suss
cum manu   koom MAH-noo
Curie, Marie   kyoo-REE, muh-REE
Cypselus   SIP-suh-luss
Daimler, Gottlieb   DYM-lur, GUT-leep
d'Albret, Jeanne   dahl-BRAY, ZHAHN
Dalí, Salvador   dah-LEE *or* DAH-lee, SAHL-vuh-dohr
Danton, Georges   dahn-TAWNH, ZHORZH
Darius   duh-RY-uss
Darmstadt   DARM-shtaht
dauphin   DAW-fin
David, Jacques-Louis   dah-VEED, ZHAHK-LWEE
Debelleyme, Louis-Maurice   duh-buh-LAYM, LWEE-moh-REESS
Debussy, Claude   duh-bus-SEE, KLOHD
décades   day-KAD
Decameron   dee-KAM-uh-run
decarchies   DEK-ar-keez
decemviri   duh-SEM-vuh-ree
de Champlain, Samuel   duh sham-PLAYN, sahm-WEL
Deffand, marquise du   duh-FAHNH, mar-KEEZ doo
de Gaulle, Charles   duh GOHL, SHAHRL
Delacroix, Eugène   duh-lah-KRWAH, ur-ZHEN
Delphi   DEL-fy
Démar, Claire   DAY-mar, CLAYR
demesne   duh-MAYN
Demosthenes   duh-MAHSS-thuh-neez
Denikin, Anton   dyin-YEE-kin, ahn-TOHN
De Rerum Novarum   day RAYR-um noh-VAR-um
Derrida, Jacques   DAY-ree-dah, ZHAHK

Descartes, René   day-KART, ruh-NAY
Dessau   DESS-ow
d'Este, Isabella   DESS-tay, ee-suh-BEL-uh
d'Holbach, Paul   DOHL-bahk, POHL
dhoti   DOH-tee
Diaghilev, Sergei   DYAHG-yuh-lif, syir-GAY
Dias, Bartholomeu   DEE-ush, bar-toh-loh-MAY-oo
Diaspora   dy-ASS-pur-uh
Diderot, Denis   DEE-droh, duh-NEE
Diocletian   dy-uh-KLEE-shun
Disraeli, Benjamin   diz-RAY-lee, BEN-juh-min
Djoser   ZHOH-sur
Dollfuss, Engelbert   DOHL-fooss, AYN-gul-bayrt
Domesday Book   DOOMZ-day book
Domitian   doh-MISH-un
Donatello, Donato di   doh-nuh-TEL-oh, doh-NAH-toh dee
Donatus   duh-NAY-tus
Donatist   DOH-nuh-tist
Dopolavoro   duh-puh-LAH-vuh-roh
Dorians   DOR-ee-unz
Doryphoros   doh-RIF-uh-rohss
Dostoevsky, Fyodor   dus-tuh-YEF-skee, FYUD-ur
Douhet, Giulio   doo-AY, JOOL-yoh
Dreyfus, Alfred   DRY-fuss, AL-fred
Dubček, Alexander   DOOB-chek, ah-lek-SAHN-dur
Du Bois, W. E. B.   doo-BOISS
Dufay, Guillaume   doo-FAY, gee-YOHM
Duma   DOO-muh
Dürer, Albrecht   DOO-rur, AHL-brekht
Ebert, Friedrich   AY-bert, FREE-drikh
ecclesia   ek-KLEE-zee-uh
Eckhart, Meister   EK-hart, MY-stur
Einsatzgruppen   YN-zahtz-groop-un
Einstein, Albert   YN-styn *or* Yn-shtyn, AL-burt
Ekaterinburg   i-kat-tuh-RIN-burk
encomienda   en-koh-MYEN-dah
Engels, Friedrich   ENG-ulz, FREE-drikh
Enki   EN-kee
Enlil   EN-lil
Entente Cordiale   ahn-TAHNT kor-DYAHL
Epaminondas   i-PAM-uh-NAHN-duss
ephor   EFF-ur
Epicurus   ep-i-KYOOR-uss
Epicureanism   ep-i-kyoo-REE-uh-ni-zum
episcopos   i-PIS-kuh-puss
equestrians   i-KWES-tree-unz
equites   EK-wuh-teez
Erasistratus   er-uh-SIS-truh-tuss
Erasmus, Desiderius   i-RAZ-mus, dez-i-DEER-ee-uss
Eratosthenes   er-uh-TAHSS-thuh-neez
eremitical   er-uh-MIT-i-kul
Erhard, Ludwig   AYR-hart, LOOD-vik
Estonia   ess-TOH-nee-uh
Etruscans   i-TRUSS-kunz
Euclid   YOO-klid
Euripides   yoo-RIP-i-deez
exchequer   EKS-chek-ur
Execrabilis   ek-suh-KRAB-uh-liss

Eylau   Y-low
Falange   fuh-LANJ
fasces   FASS-eez
Fascio di Combattimento   FASH-ee-oh dee com-bat-ee-MEN-toh
Fatimid   FAT-i-mid
Fedele, Cassandra   FAY-duh-lee, kuh-SAN-druh
Feltre, Vittorino da   FEL-tray, vee-tor-EE-noh dah
Ficino, Marsilio   fee-CHEE-noh, mar-SIL-yoh
Fischer, Joschka   FISH-ur, YUSH-kah
Flaubert, Gustave   floh-BAYR, goo-STAHV
Fleury, Cardinal   floo-REE, KAHR-di-nul
Floreal   floh-ray-AHL
fluyt   FLYT
Foch, Ferdinand   FUSH, fayr-di-nawnh
Fontainebleau   fawnh-ten-BLOH
Fontenelle, Bernard de   fawnt-NEL, bayr-NAHR duh
Foucault, Michel   foo-KOH, mee-SHEL
Fouquet, Nicolas   foo-KAY, nee-koh-LAH
Fourier, Charles   foo-RYAY, SHAHRL
Francesca, Piero della   frahn-CHESS-kuh, PYAY-roh del-luh
Frequens   FREE-kwenss
Freud, Sigmund   FROID, SIG-mund *or* ZIG-munt
Friedan, Betty   free-DAN
Friedland   FREET-lahnt
Friedrich, Caspar David   FREED-rikh, kass-PAR dah-VEET
Frimaire   free-MAYR
Froissart, Jean   frwah-SAR, ZHAHNH
Fronde   FROHND
Fructidor   FROOK-ti-dor
fueros   FWYA-rohss
Führerprinzip   FYOOR-ur-prin-TSEEP
gabelle   gah-BEL
Gaiseric   GY-zuh-rik
Galba   GAHL-buh
Galilei, Galileo   GAL-li-lay, gal-li-LAY-oh
Gama, Vasco da   GAHM-uh, VAHSH-koh dah
Gandhi, Mohandas (Mahatma)   GAHN-dee, moh-HAHN-dus
    (muh-HAHT-muh)
Garibaldi, Giuseppe   gar-uh-BAHL-dee, joo-ZEP-pay
Gasperi, Alcide de   GAHSS-pe-ree, ahl-SEE-day day
Gatti de Gamond, Zoé   gah-TEE duh gah-MOHNH, zoh-AY
Gaugamela   gaw-guh-MEE-luh
Gelasius   juh-LAY-shuss
Gentileschi, Artemisia   jen-tuh-LESS-kee, ar-tuh-MEE-zhuh
Geoffrin, Marie-Thérèse de   zhoh-FRANH, ma-REE-tay-RAYZ duh
Germinal   jayr-mee-NAHL
gerousia   juh-ROO-see-uh
Gesamtkunstwerk   guh-ZAHMT-koonst-vayrk
Gierek, Edward   GYER-ek, ed-VAHRT
Gilgamesh   GIL-guh-mesh
Giolitti, Giovanni   joh-LEE-tee, joh-VAHN-nee
Giotto   JOH-toh
Girondins   juh-RAHN-dinz
glasnost   GLAHZ-nohst
Gleichschaltung   glykh-SHAHL-toonk
Goebbels, Joseph   GUR-bulz, YOH-sef
Goethe, Johann Wolfgang von   GUR-tuh, yoh-HAHN
    VULF-gahnk fun

Gömbös, Julius   GUM-buhsh, JOOL-yuss
Gomulka, Wladyslaw   goh-MOOL-kuh, vlah-DIS-lahf
gonfaloniere   gun-fah-loh-NYAY-ray
Gonzaga, Gian Francesco   gun-DZAH-gah, JAHN frahn-CHES-koh
Gorbachev, Mikhail   GOR-buh-chof, meek-HAYL
Göring, Hermann   GUR-ing, hayr-MAHN
Gottwald, Clement   GUT-vald, kleh-MENT
Gouges, Olympe   GOOZH, oh-LAMP
Gracchus, Tiberius and Gaius   GRAK-us, ty-BEER-ee-uss and GY-
    uss
grandi   GRAHN-dee
Grieg, Edvard   GREEG, ED-vart
Groote, Gerard   GROH-tuh
Gropius, Walter   GROH-pee-uss, VAHL-tuh
Grossdeutsch   GROHS-doich
Groza, Petra   GRO-zhuh, PET-ruh
Guicciardini, Francesco   gwee-char-DEE-nee, frahn-CHESS-koh
Guindorf, Reine   GWIN-dorf, RY-nuh
Guise   GEEZ
Guizot, François   gee-ZOH, frahnh-SWAH
Gustavus Adolphus   goo-STAY-vus uh-DAHL-fuss
Gutenberg, Johannes   GOO-ten-bayrk, yoh-HAH-nuss
Guzman, Gaspar de   goos-MAHN, gahs-PAR day
Habsburg   HAPS-burg
Hadrian   HAY-dree-un
Hagia Sophia   HAG-ee-uh soh-FEE-uh
hajj   HAJ
Hammurabi   ham-uh-RAH-bee
Handel, George Friedrich   HAN-dul, JORJ FREED-rik
Hankou   HAHN-kow
Hannibal   HAN-uh-bul
Hanukkah   HAH-nuh-kuh
Harappa   huh-RAP-uh
Hardenberg, Karl von   HAR-den-berk, KAHRL fun
Harun al-Rashid   huh-ROON ah-rah-SHEED
Hatshepsut   hat-SHEP-soot
Haushofer, Karl   HOWSS-hoh-fuh, KAHRL
Haussmann, Baron   HOWSS-mun, BAR-un
Havel, Vaclav   HAH-vul, VAHT-slahf
Haydn, Franz Joseph   HY-dun, FRAHNTS YO-zef
hegemon   HEJ-uh-mun
Hegira   hee-JY-ruh
Heisenberg, Werner   HY-zun-bayrk, VAYR-nuh
heliaea   HEE-lee-ee
Hellenistic   hel-uh-NIS-tik
helots   HEL-uts
Herculaneum   hur-kyuh-LAY-nee-um
Herodotus   huh-ROD-uh-tuss
Herophilus   huh-ROF-uh-luss
Herzegovina   HURT-suh-guh-VEE-nuh
Herzen, Alexander   HAYRT-sun, ah-lek-ZAHN-dur
Herzl, Theodor   HAYRT-sul, TAY-oh-dor
Hesiod   HEE-see-ud
Hesse, Hermann   HESS-uh, HAYR-mahn
hetairai   huh-TY-ree
Heydrich, Reinhard   HY-drikh, RYN-hart
hieroglyph   HY-uh-roh-glif
Hildegard of Bingen   HIL-duh-gard uv BING-un

Hindenburg, Paul von   HIN-den-boork, POWL fun

Hiroshima   hee-roh-SHEE-muh

Hitler Jugend   HIT-luh YOO-gunt

Ho Chi Minh   HOH CHEE MIN

Höch, Hannah   HURKH, HAH-nuh

Hohenstaufen   hoh-en-SHTOW-fen

Hohenzollern   hoh-en-TSUL-urn

Hohenzollern-Sigmaringen   hoh-en-TSUL-urn zig-mah-RING-un

Holtzendorf   HOHLT-sen-dorf

Homo sapiens   HOH-moh SAY-pee-unz

Honecker, Erich   HOH-nek-uh, AY-reekh

Honorius   hoh-NOR-ee-uss

hoplites   HAHP-lyts

Horace   HOR-uss

Horthy, Miklós   HOR-tee, MIK-lohsh

Höss, Rudolf   HURSS, ROO-dulf

Hoxha, Enver   HAW-jah, EN-vur

Huayna Inca   WY-nuh INK-uh

Huguenots   HYOO-guh-nots

Husák, Gustav   HOO-sahk, goo-STAHV

Hydaspes   hy-DASS-peez

Ibn Sina   ib-un SEE-nuh

Ictinus   ik-TY-nuss

Ignatius of Loyola   ig-NAY-shuss uv loi-OH-luh

Il Duce   eel DOO-chay

Île-de-France   EEL-de-fronhss

illustrés   ee-loo-STRAY

illustrissimi   ee-loo-STREE-see-mee

imperator   im-puh-RAH-tur

imperium   im-PEER-ee-um

intendant   anh-tahnh-DAHNH *or* in-TEN-dunt

Isis   Y-sis

Issus   ISS-uss

ius civile   YOOSS see-VEE-lay

ius gentium YOOSS GEN-tee-um

ius naturale   YOOSS nah-too-RAH-lay

Jacobin   JAK-uh-bin

Jacquerie   zhak-REE

Jadwiga   yahd-VEE-guh

Jagiello   yahg-YEL-oh

Jahn, Friedrich Ludwig   YAHN, FREED-rikh LOOD-vik

Jaufré Rudel   zhoh-FRAY roo-DEL

Jaurès, Jean   zhaw-RESS, ZHAHNH

Jena   YAY-nuh

jihad   ji-HAHD

Joffre, Joseph   ZHUFF-ruh, zhoh-ZEF

Journal des Savants   zhoor-NAHL day sah-VAHNH

Juana Inés de la Cruz, Sor   HWAH-nuh ee-NAYSS day lah KROOZ, SAWR

Judaea   joo-DEE-uh

Judas Maccabaeus   JOO-dus mak-uh-BEE-uss

Jung, Carl   YOONG, KAHRL

Junkers   YOONG-kers

Jupiter Optimus Maximus   JOO-puh-tur AHP-tuh-muss MAK-suh-muss

Justinian   juh-STIN-ee-un

Juvenal   JOO-vuh-nul

Ka'ba   KAH-buh

Kádár, János   KAH-dahr, YAH-nush

kamikaze   kah-mi-KAH-zay

Kandinsky, Wassily   kan-DIN-skee, vus-YEEL-yee

Kangxi   GANG-zhee

Kant, Immanuel   KAHNT, i-MAHN-yoo-el

Karlowitz   KARL-oh-vits

Karlsbad   KARLSS-baht

Kaunitz, Wenzel von   KOW-nits, VENT-sul fun

Kemal Atatürk   kuh-MAHL ah-tah-TIRK

Kenyatta, Jomo   ken-YAHT-uh, JOH-moh

Kerensky, Alexander   kuh-REN-skee, ah-lek-SAHN-dur

Keynes, John Maynard   KAYNZ, JAHN MAY-nurd

Khanbaliq   khahn-bah-LEEK

Khomeini, Ayatollah   khoh-MAY-nee, ah-yuh-TUL-uh

Khrushchev, Nikita   KHROOSH-chawf, nuh-KEE-tuh

Khubilai Khan   KOO-bluh KAHN

Kikuya   ki-KOO-yuh

Kleindeutsch   KLYN-doich

Kohl, Helmut   KOHL, HEL-moot

koiné   koi-NAY

Kolchak, Alexander   kul-CHAHK, ah-lek-SAHN-dur

Kollantai, Alexandra   kul-lun-TY, ah-lek-SAHN-druh

Königgrätz   kur-nig-GRETS

Kornilov, Lavr   kor-NYEE-luff, LAH-vur

Kosciuszko, Thaddeus   kaw-SHOOS-koh, tah-DAY-oosh

Kosovo   KAWSS-suh-voh

Kossuth, Louis   KAWSS-uth *or* KAW-shoot, LOO-iss

Kostunica, Vojislav   kuh-STOO-nit-suh, VOH-yee-slav

kouros   KOO-rohss

Koyaanisqatsi   koh-YAH-niss-kahts

Kraft durch Freude   KRAHFT doorkh FROI-duh

Kreditanstalt   kray-deet-AHN-shtalt

Kristallnacht   kri-STAHL-nahkht

Krupp, Alfred   KROOP, AHL-fret

Kuchuk-Kainarji   koo-CHOOK-ky-NAR-jee

kulaks   KOO-lahks

Kulturkampf   kool-TOOR-kahmpf

Kun, Béla   KOON, BAY-luh

Kundera, Milan   koon-DAYR-uh, MEE-lahn

Kursk   KOORSK

Kwasniewski, Aleksander   kwahsh-NYEF-skee, ah-lek-SAHN-dur

la belle époque   lah BEL ay-PUK

Lafayette, marquis de   lah-fay-ET, mar-KEE duh

laissez-faire   less-ay-FAYR

Lamarck, Jean-Baptiste   lah-MARK, ZHAHNH-bah-TEEST

Lancaster   LAN-kas-tur

La Rochefoucauld-Liancourt, duc de   lah-RUSH-foo-koh-lee-ahnh-KOOR, dook duh

Las Navas de Tolosa   lahss-nah-vahss-day-toh-LOH-suh

latifundia   lat-i-FOON-dee-uh

Latium   LAY-shee-um

Latvia   LAT-vee-uh

Launay, marquis de   loh-NAY, mar-KEE duh

Laurier, Wilfred   LOR-ee-ay, WIL-fred

Lavoisier, Antoine   lah-vwah-ZYAY, ahn-TWAHN

Lazar   lah-ZAR

Lebensraum   LAY-benz-rowm

Les Demoiselles d'Avignon   lay dem-wah-ZEL dah-vee-NYOHNH

Lespinasse, Julie de   less-pee-NAHSS, zhoo-LEE duh

Le Tellier, François Michel   luh tel-YAY, frahnh-SWAH-mee-SHEL

Lévesque, René   luh-VEK, ruh-NAY

Leviathan   luh-VY-uh-thun

Leyster, Judith   LESS-tur, JOO-dith

Licinius   ly-SIN-ee-uss

Liebenfels, Lanz von   LEE-bun-felss, LAHNTS fun

Liebknecht, Karl   LEEP-knekht, KAHRL

Liebknecht, Wilhelm   LEEP-knekht, VIL-helm

Lindisfarne   LIN-dis-farn

Lionne, Hugues de   LYUN, OOG duh

List, Friedrich   LIST, FREED-rikh

Liszt, Franz   LIST, FRAHNTS

Lithuania   lith-WAY-nee-uh

Livy   LIV-ee

Li Zicheng   lee-zee-CHENG

L'Ouverture, Toussaint   loo-vayr-TOOR, too-SANH

Louvois   loo-VWAH

Lucretius   loo-KREE-shus

Luddites   LUD-yts

Ludendorff, Erich   LOO-dun-dorf

Lueger, Karl   LOO-gur, KAHRL

Luftwaffe   LOOFT-vahf-uh

l'uomo universale   LWOH-moh OO-nee-ver-SAH-lay

Lützen   LOOT-sun

Luxemburg, Rosa   LOOK-sum-boork, ROH-suh

Lyons   LYOHNH

Lysias   LISS-ee-uss

Maastricht   MAHSS-trikht

Ma'at   muh-AHT

Machiavelli, Niccolò   mahk-ee-uh-VEL-ee, nee-koh-LOH

Maginot Line   MA-zhi-noh lyn

Magna Graecia   MAG-nuh GREE-shuh

Magyars   MAG-yarz

Maimonides   my-MAH-nuh-deez

Maistre, Joseph de   MESS-truh, zhoh-SEF duh

maius imperium   MY-yoos im-PEE-ree-um

Malaya   muh-LAY-uh

Mallarmé, Stéphane   mah-lahr-MAY, stay-FAHN

Malleus Maleficarum   mal-EE-uss mal-uh-FIK-uh-rum

Malthus, Thomas   MAWL-thuss, TAHM-uss

Manchukuo   man-CHOO-kwoh

Manetho   MAN-uh-thoh

Mao Zedong   mow zee-DAHNG

Marcus Aurelius   MAR-kuss aw-REE-lee-uss

Marcuse, Herbert   mar-KOO-zuh, HUR-burt

Marie Antoinette   muh-REE an-twuh-NET

Marius   MAR-ee-uss

Marquez, Gabriel Garcia   mar-KEZ, gab-ree-EL gar-SEE-uh

Marseilles   mar-SAY

Marsiglio of Padua   mar-SIL-yoh uv PAD-juh-wuh

Masaccio   muh-ZAH-choh

Masaryk, Thomas   MAS-uh-rik, toh-MAHSS

Mästlin, Michael   MEST-lin, mee-kah-EL

Matteotti, Giacomo   mat-tay-AHT-tee, JAHK-uh-moh

Mauryan   MAWR-ee-in *or* MOW-ree-in

Maxentius   mak-SEN-shuss

Maximian   mak-SIM-ee-un

Maya   MY-uh

Mazarin   maz-uh-RANH

Mazzini, Giuseppe   maht-SEE-nee, joo-ZEP-pay

Megasthenes   muh-GAS-thuh-neez

Mehmet   meh-MET

Meiji   MAY-jee

Mein Kampf   myn KAHMPF

Melanchthon, Philip   muh-LANK-tun, fil-LEEP

Menander   muh-NAN-dur

Mendeleyev, Dmitri   men-duh-LAY-ef, di-MEE-tree

Mensheviks   MES-shuh-viks

Mercator, Gerardus   mur-KAY-tur, juh-RAHR-dus

Merian, Maria Sibylla   MAY-ree-un, muh-REE-uh suh-BIL-uh

Merovingian   meh-ruh-VIN-jee-un

Mesopotamia   mess-uh-puh-TAY-mee-uh

Messiaen, Olivier   meh-SYANH, oh-lee-VYAY

Messidor   MESS-i-dor

mestizos   mess-TEE-ZOHZ

Metaxas, John   muh-tahk-SAHSS, JAHN

Metternich, Klemens von   MET-ayr-nikh, KLAY-menss fun

Michel, Louise   mee-SHEL, loo-EEZ

Michelangelo   my-kuh-LAN-juh-loh

Mieszko   MYESH-koh

Millet, Jean-François   mi-YEH, ZHAHNH-frahnh-SWAH

Milo_evi_, Slobodan   mi-LOH-suh-vich, sluh-BOH-dahn

Miltiades   mil-TY-uh-deez

Mirandola, Pico della   mee-RAN-doh-lah, PEE-koh DEL-uh

missi dominici   MISS-ee doh-MIN-i-chee

Mitterrand, François   MEE-tayr-rahnh, frahnh-SWAH

Moctezuma   mahk-tuh-ZOO-muh

Mohács   MOH-hach

Mohenjo-Daro   mo-HEN-jo-DAH-roh

Moldavia   mohl-DAY-vee-uh

Moldova   mohl-DOH-vuh

Molière, Jean-Baptiste   mohl-YAYR, ZHAHNH-bah-TEEST

Molotov, Vyacheslav   MAHL-uh-tawf, vyich-chiss-SLAHF

Monet, Claude   moh-NEH, KLOHD

Montaigne, Michel de   mahn-TAYN, mee-SHEL duh

Montefeltro, Federigo da   mahn-tuh-FEL-troh, fay-day-REE-goh dah

Montesquieu   MOHN-tess-kyoo

Montessori, Maria   mahn-tuh-SOR-ee

Morisot, Berthe   mor-ee-ZOH, BAYRT

Mozambique   moh-zam-BEEK

Mozart, Wolfgang Amadeus   MOH-tsart, VULF-gahng ah-muh-DAY-uss

Muawiya   moo-AH-wee-yah

Mudejares   moo-theh-KHAH-rayss

Mughal   MOO-gul

Muhammad   moh-HAM-mud *or* moo-HAM-mud

Mühlberg   MOOL-bayrk

mulattoes   muh-LAH-tohz

Müntzer, Thomas   MOON-tsur

Murad   moo-RAHD

Muslim   MUZ-lum

Mutsuhito   moo-tsoo-HEE-toh

Myanmar   MYAN-mahr

Mycenaean   my-suh-NEE-un

Nabonidas nab-uh-NY-duss
Nabopolassar nab-uh-puh-LASS-ur
Nagasaki nah-gah-SAH-kee
Nagy, Imry NAHJ, IM-ray
Nanjing nan-JING
Nantes NAHNT
Nasser, Gamal Abdel NAH-sur, juh-MAHL ahb-DOOL
Navarre nuh-VAHR
Nebuchadnezzar neb-uh-kud-NEZZ-ur
Nehru, Jawaharlal NAY-roo, juh-WAH-hur-lahl
Nero NEE-roh
Nerva NUR-vuh
Neumann, Balthasar NOI-mahn, BAHL-tuh-zahr
Neumann, Solomon NOI-mahn, ZOH-loh-mun
Neustria NOO-stree-uh
Nevsky, Alexander NYEF-skee, ah-lek-SAHN-dur
Newcomen, Thomas NYOO-kuh-mun *or* nyoo-KUM-mun, TAHM-
    uss
Ngo Dinh Diem GOH din DYEM
Nicias NISS-ee-uss
Nietzsche, Friedrich NEE-chuh *or* NEE-chee, FREED-rikh
Nimwegen NIM-vay-gun
Ninhursaga nin-HUR-sah-guh
Nivose nee-VOHZ
Nkrumah, Kwame en-KROO-muh, KWAH-may
nobiles no-BEE-layz
Nogarola, Isotta NOH-guh-rol-uh, ee-ZAHT-uh
Novalis, Friedrich noh-VAH-lis, FREED-rikh
Novotny, Antonin noh-VAHT-nee, AHN-toh-nyeen
novus homo NOH-vuss HOH-moh
Nystadt NEE-shtaht
Octavian ahk-TAY-vee-un
Odoacer oh-doh-AY-sur
Olivares oh-lee-BAH-rayss
optimates ahp-tuh-MAH-tayz
Oresteia uh-res-TY-uh
Osama bin Laden oh-SAH-muh bin LAH-dun
Osiris oh-SY-russ
Ostara oh-STAH-ruh
Ostpolitik OHST-paw-li-teek
ostrakon AHSS-truh-kahn
Ostrogoths AHSS-truh-gahthss
Ovid OH-vid
Oxenstierna, Axel OOK-sen-shur-nah, AHK-sul
Pachakuti pah-chah-KOO-tee
Paleologus pay-lee-AWL-uh-guss
Panaetius puh-NEE-shuss
Pankhurst, Emmeline PANK-hurst, EM-muh-lyn
papal curia PAY-pul KYOOR-ee-uh
Papen, Franz von PAH-pun, FRAHNTS fun
Paracelsus par-uh-SEL-suss
Parlement par-luh-MAHNH
Parti Québécois par-TEE kay-bek-KWA
Pascal, Blaise pass-KAHL, BLEZ
Pasteur, Louis pas-TOOR, LWEE
paterfamilias pay-tur-fuh-MEEL-yus
Pensées pahn-SAY
Pentateuch PEN-tuh-took

Pepin PEP-in *or* pay-PANH
perestroika per-uh-STROI-kuh
Pergamum PURR-guh-mum
Pericles PER-i-kleez
perioeci per-ee-EE-see
Pétain, Henri pay-TANH, ahnh-REE
Petite Roquette puh-TEET raw-KET
Petrarch PEE-trark *or* PET-trark
Petronius pi-TROH-nee-uss
phalansteries fuh-LAN-stuh-reez
philosophe fee-loh-ZAWF
Phintys FIN-tiss
Phoenicians fuh-NEE-shunz
Photius FOH-shuss
Picasso, Pablo pi-KAH-soh, PAHB-loh
Pietism PY-uh-tiz-um
Pilsudski, Joseph peel-SOOT-skee, YOO-zef
Piscator, Erwin PIS-kuh-tor, AYR-vin
Pisistratus puh-SIS-truh-tuss
Pissarro, Camille pee-SAH-roh, kah-MEEL
Pizan, Christine de pee-ZAHN, kris-TEEN duh
Pizarro, Francesco puh-ZAHR-oh, frahn-CHESS-koh
Planck, Max PLAHNK, MAHKS
Plantagenet plan-TAJ-uh-net
Plassey PLA-see
Plato PLAY-toh
Plautus PLAW-tuss
plebiscita pleb-i-SEE-tuh
Pluviose ploo-VYOHZ
Poincaré, Raymond pwanh-kah-RAY, ray-MOHNH
polis POH-liss
politiques puh-lee-TEEKS
Pollaiuolo, Antonio pohl-ly-WOH-loh, ahn-TOHN-yoh
Poltava pul-TAH-vuh
Polybius puh-LIB-ee-uss
Pombal, marquis de pum-BAHL, mar-KEE duh
Pompadour, madame de POM-puh-door, ma-DAM duh
Pompeii pahm-PAY
Pompey PAHM-pee
pontifex maximus PAHN-ti-feks MAK-si-muss
populares PAWP-oo-lahr-ayss
popolo grasso PAWP-oo-loh GRAH-soh
Poseidon poh-SY-dun
Postumus PAHS-choo-muss
Potsdam PAHTS-dam
Poussin, Nicholas poo-SANH, NEE-koh-lah
Praecepter Germaniae PREE-sep-tur gayr-MAHN-ee-ee
praetor PREE-tur
Prairial pray-RYAL
Pravda PRAHV-duh
Primo de Rivera PREE-moh day ri-VAY-ruh
primogeniture pree-moh-JEN-i-choor
princeps PRIN-seps *or* PRIN-keps
Principia prin-SIP-ee-uh *or* prin-KIP-ee-uh
Procopius pruh-KOH-pee-uss
procurator PROK-yuh-ray-tur
Ptolemy TAHL-uh-mee
Ptolemaic tahl-uh-MAY-ik

Pugachev, Emelyan poo-guh-CHAWF, yim-yil-YAHN
Punic PYOO-nik
Putin, Vladimir POO-tin, vlah-dyim-YEER
Pyrrhus PEER-uss
Pyrrhic PEER-ik
Pythagoras puh-THAG-uh-russ
Qianlong CHAN-lung
Qing CHING
quadrivium kwah-DRIV-ee-um
quaestors KWES-turs
querelle des femmes keh-REL day FAHM
Quesnay, François keh-NAY, frahnn-SWAH
Quetzelcoatl KWET-sul-koh-AHT-ul
Quran kuh-RAN or kuh-RAHN
Racine, Jean-Baptiste ra-SEEN, ZHAHNH-buh-TEEST
Rahner, Karl RAH-nur, KAHRL
Rameses RAM-uh-seez
Raphael RAFF-ee-ul
Rasputin rass-PYOO-tin
Rathenau, Walter RAH-tuh-now, VAHL-tuh
Realpolitik ray-AHL-poh-lee-teek
Realschule ray-AHL-shoo-luh
Reconquista ray-kawn-kiss-TAH
Reichsrat RYKHSS-raht
Reichstag RYKHSS-tahk
Rembrandt van Rijn REM-brant vahn RYN
Renaissance REN-uh-sahnss
Renan, Ernst re-NAHNH, AYRNST
Ricci, Matteo REE-chee, ma-TAY-oh
Richelieu REESH-uh-lyoo
Ricimer RISS-uh-mur
Rikstag RIKS-tahk
Rilke, Rainer Maria RIL-kuh, RY-nuh mah-REE-uh
Rimbaud, Arthur ram-BOH, ar-TOOR
risorgimento ree-SOR-jee-men-toe
Robespierre, Maximilien ROHBZ-pyayr, mak-see-meel-YENH
Rococo ruh-KOH-koh
Rocroi roh-KRWAH
Röhm, Ernst RURM, AYRNST
Rommel, Erwin RAHM-ul, AYR-vin
Romulus Augustulus RAHM-yuh-luss ow-GOOS-chuh-luss
Rossbach RAWSS-bahkh
Rousseau, Jean-Jacques roo-SOH, ZHAHNH-ZHAHK
Rurik ROO-rik
Ryswick RYZ-wik
Sacrosancta sak-roh-SANK-tuh
Saint-Just sanh-ZHOOST
Saint-Simon, Henri de sanh-see-MOHNH, ahnh-REE duh
Sakharov, Andrei SAH-kuh-rawf, ahn-DRAY
Saladin SAL-uh-din
Salazar, Antonio SAL-uh-zahr, ahn-TOH-nee-oh
Sallust SAL-ust
Samnites SAM-nytss
San Martín, José de san mar-TEEN, hoh-SAY day
sans-culottes sahnh-koo-LUT or sanz-koo-LAHTSS
Sartre, Jean-Paul SAR-truh, ZHAHNH-POHL
satrap SAY-trap
satrapy SAY-truh-pee

Satyricon sat-TEER-i-kahn
Schaumburg-Lippe SHOWM-boorkh-LEE-puh
Schleswig-Holstein SHLESS-vik-HOHL-shtyn
Schlieffen, Alfred von SHLEE-fun, AHL-fret fun
Schliemann, Heinrich SHLEE-mahn, HYN-rikh
Schmidt, Helmut SHMIT, HEL-moot
Schönberg, Arnold SHURN-bayrk, AR-nawlt
Schönborn SHURN-bawn
Schönerer, Georg von SHURN-uh-ruh, GAY-ork fun
Schröder, Gerhard SHRUR-duh, GAYR-hahrt
Schurz, Carl SHOO-utss or SHURTS, KAHRL
Schuschnigg, Karl von SHOOSH-nik, KAHRL fun
Schutzmannschaft SHOOTSS-mun-shahft
Scipio Aemilianus SEE-pee-oh ee-mil-YAY-nuss
Scipio Africanus SEE-pee-oh af-ree-KAY-nuss
scriptoria skrip-TOR-ee-uh
Ségur say-GOO-uh
Sejm SAYM
Seleucid suh-LOO-sid
Seleucus suh-LOO-kuss
Seljuk SEL-jook
Seneca SEN-uh-kuh
Sephardic suh-FAHR-dik
Septimius Severus sep-TIM-ee-uss se-VEER-uss
serjents sayr-ZHAHNH
Sforza, Ludovico SFORT-sah, loo-doh-VEE-koh
Shalmaneser shal-muh-NEE-zur
Shang SHAHNG
Shari'a shah-REE-uh
Sieveking, Amalie SEE-vuh-king, uh-MAHL-yuh
Sieyès, Abbé syay-YESS, ab-BAY
signoria seen-YOR-ee-uh
sine manu sy-nee-MAY-noo
Slovenia sloh-VEE-nee-uh
Société Générale soh-see-ay-TAY zhay-nay-RAHL
Socrates SAHK-ruh-teez
Solon SOH-lun
Solzhenitsyn, Alexander sohl-zhuh-NEET-sin, ah-lek-SAHN-dur
Somme SUM
Sophocles SAHF-uh-kleez
Sorel, Georges soh-REL, ZHORZH
Spartacus SPAR-tuh-kuss
Spartiates spar-tee-AH-teez
Speer, Albert SHPAYR, AHL-bayrt
Speransky, Michael spyuh-RAHN-skee, mee-kah-EL
Spinoza, Benedict de spi-NOH-zuh, BEN-uh-dikt duh
squadristi skwah-DREES-tee
Srebrenica sreb-bruh-NEET-suh
stadholder STAD-hohl-dur
Staël, Germaine de STAHL, zhayr-MEN duh
Stakhanov, Alexei stuh-KHAH-nuf, uh-LEK-say
Stasi SHTAH-see
Stauffenberg, Claus von SHTOW-fen-berk, KLOWSS fun
Stein, Heinrich von SHTYN, HYN-rikh fun
Stilicho STIL-i-koh
Stoicism STOH-i-siz-um
Stolypin, Peter stuh-LIP-yin, PYOH-tur
strategoi strah-tay-GOH-ee

Stravinsky, Igor   struh-VIN-skee, EE-gor
Stresemann, Gustav   SHTRAY-zuh-mahn, GOOS-tahf
Strozzi, Alessandra   STRAWT-see, ah-less-SAHN-druh
Struensee, John Frederick   SHTROO-un-zay, JAHN FRED-uh-rik
Sturmabteilung   SHTOORM-ap-ty-loonk
Sudetenland   soo-DAY-tun-land
Suger   soo-ZHAYR
Suharto   soo-HAHR-toh
Sukarno   soo-KAHR-noh
Suleiman   soo-lay-MAHN
Sulla   SUL-uh
Sumerians   soo-MER-ee-unz *or* soo-MEER-ee-unz
Summa Theologica   SOO-muh tay-oh-LOG-jee-kuh
Suppiluliumas   suh-PIL-oo-LEE-uh-muss
Suttner, Bertha von   ZOOT-nuh, BAYR-tuh fun
Symphonie Fantastique   SANH-foh-nee fahn-tas-TEEK
Taaffe, Edward von   TAH-fuh, ED-wahrt fun
Tacitus   TASS-i-tuss
taille   TY
Talleyrand   tah-lay-RAHNH
Tanzania   tan-zuh-NEE-uh
Tenochtitlán   tay-nawch-teet-LAHN
Tertullian   tur-TUL-yun
Thales   THAY-leez
Theocritus   thee-AHK-ruh-tuss
Theodora   thee-uh-DOR-uh
Theodoric   thee-AHD-uh-rik
Theodosius   thee-uh-DOH-shuss
Theognis   thee-AHG-nuss
Thermidor   TAYR-mi-dor
Thermopylae   thur-MAHP-uh-lee
Thiers, Adolphe   TYAYR, a-DAWLF
Thucydides   thoo-SID-uh-deez
Thutmosis   thoot-MOH-suss
Tiberius   ty-BEER-ee-uss
Tiglath-pileser   TIG-lath-py-LEE-zur
Tirpitz, Admiral von   TEER-pits, AD-mi-rul fun
Tisza, István   TISS-ah, ISHT-vun
Tito   TEE-toh
Titus   TY-tuss
Tlaxcala   tuh-lah-SKAH-lah
Tocqueville, Alexis de   tawk-VEEL, al-lek-SEE duh
Tojo, Hideki   TOH-joh, hee-DEK-ee
Tokugawa Ieyasu   toh-koo-GAH-wah ee-yeh-YAH-soo
Tolstoy, Leo   TOHL-stoy, LEE-oh
Topa Inca   TOH-puh INK-uh
Torah   TOR-uh
Tordesillas   tor-day-SEE-yass
Trajan   TRAY-jun
Trevithick, Richard   TREV-uh-thik, RICH-urd
Tristan, Flora   TRISS-tun, FLOR-uh
trivium   TRIV-ee-um
Trotsky, Leon   TRAHT-skee, LEE-ahn
Troyes   TRWAH
Trudeau, Pierre   troo-DOH, PYAYR
Trufaut, François   troo-FOH, frahnh-SWAH
Tsara, Tristan   TSAHR-rah, TRISS-tun
Tübingen   TOO-bing-un

Tutankhamun   too-tahn-KAH-mun
Tyche   TY-kee
Uccello, Paolo   oo-CHEL-oh, POW-loh
uhuru   oo-HOO-roo
Ulbricht, Walter   OOL-brikkt, VAHL-tuh
Umayyads   oo-MY-adz
Unam Sanctam   OO-nahm SAHNK-tahm
universitas   yoo-nee-VAYR-see-tahss
Uzbekistan   ooz-BEK-i-stan
Valens   VAY-linz
Valentinian   val-en-TIN-ee-un
Valéry, Paul   vah-lay-REE, POHL
Valois   val-WAH
Van de Velde, Theodore   vahn duh VEL-duh, TAY-oh-dor
van Eyck, Jan   vahn YK *or* van AYK, YAHN
van Gogh, Vincent   van GOH, VIN-sent
Vasa, Gustavus   VAH-suh, GUSS-tuh-vuss
Vega, Lope de   VAY-guh, LOH-pay day
Vendée   vahnh-DAY
Vendemiaire   vahnh-duh-MYAYR
Venetia   vuh-NEE-shuh
Ventose   vahnh-TOHZ
Verdun   vur-DUN
Vergerio, Pietro Paolo   vur-JEER-ee-oh, PYAY-troh POW-loh
Versailles   vayr-SY
Vesalius, Andreas   vuh-SAY-lee-uss, ahn-DRAY-uss
Vespasian   vess-PAY-zhun
Vespucci, Amerigo   vess-POO-chee, ahm-ay-REE-goh
Vesuvius   vuh-SOO-vee-uss
Vichy   VISH-ee
Vierzehnheiligen   feer-tsayn-HY-li-gen
Virchow, Rudolf   FEER-khoh, ROO-dulf
Virgil   VUR-jul
Visconti, Giangaleazzo   vees-KOHN-tee, jahn-gah-lay-AH-tsoh
Visigoths   VIZ-uh-gathz
Voilquin, Suzanne   vwahl-KANH, soo-ZAHN
Volk   FULK
Volkschulen   FULK-shoo-lun
Voltaire   vohl-TAYR
Wafd   WAHFT
Wagner, Richard   VAG-nur, RIKH-art
Walesa, Lech   vah-WENT-sah, LEK
Wallachia   wah-LAY-kee-uh
Wallenstein, Albrecht von   VAHL-en-shtyn, AWL-brekht fun
Wannsee   VAHN-zay
Watteau, Antoine   wah-TOH, ahnh-TWAHN
Weill, Kurt   VYL, KOORT
Weizsäcker, Richard von   VYTS-zek-ur, RIKH-art fun
wergeld   WURR-geld
Windischgrätz, Alfred   VIN-dish-grets, AHL-fret
Winkelmann, Maria   VINK-ul-mahn, muh-REE-uh
Witte, Sergei   VIT-uh, syir-GYAY
Wittenberg   VIT-ten-bayrk
Wojtyla, Karol   voy-TEE-wah, KAH-rul
Wollstonecraft, Mary   WUL-stun-kraft, MAY-ree
Würzburg   VOORTS-boork
Wyclif, John   WIK-lif, JAHN
Yersinia pestis   yur-SIN-ee-uh PESS-tiss

Xavier, Francis   ZAY-vee-ur, FRAN-siss

Xerxes   ZURK-seez

Xhosa   KHOH-suh

Ximenes   khee-MAY-ness

Yahweh   YAH-way

Yangtze   YANG-tsee

Yeats, William Butler   YAYTS, WIL-yum BUT-lur

Yeltsin, Boris   YELT-sun, bur-YEESS

yishuv   YISH-uv

Zasulich, Vera   tsah-SOO-likh, VAY-ruh

Zemsky Sobor   ZEM-skee suh-BOR

zemstvos   ZEMPST-vohz

Zeno   ZEE-noh

Zenobia   zuh-NOH-bee-uh

zeppelin   ZEP-puh-lin

Zeus   ZOOSS

Zhenotdel   zhen-ut-DEL

Zhivkov, Todor   ZHIV-kuff, toh-DOR

ziggurat   ZIG-uh-rat

Zimmermann, Dominikus   TSIM-ur-mahn, doh-MEE-nee-kuss

Zinzendorf, Nikolaus von   TSIN-sin-dorf, NEE-koh-LOWSS fun

Zola, Émile   ZOH-lah, ay-MEEL

zollverein   TSOHL-fuh-ryn

Zoroaster   ZOR-oh-ass-tur

Zwingli, Ulrich   TSFING-lee, OOL-rikh

DOCUMENTS

Continued from Page xxii

PHOTO CREDITS

These pages constitute an extension of the copyright page. We have made every effort to trace the ownership of all copyrighted material and to secure permission from copyright holders. In the event of any question arising as to the use of any material, we will be pleased to make the necessary corrections in future printings. We thank the following authors, publishers, and agents for their permission to use the material indicated.

CHAPTER 1

1 © Nik Wheeler/CORBIS; **4** Erich Lessing/Art Resource, NY (Archaeological Museum, Amman, Jordan); **bottom** From Michael Roaf, *Cultural Atlas of Mesopotamia & the Ancient Near East*, published by Andromeda Oxford Limited, Oxford, England; **8** The Bridgeman Art Library International (British Museum, London, UK); **11 top** Hervé Lewandowski/Réunion des Musées Nationaux, Louvre, Paris, France/Art Resource, NY; **17** © British Museum, London, UK/HIP/Art Resource, NY; **18** © Will and Deni McIntyre/Photo Researchers, Inc.; **19 left** Werner Forman/Art Resource, NY (British Museum, London, UK); **19 right** Erich Lessing/Art Resource, NY (Tomb of Mennah, Sheikh Abd el-Qurna, Tombs of the Nobles, Thebes, Egypt)

CHAPTER 2

23 Alinari/Regione Umbria/Art Resource, NY (Initial O, Ms. E2, *The Judgment of Solomon*, Archivio di Stato, Gubbio, Italy); **24** © Adam Woolfitt/CORBIS; **26** Erich Lessing/Art Resource, NY (British Museum, London, UK); **29** Bridgeman-Giraudon/Art Resource, NY (National & University Library, Jerusalem, Israel); **33** Werner Forman/Art Resource, NY (British Museum, London, UK); **35** The Art Archive/Dagli Orti; **37** Chuzeville/Réunion des Musées Nationaux/Art Resource, NY (Louvre, Paris, France)

CHAPTER 3

40 British Museum, London, UK/The Bridgeman Art Library International; **43** © AAAC/Topham/The Image Works; **46** Scala/Art Resource, NY (Museo Nazionale di Villa Giulia, Rome, Italy); **53** © Art Resource, NY; **54** Scala/Art Resource, NY (Museo Archeologico Nazionale, Naples); **54** © Photodisc/Getty; **57** Erich Lessing/Art Resource, NY (Louvre, Paris, France)

CHAPTER 4

60 Erich Lessing/Art Resource, NY (Museo Archeologico Nazionale, Naples, Italy); **61** © British Museum, London, UK/HIP/Art Resource, NY; **63** Erich Lessing/Art Resource, NY (Museo Archeologico Nazionale, Naples, Italy); **66** © Araldo de Luca/CORBIS (Museo Nazionale Romano (Palazzo Altemps), Rome,

Italy); **69** Scala/Art Resource, NY (Museo Gregoriano Egizio, Vatican Museums, Vatican State); **70** © Araldo de Luca/CORBIS; **71 left** Borromeo/Art Resource, NY (National Museum of Pakistan, Karachi, Pakistan); **71 right** The Art Archive/Dagli Orti (Kanellopoulos Museum, Athens, Greece)

CHAPTER 5

76 Dulwich Picture Gallery, London, UK/Bridgeman Art Library; **78** Scala/Art Resource, NY (Tomb of the Leopards, Tarquinia, Italy); **81** © Archivo Iconografico, S.A./CORBIS **84** Alinari/Art Resource, NY (Mostra Augustea, Rome, Italy) **85** Scala/Art Resource, NY (Forum Boarium, Rome, Italy) **86** Erich Lessing/Art Resource, NY (Museo Archeologico Nazionale, Naples, Italy); **91** Scala/Art Resource, NY (Museo Archeologico Nazionale, Naples, Italy)

CHAPTER 6

96 Nimatallah/Art Resource, NY (Palazzo dei Conservatori, Rome, Italy); **97** Scala/Art Resource, NY (Braccio Nuovo, Vatican Museums, Vatican State); **101** © Vanni Archive/CORBIS; **102** The Art Archive/Bardo Museum, Tunis, Tunisia/Dagli Orti; **107** Scala/Art Resource, NY (Galleria Borghese, Rome, Italy); **108** Bildarchiv Preussischer Kulturbesitz (Johannes Laurentius)/ Art Resource, NY (Antikensammlung, Staatliche Muséen zu Berlin '31329, Berlin, Germany); **111** Scala/Art Resource, NY (Catacomb of S. Domitilla, Rome, Italy)

CHAPTER 7

115 Giraudon/The Bridgeman Art Library International (Fol.11r, detail of 192489, vellum, French School, 14th century, Bibliotheque Municipale, Castres, France); **118** Scala/Art Resource, NY (Palazzo dei Conservatori, Rome, Italy); **121** Bridgeman-Giraudon/Art Resource, NY (Ms Nouv. Acq.FR. 1098, Bibliotheque Nationale, Paris, France); **124** Snark/Art Resource, NY (Ms. lat. 10062, f. 98, Initial A, Bibliotheque Nationale, Paris, France); **128** Scala/Art Resource, NY (S. Vitale, Ravenna, Italy); **130** © Digital Vision/Getty Images; **131** Bibliotheque Nationale (Ar 5847 f.19 from *Maqamat*, "The Meetings," by Al-Hariri, vellum, Persian School, 13th century) Paris, France/The Bridgeman Art Library

CHAPTER 8

137 Scala/Art Resource, NY (Bibliotheque de l'Arsenal, Paris, France); **141** Bridgeman-Giraudon/Art Resource, NY (Musée Goya, Castres, France); **143** Giraudon/The Bridgeman Art Library International (Castello di Issogne, Val d'Aosta, Italy); **145** The Pierpont Morgan Library (MS M.736, f.9v.), New York, USA/Art Resource, NY; **146** Alinari/The Bridgeman Art Library International (Museo Nazionale del Bargello, Florence, Italy); **148** © British

Library (Queen Mary Psalter, early 14th century)/The Art Archive; **154** © Photodisc/Getty Images

C H A P T E R   9

157 © Mary Evans Picture Library/The Image Works; **160** Art Resource, NY (R.G. Ojeda, Réunion des Musées Nationaux, Musée Condé, MS.340, f.303v, Chantilly, France); **161** Art Resource, NY (R.G. Ojeda, Réunion des Musées Nationaux, Musée Condé, Ms.65, f.4v, Chantilly, France); **166** Snark/Art Resource, NY (Bibliotheque de l'Arsenal, Paris, France); **168** Joerg P. Anders/Bildarchiv Preussischer Kulturbesitz/Art Resource, NY (Kupferstichkabinett, Min. 1233, Staatliche Muséen zu Berlin, Berlin, Germany); **171** © The Art Archive/Dagli Orti; **172** Scala/Art Resource, NY (Notre-Dame, Paris, France); **172** © The Art Archive/Dagli Orti

C H A P T E R   1 0

175 © British Library (Harl.1498. Folio No 76 Min.), London, UK/HIP/Art Resource, NY; **176** Bridgeman-Giraudon/Art Resource, NY (Musée de la Tapisserie, Bayeux, France); **182** Giraudon/Art Resource, NY (Musée Condé, Ms.722/1196, f.392r, Chantilly, France); **185** Scala/Art Resource, NY (Sacro Speco S. Scolastica, Subiaco, Italy); **186** Archives Charmet/The Bridgeman Art Library International (Musée de l'Assistance Publique, Hopitaux de Paris, France); **188** © British Library (Cott Nero E II pt2 f.20v), London, UK/The Bridgeman Art Library; **193** © Bettmann/CORBIS

C H A P T E R   1 1

196 Snark/Art Resource, NY (Bibliotheque Royale Albert I, Ms. 13076-77, c.24t, Fol. 24v, Brussels, Belgium); **200** Image Select/Art Resource, NY; **201** The Art Archive/Bibliothèque Nationale Paris/ Eileen Tweedy; **202** Bridgeman-Giraudon/Art Resource, NY (Musée de l'Histoire de France aux Archives Nationales, Paris, France); **207** © British Library (Ms Add 23923 f.2), London, UK/The Bridgeman Art Library; **211** Scala/Art Resource, NY (Scrovegni Chapel, Padua, Italy); **212 top** Scala/Art Resource, NY (Palazzo Borromeo, Milan, Italy); **212 middle** The Art Archive/ Bodleian Library (Douce 276 folio 124v), Oxford, UK; **212 bottom left** British Library (Roy 6 E VII f.67v), London, UK/The Bridgeman Art Library International; **212 bottom right** The Art Archive/Bibliothèque Universitaire de Mèdecine, Montpellier, France /Dagli Orti

C H A P T E R   1 2

215 © Vatican Museums and Galleries, Sistine Chapel Ceiling (1508-12), Vatican City, Italy/Bridgeman Art Library; **220** Private Collection/The Bridgeman Art Library; **222** © AKG/Photo Researchers, Inc.; **226** Scala/Art Resource, NY (Brancacci Chapel, S. Maria del Carmine, Florence, Italy); **227 left** Scala/Art Resource, NY (Museo Nazionale del Bargello, Florence, Italy); **227 right** Scala/Art Resource, NY (San Lorenzo, Florence, Italy); **228** Scala/Art Resource, NY (S. Maria delle Grazie, Milan, Italy); **228** Erich Lessing/Art Resource, NY (Stanza della Segnatura, Stanze di Raffaello, Vatican Palace, Vatican State); **230 left** Scala/Art Resource, NY (Accademia, Florence, Italy); **230 right** Erich Lessing/Art Resource, NY (National Gallery, London, UK); **231** Alinari/Art Resource, NY (Uffizi, Florence, Italy); **234** Scala/Art Resource, NY (Uffizi, Florence, Italy)

C H A P T E R   1 3

237 Bibliotheque Nationale, Paris, France/The Bridgeman Art Library; **239** Scala/Art Resource, NY (Louvre, Paris, France); **242** Joerg P. Anders/Bildarchiv Preussischer Kulturbesitz/Art Resource, NY (Kupferstichkabinett, 1170, Staatliche Muséen zu Berlin, Germany); **244** Scala/Art Resource, NY (Alte Pinakothek, Munich, Germany); **247** © The Art Archive/University Library, Geneva, Switzerland/Dagli Orti; **251** Scala/Art Resource, NY (Il Gesu, Rome, Italy); **255** © Stapleton Collection/CORBIS

C H A P T E R   1 4

257 Knud Petersen/Bildarchiv Preussischer Kulturbesitz/Art Resource, NY (Kunstbibliothek, Staatliche Muséen zu Berlin, Germany); **259** © Huntington Library/SuperStock (The Huntington Library, Art Collections and Botanical Gardens, San Marino, California, USA); **261** Erich Lessing/Art Resource, NY (Museo Navale di Pegli, Genoa, Italy); **265** © Bibliotheque des Arts Decoratifs, Paris, France/Archives Charmet/Bridgeman Art Library; **268 top** © Private Collection/Bridgeman Art Library; **268 bottom** © The Art Archive/London; **271** Arnaudet/Réunion des Musées Nationaux/Art Resource, NY (Musée des Arts Asiatiques-Guimet, MG 18653, Paris, France); **276** © Huntington Library/SuperStock (The Huntington Library, Art Collections and Botanical Gardens, San Marino, CA, USA)

C H A P T E R   1 5

279 Hervé Lewandowski /Réunion des Musées Nationaux/Art Resource, NY (Louvre, 7492, Paris, France); **285** © Archivo Iconografico, S.A./CORBIS; **292** Joerg P. Anders/Bildarchiv Preussischer Kulturbesitz/Art Resource, NY (Gemaeldegalerie, 820B, Staatliche Muséen zu Berlin, Germany); **293** Jochen Remmer/Bildarchiv Preussischer Kulturbesitz/Art Resource, NY (National Portrait Gallery, 536, London, UK); **296 left** Jean Lewandowski/Réunion des Musées Nationaux/Art Resource, NY (Louvre, 1774, Paris, France); **296 right** Alinari/Art Resource, NY (Uffizi, Florence, Italy); **297** © SuperStock, Inc./SuperStock (Rijksmuseum, Amsterdam, The Netherlands)

C H A P T E R   1 6

303 Erich Lessing/Art Resource, NY (Private Collection, New York, USA); **306** Image Select/Art Resource, NY; **307** Image Select/Art Resource, NY; **309** Jochen Remmer/Bildarchiv Preussischer Kulturbesitz/Art Resource, NY (National Portrait Gallery, London, UK); **310** © Bettmann/CORBIS **313** Hervé Lewandowski/Réunion des Musées Nationaux/Art Resource, NY (Chateaux de Versailles et de Trianon, MV 3464, Versailles, France); **314** Gerard Blot/Réunion des Musées Nationaux/Art Resource, NY (Chateaux de Versailles et de Trianon, Versailles, France)

C H A P T E R   1 7

319 D. Arnaudet/Réunion des Musées Nationaux/Art Resource, NY (Chateaux de Malmaison et Bois-Preau, Rueil-Malmaison, France); **320** Alinari/Art Resource, NY (Archivio di Stato, Bologna, Italy); **323** Gérard Blot/Réunion des Musées Nationaux/Art Resource, NY (Chateaux de Versailles et de Trianon, MV 6101, Versailles, France); **329 top** Gérard Blot/Réunion des Musées Nationaux/Art Resource, NY (Louvre, 8525, Paris, France); **329 bottom** Courtesy of James R. Spencer; **331** Scala/Art Resource, NY (Museo di Firenze com'era, Florence, Italy); **332** © National Portrait Gallery/SuperStock

555 © Henry Diltz/CORBIS; 557 © Hans Namuth/Photo Researchers, Inc.

560 Czarek Sokolowski/Associated Press/AP Images/Wide World Photos; 566 David Brauchli/Reuters/CORBIS; 569 © Peter Turnley/CORBIS; 574 Ira Schwartz/Associated Press/AP Images/ Wide World Photos; 576 inset Carmen Taylor/© Associated Press/AP/Wide World Photos; 576 left © Jeremy Walker/Stone/ Getty Images; 576 right Graham Morrison/© Associated Press/ AP/Wide World Photos; 578 © 2006 The Estate of Jean-Michel Basquiat/ADAGP, Paris/ARS, New York // Art Resource, NY; 581 Courtesy of NASA

INDEX

Italicized page numbers show the
locations of illustrations.

Abbasid Caliphate, *152*
Abbasid rulers, 151–53, *152*, 189
Abbess, 126
Abbot, 124
Abd al-Rahman (Islamic ruler), 153
Abortion, 506, 576
Absolutism, 17th-century
    in central and eastern Europe, 287–92
    defined, 283
    limits of, 291–92
    in western Europe, 283–87
Absolutism, enlightened, 18th-century,
    337–43
    in Austrian Empire, 340–41
    in Britain, 338–39
    chronologies, 339, 343
    in France, 338
    in Prussia, 339–40
    in Russia, 341–43
Abstract Expressionism, 555
Abstract painting, 455, 509, 555
Abu al-Abbas (Islamic ruler), 151
Abu Bakr, 132–33
Achaemenid dynasty, 33
Acheson, Dean, 537
Acropolis, 44
Actium, Battle of (31 B.C.), 92
Act of 1911 (Britain), 460
Act of Supremacy, 246, 253
Adelard of Bath, 169
A Doll's House (Ibsen), 459
Adoration of the Magi (Dürer), 228, *231*
Adultery, in Roman Empire, 99
Aediles, 79
Aeneid (Virgil), 103
Aeolian Greeks, 43
Aeschylus, 52
Affonso (king of Congo), 267
Afghanistan
    British and Russians in, 464
    as buffer state, 464
    escape of colonial rule and, 468
    Hellenistic kingdoms in, 69
    war on Taliban, 575
Africa, ancient
    agriculture, 3–4
    Carthage, 29, 82, 83
    Christianity in, *126*, 127
    first humans in, 2
    Islamic expansion in, *133*, 134, 152
    Justinian in, 128, *129*
    Romans in, 82, 83, 90, 91, *98*
    Vandal invasion of, 119, *120*

Africa, modern. *See also under specific*
    African countries
    Boer War, 463
    colonization of, 462–64, 467
    decolonization, 547–48
    slave trade, 265–67, *266*
    in World War I, 479–80, *481*
    after World War I, 498
African Americans, civil rights for, 551
African National Congress (ANC), 547
Agamemnon (king of Mycenae), 42
Age of Enlightenment. *See* Europe,
    18th-century
Age of Modernity (1894–1914), 450–72
    African colonization, 462–64
    art in, 454–55, *455, 456, 457*
    Asian colonization, 464–65
    Austria-Hungary in, 461
    Britain in, 460
    Canada in, 462
    China in, 467
    chronology, 467
    France in, 460
    Germany in, 460–61
    imperialism, causes of, 462
    imperialism, responses to, 465–67
    India in, 467–68
    Japan in, 467, *468*
    Jews in European nation-state, 457–60
    literature in, 454
    maps of, *466, 469*
    Nietzche, philosophy of, 452
    physics in, 451–52
    psychology in, 452–53
    Russia in, 461
    social Darwinism and racism in,
        453–54, 462
    timeline (1894 to 1914), *471*
    United States in, 461–62
    women's rights movement in, 455–57,
        458, 459
    World War I, causes of, 468–70
Age of Pericles, 49–50
Agincourt, Battle of (1415), 202
Agora, 44
Agriculture
    in ancient Africa, 3–4
    in ancient Egypt, 13, 15
    Assyrian, 31
    Athenian, 56
    in Europe, medieval, 158–59, *159*
    in Europe, 18th-century, 346–47
    European Union and, 571, *572*
    Hellenistic, 67
    latifundia in Roman Republic, 90
    manorial system and, 147–48, *147, 148*
    in Mesopotamia, 6

Neolithic Revolution in, 3–4
    in Roman Empire, 101–3
Ahuramazda (Zoroastrian god), 36
Ain Ghazal, statue from, 4, *4*
Airplanes, 432, 579
Air travel, 508
Akbar, 269
Akhenaten (Egyptian pharaoh), 18–19
Akkadian Empire, 8
Alaric (Visigoth king), 118
Albania, 471
Albanians, 568
Alberti, Leon Battista, 216, 220
Albigensians, 187, *188*
Albuquerque, Alfonso d', 260
Alcohol, consumption of
    in Carolingian Empire, 143
    culture of modernity and, 454
    in Europe, medieval, 160
    in Europe, 18th-century, 330
    in Soviet Union, under Brezhnev, 561
Alcuin (scholars), 140–41
Alemanni, 119
Alexander I (Russian tsar), 369, 397
Alexander II (Russian tsar), 418, 447
Alexander III (Russian tsar), 447
Alexander the Great
    Aristotle and, 55
    conquests of, 61–64, *61, 62, 63*
    as pharaoh, 62
Alexander VI (pope), 222, 234
Alexandria, Egypt, 64, 67, 101, 117
Alexius I (Byzantine emperor), 190
Alfonso VIII of Castile (king of Spain),
    179
Alfonso X (Castilian king), 180
Algebra, 153
Algeria, 463, 545
Al-Khwarizmi, 153, 169
Allah, 131
All Quiet on the Western Front
    (Remarque), *480*
Al-Ma'smun (Islamic ruler), 152
Alphabets, 29, 151. *See also* writing
Al-Qaeda, 575
Alsace and Lorraine, 490
Alva, duke of, *253*
Amenhotep IV (Egyptian pharaoh), 18
American Civil War (1861–1865), 422
American Revolution (1775–1783),
    355–56
Americas, ancient
    agriculture in, 4
    Mesoamerica, 262–64
    South America, 6, 21
Amores (Ovid), 104
Amorites, 8

Gagarin, Yuri, 581
Gainsborough, Thomas, *350*
Gaius Cassius, *92*
Gaius Gracchus, 90
Galen, 304, 309
Galileo Galilei, 304, 307–8, 315
Gallipoli, in World War I, 478
Games and sports, 212. *See also* Leisure
    activities
    in mass society, 444, 508, 580
    in Middle Ages, *212*
    Olympic games, 41, 56, 85
    Roman gladiatorial, 106–7
Gandhi, Mohandas "Mahatma", 498, 549
Garibaldi, Giuseppe, 414
Gascony, duchy of, 201
Gas warfare, 478
Gaudry, Suzanne, *282*
Gaul. *See* France
Gauls, 66
*A General Theory of Employment, Interest,
    and Money* (Keynes), 497
Geneva, Calvin in, 247–48, *248*
Genghis Khan, 182, 268
Genoa, 164, 165
Gentileschi, Artemisia, 297, *297*
Geocentric conception, *305*
Geoffrin, Marie-Thérèse de, 319, 327
Geography
    of ancient Greece, 41–43
    of Roman Republic, 77–78
Geography (Ptolemy), 260
Geometry, in Hellenistic era, 70–71
George, David Lloyd, 460
George I (king of England), 338
George II (king of England), 338
George III (king of England), 339
Germania (Tacitus), 105
Germanic Confederation, 397
Germanic kingdoms, 119–22, *120*. *See also*
    Germany
Germanic peoples. *See* Germanic
    kingdoms; Vikings
Germany. *See also* Germanic kingdoms;
    Holy Roman Empire; Nazi Germany;
    Prussia; World War II
    14th-century, 205, *205*
    16th-century, 239–44
    17th-century, 287–88
    19th-century, late, government in, 446
    19th-century unification of, 415–17,
        417
    African colonies, 464
    anti-Semitism in, 199, 458, 460–61, 501,
        504, 524
    Austro-Prussian War and, 415, 416
    Balkan Wars and, 469–71
    Berlin, postwar, 536, 538–40
    Black Death in, 197
    Brandenburg-Prussia and, 287–88
    in Carolingian Empire, 138
    Christianity, conversion to, 138
    chronologies, 183, 405, 417, 448
    Cold War and, 532, 533, 534
    Congress of Vienna and, 393–95, 397,
        402
    Dawes plan and, 495
    East Germany, 538–40, 543, 566, 569
    Enlightenment in, 328–30

Franco-Prussian War, 416–17, *418*
French occupation of Ruhr Valley, 495
Germanic Confederation formation,
    397, 405
Great Depression in, 496
Green party, 577
Holy Roman Empire in, 180–81, *181*,
    182
Industrial Revolution in, 380–82
intellectual centers in medieval, *167*
manufacturing, late 19th-century, 432
maps of, *181*, *182*, *243*, *244*, *417*
medieval kingdoms in, 180–81
nationalism in, 453–54
Pan-German League, 460–61
Peasants' War, 241
racism in, 453–54
Reformation and, 239–41
Reformation in, 239–44
reunification of, 538, 566, 568–69
revolutions of 1948 and, 402–3
Romans in, 98–99, *101*
Schlieffen Plan, 476
sexual revolution and, 554
socialist party in, 435
terrorism in, 575
Thirty Years' War and, 283, *284*
trade unions in, 436
Triple Alliance of 1882, 469
unification of, 415–17, *417*
urbanization of, 432–33
Weimar Republic, 500–501
West Germany, 538–39, 541, 546
under William II, 460–61
World War I, aftermath of, 482–83
World War I, eastern front, 476, 478–79,
    479
World War I, homefront conditions,
    482
World War I, outbreak, 475
World War I, peace settlement, 488–91
World War I, western front, 476–78,
    478
World War II. *See* Nazi Germany
Ghent, 164, 165
Gierek, Edward, 564
Giotto, 205, *206*, 210, *211*
Giovanni Arnolfini and His Bride (van
    Eyck), 228, *230*
Gladiators, 106–7
Gladstone, William, 444
Glasnost, 562
The Gleaners (Millet), 428
Globalization, 581
Global warming, 579
Goebbels, Joseph, 508
Goethe, Johann Wolfgang von, 405
Gold, 258, 261, 265, 276, 464
Gold Coast (Ghana), 547–48
Golden Bull (1356), 205
Gomulka, Wladyslaw, 543
Gonzaga, Francesco, 221
Good emperors (Roman), 99–100
Gorbachev, Mikhail, 561, *563*, 574, *574*
Gore, Al, 573
Gothic literature, 406
Goths, Balkans invaded by, 108
Gottwald, Klement, 543
Gouges, Olympe de, 360

Government organization
    in 17th-century Prussia, 287
    American Revolution and, 356
    Aristotle and, 55
    in Athens, 47–48, 49–50
    in Carolingian Empire, 138–39
    under Catherine the Great, 342–43
    democracy in western Europe, 444–47
    in Dutch Republic, 292
    French Revolution and, 358–59,
        361–62, 366
    in Hellenistic world, 66
    Hobbes and Locke on, 296
    liberalism and, 398
    under Louis XIII, 285
    in medieval cities, 165
    Montesquieu on, 323
    in Persian Empire, 34–36
    Plato's ideas of, 55
    Roman Empire, 97–100, 101
    in Roman Republic, 79–80, 89–90
    Rousseau on, 325–26
    in Russia, 19th-century, 419–20
    Smith, Adam, on, 325
    in Soviet Union, 499
    in Spanish Empire, 265
    in Sparta, 47–49
Goya, Francisco, *371*
Gracchi brothers, 90
Granada, 180, 230
Grancis, Joseph (Austria-Hungarian
    monarch), 447
Grand Alliance, 521
Grand Empire of Napoleon. *See* Napoleon
    Bonaparte
Granicus River, Battle of (334 B.C.), 62
Grant, Ulysses S. (general), 422
Gratian, 162
Gray, Thomas, 330
Great Britain. *See* Britain
Great Depression, *494*, 496–99, *496*, *497*
Greater East Asia Co-Prosperity Sphere,
    520, 527
Great Exhibition, London (1851), 378–79,
    381
Great Leap Forward (China), 549–50
Great Northern War (1701–1721), 290
Great Proletarian Cultural Revolution, 550
Great Pyramid of Khufu, 17, *18*
The Great Restoration (Bacon), 313
Great Schism, 207–9
Great Society, 551
Great War for Empire (1756–1763), 345
Greece, ancient, 40–49, *42*
    chronologies, 49
    city-states and colonization, 44–49
    Dark Age of, 43–44
    geography of, 41–43
    Homer and, 43–44
    map, *42*
    timeline (1600 B.C. to 300 B.C.), *58*
Greece, classical, 49–57
    Alexander and, 61–64
    arts in, 53–55
    Athenian Empire in, 49–50
    Culture and society in, 51–57
    decline of Greek states, 50–51
    drama in, 52
    families in, 56–57

Marne, Battle of the (1914), 476
Marne, Battle of the (1918), 488
Marriage
    in 18th-century Europe, 347, 348, *348*
    in 19th-century Europe, late, 440–41
    in ancient Egypt, 19–20
    Aristotle on, 55
    Black Death and, 211
    in Carolingian Empire, 141–42
    Christianity and, 141–42
    Code of Hammurabi and, 9–10
    in Frankish kingdom, 121–22
    Islam and, 132
    manorial system and, 147
    in mass society, 440
    medieval, 160, *162*, 211
    in New World, 274
    in postwar western world, 554
    Reformation and, 240, 246, 248
    in Renaissance, 219–20, *219*, *220*
    Roman, 80, 86
The Marriage of Figaro (Mozart), 330
Marshall, George C. (general), 537
Marshall, John (Chief Justice), 405
Marshall Plan, 537
Martin V (pope), 209
Marx, Karl, 423–24, *424*
Marxism, 423–24, *423*
Marxist Social Democratic Party (Russia), 461
Mary (queen of England), 247, 253–56, *254, 255*
Mary, Virgin, 187, 227
Masaccio, 225, *226*
Massachusetts Bay Company, 273
Mass in B Minor (Bach), 328
Mass society, 436–44
    education in, 442–43, *443*
    emigration in, 436–37
    families in, 440–41, *442*
    housing and, 438, *439*
    leisure activities in, 444
    literacy in, 443
    living conditions and, 437–38
    population growth and, 436, *436*
    social structure of, 438–39, *442*
    urbanization and, 437–38
    women in, 440–41, *441*
Materialism, 425
Mathematics
    in Hellenistic era, 70–71
    Muslim contribution to, 153
    in Renaissance, 304
    Sumerian, 12
Matthias Corvinus (Hungarian king), 231
Mauryan Empire, 65
Maximilian (archduke of Austria), 413
Maximilian I (German emperor), 231
Mayan calendar, 262
Mayan culture, 262–63
May Day, 435
Mazarin, Cardinal, 285
Mazzini, Giuseppe, 404
McCarthy, Joseph R., 551
Mecca, 131
Medici, Cosimo de', 220, 223–24, *227*
Medici family, 218, 220

Medicine and medical practice. *See also* Plagues and diseases
    16th- and 17th-centuries, 309–12
    in Carolingian Empire, 143
    in Muslim world, 154
    national health insurance, 460, *461*, 546, 552
    nursing, 432, 456, 504
    Pasteur, Louis, 425
    socialized in Britain, 546
    vaccinations, 436
Medieval Europe. *See* Europe, medieval
Medina, 131
Mediterranean, conquest by Roman Republic, 82–84
Megaliths, 24, *24*
Mehmet II (sultan), 233
Mein Kampf (Hitler), 501, 515
Memoirs (Catherine the Great), *342*
Memphis, Egypt, 34
Menander (Athenian playwright), 69
Mendeleyev, Dmitri, 425
Menes (Egyptian king), 15
Mennonites, 246
Menno Simons, 246
Mercantilism, 274, 285, 325
Mercator, Gerardus, 277, *277*
Merkel, Angela, 569
Merovingian dynasty, 119, 138
Mesoamerica, early civilizations in, 261–63
Mesopotamia, 7–12, 100
    arts and sciences in, 11–12, *11*
    under Assyrian rule, 29–32
    city-states in, 6–7, *7*
    Code of Hammurabi, 9–10
    maps of, *7, 8*
    in Persian Empire, 32–33
    religion in, 10–11
Messenia, 47
Messiah (Handel), 328
Mestizos, 275
Methodism, *332*, 334
Metropolis, 45
Metternich, Klemens von, 393, *393, 395*, 397
Mexico
    Aztecs and Mayans in, 262, 263
    Cortés and, 259
    independence achieved, 395
    Mexico City, 263
    Napoleon III invasion of, 413
    New Spain and, 265
Micah, 30
Michael Cerularius (patriarch), 190
Michael III (Byzantine emperor), 148
Michel, Louise, *445*
Michelangelo, 226–28, *230*
Microprocessors, 579
Middle ages. *See* Europe, High Middle Ages; Europe, medieval
Middle classes
    in 19th-century mass society, 439–40
    education of, 442–43
    in Europe after World War II, 552
    family and, 441–42
    French Revolution and, 357
    in industrial Britain, 386
    Victorian Age and, 421–22, 439–41

Middle East, modern. *See also* Near East, ancient
    decolonization in, 549, *550*
    interwar years, 498
    Israel, formation of, 548–49
    Six-Day War, 549
    after World War I, 491
Middle Kingdom (ancient Egypt), 14–15
Middle Passage, 266
Midway Island, Battle of (1942), 521
Mieszko (Polish prince), 150
Milan, 165, 181, 206, *206*, 220
Military. *See also* warfare
    decline of Roman, 108
    English, under Cromwell, 293
    militarism prior to World War I, 474
    Portuguese fleet superiority, 261
    Prussian, 339–40
    reforms in Roman Empire, 116
    reforms in Roman Republic, 90–91
    Roman Empire, development of, 97–99
    training in medieval Europe, 161
Military inventions. *See* warfare
Mill, John Stuart, 398, *399*
Millet, Jean-François, *427*, 428
Milligen, J. G., 346
Milošević, Slobodan, 566–68
Ming dynasty, 271
Minoan Crete, 41, *42*
The Misanthrope (Molière), 300
Mishneh Torah, 29
Missi dominici, 139
Missionaries
    in Japan, 271, 275
    Jesuit, 250–52, *250*, 271, 275, *276*
    in late 19th-century, 462
    monastic movement and, 124–26
    in New World, 275, *276*
    in Vietnam, *270*
Mithraism, 109, 112
Mitterrand, François, *569*, 570
Moabites, 25
Moctezuma (Aztec monarch), 263
Modern Devotion movement, 239
Modernism, 454–55
Modernity, Age of. *See* Age of Modernity
Mohenjo-Daro, 5, *5*
Moldavia, after Crimean War, 413
Molière, Jean-Baptiste, 300
Molotov, Vyacheslav, 534
Moluccas, Dutch in, 267
Monastic movement, 125–27
    Benedictines, 124
    Cistercian order, 185
    Cluniac reform movement, 184
    Dominican order, *185*, 187, 265, 275
    education and, *167*
    Franciscan order, *185*, 187, 265, 275
    Irish, 125
    Luther on, 248
    manuscript copying and, 140, 143
    monks as missionaries, 124–26
    solitary hermits, 123
    Viking invasion and, 184
    women in, 126–27, 185–87, *186*
Money. *See* Currency and banking
Mongol Empire, 182, *183*, 196, 197
Monks, defined, 123
Monotheism, origin of, 27

Saint-Denis, Church of, 172
Saint Matthew's Passion (Bach), 328
Saint Peter's Basilica, 234, 297
Saint Petersburg (Petrograd), 290
Saints. *See also specific saints*
    elimination of, 248
    role of, 187
Saladin, 191, *193*
Salons, 327, 369
Saltaire, 369
Samaria, 26, *26*
Samnites, *77, 81*
Samurai, 467
Sanford, Elizabeth Poole, 440
Sanger, Margaret, 509
San Lorenzo, Church at, 226, *227*
San Martin, José de, 395
Sans-culottes, 361
San Vitale church (Ravenna), 128
Sarajevo, assassination of Ferdinand, 474
Sargon, 8
Sartre, Jean-Paul, 553, 556
Sassanid Persians, 108
Satellite television, 580
Satires (Horace), 104
Satrapies, system of, 35
Satrapy (Persian province), 33
Saudi Arabia, after World War I, 498
Saul (Israeli king), 25
Saxons, 120, *120*, 138
Saxony, 180
Schleswig, 416
Schlieffen, Alfred von (general), 476, *476*
Schlieffen Plan, 476, *476*
Schliemann, Heinrich, 41, 43
Schmidt, Helmut, 569
Scholasticism, 169–71
Schönberg, Arnold, 510
School of Athens (Raphael), *227*, 229
Schroeder, Gerhard, 569, 577
Schumacher, E.F., 579, *580*
Schurz, Carl, *403*
Schutzstaffel (SS), 503, 525
Schweickart, Russell, 581
Science. *See also* Scientific revolution
    in early Mesopotamia, 11–12
    in Europe, 19th-century, 425–26
    evolution, theory of, 425–26
    Hellenistic, 70–71
    medicine, 425, 436
    mid-19th-century progress and, 425–26
    Physics, 451–52
    social Darwinism, 453–54
    after World War II, 579
Science of Man, 324–25
Scientific revolution, 303–18. *See also*
    Science
    astronomy, 305–9
    background to, 304–5
    chronology, 311
    Descartes and, 312–13
    medicine and chemistry, 309–12
    Pascal on, 315–16, *315*
    religion and, 315–16
    scientific method, 313–14, 425
    scientific societies, 314
    social applications of, 314–15
    timeline (1550 to 1700), *317*
    women in, 310–12

Scipio Africanus, 83
Scotland, 338
Scott, Walter, 406
Scriptoria, 140
Sculpture
    Ain Ghazal, statue from, 4, *4*
    Assyrian, 32, *33*
    classical Greek, 53
    early Egyptian, 17–18
    Hellenistic, *61*, 70, *70*
    Indian, 70
    in Italian Renaissance, 226, *227*, *230*
    Roman, 89, *91*, *97*, *118*
Scutage, 204
SEATO (Southeast Asia Treat
    Organization), 540
Second Battle of Marne, 488
Second Continental Congress, 355
Second Estate, 178, 218, 357
Second Industrial Revolution, 431–36,
    431, 433, 435. See also Industrial
    Revolution
Second International, 435
Second Punic War (218-201 B.C.), 83, *87*
The Second Sex (Simone de Beauvoir), 553
Secret police
    in Cheka Russia, 487
    in East Germany, 566
    under Mussolini, 499
    in Nazi Germany, 503
    in Soviet Union, 543, 561
Secular humanism, 578
Secularism, 222
Seibertz, Englebert, *393*
Seleucids, 73
Seljuk Turks, 189–90, 232
Semitic peoples, 8, 18, 29, 32
Senate (American), 356
Senate (Roman), 89–90
Seneca, 105
Sennacherib (Assyrian king), 32
Separation of powers, 323
Sephardic Jews, 333
September 11, 2001 attack, 575, *576*, 579
Serbs
    Balkan Wars and, 469–71
    defeat by Ottoman Turks, 232
    independence from Ottomans, 413
    migration of, 151
    under Milošević, 566–68
    World War I and, 475–76
    after World War I, 491
    Yugoslavia, disintegration of, 566–67
    Yugoslavia, origin of, 491, 506
Serfs, 148, 160, 165
Sermon on the Mount, 109, *110*
Servian Wall, 78
Seven Years' War (1756–1763), 270,
    344–46, *344*
Severan rulers, 107
Sexual behavior
    in 1920s, 508–9
    in Athens, 57
    during Carnival, 330
    in Carolingian Empire, 141–42
    Code of Hammurabi and, 10
    homosexuality in High Middle Ages,
        188

homosexuality in post-war Europe, 554
    in Islam, 132
    in Sweden, 554
    witchcraft trials and, 281
Seyss-Inquart, Arthur, 516
Sforza, Francesco, 220
Shakespeare, William, 298–99
Shang dynasty, *5*
Shari'a (legal code), 132
Shelley, Mary Wollstonecraft, 406
Shelley, Percy Bysshe, 406–7
Sheridan, Richard, *348*
Shi'ites, 133, 189
Sicily
    14th-century, 206, *206*
    Crusades and, 192
    under Frederick II, 180
    Greek settlements in, 77
    High Middle Ages in, 180
    Italian unification and, 415
    plague in, 197–98
    Punic Wars and, 82–83
    revolt in 1848, 404
    slave revolt in, 86
    in World War II, 522
Sidon, *26*, 29
Sieveking, Amalie, 456
Sigismund (German Emperor), 209, 233
Signorini, Giovanni, *331*
Silesia, 340, 343, 344
Silk, 101, 128
Simeon the Stylite, Saint, 123
Sistine Chapel, 227
Six-Day War (1967), 549
Sixtus (pope), 234
Skepticism, religious, 321
Slavery
    abolition of, 365, 418–21
    African slave trade, 265–67
    American Civil War and, 422
    in ancient Egypt, 25
    in Athens, 47, 56–57
    Emancipation Proclamation, 422
    French Revolution and, 267, 365
    in Mesopotamia, *7*
    in Renaissance, 219
    in Roman Republic, 85–86
    in Sparta, 45–47
Slavic peoples
    in Austria-Hungary, 418
    Charlemagne and, 138
    chronology, 153
    migration of, 150–51, *150*, *152*
    in World War II, 525, 526
Slavonic (Cyrillic) alphabet, 151
Slovakia, formation of, 565
Slovenia, 566–68
Small Is Beautiful (E.F. Schumacher), 579,
    580
Smallpox, 263, 264
Smith, Adam, 325
Social classes. *See also* Nobles; Peasants;
    Workers
    in 18th-century Europe, 350, 357
    in 19th-century mass society, 438–39
    ancient Greece, 45
    in ancient Egypt, 15–16
    in Europe after World War II, 552–53
    in Industrial Revolution, 386, 387–88